DEVELOPMENTAL PSYCHOLOGY

PEARSON

At Pearson, we have a simple mission: to help people make more of their lives through learning.

We combine innovative learning technology with trusted content and educational expertise to provide engaging and effective learning experiences that serve people wherever and whenever they are learning.

From classroom to boardroom, our curriculum materials, digital learning tools and testing programmes help to educate millions of people worldwide – more than any other private enterprise.

Every day our work helps learning flourish, and wherever learning flourishes, so do people.

To learn more, please visit us at **www.pearson.com/uk**

PEARSON EDUCATION LIMITED

Edinburgh Gate
Harlow CM20 2JE
United Kingdom
Tel: +44 (0)1279 623623
Web: www.pearson.com/uk

First published 2011 (print)
Second edition published 2016 (print and electronic)

© Pearson Education Limited 2011 (print)
© Pearson Education Limited 2016 (print and electronic)

The rights of Rachel Gillibrand, Virginia Lam and Victoria L. O'Donnell to be identified as author of this work has been asserted by them in accordance with the Copyright, Designs and Patents Act 1988.

The print publication is protected by copyright. Prior to any prohibited reproduction, storage in a retrieval system, distribution or transmission in any form or by any means, electronic, mechanical, recording or otherwise, permission should be obtained from the publisher or, where applicable, a licence permitting restricted copying in the United Kingdom should be obtained from the Copyright Licensing Agency Ltd, Barnard's Inn, 86 Fetter Lane, London EC4A 1EN.

The ePublication is protected by copyright and must not be copied, reproduced, transferred, distributed, leased, licensed or publicly performed or used in any way except as specifically permitted in writing by the publishers, as allowed under the terms and conditions under which it was purchased, or as strictly permitted by applicable copyright law. Any unauthorised distribution or use of this text may be a direct infringement of the authors' and the publisher's rights and those responsible may be liable in law accordingly.

Pearson Education is not responsible for the content of third-party internet sites.

ISBN: 978-1-292-00308-5 (print)
       978-1-292-00311-5 (PDF)
       978-1-292-16327-7 (ePub)

British Library Cataloguing-in-Publication Data
A catalogue record for the print edition is available from the British Library

Library of Congress Cataloging-in-Publication Data
A catalog record for the print edition is available from the Library of Congress

ARP impression 98

Cover photo: Getty Images

Print edition typeset in 9.75/13 pt Times LT Pro by Lumina Datamatics
Printed by Ashford Colour Press Ltd.

NOTE THAT ANY PAGE CROSS REFERENCES REFER TO THE PRINT EDITION

Brief contents

Preface xi
Authors and contributors xv
Acknowledgements xviii

Section I Introduction to developmental psychology 1

Chapter 1 What is developmental psychology? 2
Chapter 2 Theoretical perspectives 12
Chapter 3 Research methods 46

Section II Cognitive and linguistic development 71

Chapter 4 Prenatal development and infancy 72
Chapter 5 Language development 114
Chapter 6 Memory and intelligence 144
Chapter 7 The development of mathematical thinking 174
Chapter 8 Theory of mind 220

Section III Social and emotional development 245

Chapter 9 Attachment and early social experiences 246
Chapter 10 Childhood temperament and behavioural development 278
Chapter 11 Development of self-concept and gender identity 314
Chapter 12 Peer interactions and relationships 346
Chapter 13 Adolescence 378

Section IV Clinical/applied aspects 407

Chapter 14 Developmental psychology and education 408
Chapter 15 Understanding bullying 442
Chapter 16 Atypical development 480
Chapter 17 Attention deficit hyperactivity disorder (ADHD) 520

Glossary 543
Bibliography 553
Index 611

Contents

Preface xi
Authors and contributors xv
Acknowledgements xviii

Section I Introduction to developmental psychology 1

Chapter 1 What is developmental psychology? 2

Learning outcomes 2
Introduction 3
The debates of developmental psychology 4
What is 'typical' development? 11
Recommended reading 11
Recommended websites 11

Chapter 2 Theoretical perspectives 12

Learning outcomes 12
Introduction 13
What is a theory? 14
Theoretical perspectives 14
Psychoanalytic perspective on development 17
Biological perspectives on development 24
Learning perspectives on development 31
Cognitive perspective on development 35
Integrative perspectives in developmental psychology 41
Summary 43
Review questions 44
Recommended reading 44
Recommended websites 45

Chapter 3 Research methods 46

Learning outcomes 46
Introduction 47
What is research? 48
The importance of understanding theoretical paradigms 48
Methods in developmental psychology research 50
Working with children 60
Summary 67
Review questions 68
Recommended reading 68
Recommended websites 69

Section II Cognitive and linguistic development 71

Chapter 4 Prenatal development and infancy 72

Learning outcomes 72
Introduction 73
How to grow a baby: the roles of nature and nurture in early development 74
Prenatal physical development 77
Prenatal development of the brain 77
Prenatal states: foetal sleep and waking cycles 81
Prenatal abilities and behaviours 82
Risks to prenatal development: environmental teratogens and genetic errors 83
Birth 85
The neonate: basic states, movements and reflexes 87
The postnatal development of the brain 88
Infant perception 91
Infant vision 91
Infant audition 95
Infant touch, taste and smell abilities 96
Motor abilities in infancy 98

Cognitive abilities in infancy: general models and approaches   99
Infant attention   101
Infant learning and memory   102
Basic knowledge and understanding in infancy   104
Categorisation in infancy   105
Reasoning and problem solving in infancy   108
Summary   110
Review questions   111
Recommended reading   111
Recommended websites   112

Chapter 5 Language development   114

Learning outcomes   114
Introduction   115
What is language?   116
What communication is there before verbal communication?   116
The four components of language   119
How do infants' early social interactions prepare them for later language?   121
Theories of development   122
Phonological development   128
Semantic development   131
Syntactic development   136
The development of pragmatics   138
Summary   141
Review questions   142
Recommended reading   142
Recommended websites   143

Chapter 6 Memory and intelligence   144

Learning outcomes   144
Introduction   145
What is memory?   146
Memory in children   148
What is intelligence?   164
Intelligence in children   164
Summary   171
Review questions   172
Recommended reading   172
Recommended websites   173

Chapter 7 The development of mathematical thinking   174

Learning outcomes   174
Introduction   175

What is mathematical thinking?   177
Understanding number   179
The number system as a tool for thinking   186
Reasoning and solving problems with numbers   193
The step into rational numbers   206
Summary   215
Answers to problems   216
Review questions   217
Recommended reading   218
Recommended websites   219

Chapter 8 Theory of mind   220

Learning outcomes   220
Introduction   221
What is theory of mind?   222
How does theory of mind fit into a developmental perspective?   230
Theories explaining theory of mind   235
Theory of mind and children with autism   239
Summary   242
Review questions   242
Recommended reading   243
Recommended websites   243

Section III Social and emotional development   245

Chapter 9 Attachment and early social experiences   246

Learning outcomes   246
Introduction   248
What is attachment?   248
Measuring attachment   257
Attachment and childcare   263
Attachment beyond infancy   270
Summary   275
Review questions   275
Recommended reading   276
Recommended websites   276

Chapter 10 Childhood temperament and behavioural development   278

Learning outcomes   278
Introduction   279
What is temperament?   280
Studying and measuring temperament   282

Explanations for differences in temperament 297
Temperament in the long term 304
Summary 310
Review questions 311
Recommended reading 311
Recommended websites 312

Chapter 11 Development of self-concept and gender identity 314

Learning outcomes 314
Introduction 315
What are self-concept and social identity? 316
Theories in the development of the self-concept 316
Understanding of gender categories: children's gender identity 322
Summary 342
Review questions 343
Recommended reading 343
Recommended websites 343

Chapter 12 Peer interactions and relationships 346

Learning outcomes 346
Introduction 348
The peer group and peer interactions 348
Play 351
Children's friendships 366
Summary 375
Review questions 376
Recommended reading 377
Recommended websites 377

Chapter 13 Adolescence 378

Learning outcomes 378
Introduction 379
A brief history of adolescence 380
Physical changes during adolescence 381
Cognitive development and changes in the teenage years 385
Social development in the teenage years 394
Mental health in adolescence 399
Sex and relationship behaviour in adolescence 401
Summary 403
Answers to puzzles 403
Review questions 404

Recommended reading 404
Recommended websites 405

Section IV Clinical/applied aspects 407

Chapter 14 Developmental psychology and education 408

Learning outcomes 408
Introduction 410
Understanding development within social contexts 410
The application of developmental theory in classrooms 412
Five themes of 'developmentally appropriate provision' 420
Summary 438
Review questions 439
Recommended reading 440
Recommended websites 440

Chapter 15 Understanding bullying 442

Learning outcomes 442
Introduction 444
What is bullying? 444
Involvement in bullying 447
Theoretical perspectives on bullying 462
Tackling bullying: methods of intervention and prevention 469
Summary 476
Review questions 477
Recommended reading 478
Recommended websites 478

Chapter 16 Atypical development 480

Learning outcomes 480
Introduction 481
What is atypical development? 482
Assessment 487
Disorders of development 496
Therapy and intervention 510
Summary 516
Review questions 517
Recommended reading 517
Recommended websites 518

Chapter 17 Attention deficit hyperactivity disorder (ADHD) 520

Learning outcomes 520
Introduction 521
Introduction to attention deficit hyperactivity disorder 522
ADHD across the lifespan 524
Co-morbidity and associated impairments in ADHD 528
What causes ADHD? 530
Treatment for ADHD 535
Future directions in ADHD research 539
Summary 541
Review questions 542
Recommended reading 542
Recommended websites 542

Glossary 543
Bibliography 553
Index 611

Preface

Developmental psychology is a core component of psychology degrees. In the UK, for a degree programme to carry the graduate basis for recognition with the British Psychological Society, students must study developmental psychology as part of their degree, at least at introductory level. However, this doesn't mean that studying developmental psychology should be a chore! In fact, we believe that developmental psychology is one of the most interesting, exciting and broad-ranging subjects within the whole academic discipline of psychology.

Developmental psychology covers all aspects of psychological development across the lifespan, from birth through childhood and adolescence, and into adulthood. Whether you are more interested in cognition or emotion; in relationships or intelligence; in language or identity – developmental psychology has something for you! Furthermore, development is something which affects all of us and so is relevant to everyone. We all began life as children and so we all have a journey that we can look back on, and experiences that we can draw upon to understand developmental psychology. We have all been shaped by the relationships and experiences that we have had across our life journey so far. We all have parents (whether biological or not) and many of us have siblings or relatives whom we can look at as we consider the roles of nature and nurture in shaping the people we have become. Some of us have children and many more of us will go on to have children in the future, and so we can use developmental psychology to explain, to understand and to guide our behaviour as parents and as children. So, developmental psychology is not just an abstract, theoretical subject – it affects us all and is directly relevant to our lives and to the lives of everyone around us.

The purpose of this book is to provide an introduction to developmental psychology for students who are studying it for the first time, usually in either the first or the second year of their university studies. We want to do this in a reader-friendly way which will engage your attention, stimulate your interest in the subject and enhance your learning. We have tried to write the book using accessible language instead of dense, jargon-laden academic text, whilst retaining the depth and scope necessary to study the subject appropriately. The book encourages you to think critically about the subject matter and also asks you to reflect on your own knowledge and experience. It pushes you to engage with empirical research as well as theory, to make links between different areas of development, and to recognise common themes which underpin the study of development overall.

Structure of the book

The book is structured into four sections. *Section I* provides you with an introduction to developmental psychology, exploring what it is, what some of the key perspectives on development are, what developmental psychologists do, why they do it, and how. This section includes a chapter about some of the key theoretical models and perspectives which have had the greatest influences on developmental psychology. Some of these are classic ideas which are important to understand because they laid the foundations for the subsequent study of developmental psychology. Some have been ground-breaking and controversial. Some have become the backbone of the study of development. These are the kinds of theories and models which you will encounter time and time again throughout the rest of the book. This section of the book also contains a chapter on research methods. Research methods are absolutely central to your studies as a psychology student. Whilst research methods are often taught within psychology degree programmes as self-contained courses or modules, they cannot be fully understood outside of the context of the different areas of psychology that you study. Within this book, we explicitly discuss research methods as part of the study of developmental psychology, through an introductory chapter and then as a boxed feature in subsequent chapters throughout the rest of the book.

Section II addresses cognitive and linguistic development, exploring the earliest stages of prenatal development and infancy, the development of language, memory and intelligence, mathematical thinking and theory of mind. This section will therefore enable you to learn about children as thinking beings across a range of areas of development.

Section III explores social and emotional development, covering attachment, temperament, the concept of self and gender identity, social interactions and adolescence. This section will therefore enable you to learn about children as social and emotional beings across a range of areas of development.

Within *Section IV* we have invited a number of guest authors to contribute chapters on applied areas of development which we hope you will find really interesting. These chapters cover education, bullying, atypical development and ADHD. They focus on very specific topics that are of contemporary relevance, and will let you see how theory and research in developmental psychology can be applied to particular contexts.

How should I use this book?

The book is not written so that it has to be read from cover to cover. You can do so if you wish, but each chapter is a self-contained unit that can be read by itself. Nevertheless, as you will see, there are many ways in which recurrent themes and key ideas are highlighted throughout the book. This means that as you read each chapter (whether in chronological order or by dipping in and out), you should begin to make connections between different topics, to see how certain aspects of development interact and overlap, and to recognise issues, ideas, theories and questions which underpin developmental psychology as a whole.

The book also has an accompanying website. The website is structured in line with the chapters within the book, and it contains various additional resources for you as a student, and also for your lecturer, should they decide to use them. Resources for students include test-yourself questions with suggested answers, web links and video clips. Use these resources on the website to complement your reading of the book, to assess your own learning and to bring children and development to life. If your lecturer makes use of the additional web-based resources available to them then the content of your lectures, tutorials and practicals can be linked directly to the book. The book should also serve as a helpful tool when it comes to essays and exams. There are many features within the book that you can use to structure your revision, to test yourself, to identify gaps in your knowledge

and to practise writing answers to questions. We have used a questioning technique throughout the book, so that you are often asked to consider your own experiences or opinions, or to consider the implications of what has been said. We hope that the book itself is written and structured in such a way that it aids your understanding and learning as you go along, and some of the specific ways in which this has been achieved are discussed next.

What features of each chapter will enhance my learning?

Pedagogy is the science of learning and teaching. In addition to all of the above, we have used pedagogical principles in the writing of the book so that it contains a number of specific features specially designed and included with your learning in mind.

Opening examples

Each chapter begins with some kind of illustration of the topic under discussion. This might be a recent case from the news or the media, a description of a particular scenario, an extract from a piece of research or something else. Before going into the detail of the chapter, these opening examples should allow you to immediately grasp something of the topic, its significance, its relevance or its interest.

Learning outcomes

Each chapter also has a number of learning outcomes at the start. These are statements about what you should be able to do by the end of the chapter, having read its content and engaged in its reflective exercises. You can use these to focus your reading of each chapter, actively looking for information relevant to each learning outcome as a way to read with a purpose rather than passively trying to take in information. You can also use the learning outcomes to guide your revision of the subject matter later on, using them as a check on your own knowledge, and helping you to identify gaps in your understanding.

Stop and think questions

Throughout the book, every chapter includes a number of Stop and Think questions. Sometimes these questions will ask you to reflect upon your own knowledge or experience, or to relate things to your own life. Sometimes they will push you to go further than the information which has been provided, perhaps by considering the implications of an idea, by engaging with a complex piece of research, by evaluating an argument or an approach, or by thinking about applications of theory.

Please do 'stop and think' when you come to these questions! They will help you to engage actively with the material within the chapter by thinking about it in a slightly different way. This should enable you to take a more critical and evaluative approach to the subject.

Glossary

Throughout the book you will see key words and phrases highlighted the first time they are used. Whilst these will be discussed within the main body of the text, you will also see definitions of them outside of the main text. These definitions should provide a quick and easy way for you to remind yourself of the meanings of key terms. All of the terms which are highlighted and defined are then pulled together in one glossary at the end of the book for ease of reference. So if you come across a term that you are not familiar with, or whose meaning you can't quite remember, use the glossary to help.

Illustrations

We know that students often find it off-putting when books are full of dense unbroken text, and so we have tried to make this book colourful and interesting visually. As with any psychology text, this one contains graphs, tables and figures throughout, which illustrate things like research findings or classifications of behaviour. But, in addition, we have included pictures and photographs of children in different situations, engaged in the kinds of behaviour being discussed, and other images, which all help to bring each chapter to life.

Case studies

Concrete, real-life examples are often easier to understand than abstract ones, and so we have tried to bring the content of each chapter to life by including a case study in each one. These case studies are real descriptions of behaviour – sometimes true and sometimes hypothetical – which bring difficult, abstract descriptions to life and make them easier for you to engage with and understand.

Cutting-edge feature

Reading recently published articles is very important for studying psychology, in order to keep up to date with new ideas and developments in the field. But the implications and significance of recent research may not be fully understood until they have been more widely read and considered, and until the findings have been replicated by other researchers to ensure that they are reliable. As with any textbook, this one provides you with an overview of each topic area, summarising the main knowledge and understanding that has been built up over many years of research in that particular field. But we have also included a cutting-edge feature in each chapter which presents some of the latest research or contemporary thinking within the topic under discussion. These should allow you some insight into things like the directions that research in the field is taking, the advances which are being made due to new technologies, or new applications of knowledge in that field. These contemporary and relevant discussions should therefore be particularly interesting.

Themes

We have selected themes that are important within developmental psychology as a whole. Throughout the book you will find text boxes which explore each of these themes within the context of the topic of that particular chapter. These themes are research methods, nature–nurture and the lifespan.

Research methods

Research methods are a core part of psychology and underpin the ways in which we investigate human behaviour. We cannot fully understand, evaluate or critique theory or research in developmental psychology unless we consider the methods that are used to study it. Research methods are the topic of Chapter 3, but you can then further develop and build on your understanding of these through the Research Methods boxes throughout the rest of the book. These boxes may, for example, explore a particular research methodology that is commonly used within research into the topic under discussion. They may show you how an established methodology has been applied to the study of a specific area of development, or present a very new methodology and explore its contribution to our understanding of a particular aspect of development. In all of these ways, the boxes should help you to grasp the significance of research methods for the study of development.

Nature–nurture

One of the key debates in developmental psychology is about the relative influences of nature and nurture: that is, the extent to which genes and biology affect our development, and the extent to which the environment (in the form of our upbringing, culture or experiences) affects our development. The relative influences of these factors, and the ways in which they interact, is a source of great interest to developmental psychologists, and is the topic of lots of research. You may also have your own intuitive ideas about this debate. The Nature–Nurture boxes throughout the book focus on this debate within the context of the topic of each chapter. They do this by discussing how the debate has manifested itself within that topic, by exploring what different views there are about it, or by discussing what a particular piece of research has contributed to the debate. In this way, the interaction of nature and nurture is a debate which you will encounter throughout the book, enhancing your understanding of its subtleties and complexity, and helping you to recognise its significance as an issue in developmental psychology as a whole.

Lifespan

Historically, developmental psychology has focused on the study of children, on the assumption that once we reach adulthood we are pretty much fully formed human beings and that the majority of significant and important developments have already occurred. The more contemporary study of developmental psychology, however, acknowledges that in fact development continues right across the lifespan; through later childhood, adolescence, early adulthood and right up into old age. The Lifespan boxes throughout the book focus on the ways in which development continues later in life, within the context of the topic of each chapter. Whilst the vast majority of research and theory in developmental psychology is still focused on children, these boxes should enhance your understanding of the ways in which development continues after childhood, and the different issues which are pertinent in studying adult development rather than child development.

Chapter summaries

Each chapter ends with a summary which is linked to the learning outcomes that were listed at the beginning of each chapter. The learning outcomes tell you what you should be able to do by the end of the chapter, and the summary provides an overview of the main topics covered, ideas explored and research discussed relating to each learning outcome. After reading the chapter, you can use the learning outcomes to test yourself and evaluate where there might be gaps in your knowledge and understanding. The chapter summary should help to show you where to look and which topics to revisit in order to address any of the outcomes that you don't feel you have yet achieved.

Review questions

Towards the end of each chapter, you will also find a list of review questions. These are designed to read like the kinds of question you might encounter in your exams or coursework. You can use these questions to test yourself by planning how you might answer them. Try working with a fellow student and then evaluate one another's planned responses. You can also use the questions to give you practice at writing essays. Try writing an answer to one of the questions under timed conditions. Or try writing an answer which keeps within the word limit that you are going to have for your coursework. All of this should give you some sense of your strengths and weaknesses in essay writing as well as in your knowledge of the subject area. Use that information to focus your study strategies accordingly.

Web links

At the end of each chapter, you will find a list of relevant and interesting websites that you can have a look at to develop, expand and enhance your knowledge and understanding of the subject matter. Some of these are directly related to the content of the chapter. Some might let you explore the topic from a different perspective, or consider a new application of the topic. As is always the case with the World Wide Web, one website usually provides a springboard to several others. Why not see where each one takes you, and what else you can find out about the subject by yourself? Use some of the other features, like review questions and learning outcomes, to guide your web surfing, though, and ensure that you remain focused on finding information about the topic you are researching. The web links are also available from the accompanying website at: www.pearsoned.co.uk/gillibrand.

Recommended reading

At the end of each chapter is a list of suggestions for additional readings on certain topics related to the subject of the chapter. Some of these readings relate to topics which have been discussed within the main body of the chapter, and which you may be interested in learning more about. Some topics may have been outside of the scope of the chapter itself, or may not have been fully discussed due to constraints of space. The further readings allow you to take control of your own learning, and will guide you about where to look to find out more about the subjects you are most interested in.

We hope that you enjoy the book and its accompanying website, that you find the book interesting and engaging, and that it helps you to recognise developmental psychology as one of the most diverse, dynamic, relevant and fascinating areas of psychology that you will come across!

Authors and contributors

Main authors

Dr Rachel Gillibrand

Rachel Gillibrand was awarded a PhD in Developmental Psychology from the University of Southampton where her early research explored decision making in teens with a chronic condition. Since then her research has evolved to explore a range of aspects in understanding the health, relationships and risky behaviour decisions made by young people entering early adulthood. She is a Chartered Psychologist, a registered practitioner Health Psychologist and a Fellow of the Higher Education Academy. Her current post is Senior Lecturer in Psychology at the University of the West of England, where she lectures predominantly on the psychological development of a person during adolescence and adulthood.

Dr Virginia Lam

Virginia Lam was awarded a PhD in Developmental Psychology from the University of London, Goldsmiths College, where she researched children's gender and ethnic identities across primary school ages. Since then she has extended her research to involve a broader age range and areas of social cognition and development, particularly pre-schoolers, adolescents and adults' national and supranational identities, ingroup/outgroup stereotyping and attitudes, intergroup relations and peer interactions. She is a Senior Lecturer in Psychology at the University of East London and, apart from teaching developmental psychology, she runs Research Methods for the Conversion Course and leads the Equality and Diversity Committee. She is a Chartered Psychologist and Fellow of the Higher Education Academy.

Dr Victoria O'Donnell

Victoria L. O'Donnell was awarded a PhD in Psychology from the University of Stirling, and her early research explored children's developing spatial cognition. Through her interests in teaching and learning, her research has become increasingly focused on psychological aspects of learning, teaching and education, and on how these affect development and identity across the lifespan. These combined interests mean that she has held posts in several UK universities in both Psychology and Education. She is a Chartered Psychologist, Fellow of the Higher Education Academy and Fellow of the Leadership Foundation for Higher Education. She is currently the Director of Learning Innovation at the University of the West of Scotland.

Contributors

Chapter 4, Prenatal development and infancy

Professor Di Catherwood, University of Gloucestershire

Di Catherwood is Professor in Psychology and Co-manager of the Centre for Research in Applied Cognition, Knowledge, Learning and Emotion at the University of Gloucestershire. She began her research-teaching career at the University of Queensland (Brisbane), then was Director of the Centre for Applied Studies in Early Childhood (research and consultancy) at Queensland University of Technology and foundation Vice-President of the Australasian Human Development Association, before moving to the UK in 1996. Her teaching and research interests are in the areas of cognitive science and developmental cognitive science. She has conducted many studies into how the infant brain deals with visual information and more recently has been studying adult response during decision making in both natural contexts and laboratory conditions using dense-array EEG technology.

Chapter 7, The development of mathematical thinking

Professor Peter Bryant and Professor Terezinha Nunes, both at Oxford University

We are very grateful to the Nuffield Foundation, whose generous support allowed us to take the time to review the research reported in this chapter. We are also very grateful to the ESRC-TLRP research programme; our grant (# L139251015) enabled the research on rational numbers described in the chapter.

Terezinha Nunes is Professor of Education in the University of Oxford and a Fellow of Harris Manchester College. She started her career as a clinical psychologist in Brazil and moved on to research after obtaining a PhD in Psychology at City University of New York. Her research analyses how hearing and deaf children learn literacy and numeracy and considers cognitive and cultural issues. Her work on 'street mathematics' in Brazil uncovered many features of children's and adults' informal mathematical knowledge and is regarded as a classic in mathematics education. Her books include *Street Mathematics, School Mathematics*; *Teaching Mathematics to Deaf Children*; *Improving Literacy by Teaching Morphemes*; and *Children's Reading and Spelling: Beyond the First Steps*. For more information, you can visit http://www.education.ox.ac.uk/research/child-learning/.

Peter Bryant is a developmental psychologist, whose research is about children's perception and their logical understanding. He is currently a Senior Research Fellow at the Department of Education in Oxford University and was previously the Watts Professor of Psychology in the Department of Experimental Psychology at the same university. He is a Fellow of the Royal Society. He was the founding editor of the *British Journal of Developmental Psychology* and later the editor of *Cognitive Development*. His books include *Perception and Understanding in Young Children*, *Children's Reading Problems* (with Lynette Bradley), *Rhyme and Reason in Reading and Spelling* (with Lynette Bradley), *Phonological Skills and Learning to Read* (with Usha Goswami), *Improving Literacy by Teaching Morphemes* (with Terezinha Nunes), *Children Doing Mathematics* (with Terezinha Nunes) and *Children's Reading and Spelling: Beyond the First Steps* (with Terezinha Nunes).

Chapter 14, Developmental psychology and education

Malcolm Hughes, University of West of England

Malcolm Hughes is Associate Director of the International Office at the University of the West of England, Bristol, UK. After 22 years of teaching in primary and secondary schools with 11 years as a deputy headteacher and headteacher, he became a teacher-trainer. At Bristol UWE, he has been responsible for the academic leadership of the continuing professional development provision for serving teachers and for a postgraduate programme of initial teacher training. His publications to date include three higher education core texts in psychology in education, and child and adolescent development.

Chapter 15, Understanding bullying

Dr Elizabeth Nixon, Trinity College Dublin and
Dr Suzanne Guerin, University College Dublin

Elizabeth Nixon was awarded her PhD at Trinity College Dublin and is currently a lecturer in Developmental Psychology in the School of Psychology and Senior Research Fellow at the Children's Research Centre at Trinity College Dublin. Elizabeth's core research interests are in parenting, children's agency in their family contexts, and international adoption, and she is currently involved in the first National Longitudinal Study of Children in Ireland.

Suzanne Guerin completed her PhD, on the topic of bullying among children, at University College Dublin. She is currently Senior Lecturer in Research Design and

Analysis with the School of Psychology, and Deputy Director of the UCD Centre for Disability Studies, both at University College Dublin. Her research interests include applied research methods, child and family wellbeing and intellectual disability.

Chapter 16, Atypical development

Dr Shabnam Khan and Dr Emma Rowley

Shabnam Khan studied for her PhD at the University of Southampton, researching the roles of racial stereotypes in perceptions of children's behaviour problems. After a spell at the Economic and Social Research Council, Shabnam gained her Doctorate in Clinical Psychology at the University of Bristol. She has worked since then as a clinical psychologist in NHS Child and Adolescent Mental Health Services (CAMHS) in some of London's more deprived boroughs. Being compelled by the typically hidden mental health problems amongst children with social communication problems, a particular interest of Shabnam's has been working with cognitively able children who exhibit difficulties that might fall on the autism spectrum disorder spectrum. Shabnam is a keen advocate of working with children and the family and school systems around them using a range of interventions from individual support through to whole-class approaches and parenting groups. She strives to help improve the understanding and management of the children's behaviours, as well as encouraging the use of a therapeutic space for parents (and professionals) to explore their meaning. Shabnam also works in the medico-legal field as a case manager, and as an independent treating psychologist with PsychWorks Associates.

Emma Rowley read Psychology at the University of Warwick before completing her clinical doctorate in Clinical Psychology at University College, London. Having worked extensively with young children with autism and developmental disorders, her research interest is the investigation of early social cognitive development in children with autism, and the clinical application of this work via screening and early intervention. She has contributed to several large-scale research projects funded by the Medical Research Council, the Wellcome Trust and the Department of Health.

Emma now works as a Clinical Psychologist within the private sector, supporting children with developmental disability, acquired brain injury and associated cognitive and emotional difficulties and their families. Her clinical interest lies in the development of a family-centred multidisciplinary model of support and intervention, focused on identifying the child and family's unique strengths and resources, and utilising these to support development and bring about meaningful change.

Chapter 17, Attention deficit hyperactivity disorder (ADHD)

Professor David Daley, Nottingham University

David Daley graduated from the National University of Ireland, University College Cork in 1993 with a BA in Applied Psychology. He completed his PhD in Child Psychopathology in 1999 at the University of Southampton and became a Chartered Health Psychologist in 2001. He was a lecturer in Psychology at Southampton University from 1999 until 2003 where he also taught within the Medical School. From 2003 until 2010 he was Lecturer, and later Senior Lecturer, on the North Wales Clinical Psychology Programme, School of Psychology, Bangor University, Wales. He is currently Professor of Psychological Intervention and Behaviour Change in the Division of Psychiatry and Applied Psychology, School of Medicine, University of Nottingham, a member of the Institute of Mental Health, University of Nottingham, and Co-director of the International Centre for Mental Health in China, based at Shanghai Jiao Tong University, Shanghai.

Acknowledgements

Authors' acknowledgements

Dr Rachel Gillibrand

My very grateful thanks go to my husband Gavin for supporting me, for encouraging me and for always having the time to discuss this book with me. Thank you also to all my friends and my students whose enthusiasm for the book has taken us into the second edition.

Dr Virginia Lam

My thanks go to my family, friends and colleagues, who have been tremendously understanding and supportive throughout the development of both editions of this book. My special thanks go to my son, Johan, who was born during the first edition's writing, my daughter, Anja, who was born during the second edition's revision, for their inspiration and humour, and their father, Michel, for being so patient and helpful as usual, so that I could keep with this project.

Dr Victoria O'Donnell

Thanks to all of my family, friends and colleagues for their support and patience whilst this book was being written. In particular, thanks to my two beautiful daughters, Matilda and Harriet, for making every day a lesson in developmental psychology, and to my husband, Chris, for making those two girls possible in the first place.

Publisher's acknowledgements

We would like to thank the principal authors for their dedication and commitment to this project and for all the hard work they have put in over the past few years.

We are very grateful to the following reviewers for their time and helpful comments and suggestions throughout the development of the first and this second edition:

Dr Barlow Wright, Brunel University London
Dr Claire Monks, University of Greenwich
Dr Elizabeth Kirk, University of York
Dr Gayle Brewer, University of Central Lancashire
Dr Jennifer Ferrell, London Metropolitan University
Dr Emma Haycraft, Loughborough University
Dr Jessica Horst, University of Sussex
Dr Siobhan Hugh-Jones, University of Leeds
Professor Marion Kloep, University of Glamorgan
Dr Fiona MacCallum, University of Warwick
Dr Lisa Reidy, Sheffield Hallam University
Dr Dawn Watling, Royal Holloway, University of London

We are grateful to the following for permission to reproduce copyright material:

Figures

Figure 2.3 adapted from *Lifespan development*, 4th ed., Allyn & Bacon (Boyd, D. & Bee, H., 2006); Figure 4.2 from O'Donnell; Figure 4.4 from *Birth Defects*, Perinatal Education Programme (Woods, D.L., 2010) p. 101; Figure 4.8 from Biases towards internal features in infants' reasoning about objects, *Cognition*, 107(2), pp. 420–32 (Newman, G., E., Herrmann, P., Wynn, K., & Keil, F.C., 2008); Figure 4.9 from Can infants make transitive inferences?, *Cognitive Psychology*, 68, pp. 98–112 (Mou, Y., Province, J. M., & Luo, Y., 2014); Figure 5.3 adapted from The child's learning of English morphology, *Word*, 4, pp.150–77 (Berko, J. 1958); Figure 8.1 from *Autism: Explaining the Enigma*, Blackwell (Frith, U. ,1989) p.83.; Figures 8.2, 8.3 from Do 15-month-old infants understand false beliefs?, *Science*, 308, pp. 255–8

(Onishi, K. H., & Baillargeon, R., 2005), Readers may view, browse, and/or download material for temporary copying purposes only, provided these uses are for noncommercial personal purposes. Except as provided by law, this material may not be further reproduced, distributed, transmitted, modified, adapted, performed, displayed, published, or sold in whole or in part, without prior written permission from the publisher; Figure on p. 259 from *AS Level Psychology Through Diagrams*, Oxford University Press (Hill, G. 2001) p.81; Figure 10.2 from Developing mechanisms of temperamental effortful control, *Journal of Personality*, 71, pp.1113–143 (Rothbart, M. K., Ellis, L. K., Rueda, M. R., & Posner, M. I., 2003); Figure 11.1 from *The development of affect*, Plenum Publishing Corporation (Lewis, M. & Rosenblum, L. A. (eds.) 1978) pp. 205–26; Figure 11.3 adapted from Children's gender-based reasoning about toys, *Child Development*, 66, pp. 1453–71 (Martin, C. L., Eisenbud, L., & Rose, H., 1995); Figure 11.5 adapted from *The foundations of child development*, The Open University/Blackwell (1994) pp. 211–58; Figure 13.2 from Dynamic mapping of human cortical development during childhood through early adulthood, *PNAS*, 101, Figure 3, pp. 8174–9 (Gogtay, N., et. al. 2004), Copyright (2004) National Academy of Sciences, USA; Figure 14.1 from *Child Development*, 4th ed., Allyn & Bacon (Berk, L.E. 1997) p. 25, 0205198759, © 1997 Pearson Education, Inc. reproduced with permission of the author; Figure 14.2 from Student-generated questions: a meaningful aspect of learning in science, *International Journal of Science Education*, 24 (5), pp. 521–49 (Chin, C. and Brown, D., 2002); Figure 16.1 from *Down's Syndrome – An Introduction for Parents*, Souvenir Press (Cunningham, C., 1988); Figure 16.1 adapted from *From Birth to Five Years*, Routledge (Sheridan, M., 2008) p. 65; Figure 17.1 adapted from Psychological heterogeneity in AD/HD – a dual pathway model of behaviour and cognition, *Behavioural Brain Research*, 130, pp. 29–36 (Sonuga-Barke, E.J.S., 2002).

Tables

Table 2.1 adapted from *Lifespan development*, 4th ed., Allyn & Bacon (Boyd, D. & Bee, H., 2006) © 2006. Reprinted and Electronically reproduced by permission of Pearson Education, Inc., New York, New York; Table 5.1 adapted from Infant vocalisation: A comprehensive view, *Infant Mental Health Journal*, 2(2), pp. 118–28 (Stark, R. E. 1981), Reproduced with permission of Wiley; Table 9.3 adapted from Cross-cultural patterns of attachment: A meta-analysis of the strange situation, *Child Development*, 59, pp. 147–56 (Van Ijzendoorn, M.H., & Kroonenberg, P.M., 1988); Table 10.3 from *Temperament: Early Developing Personality Traits*, Lawrence Erlbaum (Buss, A. H., & Plomin, R., 1984) p. 123, 9781138816640; Table 10.5 from Investigations of temperament at three to seven years: The children's behavior questionnaire, *Child Development*, 72, pp. 13941408 (Rothbart, M. K., Ahadi, S. A., Hershey, L. L., & Fisher, P., 2001); Table 11.3 adapted from *Handbook of socialization theory and research*, Rand McNally (Goslin, D.A (ed.) 1969) pp. 347–80; Table 15.5 from *'Peer Harassment in School. The Plight of the Vulnerable and Victimized'* Guilford Press (Juvonen, J. & Graham, S. (eds.) 2001) pp. 398–419; Table 16.2 from *Compulsory age of starting school in European countries*, National Foundation for Educational Research (Eurydice at NFER 2013) http://www.nfer.ac.uk/nfer/index.cfm?9B1C0068-C29E-AD4D-0AEC-8B4F43F54A28; Table 16.7 from Autism, *Lancet*, 374, pp. 1627–38 (Levy, S. E., Mandell, D. S., & Schultz, R. T., 2009).

Text

Newspaper headline on p. 443 from Merseyside schoolchildren as young as nine bullying each other on an unprecedented scale, *Liverpool Echo*, 02/03/2014; newspaper headline on p. 443 from Campaign aims to combat bullying, *Marlborough Express*, 04/03/2014, Fairfax Media NZ/Marlborough Press; Newspaper Headline on p. 443 from Cyberbullying poses greater risk of suicide among young people, study suggests, *Globe and Mail*, 11/03/2014, Copyright 2014 The Globe and Mail Inc. All Rights Reserved; newspaper headline on p. 443 from District struggles to develop policy for handling bullying *Palo Alto Online*, 13/06/2014; Case study on p. 521 adapted from Case study: ADHD medication can be tough, but it works, *The Times*, 24/09/2008.

Photographs

The publisher would like to thank the following for their kind permission to reproduce their photographs:
(Key: b – bottom; c – centre; l – left; r – right; t – top)

3 Dr Virginia Lam. 5 Alamy Images: AfriPics.com (tl). 8 Dr Virginia Lam. 9 Helen Bartlett. 15 Dr Virginia Lam. 23 Pearson Education Ltd: Gareth Boden. 25 Science Photo Library Ltd. 34 Courtesy of Albert Bandura: Stanford University. 37 Corbis: Jim Craigmyle. 53 Pearson Education Ltd. 57 Alamy Images: Photofusion Picture Library. 63 Pearson Education Ltd. 63 Getty Images: Olivier Morin/AFP (b). 77 Victoria L. O'Donnell. 90 Teri Pengilley. 116 Helen Bartlett: (tr). Comstock Images: (bl). 118 Victoria L.

ACKNOWLEDGEMENTS

O'Donnell. 120 Victoria L. O'Donnell. 149 Alamy Images. 154 Alamy Images: Picture Partners. 159 Victoria L. O'Donnell. 166 Victoria L. O'Donnell. 176 Shutterstock.com: chrisbrignell. 179 Pearson Education Ltd. 182 Pearson Education Ltd. 187 Pearson Education Ltd. 188 Dr Virginia Lam. 190 Fotolia.com. 199 Pearson Education Ltd: Jules Selmes. 206 Pearson Education Ltd: Jules Selmes. 210 Professor Terezinha Nunes 211 Professor Terezinha Nunes. 223 Corbis Patrick Kociniak/Design Pics. 225 Getty Images: Dorling Kindersley. 237 Getty Images: Blend Images LLC. 240 Helen Bartlett. 249 Pearson Education Ltd: Lisa Payne Photography (tl). 250 Dr Virginia Lam (r). Victoria L. O'Donnell (l). 257 Rex Shutterstock: Rex Features/Steve Back/Daily Mail. 268 Dr Virginia Lam. 270 Pearson Education Ltd: Studio 8 (tl). 273 Dr Virginia Lam. 281 Victoria L. O'Donnell. 287 Shutterstock.com: 2xSamara.com. 294 Brand X Pictures. 303 Corbis: Tom Stewart. 320 Dr Virginia Lam. 325 Dr Virginia Lam. 329 Dr Virginia Lam. 337 Dr Virginia Lam. 339 Dr Virginia Lam. 349 Dr Virginia Lam. 353 Alamy Images: ClassicStock. 360 Pearson Education Ltd: Photodisc/Ryan McVay. 365 Bubbles Photolibrary: Loisjoy Thurston. 381 Alamy Images: Pictorial Press Ltd. 388 Pearson Education Ltd: Studio 8. 396 Pearson Education Ltd: Tudor Photography (tr). 410 Shutterstock.com: Suzanne Tucker. 414 Pearson Education Ltd: Jules Selmes. 417 Pearson Education Ltd: Robert Harding/Bananastock. 422 Dr Virginia Lam. 424 123RF.com: stockbroker. 428 Shutterstock.com: michaeljung. 431 Shutterstock.com: Captain Petolea. 434 Shutterstock.com: racorn. 445 Pearson Education Ltd: Tudor Photography. 448 123RF.com: Ion Chiosea. 457 Fotolia.com. 458 Shutterstock.com: 2xSamara.com (tr). 462 Pearson Education Ltd: Tudor Photography. 485 Photolibrary.com. 490 Dr Virginia Lam. 492 Pearson Education Ltd: Jules Selmes. 512 Pearson Education Ltd: Jules Selmes. 516 Getty Images. 522 Getty Images: Martin Hospach. 525 Corbis: Westend61. 527 Pearson Education Ltd: Studio 8 (r). Shutterstock.com: Dmitry Kalinovsky (l). 529 Pearson Education Ltd: Jules Selmes. 534 Getty Images: Geri Lavrov.

All other images © Pearson Education

Section I
Introduction to developmental psychology

Chapter 1
What is developmental psychology?

Learning outcomes

After reading this chapter, and with further recommended reading, you should be able to:

1. Understand the history of developmental psychology.
2. Critically evaluate both the early and modern theories of developmental psychology.
3. Critically evaluate the role of developmental psychology in understanding and describing the nature of development in the child.

Introduction

When parents look proudly down at their new-born infant, many thoughts will cross their minds. What do we do now? How do we look after our baby? How will we know if we are doing this right? But once the parents settle into caring for their baby, it is likely that they will start to wonder what this child will be like and even who this child will be when he or she grows up. Developmental psychology is the branch of psychology that tries to understand how a child grows and develops, and how the role of the family and schooling can impact on this. It looks at how our behaviour, our thinking patterns, our emotions and our personalities begin and change from birth to adulthood.

Developmental psychologists are interested in all aspects of our behavioural and psychological development. We are interested in the *social* development of a child: from trying to understand the complexity of the relationship between a new-born infant and parent to the role of play in developing long-lasting friendships. We are interested in the *cognitive* development of the child: the development of language; understanding numbers; and developing an appreciation for art and poetry. We are interested too in *emotional* development and the way we make decisions and the role of parents and friends in developing our sense of morality and teenage decision making: careers, friendships, sexuality and risk taking. Developmental psychology ties together social, emotional and cognitive development through the study of the growing child. It is a wide-reaching branch of psychology and for that reason is, in our point of view, one of the most rewarding to study.

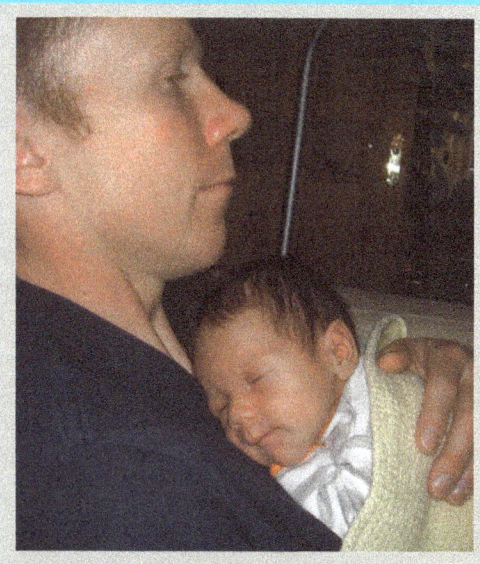

Parent holding a new-born
Source: Lam

This chapter will introduce you to both the traditional theorists and modern developmental psychologists. To help you understand the theories that are presented in this book, we will first discuss the key philosophical debates of developmental psychology and see how they have influenced the thinking of modern psychologists.

The debates of developmental psychology

Nature versus nurture

> Give me a dozen healthy infants, well-formed, and my own specified world to bring them up in and I'll guarantee to take any one at random and train him to become any type of specialist I might select – doctor, lawyer, artist – regardless of his talents, penchants, tendencies, abilities, vocations and race of his ancestors.
>
> J. B. Watson (1930), p. 104

One of the key debates in developmental psychology is that of nature versus nurture. The basic tenet of this debate is centred on whether the child is born with capacities and abilities that develop naturally over time regardless of up-bringing, or whether the child needs social interaction and society in order to shape them. Nature and nurture boxes appear in every chapter of this book, illustrating how important this debate is in developmental psychology. Look in Chapter 11, for instance, where the Baby X experiments are discussed, showing us how the adults react towards a baby wearing pink clothes and how these compare with the reactions of adults to a baby wearing blue clothes. Or for a different type of study, in Chapter 6 there is discussion of the results of twin studies in the study of intelligence. Is our intelligence affected more by our biology or by our upbringing? The question of whether we are born as social, functioning beings or whether our mind and behaviour are shaped by our interactions has long been a question for philosophers and psychologists alike.

In early literary history, little evidence remains of any research conducted into the experience of childhood as a specific period of human development. Historian Aries (1960) researched the view of childhood through the limited texts and paintings surviving from the medieval period and, based on the evidence presented there, supposed that early scientists, artists and thinkers represented children as mini-adults. Medieval portraiture of children often gives them an adult face on a small, not particularly childish, body and shows the child dressed in a miniature version of adult clothes. Texts and stories of the time reveal that children were present in all the adult places, including working in the fields and accompanying adults in bars and taverns. Although the evidence is limited from this period, it does appear to show that some children were taking a place in the adult world from the age of 6 or 7 years and all children by the age of 12 years (Shahar, 1990).

The period of Enlightenment (the late 1600s to early 1800s) brought forward great thinkers and scientists who challenged this way of thinking, and key figures such as Locke and Rousseau were enormously influential in changing our understanding of the process of learning and acquiring knowledge. Locke's writings in particular helped lay the foundations of our modern education system and set the tone of our judicial system. In order to begin to understand the complexities of the nature versus nurture debate, let us first take a look at the key principles of these philosophers and see how they have shaped our way of thinking in the new millennium.

John Locke (1632–1704)

The writings of the British philosopher John Locke described the influence of society on a person and were instrumental in the development of law and government in European society. His essay *Concerning Human Understanding* (1690) is key to the nature vs nurture debate and to understanding the principles of developmental psychology. Locke was an empiricist (someone who relies on observation and experimentation to determine the truth about something). He believed in the scientific methods of observation and systematic experimentation in finding truth and knowledge. He wrote of the *tabula rasa* – the soft or blank tablet of the mind – and applied this concept to the child. He viewed children as being born essentially as a 'blank canvas', and only through social interaction does the child learn to speak, learn emotions and morals, and learn to exist within a society that ultimately has been created for the safe keeping of its inhabitants. Is this concept, however, rather simplistic when considering the development of a child? Compare Locke's philosophy with that of Rousseau.

Definitions

Nature: the role of genetics in forming our behaviour, our personality or any other part of ourselves.
Nurture: the role of family, society, education and other social factors in forming our behaviour, our personality or any other part of ourselves.

THE DEBATES OF DEVELOPMENTAL PSYCHOLOGY

Jean-Jacques Rousseau (1712–78)

The philosopher Rousseau was keenly influenced by John Locke and closely studied his texts on the humanisation and understanding of society. Rousseau agreed with Locke that social norms and values were a strong factor in creating a person through experiences and contact with others. However, where Rousseau and Locke differed was in their vision of the new-born infant and the nature of the society he or she was born into. Locke believed the infant to be a 'clean slate' to be manipulated into a form acceptable to society. He saw value and integrity in the spirit of society. Rousseau, however, saw the role of society from a different perspective and coined the term the 'noble savage' to describe the innocent, good child who becomes corrupted by society and all that is wrong within it. For Rousseau, society was an insincere and crooked place that was harmful to children, who by sheer luck of birth he considered were almost angelic in nature.

> **STOP AND THINK**
>
> What do these early philosophers and theorists have to contribute to our understanding of the child in modern society?

Rousseau's 'noble savage'?

Source: Alamy Images/AfriPics.com

To understand the application of early philosophers to our perception of early childhood, we need to evaluate the contribution each had to the changing role of children in society. Locke believed that society tames, creates and nurtures the infant whereas Rousseau declared that the infant is corrupted by the sins and deviances of a ruthless society. Consequently, we have in place the seeds of the nature versus nurture debate. Are we born with our capabilities, knowledge, morals and values or does society shape, cultivate and support our infant into a full member of humanity? To attempt to answer this question we will look at one of the findings of the *Minnesota twin study* – a large-scale study of over 8000 twins that was begun in the early 1980s.

In 1981, Thomas Bouchard as a researcher connected with the Minnesota twin study began a study comparing the experiences of genetically identical twins raised by different parents. Theoretically, if Locke or Rousseau is correct, then twins should show considerable differences throughout their lifespan if they have been raised in different environments. The outcome of the Minnesota twin study provided evidence of slightly different outcomes for the twins, but mostly of considerable similarities in the temperaments, educational and career choices and even relationship patterns in the separated twins. Bouchard argued that this study provided evidence for the importance of genetics in determining behaviour, and his paper published later (Bouchard et al., 1990) confirmed his initial findings. This report of long-term findings on the 100 sets of twins who had been raised by different parents showed a consistent effect. Essentially, there was no significant difference in twins raised apart and twins raised together on measures of personality and temperament, occupational and leisure-time interests and social attitudes. If you look at the findings of the twin studies reported by Plomin and DeFries (1980) (see Chapter 6), you will see that Bouchard's findings are mirrored in the results on intelligence mapping across twins and other siblings.

Bouchard's conclusion was criticised for relying too heavily on the assumption that genetics were responsible for the twins' similarities in temperament, career paths and relationship choices (Joseph, 2001). Joseph argued that the twins who took part in the study were motivated by a sense of sameness and similarity, and that this bias influenced the reporting by the twins of their childhood experiences and life outcomes. Bouchard did not, however, disagree on this point and argued in the

1990 paper that the very nature of the twins' temperament could influence the environment they were raised in. For instance, Bouchard noted that twins who were considered fairly calm and easy-going as children would be more likely to report experiencing a calm and easy-going childhood, regardless of whether they were raised together or apart (Bouchard et al., 1990).

What, therefore, does this tell us about the argument of nature versus nurture? Bouchard's work appears to demonstrate that the two cannot be meaningfully separated and distinguished in research of this kind. Perhaps the nature versus nurture debate is an academic one that has little application in real-life settings. How can we truly distinguish our very own nature if it is defined by genetics, by our social environment, our upbringing and our responsiveness to events happening around us?

The twenty-first-century debate: nature versus nurture – is there another way?

In the twenty-first century, most psychologists have decided that neither nature nor nurture on its own is likely to be fully accountable for the physical, emotional and cognitive development of the child. Although some theorists may cling more tightly to one side or the other of the nature versus nurture debate, most will concede that it is likely that there is an interaction between the two that can be identified as a point on a *continuum*. Figure 1.1 represents the connection between the influence of *nature* and the influence of *nurture* on an aspect of behaviour.

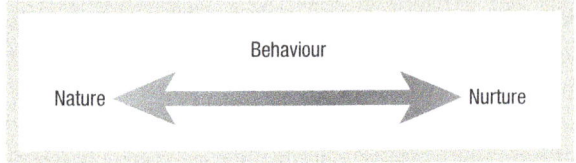

Figure 1.1 The nature–nurture continuum.

If the behaviour is 'walking', then we might represent the prominence of *nature* over *nurture* by marking the connecting line with an 'X' nearer the *nature* end of the continuum (Figure 1.2). Learning to walk requires a certain amount of physical development, but the propensity to walk present at birth combined with parental encouragement to walk is more significant in encouraging a child to walk than parental encouragement alone. Thus at the point of learning to walk, the influence of the

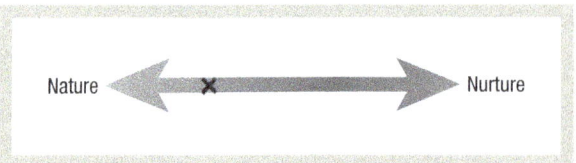

Figure 1.2 The nature–nurture continuum: *nature* is the dominant force.

natural skills a child is born with and develops is more influential than the simple *nurturing* of the parents.

Compare this to a more complex example of a young boy learning to socialise with other children and engage in play with them on his first day at preschool. In Chapter 12, the tendency to form peer groups is discussed from the perspective of the nature versus nurture debate. The author Steven Pinker in his book *The Blank Slate* (2002) proposes that our genetic make-up influences most the social groups that we form, whilst Judith Harris in her book *The Nurture Assumption* (1998) proposes that it is the peer group that is key in shaping the child's behaviour. Both authors write convincingly of their beliefs and the complexity of the behaviour. So, in this instance, Pinker might place a mark on the nature–nurture continuum towards the nature end (Figure 1.2), whilst Harris might place the mark on the continuum at the nurture end (see Figure 1.3).

Figure 1.3 The nature–nurture continuum: *nurture* is the dominant force.

The use of the arrow continuum is a simplistic way of looking at the current nature versus nurture debate, but using it to try and unpick the debate between Pinker and Harris does reveal some of the complexity of the issues at hand. When considering the role of nature and nurture in developmental psychology, we need to consider many factors: the age of the child; the biological stage or physical development; the behaviour under investigation; the social situation; and the cognitive powers present or needed in order to achieve the phenomenon under investigation. If we think again about our young boy who is standing apart from the game on his first day at preschool, can we understand his behaviour using the arrow continuum or do we need to ask further questions? Is he old enough to play with the other children, for example? Is he strong enough or tall enough to take part in the game? What is the game and could he take part? Does he know the children playing the game? Can he understand the rules of the game? In answering these questions, you may be able to come to a conclusion on the reason why the little boy is not taking part. Is it more to do with nature (not old enough, strong enough or tall enough) or is it more to do with nurture (does not know the rules of the game, is unsure how to take part, is lacking in confidence)?

The importance of early experiences

How important are your early childhood experiences in shaping the person you are in adulthood? Much of developmental psychology deals with what we can and cannot do at different times in our lives. Look at Chapter 9 on attachment and early social experiences. Some of the most discussed topics raised in the field of developmental psychology investigate questions about the importance of early experiences (Ainsworth et al., 1978). What will our adult love relationships be like if we had a close relationship to our mothers as children? How would our adult relationships be different if we had been raised without a mother; perhaps if we had been raised in institutional care? How important is that early relationship between a mother and her child in shaping who we are as adults? Equally as important, can the effects of that early relationship be changed once we reach adulthood?

One of the key factors in the argument about the importance of early experiences is whether we continue to develop socially, emotionally and cognitively into adulthood or whether we are essentially fully formed during early childhood. Although the study of developmental psychology focuses on childhood as the most important time of development, there is also a growing recognition of the nature of adulthood as a period of continuing change and development. When you read the next chapter on theoretical perspectives you will see that Jean Piaget (1952b), for instance, created a theory of cognitive development that covered the period from birth to around the late teenage years; yet Erikson, who was highly influenced by Piaget's work, argued that our psychosocial development extends from birth right through to late adulthood. Although their theories extend through different periods of our lives, both Piaget and Erikson believed that in early infancy the child learns key skills that provide the building blocks for later life. Throughout this book you will see that we begin our chapters with a discussion of what these foundation skills are, such as forming an attachment to a carer (Chapter 9), learning to make sounds (Chapter 5) or grasping wooden blocks (Chapter 4), and then we move on to show how these skills evolve. Each chapter demonstrates that skills learned in childhood are steadily built into, for example, complex attachments to friends and lovers, learning one or more languages and building play or even real houses.

Thus, early experiences in developmental psychology are considered important in moulding who we are as children and in helping us to understand who we are as adults, but it is also important for developmental psychologists to know how critical the experiences of the early years are. Watson's proposition quoted earlier that he could train any infant into any man is perhaps one of the core drivers of developmental psychology: is the child who is shaped by his early experiences a child who will continue to grow emotionally and psychologically through the teenage years and into adulthood, or are we fully formed and our personalities unchangeable by the time we go to school?

STOP AND THINK

- Are you a product of your early experiences or are you continuing to change and grow as an adult?
- What are the implications of your answer when trying to understand what type of parent you are/will be?
- Can you change who you are?

Stage theories of development

You may have noticed that parents often talk about their child as in the 'babbling' stage or the 'crawling' stage. Much of what you will also read in developmental

Definition

Attachment: a strong, enduring, affectionate bond an infant shares with a significant individual, usually the mother, who knows and responds well to the infant's needs.

psychology books talks about stages, so what does that mean? Throughout this book we describe a number of stage theories in detail, but whether we are talking about language, play or identity development, most stage theories are the same in that they break down the acquisition of a skill into age-related blocks of activity. Each of these blocks follows the same pattern. First, at a defined age, the child enters into the 'developmental stage': for example, in Chapter 5 we describe a staged process for how infants start to form sounds. At the beginning of the stage, the child cannot do the task that is described – she is perhaps making crying or cooing noises but not yet making clear letter or word sounds. When a child is in the middle of the stage, the child is picking up skills, learning to say 'ma', for instance, and developing her ability to make distinct sounds. After a period of time, the child leaves that developmental stage when she is fully competent and is ready to move on to the next stage, forming full word sounds and learning to put two or more words together.

Another behaviour that has been described as following a staged development is play (see Chapter 9). Developmental psychologist Mildred Parten (1932) described a theory of play that suggested that at the age of 2, children engage in something called *parallel play*. This is when children play beside each other but not with each other. They might use the same toys, but the children do not interact with each other and are not working together to achieve a goal. Compare this to the *cooperative play* that she saw in children aged 3 years and over, when children engage in formal games. Here children play together rather than side by side and the games have rules and boundaries. They may involve role-playing social roles (such as playing 'mummies and daddies' or 'doctor and patient') and can develop into quite complex games. This type of play is more complex than parallel play, as it involves effective communication and cooperation rarely seen before the child is 3 years of age. In this example of a stage theory, other aspects of their psychological development also determine the type of play shown by a child: the degree of language skill (so that they can convey the meaning of the game to each other), memory (so that they can remember who is who in the game and what the purpose of the game is) and an understanding of what other people do (so that 'mummies' and 'daddies' are doing the 'right things' and everyone knows who is who in the game).

Throughout this book you will see plenty of evidence supporting stage theories explaining child development. You will also see how different the rate of development can be between children. With our example of play, you have a case where certain play styles are more prominent at certain ages because of the needs for other cognitive skills to be sufficiently developed. Without the ability to communicate and remember complex game patterns, the child will be unable to engage in that game. However, if you were to observe children at play, you would see that in fact more than one style of play is taking place in a school playground. Some younger children will be playing complex games more suited to their older counterparts and some older children will be playing very simple games, better suited to the younger children.

Does this mean, then, that the different play styles do *not* follow a stage theory? Take the experience of the only child in the family and compare his play style to that of a child with many siblings. Children with older siblings often display play styles more advanced than their peers because the older siblings have taught

Definition

Stage theories: theories based on the idea that we progress through a pattern of distinct stages over time. These stages are defined by the acquisition or presence of abilities and we generally pass through them in a specified order and during a specified age range.

Role play is an important part of a child's development.
Source: Lam

them these more complex games. Stage theories generally do not account for the impact older siblings may have, for instance, on a child's play style or even their language development. Stage theories too are often seen as inflexible and uni-directional. Piaget's theory of cognitive development (Piaget, 1932) (see Chapter 2), for instance, suggests that children progress in a linear fashion through increasingly complex stages of cognitive skills. But if you look at Chapter 16, describing culture and developmental 'norms' in child development, you will see a very different story of development being told. Piaget's theory describes child development as a series of stages in which there are many phases. Each phase is characterised by the acquisition of ability – physical or mental – and only through successful completion of this phase can there be progression to the next. Piaget does not appear to make allowance for the developing child to return to a stage, or even to miss a stage out and jump to the next. Thus there is a certain rigidity to Piaget's theory that does not always reflect the individual experience of a child. However, for many psychologists, stage theories have endured as useful and often remarkably robust tools for understanding the child's social, psychological and behavioural development.

Continuous versus discontinuous development

Some developmental psychologists see children's development as a continuous process of change where the child becomes steadily more skilled at what they are doing, whilst others see children's development as a discontinuous process of change, where the child becomes skilled in a series of leaps and bounds separated by periods of calm and little change.

The stage theorists tend to hold the view that development is a discontinuous process of change. Piaget and other theorists saw children of different ages as being qualitatively different: that is, that there is a significant, remarkable difference in how the older children think and appear to make sense of the world. For example, Piaget noted that younger children were not able to complete certain tasks that an older child could, and would, with ease. Piaget demonstrated this with the *conservation of liquid* task (see Chapter 7). An experimenter has two identically shaped flasks of coloured water. She pours one into a tall, thin flask and asks the child: which has the most water in it? The 4-year-old will probably reply that the taller, thinner flask contains more water. The 6-year-old, on the other hand, will probably reply (correctly) that both flasks contain the same amount of water. Although both children see the water being poured from identical short flasks, only the 6-year-old knows that, even though the one flask looks taller, it still contains the same amount of water.

STOP AND THINK

What other tasks might you design to demonstrate discontinuous development in a child?

Piaget's work has been extremely influential and, in particular, the conservation of liquid task is still carried out to test children's level of thinking. However, recent research has shown that most of child development

Which flask has more liquid in it?
Source: Bartlett

Definitions

Continuous development: change that occurs at a steady pace, perhaps showing a constant, consistent improvement or growth.
Discontinuous development: change that occurs in what appear to be great bursts of achievement following a period of steady consolidation of perhaps knowledge or skill.

appears not to follow a discontinuous route but rather a continuous process of change. The work of modern developmental psychologists such as Dr Linda Smith at the Indiana University Cognitive Development Laboratory has revealed that, although most development occurs methodically, skill by skill, many children show discontinuous development – they develop faster in one skill than in another, resulting in asynchronous development (Fischer and Bidell, 2006).

So, which way of addressing child development is correct? Should we be striving to find clearly defined continuous stages in behaviour that we can tie to age ranges in our theories, or should we be looking at behaviour as a discontinuous learning process that progresses sometimes quickly, sometimes slowly, through childhood? The chapters in this book will help you to make up your mind. For some behaviours and skills, the stage theories work very well in helping us to understand those particular aspects of child development. For other skills, however, the stage theories do not work so well and we will consider the role of other development theories in understanding a child's behaviour. To help you evaluate the contribution a theory makes to our understanding of child development, we have produced a 'checklist' of six criteria that you should consider. Remember, a theory is never true or false, but can be considered to provide either a 'good' or a 'poor' contribution to our understanding of human behaviour.

How good is your theory?

1. *Is the theory specific to a particular behaviour or is it more generally applicable?*

   For example, a researcher wants to know whether a child knows right from wrong. Consider the theories that you might want to apply to answering this question. You could start with Piaget's theory of cognitive development. How might you use Piaget's theory to support your argument? Is Piaget's theory a general theory of cognitive development or a specific theory of moral decision making? Would Kohlberg's theory of moral development be more appropriate?

2. *Is the theory appropriate for use?*

   Find the original source of the theory – usually a paper has been written and presented in a peer-reviewed, academic journal. Is there evidence of a strong consideration of the rationale for the theory? Does it seem to have a strong evidence base? Have the theorists given sufficient thought to the strengths and weaknesses of other people's theories when developing their own?

3. *Is the theory useful? Can it be tested?*

   There should be enough detail in the theory so that you could set up a study that would allow you to test the application of the theory on a group of participants of your choice.

4. *Is the theory valid?*

   Does the theory make predictions? If so, can you work out how you might obtain the outcomes it predicts? If you were to conduct your study following the theory, would you get the same findings as the authors? Conversely, if you conduct your study and your findings are not the same as the authors' findings, can you argue that the theory is then false?

5. *Is the theory 'parsimonious'?*

   Is the theory overly complicated or does it represent the simplest (parsimonious) explanation of the behaviour or concept? If a theory comes together with a certain element of elegance, it may generally be the case that the theory has touched on the key or fundamental elements underpinning the concept and therefore has considerable 'goodness of fit'. If the theory feels complex and unwieldy, then you may want to see if it is 'missing the point' and argue that it would benefit from a reconsideration or restructuring of the key elements.

6. *Does the theory fit alongside other psychological theories?*

   Theories, like people, should not exist solely in isolation. A strong theory should be connected to other theories relating to behaviour, development or other psychological principles and you should be able to demonstrate this connection. For instance, Kohlberg's theory of moral development is strongly influenced by Piaget's theory of cognitive development and Erikson's theory of psychosocial development.

Definition

Asynchronous development: the situation that arises when a child is performing at a more advanced stage in one developmental skill and a less advanced stage in a second developmental skill: for example, the child may be performing well in Piaget's conservation of liquid task but less well in Kohlberg's Heinz dilemma task (see Chapter 13) measuring moral development (Kohlberg, 1976).

What is 'typical' development?

The final debate we are going to consider in this chapter concerns why we are interested in what 'typical' development is and how we can use this information as psychologists. Let us return to the stage theories of child development as an example. As we have briefly discussed, some behaviours fall neatly into stage theories and other behaviours do not. What we have not discussed yet is the *value* of a stage theory in describing child development. If our child develops behaviours and skills that align to a particular stage in a theory, do we say that our child is developing 'typically'? Perhaps, more importantly, if our child does *not* develop behaviours and skills in accordance to a particular stage in a theory, do we say that our child is developing 'atypically'?

In this book we have asked experts to write four applied developmental psychology chapters. These chapters cover a range of topics that you may encounter as a practising psychologist: developmental psychology and education, understanding bullying, atypical development and attention deficit and hyperactivity disorder. In each of these chapters you will find many examples of child development that may reflect either 'atypical' development or 'individual differences' in development. The authors look at whether it is possible to make a judgement on whether the child is unable to accomplish the task or whether the child will in time mature in his capabilities and 'catch up' with the other children in his class. In other chapters, such as Chapter 6 on memory and intelligence, you will see how mathematicians and psychologists have spent a lot of time creating measurement tools to see whether the child is developing normally or not. For instance, for decades now scientists have been using and modifying scales for measuring intelligence (such as the Intelligence Quotient scale) in a bid to find out what level of cognitive skills are present in most of the population at different years of age. By defining what tasks most children can do, at say age 7 years, researchers can say what is 'typically' achieved by children of age 7 years. The researchers can then also say, therefore, that a child with a level of cognitive skill above the 'norm' is achieving beyond her years and that a child with a level of cognitive skill below the 'norm' is not achieving well for her years. If used appropriately, knowing this information can help teachers provide higher-level work to the high-performing child and more support and help to the lesser-performing child. For more discussion on the range of methods developmental psychologists use to describe and measure behaviour, keep reading. In Chapter 3 we present a detailed view of how we develop and design research methods that help us measure and understand the developing child.

RECOMMENDED READING

For a critical review of modern developmental psychology:
Burman, E. (2007). *Deconstructing Developmental Psychology*. London: Routledge.

RECOMMENDED WEBSITES

The developmental section of the British Psychological Society has news and events relating to developmental psychology:

www.bps.org.uk/dps

The European Association for Developmental Psychology also has news and events relating to developmental psychology and useful resources:

www.eadp.info

Chapter 2
Theoretical perspectives

Learning outcomes

After reading this chapter, and with further recommended reading, you should be able to:

1. Critically discuss what makes a theory.
2. Evaluate the key theoretical perspectives in developmental psychology.
3. Understand the philosophical perspectives underlying key developmental psychology theories.
4. Critically evaluate the use and application of theories and perspectives in understanding real-life examples of human behaviour from a developmental perspective.

How do we know what is the 'right' way to raise a child?

Any trip into the parenting and family section of a bookshop will reveal shelves upon shelves of books telling parents what to expect during pregnancy, what to expect following the birth, how to raise a child and how to get the best from their child. New parents often receive well-meant advice from doctors, other mothers and their own families on looking after their baby: how to get him to sleep, how much she should be eating and how often, whether they should let them cry or respond to their every need. Later on, parents are often given more advice – 'read to your child every night, he should know his numbers and letters before going to school' or 'you should let your child play – there's plenty of time for her to learn to read when she goes to school'. Every week there seem to be stories in the newspapers and magazines about this or that innovation in child rearing and tips for raising a 'happy' child. It is not surprising parents often talk about being overwhelmed with information on raising their child and feeling confused about doing what is 'right'.

- Do you think you can learn to be a parent or is parenting a natural skill that comes with having a child?
- Can psychology help us to be better parents or do the day-to-day realities of parenting make it difficult to make time to change the way we do things?

Introduction

Developmental psychologists and scientists have spent decades trying to find the answers to these difficult questions. Some have made their careers observing children grow and learn, and have created developmental stage theories that describe what is 'typical' to achieve at certain ages. Some of the researchers describe the abilities that the child seems to be born with, some look at the role society has in teaching a child abilities and skills, whilst others take a combined approach and integrate what we seem to be born with and how society shapes our development over time. In this chapter, we will discuss the role of these theorists in shaping our understanding of human development. We will look in detail at the theories devised by key researchers in the field of developmental psychology and seek to understand how to relate these theories to our real-life experiences of growing up. We will then conclude this chapter by discussing the role of these theories in understanding how we develop as children and adults, and how as psychologists we might apply these theories to investigating patterns of behaviour. Throughout this chapter, we will illustrate the main points with examples of the application of theory in the real world. There will also be a few quick questions along the way to ensure that you have understood the material. This chapter will help form the foundation of your study of developmental psychology, so when you are reading the other chapters, do return to this one if you need reminding of the detail of the different approaches.

What is a theory?

A *theory* is a statement that we use to understand the world about us. We can use theories to understand why fire heats water, why people vote for particular politicians and how children learn language. A good theory begins by *describing* or *defining* the focus of the theory. In psychology it is invariably a behaviour that we are interested in. So a theory seeking to understand the way a child learns language must first define what language is. Defining the behaviour at the focus of the theory is very important. Without a good description of the behaviour we are unable to develop a good theory.

Next a theory must seek to *explain* the behaviour. Why does the child learn language in the way they do? Is it due to a biological facility in the brain or is it due to the mother talking to the child, an impact of the social environment? Look at the section on the four components of language in Chapter 5 on language development. Can each of these only be explained by biological processes or social environmental processes or is there a combination of factors at work? You will see that some theorists prefer the biological argument in understanding behaviour and some theorists prefer the social environment argument in understanding behaviour. Other theorists prefer a combination of biology and environment in understanding human behaviour.

As you study psychology, you will form an idea of which theoretical angle you align to. Often it depends on the aspect of human behaviour you study: for example, in Chapter 9 on attachment and early social experiences, you will see that the bond between a mother and child has both biological aspects and social influences. However, if you look at the theories of memory development in Chapter 6, you will see that memory has more predominantly biological influences. The choice of which theory or theoretical perspective you prefer should always be the result of a critical appraisal of the strengths and weaknesses of the theory in describing and explaining the behaviour. This appraisal process is typically centred on the ability of the theory to *predict* behaviour. Does a social learning theory explain the development of language in children raised in isolation? Does a biological theory of learning explain the ability to write poetry?

Theories are useful tools for structuring our understanding of human behaviour, but take note, theories are not necessarily exact statements – they tend to be useful for understanding a situation *most* of the time, but particularly when we are trying to understand *human* behaviour there always seem to be situations when the theory does not quite fit. This does not mean that the theory has no value or use, but often means that the human behaviour is more complex than initially thought. Many psychological theories are constantly under review – look at a selection of journals in your library to see evidence of this review process and the often lively debate surrounding it.

> **STOP AND THINK**
>
> Why do we want psychological theories not only to describe theories but to have a predictive quality too?

Theoretical perspectives

Stage versus continuous theories

The majority of theories of child development can be conceptualised as being either stage theories or theories of continuous change.

Stage theories

Stage theories tend to map out the development of competency in a pattern of behaviour that has been devised from the observation of behaviour and the calculation of what most children can do and at what age. An example

> **Definitions**
>
> Theory: a statement that we use to understand the world about us with three important component parts: it defines, explains and predicts behaviour.
> Stage theories: theories based on the idea that we progress through a pattern of distinct stages over time. These stages are defined by the acquisition or presence of abilities and we generally pass through them in a specified order and during a specified age range.

of a stage theory is Piaget's theory of cognitive development (Piaget, 1952b, 1962), described in full later in this chapter. In this theory, Piaget describes in detail what a child should be able to do at 3 months of age, 6 months, 12 months and so on. Piaget's theory evolved from observing children of all ages at play and in other interactions with each other and with their environment. He was interested in developing a statement of what was 'typical' behaviour in a child and how you could use this information to assess possible developmental delay.

There are a number of stage theories in developmental psychology but all stage theories have a number of common elements. First, the stages are precisely defined and describe very specific abilities. They may describe the ability of a child to say the letter 'b' or they may describe the young person's ability to consider the outcome of a hypothetical question, but either way, both theories will clearly define the skill being acquired. Second, the theories assume that the child enters the stage unable to accomplish the task, develops competency over a period of time and then usually is considered to have completed that stage when they demonstrate an easy familiarity with that skill or task. Third, there is an assumption that every stage will be completed in the order presented in the theory. There is no jumping ahead to a stage much later in the theory and there is no omission of a stage. Finally, there is a strong belief that every child will progress through the stages within the age ranges described in the theory.

The strengths of stage theories in developmental psychology lie in their ability to describe in detail the development of a behaviour according to age-specific 'norms'. From the psychological perspective, it is useful to know that a child is developing in line with the established 'norm', but it is perhaps more useful to know when a child is *not* developing in line with other children. Take a look at Chapter 14 on developmental psychology and education. From the educational perspective, it is also useful to know when children are ready to learn about mathematics, for instance, and when to introduce the study of poetry.

However, there are weaknesses with stage theories. For instance, consider the implications that might arise if your child does not fit into the precise age ranges for acquiring a certain behaviour, say language, and thus does not appear to be developing 'typically'? Is your child in need of further support to help her develop language at the same rate as other children, or will she just take a little bit longer? Stage theories present quite rigid, precise

Reading together helps build the bond between father and son.
Source: Lam

statements of what is 'typical' development but do not take into account the individual's rate of development. Stage theories conceptualise development as a linear, hierarchical process, but the reality is often less well defined. A child with older siblings may show advanced skills in play because he has learned advanced games from his older brothers. Another child may take longer to learn the basics of mathematics but get there in the end.

Theories that take a less rigid view of development take what we call a more continuous approach to development.

The continuous or lifespan perspective

The continuous perspective has at its core four assumptions: development is life-long, is multi-dimensional, is *plastic* and can ebb and flow across the lifespan, and can be affected by many elements, predictable and unpredictable. This perspective is gaining in popularity as it explains well the individual differences in experiences throughout life and how these experiences affect our individual course through childhood and right into late adulthood.

Definition

Continuous perspective: development is a continuous, life-long experience which does not follow specific steps and stages, but early experiences are built upon and skills expanded continuously.

The continuous perspective believes that development is life-long and does not stop as we reach adulthood. The evidence presented in the section on attachment beyond infancy (Chapter 9) shows that our emotional development begins with the formation of simple attachments driven by our need for food, warmth and security, through the formation of childhood friendships, to building on long-term emotionally rewarding relationships in adulthood. This perspective sees development as occurring in many dimensions and directions: for example, our development can occur along physical, emotional and cognitive dimensions. Whilst some development is progressive – we acquire more functions – some development is regressive – we stop studying languages in order to focus more on behavioural sciences. Often our development can show both progressive and regressive features: for example, moral development. As we get older, our decision making becomes more complex, integrating knowledge, experience and more advanced philosophical skills, and we reduce our reliance on simple, *reductionist* philosophies in everyday problem-solving activities.

In the continuous perspective, development is highly *plastic* – there may be 'bulges' of accelerated development or 'slim' periods of slow or steady development. For instance, if you look in the section on the growth of vocabulary in infancy (Chapter 5), you will see that language development in a child starts slowly in the early years and then word acquisition and grammar competence 'explode' in the pre-school years with the child learning thousands of words before the age of 6 years.

Exponents of continuous development believe that development is affected by many elements or influences. Age-related influences can be seen in the age at start of school, learning to drive, being able to vote or age at retirement. All these time-points create a specific social cohort, such as school peer group, car drivers, voters or pensioners, all of whom usually have a certain status attributed to them. These cohorts may be used as population identifiers for government purposes, such as distributing school attainment tests or public policy on road tax or pension provision, or could be used for marketing purposes, such as cartoon character detailing on school lunch boxes, advertising campaigns for particular brands of cars or developing promotional material for life insurance products.

This perspective also takes into account cohort effects of 'history-graded influences'. Thus, those people born in the 1930s have had the similar experience of childhood and early adulthood being influenced by the Second World War and periods of food rationing. Their 'make-do' philosophy is very different from that of people born in the 1980s – a period of financial growth and technological advancement. These people are more likely to have a 'use it and throw it away' philosophy and may find it difficult to empathise with the older generation's belief that things, once broken, can be repaired and re-used.

In the continuous perspective, development can also be affected by what may be called 'non-normative' influences. These are influences that occur to an individual or small group of individuals that perhaps cannot be predicted or their effect pre-determined. An example of this might be the experience of a visit to a place of particular historical interest that triggers a life-long interest in studying history, or becoming a home-carer looking after a poorly elderly parent or child with severe disabilities. None of these events could perhaps be predicted in the person's developmental life path, but they are important and have a significant impact on the direction in which that person's life experiences head. As we get older, these non-normative influences become much more important in steering our developmental path and age-related effects become much less influential.

The continuous approach also suggests that many of these influences work in conjunction with each other: for example, look at the position of puberty in our physical development. In Chapter 13 on adolescence, we look at the impact of physiological changes in the teenage years and conclude that the timing of onset of puberty can be determined by a combination of three factors: biological triggers; quality of diet and level of fitness; and environmental stressors. Those with a good, healthy diet, living in a low-stress environment and taking plenty of exercise, are more likely to experience slightly later onset of puberty than those living in a high-stress environment with a high-fat diet and low levels of exercise (Graber et al., 1994).

STOP AND THINK

What are the strengths and weaknesses in adopting a stage theory approach to child development? Support your argument with reference to a particular aspect of development, such as language.

Psychoanalytic perspective on development

The key assumptions of the psychoanalytic perspective are:

- There are three levels of consciousness – the conscious, the pre-conscious and the unconscious.
- The unconscious mind is key to understanding human behaviour.
- The unconscious mind houses our instinctual drives, which strive to maximise our ability to survive.
- The core of our personality is determined by the age of 5 or 6 years and will not change after this age, even in adulthood.

Sigmund Freud (1856–1939): the psychoanalytic theory of development

Key aspects of Freud's psychoanalytic theory (Freud, 1933) stem from his work with patients who had psychological disorders like anxiety and depression that manifested in physical problems such as partial paralysis or sudden blindness – what Freud called 'hysterical' disorders. Freud thought that, as these disorders did not seem to have physical origins, they must have origins in our 'psyche' or our mind. The mind therefore had to be investigated if he was to understand why these patients were experiencing such devastating physical problems.

Take, for example, your decision to study psychology. Why have you chosen to do this? Is it to study in more detail something, human behaviour, perhaps, that fascinates you? Are you studying psychology in order to get the foundation education needed to go into a therapeutic profession? Whatever your reason, according to Freud, you will all be doing it for the fundamental motivation of encouraging pleasure (e.g. following your passion for studying human behaviour) or avoiding pain (e.g. going into a profession or career you have little interest in).

Freud's theory of psychosexual development (Freud, 1949) expanded on the nature of the pleasure/pain motivation in developing each of our personalities. Freud argued that our personality is composed of three

LIFESPAN

Word retrieval across the lifespan

A study by Kave et al. (2010) asked 1145 participants to name 48 black-and-white drawings of simple items such as a top-hat. Each participant had as much time as they needed to remember the word for each item and, if the word given was too general a term for the item (e.g. the participant named the item 'hat'), the participant was prompted for the more specific name for the item (e.g. 'top-hat'). If the name of the item could not be recalled, the researchers provided a cue either of the item's use (e.g. you might wear this on your head) or of the first letter sound of the word (e.g. this word begins with the sound 't'). Participants varied in age from 5 years to 86 years. There were roughly 50% female participants up to age 50 years and then the percentage of female participants rose to around 65% in the over-75s.

The researchers found that word recall was approximately 35% accurate in the 5- to 6-year-olds, rose steadily to 48% in the 40–60-year-olds, then returned to approximately 35% in the 75–80+-year-old participants. The researchers concluded that word recall therefore improves into middle age and then declines into older age. Wondering whether the number of words retrieved was related to the number of words known, the researchers conducted a further study. Their results showed that although the younger adults still outperformed the older adults on word retrieval, the older adults had the largest vocabulary and were better at producing word definitions (Kave and Yafe, 2014).

- Why do older adults have the largest vocabulary?
- Why were the younger adults not as good at producing accurate word definitions?

parts: the id, the ego and the superego. The id effectively reflects our basic biological impulses. It controls our sexual needs, our food and drink needs, our warmth and comfort needs. The ego describes the conscious decision-making part of us. It develops in the first few years of life to manage and deliver the needs of the id. The third part of the personality, the superego, reflects the social norms of the community the child is growing up in. This part of the personality naturally becomes more sophisticated as the child ages and is exposed to more rules and regulations.

The job of the ego becomes much harder, the older the child is and the more aware they are of the social norms regulating their behaviour. Its role is to satisfy the id (the biological urges) whilst satisfying the needs of the superego (the social regulations of behaviour). When the ego is successful at balancing the needs of both the id and the superego, the person feels content. However, when the ego is unable to balance the needs of the id and superego, Freud argues that the person feels anxious. It is these feelings of anxiety that Freud explored with his patients. Freud felt that high levels of anxiety were causing his patients to have physical manifestations of problems for which there were no other apparent causes.

Freud described the number of ways in which people try to cope with anxiety as defence mechanisms. If you were unable to cope with the anxiety of unresolved libido, then you would experience psychological tensions – anxiety, depression and other mental illness – whether that anxiety stemmed from events recently or events a long time in your past. What type of mental illness you experienced could be linked to the age at which you experienced the anxiety induced by an unsuccessfully acting ego and the defence mechanisms or manner in which you tried, also unsuccessfully, to cope.

Freud described a number of key stages in a person's life that corresponded with different demands of the pleasure/pain motivation, the libido. Freud believed from talking to his patients that the main driving force behind the libido was not satisfying the survival needs of hunger, thirst and warmth, but sexual satisfaction. Thus, his theory is called the *theory of psychosexual development*: see Table 2.1 for a brief description of the stages.

Freud's theory of psychosexual development gave him a framework for understanding the sources of his patients' anxiety. The patient who presented as obese and found herself feeling socially ostracised because of it he described as having unresolved issues at the *oral* stage of development. Her *id* wanted food and experienced pleasure with eating. The *superego* was constructed of the social norm possibly based in the religious ideal of slim body shape and the rejection of overeating as the sin of gluttony. Her *ego* could not resolve the conflict between her hunger and pleasure from eating and her religious beliefs of moderation and thus she experienced a high level of anxiety.

> **Definitions**
>
> Id: our biological impulses.
> Ego: our conscious decision-making process.
> Superego: our sense of morality and social norms.
> Defence mechanisms: coping styles used during moments of anxiety brought on by unresolved libidinous urges.

Table 2.1 Freud's stages of psychosexual development.

Stage	Approximate age	Focus of libido	Developmental task associated with this stage
Oral	0–12 months	Mouth	Feeding: moving from breast and other forms of milk on to solid foods.
Anal	12–36 months	Anus	Toilet training: moving from passing urine and faeces without control to manipulating the need to go to the toilet and using a potty rather than a diaper or nappy.
Phallic	36 months–6 years	Genitals	Gender: gender awareness, genital stimulation and resolving anxiety by identifying with same-sex parent.
Latent	6–12 years	No focus	This is a period of calm and resolution of the previous stages. No dramatic development occurs.
Genital	12 years onwards	Genitals	Sexuality: becoming sexually aware of self and others, sexual stimulation and formation of intimate relationships.

Source: adapted from Boyd and Bee (2006)

The patient who found himself unable to settle into relationships and experience sexual intimacy with his wife had unresolved conflict at the phallic stage. He had not been able to identify well with his father as a child and had not developed a stable sexual identity for himself and others. His *id* wanted sexual satisfaction at any cost and his *superego* required sexual behaviour within the realms of marriage. His *ego* struggled to moderate his sexual libido and he therefore experienced anxiety within his relationship and sought satisfaction outside the marriage.

Freud's interest in the causes of his patients' anxiety developed into an interest in the coping strategies his patients used to alleviate the anxiety. Rather than resolving the sources of the emotional upset, all his patients used what Freud called *defence mechanisms* to 'cover up' their feelings. Some patients used *denial* and behaved as if the problem did not exist. Others used *repression* and pushed the memory away to the back of their minds or *rationalised* their behaviour to justify their feelings. Other defence mechanisms reported were *projecting* the beliefs of yourself onto others or *displacing* emotions onto someone else instead of the person the anger or anxiety was provoked by, and some patients even *regressed* their behaviour to a younger age (such as sucking their thumb as an adult in the face of adversity).

Critique

Freud's writing on the theory of the conscious and unconscious mind initiated discussion and research into understanding the motivations for behaviour and the causes of emotional upset in people. Other theorists discredited him for his lack of academic rigour in constructing and presenting his theories and many people believe his theory to be lacking in empirical evidence. In Chapter 3, you will discover the importance of research methodologies in providing academic rigour in the form of an evidence base for our understanding of human behaviour. That chapter will show you how we use a range of techniques to acquire knowledge and understanding of the developing child. However, it is important to know Freud's work as many other more critically acclaimed developmental theories arose from his work, and his notion of age-related stages of development forming a hierarchical model of behavioural achievement is evident in many developmental scientists' work.

Erik H. Erikson (1902–94): the psychosocial theory of development

Erik Erikson was born in Germany during a period of intense social and economic change. As a young adult he was heavily influenced by the work of Sigmund Freud and studied psychoanalytic theory alongside Sigmund's daughter, Anna, in Vienna, Austria. The events of the Second World War forced Erikson and his wife to relocate to America where he wrote his seminal text *Childhood and Society*, published in 1950 (2nd Ed. published 1963). This book contained his detailed observations on the psychological changes we experience in the period from infancy to late adulthood – changes he described as the *eight ages of man*.

Erikson, like Freud, saw child development as following a specific pathway through a series of stages that reflect our ability to achieve a certain task. Table 2.2 demonstrates how similar Freud and Erikson's theories are. Erikson believed that each of us follows the same pathway through these stages. The route is linear and uni-directional: we do not double-back on ourselves, miss any of the stages or skip ahead. Erikson's proposed stages of child development map neatly onto Freud's theory of psychoanalytic development and expand on it into adulthood and old age.

Each of Erikson's stages is described as a *crisis* between our biological or psychological needs and the experiences we have with others and our social world. This crisis is fought in a similar way to the way that Freud describes in the role of the *ego*. We have 'wants' that need fulfilling but we need to acknowledge the role of our environment and the people around us in setting parameters for our desires. The end of each stage is marked by a state of *resolution*. The child learns to balance their own needs with those of the people around them. For some children there is a satisfactory resolution of their needs and they come out of a stage with what Erikson described as certain positive personal characteristics. For other children there is an unsatisfactory resolution of a stage and they may display difficulties in moving onto the next stage and 'problematic' personal characteristics. Erikson wrote that each stage has its own unique personal characteristic associated with it and it is possible that problems reported in adulthood may relate to difficulties experienced at a particular developmental stage in childhood.

Table 2.2 Comparison of the age-related stage theories of Freud and Erikson.

Freud	Age of child	Erikson	Personal characteristic
Oral stage	Infancy to 12 months	Trust vs mistrust	Hope
Anal stage	12 months to 3 years	Autonomy vs shame	Will
Phallic stage	3 to 6 years	Initiative vs guilt	Purpose
Latency stage	6 years to puberty	Industry vs inferiority	Competence
Genital stage	Adolescence	Identity vs role confusion	Fidelity
	Young adulthood	Intimacy vs isolation	Love
	Middle adulthood	Generativity vs stagnation	Care
	Older adulthood	Ego integrity vs despair	Wisdom

Source: After Crain (2005)

Erikson's eight-stage theory of development (Erikson, 1950, 1963)

Trust versus mistrust – infancy to 12 months

In the very earliest stage of life, Erikson proposed that we must learn to trust both ourselves and the people around us. We are born with basic needs, such as food and warmth, and need to have these satisfied. If we receive regular care and attention, we learn to trust that others will care for us and will fulfil our need for food or blankets. Erikson did not write that any particular style of parenting (whether it was child-centred or not) was any better for the child, just that there needed to be consistency and predictability to the care. Without predictability, Erikson argues, the child cannot learn to trust that the parent will be there when needed and thus develop a sense of contentment and safety. The baby must also learn to trust himself. During breastfeeding, the baby has to learn that sucking too hard or too softly will affect the rate at which milk is released. When the baby grows teeth, he has to learn to feed without hurting the mother. Babies who have learned to trust themselves and their parents to provide adequate care will often be calm and comfortable in the presence of others and show low levels of upset when the parent leaves the room. In contrast, babies who have not found predictability in their parents' care and have not built up a level of trust are more likely to show distressed behaviour and to become very upset when the mother leaves the room.

This is not to say, however, that the child should not learn some mistrust. Erikson argued that it is important that the baby learns that others (and possibly himself) are not always trustworthy. Without knowing *mistrust* our baby cannot regulate his feelings of trust and would become vulnerable to others and not wary of the dangers society can hide. The optimum outcome, then, for this stage of development is to experience high levels of trust, tempered by awareness of mistrust. A child who succeeds in achieving this state will then, according to Erikson, develop a core personal characteristic that he labelled *hope* – hope that the world is generally a good and safe place to be and that all obstacles can be overcome. With a strong feeling of hope, the infant is now ready to progress into the next stage of development: the crisis between autonomy and shame.

Autonomy versus shame – 12 months to 3 years

During this stage of development the infant learns to control their actions. Freud described this stage as the anal stage when the child experiences pleasure at defecation. During this stage the child learns to control when they need to use the toilet and progresses from using nappies to a potty and then a full toilet. Erikson agreed with Freud that the child's development is dominated by toilet training at this age but developed the notion of learning control further. It is typical for children at this age to use the word 'no' more than the word 'yes', for instance. Erikson argues that the child is developing the notion of control over objects and events in their world and by saying 'no' the child is developing a sense of *autonomy*.

Autonomy can be seen in other behaviours of a child. The child may grab a toy from a sibling and not give it back under pressure from their brother or their parent. They may demand to be held by a parent or to be let down, seemingly at random. As the child's expression of need for control increases, however, so the parent starts to set parameters of what they consider acceptable behaviour. The development of gender identity (discussed in

Chapter 11) is a good example of the autonomy versus shame conflict. Parents start to use phrases such as 'be a good boy for Mummy' or 'be a nice girl for Granny now' to encourage the display of socially acceptable behaviour. Through this process, Erikson suggests that the child learns to feel *shame* and doubt about some of the ways in which they want to act, and develops sensitivity to the needs of behaving in accordance with the rules of society or their social *norms*.

Again, the child is engaged in a crisis. This time the crisis is to develop independence and autonomy from their parents and to engage in behaviours they enjoy whilst at the same time doing so within a pattern of social norms and avoiding the feelings of shame. Resolving this crisis successfully will develop the core personal characteristic of *will*. Erikson purported that the development of *will* at this stage will result in an adult who in a social context is able to restrain him or herself from making poor choices, but who also is independently able to make decisions that satisfy him or herself.

Initiative versus guilt – 3 to 6 years

Children of early school age start to introduce an element of competitiveness in their activities. They want to know who is the tallest, who can run the fastest and who is their 'best' friend. Children at this stage often talk in hierarchies, such as 'I'm the tallest, Sally is shorter than me and John is the shortest', and make games of building the highest tower from blocks and bricks. This stage demonstrates the child's need for *initiative*, Erikson writes, in that their play becomes goal oriented and more spirited. Their play can swiftly get out of hand, however, and anyone who has ever looked after a 4- or 5-year-old will know that this can happen. For instance, what starts as a simple game of jumping off a step to the ground can soon escalate to the child wanting to jump off a higher then a higher step, until they start to put themselves in danger of falling and hurting themselves.

This desire to go higher and higher drives the child to accomplish more and more, but at some point the adult or carer will aim to put a stop to it, often mindful of the safety of the child. Curbing the activity, for whatever reason, then provides the child with their third crisis, Erikson argues, that of *guilt*. By controlling the degree to which the child can show initiative, the parent is introducing more parameters to the child's behaviour. Telling the child 'Mummy wants you to stop that or you will hurt yourself' means that the child has to weigh up their desire to continue jumping from a high step with the guilt of upsetting their mother and even hurting themselves. Erikson believed that limiting activity at this stage of life really has a negative effect on the child and he felt that, after the age of 6 years, the child will have lost all their natural drive and energy and become a more staid, less inventive person. Later, Erikson wrote that this stage might in fact not be all bad. With the right balance of parenting and instruction, Erikson conceded that the energies of *initiative* could be focused into activities that are more appropriate and that children of this age could be encouraged to find artistic or sporting outlets that allowed them to develop the personal characteristic of *purpose*.

Industry versus inferiority – 6 years to puberty

So far, our child has gained to a greater or lesser degree the personal characteristics of *hope, will* and *purpose*. Our child has developed a sense of trust, is gaining in autonomy and is learning to display initiative within prescribed boundaries. The next stage of development Freud called the *latent stage* and he described it as a period of time when little of any consequence happened, but the child consolidated developments in the previous years in readiness for the next stage, preparing for adulthood. Erikson, however, saw this stage quite differently (Erikson, 1968). He saw the pre-pubertal years as being of increasing *industry*. In many cultures, these years are ones of learning – whether this occurs within the family unit or within a structured schooling system, the child is taught necessary skills in preparation for independent adult living. Erikson's theory has been influential in determining the types of teaching method and assessment that are most appropriate for children at school. If you have a look at the Lifespan and Case Study boxes in Chapter 14, you will see a full discussion of how Erikson's theories can be applied effectively in the classroom.

The crisis at this stage comes from the interactions with the tutor of those skills. How many of us remember the shame of being criticised for our lack of achievement in a task at school or the pleasure of receiving a commendation? Teachers use verbal praise, sticky coloured stars and league tables to reward their pupils and to encourage them in their work, but the down side of schooling can be felt when you do not receive that praise and are ridiculed for your poor performance in sport or art, writing or mathematics. These feelings of *inferiority* last a long time. We can probably all recall failing at a task or feeling embarrassed and still perhaps now do not follow pursuits that we were discouraged from at such an early age. However, with the right encouragement Erikson argues that we can all succeed at our talents, and by achieving the right balance between our *industry* and our feelings of *inferiority*, we develop a sense of *competence*, our fourth personal characteristic.

Identity versus role confusion – adolescence

Erikson described this stage as a period of intense energy and drive. In Chapter 13 on adolescence we discuss in full the physical and psychological experience of adolescence. Freud described this period as being one of striving for sexual identity but Erikson went further than that in his theory. Erikson saw the focus of energy in adolescence as being directed at all aspects of life. He saw teenagers becoming upset and confused at all the new demands on them. Teenagers are keen to establish a more permanent sense of *identity* that is more complex than ever before, at a time when even their very physical shape is changing on what can seem like a weekly basis.

Teenagers, Erikson argued, have to deal with creating an identity based on a new physical self, a new sexual self and a self that is concerned with other, more worldly worries such as religious belief and political persuasion. The teenager changes at such a rate that the only way they can cope with this sudden loss of the old self is to try and identify with others. This drive towards identification takes the teenager to different styles of music, clothes and activities in their need to feel like they belong, somewhere.

For many, the pursuit of identity continues through adulthood, but nowhere is it as painful or acute as in the teenage years. As more social, educational and other options open up to the teenager, so some may feel ill-equipped to deal with this wide choice and, rather than embrace the opportunities, they withdraw and settle into a state of impasse. This crisis of *role-confusion* means that the young person may not be able to assimilate these choices into their identity and instead may feel as if they have fallen off the track or that life is passing them by. Many teenagers take 'time out' from their studies and spend a period of time travelling, trying different jobs or even in a complete state of inertia until they are ready to cope with the adult world ahead of them.

As the young person works towards developing their sense of *identity* and reducing the amount of *role-confusion* she feels, the teenager is building on her ability to achieve long-term goals and developing the ability to make decisions with far-reaching consequences (Erikson, 1974). Without this newfound skill, she will not develop the personal characteristic of *fidelity*, the ability to pursue a goal to its conclusion and will find it difficult to make long-term commitments in adulthood.

Intimacy versus isolation – young adulthood

Where the teenager takes the self-centred approach and strives for a sense of identity based on who they are, what they like and what they believe in, the young adult changes the focus of that drive for identity by searching for intimacy with another. Erikson believed that the teenager is too caught up in finding out about herself to engage in true intimacy with another person. Only in adulthood when the sense of self is robust and your identity firmly held can you start to develop a relationship that encourages intimacy, whilst also allowing for both your and the other person's strengths and weaknesses.

Erikson believed that the adult who has a poorly defined identity and has not yet been able to settle their role-confusion is unlikely to form a satisfactory intimate relationship. Erikson keenly advocated the delay of marriage until both partners had developed full identities, for without them he saw that the marriages often failed as the man and woman grew emotionally in different directions. Erikson's proposition that you cannot be comfortable with another person until you are comfortable with yourself seems to have become the foundation stone of many marriage and relationship counsellors and probably for good reason. True intimacy in adulthood means accepting each other's strengths and faults and sharing many aspects of your lives. If you are uncomfortable with yourself, you are unlikely to be able really to accept your partner's perceived failings.

The crisis facing young adults at this time is that of *isolation*, of being alone and without experiencing an intimate relationship with another. It is perhaps this fear of being alone that drives many young people into relationships that they are not ready for or able to succeed with. However, with time many adults do maintain successful, intimate relationships that are emotionally and sexually rewarding and they experience the personal characteristic of *love*.

Generativity versus stagnation – middle adulthood

Erikson described the purpose of middle adulthood as to be focused on care and nurturing, particularly of children. He proposed that success at this stage involved the giving of yourself and your priorities to the raising of children. It is not simply enough, he argued, to have children in order to be *generative*, but the children you have must be nurtured and you must sacrifice some of your own needs in order to satisfy theirs. Without giving to others, Erikson believed that an adult becomes *stagnant* and self-absorbed.

Although Erikson's theory was child-focused at this stage, he did write that childless couples and other adults without children did not necessarily have to become stagnant. *Generativity* could come through working with others or caring for others and through roles such as teacher, nurse or priest, but the essential element for Erikson is that these roles require you to change the focus of your efforts away from yourself to the care of others. Without the experience of nurturing and encouraging others, you are left unable to develop fully your potential personal characteristic of *care*.

Ego integrity versus despair – older adulthood

Once the children have left home and are happily settled on their own life path, Erikson wrote that the older adult begins a journey of reflection on their past and a reconciliation of the past on the present and future. As we get older, we begin to make comparisons between what is now and what was before. It is common to hear members of the older generation passing comment on how 'things aren't like they used to be' and 'life's changed'. Erikson believed that adults who can look back on their lives with happiness and contentment are more likely to see the future more positively and to feel satisfied. If the older adult feels that they have achieved what they wanted to and have been able to satisfy their needs, they are more likely to have *ego integrity* and to accept that their life has panned out the way it was intended.

Adults who are not able to do this are more likely to experience *despair* and disappointment and to fear getting older. Such adults may become aggressive and dispassionate. They may complain about all the changes and about the failings of people around them. This is likely to reflect the disappointment they feel in themselves for not having had what they perceive as a satisfactory and fulfilling life. The internal struggle of coming to terms with what has been and that perhaps there is little time left for them to make amends is often forgotten in our perception of the older adult. We are quick to note physical and possibly mental deterioration, but we rarely make the effort to understand the role of reflection on the past and its integration into the present. With successful reflection and the development of strong *ego integrity*, the older adult is rewarded with the personal characteristic of *wisdom*, the personal reflection on the meaning and value of life, but it can be difficult to achieve if all you feel is *despair*.

This child is likely to benefit from growing up in a large, diverse family.
Source: Pearson Education Ltd/Gareth Boden

Critique

Erikson's theory depends highly on the resolution of your personal sense of identity as the main thrust of human development. Compared to many other theorists, Erikson's theory is unique in describing development beyond the years of childhood and right through into older adulthood. Its strengths lie in the consideration of the full lifespan in personal development and that it does not assume we are 'complete' or unchangeable after the adolescent years. Erikson's theory allows us scope to evolve complexity in our identity as we age and to keep assimilating new experiences.

The weaknesses of Erikson's theory stem from his stage-theory approach to identity formation. In using Freud's psychoanalytic theory as a foundation for his own theory, he is very clear which personality characteristics we attain at different ages. However, consider the individual differences in development and thus the implications of this approach in understanding your own personal development. Is it possible to be so strictly adherent to the stage-theory approach when we are talking about personality development?

> **STOP AND THINK**
>
> - Think about Erikson and Freud.
> - How closely is Erikson's psychosocial theory of development related to Freud's psychoanalytic theory of development?
> - What distinguishes them from each other?

Biological perspectives on development

The key assumptions underlying the biological perspective are:

- Psychologists should study observable and measurable behaviour only.
- All behaviours are learned; we are not born with any set of behaviours.
- Mental process cannot be observed or measured and therefore cannot be studied scientifically.
- The adult personality can change but only as a result of exposure to different experiences.

Arnold Gesell (1880–1961): Gesell's maturational theory

The biological perspective on development suggests that all physical and psychological changes occur because they are biologically and genetically pre-ordained to do so. Thus, we are born with a developmental 'clock' inside that will determine at what age we will sit, walk, talk and make decisions. We cannot rush our child into walking before they are physically able, or into talking before they are biologically ready. The role of *nature* is dominant in this perspective and the first proponent of this perspective was Arnold Gesell.

Gesell believed that a child is the product of his or her environment but also that a child's development is genetically determined (Gesell, 1933). His theory describes child development as a series of stages that are defined by our biological make-up. Thus, we will learn to sit when our bodies are physically strong enough and we will stand when we are physically able to. Gesell saw that children followed the same pattern of achievements – we learn to sit, then stand, walk and then run – but that children learn these skills at different rates. Gesell believed that the reason for this was our individual genetic make-up. Gesell also believed that, since our individual rate of development is pre-determined by our genetics, we cannot force advancement ahead of schedule. There is therefore no point in trying to teach a child to walk before he or she is physically able to do so.

Gesell's work was extremely influential in child-rearing books written during the 1940s. He believed that children were born with an internal body clock developed over millions of years of evolution which determines what is best for that child. Gesell pioneered the debate that parents should respond to the needs of the child as they arise and not force the child into following the schedule of the household. This meant that new parents were to feed the baby when the baby wanted to be fed, let the baby sleep when it wanted to sleep, and play when the baby wanted to play. By responding to the baby's demands, Gesell argued that the parents would learn more about the individuality of their child and be more sensitive to his or her needs in childhood.

You might think that full on-demand parenting might lead to very spoiled children, and if pursued through childhood, it almost certainly would. What Gesell argued was that on-demand parenting was only necessary in the early months, and as the child grew physically so its concern with immediate satisfaction lessened. When the baby is new-born, it does not have the ability to wait for

BIOLOGICAL PERSPECTIVES ON DEVELOPMENT

Konrad Lorenz with single file of geese
Source: Science Photo Library Ltd

feeding and will cry until food is presented. As the baby grows older, so his or her needs become less intense and the baby learns to cope with a delay in gratification. As the child gains in language proficiency, he or she will understand when the parent says 'later' or 'in a minute' and will wait contentedly for longer periods before food is produced.

Critique

Gesell's work produced a number of 'norms' – behaviours that children *should* be carrying out at quite specific ages. For this he has often been criticised. Given that his theory seeks to explain the individual differences in children's maturational processes, it seems odd that he would report child development as a series of norms. However, there has been (and still is) a large body of researchers who acknowledge his theory and some have found evidence that on-demand parenting, particularly in the early months, results in satisfied, content infants and toddlers (Ainsworth and Bell, 1969).

Konrad Lorenz (1903–89): modern ethology

Lorenz was trained primarily as a medical doctor but was fascinated also by the study of human behaviour or ethology. Lorenz was highly influenced by Darwin's writing on the evolution of species and thought that you could see evolution not only in a person's biology but also in a person's behaviour (Lorenz, 1952). Lorenz was particularly interested in what we call innate behaviour – those abilities we appear to be born with and do not have to learn. He was keen to understand behaviour in its natural environment and was therefore an *ethologist*.

Ethologists believe that many behaviour patterns we see in animals and humans are *instinctive* and serve a number of functions. One such instinct might be a specific behaviour pattern in response to a threat or stressor. An example of this could be a duck quacking loudly and drawing her ducklings close to her when a cat or fox is nearby. In humans this could be the start of an aggressive response in a man when his children are threatened or a mother pulling her children near when a large dog bounds over during a picnic. Instincts are considered *species-specific* by ethologists and, although many patterns of behaviour seem similar across the animal kingdom, each species will have a unique signal (display of a puffed throat in a toad, a verbal call in a human) that can be understood only by its members. Importantly, instincts have a particular *motivation* or drive (e.g. reproduction or communication) and all have *survival value*.

Definitions

Ethology: the study of behaviour in its natural setting. Ethologists do not conduct experiments on behaviour in non-naturalistic settings; they prefer to observe and catalogue behaviour as it occurs naturally and without intervention from the researcher.

Innate behaviour: behaviour that appears instinctive, and is natural and not learned; behaviour or abilities that we are born with.

CUTTING EDGE

Biological influences on intellectual ability

In England and Wales, Standard Assessment Tests are distributed in school to children at the ages of 7 years, 11 years and 14 years. These tests examine each child's ability in a range of subjects including reading, writing and mathematics, and indicate how well each child is performing in school. Scores are compared to a mean of 100 points with a standard deviation of 15 points. Thus, achieving a score between 85 and 115 points suggests that the child is performing well at school. Below 85 and the child might need further support in school and beyond 115 the child could be considered particularly able.

The use of norms to calibrate performance on these tests suggests that most children will achieve an average grade, but could you improve your child's performance? There are many websites available with example test sheets for you to use with your child to help him prepare for the tests. Schools devote a large amount of time to studying the subjects covered by these tests and also use practice test sheets in the hope that each pupil will perform as well as can be expected on the day of the formal test. However, what if performance on these tests can be attributed not only to practice and schooling, but to biological factors? In Chapter 4 we discuss the role of environment in early development, and a study conducted by Dr Mark Brosnan at the University of Bath has provided further evidence that the environment of the womb can have a significant effect on the developing child.

The research carried out by Dr Mark Brosnan (2008) shows that performance on the Standard Assessment Tests could be predicted by the chemical environment of the womb during pregnancy. In Brosnan's study of 75 children, he found a clear link between the child's performance in these tests and the ratio of finger length between the first and third fingers. Children with longer third fingers (and therefore a smaller ratio between the lengths of the first and third fingers) were more likely to do well in tests of literacy and mathematics. Research has shown that if the chemical environment of the womb is high in testosterone, then the child will be born with a longer third finger. Thus, the research team concluded that greater exposure to testosterone in the womb predicts better performance in reading, writing and mathematics. When seeing if this effect was different for boys and girls, the research found that mathematical performance is most influenced for boys. Interestingly, exposure to low levels of testosterone in the womb was more likely to predict high levels of literacy in girls.

So what can we take from the findings of this study? Intellectual development and performance are affected by the level of exposure to testosterone in the womb. Is there any point in studying to improve performance in these tests? Well, the brief answer is yes. This research is important in helping us to understand the individual differences in attainment in all our children, but the research is still in its early stages. Until we fully understand the biological influences on our intellectual ability, we will continue to set goals for educational performance and encourage our children to study hard.

Lorenz is particularly well known for his study of *imprinting* (Lorenz, 1952). Ethologists have found that anything remotely like the intended trigger can act in its place. The trigger could be the presence of another animal to trigger bonding and the development of a nurturing relationship between adult and offspring. In cases of orphaned offspring, often another adult animal will successfully take on the role of parent and the infant animal will bond with that adult and follow it. When raising geese, Lorenz found that when he was the first face the goslings saw, they appeared to imprint him as 'mother' and followed him about wherever he went. The goslings' instinct was to follow the 'mother' in single file and to ignore other geese, responding only to their

> **Definition**
>
> **Imprinting:** a process in which new-borns of most species will recognise and seek proximity with the first object they encounter (usually the primary caregiver) following the activation of a trigger during a critical period after birth.

'mother'. In this situation, Lorenz's face had been the trigger for this instinctive behaviour and he had been imprinted by the goslings into the role of 'mother'. Lorenz proposed a critical period when imprinting would occur, after which no imprinting and therefore no bond would happen. This idea was taken by the researcher John Bowlby to address the situation with humans.

> **STOP AND THINK**
>
> - How do the theories of Gesell and Lorenz help us to understand human behaviour?
> - What is the value in understanding about the biological nature of development?

John Bowlby (1907–90): attachment theory

John Bowlby (1953, 1969) was influenced highly by the work of Konrad Lorenz and suggested that humans also have an innate ability to imprint a carer soon after birth. Previously it had been believed that babies would form a bond or an attachment to any adult who satisfied their needs – for food or warmth. However, Bowlby suggested that there was more to it than that. He believed that infants have a biological pre-disposition to attach to their mother for not just practical reasons but also emotional reasons. Bowlby's work has been very influential in the treatment of mothers and children following birth and encouraged midwives and hospital staff to put the baby in the mother's arms immediately in order for bonding to begin as soon as possible. In Chapter 10 there is a full discussion of attachment theory, but here is an overview of the key theories.

> **Definitions**
>
> Critical period: the time period that was thought to be critical for the formation and development of any attachment relationship, hypothesised to be 6 months to 3 years, beyond which it is seen as highly difficult for such a bond to be formed.
>
> Attachment: a strong, enduring affectionate bond an infant shares with a significant individual, usually the mother, who knows and responds well to the infant's needs.

Bowlby and Lorenz believed very much in the idea of a critical period for imprinting or forming a bond with a parent or carer. Whilst Lorenz believed that the moments immediately after birth were the most important, Bowlby thought that in humans the critical period for healthy emotional growth required a strong sense of a bond or attachment to a parent or carer that extended well into the toddler years, from 6 months to 3 years of age. Bowlby came to this conclusion after working as a psychiatrist with children who had been raised in orphanages during and after the Second World War. These children were orphaned from their parents and cared for by a raft of nurses and orphanage staff who took on no particular responsibility for any one child. These children had lost any feeling of a strong emotional bond to a single person and as a result, Bowlby concluded, displayed distressing, highly volatile behaviour.

Bowlby wrote that the existence of a strong, emotional bond was essential in producing emotionally stable, happy children (Bowlby, 1953). Without this bond, perhaps through experiencing the death of a parent, long periods of hospitalisation or long periods of time spent in nursery care, the child would experience *maternal deprivation* and the child would be damaged for ever. Bowlby, as with many developmental theorists, proposed a stage theory of attachment: the formation of a bond between a child and its mother.

The first stage in his attachment theory is called the *pre-attachment* stage. From birth to 2 months of age, Bowlby says that the infant is socially responsive to anyone and shows no preference for one person over another. If the person provides food and warmth, the baby is happy. It is only in the second stage, the *early attachment* stage, that the baby learns to discriminate his mother from the other adults around him. By the time the baby is 7 months old, he will turn towards his mother's voice, smile more at her face and be more easily comforted when crying. It is not until the baby is 8 months old or more that Bowlby believes the baby forms a real and strong attachment to his mother. In this stage, the *attachment* stage, babies show a much stronger preference for their mothers and will now cry when the mother leaves the room. This separation anxiety can be

> **Definition**
>
> Separation anxiety: the anxiety a child experiences when separated from the mother or primary carer.

seen quite clearly in infants when the parent walks away after dropping the child at day care. It takes a while for the child to learn that the mother will return for them and, until that happens, the child will often show signs of visible distress on parting.

During the attachment stage, the infant will also show signs of wariness around people they do not know. This *stranger anxiety*, like separation anxiety, is perfectly typical and can also be seen quite frequently in common interactions. Think about a time perhaps when you met a family friend in the street and you were introduced to her young child. The child probably suddenly became shy, hid partially behind her mother and held onto her clothes for comfort. In these situations it can seem to take a lot of coaxing from the mother for the child to step out and say hello! Later, when the child is a little older at about 2 to 3 years of age, the child becomes aware that the attachment can work in two directions.

The *partnership* stage is the last stage in Bowlby's theory of attachment and describes a process whereby the child learns that other people have needs too. Children's play activity at this stage is much more likely to involve working together to build a bridge or a sandcastle and, with encouragement, children of this age will share their pencils and crayons. In this way they discover that relationships are not simply about seeing another person as a source of everything you need, but that you can help others and experience enjoyment when there is 'give and take' on both sides.

Critique

There are criticisms of Bowlby's work. First, there seems to be no evidence for the imprinting of a parent's face in the hours immediately after birth. However, as Bowlby suggests in his theory, this is not a problem as he believes that attachments form over a much longer period of time. Does the attachment have to happen only with the mother? Well, in practice, no. Many children are raised by fathers, grandparents and nannies, and many of these children form stable attachments to these carers. What does seem to be important to the emotional welfare of the child is that the carer provides a steady and dependable presence in the child's early months and years, regardless of who they are.

Second, Bowlby believed that without a stable attachment figure (usually the mother) in the first 3 years of life, the child would be irreparably damaged emotionally. This, however, does not seem to be the case. Parents who use childcare facilities when the mother and father both work still form strong attachments to their children, even though the child spends fairly long periods of time with other carers. The current belief is that, if the time you spend with your child is well spent, the child will be able to adjust to childcare comfortably. What is time 'well spent', however? Some people advocate intense periods of child-centred activity in order to 'make up' for the absence of both parents during the day. Other researchers advocate the maintenance of a stable and predictable structure to family life so that the child feels safe and secure at home. What is known, however, is that what really affects the child's ability to settle into day care and separation from his parents is the *quality* of the day care. With a regular pace to the day, a wide range of activities and staff who take a personal interest in the children, the child is much more likely to thrive (e.g. De Schipper et al., 2004).

Bowlby's work on attachment has dominated research into early child development and is highly influential in modern childcare practice and the provision of care facilities. Bowlby's stage theory of attachment has support from Mary Ainsworth, who saw evidence of children passing through these stages in a wide range of cultures and social contexts (Ainsworth et al., 1978). It therefore has universal appeal to people working with children across the board for its ability to clarify how our early experiences can have a quite considerable impact on our development across the lifespan.

Mary D. S. Ainsworth (1913–99): patterns of attachment

The work of Mary Ainsworth followed on naturally from that of her peers in developmental research. Ainsworth sought to find a way to measure the emotional state of a child and to illustrate the effects of parenting on child behaviour. Ainsworth began her research by observing

---

Definition

Stranger anxiety: the wariness or fear of an infant when encountering those who are unfamiliar, often characterised by the seeking of proximity to the caregiver.

parent and child interactions in Africa and noted similarities with what she had seen in Europe. This caused her to think that there could be patterns to this behaviour that are common across all cultures. What particularly interested her was observing what behaviour the child displayed when the parent left the room and what behaviour was displayed when the parent returned. This observation of parent–child interaction grew into a formal study of parent and child separation and reunification called the Strange Situation study (Ainsworth et al., 1978) (described in full in the section 'Measuring attachment' in Chapter 9 of this book).

The Strange Situation study

This is a seven-phase study designed to reflect the naturalistic observations Ainsworth had made of parent–child daily interaction. Usually it is conducted in a comfortable room in a research centre where the psychologist can watch events happen through a two-way mirror or via a camera projected onto a screen in a room next door. In the Strange Situation study, the parent and child are introduced into a plain room containing toys and asked to play together for 3 minutes (phase 1). A stranger (usually a research assistant) then enters the room, sits down for 1 minute, talks to the parent for 1 minute and then plays with the child for 1 minute (phase 2). The parent then leaves, and the stranger then plays with the child for up to 3 minutes and sits back on the chair (phase 3). In phase 4, the parent returns and the stranger leaves. The parent then settles the child down and sits with them for 3 minutes. After this, the parent leaves the room and the child is left alone for up to 3 minutes (phase 5). The stranger then comes into the room and tries to settle the child (phase 6). Finally, the parent returns and the stranger leaves. The parent settles the child down and sits with them (phase 7). The whole process takes around 20 minutes but it can be shorter if the child becomes distressed at any time and a phase is then cut short.

How can this study tell us anything about the attachment behaviour of the child? Ainsworth hypothesised that if the child is secure and content within the relationship, then in phases 1, 2 and 4 the child will use the parent as a base to explore the room and the toys within it. When the mother is absent (phases 3, 5 and 6) the child should become distressed – but not too much; in this case the mother will return before the 3 minutes are up. What Ainsworth was really interested in was the behaviour of the child when the parent returned after the period of absence (in phases 4 and 7). She observed many instances of this Strange Situation study and as a result compiled four main categories of the parent–child attachment relationship according to the way in which the child behaved when the parent returned (see Chapter 10 for a full description of them).

Attachment types

- *Type A form of attachment – avoidant attached.* If the infant shows few or no signs of missing the parent and actively ignores and avoids her upon reunion, the infant is said to show *insecure-avoidant attachment*.
- *Type B form of attachment – secure attached.* Some children showed signs of missing the mother when she left, and when she returned, the child made efforts to reunite with the mother. Satisfied that the mother was back to stay, the child returned to playing with the toys. Mary Ainsworth called this behaviour a sign of *secure attachment*.
- *Type C form of attachment – ambivalent attached.* If the infant becomes distressed when the mother leaves but cannot be settled by the parent on reunion, the infant is said to show *insecure-ambivalent attachment*.
- *Type D form of attachment, disorganised attached.* These infants were considered unclassifiable as they seemed to show reunion behaviours that could not be included in the other categories.

Critique

Why would these different attachment types come about? Is our attachment style pre-determined at birth? If this were so, then a family of both biological and adopted children would display very different attachment behaviours with their mother. However, research has shown this not to be the case. A study by Dozier et al. (2001) found that the attachment behaviours of adopted children were very similar to those of the biological children, demonstrating that the nurturing environment the children were raised in was more important in determining attachment behaviour than any biological factors. Why is this? Ainsworth proposed the *maternal sensitivity hypothesis*.

The *maternal sensitivity hypothesis* states that the more in-tune the mother is with her infant's emotional state, the more likely the child is to grow up with a secure attachment. So if a mother is responsive to her child and encourages him to play when he wants to play, and sleep when he wants to sleep, that child will grow up feeling a strong, stable and nurturing relationship with his mother. If the mother is discordant with her infant and is unable to understand her child's moods, then that mother is less likely to build a satisfying relationship with her child and the child is more likely to grow up showing an *avoidant* or *disorganised* style of attachment.

> **STOP AND THINK**
>
> How might understanding Ainsworth's description of attachment behaviour help you to improve the experience of a young child attending school for the first time?

NATURE–NURTURE

Attachment

It can be difficult finding the research tool to identify whether something like the ability to form relationships is present from birth or is something we learn in the years following. After all, we may be able to assess the type of upbringing someone has and whether they have experienced good or bad relationships, and even make changes to their environment to improve their experiences, but what we cannot do is make any kind of assessment based on their genetic make-up. We cannot investigate what biological factors there are in attachment or even locate some kind of genetic marker for defining someone who is 'good at making friends' or someone who is 'bad at making friends'. Any kind of research we conduct into attachment has effectively to ignore the biological aspects of this behaviour.

However, there is a research method that allows us to *control* for the biological aspects of behaviour and to determine whether the social environment someone is raised in is *wholly* responsible for their attachment behaviour or whether biology does have a part to play. This research method is called a 'twin study'. Twins are useful to study because if they are identical twins (in that they appear identical in looks and build) then they are monozygotic twins (twins from the same maternal egg) and therefore share the same genetic code. Thus, any differences seen between twin siblings could be argued to be a result of environmental factors, not biological ones.

A study by Fearon et al. (2006) investigated attachment behaviours in 136 pairs of twin infants from either Leiden (the Netherlands) or London (the UK). When the infants were 9–10 months old the mothers were assessed for their ability to respond to the twins' emotional and physical needs and given a score of *maternal sensitivity*. At 12 months, the mothers and children were assessed for attachment behaviours. Research had suggested that the reason why different children within a family could display different attachment behaviours was that the mother showed a different level of sensitivity to each child's needs because the children were different genetically and thus in personality and temperament. If this was the case, then the mothers of the infant twins should have shown similar sensitivity to their needs, regardless of which child she interacted with.

The results of the study showed that there were differences in maternal sensitivity to each of their twin infants – a finding that could not be explained genetically. When the mother showed equal sensitivity to each child, the attachment rating between her and her children was the same for each child. When there were differences in the attachment rating between her and each of her children, it appeared that this was affected by how the child saw the mother interacting with the other twin. The researchers conclude that attachment *is* affected by the environment the child is raised in, and that even with twin children the mother may be more sensitive to the needs of one over the other and this discrepancy will result in a difference in attachment experience for both children. Thus, biological differences in children are not what accounts for differences in attachment with their mothers; it is the nurturing environment that impacts the most.

Learning perspectives on development

So far we have discussed two perspectives on development. The psychoanalytic theories of Freud and Erikson take the view that developmental change comes from the balancing actions of our *psyche* on our emotional needs and social requirements. In contrast, the works of Gesell, Bowlby and Ainsworth have proposed that it is our pre-determined biological 'clock' that provides the foundation for our developmental changes. Both these perspectives address *internal* motivations for change. There are other perspectives, however, that address *external* motivations for our development.

The key assumptions of the learning perspectives on development are similar to the assumptions of the behaviourist perspective and are:

- Behaviour change results from our interactions with the world about us.
- Anyone can be trained to do anything.
- With the right system of reward, a behaviour can be encouraged, and with the right system of punishment, a behaviour can be inhibited.
- The strong focus on the manipulation of behaviour in these perspectives puts them in the *learning* or *behaviourist* category of theories of developmental change.

Ivan Pavlov (1849–1936): classical conditioning

Pavlov coined the term classical conditioning to describe the process of learning an association between two stimuli. He discovered that you can teach an animal to connect two previously unconnected stimuli – a bell and food – and produce the same response, saliva. Pavlov was conducting an unrelated study with dogs in his laboratory when he became interested in the response the dogs made at mealtimes. He noticed first that when you present a dog with food, the dog produces saliva in response. However, what was more interesting to Pavlov was the reaction the dogs made when the researchers were bringing the food to them. Pavlov noticed that when the technician who typically fed them walked up to the dogs, the dogs started making saliva whether or not the technician had food in his hands. The dogs had associated the technician with the food and had therefore learned to associate two previously unconnected stimuli. Figure 2.1 shows the process of classical conditioning experienced by the dogs.

How, though, does an understanding of the process of classical conditioning help us to understand human behaviour? Consider the way you felt when you first went to university. Did you feel uncomfortable in the new and often noisy environment? Did you take photos of your family and friends or your favourite teddy bear with you to keep in your bedroom? Did looking at the photos or bear help you to feel secure? The theory of classical conditioning suggests that as infants we associated warmth, comfort and security with a mother who held us and soothed us, or who tucked us up in bed with our teddy bear when we were tired or frightened by the dark. The associations we learned as children hold strong for us as adults when we seek comfort in looking at photographs of family members or feel strong emotions when we find our old teddy bear hidden away in a forgotten box.

Critique

Pavlov's theory of classical conditioning presents us with a model for understanding how we make emotional associations between a number of stimuli, but it is a limited theory in its application in developmental psychology. It was the slightly later work of B. F. Skinner that took this theory further and demonstrated how these associations can be manipulated by external events and forces.

B. F. Skinner (1904–90): operant conditioning

B. F. Skinner wrote that behaviours can be encouraged or inhibited by the effective use of reward or punishment (Skinner, 1957). The reward can be anything that *reinforces* the repetition of a behaviour. This *reinforcement* of behaviour can be achieved by positive means or negative means. A *positive reinforcer* could be giving someone a smile, verbal

> **Definition**
>
> Classical conditioning: describes the process of learning an association between two stimuli.

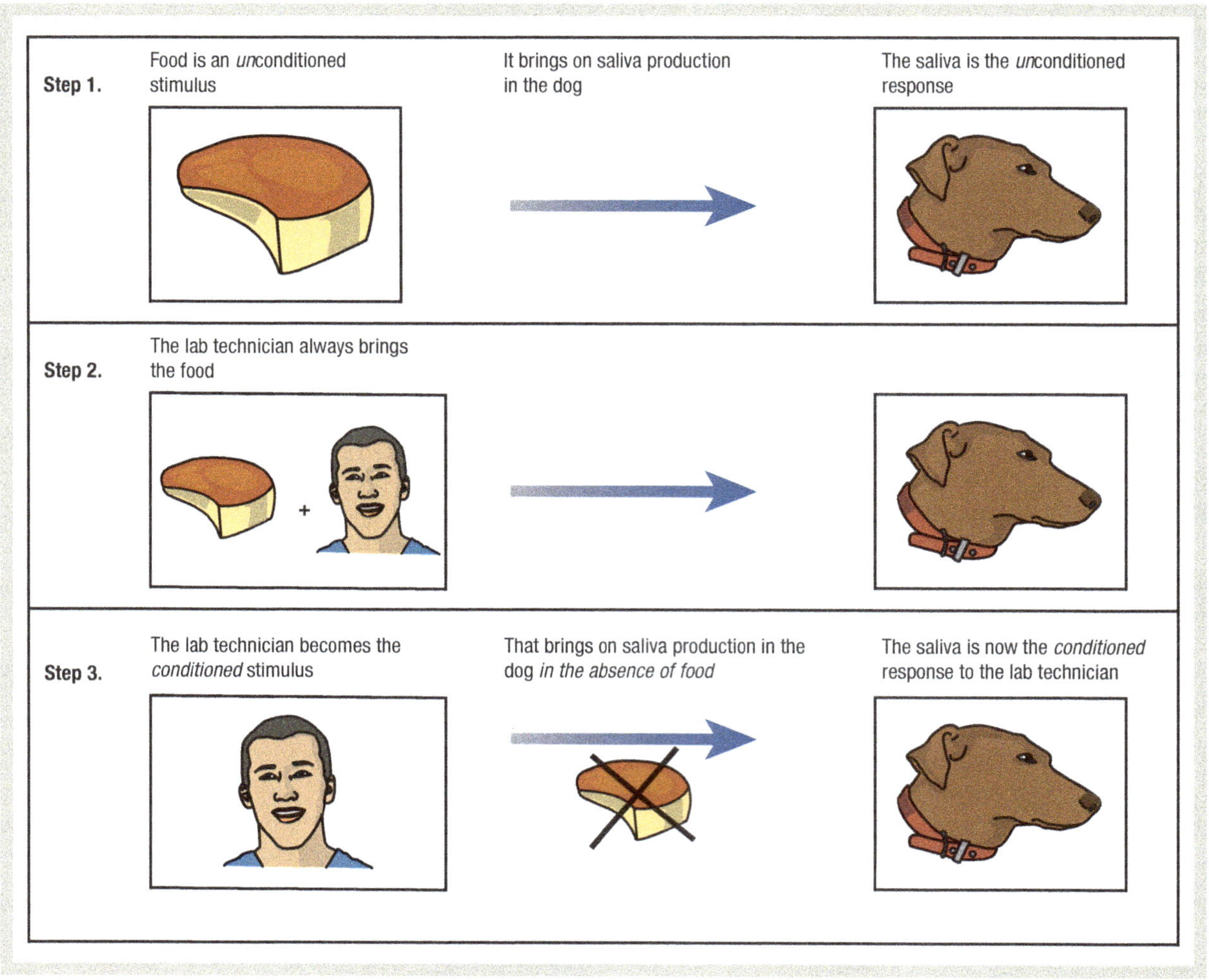

Figure 2.1

Step 1. Food is an *un*conditioned stimulus → It brings on saliva production in the dog → The saliva is the *un*conditioned response

Step 2. The lab technician always brings the food →

Step 3. The lab technician becomes the *conditioned* stimulus → That brings on saliva production in the dog *in the absence of food* → The saliva is now the *conditioned* response to the lab technician

Figure 2.1 The process of classical conditioning.

CASE STUDY

Little Albert

In 1920, researcher John Watson conducted an emotional conditioning experiment based on the principles of classical conditioning as described by Pavlov. Watson introduced a 9-month-old child called 'Albert' (not his real name) to a white rat, which the child enjoyed playing with. After a while, Watson started making loud sounds behind Albert's head whenever he played with the rat, scaring Albert. Eventually, whenever Watson presented Albert with the rat to play with, Albert would show signs of fear even in the absence of the loud noise. It appeared that Albert had been conditioned to feel fear when he saw the white rat.

- Why did Albert feel fear when he saw the white rat?
- Describe the process of conditioning that might explain his newly developed fear.
- What are the ethical implications of a study like this?
- What might be the long-term implications for Albert?

encouragement or pat on the back, as long as it is something which makes the person experience pleasure. A *negative reinforcer* is something that takes away discomfort or displeasure, such as using a painkiller to take away the pain of a headache or using a cold cloth to soothe a bump or graze of the knee. As the end-result of these actions is a reduction in pain and discomfort, we learn to use a painkiller or cold cloth when we experience a headache or bumped knee through the use of negative reinforcement.

A *punishment* is something that follows a behaviour and causes it to stop. A punishment can be many things but often takes the position of the removal of a reward. A mother may stop smiling or playing with her child and remove the reinforcement of attention that the child has previously been getting for her behaviour. A father might remove the favourite toy from the child until the unwanted behaviour stops. Effective punishment can cease an unwanted behaviour such as crying, pinching or having a temper tantrum quite quickly.

We can observe parents using operant conditioning techniques with their children – often perhaps unwittingly – as they coax and cajole their infants into complying with a request. Parents might use positive reinforcement to encourage the child to climb or jump, saying 'See, I knew you could do it!' or perhaps to eat their vegetables: 'What a good girl you are for eating those carrots.' Parents use positive reinforcement a lot with their children in all sorts of situations, but they also use negative reinforcement with them. Do you remember these phrases: 'If you eat your greens, you can have ice-cream for dessert!' or perhaps 'You can play outside when you've finished tidying your room'? In Chapter 14 on developmental psychology and education, there is a section on developmentally appropriate behaviour management. Have a look at the techniques described there. Do you remember your teachers using these techniques of punishment and reward in your class? Operant conditioning can be a very effective method of manipulating behaviour in children and the messages can stay with us for a long time and into adulthood. How often did you think during school, 'I can't go out until I've finished my revision'?

Some of the techniques of operant conditioning can be used to *shape* more complex behaviour over a period of time. When we are learning to write, we first need to learn our letters. Our parents and teachers will use reinforcement to encourage the accurate drawing of all the letters of the alphabet. Later on, we learn to spell our names and, again, our parents and teachers give us praise when we have written our names correctly. As we progress through school, we develop our abilities in writing and begin to construct sentences and then stories, all the while receiving feedback on our performance. With the correct use of reinforcement even the child with the worst spelling or the messiest handwriting will gain confidence. Rewarding the steady progression from holding a pen to writing a poem reinforces the child at each step and *shapes* their acquisition of a complex skill.

Sometimes, however, we all get the technique wrong. Take the example of a child who wants attention and calls out to his father repeatedly. Initially the father, who is engaged in conversation, wants to reduce this kind of behaviour from the child and ignores his requests. After a while, however, the father gives in and turns to the child and replies. The father's intention has been to inhibit the child's repeated calling of his name to get attention and he thinks that by not responding immediately, the child will learn to wait for a response. However, as a method of operant conditioning, this is the wrong way to go about it. What the father has now done is teach the child that he will respond on the child's tenth or so request for attention. He has positively reinforced the child's tenth attempt to get attention and not, as he supposed, inhibited his behaviour. If he persists in this method of response to the child, the child will simply learn that if he keeps calling out to his father, he will eventually respond.

The father in this situation could have used an alternative method of behaviour change, that of *extinction*. The *extinction* of a behaviour results from repeated non-reinforcement. In this example the father might have chosen to distract the child from the repeated name calling and instead asked him to wait a moment until he was able to respond to the child. By doing this, the father might have been able to eliminate the repetitive behaviour and taught the child a lesson in waiting a short while for attention whilst his father is talking.

Critique

Operant conditioning is a technique that can be replicated very well in a laboratory setting, but in the real world, the use of reinforcement and punishment in moderating a child's behaviour can be sporadic at best. Very often

---

Definition

Operant conditioning: the process that describes how behaviours can be encouraged or inhibited by the effective use of reward or punishment.

behaviours that might be tackled regularly at home might go unrewarded or unpunished when at a friend's house and the use of *partial reinforcement* is much more common. Under these conditions, behaviours are modified much more slowly than under laboratory conditions, and it will be near impossible to actually extinguish in full some unwanted behaviours. The father in our example above is actually engaged in a form of partial reinforcement of his son's repetitive behaviour and he will now find it difficult to stop it fully.

Albert Bandura (1925–): social learning theory

Bandura believed that very few of us were raised under the near-perfect conditions of reinforcement and punishment that operant conditioning requires and that many of us experienced moments of partial reinforcement during childhood. In fact, Bandura extended his theory beyond partial reinforcement and suggested that we learn to moderate our behaviour by observing social norms. His *social learning theory* proposes that we learn from seeing someone else's behaviour reinforced or punished (Bandura, 1969).

One of Bandura's key studies was that concerning the use of the *Bobo doll*, an inflatable doll painted to look like a clown, 'Bobo'. Bandura asked one of his research associates to go up to 'Bobo' and shout at it, punch it and kick it to the ground. Bandura video-taped the researcher and the doll and then showed it to some pre-school children. He then gave the children a Bobo doll to play with and watched their behaviour. Bandura noted that the children's play was much more aggressive than it had been previously and involved much more shouting and physical contact with the doll. The children had observed the researcher's violent behaviour towards the doll and had copied it.

Bandura argued that children learned a lot of behaviour from the imitation of others, whether the behaviour was playful or aggressive. His theory has been extremely influential in forming the basis of arguments on topics ranging from the causes of street violence to gender role identity and the choice of toys in boys and girls. As a theory it has perhaps been treated too simplistically and possibly been given rather too much weight in 'proving' the causes of behaviour. Certainly many of us have observed people behaving in an aggressive way but do not behave aggressively ourselves, for instance. When we look into the detail of Bandura's theory, however, we see that he does

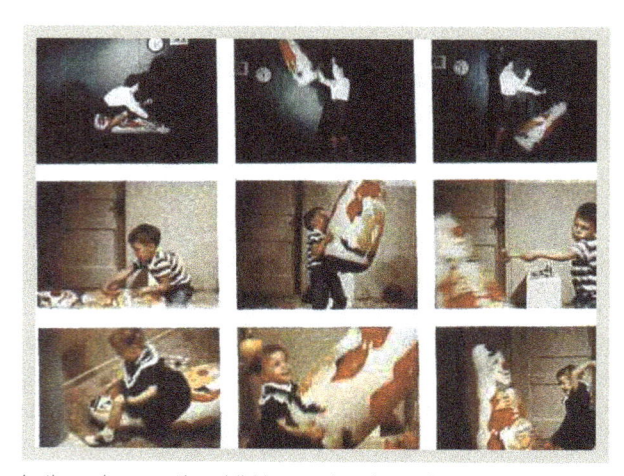

In these images the child is copying the actions of the adult researcher and hitting the toy.
Source: Professor Albert Bandura/Stanford University

not believe that imitation of behaviour happens necessarily or automatically. Bandura proposes that a behaviour will only be imitated when four conditions are satisfied: what aspect of the behaviour the child focuses on; how much of the behaviour the child is able to remember; whether the child is physically capable to carry out the behaviour; and finally, whether the child is actually motivated to carry out the behaviour. If the child does not *want* to act aggressively towards the clown doll, then even if she can remember what the researcher did and how the researcher did it, and if she is strong enough to copy the aggressive behaviour, the child will probably *not* act aggressively under these circumstances. In this situation, the child has learned self-efficacy – the ability to choose how to behave in the circumstances according to her own expectations, her understanding of social norms and her belief in the appropriateness of aggressive behaviour (Bandura, 1989).

Critique

Social learning theory is popular with developmental psychologists as it encompasses the role of parents in setting social norms for behaviour and in providing examples of behaviour for the child to copy whilst also

Definition

Self-efficacy: a person's belief about how effectively he or she can control herself, her thoughts or behaviours, particularly when intended to fulfil a personal goal.

RESEARCH METHODS

Ecological validity

Pavlov's research investigated how unrelated objects could, under certain conditions, become linked in a process he coined *classical conditioning*. This work was conducted with dogs and the research was carried out in a laboratory setting. What can Pavlov's research tell us about human behaviour in a real-life setting? The notion of *ecological validity* is important here. Criticism of a research report will often be directed at the method of the research carried out when there appears to be no real-world application. For the research to have *ecological validity*, it must be carried out with the right participants in what resembles a real-world setting.

It is a common mistake to over-generalise the findings of scientific research that has been carried out in a laboratory setting into the real-world setting. A paper that reports the impact eating a specified dose of a specific food additive has on pre-schoolers' behaviour may be reported in the press as evidence of the effect of food additives on children generally, without consideration of the dose given to the children or the effect of combining that additive with other foodstuffs. Bandura's study of mimicry and the children copying the adult hitting the Bobo doll has been reported as evidence that children copy everything they see, but how true is this? As Bandura himself reported, there are many mechanisms and intricacies that affect the process of mimicry, perhaps none more important than the evidence provided by the event itself. Is hitting an inflatable toy doll in an experimental setting wrong? Hitting a child in the playground is, but that is not what the children did. The children simply copied the researcher carrying out an act that had no real-life connotations in that context.

putting the responsibility for behaviour in the hands of the child. Look at the use of social learning theories in explaining how we acquire language in Chapter 5 or how we assemble a gender identity in Chapter 11 for examples of how social learning theory has been used to understand the development of a range of behaviours in childhood. However, in practice, Bandura's studies revealed that imitation of behaviour only occurred in approximately 10% of the research participants. This small effect can be explained by Bandura suggesting that children do not simply mimic behaviour they have seen in others, but make a personal judgement on whether to carry out the behaviour or not. This judgement can be affected by the moral teaching of the parents or teachers, the child's ability to carry out the behaviour and, ultimately, the child's internal motivation.

STOP AND THINK

How can an understanding of the method of social learning help a social worker to understand truancy behaviour in a school child?

Cognitive perspective on development

The key assumptions of the cognitive perspective on development are:

- Child development occurs through a series of mental processes such as problem solving, memory and language.
- These processes have to be learned.
- These processes become more complex with increasing age and experience.

Jean Piaget (1896–1980): cognitive development theory

Of all the theories of developmental change, Piaget's *cognitive development theory* (Piaget, 1962) has been the most influential. What distinguishes Piaget's work from that of the researchers we have just reviewed is both the methodology he used in constructing his theory and the dedication to detail in compiling a comprehensive stage theory of child development through to entry into adulthood. Freud and Erikson, for example, both developed detailed theories of internal drives and motivations to change, but one of the key weaknesses of these theories is the lack of any physical evidence for the presence of the id, the ego or the superego, or any detailed studies measuring the conflicts between these at different stages in life. The work of Pavlov and Lorenz was based almost exclusively on work in artificial laboratories with animals, not humans, and thus the application of their theories to understanding human behaviour is limited to say the least. Bowlby and Ainsworth produced theories based on their observations and experiments with children and adults in a naturalistic environment, but both have a tight focus on the issue of attachment in describing child and possibly future adult behaviour and do not look more generally at child development as a whole.

Piaget's interest in child development stemmed from an early position at the Binel Laboratory in Paris where he was required to work on developing an intelligence test for children. After working on this during the 1920s, Piaget found that what interested him the most was not when the children answered questions correctly, but when they made mistakes. He noticed that the children made similar errors and that these errors might reflect the child's specific way of thinking. Piaget began to catalogue the children's errors and devised a method of testing their abilities with a view to producing a statement of 'typical' child behaviour. It was not until after the Second World War, however, that Piaget began his work in earnest and published his theory of cognitive development in 1952.

Piaget's theory of cognitive-developmental change can be divided into four main stages: stage 1, *sensorimotor intelligence* (from birth to 2 years); stage 2, *preoperational thought* (age 2–7 years); stage 3, *concrete operations* (age 7–11 years) and stage 4, *formal operations* (age 11 to adulthood). Within each stage there are many phases which describe in detail our progression through the stage. Each phase is characterised by the acquisition of an ability – physical or mental – and only through successful completion of this phase can there be progression to the next stage. Piaget's cognitive development theory has been the most influential theory informing educational policy and practice (see it in use in Chapter 14). It has been used to illustrate how children understand numbers (see Chapter 7) and develop mathematical thinking, and it has also been used to describe how in adolescence we learn how to complete a sudoku or other logic-based problem (see Chapter 13).

Stage 1 Sensorimotor intelligence (birth to 2 years)

Phase 1 The use of reflexes (birth through first month)

The earliest ability seen in an infant is described by Piaget as *sucking*. The new-born child makes a sucking motion at the mother's breast, to her finger or indeed to any object placed near the infant's mouth. Later in the month the infant will also incline his head, raise his mouth towards his mother's breast or milk bottle and appear to actively seek the opportunity to feed.

Phase 2 Primary circular reactions (1 to 4 months)

In this phase the infant begins to repeat actions. The infant may find her hand and start to suck on it apparently by chance, but will then repeat the action later and more frequently as she progresses through this stage. The actions become more deliberate in this phase and more coordinated.

Phase 3 Secondary circular reactions (4 to 10 months)

Now the infant is making more deliberate actions, his behaviour starts to show connections with objects. Children in this phase begin to kick their legs and see how this causes the blanket to come off in the pram, or they see that shaking a toy makes the bell tinkle in response. This phase also coincides with the development of smiling and expressions of joy at being able to make noises with a toy or being able to kick.

Phase 4 The coordination of secondary schemas (8 to 12 months)

As the child reaches the later part of her first year in life, she begins to demonstrate more complicated behaviour. Having learnt the connection between an action and a response (such as shaking the toy to hear the bell tinkle), the child now starts to put different actions together in goal-oriented behaviour. An example of this could be seen in a simple game. Sit the child down and, whilst they are watching, hide the child's favourite toy under a cloth. A child engaged in this phase will use two schemas to achieve what they want: reaching for the cloth and lifting it away (one schema) then reaching for their toy and grasping it (second schema). By the age of 12 months, Piaget argues that the child is coordinating their behaviour to achieve what they want.

Phase 5 Tertiary circular reactions (12 to 18 months)

In this stage the child begins to experiment with their learned schema. If you present a toy drum to an 18-month-old boy, for instance, you will see that he tries different ways of playing with it. Six months earlier he may have only played with the toy in one way; now he is older, he will test out different uses for the toy – banging it softly and much harder, turning it on its side, banging the top and side, holding it by the carry-strap or rolling it along the ground. This phase is very much one of exploration of the elements of their world.

In the earlier months of the preoperational thought stage, the child learns something called object permanence. In the later part of the first year of life we have proposed that the child will use schemas to locate a toy hidden under a cloth. The assumption Piaget makes is that the child will only attempt to lift the cloth to reach the toy if she believes that the toy is under the cloth. In the early months of development, placing a toy under a cloth will result in the child losing all interest in the toy. If she cannot see the toy, the suggestion is that she believes the toy is no longer there. Later, the child develops a sense of object permanence. Now the child knows that even though the toy is covered by a cloth, it has not disappeared and lifting the cloth will reveal the toy.

This mother and baby are playing 'peek-a-boo'. The child is 'hiding' from his mother by covering his eyes with his hands.
Source: Corbis/Jim Craigmyle

Phase 6 The beginning of mental representation (18 months to 2 years)

Now that they know that the object remains even when hidden out of view, children in phase 6 start to form mental images of routes to getting what they want and will climb out of and onto anything to reach it. All kinds of mental representations develop at this point and children begin to put words together and to make decisions without needing to have tangible examples put in front of them. They decide what they want to eat, what they want to do and how they want to do it. The child is becoming stronger and more physically active and will run further and climb higher in order to attain their goal.

Stage 2 Preoperational thought (2 to 7 years)

The next stage of cognitive development that Piaget describes for young children is that of *preoperational thought*. This stage describes the child's burgeoning abilities in imaginative play and the use of symbols. By the age of 2 years children often engage in s*ymbolic play*: play that represents real life. They may play 'mummies and daddies' with a toy doll, feeding the doll with a miniature bottle and pushing it around in a toy pushchair, for example; or they may play 'doctors and nurses' and pretend to fix problems in their dolls or other children such as a bumped head or a scraped knee. Symbolic play is an important part of development and reflects the child's ability to observe and copy what is happening in the world around him. Other symbols that children use as they progress in the preoperational thought stage are letters and words, and children show an enormous capacity for learning new words in these years of development.

Children in the preoperational thought stage of development are egocentric: they understand the world from their own perspective and find it difficult to understand the point of view of another person. Piaget demonstrated this egocentrism with his now-famous Three Mountains

Definitions

Object permanence: knowing that even when something has disappeared from view, it has not necessarily actually disappeared.
Egocentric: understanding the world only from your own perspective and finding it difficult to understand the point of view of another person.

study (Piaget and Inhelder, 1956). Piaget and Inhelder constructed a three-dimensional model of three differently sized and shaped mountains (see Figure 2.2 below), placed a doll on one side of the model and stood the child on the other side. The researchers then asked the child to describe the scene that the doll could see and to select from a series of pictures the doll's view of the mountains. The 4 and 5-year-old children described their own view of the mountains when describing the doll's view, as the children were not able to mentally construct the doll's perspective of the model.

Another feature of this stage in development is the child's inability at first to complete conservation tasks (Piaget, 1981). Conservation is the principle that the shape or appearance of something can change without there being a change in quantity. For example, if you were to put two short tumblers of water next to each other and ask the child if they were equal, the child would confirm this. However, if you poured the contents from one of the tumblers into a thinner, taller glass and asked the same question, the pre-school child would say that no, there was more water in the taller glass. Similarly, if you took two equal balls of plasticine dough and rolled one into a long thin shape, the pre-school child would again assert that the longer, thinner shape contained more dough than did the round ball of dough. Children frequently make the mistake of thinking that the taller or longer item has more content and do not acquire the ability to make the mental transformation of mass or volume until around the age of 7 years.

During the preoperative stage of thinking, the child progresses their cognitive abilities remarkably quickly. In these five years of development the child will learn to use symbols in play and language, she will learn about

Definition

Conservation: the principle that the shape or appearance of something can change without there being a change in quantity.

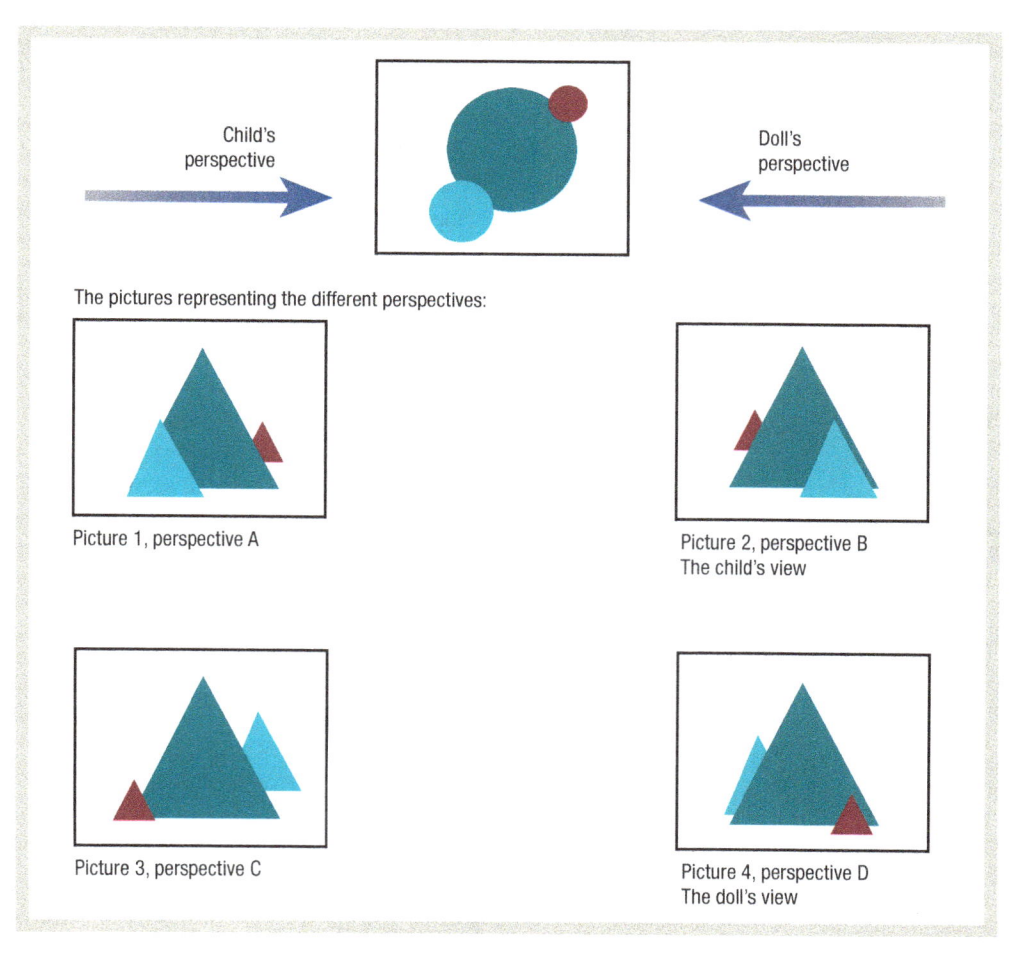

Figure 2.2 The Three Mountains study.

the different perspective of other people and understand the principles of mass and volume conservation. At around the age of 7 years the child will move into the stage of concrete operational thought and start to lose their egocentric way of thinking, beginning to look at problems from another person's perspective and to use this information in making decisions.

Stage 3 Concrete operational thought (7 to 11 years)

At around the age of 7 years the child enters into the stage Piaget called *concrete operational thought*. This stage is dominated by learning to use logic to solve real, actual problems. There are many types of logical thinking that the child will learn (see Table 2.3). For instance, the child will learn to sort objects into a hierarchical order based on their size or shape – for instance, from smallest to largest. Ask children of this age to line up in order of size and they will quickly place themselves in order of the shortest child up to the tallest child, a process called *seriation*.

Other abilities include learning to name and sort objects into categories based on similar characteristics. This ability to categorise objects is known as *classification* and allows the child to make certain assumptions about objects based on their membership to a particular category. For instance, if you know that all mammals are warm blooded, then if you read in school about an animal you have not encountered that is a mammal, then you can assume that the animal is warm blooded.

Children at this stage are able to begin to use complex mathematical skills. They have already used symbols to reflect numbers in class, but by the age of 8 or 9 years they are able to complete mathematical equations. Thus the child will be able to do simple additions such as 5 + 5 = 10, but will also be able to reverse the sum and do subtractions such as 10 − 5 = 5. This ability to understand that numbers can be changed and then returned to their original state is known as *reversibility* and is more than being able to simply do the sums, but reflects an understanding of the mathematical flexibility of numbers.

Stage 4 Formal operations (11 to adulthood)

Piaget's final stage of development, the formal operations stage, signifies a move from being able to consider the *concrete* (or real, physically present) concepts in problem solving, to being able to consider *abstract* concepts. These abstract concepts could be the use of letters to solve algebraic mathematical equations or could be the discovery of the meaning behind the words of poetry or song lyrics. From the age of 11 years the young person begins to comprehend a world where sometimes what is said does not match what is meant in a conversation, a poem or a song and, most importantly, why someone would mislead you in this way. Piaget described the key skills emerging during this stage as logical thought and deductive reasoning, abstract thought and systematic problem solving.

Logical thought and deductive reasoning

Prior to this stage, children have developed the ability to categorise and classify information and to do simple mathematics. Now, in the formal operations stage, the young person learns that you can use letters to represent missing numbers and use your knowledge of reversibility to work out which number the letter represents. Learning the skills of algebra is not possible until the child enters into this stage as it requires him to use *deductive logic*. Deductive logic is the ability to use a general principle to determine a specific outcome. This type of thinking involves the manipulation of hypothetical situations – an ability not seen until now.

Abstract thought

The ability to think about abstract concepts emerges during the formal operational stage. Previously the child was able to consider solving problems only in terms of their experiences. The child had to learn to take the

Table 2.3 Summary of the main abilities learnt during the concrete operations stage of development.

Piaget's logical task	Child is able to convert this....	To this....
Seriation	A A A A A A	A A A A A A
Classification	ABBBAABABA	(AAAAA) (BBBBB)
Reversibility	5 + 5 = 10	Therefore, 10 − 5 = 5

perspective of another person. Now, however, the young person is able to consider possible outcomes and consequences of actions for which they have no life experience. Take, for instance, a class discussion on the value of volunteering at a home for adults with various forms of dementia. Although none of the class might have direct experience of this type of work, each student will be able to consider hypothetically the need for this type of home facility, the care needs of the older adults and the value to him or herself of gaining work experience in this type of environment. The young person initially will find this type of discussion difficult when asked to consider the perspectives of everybody involved: for instance, the different needs of the adult with dementia, his wife and close family, the carer and the needs of the wider society. Often she will over-emphasise the impact on herself when considering this hypothetical question and focus on her personal development needs. However, with time and practice she will be able to make decisions that have long-term consequences not just for herself but for others and society as a whole. Developing this type of thinking is important for long-term planning, such as making decisions on what course to study to prepare you for a future career, and it is not something that happens overnight. Many young people entering university, for instance, have no real idea of what career path they desire, but still understand the important of higher study in creating career choices.

Systematic problem solving

For children in the earlier stages of development, problem solving was often a matter of trial-and-error rather than the use of any structured strategies. During the formal operational stage however, the young person develops the ability to systematically solve a problem in a logical and methodical manner. Piaget gave young people the 'pendulum problem' to see what strategies they used to solve it. The young people were given different lengths of cord and different weights and were asked what affected the rate of swing of a pendulum. Children in the concrete operations stage of development tend to approach this task quite randomly and change two or more features of the pendulum in trying to answer the question. Young people in the formal operations stage of development, however, approach the task systematically, testing each variable in turn: dropping the pendulum from a greater height, changing the length of the string (correct answer) and changing the weight of the pendulum itself.

> **STOP AND THINK**
>
> Use Piaget's theory of cognitive development to decide at what age a child should be able to study poetry effectively in school.

Critique

Piaget's theory of cognitive development is highly thought of and used frequently in understanding children's development both in the field of educational policy and in psychology. However, there are a few criticisms of his theory. First, research has shown that the stages are not as age related as previously thought. Children develop at their own pace and do not necessarily achieve proficiency in each stage at exactly the age Piaget describes. However, it is agreed that children do progress through the stages in just the order that Piaget has written.

Another criticism is directed at Piaget's belief that we all engage in the formal operations stage of development and acquire proficiency in hypothetical deduction, logic and systematic problem solving, and the ability to understand the abstract nature of life. However, research has shown that not everyone acquires these skills and, certainly, not everyone uses these skills in everyday life. Some adults will often fall back on concrete principles when considering matters of political or ethical importance and rarely show competence in highly abstract thinking. Others may never have understood the principles of algebra at school and find the use of mathematical symbols difficult.

Further criticism has been directed at Piaget's theory for underestimating the abilities of children. Piaget asserts that children in the preoperational stage of development are unable to consider another person's perspective (in the Three Mountains Task, for instance). However, children in this stage will often tailor their language and behaviour to the appropriate level for a young sibling when necessary, and must therefore be demonstrating an awareness of the limitations in the ability of that younger brother or sister. This appears to be evidence counter to Piaget's theory of cognitive development – certainly in the ability to empathise with another. Piaget's theory of cognitive development has been interpreted more recently within an information-processing framework that places greater emphasis on the changes in cognitive processing than on maturational changes. The section on neo-Piagetian theory in Chapter 14 discusses the development of Piaget's theory and illustrates how it is still considered highly useful in understanding cognitive development in children and continues to be used as the foundation stone of research by developmental psychologists.

Integrative perspectives in developmental psychology

There are other theories and perspectives of developmental psychology that are gaining in popularity as psychologists and other human and behavioural scientists search for theories that integrate the biological, physiological effects of development with social and environmental factors. Some researchers use a combination of approaches to help understand very specific behaviours. For example, a psychologist wanting to understand why a young boy set fire to a car might want to call upon many theories to create an holistic view of the influential factors involved in the onset of that act. The psychologist might invoke the use of social learning theories (does the child come from a dysfunctional family?); cognitive theories (is the child unable to understand consequences of that action?); environmental factor theories (does the child come from poverty or a home physical environment that is unpleasant?); and biological development theories (is the child experiencing strength and conflict from early-onset puberty?). Using perspectives from all these theories will provide a full picture of the young boy sitting in front of her and help her to target therapeutic intervention.

Lev Vygotsky (1896–1934): sociocultural theory

A key researcher supporting an integrative approach in developmental psychology is the Russian, Lev Vygotsky. Vygotsky was heavily influenced by the works of Gesell, Freud, Pavlov and Piaget, and his theory combines the two approaches: the biological nature or 'natural line' of development with the 'social-historical' influences from family, friends and society generally. He unfortunately died at a young age and did not have time to develop his theory in detail, but following the release of his writings after the end of the Cold War in Europe, we have some insight into what he proposed.

Vygotsky's *sociocultural theory* of development (Vygotsky, 1978b) suggests that we develop as children as a result of our biological drive to do so, but also as a result of our social interactions. Without contact with other people, Vygotsky believed we would not progress beyond very primitive patterns of thinking (Vygotsky, 1962). Vygotsky introduced a concept called *scaffolding* that describes how adults and older children try to advance the child's abilities – by correcting his language use or encouraging him with his homework. Vygotsky believed that we each advance by working in the *zone of proximal development*. When we find a task difficult to do but with help from a parent or older sibling, for example, we find we are able to complete it, then we are said to be in the zone of proximal development. According to Vygotsky, we do not develop as children or adults without the help of others, whether we are learning our alphabet or learning to drive. Without guidance and support from our social community, we can only develop our skills and abilities so far. There are, therefore, important implications of Vygotsky's work for education: in particular, the role of the teacher in structured learning. In Chapter 14, you can see many examples of how Vygotsky's theory has influenced the classroom and you can compare his contribution with Piaget's in building the framework for an effective learning environment.

Urie Bronfenbrenner (1917–2005): bioecological theory

Urie Bronfenbrenner's bioecological theory expands on the influences of other people and the social environment in shaping our development. Bronfenbrenner's theory describes social influence as a series of concentric circles with the person at the centre (see Figure 2.3). Bronfenbrenner's theory was initially described as an ecological theory (1979, 1986) based on its reliance on socialisation as a powerful factor in the young child's development, but in his paper in 2000, Bronfenbrenner

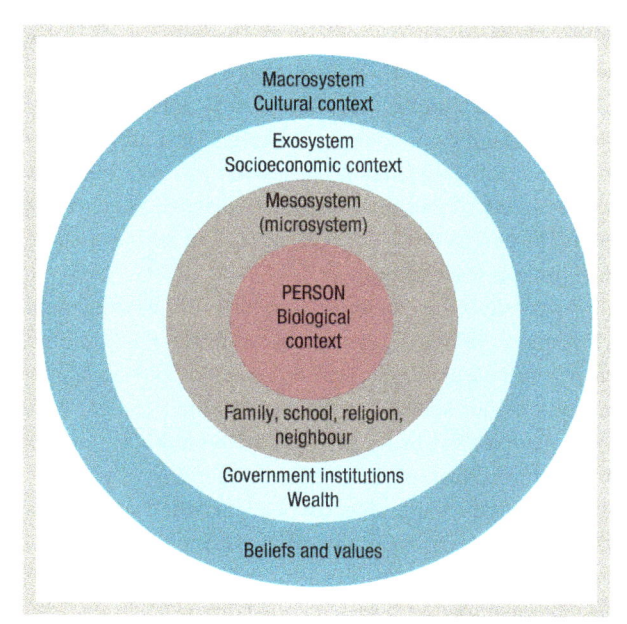

Figure 2.3 Bronfenbrenner's bioecological theory of the social influences on our development.
Source: adapted from Boyd & Bee (2006)

reworked his theory to take into account the influence a child's biology has on her development, and his theory is now called the *bioecological model* of human development (Bronfenbrenner and Evans, 2000).

Bronfenbrenner sees the child at the centre of his model existing within a microsystem of daily activities and interactions. The child is an active part of these activities and interactions: for example, if the child is hungry, he will cry and cause other people around him to come to him and bring him food. The parents too may come to him and smile, tickle him or present toys to him, encouraging the child to smile back and engage in the games. The relationships are therefore bidirectional: the child and the parents are both active in these daily interactions. The microsystem can also be affected by the nature of the child and the quality of the parents' relationship. A placid, smiling child will probably elicit calm, smiling reactions from the parents, whereas an active, distracted or fussy child might elicit quite different behaviour from his parents. Similarly, if the parents are content and supportive in their relationship, their ability to respond to the child is enhanced and both the child and the parents experience a positive interaction. However, if the parents are in conflict and are unable to provide consistent parenting, the child may experience hostile parenting and develop a hostile perspective himself (Hetherington and Stanley-Hagen, 2002).

Bronfenbrenner saw connections between each of the elements of the microsystem which he called the mesosystem. If the child's microsystem consisted of parents, a neighbour and children attending the same pre-school, then the child was not only influenced by each of these people separately, but was influenced by how all these people worked together. For example, one day the neighbour might help out and pick up the child from the pre-school and notice that she is being bullied by another child. The neighbour then tells the parents, who then work together with the pre-school to get the bullying stopped. The mesosystem, the connections between elements of the microsystem, has therefore affected the child's development by working to bring about change in the child's experience of pre-school.

As the child gets older, so Bronfenbrenner's exosystem becomes more important in the child's development. The exosystem consists of a formal structure of school governors, the board of directors in the workplace, health services and community welfare systems (Boyd and Bee, 2006). For example, the child is not directly aware of or knowingly affected by their local health authority's policy on early years parenting classes, say, but she will benefit indirectly by having parents who, early on in her lifetime, have access to parenting resources and other coping strategies to help them foster a strong, supportive home environment. The exosystem can also include the wider family unit and circles of friends. The child raised in a large, welcoming, extended family, for instance, has access to cousins, aunts and uncles, grandparents and possibly great-grandparents, all of whom will be important people throughout the child's life.

Finally, Bronfenbrenner's macrosystem describes the cultural values, norms, laws, customs and other social influences that will guide the child's development.

Definition

Microsystem: the activities and interactions immediately surrounding a person.

Definitions

Mesosystem: the connections between elements of the microsystem.
Exosystem: the social settings that do not immediately impact on a person, but surround them and are important to their welfare.
Macrosystem: the cultural values, laws, customs and resources available to a person.

A child raised in a culture that values children and supports the parents with childcare facilities and flexible working hours will experience a more positive socialisation process, and his parents too will feel more valued and supported in raising their child.

If you look at the beginning of Chapter 14 on developmental psychology and education, you will see an excellent example of Bronfenbrenner's bioecological theory being applied to the child's experience of school. Bronfenbrenner's bioecological theory of development does not just apply, though, to the experiences of the child, but is a flexible, dynamic theory that accounts for the experiences of all of us right up to old age. The quality of our social care and welfare systems has an impact on us whatever our age, and the ability to adopt flexible working patterns is just as important as we head towards retirement as it is when we have a young family in tow. Bronfenbrenner's theory integrates our biology with our social upbringing and does not see one as being more important than the other. Importantly, Bronfenbrenner described us all as being both products and producers of our environments, as dynamic drivers of our personal development and influencers of social change (Bronfenbrenner, 1986).

SUMMARY

We began our introduction to the theoretical perspectives of developmental psychology by providing you with four learning objectives. Now you have completed this chapter, let us return to them in turn. First, in order to be able to discuss critically what makes a theory, we need to know what the three main factors are that comprise a theory: define, explain, predict. Do all the theories presented here do this to your satisfaction? Are the behaviours at the focus of each theory well described and defined? Do the theories explain the changes in development sufficiently? Do any of the theories have predictive value, or some sort of discriminative value? Can you use the theory to discriminate between those children who are developing in line with their peers and those children who are not? Can you predict adult relationship behaviour from an understanding of their social development as a child and the attachment formed with their mother or primary carer? The next factor that needs to be considered when evaluating a theory is whether the theory describes development occurring as a process of continuous change or whether it happens in distinct stages. For instance, does language development happen in successive, age-specific incremental stages or is it a more fluid process that each child works through in their own time?

The second learning objective, to evaluate the key theoretical perspectives in developmental psychology, requires you to be able first to list the four main theoretical perspectives in developmental psychology, then to describe the key assumptions underlying these perspectives. Take, for example, the biological perspective. What are the key assumptions underlying this perspective? Psychologists should study observable and measurable behaviour only; all behaviours are learned – we are not born with any set of behaviours; mental process cannot be observed or measured and therefore cannot be studied scientifically; and the adult personality can change but only as a result of exposure to different experiences. What did you learn about the works of Gesell, Lorenz, Bowlby and Ainsworth that supported these assumptions? What did you learn that went counter to these assumptions? Consider comparing the biological perspective to the social learning perspective: what are the strengths and weaknesses of each approach? How do they compare with each other?

The third learning objective requires you to understand the philosophical perspectives underlying key developmental psychology theorists. This builds on the second learning objective. So, think about these questions. Which theories take the biological perspective? Which theories take the social learning perspective? Which theories take the psychoanalytic perspective? What theory takes the cognitive-developmental perspective? Knowing the underlying perspective to each of the theories will help you to understand the application of these theories to real-life situations and help you in your essays when you are asked to compare and contrast the different theorists.

Finally, the last learning objective requires you to critically evaluate the use and application of theories and perspectives in understanding real-life examples of human behaviour from a developmental perspective. The boxed features are each aimed at helping you to understand the application of theories to real-world psychology. How do each of the features help us to decide how much of development is biologically driven (or 'nature') and how much of development is learned (or 'nurture')? Take, for example, the case study 'Genie', described in Chapter 5 (page 127). What can the study of children raised in isolation tell us about the nature of the 'critical period' in child development?

To conclude this chapter, the theories and perspectives we have learned about here all help us to describe and explain human development. Some of the theories, such as Bowlby's theory of attachment, are quite specific and focus on the development of one particular behaviour. These theories can be called *micro theories* in that they are focused tightly on understanding very specific elements of behaviour. Others are more general, such as Piaget's cognitive development theory and Erkison's theory of psychosocial development, and focus on our development across the lifespan. These theories can be called *grand theories* in that they seek to explain human behaviour in all or many aspects of life, such as personality development, memory and decision making, social development and play behaviour. Throughout this chapter we have highlighted some examples of these theories 'at work'. There are other examples of these theories in action too, and when you are reading the remainder of this book, consider whether the behaviour could be understood within the context of a grand theory of development or within the context of a micro theory of development.

REVIEW QUESTIONS

1. What makes a good theory?
2. How do stage theories differ from continuous or lifespan perspective theories?
3. How have the works of Rousseau and Locke influenced our understanding of child development?
4. What contribution have Lorenz and Pavlov made to our understanding of human development?
5. What contribution do the integrative theorists make to our understanding of child development?

RECOMMENDED READING

Further reading on the critical evaluation of Piaget and other developmental theorists can be found in the excellent book:

Crain, W. (2010). *Theories of Development: Concepts and Applications* (6th Ed.). Englewood Cliffs, NJ: Pearson Prentice Hall.

Further reading on the 'nature versus nurture' debate in developmental psychology can be found in:

Ceci, S., & Williams, W. (Eds.). (2000). *The Nature–Nurture Debate: The Essential Readings*. New York: Blackwell.

Goldhaber, D. (2012). *The Nature–Nurture Debates: Bridging the Gap*. Cambridge: Cambridge University Press.

Further reading on Bronfenbrenner's bioecological theory of development can be found in:

Bronfenbrenner, U., & Evans, G. (2000). Developmental science in the 21st century: Emerging questions, theoretical models, research designs and empirical findings. *Social Development, 9*, 115–125.

RECOMMENDED WEBSITES

Useful websites aimed at furthering your knowledge of the theoretical perspectives and examples of their application in developmental psychology:

Jean Piaget Society
http://www.piaget.org

Erikson Institute
http://www.erikson.edu

Anna Freud Centre
http://www.annafreud.org

Bronfenbrenner Centre for Translational Research
http://www.bctr.cornell.edu

Chapter 3
Research methods

Learning outcomes

After reading this chapter, and with further recommended reading, you should be able to:

1. Understand how theoretical paradigms apply to children in a research setting.
2. Understand the range of research methods available for the study of child development.
3. Critically evaluate what the ethical issues are of conducting research with children.
4. Critically evaluate what the practical issues are of conducting research with children.
5. Critically evaluate the research methods of studies reporting research with children.

On 18 March 2015, researchers in Brazil issued a press release reporting that infants who were breastfed were more likely to be well educated and earn higher salaries than infants who were not (Victora et al., 2015). The researchers followed nearly 6000 babies over a period of 30 years to get an idea of the long-term effects of breastfeeding. So how did the researchers set up their study and come to these conclusions? This chapter is designed to help you understand how we research children and how we, as developmental psychologists, can work rigorously and ethically in our pursuit of knowledge.

Introduction

If we think back to Chapter 2, 'Theoretical perspectives', you will remember that we discussed a number of quite varied theories of human development. We looked at Gesell's maturational theory with a biological underpinning, which explained our psychological development occurring alongside our physical development. We reviewed Freud's theory of the psychosexual development of the child. Erikson's theory looked at the psychosocial development of the child whilst Piaget looked at understanding the cognitive development of the child. All these theories, although quite different in their theoretical perspective, together helped us to understand the wider picture of the personal and psychological development of the child. Whilst all these theories have a strong philosophical base, they also have a strong experimental or research base. That is, these theories are all the result of research studies of children in various settings. Some, like Jean Piaget, conducted hours of research observing children in their natural environment, at play, looking for patterns of behaviour, which he noted down meticulously. Others, like Mary Ainsworth, set out to test her ideas, based on her observations of mother and child behaviour, in a laboratory setting where she could control what events occurred and, again, record her findings in great detail.

Without such painstaking record keeping by Piaget and Ainsworth, as well as all the other researchers of the twentieth century, we would not have the great understanding of children that we currently have. Through reading the detailed papers of studies conducted by key developmental psychologists, education specialists and family therapists, we are able to understand the key issues in researching children and to make use of their recommendations for best practice. Research in developmental psychology generally fits into a number of themes: understanding children's social development (e.g. attachment and bonding behaviour, play and relationship behaviour); understanding their cognitive development (e.g. the development of skills such as language, memory and empathy); and understanding children with differences (e.g. children who are very high achievers, children with developmental delay, children with other learning difficulties). In order to make sense of these theories and studies, we need to understand how research is conducted on children and why the study of children presents quite different challenges to the study of adults.

What is research?

The term research refers to the series of activities we carry out when we want to find out the answer to a question or a problem. Sometimes the questions are set for us by our teachers and work colleagues, sometimes the questions come from reading and reflect our interest in a topic, and sometimes the questions come when we see something happen and want to know why it occurred. Although on occasion we may think we intuitively know the answers to the questions, using appropriate research methods to solve the question or the problem can allow us to state the answer with a reasonable amount of certainty.

Research can therefore be carried out for many reasons. It can be *exploratory* and seek to understand something that we know little about. It can be *speculative* and try to work out what might be the long-term implications of changing, say, a policy on health care, education or funding. It can be *descriptive* and aim to show patterns and connections in behaviour. It can be *explanatory* and show why those patterns and connections exist. Research can also be *predictive* and be used to develop and test a model that aims to predict what circumstances result in a certain behaviour or other outcome. Finally, research can be *evaluative* and seek to measure the impact of a change in, say, policy, illness medication or educational technique (Leary, 2008).

The importance of understanding theoretical paradigms

When thinking about conducting research in developmental psychology, we need to consider first your position in a key research paradigm, positivism versus constructivism. Do you think that it is possible to know and measure a child, for them to be investigated in a structured, scientific way that tests hypotheses and factual statements (a positivist approach)? Or do you think that children are part of the social fabric of life, dynamic and interactive? Can children only be understood in the context of being active members of relationships which are both proactive and responsive (a constructivist approach: Grieg et al., 2007)?

According to the positivist assumption, research with children can be carried out in the same way as research in the fields of chemistry, geology or plant biology. Children are biological beings that fit into the fundamental laws of science and can therefore be tested in exactly the same way. A researcher can set a hypothetical question and then test it to see if the statement is true or false. Positivist researchers thus use experimental hypotheses in their research and design studies to test the truth of them. For example, a positivist might set the hypothesis that children who are good at mathematics are poor at learning a second language. The researcher will then measure a number of children's ability in maths and in a second language and run statistical analysis to determine if the hypothesis is true. The researcher can control the test conditions of the children, make sure that the study is carried out systematically and test enough children to state confidently that his research findings indicate that the statement is true.

The difficulty with this approach is that the researcher, although controlling the test conditions, cannot control for any other external factors, known

> **Definitions**
>
> Research: (a) the systematic investigation into and study of materials, sources, etc., in order to establish facts and reach new conclusions; (b) an endeavour to discover new or collate old facts, etc. by the scientific study of a subject or by a course of critical investigation (Oxford Dictionaries, 2008).
> Positivism: (concept) a system recognising only that which can be scientifically verified or logically proved, and therefore rejecting metaphysics and theism (Oxford Dictionaries, 2008).
> Constructivism: a philosophy of learning founded on the premise that, by reflecting on our experiences, we construct our own understanding of the world we live in (Piaget, 1967).

as confound variables. For instance, one example of a confound variable happens as soon as the research takes place, as both the researcher and the child know that they are in an artificial situation that has been created for a purpose. The child and researcher may have quite different ideas on what that purpose is, but it is likely that both will change their natural behaviour as a result, affecting the validity of the study. Confound variables can be found in the interpretation of both the process and the outcome of the research study. In everyday life, each of us individually interprets the meaning of the words, actions and gestures of others, and it is no different in the research setting. As researchers, we think we know what message we are putting across when we describe the aims of the research to the child and we think we are making accurate interpretations of the data we collect. However, what we often fail to consider is the context of that language and behaviour. As researchers, we are accustomed to using language in a particular way, are familiar with research techniques and we have an expectation of the findings of the study. The child, however, does not have those influences, and may indeed see things quite differently. Take, for example, research conducted by Herbert P. Ginsberg (1997). Ginsberg asked a child to 'count the toys out loud'. The child patiently named all the toys in front of her. When he asked instead 'How many toys are there?' the child accurately counted all the toys. Ginsberg concludes that by not asking the right question, he would have thought that this child could not add, but in fact she could; she had simply misunderstood the question (Ginsberg, 1997, p. 11).

This also illustrates a further confound variable, which is the ability of the child to understand what is required of him or her in the research setting. A researcher who has decided to investigate, say, children of 7 years of age needs to be aware that the development of language, empathy, other cognitive and even motor ability varies from child to child and what might be understood by one child may not be understood by the next. The positivist researcher may have to develop research methods that will test effectively children of all abilities and to devise a measure that is suitable not just for a range of age groups, but also for the range of abilities within those age groups.

The constructivist approach sees children very differently. Constructivists see children and their parents and carers, teachers and peers as working in a dynamic way. Children and the people around them interact by talking, playing, crying and caring, and construct the meaning of these events from the context where they occur. The constructivist approach sees children and the people around them as a network of relationships where all players are important. The context of the interaction is also very important to the constructivist approach, as it is the context (history, time, culture) that gives meaning to the behaviour. Constructivist researchers try to understand as much about the behaviour as they possibly can by investigating smaller groups of people in detail, trying to enter the world of the child to see what his or her perspective is, who the important people are and where behavioural influences come from. Constructivist researchers do not try to generalise their findings on a small group to the population as a whole and, from this methodological perspective, their findings can be limited in their application. However, the constructivist argument supports the notion that findings from such detailed, individualist research have a great deal of validity when the whole social, cultural and historic context of the child is understood as, without this, the researcher's ability to describe and interpret the behaviour is highly restricted (Hatch, 1995).

Therefore, depending on your perspective, you may see children as readily testable and measurable, participants whom you can conduct your research *on* (positivist), or you may see children as people you can learn from, who need to be understood in context, participants that you can conduct your research *with* (constructivist). To understand the importance of understanding, questioning and debating the positivist–constructivist research paradigm, think about the implications for your research method. To put it simply, if your theoretical perspective is positivist, you are more likely to find using quantitative methodologies appropriate to answer your research question, whilst, if your theoretical perspective is constructionist, you are more likely to find the use of qualitative methodologies more appropriate in answering your research question.

Definition

Confound variables: extraneous factors in a research study that are not specifically measured or manipulated and that may affect the results of that study.

Methods in developmental psychology research

The research methods used in developmental psychology research have evolved to take into account the particular difficulties of investigating behaviour and other phenomena in infants and young children. A questionnaire might be a suitable tool to use with the adult population to measure, for example, voting behaviour, choice of washing powder or even emotional states. However, when dealing with young children, developmental psychologists need to consider other factors, such as reading ability, comprehension and linguistic capability. A 4-year-old child, for instance, may not be able to read the questions, or write an answer, but if asked the questions by the researcher, it is possible that the child will be able to reply verbally. Developmental psychologists employ a number of research methods to aid them in answering their research questions, but the most commonly used are observations, case studies, questionnaires and experimental methods. All of these methods are used by psychologists and other behavioural scientists but, for developmental psychologists in particular, the methods are often refined for use with very young participants. Whichever method is used, it tends to fall into one of two categories: either it is a longitudinal or cross-sectional study design or it involves quantitative or qualitative research. These reflect the ideology behind the research question and, often, the researcher himself.

Cross-sectional and longitudinal research designs

As part of the process of designing your research method, you need to consider how much time you have to complete the research. For much of your research carried out as part of your degree studies, you will only have a very short period of time to complete your work. In the first year of study, you may find you have less than an hour to collect your data, whilst in your final year you may find yourself able to devote perhaps a longer period of, say, three to four months. Evidently, the type of method you choose to collect data in these circumstances is dependent on the time available. However, in larger-scale research projects, the method design can be directed more easily by the needs of the research question. Take, for example, the following research questions:

- What is the average score in a maths test given to 7-year-old children?
- Does maths score at age 7 years predict ability in maths at age 16 years?

To answer the first research question, you will need to design a research project that measures every 7-year-old child's ability in mathematics. One way of doing this would be to go into all the schools in the region, hand out the same maths test to all the 7-year-old children there and collect in their scores. When you have retrieved all the scores, you can then work out what the average score in the maths test is for this age group and confidently report your findings. The research design you have used here is a cross-sectional research design.

Cross-sectional research design

The cross-sectional research design allows researchers to collect data that describe the current situation – in our example, mathematical ability. Data collected in this way can reveal the lowest and highest score, the most common score (the modal score), the mid-point score (the median score) and the average score (the mean score).

Definitions

Cross-sectional research design: a method of collecting data that administers a test or series of tests to a participant or group of participants on one occasion only.

Mean: a statistical term which refers to the numerical average of a set of numbers. To calculate the mean, add all of the numbers in the set and divide by the number of items in the set.

Median: the mid-point in the range of scores that the participants received on a measure. If we place our participants' maths scores in ascending order (5, 5, 5, 7, 8), we can see that the score at the mid-point in the range from 5 to 8 is the third 5 and the median score is therefore 5.

Modal: the most frequently obtained score that the participants received on a measure. In our example, the most frequently obtained score is 5 (5, 5, 5, 7, 8) and the modal score is therefore 5.

All of these scores are useful indicators of performance and are frequently used to create statements of norms of behaviour and ability. In this example, the research design will allow you to calculate the norm or average maths ability in 7-year-olds and to show what the range of ability in 7-year-olds might be. This information could then be used by educators to identify children who are particularly able in maths, who might be encouraged to study more difficult problems, and children who are struggling with maths and who might need more help.

The cross-sectional research design is, therefore, a useful way of conducting research, but it does have its weaknesses. This research method only allows us to calculate mathematical ability in children aged 7 years at one point in time. It does not allow us to calculate whether maths scores in children aged 7 years have changed over time and it does not tell us whether maths ability at age 7 years predicts maths ability (or any other type of ability) at a later age. The research design has only allowed us to see a 'snapshot' of mathematical ability. Like a photograph, the research can only provide us with information on one form of ability in one age group of children at one point in time. Thus, the researcher is limited in what she can infer from her findings.

Longitudinal research design

The longitudinal research method, however, allows the researcher to measure change over time and to find evidence of strong associations or predictors of this change.

The second research question (does maths score at age 7 years predict ability in maths at age 16 years?) requires a longitudinal research design. To answer this question, you need to start in the same way as before and hand out a standard maths test to all the 7-year-old children in a region and collect in all their scores. At this point, however, the method of data collection changes. You must then return to the same children when they are 16 years old and collect their scores in another standard maths test. By comparing the children's scores when they are 16 years of age to when they were 7 years of age, you will be able to see if there is any connection between the two and, indeed, if maths ability at age 7 years predicts maths ability at age 16 years. By administering the same test to the same participants at two different points in time, this research question can be answered quite effectively.

The longitudinal research design is an extremely useful tool for measuring change over time. It does, though, like the cross-sectional research design, have its limitations. Longitudinal research relies on testing the same participants on at least two time points using the same test of measurement. It can be carried out over a couple of days or, as in this example, over a number of years. If the research is to be carried out over a couple of days, it is usually achieved with only a minimal number of participants failing to return for the second data collection. However, if the research is carried out over a number of years, quite often a fairly large number of participants are not present for the second data collection point. In our example, 9 years pass between data collection point 1 (children aged 7 years) and point 2 (children aged 16 years). During this time, some families may move away from the area and the children change school, or some children may not be present due to illness or other changed circumstance. Thus, your participant group at the end of the study might be fewer in number than at the beginning, making it difficult to see patterns and connections in the data.

A second weakness of this method that particularly applies in developmental psychology research is that of developmental change in ability. If you were to give the 16-year-old children the same maths test as you gave the 7-year-old children, then we might predict that after nine years of cognitive development and education in mathematics, all the 16-year-old children will obtain near-maximum scores in the test and render the findings of the study void. With a nine-year age gap, therefore, you will need to select a standard test of maths ability that is appropriate for 16-year-olds. However, complications in forming conclusions can arise by changing the test of maths ability. This test will now in all likelihood test ability in more complicated problem-solving skills and more sophisticated analytical techniques such as algebra and geometry as well as arithmetic. Many people will struggle to attain these complex cognitive skills, even though they may be quite proficient in more simple arithmetic. The researcher

---

Definition

Longitudinal research method: a method of collecting data that administers a test or series of tests to the same participant or group of participants on a number of occasions.

is in danger then of measuring not a developing ability in maths, but a different cognitive process altogether. By introducing the different test, you have now altered a fundamental part of your research study and will have to consider this in your report, as you now have a factor that limits your ability to state with confidence whether maths ability at age 7 years predicts maths ability at age 16 years.

Quantitative methods

Quantitative methods can be described as methods that use numbers to describe and define concepts (Neuman, 2007). A typical quantitative method would use a survey or questionnaire to collect numerically coded data.

Quantitative methods have the advantage of being quick and easy to carry out. This also means that quantitative methods can often be a fairly inexpensive way of collecting large quantities of data. Another advantage of quantitative methods is that the data collected can often be analysed mathematically and statistically to provide information on norms and variation within the studied population.

Commonly used quantitative methods

Questionnaires and surveys

A questionnaire or survey is a quick way of collecting a lot of information. It comprises simply a list of questions that could be derived from the background literature search you have carried out, or which may come from a measure that has been through a process of validation and publication. Questionnaires usually require answers to be collected in a structured format. Thus you can collect yes/no answers, answers on a scale of 1 to 5, answers that fall into categories and answers on a continuous scale. Inventories are a little different from questionnaires in that they do not measure opinions but are composed of questions measuring aptitude and ability.

> **Definitions**
>
> Quantitative methods: use a systematic approach for collecting data that have or are assigned a numerical value.
>
> Pilot study: a small-scale, preliminary run of a study that aims to test, for example, the appropriateness of the measurement tools, methods used and then the quality of the data collected. A pilot study is usually conducted to refine the full-scale run of a study.

You can, if you choose, create your own scientific method in order to create a good quality measurement tool. A good discussion of how to develop a questionnaire can be found in chapter 11 of Breakwell et al. (2006), but briefly, first, you need to formulate a good research question and identify precisely what information you want to get from the measure. Then the individual questions or items need to be written based on a comprehensive background literature search and/or from personal and professional experience. The questions should then be reviewed by other experts in the field and rank ordered for how well they relate to the research question. The researcher then selects the questions or items with the highest ranks and tests the measure on a few people. Only by analysing the results of this pilot study can the researcher know how effective the measure is in collecting the information needed to answer the research question. When the researcher is satisfied, he or she can then start testing the questionnaire or inventory on a larger population. It can take a long time to produce a good-quality questionnaire or inventory, and many of the 'standard' measures currently used by psychologists have undergone modifications and revisions to become the version that we use today.

Inventories in developmental psychology

An example of an inventory used in developmental psychology is the MacArthur–Bates Communicative Development Inventories (CDI). The MacArthur–Bates CDI forms are parent-based forms for assessing a child's language and communication abilities. There are versions for infants aged 8–16 months, toddlers aged 16–30 months and children aged 30–37 months. The CDI form for infants measures their ability to understand words and gestures, whilst the CDI forms for toddlers and children measure their ability to say as well as understand words and short sentences. There are then two further versions of each of these inventories, the long version and the short version. The long version can take up to 40 minutes to complete and provides a comprehensive view of the child's language and communication abilities, whilst the short version takes much less time but can still provide a good indication of language and communication ability. The parent simply works through the form, marking which words and gestures the child understands and, for the older ones, speaks, then the inventories are scored by a qualified professional. The short form is a one-page document where the parent marks how many of the 89 words (infant version) or 100 words (child and toddler version) and a few phrases that the child understands and/or says. The short version is particularly useful as an alternative to the long version in cases when a quick assessment of the child is needed or the parent has low literacy skills. The CDI is an excellent way of collecting data on language vocabulary, comprehension and sentence construction in young children. It allows the parents to have some input in the assessment of their child, but there can then be reporting bias. A parent may mark a word as 'spoken' when the child repeats a word they have heard but without any understanding of its meaning. However, these tools have proven extremely useful in developmental psychology, and many versions now exist in both the English and the Spanish language. Published norms for the different age groups are widely available for comparison purposes.

Quantitative measures have to follow a strict process of development to ensure the validity of their use (see Recommended Reading at the end of this chapter) but, when complete, these tools can provide a wealth of information to the researcher. There are, however, factors that need to be considered when collecting quantitative data in research and limitations on the interpretation the researcher can give to his or her findings. Quantitative methods provide numerical data on behaviour but rarely provide a satisfying answer to why the behaviour occurs. The methods are good for listing opinions, beliefs and knowledge but are unlikely to help you truly understand why a person thinks the way they do or how events in their past have affected the person they are now. Thus, quantitative methods are useful for providing an overview of behaviour but are unable to reveal the personal, in-depth experience of your participants.

Reading and comprehension tests are common in schools.
Source: Pearson Education Ltd/Jules Selmes

> **STOP AND THINK**
>
> This is just a short list of the limitations associated with quantitative methods. Can you think of others that particularly relate to working with children?

Experimental methods

Experimental methods in psychology refer to a manipulation of behaviour, usually in a laboratory setting but also recently in more naturalistic settings. Just like in science classes at school, where you set up an experiment to assess the effect of adding one chemical to another, in psychology an experiment can be set up to assess the effect of adding or changing a variable on certain types of behaviour.

Examples of experimental methods are measuring recall of a list of words under conditions of silence or noise, measuring mathematical performance under conditions of high or low stress, and measuring young babies' responses to their mother's and other faces. All of these experiments involve the manipulation of a variable (silence or noise, high or low stress, mother's or other's face) on a type of behaviour – memory, maths ability and face recognition. The environment in which these experiments occur can be anything from a laboratory at the university, to a schoolroom or comfortable living room. There are pros and cons, of course, of using a laboratory setting over a naturalistic setting for your experiment. Regarding the validity of the setting, you need to consider the value of each against the quality of the data you will be able to collect. For instance, using a natural or near-natural setting to observe and measure change in behaviour increases the likelihood of finding accuracy in the results and improves the ecological validity of the experiment. However, using a sound-proofed laboratory setting can help distinguish, for instance, the effect of the variable being manipulated (silence versus noise) from the effect of confounding variables (e.g. background noise).

> **Definition**
>
> Experimental methods: the manipulation of events to see if change in one variable effects change in another variable.

NATURE–NURTURE

A born musician?

A paper by Ericsson et al. (2005) proposed that the key to becoming a specialist in a field of study, such as music, was not natural talent but, more mundanely, repeated hours of structured practice. The authors cite studies of 1993 and 1996, respectively, that demonstrated that expert violinists based at the Music Academy in Berlin had spent more time than other, even excellent, violinists in practice by the age of entry to the academy at 18 years (Ericsson et al., 1993). Using a survey methodology to record the number of hours each person had put in to practising, the authors concluded that by the age of 20, the very best musicians at the academy had put in more than 10 000 hours of practice compared with the 5000–7500 hours of practice that the less accomplished violinists had completed and the average of 2000 hours of an amateur musician (Krampe and Ericsson, 1996).

However, Ruthsatz et al. (2008) challenge this pure nurture perspective. They believe that confound variables relating to other aspects of musical ability were not being tested by the methods of Ericsson et al. Ruthsatz et al. used a survey technique to count the number of practice hours but supplemented it by using questionnaires and inventories to measure the effects of some of their proposed confound variables (intelligence and other musical skills) on acquiring expertise. Their study of 178 high school band members and 83 classical music students found that, although practice hours had a significant effect on developing expertise in musical ability, only those students with high general intelligence and a good aptitude for music became what might be considered accomplished musicians. The authors therefore conclude that, even with unlimited practice hours, few if any of us have the innate abilities that will make us expert musicians. Thus, by looking at studies using one methodology, a survey of practice hours, papers by Ericsson et al. (1993) and Krampe and Ericsson (1996) were only able to tell part of the story. However, by supplementing their approach with measures of other abilities, Ruthsatz et al. were able to build a much bigger picture of how musical ability is influenced and the researchers were able to take into account the confound variables present (but not measured) in the Ericsson papers.

Interpretation and use of the data

The research methods we have described here will all elicit numerical data that need to be interpreted. Most if not all published standardised measures come with instructions for coding and scoring the child's results and present a range of outcome scores that fall within the 'normal' range for children of different ages. For example, if we were to administer the MacArthur–Bates scale to a 24-month-old child and record a score of 200 words, then looking at the accompanying notes for the scale, we can see that the MacArthur–Bates scale tells us that a score of between 150 and 300 words is 'normal', fewer than 150 words is 'low' and over 300 words is 'high' for a 24-month-old (Fenson et al., 1994). Therefore, the score we have for our child falls into the 'normal' ability for language. However, what use is that knowledge?

Perhaps when you consider that our child's result falls into the 'normal' range for language, we can suggest that this information is only moderately useful. However, if the score we had collected placed the child in the 'low' range for language, what then? The researcher has always to remember that she has a responsibility for the data that she has collected and the interpretation she subsequently makes. Are the data being collected for the purpose of measuring language ability across a number of 24-month-old children within a pre-school facility, or are the data being collected for a diagnostic purpose, perhaps to begin the process of identifying children with language difficulties? Either way, the researcher needs to be confident of how the data were collected from the child, in what setting, what the data collected and how the data were recorded. Only when these concerns are addressed can the researcher state that the score is an

LIFESPAN

The Avon Longitudinal Study of Parents and Children

The Avon Longitudinal Study of Parents and Children (ALSPAC) is a long-term health research project that recruited more than 14 000 mothers during pregnancy from the Bristol and Bath area of England in 1991 and 1992. The purpose of the study is to measure the physical and psychological health of the children through to adulthood and beyond, and the study has so far provided a vast amount of information on these families. Some of the published key findings are listed here:

- Women who take the contraceptive pill for a long time get pregnant more quickly than the average when they stop taking it.
- Babies of mothers who smoke cannabis tend to be smaller at birth.
- Laying babies to sleep on their backs has no harmful effects and can reduce the risk of cot death.
- Eating oily fish when pregnant improves the child's eyesight.
- Eating fish in pregnancy improves a child's IQ and communication skills.
- Peanut allergy may be linked to the use of certain nappy rash and eczema creams.
- Children brought up in very hygienic homes are more likely to develop asthma.
- Use of air fresheners and aerosols is associated with more diarrhoea and earache in babies, and more headaches and depression in mothers.
- The discovery of a gene associated with a tendency to be overweight.
- Just 15 minutes of moderate or vigorous exercise a day cuts the risk of obesity by 50%.
- Less than 3% of 11-year-olds do the 60 minutes of exercise a day recommended by the government.

Source: http://www.bristol.ac.uk/alspac/

---

accurate reflection of the ability of the child. If the data are being used as part of a diagnostic process, then the researcher needs to consider how to use these data, keeping in mind the best interests of the child and the implications for the child, his family and his schooling.

In the Lifespan box, we describe an important longitudinal study of children and young people conducted in the south-west region of England. The researchers are using a wide range of methods to collect information on their participants: postal questionnaires, biological samples taken in a clinic and interviews conducted at home, to name a few. They have involved ethical committees in every decision and plan of research they have made, as there are important issues to consider when engaging in research of this nature. Here are some of the issues for you to think about relating to the methods employed in this study. First, it uses questionnaires completed by both the parent and child, to assess a variety of psychological and behavioural factors, such as eating behaviour and feelings of anxiety and depression. Using questionnaires in this way can have limitations, as there is a reliance on the parent and child to understand the nature of the questions fully so that they can fill them in the questionnaire accurately. Also, if the parent completes the questionnaire for the child, then the parent will probably interpret the questions for the child, interpret their answers given and/or interpret the behaviour under investigation for the researcher, thus reducing the validity of the measure.

Second, the research medical team collect blood, urine and other samples in the clinic setting. This method follows standard medical procedure and provides objective data. The interviews are carried out by a number of trained researchers in the family home. The interviewers follow a standard interview template, but the advantage of this method is that the interviewers can check that the participant has fully understood the question and encourage them to give a full answer. The limitations of this approach are the privacy restrictions on carrying out research by asking children and teens about possibly risky behaviours in earshot of their parents.

A further consideration of this study is that, to date, the parents have given consent for data to be collected from the children. Now that they are aged 18 years, the young people are being asked to consent to the study for themselves. It is important to question this approach to gaining consent. First, it is unlikely that when they were young the children were able to comprehend the needs and demands of the research and could not be said to have provided informed consent for the study – indeed, as they were recruited during pregnancy, they were unable to consent at all initially. As the children grew older, they could give verbal assent to the measures being taken, but there is an issue of coercion to be addressed – would the children really be able to refuse to take part in the study if their parents were taking them to the clinic? Power relationships are strong for children as they look to adults for their care, for guidance, for reward and for punishment (Piaget, 1962). Now the children are adults, what pressures will they feel to continue with this study? If you had been part of a study for 18 years, would you feel a personal obligation to continue as a participant even if you did not want to? All of these questions are important to consider when planning any research involving children and young people.

> **STOP AND THINK**
>
> The ALSPAC group publishes its findings on a regular basis both in academic journals and in published press releases. What are the implications of releasing the results of a study when the study itself is still ongoing?

> **Definitions**
>
> Qualitative methods: methods that describe and define concepts, *without* the use of numbers, and are usually conducted with smaller participant numbers.
>
> Observation study: the researcher views behaviour in either a laboratory or a natural setting and records events that take place. The researcher generally tries not to influence events unless this is a necessary feature of the study design.

Qualitative methods

Qualitative methods can be described as methods that describe and define concepts, *without* the use of numbers. A typical qualitative method involves observing behaviour or, more commonly, talking to individuals or groups to discover their personal experiences.

Neither quantitative nor qualitative methods exist in isolation. The researcher will decide which method will most effectively answer the research question. In our example of measuring communication ability in children with the MacArthur–Bates CDI forms, quantitative methods were appropriate as the researcher wanted to obtain numerical scores of linguistic ability and to compare the scores with published norms. If the researcher wanted to discover why, for instance, one child did not fit the pattern in the data, it might be appropriate to use a qualitative methodology. To understand the unique experience of that child, the researcher might consider talking to the child, his parents and schoolteacher. By adopting a qualitative approach, the researcher can seek to understand the personal experiences of the child and parents without making any prior assumptions as to why that child was different from his peers in language and communication ability from the same environment. The researcher can also discover particular circumstances that led to the child having a lower score and carefully assemble the data into a coherent 'story' of that unique case.

Commonly used qualitative methods

Observations

Using an observation study essentially involves watching a person or group of people in a particular situation. The researcher can use observation to *develop* a strong research question or the researcher can use observation to *answer* their research question.

A good example of the use of observation in developmental psychology comes from the work of Mary Ainsworth and Sylvia Bell in 1970. Researchers Schaffer and Emerson had reported in 1964 that some babies seemed to be more sociable than others, and that they displayed differences in attachment, with some liking to be cuddled more than others. The babies demonstrated this preference at a very early age, leading Schaffer and Emerson to conclude that this was an example of innate (natural or instinctive) differences in children.

This researcher is carefully taking notes while watching mother and daughter at play.
Source: Alamy Images/Photofusion Picture Library

Noting that the babies were unable to explain their differences in sociability, Ainsworth devised an observational study to detect the individual differences in attachment behaviours of children, and this was called the 'strange situation' study.

The Strange Situation study is described in detail in Chapter 9, Attachment and Early Social Experiences; however, the basic details are this. The observation occurs in a laboratory setting, usually a room with a one-way mirror that is set up to resemble a family living room. The observer views a series of behaviours involving the mother, the child and a 'stranger' (another researcher). Each event lasts for three minutes and follows a set format:

1. Parent and infant alone.
2. Stranger joins parent and infant.
3. Parent leaves infant and stranger alone.
4. Parent returns and stranger leaves.
5. Parent leaves; infant left completely alone.
6. Stranger returns.
7. Parent returns and stranger leaves.

Throughout these events, the observer records the infant's separation anxiety, stranger anxiety and behaviour when reunited with the parent. Ainsworth and Bell's observations of 100 children and parents allowed them to develop a classification of attachment according to the behaviour of the child during these 'strange' situations.

The observation research method is an excellent way of collecting descriptive information and is considered to have good research validity. It can be a difficult method to master, however, and it is time consuming. One of the key problems with carrying out an observation is maintaining an objective viewpoint, as it is easy to become involved in the events you are observing and to frame your observations within your own social and cultural norms, not necessarily those of the person observed. Yet, if the observation is carried out well, the information collected can provide the researcher with a solid base from which to begin developing a theory or model of behaviour (Breakwell et al., 2006).

Interviews

There are two main types of interview used in psychology, the structured and the open interview. The structured interview is useful for collecting opinions and preferences or data that require the respondent to answer every question from a pre-planned list. The data collected are useful for market analysis purposes and usually respond well to quantitative as well as qualitative analysis. Whilst the structured interview ensures that all respondents answer all the same questions, the open interview allows the interviewer and respondent the flexibility to explore the answers given and the issues raised within them. Neither the interviewer nor the participant is required necessarily to answer a set of questions and the flow of the interview depends on the answers given. It takes time to train to become fully competent in hosting an open interview, but the quality of data collected is usually vastly superior to that of the structured interview. Some researchers employ a combination of methods in their interviews, using a closed format to obtain data on participant age, sex and other factual characteristics, and then invoking a more open format when asking about opinions and beliefs or descriptions of events and so on. In this way, the researcher attempts some standardisation of the process of the interview and can collate enough information to group the participants according to common features. The researcher can, if she chooses, then consider the individual participant's experiences alongside those of other similar respondents.

Definition

Interview: the interview is conducted by the researcher following either a strict list of questions (a closed or structured interview) or an open format that evolves from the answers the respondent gives (an open interview).

Lawrence Kohlberg (1963) used interviews in his famous paper on moral development (see Chapter 13, Adolescence, for a full discussion of his theory). Kohlberg was a researcher highly influenced by the works of Jean Piaget on the stages of cognitive development in children. Kohlberg believed that as part of our cognitive development we also show a development in our ability to think morally or ethically about real and hypothetical dilemmas. In order to test this, Kohlberg set up interviews with a number of children, young people and adults. Each interviewee was presented with a series of hypothetical situations and asked to describe whether he thought the person in the situation had acted rightly and to explain why he thought this. Kohlberg was interested not so much in whether the interviewee thought the person had acted rightly or wrongly, but in the reasoning behind the decision made. In using an interview method, Kohlberg could address many of the limitations of a self-complete questionnaire type of study. It would have taken less time and fewer resources to distribute questionnaires with copies of the dilemmas, asking participants to make decisions and explain their reasoning. However, one limitation of the questionnaire method used in this way is that people completing them often miss out questions (usually by mistake) or do not give full answers to the questions. You also have to assume that each of your participants has interpreted the dilemmas and subsequent questions in the way you intended. You can rarely go back to a participant after reading their completed questionnaire and ask them, 'Did you mean to say this or did you misread the question?'

Kohlberg, however, could discuss each hypothetical situation with each participant and make sure that every participant had understood the dilemma posed and the nature of the moral question. He could also ensure that the participants did not reply simply 'yes' or 'no' to the questions, but gave detailed answers, rationalising their interpretation of each dilemma posed. If the participant said something that Kohlberg did not fully comprehend, he could ask the participant to expand, to clarify and to confirm their response. The interview method allowed Kohlberg to collect a vast amount of good-quality data that he subsequently categorised into three main types of moral decision making and thus began his theory of moral development.

Case studies

The case study approach to research might be employed in a number of situations but invariably because the researcher notes something unique or interesting about a person or situation that warrants further investigation. The researcher may have collected data from a number of participants and, on analysing those data, found that one of the participants is unusual in some way. Perhaps that person had a significant emotional response to the study or had a particularly interesting story to tell. In this case, the researcher may decide to approach that participant to carry out a detailed investigation, or case study.

Case studies can provide a wealth of information if carried out accurately. The researcher may use this method to report the effectiveness of a particular counselling technique or teaching method that brought about significant behavioural change in the participant. The detail that can be elicited from devoting time to a case study can reveal information that might expand or elucidate a theory or process that has previously been poorly understood. However, the downside of the case study approach is that it simply reveals the experiences of the person under investigation. It is difficult to extrapolate the research findings to make sense of behaviour in a large population when the research has only investigated one person. Case study researchers would argue that this is not the point of the approach and that a carefully planned and executed case study can add to the understanding of a phenomenon, but it is not designed to explain the experience of the masses (Neuman, 2007).

An example of case study work comes from some of the most influential work on child–mother attachment and the effects of periods of brief separation carried out in London in the 1960s and early 1970s by researchers James and Joyce Robertson (Robertson and Robertson, 1989). Highly regarded by both John Bowlby and Mary Ainsworth, the Robertsons are probably best known for their work in revolutionising the way that children are cared for in hospitals. In their book titled *Separation and the Very Young*, the Robertsons describe their efforts to

Definition

Case study: the detailed investigation of the experience of one person or of a small group of people.

understand the psychological effects on a child of being separated from his mother. Prior to their work, parents were actively discouraged from visiting their children in hospital as it was felt to be upsetting for the child and detrimental to their recovery. The Robertsons conducted a series of studies observing and filming children aged from 17 months to 2 years and 5 months, experiencing separation ranging from 10 to 27 days. The experience of each child is presented as a case study and arguably the most famous of these is the study of John.

John was placed in a residential nursery for nine days at the age of 17 months whilst his mother stayed in hospital for the birth of his brother. During this time, James Robertson filmed John's experiences and Joyce watched him carefully, noting down his behaviour, temperament and mood. Over the course of the nine days, John's behaviour changes and he shows distress, eventually rejecting his mother when she returns to collect him. At no point does Joyce Robertson deliberately interact with John, leaving his care to the nurses. A couple of times, John does try to make contact with Joyce, but during those episodes, she busies herself with other activities and sometimes looks away.

The value of the case study approach here is the detailed information the Robertsons were able to collect on John's experiences. The careful use of filming allows the objective observer to discuss the interpretations offered by the Robertsons and to see the changes in John during his time in the nursery. He was only filmed for four minutes each day due to the expense of filming at the time of the study, but the visual impact of the brief clips is a powerful illustration of Joyce Robertson's written observations. The case study approach allows us to focus completely on John's experiences and to interpret them in relation to the sequence of events for John. Therefore, we can see evidence of his strong, secure attachment to his mother prior to her entering hospital. We then follow him after he enters the care facility, day by day, as he finds himself in an unusual, frightening situation, surrounded by noisy, boisterous children without his mother offering him safety and support. Finally, we are able to monitor the reunion with his mother and observe how he rejects her and finds no comfort in her presence. Without this and the other case studies conducted by the Robertsons, we would not be able to see the short- and long-term effects of brief separation on children or to seek ways of improving their experiences.

The case study approach provides a wealth of information on a person's experiences, perhaps following them as they prepare and experience a major event and then observing the psychological processes involved. However, the limitations of the case study approach prevent generalisations of experience to the wider population. Information gleaned from a case study can help you interpret another's behaviour and experiences, but cannot be used to predict their response or to completely inform your interpretation.

When to bring the study to a close?

As with adults, qualitative research in the form of observations, interviews and case studies with children needs to be carried out carefully. Observations, for example, need to be prepared for well in advance so that any cameras required can be maximally placed to collect as much data as possible. The participants, adults and children, need to be aware of the purpose of the study and give their consent for the observation to take place. The researchers need to have developed and tested a schema for coding what takes place and how to make sense of it. When children are involved, the researcher needs to pay close attention to what she is observing. All researchers need to consider whether the child is becoming tired or distressed, whether the child needs to take a break for some reason, and whether the child's experiences are wholly necessary for the research.

The Stanford prison study in the Case study box (page 60) describes an experimental situation that got out of control, even with a number of researchers observing the events and recording them. It took an outsider to step in and bring the study to a stop. The participants in the Stanford prison study were all adults and were able to voice their concerns about how the study was progressing, but were unable to convince the researchers to cut short the experiment. We can see from this study that it takes a great deal of researcher sensitivity to note signs of distress in their participants, and a great deal of objectivity to position the needs of the participant above the demands of the study and bring it to a close. When conducting research with children it is even more important to develop a sensitivity to your participants; very young infants will not be able to tell you that they want the study to stop – you will have to look for signs of tiredness or distress and guidance from the parent when deciding whether to continue the study or not. At all times, the needs of the children come first, the needs of the study come second.

CASE STUDY

The Stanford prison experiment

Researchers recruited 24 male college students to take part in what was intended to be a two-week study of the psychology of prison behaviour. The students were randomly allocated to either the 'prisoner' group or the 'prison warden' group.

The 'prisoners' were arrested at home and handcuffed by real police officers. The prisoners were then taken to a police station, warned of their rights, fingerprinted and taken to a holding cell. The 'prison wardens' were given uniforms and mirrored sunglasses and had a truncheon each. The wardens were given the instruction to 'do whatever they thought was necessary to maintain law and order in the prison and to command the respect of the prisoners' and so the study began.

The prisoners were spoken to not by name but as the inmate number printed on their clothes. They were woken at 2.30 a.m. for a roll-call, made to do lots of press-ups for minor infringements and given plain, basic meals. Over a period of five days the behaviour of the wardens steadily became more controlling and aggressive. On the sixth day Christina Maslach, a recent Stanford Ph.D. graduate, walked into the researchers' observation suite, was horrified by what she saw and demanded an immediate stop to the study.

During the study, friends and family of the prisoners, a Catholic priest and a number of professional psychologists had all visited the prison and seen what was going on, yet none of them requested that the study be stopped. Maslach was the only person who protested on moral and ethical grounds (Blass, 2000, p. 18).

- How could you introduce measures in your own study that will protect your participants?
- How would you monitor the effectiveness of these measures in discontinuing a study that is causing your participants distress or harm?

Source: http://www.prisonexp.org

Working with children

When working with children, it is particularly important to consider how, where and when the research is going to take place. How will the data be collected? Will the parent or researcher rather than the child complete the measures or observations? Where do you want to collect the data? Do you want to go into the family home or into the school classroom? When do you want to collect the data? Is it important if the data are collected during the day, in the evening, during the week or at the weekend?

Before data collection can commence, the researcher needs to have a good understanding of the development capacity of the child. She needs to consider whether the child can understand the questions or tasks she wants to use. She also needs to consider if she wants to speak with the child directly, or does she want to speak about the child with a parent or teacher? According to Grieg et al. (2007), depending on the age of the child, the types of question that can be understood will vary.

Very young children can usually understand questions such as 'Who?', 'What?' and 'Where?' If the child cannot verbally identify, he can usually point to people or objects in response to these questions. Early school-age children can usually answer more complex questions such as 'Why?', 'When?' and 'How?' Until children enter schooling, they often refer to time in relation to activities and events. Morning, for instance, means 'after breakfast', afternoon could be 'after lunch' and evening is characterised by bath time and bed. Young children's lives are structured around meals and activities and it is not until they learn about clocks and how that relates to time that they can offer a more precise indication of when something occurred.

More complex questions relating to memory and recall need to be handled carefully in children. Memory in children is affected (just as in adults) by the social and emotional context of the event. As a researcher, you can help facilitate detailed recall of events by encouraging the child to re-enact the events with toys or through drawing. However, long-term memory in young children can be difficult to elicit. The ability of young children to remember events that happened a long time ago is limited and accuracy can be poor.

When thinking about where the research will take place, we need to consider the many contexts of children's lives and how those contexts will affect the types of response we might achieve. For instance, children may spend their early years in and around the family home, visiting relatives, playing in the park and attending kindergarten. The mealtimes, play and learning opportunities in each of these places are quite different and, if the researcher is interested in one particular aspect of the child's development, only one or two of the locations will be appropriate for the study.

To appreciate the complexity of choosing the right methodology when researching with children, consider, for example, a researcher interested in measuring language ability in a child: what research method could he use? Take, for instance, a measure of vocabulary to answer the question of how many different words a child might use in a day. One way of measuring this could be to ask the parent to record each night what words a child has used that day and when. This method is highly dependent on the parent being in the unlikely position of remembering every word the child has used throughout the day and also of being present every time the child speaks. Language use is highly context-dependent, so you might want to make the task easier by asking the parent to think about what they did with the child during the day and what words the child used during those activities. Of course, then you may not get a full record of the child's vocabulary, as the parent may not write down other words spoken outside of the activities. An alternative method could be to ask the parent to take five minutes at regular points during the day to write down every different word the child has spoken up to that point. However, if the telephone rings, the child falls over or something else distracts the parent during this process, it is likely that you will not get a full record of the child's vocabulary using this technique either.

Research of this nature is extremely difficult and, rather than depend on the parent to collect the data, you may prefer to carry out the data collection yourself. In this case, do you go into the family home or the classroom, or simply follow the child around all day recording their word use? Following and observing a child for a full day might seem like a very time-intensive approach, but think of the alternatives. If you arrive at the house in the morning whilst everyone is having breakfast, it is highly likely that the conversation around the table will revolve around food, getting dressed for school, checking school bags, arranging pick-up after school and the parents discussing their plans for the day. Thus, the vocabulary you will be able to collect will relate to words on these quite specific topics. Likewise, if you drop into a classroom to collect data and the conversation is about Tudor kings and queens, then the vocabulary you will collect will relate to another very specific topic. In order to gain an idea of the range of vocabulary a child has, you will therefore need to assess them in a wide range of contexts, which will take time and probably more resources than you have available. Researchers have therefore been working on developing measures that allow for a comprehensive assessment of vocabulary in a child, which can be completed by the parent or teacher or even, at a later age, by the child him or herself. These measures – for example, the MacArthur–Bates CDI that we discussed earlier – have become invaluable in research studies with children. However, although it may appear that a quantitative measure is the solution to this research problem, quantitative research methods are not necessarily a quick fix for all qualitative problems, as you will see in examples of research presented throughout this book.

Addressing the subject of norms and typicality

Much research in developmental psychology is aimed in one of two directions: measuring and describing 'normal' or 'typical' behaviour or investigating 'unique' or 'individual' behaviour. Choosing the appropriate method to answer research questions of this nature is vital and, simply speaking, quantitative methods are useful for identifying norms and typical behaviour whilst qualitative methods are useful mostly for investigating unique and individual behaviour. The danger in describing typical behaviour patterns in children lies with the wide range of variance in each child's abilities. As children develop, some forge ahead and acquire some skills such as language ahead of others, whilst others are slower to develop language but faster at developing, say, their sensory-motor skills. Although developmental psychologists can collect data that describe the 'normal' age at which, say, two-word utterances are used by most children, it is important to recognise that these norms are actually statistical average points in the data and not to get too caught up in seeing these points as deadlines for skills acquisition. For example, if a child is not yet using two-word phrases at the age of 18 months when her sister was happily using them at that age, it is crucial that, rather than worrying that the child has not reached that developmental milestone, the developmental psychologist should reassure the parent that each child develops at a different pace and that her daughter will probably catch up by the time she is 2 years of age.

However, with such variation in individual development, it becomes difficult for the developmental psychologist to identify areas where the child is not developing at a typical pace and where the child is therefore unique in his or her abilities. Some children who show particular ability at school might be considered atypical by teachers, parents and psychologists alike and be encouraged to follow an advanced stream in education, separate from their peers. However, this action might isolate the child from children his own age and he may experience difficulties making friends and building relationships. Other children, on the other hand, may find certain aspects of school particularly difficult and be considered for separate schooling with extra support. These children, too, might experience isolation and problems forming friendships. Chapter 16, Atypical Development, discusses these issues in more detail and, in particular, the difficulties that parents, teachers and psychologists face when making these types of decision. When you are reading this chapter and others throughout the book, consider the implications of theories that state age norms of ability for children, whether in the school classroom or in the family home, and reflect on what this knowledge can mean for parents, teachers and developmental psychologists.

Cohort effects

A cohort is a group of people who have something collectively in common. This could be the same year of birth, the same year of entry to school or the fact that they have all passed their driving test. On a larger scale, a cohort might be defined as people who were children during the Second World War, children who were born in the 'Swinging Sixties' or people who are now all retired from work. Researchers from the many fields of social and behavioural studies all make use of cohorts in defining their activities. For example, a company that is trying to sell a new alcoholic drink will identify the target cohort drinkers for advertising and use that information to develop its marketing campaign. In another example, a government agency for health awareness that wants to reduce deaths from lung cancer will identify a target cohort of people who smoke and direct its promotional campaign at these people in order to encourage them to quit smoking and reduce their chances of getting lung cancer. In developmental psychology, just as in these other examples, researchers define their research target population by the use of cohorts in order to obtain the most relevant findings. Although we present many theories and principles of developmental psychology according to chronological age, age in itself is not necessarily a cohort. Take, for instance, the first year of formal schooling. In the UK, that classroom will have children whose ages range from 4 to 5 years of age, yet, in most of Europe, compulsory schooling does not begin until the age of 6 years (Sharp, 2002). Thus if we are to conduct a study that requires children to be in their first year of formal education, we should choose our children based not simply on their age but on whether or not they are actually in school and what year of school they are in.

Cohort groups have the advantage of being identified by factors that are perhaps more descriptive of the similarities of the group members (e.g. children of refugee parents) rather than mere demographic data (e.g. born in the year 1971), the risk of course being that too much emphasis is placed on the supposed similarities of the cohort without an understanding of the differences between members. Yes, the children in the example of refugee parents have all been born to parents for whom the country is not their natural home, but the experiences of children whose parents have fled war-torn nations might be very different from the experiences of children whose parents fled due to a change of political leadership. However, cohort effects are an extremely useful way of identifying similarities in a target research group and can be much more meaningful than group membership by any other means, such as random or convenience selection methods (Neuman, 2007).

> **Definition**
>
> Cohort: a cohort is a group of people who are defined by having something collectively in common.

A cohort of World War survivors.
Source: Pearson Education Ltd/MindStudio

A cohort of teenagers born into the technological age.
Source: Getty Images/Olivier Morin/AFP

Ethical working practice

Ethical working practice in developmental psychology is usually regulated not just by the university where the researcher is resident, but also (and for practitioners and researchers not resident in a university) by the regulatory body of the profession. In the EU, these professional bodies are members of the European Federation of Psychologists Associations (EFPA). In the UK the professional body is the British Psychological Society, in Iceland it is the Icelandic Psychological Association, in Luxembourg it is the Société Luxembourgeoise de Psychologie, in France it is the Fédération Française des Psychologues et de Psychologie, and so on. A full list of the members of the EFPA according to member nation of the EU is available at http://www.efpa.eu/members. When you have located the relevant professional body for your country of registration, you can follow the links to the specific details of ethical practice that you need to observe. In the meantime, common threads of ethical working practice for psychologists registered all over the world are discussed here in relation to working with children in particular.

Consent and assent

An important part of research is to make sure that your participants are aware of your project and that they choose to take part in the full knowledge of what they will be asked to do. This is known as informed consent: the participants know what the study is about and what type of activity they will be involved in, and agree to take part, usually signing a form confirming this. With children under the age of 16 years, you have to get permission not only from the children but also from their parents to approach them for your study, and if you are conducting the study in a school, from the teachers and head teacher. In the UK, children under the age of 16 years are considered one of the vulnerable groups for research purposes (another is people with learning difficulties) and cannot truly give informed consent until they have attained adult status, so a written or verbal statement of agreement from them to taking part in the study is known as *assent*, whilst the agreement of the adult teachers and parents to the children taking part in the study constitutes informed *consent*.

Power relationships, demand characteristics and coercion

One of the concerns with research is the power relationship that can exist between researcher and participant. We discussed the issue of the impact of the research on the behaviour of your participants earlier in the chapter and, in particular, we discussed the idea of demand characteristics in your participants. This is where the participant feels under pressure to act in a certain way either as a result of simply taking part in the research, or because they want to please the researcher. The researcher therefore needs to be aware of the impact they may have on the behaviour of the participant and to work hard to provide a suitable atmosphere for the research that will encourage an honest reaction from the participant. Related to this concept is the notion of coercion. Offering a financial reward or some other benefit for completing a study may convince a participant to continue with a study that is making them feel uncomfortable rather than legitimately asking to withdraw from the study. Researchers commonly offer to pay travel and other expenses to their participants rather than a fee for completing the work, and it is vital that the researcher makes the participant (especially a child) aware that they can withdraw from the study at any time. It is good practice to provide breaks in the study so that the participant can be offered the opportunity to discontinue the research project. No participant should feel that they have been forced either to take part in the study or to continue with the study beyond a point where they feel uncomfortable.

Deception and debriefing participants

Occasionally you may want to introduce a factor into your research project that you do not want your participants to know about in advance. For example, you may think that if the participant knows everything about your study, then the knowledge she has will change her behaviour. So in order to counteract this, you may want

> **Definitions**
> Informed consent: agreeing to take part in a study whilst knowing as far as possible the details of the study methodology, including all possible risks and benefits of taking part.
> Demand characteristics: when a participant anticipates what the researcher wants from them and changes their behaviour to conform to that perceived desirable performance.

to introduce an element of deception into your study. If the participants have to know all the details of the study in advance in order to give informed consent, then how do you do this and still follow ethical working practices?

The rules of research state that 'deception is acceptable only if the researcher can show that it has a clear, specific methodological purpose, and . . . [they] should use it only to the minimum degree necessary' (Neuman, 2007, p. 49). Researchers using deception must obtain informed consent from their participants (describing the fundamental details of the research study), make use of deception safely and always debrief the participants afterwards to explain the use of the deception and the purposes for which it was used (Neuman, 2007). It is important to think through how you might use deception in your study and, in particular, how child participants might be affected by it. If you are in any doubt as to its purpose, it is usually best to redesign your study and remove the deception completely.

STOP AND THINK

- Think of a study design that would use deception in order to get the result you want.
- How could you now redesign the study so that you still answer your research question effectively, but in a way that is agreeable to your university ethics committee?

Protection from physical harm and psychological harm – distress, upset, guilt, loss of self-esteem

The fundamental principle underlying all these considerations is the safety of you and your participants. All universities require a statement of ethical working practice to be submitted for consideration for all research projects, whether the researcher is an undergraduate student, a lecturer planning a practical workshop session for her students or a researcher involved in a large-scale project.

Definition

Deception: the deliberate act of creating false knowledge in your participants for the purpose of influencing the outcomes of the research study.

It may seem like an arduous and probably slightly dull part of the research process, but it will help you to consider all the ways in which you can protect everyone involved in the study.

Care must be taken to prevent both physical and psychological harm. Physical harm may come from the use of apparatus in your study, but also from furniture in the study area. Researchers working with young children also need to be aware of sharp objects and keeping an eye on young children who may put things in their mouths. It is the researcher's responsibility to ensure that the study is conducted in a safe environment and to stop any study when harm occurs or the researcher sees a potentially harmful situation arise (Neuman, 2007).

Part of ethical working practice is to consider whether psychological harm could occur to your participants in any way as a result of carrying out your research study. Take some of the examples of studies we have considered in this chapter and think about how they could possibly cause psychological distress to the participants. The Stanford prison study illustrates the importance of the researcher taking the responsibility for maintaining control and even stopping the study when faced with risk of distress to the participant. This study shows how even a team of experts can be drawn into fascinating details of a study, yet remain unaware of the broader impact of its workings on the participants. When you are working with children and infants, it is imperative that the children are not placed under any undue stress and that, if the child or the parent requests the study be stopped, then it is stopped.

Another case in point showing the importance of protecting children and young people from the effects of psychological harm is the Robertsons' observations of children experiencing brief separation. Although it now seems common-sense to stay with a child during hospital treatment, it is largely due to the Robertsons challenging the practice of keeping parents away that we are now encouraged to do so. However, when watching the films and reading the reports on the experiences of the child John in particular, it feels that the children experienced a significant amount of emotional distress during the studies. Could the distress have been avoided? In terms of research, the Robertsons were merely observing the experience of a child put into care whilst his mother was in hospital. They did not ask his parents to put him into care or ask them to have little contact with him, and they did not therefore manipulate John into the situation he found himself in.

Were they therefore responsible for his emotional distress? As far as the parents were concerned, they were doing the best they could for John. His father worked and could not take the time off to care for him whilst his mother was in hospital. He visited John every day and played with him. Could he have done more? The care facility provided meals and toys as well as a bed to sleep in and nurses to care for the children. They were unable to give John the one-to-one attention he had been accustomed to at home, as they had a number of children to look after, but again, they were doing the best they could. It is important to remember when looking at studies such as this, conducted 50 years ago and more, that everyone was working within their understanding of best practice at the time. It is because of studies like these that we now have a better understanding of childhood and the importance of strong attachments to a child's wellbeing. It is also because of studies like these that we are able to work more ethically, both as researchers and carers, with children and young people.

A current example of working with children and young people, the Avon Longitudinal Study of Parents and Children (ALSPAC), shows how far we have come as researchers in understanding good working and ethical practice. This study is producing a vast amount of data on the biological, social and psychological experiences of children and young people, and, through its longitudinal study design, is looking for connections between early and late experiences and between the effects of nature and nurture. The researchers have a rare and exciting opportunity to carry out a truly long-term study on a wide range of participants, collecting samples as they go and employing a range of experts to interpret the findings. The difficulty with a study this large, however, is making sure that you are constantly working within changing ethical guidelines. As our understanding of ethical practice deepens, so changes have been made to the way we work with children and young people. At first, when the study began, parents were responsible for giving consent for their child to take part in research. Now we make sure that we not only ask the permission of parents (and teachers if we are collecting data in a school setting) to work with children, but ask permission of the children too. Currently it is considered that young children are unable to give fully informed consent to a study. This is because our understanding of the way that cognitive development occurs during childhood indicates that the child is prevented from understanding the main concepts of consent, such as the right to withdraw at any time or the subsequent use and publication of the data collected. It is also important to consider that the child is unlikely to be able to make an informed decision to take part in research, as it is unlikely that they will fully understand what the research is about and what it is you want them to do. However, that does not mean that we do not ask the child if they assent to taking part in the research. We ask the parent (and teacher) to decide whether their child can be approached to take part in the study and the parent signs an agreement of fully informed consent. Then, when the study is about to begin, we ask the child if they would like to carry out the study, telling them they can stop the study at any time. It remains, however, the responsibility of the researcher to ensure that the child is safe and not experiencing distress, and to bring the study to a close if required.

Participant confidentiality

Finally, when conducting research in an ethical manner, it is necessary to consider the issue of participant confidentiality: that is, how to maintain the privacy of the participant and the confidentiality of data you collected so that readers cannot identify any participants or their individual responses in the research report. It can be difficult to do this if you also want to publicly thank the school, say, for taking part in the study or perhaps your participant group comes from a fairly rare cohort. However, by keeping individuals' names and personal details out of the report write-up and by taking considerable care in storing your data, you can minimise the risk that people might be identified as participants in your study (Neuman, 2007).

STOP AND THINK

- What do you think of the research findings presented in the Cutting Edge box (page 67)?
- What methodology would you use to explore the reasons why the teenagers are engaged in risky online behaviours? Critically evaluate your choice of method.

Definition

Participant confidentiality: the treatment of any data collected on a participant to prevent the identification of the participant.

CUTTING EDGE

The EU Kids Online project

The EU Kids Online project is using the internet as a research tool for investigating how children and young people use the internet. The research project was set up in 2006 and aimed to collect data over three years from people in 21 countries across the European Union. The site **http://eukidsonline.net** provides a searchable database of European research on children's experiences of using the internet and provides some examples of best practice, FAQs and other resources of interest to researchers. Participating countries are:

Austria	Ireland
Belgium	Italy
Bulgaria	Netherlands
Cyprus	Norway
Czech Republic	Poland
Denmark	Portugal
Estonia	Slovenia
France	Spain
Germany	Sweden
Greece	United Kingdom
Iceland	

The research uses a survey method to measure the experiences of children and young people across Europe, to draw conclusions about the safe use of the internet by children and the cultural context of using the internet, and to make recommendations to policymakers and parents alike. The most recent publication from this study reveals that the more parents use the internet, the more children will do so. Teenagers are quickest to take up advancements in digital media, but most parents are able to understand the internet sufficiently to guide appropriate use. The researchers also state that children use the internet as an educational resource but also for fun and games. Boys think they are better at using the internet and certainly use it for longer than girls, and use of the internet increases with age for both sexes. Approximately 15–20% of the teenagers questioned were engaging in risky online behaviours, such as giving out personal information, seeing pornography and violent content, or receiving unwanted bullying, harassing or sexual comments (Hasebrink et al., 2008).

SUMMARY

Our discussion of different methods should help you decide which is most appropriate for answering your research question and allow you to produce a good critical evaluation of the limitations each method has. You should now be aware that each method has its strengths and can be applied effectively in the right situation. However, you should also now be able to consider the weaknesses of each method and how this can limit the interpretation of your findings.

This chapter has also introduced you to the notion of good working practice and some of the key ethical issues of conducting research in developmental psychology. It is important to remain sensitive to the particular needs of children and young people in research settings and to check carefully that your study is designed to care for and protect your participants.

This chapter serves to introduce you to the key issues in research design when applied in the field of developmental psychology but does not profess to be a full review of research methods. There are many excellent books available that focus purely on research methods in psychology and a few are listed in the Recommended Reading section at the end of this chapter.

REVIEW QUESTIONS

1. In the Nature–Nurture box (page 54), the studies presented discussed the nature of musical ability. What are the practical implications of the research findings?
2. In the Lifespan box (page 55), the ALSPAC study was briefly described. What type of research methodology does this study represent? What are the strengths and weaknesses of this methodology? List three of each.
3. The Stanford prison study was described in the Case study box (page 60). What have we learnt as researchers from the conduct of this study? Answer with reference to:
   a. Informed consent
   b. Good working practice
   c. Ethical considerations
4. In the Cutting edge box on page 67, we listed an example of an internet-based study. What are the limitations to conducting research in this way? List at least three.

RECOMMENDED READING

For a clearly presented, informative book on all aspects of research planning and design:

Leedy, P., & Ormrod, J. (2004). *Practical Research Planning and Design: International Edition* (8th Ed.). London: Pearson Education.

Offering a good resource for new researchers that will guide you through designing your own research project:

Cresswell, J. W. (2008). *Research Design: Qualitative, Quantitative and Mixed Methods Approaches* (3rd Ed.). Thousand Oaks, CA: Sage.

A good resource for learning about all the methods of research included in this chapter, especially questionnaire design:

Breakwell, G. M., Hammond, S., Fife-Schaw, C., & Smith, J. A. (2006). *Research Methods in Psychology* (3rd Ed.). London: Sage.

An excellent investment resource that will take you through all the analytic processes step by step:

Keppell, G., & Wickens, T. D. (2007). *Design and Analysis: A Researcher's Handbook* (5th Ed.). Englewood Cliffs, NJ: Pearson Prentice Hall.

An excellent resource on how to conduct research with children's needs in mind:

Grieg, A., Taylor, J., & MacKay, T. (2007). *Doing Research with Children* (2nd Ed.). London: Sage.

RECOMMENDED WEBSITES

A good resource of materials describing the scientific method and worksheets to help you design your own project:

http://www.scientificmethod.com

The following is a good starting point to research academic materials. The Scholar version of Google currently scans peer-reviewed and published papers and books etc., only:

http://scholar.google.com

A good resource to help you locate the webpage of your national professional body and the ethical and practical guidelines of working as a psychologist:

http://www.efpa.eu/members

Full details of the Avon Longitudinal Study of Parents and Children:

http://www.bristol.ac.uk/alspac/

Section II
Cognitive and linguistic development

Chapter 4
Prenatal development and infancy

Di Catherwood

Learning outcomes

After reading this chapter, and with further recommended reading, you should be able to:

1. Describe the process of human development from zygote through to birth and infancy, particularly in relation to the development of the brain.
2. Discuss the close interaction between genes and environmental factors in prenatal development and infancy.
3. Describe and evaluate the different research methods which are used to explore prenatal abilities and behavioural capacities *in utero* and in infancy.
4. Critically discuss the evidence surrounding infants' sensory-perceptual capacities (vision, audition, touch, taste and smell).
5. Evaluate classic and contemporary evidence, theory and debates about infant cognition (attention, learning and memory, basic knowledge, categorisation, reasoning and problem solving).

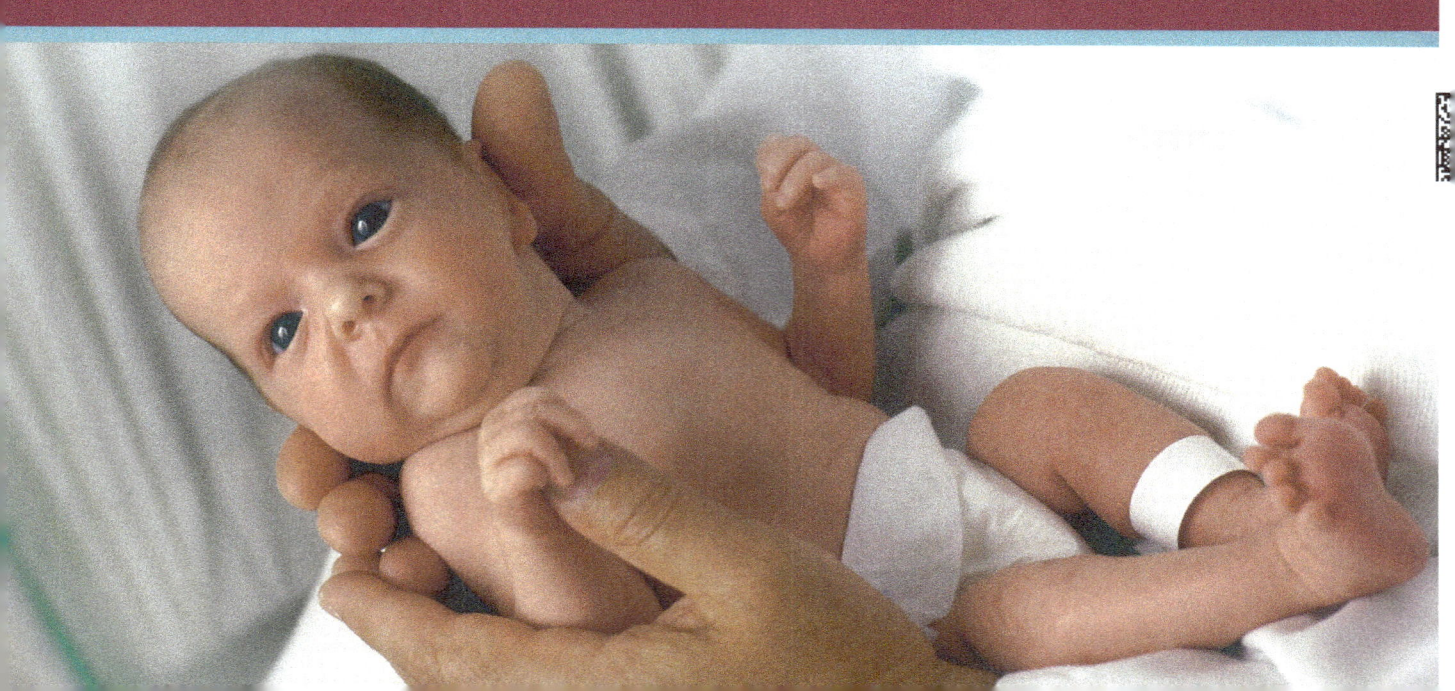

No 'blooming, buzzing, confusion': babies separate birds and fish!

Recent work has used electroencephalography (EEG) equipment (Grossmann et al., 2009) to record the brain waves of infants watching pictures of birds or fish or cars. This has shown, for example, that after seeing many examples of birds, the 6-month-old brain will show a different pattern of response when then presented with a fish, indicating that the infants treated these items as categorically different. Moreover, infant brain activity for distinguishing between these different categories differed from that for simply distinguishing items from the same category. This pattern of brain activity is not consistent with the chaotic, jumbled or fleeting experience of the world proposed in older views of infant capacities. The well-quoted 'blooming, buzzing confusion' proposed by James in 1890 is not an accurate portrayal of the infant's impression of the world. Even if not mature, perception and cognition are orderly and structured at birth and provide the basis for subsequent understanding and learning.

- What might be the implications for our interactions with infants, if their perception is orderly and structured from birth?
- How might we alter the way that we engage with them?
- Do you have any personal experience with infants that would support the findings from this research?

Introduction

This chapter will chart the remarkable development of the human infant from the humble beginnings of a single cell. This event-filled journey provides a basic roadmap for the rest of the human lifespan, so it is critical to understand these early beginnings. For other texts which focus specifically on infant development, see the Recommended Reading at the end of this chapter. This period of life was once considered to be limited to 'sensorimotor' experience (Piaget, 1952b, 1958) with no true cognitive activity and only fractured and fragmentary impressions of the world (James, 1890). This portrayal under-estimates infant capacities, and decades of more recent research confirm that infant experience is richer and more coherent than previously proposed (Bremner and Fogel, 2001; Johnson et al., 2002; Slater and Lewis, 2002; Keil, 2006). This chapter will focus on this updated portrayal of infant capacities.

Other chapters in this book will cover topics and material that overlap with this to some extent: for example, Chapter 7, The Development of Mathematical Thinking, provides further discussion of knowledge in infancy and its relationship to the development of scientific and mathematical thinking in children, and Chapter 2, Theoretical Perspectives, provides a broader background to the debate on early cognitive competence. The theme of the interaction between nature and nurture in human development is explored throughout this book and so it is useful to begin by considering how these forces work together from the very moment of conception to shape infant development.

How to grow a baby: the roles of nature and nurture in early development

Human development at all ages depends on the close interaction of two powerful sets of forces: nature (the processes controlled by our genes) and nurture (input from the environment and experience). These forces guide and direct development over the human lifespan. One of the oldest debates in psychology is about the relative contribution of nature and nurture to human development, but contemporary research with humans and other animals makes it clear that these factors are so closely intertwined in shaping human growth and capacities that it is almost nonsensical to ask which is more important. To find out more about recent developments in how nature and nurture interact in development, see the Recommended Reading. Before considering how this close relationship operates, it is useful first to describe how nature and nurture can each influence early human development.

How does the environment affect early development?

Environmental factors affecting early development are the physical, cognitive, linguistic, social and emotional stimuli that impact on the child. The physical environment can include nutritional factors affecting physical growth, and sensory stimulation affecting the development of perceptual and cognitive abilities. The child's cultural–social–interpersonal environment also provides experiences influencing many aspects of early development (Bronfenbrenner and Morris, 1998). The environment can have a lasting impression on the child's capacities via memory and learning, leaving a residue in the brain circuitry (see 'Prenatal abilities and behaviours', pages 82–3). In prenatal life, the maternal environment is the conduit for the external world to impact on the developing child. Maternal diet or habits can influence the child's physical growth (see 'Risks to prenatal development', pages 83–5) and sensory input can permeate the uterine environment and stimulate the growing sensory organs and systems, possibly even providing content for earliest memories and learning (see 'Prenatal abilities and behaviours', pages 82–3). Maternal emotional state can also provide environmental shaping of the child's development *in utero*. For example, maternal stress gives rise to cortisol, a hormone that is released into the mother's bloodstream, reaching the infant and possibly affecting subsequent brain and emotional development (Mennes et al., 2009). Such environmental factors, however, invariably work in close relationship with the child's genetic endowment in a two-way dialogue that allows genes to modify the effects of environmental experience and allows experience to influence the activity of genes directly (Diamond, 2009a).

How do genes affect early development?

To find out more about human genetics generally, see Recommended Reading. Genes are strings of biochemical material called DNA (deoxyribonucleic acid) found in all body and brain cells. They influence the way in which all body and brain cells grow and function. Like beads on a necklace, genes are arranged on strands called *chromosomes* that are found inside each cell, so that one gene is one segment of the chromosome (see Figure 4.1). Each gene has its own DNA pattern, with this providing the biochemical plan for building and copying the cell in the correct way like the blueprints or designs for building a house.

In all human cells there are 23 pairs of chromosomes and there are collectively tens of thousands of genes along all of these chromosomes. Genes are passed from parent to infant and each human cell generally has two versions (*alleles*) of each gene. This is because chromosomes come in pairs (one from each parent) and so we have two versions of each gene. These alleles may be the same or different, with any difference resulting either in a mixture or with one dominating the other (such as happens with dark hair genes over fair hair genes).

All cells have the same set of genes, but only certain ones need to be turned on for any particular cell and then only at the correct time. For example, you wouldn't want

> **Definition**
>
> DNA (deoxyribonucleic acid): strings of biochemical material that provide the code for genes.

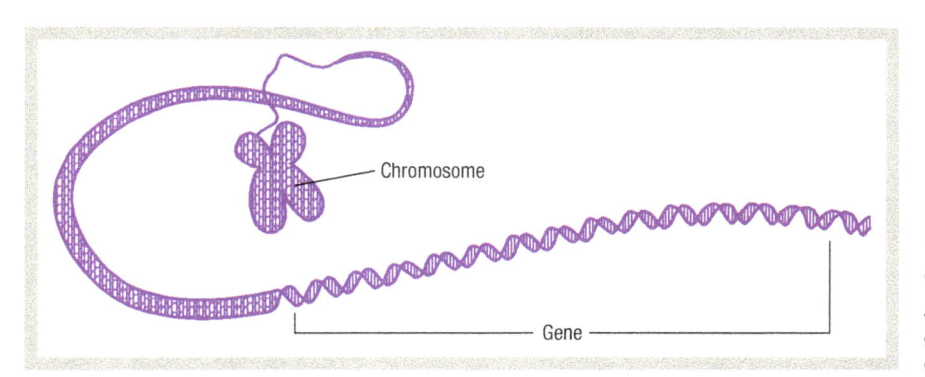

Figure 4.1 Illustration of a 'gene' as one section of a chromosome.

Source: http://ghr.nlm.nih.gov/handbook/illustrations/geneinchromosome

to have a brain cell gene switched on in the cells that make up your feet! Nor would you want the genes controlling the hormones of puberty to turn on in infancy. To make sure that the correct genes are active in the correct cells at the correct time, there are 'operator' or 'boss' genes that control where and when the 'builder' or 'worker' genes do their job.

The timetable and direction of prenatal growth of brain and body is controlled by switching on and off the correct genes at the appropriate time in this way. The Human Genome Project (http://www.yourgenome.org/hgp) has indicated that 40% of our genes are specialised for brain growth and function (Pennington, 2002). For example, prenatal brain development is known to be affected by a gene called *PAX-6* (Mo and Zecevic, 2008). For more information about the ways in which genes control the early development of brain structures and regions, see Recommended Reading.

Does this mean that our brains are simply the product of our genes then? There is certainly a growing list of psychological functions considered to be influenced by genes, including both cognitive processes and emotional tendencies in regard to stress, anxiety, depression or happiness (Caspi and Moffitt, 2006; Ramus, 2006; Hariri and Forbes, 2007). Even the ways we cope with attachments and loss are associated with particular genes (Caspers et al., 2009).

Nonetheless, most human capacities or characteristics are unlikely to be due to simple links to one gene or another. Most psychological functions are likely to involve many genes (polygenic) and complex genetic–environment interactions. It is important to stress the difference between *genotype* (the basic genetic blueprint) and *phenotype* (the expression of the gene in actual development). Phenotype may differ from genotype because of the influence of environment that can modify, add to or even inhibit the action of genes.

How do genes and environment interact in early development?

Nature and nurture are clearly both required in development and interact with each other in direct and indirect ways. A classic example of this mutual relationship comes from cases of phenylketonuria (PKU), in which a faulty gene impairs the ability to process protein, with devastating effects on the development of the brain (Diamond et al., 1997). The condition can be contained by restricting the dietary intake of protein – a clear instance of interaction between nature and nurture. Such interactions can take different forms, however. It may not be that genes contribute $X\%$ and the environment contributes $Y\%$ to development. There may be an actual interface between experience and genes, so they can directly impinge on each other's activity or effects.

On the one hand, nurture (experience) can turn nature (genes) on or off. The direct activation or conversely deactivation of genes by environmental factors (called *epigenetic* effects) has been shown in many animal studies. Many genes are inactive and are only switched on by particular environmental triggers. For example, research with laboratory rats or rhesus monkeys (Meaney, 2001; Weaver et al., 2004) has confirmed that maternal stress or styles of care directly affect the expression (switching on or off) of genetic factors linked to the response to stress in the offspring, with this being further modifiable by additional experiences over the lifespan. There is even a suggestion that maternal stress prior to the conception of offspring can alter genes in the maternal ova, with this altered genome passed on to any offspring (Diamond, 2009a). Epigenetic interactions of this type are yet to be explored in human development, but there is evidence which suggests such effects. For example, adolescents who have a short version of the *5-HTTLPR* gene linked to the neurotransmitter serotonin (5HT) are prone to develop antisocial behaviour – but not if they have supportive parenting (Brody et al., 2009), indicating that the parental environment may influence this gene expression.

On the other hand, there is growing evidence for human development of the converse: that genes can alter the effects of environment (Ramus, 2006). Individuals with different versions (alleles) of the same gene may react differently to the same experiences. In other words, genes can limit or filter the effects of experience. For example, people with a particular version of the *5-HTT* gene involved in making the serotonin neurotransmitter are more likely to develop depression after stressful life events than those with a different allele of this gene (Caspi and Mofitt, 2006). Likewise, abused children are more likely to develop antisocial personality traits if they have a particular version or allele of a neurotransmitter (*MOAO*) gene than if they have a different allele (Caspi and Mofitt, 2006).

The relationship between genes and environment is thus a very intimate one. This is apparent in regard to the development of attachment in early life (see the Nature–Nurture box).

Nature and nurture are thus knitted together in an almost seamless way to direct the course and pattern of early development, with this mutual relationship taking a range of possible forms (Karmiloff-Smith, 1999; Ramus, 2006; Pennington et al., 2008). Genes and environment may interact directly as in the epigenetic processes described above or more indirectly. For example, children with genes involved in musical skills may seek out or be offered music experiences which reinforce these tendencies. To find out more about human genetics, see Recommended Reading. In any case, the dividing line between the effects of genes and those of environment may well be undetectable, since both forces are so closely intertwined in shaping human development. We can now explore the way in which this close link between nature and nurture builds a human being in prenatal life and infancy.

STOP AND THINK

Reflection

Choose some aspect of your own development. How do you think this has been influenced by your genetic endowment from your parents and/or your early childhood experiences?

NATURE–NURTURE

How genes and parenting influence early attachment patterns

New evidence on the close dialogue between nature and nurture comes from research into how genes and parenting interact in producing patterns of infant attachment. It is well established that early parenting style or environments directly affect attachment patterns in children (see Chapter 9 for details). Nevertheless, there is also evidence of genetic factors in this regard as well. In particular, shortened alleles (versions) of genes linked to the neurotransmitters dopamine and serotonin (namely the *DRD4* and *5HTTLPR* genes, respectively) are associated with disorganised or dysfunctional attachment in children and unresolved attachment in adults (Gervai et al., 2007; Caspers et al., 2009), possibly indicating the role of these neurotransmitters in aspects of emotion in attachment. Further research, however, shows how both parenting environment and genes work hand-in-hand to shape the final form of children's development. Inconsistent or disrupted maternal behaviour may only have an impact on children's attachment if they have the short version or allele of the *DRD4* gene (Gervai et al., 2007). Nature and nurture work very closely together to produce the patterns of early attachment.

Prenatal physical development

The 40-week journey from a single-cell zygote to the complex structures and systems that comprise the newborn human involves many steps and processes under the influence of both genetic and environmental forces. There are three main phases in prenatal life: the *germinal period* (0–2 weeks), the *embryonic period* (3–8 weeks) and the *foetal period* (9–40 weeks) (see Figure 4.2). The main features of physical development in these periods are summarised in Table 4.1 below. Another mapping of prenatal life is by trimesters: (0–3 months, 4–6 months and 7–9 months). You can read in more detail about landmark events and features of the physical aspects of prenatal development elsewhere (Moore et al., 2000; Moore and Persaud, 2003) (see Recommended reading or see http://www.visembryo.com/baby/index.html for a graphic representation of weekly stages of prenatal growth).

Definition
Zygote: the single cell formed from the union of sperm and ovum.

Prenatal development of the brain

Before considering how the brain develops *in utero*, it is useful to describe some of the main brain features and structures.

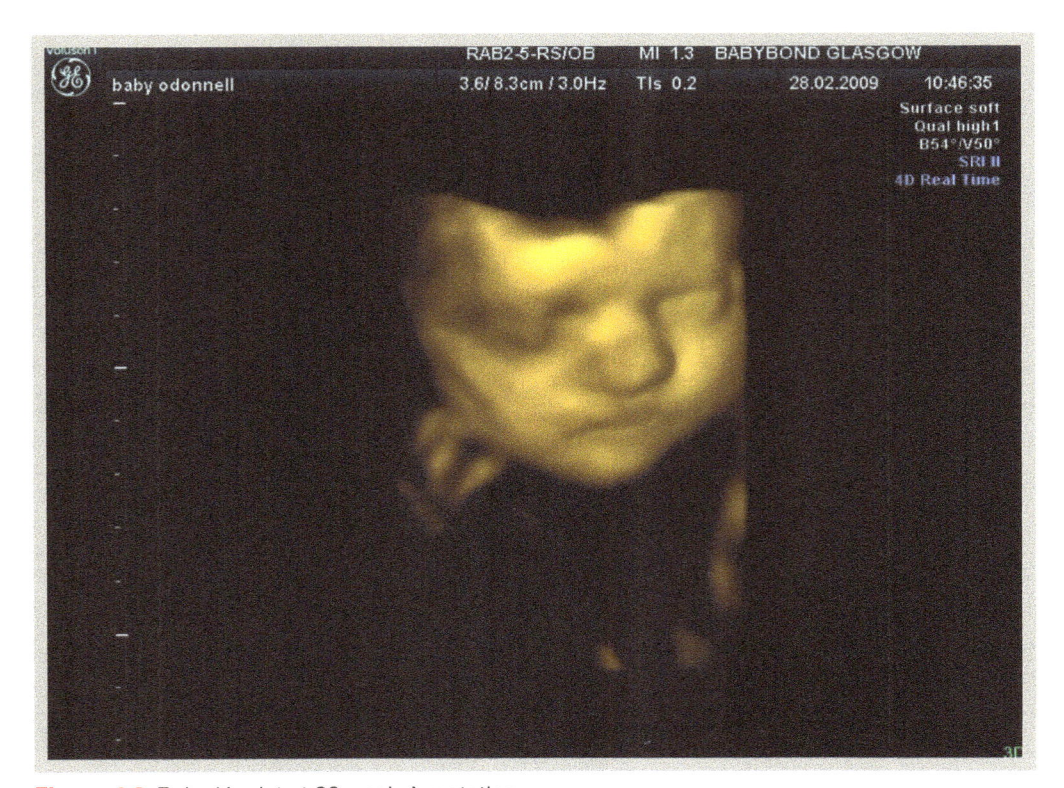

Figure 4.2 Baby Harriet at 28 weeks' gestation.
Source: O'Donnell

Table 4.1 Major physical developments during the prenatal period.

Prenatal phase	Weeks of gestation	Key features at beginning of phase	Key features at end of phase	Main developments during phase
Germinal period	0–2 weeks	Single-cell zygote	Ball of 60–70 cells called a blastocyst	Creation of embryonic disc inside the blastocyst, which will form the human being, whilst an outer shell protects it.
Embryonic period	3–8 weeks	About 2 mm long	About 2.5 cm long, weighing about 4 g. Looks human. Eyes are open. Shows reflexive response to touch.	Heart begins to beat. Not yet a viable organism outside the uterus. Development of neural tube which will eventually form brain and spinal cord. Neuron production begins and neurons migrate to correct parts of body and brain. Development of buds for arms, legs, fingers and toes.
Foetal period (see Figure 4.2)	9 weeks onwards	7.5 cm long, weighing 20 g in third month	Average length 50 cm, weighing 3.2 kg	Body and nervous system begin to operate in an organised way, 'breathing', swallowing and urinating. Frequent movements of limbs.
				Sex can be determined.
				May survive premature birth from 21–22 weeks. By week 24 most brain neurons are formed. Massive growth.

A quick tour of the brain: some important brain features and landmarks

The human brain consists of billions of tiny cells called *neurons* that transmit signals to one another in organised networks. They have a typical shape that helps them communicate with each other, looking a lot like tiny trees, comprising a head or cell-body, with branches called dendrites, a tail or trunk called the *axon* and root-like extensions called *terminals*. When stimulated, neurons propel a tiny charge or impulse (the *action potential*) from the head to the terminals. This impulse passes from one neuron to another across tiny gaps called synapses, with each neuron potentially having thousands of such connections. Chemicals called *neurotransmitters* (e.g. serotonin or dopamine) are needed in most cases to help pass the message over the synapse. These connections allow complex networks of neural activity that underlie the functions of the brain and nervous system (see Pinel, 2008; Purves et al., 2008).

The older hindbrain regions are responsible for basic survival functions, states of alertness and well-learned movements, and the midbrain for rapid response to sensory signals. The forebrain has internal structures such as the hippocampus for working memory and aspects of emotional processing, and a thin wrinkled outer layer, the cortex, for most higher-level perceptual, cognitive and emotional analysis and for complex aspects of memory and learning. These areas of the brain are illustrated in Figure 4.3(b). The cortex is described in four lobes corresponding to the skull bones, as illustrated in Figure 4.3(a) – frontal, parietal, occipital and temporal – and to some degree, there is specialisation of functions in different regions of the cortex (e.g. primary visual processing occurs in the occipital cortex) (see Pinel, 2008 or Purves et al., 2008 for more details).

Definitions

Dendrites: the branches or extensions at the top of neurons that allow contact with other neurons and so form neural networks.
Synapse: the gap between neurons across which the neural signal is passed.

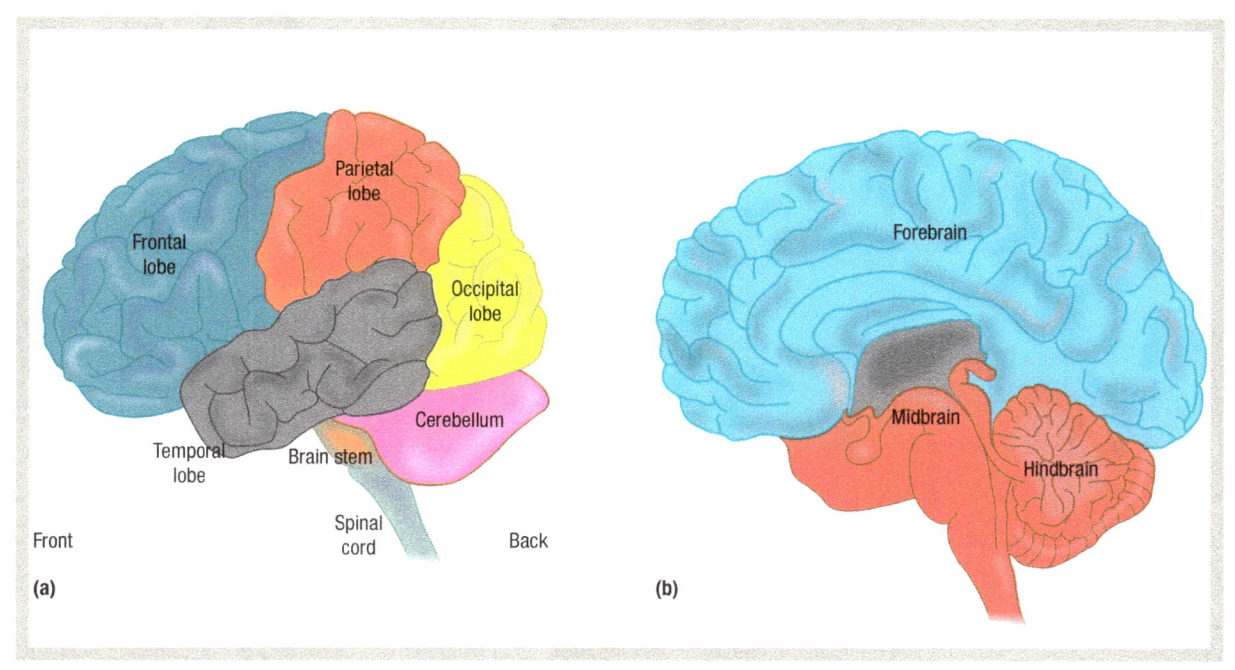

Figure 4.3 Basic regions of the human brain.

Stages of prenatal brain development

The brain develops very early *in utero* in stages (Huttenlocher, 1990; Johnson et al., 2002; Nowakowski and Hayes, 2002; Strachan and Read, 2003; Rosenzweig et al., 2005). The basic pattern and timetable is under genetic control: about 40% of the structural or worker genes in the human genome are exclusively involved in brain growth and maintenance, while the other 60% are also involved to some degree as well (Pennington, 2002; Ramus, 2006), but prenatal environment can also impact on this early development of the brain.

During the embryonic period, the embryonic disc develops into a three-layered sandwich of cells comprising an outer layer called the *ectoderm*, a middle layer called the *mesoderm* and an inner layer called the *endoderm*. The ectoderm will eventually form the skin, hair and nervous system. By day 15, a small group of cells begins to grow rapidly at one end of the ectoderm, creating a primitive basis for the head and brain.

By weeks 3–4, the development of the nervous system begins in earnest. By day 18, chemical signals are sent to the ectoderm from the layer below, causing the growth of a thick *neural plate*. The cells in this plate continue to multiply rapidly, although at uneven rates, so that by about day 20, the plate has a groove all along its midline with folds of tissue either side (like a river bed with canyon walls) (see Figure 4.4).

By the start of week 4 (about day 22), these folds arch over the groove, wrapping around to form a hose-shaped structure, the neural tube, the precursor to the brain and spinal cord. This folding starts at the middle of the groove, moving towards each end in a 'zipping' manner until the tube is sealed except at the ends. The tube opening at the anterior (head) end now closes, followed by that at the tail end. In about 1 in 1000 births (Bukatko and Daehler, 2004), the neural tube fails to close – either at the head end, resulting in *anencephaly*

Definition

Neural tube: hose-shaped structure forming the basis of the brain and spinal cord in the embryo.

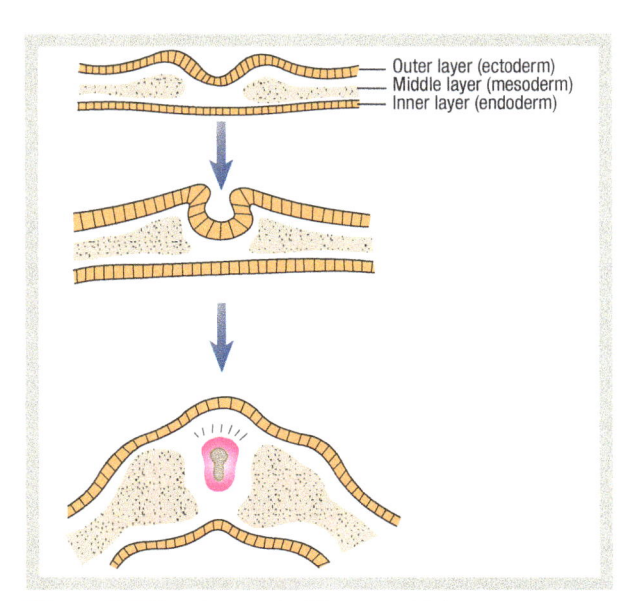

Figure 4.4 Development of the neural tube.
Source: http://www.sciencemuseum.org.uk/on-line/lifecycle/11.asp

(a severe impairment of brain development usually fatal after birth), or at the tail end, producing *spina bifida*, which can result in paralysis.

By about 3½ weeks, there is a defined swelling at the top end of the tube and by week 4, this shows three clear divisions corresponding to the future forebrain, midbrain and hindbrain. The entire nervous system becomes a clearer structure as the neural tube separates from the surface ectoderm. Many different genes control this process: for example, forebrain development involves genes from the E_{mx} family.

After the closure of the tube in week 4, neural development proceeds frantically in several phases which can overlap in different brain areas. The first phase is neurogenesis, the rapid and teeming production of neurons within the neural tube. Neurons cannot copy themselves but are made from other cells in the neural tube that rapidly divide to form more cells, which are in turn changed under genetic control into neurons. Neurogenesis begins in weeks 3–4 and is especially active up to week 16, with hundreds of thousands of neurons being made each minute and most of the brain neurons formed by about week 24. This frantic proliferation of neurons is reflected in the corresponding growth in the size of the infant brain, with the head enlarging to one-half of the body size by week 8. Neuron production generally ceases at birth, although some new neurons may be made in the adult brain (possibly in the hippocampus, the part of the brain important in making new memories) (Erikson et al., 1998). Most brain development in the final months of prenatal life (and after birth) consists of the growth of connections (synapses) between neurons and of the myelin tissue that coats the neural membrane (see below), leading to a tenfold increase in brain weight from 20 weeks to birth.

The second important phase is neuronal migration, in which the neurons move to different locations in the emerging brain and nervous system. Some only go short distances but others have to travel far. By a pushing or pulling process under the control of genetic and biochemical factors, they move along fine filaments sometimes swinging like monkeys from one filament to another (Feng and Walsh, 2001; Hatten, 2002) (see Figure 4.5 and for 'movies' of migrating neuronal cells, see: http://hatten-server.rockefeller.edu/HattenLab/movies.html). Migration begins in earnest after the final sealing of the ends of the neural tube. This exodus of neurons establishes different neural groups or populations that will eventually contribute to different structures and systems in the brain and nervous system. If this migration is disrupted for any reason (genetic or environmental), then there may be impairment of subsequent brain function. Numerous disorders such as *dyslexia* and *autism* have been linked to the impairment of neuronal migration in the prenatal brain (Watts, 2008) (see Chapter 16, Atypical Development, for more on autism).

The third phase – *neuronal differentiation* – begins when genes further modify the newly arrived cells to make them specialised for their future roles in the brain regions and systems.

During the process of embryonic cell differentiation, two other 'phases' also occur at the same time. One of these is synaptogenesis: the development of potential connections or synapses amongst the emerging neurons due to the growth of extensions or branches at the top of the neuron called dendrites and at the bottom called terminals. There is also the beginning of myelinisation or myelination – the coating of the axons in fatty insulating

Definitions

Neurogenesis: the production of neurons in the embryo.
Neuronal migration: the movement of neurons to appropriate locations in the brain and body.
Synaptogenesis: rapid growth of dendrites to form neural connections or synapses.
Myelinisation: the growth of fatty insulating coating along the axon of the neuron.

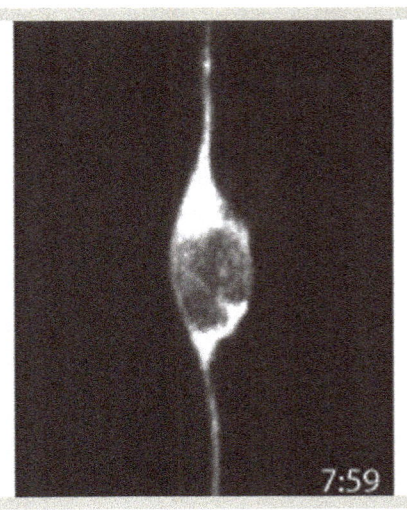

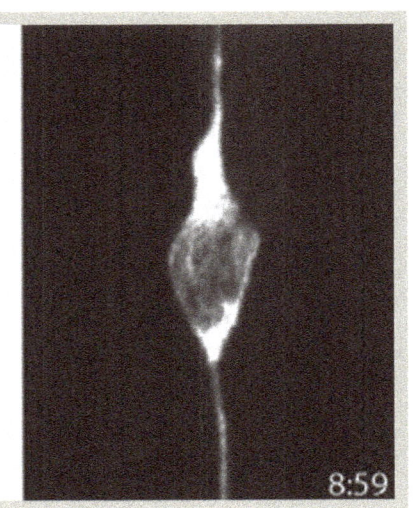

Figure 4.5 Images of a migrating neuronal cell.
Source: Courtesy of the Hatten Laboratory at Rockefeller University

material to improve their efficiency, although this process increases markedly after birth with use of the brain (see 'The postnatal development of the brain', pages 88–90).

In the prenatal brain there is considerable over-supply of synapses. This leads to the final phase or aspect of neural development, involving 'pruning' of connections and rivalry amongst neurons for target neurons. Success in this regard may be due to good availability of connections or even to repeated stimulation of the 'lucky' neural pathways by environmental factors such as sensory input (see next section). This whole process of synapse building and pruning does not only occur *in utero*, but will also continue vigorously after birth (and to some extent across the lifespan) in response to input from new learning and experience (see 'The postnatal development of the brain', pages 88–90).

The basic brain structures are in place early in the foetal period by weeks 9–10, with the main aspect of development thereafter being the growth in brain mass. During the last few months of prenatal life, the cerebral cortex of the brain shows increasing folding due to neuron production and growth of synapses and myelin. Not all regions of the brain develop at the same pace and, even within the cortex, there are different timetables for different regions with these discrepancies continuing after birth (see 'The postnatal development of the brain', pages 88–90). As a result of this rapid development of the brain and nervous system, even the embryo soon displays basic behaviours and responses reflecting organised neural activity.

> **STOP AND THINK**
>
> **Reflection**
>
> The development of the brain *in utero* is an amazing achievement under the control of genes, biochemical factors and even environmental factors. Imagine the whole sequence as a movie, from start to finish. Could you draw and label rough diagrams for yourself about each step of the way?

Prenatal states: foetal sleep and waking cycles

By the end of the first trimester, the foetus shows daily (24-hour or *Circadian*) rhythms of heart and lung activity, and hormone release. The brain centre that is critical to Circadian rhythms (the suprachiasmatic nuclei) is present by the middle of prenatal life, although Circadian rhythms continue to develop after birth (Rivkees and Hao, 2000. Most importantly, sleep–wake cycles have begun. Sleep cycles with rapid eye movements (*REM sleep*) appear at about 28 weeks gestational age, with REM accounting for most sleep cycles at this time, declining to about 50% by birth (Graven and Browne, 2008). Sleep is not just a passive process. REM sleep is critical to the early development of the brain, especially the organisation of the visual, auditory and touch systems and the ability to form long-term memories (Graven and Browne, 2008). REM sleep deprivation in foetal and early postnatal life is associated with delayed or disrupted development of these capacities.

Prenatal abilities and behaviours

One of the most fundamental human capacities is the ability to sense and respond to a stimulus external to the body. Imagine how isolated you would be without your senses to connect you to the world, or how frustrating it would be not to be able to react to some stimulus. But what is it like for the developing foetus? Is there any sign that the foetus can 'sense' and react to the world? Indeed there is: the rapid development of the brain and nervous system supports the early emergence of sensory capacities and behavioural responses, and even within the cloistered world of the uterus, these basic abilities are exercised and refined as the infant develops.

By the end of the embryonic period, there is already the capacity to react to external stimulation, initially with simple *reflex* responses (not engaging the brain), but increasingly with responses under brain control. The five main sensory systems of vision, touch, audition, taste and smell all begin to develop in the embryo. All such channels involve bodily receptors (eyes, ears, etc.), as well as specialised neural pathways and brain regions. For example, processing in the visual system begins with the components of the eye (lens, retina, etc.), continues along the optic tracts to the brain and involves further processing in the visual cortex and other subsequent brain areas (see Figure 4.6). These systems operate to some extent and provide channels for perceiving even in foetal life (Hepper, 1996). Moreover, as the brain develops across the foetal period there is an increasing ability to retain this sensory information, which shows the capacity for memory and learning (Hepper and Leader, 1996).

Foetal touch, taste and smell perception and memory

The earliest sensory channel to develop is that of touch. During intrauterine diagnostic procedures, it has been established that by 8 or 9 weeks, the foetus moves its head if touched in the mouth region and by 12 weeks will grasp at anything touching the fingers (Fifer et al., 2001). The foetus regularly receives tactile stimulation via the maternal abdominal wall and will show increased activity if this is touched (Lagercrantz and Changeux, 2009). The taste systems and receptors (taste buds) are formed in the foetus by about 18 weeks and the smell system by about 15 weeks, although it may be 6 months before the nasal passage is free to 'inhale' (Browne, 2008) (although it is somewhat difficult to distinguish between these senses in the watery world of the foetus, since substances can enter both nose and mouth). Ultrasound images, however, clearly show the reaction of the baby to substances introduced into the uterine environment. The foetus becomes familiar with the smell and taste of the amniotic fluid environment, as shown by preference for own mother's amniotic fluid at birth (Browne, 2008). The maternal diet also conveys odours and tastes into the amniotic fluid, which are detected by the foetus as shown by preferential response (head turning etc.) at birth – for example, to maternal diet odours such as anise or garlic (Schaal et al., 2000; Browne, 2008). The foetus is also more likely to swallow a sweet substance in the amniotic fluid than an unpleasant one, suggesting innate preferences for sweet flavours (Liley, 1972; Hepper, 1992) and, of more concern, is likely to increase swallowing if alcohol is in the amniotic fluid (Molina et al., 1995). The foetus is clearly immersed in a world of touch, smell and taste.

Foetal hearing and auditory memory

The auditory system is also functional to some extent by about 20 weeks, even though the ear and auditory brain regions are not yet mature. The foetus will respond to loud sounds with movements, perhaps showing a *startle reflex* (Zimmer et al., 1993). By 22 weeks, the foetus will show a more sophisticated reaction by orienting or attending to sounds, as evidenced by movement and a decline in heart rate. Furthermore, if the tone or sound is repeatedly presented, the foetus will eventually show *habituation* or a decline in responsiveness, evidence of simple learning or memory (Dirix et al., 2009; Leader et al., 1982). The foetus is capable of simple associative learning in regard to the pairing of a sound with a touch stimulus

(Hepper and Leader, 1996), but is also able to learn and remember complex sound patterns from the external world. Many natural sounds penetrate the uterine environment, and the foetus can not only hear them but also learns about or remembers them. In particular, new-borns show preferential response to the maternal voice (DeCasper and Fifer, 1980) and even to theme tunes from television shows watched by the mother during pregnancy (Hepper, 1988), indicating perception and learning of these sounds during foetal life. There is even remarkable evidence of new-born preference for the sound patterns of nursery rhymes (DeCasper et al., 1994) or Dr Seuss stories presented during pregnancy (DeCasper and Spence, 1986). More recently there has even been more direct evidence of foetal learning, in that foetuses of 8–9 months familiarised to either their mother or a female stranger reading a passage showed a reaction when the opposite voice was then used (Kisilevsky et al., 2009). Some of this research, and its role in helping us to understand the development of memory from infancy, is explored further in Chapter 6, Memory and Intelligence.

Foetal vision

The least developed of the sensory channels in prenatal life is vision. The murky light of the uterine world is not optimal for vision, so it is probably just as well that the visual system does not operate fully, or else it may become attuned to poor lighting levels and become ill-equipped to deal with the more intense light outside the uterus. Nonetheless by about the fourth month, although the retina is still immature, the main parts of the eyes have developed and the next month sees the specialisation of cells along the visual pathways for colour and spatial detail. A foetus of 6 months will try to shield its eyes with its hands if a bright light is introduced into the mother's abdomen in diagnostic procedures (Nilsson and Hamberger, 1990) and by the seventh month, the visual region of the brain (the *visual cortex*) has developed its basic structure with the capacity for analysing the main features of the visual world, as shown by studies of post-mortem tissue (Huttenlocher, 1990).

It is thus clear that basic abilities for sensing, perceiving, remembering and learning operate in foetal life and that the life-long task of the brain to detect, process and retain information from the external world begins even before birth.

Risks to prenatal development: environmental teratogens and genetic errors

Regrettably, not all prenatal development runs smoothly according to the plan outlined so far. It is estimated that about 3% of new-borns have some congenital malformation – that is, a problem present at birth (Kalter, 2003). These are due either to noxious or damaging environmental factors known as teratogens (such as maternal disease or environmental pollutants), or to failures in genetic processes. About 10% of congenital problems are due to environmental teratogens and 15–25% involve genetic problems (with the causes of the rest being undetermined) (Kalter, 2003; Reece and Hobbins, 2006).

Environmental teratogens

The embryonic period is the most vulnerable to the effects of teratogens as this is the time in which all the basic organs and structures including the nervous system and brain are being formed (see above), and so teratogens at this time can be particularly destructive. In contrast, there is little effect in the germinal period. The effects in the foetal period are less severe than in the embryonic period, but nonetheless the sensory organs (especially the eyes) and the central nervous system are still susceptible right across the foetal period up until birth (Moore and Persaud, 2003).

Most teratogens either involve maternal conditions or behaviour (nutritional insufficiency, stress, ingestion of alcohol, smoking, caffeine intake, etc.) or derive from wider environmental factors (such as radiation) (Kalter, 2003; Brent and Fawcett, 2007).

Malnutrition

One of the most common teratogens is maternal malnutrition. There are many nutrients that are essential to

Definition

Teratogen: an environmental hazard to prenatal development.

healthy prenatal development, although lack of folic acid (vitamin B9) seems especially serious as it is essential for producing the genetic material (DNA) used in the formation of new cells, including neurons and blood cells. Lack of folic acid is a key factor in neural tube defects, for example (Brent and Fawcett, 2007).

Maternal drug use

Legal drugs can be of equal or greater concern than illegal drugs in regard to effects on the developing child. Even the caffeine in a few cups of coffee a day may have harmful effects such as poor growth and high excitability in the infant (Scheutze and Zeskind, 1997), and some of the most disabling effects have come from the use of prescribed medications, such as the 1960s sedative thalidomide that produced major deformations of the limbs in the developing embryo (Moore and Persaud, 2003). The most commonly available legal drugs are, of course, alcohol and nicotine, and both of these can have profound effects on the developing brain and body (Alati et al., 2013; Dejin-Karlsson et al., 1998; Mattson et al., 2011) (see the Case Study box).

The evidence on the effects of illegal drugs such as cocaine is not as clear-cut because their use may be linked to other risk factors such as poverty and use of other drugs which also have an impact on the developing child. However, maternal use of illegal drugs such as heroin or cocaine is generally considered to lead to low birth weight and disruption of 'state' in the infant, such as poor sleeping patterns, under- or over-excitability (Friedman and Polifka, 1998).

Maternal disease

Maternal disease is also another risk factor in prenatal development. There are a number of teratogenic viruses. Rubella is especially destructive in the first few months of prenatal life, when it can cause damage to the developing eyes and ears, heart and brain, resulting in visual and auditory impairments and heart and brain abnormalities (Moore and Persaud, 2003; Reece and Hobbins, 2006).

CASE STUDY

Baby shares a drink with Mother

In May 2007, the Department of Health in the UK issued new guidelines for women, advising that they should avoid alcohol altogether during pregnancy. This is because of the risks which alcohol poses to the developing foetus. Alcohol readily crosses the placenta and affects the infant, potentially impacting on the generation, differentiation and migration of neurons and growth of synapses in the developing brain. This can result in disordered foetal brain development such as a sheet of aberrant cells over parts of the brain surfaces (Kumada et al., 2011). As noted in 'Prenatal abilities and behaviour', the foetus will swallow more of the amniotic fluid if alcohol is present (Molina et al., 1995).

Even moderate maternal alcohol consumption may lead to a condition known as *Foetal Alcohol Syndrome (FAS)* or to a range of impairments known as *foetal alcohol spectrum disorders* (Alati et al., 2013; Kumada et al., 2011; Mattson et al., 2011). FAS is associated with brain and facial abnormalities, poor growth and cognitive, motor, language learning impairments in childhood (Mattson et al., 2011). There is ongoing debate about the precise levels of alcohol consumption resulting in such disorders (Mattson et al., 2011), as there is evidence that low levels of maternal alcohol consumption do not necessarily have any long-term effects on cognitive, motor or language performance and there may be confounding factors such as socioeconomic status in some studies (Alati et al., 2008, 2013; O'Leary et al., 2009). Nevertheless there is robust evidence that moderate maternal alcohol consumption increases the risk of FAS and this is clearly a major concern: for example, three to four out of every 1000 babies born in the USA are considered to be affected by FAS (Streissguth et al., 1994; Carr and Coustan, 2006).

- Have you read or heard any recent press reports about alcohol or drug use in pregnancy?
- How do they compare with the research reported here?
- What advice might you give a pregnant woman concerned about the effects of alcohol on her unborn baby?

Maternal psychological state

It is not only maternal physical state that can affect prenatal development. Maternal psychological or emotional state also appears to have an impact. Maternal stress or anxiety produces high levels of cortisol linked to growth problems and postnatal cognitive problems (Bergman et al., 2007). For example, extreme maternal anxiety in pregnancy is linked to brain activity reflecting poor cognitive control in the offspring in adolescence (Mennes et al., 2009). It is difficult, however, to be certain that it is prenatal stress alone that is the causal factor in such studies. A stressed pregnant woman may continue to be stressed after the child is born, thereby affecting the child in this way beyond the prenatal period. Nonetheless, animal research has confirmed that maternal stress can affect prenatal development in two direct ways: either via the effects of maternal stress hormones on the developing brain circuitry of the offspring (Nathanielsz, 1999) or by actually influencing the activity of genes in the embryo or foetus (Gluckman et al., 2007) (see 'How to grow a baby', pages 74–6).

Environmental toxins

Pollutants and toxins in the natural environment may also impact on the prenatal infant, although the evidence in this regard is sometimes controversial (Kalter, 2003). One of the confirmed cases of environmental teratogens occurred in Minimata in Japan in the 1950s, when industrial mercury waste was released into the food chain and water supply, causing prenatal brain damage that resulted in physical and cognitive impairments (Clarkson et al., 2003).

There are many environmental teratogens but, as noted above, a greater percentage of problems in prenatal development are due to the effects of faulty genetic processes.

Genetic factors that impair prenatal development

As explained in 'How to grow a baby', genes influence prenatal cell growth and development, but there can be errors in this process. For example, a mutation in the *Sonic Hedgehog* gene that controls the left–right organisation of the neural pathways can lead to the development of a single eye in the centre of the face (Gilbert, 2000). One of the most common genetic errors, however, leads to the condition known as Down or Down's syndrome or Trisomy 21 (Tocci, 2000). This occurs for about one in every 800 births, with risk increasing markedly with maternal age or most probably the age of the maternal ova which are formed in infancy (the risk rising from 1 in 1900 at 20 years to 1 in 30 at 45 years: Halliday et al., 1995). Most cases are due to the failure of the twenty-first pair of chromosomes to separate properly during cell replication (usually in the copying of the ovum), so that the new cells have three chromosomes for this twenty-first pair instead of the usual two. This causes abnormalities in both body and brain, with impairments in cognition, speech and motor capacities, though less severe forms from only a partial failure of chromosomal separation are associated with less marked impairments.

Although this list of potential hazards seems daunting, by and large most new-borns are not affected by them and make the journey from zygote to neonate intact.

STOP AND THINK

Reflection

- Think about the factors that can penetrate the uterine world.
- Which can have beneficial effects on the development of a baby's brain?
- Which can have detrimental effects?

Birth

The social and cultural practices surrounding labour and birth vary considerably. For example, the presence of the father is welcomed in some societies but forbidden in others (Read, 1968). Nonetheless, in physical terms, the birth process is universal, following clear phases or stages as described below.

Why does birth begin?

After about 38 weeks or 266 days, the foetus is ready to arrive in the world. Birth is initiated by chemical communication between mother and baby. The foetus sends hormonal signals causing the uterus to contract and also produces 'stress' hormones such as adrenaline that enhance labour contractions and help the infant prepare for birth by clearing the lungs and improving alertness (Emory et al., 1988; Hepper, 2002). The mother then begins labour, which averages about 12+ hours for a first baby and half that for subsequent babies (Niswander and Evans, 1996).

Stages of labour

Labour proceeds in three stages. Stage 1 (eight + hours) involves rhythmic uterine contractions increasing in strength and frequency and causing the dilation of the cervix (the narrow opening of the uterus into the birth canal). In Stage 2 (about one to two hours) the baby's head enters the cervical opening and the mother pushes the baby out into the world. In the final stage (about five minutes) the placenta is expelled.

Complications

There can be complications with labour, and protracted deliveries can lead to possible brain damage in the infant due to *anoxia* – the loss of oxygen – but nonetheless most infants whose mothers have had good care arrive intact without problems.

The importance of birth weight for gestational age

As noted in Table 4.1 earlier, the 'average' neonate weighs about 3.2 kg (7 lbs) and is 50 cm (20 inches) long, with boys slightly heavier and longer than girls on average. Birth weight is a key factor in postnatal survival, since low birth weight may be associated with immaturity in the lungs and other organs. An optimal weight-range is about 3–5 kg (6.6–11 lbs) (Rees et al., 1996), although 2.5 kg (5.5 lbs) is within normal range and rare birth weights of 9 kg (20 lbs) have been recorded (Smolak, 1986). The survival chances of babies with birth weight lower than 2.5 kg have improved markedly and even babies weighing as little as 700–800 g may have a good chance of survival with intensive support (Macdonald, 2002). However, low birth weight can occur if infants are pre-term (three or more weeks premature) or small-for-gestational-age (SGA) – or both. Babies who are pre-term, but within the expected weight range for their gestational age, are more likely to survive and make better developmental progress after birth than SGA infants (McCormick et al., 1993; Macdonald, 2002).

Is the new baby in good shape?

To ensure that the infant has arrived in good order, physical condition and state may be assessed by a number of means (Lipkin, 2005), such as one-minute and five-minute ratings against the Apgar scale, estimating aspects of the infant's condition (see Table 4.2). An overall score of 7 or better reflects good condition, but scores of 4 to 6 indicate that the baby may require breathing support, and 3 or below, that the baby is in urgent need of assistance.

Definitions

Placenta: the organ which connects to the wall of the mother's uterus, and which connects to the foetus by the umbilical cord. It allows for the uptake of nutrients by the foetus, and for the elimination of waste.

Apgar scale: a rating scale for the condition of the new-born.

Table 4.2 Features used in Apgar scale scoring (a total score out of 10 is derived by adding the ratings for each of the five features).

Breathing	Skin colour	Heart rate	Reflexes	Muscle tone	Rating scale
None	Grey/blue	None	None	None	0
Shallow and irregular	Grey extremities/ body appropriate colour for ethnicity	< 100 bpm	Slow or moderate	Weak or moderate	1
Regular with crying	Appropriate colour for ethnicity	100–140 bpm	Clear and strong	Flexed limbs, strong movements	2

Source: After Apgar (1953)

> **STOP AND THINK**
>
> **Reflection**
>
> - Is there someone you know who has had a baby?
> - If (*and only if*) they are happy to talk about it, ask them to tell you about the experience.

The neonate: basic states, movements and reflexes

No blooming or buzzing confusion?

The neonate arrives with a functional brain and nervous system, allowing a coherent experience of and response to the world. Indeed, for about 30 minutes after birth most infants show a period of 'quiet alertness' when they appear to scan the world into which they have arrived (Klaus et al., 1995). Decades of research (Bremner and Fogel, 2001; Slater and Lewis, 2002) have overturned Piaget's view that the new-born has only disjointed and momentary impressions, limited to representing the world in terms of actions upon it, rather than by its features and properties. William James' similar opinion (1890) that the neonate exists in a 'blooming, buzzing confusion' has also been shown to be inaccurate. Contrary to these perspectives, more recent research confirms that the neonate is capable of organised sensation, perception, attention, memory and learning, and displays not only simple reflexes but also voluntary responses relying on complex brain functions. This is not to say that the neonate is fully developed in these terms, but rather that the basic mechanisms for registering and reacting to the world are in place and operate in a coordinated manner to provide a springboard for further development.

Neonatal states of arousal

One of the key signs that the neonatal nervous system is operational is that after an initial state of quiet attentiveness following birth, new-borns show six different states of arousal or alertness (Wolff, 1966): deep sleep, light sleep, drowsiness, quiet alertness, alert activity (awake but restless) and, finally, crying (often to signal discomfort such as hunger). Sleep in the newborn is influenced not only by internal factors but also by the environment and is related to development of brain function (Graven and Browne, 2008). The neural centre for Circadian (daily) rhythms develops prenatally (Rivkees and Hao, 2000) with further maturation after birth. New-borns sleep about 16–18 hours a day, though in shorter intervals and with more REM (rapid eye movement) sleep than for adults (Louis et al., 1997). REM accounts for about 50% of sleep at birth, declining to adult levels (about 20%) by about 9 months. As noted, REM sleep is critical to brain development in foetal and early postnatal life, and deprivation of REM sleep at these times is associated with disruption or delay in development of the sensory systems and long-term memory ability (Graven and Browne, 2008).

Neonatal movement and reflexes

Neonates have relatively poor control of body movement, but can move their heads and kick their feet when lying on their stomachs, and studies of the trajectories of neonatal arm movements indicate that they have some visual control of arm movements (Von Hofsten, 1982). They also show many reflex reactions which are an indicator of the maturity of the nervous system, as is their eventual disappearance in the first year of life. A few reflexes continue across the lifespan (e.g. eye blink reflex), but most should vanish in the first year of life as higher brain centres take control of movement. The Moro Reflex is a good example: neonates will react to a sudden stimulus by a startle response, throwing their head and limbs back and then retracting them. This is a healthy sign that the nervous system is functioning well at birth, but it should disappear by about 4–6 months (Hepper, 2002). Infants are able to moderate reflex movements to some extent, such as adjusting the sucking reflex relative to the flow of breast milk (Craig and Lee, 1999), with this reflecting more deliberate control of action that will increasingly develop after birth (see 'Motor abilities in infancy', pages 98–9).

> **STOP AND THINK**
>
> **Reflection**
>
> The human neonate is relatively helpless in terms of movement control. What do you think the effects of this might be for the overall development of a child?

The postnatal development of the brain

The new-born brain is relatively mature in some ways, but undeveloped in others. Many basic aspects of brain development are under genetic control. For example, the structure of the cortex in many areas seems to be 'inherited' via genes (Ramus, 2006), but there is also considerable room for change and plasticity.

Many of the brain systems for sensation and perception of the world are functioning well at birth, as is the basic ability to learn and store information in memory. Nonetheless, these basic competencies undergo refinement in the months after birth and some aspects of the brain require many months or even years to reach full function. The neonatal brain is therefore sufficiently developed to allow the infant to perceive and learn about the world, but also sufficiently pliant to allow adaptation to the context for development.

The neonatal brain resembles the adult brain apart from being only about 25% of its weight (Thatcher et al., 1996). The main structures and all of the 100 billion neurons are present, having been produced in foetal life (see 'Prenatal physical development', pages 77–81). However, the neonatal brain differs from that of the adult in two main ways, as discussed in the next two sections.

Connecting and pruning the brain after birth

One difference is that the new-born brain only has about one-sixth of the connections or synapses of the adult brain, but then, in the months after birth, the synaptogenesis that began in prenatal life (see 'Prenatal physical development', pages 77–81) increases in earnest. There is now a massive increase in the number and length of dendrites and terminal branches, leading to such a rapid increase in number of synapses that by about 12 months of age, the infant brain has twice as many as the adult brain (Huttenlocher, 1990; Casey et al., 2000; Gogtay et al., 2004). It is as if the brain has generated maximum material to ensure that its messages are transmitted. This over-production is eventually corrected or refined as neurons compete with each other for favoured pathways and connections, leading to severe pruning of the connections. Only the most used connections survive this trimming process (Eisenberg, 1999).

Synaptogenesis and pruning do not occur uniformly across brain areas and are linked to the usage of the brain region. The earliest regions to show these processes are the brain areas for sensory processing. For example, there is rapid synaptogenesis in the visual cortex after birth, peaking at about 8 months, before falling to adult levels by the end of childhood (Huttenlocher, 1990; Dubois et al., 2014). In contrast, synaptogenesis occurs later in the language areas (Thatcher, 1991). The frontal lobes are the last of all to develop in this way, showing a high level of synaptic growth throughout childhood, with a peak in synaptic density around 2 years and pruning ongoing across childhood (Johnson, 2001; Gogtay et al., 2004; Lenroot and Giedd, 2006). Chapter 14, Developmental Psychology and Education, explores some recent research which points to other periods of over-production and rapid synaptic pruning in adolescence, and the implications of these for education.

Coating the neurons: myelinisation

The usage of the brain is also reflected in increased myelinisation (the coating of neurons in fatty myelin), which begins in prenatal life (see 'Prenatal physical development', pages 77–81) but expands rapidly after birth, not slowing until adolescence. It occurs first of all in the spinal cord, then the hindbrain, midbrain and forebrain, enabling the increasingly efficient use of these regions. In the cortex, it occurs firstly in the sensory areas (Huttenlocher, 1990) and appears in brain areas for controlling the arms and trunk at about 1 month of age and later for areas controlling the legs, fingers and hands (Tanner, 1990). Myelinisation of the frontal lobes begins in infancy but continues throughout childhood to adult life (Nelson, 2002a).

Lateralisation: how the left and right brain grows after birth

The neonatal brain also shows some lateralisation of brain function (differences in function across the two halves or hemispheres) that continues to develop after birth. For example, in anticipation of later hemisphere differences in adults, there is a left hemisphere bias in new-born speech perception (Davidson, 1994) and some movement control (Grattan et al., 1992) and, by 12 months or so, most infants show a right-hand preference reflecting control by the left hemisphere (Hinojosa et al., 2003). There is also left hemisphere bias for positive emotions such as happiness in 4-month-olds (Hane et al., 2008) and for the categorical perception of orientation in 5-month-olds (Franklin et al., 2010). The right hemisphere shows early dominance for processing the relational aspects of facial patterns (de Schonen and Mathivet, 1990; Catherwood et al., 2003), colour categorisation (Franklin et al., 2008) and negative emotional arousal such as fear or sadness (Hane et al., 2008).

Although basic left–right organisation of the brain may be in place early in infancy, there is nonetheless still considerable plasticity. One big change comes with the onset of language, mainly handled by the left hemisphere. This can have effects on other functions. For example, in infants the right hemisphere is especially sensitive to the main differences between hues or colours but, as colour naming abilities develop, the left hemisphere becomes more dominant in this regard (Franklin et al., 2008). While lateralisation develops over childhood, so does communication between the two hemispheres. The latter occurs with the myelinisation of the corpus callosum, the nerve fibres connecting the hemispheres, with this process starting by 12 months of age, increasing between 3 and 6 years of age, and slowing in adolescence (Giedd et al., 1999).

Mapping activity in the infant brain: developmental neuroscience

A most promising future direction for studying the infant brain and its abilities is that provided by research approaches in developmental neuroscience (studying brain regions and systems) and developmental cognitive neuroscience (studying the brain during different states and activities related to perceptual–cognitive processing). To find out how our understanding of the brain and cognitive development has been informed by neuroscience research, see Recommended Reading. These approaches use brain mapping and imaging technology such as functional magnetic resonance imaging (fMRI) and EEG (electro-encephalography). For example, a longitudinal fMRI study of the infant brain from 4 to 9 months of age revealed increasing long-range connections from the frontal cortex to visual and sensorimotor areas (Damaraju et al., 2014), consistent with greater control over these capacities over this timespan. Patterns of EEG activity in the resting brain also undergo development in the first 12 months, becoming adult-like during that time (Chugani, et al., 1987; Szücs, 2005), and studies with infants around 7–8 months have found infant EEG patterns to be indicative of infant cognition (e.g., Szücs, 2005; Orekhova et al., 2006; Csibra and Johnson, 2007) (see 'Cognitive abilities in infancy', pages 99–101, for more details on this).

EEG is being increasingly used to map infant brain activity during different states and cognitive tasks. In infants, as for adults, brain activity in the form of 'waves' from the scalp can be detected by EEG technology and 'dense-array' sensor-nets have made it easier to apply this technique to young infants.

A very recent EEG approach is to search for bursts of activity in particular frequencies in the EEG waves that have been linked to different types of cognitive processing. EEG frequencies are conventionally grouped in bands related to how frequently the waves occur (like fast or slow ripples on a pond), with these bands denoted by Greek letters: δ

> **Definition**
>
> EEG (electroencephalogram): record of brain activity recorded by means of electrodes placed around the scalp.

(delta: very slow: 0–4 Hz or cycles per second), θ (theta: 4–8 Hz), α (alpha: 8–12 Hz), β (beta: 12–20 Hz), γ (gamma: fastest of all: 30+ Hz) (Purves et al., 2008).

In adults, for example, the brain shows theta waves when holding items in working memory, beta activity when processing information from the environment and alpha activity when awake but in relaxed mode (as with eyes closed). The superfast gamma may arise when there is a need to synchronise processing across different brain regions – for example, when different visual features of an object such as colour and shape need to be bound together. There is growing evidence of similar types of EEG activity in the infant brain (Szücs, 2005; Orekhova et al., 2006; Csibra and Johnson, 2007; de Haan, 2008) (see the Cutting Edge box, page 100, and 'Infant vision', pages 91–5, and 'Cognitive abilities in infancy', pages 99–101, for more detail).

Nature and nurture in postnatal brain development

Nature and nurture work in harmony in early brain development. Although the basic processes in growth of synapses are under genetic control (Li et al., 2000), paradoxically this growth also reflects the plasticity and adaptability of the human brain to learning and experience. Input to the brain from learning and experience directly affects synapse growth. New brain pathways and patterns are built to encode new memories and learning, not just in infancy but right across the lifespan. Synaptogenesis is the perfect example of genes and experience working together to create human capacities. As studies with other animals show, even innate brain capacities can be either strengthened or weakened by early experiences. For example, rats raised in enriched environments (with lots of toys, handling and stimulation) show richer development of the visual cortex (Rosenzweig, 1984), while monkeys and cats raised under restricted visual conditions suffer impairments in innate visual abilities (Held and Hein, 1963; Sugita, 2004).

For humans, studies of institutionalised infants have shown that highly impoverished early environments can have a deleterious effect on natural perceptual–cognitive ability while moderate stimulation can enhance it (White and Held, 1966). Early musical training increases the cortical area devoted to musical processing (Pantev et al., 2003) and early blindness can lead to the expansion of auditory cortical areas to nearby brain regions to enhance the processing of sounds (Rauschecker and Henning, 2000).

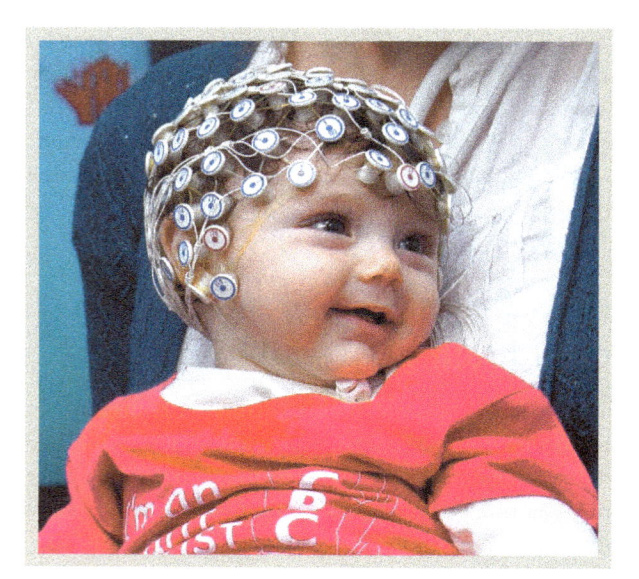

An infant wearing a dense-array EEG (electroencephalograph) net for testing infant brain activity in research at the Centre for Brain and Cognitive Development, Birkbeck, University of London
Source: Teri Pengilley

Critical periods for brain plasticity?

The brain is thus adaptable in infancy, but there are also limitations or 'critical periods' for major changes in brain organisation. In general, the brain is less plastic in later childhood and adulthood (Banich, 2004). Earlier-maturing areas such as the visual cortex may be more plastic and resilient to early damage since they can 'poach' or borrow brain power from nearby regions. This comes at a cost, though. The 'crowding hypothesis' (Teuber and Rudel, 1962) suggests that later-maturing functions such as language and movement control may be affected as a result (since their intended brain territory has already been used). Hence late-maturing functions like language are more vulnerable to damage in early life.

The infant brain has many basic systems and structures already in place by birth and shows rapid development with increasing brain usage, but to what extent do these systems support useful functions and operations? One key source of information on this issue is research into the infant ability to sense and perceive the world. We will consider this in the next section.

> **STOP AND THINK**
>
> **Reflection**
>
> How do we know that the infant brain is 'turned on' at birth or in the early months of life?

Infant perception

Sensation involves activity in special body receptors (such as the tiny rods and cones lining the retina of the eye) and in special channels in the nervous system that enable us to detect stimulation from the environment (light, sound waves, etc.). Perception is the additional processing in these neural pathways and brain regions providing a more complete or coherent impression of the nature of the stimulus. The five main sensory–perceptual systems: visual, auditory (hearing), tactile–haptic (touch), olfactory (smell) and gustatory (taste), operate from birth (or before). Decades of research (Bremner and Fogel, 2001; Slater and Lewis, 2002) have overturned earlier views (Piaget, 1952b, 1958; James, 1890) and confirmed that, while perception undergoes development and refinement after birth, even in neonates it is operational and largely 'coherent', providing structure to the flux of stimulation arriving from the outside world. As for adults, different sensations are processed as separate from each other, but sensations can also be bound together into unified wholes where necessary. For example, for adults, the colour blue can be distinguished from green but can also be linked to a round shape as in a blue balloon. Young infants appear to have similar capacities.

Infant vision

What visual equipment do new-borns have?

Visual sensation and perception relies on the response of the nervous system to light emitted or reflected from objects. The main components of the visual system include: the eyeball(s) for collecting light; a lens for focusing the light by 'accommodation' (bulging for close things, flattening for far objects); the retina lining the inner eyeball with neural pathways from the retina to the brain; and the visual (occipital) cortex (with ordered groups of neurons for analysis of the visual signals). These are illustrated in Figure 4.6.

New-borns have this basic visual kit, although some components are still immature for the first year, with some lingering development across childhood (Hainline, 1998). In particular, the cones are not in their final place in the fovea and the lens may not readily focus at a range of distances. It was once considered that the infant lens was fixed to focus at about 20 cm; however, even new-borns can focus on objects 75 cm away (Hainline, 1998) but may not do so, often under- or over-accommodating. The lens and brain need to cooperate for correct focusing, and it takes a few months of practice before this fine-tuning works smoothly.

How strong is infant vision?

The power of this infant visual system to see fine detail (visual acuity) has been assessed. Adult visual acuity is usually tested by reading a Snellen chart with rows of letters of diminishing size. You will have seen this kind of chart if you have ever had your eyes tested. The limit of acuity is the line of the letters that cannot be clearly read (e.g., where 'P' is read as 'R'). An estimate of 20/20 vision means seeing as well as the 'average' person at 20 feet (or 6/6 in metres). If vision is weaker than the average then the number on the right side will be bigger than 20. For example, 20/600 vision means seeing at 20 feet what the average observer sees at 600 feet (so you would have weak vision).

Infant acuity obviously cannot be measured with Snellen charts, but it can be measured in a similar way with the preferential looking method (Fantz, 1964; Dobson and Teller, 1978; Atkinson, 2000), based on the idea that babies (like adults) prefer to look at something rather than nothing. The baby is observed while being shown a black-and-white striped pattern on one side and a blank display on the other. If the baby prefers to look towards the stripes then she or he must be able to see them. At first, patterns with thick stripes are shown and then progressively finer ones – like the rows of Snellen letters. Eventually the baby won't show a clear preference for the pattern, with this taken as the limit of the baby's

> **Definition**
>
> **Preferential looking method:** a procedure for testing infant perceptual and cognitive skills by observing infant viewing preferences to two or more items.

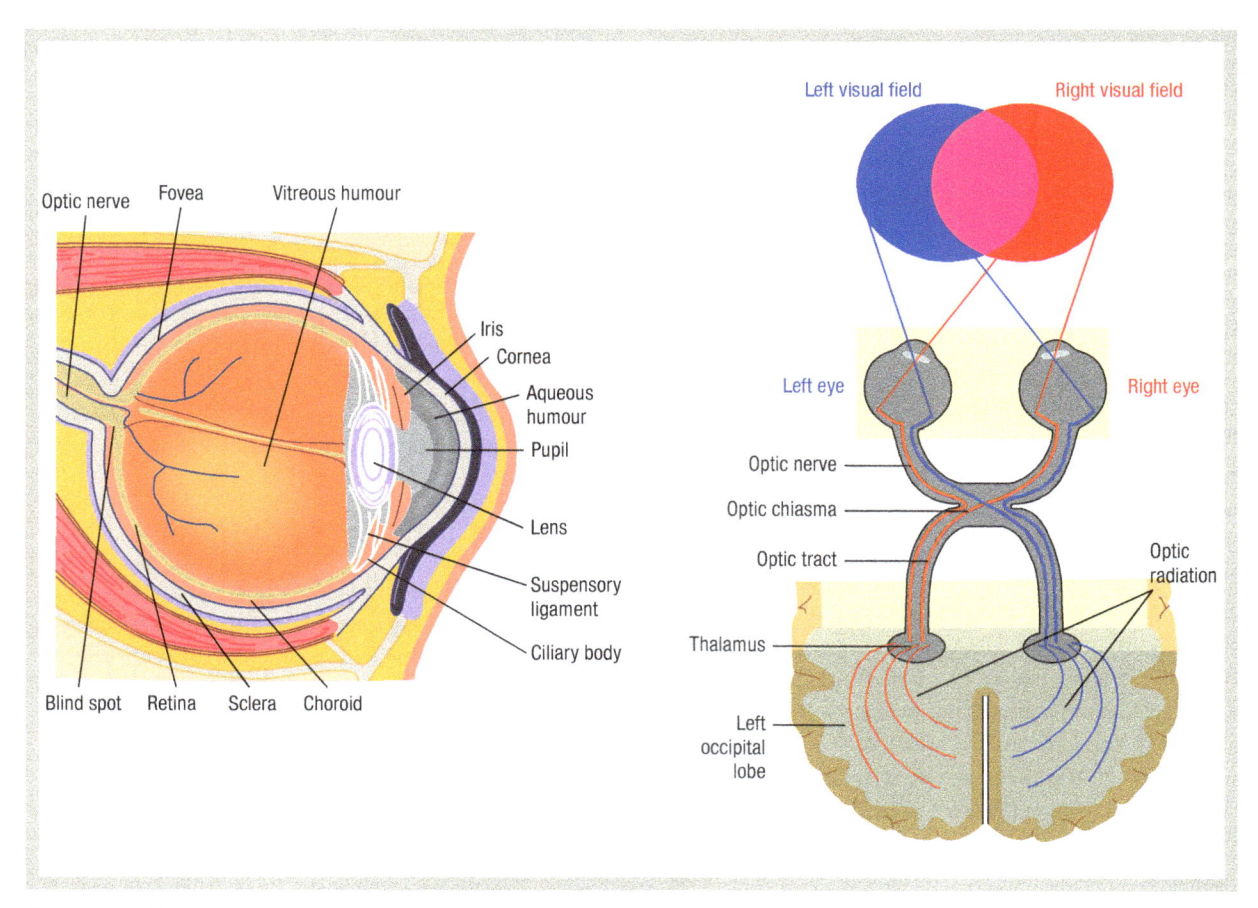

Figure 4.6 The eye and visual pathways.

acuity – just as the lowest readable line of the Snellen chart is for adults. A more sensitive test uses VEPs (visually evoked potentials) or EEG measures of brain activity that arise as the baby views striped patterns. From both preferential looking and VEP methods, the estimate of new-born visual acuity is about 20/600. New-borns can certainly see important aspects of their world, including the main features of faces 50 cm away (Atkinson and Braddick, 1981). Visual acuity improves rapidly to about 20/60 by 6 months and adult levels (20/20) by about 9 months, though precise estimates vary with different methods (Atkinson, 2000; Gwiazda and Birch, 2001). Small improvements continue across childhood but 10–12-month-olds see about as well as adults.

Do infants see a 'coherent' world?

So infants can 'see', but do they do so in a coherent or sensible way? That is, do they distinguish one thing from another or is everything a chaotic jumble? And if so, when does the shift from chaos to coherence occur? This question has been answered by preferential looking, habituation-recovery and familiarisation procedures (see the Research Methods box).

Definitions

Habituation-recovery: a procedure for testing infant perceptual and cognitive skills by repeatedly presenting an item until the infant's interest drops to some criterion or set level, then presenting a novel item to see if the infant shows refreshed interest and so can distinguish it from the familiar one.

Familiarisation: a procedure for testing infant perceptual and cognitive skills by presenting an item for a set number of times or trials and then comparing infant interest in the familiar item with interest in a novel one.

RESEARCH METHODS

Windows on the infant brain and mind

Several procedures developed since the 1970s have been especially powerful as tools for appraising infant abilities, and in later chapters you will come across examples of research which has used these methods. For example, in preferential looking tasks, infants are presented with different stimuli simultaneously and observed to see which ones they look at longest (Fantz, 1964; Adams and Courage, 1998).

Habituation-recovery methods (Slater et al., 1983) involve repeatedly showing an infant some item until some preset criterion is reached (e.g. until the baby is looking 50% of the time compared to the amount that they were looking during the initial trial or baseline) and then measuring the baby's fixation to a 'novel' item. If infants can perceive the change to this novel stimulus, they may show 'recovery' of interest, looking longer at the novel item than on the previous trials of the old item. If they can't see any difference, they won't show refreshed interest. An alternative method, called the familiarisation approach (Catherwood et al., 1996), is usually faster to complete since the first item is presented for a set time or for a set number of trials determined by the experimenter in advance, instead of being determined by the infant's level of fixation on the trials. The 'test' phase in these methods involves presenting the old and new items either together or one after the other (with the order random or balanced out to avoid order or carryover effects). These approaches have been used in many studies to confirm that neonates and older infants see basic visual features such as shape and colour in an ordered way.

Do young babies see shape in a coherent way?

New-borns who are habituated to one shape show recovery to a different shape – for example, neonates habituated to a square showed recovery to a rectangle and vice versa (Slater et al., 1983). New-borns also show visual preference for certain shapes, indicating that they can discriminate them. They have a particular bias for facial shape (Dannemiller and Stephens, 1988; Leo and Simion, 2009) and, after only four hours of exposure to the mother, show preferential fixation for their mother's face (Field et al., 1984). Importantly for socio-emotional development, they can also distinguish between basic emotional expressions such as happiness or sadness at about 2 days old (Field et al., 1983).

This evidence suggests that the ability to see shapes in a structured way depends either on innate mechanisms in the visual system or rather on mechanisms that can be fine-tuned with minimal experience after birth (Morton and Johnson, 1991). Animal research has confirmed, however, that even innate mechanisms can be undone by postnatal environments that are poor in visual stimulation (see 'The postnatal development of the brain', pages 88–90, for further details).

When can babies see colours?

The research on infant colour vision and perception has been somewhat more contentious. Nonetheless, the current view is that neonates have at least some functional colour vision and this develops rapidly in the first 3 months after birth. Infant colour vision has been revealed by various methods such as observation of whether infants show 'preferential looking' to coloured as opposed to achromatic (uncoloured) stimuli or to a coloured item on an achromatic background, with some studies also recording associated brain activity (visually evoked potentials or VEPs). Colour vision involves the cone cells of the retina as well as neural pathways to the brain and regions in the cortex. By about 1–2 months, infants appear to have the retinal apparatus for distinguishing colours and also the brain pathways for perceiving at least greenish and reddish colours, although bluish colours may develop somewhat later (Knoblauch et al., 1998; Adams and Courage, 2002; Suttle et al., 2002). By 3–4 months infants can perceive all four basic colours or hues perceived by adults (broadly corresponding to the labels: blue, green, yellow and red) (Hainline, 1998; Teller, 1998; Teller and Bornstein, 1987; Bornstein, 2006a; Brown and Lindsey, 2013).

By 3–4 months, infants also seem to see colour *categorically* as adults do. This is shown by the fact that 3–4-month-old infants habituated to one hue (e.g. a blue) show more recovery of interest to hues from different categories (e.g. green) than a new hue from the same category (i.e. another blue) (Franklin and Davies, 2004; Bornstein, 2006a) (see the Research Methods box). Colour vision and categorisation would seem to depend on innate processes or ones that mature early in life, but nevertheless such natural abilities require environmental stimulation in infancy to be sustained. Research with young monkeys has shown that they can lose natural colour vision if raised in environments with limited colours (Sugita, 2004).

Do infants see in 3-D or do they see a flat world?

Another key aspect of visual perception is that we use cues to see the world in depth or 3-D (e.g. nearby objects and patterns look bigger than those far away). Infants display early preference for 3-D over 2-D versions of objects. Habituation and preferential looking and reaching studies as well as studies measuring brain response (VEPs) have shown this to be the case, indicating that infants start to perceive the world in depth by about 2–3 months with this developing rapidly over the first year (Birch and Petrig, 1996; Sen et al., 2001; Slater and Lewis, 2002; Brown and Miracle, 2003; Kavšek et al., 2012; Giaschi et al., 2013). Infants use 'stereoscopic' cues to depth (different views from the two eyes) by 4–5 months of age and 'pictorial' cues to depth (texture gradients, linear perspective, etc.) soon after.

A classic method to test infant depth perception employs an illusory depth apparatus (the 'visual cliff': Gibson and Walk, 1960; Adolph, 2000) comprised of a table with a transparent surface or top. The illusion of depth (a 'visual cliff') is provided by attaching a patterned checked material to the under-surface of one half of the table-top and using the same patterned material on the floor under the other half. The difference in pattern size on the shallow and deep sides provides a strong illusory impression of depth (the 'cliff'). Babies old enough to crawl (around 7 months) who are placed on the 'shallow' side will stop at the cliff in distress. On the other hand, 2-month-olds may show a decline in heart rate if placed on the cliff side, suggesting they are processing the depth cue but in an interested rather than fearful way (Campos et al., 1978).

Do infants see 'constant' objects?

More complex aspects of visual perception have also been confirmed in infants. Infants perceive that the same object can appear different from different angles or distances – that is, they have both shape constancy and size constancy, respectively. Piaget would not have credited new-borns with these abilities (Piaget, 1952b, 1958), but neonates showed size constancy in a study that habituated them to a small cube-shaped item then showed this old shape in comparison with a new larger copy (Slater et al., 1990). The new larger shape was shown further away than the old smaller shape, so that the two shapes were the same size on the infant's retina. The infants still showed more interest in the new shape, however, indicating that they could distinguish actual changes in size from apparent changes in size. In a similar habituation procedure, neonates also showed evidence of shape constancy (Slater and Morison, 1985).

This ability to see 'constant' objects suggests that infants do appreciate the wholeness of objects. This is at odds with the proposal from Piaget (1952b, 1958) that in the first 12 months or so infants perceive only fragmentary and disjointed impressions of objects not combined into wholes (infants would think they had many mothers according to this view of their abilities). Infants also seem to see objects as 'wholes' in other ways too.

Babies 'join up' the parts of an object

Objects consist of many features such as colour, texture and size, and these need to be 'bound' together to form a whole impression of the object. Evidence from habituation and familiarisation studies confirms that young infants do bind together such features into a 'whole' object, given sufficient time (Catherwood et al., 1996). Recent research using EEG data shows brain activity in 8-month-olds suggestive of this binding together of object features (Csibra and Johnson, 2007).

This 'whole' view of objects also involves joining up information from different senses. Even in the early months, infants act as if they 'expect' visual and auditory aspects of the same object to link up. For example, babies of 3 months will show a distress or indifference reaction if there is a mismatch between vision (lip movements) and sound (the voice of adult speakers) (Broerse et al., 1983). This resembles adult discomfort at watching asynchronised films and soundtracks. Likewise 4-month-olds prefer to look at synchronised puppet displays (i.e. puppets jumping in rhythm with a sound) than asynchronised ones (Spelke, 1979). Such studies are consistent with infant expectations of a coordinated sensory world.

> **STOP AND THINK**
>
> **Reflection**
> Why do psychologists no longer think that the infant sees a disordered jumble of visual impressions?

Infant audition

The auditory system is more developed physically than the visual system at birth, and coherent auditory perception may emerge even before birth (see 'Prenatal abilities and behaviours', pages 82–3). The contemporary view is therefore that neonates can distinguish between sounds (pitch and loudness) as well as being able to perceive similarities and patterns among sounds, but that auditory sensitivity (Trehub et al., 1991) improves over childhood. Much of auditory development in childhood in fact consists of the loss of neonatal auditory capacities, in regard to the shaping of sensitivity to speech and musical patterns of the surrounding environment.

How do we know that the infant auditory channels are working?

Infant audition can be tested for basic operation at birth using evoked otoacoustic emissions (EOAE), in which a tiny microphone in the infant ear picks up 'feedback' if hearing is functional (Chabert et al., 2006). A simpler method is to observe whether the baby orients towards a sound. Neonates will turn their eyes and head towards sounds if they are presented for long enough and are pleasant or interesting (e.g. voices or rattles).

More complex auditory capacities are often measured with the 'high-amplitude' sucking (HAS) or 'non-nutritive' sucking procedure (Eimas, 1975; Nazzi et al., 1998). Babies are given a dummy or pacifier linked to equipment that controls the production of some sound such as music. The sound will turn on when the baby's sucking increases to a certain rate (amplitude). If the baby can and wants to hear the sound, she or he will keep sucking at this elevated rate, but if the baby habituates to the sound then the sucking rate will decline. At this point, another sound is played to the baby. If the sucking rate returns to the high level, then the baby has perceived that sound as different from the old one. The non-nutritive dummy method can be used to assess infants' responses to visual as well as auditory displays, and is discussed further in Chapter 6, Memory and Intelligence.

As discussed in 'Prenatal abilities and behaviours' (pages 82–3), the auditory system is functional to some degree by the fifth month after conception, so that even the foetus can 'hear' through the medium of the amniotic fluid. EEG methods show that new-borns detect changes in the pitch, loudness and duration of a sound stream (Sambeth et al., 2009). Infants in general are less sensitive than adults so sounds need to be louder, but this is less so for high-frequency sounds. Sensitivity to these actually declines before adolescence, and adults are less sensitive than infants to higher-pitch sounds (Trehub et al., 1991).

Do babies hear sound patterns or is it all just noise for them?

The new-born hears sounds, but is this coherent perception? Do babies hear organised sound patterns as in speech or music? Research using observation of infant preferences and HAS methods suggests that they do. Babies show preferential orientation to speech and music (Kuhl and Rivera-Gaxiola, 2008) and, as described in 'Prenatal abilities and behaviours', even the foetus seems capable of some processing of these sounds, as

> **Definition**
>
> **High-amplitude sucking (HAS) method:** a procedure for testing infant auditory skills (especially in regard to speech and music), in which infants suck on a dummy or pacifier to maintain a sound if interested.

evident from new-born preference for the mother's voice (DeCasper and Fifer, 1980), her favourite TV theme tunes (Hepper, 1996), her native language (Mehler et al., 1988) and Dr Seuss stories heard while *in utero* (DeCasper and Spence, 1986). So the new-born arrives with a bias to speech and music, and the research described next indicates that this reflects coherent perception.

Infants show better ability than adults to detect the basic speech sounds

Brain imaging (Kuhl and Rivera-Gaxiola, 2008) and the HAS method have confirmed that young infants are highly responsive to the language environment around them. Neonates arrive with a strong natural ability to detect speech patterns. In fact, studies using the HAS method (Eimas et al., 1971; Ramus, 2002) have shown that very young infants can discriminate or perceive the basic sounds (phonemes) from a wider range of languages than adults can.

This remarkable ability is, however, lost by 12–18 months as the native language environment takes over and the ability to hear non-native speech sound differences is reduced. For example, in the first 6 or so months of life, Japanese babies can hear the difference between 'l' and 'r', but by 12 months they – like Japanese adults – cannot detect this difference (Jusczyk et al., 1998). Similarly, babies in English-speaking families can distinguish Hindi and North American Indian (Salish) language sounds at 6–8 months, but not at 12 months (Werker and Tees, 1984).

Kuhl and Rivera-Gaxiola (2008) describe this trend as an example of how experience (nurture) can in fact both strengthen and curtail natural abilities (nature). This shaping begins early, with recent evidence (Mampe et al., 2009) that even new-born crying has an intonation pattern (rising or falling) shaped by the native language. The development of speech sound perception and its role in language is explored more fully in Chapter 5, Language Development.

Babies can also detect musical patterns

A similar pattern of development occurs for the perception of musical sounds. Even neonates perceive basic features of music such as rhythm in a coherent way (Winkler et al., 2009). Older infants of 8 months can recognise changes in pitch for a single note in six-note melodies (Trehub et al., 1985). Even more remarkably, 4–6-month-olds can distinguish typical and atypical versions of musical pieces by Mozart (Trainor and Heinmiller, 1998), while 7-month-olds can distinguish between two Mozart sonatas after a few weeks of exposure and can still do so two weeks later (Saffran et al., 2000). Infants also have a better ability to detect musical patterns in foreign music than adults do (Hannon and Trehub, 2005). Music perception is thus another example of how natural abilities can be curtailed by the prevailing environment (see the Lifespan box).

> **STOP AND THINK**
>
> **Reflection**
>
> Given what you have read about infants' auditory abilities, when do you think might be the best time to learn another language?

Infant touch, taste and smell abilities

Vision and hearing are key perceptual abilities, but neonates also rely heavily on the other sensory–perceptual channels to engage with and learn about their world.

Using touch to learn about objects

Touch is critical to infant development in two ways. Firstly, tactile contact is essential for infant well-being: skin-to-skin (kangaroo) contact improves development for pre-term or low-birthweight babies and gentle touch reduces stress and stimulates the prefrontal cortex in infants (Field, 2010; Kida and Shinohara, 2013). Secondly, touch is an important medium for infant perception and learning. Basic aspects of touch perception operate early, since the embryo, foetus and neonate show clear reflex reactions to touch

LIFESPAN

The musical brain

As the research discussed in 'Infant audition' (pages 95–6) shows, infants show an early capacity to detect musical patterns and are better at this than adults for a wider range of musical forms, apparently because the brain becomes accustomed to the dominant musical forms of the culture in which the child is raised. This research highlights the general issue of brain plasticity. The infant abilities suggest innate programmes or processes that allow the detection of musical patterns, but the curtailment of this early ability by the dominant musical culture also shows the plasticity of the brain.

This could be seen as a case of negative plasticity – of restriction of early abilities – but research into musical training also reveals positive plasticity across the lifespan. Brain reactions change with musical training in childhood. For example, Shahin et al. (2008) found that 4–5-year-olds who had piano training showed higher rates of gamma-band EEG activity in response to piano tones than untrained children. Adults showed a similar response to tones from instruments on which they had been trained.

The gamma activity suggests that musical training can directly influence how well the brain binds musical sounds together. The effects of training, though, are not limited to childhood: even short-term training of adults in aspects of musical perception has been shown to produce changes in brain response (Pantev et al., 2003; Trainor et al., 2003). Such research into the response to music thus shows how the human brain arrives with natural abilities that can nevertheless be shaped and moulded at least to some degree by experiences across the lifespan.

(see 'Prenatal abilities and behaviours', pages 82–3). However, new-borns also use touch in a 'haptic' way: that is, using touch to get 'information' about the world – for example, by altering their sucking or mouthing responses to dummies with different textures or showing differential grasping of tubes of different temperatures or weights (Hernandez-Rief et al., 2000; Field, 2010). The pathways for painful touch also seem to develop in the foetus around 25 weeks, and the neonate responds to medical procedures such as circumcision with distress (Jorgensen, 1999). More complex haptic perception has been examined by habituation or familiarisation methods. Babies allowed to explore a stimulus through touch alone (either in the dark or with a bib covering their hands) will subsequently show more manipulation for a novel item that varies from the familiar one in texture, shape, rigidity and so on (Streri and Spelke, 1988; Catherwood, 1993). Such evidence confirms that touch can be used by infants to acquire knowledge or information about important properties of objects.

How babies can use taste and smell to 'know' the world

Taste and smell (gustatory and olfactory perception, respectively) are perhaps most closely related to early survival and so mature early. Taste sensitivity actually weakens with age. Neonates react as if they perceive the four basic tastes of sweet, sour, salty and bitter as shown by their facial expressions, sucking rate and swallowing when solutions are placed in their mouths (Browne, 2008). They prefer sweet tastes and dislike bitter, sour and strong salty tastes (Rosenstein and Oster, 1988; Harris, 1997), but taste is affected by subsequent learning, and taste preferences can and do change with age and experience.

Smell (olfactory) perception is also well developed in new-borns and may help them to identify the familiar or safe things and people in their world. New-borns show an apparently innate bias to odours considered pleasant by adults (e.g. banana, vanilla, strawberry) and avoidance of odours considered unpleasant or noxious (disinfectant, fish or rotting eggs) (Crook, 1987; Lagercrantz and Changeux, 2010). There is also an innate bias to breast milk. The Near-Infrared Spectroscopy (NIRS) method, which maps blood flow and hence neural activity of the brain, reveals more activity in the newborn's orbitofrontal cortex (an area linked to 'reward') for breast milk compared to formula milk (Aoyama et al., 2010). Nevertheless this innate preference is rapidly influenced by early experience, as shown by research in which breast milk from the baby's own mother was presented on a pad and another mother's milk on another pad. By 4–6 days of age, babies oriented to, and so were able to identify, their own mother's milk (Browne, 2008; MacFarlane, 1975; Cernoch and Porter, 1985). Neonates also indicate recognition of odours experienced from the prenatal maternal diet and show preference for their own mother's amniotic fluid (Browne, 2008; Schaal et al., 2000). Foetal familiarity with the tastes and smells of the maternal diet may provide a foundation for postnatal socialisation into the dietary culture after birth (Browne, 2008). As well as showing the effects of experience on taste and smell, taste and smell perception clearly operate at a sensitive level in new-borns, giving them an important basis for coherent experience of one very important aspect of the world, namely food, but also for identifying familiar aspects of their environment.

STOP AND THINK

Reflection

Consider how babies make maximum use of the senses other than vision to learn about the properties of objects. Do you think these are as important for them as visual learning? Why/why not?

Motor abilities in infancy

Although new-borns arrive with good sensory–perceptual abilities, their movement (motor) capacities are much weaker. Control over body posture, gross limb movements and fine movements of hands and fingers takes considerably longer to develop. New-borns have many reflex movements and some basic abilities for acting on and reacting to the world (see 'The neonate: basic states, movements and reflexes', page 87), but after birth, motor control develops in both *cephalo–caudal* (head-to-toe) and *proximo–distal* (midline-to-extremities) directions with each new skill building on the previous one and contributing to the next.

This kind of control is essential for effective action on and reaction to the environment, but presents a considerable developmental challenge. Mastery of body and hand movement involves both higher and lower brain centres that communicate via the spinal cord with the muscles of the body (Purves et al., 2008). Effective initiation and control of action and movement therefore requires coordination across many brain regions, and it takes considerable time in infancy and early childhood to achieve this efficiency.

The development of gross-motor and fine-motor control depends on innate routines for action that mature in conjunction with stimulation from the environment. It is also closely tied to the infant's perceptual, cognitive and communicative abilities and motivational states (Thelen and Smith, 1994; Goldfield and Wolff, 2002; Diamond, 2009b; Gallese et al., 2009). For example, infants may grasp at desired objects or point to an object to draw attention to it.

Typical patterns of gross-motor development are shown in Table 4.3, but there are wide individual variations in the timing and even the sequence of these achievements (Goldfield and Wolff, 2002; Bukatko and Daehler, 2004; Bayley, 2005).

Fine motor development also reflects the integration of both innate programmes and feedback from experience and learning. The primary focus for fine-motor development is the growth of control over the hands and fingers, especially in the act of reaching for and grasping

Table 4.3 Major developments in gross motor abilities in infancy.

Approximate age	Gross motor developments
1–4 months	Reflex movements, lifts head when prone on stomach, sits with support
5–9 months	Sits without support
5–10 months	Pulls self to standing position
5–11 months	Crawls
10–17 months	Stands then walks alone
18–30 months	Runs, jumps, etc.

objects. This skill is critical to infant exploration of the properties of objects, an essential basis for all knowledge and understanding about the physical world.

Visual control of reaching seems to be present at birth (Van der Meer et al., 1996) as neonates show 'pre-reaching' – poorly coordinated swiping at objects that they can see. This quickly improves, though, so that by about 5 months infants can accurately reach for an object even in the dark (McCarty and Ashmead, 1999). In general, however, reaching improves as it becomes increasingly under visual control. Accurate visual guidance of reaching with adjustments to the size and shape of objects develops between 4 and 6 months (McCarty and Ashmead, 1999; Newman et al., 2001).

It takes time for hand movements to become efficient. Even the 22-week-old foetus may exercise a degree of control over their hand movements (Zoia et al., 2002), but neonatal hand control is generally poor (Von Hofsten, 1984). Initially infants may hold objects in a clumsy '*ulnar*' grip, that rigidly holds the object between fingers and palm. By about 9 or 10 months, infants are using a more mature '*pincer*' grip with coordination of thumb and fingers, and by 12 months children are so adept at this that they can pick up all manner of debris from carpets or floors!

STOP AND THINK

Reflection
How do you think infants' changing motor abilities allow for increasing learning about and exploration of the world as they get older?

Cognitive abilities in infancy: general models and approaches

The word *cognition* refers to thinking or brain processes which go beyond sensory–perceptual encoding, and allow for further analysis of information. Depending on the model of cognition, there are differing views as to how cognitive development occurs. In Chapter 2, Theoretical Perspectives, we learned about Piaget's influential theory of cognitive development, in which cognition is defined as 'operations on mental structures'. From this perspective, the child's action on and exploration of the world leads to the assimilation of new information into older structures and the accommodation or revision of older structures in light of new information. According to Piaget, cognitive development moves through four stages with the period of infancy being the sensorimotor stage, and true cognitive function or formal operations are not attained until adolescence. More recent research has, however, established that this view underestimates the cognitive and perceptual capacities of infants and young children. Furthermore, from contemporary perspectives on cognition, the mental operations described by Piaget do not sufficiently resemble actual brain processes or the way that cognition typically operates even in adults.

To find out more about current debates in infant cognition, see Recommended Reading. Most current views of cognitive development (e.g. Karmiloff-Smith, 1999; De Haan and Johnson, 2003; Keil, 2006; Nelson et al., 2006) are based on contemporary models of cognitive processing that relate more closely to actual brain functions and systems. These models draw on information-processing, neural network and neuroscience approaches which describe cognition in terms of the brain processes for handling information, with this involving the activity of many groups or networks of neurons, often distributed across many regions and pathways in the brain (Atkinson and Shiffrin, 1968; Rummelhart et al., 1986; Baddeley, 2003; Purves et al., 2008). Even for adults, contemporary models of cognition acknowledge that we have a tendency to rely on past knowledge (or even biases) rather than abstract logical streams of thought (Tversky and Kahneman, 1973), and that there are important influences of emotional and unconscious processing on cognition (Libet et al., 1979; Le Doux, 1999).

Definitions
Assimilation: within Piagetian theory, this is the process of taking new information into existing knowledge structures.
Accommodation: within Piagetian theory, this is the revision of older knowledge structures to take account of new information.

In such contemporary models, cognition is defined in terms of basic processes such as attention, working memory, long-term memory and categorisation, which are more readily linked to patterns of brain activity than the 'operations' described by Piaget. Some of these processes are discussed in more detail in Chapter 6, Memory and Intelligence. Higher-order cognition (thinking, reasoning, problem solving) uses these basic processes to combine information within or across the neural networks of the brain. A thought is not a static well-defined 'structure', but rather involves dynamic, shifting webs of brain activity, with groups of neurons working in concert like the sections of a large orchestra, representing sensory–perceptual information as well as more abstract–symbolic content (e.g. words) and even motor or emotional responses.

These contemporary views differ considerably from those of Piaget. From this current frame of reference, infants are seen as capable at least of basic cognitive function and are not limited to the essentially 'pre-cognitive' existence defined in Piaget's sensorimotor period. This view of infant cognition is being confirmed by studies using neuroscience methods reflecting infant brain activity during cognitive tasks (see the Cutting Edge box). Moreover, the gap between adult and child thinking may not be as wide as proposed by Piaget. For example, neuroimaging evidence suggests that there are child-like tendencies in

CUTTING EDGE

Using EEG and neuroscience methods to explore the infant 'mind'

Contemporary neuroscience evidence, such as from research using EEG, shows infant brain activity consistent with cognition far beyond the sensorimotor abilities which Piaget associated with infants. EEG can reveal sources and patterns of brain activity associated with cognitive performance. A common approach is to examine brain activity in terms of EEG 'frequency' bands, which have been long associated with aspects of cognitive performance in adults. For example, there are changes in infant brain activity in the theta frequency band during correct eye movements to the location of a hidden object (Bell, 2002), and changes in alpha activity during anticipation of the appearance of an adult in a peek-a-boo game (Orekhova et al., 2001). There is an increase in gamma activity during the viewing of illusory figures, or in object permanence tasks or when there is a mismatch between current information and that sustained in working memory (Kaufman et al., 2003a; Csibra and Johnson, 2007). These responses are consistent with cognitive responding in infants.

Kaufman et al. (2003a) showed 6-month-old infants videos of a toy train moving into a tunnel and then either staying inside or passing out of the tunnel. The tunnel was then lifted. If the train should still have been inside the tunnel but was not, there was a burst of gamma activity in the infant EEG record. This activity did not occur if the train was where it should have been. Such activity is strongly suggestive that the infants held a representation of the train in memory, despite it being hidden in the tunnel, and the researchers suggest that there was consequently brain activity to resolve the mismatch between this mental expectation and the disappearance of the train. This was taken as evidence of expectation of object permanence in the infants.

All of this evidence is counter to Piaget's traditional views about infants' cognitive limitations, and suggests that infants have brain activity even in the absence of a currently visible stimulus. Moreover, in denial of the infant confusion posed by James and Piaget, 8-month-olds show distinctly different EEG patterns to ordered as opposed to random visual stimulation (Van der Meer et al., 2008), which suggests an ability to distinguish a chaotic world from an ordered one. This fits with EEG evidence on infant response to different categories such as cats versus dogs that also points to order in infant cognition (Quinn et al., 2006; Grossman et al., 2009) (see 'Categorisation in Infancy', pages 105–6). Contemporary neuroscience methods such as EEG in conjunction with behavioural measures are thus helping to open a new window on the infant mind that was not feasible in the past.

adult thinking (such as judging quantity by appearance), and that adults then have to inhibit these initial reactions (Daurignac et al., 2006; Leroux et al., 2009), which suggests a continuity between child and adult cognition.

Contemporary views of cognition (e.g. Karmiloff-Smith, 1999; Spelke, 2000; Slater and Lewis, 2002; Onishi and Bailargeon, 2005; Rose et al., 2005; Goswami, 2006; Keil, 2006) in general propose that infants display basic cognitive abilities, although the use of these improves over childhood, due to:

- the acquisition of a more extensive and interconnected knowledge base which provides more efficient attention and memory; and
- more efficient control of cognitive processes, or metacognition, due to developing frontal lobe capacity for inhibiting irrelevant responses and promoting better attention, awareness and organisation of knowledge (Johnson, 2001).

There is ongoing debate about the continuity of cognitive function from childhood to adulthood, with some views suggesting that infant and adult thinking is fundamentally and qualitatively different in character (e.g. Haith, 1998; Mandler, 2003) and others proposing a more continuous developmental pathway (e.g., Keil, 2006, 2008). Nevertheless, there is at least widespread consensus that infant cognitive capacities far exceed those proposed by Piaget or James. Piaget's under-estimation of the cognitive capacity of infants and children and the implications of this for education are discussed in Chapter 14, Developmental Psychology and Education.

> **STOP AND THINK**
>
> **Reflection**
>
> - Given the material in this last section, how do you think that infants 'think'?
> - Do you think that there is genuine cognitive activity in the infant brain before language develops?

Infant attention

Attention is the selective processing of some stimulus or event and is essential for acquiring information about the world. It can be covert attention or overt attention (apparent in behavioural reactions such as eye movements) and measured by physiological responses such as decline in heart rate (a sign of attention). It can involve sudden orienting to a stimulus or a more sustained focus, with these two aspects calling on different brain systems.

The attentive new-born?

New-borns show basic attentional responses adapted to the requirements of the situation. These can be defensive reactions to threatening stimuli (e.g. increased heart rate) or an orienting reaction (visual fixation, decline in heart rate) to non-threatening stimuli such as a coloured pattern (Sokolov, 1963; Finlay and Ivinskis, 1984). More sustained attention is also shown by new-borns through their preferential or prolonged fixation to particular stimuli, especially human faces (Slater and Johnson, 1999; Slater and Lewis, 2002). Even just after the rigours of birth, neonates will turn their heads and fixate on visual stimuli like moving facial patterns (Morton and Johnson, 1991) or orient towards sounds (Morrongiello et al., 1994). New-borns therefore show a clear capacity for selectively orienting and attending, which is an essential tool for all cognitive activity.

What attracts the attention of babies?

Preferential looking, habituation and familiarisation studies show that many sensory features can elicit sustained attention in infants. For example, infants prefer coloured stimuli to those in greyscale (Bornstein, 2006a), they prefer red and blue and purple to greens and yellows

> **Definitions**
>
> **Metacognition:** a person's knowledge or awareness of their own cognition; sometimes referred to as 'knowledge about knowledge' or 'cognition about cognition'.
> **Covert attention:** the act of mentally focusing on one of several possible stimuli.
> **Overt attention:** the act of directing the senses towards a particular stimulus.

(Zemach et al., 2007), and they prefer facial patterns to most other patterns (Pascalis and Slater, 2003). In general, older infants have more efficient attention than younger babies (Rose et al., 2004b). Indeed, babies showing unusually longer attention time than others in the same age group may actually have poorer information-processing skills and show lower cognitive competence in later childhood (Colombo, 2001; Reynolds, et al., 2011; Rose et al., 2004b). Nonetheless, attention at all ages is affected by factors such as knowledge, interests and emotional state. For example, one study showed that older infants looked longer than younger babies at items from the *Sesame Street* TV programme, possibly reflecting the personal experience of the former group (Valkenburg and Vroone, 2004; Courage et al., 2006).

Different aspects of attention may develop at different rates

There may be also different rates of development for different aspects of attention (Ruff and Rothbart, 1996; Colombo, 2001; Johnson 2002; Bartgis et al., 2008; Richards, 2010). Rapid orienting may develop sooner due to the earlier development of the posterior (rear) attentional systems of the brain (in the parietal cortex and brainstem: see Figure 4.3) (Posner and Rothbart, 1981; Johnson, 2002). In contrast, sustained attention requires the involvement of more anterior (frontal) regions of the brain, which are especially important in the ability to resist distraction, and these take longer to mature (see 'The postnatal development of the brain', pages 88–90). Infants also show increasing attention from 6 months or so to more complex audio-visual stimuli (e.g. children's television material) (Richards, 2010).

Infant learning and memory

Memory and learning are different views of the same phenomena. Memory is the set of processes for storing information in the networks of the brain and for later being able to retrieve or reactivate that stored information by either recognition (if the item is present again) or recall (if the item is not actually present and must be located in long-term memory). As the result of memory, we 'learn' or show enduring and obvious changes in our behaviour, capacities and responses. Most models (e.g. Baddeley, 2003) propose different phases of memory: *sensory memory* (brief persistence of sensory impressions), *working memory* (the temporary maintenance of information in an active state) and *long-term memory* (enduring biochemical and structural changes in brain connections or synapses). Contemporary accounts propose that these aspects of memory may work in parallel (at the same time) or that working memory is simply the currently active part of long-term memory (Cowan, 1999). The development of memory across childhood is discussed in Chapter 6, Memory and Intelligence.

As noted, even the foetus displays simple memory such as habituating to a repeated tone or retaining the sound patterns of songs or stories read by the mother. There is also longstanding evidence that new-borns have recognition memory ability. One of the classic demonstrations of this was by Friedman (1972) who habituated new-borns to chequerboard patterns and then showed them a novel chequerboard pattern. The infants showed recovery of visual interest to the novel pattern but not the familiar one, which was only feasible if they had in fact detected the familiarity of the old one. Many more recent studies using habituation and familiarisation methods have confirmed recognition memory even in neonates (e.g. Slater et al., 1983) for all manner of sensory information (auditory, tactile, etc.). It would thus seem that recognition memory develops early and, indeed, children's recognition memory can match that of adults (Siegler, 1996).

Infant recall of absent items

As noted above, memory may involve either recognition of an item that is present or recall of one that is absent. It is more challenging to study recall in infants. Tasks requiring memory for a hidden object (see 'Basic knowledge and understanding in infancy', pages 104–5) show that 6–12-month-olds look at the location of hidden items (Ahmed and Ruffman, 1998) or show associated EEG brain activity (Bauer, 2007; Csibra and Johnson, 2007), suggesting recall of the items. In more natural surroundings, 2-year-olds can easily find a hidden toy after delays of an hour (Deloache and Brown, 1983) and infants of 12–20 months will continue to search for all items in a set of three hidden objects until they have located the last item (Feigenson and Halberda, 2008). Delayed imitation may also reflect elementary recall ability, and infants can imitate the movements of others possibly even at birth (Meltzoff and Moore, 1977). In one study (Giles and Rovee-Collier, 2011), two puppets were shown in the background for 30 minutes over two days while 6-month-old infants did other activities. Up to 28 days later, an action modelled on one puppet by the experimenter was copied with the other puppet the next day by the infants, indicating not only recall of the action, but an association between the visible and the absent puppet in the infant's memory.

The mobile conjugate reinforcement paradigm (Rovee-Collier and Cuevas, 2009) has also offered evidence on infant recall. Using this method, one end of a ribbon is attached to a baby's ankle and the other end to a mobile. The baby soon learns to kick to make the mobile move, but if the mobile is changed to a new one, the baby does not kick, suggesting recall of the old absent mobile. There is also evidence of more active recall capacity in older infants who have been trained to perform a lever-pulling action that operates a toy train. For example, 6-month-olds show recall of the action after delays of two weeks and 12-month-olds after delays of two months (Rovee-Collier and Boller, 1995). This research is discussed further in Chapter 6, Memory and Intelligence.

Are there individual differences in infant memory?

It has been known for some time that some babies are 'short-lookers', appearing to process visual items faster than other babies, since short looking is related to better subsequent memory and better cognitive performance in general in infancy (Colombo and Mitchell, 1990; Reynolds et al., 2011). Recent research using EEG has also shown that for short-lookers, a particular brain pattern (a Late Slow Wave) is stronger for new versus familiar objects – a pattern that is not apparent for long-lookers. This pattern may reflect greater initial depth of encoding of the familiar object by the short-lookers (Reynolds et al., 2011). The significance of such early memory differences is still under investigation but it is clear at least that not all infants display the same patterns in memory performance.

Is infant memory the same as that of adults?

Memory and learning clearly operate from birth, but there is disagreement about the exact nature of this early memory. Neuroscience methods such as EEG are helping to shed light on how or whether brain activity associated with memory processes changes during infancy and childhood (e.g. Cuevas and Bell, 2011). In general, however, it is considered that, by about 6 months, infant memory resembles the explicit declarative memory of adults (Rose et al., 2004a) with both using similar brain structures. In particular, the hippocampus (see Figure 4.7) is essential in explicit memory and in the transfer of information from working memory to long-term store (Purves et al., 2008), and this appears to develop early in infancy (even before the visual cortex) (Nelson, 2002b). However, parts of the hippocampus and its connections to the prefrontal cortex of the brain, which are important in consolidating new memories, may not reach functional maturity until 20–24 months of age (Bauer, 2007). Hence, there is ongoing debate about whether

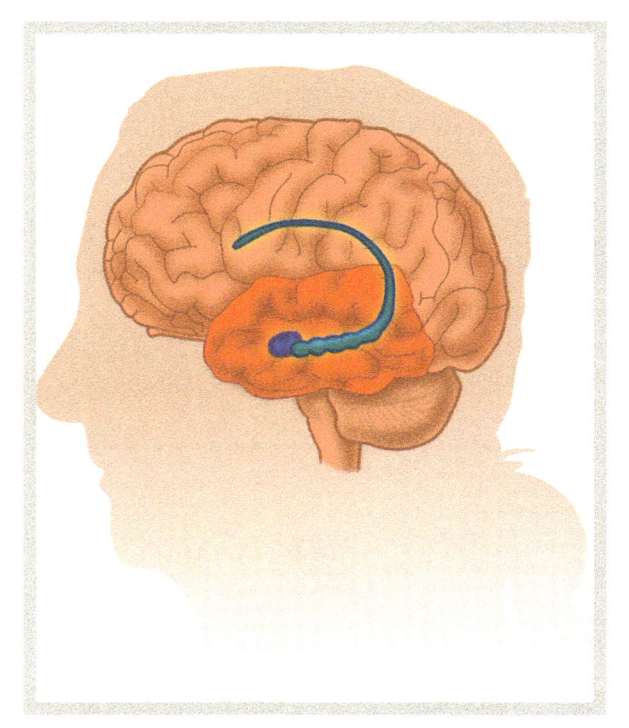

Figure 4.7 The hippocampus is a brain structure important in consolidating memories and a focus for debate about infant memory.

infant memory in the first six or so months of life is in fact 'explicit'.

One view is that early memory is implicit and procedural, with explicit memory developing at 6–12 months, especially with the increasing involvement of the prefrontal cortex (Nelson, 2002b). However, recent evidence using a brain-imaging method called *near-infra-red spectroscopy* does not fit with this view, since it showed activity in the prefrontal cortex of 3-month-olds in response to novel stimuli during memory tasks (Nakano et al., 2009).

Moreover, the implicit-to-explicit account of memory development is at odds with infant performance in the conjugate reinforcement paradigms (Rovee-Collier and Cuevas, 2009). Infant memory and learning in such contexts is often rapid and does not reflect the extensive trials often required for procedural learning. For example, adult cats require over 1300 trials to learn a limb-flexion movement while 3-month-old human infants can learn to kick to a mobile in minutes. Rather than infant learning being seen to develop from implicit to explicit knowledge then, infants may simply display the type of memory and learning most adaptive for the circumstances (Rovee-Collier and Cuevas, 2009).

In any case, whatever the exact nature of early infant memory and learning, it is clear that from birth, memory operates well enough to allow infants to learn and build up a storehouse of knowledge about the world.

> **STOP AND THINK**
>
> **Reflection**
>
> Try to design a simple study to see whether infants can recognise a colourful toy after a delay of a few minutes.

Basic knowledge and understanding in infancy

Cognition is defined not only in terms of these basic processes that we have been discussing, but also in terms of its content or knowledge. Initial knowledge or understanding about the properties of people, other animals, objects, places and events arises in the first instance from the sensory–perceptual channels. There is ongoing debate about whether such early knowledge is innate or acquired and whether it is used in an aware manner by infants (Haith, 1998; Karmiloff-Smith, 1999; Spelke, 2000; Müller and Giesbrecht, 2008; Rovee-Collier and Cuevas, 2009), but it clearly provides the foundation for subsequent and more complex networks of understanding.

Object permanence?

One fundamental aspect of knowledge and understanding that was a focus in Piaget's work, and which we discussed in Chapter 2, Theoretical Perspectives, is whether infants have an understanding of object permanence: that is, that objects continue to exist independently from our perception of them. This is a more complex concept than the other aspects of object identity discussed in infant vision, and may be harder to develop simply because the world offers contradictory information. Objects can disappear from view in many ways. They can go behind or inside other objects or can be projected out of visual range altogether. They may or may not reappear and if they do reappear, they may be either intact or in an altered form. For example, while a train speeding behind a mountain will (hopefully) reappear in the same form on the other side, does a sweet that is swallowed and so vanishes from view continue to exist as such? It certainly won't reappear in the same form!

Piaget's conclusion was that for children younger than 18 months, objects are linked to actions and so for these infants they do not exist permanently or independently of such actions. This conclusion was founded on infant performance in tasks requiring searching for a hidden toy. Infants of 8–12 months may search for a toy at one location (A), but when the object is then moved to a new location (B), the infants may still return to search in the first hiding place. This is therefore known as the *A not B error*.

More recent studies have used approaches which don't rely on infants having to search for objects. In particular, infant responses to impossible events have been assessed. In one example (Baillargeon and DeVos, 1991), infants observed two carrots moving behind a wall, or behind a screen with a window opening. One of the carrots was short and so not visible at the window, whilst the other one was tall and so should have been visible, but it wasn't. This was therefore an 'impossible' event, violating the idea of object permanence.

Infants of 3½ months showed more visual interest in this impossible event than the former. In another example, 2–3-month-olds showed more interest when a container that had covered a moving toy duck was subsequently lifted to reveal the duck was absent (Baillargeon, 2004). The conclusion from such studies is that infants' responses reflect their expectations about object permanence. Some studies using this approach have had more mixed results (Cashon and Cohen, 2000), and there is continuing debate about whether object permanence is innate knowledge (Karmiloff-Smith, 1999).

Nevertheless, recent evidence from EEG studies has provided a fresh perspective with compelling indication of expectations about object permanence in young infants. Even 6-month-old infants show high-frequency (gamma) brain activity while observing locations of hidden objects or when confronted with the unexpected disappearance of objects (Csibra et al., 2000; Csibra and Johnson, 2007), and this gamma activity in adults is linked to maintaining an item in working memory (Tallon-Baudry et al., 1998). Other studies using EEG have also linked developmental improvements in the A not B task to brain activity associated with working memory (e.g. Cuevas and Bell, 2011). These methods will undoubtedly help to clarify how the infant brain develops the capacity to retain object information in memory and understand object permanence.

In general, studies requiring infants to search for hidden objects are less likely to confirm the early development of understanding of object permanence. The ability to search requires the coordination of motor skills, memory and attention systems that may not be easily achieved in infancy. For example, 6–12-month-olds will look at the correct location in the A not B task even while reaching to the wrong location (Ahmed and Ruffman, 1998), and infants may have difficulty preventing themselves from reaching to a previously rewarded location (Diamond et al., 1994). So infants may well have more understanding about object permanence than they can reveal in search tasks.

Categorisation in infancy

A central aspect of knowledge development in infancy (and indeed over the lifespan) is categorisation, which allows for the grouping or organisation of items based on similarity, and concepts, which are the defining representations on which categories are based. For example, instead of knowing about their own dog Pluto and their neighbour's dog Saturn, infants evolve a concept about dogs in general. Dogs are items that bark, have tails, have fur, etc. Infants also evolve a category associated with that concept (e.g. including poodles, collies, boxers, etc.). This process enables them to classify new dogs in that category, but to exclude other animals such as cats (see Chapter 5, Language Development). This process is a powerful cognitive tool, enabling the efficient organisation of knowledge. In fact the tendency to categorise is so potent that infants, like adults, will even classify fabricated objects (Younger and Cohen, 1986; Gauthier et al., 1998). Categorisation is also important within the development of maths skills, which is explored in Chapter 7, The Development of Mathematical Thinking.

All categories are based on similarities, but this can involve different levels of obvious similarity, ranging from superordinate or global categories where there is low similarity amongst items (e.g. 'living things' or 'animals') to subordinate categories where there are high-similarity items (e.g. 'poodles'). Somewhere in between these extremes are basic categories with moderate similarity in item appearance (e.g. 'dogs'). Some items will be better examples of a category than others. For example, a robin is a better example of the category 'bird' than a penguin is (Rosch, 1978). The best example and/or a prototype (an abstraction of main properties of the examples) may be stored in memory. When new items are experienced, any overlap with these leads to inclusion in the category and any dissimilarity to exclusion.

Do infants detect categories?

A number of different research methods confirm that categorisation does occur in infancy (Quinn, 2002). A common method is to habituate or familiarise infants to items from the same category (e.g. different pictures

Definitions

Categorisation: the grouping or organisation of items based on their similarity.
Concepts: mental representations upon which categories are based.

of dogs) and then present two new items: one from the familiar category (e.g. a new dog) and one from a new category (e.g. a cat). Greater fixation to the new category item is evidence that infants can distinguish the two categories as different. This method has indicated that infants as young as 3–4 months detect basic categories such as the four hues (Franklin and Davies, 2004; Bornstein, 2006a) and natural-kind categories such as cats and dogs (Quinn and Eimas, 1996). Recently, brain activity in 6-month-olds has also been measured using EEG to confirm that such categories are processed distinctly by infants (Grossmann et al., 2009; Quinn et al., 2006).

Other behavioural methods involve observing older infants playing with toys from different categories. 'Sequential touching' of items from the same category indicates that the category similarities have been detected (Rakison and Butterworth, 1998). For example, 9–10-month-olds showed more serial touching of bird items after they had played with or touched a series of toy planes and vice versa, suggesting that the categories were guiding responses (Mandler and McDonough, 1993).

Infants also show responses consistent with subordinate categorisation such as *Tabby Cat* (Quinn, 2004) and, at the other extreme, of broad superordinate categories. For example, in contrast to Piagetian proposals (1952, 1958), 3–4-month-olds categorise 'animate' things as different from 'inanimate', especially if these have clearly different features such as legs versus wheels (Quinn, 2002). Indeed, infants show quite subtle understanding about animacy (Keil, 2008) (see the Stop and Think box, page 107).

Infant categorisation isn't just applied to things. Studies using familiarisation and habituation methods have shown that as 3-month-olds have begun to categorise faces by gender and 9-month-olds by ethnicity (Anzures et al., 2010; Quinn et al., 2002). Categorisation is clearly a key aspect of infant cognitive experience.

Issues about infant categorisation

There are, however, three debates about infant categorisation. The first is about whether basic categories develop before superordinate ones or vice versa (Quinn and Johnson, 2000; Mandler, 2003; Keil, 2006, 2008; Quinn, 2008). As noted above, many basic categories do appear early, but some broader categories may precede them. For example, in one study, 2-month-olds seemed to learn the category of 'mammal' more readily than that of 'cat' (Quinn and Johnson, 2000). It may be that infants will use whatever level is fit-for-purpose, and even adults may be flexible and use different categorical levels depending on their needs. For example, a hungry adult may seek any food (superordinate), but a well-fed person may want caviar (subordinate). Such flexibility has also been shown in infant cognition. For example, infants attend to the colour or shape of two-dimensional objects, but attend to the location of three-dimensional objects they can pick up (Kaufman et al., 2003b).

The second debate is about whether infant categories are the same as adult categories. One view is that for infants, even superordinate categories are more perceptually based than those of adults (Rakison, 2000). An alternative view is that infant categories are too general, and require further enrichment to achieve maturity (Mandler, 2003). In contrast to these views is the proposal that, although early categories may not have the full semantic richness of adult categories, they are basically similar with continuity between early categories and later ones (Carey, 2002; Keil, 2006, 2008). This debate is ongoing in developmental psychology.

The third debate is about whether categories need language. A traditional view, called the *Whorfian Hypothesis*, is that language is needed for categorisation. Clearly this is not the case, as shown by the research with very young infants cited above, but, nonetheless, language helps to enrich and refine categories. Older infants are more likely to show categorical responses to items with a common name (Graham and Kilbreath, 2007) and language links up with pre-language categories. For example, the basic hue categories emerge prior to language development (see 'Infant vision', pages 91–5), but with the development of colour naming, hue categorisation moves from the right to left hemisphere of the brain, which reflects the left hemisphere's verbal enrichment of these basic concepts (Franklin et al., 2008). In addition, there is evidence that more sophisticated categorisation abilities may be linked to vocabulary growth in older infants, and this is explored further in Chapter 5, Language Development.

Overall there is sound evidence that infants begin to categorise the objects and people around them from an early age, although language and experience serve to refine and further develop these early classifications.

STOP AND THINK

Going further

Piaget proposed that the concept of **animacy** did not develop until after infancy, but this study shows that 14-month-olds can respond in terms of object features essential in a concept of animacy. In one experiment, Newman et al. (2008) familiarised children to computer animations showing two moving 'cats in hats' – a cat with a blue stomach and blue hat and one with a red stomach and red hat. The stomach was a fixed feature but the hats were shown to be removable. The cat in the blue hat moved backwards and forwards while the other one jumped up and down. This is shown in Figure 4.8.

In two test events, the infants were then shown two new cats whose stomach and hat colour now did not match to the previous displays (i.e. blue hat–red stomach and red hat–blue stomach). In one test trial, the cat's motion was the one previously linked to the hat colour, while in the other test trial, the motion was the one previously linked to the stomach colour (see Figure 4.8). The toddlers showed more interest when the stomach colour and motion did not match up than when the hat colour and motion did not match. This suggests that the toddlers were rating the cat's body feature as more important in regard to the cat's motion than the external feature of hat colour, and so were more interested when this association between internal features and movement was violated than if the link between external features and motion was changed. A second experiment confirmed that 14-month-olds only responded this way when an object's motion was self-generated. In other words, 14-month-olds especially tied the internal features of an object to motion only when the object was able to move under its own power.

This pattern of response could reflect the foundations of an animacy concept – that internal characteristics are linked to animate identity and the ability to move. While this may not reflect a mature concept of animacy, it nonetheless suggests a level of inference about animate objects that goes beyond the approach proposed for young children in Piagetian theory.

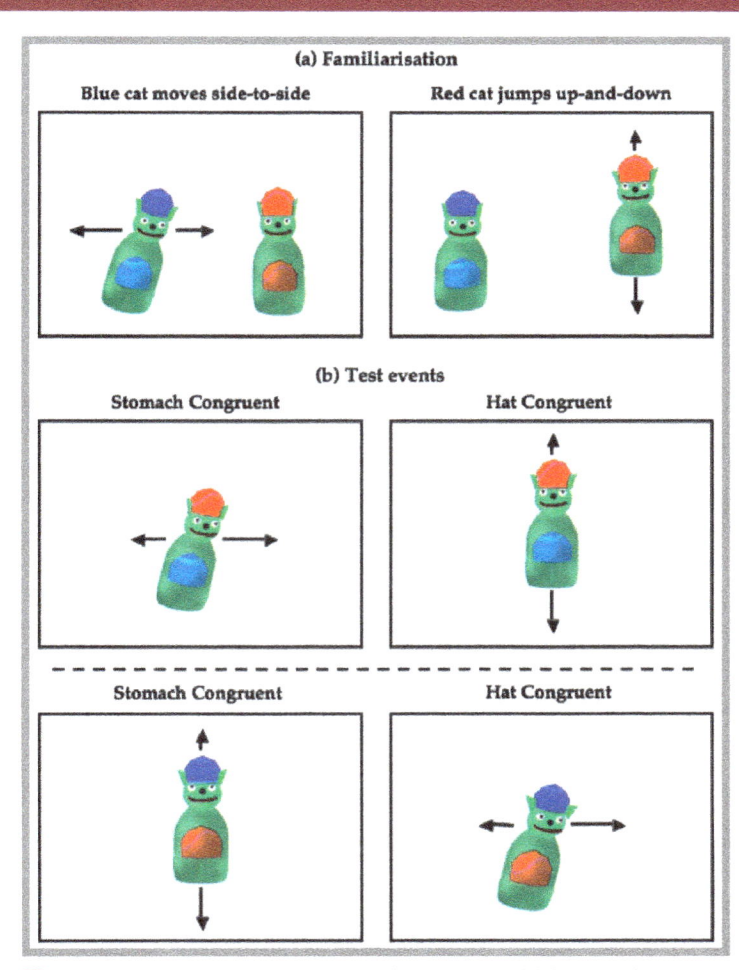

Figure 4.8 Newman et al.'s study of 14-month-olds' reasoning about object identity.

Source: Newman et al. (2008, p. 423)

Although there is ongoing discussion about the precise nature of early categorical abilities, it is clear that infants can and do respond categorically, and that this is a powerful tool for building knowledge and understanding, especially when it integrates later with language.

Definition

Animacy: the concept of animacy refers to an understanding of the difference between living (animate) and non-living (inanimate) things.

Reasoning and problem solving in infancy

So far we have considered how attention, memory and categorisation develop in infancy. All of these work together to support the most complex cognitive activities of the human brain – reasoning and problem solving – the processes involved in combining information from the external world or from memory to produce a solution to a problem. There is ongoing debate (e.g., Haith, 1998; Keil, 2006; Kagan, 2008; Quinn, 2008) about whether infant problem solving is essentially similar to or different from that of adults. Piaget proposed that there is a qualitative difference in the ways in which children and adults reason, with adults using formal operations in accordance with the principles of logical deduction, but is this a fair standard against which to judge children's reasoning?

How do adults reason?

Adult reasoning can in fact take two quite different forms. Deductive reasoning is consistent with logic, and provides a certain or definite conclusion. Inductive reasoning uses knowledge or information beyond that which is given and provides less certain conclusions.

Adults are, of course, capable of reasoning deductively, but may fail to do so, even on Piagetian tasks (Merriwether and Liben, 1997). In fact adults often sidestep logical deduction altogether and rely on 'fuzzier' or knowledge-based reasoning or use probabilities rather than the certainties afforded by logical reasoning. For example, they may solve a problem by analogical reasoning based on its similarity to a previous problem, or use mental shortcuts called 'heuristics', such as drawing conclusions based on how readily they come to mind (Tversky and Kahneman, 1973). Deductive and fuzzy approaches use different brain regions, with the right hemisphere more active in deduction and the left hemisphere in knowledge-based reasoning (Parsons and Osherson, 2001), so even the adult brain can use different pathways to reason and solve problems.

Adults are also said to use more abstract information while children rely on perceptual properties such as size or shape (Piaget, 1952b, 1958), but, as mentioned earlier, neuroimaging research shows that adults firstly respond in terms of appearances in Piagetian-type tasks, and that these reactions then have to be inhibited (Daurignac et al., 2006; Leroux et al., 2009). It may be therefore that there is closer overlap between child and adult thinking than might be predicted. The yardstick for comparing child to adult reasoning might need to include knowledge-based or heuristic approaches as well as the deductive processes identified in Piagetian theory.

So do infants 'reason' or 'solve problems'?

Using the 'fuzzier' view of adult reasoning, infants can be said to 'reason' within the bounds of their motor and sensory abilities and their knowledge of the world. Young infants are certainly capable of inductive processing to develop new knowledge and information, as shown in the evidence on infant categorisation and concept formation (see 'Categorisation in infancy', pages 105–6). These are relatively passive modes of processing that arise out of sensory-perceptual channels, but there is evidence of more active problem solving. For example, infants of 14 months adopt different strategies to achieve the goal of feeding themselves with a spoon presented in awkward orientations (McCarty et al., 1999).

There is also evidence that infants, like adults, are able to solve problems and reason by using prior knowledge in an analogical way. For example, 10- and 12-month-olds were tested in a task in which they had to retrieve a toy from behind a barrier and then repeat this with different toys and barriers (Chen et al., 1997). They showed increasing efficiency with each retrieval, reflecting an analogical-type approach to the problem. Another study (Holyoak et al., 1984) showed that children as young as 2 years could use analogy to solve a problem with more abstract information. After being told stories, such as that of a genie who retrieved a precious jar without leaving his lamp by using a magic staff, the children solved problems in an analogous way. They had to reach some sweets without moving from their chair and did so by using items like the staff used by the genie.

> **Definition**
>
> **Analogical reasoning:** a method of problem solving which makes use of the similarity of a new problem to some previously solved problem.

Infants have also been shown to respond in a way consistent with reasoning by probability (Denison et al., 2013). Six-month-old infants were familiarised to two boxes of ping-pong balls: one box with mostly pink balls and some yellow and the other the converse. They looked longer when the experimenter drew a sample of balls from a box with a ratio of pink to yellow balls that was inconsistent or 'improbable' based on the overall ratio in the respective box (e.g. if she drew four yellow and one pink from the box with mostly pink balls).

Such evidence points to the emergence of abilities that contribute to inductive or heuristic reasoning. There is also evidence that logical reasoning may be used earlier than previously believed. For example, children younger than 7 or 8 years often fail Piaget's test of 'transitive inference' (if told that $A > B$ and $B > C$, they may not deduce that $A > C$), but recent evidence indicates precursors to this ability in 16-month-old infants. The infants watched an actor touch a red football in preference to a yellow one and then the yellow one in preference to

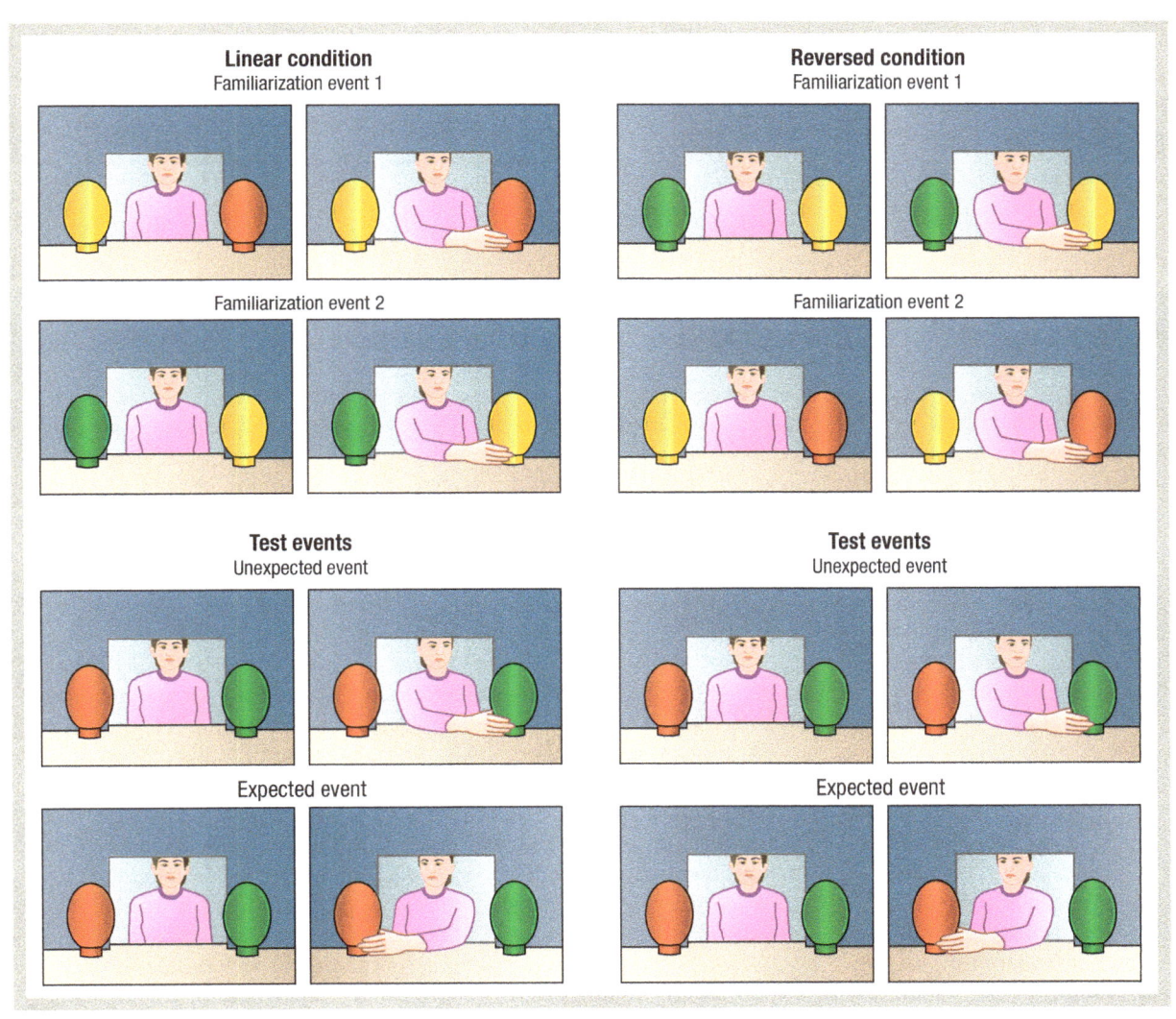

Figure 4.9 Sixteen-month-old infants watched an actor touch a red football rather than a yellow one and then the yellow rather than a green one (see left-hand images). By transitive inference the red football should then be preferred by the actor over the green. When the actor violated this inference by unexpectedly touching the green preferentially to the red, the infants showed more interest than when the expected preference was shown. This was not the case in a more difficult condition when the order of the initial 'premises' was reversed (see right-hand images), but the response in the first condition was consistent with transitive inference.

Source: Mou et al. (2014)

a green one, with the transitive inference being that the actor would then prefer the red to the green. Consistent with transitive inference, the infants showed more interest if the actor then showed the unexpected pattern of touching the green one in preference to the red one (Mou et al., 2014).

Young children may especially show logical reasoning if they can picture the context. For example, in one study of reasoning, 2-year-olds were able to respond correctly to logical problems such as '*All sheep ride bicycles. Bill is a sheep. Does Bill ride a bicycle?*', so long as they were encouraged to imagine the contexts. This is despite the fact that the problems involved hypothetical information counterfactual to real life (Richards and Sanderson, 1999). The correct answer here, by the way, is that Bill does ride a bike!

The debate continues about whether infants are explicitly aware and in control of their reasoning. However, the range of evidence suggests that within the limits of their physical and motor development, and of their knowledge, attention and working memory, infants certainly exhibit behaviours and responses consistent with elementary reasoning and problem-solving abilities.

STOP AND THINK

Reflection

- Can you think of a routine problem that an infant might solve in everyday life?
- What cognitive processes might be used by the infant to solve this problem?

SUMMARY

The remarkable body of research described in this chapter highlights major routes and landmarks along the pathway from zygote to birth and through infancy, the significance of the prenatal period in understanding development, the interaction of nature and nurture and the ways in which early research and theory have under-estimated infants' abilities to learn and know about the world. Many of the topics explored here will be developed in later chapters in the book.

Development begins from the moment of conception. We have learned that the brain begins to develop very early in the embryonic period and that this development continues through infancy. The developmental pathway can be affected by genetic factors and environmental factors in the prenatal period as well as in infancy, and so to understand the psychology of a child we have to understand what happens *in utero* as well as what happens after birth.

Much of the research which this chapter has considered indicates the interweaving of nature and nurture in early development. Genetic and environmental factors interact to affect development in the prenatal period, and this interaction continues after birth. The infant is born with certain basic capacities for learning about the world, but the brain is still highly plastic in infancy and experiences can turn genes on or off and, vice versa, genes can limit or influence the impact of experiences. There is an ongoing dialogue over the human lifespan between our innate abilities and our environmental experience, and the Nature–Nurture boxes, which you will find in every chapter of this book, highlight this interaction.

Researchers have had to be extremely inventive in coming up with methods that will allow for the study of prenatal and infant development. In this chapter, we have explored some of the classic and the cutting-edge methods which have all contributed to the body of knowledge that we have about this period of development. These include contemporary methods such as EEG (electroencephalography), VEP (visually evoked potentials) and EOAE (evoked otoacoustic emissions), as well as methods like preferential looking, habituation-recovery, familiarisation, high-amplitude sucking and the visual cliff. Some of these methods will be explored in other chapters throughout the book.

The new-born arrives with many basic capacities for sensing, perceiving and knowing the world using vision, audition, touch, taste and smell.

The evidence we have considered in this chapter certainly does not suggest that infants experience the chaotic, transient and 'non-cognitive' universe which was proposed by James and Piaget. In fact, it seems as though infants have a richer and more coherent early experience of the world than these authors ever proposed.

Piaget believed that the world of an infant was limited to sensory and perceptual experience. The research and theory considered in this chapter contrasts with this view. We have seen that infants' abilities include attention, learning and memory, basic knowledge about the world, categorisation, reasoning and problem solving. The evidence we have explored therefore suggests that infants are capable of cognition and the analysis of information beyond the stage of mere sensory-perceptual encoding.

REVIEW QUESTIONS

1. Discuss how genes and environment work together to influence infant development, making reference to recent research with humans and other animals.
2. Describe the key features of the physical development of the brain in prenatal life and in the first year after birth.
3. Critically evaluate Piaget's and James's view of early infant perception in the light of some recent evidence on infant visual abilities.
4. Describe one of the methods used to study infant memory.
5. Do infants have explicit and aware cognitive capacities? Justify your answer with reference to recent research on infant categorisation and problem-solving abilities.

RECOMMENDED READING

For a more general overview of infant development, see:

Bremner, J. G., & Wachs, T. D. (Eds.) (2010). *The Wiley-Blackwell Handbook of Infant Development: Vol. 1, Basic Research*. Oxford: Wiley-Blackwell.

Slater, A., & Lewis, M. (2007). *Introduction to Infant Development*. Oxford: Oxford University Press.

For more information on the brain and cognitive development from contemporary perspectives, see:

Bornstein, M. H., & Lamb, M. E. (2011). *Cognitive Development: An Advanced Textbook*. Hove, East Sussex: Psychology Press.

De Haan, M., & Gunnar, M. R. (2009). *Handbook of Developmental Social Neuroscience*. New York: Guildford.

Goswami, U. (Ed.) (2011). *Wiley-Blackwell Handbook of Childhood Cognitive Development*. Oxford: Wiley-Blackwell.

Johnson, M. H., & de Haan, M. (2011). *Developmental Cognitive Neuroscience*. Oxford: Wiley-Blackwell.

Luciana, M. (2007). Special issue: Developmental cognitive neuroscience. *Developmental Review*, 27, 277–282.

Nelson, C. A., & Luciana, M. (2001). *Handbook of Developmental Cognitive Neuroscience*. Cambridge, MA: MIT Press.

Nelson, C. A., de Haan, M., & Thomas, K. M. (2006). *Neuroscience and Cognitive Development: The Role of Experience and the Developing Brain*. New York: Wiley.

For more information about physical development during the prenatal period, see:

Moore, K. L., & Persaud, T. V. N. (2003). *The Developing Human: Clinically Oriented Embryology*. Philadelphia, PA: Saunders.

Moore, K. L., Persaud, T. V. N., & Shiota, K. (2000). *Colour Atlas of Clinical Embryology*. Philadelphia, PA: Saunders.

Tanner, J. M. (1990). *Foetus into Man: Physical Growth from Conception to Maturity* (2nd Ed.). Cambridge, MA: Harvard University Press.

For more information about human genetics, see:

Strachan, T., & Read, A. (2003). *Human Molecular Genetics*. New York: Wiley.

For more information about the interaction between nature and nurture, see:

Diamond, A. (2009). The interplay of biology and the environment broadly defined. *Developmental Psychology*, 45, 1–8.

For more information on current debates about infant cognition, see:

Haith, M. M. (1998). Who put the cog in infant cognition? Is rich interpretation too costly? *Infant Behavior and Development*, 21, 167–179.

Keil, F. (2006). Cognitive science and cognitive development. In W. Damon & R. Lerner (Series Eds.) and D. Kuhn & R. S. Siegler (Vol. Eds.), *Handbook of Child Psychology: Vol. 2, Cognition, Perception, and Language* (6th Ed.) (609–635). New York: Wiley.

For more information on the relationship between genes, brain development and cognition, see:

Johnson, M. H., Munakata, Y., & Gilmore, R. O. (2002). *Brain Development and Cognition: A Reader*. Oxford: Blackwell.

Ramus, F. (2006). Genes, brain, and cognition: A roadmap for the cognitive scientist. *Cognition*, 101, 247–269.

RECOMMENDED WEBSITES

For a detailed account of prenatal growth, click on the circular chart at:

http://www.visembryo.com/baby/index.html

For ongoing updates on the Human Genome Project:

http://www.ornl.gov/sci/techresources/Human_Genome/home.shtml

http://www.genome.gov

http://ghr.nlm.nih.gov/handbook

To see 'movies' of neuronal cells migrating, go to:

http://hatten-server.rockefeller.edu/HattenLab/overview.html

Chapter 5
Language development

Learning outcomes

After reading this chapter, and with further recommended reading, you should be able to:

1. Explain what language is, and describe its four major component parts.
2. Discuss some of the ways in which infants' early communicative and social interactions pave the way for later language development.
3. Compare some different theoretical explanations for the development of language.
4. Explain how development occurs in the four major parts of language.

Talk to your baby

In 2008, Suzanne Zeedyk, a psychologist at the University of Dundee in the UK, published the findings of research carried out in collaboration with a UK organisation called the National Literacy Trust (NLT). The article is entitled, 'What's life in a baby buggy like? The impact of buggy orientation on parent–infant interaction and infant stress'. The research was carried out as part of the NLT's 'Talk to Your Baby' campaign (http://www.literacytrust.org.uk/talk_to_your_baby), which is aimed at encouraging parents and caregivers to talk more to children from birth to 3 years. 'Buggy orientation' is the way the buggy faces: towards the person pushing it, or away from them. You might wonder why the orientation of a buggy is important in considering language development. Well, the research showed that mothers spoke much more to their infants when using a toward-facing buggy. In fact, when infants were in away-facing buggies, the amount of speech that mothers directed towards them dropped by half. Consider the following questions:

- Do we talk less to our children than we used to and, if so, why might that be?
- Can talking to babies before they can talk themselves really facilitate language development?
- Could something as seemingly simple as a pusher-facing baby buggy really have a significant effect on a child's language development?

A full report of Suzanne Zeedyk's findings can be downloaded from http://www.literacytrust.org.uk/assets/0000/2531/Buggy_research.pdf

Introduction

Language is a system of symbols that we use to communicate with one another. It consists of sounds, which can be combined in various ways to make words, and those words each carry their own meanings. There are grammatical rules which govern how those words may be combined in order to construct sentences correctly, and social rules which govern how language is used appropriately in different situations. The foundations of this complex system of communication are laid well before a child even utters his first words. This chapter will explore the process of developing language, beginning in the pre-verbal stage and following children's progress through childhood to the point where they can use language very effectively to communicate and engage in social interactions. (For a consideration of speech and language disorder in childhood, see Chapter 16, Atypical Development.)

What is language?

Language is a system of communication, although not all communication occurs through language. We will see later in this chapter that, before they are able to understand or produce words, infants can communicate quite effectively with us. Language is a symbolic system. That is, each word (and sometimes even parts of words) means something, stands for something or refers to something else. So long as we all share a common understanding of what words refer to then we can communicate. The precise word that we choose to represent something is to a certain extent unimportant. Take, for example, the word 'bed'. This is the word which we use in the English language to refer to objects like the one in the photograph.

However, if we were speaking German, we would use the word 'Bett'. If we were speaking French we would say 'lit' and if we were using British Sign Language then we would make the sign pictured on the right. The relationship between the object and the word which we use to refer to it is, therefore, not a necessary one – there is no intrinsic reason why another word could not be used. From now on, we could all use the word 'kofu' to refer to objects like that in the photo. So long as everyone did it, and we all understood what we were referring to, kofu would serve as just as adequate a symbol for such objects as the word 'bed'.

The individual words themselves, though, are only the building blocks of language. There are rules which children must learn about how those words can be combined, and these serve as the cement which holds the words together. There are also rules about how words can be altered to make, for example, different tenses or to create plurals. Again, these rules differ between different languages. What is amazing about language is that, although there are only a finite number of words and rules available to us, there are a potentially infinite number of ways in which those words may be combined. Young infants use words to communicate only their basic needs but, by adulthood, we can talk about abstract ideas and concepts meaningfully. As children begin to develop language, they start by naming and describing objects. Eventually, though, they will be able to discuss how they feel and what they like, and will not rely upon the immediate environment for communication. Developing language enables us to talk about the past and the future. Language is therefore incredibly creative and productive.

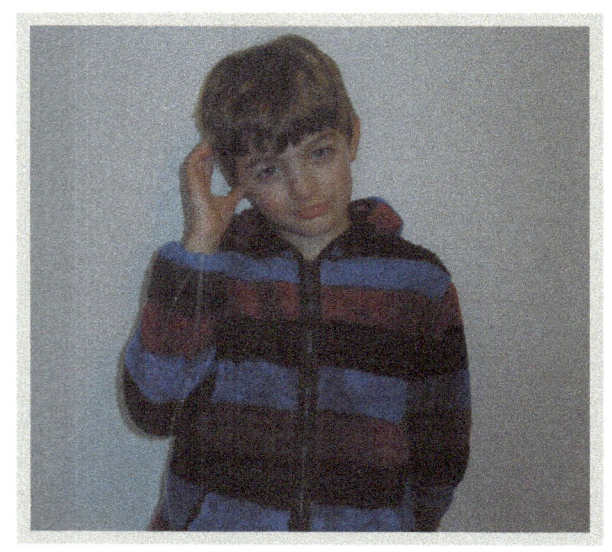

British Sign Language for 'bed'.
Source: Bartlett

An object which may be referred to using many different words.
Source: Pearson Education Ltd/Comstock Images

What communication is there before verbal communication?

We have referred to the fact that language is a system of communication, but that not all communication occurs through language. In this section, we will consider some of the ways in which early communication occurs even before spoken language.

Infants are social and emotional beings, and are able to send emotional messages from the time that they are born. Using facial expressions and early vocalisations such as crying, screaming, smiling or laughing, we can interpret an infant's emotional state. In fact, some researchers suggest that there is a universal repertoire of facial expressions that infants are born with, so that regardless of culture they are able to communicate their basic emotions and their primary physiological needs (Izard, 1994). Crying has received particular attention from researchers as a key way in which infants communicate. However, there has been controversy in the research literature about the exact purpose and function of a baby's cry. The next 'Stop and think' box explores some of the arguments which have arisen from recent research exploring infants' crying – an interesting and controversial topic in understanding language development.

There are disagreements about whether crying should be viewed as an attempt to communicate some physiological need, a way to manipulate parents and caregivers or a way for an infant simply to signal that she is healthy and strong. In Chapter 9, Attachment and Early Social Experiences, we discuss the development of a healthy mother–infant bond. The work of John Bowlby (1969, 1982) in the field of attachment suggested that crying has an important function for infants since most mothers will return to an infant if she begins to cry, and thus crying can restore the infant's proximity to her mother. This is important since the infant is more likely to remain fed and warm, but also because proximity to the mother is important for the development of that infant's social and emotional wellbeing. Bowlby believed that crying may have developed as part of infants' behavioural repertoire through the process of human evolution. Remaining close to her mother will have made the early human infant less vulnerable to predators and thus will have served an important function in evolutionary terms in ensuring the continuation of the species.

Lummaa et al. (1998) suggest that excessive crying on the part of an infant is a manipulative signal and would have us believe that on some level there is an intent to 'send' a message. Research by Lorberbaum et al. (2002) suggests that when infants cry, their mothers are 'receiving' information. They used functional magnetic resonance imaging (fMRI) to examine the brain activity of first-time mothers whilst listening to infant crying, and compared this to their brain activity during a control condition where they listened to white noise and to a third condition where they heard nothing. Some previous research by the neurologist Paul MacLean (see Recommended Websites) had suggested that a part of the brain called the thalamocingulate division would be important in mother–infant attachment behaviour (MacLean, 1990). If there are particular parts of the brain which are involved in maternal behaviour then clearly it is important to investigate which parts these are in order to better understand normal mothering and also potentially to understand what might underpin some instances of abnormal, neglectful or abusive mothering. The fMRI study showed that parts of the brain within the thalamocingulate division were indeed more active when mothers heard infants' crying than in the control conditions. Overall the results were consistent with other research which has identified areas of the brain involved in maternal behaviour with non-human mammals.

Interviews with the mothers in that research also asked them to report their emotional reactions to the different stimuli which they had heard, and the results of these interviews showed that hearing infants' crying resulted in the mothers experiencing significantly more sadness, and significantly more 'urges to help' than the control conditions. This evidence using fMRI techniques and interviews indicates that, merely by crying, infants elicit a consistent response in particular parts of mothers' brains and an accompanying desire on the part of the mothers to behave in a certain way (to help). It could therefore be argued that complex pre-verbal communication is occurring. This research shows how infants' crying can have a very real physiological effect on mothers, and supports the very early view of Bowlby that crying may have a survival function by ensuring that an infant remains in close proximity to its mother.

Should we really consider these early emotional expressions to be communication, though? Are infants and mothers really sending and receiving messages (see the next photo)? What is generally agreed is that in the very earliest days of life these kinds of emotional expression do

Definition

Thalamocingulate division: part of the human brain suggested within Paul MacLean's 'Triune Brain' theory (that we have three brains, each developed from the preceding ones through evolution) as important in family-related behaviour.

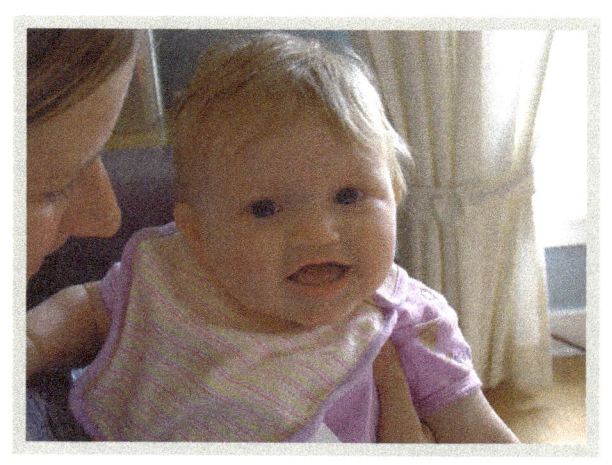

Mother–infant smiling. What is being communicated?
Source: O'Donnell

not occur as deliberate attempts on the part of the infant to communicate something to someone. At first they are merely reactions to physiological states. For example, new mothers may mistake an attack of wind for their baby's first smile! It is not until around 6 weeks of age that smiling begins to occur in response to something in the child's external world (Emde et al., 1976). By 12 months of age it seems as though infants are able to use smiling as a much more complex device, to communicate their positive feelings about an object to a social partner. For example, Venezia et al. (2004) observed a group of normally developing infants of between 8 and 12 months in situations where they had both an object and a social partner to attend to. The amount that these infants smiled in these situations did not increase during the four months that they were studied, but the amount that they smiled and then immediately made eye contact with their social partner did increase significantly and suggests that, even at 12 months of age, infants have already made some important progress in using facial expressions deliberately to communicate.

Definitions

Infanticide: intentionally causing the death of an infant.
Colic: a condition where babies cry for long periods of time (most commonly in the first three months of life) without obvious reason, but possibly due to trapped wind or infant temperament.
Shaken baby syndrome: a type of child abuse which occurs when a baby is vigorously shaken; it can result in neurological damage and may be fatal.

STOP AND THINK

Going further

In 2004 the journal *Behavioural and Brain Sciences* published an article by Joseph Soltis (a researcher in vocal communication). This suggested that infant crying is a behaviour which has evolved in human babies as a way of ensuring their survival (Soltis, 2004), but for slightly different reasons to Bowlby. Using evidence from research with a variety of different species of animals, Soltis argued that crying is a sign of physical strength and health. After discussing cross-cultural evidence from communities where there are instances of infanticide, and from research with a variety of non-human species, Soltis suggests that a crying infant is less likely to be killed by its family. This is because by crying he advertises himself as a healthy and viable specimen. If for some reason parents cannot support all of their offspring, then they will be more likely to spare the healthiest whilst weak or injured offspring will be killed or allowed to die. Crying is therefore a way of signalling physical vigour. This suggests some sort of communicative function, given that the infant's caregiver responds to the crying and acts a certain way as a result of it.

In a response to Soltis' article, Barr (2004) suggests an alternative account of crying, and argues that during the first three months crying is a behavioural state, in the same way as an infant may be described as being 'awake' or 'asleep'. Barr agrees that caregivers may respond to the crying in particular ways, but argues that this result of the crying 'signal' is secondary only and not a primary function of crying.

Another important point to note about crying is that, in spite of the positive effects it may have in terms of ensuring an infant's survival or psychological health, there may be some negative effects, particularly when the amount of crying an infant does is perceived to be excessive or abnormally high. In such cases, the infant's crying may lead to abuse or neglect. Infants suffering from colic engage in prolonged bouts of crying. Yet instead of eliciting positive maternal behaviour, Hagen (2002) found that the opposite was true. He surveyed 129 mothers of babies between 3 and 32 weeks of age and found that the more the infants cried, the less positive emotions the mothers experienced towards the infant. Even more worrying is that some anecdotal reports from perpetrators of shaken baby syndrome (see Recommended Reading) suggest that in some cases an infant's crying may be an important trigger for this kind of child abuse. Research published in the medical journal *The Lancet* supports this, by showing that 5.6% of parents reported having smothered, slapped or shaken their baby at least once because of its crying (Reijneveld et al., 2004).

- Should we view crying as an important part of infants' early communication, or as a normal behavioural state like waking or sleeping?
- Is the communicative function of crying merely a side effect of evolutionary processes, or does it still have an important function in developing the mother–infant bond and ensuring healthy psychological development?
- Or does crying do more harm than good?

The four components of language

Language is made up of four main component parts. These four components are: phonology; semantics; syntax; and pragmatics. We will now consider each of these in turn in order to get a better understanding of this complex system, and how the different parts of it develop.

What is phonology?

When we talk about phonology, we are talking about the sound system of a language. Different languages contain different sounds, and if you have ever learned another language then you will know that just mastering the speech sounds that you need to be able to pronounce certain words can be a big challenge. In fact, there are significant phonological differences even between different dialects of the English language. The Scottish word 'loch' contains the phoneme /ch/ which does not feature in other English speakers' repertoire of sounds, and which they may therefore struggle to pronounce. In contrast, that same phoneme is a key part of the phonology of the German language, and Scottish students may find mastering the sounds necessary to pronounce German words easier than their traditional-English-speaking counterparts. Phonology also determines which sounds can precede or follow other sounds in a given language. For example, in English /s/ can be followed by /t/ as in the words 'star' or 'fast'. However, the sound /z/ cannot be followed by /x/, nor /p/ by /q/.

It is important to note that it is not just the ability to produce the speech sounds of a language which is important in understanding children's phonological development, but also the ability to recognise and to tell the difference, or discriminate, between different phonemes within a language. For example, in spoken English the /k/ sound in the word 'cat' actually sounds different to the /k/ sound when it appears in the spoken word 'ski'. However, if we get speakers of English to listen to different instances of the /k/ sound (say, by different speakers or taken from different words), they are unable to tell the difference between them. This means that these different instances of the speech sound /k/ all form one category of sound within spoken English. English speakers do not discriminate between different instances within the category of speech sound /k/. In contrast, speakers of Arabic can readily discriminate between different instances of the /k/ sound, because in Arabic these constitute different phonemes. Later in this chapter we will see how the ability to produce the sounds of a language develops, as well as the ability to perceive the sounds of language.

What are semantics?

Semantics refers to the part of language to do with the meanings of words, and also of sentences. As children learn language, they develop a vocabulary of words to

> **Definitions**
> Phonology: the sound system of a particular language.
> Semantics: the part of language concerned with the meanings of words and parts of words.
> Syntax: the part of language concerned with the rules which govern how words can be combined to make sentences.
> Pragmatics: the part of language concerned with its use in social contexts.
> Phoneme: the smallest units of sound in a language.
> Discriminate: in speech-sound perception, to be able to tell the difference between speech sounds of a language.
> Category: a set of sounds or words perceived as belonging to the same group (e.g. all instances of the sound /s/ or all words relating to female humans).

which they attach certain meanings (not always correctly at first, as we will see later on). As children's vocabularies grow, they are able to organise the words they know into groups of words which are semantically related. The words 'cat' and 'kitten' have a lot in common in terms of their meanings and the animal to which they refer. They are therefore semantically related, but have key semantic differences in terms of the age of the animal. Nevertheless, recognising that there are commonalities in their meanings is important in language development.

Even sentences which are grammatically correct may not be semantically accurate, if they do not make sense. For example, the sentence 'The carrot sang to the boy' is constructed correctly from a grammatical point of view, but it contradicts our semantic knowledge that the word 'carrot' denotes a vegetable which cannot sing.

A cat or a kitten?
Source: O'Donnell

What is syntax?

Syntax refers to the way in which words can be acceptably combined to create sentences or phrases in a given language. The sentence 'I am going to the shop' is syntactically correct in English, but combining the same words in a different way to say, 'I am to the shop going' is syntactically incorrect. Nevertheless, we may still be able to infer the meaning of what someone is trying to say from a sentence which is syntactically incorrect. The character Yoda in the *Star Wars* movies constructed sentences in this way and yet we are still able to follow what he is trying to say!

What are pragmatics?

Pragmatics refers to the social part of language and determines how language can be used appropriately in different contexts, and how meanings can be conveyed which go beyond the words themselves. For example, the convention of taking turns during conversations is part of the pragmatic system, and this begins to develop even before children have developed any spoken language, as we will see later in the chapter. Telling jokes, or using language deliberately to make people laugh, is part of this system as well, as is the ability to modify the way we use language depending upon whom we are talking to.

STOP AND THINK

Reflection

- Have you ever heard anyone refer to things children say as 'refreshingly honest'?
- Young children often say things which we, as adults, may be thinking, but would not dream of saying out loud. Can you think of occasions where you have not said something, perhaps because of concern for causing embarrassment or insulting someone?
- How do you think a child learns the 'rules' concerning these aspects of language?

Consider the way that you might talk to a group of close friends when you are on a night out, and compare it to the way you might talk to your lecturer or to your grandparents. What are the differences between these different ways in which you use language? Knowledge and understanding of social contexts and of the effects of using language in different ways allows us to modify and adapt what we say and how we say it, to different situations.

Definition

Semantically related: words which have something in common in terms of their meaning.

How do infants' early social interactions prepare them for later language?

Turn taking in feeding

Earlier in the chapter, we mentioned the importance of turn taking for successful conversations to occur. This is a social aspect of language and researchers have found evidence that early social interactions which infants have with their caregivers may be important in preparing them for turn taking in formal conversations later on. When they are feeding, infants fall into a rhythmic pattern which includes bursts of sucking separated by pauses. It seems as though these pauses are unique to human babies, as they have not been found in other mammals' feeding patterns (Wolff, 1968a, 1968b). The purpose and function of the pauses is not clear, as there does not seem to be any logical reason for them to occur. Infants are perfectly able to suck continuously without needing to take a break in between. They can suck and breathe at the same time and, although their bouts of sucking may get shorter over the course of a feed, the pauses stay at roughly the same length (Kaye and Brazelton, 1971). This is curious and has led researchers to investigate what happens during these pauses in order to try to explain what purpose they might serve.

It seems as though the infant's mother matches her own cycles of activity and rest with the infant's burst–pause sequences, by remaining passive whilst the infant is sucking, and then inserting dialogue or 'jiggling' the baby during the pauses (Kaye, 1977; Kaye and Wells, 1980). This mirrors the conventional patterns of language that occur during conversational exchanges in later life, which require us to be attuned to the people around us. These cycles of resting and feeding may therefore play a part in the development of reciprocal turn taking as part of the development of the pragmatic system.

Interestingly, some research has compared these rhythmic exchanges between infants and their mothers in babies who were born prematurely and those who were born after a full-term pregnancy (Lester et al., 1985). This research showed that these mother–infant interactions are less well synchronised in premature babies than in babies born at full term. Other research has reported that children born prematurely show some delays in language development (e.g. Friedman and Sigman, 1981). Lester et al. (1985) suggest that this lack of synchrony in the earliest interactions between infants and their mothers may be at least partly responsible for the delays in language development seen in children who were born prematurely. If this is the case then it shows how important these early social interactions can be for later language development. These cycles and rhythms of social interaction also occur in contexts other than feeding, as the next section shows.

Cycles of attention

In other interactions between infants and their caregivers, there is evidence of the same kinds of rhythm as discussed in the previous section. For example, studies of mother–infant gazing show that babies will engage in cycles of attention and looking away. In adult communication, meeting someone's gaze is interpreted as an invitation to engage socially, and this seems to be mirrored in these infant interactions, where babies are able to indicate their willingness to engage socially by attending visually to their mother or other caregiver. They can control the amount of interaction that takes place by then looking away. Interactions between babies and their caregivers are very stimulating for babies and too much attention can lead to over-stimulation and upset. Babies can therefore use these cycles of attention and looking away to regulate their level of excitement. Nonetheless, caregivers also need to be sensitive to the baby's state. Understanding the need to lower the level of stimulation when a baby looks away is an important part of the parent's role in an interaction, as persisting in trying to engage a baby who is not receptive to interaction can have adverse effects.

Where mothers are not attuned to their infants, the development of an attachment bond may be disrupted and so these early communicative interactions may be important for a child's social development, as well as for the development of language (Murray and Cooper, 1997). Chapter 9, Attachment and Early Social Experiences, explores the development of an infant's bond with her mother or primary caregiver. It is interesting to note that parental sensitivity to infants may play an important part in the development of a child's attachment style (for more information about attachment styles in general, see Recommended Reading), and this sensitivity to an infant's cycles of attention regulation in pre-verbal interactions may indicate a parent's sensitivity to the infant.

For both parties, engaging in this kind of social interaction provides a positive shared experience. We will see later in this chapter how learning theorists' accounts of language development would conceptualise the importance of this kind of positive reinforcement for language development. But equally, if the interaction produces negative effects for the infant, it may lower the likelihood of the infant engaging in this kind of interaction again. Thus, these early social interactions pave the way for later communicative exchanges and language.

Infant-directed speech

In the literature you may see this referred to as mother–child speech, parentese, baby talk, motherese or infant-directed speech. What we are talking about here is the kind of speech that is heard when adults talk to infants. This kind of speech has a number of distinct characteristics which make it quite different from normal adult-to-adult speech. It is generally of a higher pitch. It also tends to use a greater range of pitch, from high to low, which sounds exaggerated. This kind of speech is often slower, and words are articulated much more clearly. It is also simpler, using less complex words as well as less complex clauses and phrases. There is also more repetition than is usually heard in adult-to-adult speech.

Adults seem to make use of this kind of speech, almost without realising it, in their interactions with infants. There is evidence from research which shows that infant-directed speech exists in many different languages, even sign language (for more information on this, see Recommended Reading). Acquiring the speech sounds (phonology) of a language may be facilitated by the use of infant-directed speech, which exposes babies to their language in an exaggerated and simplified form, and this may therefore prepare them for its more complex forms later on. Having said this, it is important to note that exposure to infant-directed speech is not something which is necessary in order for language development to occur, as studies of different cultures have shown us that in some communities this special way of interacting with infants does not happen, and yet children in those communities develop in approximately the same ways and at the same rates as children who are exposed to infant-directed speech.

In one Mayan society, parents have been observed not to use infant-directed speech at all and yet children seem to acquire language quite normally (Pye, 1986). In Papua New Guinea, the Kaluli tribe treat children as though they do not have any understanding and so parents do not really address children verbally at all until later in life (Schiefflin and Ochs, 1983). Again, these children still go on to acquire language normally. So in spite of these examples of cultures where children's earliest exposures to the phonology, syntax and semantics of their language are not especially simplified, such children are nevertheless able to develop language normally, suggesting that whilst infant-directed speech may facilitate the development of language, it is not strictly necessary for development as a component of a child's early exposure to language.

Theories of development

Having established what language is, what its component parts are, and how some of the foundations of language may be laid in infants' earliest social interactions, we will now explore some of the theoretical perspectives which try to explain how language develops. Before reading on, stop and think about your own beliefs regarding language.

> **STOP AND THINK**
>
> ### Reflection
> - How significant is language as a feature of what makes humans different from other animals?
> - Is there something 'special' or 'different' about language, or is it just one of many abilities that we have? What makes you think so?
> - What do you think would happen to a child's language development if they had no contact with other people? What makes you think so?

Learning theory accounts

Learning theorists argue that language is just another kind of behaviour which we learn, albeit a verbal behaviour. If we accept this account then it implies that there are no in-born language abilities. This contrasts with Nativist accounts of language, which we will discuss in the next section, and which suggest that there are some abilities or aptitudes that infants are born with, which allow for the development of language.

> **STOP AND THINK**
>
> ### Reflection
>
> Consider some of the research we have already discussed in this chapter about children's earliest communicative encounters. Would these fit with the view that children are not born with any specific language abilities?

Learning theorists point out that from the time they are born, children are surrounded with language. We talk to babies all the time, even though we know that they cannot respond or even understand us. For example, Rheingold and Adams (1980) collected samples of speech which was directed to new-born infants by staff in a hospital neonatal nursery over a period of two months. Ten two-hour samples of speech were collected and analysed in terms of their grammatical characteristics, topic and whether they expressed warm regard or instructions. The researchers found that the speech which was directed to these infants was extensive and grammatically well formed, and occurred from the day the infants were born. This suggests that infants have ample opportunities to learn language quickly after birth without us needing to believe in the existence of abilities that are present within the child from birth.

The discussion in the previous section about the use of motherese is another way in which exposure to language after birth could arguably provide opportunities for infants to be exposed to their native language and thus learn it from an early age. Perhaps infants imitate the sounds of language to which they have been exposed, and learn the words and the grammatical rules by copying what they have heard. Social learning theorists emphasise how important parental approval and positive regard are in the process of language development, by influencing which sounds, words and sentences are repeated in future and thus *shaping* a child's language development. Consider this example taken from an observation of a mother as she holds her 7-month-old infant on her knee:

Baby Ivor:	*Baba ba ba na na*
Mum:	*(smiles) What are you saying baby?*
Ivor:	*Ba ba ba na*
Mum:	*Yes, I know (kisses baby on the nose)*
Ivor:	*Ba ba ba da*
Mum:	*(eyes wide, big smile) What did you say? What did you say?*
Ivor:	*Ba ba ba da*
Mum:	*Da! Did you say Da! Clever boy! What a clever boy! (touches nose to nose)*
Ivor:	*Bababa da*
Mum:	*Da! Yes baby! Yes! Dada! What a clever boy!*
Ivor:	*Da da da da (jiggles)*
Mum:	*Dada! (excited voice) That's a clever boy! You love your dada? Yes, you love your dada! Where's your dada? Where is he?*
Ivor:	*Da da da da (big smile)*
Mum:	*Dada! That's my clever boy! (three kisses) Dada! What a beautiful boy!*

It is likely that Ivor's vocalisation of the 'da' sound was produced as part of his expressive experimentation with speech sounds, along with 'ba' and 'na' sounds which were also produced in the early part of the exchange above. But clearly Mum picks up on the 'da' sound and repeats that particular sound to Ivor rather than the others. She also responds much more positively and enthusiastically to his production of the 'da' sound and by the end of this exchange we can see that Ivor is making that sound to the exclusion of others which were present at the beginning. Ivor therefore received a great deal of positive reinforcement from his mother for producing the 'da' sound, making it much more likely that this sound would be produced again. It is unlikely that Ivor actually

> **Definition**
>
> **Shaping:** a process by which children's utterances move closer to correct speech as the result of positive reinforcement, which leads to a series of successive approximations.

intended to say 'Dada' (meaning Dad), but the likelihood of Ivor now saying 'Dada' in the future is increased. In this way, social learning theorists suggest that language is learned through a process of gradually shaping sounds into word-like sounds, which will eventually become words associated with specific meanings. So do we really need to believe in any in-born language abilities to be able to explain how the process of language develops? Well, some people suggest that learning in infancy is not enough to account for all of the aspects of language development, as we will see in the next section.

The Nativist account

Noam Chomsky (see Recommended Websites) is a leading linguist who has suggested that humans are born with something called a language acquisition device (LAD). Chomsky does not believe that learning in infancy can account for all of the different aspects of language development. In particular, the suggestion that children can develop an understanding of the complex rules of grammar or syntax of a language through simple learning by imitation and reinforcement is unlikely. If you listen to adults talking, it is rare that they speak in fully formed, grammatically correct sentences, making it improbable that children would be able to learn the rules which govern language in this way.

Figure 5.1 gives an excerpt from a transcript of a conversation between two colleagues at work and illustrates the fact that adult language does not always involve grammatically correct sentences. Adult conversation is quite messy, with lots of hesitation and unnecessary or superfluous words. Exposed to this kind of language, it is difficult to imagine how infants could make sense of what they heard to such an extent that they could work out what was correct and incorrect syntax. Perhaps infant-directed speech helps with this, by exposing babies to exaggeratedly simplified speech which cuts out the unnecessary aspects of adult speech.

> A: So it's just like (1) I don't know (.) you know the thing is (1) um (1) it's like there's no appreciation of what they have to
> B: I know (.) I know how you feel (.) I feel the
> A: I know (1) and so I think we have to (.) like
> B: We do (.) say something about it
> A: Yeh because otherwise it's just gonna keep on and (.) there's never gonna be
> B: I know (.) it'll just be the same again
> A: And it's not even just about him (.) it's a general
> B: I know (.) like principle
> A: Yeh the principle or something (.) I don't know
> Key: (.) = short pause; (1) = 1-second pause

Figure 5.1 Excerpt from transcript of a conversation between colleagues.

Yet we have already considered evidence from other cultures which shows that even when the different kind of infant-directed speech does not feature in a society's interactions with infants, they develop language in approximately the same ways, so even the use of motherese cannot account for the learning of syntax.

Chomsky has also pointed out the predictability of the way in which language develops, and the fact that, regardless of country, culture or which specific language is to be learned, children reach certain developmental language milestones at roughly the same points in development. In fact, there are numerous websites that parents can visit which contain information on the speech and language abilities that typically developing children are expected to reach at different ages (see Recommended Websites). This lends further weight to the argument that learning from environmental influences and behaviour cannot be solely responsible for language development. If it were then we would expect to see far more variation in language development as a result of variations in the learning environment.

Studies of the kinds of mistakes which children make in their attempts to master language suggest that instead of learning syntax directly from speech, a LAD which they are born with enables children to pick up on the regularities that do exist in everyday speech. On the basis of these regularities, the LAD comes up with mini-theories about the rules which govern speech. For example, children may say 'mouses' instead of mice, and yet it is very unlikely that they would have learned to say 'mouses' as the result of hearing it said by

Definition

Language acquisition device: a hypothetical cognitive structure predisposed towards the acquisition of language and sensitive to rule-based regularities in everyday speech, therefore allowing for the development of grammar and syntax.

other adults. An adult would not make this error in the construction of this plural noun, and so learning theories of language cannot account for these kinds of mistakes in children's development. But if there is a LAD which has generated a mini-theory (based on lots of instances of pluralised nouns in the English language) that you make a plural by adding an /s/, then it is possible to understand how this error (of saying 'mouses') might have come about. It is only after more exposure to language that children's mini-theories will be modified, as they come across instances of plurals which contradict their existing theory. Eventually they will arrive at a more sophisticated understanding of the rules that govern the pluralisation of nouns, which incorporates some of the exceptions too. We will be looking at some other kinds of errors that children make in their developing language later in this chapter, because they can offer us useful insights into the way in which language is acquired, the mini-theories that children have about language at different stages of development and the way in which they come to appreciate the relationship between words and their referents.

A LAD, if there is such a thing, would have to have some sort of biological basis, but it is not entirely clear what this might be. It is possible that the LAD might represent a particular part of the brain, and there is certainly evidence that there are particular parts of the brain which are involved in language. It is widely understood that in adults the left hemisphere of the brain is important for language, and in 1987 a review of the literature about lateralisation of brain functioning confirmed that this is also the case for children from birth (Hahn, 1987). Evidence from patients who have suffered brain injuries has helped us to understand which parts of the left hemisphere may be implicated in language.

Pierre Paul Broca, a French neurosurgeon and pathologist, was the first to identify a specific part of the left hemisphere which is involved in language. In 1961 Broca conducted an examination of a patient with a specific language impairment following that patient's death, and found lesions in a particular part of the posterior of his left hemisphere which has come to be known as 'Broca's area'. This part of the brain is important for the production of speech (and is sometimes referred to as the speech centre). Individuals whose speech and language is affected by damage to this area are often referred to as suffering from Broca's aphasia, which means that they have problems with expressive language, their sentences will be short and their speech very broken and sometimes distorted (for more information, including classic and contemporary papers about Broca's area, see Recommended Reading). Broca's area is connected by a pathway of nerves to another part of the brain implicated in language, called Wernicke's area. The location of these two areas of the brain is illustrated in Figure 5.2.

Wernicke's area is most important for the comprehension of language, and is named after the German psychiatrist and neurologist Carl Wernicke who first described the symptoms associated with damage to the area, in 1908. Individuals with damage to this area are able to produce speech that has the same kind of sound and rhythm as normal speech, but which does not have any real meaning, and they have difficulty in understanding language. Such symptoms are known as Wernicke's aphasia.

It is thought that Wernicke's area is important for language development. Damage to the area means that children will be unable to make sense of the language that they are exposed to, thus seriously impairing its development. Figure 5.2 illustrates the connection between

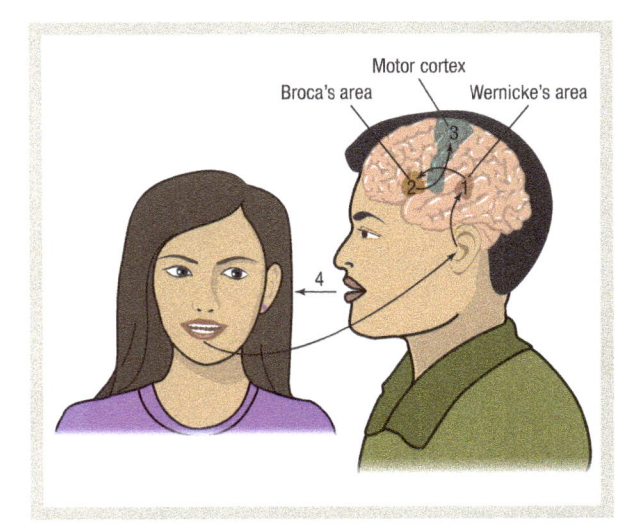

Figure 5.2 Broca's area and Wernicke's area are both important for language.

Definition

Lateralisation: the principle that some specific psychological functions are located in one or the other side of the brain's two cortical hemispheres.

Broca's and Wernicke's areas, and their involvement in language, from comprehension to production.

Contemporary research into these biological bases for language have lent support to the *critical period hypothesis*, through studies of children who have suffered traumatic brain injuries. Adults who develop language impairments following these kinds of injuries are likely to be permanently impaired, and some research with children suffering head injuries has also found long-lasting effects on language for at least some children. For example, Jordan and Murdoch (1993) studied 11 children over a period of 18 months following head injuries, assessing various different aspects of their language abilities, and found that few of them recovered to what would be considered 'normal' levels on all of the measures after 18 months. However, the youngest child in that study was 7 years old at the time of their injury. Another longitudinal study, this time of an infant who was 17 months and 10 days old when she suffered a head trauma, suggests that despite an initial decline in her language ability immediately following the injury, six months after her injury there were no longer any significant impairments on any of the measures of language that were used (Trudeau et al., 2000). This kind of evidence supports the idea that there may be a period in the early part of a child's life where parts of the brain develop specifically for language but that, if there is damage to those parts of the brain, there can be some compensation and other parts of the brain may be recruited for language. This ability of brains to recover their functioning is referred to as *plasticity*.

In the 1960s, Eric Lenneberg suggested that the critical period for children's language learning was between 18 months of age and the onset of puberty (Lenneberg, 1967). This original suggestion was based on the fact that language develops quickly during the early years of a child's life, and Lenneberg believed that there was a biological basis for this, in that language develops due to the development of the brain as children mature. The fact that more contemporary research has shown that brain damage in children over the age of 5 typically leads to at least some long-term effects on language, though, suggests that the critical period for language development has passed by this time, and that the opportunity for the brain to recover its functioning in this area is lost.

Overall, the ideas which Chomsky put forward about a possible LAD and the research from neuroscience regarding the importance of certain parts of the brain for language do suggest that external input and learning alone cannot account for how language is acquired and develops. Yet it is clear from the evidence regarding learning and the social world that environmental influences do affect how language develops too. Alternative accounts of language have evolved which emphasise the interaction between in-born abilities with a biological basis and input from the environment. These 'interactionist' accounts suggest that language can be understood best as an interaction between these two factors, and they are explored in the next section.

Interactionist accounts

Some interactionist accounts of language development make us think about the interaction between the development of language and the development of cognition and thinking abilities in general. For example, if we consider Piaget's theory of cognitive development (explored in Chapter 2, Theoretical Perspectives) then we recall that he believed in a progression through stages of development for children. Each stage means that a child is able to think and interact with the world in a particular way, which is fundamentally different to the way in which they thought about and interacted with the world in the previous stage. Early on in the present chapter, we discussed the fact that language is a symbolic system, where words represent things in the world. Language development can therefore be seen as part of a child's broader representational development, as they move into Piaget's later stages of development (see Chapter 2), where language and thinking are no longer dependent upon the immediate environment. Acquiring language allows us to think

Definitions

Critical period hypothesis: the suggestion that there is a specific period of time in the early part of a child's life (suggestions about when this begins and ends vary), during which language learning should occur in order to develop normally.

Plasticity: the ability of the brain to reorganise neural pathways either to recover lost functioning due to damage, or in response to learning from new experiences.

and talk about objects, people or events which are not present in our environment. Eventually, more sophisticated language allows us to talk and think about abstract concepts like justice or truth, which have no concrete referents in the external world. An 18-month-old infant has not yet reached the stage of cognitive development where thinking about such abstract concepts is possible. At this age, infants' thinking is focused on basic concepts like 'mummy' or 'food', 'hot' or 'sad' – these are things that they know about, and their language reflects the level of development of their knowledge and thinking. As children encounter new concepts, they will learn new words to associate with those concepts and then they will be able to talk about and think about the new concepts. Learning a new word which does not fit with any existing concepts will mean that a new concept is constructed (Kuczaj, 1982).

One of the Stop and Think boxes earlier in this chapter asked you to think about how important language really is, and whether you think it is much different from some of the other abilities we develop. In this particular theoretical framework, we can see that language is presented as part of the process of cognitive development, which means that we should not regard it as a special or significantly different aspect of development.

Other interactionist accounts emphasise the fact that children do not develop language in isolation, and allow us to consider how input from the external world works with innate abilities that a child brings into the world. Looking at some of the cases of children who have developed without input from the external world can help to illustrate this.

In 1992, an American journalist called Russ Rymer published a book called *Genie: A Scientific Tragedy*, one of many such books which tells the true and harrowing story of a young girl who was discovered aged 13 years of age, locked away in her parents' home in California, USA. She had spent her entire childhood strapped to a chair and was kept almost completely isolated during this time. Her father subjected her to physical beatings if she made any sounds, and when she was rescued, as well as having various physical problems, she could not speak. For many years after she was found, Genie was surrounded by therapists of many kinds, and although she did eventually learn some basic words and word combinations, she did not develop normal language abilities and in particular she did not acquire an understanding of grammar or syntax. Sadly there have been other instances of children who for various reasons have lived the early parts of their lives without being exposed to language.

The study of an individual child like Genie represents a case study. The use of case studies as a research method in developmental psychology is discussed in more detail in Chapter 3 (Research Methods). Case studies do not necessarily allow us to generalise to an entire population. The fact that Genie's language was affected in certain ways by her deprivation does not mean that any child subject to the same circumstances would develop in the same way. However, case studies like this do allow us to carry out in-depth studies of naturally occurring phenomena which would simply not be possible to manipulate artificially for the purposes of an experiment. Obviously we could not remove infants from their families and keep them in conditions similar to those which Genie experienced, merely for the purposes of studying the effects on their development. But when cases like these occur, tragic though they are, they provide an opportunity for psychologists to learn something. What is crucial, though, is that the welfare of the child is always paramount, and that the researchers' interests are always secondary to the need to provide the best possible support and care for the child. Genie's case lends weight to the critical period hypothesis discussed previously, which suggests that language needs to develop within the first few years of life if a typical developmental pattern is to be established (see Recommended Websites for a link to a site devoted to cases of these kinds of children).

In these ways, then, interactionist approaches to understanding and explaining how and why language develops allow us to think about how abilities which are specific to language may interact with other cognitive abilities, and also how they may interact with input from the social world. Having explored these three major theoretical explanations for language development, the next part of this chapter will focus on the four component parts of language (phonology, semantics, syntax, pragmatics), and will describe what developments occur in those four domains across childhood, so that we can start to build up a picture of what language looks like (or, more accurately, *sounds* like), at different stages of development.

RESEARCH METHODS

The use of language in researching children's cognitive development

One of the major challenges facing researchers in developmental psychology is how to assess children's thinking in the pre-verbal stage. Once children have developed enough language to provide verbal responses or explanations, things seem a little more straightforward. Chapter 4 (Prenatal Development and Infancy) explores in more detail some of the methods that researchers have developed which allow them to assess psychological development in infancy, and Chapter 6 (Memory and Intelligence) explores some of these as well. Chapter 8 discusses the development of Theory of Mind, which is significant for understanding children's development. Developing a theory of mind is about developing the ability to recognise the mental states of others, and how these mental states relate to people's behaviour.

You will see in Chapter 8 that researchers have developed false-belief tasks to assess whether a child can correctly identify that someone else holds a belief about something, which the child themselves knows to be false. For example, the child might know that the chocolate is in the cupboard because they moved it there from the table. But do they understand that if their mother came into the room, she would look on the table for the chocolate? Understanding that someone else can hold a belief which is false, and that their false belief will influence their behaviour, is not easy for young children. Presenting children with scenarios like this one and asking them how someone else would behave allows us to judge children's theory of mind. These kinds of traditional false-belief tasks require verbal responses on the part of the child, and generally children cannot successfully complete such tasks until they are around 4 years of age (Wellman et al., 2001). However, researchers have developed other tasks which do not require verbal responses, since they assess implicit theory of mind rather than explicit theory of mind. Using such tasks, researchers have been able to demonstrate implicit theory of mind in much younger infants (e.g. Baillargeon et al., 2010). We may underestimate children's cognitive abilities because the tasks children complete require verbal responses that they are not capable of. Recent research suggests that understanding verbs to do with knowledge (such as 'know' and 'think') may be part of the explanation for the shift from implicit theory of mind in infants to explicit theory of mind in older children (San Juan and Wilde Astington, 2012). This supports the interactionist approach to language development, and shows just how closely linked the development of language and cognition are.

These ideas, and the link between language development and theory of mind, are discussed more fully in Chapter 8. The study of language is important as an area of developmental psychology in itself, but understanding how language develops is also important for how we carry out research with children into other areas of their development, and how we interpret the results of research.

Definitions

False belief: the wrongly held belief that something is true.
Implicit: implicit knowledge comes from an understanding of what is meant or suggested even when it has not been directly stated.
Explicit: explicit knowledge is that which has been stated clearly and in detail, and where there is no room for misunderstanding, confusion or doubt.

Phonological development

The development of speech-sound perception

In order to use language, we need to be able to understand the spoken words that we hear, as well as to be able to produce words ourselves. Hearing and understanding spoken words requires auditory perceptual abilities, and this section explores some of what we know about how the ability to perceive speech sounds develops in children. For adults to use language effectively, it is important to be able to discriminate (to hear the difference) between different categories of speech sound, and there is little point in us being able to discriminate between different sounds *within* a category of speech sound. As discussed earlier, in Arabic, it is important to be able to discriminate between the different categories of /k/ sound, because these constitute different phonemes in Arabic. However, when speaking English there is little advantage in being able to discriminate within the single category of /k/ sound, since these are perceived by English speakers as belonging to the same category of phoneme.

In a piece of ground-breaking research published in the esteemed journal *Science* in 1971, four psychologists presented convincing evidence that children are able to make these kinds of discriminations between categories of speech sounds, yet not within categories of speech sound, at a surprisingly early age (Eimas et al., 1971). Using a habituation technique and a non-nutritive dummy, infants from English-speaking families aged just 1 and 4 months of age were exposed to the phonemes /p/ and /b/. By measuring changes in the infants' rates of sucking, these psychologists were able to establish that even at 1 month of age infants could tell the difference between /p/ and /b/ and would respond to them as different sounds, but that they did not discriminate within the categories of /p/ and /b/. For infants' speech-sound perception to so closely mirror that of adults was very surprising, given that at such a young age these infants will have had only a very limited exposure to spoken language. This evidence suggests that from early in the very first year of life, children can already make important distinctions between the sounds which, in their native language, constitute different phonemes. This evidence of infants' early abilities to discriminate between different phonemes has been shown to extend beyond the languages to which an infant has been exposed. Streeter (1976) found that Kenyan infants aged around 2 months were able to discriminate between phonemes which are not distinct in their own native language. This may indicate that the ability to perceive differences in speech sounds is in-born, rather than learned as a result of exposure to language. The Nature–Nurture box considers what the implications of these sorts of findings might be for the different theories of language development considered earlier, and how the conclusions which we draw might be affected by other research.

In terms of the continued development of speech-sound perception, it is interesting that despite the very good abilities which young infants have to discriminate between different phonemes as mentioned above, their abilities have actually been shown to diminish as they get older, as discussed in Chapter 4, Prenatal Development and Infancy. This is an interesting phenomenon as we tend to assume that, as a general rule, children get better at things as they get older. In the area of speech-sound perception, though, they get worse as they get older. Can you think of why this might be the case? Consider Chomsky's ideas about the existence of a language acquisition device. If all humans are born with one of these then it must be capable of facilitating the development of whichever language a child is exposed to, since we can assume that the LAD would not know in advance which language to prepare for. Yet it then needs to be able to respond specifically to whichever language the child needs to learn. Perhaps, then, the LAD comes equipped with generic capacities to respond to all possible languages, but as it begins to specialise in a particular language it develops an expertise in hearing and responding to the sounds of that language at the expense of others. In some ground-breaking research in the 1980s, an American child psychologist Janet Werker investigated exactly this possibility and was able to show that the decline in infants' abilities to perceive differences between different categories of speech sounds in languages other than their own occurs between 6 and 12 months of age (Werker, 1989). This seems to be one area of children's development, then, where their abilities are actually considerably better than those of adults, and reminds us that understanding children's development is more complicated than just following improvements in their abilities over time.

The development of speech-sound production

Having looked at some of what we know about children's developing abilities to perceive speech sounds, we will now explore the pattern of development which characterises children's speech-sound production. Following a Piagetian approach to development in this area, initial research identified a series of stages through which children's vocalisations progress, and which seem to be remarkably similar across children despite differences in language, culture and context (see, for example, Oller, 1980; Stark, 1980, 1981). Table 5.1 (page 131) presents an overview of the main stages. Physical maturation in the child's vocal system was thought to underpin the development of vocalisation through these stages, as infants then explore their developing abilities in interaction with others. We will see a little later that more recent research places greater significance on the influence of social interaction on the development of speech-sound production than previously.

Infants' earliest vocalisations include burping, crying, coughing and sneezing, all of which are produced in

NATURE–NURTURE

Is speech-sound perception innate?

Let's consider what the significance of this evidence from Eimas et al. (1971) might be to our understanding of how children develop language. Earlier on in this chapter we considered different theoretical approaches to the understanding of language development, and one of the key questions was about whether children are born with innate language abilities, or innate predispositions towards language acquisition, or whether learning is more responsible for language development. What do you think this key piece of research suggests in terms of language development? Could it be that infants of just 1 month old have already learned which speech sounds belong to one category and which represent different categories, as a result of their limited experience with spoken language? This seems unlikely to explain the results, and the original authors suggested that the evidence supported a view that some aspects of language development are 'part of the biological makeup of the organism' (p. 306) and that children are therefore born with innate language abilities. Some more recent research suggests that it is unlikely to be this straightforward either, though.

Patricia Kuhl, a professor of Speech and Hearing Sciences, did several pieces of research in the 1970s and 1980s which suggest that animals such as chinchillas and macaques are able to make the same kinds of categorical discriminations between human speech sounds as infant children and adult humans can (see Recommended Reading). It is difficult to see why these kinds of animals would also have a built-in capacity for perceiving human speech sounds. What seems more likely is that humans (and other animals) are born with some innate mechanism for making sense of sounds generally, but that this is not exclusively for the purposes of developing language. This mechanism is likely to be sensitive to auditory information generally, and for human infants would then provide the basis for the categorisation of speech sounds specifically.

The particular language to which an infant is exposed in infancy would then allow for the development of categorical discrimination between the sounds of that language, suggesting an interaction between children's in-born abilities and learning from the world around them. This suggestion is supported by the fact that infants' ability to discriminate between phonemes is one of the few areas of development where children get worse as they get older! Infants at 6 months of age are able to discriminate more phonemes than they can at 12 months. This seems to reflect the effects of environmental input on infants' initial auditory processing abilities, which leads to a gradual specialisation that enables the discrimination of phonemes from the child's native language, and a decrement in the ability to discriminate phonemes from other languages.

These pieces of research therefore lead us towards an understanding of the development of language which stems not from innate language abilities per se, but from innate mechanisms or abilities to process certain types of information. Development occurs as the result of the interaction between those mechanisms and the particular information which infants are then exposed to.

---

response to physiological or emotional states. An infant may be able to communicate some physiological need to us through crying, and in the first two months of life these vocalisations are referred to as 'reflexive' and are not viewed as language proper. Earlier in this chapter, we explored what kinds of communication can occur before verbal communication, and we discussed the significance of crying in particular. One study has found that new-born infants' crying seems to reflect the exposure which they have had in the womb to the sounds of their native language (Mampe et al., 2009). The pitch and contours of two groups of new-borns (a French group and a German group) were compared. The researchers found that French new-borns produced cries which had rising melody contours, whereas the German new-borns cries had falling melody contours. This indicates that, even before birth, human babies must be able to perceive the sounds of their native language, and that the production of even their earliest vocalisations reflects those sounds.

The amount of crying which infants do seems to decrease after the second month of life, and it is then that more speech-like vocalisations occur. Cooing and laughing characterise a great deal of the vocalisations of infants between 2 and 4 months of age. The third stage is characterised by what is referred to as *babbling* or *vocal play* and features between 4 and 6 months. During this stage, infants begin to master some of the physical movements and manipulations which are required to make sounds (such as moving their lips and tongue and making their vocal chords vibrate) and they begin to play, explore and experiment. This is the vocal equivalent of exploring a new object which they have begun to be able to grasp – to see what it does, how it feels and what they can do with it. The next stage, *canonical babbling*, features sounds and combinations of sounds which actually sound like words (such as mama or dada, as seen in the example of Baby Ivor's exchange with his mother earlier in the chapter), though it is unlikely that infants are attaching any meaning to the word-like sounds that they produce during this stage. Next comes more complex babbling which is often referred to in the literature as *modulated babbling*, and which features between 10 and 15 months. During this stage, infants begin to play and explore the patterns of intonation, stress, pitch and tone which characterise more adult speech. This is the final stage before proper articulation and the use of referential words occurs at between 12 and 15 months. These stages are summarised in Table 5.1.

Definition

Referential words: common nouns used to denote real objects.

Semantic development

The growth of vocabulary in infancy

Once a child produces her first referential words, her vocabulary begins gradually to grow. This process is fairly slow for the first three or four months, adding just a few new words to her vocabulary each month. Once her vocabulary has reached between 50 and 100 words, however, the process of vocabulary growth accelerates rapidly. This is commonly referred to in the literature as the vocabulary spurt. Different authors disagree as to the exact rate at which a child's vocabulary grows during this spurt period, but some have reported cases where a child's vocabulary growth has increased from learning fewer than 10 new words one week, to learning as many as 40–70 new words the next week (e.g. Dromi, 1987; Mervis et al., 1992). The vocabulary spurt often occurs at around 18 months of age, but the exact point varies between children, and some children may not display a spurt at all (see, for example, Ganger and Brent, 2004).

There is a subtle but important distinction to be made between the size of a child's vocabulary and the rate of their vocabulary growth. Think about a Porsche Carerra driving down the M1 motorway. As it joins the motorway at junction 26 the Porsche is doing 57 miles per hour (mph), and by the time it reaches junction 27

Definition

Vocabulary spurt: a point in language development where the rate of acquisition of new words is thought to accelerate rapidly.

Table 5.1 Stages of infant vocalisation.

Stage	Main features	Approximate age range
I: Reflexive vocalisation	Crying, burping, coughing, sneezing	0–6/8 weeks
II: Interactive sound making	Cooing, laughing	6–19 weeks
III: Vocal play	Deliberate exploration of sounds	18–30/35 weeks
IV: Canonical babbling	Sounds and sound combinations which begin to sound like words	35 weeks–1 year
V: Complex/modulated babbling	Interactive use of babbling; exploration of stress, intonation, etc.	10–15 months
VI: Referential words	First words used to refer to things	12–15 months

Source: adapted from Stark (1981)

it is doing 70 mph. This tells us the absolute speed at which the Porsche was travelling at these two points, but it doesn't tell us about the Porsche's rate of acceleration between those two points. A Ford Fiesta could also join the M1 at junction 26 doing 57 mph, and could have reached 70 mph by junction 27, but we would imagine that the Porsche's rate of acceleration would have been greater than the Fiesta's, and that this would be due to differences in the engine capacity of the two cars. The spurt which is seen in children's vocabulary growth is evidence to many psychologists that there is suddenly a different 'engine' powering the process of word acquisition – that there has been some fundamental change in children's language abilities which allows for a much faster rate of vocabulary growth. In other words, it is suggested that some kind of underlying cognitive developments may be responsible for the spurt. This possibility is explored in the next section.

Cognitive development and semantic development

One suggestion as to what fundamental cognitive change might underlie the dramatic increase in vocabulary growth seen in the second year of a child's life is that they experience what is known as the naming insight. The majority of infants' first words are nouns which refer to objects or people. The naming insight theory suggests that at first infants associate words with particular objects, activities, people or routines in their lives, but they do not yet realise that in fact every thing has a name, and conversely that every name refers to some thing (Reznick and Goldfield, 1992). Once they experience this realisation, their interest in naming things and their ability to learn new names for things increases. This may be why the vocabulary spurt often coincides with children beginning to ask the question 'What's that?' as they start to realise that everything that they encounter has a name.

Another feature of this period of development is the development of semantic relations – grouping words together according to their common membership of some kind of group or category. The development of early categorisation in infancy is discussed in Chapter 4, Prenatal Development and Infancy, and its role in mathematical thinking is explored in Chapter 7, The Development of Mathematical Thinking. Alison Gopnik and Andrew Meltzoff are both eminent developmental psychologists who have carried out some research into the role of categorisation in children's language development. In one study, infants between 15 and 21 months of age were observed playing with different sets of objects (Gopnik and Meltzoff, 1987). Each set of eight objects consisted of four objects of one type (e.g. four plastic boxes) and four objects of another type (e.g. four balls). The infants' behaviour as they played with and manipulated these objects was observed, with the researchers paying particular attention to whether the infants exhibited any of three different levels of grouping behaviour: (1) single category grouping – this is when a child systematically displaces four objects of one type and groups them together. The other type of object does not need to have been manipulated in order for single-category grouping to be said to have occurred; (2) serial touching of both object types – this is when a child touches the four objects of one type one after the other, and then touches the four objects of the other type one after the other; (3) two category grouping – this is when a child moves all eight objects from their original locations and systematically sorts them into two distinct groups. This was the highest level of categorisation to be observed. They observed each infant on these categorisation tasks at three-weekly intervals until he or she had passed all of the tasks. In addition to the infants' categorisation, the researchers were also interested in their vocabulary development, and noted when each infant's vocabulary spurt occurred.

They found quite a lot of variation in the ages at which individual infants each began to produce the three levels of categorisation behaviour, but the mean age at which level 3 categorisation was observed was 17.24 months. They also found a great deal of individual variation in the age at which the vocabulary spurt occurred, but the mean age at which it happened was 18.33 months. What was particularly interesting, though, was that these researchers found a strong correlation between the age of the vocabulary spurt and the age of the development of level 3 categorisation. None of the infants in this study had a vocabulary spurt before they were able to make

> **Definition**
>
> Naming insight: the realisation that all things have names, leading to a fundamental change in the way children think about the world.

level 3 categorisations. This makes it seem as though the development of this understanding of semantic relations or category membership is a necessary prerequisite to the spurt in vocabulary which is seen in children at around this point in their development. None of the infants in this study had a vocabulary spurt before they reached level 3 categorisation, and the mean amount of time which elapsed between this kind of categorisation and the vocabulary spurt was 33 days, which again suggests that the two are closely linked developmentally. Think again about the different theories of language development which were considered earlier in this chapter. This kind of evidence seems to lend support to the interactionist accounts of language development, which emphasise the interrelationships between the development of language and the development of other more general cognitive abilities.

An interesting, and somewhat controversial topic in contemporary language development is that of baby signing. The underlying symbolic nature of language means that, for hearing-impaired children and adults, signing can be used as a form of communication, and this has been extended to pre-verbal infants on the assumption that whilst they may not yet be able to use words, symbols of a visual form can be learned (Doherty-Sneddon, 2008).

Learning the meanings of words

After the vocabulary spurt, children's vocabularies continue to grow, so that by the time they reach 6 years of age some estimates suggest that their vocabularies may be as large as 14 000 words. Initially, the words which infants produce are primarily common nouns and action verbs, but they also include sound effects such as animal noises (e.g. 'moo') and people words (e.g. 'Daddy'). Common nouns include animals, vehicles, toys and food, such as 'dog' or 'ball'. Action verbs include words such as 'go' and 'give'. One cross-cultural study of English-speaking infants, Mandarin-speaking infants and Cantonese-speaking infants found that there were a lot of cross-cultural commonalities in the first words which are produced, and that six of the top 20 first words produced by infants are shared across all three of these languages (Tardif et al., 2008). These were 'Daddy', 'Mommy', 'Bye', 'Hi', 'UhOh' and 'WoofWoof'. These are the kinds of words which reflect objects or people that are immediately present in infants' environments, or which reflect infants' routines. This is consistent with theories of development such as Piaget's (explored in Chapter 2, Theoretical Perspectives) which suggest that at this stage infants' cognitive development reflects a reliance upon the immediate environment. Their language development here allows them to interact with their environment and is limited to that with which they have had direct experience.

Learning a new word is not as easy as you might think, though. Imagine you are walking down the street with a young child in a buggy, and the child points across the road and asks, 'What's that?' As you look across the street, you see a man walking a dog, and you reply, 'Doggy.' The first thing to consider here is whether your assumption about what the child was pointing to is correct. Perhaps the child was pointing at a bus stop or a tree! What effect is this exchange going to have on the child's word learning, do you think? In another situation, you might point to a dog and say to a child, 'There's a doggy!' The child may look in that direction, but do they really understand the communicative function of pointing? In other words, do they understand that by pointing at something you are trying to convey some information and not just direct their attention? Some researchers have tried to establish the age at which infants are really able to understand the communicative function of pointing, and the age at which they are able to produce communicative pointing themselves (e.g. Behne et al., 2012; Grafenhain et al., 2009). There is evidence that some, but not all children have developed these abilities at 12 months of age. Therefore it is important to bear in mind that when we use pointing with children, they may or may not be able to interpret what we are trying to communicate.

And how will we know whether the child has successfully learned a word or not? What would 'count' as successful word learning? When dealing with common nouns like 'dog', 'daddy', 'apple' or 'train', we want children eventually to arrive at an understanding of the appropriate object or category of objects, to which the referential word applies. In the example above, we want the child to use the word 'doggy' to refer to all dogs, but not to cats or cows. We would not want them to use the word 'doggy' to refer to bus stops or trees! But when children do use words incorrectly, it provides us with an insight into how their learning of that word has occurred. The next section explores what kinds of errors commonly occur in children's word learning, and what these can tell us about the process of learning words.

CUTTING EDGE

Immigrant children and second language acquisition

When they arrive in a new country one of the main barriers immigrant children must overcome is to learn a second language. A wealth of research exists exploring the process by which second languages are acquired (see Dixon et al., 2012, for a review), and it is clear that this is a challenging process in itself. Immigrant children may be at increased risk of social and family disadvantages (OECD, 2006) which may adversely affect their development in a variety of ways, but some recent research has suggested that for immigrant children with certain personalities, the acquisition of a second language may be even more of a challenge.

Chapter 10, Childhood Temperament and Behavioural Development, discusses the ways in which children's temperaments may differ, and how such differences manifest in tendencies to behave in certain ways. Previous research has shown that shy, inhibited children face particular social or emotional challenges (Letcher et al., 2009; Gazelle and Spangler, 2007) (see Chapter 16, Atypical Development, for a more detailed discussion of children and mental health). There are also various ways in which the development of shy children's first languages may differ from other children's (Evans, 2010).

However, one recent study has specifically explored the impact of shyness on second language acquisition in a group of preschool-age immigrant children (Keller et al., 2013). Standardised tests of language and an assessment of shyness were applied to a group of 330 preschoolers in Switzerland. Then 130 of these children were followed up 16 months later, giving the researchers longitudinal as well as cross-sectional data (see Chapter 3, Research Methods). The results showed that shy immigrant children's second language skills were significantly lower than their non-shy counterparts. When the follow-up tests were carried out 16 months later, all of the children's second language abilities had improved, but the shy children had improved less than the non-shy children.

Chapter 13, Adolescence, discusses the issue of identity and immigration. But the research discussed here has revealed other challenges which may be faced by some immigrant children in development. In second language learning, as in first language development, social interactions play a crucial role. A child's temperament is important for social development, and here we see how it can affect other aspects of development too.

Using children's errors to understand referential word learning

There are four common types of error which children make in their learning of referential words. These are underextension, overextension, overlap and mismatch.

Underextension

Underextension is when a child uses a word to refer to only a sub-group of the category of objects to which that word applies. For example, in the case of the situation described above, underextension would occur if the child subsequently uses the word 'doggy' to refer to that particular dog, each time he encounters it on the street, but does not apply it to any other dog that he comes across. This might seem odd, but let's think about what else could have happened in the example above. Imagine once again that you are walking this child in his buggy and he points across the road and says, 'What's that?' As you look across the road, you see your neighbour walking his dog, Buster. You respond, 'Buster.' In actual fact, Buster is just one exemplar of the broader category of dogs. Saying 'Buster' is correct, but saying 'Doggy' is also correct. How is the child supposed to understand the difference between these two possible responses, and recognise that the two words 'Buster' and 'Doggy' should be applied to a different range of objects? Clearly the process of learning a word and what it refers to is not as simple as it seems.

When children underextend their use of a word, then, we know that in the process of learning the word they have mistakenly associated it with only a sub-group of the category of objects to which it actually refers.

Overextension

Overextension is almost the opposite of underextension, and occurs when a child uses a word to refer to the whole category of objects to which it refers, but more besides! Again, let's think about the example above, and assume that you have responded, 'Doggy' when the child points across the road. Some time later, you pass another dog on the street, and the child shouts, 'Doggy!' But later still, you pass a cat and the child shouts, 'Doggy!' And when the child sees a goat on television the following day he shouts, 'Doggy!' These are examples of overextension.

Think back to when the child initially pointed across the road and said, 'What's that?' Your interpretation of the question was 'What's the name for that particular kind of animal?', and so you answered, 'Doggy.' It is possible, though, that to the child, the question 'What's that?' meant 'What's the name for hairy things with four legs?' and so your answer 'Doggy' is now the word that the child applies to refer to all instances of hairy things with four legs. The difficulty for us in interpreting the child's question 'What's that?' is that this simple two-word question could potentially mean many different things. This is something that we will explore more fully in the next section on the development of syntax. But when children overextend a word, we know that in the process of learning that word they have mistakenly associated it with more than just the category of objects to which it refers.

Overlap

Overlap can be thought of as a cross between underextension and overextension. Let's use a different example this time. Imagine you are with a young child at home and the child points to the mug of coffee you are holding and says, 'What's that?' You reply, 'Coffee.' The child then correctly says, 'Coffee' whenever she sees someone with a mug of coffee, but not when she sees someone with coffee in a cup or in a Styrofoam container. However, the child also says, 'Coffee' whenever she sees someone with a mug of tea. In this way the child is correctly using the word 'coffee' to refer to some appropriate referents, but not all appropriate referents (this is underextension) whilst also using the word to refer to some inappropriate referents as well (this is overextension). This tells us that in learning the meaning of the word 'coffee' this child has correctly associated it, but with only a sub-set of the category to which it refers, whilst simultaneously incorrectly associating it with referents from other categories as well.

Mismatch

Mismatch occurs when there are no correct associations between a word and its category of referents. For example, in the example above when the child pointed and said, 'What's that?', you answered, 'Coffee.' Let's imagine, though, that the child was not pointing at your coffee mug at all, and was instead pointing at the window behind you. If the child subsequently used the word 'coffee' to refer to windows, then this would be an example of mismatch.

When we think of examples like these, it is surprisingly easy to see how these kinds of errors could occur in the process of children's learning of referential word meanings. It is clear that children may initially simply associate words with specific instances of categories of objects, like when the child used the word 'doggy' to refer only to one particular dog that he encountered regularly on the street. To arrive at a more sophisticated understanding that the single word 'doggy' should be used to refer to an entire category of a particular type of animal, children need to be able to group words together and to recognise that some words refer to whole sets of related objects. This means that upon encountering any new dog that they have never seen before, they will nevertheless be able to name it correctly, and this allows their language to move beyond the world which is immediately surrounding them. This is why the kinds of conceptual insights which children achieve with things like the naming insight or an understanding of semantic relations, as discussed above, mean that children's language development can move beyond their immediate environment, and this is reflected in a more sophisticated understanding of language and words. Learning that words can be related to one another in groups provides a framework within which children can organise their words.

We also need to bear in mind that children may infer the meaning of new words from the language which surrounds them in everyday life, and not just from situations where they have directly asked for the meaning of an object. This leaves even more room for potential errors in word learning, but research has also shown that the more speech which surrounds a child, the better their vocabularies, so we should probably not worry too much about the possibilities which exist for errors, and view these as a normative part of the development of language.

For example, Huttenlocher et al. (1991) studied 22 children from the age of 14 months to 26 months. They observed the children in their daily activities with their mothers and took measures of the children's vocabularies as well as the amount of exposure to their parent's speech which each child had. The results of this study showed that the amount of exposure to their parent's speech was very important in explaining differences in vocabulary growth which were observed between different children. Think back to the example at the beginning of this chapter. If it is the case that children's vocabulary development is better if they have more exposure to speech then this might be an argument in favour of using buggies which face towards the person pushing them.

Syntactic development

Single-word utterances

Once infants have produced their first words, we have seen that their vocabularies then continue to grow. However, there comes a point where language development moves beyond just the accumulation of single words to the production of phrases where words are combined, and also to the application of rules to individual words. In this section, we will explore the development of the rules of grammar, which govern how words can be changed within a language and how they may be combined.

The period before children start to combine words is known as the one-word period. However, there is evidence to suggest that, even in this period, children are condensing more complex meanings into their single words, which go beyond just naming objects or labelling things. When words condense more complex meanings in this way they are known as holophrases. This is a difficult issue because ultimately it is difficult to know whether children intend to convey more complex meanings with their single-word utterances. Imagine, though, that a child is sitting in his high chair with his favourite toy, which then drops on to the floor. He points down at it on the ground and shouts, 'Teddy! Teddy!' Is this a simple case of his naming and labelling his toy, or is it possible that he is actually trying to convey something like 'I've dropped my teddy!' or 'I want my teddy back!'? The problem with these possible interpretations of a single-word utterance is where we draw the line. For example, could it be that the child is actually trying to convey, 'My favourite teddy has fallen on the floor and I can't reach it. Could someone pick it up and give it back to me?' Something this complex seems unlikely. However, if we are prepared to attribute some more complex meanings to holophrases then we need to beware of the dangers of over-estimating the complexity of what they are likely to mean. In other words, in doing so we are attributing children with an understanding of language (comprehension) which far exceeds their ability to themselves produce language (production). Having said this, it is generally accepted that production does lag behind comprehension, at least during the second year of life, and some psycholinguists suggest that children may comprehend between five and ten times as many words as they actually produce (Benedict, 1979).

Combining two words

Children begin to put words together in combinations from about 18 months of age. Slobin (1972) reported that children are able to convey an immense amount of meaning with just two words, through the use of accompanying gestures and by their tone. For example, two words allow a child to indicate possession by saying 'My sweets', or to attribute features to something by saying, for example, 'Big car'. Children can convey information about location, by saying 'Book there' or can attribute someone with an action, like 'Mama walk'. The phrase 'Hit you' conveys a direct action of theirs to someone else, whilst saying 'Give papa' conveys an indirect action towards someone else. They can also ask simple questions, like 'Where ball?' and reveal an understanding of negation, through phrases such as 'Not wolf'.

> **Definition**
>
> Holophrase: a single word which expresses some more complex idea.

These sorts of two-word phrases were observed by Slobin (1972) in children from a variety of countries whose first languages included English, Samoan, Russian and Finnish, and the similarity of this process of development between children speaking a variety of languages lends support to those theories which argue that there is some sort of universal form underlying the development of language generally. Such two-word phrases carry a significant amount of meaning because the words which are combined tend to be nouns, verbs and adjectives. Words like 'in', 'on', 'the' and 'and' are not generally featured in these two-word combinations, but despite their omission children are able to communicate very effectively. For this reason, such speech is often called telegraphic speech because of its similarity to old-fashioned telegrams, where unnecessary words are omitted yet a great deal of meaning is retained.

Combining three and four words

After the end of the second year, children begin to put three and four words in combination. Their word combinations are still condensed and telegraphic in nature, and are not yet grammatically correct. However, it is interesting that despite this their speech contains evidence that they already understand some of the rules which govern their language. Earlier in this chapter we saw that some of the mistakes which children make in their use of referential words are useful in helping us to understand the process of acquiring new words. In terms of syntactical development, once again the errors which children make provide us with insights into the process of learning the rules of language. For example, in this stage of development we would not be surprised to hear a child say 'sheeps' or 'mouses' as the plural forms for these animals. To us this may seem like an amusing and insignificant mistake, but actually it tells us that the child has learned a rule – namely that adding /-s/ to the end of a noun makes it into a plural. The child has not yet learned that in English there are exceptions to this rule which need to be learned separately, but her error tells us that she is already making progress in the learning of the rules which govern the English language. Jean Berko Gleason, a well-known psycholinguist, carried out a classic study in this area in 1958, where she developed a test commonly known as the Wug Test, which allows for an understanding of how children develop their rules of word formation.

In the Wug Test, children are shown a picture of a single creature with a fictional name. Next, they are shown more of these creatures and asked what they are. The child is therefore forced to produce a plural version of a noun which they could never have heard before since it is fictional, and their answers allow for an insight into how they understand the rules which govern, for example, the construction of plurals. Figure 5.3 shows an example of a stimulus used in Berko's (1958) original study. The results showed that the majority of children correctly produced the word 'wugs' as the plural form of the fictional word 'wug'.

Figure 5.3 Example of stimulus from Berko's (1958) Wug Test.

Source: http://childes.psy.cmu.edu/topics/wugs/01wug.jpg

Definition

Telegraphic speech: speech consisting of phrases of a small number of words (usually nouns, verbs and adjectives) combined to make sense, but without complex grammatical forms.

Similar errors are made in verb construction, and particularly in the creation of the past tense. For example, you might hear a child say 'I runned' or 'we swammed'. Again, this reveals an understanding that adding /-ed/ to the end of a verb makes it into the past tense, although the child once more has not yet learned that there are exceptions to this rule where verbs are constructed differently.

> **STOP AND THINK**
>
> **Going further**
>
> Think about how these kinds of errors relate to different theories of language development considered earlier.
>
> - Could such errors be the result of simple learning or imitation?
> - Does it seem likely that something like a LAD could account for these kinds of rule-based errors?
> - What other cognitive developments do you think a child would need to have undergone before reaching this level of language ability?

It is interesting that, in many aspects of semantic and syntactic development discussed so far, there seems to be a difference between boys and girls. One recent study which examined data from more than 13 000 children under the age of 3 years, found that girls are ahead of boys in terms of their use of early communicative gestures, their productive vocabulary and their word combinations (Eriksson et al., 2012). The data came from children in ten different language communities (including French, Swedish, Croatian and Basque), and the difference between the genders was apparent across all of the languages. In addition, whilst the gender difference was only small for the youngest children, it seems to get bigger as children get older. You might want to think about what could be responsible for these differences between boys and girls.

A later development in syntax comes when children begin to re-order their sentences to construct questions. For example, a younger child may say, 'Mummy eat?' as a question, by raising his pitch at the end of the phrase. By 3 or 4 years this may have developed to something like 'What Mummy is eating?' which represents a syntactical development with the inclusion of 'what' at the beginning of the phrase to denote a question. However, this child has still yet to learn that the auxiliary verb needs to be 'inverted' and exchanged with the subject of the sentence so that it is transformed from 'mummy is eating' to 'is mummy eating' when forming a question. By the time children move into their early school years, their use of irregular verbs and grammatical rules in general will have increased dramatically, so that they are now competent language users capable of constructing complex utterances which convey complex ideas and meanings.

The development of pragmatics

The pragmatic system is that part of language concerned with its appropriate use in social situations, our ability to extract and to convey meaning which goes beyond just syntax and semantics (for more information on pragmatics, see Recommended Reading). As this develops, children become more sensitive to the needs of other people in conversations, and show a greater awareness of, for example, what other people know and do not know. This may be linked to developments in other areas of cognition, such as theory of mind (see Chapter 8, Theory of Mind), and in Piagetian theory the development of non-egocentric thought. One clear example of this is when children begin to show an awareness of the difference between 'a' and 'the' in their conversations with others. Let's imagine you were having a conversation with your friend. They say, 'I was sitting at the bus stop last night, and the man just started laughing.' Your immediate response might be to ask, 'What man?' Since your friend had not introduced a man into the story previously, you could not have known that there was even a man there, and so it feels as though there is a step missing in the chronology of the tale. Yet this use of 'the man' or 'the dog' is common in younger children's speech, and seems to be the result of their assumption that other people know what they know. In Piaget's theory of development this may be due to egocentrism, and reflects a younger child's lack of awareness that other people have thoughts, ideas and perspectives which are different from their own. Once children develop this awareness,

LIFESPAN

Pragmatics and working memory

Some researchers have discussed the importance of working memory to understanding the pragmatic aspects of language, and have found that adults with damage to their brain's right hemisphere have problems with their pragmatic skills because of difficulties with their working memory capacities (e.g. Tomkins et al., 1994; Stemmer and Joanette, 1998). Pragmatics involve awareness and understanding of the particular context in which we find ourselves, in order to infer some of the meaning of conversations. Inferring that someone is joking or being sarcastic, for example, requires that we integrate several varied aspects of the context in which we find ourselves. It is thought that this places complex demands on working memory, and that this therefore affects the pragmatic aspects of language.

Previous research has shown that people with dyslexia also have a reduced working memory capacity (e.g. Baddeley, 1998), and several studies have found lower pragmatic competence in adults with dyslexia. For example, Griffiths (2007) compared groups of dyslexic and non-dyslexic adults' on four tests from the Right Hemisphere Language Battery (Bryan, 1995), which assess pragmatic competence, as well as on a self-report pragmatic competence questionnaire and on the Dyslexia Adult Screening Test (DAST). Participants ranged in age from 18 to 45 years and had to show their understanding of metaphorical (as opposed to literal) information, inferential storylines (where they had to extract information from stories which had not been made explicit) and joke punch lines (where they had to choose the correct one from four possibilities). All of these are examples of pragmatic understanding.

Griffiths found that the dyslexic group consistently misunderstood aspects of pragmatics more often than the non-dyslexic group. She also found that there was a correlation between increasing pragmatic impairment and performance on the part of the DAST which tests working memory: the poorer the working memory, the greater the pragmatic impairment. The study of pragmatics therefore clearly demonstrates the ways in which language and cognition interact across the lifespan.

Definition

Dyslexia: a learning difficulty which affects a person's ability to read despite otherwise normal levels of intelligence.

---

they seem to recognise the need to introduce 'a man' into a story before then referring to 'the man' and this represents a significant improvement in the success of their conversations. Even so, some 5-year-olds still do not consistently use 'a' before 'the'. It is therefore an important part of the development of pragmatics, and another example of the ways in which language and cognition may interact.

The ability to repair faulty communications or to put right misunderstandings is a part of the pragmatic system which has been observed in children as young as 33 months. When there is a breakdown in communication, a sensitivity to the amount of information needed to put things right provides an important indicator of the maturity of the child's pragmatic system. For example, imagine you approach a woman on the street to ask for directions. You say, 'Where is the nearest tube station?' If she replies, 'What?', how will you respond? It is likely that you would interpret her response as indicating that she has generally failed to understand you at all, and that you would therefore repeat the whole of your question. On the other hand, if she responded by saying, 'Where is the nearest what?', you would interpret this as indicating that she had simply failed to understand a part of what you had said, and that you would therefore repeat just that part, by saying, 'Tube station.' Your mature pragmatic system therefore enables you to appreciate the difference between general and more specific queries for information, and to modify your provision of additional information based on those differences. In one study of how this sensitivity to conversational queries develops, researchers used a talking toy robot who responded to children's utterances with either general or specific queries (e.g. 'What?' or 'Baby's eating what?') (Ferrier et al., 2000). The researchers found that at 27 months of age, children were more likely to respond to both of these types of query with complete repetitions of their previous utterances, whilst at 33 months of age, children would respond to general queries with complete repetitions, and would give only the necessary partial information in response to specific queries. This illustrates an important development in children's pragmatics within the third year of life.

By the time they reach school age, children already have a well-developed pragmatic system, but there are still ways in which this continues to develop further. For example, some recent research showed that between the ages of 5 and 10 years, children's ability to recognise others' emotions from vocal cues improves considerably (Sauter et al., 2013). Non-verbal vocalisations (such as laughs, sighs and grunts) and speech (spoken three-digit numbers) inflected with a variety of emotions (such as amusement, relief, anger, surprise and fear) were presented to children as auditory stimuli. The children had to select an appropriate picture showing the corresponding facial cues to what they had heard. Performance was already good for 5-year-old children (average score of 78% correct for non-verbal vocalisations and 53% for speech), but continued to get better with age so that by 10 years the average scores were 84% correct for non-verbal vocalisations and 72% for speech. So the ability to understand the emotional content of words, irrespective of their meaning, continues to improve through the school years.

Another way in which the pragmatic system develops is in relation to the use of language and humour. Learning to tell jokes or funny stories, as well as the ability to understand when someone else is using humour, requires the ability to use language more creatively, and goes beyond just an understanding of word meaning and grammar. Telling jokes often requires a more subtle understanding of the ways in which words can have double meanings. Some types of joke (like knock-knock jokes, for example) have a very structured form whereby two individuals engage in a back-and-forth exchange with five stages. Learning these five stages of a knock-knock joke represents an important development in the child's learning of the 'rules' of conversation. The child is learning that words and sentences need to follow certain patterns and sequences in order for successful social exchanges to take place. Some differences have been found in the use of verbal humour in children with and without hearing loss (Nwokah et al., 2013), and this is thought to be because children with hearing loss will have had fewer opportunities to be exposed to the subtleties of language. Another study (Hoicka and Gattis, 2012) suggests that the special infant-directed speech we use with young children might reflect humorous content. When mothers read stories or picture books to their infants, visual humour and sentences with humorous content were communicated using speech that was louder, of a higher pitch and slower, than with pictures or content that were sincere. Motherese may therefore help with the development of the pragmatic system, as well as just with word learning. And once again we can see how the earliest interactions between infants and caregivers pave the way for later, more complex developments in language ability.

Earlier in this chapter, we discussed the ways in which early social interactions assist with the later development of children's language, and in this context we explored how children may be prepared for turn taking in conversations through some of their earliest interactions with their caregivers. Turn taking is an important part of pragmatics, since conversations are generally quite well-organised interactions, and research has shown that normal adult conversation contains very few noticeable overlaps or interruptions (see, for example, Levinson, 1983). Understanding the rules which govern turn taking in conversation is important for successful conversations. For example, knowing when in a conversation it is possible and appropriate for there to be a change in speaker, how to go about taking your turn in a conversation and what to do to correct mistakes in the turn-taking sequence, all enable there to be fairly trouble-free transitions between speakers (Sacks et al., 1974). Infants' early interactions lay the groundwork for later social interactions, including conversations, and as such are an important part of the development of the social side of language.

Earlier in the chapter we discussed the lateralisation of brain function in relation to language. One interesting point to note here is that in fact not all language abilities are located in the left hemisphere. When it comes to pragmatics and the social side of language, the right hemisphere is involved. The fact that both 'sides' of the brain are involved in language emphasises just what a complex human function it is.

CASE STUDY

Early pragmatics in everyday life

Louise is 4½ years old and enjoying a day at home with her mum. Mum's friend, Alison, pops round and the three of them decide to take a walk to the park. Whilst pushing Louise on the swings, Mum and Alison carry on a conversation. After a few minutes, Louise asks to get off the swing and then says, 'Mummy, I want to talk to you.' She motions for Mum to bend down and then whispers in her ear, 'When you are talking to Alison, I think you have forgotten about me.'

- Why did Louise whisper instead of talking out loud?
- What does this tell us about her understanding and awareness of other people?
- What could we say about the development of Louise's pragmatic system on the basis of this example?
- How might this link to other aspects of Louise's cognitive development that you have read about elsewhere in the book?

SUMMARY

At the beginning of this chapter, we set out to discover what language is and what elements it comprises. We have seen that language is more than just speech and grammar. It is a logical yet creative symbolic system, and its development is a complicated business, dependent upon developments in four component parts: phonology, semantics, syntax and pragmatics.

The foundations of language are laid in infants' earliest social interactions in the pre-verbal stage, and these may pave the way for later developments. Early exposure to language assists with the specialisation of infants' phonological awareness so that they can discriminate between categories of sounds in their native language. The special kind of speech which adults direct towards infants may also help with developing language by exposing children to it in a simplified and more accessible form. Infants may get some preparation for the social side of language through patterns of turn taking which are established during feeding or activities which involve joint attention.

The abilities of infants in the first months of life force us to consider what language abilities or capacities children enter the world with, and how much of language is learned. Some of the mistakes which children make during the process of learning language may suggest the existence of an innate mechanism which allows for the acquisition of language generally, but which depends upon input from the external world to fuel the acquisition process. The language which children are exposed to from infancy affects the development of language in various ways, but there is also evidence that developments in cognition and thinking more generally may underpin the development of language.

Before children can begin to learn words, they must be able to recognise and produce the speech sounds of their language. The learning of referential words is a complicated process, with lots of room for errors. It may be facilitated by more general cognitive developments which allow for a dramatic acceleration in vocabulary growth in the second year of life, and other cognitive developments may be necessary before children can learn and understand words which relate to abstract concepts. Even once children have learned lots of words, there is still work to be done in learning how to combine those words in grammatically correct ways. Children progress through combinations of two, three and four words, using condensed and telegraphic forms of speech, before eventually being able to produce fully formed grammatically correct sentences. The rules of grammar may be acquired through some innate language acquisition device which is sensitive to the regularities in the adult language which children are exposed to, and some of the mistakes which children make as they move towards a full grasp of the rules of syntax can provide us with useful insights into the process that they go through. How to use language appropriately in different social contexts and how to interpret and communicate meanings which go beyond the mere semantics of the words themselves is another important aspect of the development of language. Speech and grammar alone cannot ensure successful communication, but the development of pragmatics enables children to be confident and competent users of language in the social world.

REVIEW QUESTIONS

1. Discuss what the possible benefits to children's language development might be of backward-facing prams and buggies.
2. In what ways might infant-directed speech or 'motherese' facilitate children's language development?
3. Compare and contrast Nativist with learning theory explanations of language development. Which do you think is more convincing, and why?
4. Discuss some of the ways in which cognitive development and the development of language may interact.

RECOMMENDED READING

To read more about Patricia Kuhl's work on the perception of speech sounds by non-human animals, see:

Kuhl, P. K. (1988). Auditory perception and the evolution of speech. *Human Evolution*, 3, 19–43.

Kuhl, P. K., & Miller, J. D. (1975). Speech perception by the chinchilla: Voiced–voiceless distinction in alveolar plosive consonants. *Science*, 190, 69–72.

Kuhl, P. K., & Padden, D. M. (1982). Enhanced discriminability at the phonetic boundary for the voicing feature in macaques. *Perception and Psychophysics*, 32, 542–550.

Kuhl, P. K., & Padden, D. M. (1983). Enhanced discriminability at the phonetic boundaries for the place feature in macaques. *Journal of the Acoustical Society of America*, 73, 1003–1010.

For more information about infant-directed speech or 'motherese' in different languages and cultures, see:

Lieven, E. V. M. (1994). Crosslinguistic and cross-cultural aspects of language addressed to children. In C. Gallaway & Brian J. Richards (Eds.). *Input and Interaction in Language Acquisition* (56–73). Cambridge: Cambridge University Press.

For more information about Broca's area, see:

Grodzinsky, Y., & Amunts, K. (Eds.) (2006). *Broca's Region*. Oxford: Oxford University Press.

For more information about the development of pragmatics, see:

Ninio, A., & Snow, C. E. (1996). *Pragmatic Development*. Boulder, CO: Westview Press.

RECOMMENDED WEBSITES

To find out more about Paul MacLean's Triune Brain theory, see:

http://www.kheper.net/topics/intelligence/MacLean.htm

To find out more about the ideas of linguist Noam Chomsky, see:

http://www.chomsky.info/

To find out more about the developmental milestones which typically developing children are expected to reach at different ages, see:

http://childdevelopmentinfo.com/child-development/language_development

To find out more about cases of children who develop without the influence of human interaction, see:

http://www.toptenz.net/top-10-feral-children.php

On the importance of language development from birth to age 3:

http://www.literacytrust.org.uk/talk_to_your_baby

Chapter 6
Memory and intelligence

Learning outcomes

After reading this chapter, and with further recommended reading, you should be able to:

1. Explain what memory is, what processes it consists of and what different types of memory children have.
2. Describe research into memory abilities in infancy, and explain how memory develops through childhood, and what might be responsible for different instances of children's forgetting.
3. Discuss the difficulties which are associated with traditional approaches to intelligence testing in children.
4. Compare and contrast some different conceptualisations of intelligence.
5. Discuss some of the ways in which memory and intelligence develop and change across the adult lifespan.

The pub quiz

Karen, Raymond and Paul have formed a team called 'The Fourth Floor' and are taking part in a pub quiz. The quizmaster asks questions about subjects such as music, sport, history, entertainment, geography, the human body, animals and food. For example, which composer's eighth symphony is also known as the 'Unfinished Symphony'? Which country hosted the World Cup Soccer Finals in 1930? All three members of 'The Fourth Floor' have university undergraduate degrees, and between them they also have several masters and even a doctoral degree. Yet they struggle to answer many of the questions!

- What explanations could there be for their difficulties?
- Do these well-educated individuals lack intelligence?
- Perhaps they simply cannot remember the answers?
- Would winning this quiz make you the most intelligent person in the pub?
- Does remembering the details of every World Cup final make you intelligent?

Introduction

Cognitive psychologists study the way in which we process information from the world around us. To understand cognitive development, we need to study the development of memory and intelligence as these are important parts of cognition. Our memory can be thought of as a database within which knowledge and information are stored. Prior to storage, information has to be processed. This can be thought of as similar to identifying what the content of a particular piece of data is and what it means, and deciding how it should be entered into the database. Then we have to be able to get information back out of the database when it is required. This will depend on how efficient our original entering and recording of the data was, how good a system of cross-referencing we have and how easily we can track down a particular source of data when we want it. Intelligence is a general term used to describe how efficiently we are able to process information and includes, for example, how quickly we can solve problems or respond to a new situation and how fast we can get information out of storage when required. Memory and intelligence are therefore closely linked to one another, and this chapter will explore how each of them develops.

What is memory?

Memory is an important part of our cognitive processes, as mentioned above. It has been said that our individual identities are made up of the sum total of all of our experiences. If this is true then who would we be if we could not remember any of those experiences? Piaget's theories of cognitive development (referred to previously in Chapter 2, Theoretical Perspectives) continue to dominate developmental psychology. He suggests that for infants, the primary focus is on the world which is immediately present to them, and that previously stored information does not influence their behaviour until late infancy or early childhood. In the first part of this chapter, we will explore what more contemporary research has revealed about the memory abilities of infants. By adulthood, we have a sophisticated memory system which stores all sorts of knowledge and information of many different types (see Table 6.1). For example, our memories may contain factual information, such as the date of the Battle of Trafalgar or how many players make up a football team. This kind of stored knowledge is called semantic memory. Our memories also contain knowledge about ourselves, our past experiences and lives and things which have happened to us. This is known as autobiographical memory.

Some of the memories we have are explicit, in that we can talk about them and declare what we remember. We also have implicit memories, such as procedural memories for skills and abilities, like riding a bike or driving a car. Our memories also contain scripts for procedures or events – for example, what happens at a dinner party or a university lecture. All of these memories make up who we are and what we know and will be discussed in the first part of this chapter, which provides an introduction to the processes involved in memory, explores research on the memory abilities of children from infancy onwards, and discusses how these processes develop through childhood.

Memory is not just one thing, and it is more useful to think of memory as a system made up of several different component processes (see Figure 6.1). At its most basic level, our memory system consists of three major component processes. Information is taken in from the

STOP AND THINK

Reflection

- What is your earliest memory? How old were you then?
- Are you sure that you really remember this, or do you really just remember what other people have told you about this? Is there any way that we could tell the difference?
- Do you think you have any memories prior to that which could be accessed?

Definitions

Semantic memory: long-term memory for facts, concepts and meanings.
Autobiographical memory: an individual's personal memory for their life experiences and events and for information about themselves.
Procedural memory: implicit, unconscious long-term memory for skills or how to do things.
Scripts: mental representations which we have of certain types of event, which include our general expectations of such events based on prior experience.

Table 6.1 Key features of some of the main types of memories.

Type of memory	Explicit or implicit?	Main features	Example
Episodic	Explicit	Memory for events or episodes	Remembering what you had for breakfast this morning
Semantic	Explicit	Memory for knowledge and facts	Remembering the date of the Great Fire of London
Procedural	Implicit	Memory for skills or procedures	Sitting down at a computer and remembering how to type
Autobiographical	Explicit	Memory for our own life experiences, our interpretations of those experiences and personal facts about ourselves	Remembering the events of your wedding day, how you felt and what it meant to you; also being able to answer 'yes' to the question, 'Are you married?'

WHAT IS MEMORY?

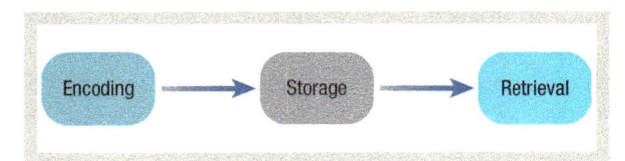

Figure 6.1 The three stages of memory.

world around us, and this process is the part of memory known as *encoding*. That information then needs to be kept, which is the process known as *storage*. Initially, information enters our short-term memory store, but may eventually pass on to our long-term memory store. Finally, we need to be able to bring that information back out of storage when it is required, and that process is known as *retrieval*. Cognitive psychologists also talk about information being held in *working memory* – this is the idea that new and existing information often needs to be manipulated, re-organised and processed in various ways in order for us to understand things, solve problems or make decisions. Our working memory may therefore determine how successfully we can do these things.

Not only are there these three processes involved in memory, but there are several different types of information which our memory systems deal with, as we have mentioned already. Imagine bumping into someone in the street that you recognise. You may remember their name as well as other information about them, such as where you know them from, what they do for a living or what colour their hair was the last time you saw them. Whether you were aware of it or not prior to bumping into them, if all those things came to mind when you met them, then all of that information about that person must have been encoded and stored in your memory.

In contrast, each time we get into a car and drive off, we are accessing a different type of memory again. When driving, we do not search our memories for knowledge and information about cars, gears and motion. Imagine what a complex process driving would be if we did! Instead we access procedural memories – implicit memories that we have for actions or procedures which we have learned at some point, but which have now become automatic

Definitions

Encoding: the first stage of information processing in memory, where information is taken in via the senses.
Storage: the second stage of information processing in memory, by which information is retained for short or long periods of time.
Retrieval: the third stage of information processing in memory, by which information is brought back out of storage and recalled.
Working memory: a theoretical set of structures and processes where information is temporarily stored and processed.

CASE STUDY

Early memory in everyday life

Baby Ella is 5 months old. Her mum and dad have gone out for the evening, leaving Ella in the care of Marie, a family friend who has agreed to babysit. Ella sleeps for most of the evening. When she wakes up crying, she is easily comforted by Marie, despite the fact that the two of them have met only six or seven times in Ella's short life. Marie feeds Ella a bottle and then they play together and watch television until Ella's parents return home. As her mum enters the living room, Ella catches sight of her and immediately her face breaks into a smile. Dad enters the room behind Mum, and when Ella sees him her smile broadens. She gurgles and begins to kick her legs and, as Dad lifts her from the babysitter's arms, Ella lets out a squeal.

- What does all of this mean in terms of Ella's memory?
- Does baby Ella really recognise her mother and father?
- At what age would she first have been able to do this?
- What kinds of knowledge and information about her parents does Ella really have stored in her memory?

and can be carried out without information needing to be consciously retrieved. Our memories also store *episodic memories* for events or occurrences which have happened in the past. Remembering your tenth birthday party or your first day at school would be examples of episodic memories. So our memory systems enable the encoding, storage and retrieval of very different types of information, all of which are vital for our functioning in the human world. Yet memory is like an iceberg, in that the parts which we can easily retrieve are often only a very small proportion of what there actually is. Much of it is hidden from view or not easily accessible, and the problem may be in trying to get to it.

When we forget something, that forgetting may be due to a failure in any one of the three major parts of our memory system mentioned already, and it is not always obvious which one of the three is responsible for the failure. If we are unable to recall the name of the person we bumped into in the street, is it because their name was never successfully encoded in the first place? Or could it be that the information was encoded, but that there has been a failure in its storage? Or alternatively, could it be that the information was encoded and has been stored, but that we are experiencing problems in retrieval and are unable to get it out of storage? Difficulties in separating out these three parts of memory can make it tricky to study how children's memory develops too. With children who are not yet able to talk, this is even more difficult. The lack of language ability in infants and young children means that researchers have had to develop novel and innovative ways of studying memory that do not rely upon the ability to communicate verbally. We will explore all of these issues in the development of memory within the first part of this chapter.

research technique which would enable infant memory to be studied systematically for the first time. Fantz noticed that when presented with pairs of *stimuli*, chimps spend different amounts of time looking at each member of the pair (Fantz, 1956). Secondly, he noticed that infants' preferences for different stimuli change over periods of time, so that eventually familiar stimuli are given less attention and new or unfamiliar stimuli are given more attention (Fantz, 1964). These influential observations by Fantz provided a method of judging whether infants remember things which they have seen before, even before those infants are able to talk, and is called the *preferential looking method* (see Chapter 4, Prenatal Development and Infancy). This pioneering work on *visual recognition memory* led to the development of the visual paired comparison (VPC) task, which has paved the way for a wealth of infant memory research subsequently. The Research Methods box explains this particular task in more detail.

Using techniques such as these, it has been possible to gain some insights into the memory abilities of even new-born infants. Joseph Fagan, a colleague of Fantz, first used the VPC task and presented infants of between 3 and 6 months of age with a target visual stimulus (a black and white pattern) (Fagan, 1970). He then tested the infants' recognition memory by presenting a pair of stimuli, including the original target, and measuring how long the infants looked at each one. Because they looked longer at the novel stimulus, Fagan inferred that infants recognised the target as familiar and that they therefore have a recognition memory for it. You may want to refer back to Chapter 4 to remind yourself of other research methods which have been used by developmental psychologists to study infants.

Memory in children

What can infants remember?

In the 1950s and 1960s, Robert Fantz, a psychologist studying both chimpanzees and infants, came up with a

Definition

Episodic memory: memory for specific events or occurrences, including details of time, place and emotions associated with it.

Definitions

Stimulus (plural stimuli): anything which elicits or evokes a response, such as a sound, a picture, a taste or a smell.
Preferential looking method: a procedure for testing infant perceptual and cognitive skills by observing viewing preferences for two or more items.
Visual recognition memory: memory for a visual stimulus which has been seen before. This type of memory can be assessed from very early in life and so is often used in infant memory research.

RESEARCH METHODS

Exploring infant visual recognition memory

Visual recognition memory can be assessed by placing an infant in front of a single visual display. In recent research, such displays are usually on computer screens, and so the amount of time which the infant spends looking at the display can be carefully controlled (see the photo below for an example).

In visual paired comparison (VPC) tasks, after the infant has viewed a display there is a delay, and they are then presented with two displays at the same time, one of which is the familiar one, and one of which is new. The time which the infant spends looking at each of these two displays can be measured. Since Fantz and others' pioneering work has shown that infants have a preference for, and look longer at, novel or unfamiliar stimuli, it is possible to infer whether an infant perceives one of the displays to be familiar. If so, then we can judge them to have retained some sort of memory for that display.

It is important to recognise that this research method assesses recognition memory. Responses to a stimulus which has been seen before allow us to judge that the child recognises it and we can infer that they have a memory of it. It is an appropriate method to use with pre-verbal infants because it does not rely upon their ability to tell us what they remember. In contrast, asking a child to tell us as many words as they can remember from a previously presented list would be an example of free recall. Here the onus is on the child to retrieve as many items as they can from memory without being provided with any additional cues as to what may or may not have been on the original list. Sometimes participants in memory research will fail to remember things using recall, but using a recognition technique they will be able to identify more items correctly.

Another technique which assists psychologists in research with infants is the use of a specially designed non-nutritive dummy which infants can suck. Non-nutritive sucking is sucking which occurs without any milk being given. The rates at which infants suck can be carefully measured. For example, Wolff (1968a) found that 4-day-old infants' baseline suck-rate was 2.13 sucks per second. Researchers have found that suck-rates decline when infants become familiar with a stimulus. Their suck-rate can therefore be measured to assess whether they perceive something to be familiar or unfamiliar. It is also possible to link the dummy to visual or auditory displays in such a way that infants can themselves control what they see or hear, by varying their suck-rate.

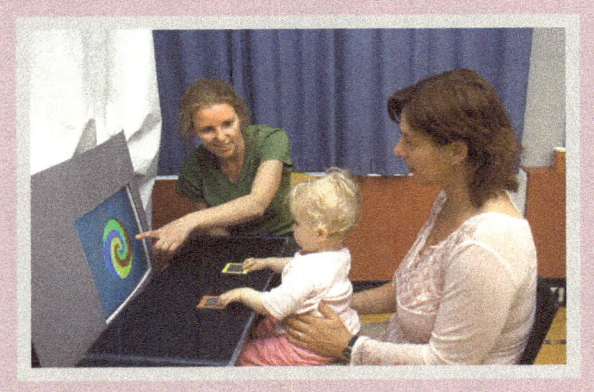

Infant viewing a visual display.
Source: Alamy Images/Picture Partners

Other research has since suggested that this kind of recognition memory exists in infants even younger than 3–6 months. It has also been shown to extend to senses other than just vision, as explored in Chapter 4. For example, DeCasper and Fifer (1980) carried out an important piece of research using the non-nutritive dummies, discussed in the Research Methods box, with infants who were no more than 3 days old. The dummies were linked to recordings of both the infant's own mother and another infant's mother. Depending on how fast they sucked, the infant could control whose voice they heard. Each infant in this study had had less than 12 hours' contact with their mother since birth (they spent most of their time in a nursery and were cared for primarily by staff), yet they still showed a clear preference for their own mother's voice, and would modify their rate of sucking in order to hear her rather than another mother. This suggests that these infants at just 3 days old already recognised their mother's voice and could distinguish it from another voice. This would not have been possible if the infants did not have some stored memory for their mother's voice.

DeCasper and Fifer (1980) suggested that it could have been exposure to their mothers' voices whilst in the womb which led to these findings. Many researchers have shown that to understand the development of infant memory, we have to go back even further, to the prenatal period (see Chapter 4). For example, DeCasper and Spence (1986) asked pregnant women to read a particular piece of text aloud twice a day during the last six weeks of their pregnancy. When their infants were 2 or 3 days old, a non-nutritive dummy was linked to audio recordings of the piece which had been read to them, as well as to an unfamiliar piece. The infants could control which one they heard by adjusting their suck-rate. It was found that infants would alter their suck-rate to hear the familiar piece of text, and that this was the case regardless of whose voice was on the recording reading the text. In other words, it did not matter whether their mother was the one reading the piece or not, they would alter their suck-rate to hear the familiar one. They were not just showing a preference for a familiar voice, but had encoded complex verbal information prior to their birth. The fact that the study took place two or three days after birth tells us that these infants had the capacity for memory storage for at least that long, as well as encoding and retrieval capabilities.

In addition to auditory and visual memories, some research suggests that infant memory extends to touch and feel (e.g. Catherwood, 1993) as well as to smell (Cernoch and Porter, 1985). All of this shows that infants have the ability to encode information even before birth, that they can store information for at least a couple of days even just after birth and that they can access that stored information sufficiently to be able to recognise familiar stimuli straight from birth.

The exact nature of the memories which infants have is not known, and neither is it clear whether an infant is aware at a conscious level of having viewed a particular display or having heard a particular piece of prose being read before. In studies of adult memory, a distinction is made between explicit memories and implicit memories. Explicit memories are those which we can consciously and deliberately recollect, such as our date of birth or the offside rule. Implicit memories are those which we know must be stored because our behaviour reveals them, but which we are not necessarily conscious of having. For example, I can't consciously remember what my neighbour's living room wallpaper is like and so I can't describe it; but when I am visiting someone else's house I suddenly recognise that the wallpaper in their dining room is the same as my neighbour has in her living room. My recognition of this means that I must have stored the information about my neighbour's wallpaper, even though I could not consciously recall it. Because their language abilities have not developed enough for them to be able to articulate what they can and what they cannot remember, it is very difficult for us to make judgements about the exact nature of very young children's memories, and how they compare with the kinds of memory that we have as adults.

How does memory develop with age?

The section above suggests that even very young infants have some memory abilities, and this section explores what it is within the memory systems of children that changes over time, and what gives rise to improvement in memory abilities from childhood to adulthood. To better understand this process of development, we need to look once again at the different processes which make up memory – encoding, storage and retrieval – and examine whether children get better at taking information in as they get older, whether they get better at retaining it, whether they get better at retrieving it or whether improvements in all of these areas of memory occur.

Developments in encoding

Encoding and retrieval are closely linked and so, as we discuss one, we will inevitably discuss the other. This is because we can only really assess how things are encoded into memory by looking at how they are subsequently retrieved from memory. One aspect of encoding which may improve memory as children get older is the speed at which it happens. Using visual recognition memory techniques, such as the VPC task explored earlier in this chapter, research has shown that younger infants need longer periods of time for initial encoding to occur before they will show the kinds of preference for novel stimuli we discussed previously, thus demonstrating memory for the previously viewed stimulus. For example, Morgan and Hayne (2006) showed children visual displays with two identical stimuli. Children therefore became familiar with that stimulus during this familiarisation phase. In the subsequent test phase of the experiment, the familiar stimulus and a novel stimulus were presented and the researchers measured how long they spent looking at the novel stimulus. Two groups of children took part – one group of 1-year-olds and a second group of 4-year-olds. The length of the familiarisation phase was either 5 seconds, 10 seconds or 30 seconds, and their memories for the stimuli were tested either immediately, after a delay of 24 hours or after one week. The results showed that when tested immediately, encoding occurred for the older children with a familiarisation phase of just 5 seconds. In contrast, the younger infants required 10 seconds of familiarisation in order to encode information. This suggests that older children take shorter times to encode information successfully.

In addition, as we have mentioned above, encoding and retrieval are very closely linked. One way in which this has been demonstrated is through research which shows that the amount of time available for initial encoding affects the length of time for which information will be retained and then successfully retrieved. Morgan and Hayne's (2006) work showed that not only did older children require shorter encoding times overall, but that for all children, the longer the encoding time, the longer the time for which information will be retained. The 1-year-olds in their study showed retention times of 24 hours with the longest (30 second) familiarisation phase, but not with the familiarisation phase of 10 seconds. These kinds of change in encoding and retention with age have been demonstrated by other research studies as well (e.g. Hayne, 2004; Rose et al., 2004a).

From a wealth of research on adult memory, we also know that not all of the information which our senses are exposed to will be encoded at all. Imagine that you spend the evening in a restaurant with friends. Upon leaving the restaurant, one of your friends comments on how much he liked the tablecloth. You realise that you cannot even recall what colour the tablecloth was. You would certainly have seen it, so the information about the tablecloth must have filtered through your visual system, but it has been encoded in such a way that it is not available to you later for conscious recall (although the next Stop and Think box touches upon one method by which this could be addressed). In this way, the nature of the initial encoding affects how easily that information is available for recall. The world around us contains far too much information for us to be able to take all of it in, and so attention allows us to focus on certain things, to the exclusion of others. This means that we make judgements, consciously or unconsciously, about what is most important in a given situation. At the restaurant, if you focused on the conversation and the food, then other information about the decor may simply not have been attended to. It is possible, then, that children get better at focusing their attention on what is important as they get older, leading to more efficient encoding. Perhaps this explains some aspects of the development of memory.

To be able to focus on what is important, children need to have learned what kinds of things are important in given situations. Without this knowledge they will be none the wiser as to what is important and what is unimportant (see Recommended Reading for advice on where to look for a thorough review of the development of selective attention). Making links between new information and information already stored in memory may also lead to better encoding of that new information, making it more likely that it will be recalled at a later date. If we think of the storage part of memory as a system within which information is stored, then we can begin to see how this might work. Paperwork is not just dumped randomly into a filing cabinet, but is filed away in different drawers or within different hanging files based on a system of organisation. New papers are filed away alongside other, related papers, and this means that information on a particular topic can be more easily retrieved when needed than if the drawers just contained piles and piles of unorganised paperwork. It also means that other related information can be accessed alongside the 'target' information when that is retrieved. There might also be overlaps or relationships between information

> **STOP AND THINK**
>
> **Reflection**
> - What are your views on hypnosis?
> - Could this be a way of accessing information which has been encoded on some level, but is not available for conscious recall?
> - What do you think might be the potential problems with such methods?

Definition

Attention: the part of our cognitive processes which controls ability to focus efficiently on specific things and ignore others.

STOP AND THINK

Going further

Repeating something over and over again (rehearsal) is an encoding strategy which may increase the likelihood of it being remembered later. Why might this be the case? As mentioned earlier, the three-stage model of memory as represented in Figure 6.1 is a simple view of that system. In cognitive psychology, the 'storage' part of memory is thought to comprise several separate but interrelated sub-systems. In particular, there is a distinction between short-term memory, working memory and long-term memory. Alan Baddeley (Baddeley and Hitch, 1974; Baddeley, 1986, 1992), a leading researcher in the field of memory, suggests that working memory mediates between encoding and long-term storage, and consists of a 'central executive' (which controls the activities of working memory and allocates processing resources accordingly), as well as two 'slave' systems, one dealing with verbal information and the other with non-verbal (visuo-spatial) information. Some researchers suggest that there are even more specialist systems within these two general systems. For example, Piccardi et al. (2014) explored the development of navigational working memory, studying children's ability to learn complex environments. In any case, new information can be maintained and manipulated within working memory for a relatively short period of time, and may then pass to the long-term store. Verbal information, in particular, requires rehearsal in order for it to be maintained in working memory, otherwise it decays quite rapidly. Working memory can also maintain information which has been re-acquired from long-term storage when it is needed for some additional processing.

The way in which working memory operates is of interest within cognitive psychology generally, but in developmental psychology research has begun to explore the development of working memory in children (the implications of developments in working memory capacity for learning and teaching are explored in Chapter 14, Developmental Psychology and Education). Simpson and Riggs (2005) tested children on a modified version of a game called the 'day–night task' (Gerstadt et al., 1994) which requires children to respond 'day' to a picture of the moon and stars and to respond 'night' to a picture of the sun. This requires two things of the child. First, they need to inhibit their usual response of 'day' or 'night' to the appropriate picture and respond instead the opposite way around, but second, they need to maintain information about the rules of the game within working memory whilst they complete the task. In general, children's performance improves on this task between 3½ and 5 years of age. Could this be due to developments in working memory during this period? In a comparison task, the researchers tried to remove the 'inhibitory' demands of the task so that children had to respond 'night' to one abstract picture and 'day' to another abstract picture. In this case children still had to maintain the rules of the game in working memory, but since there was nothing intrinsic to the abstract pictures which would require the inhibition of an 'opposite' response, there should be no inhibitory demands on the children. The results suggested that the improved performance on the day–night task with children between 3½ and 5 years is actually associated with improvements in inhibitory control rather than in working memory.

One way in which working memory does seem implicated in memory improvements more generally, though, is through children's use of memory strategies like rehearsal. These kinds of strategy allow for information to be manipulated in some way prior to storage, and can increase the likelihood of retention and therefore subsequent retrieval. Have you ever tried to remember a phone number when you do not immediately have a pen and paper to hand? How would you go about this? Do you have any other 'tricks' which you like to use as aids to your memory?

Children's use of strategies increases as they get older, and the complexity of the strategies used also seems to increase. The next section of this chapter looks at some of these developments.

stored in different parts of the system which necessitate a system of cross-referencing.

As children get older, they accumulate knowledge and information which means that new information can be linked with existing information as it is encoded. Perhaps it is this accumulation of knowledge which improves memory through childhood then, by allowing information to be organised more efficiently as it is encoded, and as a more complex system of cross-referencing develops, there are more possible routes through which a target piece of information can be reached. Some specific ways in which prior learning may affect memory through encoding are explored

Definition

Rehearsal: the repetition of information in a deliberate attempt to aid memory.

later in this chapter (see 'The influence of prior knowledge and expectations', pages 158–9). When prior knowledge or information affects the encoding of new information as it comes in, this is known as top-down processing.

Rehearsal is just one of a whole variety of memory tricks or mnemonics, which as adults we use regularly, and which may also contribute to improvements in memory abilities across childhood. Mnemonic devices are important strategies which act as memory aids, and so it may be that improvements in children's memory are the result of their increased use of such encoding strategies. Rehearsal is a fairly simple strategy, but there are much more complex strategies which can be used as well.

For example, as a child, did you learn a rhyme or a song to help you remember how many days are in each month of the year? If so, then you encoded that information more elaborately than if all you had learned were mere numbers and months. More elaborate encoding means taking information (in this case, months and numbers) and expanding it into a more meaningful format (in this case, a rhyme or a song). You are more likely to be able to recall the information at a later date if it has been elaborately encoded than if you had just tried to rote learn it.

One good example of how elaborate encoding can assist children's recall is that of paired-associate tasks. Paired-associate tasks are used to test children's ability to recall pairs of items – usually pairs of words. Children are encouraged to learn the word-pairs by linking them together, often using visual imagery. So if the pair of words was 'kite–tiger' then the child might imagine a tiger standing on its hind legs in a park, flying a kite. After learning the words by linking each pair together in this way, children are prompted with one of the pair, and then have to remember what its partner was. If prompted with the word 'tiger' the correct response would be 'kite'. The prompt word should generate the image of the tiger flying a kite which the child had previously created, and help them to correctly recall the word which they are trying to remember. In this way, elaborating the information being encoded can improve recall. Very early research suggests that using this kind of imagery technique can improve children's recall between the ages of about 6 and 12 (e.g. Levin, 1976), but that at the younger end of this age range children only really benefit if they are given additional instructions to help them use the strategy (e.g. Varley et al., 1974; Bender and Levin, 1976). In other words, younger children cannot spontaneously elaborate information during the encoding process without more concrete help.

Simpler memory strategies like rehearsal are spontaneously used by children as young as 10 years of age (e.g. Beuhring and Kee, 1987), but as they get older children seem to rely less and less on such simple strategies, and instead use more complex strategies like elaboration and association (Pressley, 1982). Younger children do not make use of these more complex strategies themselves unless they are prompted or trained to do so. The use of memory strategies and the increasing complexity of those strategies may therefore lead to improvements in memory as children get older.

Recently, psychological research has begun to make use of advances in technology which allow us to study which parts of the brain are activated under certain conditions, by showing images of which parts of the brain 'light up' when we are engaged in certain mental tasks. These are known as neuroimaging techniques, and one such technique which has recently been applied to the study of children's memory is fMRI (functional magnetic resonance imaging).

Chiu et al. (2006) were particularly interested in the encoding of episodic memories by children. They studied which parts of the brain were involved when children attempted to encode episodic memories, and compared these to the parts of the brain which are involved when adults encode episodic memories. Using fMRI, the authors were able to identify which parts of the brain were active when children attempted to encode information. Two tasks were carried out by the children – one where they had to generate a verb from a noun that they had heard, and a second where they listened to short stories. During a subsequent test phase, the researchers assessed children's recognition memory for the information presented (i.e. whether the children recognised stimuli as having been presented previously or not). By analysing which information was successfully remembered by children, and examining which parts of the brain had been active during

Definitions

Top-down processing: when the processing of information coming in via the senses is heavily influenced by prior knowledge.
Mnemonics: memory aids which are used to assist with the learning or memorisation of information.
Neuroimaging: techniques which provide images of the structure and/or functioning of the brain.

the encoding of that information, the authors were able to conclude which parts of the brain had been involved in the successful encoding of episodic memories in children of different ages, and how this compares to the activity of adults' brains during such encoding.

In adults, the prefrontal cortex and the medial temporal lobe (MTL) have been shown to be associated with encoding episodic memories. The researchers in this study found that with children, the left prefrontal cortex was involved in the verb generation condition, but the MTL was not. For the story comprehension condition, activation of the left posterior MTL was found to be involved in encoding episodic memories, but the left anterior MTL and the prefrontal cortex were only involved in encoding for older children (10 years plus).

More traditional research methods tell us about what children can or cannot do in terms of the memory-related performance and behaviour which we observe. This cutting-edge technique allows a new dimension to be added to our understanding of how children's memory develops, by indicating which parts of the brain are involved. By comparing children's brain activity to that of adults, and by examining the brain activity of children of different ages, we can start to build up a picture of the neurological changes which take place during development.

Such techniques have their limitations, however. The photo shows a scanner. Children are required to lie on a moveable table which slides in and out of a large, cylindrical tube. Whilst this occurs, they are instructed to carry out whichever mental tasks or activities are required. In the study we are discussing here, the task required children simply to listen to auditory stimuli which they heard through headphones. However, it is important to note that the scanner itself makes a considerable amount of noise, not all of which will be eliminated by headphones. In addition, someone undergoing an fMRI scan has to lie as still as they possibly can. Even adults find this uncomfortable and difficult. This makes fMRI scanning virtually impossible to use with very young children, and the whole experience is likely to feel very strange for children of any age.

It is worth thinking about how demanding even a short scanning session like this is likely to be for a child. Nonetheless, as advances in such neuroimaging technologies continue, more 'user-friendly' versions may appear. Already there are variations of the traditional scanners available (e.g. open MRI machines) which are open on all sides and therefore feel less threatening. In the future, perhaps, researchers will be able to make more use of these, particularly for research with young children.

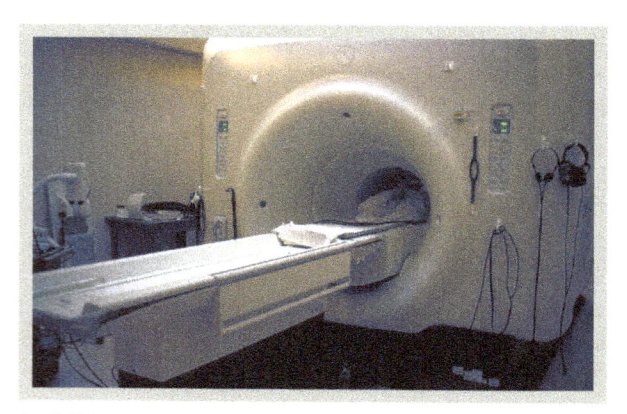

An fMRI scanner.
Source: Alamy Images/Tina Manley

Some recent research suggests that memory development may be closely linked to developments in other areas of cognition, such as theory of mind (ToM) (e.g. Perner and Ruffman, 1995; Naito, 2003). Theory of mind is the ability to attribute mental states (such as desires, beliefs or intentions) to others, and to understand that other people have mental states which differ from our own. This ability develops in children between around 3 and 4 years of age, and is discussed in full in Chapter 8, Theory of Mind. Perner et al. (2007) conducted some research which explored the relationship between ToM and memory development. Children of between 3½ and 6½ years of age had the opportunity to form episodic memories under one of two conditions. In one condition, children placed 12 picture cards into a box after looking at each picture for several seconds. This group therefore had the opportunity to directly experience the pictures themselves. In the second condition, children placed 12 picture cards into a box, but were blindfolded throughout and so did not have the opportunity to directly experience the pictures themselves. This second group were then shown a video presentation of what the 12 pictures had been. All of the children were subsequently tested on their ability to recall what pictures they had put into the box, and their ToM was also assessed. The results showed an interaction between ToM and direct experience of the events. In other words, as children's ToM scores increased, so their recall of pictures which they had directly experienced improved as compared to those which had not been experienced. On the basis of this research, the researchers suggest that recall of events which children have directly experienced is associated with the development of ToM. Fully understanding memory development then, seems to require us to look at its relationship to other areas of cognition as well.

MEMORY IN CHILDREN | 155

STOP AND THINK

Going further

The involvement of working memory and the use of strategies has been studied in relation to other areas of children's cognitive development, such as the development of mathematical or arithmetical skills (see Chapter 7, The Development of Mathematical Thinking). For example, Imbo and Vandierendock (2007) tested 10- to 12-year-old children using something called the 'dual task' method, where children are required to solve arithmetic problems (the primary task) whilst a secondary task (responding by hitting a button on a computer keyboard to indicate whether an audible tone they hear is high or low) occupies their working memories.

The results showed that children used mathematical strategies less efficiently when their working memories were loaded with the secondary task. However, the negative impact of this working memory load gets less as children get older. The authors suggest that as children get older they get better at selecting appropriate strategies, and more efficient at using those strategies, so that the impact of having their working memories loaded with another task declines. This shows how fundamental memory is to other areas of cognition and development. To find out more about the development of mathematical abilities and memory, see Recommended Reading.

LIFESPAN

Memory strategy use in adulthood

The development of strategy use seems to be something which improves children's memory as they get older, but does it continue to improve memory across the lifespan, into adulthood and old age? There are many myths and assumptions which we all have about memory across the lifespan, particularly in relation to older adults. We seem to accept the idea that becoming forgetful is simply a feature of getting older, but is this really the case? In fact, most of the research suggests that when adults are cognitively healthy (in other words, when they do not have any degenerative conditions such as Alzheimer's) their memories remain good and they can continue to improve their performance by using memory strategies, right up until they are in their 80s (e.g. Kramer and Willis, 2003).

When compared to younger adults, older adults seem to have less potential for improvement through strategy use, but nonetheless there is no reason to suppose that older adults experience poorer memory performance as a matter of course, nor is there reason to suppose that we will not be able to continue to improve our memories by using strategies or other techniques as we get older. However, the psychological studies on which we base these conclusions tend to have been carried out with one or other of these three key groups at a time: children, younger adults or older adults. By looking at the results from many different studies, we can make rough judgements about the relative memory abilities of the three groups as compared to one another. However, we cannot make direct comparisons between all three groups using exactly the same tasks under the same conditions. One area where psychological research on memory development is lacking, then, is in direct comparative research between different age groups across the lifespan.

One study which addresses this gap studied children's and adults' memory for words which they learned using a modified version of a memory technique known as the 'Method of Loci' (Brehmer et al., 2007). This is a mnemonic which works by linking targets visually with images of locations. You could try this out yourself. Make a list of six words to be learned, and then visualise the journey that you make from home to class each day. Pick six locations along the route, and mentally place one of the words at each location. Repeat the journey in your head until you are confident you have paired the words with their locations. Now do something else for an hour and after that time try to recall the six words by making the journey again in your mind.

Four groups of participants took part in the study altogether – one group of younger children (mean age 9.6 years), one group of older children (mean age 11.9 years), one group of younger adults (mean age 22.5 years) and one group of older adults (mean age 66.9 years). Using the modified Method of Loci, during the encoding phase of the study, target words were shown to participants paired with visual images of a particular location. During the test phase, participants were shown images of the locations, which served as cues to help them to remember the target words.

Before the study, each participant's baseline memory performance was measured to see how well they could remember lists of words without the use of any particular strategy. Then participants were introduced to the memory strategy over multiple sessions, and each participant received individual practice and training sessions over a period of time to try and maximise their memory ability.

The results of the study showed that younger adults had the highest level of baseline memory ability of all of the four groups, suggesting that this may be the period of our lives when our memory abilities have reached their natural optimum level. All four groups showed an improvement in memory after instruction in using the mnemonic technique, although again it was the group of younger adults who benefited most from this. Older adults seemed to be most at a disadvantage over the other groups in the extent to which they improved following the extended period of practice and training.

This study supports the view that baseline memory ability improves through childhood, peaks in younger adulthood and then declines in older adulthood. However, it also shows that even older adults have the potential to improve their memory by using specific strategies, although repeated practice and training in such strategies will have less of an effect on older adults than it will with younger adults or children. Bear in mind, too, that the 'older adults' in this study were between 65 and 78 years of age, and so these kinds of decrement in performance really are occurring only very late in the human lifespan.

Developments in storage

One of the areas in which children's memories are limited is the length of time for which information can be stored. In this section, we consider how improvements in storage affect the development of memory in childhood.

In terms of long-term memory storage, most of the research with infants which uses the visual recognition memory techniques discussed earlier in this chapter allows us to judge that infants recognise previously viewed stimuli a few seconds or minutes later. For example, Rose (1981) found that infants aged just 6 months could recognise previously viewed stimuli after delays of 5 seconds and 20 seconds. A delay of two to three minutes was problematic for the 6-month-olds, but not for infants of 9 months. This suggests that in the first 6 months, long-term storage is limited. However, some research has shown that even young infants can remember things for much longer periods than that and, during their first year, there is evidence of an improvement in the length of time for which infants can retain information. For example, early research by Fagan (1973) reveals that at 4 or 5 months of age, infants show recognition memory for images which were viewed up to two weeks previously. Some studies have shown that by 18 months of age, infants can retain information for as long as 13 weeks (Hartshorn et al., 1998).

These experimental studies of children's memories tell us about what infants can remember of carefully controlled visual stimuli in laboratory settings. Such stimuli are viewed for short periods of time, during which the infant has the opportunity to become familiar with them. This is a different situation to when infants appear to recognise their parents, with whom they have had long periods of exposure on a regular basis since birth. Think back to the example of baby Ella at the beginning of this

Definition

Mean: a statistical term which refers to the numerical average of a set of numbers. To calculate the mean, add all of the numbers in the set and divide by the number of items in the set.

chapter. Anecdotal reports of children similar to Ella's response to her parents also suggest that infants have the ability to encode, store and remember. Within cognitive psychology generally, the study of face recognition has become an important field of investigation, exploring this very specific aspect of human memory. In developmental psychology, the study of face recognition in infancy and early childhood is also now an established field of enquiry (see Recommended Reading).

There is an interesting phenomenon in the study of memory development which seems to contradict this general improvement in long-term retention, though, and this is referred to as infantile amnesia. Right at the beginning of this chapter, you were asked to Stop and Think about what your earliest memory is. The memory we have for our own lives, things which have happened to us, places we have seen and things we have done, is called *autobiographical memory*. For most of us, the first three years of our lives are simply not available for conscious recall, despite the memory abilities which infants and young children have been shown to have. So our autobiographical memories have a significant gap in them. Think back to the example of baby Ella at just 5 months of age. Despite her obvious recognition of her mother and father at that age, and the novelty of being left with a babysitter for the evening, as an adult Ella is unlikely to have any memories of that evening, or of anything else which happened to her during those first three years of her life. Much has been written about this phenomenon and the extent to which it can be explained by the research to date about developments in children's memory (see Recommended Reading), but it is still not clear whether infantile amnesia is a problem with the encoding, storage or retrieval of information. One theory put forward by several authors concerns the importance of language for recall. Perhaps in the pre-verbal stage of their lives, the absence of language somehow creates problems for children's long-term storage of information. Maybe language is necessary for long-term storage, in order to make abstract representations more concrete and meaningful. Alternatively, perhaps once language is acquired, memories which were stored during the pre-verbal stage somehow become inaccessible. This could be another example of the relationship between memory development and developments in other areas of cognition – a possibility which we discussed earlier in relation to theory of mind. There may also be links to the development of identity (discussed in Chapter 11, Development of Self-concept and Gender Identity), as some researchers suggest that a sense of self may be necessary before autobiographical memory can truly begin (Howe and Courage, 1997). In any case, this is an area of children's memory development which is still very much open to investigation, and perhaps new technologies being used in psychological research may help to shed some more light on the issue in the decades to come (see the Cutting Edge box).

Interestingly, in 2006 BBC Radio 4 broadcast a series of programmes called *The Memory Experiment*, which invited listeners to submit details of their own memories, including their earliest memory. The information has been collected and analysed in conjunction with Martin Conway, a cognitive psychologist. He reported that around 10 000 recorded memories had been received by March 2007, and this has therefore become the biggest collection of memories anywhere (Conway, 2007). Analysis of the memories supports previous research about infantile amnesia, in that when we attempt to recall things from the early part of our lives, the average age of people's earliest memories is 3½ years. So, whilst there seem to be general improvements in infants' ability to store information for longer and longer periods of time during infancy, there is very little in the way of any long-term retention of that information into adulthood. Either that, or the way in which that information is encoded during infancy makes it inaccessible in adulthood and therefore not retrievable.

Developments in retrieval

In this section, we explore the age-related improvements in retrieval which may assist with memory development in childhood. Encoding and retrieval are closely linked processes, and memory research in general supports this. Tulving's (1983) encoding specificity principle states that retrieval will be better in the presence of cues which were also present at the time of encoding. Cues may be any other stimuli which were present at the time of encoding, from the particular colour or precise

---

Definition

Infantile amnesia: a phenomenon whereby memories from the first three or four years of life are relatively scarce.

shape of the stimuli which were encoded, to the context in which encoding occurred – like the room in which it took place or the music which was playing at the time. This has been found to be particularly true of infants. So for young infants, retrieval will only occur if the cues at the time of retrieval are practically identical to those which were present at encoding. Slight variations in the cues which are present can reduce memory performance to almost nothing. One study found that just changing the appearance of an infant's playpen from a striped pattern to a squares pattern can affect the infant's memory (Borovsky and Rovee-Collier, 1990). What might this mean for infants who move house? What advice would you give a parent considering repainting their child's nursery? As children get older, though, their retrieval system becomes more flexible and they can recall information despite variations in the retrieval context and even despite variations in the stimuli presented.

There is also evidence that if certain reminders are given prior to an attempt at retrieval, these can help with the retrieval of memories which would previously have been assumed to be forgotten. In a key study, Rovee-Collier et al. (1980) used a technique known as the mobile conjugate reinforcement paradigm (mentioned in Chapter 4) to demonstrate that reminders could serve as important aids to retrieval by infants as young as 3 months. Using this technique, an infant is placed in a cot with a mobile suspended above it. The mobile is attached to the infant's leg with a ribbon, and by kicking their legs the infant can make the mobile move. Infants quickly learn that they can make the mobile move, and after training they will start to kick as soon as they are placed in the cot. However, they are quick to forget this, and after a gap of just two weeks from the end of their training, when placed back in the crib with their legs attached to the mobile, infants do not seem to remember what they had previously learned. What this study found, though, was that if an infant was given a reminder of the task the day before testing by simply being shown the mobile, then the following day their recall was much better. This suggests that the infants had not forgotten what they had learned after all. It was still stored in their memory somewhere, but they needed a reminder in order to be able to retrieve the information.

Subsequent research has shown that as children get older reminders can still be effective, even given longer gaps since the original encoding took place and also that the interval between the reminder and a subsequent successful retrieval gets shorter as children get older. Following a reminder, it takes younger children longer to retrieve the memory successfully, whilst older children can retrieve the memory more rapidly (e.g. Boller et al., 1990). As children get older, the reminder itself can be shorter and yet still be effective. Hsu and Rovee-Collier (2006) found that a two-minute reminder could reactivate the memory of 15-month-old infants, whilst a ten-second reminder was sufficient to reactivate the memories of 18-month-olds. All of this suggests that retrieval improves with age. Getting access to memories which seem to have been forgotten is possible, and children's retrieval systems seem to get more flexible as they get older.

The influence of prior knowledge and expectations

As children get older, they accumulate knowledge and information about the world. This results in children having quite well-formed expectations as to how the world works. For example, by the time baby Ella reaches 5 years of age she will have attended the birthday parties of many of her friends, and will have developed a set of expectations, or a script, for birthday parties. Based on the numerous parties she has attended, the specific details of which will have varied from party to party, Ella has developed a very generalised script for what should happen at a birthday party. Ella's script includes the knowledge or expectation that she should take a present and a card along for the child whose birthday it is. She also expects that there will be party games. Her script includes the expectation that certain types of food will be served, including jelly and ice-cream for pudding, and that at some point there will be a cake, with candles,

---

Definitions

Encoding specificity principle: a principle which states that memory is improved when contextual information present at the time of encoding is also available at the time of retrieval.

Cues: stimuli which assist with the retrieval of information from memory by providing a hint or by helping to recreate something of the original encoding environment.

which the 'birthday boy' or 'birthday girl' will blow out, whilst the guests all sing 'Happy Birthday!' Ella's script also includes the expectation that there will be 'goody bags' for all of the guests to take home with them, and that a slice of birthday cake will be included in each bag.

Children as young as 3 years of age have general scripts for everyday events such as going to the supermarket (e.g. Nelson and Gruendel, 1981). When asked what happens during an everyday event like that, children give general accounts which are organised according to the order in which things occur. 'You buy things and then you go home' is one such account which is simple but structured and general. This account is not referring to a specific instance of going to the supermarket yesterday, but reveals that the child has a more generalised understanding of what happens every time one goes to the supermarket. The fact that children tend to use the impersonal pronoun 'you' in these accounts, rather than the personal pronoun 'I', further supports the assumption that their understanding of a trip to the supermarket goes beyond any specific instance of that event.

Each party Ella attends will lead to the encoding of lots of new information specific to that particular party: for example, what colour the goody bags were, or which particular party games were played. These details vary from event to event, but Ella's script for birthday parties means that all of that information can simply be slotted in to the appropriate part of the script, to fill in the blanks. The script serves almost like a box within which there are various compartments for organising specific information. New information is placed into the appropriate compartment within the box, and can be stored and subsequently accessed if required, in a much more structured way than if there were no script. As children get older, then, the development of scripts is one way in which prior knowledge and expectations may help with the encoding, storage and subsequent retrieval of information. For more information on scripts, see Recommended Reading.

Some more recent research also shows that children's long-term semantic knowledge (knowledge about the meanings of words; see Chapter 5) can influence their short-term memory performance. Monnier and Bonthoux (2011) tested children's recall of lists of words. Some lists contained words that were from the same semantic categories (e.g. animals, food) and some contained unrelated words. Children's recall was better for words from the same semantic categories, which seems to suggest that their knowledge of the meaning of words influences their short-term memory performance.

What is responsible for 'forgetting'?

It is clear from the previous section that all three parts of memory develop across childhood, and that when a child is unable to recall something, it is often difficult to separate out the role of the three different memory processes in forgetting. It could be that information was never encoded successfully in the first place. It could be that it has been lost from storage. Or it could be that the information is stored, but the child is unable to retrieve it. It could be that children's developing working memory affects how information is used and processed to solve problems or answer questions, and that this holds the key to understanding what may seem to be instances of 'forgetting'. The mystery of infantile amnesia shows us that it is possible for large chunks of information to have been forgotten, and yet for us to have only a limited understanding of why this might be the case. However, there are certain instances of forgetting or incorrect remembering which are worthy of some special consideration – post-traumatic amnesia and false memories. Post-traumatic amnesia is when memories are forgotten or repressed following some traumatic event, and so it occurs when real memories appear to be lost. False memories occur when children report something which did not actually happen.

Eating cake will be a feature of children's experiences of birthday parties from early in life.
Source: O'Donnell

Post-traumatic amnesia

Repression is a feature of human memory which some psychologists believe allows memories for difficult, troubling or traumatic events to be hidden from our conscious minds, sometimes for decades, before emerging from the unconscious and making themselves known to us consciously. The very idea that human memory is capable of repression forms the basis for psychoanalysis; however, it is a hotly contested issue (e.g. Holmes, 1990). Loftus (1993) published a ground-breaking review of the evidence for how real such repressed memories are, in the light of increased numbers of alleged cases of childhood sexual abuse which were being reported by people many years after the abuse was said to have occurred. Loftus concluded that memory is incredibly malleable, and that in fact it is possible for our minds to create entirely false memories for traumatic events which in fact never took place. Nonetheless, as Loftus pointed out, that does not mean that all memories for traumatic events are false, and nor does it help us to distinguish between real repressed memories and false memories.

Childhood sexual abuse is one of the most difficult and sensitive issues in the study of children's memory for traumatic events, and some research has focused specifically on the forgetting of child sexual abuse (e.g. Ghetti et al., 2006). However, the study of post-traumatic amnesia has also included cases of repressed memories for other events, including witnessing a murder. The evidence suggests that there is no good reason to suppose that at least some of the reported cases of repression and subsequent recovery of traumatic memories are not genuine. For example, Ghetti et al. (2006) interviewed adults who were known to have been victims of child abuse as children, and found that 15% of those adults reported having experienced a complete forgetting of the abuse at some point in their lives. Even now we cannot be sure which memory processes are involved in repressing these memories. However, there is certainly enough evidence to suggest that something different is happening when traumatic childhood memories are repressed, as compared to the forgetting of ordinary memories, and that this may involve specific mental processes which affect our memories in order to defend us against the possible negative effects of traumatic events (see Brewin (2007) for a comprehensive review of the empirical research in this area). Nevertheless, many psychologists are uncomfortable with accepting the notion of repressed memories because there seems to be no rigorous, scientific way to validate their authenticity. In fact, one psychologist has remarked, 'Warning. The concept of repression has not been validated with experimental research and its use may be hazardous to the accurate interpretation of clinical behaviour' (Holmes, 1990, p. 97).

False memories

A false memory occurs when someone recalls something which did not actually occur, or recalls the details of it incorrectly. False memories represent a different kind of failure of memory from those referred to in the previous section. However, false memories and recovered memories pose similar questions for psychologists. When someone tells us that they remember something happening, how can we possibly know whether their recall is accurate or not? Children's memories appear to be particularly susceptible to false memories. They will often tell far-fetched and fantastic stories about things they have seen or done, with amazing conviction and detail. Imagine, for example, a 5-year-old boy on the journey home from nursery with his dad, explaining clearly the details of the trip he made to the moon that afternoon! Whilst we might generally find such tall tales charming and entertaining, what should we do if a child tells us something which we find disturbing? Can we ever know whether a child's stories are fact or fiction?

There is an important distinction to be made between the deliberate reporting of false memories by children, and the incorrect reporting of false memories. If a child reports false information knowing that it is false, then this constitutes lying, deceit or sometimes storytelling. However, what is of interest in the study of memory development are instances of children reporting information which is false, but which they believe to be true.

> **Definition**
>
> Repression: a psychological defence mechanism which allows uncomfortable memories to be stored in the unconscious mind.

STOP AND THINK

Going further

Within the study of memory in mainstream cognitive psychology, 'fuzzy trace theory' (FTT) offers a framework for understanding how information is processed and stored (Brainerd and Reyna, 1990). When applied to the area of false memories in both adults and children, it offers one possible explanation of how and why these might occur. FTT suggests that two types of memory trace are represented or stored – gist traces and verbatim traces. Roughly speaking, verbatim traces are representations of the specific details of target information, whilst gist traces are representations of more general meanings or things associated with the target. Think of someone you have recently met. You might have specific memories of their name and what they were wearing or what they looked like, but you might also have memories for how you feel about them, places you associate them with, knowledge of how you met or things you have in common. Verbatim traces are internal representations of your actual experience with that person, and could therefore be shared by anyone else who was also there at the time; gist traces are the representations which you have added to your memory, through your understanding of the person and what that encounter meant to you.

Memories can be accessed through either gist or verbatim traces, depending upon the retrieval cues, and the processing of both verbatim and gist information generally improves with age (Bjorklund and Jacobs, 1985; Brainerd and Reyna, 2001). Younger children are more suggestible when it comes to accepting gist-consistent false information. Imagine a young child who was wearing a blue dress the day before, but to whom we say, 'That was a lovely red dress you were wearing yesterday.' Our statement is gist-consistent (in that the child was indeed wearing a dress the day before) and that child is more likely than an older child to falsely remember wearing a red dress when tested subsequently on recall or recognition. This general pattern of younger children being more susceptible to false information has been observed in many studies (see Bruck and Ceci, 1997, for a review).

Interestingly, FTT suggests that the increase in gist processing as children get older may actually make older children and adults more susceptible than younger children to certain types of false memory (Brainerd and Reyna, 2004). When presented with a list of words which overlap in meaning (gist) or are semantically related (see Chapter 5, 'Language development'), adults and older children will be more likely to incorrectly remember a semantically related word which was not on the list (Brainerd et al., 2002).

- Can you recall an instance where you or someone else incorrectly remembered something?
- Think about some of the issues we have covered in this chapter to do with encoding, storage and retrieval. What do you think might have been responsible for your false memory?

Suggestibility is the term which is used to refer to how likely a child is to report false memories. A child may be suggestible because of cognitive and/or social factors (Ceci and Bruck, 1993; Reyna et al., 2002). Cognitive factors relate to the memory system itself – in other words, the processes of encoding, storage and retrieval. Social factors require us to look at the context in which the child's report is made, in order to understand their false memories. For example, we know that children are suggestible to reporting false memories if they are asked leading questions. Let's consider a child who has been on a day trip to a farm, where they saw pigs, cows and sheep. Asking the question, 'What colour was the gorilla?' itself suggests that there was in fact a gorilla, even though there wasn't! This kind of question is difficult for a child to respond to adequately, and is likely to lead them to respond with a colour. Even to understand the question, the child needs to imagine a gorilla at the farm, and merely by doing so they have incorporated a gorilla into their memory of the day at the farm, making them more susceptible to reporting falsely

Definition

Suggestibility: how susceptible someone is to ideas or information presented by others.

that they saw a gorilla at the farm when they are asked about it later.

Scripts, which we discussed earlier in the chapter, may also affect children's suggestibility, because a child's expectations of an event may influence their recall of the reality of that event. Let's think again about Ella's script for birthday parties. Part of her script includes the expectation that at parties there is jelly and ice-cream for pudding. After attending yet another party, her mum asks what she had for pudding, to which Ella responds, 'Jelly and ice-cream'. In fact she had Angel Delight! This incorrect report is not due to any deliberate attempt on Ella's part to mislead her mother, but simply because her recall of an event is highly influenced by her prior knowledge and expectations of birthday parties. In this way, a script can impose itself upon children's memories in a top-down way, and can influence the information which is recalled. For much more information about false memories, see Recommended Reading.

Cognitive interviews

In recent years, the incidence of children giving evidence in court has increased. Video-recorded or video-linked evidence from children has become admissible (e.g. Home Office and Department of Health, 1992), and the age at which children are permitted to give evidence is getting lower. In Scotland, there is no legal minimum age at which a child may be considered capable of giving evidence. All of this brings other important reasons to research the nature of false memories. Judges and juries need to know what the likelihood is of a child being able to give an accurate account of things which have happened to them, or which they have witnessed, and those interviewing children for such purposes need to know how to go about this in such a way that it maximises the chances of children providing accurate accounts. For this reason, a technique is used called the cognitive interview (CI), which is described in full by Milne and Bull (1999) (see also Recommended Reading). There are four key elements to the cognitive interview. Firstly, the interview should entail context reinstatement. In other words, instead of the child being encouraged simply to recall a small amount of 'target' information, the interviewer should assist the child to reconstruct mentally the physical and personal context which surrounded the event. Where did it take place? What was the weather like? What else could you see? What noises were there? How were you feeling? Where had you been previously? What were you planning for that day? Secondly, the child should be encouraged to recall everything. In other words, no attempts should be made to filter out information which is perceived to be irrelevant. The child should be encouraged to recall as much detail as possible. The reason for these first two elements of the CI links back to the discussion of encoding specificity earlier in this chapter. The principle of encoding specificity states that information is more likely to be successfully retrieved if the specific context in which it was encoded can be replicated. By getting children to remember as much as they can about the circumstances surrounding the 'target' information in a CI, it is hoped that the original encoding context can be re-created, and that this will help with accurate recall.

The third key element of a CI is that the child should be encouraged to change their perspective. In other words, the interviewer should try to facilitate the child recalling what events or things would have looked like, or sounded like, from the perspective of someone else who was involved in the situation, or from a different position in the situation. In much research into these interview techniques, psychologists have had to make use of events or situations which children have been routinely involved in, such as eye tests or doctors' examinations, and then interview children about these events. So a child could be asked to think about what the receptionist would have seen from her seat, or what something would have looked like from the opposite side of the room to that on which the child was sitting herself. Fourthly, the CI attempts to get the child to remember things in a different order to the chronological order in which they actually happened. These third and fourth elements of the CI are included in order to vary the way in which information is retrieved. Retrieval can be thought of as the process of following a route which eventually leads to a memory. Most memories have several such routes which we could follow in order to gain access

Definition

Cognitive interview: a technique developed specifically for interviewing witnesses in legal situations, using principles of memory from cognitive psychology, to maximise the amount of information which is accurately recalled.

to them. For example, FTT suggests that memories can be accessed through verbatim and gist information, as discussed earlier in the chapter. This is known as varied retrieval. Some routes are faster, some are slower; some are more accessible than others whilst some are very difficult to follow. By attempting to access a memory via alternative routes, recall is less likely to rely upon a child's prior knowledge or expectations of the situation (such as scripts, which were discussed earlier).

Milne and Bull (2002) provide an overview of these four components of the CI, and report the results of a study which they conducted to determine whether any one of these four on their own improves recall more than the others. Three groups of participants (adults, 8/9-year-olds and 5/6-year-olds) took part in the research, and were interviewed after viewing a video of an accident. The participants were allocated to groups, each of which was interviewed according to just one of the four elements of the CI. A fifth group were interviewed using a combination of the 'report everything' and 'context reinstatement' components, and a sixth (control) group were simply asked to 'Try again'. The results showed that each of the four components of the CI were of equal benefit to participants' recall, and that there were no age-related differences in the extent to which recall improved using each of the four components.

To find out the truth about what Ella really had for pudding at the birthday party using the CI technique, an interviewer might try asking her to recall the meal from the perspective of one of the other children at the party, or from the point of view of the 'birthday boy's' mum. This should allow access to the memory of what was eaten via a route which is free from Ella's own general knowledge and expectations about what one eats at a party. By reconstructing an event from someone else's point of view, or in a different order from that which actually took place, a child should be able to recall without the influence of additional information which is imposed onto their memory of the event, and it is hoped that their recall will be closer to the event as it actually occurred.

Memory is a key part of a child's cognitive processes, and memory tasks often feature in tests of intelligence. If we think back to the case study of baby Ella at the beginning of the chapter, we might consider her to be

CUTTING EDGE

Contemporary research into the development of memory now often attempts to apply theoretical knowledge to understanding complex, real-life situations. Chapter 14 further explores the impact developmental psychology has on education, and one recent study presents a good example of how memory research can help us to better understand children's experiences in the classroom. Wang and Shah (2014) studied how third-grade and fourth-grade school children performed on tasks of mental arithmetic. They found that performance was affected by whether the children had high or low working memory abilities, but that it was further affected by whether the tasks themselves could be solved using basic heuristic strategies or whether they required more complex strategies to be applied. On top of these factors, performance was further affected by whether the tasks were carried out in a high-pressure environment or a low-pressure environment.

The results of the study showed that where tasks could be solved using basic strategies, children's working memory abilities made no difference to performance, and neither did the pressure of the environment. However, when the tasks required more complex solutions, even in a low-pressure environment, children with low working memory abilities performed worse than those with high working memory abilities. In a high-pressure environment, the negative effect of complex tasks on children with low working memory abilities was even more pronounced.

This kind of research applies theoretical knowledge about memory functions to complex, real-life situations, and enables us to understand how children's behaviour is affected by both their cognitive skills and the environment.

an intelligent baby, due to the fact that she showed some recognition of her parents at such a young age, but as she gets older, how might Ella's intelligence be tested more formally? How might our expectations of her as an intelligent child change as she grows up? What would she have to do to impress us and convince us of her intelligence at the age of 5, for example? The rest of this chapter considers the nature of intelligence and intelligence testing, in order to understand the development of intelligence.

What is intelligence?

When we talk about someone being intelligent, or make judgements about one person being more or less intelligent compared to another, what is it that we are actually talking about? This is a contentious issue, and not all psychologists agree with one another about what constitutes intelligence. We will explore some of these different perspectives in the rest of this chapter. Generally speaking, intelligence is thought to be made up of the cognitive processes of memory, problem solving and thinking. How intelligent a person is, is an indicator of how well they process information, solve problems and adapt or learn from experience. The developments in memory which have been explored in the first part of this chapter are therefore a part of the development of intelligence.

> **STOP AND THINK**
>
> ### Reflection
> - Which of these four men would you consider to be the most intelligent?
>   Bill Gates
>   Gandhi
>   Stephen Hawking
>   William Shakespeare
> - Rank them in order from the one you would consider to be the most intelligent, to the least intelligent.
> - What is it about each of them which led you to rank them as you did?
> - What does this tell you about your own personal ideas regarding the nature of intelligence?

Intelligence in children

What makes for an intelligent child? How intelligence is defined, and the importance of this for education and schooling, are discussed in Chapter 14, 'Developmental psychology and education'. Should we be looking for the same kinds of behaviour or ability that we have considered in the men above, just on a smaller scale? Or does intelligence in children manifest itself in different ways? In adults, as we have considered above, intelligence is generally judged on the basis of things like what they say, their ability to answer different questions or solve problems, and the way they express themselves and interact with others. One particular challenge for developmental psychologists studying intelligence in children is that their language abilities may be limited or even absent, depending upon their age. Children's answers to questions might be affected by their language development rather than a reflection of their intelligence. In the remainder of this chapter, we will consider various issues relating to the study of intelligence in children, including how intelligence testing has been approached, how it has been conceptualised, and how nature and nurture interact in its development.

Approaches to intelligence testing

When thinking about testing intelligence, what most frequently comes to mind is the notion of IQ, which stands for 'intelligence quotient'. A person's IQ is calculated by assessing their mental age, dividing it by their chronological age (their age in years) and multiplying by 100. The very notion that there is such a thing as mental age originated from the French psychologist Alfred Binet in the early 1900s, and his work with children. Binet was asked by the French government to come up with a way of identifying children who would not benefit from education within a standard school setting. Binet thought that a mentally retarded child would perform at the level of a younger child, and so he tested a number of normally developing children aged between 3 and 11 years on a variety of different tasks, to establish what would constitute normal performance for children of different

> **Definition**
>
> IQ: abbreviation for intelligence quotient – a score obtained from an individual's performance on tests designed to measure intelligence.

ages. Subsequently, any child could be tested and their results compared to these norms, and a judgement then made about their mental age. The use of intelligence tests in education is discussed further in Chapter 14.

William Stern then took the idea of mental age and came up with the specific formula for calculating IQ explained above. If a child performs at the appropriate level for their age (for example, if a 6-year-old child performs at the level of a 6-year-old) then their IQ should be 100 because (6/6) × 100 = 100. A child performing above the normal standards for their age would therefore have an IQ of above 100, and a child with an IQ of below 100 would be considered to be below average for their age.

Over the years, substantial revisions to Binet's intelligence test have been carried out, to incorporate some of the ideas about IQ, but also to enable an individual child's performance on the different tests to be broken down into four separate areas. These revisions were done at Stanford University in the USA and, because of this, the test is now known as the Stanford–Binet. The four areas in which we can now assess a child's performance are quantitative (numerical) reasoning, abstract/visual reasoning, verbal reasoning and short-term memory.

STOP AND THINK

Reflection

- What makes an intelligent baby? Think back to what you have read about infancy in Chapter 4, Prenatal Development and Infancy, about language in Chapter 5, 'Language development', and about memory in the earlier part of this chapter. Think about your own children or talk to someone who has children. Did they consider their babies to be particularly 'bright'? What did they base their judgements on?
- How reliable are these kinds of parental report?
- How else might we explore whether one baby was more intelligent than another?
- What kinds of behaviour would you look for if you wanted to investigate intelligence in babies?

CASE STUDY

Interpreting IQ

Consider the case of two children, both of whom have been identified by their teachers as particularly able in class. Both children have been IQ tested, and both have IQs of 125, calculated as follows:

James: Mental age = 5
         Chronological age = 4
         IQ = (5/4) × 100 = 125

Inanya: Mental age = 10
         Chronological age = 8
         IQ (10/8) × 100 = 125

The fact that both children have the same IQ might lead you to believe that they both have the same level of general intellectual ability. In fact these two children's IQs reveal some important individual differences. James' mental age is one year greater than would be expected according to his chronological age, whilst Inanya's mental age is two years greater than her chronological age. Thus, their level of intellectual superiority is quite different.

In addition, whilst their overall IQ may be the same, when broken down into the four subscales defined by the Stanford–Binet test, we may discover very different patterns of ability in these two children. James may score very highly on verbal and abstract reasoning, and less well on memory and numerical reasoning. Inanya's score may reflect the opposite pattern. Taken in isolation, a child's IQ may not provide us with enough information to give a clear insight into the nature of their intelligence, but the more contemporary revisions to Binet's tests can provide useful information, not just about a child's intelligence relative to other children, but about their own intellectual strengths and weaknesses.

- How would you explain the differences between these two children's level of intellectual ability to someone who didn't know them?
- What do you think might be the benefits of using IQ as a measure of children's intelligence?
- What are its limitations?

One criticism which has been levelled at traditional tests of IQ is that from the normative data we know that mental age plateaus in our mid-teens. This means that there comes a point in development where the mental age part of the calculation will not increase much more. Yet our chronological age continues to increase across the lifespan. It has been argued that this puts adults at a disadvantage when calculating IQ and suggests that such tests ought to be used only with children. To address this, there are intelligence tests which have been devised specifically for use with adults, such as the Wechsler Adult Intelligence Scales.

One intelligence or many?

So far, although it is clear that there is some disagreement about what intelligence is and how it ought to be measured, there is still an assumption that when we talk about intelligence, we are talking about just one thing. Is it more useful to think of there being different types of intelligence? Consider your assessments of the different intelligences of the four famous men previously. Some standard IQ tests do have several sub-tests embedded within them. For example, the Stanford–Binet test includes sub-tests for verbal ability and for numerical reasoning, as we have already discussed. Instead of looking at these as constituent parts of one general intelligence (sometimes referred to as 'G'), maybe it would be more helpful to think of these as two completely separate intelligences. Gardner (1993) suggested exactly that, and in fact he argued that there are eight different types of intelligence.

The eight types of intelligence which Gardner proposed are: (1) verbal; (2) mathematical; (3) spatial; (4) bodily-kinaesthetic; (5) musical; (6) interpersonal; (7) intrapersonal; (8) naturalist. There is certainly an appeal to thinking about children's intelligence in this kind of way. Instead of labelling a child as having either a high or a low level of intelligence, this approach allows us to consider each child's unique set of strengths and weaknesses. To be labelled as having below average intelligence as a child carries a considerable stigma and the effects of that may lead to a lowering of a child's self-esteem or motivation to succeed. In contrast, using a multiple intelligences approach removes the dangers inherent in this kind of labelling and allows each child to be considered as simply different.

As well as tests of general intelligence, which have sub-tests within them, there are other specific standardised tests such as the British Picture Vocabulary Scale, the Test Reception of Grammar, the Digit Span Test and the Test of Pattern Construction. When children's development does not follow a typical pathway, such tests may help to evaluate which specific domains of their cognitive development are affected. Chapter 16 explores atypical development in more detail. Nevertheless there is still disagreement in some of the research literature where standardised tests have been employed, in terms of what they tell us about the exact nature of differences between typically and atypically developing children's abilities. Previous studies of children with Williams syndrome

Definition

G: an abbreviated way of referring to general intelligence, the common factor believed by some to underpin performance on all intelligence tests.

Is musical ability a kind of intelligence?
Source: O'Donnell

(a condition described in detail in Chapter 16) have suggested a lot of variability in their performance on verbal and non-verbal standardised tests – more than we would expect to see in a typically developing population. However, when children's chronological age was controlled for, Van Herwegen et al. (2011) did not find differences between Williams syndrome children and typically developing children in terms of the variability in their performance on such tests. So even the use of standardised tests does not allow for consensus and agreement about what the results mean and how they are interpreted.

Another school of thought suggests that other theories of intelligence fail to recognise the importance of children's *emotional intelligence*. Emotional intelligence includes children's ability to interpret the emotions of others and the ability to manage their own emotions. Goleman (1995) suggests that emotional intelligence is a far better predictor of someone's actual competence in the real world than more traditional tests of IQ.

However, critics of these multiple intelligence theories ask where we should draw the line in identifying different types of intelligence. For example, if musical ability is to be considered a specific type of intelligence, then why not also writing ability? Should we be adding poetic intelligence to the list? There is an argument that things like musical and artistic abilities should be considered under the banner of creativity, not intelligence, and creativity is explored in the next section. More important is the question of whether the belief that there is only one type of intelligence and only one way of measuring it is actually helpful to understanding children and their development. Using traditional IQ tests allow us to compare children to one another, and to the levels of ability which would normally be expected from a child of their age, and can potentially assist with the identification of children who may require additional support for their learning or development. However, they do not allow us to acknowledge that different children may have different strengths and weaknesses in terms of their abilities. More and more, there seems to be an acknowledgement that there is more than one way in which a child can be intelligent.

Definition

Creativity: the ability to think in new or different ways or to come up with original ideas, concepts or solutions.

Intelligence versus creativity?

The word 'creativity' refers to the ability to think about something in an original or unique way, or in a way which differs from how the majority of other people would think about it. Sternberg (1985) developed another theory of multiple intelligences, but one which included just three types as opposed to Gardner's eight types. Referred to as the 'triarchic' theory of intelligence, it includes (1) analytical intelligence; (2) creative intelligence; and (3) practical intelligence. Children who are creatively intelligent might not perform well on standard tests of IQ but they are quick to come up with solutions to novel questions or problems, or to come up with novel solutions to standard questions. Analytically intelligent children are those who would score highly on traditional IQ tests and would do well on standard maths or verbal problems. Practically intelligent children are good at many of the kinds of things which are not taught at school. Such children might be 'streetwise' and have a good understanding of people, or be good with their hands. Viewed in this way, children who score highly on standard tests of intelligence may not be at all creative, yet creativity is often associated with high intelligence or even genius (see also 'Gifted children', pages 168–70).

STOP AND THINK

Reflection

- Consider some of the great artists or musicians throughout history. Would you consider them to be unintelligent because of the nature of their particular abilities?
- Think again about Bill Gates, Ghandi, Stephen Hawking and Shakespeare, who featured earlier in this chapter. Which one did you consider to be most intelligent, and why? Which one would you judge to be most creative?

Culture-fair intelligence testing

Another criticism which has been levelled at traditional intelligence tests is that success on them is dependent upon a child having prior knowledge and experience with a particular culture. Success on traditional tests often relies upon knowledge of the language in which they were constructed – usually English – because the questions require verbal responses. Western cultural norms and expectations also dominate traditional tests, which means that children from different cultures may interpret a particular question differently and give a response which lowers their score on the test, but which is in no way due to their lack of intelligence. In fact, it is interesting that within educational psychology there is a particular phenomenon called divergent thinking which is often seen in gifted or able children (see 'Gifted children') and is a particular feature of creativity, as explored in the previous section. Thinking about something in a way which differs from the way everyone else thinks about it could actually be an indication of high intelligence. Yet using traditional tests of intelligence, able children as well as non-white children and non-English-speaking children may be at a disadvantage. For that reason, culture-fair intelligence tests have been developed.

Cattell's (1940) Culture Fair Intelligence Test (CCFIT) is one example of such a test. It relies mainly on non-verbal test items and uses things like mazes, classification tasks and mirror-images as alternative ways of assessing intelligence which do not depend upon language and culture. For example, after viewing a series of abstract geometric forms, you might then have to select from a set of five other abstract geometric forms the one which completes the progressive series.

STOP AND THINK

Reflection

- Can any test can be truly culture fair?
- The CCFIT is a timed test, so children must attempt to complete the various tasks as quickly as they can within the permitted time. Is the ability to work as quickly as possible really valued equally in all cultures?
- Is it really a marker of intelligence at all?

Definition

Divergent thinking: the type of thinking which is usually the product of creativity and is therefore original.

Gifted children

Having considered several different approaches to understanding and testing intelligence, this section considers the case of children who, for one reason or another, stand out from the rest in terms of their high level of intelligence or ability. Such children are referred to as gifted, talented or able children. The precise definition of giftedness varies depending upon where you look, but traditionally a child will be considered to be gifted if their IQ is measured at 130 or more. Gifted children may also have a special talent for something, or a particular area in which they excel.

It is important to consider what is responsible for giftedness. Do gifted children have better memories, for example? Or does creativity, which has been discussed earlier in this chapter, have a role to play in explaining giftedness? One study found that mathematically gifted children did not differ from their non-gifted peers in terms of memory ability, but that the conceptual structures they were using were equivalent to those of children about a year older than them (Okamoto et al., 2006). These gifted children were thinking about maths in a way which was fundamentally different from their peers. This can be viewed as the kind of divergent thinking referred to earlier in the chapter, and indicates that creativity, or the ability to think about things in novel ways, may be what is important in understanding giftedness in children.

A focus on understanding children's cognitive development, as is the case in studies of gifted children, may lead to a neglect in consideration of their social or emotional development (see Section III of this book). Parents and teachers of gifted children may express concern about this. For example, should a gifted child be accelerated through school or left in a class with children of the same age? What impact might this have on their ability to make friends? If they are in a class with children who are older than them, albeit of an approximately equal intellectual level, will the gifted child 'fit in'? Hoogeven et al. (2012) investigated the social-emotional characteristics of over 200 gifted children and found no differences between the self-concepts and social contacts of those who had been accelerated through school and those who had not. This kind of research could be helpful for parents and teachers in making decisions about how to support gifted children, and illustrates the importance of developmental psychology for the everyday lives of children. It also illustrates how important it is to consider the integration of social, emotional and cognitive aspects in understanding children, instead of focusing on these as separate aspects of development.

NATURE–NURTURE

'Twin' research in the study of intelligence

The issue of how children are affected by the interaction of 'nature' and 'nurture' is a recurring theme in developmental psychology, and nowhere is it a more important or interesting area of investigation than in the study of intelligence. Having explored the question of what intelligence is and how it is measured, this box considers what is responsible for the level of a child's intelligence. Putting aside the questions we have considered about the extent to which various tests are effective measures of intelligence, we now turn to the question of what factors influence or affect intelligence.

Ask yourself: How intelligent am I? Where do I get this intelligence from? Do you think that you have inherited your intelligence from one or both of your parents? How similar to or different from the intelligence of your siblings do you think your intelligence is?

As has been apparent throughout this book, it is difficult to disentangle the influences of heredity in development from the influences of the environment. Research which has been carried out in an attempt to disentangle these two factors has often made use of twins. This is because identical twins share exactly the same genetics. If intelligence is strongly influenced by genetics then identical twins would be expected to have very similar levels of intelligence. In contrast, non-identical twins share only about half their genetic material. If intelligence is strongly influenced by genetics then non-identical twins would be expected to have less similar levels of intelligence when compared to identical twins.

As well as the influence of genetics, twins (identical and non-identical) will have a certain amount of their environmental influences in common, through being raised in similar environments. Non-identical twins will also have had some unique experiences which differentiate them from their twin. For these reasons, studies of the intelligence of twins who were separated at birth and raised in different environments altogether have been important. If there are large differences between the intelligence of identical twins who were raised separately, then this would suggest that intelligence is strongly influenced by the environment. If, on the other hand, such twins' intelligence remains similar despite their separate upbringings, then the influence of the environment is likely to be weak.

The results of a variety of studies over the years indicate that the influence of genetics is quite strong. Plomin and DeFries (1980) took the results from lots of such studies, combined them, and then analysed them all together – a technique known as a meta-analysis. The results of this meta-analysis showed that pairs of identical twins who were brought up together had IQ scores which were most closely related to one another. Identical twins that were brought up separately showed the next most closely related IQs. Non-identical twins brought up together were next, and then came ordinary siblings brought up together. After them came ordinary siblings who had been brought up separately, and finally came adopted siblings who were brought up together but were not genetically related to each other.

The results from ordinary siblings add another dimension to this kind of research because they share approximately half of the same genetics, which is the same proportion as non-identical twins. But crucially, ordinary siblings will have had more unique environmental experiences than non-identical twins so, whilst the influence of genetics will be approximately the same for these two groups, there will be more variation due to environmental factors.

These results allow us to begin the process of disentangling the relative effects of genetics and the environment, but it is quite clear that both factors do influence intelligence. The fact that identical twins' IQs are more closely related than non-identical twins, regardless of whether those identical twins have been brought up separately or together, shows us that the genetics which we inherit from our parents have a large effect upon our intelligence. Yet the fact that there is still a relationship, albeit a much weaker one, between the IQs of adopted siblings that have no genetic material in common at all shows that the environment does have some effect on intelligence.

Definition

Meta-analysis: a method of statistical analysis which combines the results of many studies to identify an overall effect or change, often in an attempt to overcome problems of small sample sizes in research.

In early 2008, the digital television channel E4 launched a new series called *Big Brother: Celebrity Hijack*, where 12 young people who each had an exceptional level of ability in a particular field moved into a house together for just over three weeks. These included: Victor, a circus performer; John, a politician; Amy, an artist; and Calista, a singer–songwriter. It is interesting to consider how each of these young people would fare on a 'traditional' test of IQ. Could creativity be an alternative way to think about their exceptional talents? Or would the theory of multiple intelligences be the best way to account for the abilities each of them has?

Interactions between heredity and environment in development

The information in the Nature–Nurture box allows us to make some judgements about the relative effects on intelligence of genetic material which children inherit from their parents and the environment in which they grow up. Yet one interesting finding to emerge is that the effects of heredity and the environment do not necessarily remain the same across the whole of childhood, or across the whole of a person's lifespan.

As children get older, they accumulate life experiences. By the time they reach adulthood they will not only have had more experiences, but they are likely to have gained a considerable amount of independence. We would probably expect that as twins get older, the number of experiences which each of them have had which are unique to them as individuals and not shared with their twin, will also be greater. Intuitively, we might expect that young children's intelligence will be strongly affected by genetics, in the absence of a great deal of environmental experience. Older children's and adults' intelligence might then be expected to be influenced more by experience and less by genetics. In fact, the opposite pattern seems to be true (e.g. McClearn et al., 1997) in that the older we get, the more influenced by genetics our intelligence is. Maybe you can think of some possible explanations for this? One suggestion from those working in this field is that as we get older we are more able to live the kind of life and have the kinds of experience that our genetic inheritance was always pushing us towards. For example, whilst genetically we might be driven towards experiencing rural living, the influence and control which our parents have over us as children means that we nevertheless spend our childhood living in a city. As we get older, we have more control over our own lives and can follow the direction in which our genetics are pushing us.

This means that the older we get, the more our environments are actually the product of the genetics we have inherited (see Recommended Reading). It is almost certainly true that the older we get, the more environmental influences we will have had, but if those environmental influences are themselves the product of our genetics then this could explain the greater influence which genetics seem to have as we get older. Some longitudinal research conducted in Scotland supports this, and is discussed below.

The Scottish mental surveys

On Wednesday, 1 June 1932, almost every child attending school in Scotland who had been born in 1921 took the same test of mental ability. The same thing happened in 1947, when every child attending school who had been born in 1936 was tested. In 1932, a total of 87 498 children were tested, and in 1947, 70 805 children were tested. The Scottish Mental Surveys are described in more detail by Deary et al. (2004). The test used was called the Moray House Test, and for each child their performance on the test generated a single score out of a total possible score of 76. The test included questions assessing various aspects of intelligence, including following directions, opposites, word classifications, analogies, reasoning, proverbs, arithmetic, spatial abilities and practical issues. In 1947, data were also obtained for each child tested about their school, its size and location and the number of teachers it had. In addition, specific details including each child's position in their family, date of birth, gender, the size of their family and their attendance at school were obtained.

Deary et al. (2004) report on follow-up data which they obtained between 1999 and 2001, from a sub-set of those individuals who, as children, had participated in the 1932 survey. Participants in this follow-up research were tested using the original Moray House Test, but also using an array of other cognitive tests (including a sub-scale of the Wechsler Memory Scale, the National Adult Reading Test and a test of verbal fluency) as well as the hospital anxiety-depression scale and various physical tests. Many other articles have published findings from follow-up studies of other sub-sets of individuals who participated in the original surveys (e.g. Deary et al., 2000, 2003).

The results from the 2004 study show that there is a great deal of stability in measurements of intelligence, in that an individual's intelligence as measured at the age of 11 would be similar to that at the age of 80. When compared to follow-up data obtained from a sub-set of the 1947 survey, the results also showed that general intelligence (G) plays a greater role in intelligence as we get older.

SUMMARY

Within this chapter we have explored two aspects of cognition – memory and intelligence. Memory is a system, made up of three major component parts – encoding, storage and retrieval. Encoding is the process by which information is taken in from the world around us; storage concerns the way that information is then kept; and retrieval is the process of getting information back out of storage when required. Working memory is where information is manipulated and processed for a short period of time in order to solve problems. There are different types of memory which children may have. From the earliest days of life, they demonstrate recognition memory for visual and auditory stimuli. As they get older, children demonstrate that they have semantic memories for factual information, and develop autobiographical memories about themselves and their lives. They have implicit memories for skills like riding a bike, and they have scripts for procedures or events.

Researchers face difficulties in trying to study infant memory, because infants cannot tell us what memories they have or what the nature of those memories is. Techniques which enable us to make some judgements about memory abilities in infancy include the visual paired comparison task, the mobile conjugate reinforcement paradigm and the use of non-nutritive dummies. At just a few days old, infants can encode information, store it for at least a couple of days and retrieve it. Younger infants take longer to encode information than older infants, and during their first year the length of time for which infants can store information increases. All three parts of the memory system develop through childhood, so that the general improvements we see as children get older are likely to be due to a combination of the improvements which take place in all three areas. The development of working memory and the use of memory strategies may also help with encoding and subsequent retrieval. Encoding and retrieval are closely linked, and the way in which something is initially encoded can affect how it is subsequently retrieved. Overall, as children get older they have more tools at their disposal to help with encoding, and forgetting may occur if encoding is not successful.

Children can generally maintain information in memory for longer periods as they get older. However, this is contradicted somewhat by the infantile amnesia phenomenon, which affects autobiographical memory. This type of forgetting is still not fully understood, but theories suggest that the lack of language in the first years of life may create storage or retrieval difficulties for children, or that true autobiographical memory cannot develop prior to a child's sense of self.

Older children are less sensitive than younger children to differences between the encoding context and the retrieval context. Forgetting may occur in younger children if there are not enough retrieval cues to allow access to the memory. In addition, reminders are more effective with older children even with long gaps since the original encoding, and those reminders can be shorter and still have the desired effect.

The fact that sometimes our memories can be hidden from our conscious mind suggests that additional memory processes may exist to protect us against the potentially damaging psychological effects of a negative event. However, when these kinds of repressed memory subsequently come to light, it can be difficult to validate them and establish whether they are accurate or not. This is because we know that sometimes people recall things which did not actually happen, and children are particularly susceptible to this. Leading questions can cause false information to be incorporated into a child's memory, and prior knowledge and expectations may influence their recall of reality. Cognitive interviews put the knowledge and understanding which we have of children's memory systems to use in order to maximise the amount of accurate information which a child is able to recall.

Traditional tests of intelligence measure IQ, assess a child's mental age as compared to their chronological age and suggest that general intelligence (G) is one thing. Tests of IQ measure a child's overall intelligence using sub-tests of (for example) verbal ability and numerical ability, but have been criticised for being culture-specific, asking questions which assume a certain way of looking at the world, and asking questions in such a way that children from minority backgrounds may understand and respond to them differently. IQ tests have also been criticised for their assumption that children's responses to a variety of different questions are indicative of one underlying level of general intelligence.

Traditional IQ tests may disadvantage children who take novel or creative approaches to solving problems. Creativity and divergent thinking are often associated with highly intelligent or gifted children, yet this type of thinking may lead to lower scores on traditional tests of IQ.

Alternative perspectives suggest that tests of verbal and numerical ability should be considered to be measuring fundamentally different types of intelligence. However, critics ask where we should draw the line in associating particular abilities with different intelligences. More recently, theories have been developed which suggest that emotional intelligence should be considered another kind of intelligence. Supporters of multiple intelligences point out that this way of thinking allows us to acknowledge individual differences which exist between children in terms of their strengths and weaknesses, instead of labelling children as above or below some normal level of intelligence.

Despite developmental psychology's focus on childhood, we have seen that in both of these areas of cognition there are changes through adulthood as well. Research suggests that we reach the peak of our memory abilities in young adulthood, at which point it appears to plateau before declining in older adulthood. For adults who remain physically healthy, a general deterioration in memory may be due to loss of ability in any of the three sub-systems. However, recent research seems to point to encoding as the part of memory where a decline in ability is particularly apparent, because older adults appear less able to benefit from the use of memory strategies.

Mental age increases through childhood and then plateaus in the mid-teenage years, whilst chronological age continues to increase right through the lifespan. When calculating IQ, adults will therefore be at a disadvantage as they get older. This has led to the development of intelligence tests specifically for adults. Twin studies have led researchers to believe that, whilst our genetic inheritance is largely responsible for intelligence, the influence of the environment is still important. So intelligence comes about as the result of interaction between these two factors.

REVIEW QUESTIONS

1. Compare and contrast three different types of memory which children may have.
2. Explain the encoding specificity principle, and describe the changes in encoding specificity in children's development.
3. Describe one method designed to research infant memory.
4. In what ways might top-down processing affect children's memory?
5. What is a cognitive interview? Explain the rationale for its different components.
6. How many different intelligences do you think there are, and why?
7. What are the pros and cons of using traditional IQ tests to measure intelligence?

RECOMMENDED READING

For a comprehensive review of the research on infant memory development specifically, see:

Hayne, H. (2004). Infant memory development: Implications for childhood amnesia. *Developmental Review*, 24, 33–73.

This paper also contains a useful review of comparisons between adult memory research and infant memory research, which may help to answer these questions.

To read other research about the development of children's mathematical abilities and the role of working memory, see:

Barrouillet, P., & Lepine, R. (2005). Working memory and children's use of retrieval to solve addition problems. *Journal of Experimental Child Psychology*, 91, 183–204.

For a thorough examination of the development of children's ability to attend selectively, see:

Miller, P. H. (1990). The development of strategies of selective attention. In D. F. Bjorklund (Ed.), *Children's Strategies: Contemporary Views of Cognitive Development* (157–184). Hillsdale, NJ: Erlbaum.

For more information on the field of face recognition in children, see:

Pascalis, O., & Slater, A. (Eds.) (2003). *The Development of Face Processing in Infancy and Early Childhood: Current Perspectives*. New York: Nova Science.

For a consideration of memory research and how it helps us to understand the phenomenon of infantile amnesia, see:

Hayne, H. (2004). Infant memory development: Implications for childhood amnesia. *Developmental Review*, 24, 33–73.

For an overview of the foundations of research into the role of scripts in the development of memory, see:

Nelson, K., & Gruendel, J. (1986). Children's scripts. In K. Nelson (Ed.), *Event Knowledge, Structure and Function in Development* (231–247). Hillsdale, NJ: Erlbaum.

For further reading about false memories, see:

Brainerd, C. J., & Reyna, V. F. (2005). *The Science of False Memories*. Oxford: Oxford University Press.

For a detailed exploration of the development of cognitive interviewing as a technique for improving the witness testimony of children, see:

Fisher, R. P., & Geiselman, R. E. (1992). *Memory Enhancing Techniques for Investigative Interviewing: The Cognitive Interview*. Springfield, IL: Charles C. Thomas.

Geiselman, R. E., & Fisher, R. P. (1997). Ten years of cognitive interviewing. In D. G. Payne & F. G. Conrad (Eds.), *Intersections in Basic and Applied Memory Research* (291–310). Mahwah, NJ: Erlbaum.

For a consideration of the influences of heredity and the environment on cognition right across the lifespan, see:

McGue, M., Bouchard, T. J., Iacono, W. G., & Lykken, D. T. (1993). Behavioural genetics and cognitive ability: A lifespan perspective. In R. Plomin & G. E. McClearn (Eds.), *Nature, Nurture and Psychology* (59–76). Washington: APA.

RECOMMENDED WEBSITES

Human memory: test yourself:

http://www.psychologistworld.com/memory/test1.php

Cognitive interviewing: a 'how-to' guide:

http://appliedresearch.cancer.gov/archive/cognitive/interview.pdf#search=cognitive%20interview

Mnemonics: fun with words:

http://www.fun-with-words.com/mnemonics.html

The mystery of infant memories:

http://brainconnection.brainhq.com/2013/04/22/gone-but-not-forgotten-the-mystery-behind-infant-memories/

fMRI:

http://www.radiologyinfo.org/en/info.cfm?pg=fmribrain&bhcp=1

Take an IQ test online:

http://www.free-iqtest.net/iq.asp

National Association for Able Children in Education:

http://www.nace.co.uk/

Chapter 7
The development of mathematical thinking

Terezinha Nunes and Peter Bryant

Learning outcomes

After reading this chapter, and with further recommended reading, you should be able to:

1. Explain the difference between mathematical concepts and categorical concepts.
2. Discuss the difficulties in learning the meaning of numbers, both whole and rational numbers, and the connections between numbers and quantities.
3. Describe research into children's learning of number meanings, including whole and rational numbers.
4. Explain the connection between schemas of action and children's understanding of arithmetic operations.
5. Design theoretically driven assessments of children's understanding of additive and multiplicative reasoning.
6. Use research to argue that there is a crucial difference between knowing how and knowing when to do sums.

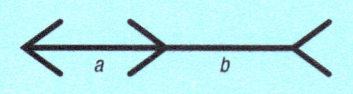

The power of maths

It is most likely that you have seen this picture in other psychology texts. It is called the Müller-Lyer illusion (Müller-Lyer, 1890). The horizontal line is divided in two segments, *a* and *b*, by the arrow head. Are the segments the same size? When you look at them, you see them as different, but if you take a ruler and measure them, you will find that they are the same. This is an example of the power and also of the intellectual demands of mathematics.

The power of mathematics in this example is that it allows you to go beyond perception: you don't see the segments as the same, but you know that they are the same. You use something to represent the size of the segments, compare the representations and draw a conclusion from the representations. Much of mathematics is about using signs, such as numbers or letters, to represent something like a quantity, a relation or an unknown value, and about manipulating these signs to arrive at conclusions about what is represented. Mathematics therefore allows us to go beyond mere perception in understanding the world around us.

- What numbers, letters or symbols can you think of that are used in mathematics?
- Think back across the course of the last couple of days. How many times have you used maths in your everyday life?
- What problems, questions or challenges has maths allowed you to solve?

Introduction

Mathematical thinking has been of interest to developmental psychologists for about a century and it still fascinates cognitive development researchers. There are many reasons for the continued interest in how children's mathematical thinking develops. Some people become interested in how children learn mathematics because they are, themselves, very fond of mathematics. Others are fascinated by children's mathematical thinking because of the ingenious ways in which some children solve mathematical problems, drawing on resources that might not have occurred to us adults. Still others are interested in children's mathematical thinking because of the amazing misconceptions and deductive failures to which children seem to be prone.

Besides all of these somewhat personal reasons, there is one really good reason for developmental psychologists to be interested in mathematics: mathematics is such an important part of our culture that everyone who goes to school is required to learn mathematics. The universal aim of learning mathematics is matched only by one other learning aim, which is learning to read and write. It is obvious why every child is required to learn to read and write: reading gives people access to books and to the internet, from which we can all learn a great deal, and it enables us to learn on our own. Reading gives us a ticket to ideas and information, ways of thinking and arguing, and communication that is not bound by things that are immediately present in our physical environment.

Most people would readily agree that mathematics is just as necessary for everyone as reading, but their reasons may differ. Some people think that mathematics is important for everyone because it is a skill that we all need in daily life. People need to know the arithmetic operations required to get on in life. For example, we need to calculate prices and change; to estimate how long we need to get somewhere; to determine when we should leave the house if we do not want to be late for a meeting; to figure out how much medicine to give our pet if the dosage depends on body weight.

If all we needed to know about maths were computations then we wouldn't need much more than just a calculator.

Others might argue that, whilst all of this is true, it is not the whole story. Mathematical skills are certainly important for daily life, but mathematics is much more than this, and everyone needs much more than computation skills. Galileo (whose father did not want him to become a mathematician because this was such a poorly paid career) saw mathematics as a way of understanding

> this great book of the universe, which stands continuously open to our gaze [but which] cannot be understood unless one first learns to comprehend the language and to read the alphabet in which it is composed. It is written in the language of mathematics. (Sobel, 2000, p. 16)

If all we needed to know about mathematics were computation skills, we would not need to learn mathematics nowadays: anyone can afford a calculator today, and this would solve the problem. However, each time we use a calculator, we need to make a choice about which calculation is the right one to use. The understanding behind this choice is much more than a skill; it involves insight into the relationship between numbers and the world. This chapter is about how children develop insights into the relationships between numbers and the world; it is not about calculation skills. It encompasses calculation only in so far as the way in which children calculate tells us something about the way they think about, and with, numbers.

CASE STUDY

The complexity of understanding relations

Megan, Alice and Deborah, aged 4, meet in the playground. Alice points to a boy on a tricycle and says: 'That's my brother.' Deborah points to a boy climbing a frame and says: 'That's my brother'. This is the first time Megan has come across the word 'brother'. Megan's mum comes over to give her a drink. Megan says, as she points to the correct boys: 'Mummy, that is Alice's brother and that is Deborah's brother'. She used the word correctly.

- Does Megan know what the word 'brother' means?
- What is difficult about the meaning of the word 'brother'?
- In what way is it different from words like 'cat' and 'car'?

What is mathematical thinking?

The development of mathematical thinking is in some ways similar (but of course not identical) to language learning. In order to progress in mathematical thinking, children must learn mathematical symbols and their meanings, and must be able to combine them sensibly, just as they learn to combine words sensibly in sentences. Learning meanings for mathematical symbols is often more difficult than one might expect. Think of learning the meaning of the word 'brother', in the example above. Megan was able to tell her mother correctly that the two boys in the playground were Alice's and Deborah's brothers. But this does not necessarily mean that she knows the meaning of 'brother'. 'Brother of' is an expression that is based on a set of kinship relationships; in order to understand its meaning, we need to understand other relationships, including 'mother of' and 'father of'. We could test whether Megan really understood the meaning of the word 'brother' in several different ways. For example, if she found out that another little girl in the playground, Emma, was Alice's sister, she should be able to know that Alice's brother is also Emma's brother.

Think back to the Müller-Lyer illusion from the beginning of the chapter, which illustrates how we can use mathematics to understand space. The intellectual demand here is that you need to understand transitivity. In other words, if two elements A and B have a relation to each other, and B and C also have the same relation, this relation is transitive if it implies that A and C also have the same relation to each other. In the illusion, if a is equal to 3.3 cm and b is equal to 3.3 cm, then $a = b$. Equality and equivalence are transitive relations. (Note, however, that if $A \neq B$ and $B \neq C$, this does not imply that $A \neq C$. Non-equivalence is not a transitive relation.) This illustrates the core intellectual demand that mathematics makes of us: the need to understand relations between things, rather than just understanding things in isolation.

Understanding relational concepts, such as 'brother of', is different from learning the meanings of words like 'cat' and 'car' for two main reasons. Firstly, when children learn words like 'cat' and 'car', they develop perceptual prototypes for cats and cars and use these prototypes to identify other exemplars of these categories. Chapter 5, Language Development, explores the

Definitions

Transitivity: a property of relations where new logical conclusions about one relation can be reached on the basis of premises about two other relations. For example, if $A = B$ and $B = C$, then $A = C$.

Relations: the positions, associations, connections, or status of one person, thing or quantity with regard to another or others; relational statements have an implied converse, so that (for example) if A is greater than B, then B must be less than A.

Prototype: a person or a thing that serves as an example of a type.

importance of the development of such category prototypes for language learning. A prototype for the category 'cat' might be a small, furry animal with four legs, a tail and pointy ears that says 'miaow', but there are no prototypes for relational words like 'brother'. Brothers have their gender in common (since all brothers are male), but being male does not define someone as a brother. Secondly, relational concepts allow for deducing new knowledge, whereas categorical concepts do not allow for generating new knowledge through inferences. Leaving aside reconstituted families, if we know that Tom is Megan's brother, and that Emma is Megan's sister, we can deduce that Tom is Emma's brother, thus generating new knowledge about the world.

The meanings of mathematical symbols, such as numbers, are based on relations and we can test whether children understand number by testing whether they understand the relations implied by the use of numbers. In the same way that Megan pointed to her friends' brothers and used the word 'brother' correctly, Megan could count a set of pens and say: 'five'. After going through the counting words, she could say the number 'five' to indicate correctly how many pens there are, but this does not assure us that she knows the meanings of numbers. 'Five' in mathematics does not just refer to the result of counting a set: 'five' also means something about which sets are equivalent to this one, and which sets are not. Understanding equivalences between sets (or, more generally, between quantities) is often referred to as the cardinal concept of number, or cardinality (this is closely related to the idea of cardinal numbers). If the items in one set can be paired up one-by-one with the items in another set, and neither set has any items left over, then the sets are equivalent and so have the same cardinality.

RESEARCH METHODS

Using puppets to explore children's understanding of cardinality

Gelman and Meck (1983) introduced the method of asking children to judge whether a puppet had counted correctly as a way of testing children's knowledge of counting principles. This method has been extended to the analysis of the inferences that children make about cardinality when they watch someone else counting. Bermejo et al. (2004) argued that if children really understand cardinality, they should be able to draw inferences about the number of objects in a set even if the researcher counts backwards while pointing to the objects. For example, if you count a set by saying 'three, two, one', and you reach the last item when you say 'one', you know that there are three objects in the set, not one, despite the fact that 'one' was the last counting word (number label) used. When you count a set of three backwards from four, the last number label used is 'two'. But you know that the set does not have two objects because you ran out of objects before reaching 'one', and you also know that it does not have four objects.

Bermejo and colleagues carried out research with 4- and 6-year-old children. These children could count correctly up to three and they could say that there were three objects in a set. The children were asked to say how many objects were in the set when the puppet counted in different ways, as outlined above. Many of these children answered that there were two objects in a set of three when the puppet counted backwards from four and the last number label was 'two'. In fact, many children did not realise that there was a contradiction between the two answers: for them, the set could have three objects if you counted one way and two if you counted in another way.

They then gave the children the opportunity to discuss what the cardinal was for the set when the counting was done backwards. Children who understood why the cardinal could be neither four nor two also showed progress in another task in which they had no practice: for example, knowing the cardinal for the set when the experimenter started to count from two, rather than from one.

- What does this tell you about the difference between knowing how to count and reflecting about the connection between counting and cardinality?

UNDERSTANDING NUMBER | **179**

Knowing how to count doesn't necessarily imply a full understanding of number.
Source: Pearson Education Ltd

Let's imagine that, having counted her set of pens, Megan then gives one pen to each one of her dolls. Each doll then has a pen. There are no pens left, and no dolls without a pen. Our mathematical abilities and our understanding of equivalences mean that we know that Megan must therefore have five dolls. But without actually counting the dolls, would Megan know this too?

Understanding number

What constitutes a true understanding of number?

From our discussion of Megan, it would seem that true mathematical thinking requires an understanding of number which goes beyond just the basic principles of counting. Some researchers (e.g. Gelman and Gallistel, 1978) do believe that number knowledge is demonstrated just by children's ability to count correctly, using all the number labels in the right order and in one-to-one correspondence with the objects they count, plus the ability to use the last number word in the counting sequence to say how many items are in a set. In contrast, Piaget (1952a) argued that, in order to credit children with an understanding of number, we need to check whether they understand the equivalence between sets. In other words, Megan should recognise that she had five dolls as well as five pens, in the examples given above. To place one of Piaget's studies in the context of this discussion: suppose that Megan exchanged with Alice each pen that she had for a sweet. We would expect Megan to know by the end of this exchange, without having to count, that she had five sweets; this would show that she understands something about cardinality. Piaget (1952a) and later Frydman and Bryant (1988) tested whether all children who can count a set can infer the number in another set, which they themselves said is equivalent to the first one. Both studies showed that not all the children who could count the first set correctly could say how many items were in the equivalent set without counting it as well. Frydman and Bryant reported that all the 4-year-olds in their study attempted to count the second set when asked how many items there were, even though they already knew the number in the equivalent set. The researchers then covered the second set up and encouraged the children to say how many items were in the set without counting: only 40% of the 4-year-olds answered the question correctly without counting.

Cardinality is important, but there is another meaning of number, the ordinal aspect, that we would want to test for in order to credit Megan with a sound understanding of number. In studying sets, ordinality is about the use of number words to indicate their order in relation to one another. For instance, the number six is higher relative to the number three, and so a set with six items or more in it will always be larger than a set with three items in it. The number two is less than the number three, though, and so a set with two items or fewer in it will always be smaller than a set with three items. Megan should know that a set with five pens has fewer pens than any set with six or more, and has more pens than any set with four

> **Definitions**
> Quantity: a property of magnitude or multitude used to express how much or how many of something there is.
> Cardinality: the property of being represented by a cardinal number.
> Cardinal numbers: numbers used in counting, to denote how many items are in a set.
> Ordinality: in set theory, this is the use of numbers to measure the position of a number in an ordered set.

or fewer. This aspect of number knowledge is known as the ordinal concept of number. In the context of mathematical thinking, in order to say that Megan understands numbers, we expect some demonstration that she understands the relational meanings of number words, and the cardinal as well as the ordinal aspect of number.

> **STOP AND THINK**
>
> **Going further**
>
> The inference that two sets have the same cardinal number does not depend on counting: if we can think of how sets could be placed in correspondence with one another, we can make inferences about the cardinal relation between the sets. You cannot count two infinite sets, but you can think of whether they could be placed in correspondence. Thinking about infinite sets is an intriguing aspect of cardinality. For example, think about the set of positive whole numbers. This is an infinite set. Now think about the set of odd positive whole numbers. This too is an infinite set. But could you place these two sets in one-to-one correspondence? Are they the same size – in other words, are they equivalent in cardinality?

Finally, in order to credit Megan with number understanding, we would also expect her to know that the number of pens does not change if we don't add pens to her set and we don't subtract pens from her set. We would also expect her to know that there would still be five pens if we added and then subtracted the same number of pens to and from the set. If she believed that the number changed without any addition or subtraction, and that it also changed after we added and subtracted the same number to the set of pens, we would conclude that she does not yet understand the meaning of numbers. Understanding the relationships between addition, subtraction and numbers is crucial because whole numbers are like points embedded in a network of additive relations. Additive relations are relations between quantities where those quantities are defined in the context of parts and wholes: for example,

> **Definition**
>
> Additive relations: relations between quantities defined within a part–whole schema.

knowing that a whole is equal to the sum of its parts, or knowing that the whole minus one part is equal to the other part. This kind of knowledge about the relations between parts and wholes is part of an understanding of additive relations.

As we have seen, whilst some researchers believe that number knowledge is demonstrated simply by children's ability to use counting principles correctly, others, such as Piaget (1952a), believe that it is an ability to make relational inferences which demonstrates true number knowledge. That is, that no-one can understand the meaning of number unless they can make certain inferences: inferences about the relations between quantities, from the numbers that represent quantities; and inferences about the numbers that represent quantities, from the relations between quantities.

One of Piaget's colleagues, Pierre Gréco (1962), set out to test whether children who could count realised that if two quantities are labelled by the same number, then they are equivalent quantities. He asked children to count two arrays of objects that had the same number. The objects in the arrays were not set up in visual correspondence, because one set was more spread out than the other, forming a longer row. All the children in his study could count the objects correctly and labelled the quantities by the same number, but this did not compel them to infer that the two quantities were equal. Instead, most went on to say that there were more objects in the row that was spread out more. So, for these children, the same number did not imply the same quantity.

Sarnecka and Gelman (2004) observed that children do not see the converse of this relation to be necessary either. In other words, they do not realise that the same quantity should imply the same number. The children first compared the number of snacks that a frog and a lion would be given (a task that could be carried out visually because of the way the snacks had been set up) and stated whether the animals had the same amount or had different amounts. The arrays of snacks were then set aside and, in their absence, the children were told, for example, that the frog had five strawberries. They were asked whether the lion had five or six strawberries. The children should answer 'five' if they had previously said that the animals had the same amount of snacks, but with a different number if they had said that they did not have the same amount.

In fact, not all of the children who had originally said that the quantities were the same inferred that the number should therefore also be the same. Even children who had shown in another task that they could correctly recognise five and six objects were not perfect in answering this question: they were on average correct in 80% of the trials. Children who could not recognise five and six objects correctly, but who could recognise two and three, performed at chance level (i.e. no better than someone who was just guessing) when both animals had five or six snacks.

This study adds an interesting piece of information to our understanding of the connections that children make between numbers and quantity. If a child knows the number of objects in a box, then they can correctly predict that that number will stay the same if nothing is added or taken away (and most of the time, they can also correctly predict that the number will change if one item is taken away or added). So for the same single quantity, they can predict that the number will not change if the quantity does not change. However, if there are two boxes then they cannot make a parallel inference about number from one box to the other. In other words, they cannot make parallel inferences when comparing two quantities. What does this tell you about using a number to label a quantity, as opposed to using numbers to think about relations between quantities?

In summary, if a child can count correctly – that is, can use number labels in the correct order, establish a one-to-one correspondence between number labels and objects, and say that the last number label is the number of objects in the set (see Gelman and Gallistel, 1978) – then we can credit this child with having good counting skills. However, we have argued that this is not sufficient to credit this child with a good understanding of number. Number knowledge can be used to generate further knowledge because of its relational nature.

Current theories about the origin of children's understanding of the meaning of cardinal and ordinal number

There are currently three main theories about how children come to understand the meaning of numbers. These theories illustrate well the nature–nurture debate in mathematical development and are briefly summarised here (also see the Nature–Nurture box on page 186).

Piaget's theory: the interactionist view

We have seen that Piaget's theory defines children's number competence on the basis of their understanding of relations between quantities; for him, cardinality is not just saying how many items are in sets, but is about grasping that sets which are in one-to-one correspondence are equivalent in number and vice versa. He argued that children could only be said to understand numbers if they made a connection between numbers and the relations between quantities that are implied by numbers. He also argued that this connection was established by children as they reflected about the effect of their actions on quantities. Setting items in correspondence, or adding and taking items away, are *schemes of action* which form the basis for children's understanding of how to compare and to change quantities. Imagine two young brothers comparing their collections of sweets after a Halloween evening spent trick or treating! By lining up their swag in two rows along their bedroom carpet, they could work out who has more even without being able to count correctly.

> **STOP AND THINK**
>
> ### Reflection
>
> In order to learn to count, respecting the counting principle, children need to establish a one-to-one correspondence between number labels and objects and to say the number labels always in the same order. So, in order to count 100 objects, you would need to know 100 number labels and always be able to say them in the same order.
>
> - How difficult do you think it is to learn 100 words in a fixed order by memory?
> - Do you think that children learn to count to 1000 by memorising 1000 words in a fixed order?
> - What other strategies might they use?

> **Definition**
>
> *Schemes of action:* representations of actions that can be applied to a variety of objects leading to predictable outcomes independent of the objects.

Piaget (1952a) acknowledged that learning to count can accelerate this process of reflection on actions, and so can some forms of social interaction. These may help children to realise the contradictions that they fall into when they say, for example, that two quantities are different even though they are labelled by the same number. However, the process that eventually leads to their understanding of the meanings of numbers and the implications of these representations of numbers is the child's growing understanding of relations between quantities.

Piaget's studies of children's understanding of the relations between quantities involved three different ideas that he considered central to understanding number: equivalence, order and class-inclusion (which refers to the idea that the whole is the sum of the parts, or that a set with six items comprises a set with five items plus one). The methods used in these studies have been extensively criticised, as has the idea that children develop through a sequence of stages that can be easily traced and are closely associated with age. However, the core idea that children come to understand relations between quantities by reflecting upon the results of their actions is still a very important hypothesis in the study of how children learn about numbers (see Recommended Reading). Later sections of this chapter will revisit Piaget's theory and discuss related research.

Piaget believed that reflecting upon the results of their actions is key to the development of children's understanding of relations between quantities.

Source: Pearson Education Ltd

The Nativist view

Piaget's is not the only theory about how children come to understand the meaning of cardinal numbers. Nativist theories are those which suggest we have certain in-born capacities, and one alternative theory about understanding number is a Nativist one, which proposes that children have access from birth to an innate, inexact but powerful analogue system (Dehaene, 1992, 1997; Gallistel and Gelman, 1992; Wynn, 1992, 1998; Xu and Spelke, 2000; Gelman and Butterworth, 2005). To understand this, think about a traditional analogue clock, with a face and two hands. This provides a concrete visual representation of time, where each one of the 60 minutes in an hour is represented as being a fixed distance apart, and where the minute hand travels around the clock face once every hour. The interval between one o'clock and two o'clock is the same as the interval between four and five o'clock. So time can be measured as a relation between distance and speed. In contrast, on a digital watch the time changes from 1:59 to 2:00 without giving us any clue as to why this change has taken place.

The Nativist theory proposes that we all have an in-built system which gives us the ability to make approximate judgements about numerical quantities. The system allows us to map the number labels that are used in counting onto corresponding points with discrete quantities (like the minutes on an analogue clock). It may not be precise or exact, but this system allows us to make judgements about numerical quantities, much like the judgements we make along other continua, such as loudness, brightness and length. Have you ever walked into a room and been struck by how bright it was? You made this judgement without needing a light meter and without knowing exactly how many lumens it was. Do we have an in-born system which allows us to make the same sorts of judgement about numerical quantity?

On this Nativist account, children also have innate knowledge of counting principles and they attach number words to the properties occasioning those magnitudes. One feature of all these kinds of judgement is that the greater the quantities (the louder, the brighter or the longer they are), the harder they are to discriminate between. This is known as the 'Weber function', after the great nineteenth-century psycho-physicist who meticulously studied perceptual sensitivity, and you can explore this yourself by carrying out a simple exercise, which is adapted from Carey (2004).

You are going to tap a certain number of times on the table without counting. To prevent yourself from counting, you should think 'the' with each tap. Get a friend to note silently how many times you actually tap. Tap out as fast as you can, whilst thinking 'the', the following numbers of taps: 4, 15, 7 and 28. Do this several more times, each time thinking 'the' with each tap, and getting someone else to note how many taps you actually make.

Have a look at the number of taps you actually made. Usually we would expect the average numbers of taps that were made to be 4, 15, 7 and 28, but it is the range of variation which is interesting. The range of variation is usually very tight when the target number of taps is 4 (usually there are 4 taps, occasionally 3 or 5), but very great when the target is 28 (anything from 14 to 40 taps). The Weber function predicts, then, that it is more difficult to discriminate 28 from 30 than it is to discriminate 4 from 6. This prediction is supported in studies of the discriminability of a number of dots randomly spread on a background (Dehaene et al., 1998) and in the study of the number of taps that we can distinguish from each other without counting (Carey, 2004).

The evidence for this analogue system being an innate one comes largely from studies of infants (Xu and Spelke, 2000; McCrink and Wynn, 2004) and, to a certain extent, from studies of animals as well, and is beyond the scope of this chapter (see Recommended Reading if you want to know more). The evidence for its importance for learning about number and arithmetic comes from studies of developmental or acquired dyscalculia (see Recommended Reading). However important this basic system may be as a neurological basis for number processing, it is not clear how the link between an imprecise analogue system, and a precise system based on counting, can be forged. 'Ninety' does not mean 'approximately ninety' any more than 'eight' could mean 'approximately eight'. In fact, as reported by Sarnecka and Gelman (2004), 3- and 4-year-olds know that if a set has six items and you add one item to it, it no longer has six objects: they know that 'six' is not the same as 'approximately six'.

The empiricist view

A third well-known theoretical alternative, which starts from a standpoint in agreement with Gelman's theory, is Susan Carey's (2004) hypothesis about three ways of learning about number. Carey accepts Gelman and Gallistel's (1978) limited definition of the cardinality principle, but rejects their conclusions about how children first come to understand this principle. Carey argues that initially (by which she means in the first three years of life), very young children can represent number in three different ways (LeCorre and Carey, 2007). The first is through the analogue system, described in the previous section. However, although she thinks that this system plays a part in people's informal experiences of quantity throughout their lives, she does not seem to assign it a role in children's learning about the counting system, or in any other part of the mathematics that they learn about at school.

In her theory, the second of her three systems, which she calls the 'parallel individuation' system, plays the crucial part in making it possible for children to learn how to connect number with the counting system. This system makes it possible for infants to recognise and represent very small numbers exactly, not approximately like the analogue system. The system only operates for sets of one, two and three objects, but even within this restricted scope there is marked development over children's first three years.

Initially the parallel individuation system allows very young children to recognise sets of one as having a distinct quantity. The child understands 1 as a quantity, though he or she does not at first know that the word 'one' applies to this quantity. Later on the child is able to discriminate and recognise – in Carey's words, 'to individuate' – sets of one and two objects, and still later, around the age of 3 to 4 years, sets of one, two and three objects as distinct quantities. In Carey's terms, young children progress from being 'one-knowers' to becoming 'two-knowers' and then 'three-knowers'. It should be noted that this knowledge is categorical, not relational: the children

> **Definition**
>
> **Dyscalculia:** impaired number comprehension, number production or calculation. When attributed to brain damage, it is known as acquired dyscalculia. With no evidence of brain damage, and a discrepancy between number abilities and general intelligence, it is known as developmental dyscalculia.

know 'one', 'two' and 'three' from perception as distinct categories, but have not established necessary connections or understanding of the relations between these numbers.

During the same period, these children also learn number words and, though their recognition of 1, 2 and 3 as distinct quantities does not in any way depend on this verbal learning, they do manage to associate the right counting words ('one', 'two' and 'three') with the right quantities. The association between parallel individuation and the list of counting words eventually leads to what Carey (2004) calls 'bootstrapping': the children lift themselves up by their own intellectual bootstraps. They do so some time in their fourth or fifth year, and therefore well before they go to school.

This bootstrapping takes two forms. First, with the help of the constant order of number words in the count list, children begin to learn about the ordinal properties of numbers: for example, that 2 always comes after 1 in the count list and is always more numerous than 1; 3 is more numerous than 2 and always follows 2. Second, since the fact that the count list that the children learn goes well beyond 3, they eventually infer that the number words represent a continuum of distinct quantities which also stretches beyond 'three'. This inference is based on induction in that from a limited number of examples the children reach a conclusion about an infinite sequence of numbers. They also begin to understand that the numbers above 3 are harder to discriminate from each other at a glance than sets of one, two and three are, but that they can be identified by counting. In Carey's words:

> The child ascertains the meaning of 'two' from the resources that underlie natural language quantifiers and from the system of parallel individuation, whereas she comes to know the meaning of 'five' through the bootstrapping process – i.e., that 'five' means one more than four, which is one more than three – by integrating representations of natural language quantifiers with the external serial ordered count list.

Carey called this new understanding 'enriched parallel individuation' (Carey, 2004, p. 65).

Definition

Induction: a type of reasoning where a factual conclusion is reached on the basis of empirical evidence, but need not necessarily be true.

Her main evidence for parallel individuation and enriched parallel individuation came from studies in which she used a task, originally developed by Wynn, called 'Give a number'. In this task, an experimenter asks the child to give her a certain number of objects from a set of objects in front of them: 'Could you take two elephants out of the bowl and place them on the table?' Children sometimes put out the number asked for and sometimes just grab objects apparently randomly. Using this task, Carey showed that different 3-, 4 and 5-year-old children can be classified quite convincingly as 'one-' 'two-' or 'three-knowers' or as 'counting-principle-knowers'. The one-knowers do well when asked to provide one object, but not when asked the other numbers, while the two- and three-knowers can, respectively, provide up to two and three objects successfully. The 'counting-principle-knowers', in contrast, count quantities above three or four. The evidence for the existence of these groups certainly supports Carey's interesting idea of a radical developmental change from 'knowing' some small quantities, to understanding that the number system can be extended to other numbers in the count list.

STOP AND THINK

Going further

Developments in 3- to 5-year-olds' understanding of number

Freeman et al. (2000) assessed 3- and 5-year-olds' number understanding by asking them to watch a puppet counting arrays of three or five items. Sometimes the puppet miscounted, by counting an item twice or by skipping an item. The puppet was then asked how many items were in the array. The puppet's answer was the last number word he had said when he counted – that is, the puppet correctly used Gelman's cardinality principle after counting the array, whether he had counted correctly or not. The children were asked whether the puppet had counted correctly and, if they said that the puppet had not, they were asked: 'How many does the puppet think there are?' and 'How many are there really?'

All the children had shown that they could count five items accurately. However, their competence in counting was no assurance that they realised that the puppet's answer was wrong after miscounting.

> Only about one-third of the children said that the answer was not right after they had detected the error, even if the number of items was only three. The children's rejection of the puppet's wrong answer increased with age, but not all 5-year-olds correctly rejected the puppet's answer in all three trials when the puppet made a counting error: only 82% did so. When the children were asked, 'How many are there really?', the majority could not say how many items were in the array without recounting. For example, they did not conclude that there were three if the puppet had skipped one item and had answered that there were two.
>
> - What does this tell you about 5-year-olds' ability to infer that '3' is one more than '2' from their knowledge of counting?

The third way in which children learn number, according to Carey's theory, is through a system which she called 'set-based quantification'. This is heavily dependent on language and particularly on words like 'a' and 'some' that are called 'quantifiers'. So far the implications for education of this third hypothesised system are not yet fully worked out, and so we won't discuss it any further.

The value of Carey's work is that it shows developmental changes in children's learning about the counting system. These had been by-passed by Piaget and his colleagues because their theory was about the underlying logic needed for this learning and not about counting itself, and also by Gelman, because her theory about counting principles was about innate or rapidly acquired structures and not about development. Carey's theory aims to explain children's understanding of ordinality – that is, the sequence of numbers and the increase of one from one number to the next in the sequence. However, her explanation of children's counting in terms of enriched parallel individuation suffers a limitation that we have already discussed in relation to Gelman: it does not measure children's understanding of cardinality in its full sense. Just knowing that the last number that you counted is the number of the set is not enough. Even when children achieve the insight that 2 is 1 more than 1, and that 3 is 1 more than 2, and extend this insight to other numbers in counting, they will not necessarily have understood that all sets with the same quantity are represented by the same number and vice versa.

Carey's theory has been subjected to much criticism for the role that it attributes to induction or analogy in children's learning about 'next numbers', and to language. Gelman and Butterworth (2005), for example, argue that groups which have very restricted number language still show understanding of larger quantities; their number knowledge is not restricted to small quantities as suggested in Carey's theory. Others have critiqued Carey from a more theoretical standpoint and argued that the bootstrapping hypothesis pre-supposes the very knowledge of number that it attempts to explain (see Recommended reading to learn more about this critique).

Which of these three approaches is right? There is not a simple answer. If understanding number is about understanding an ordered set of symbols that represent quantitative relations, Piaget's approach definitely has the edge. Neither Gelman's nor Carey's theory entertains the idea that numbers represent quantities and relations between quantities, and that it is necessary for children to understand this system of relations in order to understand what numbers mean. Their research did nothing to dent Piaget's view that children are still learning about very basic relations between numbers and quantities at age 5.

In summary, it is important to remember that numbers and quantities are not the same thing. Numbers can be used to represent quantities, but this is not obvious to children from the time they can count correctly. Gelman's studies of children's counting established that even very young children count correctly when they do count. However, this does not indicate that they understand cardinality or ordinality. Carey's theory attempts to explain how children combine their initially categorical perception of number with learning to count, in order to understand that any number in the counting string is one more than the preceding number. However, even at age 5 children still seem unable to predict that if you counted a set wrongly by skipping an item and said that there were two items, the number in the set would be three. Piaget's theory proposes that understanding number must be grounded in children's understanding of quantities, which is attained through their schemes of action. Children's actions on quantities, changing and comparing them, lead them to understand relations between quantities, and these will provide the basis for their understanding of number. Learning the number string in and of itself does not lead to understanding the relations between numbers.

NATURE–NURTURE

Where does the meaning of numbers come from?

On the Nativist view, exemplified in the work of Gelman and Gallistel and also of Dehaene, we are born with mechanisms that allow us to perceive quantities as well as with mechanisms that allow us to count in a principled way (i.e. following the counting principles). These innate mechanisms come together so that the number labels acquire meaning by their connections with the quantities that we distinguish perceptually. Although it is not clear in the theory how the two come together, it is quite clear that the theory endows the mind with innate mechanisms that are crucial to the acquisition of number knowledge. These theories represent the idea that in mathematical thinking, nature underlies development.

In the empiricist view, illustrated by Carey's theory, the meaning of number words comes from perceiving the differences between small sets and connecting these differences to the perceived sequence of number words. The existence of 'one-knowers' who differ from 'two-knowers' who also differ from 'three-knowers' speaks against innate mechanisms in her theory. The inference that there is a difference of one between each number label and the subsequent number label throughout the whole counting sequence is made by induction, which is the mechanism of learning typical of empiricist theories, although Carey refers to it as 'bootstrapping'. Both mechanisms of development in her theory – noticing that there is a difference of exactly one between one and two and also between two and three, as well as the inference made from learning the counting sequence – are derived from experience. This places Carey's theory in the nurture territory, by comparison with Gelman and Dehaene.

The interactionist view is illustrated by Piaget, who argued that mathematical relations are not reducible to mere biology. In his theory, babies are born with reflexes (e.g. sucking and grasping) that become schemes of action through their use and adaptation to objects to which they are applied. Schemes of action become progressively coordinated with each other and eventually with signs and symbols. The meaning of numbers is constructed through schemes of action such as addition and subtraction, and through reflection about the consequences of adding or subtracting elements from a set. According to Piaget, learning to count can accelerate this process of construction because the use of signs to represent the sets supports reflection about the effects of the child's actions.

No crucial research exists that directly contrasts these different views. A direct contrast would take the form of an experiment in which two (or more) of the theories would make contradictory predictions about the same situation. Currently, an evaluation of these theories relies much more on their value in guiding new discoveries about children's mathematical development. In that respect, there is little doubt that much more research about children's mathematical development has been prompted by Piaget's than any other theory at present.

The number system as a tool for thinking

So far we have focused only on small numbers and, more specifically, on the relations between consecutive numbers, such as 2 and 3, or 5 and 6. These numbers represent small quantities, which one can often discriminate without having to count. Learning to count undeniably extends our ability to make comparisons between quantities to values beyond those that we can discriminate perceptually. Children may not be able to look at a pile of books and tell without counting that the one with 17 has more books than the one with 15; indeed, the thickness of books varies and the pile of 15 books could well be taller than the pile with 17. By counting, they can know which pile has more books, but that presumes that children know that counting is a good way of comparing two quantities. This section addresses two questions: the first

When do children learn that counting is a tool for thinking?
Source: Pearson Education Ltd/Brand X Pictures/Joe Atlas

Children often rely on perceptual cues rather than counting, to compare quantities.
Source: Photolibrary

is whether children who can count realise that counting is a tool for comparing quantities – a tool for thinking; the second is what seems to be required for children to learn to say counting labels beyond the limits of their memory for a series of words in a fixed order.

Do children know that counting is a tool for comparing quantities?

Most of the research on this topic suggests that it takes children some time to realise that they can, and often should, count to compare. Certainly many pre-school children seem not to have grasped the connection between counting and comparing even if they have been able to count for more than one year.

It seems that even at school age many children do not fully understand the significance of numbers when they make quantitative comparisons. It has been observed in many studies (Michie, 1984; Saxe et al., 1987; Cowan and Daniels, 1989) that children who can count quite well nevertheless fail to count the items in two sets that they have been asked to compare numerically; instead they rely on perceptual cues, like length, which of course are unreliable. Children who understand the cardinality of number should understand that they can make reliable comparisons between larger sets only by counting or using one-to-one correspondence, and yet at the age of 5 and 6 years most of them do neither, even when, as in the Cowan and Daniels study, the one-to-one cues are emphasised by lines drawn between items in the two sets that the children were asked to compare.

Another source of evidence comes from the way children use counting to solve different problems. Counting does not always have to follow the same routine. If you are counting two rows of objects to find out which one has more, you need to count one row and start again from the number one when you count the other row. If you are counting two rows to find out how many items there are altogether, you count one row and continue from the next number when you go on to the second row. Sophian (1988) asked children to judge whether a puppet was counting the right way in order to answer these two different questions. Sometimes the puppet did the right thing, which was to count the two sets separately when comparing them and to count all the items together when working out the grand total. At other times he got it wrong: that is, he counted all the objects as one set when asked to compare the two sets. The main result of Sophian's study was that the pre-school children found it very hard to make this judgement. The most common pattern of responses was for the 3-year-olds to judge counting each

Definition

Tool for thinking: a culturally developed system of signs that allows the user to represent something and operate on the representations in order to reach a conclusion about the represented reality.

set separately as the right way to count in both tasks and for the 4-year-olds to judge counting both sets together as the right way to count in both tasks. Neither age group could identify the right way to count reliably.

So the use of counting as a tool for comparing quantities requires knowing how to use counting in ways that depend upon the task. A routine-like approach to implementing counting does not work when what we want to do is to use counting as a thinking tool. Pre-school children, aged 3 and 4 years, who know how to count, don't necessarily know how to use counting as a tool for thinking.

How do children learn the number system beyond the initial string of numbers?

Learning to count to 100 is a task that taxes our memory for serial recall. In order to count correctly, we need to say all the number labels in a fixed order. Remembering 100 words in a fixed order is a challenging task. Fortunately, we do not have to master this task as a memory task. Number systems are created by cultures in a rule-like fashion, which requires more understanding than memory. (For more information about the role of culture and symbols in mathematical reasoning, see Recommended Reading.)

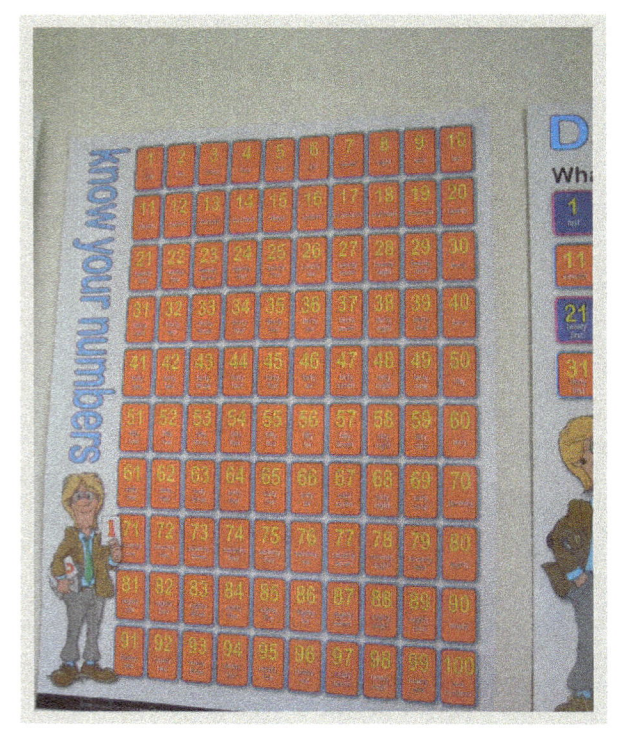

Does learning to count to 100 require memorising a list of 100 numbers?
Source: Lam

> **STOP AND THINK**
>
> ### Reflection
>
> When young children are learning to count, they may proudly tell an adult how far they can count. If a child says to you, 'I can count up to 24!' and then shows this to be true, you could encourage the child to think about what number comes after 24.
>
> - What could you infer about the way this child is learning to count if the child just could not think what number comes after 24?

A number system can be a simple string of numbers, without any recursive use of number labels, or it can be structured by one or more values that allow for the recursive use of number labels. The Oksapmin, an indigenous group in Papua New Guinea, use a number system based on body parts, in which the names of body parts are used as number labels (Saxe, 1981). You start counting by using the name for 'right thumb' as the word corresponding to 1, followed by 'right index finger' to correspond to 2, etc., going on through the fingers, up the arm and so on until you reach the left little finger, which corresponds to 27. This system is non-recursive and finite. This contrasts with numeration systems that have a base, which marks the grouping of units and the recursive use of number labels. In English, 10 is used as a base, so when we reach 10 units we start repeating the number labels. The words between 11 and 19 do reveal this, but the use of repetition in number words is more transparent after 20.

The number words used in English rely on two principles: one is additive and the other multiplicative. The additive principle is very clear in number words like 'twenty one', 'twenty two', 'twenty three', etc. We do not say 'twenty plus one', 'twenty plus two', 'twenty plus three', but this addition is part of understanding the system. The multiplicative principle is more transparent in counting words with hundreds and thousands: the words 'two hundred', 'three hundred', 'four hundred', etc. mean 2 × 100, 3 × 100, 4 × 100 and so on. But the multiplicative principle is also applied to decades, even if the words do not indicate this as clearly: twenty mean two tens, thirty means three tens, forty means four tens, etc.

Understanding these principles is taxing because two insights are necessary. The first is called the additive composition of number. To put it simply, additive composition means that any number can be seen as the total of two other numbers. Researchers such as Piaget and Resnick (e.g. Resnick and Ford, 1981), who held different views about many other aspects of mathematical development, agree about the importance of additive composition for understanding number (which Resnick and Ford refer to as part–whole relations).

The second insight is the multiplicative idea required to understand that units can have different values; in our number system, they can have the value of one, ten, hundred, thousand, etc. This idea is also used in written numbers. In the Hindu–Arabic number notation that we use, each digit's value depends on its position, from right to left. So the number 222 has the digit '2' representing three different values, ones, tens and hundreds.

Children seem to learn to count initially by what one could call 'brute memory'. But this way of learning to count has limits; they may, for example, stop at 24 and find it difficult to answer the question 'what number comes after 24?' Once they understand additive composition, they can always count up within a decade, but may get stuck when they come, for example, to 29 and find it difficult to say what comes after 29. Once they understand the multiplicative principle and realise that there is a connection between the decades and the beginning of the counting string, they can suddenly count on to 100, as they know how to find the transition from one decade to the next. However, they may do this at a verbal level, establishing connections between the number words and their sequence, without an insight into the representation of quantities.

Definitions

Decades: values in a numeration system with a base 10 that include one or more groups of 10 units. In English, twenty, thirty, forty, etc. up to ninety are the number labels for decades.

Additive composition: the property of numbers that allows any to be defined as the sum of two other numbers.

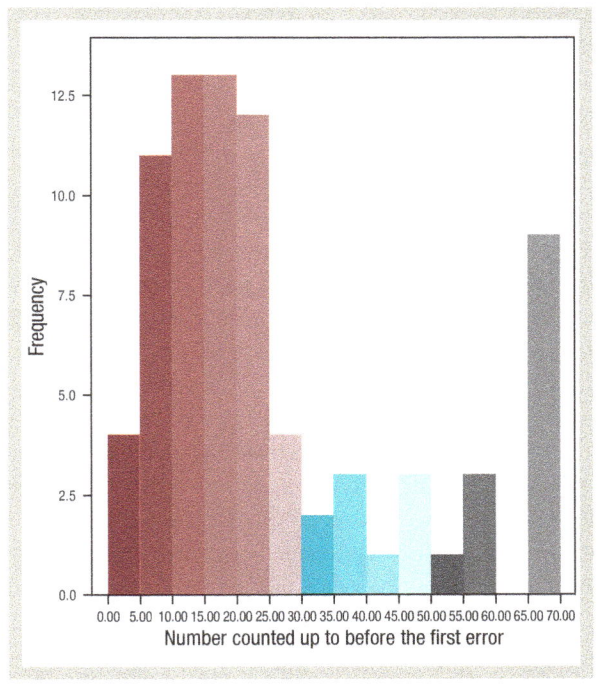

Figure 7.1 The stopping points in children's counting ability by frequency.

When we looks at graphs which describe the frequencies for the different stopping points in children's counting ability, an interesting pattern emerges. Look at Figure 7.1 and think about what the pattern tells you about how children learn to count.

Eighty children of around 6 years of age, in their first year of school, were asked to count a row of 70 monkeys. Sometimes they made mistakes, but did not stop counting; sometimes they stopped and said that they did not know what the next number was. Figure 7.1 shows the frequencies of children who counted correctly up to each number. The numbers are grouped in sets of five to make the graph easier to read. What might explain the fact that the majority of the children made their first error before the number 30? What might explain the fact that, after the number 30, more children make a mistake in the transition to the next decade (i.e. between 35 and 40 or between 45 and 50) than at the beginning of the decade (i.e. between 30 and 35 or between 40 and 45)?

Additive composition is also at the root of our ability to count money using coins and notes of different denominations, and so we can use money counting as a means to test children's understanding of how the principles for counting labels relate to quantities. When we have, for

CHAPTER 7 THE DEVELOPMENT OF MATHEMATICAL THINKING

example, one 10p and five 1p coins, we can only count their value together if we understand something about additive composition. Nunes and Schliemann (1990) drew on this idea to devise the 'shop task', which allowed them to see how well children were able to combine units of different values additively with their knowledge of the counting string. In the shop task, children are shown a set of toys in a 'shop', are given some (real or artificial) money and are asked to choose a toy that they would like to buy. Then the researcher asks them to pay a certain sum for the toy of their choice. Sometimes the child can pay for this with coins of one denomination only: for example, the experimenter charges a child 15p for a toy car and the child has sufficient 1p coins to make the purchase. In other trials, the child can pay only by combining denominations: the toy costs 15p and the child, having fewer 1p coins than that, must pay with the combination of a 10p and five 1p coins. Although the values that the children are asked to pay when they use only 1p coins and when they must use combinations of different coins are the same, the mixed denomination trials are significantly more difficult than the other trials in the task. There is a marked improvement between the ages of 5 and 7 years in children's performance in combining coins of different denominations. This work was originally carried out in Brazil, but the results have been confirmed in research carried out in the UK (Krebs et al., 2003; Nunes et al., 2007a).

Figure 7.2 displays the frequencies of children with different proportions of responses correct when the trials

Tasks using money of different denominations help us to explore children's understanding of additive composition.
Source: Fotolia

in the shop task involved counting only 1p coins, and in additive composition trials when the children had to combine coins of different values. The 40 children were in their first year in school; their mean age was 5 years

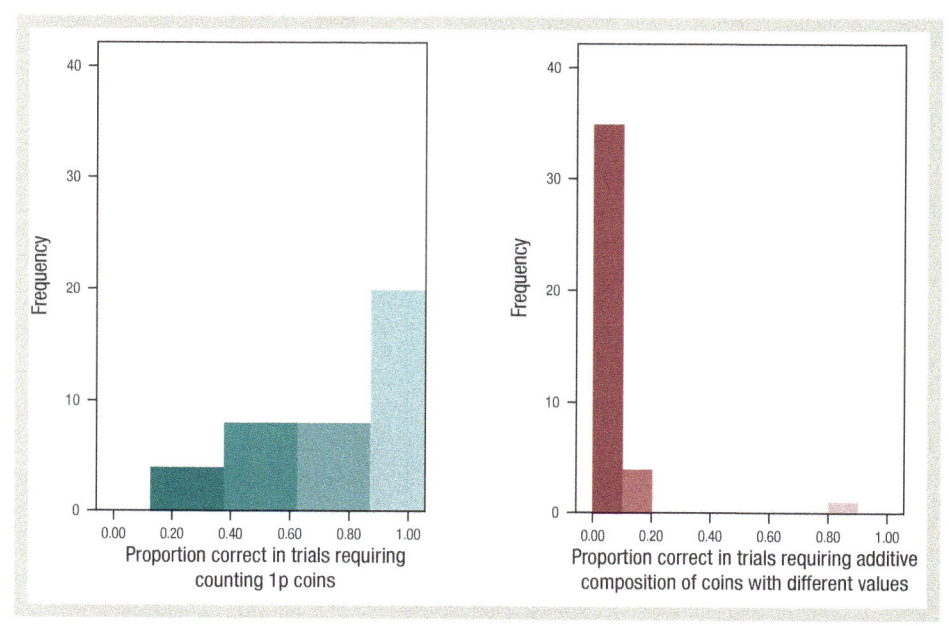

Figure 7.2 Frequency of children showing different proportions of correct responses in the two types of trial in the shop task.

and the age range was from 4½ to 5½ years. Note that the children in this study are younger than those in the previous study because the age of entry into school in the UK was lowered between the two studies. The total that the children had to pay was the same in the two types of trial. In the additive composition trials, they were asked to combine: (a) 2p and 1p coins to pay values up to 5p; (b) 5p and 1p coins to pay values up to 9p; (c) 10p and 1p coins to pay values up to 19p; and (d) 20p and 1p coins to pay values up to 29p.

What do these results suggest to you about the difference between children's counting skill and their ability to understand additive composition of number?

When children succeed in the shop task in combining, for example, 10p and 1p coins, they point to the 10p coin and say 'ten', and then go on to say 'eleven, twelve, thirteen', etc. until they reach the value they have been asked to pay. Children who do not succeed in the task point to the 10p coin and say 'ten', but do not carry on with the counting when they point to the 1p coins. They either start from one or they count in tens as they point to the 1p coins ('10, 20, 30 . . .'), as if 'ten' triggered their memory for a different counting string that refers to decades only. So children who fail this task simply use two counting strings, one that increases by one unit and the other that increases by 10 units, but do not combine the tens and ones to compose a number such as 15. Children who succeed in this task at the time when they start school perform significantly better in mathematics assessments at a later age, when they have had two years of mathematics instruction (see Nunes et al., 2007a).

A fascinating observation in the shop task is that children seem to go through an intermediary phase between being unable to use additive composition and succeeding in the task. This intermediary phase involves trying to represent all the units 'hidden' in the 10p coin: they may point to the 10p coin 10 times as they count from one to ten, and then go on to count the 1p coins, or they may lift up 10 fingers and say 'ten', and only then go on to count 'eleven, twelve, thirteen', etc. This repeated pointing to count invisible objects has been documented also by Steffe and his colleagues (e.g. Steffe et al., 1983). It has been interpreted as a significant step in understanding how addition is part of composing numbers. The restriction that the children experience is that they want the parts that they are adding to be 'visible' to them in some way, and so they use gestures or fingers to represent them in a perceptible format.

> **STOP AND THINK**
>
> **Reflection**
>
> Chris, aged 5, is a good counter: he can count sets correctly up to 30. He counted his marbles and knew that he had eight marbles in his pocket when he walked with his parents down the road to visit his uncle. They stopped at the park and he played on the climbing frame. When he got to his uncle's house, he wanted to show off his marbles and was upset to find that some marbles were missing. He remembered the nice shiny one he had got the day before and it was not there. His uncle said he would give him the same number of marbles that he had lost; all Chris had to do was to tell him how many marbles he had lost. Chris counted his marbles and said he had six now. Then he said he could not know how many marbles he had lost because he could not count them – *he had lost them*!
>
> - How would you describe Chris's knowledge of number?

In a recent study, Nunes et al. (2008b) encouraged children who did not succeed in the shop task to use the transition behaviour observed previously. The researchers asked the children to show ten with their fingers; they then pointed to their fingers and to the 10p coin and asked the children to say how much there was in each display. Finally, the researchers encouraged them to go on and count the money. This study showed that some children seemed able to grasp the idea of additive composition quite quickly after this training and still performed well on the task after a two-week delay since training had been completed. Others did not benefit significantly from brief training sessions using this procedure. Figure 7.3 presents a comparison between the training (intervention) group and the control (no intervention) group at the immediate post-test and the delayed post-test. Although the groups had not differed at pre-test, they differed significantly at both post-tests.

Since children appear to be finding out about the additive nature of the base 10 system and at the same time (their first two years at school) about the additive composition of number in general, one can reasonably ask what the connection between these two is. One possibility is that children must gain a full understanding of the additive composition of number before they can understand the decade structure. Another is that instruction about the

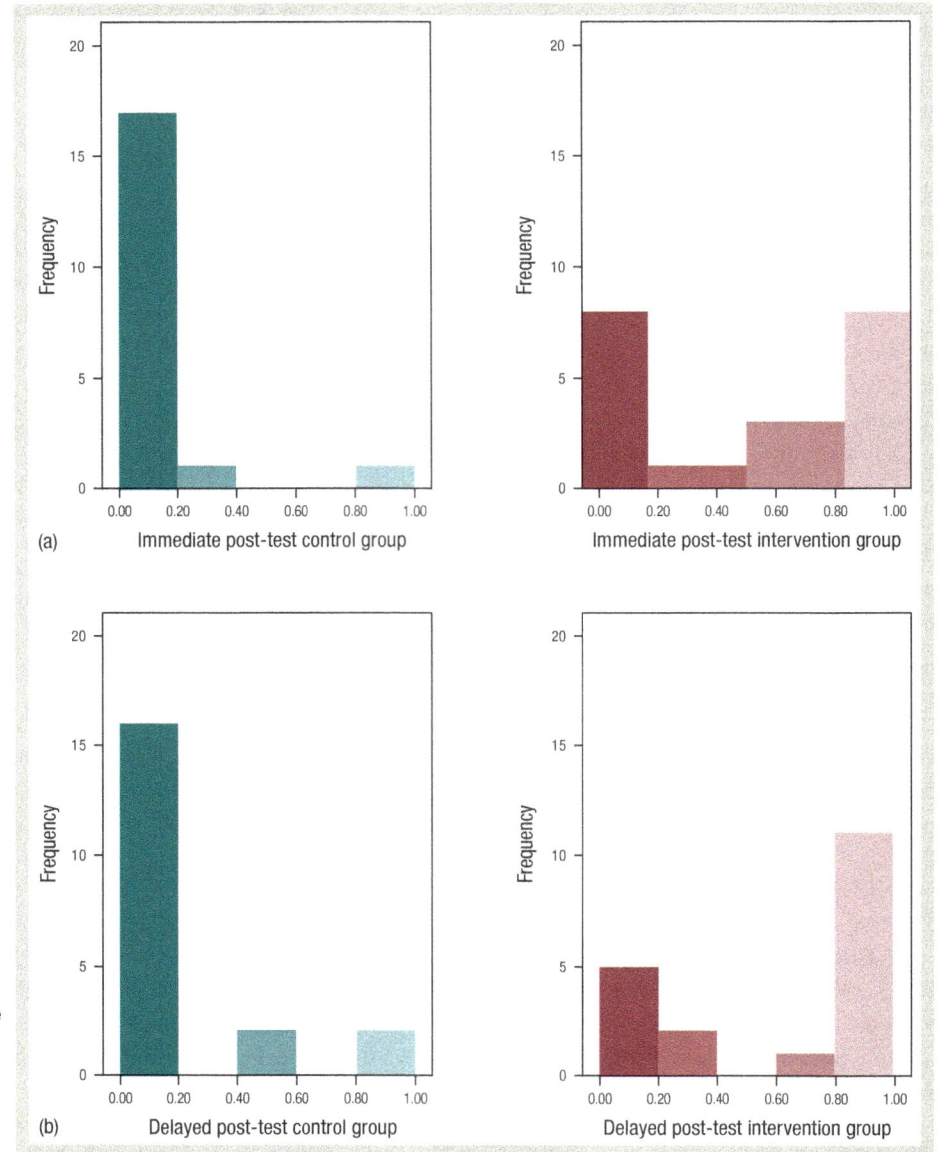

Figure 7.3 Frequency of children showing different proportions of correct responses in the shop task by group. Part (a) shows the results in the immediate post-test, given right after training. Part (b) shows the results in a delayed post-test, given about two weeks later.

decade structure is children's first introduction to additive composition. First they learn that 12 is a combination of 10 and 2 and then they extend this knowledge to other combinations (e.g. 12 is also a combination of 8 and 4). The results of a recent study by Krebs et al. (2003), in which the same children were given the shop task and counting all/counting on tasks, favour the second hypothesis. All the children who consistently counted on (the more economic strategy because it does not require counting all the items) also did well on the shop task. Some children scored well in the shop task, but nevertheless tended not to count on. However, no child scored well in the counting on task but poorly in the shop task.

Definitions

Counting all: term used to describe behaviour in addition tasks whereby children join sets and start counting from one, e.g. when adding seven and five tokens, they count all the items in the first set starting from one and then continue counting as they point to the items in the second set.

Counting on: term used to describe behaviour in addition tasks whereby children start counting from the number after the value of one set, e.g. when adding seven and five tokens, they point to an item in the second set and start to count from 8.

This pattern suggests that the cues present in language help children learn about the base 10 system first and then extend their new understanding of additive composition to combinations that do not involve decades.

In summary, it seems that counting systems are thinking tools for solving problems. They can be used by children to compare sets or to find how many items are in two sets altogether, but in order to do so the children must know how to use counting in different ways. The number system that we use is a good example of an invented and culturally transmitted mathematical tool. It frees us from having to remember extended sequences of number and enhances our power to compare quantities and to calculate. Once we know the rules for the decade system and the names of the different classes and orders (tens, hundreds, thousands, etc.), we can use the system to count by generating numbers ourselves. However, the system also makes some quite difficult intellectual demands. Children find it hard at first to combine different values, such as tens and ones. The ability to combine different values rests on a thorough grasp of additive composition. There is some evidence that experience with the structure of the base 10 system enhances children's understanding of additive composition. There is also evidence that experience with money may play a role in children's progress in understanding additive composition.

Reasoning and solving problems with numbers

> **STOP AND THINK**
>
> **Reflection**
>
> One might think that a natural progression in development is that children first learn about numbers and then learn to use numbers to solve addition and subtraction problems. However, the previous discussion suggests that children need to learn about addition and subtraction in order to understand numbers, because the meaning of numbers is based on additive relations.
>
> - Is it possible that there is a mutual influence between children's understanding of additive relations and their understanding of number?
> - If so, what might this idea of mutual influence mean in practice?
> - What might it mean for mathematics teaching?

Additive reasoning

Additive reasoning refers to reasoning used to solve problems where addition or subtraction is the operation used to find a solution. The expression 'additive reasoning' is used rather than addition and subtraction problems, because it is often possible to solve the same problem either by addition or by subtraction. For example, if you buy something that costs 35 pounds, you may pay with two 20 pound notes. You can calculate your change by subtraction (40 – 35) or by addition (35 + 5). So problems are not addition or subtraction problems in themselves, but they can be defined by the type of reasoning that they require: additive reasoning.

Pre-schoolers' knowledge of number and additive reasoning is limited, but it is clear that their understanding of number and additive reasoning develop simultaneously rather than in succession. Martin Hughes (1981) was the first researcher to document that pre-schoolers find purely numerical problems like 'what is 2 and 1 more?' a great deal more difficult than problems that involve concrete situations, even when these situations are described in words and left entirely to the imagination. For example, 3- and 4-year-old children are much more successful in answering a question about an imaginary box ('imagine that I have a box, and put two bricks into it; then I put one brick into the box; how many bricks are in the box?') than a question purely about number. This suggests that children build their understanding of relations between numbers on their everyday experiences with putting things together or taking out elements from one set. As we have already discussed earlier in this chapter, these actions – putting items together or separating them – are referred to as schemes of action because they refer to actions that can be applied to many different objects; the result of the action does not change as a function of the object to which the action applied. For example, it does not matter whether you put together three cars or pencils or sweets with two cars or pencils or sweets; the result is always the same. Young children, from the age of about 4 years, can use these schemes of action to solve additive reasoning problems when these are presented in the context of stories.

Researchers studying children's problem solving have classified additive reasoning problems into three main kinds, which are presented in Table 7.1. This sort of analysis has resulted in relatively complex problem classifications that take into account which information is given and which information must be supplied by the children in

Table 7.1 A summary of the different types of additive reasoning problem.

1. **Change problems**   (Bill had eight apples and then he gave three of them away. How many did he have left?).

   There are three possible types of Change problem:

   (a) end result unknown, as in the example above

   (b) start unknown (Bill had some apples and then he gave three of them away. Now he has five. How many did he have before?)

   (c) transformation unknown (Bill had eight apples and then he gave some of them away. Now he has five. How many did he give away?)

2. **Combine problems**   (Jane has three dolls and Mary has four. How many do they have altogether?)

   There are two possible types of Combine problems:

   (a) you know the two parts and are asked about the whole, as in the example above

   (b) you know the total and one part and are asked about the other part (Jane and Mary together have seven dolls. Jane has three dolls. How many does Mary have?)

3. **Compare problem**   (Sam has five books and Sarah has eight. How many more books does Sarah have than Sam?)

   There are two different types of Compare problem:

   (a) you know the quantities and are asked about the relations, as in the example above

   (b) you know one quantity and the relation and are asked about the other quantity (Sarah has eight books. Sam has three books fewer than Sarah. How many books does Sam have?)

---

the answer. Combine and Change problems can be solved by the same action schemes of joining or separating, but there is a difference between them. As shown in Table 7.1, there are only two questions one can ask in a Combine problem, but there are three types of Change problem.

The different problems shown in Table 7.1 can be phrased in different ways because a relation has a converse: they can be phrased as, for example, Sarah has three more books or Sam has three fewer books. A great deal of research (see Recommended Reading) has shown that, in general, the Change and Combine problems are much easier than the Compare problems. The most interesting aspect of this consistent pattern of results is that problems that are solved by the same arithmetic operation – in other words, by the same sum – can differ radically in how difficult they are.

STOP AND THINK

Going further

In order to investigate children's growing understanding of additive relations, researchers create story problems and analyse the difference between them. They design the studies in such a way that story problems can be solved by the same arithmetic operation. If there is a difference in the percentage of correct responses across the problems, it can be concluded that the difference between the stories has an effect on problem difficulty. Think about the three problems below:

1. Tim had 11 sweets; he gave Martha 7 sweets; how many does Tim have now?

2. Tim has 11 sweets; Martha has 7 sweets; who has more sweets? [this is usually an easy question]; how many more sweets does Tim have than Martha? [this is much harder]

3. Tim has 11 sweets; he has 4 sweets more than Martha; how many sweets does Martha have?

   - What differences between these three problems could affect the level of problem difficulty?
   - Which problem do you find easiest and which do you find hardest? Why?

Combine and Change problems

Usually pre-school children do make the appropriate moves in the easiest Change and Combine problems: they put together and count up and separate and count the relevant set to find the answer. Very few pre-school children seem to know addition and subtraction facts, and so they succeed considerably more if they have physical objects (or use their fingers) in order to count. Research in the USA by Carpenter and Moser (1982) gives an indication of how pre-school children perform in the simpler problems. They interviewed children (aged about 4 to 5 years) twice before they had had been given any instruction about arithmetic in school; we give here the results of each of these interviews, as there is always some improvement worth noting between the testing occasions.

For Combine problems (given two parts, find the whole), at the beginning and end of pre-school, respectively, 75% and 82% of the answers were correct when the numbers were small (always less than 10) and 50% and 71% when the numbers were larger. Only 13% of the responses with small numbers were obtained through the recall of number facts, and this was actually the largest percentage of recall of number facts observed in their study. For Change problems (Tim had 11 sweets; he gave 7 to Martha; how many did he have left?), the pre-schoolers were correct 42% and 61% with larger numbers (Carpenter and Moser do not report the figures for smaller numbers) at each of the two interviews. Only 1% of recall of number facts is reported. So, pre-school children can do relatively well on simple Change and Combine problems even before they know arithmetic facts. They do so by putting sets together or by separating them and counting.

Stories that describe a situation where the quantity decreases, but have a missing initial state (e.g. Tim had some marbles; he lost seven in a game and he has four left; how many did he have before he played the game?) can most easily be solved by an addition. The apparent conflict between the decrease in quantity and the operation of addition can be solved if the children understand the inverse relation between subtraction and addition: that by adding the number that Tim still has and the number he lost, one can find out how many marbles he had originally. (See Recommended Reading for more on the development of children's strategies for solving problems using an understanding of the inverse relation between addition and subtraction.)

Gérard Vergnaud, a French psychologist who studied with Piaget, carried out the most complete comparisons between these different types of story. His analysis can help us understand the level of difficulty of further types of additive reasoning problem, involving not only natural numbers, but also whole numbers (i.e. positive and negative numbers).

Vergnaud (1982) distinguishes between numerical and relational calculation. Numerical calculation refers to the arithmetic operations that children carry out to find the answer to a problem. In the case of additive reasoning, addition and subtraction are the relevant operations. Relational calculation refers to the operations of thought that the child must carry out in order to handle the relations between quantities in the problem. Consider the following problem: 'Bertrand played a game of marbles and lost seven marbles. After the game he had three marbles left. How many marbles did he have before the game?' Here, the relational calculation is the realisation that the solution requires using the inverse of subtraction to go from the final state to the initial state. The numerical calculation would be 7 + 3.

Vergnaud proposes that children perform these relational calculations in an implicit manner. To use his expression, they rely on theorems in action (Vergnaud, 2009). The children may say that they 'just know' that they have to add when they solve the problem, and may be unable to say that the reason for this is that addition is the inverse of subtraction. Vergnaud reports approximately twice as many correct responses by French pre-school children (aged about 5 years) to a problem that involves no relational calculation (about 50% correct in the problem: Pierre had 10 marbles; he played a game and lost three; how many did he have after the game?) as compared to the problem above (about 26% correct responses), where we are told how many marbles Bertrand lost and asked how many he had before the game.

Definitions

Natural numbers: the set of counting numbers. Does not include negative numbers, but some people include zero as a natural number. The cardinality of a finite set will be a natural number.

Whole numbers: also referred to as directed numbers. The natural numbers together with the negatives of the non-zero natural numbers (–1, –2, –3, . . .).

Numerical calculation: the arithmetic operations that children carry out to find the answer to a problem.

Relational calculation: the operations of thought that children must carry out in order to handle the relations between quantities in the problem.

Theorems in action: propositions held to be true which are only implicitly known to the person who holds them.

Vergnaud also distinguished three things that can be represented by natural numbers: quantities (which he calls measures), transformations and relations. This distinction has an effect on the types of problem that can be created starting from the simple classification in three types (Change, Combine and Compare) and their level of difficulty.

First, consider the two problems below, the first which involves a quantity and a transformation, and the second which involves two transformations:

- Pierre had six marbles. He played one game and lost four marbles. How many marbles did he have after the game?
- Paul played two games of marbles. He won six in the first game and lost four in the second game. What happened, counting the two games together?

French children, who were between pre-school and their fourth year in school, consistently performed better on the first than on the second type of problem, even though the same arithmetic calculation (6 − 4) is required in both problems. By the second year in school, when the children are about 7 years old, they achieve about 80% correct responses in the first problem, but they only achieve a comparable level of success on the second problem two years later. So, combining transformations is more difficult than combining a quantity and a transformation.

Brown (1981) confirmed these results with English children in the age range 11–16. In her task, children were shown a signpost indicating that a town called Grange is 29 miles to the west and Barton is 58 miles to the east. The children were asked how they would work out how far they need to drive to go from Grange to Barton. There were eight choices of operations connecting these two numbers from which the children chose what they considered to be the correct one. Note that driving from the signpost to Grange or to Barton are transformations in space: you go from 0 (the signpost) to the destination. The rate of correct responses to this problem was just 73%, which contrasted with 95% correct responses given to a Combine problem (which they did not describe in the report).

The children found problems even more difficult when they needed to de-combine transformations than when they had to combine them. Here is an example of a problem in which they needed to de-combine two transformations, because the story provides the result of combining operations and the question that must be answered is about the state of affairs before the combination took place:

- Bruno played two games of marbles. He played the first and the second game. In the second game he lost seven marbles. His final result, with the two games together, was that he had won three marbles. What happened in the first game?

In order to solve this problem, children need to think that at the end of the second game, Bruno had −7 marbles and his final result was +3; so in the first game he must have won sufficient marbles to compensate for the seven he lost in the second game and still have a won three at the end: that is, he must have won ten in the first game. This de-combination of transformations was still very difficult for French children in the fourth year in school (aged about 9 years). They attained less than 50% correct responses.

Vergnaud's hypothesis is that when children combine transformations, rather than quantities, they have to go beyond natural numbers: they are now operating in the domain of whole numbers. Remember that natural numbers are counting numbers, whilst whole numbers also include negative numbers. You can certainly count the number of marbles that Pierre had before he started the game, count and take away the marbles that he lost in the second game, and say how many he had left at the end. However, in the case of Paul's problem, if you count the marbles that he won in the first game, you need to count them as 'one more, two more, three more', etc. In other words, you are not actually counting marbles, but measuring the relation between the number that he has now and the number he had to begin with. So if the starting point in a problem that involves transformations is not known, the transformations have to be treated as relations. Of course, children who do solve the problem about Paul's marbles may not be fully aware of the difference between a transformation and a relation; the comparison between their level of success in these problems tells us something about what is more difficult for them, but not about whether they can explain the difference between the problems themselves.

> **Definition**
>
> Transformations: changes in the number of a set resulting from an event (e.g. an increase in the number of marbles you have due to winning a game). May also refer to changes of position (e.g. if you walked 2 km away from a house, your position changes).

Compare problems

Problems where children are asked to quantify relations are usually difficult. For example:

- Peter has eight marbles. John has three marbles. How many more marbles does Peter have than John?

The question in this problem is neither about a quantity (i.e. John's or Peter's marbles) nor about a transformation (no-one lost or got more marbles): it is about the relation between the two quantities. Although most preschool children can say that John has more marbles, the majority cannot quantify the relation (or the difference) between the two. Carpenter et al. (1981) observed that 53% of the first-grade children whom they assessed in Compare problems answered the question 'how many more does A have than B?' by saying the number that A has. This is the most common mistake reported in the literature: the relational question is answered as a quantity mentioned in the problem. The explanation for this error cannot be children's lack of knowledge of addition and subtraction because about 85% of the same children used correct addition and subtraction strategies when solving problems that involved joining quantities, or a transformation of an initial quantity.

If the children are asked, in the same problem, who has fewer marbles and how many fewer, their most common answer is three. They do not realise that the relation between the sets is the same, irrespective of the question: '*x* more than *y*' and '*y* more than *x*' are expressions about the same relation, so the use of one or the other expression should not affect the answer. However, it does take some time for children to understand that a relation such as '*x* more than *y*' and its converse, '*y* more than *x*', mean the same thing.

Compare problems can state how many items A has, then the value of the relation between A's and B's quantities, and then ask how much B has. Two examples from Verschaffel's work (1994) will be used to illustrate this problem type. In the problem 'Chris has 32 books. Ralph has 13 more books than Chris. How many books does Ralph have?', the relation is stated as '13 more books' and the answer is obtained by addition. This problem type is therefore referred to by Lewis and Mayer (1987) as involving consistent language (since 'more' intuitively implies addition). In the problem 'Pete has 29 nuts. Pete has 14 more nuts than Rita. How many nuts does Rita have?', the relation in the problem is stated as '14 more nuts', but the answer is actually obtained by subtraction. This problem type is therefore referred to as involving inconsistent language. Verschaffel found that Belgian children in sixth grade (aged about 12) gave 82% correct responses to problems with consistent language and 71% correct responses to problems with inconsistent language. The operation itself, whether it was addition or subtraction, did not affect the rate of correct responses.

Verschaffel (1994) also asked the children in his study to retell the problem after they had already answered the question. In the problems where the language was consistent, almost all the children who gave the right answer simply repeated what the researcher had said. In the problems where the language was inconsistent, about half of the children (54%) who gave correct answers retold the problem by rephrasing it appropriately. Instead of saying that 'Pete has 14 nuts more than Rita', they said that 'Rita has 14 nuts less than Pete', and thus made Rita into the subject of both sentences. Verschaffel then showed these children the written problem that he had originally read out and asked them whether they had said the same thing. Some said that they changed the phrase intentionally because it was easier to think about the question in this way; they stressed that the meaning of the two sentences was the same. Other children became confused, as if they had said something wrong, and were no longer certain of their answers. Thus, some children reinterpret the sentences and recognise that

> **STOP AND THINK**
>
> **Reflection**
>
> Thompson (1993) gave children aged about 11–12 years this problem: 'Tom, Fred and Rhoda combined their apples for a fruit stand. Fred and Rhoda together had 97 more apples than Tom. Rhoda had 17 apples. Tom had 25 apples. How many apples did Fred have?' (p. 167).
>
> - What is the answer to this problem?
> - What other answers do you think would be given and why?
>
> If you want to use a schematic representation to help you think of possible errors, see Figure 7.12 on page 216.

the two expressions mean the same thing, but almost as many children seem to reach the correct answer without rephrasing the problem into consistent language, and may not be completely aware of the equivalence of the two expressions. In Vergnaud's terminology, these latter children may hold that the expressions are equivalent only as a theorem in action.

In summary, this section has described the use of arithmetic word problems to investigate children's understanding of different aspects of additive reasoning. In arithmetic word problems, children are told a brief story which ends in an arithmetical question. These problems are widely used in school textbooks and also as a research tool. There are three main kinds of word problem: Combine, Change and Compare. Vergnaud argued that the crucial elements in these problems are quantities (measures), transformations and relations. On the whole, problems that involve relations are harder than those involving quantities and transformations. However, in a Change problem, if the initial state is missing in the story, the transformation has to be treated as a relation. Problems that involve combining and de-combining transformations are as challenging for children as problems about relations. One type of relational calculation that children may need to draw on to solve story problems is the inverse relation between addition and subtraction; they may also need to draw on the idea that a relational statement and its converse are equivalent. Many children use this knowledge without being able to express it in words. Vergnaud refers to these forms of knowledge as theorems in action.

Overall the extreme variability in the level of difficulty of different problems, even when these demand exactly the same mathematical solution (the same simple additions or subtractions), leads to the conclusion that reasoning about a problem and carrying out an arithmetic operation are two quite different things. Vergnaud emphasised this difference by calling the first relational calculation, and the second arithmetic calculation. There is therefore a great deal more to mathematical development than knowing how to carry out particular operations. This research suggests that mathematical development depends on children making a coherent connection between quantitative relations and numbers. As children establish these connections, they become better able to solve problems and also improve their understanding of number.

Multiplicative reasoning

We made the claim earlier that the ability to write numbers in a place value system, as we do, requires a multiplicative idea because the units in the different places have different values – such as tens, hundreds, thousands, etc. This can seem a wild claim to some, who would argue that children learn to read and write numbers well before they learn about multiplication in school. However, one needs to be careful about inferring that the order in which children are taught about things in school, and also the timing of teaching, tells us something about children's development. It is quite possible for children to have some very good ideas about mathematical concepts that are not recognised in school because the curriculum does not draw on them (see Chapter 14, 'Developmental psychology and education)'. The remainder of the present chapter deals with two aspects of children's mathematical development that are not in tandem with current school instruction: multiplicative reasoning and rational numbers. There is evidence that children have some understanding of both these aspects of mathematics well before they are taught about them in school.

We use the expression 'multiplicative reasoning' to refer to problems that can be solved by multiplication or division. The hypothesis that we analyse in this chapter, following authors such as Thompson (1994) and Vergnaud (1983), is that additive and multiplicative reasoning have different origins. Both originate from children's schemes of action, but from different schemes. Additive reasoning stems from the actions of joining, separating and placing sets in one-to-one correspondence. Multiplicative reasoning stems from the action of putting two quantities in one-to-many correspondence – an action that keeps the ratio between the variables constant.

Additive and multiplicative reasoning problems are fundamentally different. Additive reasoning is used in one-variable problems, when quantities of the same kind are put together, separated or compared. In contrast,

Definitions

Rational numbers: numbers which can be expressed as a simple fraction.
Variables: has different meanings in different contexts. Here it is understood as quantities that we can measure through counting or using conventional measuring tools.

multiplicative reasoning involves two variables in a fixed ratio to each other. Even the simplest multiplicative reasoning problems involve two variables in a fixed ratio. For example, in the problem 'Hannah bought six sweets; each sweet costs 5p; how much did she spend?' there are two variables: the number of sweets and the price per sweet. The ratio of sweets to pence is 1:5. The problem is solved by a multiplication if, as in this example, the total cost is unknown. The same problem situation could be presented with a different unknown quantity, and would then be solved by means of a division: for example, 'Hannah bought some sweets; each sweet costs 5p; she spent 30p; how many sweets did she buy?'

One-to-many correspondence problems

Even before being taught about multiplication in school, children can solve multiplication problems such as the one about Hannah and the sweets that she bought. If they have objects to represent the problem, they can set each sweet in correspondence with 5p and solve the problem. This illustrates the use of the schema of one-to-many correspondence. Similarly, even before being taught about division in school, children can solve some division problems. If asked to share six sweets among three friends, they can distribute the sweets equally and find that each friend gets two sweets. Fair sharing also involves setting two variables in a fixed ratio and is usually carried out by children using procedures that set the sweets in correspondence with the recipients, following a one-for-you, one-for-me routine.

Different researchers have investigated the use of one-to-many correspondences by children to solve multiplication and division problems before they are taught about these operations in school. Piaget (1952a) pioneered these studies by asking pre-school children to solve problems, always using objects. In one study, he asked the children to place a red flower in each vase of a set of vases. He put these flowers aside and then asked the children to place a yellow flower in correspondence with each vase. Next, he asked the children to place both sets, the red and the yellow flowers, in the vases, thus allowing the children to establish that there was a 2:1 ratio between flowers and vases. Finally, he put the flowers aside, leaving only the vases on the table, and asked the children to take from a box the exact number of straws they would need in order to place each flower in one straw. In order to solve this problem, the children could reason that there was a 2:1 ratio between the flowers and the vases so there should be a 2:1 ratio between the straws and the vases for the number to be the same. Piaget noted that many 5-year-olds were able to use this reasoning and successfully take the right number of straws from the box.

Frydman and Bryant (1988, 1994) also showed that young children can use one-to-many correspondences to create equivalent sets. They used sharing in their study because young children seem to have more experience with correspondence when sharing. In a sharing situation, children typically use a one-for-you, one-for-me procedure, setting the shared elements (sweets) into one-to-one correspondence with the recipients (dolls). Frydman and Bryant observed that children in the age range 5 to 7 years became progressively more competent in dealing with one-to-many correspondences and equivalences in this situation. In their task, the children were asked to construct equivalent sets, but the units in the sets were of a different value. For example, one doll only liked her sweets in double units and the second doll liked his sweets in single units. The children were able to use one-to-many correspondence to share fairly in this situation: when they gave a double to the first doll, they gave two singles to the second. This flexible use of correspondences to construct equivalent sets was interpreted by Frydman and Bryant as an indication that the children's use of the procedure was not merely a copy of

Even before being taught division, children can divide quantities by sharing.
Source: Pearson Education Ltd/Jules Selmes

Ratio: expresses the magnitude of one quantity relative to another.

previously observed and rehearsed actions: it reflected an understanding of how one-to-many correspondences can result in equivalent sets. They also replicated one of Piaget's previous findings, in that some children who succeeded with the 2:1 ratio found the 3:1 ratio difficult. So the development of the one-to-many correspondence schema does not happen in an all-or-nothing fashion, and it is necessary to consider the role of task variables in understanding children's performance.

Kornilaki (1999) replicated Piaget's findings using a modified assessment of children's understanding of correspondences with a sample of children in London. She placed three rabbit hutches in front of pre-school 5-year-old children and told them that in each hutch lived four rabbits. She then asked the children to pick from a box the right number of pellets so that each rabbit could have one pellet. As in Piaget's study, there were no visible rabbits, but the children knew the rabbit-to-hutch ratio, which was 4:1. She observed that 57% of the children were able to pick up the correct number of pellets of food by establishing correspondences between the hutches and the pellets.

Such surprising results about young children's ability to think in multiplicative terms are not restricted to children in the UK. Becker (1993) asked kindergarten children in the USA, aged 4 to 5 years, to solve similar types of problem in which the ratios were 2:1 or 3:1. As reported by Piaget and by Frydman and Bryant, the children were more successful with 2:1 than 3:1 correspondences, and the level of success improved with age. The overall level of correct responses by the 5-year-olds was 81%. Carpenter et al. (1993) also gave multiplicative reasoning problems to US kindergarten children involving correspondences of 2:1, 3:1 and 4:1. They observed 71% correct responses to these problems overall.

These success rates leave no doubt that many young children start school with some understanding of how to use one-to-many correspondences to solve multiplicative reasoning problems. It does not seem that these children consciously recognise that in a multiplicative situation there is a fixed ratio linking the two variables. Their actions maintain the ratio, but it is most likely that the invariance of the ratio is a theorem in action, and thus not explicitly known by them.

Finally, it should be noted that one important task variable is whether the children have materials at their disposal to answer the question. Nunes et al. (2007a) presented children in their first year in schools in Oxford (aged 5½ to 6½ years) with a problem in which they showed children a row of four houses and told them that three dogs lived in each house. The children were asked how many dogs live in that street. The children could point to the houses as they counted the dogs, which were not visible, but could be imagined. The rate of correct responses was 40%. In another study, Nunes et al. (2008a) asked a similar question to a sample of 5-year-olds in Oxford schools, but this time there were no objects for the children to work with. Instead the children saw three tubs on a computer screen and were told that the researcher was going to place three apples in each tub. This was followed by a computer animation which showed the apples disappearing in the tubs. The children were asked how many apples were needed so that there would be three in each tub. The children were much less inclined to point to the tubs on the computer screen and count. Many children simply answered 'three', which was the number of apples they had seen on the screen, and did not attempt to establish the correspondences between tubs and apples. Only 15% of them answered this problem correctly.

These differences in success rates could result from differences in sampling. In other words, there might have been some fundamental difference between the two groups of children in the two studies which led to their differences in performance. So in a later study Bryant et al. (2008) made a direct comparison between giving children all the materials they needed to solve a problem (e.g. objects to represent both houses and dogs) and only giving some of the materials (e.g. offering the children only cut-out paper houses to solve the problems). The children in this study were slightly older, with a mean age of 7 years and 4 months. They were just starting their third year in primary school and had not been taught multiplication tables. They were randomly assigned to the two testing conditions, so that if they showed different success rates, the differences could not be explained by sampling variation. The children who had all the materials to solve the problems at their disposal did in fact perform better than the others: their mean number of correct responses (out of 12) was 10.5 whereas the children who only had some of the materials attained a mean of 7.25 correct. This difference, which was statistically significant, shows that children do solve multiplication problems in action before they can solve the same problems only with numbers.

The results also show quite clearly that children can succeed in multiplicative reasoning problems before they are taught about multiplication in school. Many 5- to 7-year-olds have an understanding of the relations between the quantities in multiplication situations and can establish fixed ratios between quantities in action, although at such an early age they do not know multiplication tables.

> ### STOP AND THINK
>
> #### Reflection
>
> Children sometimes use the wrong operation to solve problems. Cramer et al. (1993) asked some young adults to solve this problem: 'Sue and Julie were running equally fast around a track. Sue started first. When she had run nine laps, Julie had run three laps. When Julie completed 15 laps, how many laps had Sue run?'
>
> - What is the answer to this problem?
> - What is the ratio between Sue's and Julie's number of laps?
> - What other answers do you think would be given and why?
> - If you want to know more about this problem, go to Figure 7.13 on page 217.

Sharing problems

Multiplicative reasoning involves correspondences in two ways: the one-to-many correspondence problems, that we have been discussing, and also correspondences established in sharing situations, in which the children may use a one-for-you, one-for-me procedure to create fair shares for different recipients.

Most people would not be surprised that children can share fairly using such procedures. The finding that does surprise many people is that children can also understand something that is not very obvious about the relation between the three terms in a division. In a division situation, we typically have three terms: the quantity to be shared (e.g. 12 biscuits), the number of sharers (e.g. four children) and the quota that each one receives (in this case, three biscuits). These terms are referred to as dividend, divisor and quotient, respectively. The relationship between these terms is not obvious: there is a direct relation between the dividend and the quotient (the greater the quantity to be shared, the larger the quota), but an inverse relation between the divisor and the quotient (the larger the number of sharers, the smaller the quota).

Correa et al. (1998) used a set of experiments to test whether young children understand the inverse divisor–quotient relation. The children were asked to imagine that the same amount of sweets was being distributed to different numbers of recipients. In this case, teddy bears were organised in two separate groups, one group with three and the other group with four teddies. The children did not see the sweets. These were shared by the experimenter and placed inside small bags on the backs of the teddies, but the teddies were in full view. The children were asked whether each teddy in one group would receive the same amount of sweets as each teddy in the other group. Sometimes the number of recipients was different in the groups, as in this example, and sometimes it was the same.

About two-thirds of the 5-year-olds realised that if the dividend is the same and number of recipients is also the same, each teddy in one group will get the same number of sweets as each teddy in the other group. When the dividends were the same, but the divisors were different, the problems were more difficult. Even so, about half of the 5-year-olds realised that the larger the number of recipients, the smaller their share. It seems quite remarkable that such young children realise that there is an inverse relation between the divisor and the quotient in a division situation.

Kornilaki and Nunes (2005) replicated this study with 5- and 6-year-old children and compared the success rates across problems that used either discrete quantities, such as sweets, or continuous quantities, such as cakes. The problems with discrete quantities were similar to those used by Correa et al. (1998) described previously.

> #### Definitions
>
> Dividend: in division, the quantity that is being divided.
> Divisor: in division, the quantity by which another quantity (the dividend) is to be divided.
> Quotient: in division, the number of times by which the dividend is divisible by the divisor.
> Discrete quantities: quantities which can be counted using natural numbers –1, 2, 3, etc.
> Continuous quantities: quantities to which one must apply a unit of measurement in order to determine their magnitude, such as length, mass, time, etc.

In the problems about continuous quantities, the children were shown two groups of recipients (cats) and asked to imagine that identical fish cakes were being distributed to cats in the two groups. One group with three cats would be sharing a fish cake and the other group with four cats would be sharing an identical fish cake. The rate of success observed by Kornilaki and Nunes was more modest than in the study by Correa et al. – 35% correct among the 5-year-olds and 53% correct among the 6-year-olds in the problems with discrete quantities. However, the children were just as successful in problems about continuous quantities: 31% of the 5-year-olds and 50% of the 6-year-olds correctly responded that if there were more recipients sharing a cake, each one would receive less.

In conclusion, many children as young as 5 and 6 years are able to solve multiplicative reasoning problems in action. They use the scheme of correspondences to solve these problems in action and some can also make explicit judgements about the relations between the different quantities in a division situation. These results should inspire schools to make better use of children's growing reasoning skills, but currently the teaching of mathematics has not matched the pace of children's development in the domain of multiplicative reasoning. There is evidence (Nunes et al., 2007a, 2009, 2010) that it is entirely possible to promote children's multiplicative reasoning further through teaching, and hopefully this will happen as these findings become better known. See also Chapter 14 for discussions of how schools might develop more developmentally appropriate teaching.

Product of measures problems

In the multiplicative problems that we have discussed so far, there are two variables or quantities represented by numbers that have a fixed ratio to each other. For example, the price that Hannah pays for the sweets stands in a 5:1 pence per sweet ratio. These problems have been termed co-variation (Nunes and Bryant, 1996) or isomorphism of measures problems (Vergnaud, 1983). There is another type of multiplicative reasoning problem that also involves fixed ratios and can be understood by means of correspondences, but which involves three quantities. For example, Susan has three T-shirts (one green, one white and one black) and two pairs of shorts (one blue and one black). If she matches each T-shirt with each pair of shorts, how many different-looking outfits can she wear? In this problem there are three

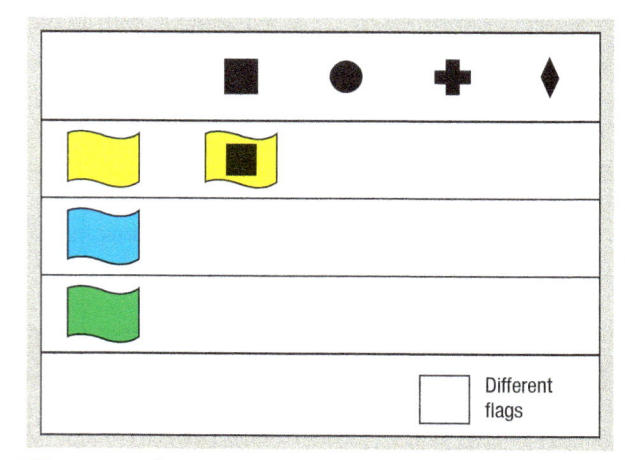

Figure 7.4 A product of measures problem.

quantities: the number of T-shirts, the number of shorts and the number of outfits. The number of outfits is simultaneously in a fixed ratio to both the number of shorts (one outfit for each shorts, so 1:2) and to the number of T-shirts (one outfit for each shirt, so 1:3). Thus the number of outfits can be calculated by multiplying the number of T-shirts by the number of shorts. Because the result of a multiplication is called 'product', this type of problem was called by Vergnaud (1983) product of measures problems.

Figure 7.4 shows an example of a product of measures problem that we have used in our studies. Children are presented with a problem concerning school flags. In the Pear Tree school, the teacher brought three different cloths and four different emblems for the children to use to make flags for their sports competition. There are eight teams playing and the children don't know whether they will be able to make eight different flags. One flag is drawn as an example. How many different flags can they make? The number of different flags that they can make is the number of different cloths times the number of emblems.

Definitions

Co-variation or isomorphism of measures problems: multiplicative reasoning problems in which there is a fixed ratio between two quantities or two measures. For example, there is usually a fixed ratio between the number of sweets you buy and the price you pay.

Product of measures problems: multiplicative reasoning problems that involve three variables, where the third one is the product of the first two.

Most of the research on multiplicative reasoning is about the previous type of problems. There is comparatively little research on these product of measures problems. But the results of what research there is are very consistent (Brown, 1981; Vergnaud, 1983; Bryant et al., 1992): product of measures problems are significantly more difficult than the previous types of problem. In the study by Bryant et al., 8-year-olds obtained 85% correct responses in multiplicative problems of the previous types and only about 4% correct responses in product of measures problems; for the 9-year-olds, the rates of success were 92% and 50%, respectively.

Figure 7.5 presents three problems that were given to approximately 5000 children in the county of Avon (in the west of England) when they were in their fourth year in school and were between 8 and 9 years of age. Two of these we have already encountered in this chapter.

Almost all of the children answered correctly to the question of how many rabbits live in the street. The question about the sweets is more complicated, but it is also more comparable to product of measures problems in terms of the number of reasoning moves that the children have to make. The children are not given the basic ratio 6:1 (i.e. six sweets to each section in the roll). They have to work this out and then use the 6:1 ratio to figure out the answer. The bottom roll has two sections, so they need to multiply 6 by 2. In this problem, 54% of the children answered correctly, a rate of success that is lower than that in a problem in which the children are told the unit ratio between the quantities. This rate of correct responses was still significantly better than the results for the product of measures outfits question, though, which only 27% of the children answered correctly.

In each house in this street live 3 rabbits.
How many rabbits live in this street?

The top roll has 18 sweets.
How many sweets are in the bottom roll?

Different outfits

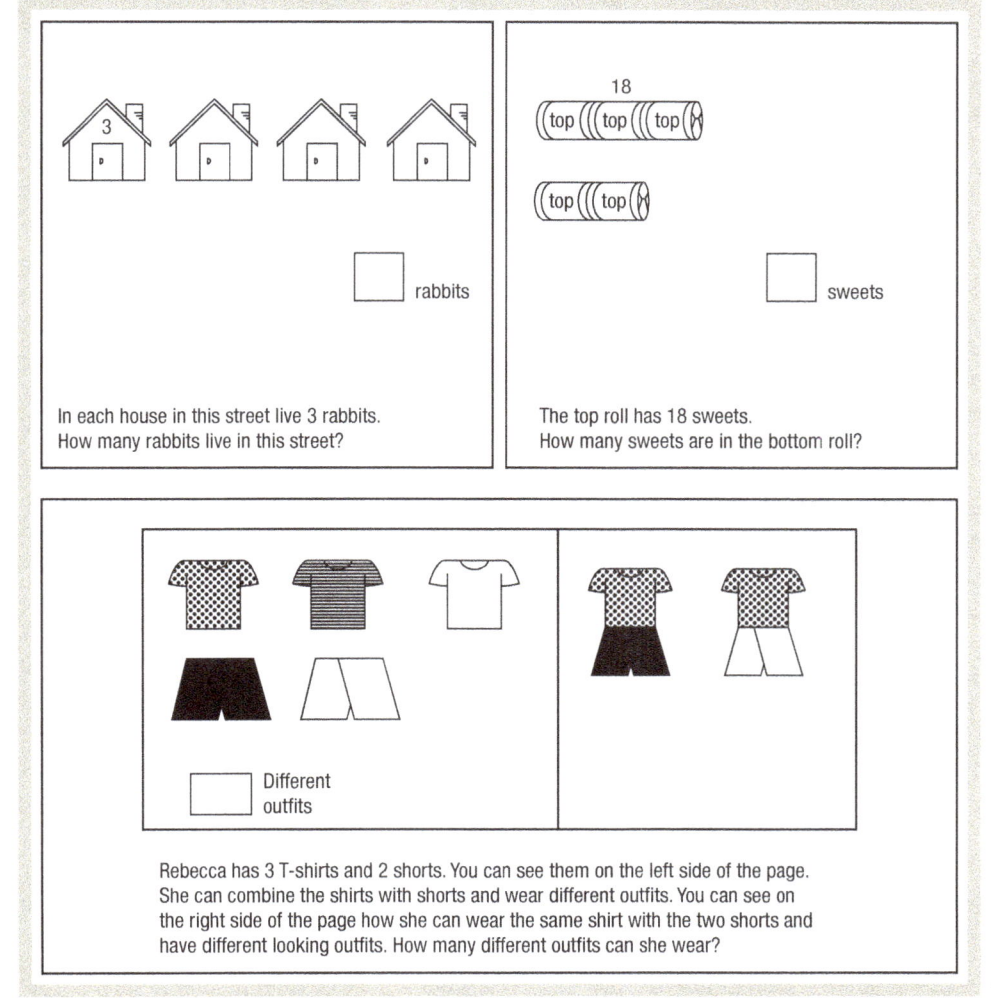

Rebecca has 3 T-shirts and 2 shorts. You can see them on the left side of the page. She can combine the shirts with shorts and wear different outfits. You can see on the right side of the page how she can wear the same shirt with the two shorts and have different looking outfits. How many different outfits can she wear?

Figure 7.5 Examples of multiplicative problems of different types.

Product of measures problems are an important part of reasoning about many situations. They involve a form of reasoning that is called *multiple classification*: the child has to think that each exemplar (e.g. each outfit) is the result of a classification by shorts combined with a classification by T-shirts. Working out the different possible classifications is often the first step in solving probabilities problems; in this context, we talk about working out the 'sample space'. Once we know the total number of possible outfits, we can then work out the probability of Rachel wearing a black T-shirt and black shorts. Because probabilities are at the heart of so many mathematical models that we use to think about the world, there are strong reasons for children to learn more about product of measures problems and for researchers to investigate how children make progress in understanding them. Therefore this type of problem should not be neglected, as it has been, in research on cognitive development.

> **STOP AND THINK**
>
> **Reflection**
>
> Imagine that you are throwing two dice. You want to know how likely it is that you would throw the same number on both. How do you work out this probability?
>
> Try to use the organisation presented in Figure 7.4 for the problem about flags to help you answer this question more efficiently and with greater certainty.

Bryant et al. (1992) investigated whether children who solve product of measures problems correctly interpret them as multiple correspondence problems, first establishing one ratio and then considering the second ratio. The children were given the materials they needed to represent the problem situation and were asked to explain their solutions. One example of the explanations observed in this study is presented here. In this problem, the children were asked how many different outfits could be formed with six different pairs of shorts and four different T-shirts.

Interviewer: And if she changed them all around, had all the shorts on with the different T-shirts, how many different ways would she look, how many different outfits?

Sarah: [First moves all the shorts and puts them next to the blue T-shirt]: Six.

Interviewer: [mistaking the child's comment for the final answer]: How do you know. . . .?

Sarah: With the blue T-shirt [the child indicates here clearly that she established the first correspondence, between the six shorts and the blue T-shirt].

Interviewer: And with all of them?

Sarah: Twenty-four.

Interviewer: How do you know it is twenty-four?

Sarah: Six times four.

(*Source*: Nunes and Bryant, 1996, p. 166)

Sarah's approach illustrates the systematic use of correspondences in combination with a double-classification, once by T-shirts and then by shorts. First all the shorts are placed in correspondence with one T-shirt, and the 6:1 ratio of outfits to shirts is identified when only one T-shirt is considered. Because there are four T-shirts, there should be a 4:1 ratio between outfits and T-shirts. Sarah is immediately able to conclude that the number of outfits will be 6 times 4.

It is likely that children can be helped to recognise that the scheme of correspondences in combination with this double-classification of the outfits leads to the solution. This teaching procedure has been included in a more general programme to improve deaf children's understanding of multiplicative relations (Nunes and Moreno, 2002), but that study cannot provide solid evidence to say whether it really works because it was only one among many aims of the teaching programme.

To summarise, this section has shown that young children have some understanding of multiplicative reasoning, which is manifested in the way they solve these types of problem using the scheme of one-to-many correspondences. This scheme of action differs from those used in additive reasoning problems, which are joining and separating. Children's rate of success in multiplicative reasoning problems varies with the ratio in the problem – smaller ratios, such as 2:1, are easier than larger ratios. The rate of success also varies with the materials that they can use to solve the problems, because young children solve problems in action and not by using knowledge of multiplication tables. By using their schemes of action, they can establish relations between quantities, and this guides their problem solving.

LIFESPAN

Developments in multiplicative reasoning in later childhood

Multiplicative reasoning, as we have seen, starts to develop from the time children are quite young. However, by the time they finish primary school, there is still room for much more development. Different researchers (e.g. Vergnaud, 1983; Nunes et al., 1993; Nunes and Bryant, 2010) have analysed children's reasoning about proportionality and distinguished two ways in which this reasoning is used: *scalar reasoning* and *functional reasoning*. Scalar reasoning refers to parallel calculations within the same variables. For example, if 2 kg of fish costs £11, then 6 kg (i.e. three times as much fish) costs £33 (i.e. three times as much money). Functional reasoning is based on the ratio between two quantities. For example, if 2 kg of fish costs £11, then the price per kilo (the relation between the two quantities) is £5.50. Scalar reasoning is often observed amongst children, and amongst adults with low levels of schooling. No examples of functional reasoning have been reported amongst adults with low levels of schooling. Research that clarifies the role of schooling – whether it is necessary for functional reasoning and how it can best be taught – should help us understand more about the development of multiplicative reasoning from a lifespan perspective. Although many studies have been carried out, this is still a poorly understood aspect of development.

Whilst this chapter focuses on children's understanding of relations between quantities, numerical signs and problem solving, as they get older and are introduced to algebra, they learn to use letters to represent unknown quantities and relations. Algebra should therefore help older children take a major step in using mathematics to understand the world. However, research on children's mathematical difficulties has suggested that a major obstacle in learning algebra is not understanding algebraic equations as ways of representing relations. For example, many students think of the sign '5' as expressing a sort of command to carry out a computation. $5 + 3 =$ is seen as the command, 'calculate the result of 5 add 3', instead of something like 'what number is equivalent to 5 add 3?'. In expressions such as $5x + 2 = 8x$, students need to think differently: they need to think about how they can manipulate this expression without destroying the equivalence.

Filloy and Rojano (1989) suggested an interesting way to help older students understand the manipulation of unknown quantities. They suggested that students could start by working on a model of a two-pan balance scale, and try to understand the relations between quantities in this context. In two-pan balances, previously very common in markets, you set the weight on one plate – for example, 1 kg – and add tomatoes to the other plate on the opposite side until the scale is in equilibrium. If you have five packages of unknown, but equivalent, weight plus a 1.5 kg weight on one side, and this balances with eight equal packages on the other side, the way to find out their weight and maintain the balance is to remove five packages from each side. This would leave you with three packages on one side and the 1.5 kg weight on the other. From this equivalence, you can ascertain that $3x = 1.5$ kg, which means that $x = 0.5$ kg: in other words, one package weighs 0.5 kg. Filloy and Rojano observed that students can learn from this example that if you carry out the same operation on both sides of an algebraic expression, the equivalence between the two sides of the equation is not destroyed – that is, if you have $5x + 1.5 = 8x$, and you subtract $5x$ from both sides of the equation, you end with $1.5 = 3x$ and can solve the problem.

Definition

Algebra: a domain of mathematics that involves representing quantities and relations by letters, rather than numbers, and operating on these in ways that respect the properties of the operations and the relations.

Balance scales can serve as a useful tool in helping older students understand the equivalence between the two sides of algebraic equations.
Source: Pearson Education Ltd/Photodisc/C. Squared Studios

Sharing is one way in which children use the schema of correspondences to solve some division problems. Many children in pre-school and in their first year of primary school already have some insight into the relations between quantities in division situations. Many understand that, if the dividend in two problems is the same and the divisor is the same, the quotient will also be the same. A sizeable group (which in our studies varied between about one-third and one-half of the 5-year-olds) also realises that there is an inverse relation between the divisor and the quotient: they know that the more people sharing, the less each one will receive.

Children's development of multiplicative reasoning receives little input from school in these early years. It seems that this aspect of children's development is left to less systematic influences than those that one would expect to take place in school. Thus rates of success could increase significantly if schools were to include multiplicative reasoning in the curriculum for young children. (See Chapter 14 for more discussion of how schools could develop developmentally appropriate curricula.) Product of measures multiplicative reasoning is less well researched in cognitive development. In this type of problem, one quantity has a fixed ratio at the same time to two other quantities. This problem type is more difficult than the more commonly used multiplicative reasoning problems. The reasoning used in product of measures problems forms the basis for understanding a whole set of mathematical situations in the domain of probabilities. More research on this topic could contribute to a better understanding of how children's mathematical development takes place in the domain of probabilistic thinking, which is so often used as a model to understand the world when events cannot be predicted with certainty.

The step into rational numbers

So far in this chapter we have discussed a fairly simple mathematical world, one that can be represented with whole numbers. But even very young children encounter situations in the world that are not so simple, and the question is when they become able to think mathematically about these situations. Suppose you have a chocolate bar to be shared amongst four children. How can they share it? The procedure one-for-you, one-for-me does not work, unless they cut the chocolate into four equal parts. How good are young children at partitioning continuous quantities into equal parts? The amount of chocolate that each receives is less than one chocolate bar. How do young children talk about this quantity? How do they learn about the mathematical properties of fractions – or, more generally, rational numbers?

There are some quantities that cannot be represented by a single whole number and, in order to represent these quantities, we must use rational numbers. We cannot use natural numbers when the quantity that we want to represent numerically is smaller than the unit, irrespective of whether this is a natural unit (e.g. we have less than one chocolate bar) or a conventional unit (e.g. a fish weighs less than a kilo). Although there are other quantities that require the use of rational numbers (e.g. quantities that are measured by the relation between two quantities, such as the concentration of a drink, measured by the ratio of juice to water, or velocity, which is measured by the ratio of distance over time), for reasons of space this

Definition

Partitioning: the process of dividing a whole into parts.

topic will not be discussed in the present chapter (see Recommended Reading).

Situations in which a quantity is smaller than the unit can arise in two ways: (1) in a division situation, if the number of things being divided (the dividend) is smaller than the number of recipients (the divisor) (e.g. three chocolate bars are being shared by four children); or (2) in a measurement situation, when the quantity we want to measure is smaller than the standard used in measurement (e.g. we are measuring the width of a pavement with our feet and the pavement is wider than four but narrower than five feet).

In both of these cases, to find a number to describe the quantity we need to carry out a division. In the sharing situation, we need to think about how to divide the chocolate so that the children receive the same amount. In the measurement situation, we need to think about what portion of our foot best describes the bit between four and five feet – is it half, a third, a quarter or what? Researchers interested in rational numbers may not agree on many things, but there is a clear consensus among them on the idea that rational numbers are numbers that result from division – or, more technically, they are numbers in the domain of quotients (Ohlsson, 1988; Kieren, 1993; Brousseau et al., 2007) and do not result from counting.

STOP AND THINK

Reflection

Ema Mamede (2007) asked 6- and 7-year-olds in their first year in primary school in Portugal to imagine that four children were sharing three chocolates. She then asked: how much will each child receive? This question was part of a pre-test for a teaching experiment in which she planned to teach children how to represent fractions with numbers. The question 'how much' is often answered with a number. A few children said that they did not know a number to answer this question.

- What do you think the children did know in order to give this answer?

We argued earlier in this chapter that in order to make sense of numbers, children need to make connections between numbers and quantities, because the relations between quantities define the relations between numbers and vice versa. Children should be able to use numbers to know whether two quantities are equivalent or not and, if not, which one is more. This is true in the domains of both whole numbers and rational numbers. The basic relations that children must understand are essentially the same in both number domains: they need to understand the equivalence between quantities and they need to know how to order quantities by their magnitudes. However, the difficulties of understanding equivalence and order in the domain of fractions are quite different from those in the domain of natural numbers. This is quite apparent when we think of written representations of fractions. There are two widely used written notations for fractions: ½ and 0.5 are the same number with two different notations. The first, ½, is called a common fraction and the second, 0.5, is called a decimal fraction. Common fractions can be converted into decimal notation by carrying out the division indicated in the notation. For example, ½ indicates 1 divided by 2, and if we carry out this division, we can use the decimal notation 0.5, which is equivalent to ½.

In the domain of natural numbers, all sets that are represented by the same number are equivalent. Those that are represented by a different number are not equivalent. Understanding equivalence in the domain of fractions is not as simple as this because number labels do not help the children in the same way. Two fractional quantities that have different labels can be equivalent. In fact, there are an infinite number of equivalent fractions. ⅓, ²⁄₆, ⁶⁄₉, ⁸⁄₁₂, etc. are different number labels, but they all represent equivalent quantities. Because rational numbers refer (although often implicitly) to a whole, it is also possible for two fractions to have the same number label, but to represent different quantities: ⅓ of 12 and ⅓ of 18 are not representations of equivalent quantities.

The order of magnitude of natural numbers is the same as the order of the number labels we use in counting. Determining the order of rational numbers is a much more complicated matter. Think of ordering fractions

Definitions

Common fractions: notations for rational numbers that use the form *a/b*, in which *b* can have any value.
Decimal fractions: fractions in which the denominator is a power of 10. Decimal fractions can be expressed as *a/b*, but they can also have a different notation: ⁸⁄₁₀ can also be expressed as 0.8.

in common notation. If the denominator is constant, then the larger the numerator, the larger is the magnitude of the fraction. If the numerator is constant, then the larger the denominator, the smaller is the fraction. Children often order fractions wrongly when they have the same numerator, but different denominators. They indicate, for example, that ⅓ is less than ⅕ because 3 is less than 5. The use of decimal notation does not make things easier: 0.8 and 0.23, for example, are often placed in the wrong order by children, who think that 0.23 is more than 0.8 because 23 is more than 8.

All these difficulties arise because fractions are numbers that originate from division: ⅓ is more than ⅕ because if you share a cake among three children and an identical cake among five children, the children in the second group will receive less. This inverse relation between the divisor and the quotient was discussed in the previous section.

Children's ideas about quantities that are represented by fractions

In order to analyse children's insights into division situations that lead to fractional quantities (i.e. quantities represented by fractions), we need to think about what schemes of action children have for division and how these develop. Children use two schemes of action in division: partitioning and sharing. Partitioning refers to the action of cutting things up into equal parts. Problems that involve partitioning are often known as part–whole problems, because the aim of partitioning is to have a whole divided into equal parts. Sharing involves, as we saw in the previous section, establishing correspondences between the quantities being shared and the recipients. Problems that involve sharing are referred to as quotient problems, a term that emphasises the fact that the situation involves a division with three terms: dividend, divisor and quotient.

Definitions

Denominator: in the common notation of fractions (a/b), the denominator is b, which can also be conceived as the divisor in the division represented by the a/b notation.
Numerator: in the common notation of fractions (a/b), the numerator is a, which can also be conceived as the dividend in the division represented by the a/b notation.

At first glance, the difference between these two schemes of action, partitioning and correspondence, may seem too subtle to be of interest when we are thinking of children's understanding of fractions. The difference between partitioning and correspondence division is that in partitioning there is a single whole (i.e. a quantity or measure) and in correspondence there are two quantities (or measures). However, we will consider research next that shows that, from the children's point of view, these schemes of action are not one and the same. In order to investigate children's understanding of fractional quantities, researchers use the same methods described earlier on when analysing children's understanding of additive relations. They create story problems that relate either to part–whole or to quotient situations and compare children's level of success in the two types of problem.

How partitioning and sharing support children's understanding of fractions

Partitioning is the scheme of action that children use in part–whole tasks. The scheme of partitioning has also been named subdivision and dissection (Pothier and Sawada, 1983), and is consistently defined as the process of dividing a whole into parts. The most common type of fraction problem that teachers give to children is to ask them to partition a whole into a fixed number of parts (the denominator) and to show a certain fraction with this denominator. For example, the children have to show ⅗ of a pizza or of a line. This process is not understood as the activity of cutting something into parts in any old way; partitioning is understood as a process that must be guided from the outset by the aim of obtaining a pre-determined number of equal parts.

Piaget et al. (1960) pioneered the study of the connection between partitioning and fractions. They spelled out a number of ideas that they thought were necessary for children to develop an understanding of fractions, and analysed them in partitioning tasks. They suggested that 'the notion of fraction depends on two fundamental relations: the relation of part to whole . . . and the relation of part to part' (p. 309). Part-to-part relations refer to the equivalence of fractions. Piaget and colleagues identified a number of insights that children need to achieve in order to understand fractions:

1. The whole must be conceived as divisible – an idea that children under the age of about 2 do not seem to attain.

2. The number of parts to be achieved is determined from the outset.
3. The parts must exhaust the whole (i.e. there should be no second round of partitioning and no remainders).
4. The number of cuts and the number of parts are related (e.g. if you want to divide something into two parts, you should use only one cut).
5. All the parts should be equal.
6. Each part can be seen as a whole in itself, nested into the whole, but also susceptible to further division.
7. The whole remains invariant and is equal to the sum of the parts.

Piaget and colleagues observed that children rarely achieved correct partitioning before the age of about 6. There is variation in the level of success depending on the shape of the whole (circular areas are more difficult to partition than rectangles) and on the number of parts. They observed that a strategy which children often used to achieve partitioning is the use of successive divisions in two: so children are able to succeed in dividing a whole into fourths before they can succeed with thirds. Successive halving helped the children with some fractions: dividing something into eighths is easier this way. However, it interfered with success with other fractions. Some children, attempting to divide a whole into fifths, ended up with sixths by dividing the whole first in halves and then subdividing each half in three parts. Figure 7.6 presents several attempts by an 8-year-old to attain the partitioning of a 'pizza' into three equal parts.

Piaget and colleagues also investigated children's understanding of their seventh criterion for a true concept of fraction – that is, the conservation of the whole. This conservation, they argued, would require the children to understand that each piece could not be counted simply as one piece, but had to be understood in its relation to the whole. Some children failed to understand this, and argued that if someone ate a cake cut into ½ + ¾ and a second person ate a cake cut into ⁴⁄₄, the second one would eat more because he had four parts and the first one only had three. Although these children would recognise that if the pieces were put together in each case they would form one whole cake, they still maintained that ⁴⁄₄ was more than ½ + ¾. Finally, they also observed that children did not have to achieve the highest level of development in the scheme of partitioning in order to understand the conservation of the whole. Children's difficulties with partitioning continuous wholes into equal parts have been confirmed many times in studies with pre-schoolers and children in their first years in school (e.g. Novillis, 1976; Hiebert and Tonnessen, 1978; Pothier and Sawada, 1983; Miller, 1984; Hunting and Sharpley, 1988; Lamon, 1996).

A significant question in the analysis of conceptual development is about the extent to which the scheme of partitioning supports children's understanding of the equivalence between different fractions. Piaget and his colleagues suggested that at about 6 or 7 years of age, children could understand the equivalence of fractions such as ½ and ¾ when the fractions resulted from divisions of the same whole. Subsequent studies have investigated this question when the fractions are obtained from equivalent wholes. For example, Kamii and Clark (1995) presented children with identical rectangles and cut them into fractions using different cuts. For example, one rectangle was cut horizontally in half and the second was cut across a diagonal. The children had the opportunity to verify that the rectangles were the same size and that the two parts from each rectangle were the same in size. They asked the children: if these were chocolate cakes, and the researcher ate a part cut from the first rectangle and the child ate a part cut from the second, would they eat the same amount? The children in Kamii's study were in the fifth or sixth year in school (approximately 11 and 12 years). Both groups of children had been taught about equivalent fractions. In spite of having received instruction, the children's rate of success was rather low: only 44% of the fifth graders and 51% of the sixth graders reasoned that they would eat the same amount of chocolate because these were halves of identical wholes.

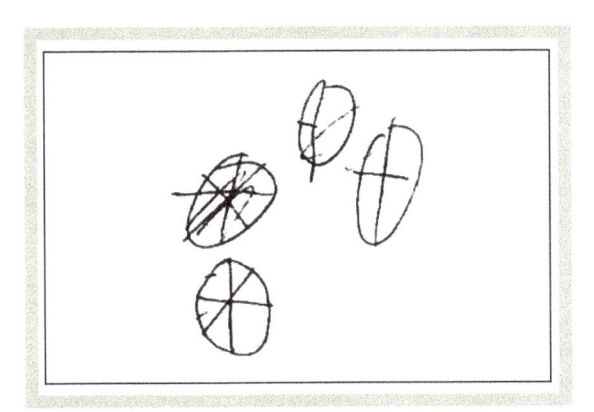

Figure 7.6 An 8-year-old attempts to partition a pizza into three equal parts.

Kamii and Clark then showed the children two identical wholes, one cut in fourths using a horizontal and a vertical cut, and the other in eighths, using only horizontal cuts. They discarded one fourth from the first 'chocolate cake', leaving ¾ to be eaten, and asked the children to take the same amount from the other cake, which had been cut into eighths, for themselves. The percentage of correct answers this time was even lower than those to the previous question: only 13% of the fifth graders and 32% of the sixth graders correctly identified the number of eighths required to take the same amount as ¾.

These studies suggest that partitioning is a scheme of action that develops slowly: it takes children some time to be able to anticipate how they should cut a whole in order to obtain equal parts. They also suggest that, even when the partitioning has been carried out by the researcher in order to make sure that the parts are the same, the scheme of partitioning does not afford insights into the part–whole relations required for a solid understanding of equivalence of fractions. It seems that children become too focused on the appearance of the parts and do not draw on the logic of successive divisions when they solve problems about partitioning. If this is the case, it would be possible to design interventions to improve their performance, but so far there has been no investigation of this possibility.

In the previous section, we described studies that showed that some 5-year-olds and most 6-year-olds realise that there is an inverse relation between the divisor and the quotient in division situations. Next we describe studies relevant to the understanding of equivalence between fractional quantities.

Mamede et al. (2005) and Mamede (2009) compared young Portuguese children's understanding of equivalence and order of fractions in problems that referred to either part–whole or quotient situations, in which they could therefore use their schemas of partitioning or sharing. The children were not required to share or partition anything: they were asked to think about the situations without carrying out the actions.

The children were asked six questions about the equivalence of fractional quantities, illustrated in Figures 7.7 and 7.8. In the sharing situation (the pictures in Figure 7.7) children were told that there were two parties. In party 1, there were three children sharing a cake. They would share the cake fairly and there would be no cake left. In party 2, there were six children sharing two cakes, which were identical to the cake in party 1. The children in party 2 would also share the cakes fairly and there would be no

Figure 7.7
Pictures illustrating the sharing situation designed to assess children's understanding of the equivalence of fractions.
Source: Nunes

Figure 7.8 Pictures illustrating the partitioning situation designed to assess children's understanding of the equivalence of fractions.
Source: Nunes

cake left. The children taking part in the study were then asked whether each child in party 1 would eat the same amount of cake as each child in party 2.

Having been asked whether the children in parties 1 and 2 would eat the same amount of cake, the girl (C) in the picture responds like this:

C: Uhm, I think this one eats a little more (pointing to the boy in the party on the left).
Researcher: How do you think they could cut the cakes and share them?
C: They could cut this cake in three and give it to these three boys and cut the other cake in three and give it to these three boys (moving the cakes as displayed on the picture on the right).
R: So you could share the cakes like this. Do you think that this boy would eat a bit more than this boy (repeating the child's previous answer).

C: (smiled): Oh, no, it's all the same in the two parties, one cake shared for three boys here and one cake for three boys here.

This brief interaction illustrates the significance of the action scheme of one-to-many correspondences for children's understanding of sharing and the equivalence of fractions. Once the child sets the cakes in correspondences with the boys, she draws the 'obvious' conclusion that it is all the same. It also illustrates the role that asking children to reflect on their actions can have in their thinking.

In the partitioning problems, the children saw drawings representing the situation in Figure 7.8. They were told that a boy and a girl had identical chocolate bars. The chocolate bars were too large to eat all at once. So the boy cut his chocolate bar into four equal pieces and ate two. The girl cut her chocolate bar into eight equal pieces and ate four. Children taking part in the study were asked whether the boy and girl had eaten the same amount of chocolate.

R: The boy and the girl each got a chocolate bar, the same size. It was a big chocolate bar, they could not eat it all at once. So the girl decided to cut her chocolate in four parts and ate two. The boy decided to cut his chocolate in eight parts and ate four. Do you think that they ate the same amount of chocolate?
C: No, the boy ate more, he ate four pieces.
R: Show me how they would cut their chocolates. How would the girl cut her chocolate?
C: (takes the chocolate, pretends to cut by using a horizontal and a vertical cut through the middle): Like this.
R: What about the boy?
C: (takes the chocolate, pretends to cut slices horizontally): Like this. He has lots of small pieces.
R: Do you think that the boy eats more than the girl (repeating the child's previous answer)?
C: I think she eats more, her pieces would have lots of those squares (referring to how some chocolate bars have squares marked in them).

This conversation illustrates the difficulty of using the scheme of partitioning to compare fractions. The child focuses on what the pieces would look like if they were cut. The child does not follow another possible line of reasoning that could be used in this situation to help them understand equivalence: the boy cut his chocolate into twice as many pieces and ate twice as many pieces as the girl, so he eats the same amount. It seems that the focus on the appearance of the pieces turns the children's attention away from this relation between the numbers of pieces. Intervention studies could explore whether teaching can help children achieve this latter insight when using the scheme of partitioning.

Nunes et al. (2007b) used the same types of problem with older children, who were in the fourth or fifth year in school; their ages were in the range 8½ to 10 years. They had received some instruction on fractions, but had only been taught in school about one pair of equivalent fractions: they were taught that one-half is the same as two-quarters. So our questions were about ⅓ and ²⁄₆ and ¾ and ⁴⁄₈. Figure 7.9 summarises the results by age and type of problem. The results for the 6- to 7-year-olds come from the study by Mamede and Nunes (2008) and are from Portuguese children; the results for the 8- to 9-year-olds are from our investigation. The rate of correct responses increases as the children get older for both types of problem. The sharing problems seem to be easier up to about the age of 9 years, and the gap between the success rates becomes smaller over time. The difference between the mean correct responses across problem type was statistically significant in both studies.

The differences between the insights that children have about fractional quantities that result from sharing or partitioning are very much the same when the questions are about ordering fractional quantities rather than equivalence. The stories that are used to investigate the order of fractional quantities are similar to those illustrated in Figures 7.7 and 7.8, but the quantities resulting from the division are not equivalent. For example, in Mamede and Nune's study, in the sharing problems children were asked to compare the quantities received by boys and girls sharing identical cakes in two parties. In one party, there were two boys and in the other party there were two girls. In the partitioning problems, the children were told a story about a cake that was too big to be eaten all at once, so one girl cut her cake in two equal parts and ate one and the other girl cut her cake in three equal parts and ate one.

The rate of correct responses is presented in Figure 7.10. It is quite clear that the questions about sharing produced a higher rate of correct responses than those about partitioning, among both 6- and 7-year-olds. The questions about ordering fractional quantities (Figure 7.10) were significantly easier than those about equivalence (Figure 7.9; compare the success rates among 6- and 7-year-olds), but the order questions only included quantities in which the dividend (the numerator in the fraction) was the same – for example, ⅓ and ⅕. In this case, the children can focus on one value only, the number of recipients or the number of parts into which the whole was cut. In equivalence problems, the children must think about two numbers, the dividend and the divisor (the denominator in the fraction).

This research tells an intriguing story about children's understanding of the equivalence and order of fractional quantities. There are significant differences between how well children reason about quantities smaller than the unit when the questions are about sharing versus about partitioning. This difference is observed even when the children do not carry out the actions of sharing or partitioning. These results are, as we hinted earlier, quite surprising: the children in Portugal had not been taught about fractions at all in school and those in the UK had only been taught about fractions in problems related to the partitioning scheme, involving part–whole relations.

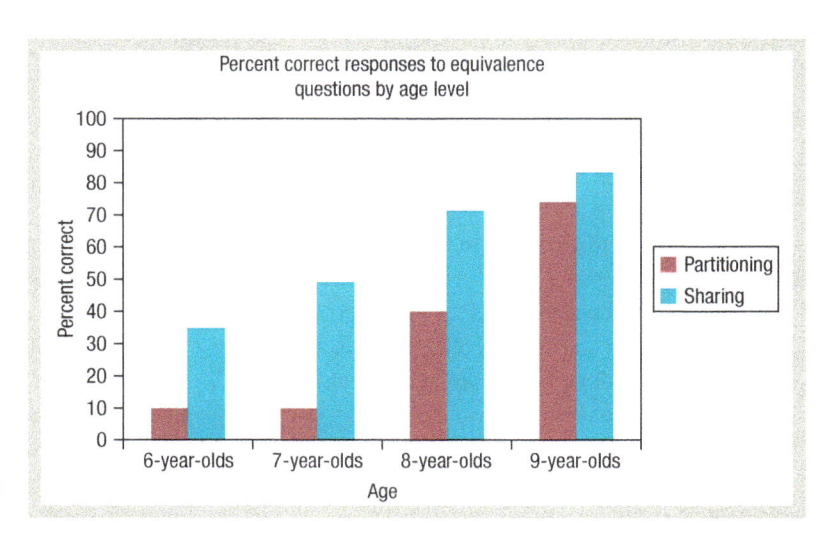

Figure 7.9 Responses to equivalence questions using sharing and partitioning tasks by children at different ages.

THE STEP INTO RATIONAL NUMBERS | **213**

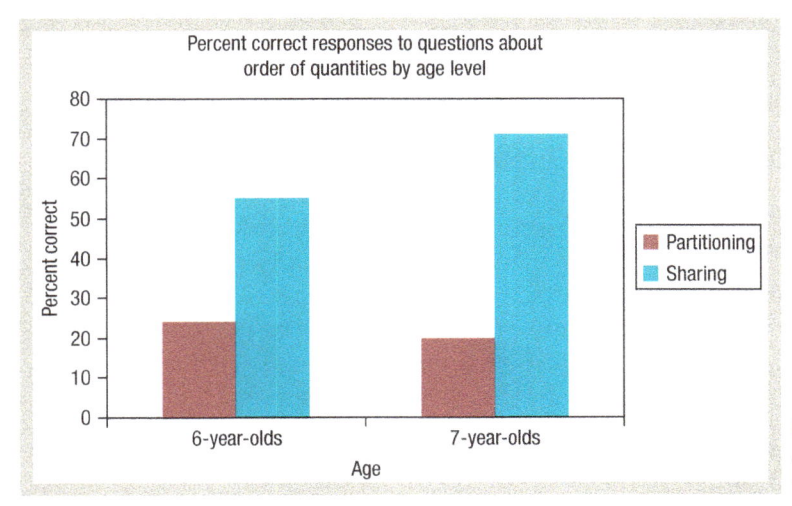

Figure 7.10 Responses to ordering questions using sharing and partitioning tasks by children at different ages.

Comparing numerically represented fractions

Researchers have asked children equivalence questions about fractions represented numerically when the notation used was common or decimal. With common fractions, the question is often about painting regions of a figure. Hart et al. (1985) asked children in London to paint ⅔ of figures that had been divided into three, six or nine sections. Note that painting ⅔ of figures divided into six and nine sections means painting an equivalent fraction, 4/6 and 6/9, respectively. The researchers found that 60% of the 11–12-year-olds and about 65% of the 12–13-year-olds were able to solve the task of painting equivalent fractions. Nunes et al. (2006) gave the same item to primary school children in years 4 and 5 in the study mentioned previously. The rate of correct responses by age level for both studies is summarised in Figure 7.11; results for 11–13-year-olds are from Hart et al. (1985).

There is little doubt that children learn how to shade ⅔ of a figure quite early on, but there is a slow and gradual development in their understanding of what it means to shade 2/3 when the figure is divided into six or nine parts and they need to shade an equivalent fraction. A comparison between Figures 7.9 and 7.11 suggests that children are better at comparing fractional quantities without any explicit reference to fractions, than they are at comparing fractions. However, it must be noted that there are task differences that make this comparison ambiguous. The Hart et al. (1985) task is a more open task because the children had to decide how many sections to shade, whereas in the Nunes et al. (2006) task of comparison of fractional quantities there were only

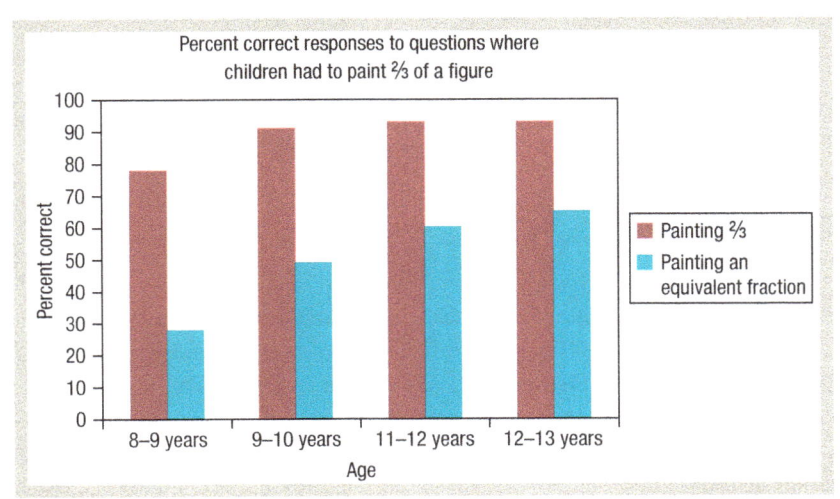

Figure 7.11 Performance on painting ⅔ of a figure at different ages.

CUTTING EDGE

Math Wars – the debate surrounding mathematics teaching

'Math Wars' is a term that was originally coined in the USA to refer to the debate between the proponents of 'traditional' or 'back to basics' approaches to teaching in mathematics, and the proponents of an approach to mathematics in which arithmetic receives less emphasis than understanding and which instead uses mathematics to solve problems. In spite of the long debate around this topic, illustrated by the coining of the term in 1989, there was until recently no research that could be used as a basis for solving the dilemma of which of these approaches is better.

The Department of Education in England supported a project that can shed light on this issue. A large-scale longitudinal study (the Avon Longitudinal Study of Parents and Children – ALSPAC) (see Golding et al., 2001, for an overview) which included a variety of measures related to health and education, provided relevant data for addressing this question. Nunes et al. (2009) analysed whether numerical skills (i.e. arithmetic) or mathematical reasoning (measured through problem-solving tasks that placed little demand on numerical skills) was a better predictor of later mathematical achievement, or whether they were equally important. If an ability is important for mathematics achievement then children's scores in measures of that ability at an early age should predict their mathematics achievement later on.

Numerical skills were measured by the arithmetic sub-test of the Wechsler Intelligence Scale for Children (WISC-III, Wechsler, 1992). Mathematical reasoning was measured by the children's scores in a problem-solving test, in which the items placed high demands on relational calculation and reduced demands on numerical calculation. The children participated in these assessments when they were between 8 and 9 years of age. The measure of their mathematics achievement was their performance in the state-designed Key Stage mathematics assessments, which they took when they were 11 (KS2) and 14 years (KS3).

When the children were between 8 and 9, they also participated in assessments of their general intelligence and working memory (see Chapter 6, 'Memory and intelligence'). General intelligence and working memory influence children's scores in measures of numerical calculation, relational calculation and their mathematics achievement as well. So, in order to know whether it was numerical skills or mathematical reasoning that was relatively more important for mathematics achievement, it was necessary to control for intelligence and working memory when analysing the relationship between the predictors and mathematics achievement.

The results of this study were clear and consistent. Mathematical reasoning was a more important predictor of children's mathematical achievement, at both age 11 and 14 years, than numerical reasoning. This was the case even after the effects of intelligence and working memory had been controlled for in the analyses. Numerical skills made a separate, but less important, contribution to the prediction of mathematical achievement at both ages.

The conclusion from this research is that if primary schools place greater emphasis on supporting the development of children's mathematical reasoning, they could well reap the benefits of this investment by finding that children achieve more in mathematics later on. Numerical skills play a role too, and there should be some time for arithmetic learning, even though more attention should be dedicated to mathematical reasoning.

---

three possible answers (A eats more, B eats more or they eat the same).

Difficulties in comparing fractions are not confined to the common fraction notation. Resnick et al. (1989) asked children to compare decimal fractions when the number of places after the decimal point differed. The samples in their study included children from three different countries: the USA, Israel and France, and in three grade levels (fourth to sixth). The children were asked to compare pairs of decimals such as 0.5 and 0.36, 2.35 and 2.350, 4.8 and 4.63 in order to say which was larger. The rate of correct responses varied between 36%

and 52% correct, even though all children had received instruction on decimals. So even children in their sixth year in school only answered about half of the questions correctly. Rittle-Johnson et al. (2001) replicated the observation of children's difficulties when comparing the magnitude of decimals. The rate of correct responses by the fifth-grade children in their study was 19%. Thus it seems that children have difficulties in comparing fractions irrespective of the type of notation used.

In this section, we have emphasised the contrast between natural numbers, which result from counting, and rational numbers, which stem from division and refer to quantities smaller than a unit which can be counted. It doesn't seem that the picture of how children's understanding of fractions develops is fully painted yet. They need to establish connections between their understanding of quantities and the notations that they use for fractions, of both common and decimal notation. We have seen that children have two schemes of action that are relevant to fractions: partitioning and sharing. Children have some understanding of equivalences between fractional quantities from about the age of 7. They seem to achieve this understanding by placing the things to be shared in correspondence with the sharers. The scheme of partitioning develops more slowly. In order to achieve correct partitioning, it is necessary to understand the relation between the number of 'cuts' and the number of parts – a problem that takes children some time to solve. Even 8-year-olds can have difficulty in partitioning wholes into an odd number of parts because of the tendency that children have to start partitioning by dividing the whole in the middle. Children's reasoning about equivalence and ordering of fractional quantities develops earlier in the context of sharing, but schools in the UK draw mostly on the partitioning scheme when children are taught about fractions. A better picture of the development of children's understanding of rational numbers would be accomplished if children's insights into sharing were also being used in schools.

SUMMARY

Mathematical development depends on both children's understanding of quantities and their ability to reason with the numbers that represent quantities. This chapter has shown that these two aspects of children's mathematical learning do not always develop at the same time. Children can learn to count quite early, but knowing how to count and reasoning about cardinality and the order of quantities represented by numbers are not the same thing. When children can say the number of objects in a set – for example, 'five' – they may be using the number label 'five' as it designates this set only. They may not realise that there is a specific relation between this set and all sets with five elements – equivalence – and also specific relations between this set and any other set that can be represented by a whole number – for example, a set with five elements has more elements than those with four, three, two and one, and fewer than sets with six or more elements. There is much research investigating the inferences that children draw from counting and also those that they can draw from equivalences between sets without having to count, that shed light on the distinction between a relational and a non-relational (or categorical) understanding of number.

Natural numbers represent quantities that can be counted. Rational numbers or fractions represent quantities stemming from division. These two different types of number make different intellectual demands on children when it comes to understanding equivalence and order. Research reviewed in this chapter shows the differences between these two types of number and the differences between the connections that children can establish between number labels and quantities for natural and rational numbers.

In order to learn the meaning of numbers, children must establish connections between number labels (oral or written) and quantities. In the domain of whole numbers, the relations that children must consider involve additive relations, because the logic of whole numbers is based on additive composition. Multiplicative relations are also involved in learning a numeration system with a base (base 10 in our system). For example, in our written place value system, the value of a digit depends on its place in the number from right to left. So in the number 256, the 6 represents units, the 5 represents tens and the 2 represents hundreds. Research reviewed in this chapter illustrates the difficulties of using this combination of additive and multiplicative reasoning and the processes that help children overcome them. In the case of fractions, children must consider division as the basis for giving meaning to numbers. They have two schemes of action that can be used to give meaning to fractions, sharing and partitioning. Research reviewed in this chapter shows that these develop at different paces even though children must sometimes attain the same insights about the relations between quantities.

Children start to solve story problems about quantities at first using schemes of action. Many can solve some additive as well as multiplicative reasoning problems from the time they start school, using actions and objects to represent quantities. This shows the role of schemes of action in children's mathematical development. Over time, they can also use reasoning based on schemes of action, but without having to carry out the actions – just thinking with numbers. Additive and multiplicative reasoning originate from different action schemes.

Children's understanding of additive and multiplicative reasoning develops over time. The use of small versus large numbers makes arithmetic problems more difficult because the numerical calculations are more difficult. However, the more important developments in solving arithmetic problems are those called by Vergnaud (1982) relational calculations, which require understanding of the relations between quantities in order to know what sort of arithmetic calculation to use. It is possible to design arithmetic problems that can be solved by the same calculations, but which have very different levels of difficulty. The variation in level of difficulty of arithmetic problems has been analysed in many studies which contribute to a better understanding of how children's mathematical concepts develop.

In many different ways, this chapter has illustrated the difference between knowing how and knowing when to do sums. This is a simple way to think of the old controversy in mathematics teaching in primary school: should children have lots of drill and practice to develop their number skills? Or should more time be allocated to promoting their mathematical reasoning? This chapter has reviewed much research that should help you reach your own conclusions about this debate.

ANSWERS TO PROBLEMS

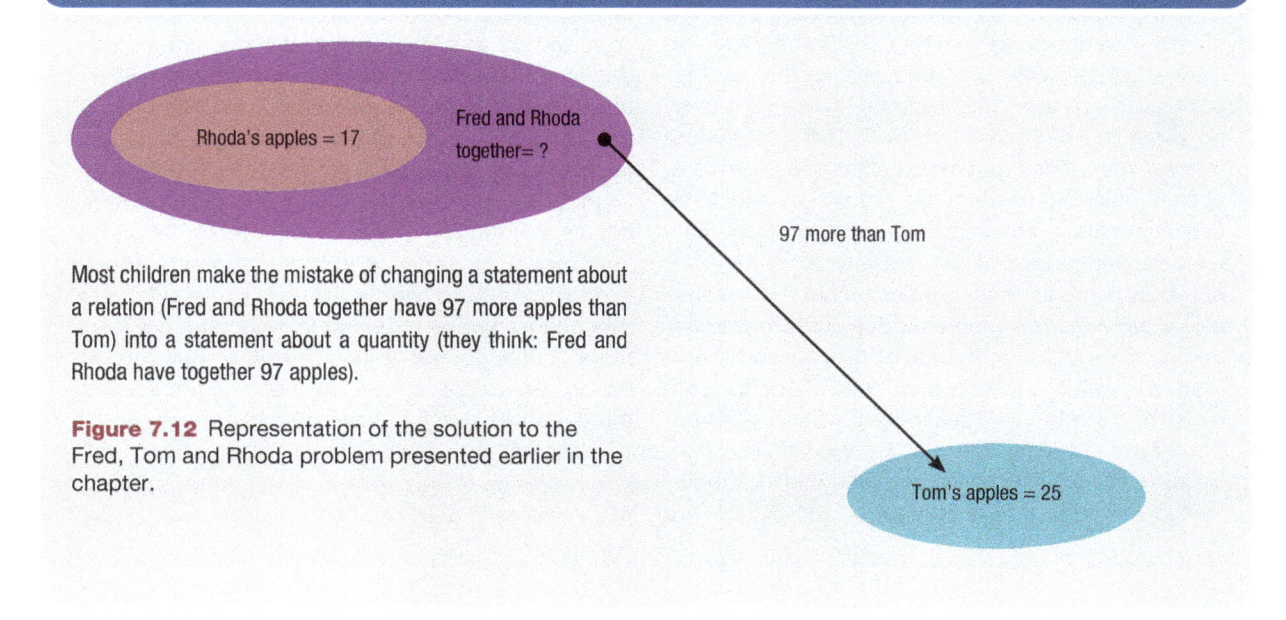

Most children make the mistake of changing a statement about a relation (Fred and Rhoda together have 97 more apples than Tom) into a statement about a quantity (they think: Fred and Rhoda have together 97 apples).

Figure 7.12 Representation of the solution to the Fred, Tom and Rhoda problem presented earlier in the chapter.

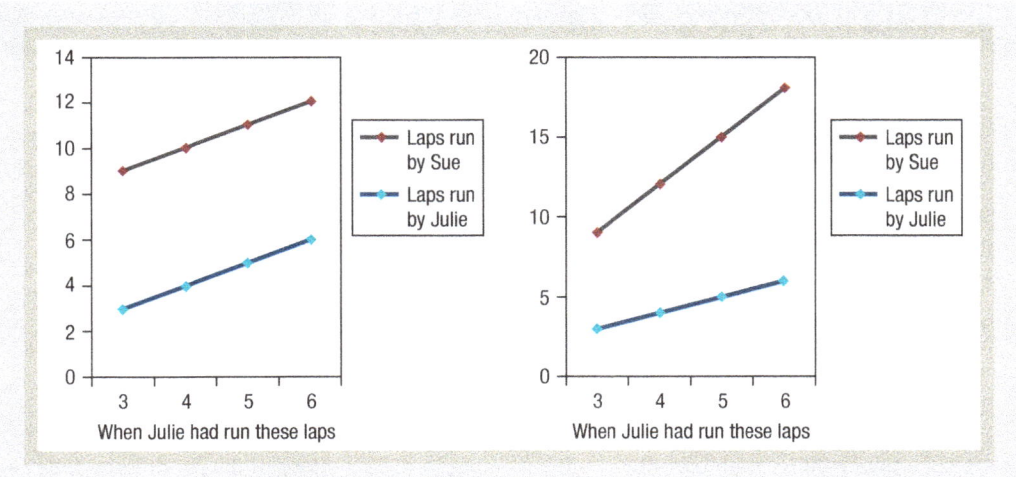

Which graph describes accurately the relation between the number of laps run by Sue and Julie? Which represents additive and which represents multiplicative relations? What is the right answer and why might people choose the other one?

Figure 7.13 Possible solutions to the 'Sue and Julie' running problem presented earlier in the chapter.

REVIEW QUESTIONS

1. Use research to argue that knowing how to count and understanding number are different things.
2. Compare and contrast Piaget's with Gelman and Galistell's work about children's concept of cardinality.
3. Discuss how the analysis of children's ability to make inferences contributes to the study of the development of mathematical concepts.
4. Compare and contrast additive and multiplicative reasoning and the origins of these in children's development.
5. Describe different types of additive reasoning problem and research that shows their different levels of difficulty.
6. How have researchers used story problems in the study of the development of mathematical reasoning? What contributions has this method made to the understanding of mathematical development?
7. Describe different types of multiplicative reasoning problems and research that shows their different levels of difficulty.
8. What are 'product of measures' problems and why should researchers pay more attention to these problems?
9. Compare and contrast the difficulties involved in understanding equivalence and order in the context of natural and rational numbers.
10. What are the pros and cons of teaching children about fractions using the scheme of partitioning as the starting point?

RECOMMENDED READING

For further discussions of the idea that children come to understand relations between quantities by reflecting upon the results of their actions, and a detailed account of how children think about different ways of counting and solving arithmetic problems, see:

Steffe, L. P., Cobb, P., & Glaserfeld, E. V. (1988). *Construction of Arithmetical Meanings and Strategies*. London: Springer.

For discussion of the evidence from humans and animals in favour of an innate analogue system, see:

Dehaene, S., DehaeneLambertz, G., & Cohen, L. (1998). Abstract representations of numbers in the animal and human brain. *Trends in Neurosciences*, 21, 355–361.

For discussions of developmental or acquired dyscalculia, see:

Butterworth, B., Cipolotti, L., & Warrington, E. K. (1996). Short-term memory impairments and arithmetical ability. *Quarterly Journal of Experimental Psychology*, 49A, 251–262.

Kosc, L. (1974). Developmental dyscalculia. *Journal of Learning Disabilities Quarterly*, 7, 164–177.

Landerl, K., Bevana, A., & Butterworth, B. (2004). Developmental dyscalculia and basic numerical capacities: A study of 8–9 year old students. *Cognition*, 93, 99–125.

McCloskey, M., Aliminosa, D., & Macaruso, P. (1991). Theory-based assessment of acquired dyscalculia. *Brain and Cognition*, 17, 285–308.

For a review of the development of arithmetical skills which complements the analysis of problem solving and understanding number presented in this chapter, and also includes a review of arithmetical disabilities, see:

Butterworth, B. (2005). The development of arithmetical abilities. *Journal of Child Psychology and Psychiatry*, 46, 3–18.

To read more about the critiques of Carey's work, see:

Rips, L. J., Asmuth, J., & Bloomfield, A. (2006). Giving the boot to the bootstrap: How not to learn the natural numbers. *Cognition*, 101, B51–B60.

Rips, L. J., Asmuth, J., & Bloomfield, A. (2008). Discussion: Do children learn the integers by induction? *Cognition*, 106, 940–951.

For a complementary analysis of the role of culture and symbols in mathematical reasoning, a topic that could not be covered within this chapter, see:

Nunes, T., Schliemann, A. D., & Carraher, D. W. (1993). *Street Mathematics and School Mathematics*. New York: Cambridge University Press.

For research which has shown that Change and Combine problems are easier than Compare problems, see:

Brown, M. (1981). Number operations. In K. Hart (Ed.), *Children's Understanding of Mathematics: 11–16* (23–47). Windsor, UK: NFER-Nelson.

Carpenter, T. P., Hiebert, J., & Moser, J. M. (1981). Problem structure and first grade children's initial solution processes for simple addition and subtraction problems. *Journal for Research in Mathematics Education*, 12, 27–39.

Carpenter, T. P., & Moser, J. M. (1982). The development of addition and subtraction problem solving. In T. P. Carpenter, J. M. Moser, & T. A. Romberg (Eds.), *Addition and Subtraction: A Cognitive Perspective* (10–24). Hillsdale, NJ: Erlbaum.

De Corte, E., & Verschaffel, L. (1987). The effect of semantic structure on first graders' solution strategies of elementary addition and subtraction word problems. *Journal for Research in Mathematics Education*, 18, 363–381.

Fayol, M. (1992). From number to numbers in use: Solving arithmetic problems. In J. Bideaud, C. Meljac, & J.-P. Fischer (Eds.), *Pathways to Number* (209–218). Hillsdale, NJ: Erlbaum.

Ginsburg, H. (1977). *Children's Arithmetic: The Learning Process*. New York: Van Nostrand.

Kintsch, W., & Greeno, J. (1985). Understanding and solving word problems. *Psychological Review*, 92, 109–129.

Riley, M., Greeno, J. G., & Heller, J. I. (1983). Development of children's problem solving ability in arithmetic. In H. Ginsburg (Ed.), *The Development of Mathematical Thinking* (153–196). New York: Academic Press.

Vergnaud, G. (1982). A classification of cognitive tasks and operations of thought involved in addition and subtraction problems. In T. P. Carpenter, J. M. Moser, & T. A. Romberg (Eds.), *Addition and Subtraction: A Cognitive Perspective* (60–67). Hillsdale, NJ: Erlbaum.

For discussion of children's discovery of strategies for solving arithmetic problems using knowledge of the inverse relation between addition and subtraction, see:

Siegler, R. S., & Stern, E. (1998). Conscious and unconscious strategy discoveries: A microgenetic analysis. *Journal of Experimental Psychology – General*, 127, 377–397.

For more information on quantities that cannot be represented by a single whole number, see:

Nunes, T., Desli, D., & Bell, D. (2003). The development of children's understanding of intensive quantities. *International Journal of Educational Research*, 39, 652–675.

RECOMMENDED WEBSITES

For a review of the topics in this chapter in greater depth and further topics in mathematics, go to:

http://www.nuffieldfoundation.org/key-understandings-mathematics-learning

To have a look at maths for children explained in easy language, plus puzzles, games, quizzes and worksheets, go to:

http://www.mathsisfun.com/

To explore the UK's National Curriculum, go to:

https://www.gov.uk/government/collections/national-curriculum

and then search by Key Stage and Subject.

The BBC's channel for young children, CBeebies, has a show called *numberjacks*. 'The series is aimed at four to five year old girls and boys and will help them develop early maths skills, knowledge and understanding.' Explore the Numberjacks website and evaluate the extent to which you think it achieves these aims, and why:

http://www.numberjacks.co.uk/kids/

For a complete report on the research featured in the Cutting Edge box on page 214, go to:

http://publications.dcsf.gov.uk/eOrderingDownload/DCSF-RB118.pdf

Chapter 8
Theory of mind

Learning outcomes

After reading this chapter, and with further recommended reading, you should be able to:

1. Describe and define what theory of mind is.
2. Critically evaluate the developmental nature of theory of mind.
3. Critically evaluate methods of measuring false beliefs.
4. Critically evaluate theories underpinning the development and existence of theory of mind.
5. Critically evaluate the research investigating theory of mind in children with autism.

What do we mean by theory of mind?

Mary finished putting her groceries into a bag. 'That will be £27.63,' said the till assistant. Mary looked in her handbag, shuffled her gloves and keys and looked thoughtful. Then she put her hand into each of her coat pockets, first the right, then the left and sighed.

What did Mary need? What did she believe was in her handbag? Why did she sigh? The ability to understand this scenario and to provide answers to these questions is an example of a concept called by some 'folk psychology' and by others 'theory of mind'. Both describe a process that connects our cognitive development with our social development, for without it we are unable to understand the meaning of other people's emotions or the focus of other people's attention. As we grow in cognitive competence, so we develop the ability to identify the goals, intentions, desires and beliefs of other people.

- Do you ever feel that you have misread a situation or perhaps you know of someone who commonly seems to misread situations?
- Sometimes these mistakes are simply due to a lapse of concentration: we are busy talking on the telephone whilst partly listening to a conversation being held in the same room. But what if you frequently misread situations? Does this have a meaningful effect on your ability to socialise?

Introduction

This scenario demonstrates that we are able to infer a person's beliefs, desires and intentions from observing their behaviour. In order to do this, we each hold a substantial amount of information about our minds and the minds of others, and this is the basic principle of folk psychology.

Folk psychology constitutes a large part of psychology, but the main discussion within cognitive science has been how folk psychology allows us to predict and explain behaviour. This ability to predict and make sense of events intrigued the cognitive psychologists in the late 1940s as a challenge to the purely behaviourist perspective that denounced all involvement of the mind in our behavioural responses to events. The influence of the psychoanalytical perspective of introspection in providing us with knowledge of the mind had also begun to lose favour, and psychologists were looking for another ▶

> **Definition**
>
> Folk psychology: the information that ordinary people have about the mind and how it works. It is usually based in a common set of traditions and customs that are used to explain people's emotions and behaviour.

way to explain our ability to infer desires and beliefs and, in turn, to predict another person's behaviour. Research has since attempted to theorise how we are able to understand and make judgements about other people's behaviour, and it is often conceptualised under the heading of a *theory of mind*. This chapter is designed to help you understand theory of mind, what it means to us and how we go about measuring this complex principle.

What is theory of mind?

The term theory of mind was first coined by Premack and Woodruff in 1978, and describes the ability to figure out what a person might believe to be the case in any given situation and, from that, to describe what that person might then do. Think of our example of Mary at the shop. You might infer that she *believes* that her purse is in her bag to pay for her shopping, but her behaviour reveals that she has forgotten her purse. If asked, you might then *predict* that Mary will ask for her shopping to be put aside until she can return with her purse. This ability to predict others' behaviour by inferring a person's motivation is an important social skill and one that uses sophisticated cognitive skills. Premack and Woodruff state that, in order to understand the mental states of others, we must first be able to understand our own mental state. Although the definition of theory of mind describes a wide range of cognitive abilities, these researchers state that most importantly, in order to be able to predict and even explain the behaviour of others, we must be able to make judgements based on two core cognitive skills. First, we must be able to judge what that other person seems to want or desire and second, we must be able to judge what that other person believes to be true. Research demonstrates that this ability to 'mind-read' follows a developmental pathway that maps neatly onto both our cognitive development and our social development. But first let's consider how theory of mind displays itself in the developing child.

The development of empathy and other 'mind-reading' skills

How, then, do we develop the ability to know what another person feels or desires? Take the following scenario. A father takes his son to the park. They walk past a pool of water and the father sees some ducks swimming. He looks at his son and says, 'Look, ducks!' As he does this, he looks away from his child and towards the ducks. His son follows his gaze towards the ducks, spots them and says excitedly, 'Ducks! Ducks!' At around the age of 8 months, when an adult looks away from the child and towards something else, the child will turn his head and look there too. At around 12 months, if the adult points at something of interest to the child, then the child will point at it too. Baron-Cohen (1995) describes these behaviours as, first, gaze following and, second, proto-declarative pointing, providing evidence that the child is learning to coordinate his own mental state (e.g. attention to the object being looked at or pointed at) with that of another person's mental state. Gaze following in the child shows that the child is aware that the adult is looking at something of interest. Proto-declarative pointing in the child then shows that the child confirms that he knows the adult is pointing at something of interest. These subtle behaviours Baron-Cohen argues are the first early signs and the building blocks of 'mind reading'.

The next step in 'mind reading' is to understand that what a person knows about a situation depends partly on what a person sees of a situation. At about age 36–48 months, the child begins to grasp the concept that what another person knows about an event of interest is based in what that person has seen of the event of interest. For example, if the child observes the adult *see* a toy being put away in a box, the child understands that the adult *knows* that the toy is in the box. This principle that

> **Definitions**
>
> Theory of mind: being able to infer the full range of mental states (beliefs, desires, intentions, imagination, emotions, etc.) that cause action (Baron-Cohen, 2001).
> Gaze following: the ability to follow where another person is looking and to look in the same direction.
> Proto-declarative pointing: the ability to point at the same object of interest as another person.

'seeing leads to knowing' is again an important part of a child's cognitive and social development. By learning this key principle, the child is able to make a judgement of what another person may know based on what that person has seen happen.

At around the same time as developing these mind-reading skills, the child begins to show 'meta-representational' or 'pretend' play. Leslie (1994) proposes that children learn to separate what is the truth of a situation from what a person may believe about a situation. For example, if you give a small child a banana, then that child may play with that banana and pretend it is perhaps a telephone, or a car, a pistol or anything else that comes to mind. Being able to separate out what is true (it is a banana) from what you can believe (it is a telephone, car or pistol) demonstrates that the child is engaging in the skill of meta-representation. Most children are able to do this by the age of 48 months and the research shows that the use of meta-representation or 'pretend' play illustrates a child's developing ability to understand that a thought can be based in fantasy and not based necessarily in reality.

All of these abilities – gaze following, proto-declarative pointing at items of interest, learning that 'seeing leads to knowing' and using cognitive meta-representations in pretend play – together complete a complex picture of the child's early cognitive development. The gaze following demonstrates the child's ability to follow the attention of another person. The proto-declarative pointing reveals that the child understands the focal point of the other person, in our example the ducks. The concept of 'seeing leads to knowing' helps the child figure out how another person knows what he knows, whilst pretend play reveals that the child understands that objects can represent other things like the banana representing a telephone, car or pistol. If you look at the section on learning the meanings of words in Chapter 5 (page 133), you will see how gaze following and proto-declarative pointing act

Definitions

Seeing leads to knowing: the principle that a person's belief/knowledge about a situation depends partly on what they have seen.

Meta-representation: (1) the ability to separate reality from fantasy, e.g. during pretend play (Leslie, 1987); (2) additionally, knowing the difference between what might be represented in a photograph or painting of an object and what the reality of that object might be (Perner, 1991).

This young boy is showing proto-declarative pointing – he is pointing at the same object as his father.
Source: Corbis/Patrick Kociniak/Design Pics

together to enable the child to talk about what he can see and show the parent what interests him. Combining these skills together, you can see that the child is beginning to learn the skills necessary for effective social awareness and social interaction. This is demonstrated neatly when observing the behaviour of young children who encounter someone showing emotional upset or distress.

From an early age (around 2 years), children appear to show an awareness of other people's feelings. If another child or an adult shows sadness or upset, a toddler may go up to them and give them a hug or even say 'there there' and offer comfort. In a paper by Cole et al. (1992), the authors discuss this awareness of emotional upset in 2-year-olds responding to two events: breaking a doll and spilling a drink. In the study, Cole et al. found that the toddlers would try and fix the problem when it occurred, either by trying to put the doll back together or by trying to mop up the spilt drink. The toddlers' responses were described as 'tension and frustration' at the break or mishap and 'concerned reparation' in trying to repair the damage. The toddlers' response also appeared to reflect the emotional response of their mothers to the mishaps. For instance, the response of the children was different if they had mothers who reported experiencing depression and anxiety. These children were more likely to respond to the incidents in a subdued way, mimicking the response of the mother, when compared to children of mothers not reporting depression and anxiety. The toddlers appeared to be responding to the physical expression of their mother's response and the authors argue that as such this demonstrated that the children had learned empathy.

> **STOP AND THINK**
>
> What other psychological theories might help to explain the subdued reaction of the child of the depressed mother to the breakage?

However, empathy is a complicated notion that describes our ability to understand that how a person feels on the 'inside' (our private self) can be expressed by how the person behaves on the 'outside' (our public self).

> **Definition**
>
> Empathy: the ability to identify with the emotions of others and to read the physical expression of emotions in others.

Were the children of depressed mothers being empathic or were they simply copying the response of the mother? For example, children learn that a person who is smiling on the 'outside' is feeling happy on the 'inside'. The ability to read feelings by the physical expression of them is important if the child is going to be able to empathise with others and have successful social interactions (Baron-Cohen, 1995). The findings of the Cole et al. study show that the children of mothers who report depression and who show sadness and disinterest on their faces pick up on this when the toy breaks and react accordingly. Also at this age, children begin to show what we call 'pro-social' behaviours, or behaviours that encourage and support social interaction. For instance, the 2-year-old begins to share her toys and snacks with other people and helps other people out. Children of this age understand that when another child is crying that child is upset and will often react to reduce this feeling of upset by giving them a hug, a toy or a biscuit. The child also at this age starts to develop an understanding of deception and will enjoy hiding objects from sight whilst professing no idea of where the objects are! All of these behaviours reflect the ability to understand the minds of others and are a sign that the child is developing a theory of mind.

Beliefs and desires

The child is developing at this time a sense of the 'private self' and the 'public self'. The 'private self' denotes how we feel 'inside' and the 'public self' denotes how we display our notion of 'self' to others. By learning the distinction between a person having a 'private self' and a person having a 'public self,' the child is gaining an important understanding of the adult world. It is a complicated cognitive skill for the child to understand that a person may act happy on the outside but that inside they might be unhappy, although the child will eventually learn to distinguish this. However, initially the child is starting to learn that if another person is acting happy on the outside, they are also happy on the inside. This ability to read feelings by the physical expression of them is important if the child is going to be able to empathise with others. The ability of children to empathise with others is discussed in Simon Baron-Cohen's work on the theory of mind (1995).

An example of theory of mind in action would be this. Show a child a picture of an event, say a girl on a bicycle and a boy on the pavement crying. If you ask the child what is happening, they might say that the girl is riding the bicycle and the boy is crying because he wants a go and she will not let him on it. Alternatively, the child might say that the boy is crying because it is his bike and she has taken it from him. In order to explain the picture, the child has to describe and understand another person's emotions, desires and intentions from this simple vignette. Thus, the child has learnt to deduce a mental state from a visual image which allows them to explain why the behaviour occurs. This is an important ability to acquire. If we were not able to infer a series of events based on key amounts of information, we would not be able to 'read' a social situation. Consequently, if we 'read' a social situation incorrectly, we might find ourselves displaying inappropriate behaviour. By behaving inappropriately in a situation we might be putting ourselves at risk – physically or, more likely, socially. None of us want to feel uncomfortable at a party because we were unable to 'read' the situational cues and see that the party was no longer 'fancy dress'!

This boy is demonstrating empathy as he seeks to console his friend.
Source: Getty Images/Dorling Kindersley

Between the age of 12 and 24 months, the child develops important social skills that correspond to the desire stage of theory of mind. The desire stage suggests that we understand that people have internal states or emotions that correspond to desire. This allows us to predict what people want from understanding their internal state or public display of emotions. For example, a child might say that the boy was crying because he was *upset* at not being able to ride the bicycle. A child who has developed the ability to predict desires from a person's behaviour would be able to understand that the boy was crying because he had the desire to ride the bicycle and for some reason could not. The next step in understanding other people's desires is to understand also that people will act to satisfy their desires. So, in our example the child might continue discussing the story and propose that the boy's crying might attract the girl's attention. If she sees that he is upset because she is riding the bicycle, she may pass it over to him, for him to ride. Thus, from this simple vignette, a child with well-developed desire stage of theory of mind can deduce from the scenario that, by crying, the boy has communicated that he is not happy that the girl is riding the bicycle, that he wants to ride the bicycle (otherwise he would not be upset) and that his act of crying has brought about the response he wants, for the girl to hand over the bicycle and let him ride it.

By the age of 3 years, the typically developing child has developed a much more sophisticated level of social interaction. The child's language skills are improving rapidly and their vocabulary is increasing by an average of 10–20 words a week (see Chapter 5, 'Language development', pages 131–3). The child is engaging in cooperative play and has started to allocate a hierarchy to their friendships. Children of this age start to have 'best' friends – a status that may change from day to day. This hierarchy is an important part of childhood as it demonstrates the child is able to allocate greater importance to certain people and lesser importance to others. The child's ability to sympathise with other children's feelings expands to an ability to *empathise* with other children (see Chapter 12, 'Peer interactions and relationships', for a full discussion of the development of play

Definition

Desire stage of theory of mind: the ability to detect in someone a strong feeling of wanting to have something or wishing for something to happen.

and interaction in young children). The child can understand what the other child is thinking and act accordingly. An important part of this learning is that the child is also beginning to understand deception. The child might, for instance, be able to keep a birthday party a secret from a younger sibling, knowing that part of the act of surprise is that the recipient does not know that the event is about to happen.

The child's ability to empathise and to predict how another person might act is known as the belief-desire stage of theory of mind. In this stage, the child understands that a person has both *beliefs* as well as desires. Thus using our example, the boy might have a desire to ride the bicycle and may also have the belief that he is allowed to ride the bicycle. If the beliefs match the desires then the subsequent action will have the goal of resolving those desires. For example, the boy will go to the bicycle, pick it up and ride it. However, what children of this age are also beginning to understand is that someone may have a desire for something but have a conflicting belief. In our example, the boy might have the desire to ride the bicycle but has the belief that he is *not* allowed to ride it, perhaps as he is too small or too young to do so. As a result, the child learning that the boy might have a conflicting belief might interpret the vignette as the boy, although upset because he wants to ride the bicycle, does not do so as he knows he is not allowed to ride the bicycle. Children at age 3 are beginning to understand that you might not act on your desire if it goes against your beliefs. However, they do not understand yet that the beliefs may be false. In our example, the child interprets the picture as the boy not riding the bicycle because he believes he is not allowed to. However, it may be that he is not allowed to ride the bicycle on the road because it is deemed dangerous, yet he is allowed to ride the bicycle in the relatively safe garden. The child cannot make the judgement yet that the boy's belief might be false.

False beliefs in theory of mind

Daniel C. Dennett proposed in his essay on the philosophies of the mind that the only way to test the ability to impute mental states is to test the understanding of false belief (1978). This theory was tested by Wimmer and Perner (1983) who constructed a test of the child's understanding of false beliefs called the *Maxi and the chocolate* task. In this task, the child is talked through the following scenario: Maxi has some chocolate. Maxi puts the chocolate in a cupboard and goes out to play. Maxi's mother then moves the chocolate to the refrigerator. Maxi comes in from playing and wants his chocolate. The researcher then asks the child: 'Where does Maxi look for his chocolate?' The researchers found that a child of 3 years of age is likely to answer 'refrigerator' whereas a child of 4 years of age is likely to answer 'cupboard'. The authors suggest that the 3-year-olds have not yet understood that Maxi's belief about where the chocolate is to be found is different from where the chocolate really is. Maxi has a false belief about the location of the chocolate, one that the older children only are able to recognise. At age 4, the child is considered to be at the representational stage of theory of mind. The child has learnt that beliefs may be false and that someone might misrepresent a situation because of these false beliefs. However, some researchers have criticised the Maxi and the chocolate story for being overly complicated for children of 3 years of age, reporting instead that the younger children may have simply been confused by the story length rather than being unable to comprehend the perspective of Maxi.

So to address this limitation, Baron-Cohen et al. (1985) proposed a simplified story to test a child's recognition of false beliefs. The Sally-Anne task requires the researcher to show a child a card (Figure 8.1) and to talk her through the following scenario.

The researcher points to each of the figures and names them 'Anne' and 'Sally' and explains the scene. To paraphrase the card, Sally puts her marble in the basket and leaves the room. Anne moves the marble to the box. Sally returns to get her marble and the researcher asks the

---

Definitions

Belief-desire stage of theory of mind: the ability to make a mental representation of the world.
False belief: the wrongly held belief that something is true.
Representational stage of theory of mind: the ability to know that someone may believe something is true even when it is not and understand that the mistake happens because they are relying on incorrect or false knowledge.

WHAT IS THEORY OF MIND? | **227**

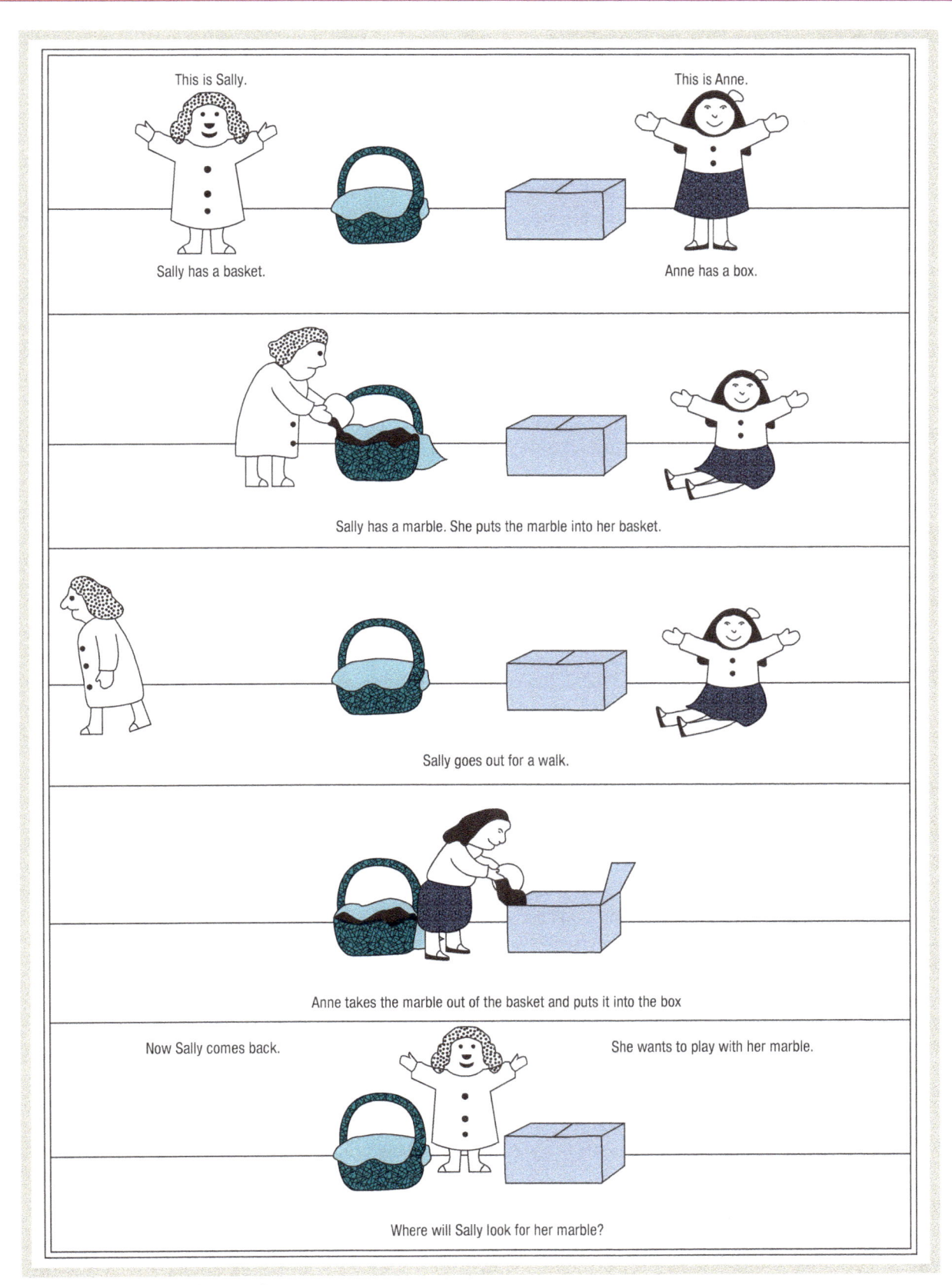

Figure 8.1 The Sally-Anne task.
Source: Frith, U. (1989) *Autism: Explaining the Enigma* (Oxford: Blackwell Ltd)

child a number of questions. First, the researcher asks the child where Sally will look for her marble. This question tests the child's ability to understand Sally's *belief* about the marble, the correct answer being 'in the basket'. The researcher then asks the child where the marble actually is. This question tests the child's understanding of *reality*, the correct answer being 'in the box'. Finally, the researcher asks the child where the marble was in the beginning. This is a *memory* question that tests the child's ability to recall events and the correct answer is 'in the basket'. These are all critical skills – skills that Baron-Cohen (1995) calls 'mind reading' – that the child needs to learn in order to function well in a social environment. The authors in the 1985 study found that all 27 of the children (age range 3.5 years to 5.9 years) were able to answer the reality and memory questions accurately and that only 23 were able to answer correctly the belief question. The children who could not answer the question correctly were all under the age of 4 years. Baron-Cohen et al. suggest that this shows that the children understood the task, but that the children under the age of 4 years were unable to recognise or identify with the false-belief part of the test.

Other studies have produced similar results. A study by Perner et al. (1987) shows this in what is called the 'Smarties task'. In this test, the researcher shows a tube of Smarties (coloured chocolate buttons) to a 4-year-old and asks them what is in the tube. The 4-year-olds always reply, 'Smarties.' The researcher then opens the tube and shows the child that what are in the tube are actually pencils. The researcher asks the child what they think the other child would say when asked what is in the tube. Again, there appears to be a distinct difference in what children of different ages will say. The 4-year-old will generally answer, 'Smarties.' The 4-year-old knows that pencils are in the tube but appears to understand that another child does not know this and will assume the tube contains sweets. It appears that the 4-year-old child understands the nature of false beliefs. However, when the researcher asks a 3-year-old child what is in the tube, the 3-year-old will invariably say, 'Pencils.' The implication here is that the 3-year-old does not understand the nature of false beliefs. Studies like this appear to show the developmental nature of understanding the perspective of others' beliefs, desires and behaviour in young children. However, the findings of studies like these are not without criticism.

Siegal and Beattie (1991) argue that the reason the 3-year-old children fail on this task is because the children make a mistake in understanding the question, 'Where will Sally look for her marble?' The authors argue that, with this standard question, approximately 35% of the children answer correctly. However, if the question is changed to 'Where will Sally look *first* for her marble?', the children perform better and just over 70% are able to answer this question correctly. Does changing the question in this way mean the children are now able to understand the story better or is the question now simply easier to answer? Surian and Leslie (1999) first replicated a false-belief task then adapted it to investigate this point with a group of 3-year-olds. Surian and Leslie chose a slightly different story based on Leslie and Thaiss's (1992) story of a boy Billy, a ball and three items of furniture: a bed, a dressing-table and a toy-box. The children were told that Billy puts his ball on the dressing-table. Billy leaves the room and his mother enters, picks up the ball and puts it away in the toy-box. The researchers then asked the children a series of questions.

Know question:	'Does Billy know where the ball is?'
Think question:	'Where does Billy think the ball is?'
Memory question:	'Where did Billy put the ball in the beginning?'
Reality question:	'Where is the ball now?'
Look-first question:	'When he comes back, where is the *first* place Billy will look for his ball?'

(*Source:* Surian and Leslie, 1999, p. 148)

This series of questions was designed to test how much the child understands of the story as well as how able the child is to understand the perspective of the boy Billy. Surian and Leslie found that the 3-year-olds were more likely to answer the look-first question accurately than the think question, suggesting that the method of asking is important in gauging whether or not the child has developed the ability to detect false beliefs. The authors propose that, by being able to answer the look-first question more accurately than the think question, the children demonstrate that they have some burgeoning understanding of the concept behind the false-belief task without yet having a full understanding of it. Perhaps, too, there is more to these tasks than that of understanding beliefs? The task itself describes a hypothetical event and therefore requires the child to consider what an imaginary child might do in an imaginary situation. Possibly the child needs to develop the appropriate cognitive skills necessary to consider this supposed event mentally, and that this cognitive ability may develop *after* the ability to know about beliefs in a real-life situation. The argument in this case suggests that performance on the false-belief tasks might have more to do with a child's developing cognitive skills than their capacity for mind reading.

Wellman et al. (2001) conducted a meta-analysis on a wide range of papers published on the theory and measurement of false belief. The meta-analysis sought to find patterns of consistency in 178 studies reporting on the false-belief task and found that, even when accounting for age, country of origin and the type of task described (the Sally-Anne task, Maxi and the chocolate task, Billy and the ball, etc.), there is a clear pattern in the development of understanding the conceptual nature of false beliefs in young children. The data showed that there is a true change in the understanding of false beliefs that is unrelated to the limited ability to process such complex information in the very young. The authors report that manipulation of the style in which the questions were asked (such as by Surian and Leslie) improved the performance of children of all ages and not just of the younger children. They conclude that none of these studies actually provides evidence of early development of competence: that older children were simply better at the false-belief tasks than younger children. The analysis also showed that prior to developing the understanding of false beliefs, the children performed at 'chance' levels of accuracy: that is, their responses were 50/50 right or wrong. Thus the children could not be considered to be making false-belief mistakes on these tasks; rather they failed to understand the concept of false belief altogether and understand human behaviour in other, different ways.

It is important to note that performance on false-belief tasks does not in itself indicate a child's development of theory of mind: however, false-belief tasks do illustrate an important part of a person's early cognitive development. Theory of mind continues to develop in young to middle childhood at the same time as the child's social behaviour becomes more complex. By the time the child reaches the age of 6 years, there is a sharp increase in the amount of time they spend with their peers (see Chapter 12, 'Peer interactions and relationships'). The number of friends a child has increases in number and their peer interactions start to occur in a number of different situations: for example, in their own home, in a friend's home and at school. A developing theory of mind helps to facilitate the child's ability to understand the emotional and practical implications of these friendships. For instance, the child's friendships begin to be based on shared interests and their play style is coordinated and involves rules and role-play. Without theory of mind, the child would not be able to infer a child's interests from their choice of toy or game, or to pick up the subtle rules of play.

Theory of mind researchers explain this development in play by describing the children's stage of theory of mind as *second-order states*. This means that the children understand that people may want to evoke an emotion in another person and that we might say or do something to make someone feel good or bad. For example, children understanding second-order states will be able to make sense of this scenario: Fred wants Bill to think he has a present waiting for him at home. The child will understand that Fred has a desire to make Bill believe he is being rewarded. Alternatively, if presented with the scenario: Susan tells Mary that no-one wants to play with her, the child will understand that Susan has a desire to make Mary believe she is unpopular. Children of this age also develop an understanding that people sometimes say things that mean the opposite of what they want to convey and they begin to understand sarcasm. Children of age 6 will understand when, for instance, the following story is told to them. 'Fred won the lottery, passed all his exams and got lots of presents. Fred said, "I had a really bad day."' Until the child understands that people sometimes say the opposite of what they mean, they will not be able to make sense of Fred's statement at all.

Definition

Meta-analysis: a method of statistical analysis which combines the results of many studies to identify an overall effect or change, often in an attempt to overcome problems of small sample size in research.

How does theory of mind fit into a developmental perspective?

As our discussion of theories shows, certain cognitive abilities have to be in place before the child is able to empathise with the viewpoint, the beliefs and behaviours of another. The Wellman et al. paper presented the results of a meta-analysis of 178 studies showing that there is definitely a trend in developing theory of mind in young children. Wellman argued that fewer than 20% of children aged 2 years and 6 months could complete the false-belief task compared with 50% of children aged 3 years and 8 months and with 75% of children aged 4 years and 8 months. Thus theory of mind fits into a similar trajectory of development as other cognitive abilities, such as language and reasoning. Although small changes to the methods used in the false-belief tasks improved performance slightly, change was only seen in those children on the 'cusp' of acquiring theory of mind: that is, changing the wording of the task helped those children who had a partially developed sense of theory of mind. However, even with changes to the wording of the task, none of the children aged 3 years and under showed anything other than chance rates of performance when given repeated testing.

Theory of mind and the development of language

The false-belief tasks described by Baron-Cohen et al. (the Sally-Anne task), Wimmer and Perner (Maxi and the chocolate) and Perner et al. (the Smarties task) all rely on the child understanding what the experimenter is asking him to do. All of these studies revealed that there was a developmental aspect to theory of mind, but as Siegal and Beattie suggest, perhaps the studies actually measured development in language competence instead. Siegal and Beattie's study changed the wording in the Sally-Anne task to ask, 'Where will Sally look *first* for her marble?' and recorded a significant improvement in the accuracy of the children's responses. Similarly, the Surian and Leslie study asked the children a number of questions leading up to the 'look *first*' question and, again, noted an improvement in the children's performance.

All of these studies connect the child's linguistic ability with their theory of mind status, but what if language is a separate cognitive ability to theory of mind? De Villiers and de Villiers (2000) propose just this, that perhaps those children who perform less well on the false-belief tasks do so because they do not understand fully what is being asked of them? In Chapter 5, Language Development, there is a good discussion on the relationship between cognitive development and semantic development in language, which will help you to understand this debate.

There is certainly evidence that children who are more linguistically competent perform better on false-belief tasks and that language training can improve performance on these tasks. Hale and Tager-Flusberg (2003) worked with 60 children between the age of 3 and 5 years who had previously made mistakes on the false-belief tasks. Over a period of two weeks, the children were told false-belief stories using phrases such as '_ said he hugged _ but actually he hugged _. Who did _ hug?' For each incorrect answer, the children were corrected and the scenario was played out again with emphasis on where the children had made their mistake. The children were tested on standard false-belief-type tasks between three and five days after completing the training. Hale and Tager-Flusberg found that the children's performance on these tasks significantly improved from an initial accuracy of approximately 10–20% to a final accuracy of approximately 70%. This suggests that by helping the children understand the language used, their performance in false-belief tasks improved and therefore their understanding of theory of mind.

As the child's language abilities become more complex, so then it appears does their understanding of theory of mind. What happens, however, if the child does not hear or speak? A study by Meristo et al. in 2007 compared the development of theory of mind in deaf children from Italy learning Italian sign language to hearing children. The deaf children in this study had either been taught sign language from birth (native signers) or been introduced to it at school (late signers). All the native signers had at least one deaf parent who used sign language whilst the late signers had parents who could hear and who were not proficient in sign language. The findings of the study showed that deaf children who had been introduced to sign language from birth had theory of mind skills comparable to the hearing children, whilst those children who were late signers had a much poorer score on the false belief tasks.

CUTTING EDGE

Development of theory of mind in children

A paper by researchers at the Radboud University of Nijmegen, the Netherlands, has found evidence that a person's ability in theory of mind tasks at age 5 years appears to predict their ability later on in life. The authors followed 77 children aged 5 years old for three years and found that their theory of mind relating to understanding false beliefs and emotions continued to develop over the three years. The children were given a series of theory of mind-related tasks to complete as well as measures assessing language development. Ketelaars et al. (2010) found that increased ability in the false-belief tasks was correlated with the child's ability to understand complex emotions and that both these theory of mind-related abilities developed alongside the child's linguistic capabilities, thus supporting the theory that language and theory of mind are closely connected in child development. This important study is one of few longitudinal designs that attempts to plot theory of mind development in children and it will be interesting to follow this study to see if there is support for the lifespan theory of development of theory of mind proposed by Pardini and Nichelli (2009).

STOP AND THINK

Why do children classed as native signers show better performance on false-belief tasks than children who are late signers?

In further research connecting language development to theory of mind, Peskin and Ardino (2003) report that children start keeping secrets at about the age of 4 years and those children able to keep secrets perform better at the false-belief tasks. At this age, too, children begin to show the ability to detect another person's perspective. Astington (1994) proposed that 4-year-olds can understand that their interpretation of a picture and someone else's interpretation of a picture can be two very different things. In a study of child delinquency, researchers found that children of 4 years of age begin to lie and not tell the truth, which is another expression of the ability to understand that a person's behaviour is related to their interpretation of events (Stouthamer-Loeber, 1986). All of these cognitive developments relate very much to the child's ability to use language. Thus all the measures of the false-belief task are reliant on the child's linguistic skills, and a child with poorly developing language may not be able to vocalise their thoughts and beliefs.

Clements and Perner (1994) set out to investigate just this: whether theory of mind was present in young children unable to express their beliefs verbally. Their argument was that theory of mind might still be present in the younger children, but present as an *implicit* (not-conscious) concept rather than as an *explicit* (conscious) concept. As the child learns syntax and semantics in language, so these researchers argue that the child is able to understand another person's beliefs and behaviour. Without the ability to construct meaning from language, the child is unable to make sense of the behaviours of others. Yet, what if the child was able to understand behaviour before she developed the ability to understand language? Clements and Perner set up a study to test whether theory of mind is implicitly present in children and whether this is reflected in their vocal responses. The children were shown a scenario where a doll placed a

Definitions

Implicit: implicit knowledge comes from an understanding of what is meant or suggested even when it has not been directly stated.
Explicit: explicit knowledge is that which has been stated clearly and in detail and where there is no room for misunderstanding, confusion or doubt.

toy in a box on the left-hand side, the doll left the room and, whilst it was absent, the toy was moved to a box on the right-hand side. The children were then asked where the doll would look for the toy and their answers were recorded. When the doll returned, the child's visual gaze was measured. When the researchers asked the children, 'Where will the doll look?', they recorded whether the children looked at the box on the left or looked at the box on the right. The researchers proposed that where a child looked during this task indicated where the child implicitly believed the doll would look. Where the child said the doll would look indicated where the child explicitly believed the doll would look. The results of their study show that children under the age of 2 years and 11 months looked at neither the box on the left nor the box on the right. However, children of approximately 3 years and 7 months looked to the box on the left (the correct answer in the false-belief task), yet only 23% of them spoke the correct answer. The researchers suggested, therefore, that these younger children knew where the doll would look (showing an implicit understanding of the task) but were unable to represent the doll's behaviour explicitly.

This study by Clements and Perner suggests that these younger children were able to understand the demands of the task and that the incorrect answers given in previous studies actually reflect the immature language abilities of the child rather than an inability to complete the task. By modifying the task to include measurements of eye-gaze, Clements and Perner introduce a refinement to the experiment that detects more sensitively the child's abilities. Since this study was published, many other researchers have attempted to refine the design of their studies to improve the sensitivity of their experiment. In particular, a key paper published by Onishi and Baillargeon in 2005 has shed light on the ability of infants to understand false beliefs from the age of 15 months. Onishi and Baillargeon used a simple yet sophisticated design involving a cream box, a black box and a plastic slice of watermelon. The infants were sat in front of a small stage, and the two boxes were placed side by side with their openings (covered with a fine fringe) facing each other. The slice of watermelon was placed between the two boxes and behind these objects were doors that were opened and closed during the experiment (see Figure 8.2).

First, the infants were shown two scenes that familiarised them with the nature of the event. First, the infants saw the stage set with the two boxes and piece of watermelon. An actor opened the doors behind the boxes, played with the toy watermelon and then placed it in the black box on the right. The scene ends with the actor keeping her hand in the black box and a curtain falls in

Figure 8.2 The familiarisation trials.
Source: Onishi and Baillargeon (2005)

front of the stage. The second scene opens to show the cream box and the black box, the actor opens the doors behind the boxes and reaches inside the black box (as if to take the watermelon out). The scene ends with her hand in the black box and a curtain again falls in front of the stage. These trials help the infant become accustomed to the objects and scenarios being played out in front of them.

Next, the researchers created a number of conditions to test whether the infants could detect false belief in the actor (see Figure 8.3). The first two conditions create true beliefs in the actor. In condition A the doors open and the actor looks at the boxes and watches the yellow box move towards the green box and return to its original position. The actor in this condition has the true belief that the watermelon is in the green box. In condition B the doors open and the actor looks at the boxes and watches the watermelon move from the green box to the yellow box. The actor in this condition has the true belief that the watermelon is now in the yellow box. The third and fourth conditions create false beliefs in the actor. In condition C the doors remain closed and the actor does not see the watermelon move from the green box to the yellow box. The actor now has the false belief that the watermelon is in the green box when it is in fact in the yellow box. In condition D the doors open and the actor watches the watermelon move from the green box to the yellow box. The doors close and the watermelon returns to the green box. The actor now has the false belief that the watermelon is in the yellow box when in fact it has returned to the green box. After each of these conditions the curtain falls, signalling an end to the scenario. The curtain rises and the infants see the actor open the doors behind the boxes and reach for the toy.

Onishi and Baillargeon argue that if an infant expects the actor to reach for the watermelon on the basis of her belief about its location, rather than where the infant knows the watermelon to be, then the infant should look for measurably longer when the actor looks elsewhere and confounds the infant's expectations. So, for instance, in condition D the actor believes the watermelon is in the yellow box, but the infant knows the watermelon has returned to the green box. When the actor returns to search for the watermelon, if the infant understands the actor's perspective, she will expect the actor to look in the yellow box. If the actor looks in the yellow box, he has confirmed the infant's expectations and the infant's gaze will be relatively short. If the actor looks in the green box, then he surprises the infant and she will spend longer gazing at the green box. What the researchers found was that the infant's behaviour confirmed their hypotheses, and they argue that these 15-month-old infants were displaying representational theory of mind.

Critics of this research, however, have pointed out that these and other authors have over-stated the contribution of their work in discovering young infants' understanding of false beliefs. Perner and Ruffman (2005), for instance, believe that the infant's long attention to the task reflects not an ability to attribute beliefs to the actor, but that the infant simply notices that something unusual is happening (see the discussion on the development of infant vision in Chapter 4, 'Prenatal development and infancy', pages 91–5). However, Buttelmann et al. (2009) propose that a solution to the limitations of Onishi and Baillargeon and others' studies is to adopt a testing situation whereby the child is an active part of what is going on.

Buttelmann et al. recognise that, from the age of about 12 months, most children begin to help other people with tasks and problems (Warneken and Tomasello, 2006). Therefore, Buttelmann et al. argue, if the child goes to help another child or adult who is trying to complete a task, then that child must be able to understand what the focus of that task is and therefore be able to make a judgement on what the other person intends to happen. This, the authors say, suggests that these children are demonstrating theory of mind rather than simply noticing something unusual going on. In order to test their ideas, Buttelmann et al. set children aged both 16 months and 18 months a false-belief task that involved helping behaviour. Each child watched whilst an adult placed a ball in a basket and left the room. An experimenter then moved the ball from the basket into a box. When the adult returned to the room, he went to the basket to retrieve his ball. When he could not find it, the adult set about looking for the ball. As they expected, most of the children behaved in accordance with the nature of the false-belief task and helped the adult find the ball in the box. There was a developmental aspect to the successful completion of the task: the 18-month-old children were much more likely to successfully interpret the actor's perspective on the task, but a substantial number of the 16-month-old children managed the task too. Thus, by introducing a behavioural aspect to the false-belief task, any bias based on language abilities is eliminated and arguments suggesting that the

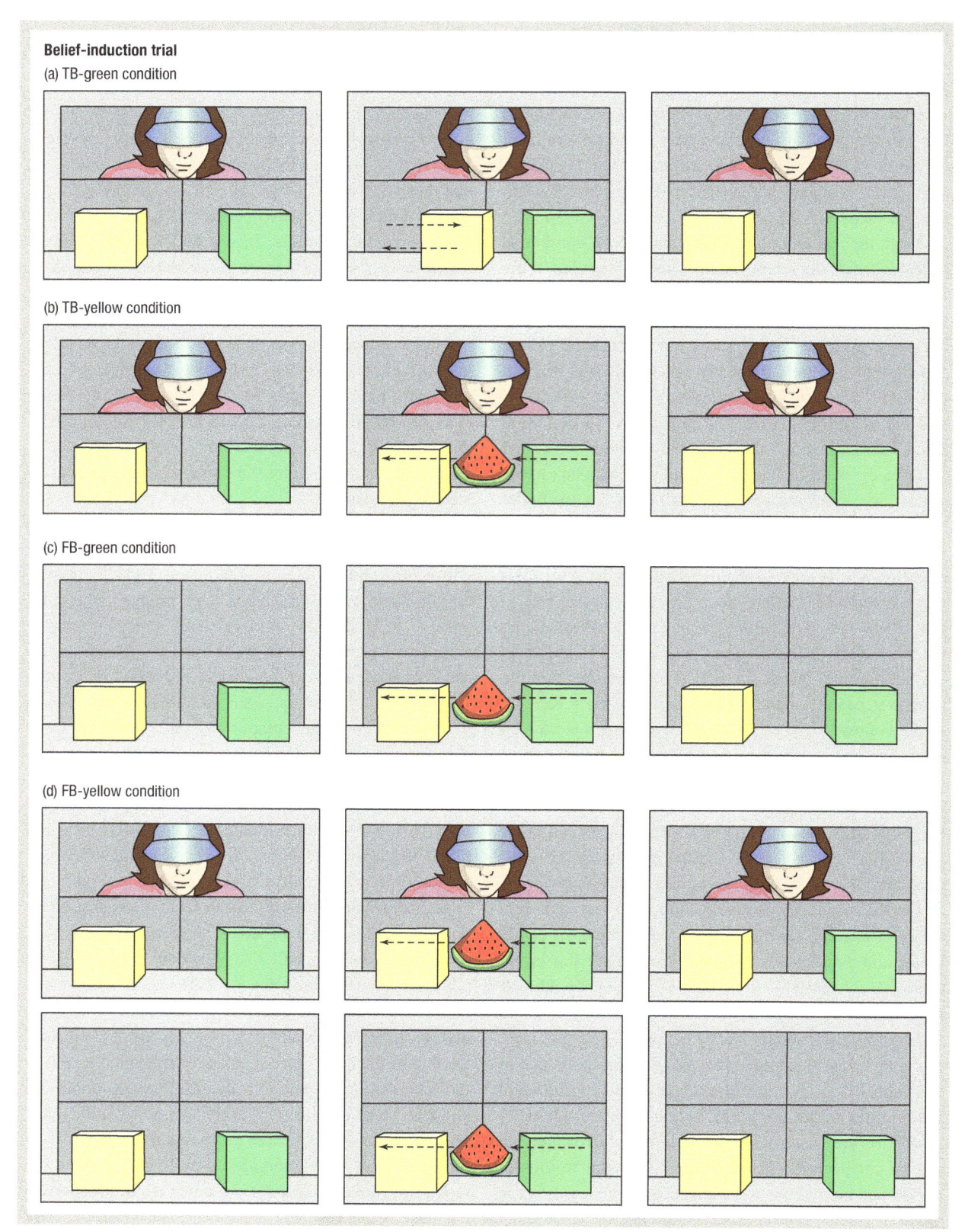

Figure 8.3 The four conditions in the false-belief task.

Source: Onishi and Baillargeon (2005)

RESEARCH METHODS

Theory of mind: research path

The papers discussed in this section are each proposing varied methods for identifying whether or not young children have theory of mind and can understand the nature of false beliefs. Following the papers in a chronological fashion, we can see that each set of authors has reflected on the limitations of the previous paper and then sought to address these either through slight changes to wording and/or the situation described or with more significant changes to the design and process of each experiment. If we take the Maxi and the chocolate task described by Wimmer and Perner (1983), we can see that the results of the paper led the authors to believe that theory of mind was not present in 3-year-old children. However, criticisms of the paper suggested that the story of where the chocolate *is* and where Maxie might *believe* the chocolate is was considered by many as too complex for young children to understand. Furthermore, criticisms of the task were also directed at the length of the story, with critics suggesting that the story was too long for 3-year-olds to understand. So in response to these criticisms, Baron-Cohen et al. (1985) proposed a shorter, simpler story (the Sally-Anne task). However, even with this change to method they were unable to detect significant evidence of theory of mind in the under-3s.

Reviewing these papers and considering the cognitive development of the child, Siegal and Beattie (1991) noted that by simply changing the question asked of the children from 'Where will Sally look for her marble?' to 'Where will Sally look *first* for her marble?' accurate performance on this false-belief task improved from around 35% to over 70% in 3-year-olds. Thus, considering the developmental stage of a child when devising an experimental technique can be crucial when you are devising the questions you might ask of her. The researchers did not stop there, however, and continued to refine and revise their methodologies in an attempt to develop a measure sensitive enough to detect the development of theory of mind in children too young to have the language ability to express their beliefs. With each paper that was published, there was evidence that the researchers were reflecting on each other's successes and failures, and each new paper pushed the boundary of our knowledge further. Thus, by reviewing previous research evidence, revising theory in the light of new evidence and devising new hypotheses, these developmental psychologists have designed new experiments to test those hypotheses. The process described here should help you to understand how developmental psychologists are continually reflecting and revising their methods in an attempt to refine their understanding of human development.

gaze-following studies simply measure the child's interest in something happening in front of them can be rejected. We can conclude, then, that a child's ability to understand and interpret others' behaviour in the context of beliefs, desires, intentions and goals can be measured using false-belief tasks and, to date, appears to be present from a very early age.

STOP AND THINK

What might be the implications for the older adult whose ability to gauge emotional states is weakening?

Theories explaining theory of mind

There are two dominant theories behind research into theory of mind: the 'theory-theory' (often abbreviated to TT in texts) and the 'simulation theory' (often abbreviated to ST in texts).

'Theory-theory' or representational account of theory of mind

The theory-theory or representational account of theory of mind suggests that a child cannot have a full

LIFESPAN

Theory of mind through adulthood

The focus so far in this chapter has been on looking at how early in life a child begins to show evidence of theory of mind, but as we get older, does our ability to infer a person's beliefs, desires and motivations change? A study conducted by Pardini and Nichelli published in 2009 used a version of the 'Reading the Mind in the Eyes Test' (Baron-Cohen et al., 2001). In this test, participants see only the eye region of the face of a person who is enacting an emotional state. The participant then has to choose from four words which emotion is being represented. The three 'incorrect' words relate to emotions that, when expressed, might have similar facial characteristics but mean the direct opposite of the target emotional state. The advantage of this method is that it does not rely on participants' working memory abilities yet is sophisticated enough to pick up on more subtle messages than the false-belief tasks directed at young children.

Pardini and Nichelli put this test to 120 people equally split into four age groups – 20–25 years old, 45–55 years old, 55–65 years old and 70–75 years old. All participants in the groups were matched for gender and education level and reported good vision. The results showed that the mean number of correct recognitions of the emotional states were 26.79, 25.3, 23.5 and 21.6, respectively, indicating that the ability to recognise emotional state declined with advancing age (ANOVA test revealed the significance of these findings: $f(3,116) = 24.5$, $p < 0.001$). The authors conducted further analysis and propose that the significant point at which a person's ability to deduce another's emotional state weakens is around the age of 55 years. Therefore, this study illustrates that, as we get older, so our ability to infer a person's state of mind becomes less accurate. Further research is needed to understand why this happens, but at present the literature suggests that although there is age-related decline on a number of cognitive skills that could be explained by subtle changes in the frontal lobes of the brain (McPherson et al., 2002), theory of mind appears to decline irrespective of these other age-related changes (Bernstein et al., 2011).

---

understanding of the nature of false beliefs until he can make a cognitive decision using meta-representation. Earlier in the chapter we defined meta-representation as (1) the ability to separate reality from fantasy – for instance, during pretend play (Leslie, 1987); and (2) additionally, knowing the difference between what might be represented in a photograph or painting of an object and what the reality of that object might be (Perner, 1991). Leslie points out that children start to engage in pretend play at around the age of 18 months – at a time when the child is learning the true words for objects (for a full discussion, see the section on cognitive development and semantic development in Chapter 5, 'Language development', pages 132–3). At a time when the child is also learning to categorise items (e.g. fruit, animals, people, furniture), pretend play should theoretically be very confusing for the child. If she is still learning that the word for a curved yellow fruit is 'banana', then to play with it and pretend it is a 'telephone' should be beyond the young child's cognitive grasp. Yet children enjoy this type of pretend play and it does not appear to have any effect on their ability to learn that the yellow fruit is called 'banana' or that the real telephone is not a yellow fruit.

The reason Leslie offers to explain this apparent discrepancy is that young children develop two types of representation during pretend play: the first, the primary representation, is 'banana' for the curved yellow fruit and the second, the secondary representation, is 'pretend-telephone' for the game of playing on the telephone. These secondary representations are what Leslie calls meta-representations and demonstrate the child's ability to fantasise in her own game. Leslie also noted that meta-representations are not solely present in the child's own fantasy game, but that the same child will successfully

This boy is having fun using a meta-representation of the box, which is now a bus.

Source: Getty Images/Blend Images LLC

'Simulation theory' of theory of mind

The simulation theory or simulation account of theory of mind proposes that we are biologically designed to understand beliefs, desires and motivations in the minds of others and that we initially do so by using our own mind as a model or template for understanding the minds of others (Apperly, 2008). By thinking that the mind of another person is similar to your own mind, you can then make predictions of that person's behaviour based on how you think you would behave under the circumstances. Thus, researchers who follow the simulation theory of theory of mind suggest that we do not need to learn other people's mental states and make judgements about them as is proposed in the theory-theory but, instead, use what Meltzoff called a 'like me' comparison (Meltzoff, 1995). Simulation theorists suggest that we are born with the ability to make the self–other comparison and indeed there is some biological evidence that supports this. Present in the brain are neurons called mirroring neurons that appear to be activated either by performing an intentional action or by observing an intentional action. Simulation theory argues that these mirroring neurons are what enables this 'like-me' appraisal to take place. For example, we see a behaviour take place, the mirroring neurons process the action and we experience empathy or resonance (Schulkin, 2000).

join another child's fantasy game, thus demonstrating that the child is aware of the meta-representation of the banana in the second child's pretend play of, say, 'cops and robbers', 'cars' or any other game that might be being played at that moment. This, Leslie argues, is evidence that the child is able to mind read and is therefore developing a theory of mind.

Perner (1991), however, disagrees with Leslie's representational account and argues that the child is not showing a meta-representation of the banana as a telephone, but is in fact simply acting out talking on the telephone using the banana as a prop. If children were truly capable of using meta-representation, Perner argues, then they would not routinely fail the basic false-belief tasks such as the Sally-Anne task or the Maxi and the chocolate task. However, since Perner's paper was published in 1991, much research has been carried out that shows that the reason children were failing these tasks was not because of a deficit in meta-representation skills but because of the way the tasks were presented to the children. Taking the examples of research presented earlier in this chapter, the Onishi and Baillargeon paper in 2005 demonstrated that children as young as 16–18 months showed differences in their gaze patterns that correlated with the nature of the false-belief task, and the paper by Surian and Leslie in 1999 found that rewording the question helped the children understand what was being asked of them and their performance on the false-belief tasks improved dramatically. Thus there appears to be evidence of some ability to form meta-representations in young, pre-verbal children, as evidenced in their pretend play and some ability to complete a false-belief task.

Both theories are well argued in the literature and many researchers believe that both theories have something to contribute to our understanding of theory of mind. Failure to understand another person's perspective and failure to predict another person's behaviour can both be explained by either theory-theory or simulation theory accounts. Theory-theory would explain these failures as not being able to fully understand the other person's beliefs and making a false meta-representation of those beliefs will lead to making a false prediction of that person's behaviour. Simulation theory would explain these failures as making a 'like-me' mistake and expecting the other person to behave 'like-me' when the person is not 'like-me' at all (Nichols and Stich, 2003). Research methods have so far failed to demonstrate the dominance of either theory-theory or simulation theory in understanding theory of mind, so it seems likely that a hybrid approach to theory-theory and simulation theory might be more influential in the future.

Debates about the origin of theory of mind

Is there an over-reliance on false-belief tasks to explain theory of mind?

As we have seen, Siegal and Beattie (1991) argue that children, rather than not having theory of mind, instead misunderstand the questions and therefore the nature of the task. This argument was supported by Freeman et al. (1991) who found that young children were unable to articulate the false belief held by the actor in a false-belief task. These arguments point to communications skills and theory of mind being tightly interconnected and lead us to the conclusion that theory of mind does not or cannot develop until the child reaches a certain level of cognitive maturity. However, Perner's counter-argument proposes that theory of mind may be present in the child before the child is able to complete these tasks and, therefore, that false-belief tasks are not suitable for picking up theory of mind in the very young. Perner noted that children engage in pretend play and use deception or lies at an early age; the key defining principle of theory of mind is that a person can understand another person's *belief* and this, he states, does not fully occur until the age of 4 years. Therefore, Perner argues, we can see evidence of theory of mind in young children unable to put into words the false belief held by the actor in the false-belief tasks.

Gopnik et al. (1994) also present the argument that pretend play, deception and lying in young children indicate a pre-theory of mind. The authors propose a four-stage model of development of theory of mind whereby, first, children aged 30 months and under have a basic level of understanding of other people's motivations based on their

NATURE–NURTURE

Is theory of mind innate?

In a paper titled 'Origins of individual differences in theory of mind: From nature to nurture?' Hughes et al. (2006) investigated the contribution of genetic and environmental influences on individual differences in development of theory of mind in the first large-scale population-based study of twins born in England and Wales in 1994 and 1995. As part of a larger study called the Environmental Risk (E-Risk) Longitudinal Twin Study, 1104 five-year-old monozygotic (MZ) or dizygotic (DZ) same-sex twins were selected for home visits, one-third of whom were born to young mothers (aged under 20 years at child's birth) and two-thirds of whom were born to mothers aged 20–48 years. The children were given four false-belief tasks to complete similar to the Smarties and pencils study, the Sally-Anne task and the Maxi and the chocolate task.

Of the twins 56% were monozygotic (sharing the same genetic make-up) and 44% were dizygotic (sharing only half the same genetic make-up): 49% of the twin pairs were male. The results of the study show that the verbal abilities of each twin per pair showed no significant difference, but there was a small but significant difference on the theory of mind tasks with girls performing slightly better than boys.

Statistical analysis of the effects of genetics and environment on the twin pairs' performance on theory of mind tasks showed that there was no significant difference in performance based on whether you were an MZ twin or a DZ twin. Further analysis revealed that only about 7% of the variation in children's ability to complete the false-beliefs tasks could be accounted for by whether you shared your full genetic make-up or only half your genetic make-up with your twin. When family socio-economic status was taken into account, the authors found that they could account for 48% of the children's performance on false-belief tasks. A child's verbal ability was significantly related to socio-economic status (SES) (a greater vocabulary was seen in children from families with higher SES) and accounted for about 50% of the impact of SES on performance on false-beliefs tasks. The authors conclude that the individual differences shown in each child's development of theory of mind can in the main be accounted for not by genetic factors but by environmental factors. This study found that approximately 48% of performance in the false-belief tasks was accounted for by family SES, but the authors acknowledge that there still remains 45% of variance accounted for by other environmental factors.

own needs (hence the child engaging in pretend play – but for his own satisfaction rather than based out of an understanding of the beliefs and motives of others). Gopnik et al. describe how by 30 months the child is able to understand that another person might see things differently and might have different desires from him. Nevertheless, it is not until the age of 3 years that the child starts to make formal connections between the other person's perspective and desires, and starts to form a more complex understanding of other people's motivations. When the child is 4 years old, however, the authors state that the child is able to make the association between other people's perspective and, in the case of the false-belief tasks, their misrepresentation of events, and to predict what behaviour might ensue. Thus, Gopnik's study reveals that, although the younger children may display evidence of a basic understanding of other people's motivations (and therefore aspects of a burgeoning theory of mind), the dramatic shift in performance accuracy on the false-belief tasks at age 4 years reflects the child's state of change in cognitive development, and a concurrent dramatic improvement in the complexity of understanding theory of mind. Therefore, although criticisms are levelled at researchers who use false-belief tasks to ascertain a child's theory of mind capability, Gopnik's work demonstrates that a limited theory of mind might be detectable in the very young child through their use of pretend play, lying and deception.

Theory of mind and children with autism

Autism spectrum disorder (ASD) occurs in 1% of the population, are strongly heritable, and result from atypical neurodevelopment. Classic autism and Asperger syndrome (AS) share difficulties in social functioning, communication and coping with change, alongside unusually narrow interests. IQ is average or above in AS with average or even precocious age of language onset. Many areas within the 'social brain' are atypical in ASD. ASD has a profile of impaired empathy alongside strong 'systemising'. Hence, ASD involves disability (when empathy is required) and talent (when strong systemising would be advantageous). Psychological interventions that target empathy by harnessing systemising may help. (Baron-Cohen, 2008)

People with autism spectrum disorder (abbreviated to 'autism' from hereon in) have difficulty in understanding the mind of others – that is, other people's perception of events, their beliefs and their motivations (for a full discussion of this condition, see the section on autism spectrum disorders in Chapter 16, 'Atypical development', pages 499–505). People with autism also find it difficult to see the context of events and are said to have poor central coherence (Happé, 1994). For example, a person with central coherence will be able to put together images such as balloons on the front door with the birthday cake on the table and the presents next to it into the context of a home hosting a birthday party. A person with autism may find this difficult and not make the connection between the balloons, the cake and the presents to form a representation of a birthday party. However, what the person with autism does have in this and other situations is the ability to note the detail of each of those items and they may be able to tell precisely the location of the balloons, how many, what is written on each, what colour they are, what colour the thread is tying them to the front door and how many knots are tied on each thread! The other key cognitive characteristic of people with autism relates to executive function: that is, control of actions. People with autism often show difficulties with their executive function: for example, in displaying repetitive behaviours or in focusing attentively on one thing to the detriment of everything else happening around them. For example, you may see a person with autism compulsively arranging their books by order of size or repeatedly drawing an action figure. The person with autism may sway from side to side or hop continuously for an excessive period of time or when they are talking to you. For more information on autism spectrum disorders, see Recommended reading.

Beliefs and mental states

There is a great deal of evidence relating autism to deficits in cognitive skills, including theory of mind, in the literature. First, children with autism fail to make the

> **Definition**
>
> Central coherence: the ability to put together information in context to form a whole picture (Frith, 1989).

distinction between what is mental (held in the mind) and what is physical. For example, a study conducted by Wellman and Estes (1986) found that typically developing children can distinguish the two quite easily at the age of 3 to 4 years. Wellman and Estes told children a story of two characters, one thinking about a dog (a mental experience) and one holding a dog (a physical experience). The authors then asked the children, 'Which character can stroke the dog?' The typically developing children aged 3 to 4 years could make this judgement quite easily, but when this study was replicated with children with autism, it was found that they frequently made mistakes in this task, despite having a mental age equivalent to the children in the other study (Baron-Cohen, 1989). Wellman and Estes also found that typically developing children knew what the brain was 'for'. The children could describe its mental functions, such as thinking, dreaming and wanting, but would also describe its physical function of making you move and so on. Yet when the children with autism were asked this question they knew about the physical activity-related functions of the brain but would say nothing of its mental functions (Baron-Cohen, 1989). Other studies have shown that children with autism find it difficult to distinguish between appearance of an object and the reality of an object. For instance, a child with autism presented with a pen in the shape of a dinosaur will decide either that it is a pen or that it is a dinosaur but, unlike the typically developing child, does not seem to appreciate the nature of the 'dinosaur pen' as a concept.

The child with autism also finds the false-belief tasks difficult. In their paper investigating whether children with autism have a theory of mind, Baron-Cohen et al. (1985) gave the Sally-Anne task to children with autism and compared their performance with that of typically developing children and children with Down's syndrome. Their results showed that 23 out of 27 typically developing 4-year-olds and 12 out of the 14 children with Down's syndrome passed the false-belief tasks. Compare that with only 4 of the 20 children with autism passing the belief question on this task. All of the 16 children who failed the task pointed deliberately at where Anne knew the marble *was* rather than where Sally would *believe* the marble was on returning to the room. The authors suggest that the children's performance on the false-belief task demonstrated an

Lining up your toys is a common behaviour seen in children with autism.
Source: Bartlett

inability to represent mental states. They argue that children with autism are therefore unable to deduce the beliefs of others and thus predict the behaviour of other people.

Why these children with autism cannot represent mental states might stem from their apparent inability to make the connection that a person knows what she knows because of what she sees. This concept of 'seeing leads to knowing' is present in typically developing 3-year-olds but is infrequently seen in children with autism. A paper published by Leslie and Frith (1988) showed this with a story of two characters, one who looked in a box and the other who merely touched the box. The children were then asked, 'Which character knows what's in the box?' The typically developing children knew that it was the character who had looked in the box. The children with autism performed at chance levels of accuracy on this task and showed no preference for the character who had looked inside the box. Thus there appeared to be no indication that the children with autism understood that knowledge comes from seeing, a precursor skill to being able to understand the concept behind the Sally-Anne task: that a person may believe a situation to be true but be proven wrong when that situation is changed without them seeing it happen.

> **STOP AND THINK**
>
> How might you explain why a child with autism finds it difficult to make friends?

Deception

Deception is essentially a skill that you need in order to change somebody else's mind. In order to be able to deceive someone, you need to understand that 'seeing leads to knowing' and that what a person knows can be proven wrong when the situation is manipulated without their knowledge (as demonstrated in the false-belief tasks). Deception also carries an element of motivation. Why else would you seek to deceive someone if you did not believe that by doing so you would benefit from the act? If, for example, there is no material or emotional gain following the deception or avoidance of punishment or emotional disappointment, what reason is there to deliberately create a false belief?

Deception appears in typically developing children around 4 years of age, and although not sophisticated, the child's attempts to cover up his actions by pointing to his infant sister or denying eating all the sweets when he is surrounded by the wrappers do illustrate the complexity of his developing theory of mind. However, the child with autism appears to find deception a difficult concept to pull off effectively. A paper by Baron-Cohen in 1992 described a 'penny hiding game' where the child is asked to hide a penny in one hand and not tell the experimenter which hand it is in when asked. The typically developing 4-year-old child is fairly proficient at this game, yet the child with autism finds this game very difficult, often revealing the position of the penny before the experimenter asks its location.

> **Definition**
>
> Deception: trying to make someone else believe that something is true when in fact it is false (Baron-Cohen, 2001).

CASE STUDY

Gary McKinnon – autism and the position of personal responsibility

In March 2002, Gary McKinnon was arrested by British police for breaking into American military computer systems. In a BBC interview in 2005 he said: 'I found out that the US military use Windows and having realised this, I assumed it would probably be an easy hack if they hadn't secured it properly.' In a later interview, he claimed that he was convinced that American government intelligence agencies had access to 'crashed extra-terrestrial technology which could . . . save us in the form of a free, clean pollution-free energy'. However, the American authorities did not accept his claim and pursued his extradition for trial on the basis of hacking into computers 'with the intention of intimidating the US government', claiming that many government files were accessed, altered and even deleted by Gary McKinnon.

In August 2008, Gary McKinnon was diagnosed with Asperger's syndrome, a form of the autism spectrum disorder. People with Asperger's syndrome share many of the same features of autism but show normal or above average IQ and show regular development in language skills (Autism Research Centre). As with autism, Asperger's syndrome has as one of its characteristics difficulties in social interaction, and people with Asperger's syndrome find it difficult to establish the consequences of their actions. Thus since his diagnosis, lawyers and other professionals have been working to prevent Gary McKinnon's extradition order to be tried in the USA, arguing that he was not fully cognisant of the implications of breaking into the computer system and was not therefore wilfully engaged in breaking the law. Specialists have also advised that a person with Asperger's syndrome would be unlikely to do well in a prison environment. In 2012, the Home Secretary decided not to extradite Gary McKinnon to the USA and, following that decision, the Crown Prosecution Service advised the Metropolitan Police not to commence a new investigation into his activities. The Assistant Commissioner of the Metropolitan Police accepted that advice.

- What do you think the decision should be in these circumstances?
- Should Gary McKinnon have been extradited to the USA to answer charges?

SUMMARY

This chapter has introduced you to the psychological concept of theory of mind. Theory of mind is very much a cognitive skill that appears to follow a developmental pathway, starting in very early infancy and progressing through to late adulthood. Research shows that using false-belief tasks can help us to understand the developmental nature of theory of mind and that skills learned in early childhood continue with us into our adult lives. Although the ability to understand a person's mental states, such as their beliefs, desires, intentions and emotions, is substantially a cognitive one, the implications for a person's social development are considerable. Without being able to make sense of someone's behaviour, their motivations and decision making, we perform poorly in social situations and may make mistakes in predicting what an outcome could be.

Researchers working with children with autism have found considerable differences in performance between these children and typically developing children. Children with autism find it difficult to understand the perspective of others and routinely fail the false-belief tasks. The large amount of evidence collected by researchers using false-belief tasks has revealed the complexity of cognitive deficit underlying autism spectrum disorder and has provided key information that underlies support and intervention programmes for these children. However, how a person learns theory of mind is still debated, and the implications for understanding the difficulties children with autism face have become apparent. The theory-theory or representational account of theory of mind requires the child to have the cognitive ability to use meta-representations; to separate reality from fantasy. This is something that the child with autism and poor theory of mind is commonly unable to do, and theory-theory seemingly accounts for this. However, simulation theory can also account for the difficulties a child with autism experiences on the false-belief tasks. Simulation theory requires the child to be able to perform a 'like-me' comparison in order to predict behaviour, and perhaps the child with autism can carry out the 'like-me' comparison but finds no-one behaves 'like-me' and is therefore unable to make appropriate judgements of that person's beliefs and desires. These and other debates continue in theory of mind research. To find out more, follow up the Recommended Reading.

REVIEW QUESTIONS

1. What are the key features of theory of mind?
2. How does theory-theory account for theory of mind and how does it differ from simulation theory?
3. Why is the false-belief task used to test for the presence or otherwise of theory of mind in the young child?
4. Why does the ability to recognise emotional states weaken as we get older? What are the implications of this for the older adult?
5. How can the use of false-belief tasks help us to understand the difficulties children with autism have in social interaction?

RECOMMENDED READING

For further information on the theory-theory versus simulation theory debate:

Schulkin, J. (2000). Theory of mind and mirroring neurons. *Trends in Cognitive Sciences*, 4 (7), 252–254.

Goldman, A., & Gallese, V. (2000). Reply to Schulkin. *Trends in Cognitive Sciences*, 4 (7), 255.

Short, T. (2015). *Simulation Theory: A Psychological and Philosophical Consideration* (Explorations in Cognitive Psychology). New York: Psychology Press.

For further information on autism and theory of mind:

Baron-Cohen, S. (2001). Theory of mind and autism: A review. *Special Issue of the International Review of Mental Retardation*, 23 (169).

Baron-Cohen, S. (2008). *Autism and Asperger Syndrome: The Facts*. Oxford: Oxford University Press.

Baron-Cohen, S., Tager-Flusberg, H., & Lombardo, M. V. (2013). *Understanding Other Minds: Perspectives from Developmental Social Neuroscience*. Oxford: Oxford University Press.

RECOMMENDED WEBSITES

The false-belief task in action:

http://www.open.edu/openlearn/body-mind/psychology/understanding-what-others-think

This page has lots of information on the Environmental Risk (E-Risk) Longitudinal Twin Study:

http://www.scopic.ac.uk/StudiesERisk.html

Section III
Social and emotional development

Chapter 9
Attachment and early social experiences

Learning outcomes

After reading this chapter, and with further recommended reading, you should be able to:

1. Evaluate the importance of a parent or consistent primary caregiver to a child's early development characterised by the concept of attachment.
2. Describe attachment theory in terms of its key features which underpin the emotional ties between the child and her primary caregiver.
3. Describe and evaluate the key procedure and assessment tools that have been used to measure attachment behaviours and relationships.
4. Apply all of the above in discussing the possible impact of changes in child-rearing practices, including paternal care and day care, on development.
5. Describe research documenting the implications of attachment relationships for later childhood and adulthood.

Description of two toddlers

Daisy, 13 months old

Daisy and her mummy have entered the room . . . Mummy settles Daisy down on the floor in front of her . . . Daisy looks cautious and, although clearly curious about the objects in front of her, she barely touches them until Mummy enthusiastically encourages her to play . . . Daisy frequently turns round to look at Mummy, to which she responds with a smile and encourages Daisy to continue to play. She gets up to reach Mummy once for a 'cuddle' . . . When the female stranger comes in the room, Daisy stares at her and then clings on to Mummy as she sits down next to Mummy . . . When Mummy gets up and goes to the door, Daisy toddles over to follow her and then gives out a loud cry as Mummy leaves, closing the door behind her . . . Daisy continues to wail and whimper as the stranger tries to comfort her and engage her to play . . . Mummy returns and promptly picks up Daisy and holds her in her arms . . . she eventually quietens down and Mummy is once again encouraging her to play . . .

Chloe, 18 months old

Chloe and her mummy have just entered the room. Chloe spots the toys straight away and goes to play before Mummy settles herself down on the chair . . . She touches each and every object before she starts playing with the trumpet with apparent interest, and Mummy quietly watches. Though facing Mummy, Chloe does not appear to make any eye contact with her during play . . . The stranger arrives; Chloe says 'Ah' and smiles at her as she goes to sit by Mummy, and Chloe 'gives' her one of the other toys . . . When Mummy gets up to leave the room, Chloe watches her throughout, but does not get up to follow or make any sound, before she starts playing again, this time ignoring the stranger . . . When the door opens again and Mummy comes in, Chloe looks at her for a few seconds before settling back to play again . . .

- What are the major differences between the behaviour of Daisy and Chloe?
- Are there any differences between the behaviour of their mothers too?
- What do you think are the reasons for such differences?
- Do you believe that their behaviour in sessions like these reflects some things about the relationship the girls have with their mothers?

Introduction

The opening examples describe two mother–infant dyads in an established procedure used to assess the nature of their 'bond' (see 'Measuring attachment', pages 257–63), involving a series of interactions, separations and reunions. It seems that there are some differences between them in things such as eagerness for closeness and reaction during separation and return. Many reasons could go to explain such differences, which might be reflective of the mother-and-child relationship.

This chapter will overview and evaluate the first relationship or bond we experience in our lives: that is, the relationship between a child and her earliest primary caregiver, typically the mother. While the importance of this early relationship to children's development is hardly ever doubted, over the years the substantial amount of work in this area has still not totally addressed many questions, from the exact origins of this supposedly one-to-one relationship to its longer-term implications. Must it be our mothers that we bond with? How do we know we have bonded strongly 'enough' with a caregiver? What about children in out-of-home care or those who are cared for by several people? Even as adults, the closeness of our relationships with our parents varies a great deal, much as that of the relationships we have with other people. Some question whether the latter goes back a long way to our childhood, concerning the quantity or quality of time that we spent with our caregivers. If so, are some of us doomed in our current and future relationships if we have missed out on a 'good start' in the form of a warm, loving relationship with our mothers? Clearly, this topic has theoretical, personal and practical significance; it may make some of us reminisce our own childhood and upbringing, and those of us who are parents may reflect on our parenting skills or re-evaluate the quality of the places or people providing day care for our children. Not giving any 'right' answers to these questions, this chapter will nevertheless explore some possibilities by looking at the work of influential figures from the past to more recent research that dissects and evaluates this highly significant relationship in our early childhood.

What is attachment?

> **STOP AND THINK**
>
> ### Reflection
>
> Try to jog your memory to as far back as you can remember in your childhood.
>
> - Who was the person you spent the most time with at home?
> - Who was the person who knew you best, whom you felt most 'safe and secure' with?
> - Was it the same person for both questions?

With increasing competence in their physical, perceptual and cognitive faculties (see Section II of this book for such development during infancy), by the latter half of the first year of life most infants can recognise the familiar people they encounter and interact with the most. It is almost invariably the case that these are the people who also know the infant better than other people in that they understand her needs and behaviours well, since they respond to these needs regularly, usually in the role of parents.

As described in the introduction, attachment is often referred to as an affectionate bond or emotional tie, which is often strong and enduring, that we have with significant people in our lives. Attachment, in developmental psychology, is typically understood as the first bond of this kind that a child has with her primary caregiver, typically the mother, since it is usually (though not always) the case that at least for some of the neonatal period post-birth the mother goes on to look after her own baby. Although numerous psychologists have explored the nature of this important relationship for over half a century, many still look to the starting points of the idea of attachment as articulated by the forefather

> **Definition**
>
> **Attachment:** a strong, enduring, affectionate bond that an infant shares with a significant individual, usually the mother, who knows and responds well to the infant's needs.

WHAT IS ATTACHMENT?

The strong affectionate bond between mother and child is often plain to see.
Source: Pearson Education Ltd/Lisa Payne Photography

of what is regarded as one of the landmark theories in developmental psychology. That is the attachment theory of John Bowlby. Below we will take a close look at Bowlby's influential theory.

Bowlby's early attachment theory

As a practising British child psychiatrist in the 1950s, John Bowlby (1907–90) drew his original ideas from various disciplines, most notably the psychoanalytic school of thought (see Chapter 2, 'Theoretical perspectives', for premises of psychoanalysis), but also evolution and ethology (see later in this chapter), as well as his own observations and clinical research with those he regarded as having inadequate attachment (see 'Maternal deprivation hypothesis', pages 251–2).

According to Bowlby (1958), our tendency to form and develop strong, enduring, affectionate bonds with certain individuals is an evolved biological 'given', in that it has critical survival and adaptation values. Because the attachment figure tends to be, or is to start with at least, the mother or someone responsible for the feeding and day-to-day care of the baby, this relationship acts to source and maintain nurturance as well as protection and security from this figure. This bond hence caters not only for the physiological needs of a child (like food), but also for the psychological needs such as comfort or the sense of a 'safe base', for the child. The latter is required as the human young (as well as the young of many other animals) also have an opposing (to attachment) tendency to explore the world around for her learning needs, taking her momentarily away from the safe base. A return to this available base is paramount when, during her exploration, the child feels threatened or distressed by an object, event, setting or experience (such as meeting a new person or animal, entering a new place or feeling illness or discomfort). To this end, this relationship will reflect certain recognisable characteristics that function to establish and maintain closeness between the mother and her child. We will first explore these characteristics one by one before structuring the key ones within the development of attachment.

Monotropism. The first step towards any attachment is the ability for the infant to discriminate between her parents and other individuals. There is evidence that babies recognise their mothers' voice by birth, and by sight and smell at just a few days old (see Chapter 4, 'Prenatal development and infancy'). Further to this, Bowlby argued that eventually most infants will become more attached to the mother or primary caregiver, and prolonged separation from or unavailability of her would have enduring serious and deleterious consequences for the child (see 'Maternal deprivation hypothesis' below, pages 251–2).

Proximity seeking. Bowlby first conceptualised early attachment as a goal-driven system that has the goal of maintaining optimum proximity with the primary caregiver, on the part of the child. The child should display a concomitant set of behaviours that draw the attention of the caregiver, who will then get close to him. The exact starting point and behaviours will depend on the age and cognitive and physical development of the child, which include recognition of the caregiver, distinguishing her from other people, representations of objects (including mother) in her absence (Piaget, 1954; see Chapter 4), and the ability to vocalise and mobilise oneself. A new baby

Definitions

Monotropism: the idea that any child only forms a strong attachment to one person.

Proximity seeking: a set of typical behaviours displayed by children to draw the attention of the primary caregiver towards themselves or reach her when separated, with the goal of restoring proximity.

Once mobile, an infant can take more active steps to restore proximity to mother.
Source: O'Donnell

Smiling to draw attention and seek proximity
Source: Lam

not long after birth may only be able to cry for attention or at most make eye contact as he feels discomfort, but later he will be able to smile or even reach out or cling to mother, and later still he can call out or follow her as a toddler. In any case, this mechanism is such that separation from the caregiver should activate this behavioural system to restore proximity.

Separation protest. His work with infants led Bowlby to notice not only the sorts of behaviour that they displayed when they were with their caregivers but, even more importantly, those behaviours that they displayed during the departure of, or separation from, the caregiver. By the time an infant has started to use his mother as a secure base from which to explore, in the second half of the first year he also starts to show some recognisable signs of 'protest' as he gets parted from her. Even a stay-at-home mother has moments where she needs to attend to other business (such as answering the phone or door, tending the cooking in the kitchen or checking on another child). On many occasions the infant will cry and may reach out in an attempt to prevent her departure as a form of protest, and may continue such behaviour in her absence.

Stranger anxiety. At around the same stage that the child shows clear regular signs of anxiety upon separation from mother, after being able to differentiate her from other people, behaviours that pertain to wariness or fear (anxiety) of unfamiliar people (strangers) also emerge. The child may wince, but will often want to cling on or stay close to mother, as if to obtain her protection from these unfamiliar human objects.

> **STOP AND THINK**
>
> **Attachment behaviours in real-life settings**
>
> Imagine yourself at a party in a friend's house. The friend has also invited many other guests, some of whom have brought along their children. You have been playing with a sociable little boy of about 18 months to 2 years for a short while in the conservatory, among other children. His mother returns with a few other women – you don't know her or the others – but you can tell immediately with some certainty that she is the mother, just from the expression and behaviour that the woman and child display.
>
> - What kind of 'expression' and 'behaviour' would you expect of the child?
> - What kind of 'expression' and 'behaviour' would you expect of the mother?

> **Definitions**
>
> Separation protest: a set of typical behaviours displayed by the infant to register a form of protest against their caregiver's departure.
> Stranger anxiety: the wariness or fear of the infant when encountering those who are unfamiliar, often characterised by the seeking of proximity to the caregiver.

Critical period. Attachment as characterised by the above features is seen to have time 'boundaries' for its formation. Based on his work with older children who had gone without this goal-driven relationship earlier on, Bowlby specified the period in which attachment ought to be strived for and achieved as being between 6 months and 3 years of age. If good parenting is not attempted until after age 2½ years, it was argued that it is immensely difficult for an attachment to be formed (see also the following sections).

Judging from the features and criteria of the above characteristics, you may find some of them reasonable or predictable while others seem slightly inflexible or unrealistic. While we will evaluate Bowlby's principles later, it should be noted that his original theory was refined several times (Bowlby, 1953, 1969, 1973, 1980). On establishing his initial theory, more work was conducted to chart the age-related stages at which the features of attachment emerge, as attachment 'phases'. These are described below.

The attachment phases

Because, as we noted above, certain attachment behaviours have prerequisites in the form of physical (mobility) and cognitive (object recognition and representation) development, Bowlby proposed that attachment develops in stages (see Table 9.1 for ages and key characteristics).

Due to the lack of differentiation between familiar and unfamiliar faces in the earliest two months, the baby is said to be in a phase with little or no recognition of mother. Even at the next phase, those prerequisites for attachment are merely getting formed as the infant begins to recognise his mother or primary caregiver, but the lack of object representation (including that of mother as a human social object) at this age (Piaget, 1954) means that separation protest is not yet evident, even if he is comforted more easily by this familiar figure.

Definition

Critical period: the time period that was thought to be critical for the formation and development of any attachment relationship, hypothesised to be six months to three years, beyond which it is seen as highly difficult for such a bond to be formed.

Table 9.1 Bowlby's attachment phases by approximate ages.

Phase	Approx. age	Key characteristics of child
Pre-attachment	0–2 months	Shows little differentiation in responses to mother and other people, familiar or unfamiliar
Early attachment	2–7 months	Begins to recognise mother, gradually more likely to be comforted by her
Separation protest	7–9 months to 2 years	Seeks to maintain proximity with mother, wary of strangers and protests when separated
Goal-corrected	2–3 years & upwards	Has more abstract representations of attachment, (trust, affection, approval), begins to understand mother's needs, with increased independence

Protesting behaviours during separation, clearer signs of proximity seeking as well as stranger anxiety will emerge from the second half of the first year in the third phase, and such behaviours will be more apparent as the child enters into the second year of his life. However, as the child grows further still, with even greater physical mobility and thus exploration, and cognitive skills such as developing language and more complex thoughts, attachment transcends into a more abstract idea or representation. This final so-called 'goal-corrected' phase signifies the more confident independent toddler, who can now better understand his mother's needs and motives apart from her availability (that she can be absent, but will return and respond). This milestone of an 'internal' representation will be explored more thoroughly later in terms of its implications for future relationships (see 'Internal working model', pages 270–1). For now, it is important to bear in mind that there is not a one-to-one mapping of behaviour to phase. Infants vary in the frequency or intensity of their attachment behaviour even though the *goal* of proximity seeking and maintenance is the same.

Maternal deprivation hypothesis

Apart from the features of 'normal' attachment, the other essential part of Bowlby's theorisation had stemmed from his work as a child psychiatrist with those who suffered the consequences of severe parental neglect or long-term separation from parental figures. Such prolonged bouts of disruption in the attachment to a mother figure are collectively known as *maternal deprivation* and can be a result of such things as illness of either the mother or the child, abandonment by or bereavement of mother during the critical period, or even becoming orphaned. The notion that deprivation of a key caregiving figure could lead to a whole host of profound negative outcomes, as widely documented at the time by Bowlby (1953), has come to be known as the maternal deprivation hypothesis.

Bowlby drew on both his clinical work and research by others with institutionalised children. For instance, well before his theory came into being, Bowlby's retrospective study (see Chapter 2) in the 1940s documented in some detail how delinquent adolescents recounted their early experiences. He wrote that many such young males shared a history of lack of consistent parenting figures; some were in serial foster care, others in impersonal institutions for most of their childhoods, and others still were periodically in transit between foster care and institutions throughout childhood. Their common outcomes and early experiences led Bowlby (1944) to his early conclusions about the ill effects that a lack of attachment relationships can bring.

At around the same time, the American psychiatrist, William Goldfarb (1947) followed up 30 children who had been given up by their mothers before 9 months of age. Whilst half of them went to foster homes, the other half were first placed at an institution until they were fostered at about 3½ years, then remained in foster care. Goldfarb carried out a batch of tests on these children between the ages of 10 and 14, including intelligence, reading and arithmetic, and also took observations and notes on the children and their caregivers and teachers. He found that those who had spent their first few years in institutions performed worse than those in continual foster care, and were reported as being more fearful and restless, while being less popular with their peers and needier with adults. Since Goldfarb evaluated the quality of foster care that the two groups had received to be comparable, like Bowlby, he attributed the formerly institutionalised children's delayed or maladaptive development to institutionalisation. From this, Bowlby (1951) further concluded that, even if an infant has undergone deprivation in the first half-year of his life, he can still be salvaged with prompt and proper care, but delayed attempts to form attachment beyond the age of 2½ years are likely to be futile.

Such reports of profound deleterious effects and stunted development led to early formulations of the maternal deprivation hypothesis. When Bowlby (1953) was invited by the World Health Organization to comment on the issues of homeless children, he asserted that the vital ingredient for healthy development for any child is a continuous, warm and intimate relationship with her mother (or a suitable mothering figure). After further years of work, he went on to articulate that there is no other childhood variable more influential on the child's later personality than her experience of a loving parental figure within her family, on which her expectations about future relationships will be based (Bowlby, 1973).

Bowlby's work with young children who had to be separated from their family due to hospitalisation was given much support by the husband-and-wife team of social workers, James and Joyce Robertson, who made a vivid series of films in 1989 illustrating children's responses beyond separation protest. The children were shown to go through a stage of being inconsolable before eventually becoming indifferent and unresponsive towards the parents upon reunion. Support for Bowlby's work did not stop here. As the next section shows, features of attachment behaviours and maternal deprivation also seem to hold for many non-human beings.

Definition

Maternal deprivation hypothesis: the notion that later serious deleterious outcomes will result from the lack of a consistent attachment figure in early childhood.

STOP AND THINK

Going further

- What are the problems with drawing the conclusion that a lack of early attachment leads to later negative outcomes from the kind of research Bowlby and others did?
- Despite these problems, why do you think his theory was so popular?

Animal research

Much of the information about the attachment relationship from non-humans is founded on a relatively modern branch of zoology called ethology. With close links to evolution, ethology is the study of natural animal behaviour primarily concerned with survival and adaptation, through a combination of outside fieldwork and laboratory settings. One of the most influential figures to inform us about attachment was Konrad Lorenz (1903–89), winner of the Nobel Prize in Physiology and Medicine in 1973.

A keen researcher of animal behaviour, Lorenz carefully observed and replicated the invariable process of imprinting, first in the new-borns of several species of birds. He found that, on hatching from the eggs, the babies will follow the first thing that they see, usually the mother, for the next few days. Lorenz discovered that if it was a human that they saw, in this case himself, they would follow him in that early period. The young offspring in this case were said to have been 'imprinted' on their surrogate human parent. In fact, the first 'thing' on which the neonate will imprint herself does not even have to be a living creature; animals can imprint on an inanimate object like a ball, a box or even a light (Ridley, 1995). Whatever the imprinted target, the infant will recognise it by its sight, sound, smell, movement, or some other distinctive features that characterise it.

The other key aspect of imprinting that Lorenz discovered was its irreversibility. That is, once an animal has imprinted itself on a certain target, it remains attached to him/her/it, and will not 're-imprint' on another. Lorenz also found this to be the case with other species that require a relatively extensive period of parental care, including mammals such as sheep. The animal would recognise the first person that handfed it and re-join that person when he/she appeared even after the animal had been weaned.

Drawing from the predictable pattern of imprinting behaviour across different species, Lorenz concluded that imprinting is an adaptive process as it enables the new offspring soon to recognise and attach themselves to, under normal circumstances, the 'right' individual: that is, the mother who will provide for and protect their young from a hostile world, which is critical for their survival.

Bowlby could draw support for his theory from the above research on several counts in terms of the observed behaviours themselves, as well as the principles that Lorenz deduced from them. The imprinting behaviours, pertaining to proximity seeking, are similar to those of human infants with the purpose of getting and staying close to the primary caregiver, who is normally the mother or the first person with whom the infant spends his early days for survival needs. The irreversibility of imprinting further offered Bowlby the impetus to propose the critical period applicable to humans as introduced by Lorenz (1966) for animals. Although, of course, the exact timeframe will differ across species, the notion that there is a limited window of opportunity in which bonding can be forged through continuous care from the same caregiver (monotropic), or beyond which any delayed attempt will probably fail, is similar between humans and their animal counterparts. In addition, comparable evidence of the deleterious impact of the failure to bond in this period on the infant's social and emotional development is available from further animal research in another setting, as described below.

STOP AND THINK

Going further

- How convinced are you by the apparent parallels between imprinting behaviours in animals and attachment behaviours in humans?
- Can you think of any species that does not go through the imprinting process?

Another notable set of research that supported Bowlby's premises came from Harry Harlow, who conducted experiments on rhesus monkeys in a controlled laboratory setting in the 1950s. Harlow (1958) separated otherwise healthy monkeys from their mothers at birth and placed them in isolated cages. At first, Harlow noticed that, like Lorenz's imprinted animals, if the monkeys obtained regular attention from a human surrogate mother who provided not only food but also warmth

---

Definition

Imprinting: a process in which the new-borns of most species will recognise and seek proximity with the first object that they encounter (usually the primary caregiver) following the activation of a trigger during a critical period after birth.

and comfort, they had a better chance of survival even when compared with monkeys that were cared for by their biological mothers in captivity.

Later on, some well-known experiments (Harlow and Zimmerman, 1959) involving other objects as the surrogate mother yielded findings that were even more revealing about the nature of the attachment relationship. In isolated cages, infant monkeys were given a mesh wire surrogate mother that held a milk bottle, and a terry cloth one that did not provide food. What Harlow discovered was that, although the monkeys used the wire model as the source of food, they used the softer cloth model as a source of comfort, like a 'mothering' figure. They would go to it and hold on tightly when they were frightened, and its presence in a new room appeared to reduce their anxiety, as if they were using this cloth surrogate as a 'secure' base from which to explore the unfamiliar environment. Essentially, feeding times aside, whenever the cloth model was available, the infants showed a preference for it as they regularly clung on to it. In fact, the monkeys actually made increasing use of this softer figure as they grew bigger. While these behaviours are strongly reminiscent of human behaviours during the mid-attachment phases, the findings also give evidence that attachment, whether in humans or non-humans, is about much more than just the bare essentials of nourishment. As Bowlby argued, it offers a safe base from which the infant explores the world and to which she can return when distressed or threatened.

Although the monkeys appeared to be able to make reasonably good progress with a cloth 'mother' as a source of comfort, once they grew into adolescence and ventured outside the confines of the cage, it was clear that the lack of any 'real' attachment figure had caused untold psychological damage to the youngsters (Harlow and Harlow, 1969). They typically appeared withdrawn, and when put in the company of same-age peers who had not been separated from mothers, they became fearful and might even attack the others. If the separated monkeys were not reunited with their birth mothers by the age of 3 months, such ill effects appeared to be irreversible, as if they had missed that critical window of opportunity for bonding. Furthermore, as adolescents, few of these monkeys were able to mate successfully, and even if they did, the females were very unlikely to provide adequate care for their own offspring, as if they were perpetuating a cycle of absent parenting.

The profound and enduring harmful consequences of animals reared apart from their mothers offer powerful support for Bowlby's maternal deprivation hypothesis. Similar to the delinquent boys whom Bowlby interviewed, or the older youth whom Goldfarb tested for delayed development, Harlow's monkeys displayed what would be expected as the 'animal-equivalent' of serious damage. Still, how far can we extrapolate from such findings with animals to humans like ourselves? Is a lack of, or inadequate, attachment totally irredeemable? With the benefit of later studies and more critical

NATURE–NURTURE

Is attachment innate?

The fact that not just humans, but various animals also display behaviours that reflect the mother–child bond functional for the survival and development of the child has led many to believe that the attachment relationship reflects an innate tendency – as Bowlby put it, a biologically driven predisposition based on our evolved needs to bond with the one who takes care of us. This is supported by neuroimaging research that demonstrates parallels between animal and human maternal caregiving responses in the brain (see the comparative review by Strathearn, 2011). Specifically, two neuroendocrine systems controlling oxytocin and dopamine are identified as the key contributors. The hormone oxytocin is important in the formation of social and spatial memories, affiliative behaviour and emotion regulation, and in several mammalian species facilitates physical proximity and nurturance between mother and infant (such as nest building, pup grooming and licking in rats). Dopamine is a neurotransmitter associated with motivated behaviour, and maternal behaviour is severely impaired in mice given a dopamine 'blocker'. Importantly, the strength of the connections between these systems is associated with levels of maternal caregiving. Infant cues such as suckling, vocalisation and tactile stimulation go to trigger oxytocin release in the brain, which leads to the activation of a dopaminergic reward pathway underpinning behavioural reinforcement and long-term conditioned preference to such cues by the mother.

A decade of fMRI studies has enabled us to see brain responses to such infant cues: mothers with secure attachment (versus those without; see 'Measuring attachment', pages 257–263) show greater activation of the dopaminergic pathways on seeing happy or crying faces of their infant. Furthermore, less securely attached mothers show lower oxytocin production when interacting with their infant, which is correlated with activation in the dopaminergic regions and may account for the reduced activation of reward processing in the brain on seeing their infant's face (Strathearn et al., 2009). Such findings shed light not only on the biological 'workings' of maternal behaviours, which will support the intergenerational transmission of attachment (see 'Attachment beyond infancy', pages 270–5), but also on how different functioning of the key systems may lead to variations in attachment. This helps to explain the neurological underpinnings of the flipside of attachment – maternal neglect – and how potentially to prevent it (by pharmacological intervention, as suggested by Strathearn, 2011).

One must note, however, that just because there are seemingly clearly defined brain pathways that underpin maternal caregiving responses, it does not prove that attachment between mother and child is a given and thus innate. Indeed, the neuroendocrine systems involved are also influenced by environmental factors, including stress during pregnancy, early caregiving experience and relationships through life (reviewed by Strathearn, 2011). For instance, it was found from rodent models that stress during pregnancy may reduce the binding of the oestrogen-receptor in key brain areas, with associated increases in maternal anxiety and decreased licking and grooming behaviour postnatally, which may then result in a similar decrease in such oxytocinergic binding in the offspring.

If attachment is innate, we should also expect it to be universal. Yet how universal are attachment behaviours? Much cross-cultural research has shown that most infants show a tendency to form close relationships with a consistent set of people, if not one person; but there are exceptions as well as differences in *how* parents relate to infants (Flanagan, 1999; see 'Attachment and childcare', pages 263–70). Recent data (Jin et al., 2012) suggest that even though the secure base function applies in both Western and 'Eastern' cultures, there are variations in the ways that infants and mothers achieve this. Western infants are generally the ones to seek proximity owing to their mothers' encouragement for them to explore independently, but Japanese and Korean mothers encourage their infants to stay close and are more likely to approach them (see also the Research Methods box on page 259). However, most infants in all cultures are able to explore and play once proximity is achieved. Even animal attachment behaviours are subject to a combination of conditions in the contact setting (e.g. the length of continuous exposure to the attachment figure and the figure's distinctiveness; Cairns and Cairns, 2008). Strathearn (2011) similarly questions whether human parallels to 'licking and grooming' or rodent models of maternal 'separation' and 'deprivation' exist where comparative studies are concerned. Therefore, even if we say that the tendency *per se* to bond with our caregiver is innate, not every characteristic of attachment, particularly by how we have defined it so far, will apply to every living being.

analysis, we will next evaluate the premises of Bowlby's original theory before we move on to cover the more recent areas of interest in attachment.

Critique of Bowlby's theory

Bowlby's theory gained a lot of momentum in the first few decades that followed its inception, in that it influenced not only the academic perspective on children's early social experiences, but also public perception of childhood and child rearing, and social policy on associated issues such as childcare provision and parenting education. However, although studies available at the time, including those we have just indicated, support Bowlby's arguments, later extensive empirical work and the social trends that followed meant that the relatively deterministic principles of his original theory were viewed in a less favourable light and some were revised by Bowlby himself.

Firstly, the maternal deprivation hypothesis received a great deal of criticism with newer waves of findings and more caution interpreting earlier findings. In the case of animals, Suomi and Harlow (1972) discovered that the appalling effects of isolation on monkeys were reversible under certain conditions. An 'intervention' which introduced the company of normal (not isolated) younger monkeys, who would 'cuddle' the older deprived peers, was reported soon to have a comforting effect. After a few weeks, the deprived monkeys started exploring their environment and playing with others, and six months on their behaviours were comparable to that of normal same-age peers. Later research echoes this as it was found that environmental enrichment later in life may compensate for (if not reverse) stress-related effects of maternal separation in rodent offspring (Francis et al., 2002). Evidence challenging the inflexibility of attachment timing led ethologists as well as Bowlby to replace the concept of 'critical period' by the more appropriate sensitive period when affectionate bonds are more readily forged than at other times in life.

In humans, early evidence, such as that of Goldfarb's study, on the effects of early separation has also been called into question. One cannot be sure that the children's negative outcomes were due to separation from the mother *per se*, instead of some of the other negative factors linked to institutionalisation, such as the quality of the institutions themselves. Indeed, places like orphanages at the time were often renounced for their unstimulating environment and high turnover of staff, who were discouraged from forming relationships with the infants (see also Chapter 16, which considers the effects of the environment on atypical development).

Since Goldfarb's work, more research with children who had been institutionalised has been published, most notably several studies by Barbara Tizard, the renowned British educationalist. Tizard followed up children who had been taken into institutional care by or within the sensitive period and who were later fostered, adopted or returned to the birth mothers. In most such cases, the children's cognitive and linguistic development was on a par with non-institutionalised children from 4½ years to late adolescence (Tizard and Rees, 1975; Tizard and Hodges, 1978) and many had settled well into family life, with affectionate relationships resembling attachment ties (Tizard, 1977; Hodges and Tizard, 1989). However, the children had in common certain social or emotional issues; some were reportedly unpopular with peers, or antisocial and aggressive, and some were seen by adults as attention seeking and over-friendly with strangers.

It should be noted that, although the conditions of the institutions were a marked improvement on those of the orphanages in Goldfarb's study, there was a large amount of shared care that saw a constant change of staff per child. On the other hand, a few studies in the 1990s of children in severely overcrowded, squalid Romanian orphanages (e.g. Chisholm et al., 1995; Chisholm, 1998) showed that, despite such conditions and their late adoption (up to 5½ years old), the children were still able to form affectionate bonds with their families, even if the strength of such bonds was less than it might have been if formed earlier. Recent research of late-adoptees, such as those placed transnationally at 3–5 years (Barone and Lionetti, 2011) and at 4–7 years after multiple difficulties or prolonged institutionalisation (Pace et al., 2012), has also produced promising findings. Within the first year of placement, the majority of children reported a secure relationship, with a significant change in the attachment behavioural patterns since their arrival, even if the adverse history persisted at a representational level in a minority (one-third in Pace et al., 2012). An important aspect was the secure state of mind in the adoptive parents as a protective factor towards resolving past traumatic experiences and emotional adjustment. Since screening for adoption has tightened from decades ago, identifying and training adoptees on key aspects of parenting and family life will help adoptees adjust and develop after their trauma.

Apart from challenging the idea of a critical period in favour of a more flexible sensitive period and raising doubts about the maternal deprivation hypothesis, such evidence also questions basic premises such as monotropism and stranger anxiety. The fact that, after deprived conditions or inconsistent care provision, human and non-human young can still go on to have functional family lives or relationships indicates that it may not be as damaging as previously thought for infants not to bond with just one person. In fact, reviews as early as the 1960s

Definition

Sensitive period: revised from critical period, the timeframe that is most conducive to forming strong attachment compared to other times in the child's life.

In a Romanian orphanage of the 1980s.
Source: Rex Features/Steve Back/Daily Mail

and 1970s had already revealed that, by 18 months, less than one-fifth of children had just one primary caregiver and that in one-third of cases the strongest tie was with someone other than the mother (Schaffer and Emerson, 1964; Gallimore and Weisner, 1977). In addition, far from being wary of new people, between 1 and 2 years old infants are perfectly able to form new relationships with others. Bowlby (1973) himself came to emphasise that, as long as ongoing and reliable care is given, attachment relationships are not limited to the birth mother, and that a variety of figures, in particular the father, complement the mothering figure well (see 'How important is father?', pages 267–8). These insights are significant in view of the social and economic shifts in the last few decades, at least in Western societies, that saw many mothers return to employment after childbirth.

> **STOP AND THINK**
>
> **Reflection**
>
> - Before and around school ages, were you only looked after by your mother?
> - If not, who else took care of you when your mother was not there?
> - How close did you feel towards that person/those people who also looked after you?

The popularity of Bowlby's original theory has to be put into its historical context, in the 1940s and 1950s, during and immediately after the Second World War. Events at the time had invariably disrupted the prior way of life in a great number of families, propelling women into the workforce to fill the gap left by men who went to war. Until then, a typical family was made up of the mother as the key, if not sole, caregiver and the man as the sole breadwinner. As the war ended, many longed for a return to the 'traditional' nuclear family, coinciding with the need for work by returning men. These social and economic pressures might have, if by accident rather than by design, added more public appeal to a theory that could be taken as promoting the mother's role back in the home whilst allowing more jobs for the male population.

Finally, as devastating as the effects of maternal deprivation may be, as we have read, since Bowlby's era, with the decline in institutionalisation and a rise in the number of working mothers and day childcare provision, research has 'moved on' from focusing on the effects of maternal deprivation. Nevertheless, Bowlby's essential ideas on the attachment experience and its functional significance are still highly regarded to this day. As the following sections of the chapter explain, rather than looking at the effect of *whether* an attachment relationship has been formed, psychologists in the past few decades have studied how strong or 'secure' a child's attachments are and the implications of the security and nature of these relationships.

Measuring attachment

The essence of Bowlby's theory concerns infants' experience of using the primary caregiver(s) as a safe base or a source of security. This is well established and easily understood by many, academics and laypeople alike. Nevertheless, we can imagine that children's experiences of this supposed early and intimate bond with their caring figures may differ somewhat, depending on the characteristics of that figure, or the child, or perhaps the dynamics of their relationship. One concept that has received a great deal of attention is the degree and pattern of 'security' in this relationship, with researchers also endeavouring to study systematically the individual (and group) differences in this relationship.

Security of attachment

The influential concept that different children may obtain different senses of security from the attachment relationship owes itself to the work of Mary Ainsworth, who had been a student of Bowlby in the 1950s.

She was particularly interested in attachment behaviours in 'action', and how they translate later into a set of internalised 'goal-corrected' representations, which Bowlby proposed, that can purportedly influence future relationships and outcomes. Ainsworth went to observe attachment behaviours among the Ganda people in Uganda in 1954, and then compared them to American samples from Baltimore (Ainsworth, 1963, 1967). She noticed certain differences in the intensity of separation protest and stranger anxiety (stronger in Uganda), but both groups showed the typical behaviours through the attachment phases, despite communal childcare among the Ganda. On the other hand, she also noticed considerable variations *within* each sample in terms of the infants' frequency and intensity of such behaviours. This prompted her to look closely at the nature of the attachment relationship, by studying how readily the infant is able to use the caregiver as a secure base, or attachment security, which should be reflected by their observed behaviour. Influenced by Bowlby's theory and drawing on her own observations, this readiness was considered to be most apparent during the critical events of separation from, and reunion with, the caregiver. It is from this starting point that Ainsworth devised the now very widely used standard experimental procedure, and its associated scheme of classification, for gauging and charting children's attachment security.

The Strange Situation

Ainsworth's procedure, known as the Strange Situation experiment, is based on a series of timed episodes that take place in an unfamiliar, but comfortable, controlled laboratory setting, while being observed unobtrusively by a researcher (or set of researchers) (see the Research Methods box on page 259). The seven episodes involved the mother (or primary caregiver) and child being together with and without the addition of a stranger, the departure of the mother in the presence and absence of the stranger, and the return of the mother in the presence of the stranger. This procedure was designed for infants in the second year of their life as it was thought that the moderate stresses inherent in such a 'strange' situation would activate the relatively obvious attachment behaviours in that phase (particularly the reunions after the mother's departures), reflecting the security of the infant's attachment to his or her primary caregiver. By gauging and charting the frequency and intensity of such critical behaviours, Ainsworth and her colleagues (Ainsworth and Bell, 1974; Ainsworth et al., 1978) highlighted the ways in which individual children differed in their attachment security with their caregivers, giving rise to the 'types' of attachment relationship they might have formed with this person.

Types of attachment

By the Strange Situation, Ainsworth identified a few patterns in which infants display signs of their differing ability and willingness to use their mother or primary caregiver as a safe base to derive a sense of security. Such patterns reveal what are commonly referred to as attachment types. The types, and their labels and behavioural descriptions, are found in Table 9.2. Ideally, if an infant has a secure attachment to the caregiver as a safe base, the procedure will see him initially stopping his exploration to draw himself closer to the mother or primary caregiver upon the stranger's entry (stranger anxiety). In particular, the departure of his mother should at least cease his exploration promptly and may trigger him to cry and to seek her (separation protest). However, her subsequent return should bring enough comfort to him to halt his distress and to restore his exploration. It can also be expected that the second separation and reunion will bring these behaviours to a greater intensity. Indeed, this general set of behaviours has been observed in roughly two-thirds of children from samples in most Western countries (e.g. van Ijzendoorn and Kroonenberg, 1988) who are seen as 'securely attached' infants (Type B).

Definitions

Attachment security: the readiness of an infant to use the primary caregiver to derive a sense of security that can be reflected in her pattern of attachment behaviours.

Strange Situation: a seven-part staged procedure employed to observe the behaviours and interactions between a child and the primary caregiver in a controlled laboratory setting, from which the type of attachment security between the dyad can be deduced.

Attachment types: patterns of behaviour observed in the Strange Situation denoting differing security of attachment to the primary caregiver as a safe base from which to explore.

RESEARCH METHODS

The Strange Situation experiment

The classic Strange Situation procedure consists of seven staged episodes, each with a set time limit of three minutes. The child is observed in interaction with either or both his mother and a stranger, as well as in solitary. The physical location is that of a room behind a one-way mirror (for the researcher to observe the participants unobtrusively) containing chairs and a rug or carpet laid with toys and objects for the child to explore.

The procedure is as follows:

1. Mother and child enter and settle in the room (three minutes).
2. Stranger enters the room and interacts with mother (three minutes).
3. Mother leaves the room – child alone with stranger (three minutes, or less if child shows excessive stress).
4. Mother re-enters the room. Stranger leaves – mother and child alone in room (three minutes).
5. Mother leaves the room – child alone in room (three minutes, or shorter if child shows excessive stress).
6. Stranger enters room (three minutes, or shorter if child shows excessive stress).
7. Mother re-enters room (stranger leaves) and remains (three minutes).

In summary, a series of entries, departures and reunions and one solitary moment are featured. Of the most interest to researchers are the child's behaviours at reunions (stages 4 and 7). It is mainly based on these behaviours that the categorisation into the attachment 'types' denoting differing attachment security is evaluated.

- **What are the main advantages of this procedure?**
- **What are the potential problems of this procedure?**

The physical setting of the Strange Situation experiment.
Source: Grahame Hill, 2001. http://books.google.co.uk/books?id=-rYkNmp4EPcC

On the other hand, a substantial minority of children do display lower readiness to use their mother or primary caregiver as a safe base and are labelled as one of the 'insecure' types depending on the behaviours observed. Type A, 'insecure-avoidant' infants, appear indifferent to the caregiver's departure (and there may even be signs of a lack of distinction between the caregiver and stranger beforehand) and will ignore or even avoid contact with the caregiver upon her return. Type C, 'insecure-resistant' (or 'insecure-ambivalent') infants, are the opposite to Type A in that they seem extremely distressed by the caregiver's departure, so that not only will they resist the stranger's effort to comfort them, but also they will be 'ambivalent' in their approach to the caregiver on her

Table 9.2 The four attachment types and key behaviours of the child towards mother during the Strange Situation experiment.

Type	Name	Key behaviours in Strange Situation
A	Insecure-avoidant	Lack/avoidance of contact with mother, treating her and stranger in a similar way; not upset by her departure and ignoring her or even turning away upon her return
B	Securely attached	Moderate amount of proximity seeking to mother, upset by her departures followed by positive greetings during reunions
C	Insecure-resistant/ambivalent	Great distress at mother's departure, resisting comfort by stranger, but difficulty in being comforted upon reunion with a mixture of proximity seeking, resistance or anger
D	Insecure-disorganised	Lack of a consistent behavioural pattern; apprehension about approaching mother; confusion about separation and reunion

return, seeking contact while rejecting her in anger. In this vein, Type A and Type C are considered to reflect the child's respective lesser willingness and ability to use the mother or primary caregiver as a source of security, and each accounts for between 10 and 20% of Western samples (van Ijzendoorn and Kroonenberg, 1988).

Later on, researchers who are interested in atypical development (Main and Solomon, 1990; see also Chapter 16, 'Atypical development') identified an additional 'insecure' type called 'insecure-disorganised', where the infant appears to have no consistent pattern of behaviours or responses in the Strange Situation procedure. These children are generally apprehensive about approaching the caregiver; they may seek some proximity and then back away, as if to avoid her with fear, among other odd, incoherent behaviours. Overall, they seem to be totally 'out of their depth' in the situation and uncertain about how to make use of the caregiver. It is said that these infants' behaviours are due to some experience of having been frightened by the caregiver or having seen the caregiver being frightened. This form of attachment (or lack of) is of obvious interest to clinicians due to its pathological nature and how it may predict future psychopathology, and some studies have attempted to trace its behavioural transmission from the caregiver before it manifests itself as 'faulty' attachment (see the Cutting Edge box). Indeed, this pattern of disorganisation is much more prevalent in infants from families with parental dysfunction or pathology such as bereavement, separation and divorce (Main and Hesse, 1990), or depression, maltreatment, neglect or abuse (Lyons-Ruth et al., 1991, 1999; for details, see 'The mother', pages 263–7).

It would appear that the relatively simple procedure of the Strange Situation allows us to distinguish different types of attachment security, by observing the behaviour of infants with their caregivers, and to even identify possible family discord or pathology. Still, how far can we really rely on this procedure and its classification system?

Critique of the Strange Situation

Before launching into criticisms, it is worth first pointing out the significant practical value of the Strange Situation research procedure. Entering new spaces, encountering new people and being temporarily separated from the key caregiver(s) are events that many children in the first years of life and most cultures go through, if some more than others. So, the procedure is not too far removed from children's experiences at the stage of development, even though it is confined to the artificiality of a laboratory. With its utility and uncomplicated set-up, both the procedure and its associated classification have been almost universally adopted to measure variations in attachment.

It is also important to identify that the attachment type a child has with a caregiver signifies more the property of the *relationship* between the child and that caregiver, than solely the general propensity of the child to bond. Thus, it is highly plausible that a child could exhibit different attachment behaviours with different people according to the kind and quality of relationship she has with each of them. As we will explore in the next section, children do seem to interact and relate rather differently to mother, father and other family and non-family caregivers, and vice versa. Differences in interaction and communication will invariably lead to differences in relationships, and this is the case not only

CUTTING EDGE

Origins of disorganised attachment? A 'microanalysis' of mother–infant interaction

Since infant attachment status assessed around age 1 by Strange Situation can already predict later development, some researchers gear their focus on how specifics within the mother–baby interactions in the earlier months may discriminate future attachment types. The large literature has tended to describe mothers of secure (versus insecure) infants as more responsive, consistent or prompt in response to infant distress, and more tactile, but less intrusive, tense and irritable (on maternal sensitivity, see 'Attachment and childcare', pages 263–70). However, similar measures have not predicted disorganised infant attachment as reliably, probably due to the diversity of parental profiles and lack of detailed behavioural coding.

Recently some researchers have turned to so-called 'microanalysis' on mother–baby interaction to gauge anomalous maternal response which is directly implicated in the development of disorganised attachment. This involves the analysis of a time-series (moment-to-moment) sequence of behaviours across an entire segment of face-to-face play. In the case of Beatrice Beebe and her large team of researchers (Beebe et al., 2012a, 2012b), this involved second-by-second analysis of videoed interactions of such things as facial affect interactive contingency, which is how closely the mother coordinates her range of facial affect changes (from positive to negative) with her infant's just-prior affect changes, 'going with' his direction of change across the session. Such contingency measures the degree to which rhythms within one partner can be predicted from those within the other. Lower contingent coordination is said to mean that the mother does not predictably adjust to her infant's just-prior behaviour.

If the infant cannot predict what her mother will do, it is argued that he will have a reduced sense of influence or 'agency' (Beebe et al., 2012a).

The researchers also analysed separately 'modalities' of the mother–infant interaction, such as orientation (from en face to arch), visual attention (gaze at or away from partner's face) and facial and vocal affect, to identify which potential discordant communication may be involved with disorganised attachment. They cite their previous work which found that depressed mothers and their infants showed a discordant pattern of lowered coordination of gaze, but heightened facial/vocal affect coordination, which they discuss would not be detectable if gaze and affect were assessed as a composite, as they are in most research.

In their two-part study, Beebe et al. (2012b) studied 84 mother–infant dyads' face-to-face interactions, noting the described qualitative features and contingency of behaviours at 4 months, before measuring attachment security using Strange Situation at 12 months. The analysis of different modalities identified the 'striking intrapersonal and interpersonal discordance or conflict' in intensely distressed infants at 4 months as a central feature of disorganised dyads later at 12 months. This is characterised by maternal withdrawal that compromises a baby's interactive agency and emotional coherence by the mother's lowered contingent coordination (as described above) and failed affective correspondence from those babies. They cite related studies where infants of traumatised mothers experienced an increased number of these 'failed bids' for maternal engagement in coordinating joint attention, and argue that such early measures can successfully predict future disorganised attachment through the infant's emerging 'internal working models' based on their expectations of sequences of events (see also 'Attachment beyond infancy', pages 270–5).

for attachment relationships, but also for other forms of relationships (such as those with siblings and peers; see Chapter 12, 'Peer interactions and relationships').

The Strange Situation was designed in such a way that the child is exposed to an increasing amount of stress, on entering an unfamiliar environment, through the entry of a stranger and absence of the caregiver, to being left alone in the unfamiliar room. As already suggested in the earlier section of the chapter, most children in the second year of life are often exposed to adults other than the primary caregiver who take care of them. It is likely that the impact of some of the 'strange' episodes is not as stressful as once thought and, by that token, classification just by the infant's responses to these events may not reflect his 'real' degree of attachment to the primary caregiver. For example, a child already used to being cared for by his father, grandparents or in a nursery may, due to his regular experience, not be unsettled by the stranger nor upset by his mother leaving. Even if the mother is still the 'primary' caregiver, and mother and child share a relatively strong relationship, his behaviour may have him labelled as 'insecure-avoidant' due to his apparent lack of distress shown upon her departure and also a lack of need to be comforted by her when she returns. This is particularly so when the classification is based solely on the limited subset of behaviours during reunions.

Not only may the Strange Situation be less accurate for use with children used to non-maternal care, whose deviations from the majority may be a reflection of relative independence rather than insecure attachment, but also such variations from the 'secure' type may in fact be a facet of cultural norms that are encouraged in some societies. Table 9.3 lists the average percentages of children placed in each of the three key attachment types from research in eight countries across Europe, America and Asia in the 1980s after Ainsworth's classification types were established. A very striking feature is the contrast in proportions of 'secure' children across countries, even though this category was still the commonest *within* each country. The UK and Sweden had the most secure children whilst only half of the Chinese sample was in that category, slightly behind Germany (although one ought to be concerned with generalising from a single study in three of these four countries). What also stands out are the contrasting figures for the 'insecure' types; Japan and Israel, though still with high proportions of secure children, also had relatively high proportions of insecure-resistant ones versus very low proportions of avoidant ones.

It is unlikely that infants of some groups have a 'naturally' higher (or lower) tendency to attach securely to the primary caregiver than those of other groups, since any pattern of highs or lows is not unique to one part of the world. It is more likely that attachment behaviours are interpreted or valued differently, thus promoted to varying degrees, between different cultures. Differences in parental attitudes and childcare practices may be translated into different styles of interaction in the setting. For instance, one possible explanation for the relatively higher rate of 'insecure-avoidant' attachment in Germany is that their traditional culture prizes and promotes independence in infants near the second year (Grossman, 1985). In contrast, in Japan infants are rarely left alone, even for a short time, in the same period. In fact, a baby in the first year is seen as a 'mono' (object), which means extension, of mother rather than a separate being (Goodman, 2000, p. 165). Mother carries him around in the day and sleeps with him at night. The Strange Situation is likely to bring great distress to him, and he will be less easily comforted

Table 9.3 Percentage of main attachment types in children across eight countries.

Country	No. of studies available	Attachment type (%) Secure	Attachment type (%) Avoidant	Attachment type (%) Resistant
UK	1	75	22	3
Sweden	1	75	22	4
Japan	2	68	5	27
Holland	4	67	26	6
USA	18	65	21	14
Israel	2	64	7	29
Germany	3	57	35	8
China	1	50	25	25
Average		65	21	14

Source: Van Ijzendoorn and Kroonenberg (1988)

after being separated from mother (Takahashi, 1990). As cited earlier in the Nature–Nurture box (page 254), Korean mothers show a similar parenting style to Japanese mothers; both are likely to approach their infants rather than encourage their infants to seek proximity as with Western mothers (Jin et al., 2012). This is seen as a key reason for the very small number of babies classified as avoidant in Japanese and Korean samples (the mothers approach the infants immediately after reunion and maintain closeness) even if the basic percentages of 'secure versus insecure' infants mirror the global distribution. Although child-rearing methods evolve over time, particularly in Asia with increasing numbers of women returning to work after childbirth, cultural specificities in parental values exist and may challenge the validity of the Strange Situation procedure (Grossman et al., 1986; Nakagawa et al., 1992; see also Chapter 16 on culture and developmental norms).

Ultimately, many shortcomings of the Strange Situation and attachment types are due to the fact that they are entirely 'behaviour-based', in that only overt behaviours and expressions 'count' towards the classification. This is because the procedure was designed for a narrow age band where infants are still in the pre-linguistic stage (see Clarke-Stewart et al., 2001, for a full review). Other methods based on the Strange Situation have been developed, most notably the 'separation–reunion' procedure for pre-school and early-school children by Mary Main (Main and Cassidy, 1988), who also derived the insecure-disorganised category. The procedure follows the basic format of free play with separations and reunions, but each with an extended duration (up to 1 hour). With the same classification as Strange Situation, this method has shown 78–90% predictability on the basis of Strange Situation classification (as reviewed by Pace et al., 2012). Yet, as we have learnt, in Bowlby's 'goal-corrected' phase the older child is supposed to 'represent' the attachment relationship 'internally' as she matures, with a greater understanding of others and more cognitive competences. One question is whether she will remain in the same attachment type years later. This concerns the stability of attachment security and its bearing on the future (Goldberg, 2000), which will be explored later. Associated with this are the variables which influence attachment relationships at the same time, and such variables inevitably involve the people with whom the child regularly engages, and the kind(s) of care that she receives. These will be covered in the following section.

Attachment and childcare

Notwithstanding the caveats and limitations of the key measurements of attachment, it suffices to say that different patterns of this relationship exist, and since attachment usually starts from home, such differences have their likely origins in the environment of the child's family. The mother is the obvious starting point; as variously mentioned so far, most children have their birth mother as the primary caregiver. However, it has become commonplace for the father or other family relations to take on at least part of the responsibility of child rearing. Additionally, more and more formal and informal out-of-home childcare arrangements such as childminding services and day nurseries have become established all over the West (as well as in many non-Western countries) in the last few decades for children as young as a few weeks old. What are the implications of such 'alternatives' for attachment security? This section will begin by first considering how some characteristics of the mother may affect her relationship with the child, before venturing into a discussion of whether and how paternal and out-of-home day childcare may have a bearing on the child's attachment security.

The mother

Despite the alternative childcare available, it is still taken for granted that the mother as primary caregiver is the best 'scenario' for both mother and child. Indeed, in most cases the child does feel closest to his mother even if he is also looked after by other adults. So, what aspects of mother are the key ingredients for such closeness?

According to Bowlby's work, and also other research, it is not so much about her 'being there' or physical availability, but that the mother's *emotional* availability or 'responsiveness' is essential for establishing that 'secure' bond with her own child. Bowlby termed this maternal sensitivity, which is the emotional sensitivity on the part of the mother (or a mother substitute) to recognise the infant's cues and respond to them

> **Definition**
>
> Maternal sensitivity: the emotional sensitivity of the mother to recognise her child's cues and to respond to them promptly, appropriately and consistently.

promptly, appropriately and consistently. A 'sensitive' mother is one who is able and willing to look out for her child, so that she can attend and cater to him when he tries to engage her in his times of needs. For example, when he cries, she picks him up, when he smiles, she smiles back, and when he babbles, she often talks to him in a high-pitched voice (see also the section on infant-directed speech in Chapter 5, Language Development). That a mother is supposedly constantly contingent to her own baby's signals has obvious implications (for working mothers, in particular); an absent mother cannot be sensitive (or sensitive 'enough') for she is not always available to observe and respond in order to meet her baby's needs on a day-to-day basis.

Ainsworth followed Bowlby's arguments while developing the concept of attachment security, adding that a secure attachment is founded on such sensitivity of the parent during the first year of life. There does seem to be overall support for a link between sensitive parenting and attachment security. By observing parent–child interactions in other settings and the child's behaviours in Strange Situation, research has shown that warm, attentive or positive parenting, usually characterised by harmony and apparent mutual enjoyment, is associated more with the 'secure' type attachment, and this is regardless of culture, socio-economic status and whether the attachment figure is the biological mother or an adoptive parent (de Wolff and van Ijzendoorn, 1997; Posada et al., 2002, 2004; van Ijzendoorn et al., 2004). Children of mothers who may at times act in a negative or rejecting manner while at others overstimulating them tend to show the 'insecure-avoidant' type of attachment, and children who receive unreliable or inconsistent care (sometimes unresponsive and sometimes overbearing) are likely to be 'insecure-resistant' (e.g. Ainsworth et al., 1978; Isabella, 1993, 1995).

There is further evidence that inadequate care is associated with the 'disorganised' type of attachment. Earlier, we already touched on some links between this type and adverse family conditions. Depression in a parent, or one suffering from bereavement, has been linked to their inadvertently showing contradictory, unpleasant or even threatening behaviours, such as looking frightened or frightening, handling the infant roughly or using the infant as a source of comfort for their own condition (Lyons-Ruth et al., 1999; Schuengel et al., 1999). In turn, the infant is likely to express more negative emotions when interacting with the affected parent and develop other problems, such as problematic feeding (Rahman et al., 2004) and night-wakings (Zentall et al., 2012), which might in turn interfere with the development of a secure attachment and so forth. Indeed, recent research has indicated that children with disorganised attachment report the most maladaptive externalising problems later in life (e.g. somatic complaints, aggressive or delinquent behaviour) compared with their securely attached counterparts, and having mothers evidencing more helplessness (Lecompte and Moss, 2014).

More worryingly, the disorganised type of attachment is over-represented by children who have been maltreated through neglect or even abuse (Barnett et al., 1999). In the extreme cases, the caregiver not only fails to provide basic security and protection, but may even do the opposite by causing emotional or physical hurt to the child (see the Case Study box). In many such cases, the attachment disorder in the child will persist and even influence her interactions and relationships with other people (including peers; see Chapter 12, 'Peer interactions and relationships') later on. Importantly, abused children are far more likely, compared with those who have never been abused, to later become abusive parents, passing down the pathological relationship across generations (Cichetti and Barnett, 1991; Barnett et al., 1999; and see 'Attachment in later childhood and adolescence', pages 271–2).

The potential consequences of maternal pathology for children's attachment seem to be as daunting, if not more so, than those of deprivation that we read earlier. Still, it is important to stress that the association between maternal sensitivity and attachment security is not a perfect one and certainly not necessarily causal. A minority of formerly maltreated children do manage to form secure attachments with caregivers and good relationships with others, and some form attachment to parents who lack sensitivity or care in an incoherent manner (Barnett et al., 1999). Not all children in such situations are condemned to a life of disorders; parental sensitivity may be a highly important ingredient, but it is not the only one necessary for secure attachments.

In addition, not only are there variations in maternal sensitivity, there is also a lot of variation in how maternal 'sensitivity' is viewed and expressed, particularly cross-culturally. We have broached this concept in a relatively 'Eurocentric' manner, based on the observable moment-by-moment responsiveness of the mother. Earlier, we read about the close physical contact between mother and baby in Japan. Such contingent interactions and overt closeness may not be the norm in other cultures, where parents respond to their children's needs in other ways, such as guiding their actions (Carlson and Harwood, 2003). Hence, it is worth remaining open-minded about what 'counts' as sensitivity – some may say warmth; others say stimulation, or simply general attentiveness.

The nature and criteria of maternal sensitivity have great implications for mothers who may have a need to return to work, and are under pressure due to the apparent need for regular availability by their young. Thus far, this kind of sensitivity has been presented as if it almost comes 'naturally' from the mother, but in reality, there is some gap between the aspiration to become a sensitive mother and the actual experience of being one, which may feature routine boredom or even occasional depressive episodes rather than mutual fulfilment (Boulton, 1983). On the other hand, it is possible to 'train' such sensitivity. Participating in even short parenting sessions for interacting with their babies identified as having an irritable temperament (see Chapter 10 on temperament) can help economically disadvantaged mothers to become more responsive, and their infants are more likely to be securely attached one year later, compared with those of mothers who do not go through training (van den Boom, 1994).

CASE STUDY

Baby P and other child abuse cases

In late 2007 a news story stunned and outraged the public in the UK and beyond. The case of 'Baby P' (later revealed as Peter Connelly), a toddler who died at the age of 17 months earlier that year, was uncovered as his mother, her partner (who moved in a few months after Peter's father left when Peter was 2 months old) and a lodger (the partner's brother) were convicted of allowing or causing Peter's death. It was reported that Peter regularly received a catalogue of neglect, physical attacks and emotional turmoil for no less than eight months; before his death he endured at least 50 injuries including a broken back and ribs, and he was losing weight in the last few months of his life. Peter's mother (and grandmother at one time) had been previously arrested for assault and neglect; he was already on the council's child protection register. In the half year before his death, Peter had been placed into the temporary care of family friends twice after alarms of abuse were raised by a GP and a social worker, but he was returned home on both occasions shortly after.

Some of the disbelief expressed by the public was based on the fact that, although the physical attacks on Baby P were caused by his mother's partner, his mother was at least complicit in such acts, because she 'stood by' when the violent abuse took place and made no attempt to prevent further abuse. She was also responsible for Baby P's maltreatment through neglect and starvation. It was reported that she spent her nights drinking and days surfing the internet for pornographic material. Additionally, she actively attempted to hide evidence of physical abuse and made up cover stories about Baby P's injuries to social workers, who visited their home over 60 times due to concerns raised by the childminder, relatives, health professionals and neighbours.

Sadly, barely four and a half years had passed before yet another high-profile child abuse case arose, ending in the death of a 4-year-old boy in 2012. Daniel Pelka had been living with his mother and his stepfather, both of whom were convicted of his murder and jailed for life. Daniel's Polish-born mother had broken up with his father in early pregnancy and moved to the UK with her new partner before giving birth to Daniel. The pair were said to have subjected Daniel to isolation, starvation, beatings and other forms of abuse; he weighed only 1 stone 9 pounds and sustained at least 30 injuries to his body when he died. Similar to Baby P's case, for a year before his death there had been numerous incidents (the police had been called 26 times to the home concerning alcohol abuse and domestic violence, and school staff had reported to the headteacher about bruising and scavenging for food), while Daniel's mother, an alcohol and drug abuser, made excuses and stories (that he had an 'eating disorder', for instance) which were accepted by agencies.

The wilful maltreatment or abuse of a young child by his own mother is beyond the imagination of most people. A film broadcast by the BBC in 2014 about Baby P's case put the estimate at over 260 for children who had died at the hands of a parent or carer since his death. Following high-profile cases, public online forums are filled with comments labelling the killers, including the mothers, as 'evil', 'sick' and suchlike, with some calling for more to be done by the Social Services and other agencies towards 'at risk' children.

Amidst the public shock and outrage and media frenzy of 'blame and shame', some psychologists responded controversially with a reminder that adults who fail dramatically in their parenting are often far from being 'evil', but were once children themselves who were not properly cared for or protected in their own childhood. Baby P's mother was born to a neglectful mother and an absent father who was a sex offender, before she went to a care home that was later exposed in a scandal involving a paedophiles' ring. Her partner, who tortured Baby P, had an IQ of 60 and a similarly abusive background. Daniel Pelka's grandmother, according to friends and neighbours, was said to have been an aggressive mother who beat her children (including Daniel's mother), and her husband was rarely at home. Daniel's stepfather was a wanted criminal in Poland; he had gone to the UK after violating the terms of his suspended sentence for an assault conviction.

As Anna Motz, a consultant clinical psychologist who has studied women who abuse or collude with a partner's abuse points out (in Laville, 2009), in such cases there is often an early experience of abuse, trauma or neglect in the mother's history. The mothers are said to develop a 'narcissistic' attitude or way of relating to their child as an 'extension of themselves and [go] on to treat the child with the cruelty, contempt and neglect that they were exposed to themselves' as their 'norms' are different from other people's. Motz goes on to assert that such cases are actually 'not rare', and that because of this the dynamics of maternal neglect, abuse or collusion in abuse should be examined further.

It has been controversially argued that, even in the face of maltreatment, removing children from their parents might not have improved their chances due to the traumatising effect of frequent changes in homes and carers within our over-burdened care systems. Baby P's case is remarked upon as 'just one of thousands of children who are vulnerable and who live with parents in need of support and greater supervision' (Boynton and Anderson, 2009, p. 8). At the same time, the UK's child protection system has seen a huge rise in the number of children being taken from their families into care, in response to the fear of a 'next Baby P', according to a *Guardian* report (Butler, 2011). Councils have been looking recently to shift their focus towards 'early intervention' policies, in terms of promoting parenting support projects, in the hope that this will reduce the number of children at risk of being taken into care. However, this might prove difficult amidst recent government cuts to public spending.

- What is your response to cases like Baby P and Daniel Pelka?
- Do you agree with the psychologists' idea that abusive or neglectful parents are likely to have been abused or neglected as children themselves? What about giving support to such parents?
- To what extent do you believe that the way we were reared by our parents can influence the way we will rear our own children?

Sources: BBC (2014); Boynton and Anderson (2009); Butler (2011); Laville (2009); Taylor (2008)

More recently, research has explored other characteristics of the mother that may go to promote secure attachment. The seasoned British psychologist Elizabeth Meins (Meins et al., 2001, 2002) first introduced the concept of mind-mindedness as the ability of a parent to look at her child as an individual with his own thoughts and feelings (similar to theory of mind; see Chapter 8,

Definition

Mind-mindedness: the ability of a parent to see and treat her child as an individual with his own thoughts and feelings, through her interactions with him, using talk to refer to mental states.

'Theory of mind'). Meins suggests that, instead of treating her infant as a vulnerable dependant with needs, a mother's ability and willingness to treat him as a person 'with a mind', as reflected by engagement with him using talk about mental states, will help him achieve secure attachment by enabling him to see others' needs and motives (building up a 'representation' of others as an achievement in the final attachment phase). Her work found that, from as young as 6 months old, mothers who made more verbal references to their infants' psychological states in their interactions were more likely to have the infants assessed with a secure attachment at 1 year old; in fact, mind-mindedness predicts attachment security better than maternal sensitivity.

Meins' recent research (Meins, 2013; Meins et al., 2011, 2012, 2013) further highlights the multidimensional nature of mind-mindedness, its antecedents and predictive power for later outcomes. Assessing mind-mindedness involves identifying content in the mother's comments on her infant as being: 'appropriate' (i.e. an accurate reflection of what he may be thinking or feeling, such as saying that he is excited if he squeals joyfully); and 'non-attuned' (a tendency to misinterpret his internal state, such as stating that he is bored when he is actively engaged in play). More appropriate mind-related and fewer non-attuned comments can independently distinguish secure type mothers from their insecure counterparts. While mothers' appropriate comments in the first year are associated with their child's theory of mind development at age 4, non-attuned comments are related to the child's lower levels of internal state language and symbolic play at age 2 (which may lead to poorer theory of mind). Crucially, such mind-mindedness dimensions are unrelated to infant temperament, maternal socio-economic status, perceived social support and depression, but are related to the obstetric history (whether the pregnancy was planned or perceived as difficult, and the birth experience). This has implications for antenatal care in terms of promoting stable cognitive-behavioural traits in the mother postnatally for secure bonding with her baby.

The idea that 'good mothering' is not about constant contingent responsiveness, but about the *quality* of interactions, is a welcome one for many in that it lessens the obligation of mothers to remain at home and gives more scope for non-maternal care. In fact, Bowlby (1969) himself did not advocate for a mother attending to all of her baby's discomfort or distress at every turn, but suggested that part of the process is to allow waiting with moderate stress to learn tolerance and independence. As covered before, Bowlby also advocated the complementary role of the father, and it is to this other key figure in modern-day parenting that we turn our attention next.

How important is father?

After a period in which the role of the father was sidelined since Bowlby's theory first emerged, by the 1990s research that included fathers as attachment figures was burgeoning. Some of the work has compared infant attachment to the father with that to the mother or the parent dyad's engagement with their infant. The pattern of findings can be summarised as indicating modest similarity in attachment security, but also clear differences in the *quality* of attachment or type of engagement between the two parenting figures. In a two-parent family, although a child with a secure attachment to her mother is likely to also have secure attachment to her father (which may signal matching characteristics between the parents), parenting factors such as sensitivity, warmth and availability, which have been identified as predicting maternal attachment, often do not predict paternal attachment (e.g. Grossman et al., 2002; Caldera, 2004; Brown et al., 2007).

> **STOP AND THINK**
>
> **Reflection**
>
> If your primary caregiver was your mother:
>
> - Did your father (at least sometimes) look after you by himself?
> - What things did you enjoy doing with your father the most?
> - Was there any difference between your relationships with your mother and father?

Recent research seems to confirm the idea that the amount of involvement aside, fathers play a differential role to mothers in that they typically have a smaller part in the practical and emotional aspects of caregiving (such as feeding and soothing the baby). Fathers tend to spend more time in play with their children, particularly sons, involving more physical activities and stimulation (see Lamb, 1997). In play, mothers tend to engage in more 'traditional' games (such as peekaboo) with affectionate interplay between mother and infant. These differences may go to explain why, in general, infants prefer to turn to their mother rather than father in times of discomfort or distress (Lamb, 1987).

Is father's playful engagement a factor contributing to paternal attachment? It is likely. Some have called this *play sensitivity*, which includes adapting his play to the infant's ability, letting her take the initiative, and responding to her facial expressions (Grossman et al., 2002). Such paternal sensitivity is argued to convey warmth and confidence to the child, and predicts attachment much better than conventional sensitivity up to the age of 16. At the same time, this image of father as a 'playmate' has been diversified to include more practical tasks, with more mothers returning to employment, but it is promising that other research has found that greater involvement in sensitive caregiving by fathers can predict secure attachment (Cox et al., 1992; van Ijzendoorn and deWolff, 1997). Even though they tend to show less affection in such tasks, fathers are just as capable as mothers in performing them, and researchers are calling for a close look at the multiple dimensions of fathering quality (Brown et al., 2007). Recent studies further highlight the differential and complex role of attachment to both parents as a potential precursor towards social competence. Insecurity with both parents ('double-insecure') promotes defiance (particularly in reactive toddlers; Lickenbrock et al., 2013) and is associated with more teacher-rated externalising problems than in those secure with one parent (Kochanska and Kim, 2013).

There is still a much richer literature on maternal attachment than on paternal attachment, and with the greater sharing of parenting today, more work is required to ascertain the nature of this relationship. Changing childcare patterns also lead to relationships with other potential caregivers, such as nursery/pre-school workers and childminders, and the impact of such changes has been debated even more as we will discover below.

Fathers spend more time in play with their infants, particularly sons.
Source: Lam

Impact of day care

The concerns about the impact of day care on attachment have also originated from Bowlby's theorisation. His work on the harmful effects of permanent placement in institutions in support of the maternal deprivation hypothesis led some to consider the possibility that placing children in non-parental care at all, particularly before the age of 3 years (the end of sensitive period), might already have adverse effects on their attachment relationship. This has provoked a great deal of debate as the need for many mothers to return to work means the need to use such day-care services, unless the father or other family members are available to provide care during her working hours.

The earliest findings, in the 1970s by the internationally renowned researcher in child development, Jay Belsky, were at first reassuring. It was concluded that there was no reason to suspect day care would disrupt the child's attachment to his mother and that children of working mothers still preferred their mothers over any other caregiver (Belsky and Steinberg, 1978). However, based on further reviews of the research, he adjusted his position accordingly (Belsky, 1988, 1992). He noticed that children who were in out-of-home care for more than 20 hours per week by 1 year of age were more likely to show insecure (usually avoidant) attachment to their mothers compared to children who had more maternal care.

Definition

Play sensitivity: responsiveness to the infant during play through cooperation and motivation by accepting her initiative, adapting play to her cognitive capability and responding to her emotional expressions.

Even though Belsky was more inclined to attribute the day-care children's attachment insecurity to their regular experience of separation from the mother, leading them to doubt her responsiveness or availability, the results may be interpreted in other ways. Earlier we analysed the Strange Situation and attachment types, and identified that events in the procedure that were supposed to cause anxiety and trigger attachment behaviours are perhaps not that distressing to some children. In the case of those who are used to multiple caregivers, their responses may be seen as reflecting independence rather than avoidance of mother (Clarke-Stewart et al., 2001). This is plausible as some evidence showed that children in different forms of non-maternal care (relatives, childminders and nursery) had similar behaviours during reunion with their mothers, and that those in nursery were more likely to show more of some desirable social traits such as empathy and sharing, if also less of others such as affection (Melhuish et al., 1990).

Methodological issues of interpreting the Strange Situation aside, it is also not possible to be sure that less secure attachment was indeed caused by being in day care as such rather than the conditions of the care provision, as found in some reviews (Sagi et al., 2002). This is similar to attributing any negative outcome of children who had been put in orphanages with appalling conditions to the fact that they were institutionalised *per se* rather than to the conditions of the institutions. This is worth considering because, overall, more of Belsky's day-care sample than not, as comparable to most American children, still showed secure attachment to their mothers (Clarke-Stewart, 1988). It is important, therefore, to consider the types of childcare available (of which parents often use a combination) and the variables that denote quality of care, such as the ratio of children to caregivers, the experience of caregivers, the structure of day-to-day routines and the physical setting. There seemed to be much variation and, unsurprisingly, with a substandard environment or higher staff–children ratio, day-care workers tended to find it difficult to interact positively with individual children (Melhuish et al., 1990).

Reassuringly, associations between high-quality day care and attachment security have been found even when full-time care is received, and in fact children in such centres may even show more secure attachment than those cared for by childminders, family or friends (Love et al., 2003). Furthermore, state-funded high-quality day care can even ameliorate the effects of poverty and associated social disadvantages (such as poor parental education) by promoting, from early on, competences in children that their families do not have the resources to promote (Lamb, 1998). However, the availability and affordability of such day care varies, and poorer families are more likely to 'settle for' poorer-quality care. Frequent and long periods spent in such care coupled with insensitive mothering due to poverty and stress makes a classic combination for insecure attachment. On the other hand, recent research shows that, if close carer/teacher–child relationships are enabled in early years, these can go to buffer against negative outcomes (such as aggressive behaviour) in those who are less securely attached to their mothers to begin with (Buyse et al., 2011). Such relationships may be fostered through the carer's sensitivity and positive caregiving behaviour, including positive physical contact or speech and responsiveness (Clasien de Schipper et al., 2008).

In 2007 Bowlby's son, Sir Richard Bowlby, president of the Centre for Child Mental Health, stated that infants in non-parental day care can develop a lasting secondary bond to a carer who is 'consistently accessible'. Still, he qualified the statement by saying that this is not the experience of many babies in some forms of day care – specified as 'group settings' – where care is not given by one individual carer. R. Bowlby wrote a list of conditions that 'attachment-based' day care should meet, such as not accepting babies until 9 months old and having mother accompany her baby for a few weeks while keeping care durations short – which gave food for thought as providing such conditions can be logistically difficult. Since then, in line with the Early Year Foundation Stage in UK, writings by practitioners have been published to approach attachment in more practical, informative ways, linking good practice to social and emotional development (such as how to greet children, the role of staff as secondary caregivers, and guidance for dealing with separation anxiety; see Read (2010)).

In sum, while day-care arrangements give relief to mothers who need to return to work, the quality of care and the conditions under which care is taken should be taken into account when choosing a provider. As we will explore in the next section, children form expectations about others and relationships from their care experiences at home and beyond that can have significant implications for their development in the long term.

A good amount of high-quality day care can be beneficial to children's development.
Source: Pearson Education Ltd/Studio 8

Attachment beyond infancy

In more recent strands of research, attachment theory has been given longer-term and potential lifespan implications, particularly for social and emotional development. In the previous section, we learnt that a mother's characteristics, including any history of abuse, can have a bearing on her child's attachment to her and the child's future parenting capacity. 'Cross-generational' factors like this give an idea of continued and discontinued patterns of relationship development within families. These patterns are said to be based on the 'notion' (representation) that the child in each generation has about her relationships with her caregivers, and how she carries forward this notion as she grows and forms new relationships with other people in her life. Below, we will first investigate the nature of this 'representation' of relationships, before moving on to complete the chapter by looking at research that has assessed its influence on the child's later development.

Internal working model

We have learnt (through the attachment phases) that a key milestone of developing attachment is that the child depends less and less on the actual physical proximity of a constantly present caregiver, but more and more on the notion that she is 'available'. We have also emphasised the child's understanding of a responsive parent or a consistent and good-quality childcare routine. The central function of this notion is that the child learns about how to 'relate'. Through these early relationships that she forms with the closest people to her, she builds up expectations about herself, others and the relationships between them which make up what Bowlby (1969, 1973) originally called the child's internal working model (IWM).

Note that, in assuming that the child is able 'internally' to represent relationships in her mind, the IWM part of attachment goes beyond the behavioural and emotional elements, and signifies a 'cognitive' side to attachment. Such a cognitive structure, or model, contains past interactions with the attachment figure(s) and incorporates new ones as the infant engages with them more and more, and this will guide her later interactions with these key figures and other people. This is why their characteristics (such as sensitivity) matter, since these get associated with her experiences as part of the working model, which informs her further actions using the expectations formed from the experiences.

Accordingly, the few different attachment types can be represented by different IWMs (Ainsworth et al., 1978). For a securely attached child, his IWM of his caregiver(s) will be one of warmth and attentiveness or of someone who is often available. He expects her to return to him after separation, which helps him become accepting of others and relationships and see himself as someone worthy of love. The IWMs of the caregiver of insecurely attached children will be either one of more coldness or even rejection (avoidant type), which leads the child to display little or no distress at separation and expect little from the reunion; or one of inconsistency and unpredictability (resistant type), leading the child initially into excessive distress, but potentially anger over time towards the caregiver. Such children are said to have a less worthy sense of self and have more difficulty building close relationships due to their pessimistic outlook towards others or their preoccupation with their relationships as a result of their experiences.

Definition

Internal working model: the mental representation about oneself, others and their relationships on which one's expectations about future relationships are based.

For the insecure-disorganised type of children, the experiences of disturbed or distorted caregiving mean that they are unable to organise a coherent set of actions towards, or coherent expectations about, their caregiver, hence the lack of a coherent IWM. This means they will lack the usual know-how for approaching or interacting with others to form new relationships, even if they still have the motivation to do so.

Obviously, to see whether the features and functions of these hypothetical cognitive models actually 'work' as they are prescribed, we need to review the evidence about the later development of children classified as different attachment types, and thus with different IWMs. We covered some indicators for the cycle of dysfunctional interactions and relationships in insecure-disorganised children through neglect or abuse earlier. Next we will examine the wider evidence base that includes the major attachment types.

> **STOP AND THINK**
>
> **Going further**
>
> Refer back to the examples at the start of this chapter.
>
> - What kind of an IWM do you think each of these toddlers has?
> - How do you imagine they may relate to other people a year later and then in school?

Attachment in later childhood and adolescence

The IWM purportedly relays children's past experiences to guide present interactions. In theory, it will equip a secure child with confidence and self-worth to develop closer relationships with family and build friendships with peers. An insecure child will lack these desirable social and emotional traits (or even bring forth their opposite) for developing healthy relationships. There is empirical support for both ideas, with some of the early research being carried out by Mary Main, who derived the insecure-disorganised attachment type.

As explained earlier, being a keen follower of Ainsworth's ideas, Main and her teams (e.g. Main et al., 1985; Main and Cassidy, 1988) devised variants (particularly the separation–reunion procedure, but also other standardised interview schedules) of the Strange Situation for measuring quality of relationships in pre-schoolers and older children. She found that children who had been securely attached at 12 months went on to show more emotional coherence and openness, whereas insecurely attached toddlers were more likely to give irrational or negative answers or stay very quiet, in an interview discussing imagined parent–child interactions and relationships at 6 years. Main noticed that secure children were more likely to see themselves as lovable and liked by peers, while insecure children had lower expectations of relationships as well as being actually engaged less in social activities. Their behaviour during reunion with parents at that age was reminiscent of their behaviour at 12 months old (such as greeting then ignoring the parent or being clingy but whiny). There were also age-appropriate signs of hostility or fear towards their parents in insecure-disorganised children, indicating maladjusted relationships. Later studies have also more or less confirmed the above pattern when using more measures of social and emotional development outcomes. For instance, Alan Sroufe, who specifically studied peer relationships (e.g. Elicker et al., 1992; Shulman et al., 1994; Carlson et al., 2003), found that from pre-school through to school, children who had been securely attached as infants showed greater skills in and enthusiasm for social play, had more close friendships, and were rated by teachers as higher in self-esteem, social competence and emotional maturity (such as showing more pro-social behaviour and empathy).

There is also evidence that attachment security can predict social adjustment further into adolescence (Sroufe et al., 1993; Ostoja et al., 1995; Carlson et al., 2004). Adolescents securely attached to their parents during infancy and adolescence (assessed by interviews) show higher self-esteem, school attainments and social skills, and more friendships than those with insecure attachments. In particular, the insecure-avoidant adolescents report less social support and being more likely to have earlier sexual experiences and riskier sexual practices. Recent research also locates children, particularly girls, with a history of insecure attachment as being at higher risk of internalising symptoms (such as loneliness, depression and anxiety) through 'preoccupation' with parental relationships (Milan et al., 2013). The risk of insecure-disorganised adolescents for externalising symptoms due to mothers' helplessness (Lecompte and Moss, 2014) was described earlier. The importance of attachment has also been identified in adoptees, where parental sensitive support from early childhood through to adolescence predicts the continuity of secure attachment up to at least 14 years old (Beijersbergen, 2012). With the extra complications of biological changes during puberty, along with cognitive and social changes, adolescence marks a critical period in which the 'balance' between consolidating relationships with the family and norms within society, whilst exploring and experimenting with more independence and autonomy, is difficult without positive, but authoritative, support by parents (Baumrind, 1991; and see Chapter 13, 'Adolescence').

It also seems that attachment security in infancy can predict development well into the future, but there are, of course, exceptions (Schneider et al., 2001; Stams et al., 2002). Insecure infants do not always end up 'worse off' than their secure counterparts (except for disorganised infants, even though some of these do develop normally as described earlier). Part of the inconsistency can be due to the stability of attachment – whether children will remain in the same attachment type. Infants tend to do this in the short to medium term as assessed by the Strange Situation. In the longer term, with the complication of different measures, and longer lapses between taking measures, more children change attachment patterns (Thompson, 2000). This is because variables such as childcare arrangements (e.g. mothers working more as children get older) and the family setting (e.g. separation, remarriage) can change (see the Lifespan box on page 274). It is also possible that a change in circumstances may lead to a change in attachment security as well as to other developmental outcomes. For instance, parental separation can lead to the child feeling less securely attached to an estranged parent, and the stress can cause him to have less positive peer interactions. On the other hand, an adoption study (Beijersbergen, 2012) shows that children who had little maternal sensitive support in early childhood, but more of it in adolescence, were able to gain more attachment security. However, although long-term secure attachment cemented by continuity of good-quality caregiving may facilitate healthy development, this does not mean that the security of attachment achieved at any point will remedy the ill effects resulting from another point in development.

Adulthood and intergenerational cycles

We have explained that if attachment security is stable alongside parenting and family circumstances, it can predict later childhood outcomes. Researchers have also explored how well it can predict outcomes in adulthood. For Bowlby, the earliest representations (IWMs) of attachment are most likely to remain stable since, drawing from psychoanalysis, he believed that these models exist outside of our consciousness and influence us through the lifespan. If that is the case, one would expect that IWMs representing different attachment types in childhood would be associated with different attachment types in adulthood. Mary Main, who introduced the concept of IWM, also devised a method that measures attachment quality in adults for this purpose.

Main and her co-workers (Main et al., 1985; Main and Goldwyn, 1994) developed a semi-structured interview schedule, called the Adult Attachment Interview (AAI) to measure how much an adult is able to integrate memories of her earliest relationships with her primary caregivers into her present state of mind concerning relationships. In this respect, the AAI is a retrospective method of tapping into former attachment security with the aim of mapping it on to present relationship quality, hence charting cross-generational patterns of attachment. Main maintains that it is not so much about 'what' the person remembers about the past, but 'how' in terms of his/her emotional openness and the coherence between former and present experiences.

Again, influenced by Ainsworth's ideas of attachment types, Main's classification of adult attachment contains three major categories plus an additional one that denotes an inability to form attachments in the person's past. Table 9.4 lists such adult attachment types, along with the infant attachment types to which each is hypothesised to be linked.

Definition

Adult Attachment Interview: a semi-structured interview method for probing into an adult's early childhood relationship experiences with attachment figures and assessing the extent to which she integrates such experiences into her current relationships.

Table 9.4 Adult attachment types and their matching infant attachment types.

Type	Characteristics	Matching
Dismissive	Dismisses the significance of (or denies or claims to forget the existence of) early experiences. Recalls events with little detail and emotion. Acknowledges the importance of relationships in past and present.	Insecure-avoidant
Autonomous	Talks frankly and in detail about both positive and negative experiences. Shows insights into others' motives and feelings.	Secure
Preoccupied	Remembers experiences in a lengthy, unstructured way, often with repetitions. Talks emotionally about events as if overwhelmed.	Insecure-resistant
Unresolved	Failed to organise mental life after a traumatic past.	Disorganised

According to Main, if the adult has positive memories of her past relationships at home, she will talk more openly about them and be more likely to build a secure attachment with her own child. If her childhood relationships were difficult and she 'blocks' them out (dismissive) or is still emotionally burdened by them (preoccupied), then she will be more likely to have an insecure attachment with her own child because she cannot draw upon and build on positive experiences. Indeed, it was found that 75% of securely attached infants had mothers assessed as 'autonomous' (Main and Goldwyn, 1994), while there was even evidence for three-generational continuity (Benoit and Parker, 1994). This indicates that the representation that the parent has of her attachment with her own parents will affect the way she interacts with her child, who will in turn form the corresponding type of attachment, which will go on to affect the way that her child interacts with her future children, within an inter-generational cycle.

Indeed, differences in parenting behaviours and parents' perceptions of their children have been associated with differences in their adult attachment model or history of attachments (van Ijzendoorn, 1995; Steele et al., 2003; Pesonen et al., 2004). Mothers who are assessed as securely attached are more sensitive towards their children, whilst those who have a history of insecure attachment are more likely to see their children negatively. In addition, the relationship that insecure parents form with their children, itself likely to be insecure, can have consequences for other relationships that the children will form as future adults, such as romantic relationships.

Longitudinal studies that followed up infants who had been assessed by Ainsworth's Strange Situation to study their adult attachment years later lend further support to Main's ideas of IWM. Some research has shown direct mapping from infant to adult attachment types, in particular when family circumstances remain stable, but change has also been detected (Hamilton, 1994). Change might be due to the predictiveness of infant attachment types, the reliability of the AAI or life events. Changes in family circumstances such as marital separation,

Representations of attachment relationships may be maintained across generations.
Source: Lam

divorce, illness and bereavement in the intervening years between assessments can exert a very significant impact on adult attachment (Zimmerman, 2000). It can be said that, apart from early secure attachment, a stable home-life is a major contributor to secure relationships in the future. Recent comparative research (tracing chimpanzees whose attachment had been assessed at age 1 when they were 20 years of age) also found both attachment organisation and rearing experience to be significant predictors of later health, wellbeing and personality (Clay et al., 2015). These patterns call for more research with parents on their own perspective and history, not just as caregivers, to examine the effects of parenting representations (Mayseless, 2006).

LIFESPAN

Intergenerational attachment across cultures, regions and family types

In recent years, researchers from non-Anglophone countries have not only translated the standard tools such as the AAI, but also used them to explore intergenerational patterns of attachment in less 'conventional' settings (such as single-parenthood or isolated rural communities). One such study by Gojman and colleagues published in 2012 made home observations using the Strange Situation procedure of 66 mother–infant dyads in Mexico, comprising 35 urban middle-class Spanish-speaking pairs and 31 rural impoverished pairs of aboriginal heritage. The AAI (with the reliability of Spanish transcripts being validated for the first time) was used to measure the mothers' attachment classification. Another measure of 'quality of caregiving' was taken, by observing maternal behaviour during activities like feeding, changing, bathing and playing.

Gojman et al. found that, although the secure-insecure AAI category distinguished caregiver sensitivity and cooperation only in the rural subsample, a good correspondence between AAI classifications and dyadic attachment classifications in the Strange Situation was supported in both subsamples. The researchers reason that this supports the cross-cultural robustness and intergenerational relationship of attachment as a pathway from an adult's state of mind (IWM) through responsive care to attachment security with the infant.

Another study published in the same year was led by Miljkovitch, who assessed adult (AAI) and child (with a verbal task as the children were older) attachment representations in 50 married couples, 43 single parents and their children in France. With family socio-economics controlled for, single-parent status itself was not related to child attachment, but children with father as the sole caregiver reported more disorganised representations. Mother–child associations in attachment representations (which indicate intergenerational transmission) were found only for intact families and not single-mother families, and there were no father–child associations found in attachment representations.

Miljkovitch et al. remind us that, although children's attachment representations vary as a function of family structure (representations are more likely to be disorganised in single-parent families), the variations may be due to the circumstances leading to single parenthood, which differ between men and women, rather than the family structure or parental gender *per se*. As mothers are the main caregiver in most family structures, following separation maternal custody (which is much more common) may affect a mother's involvement and sensitivity with her child through such challenges as dealing with the break-up or income reduction. Paternal custody is usually the consequence of major maternal shortcomings (e.g. abandonment, serious psychiatric disorder) or death, which are major risk factors in themselves for 'disorganising' attachment (as reviewed earlier in this chapter), while the main caregiving role remains vacated (as we read earlier, the father's role often differs from the mother's). These are added to the fact that children in sole custody have also witnessed marital discord and their parents' own unresolved states of mind.

Sources: Gojman et al. (2012); Miljkovitch et al. (2012)

Gathering the evidence thus far, the long-term consequences of the earliest attachment relationship that a child forms with her parents are not yet conclusive. However, this relationship is quite clearly at least relevant to the one that resembles it the most – the relationship that the child will go on to form with her own children in the future.

SUMMARY

This chapter has introduced us to the earliest social experiences that a child has in her life. From Bowlby's original theory through to intergenerational cycles of attachment security, and from the Strange Situation and AAI, we have explored the nature and origins of a highly important part of development and its implications for theoretical, personal and practical issues.

We have evaluated Bowlby's original theory and the importance placed upon the relationship with the primary caregiver in early development, considering the maternal deprivation hypothesis and animal research as well. We have also looked at more recent research which helps us to understand how other caregivers and consistent parenting allow for the development of attachment. Whether the characteristics of attachment relationships are a nature 'given' or are nurtured by our conditions, we humans, like most animals, are social creatures and, as such, have a tendency to bond with and relate to others. Exactly how this bonding is done, and the effects that the lack of bonding has, can vary across human cultures and animal species.

We have explored the key features of the attachment relationship, including monotropism, proximity seeking, separation protest, stranger anxiety and the critical or sensitive period for its formation. We have also looked at the phases of attachment which children go through at different ages in the development of attachment.

We have critically considered the Strange Situation procedure, how it works and what it is supposed to reveal about a child, as well as considering some of its potential shortcomings, alternative accounts of its usefulness and other explanations as to what it might reveal about a child's relationships.

We have looked at the reality of modern society in order to consider how optimum relationships can be achieved within its demands and constraints. Fathering, working mothers and shared care are all prevalent phenomena and whether they mean compromised attachment relationships is unclear. As such, more support might be offered to families to optimise their relationships with children.

We have discussed a great deal of research which suggests that a child's early attachment experiences can have long-term psychological impacts which may be positive and negative. We have also seen various ways in which the long-term negative effects of disturbances in early attachments can be minimised. The current and future direction of research in this field is to examine the combination of factors that lead to optimum attachment relationships and to minimise the ill effects of deprivation or disturbed attachment relationships.

REVIEW QUESTIONS

1. With research evidence, outline and evaluate Bowlby's attachment theory in relation to its implications for non-maternal and out-of-home childcare provision.
2. Describe and critically evaluate the Strange Situation procedure.
3. What is an internal working model? How does it relate to attachment relationships and predict future relationships?
4. What are the deleterious effects of maternal deprivation? Are such effects entirely inevitable once the mothering figure has been absent in an infant's life?
5. Are Bowlby's original proposals for attachment applicable to contemporary family life in Western society?

RECOMMENDED READING

For a detailed evaluation of the Strange Situation procedure:

Clarke-Stewart, K. A., Goosens, F. A., & Allhusen, V. D. (2001). Measuring infant mother attachment: Is the Strange Situation enough? *Social Development*, 10, 143–169.

For looking at the neurobiological basis of maternal attachment (as well as neglect) in humans and non-humans:

Strathearn, L. (2011). Maternal neglect: Oxytocin, dopamine and the neurobiology of attachment. *Journal of Neuroendrocrinology*, 23, 1054–1065.

For predictors of attachment and later development:

Goldberg, S. (2000). *Attachment and Development*. London: Arnold.

For workings of the internal working model of parenting and attachment:

Mayseless, O. (2006). *Parenting Representations: Theory, Research and Clinical Implications*. New York: Cambridge University Press.

For a succinct evaluation of the stability of attachment and its role as a predictor:

Thompson, R. A. (2000). The legacy of early attachments. *Child Development*, 71, 145–152.

For a review of attachment relationships in early-years settings:

Read, V. (2010). *Developing Attachment in Early Years Settings: Nurturing Secure Relationships from Birth to Five Years*. London: Routledge.

RECOMMENDED WEBSITES

The 'Attachment Theory Website' (ATWS) with regularly updated information on books, chapters, presentations, manuscripts and journal articles on attachment:

www.richardatkins.co.uk/atws

The website of a charity specialising in supporting parents and professionals who work in parenting education, with details of online, printed and multimedia resources:

www.parenting.org.uk

For some facts and figures and publications about day care:

www.daycaretrust.org.uk

Chapter 10
Childhood temperament and behavioural development

Learning outcomes

After reading this chapter, and with further recommended reading, you should be able to:

1. Describe the key features of childhood temperament and how its characteristics are expressed differently at different ages.
2. Explain the difficulty in ascribing a finite number of dimensions to the concept of temperament, and discuss research which has focused on a few dimensions.
3. Critically evaluate research findings of differences in temperament between groups of children and the explanations for these variations.
4. Explain the biological and social origins of children's behaviour and the importance of an inclusive and integrated approach to this development.
5. Discuss the complexity of the relationship between childhood temperament and later personality development and other developmental outcomes.

Description of two 2-year-olds

Sebastian

Sebastian is the only child of two upper-middle-class parents in their early 40s. His mother works part time and he goes to a private nursery three days a week. Regularly he cannot settle in bed until past 9 pm, and his parents sometimes allow him in their bed when he is particularly unsettled. He is generally pleasant in nursery, though he can be impatient and easily distracted. He does not like group activities and sharing, and sometimes he 'throws a strop' if he does not get his own way when playing with others. He eats most of his given food at meal times; however, he demands his snacks regularly and may get restless if he does not get any.

Luke

Luke is the second-youngest child among six siblings; he has a 16-year-old brother, the oldest among the six, three older sisters and a younger sister. His parents recently separated and all the children are living with their mother, who does not work, in a three-bedroom house. Luke has regular temper tantrums and is said by his mother and older siblings to be very restless ('he can hardly sit still'). He is not usually difficult with others, but can be 'wild' or 'out of control' when frustrated – especially when he is waiting his turn for toys. He is known to more than 'tease' his little sister; he has hit the 9-month-old at least once so he is never left alone with her. He is picky with food at meal times and eats very little. He cannot settle in bed for a long time and is often awake past 10 pm. He frequently wets his bed.

- What do you think are the key differences (and similarities, if you think they apply) between Sebastian and Luke?
- How would you describe their characters?
- What might be the cause of the differences in behaviour between the two children?
- Do you think the children currently have 'problems' in their behaviour?
- Whose problems are they – the child's, the parent(s), or someone/something else's?
- How likely do you think it is that their behaviour will persist into later childhood and beyond?

Introduction

The cases and questions above give us a taste of some issues that are explored in this chapter. It has often been noticed by both parents and casual observers how children of the same age and gender, and who belong to the same social-class background, can differ so dramatically from each other in their behavioural characteristics.

▶ In particular, oftentimes parents are overheard comparing their different offspring and remarking on how different they have been since a very young age. For instance, the firstborn may have been active and exuberant, if impulsive, as an infant, while their second one may have been shy and reserved, but relaxed. The two children's characters may also have remained that way well into their teens, even though the two were only separated by a year in age and the family circumstances have been similar and stable throughout their childhood.

For developmental psychologists, differences in behavioural tendencies that apparently emerge very early on in life concern what are often known as differences in 'temperament'. Researchers have for a long time been investigating whether there is a 'normal' range of childhood temperament or how enduring a child's temperament can be. The latter concerns longer-term implications in childhood outcomes. Can such early-emerging behavioural styles in children lead to their later-developing personality in adulthood? Can any pattern of temperament predispose a child to problems or aversive outcomes and failed relationships later on in life? Amongst all these questions, one important question remains: what can cause such differences in children's behavioural style in the first place? In this chapter, we will be exploring this question, and the question of whether the course of this aspect of development can be influenced or altered in any way.

Before going further, it is worth noting that for a long time temperament has been seen by numerous influential investigators to have a genetic origin and to be underpinned by biological mechanisms. Although worded differently by different people, the definitions that have been offered include 'biologically rooted individual differences' (Bates, 1989, p. 4), 'behavioural quality . . . influenced by inherited biology' (Kagan, 1994, p. xvii), and 'genetically based' or just 'innate' (Goldsmiths et al., 1987, p. 524). However, the latter was offered with the qualification that, as development proceeds, the expression of temperament increasingly becomes more influenced by experience and context. And more recent articulations have included the physiological basis for individual differences in reactivity and self-regulation that include motivation, affect, activity, and attention characteristics (e.g. Rothbart and Bates, 2006), which suggest a degree of self-control on some characteristics. Indeed, as we will see later, recent research has suggested that a more inclusive and integrated approach to studying temperament differences in children and their long-term impact is warranted.

Children from the same parents and environment may be remarkably different in temperament.
Source: O'Donnell

What is temperament?

As hinted earlier, the different ways in which different children behave and respond to things and people from infancy are often seen to characterise those children's individual style of temperament. Temperament is then not manifested in just one or two discrete behaviours, but instead a relatively consistent *set* of behavioural tendencies. Some authors have conceptualised this in terms of the child's underlying 'disposition', or tendency to act, called a 'trait'. Also, any disposition should endure over an extensive period of time (not just days or weeks, but at least months and usually years), and should affect behaviours across different settings (Rutter, 1987). These qualities, seen as the essential or even the qualifying features of temperament by many for a long time, will be specified further and discussed below. However, it is important to say that, despite the extensive research in this area which we will explore in this chapter, it has still not been conclusively shown that children's temperament reliably reflects all of these qualities and remains unchanged over time (Shiner et al., 2012).

Stability

We have just identified above that a qualifying feature of temperament is that any trait or behavioural tendency should persist over time. One way to look at this is through the notion of stability. Stability of temperament generally means that a child who shows a trait at a level that is higher or lower than other children at one point in time should also be expected to show about that level in comparison to other children after a lapse of time. So, for instance, if a 2-year-old infant is more active compared to his same-aged peers, he should also be more active compared to his peers one, two or even more years down the line, if activity is a 'stable' part of his temperament. It is likely that all children's general activity level decreases as they get older – we may say they 'calm down' a little. However, it is each individual child's *relative* level, as compared to the level of others, which is the key feature that can tell us that this aspect of his temperament is stable.

Continuity

Another notion that concerns the persistence of temperament over time is continuity. Any temperamental trait is supposed to be a fundamental underlying disposition to behave in certain ways. Therefore, even though children grow older and show different 'sets' of behaviours with age, the sets should nevertheless still reflect the same underlying trait. For example, one such trait is 'approach'. A highly 'approachable' infant at 6 months may be at ease with strangers, or later on when older she will laugh with them, and later still she will toddle towards them as she gains mobility. Thus the particular set of behaviours can change with age, but they are still indicative of the same *underlying* trait. If being approachable is indeed a 'continuous' trait then at age 3 or older, she may be expected to express this by being friendly with others, such as initiating contact with new adults and inviting play with new children. Table 10.1 charts some of the 'sets' of behaviours and expressions that may be expected for such a child at increasing ages,

> **Definitions**
>
> **Temperament:** a general underlying set of tendencies to behave in a particular way. It should show stability, continuity, context-dependence and early emergence.
> **Stability:** similar level relative to other same-age peers over time.
> **Continuity:** related ranges of behaviour appropriate to age.

Table 10.1 Behavioural and expressive responses of an approachable child by age.

Age group	Behaviours and expressions shown
Birth–6 months (new-born)	Orienting towards novel objects, people or situations; smile and laughter emerge
7 months–1 year (early infancy)	Above behaviours and expressions; emerging approach towards novel objects, people or situations; increase in frequency and intensity of seeking such approach
1–2 years (late infancy)	Above behaviours and expressions; emerging effortful control to regulate the above; emerging use of language to seek contact
3–6 years (pre-school)	Above behaviours and expressions; improving effortful control to regulate the above; improving language to seek contact and communicate interest
7–11 years (pre-adolescence)	Above behaviours and expressions; increasing use of strategies for initiating and engaging contact; continuing development in effortful control

according to what behaviours children can perform in each developmental period. We can see that, even though actual behaviours or expressions are different at different ages, because of increasing control or regulation of the responses, the sets themselves are *coherent with each other* in that they reflect the same underlying temperamental trait.

Context-dependence

So far we have seen that temperament is not just about one or two behaviours acted out at a certain time, but a *general underlying tendency or disposition* (trait) to behave in a particular fashion. It may be expected that temperament should also be consistent across places, events or situations (contexts). Indeed, it should be the case that any trait within the child influences his behaviours over a range of settings, but it is also important not to downplay the significance of objects, people and events in any given social context that can elicit or trigger different *expressions* of the same underlying feature of the child. In fact, it has been suggested (Hinde, 1989) that children will not behave in the same way in different places with different people despite their stability of temperament, but that certain characteristics shown in one setting may be related to other characteristics shown in another. For example, very active children tend to be less friendly with their parents at home than less active children and then in school they actually show more hostility to peers and teachers. In this sense, it is understandable that any given trait does not involve a 'fixed' way of responding or behaving, but a set of behaviours that may be predictably related to certain social contexts (i.e. context-dependence), because they are still underpinned by the same disposition.

Early emergence

It has been highlighted already that temperament has been widely assumed to be something that has a biological basis, or is inherited. One of the strongest indicators of this is its apparent early emergence in infancy. If something is really innate, then one will expect it to be exhibited in some way at an early age as well as to persist over time as mentioned. However, it is actually the case that some inherited characteristics are not displayed until later in development (such as sexual characteristics and mental illnesses that form or become apparent during adolescence). Furthermore, from what you have read already in this book, you should be well aware that a baby engages in interactions with mother or a primary caregiver from day one, and many other interactions soon follow. Unless these early interactions can somehow be eliminated from the picture, we cannot be certain that a temperamental pattern is not at least in part a product of these social inputs rather than being innate. The only thing we can say is that some identifiable patterns that do appear very early in life are probably indicators of temperamental traits.

Studying and measuring temperament

At this point in the chapter, we have a relatively basic, if increasingly abstract, notion of temperament being something that is expressed in 'styles' of behaviour, which are relatively stable and continuous over time and consistent between settings, as they reflect underlying dispositions or tendencies (traits). Since these can influence the child in so many ways and in so many places throughout childhood, how do psychologists actually study such a complex set of behavioural tendencies?

So far we have only considered the specific examples of 'activity' and 'approach'. As we can see from the snippets of the 2-year-olds in the opening examples in this chapter, there are far more dimensions that can be subsumed under this broad umbrella term of 'temperament'. We already know from Chapter 3, 'Research methods, that it is very time consuming (not to say expensive) to conduct research on even one or a few aspects in any area of development. So do temperament researchers cover all or most of these aspects in their investigations or do they tend to focus on one or two? Do they reduce some overall traits into a smaller set of dimensions so that

> **Definitions**
>
> Context-dependence: related sets of behaviour or expressions depending on settings.
> Early emergence: in infancy, product of biology and/or environment since birth.

they concentrate on studying a narrower range of behaviours? Are the dimensions separate from each other or do they overlap as sets of behaviours? For example, the opposite of being 'approachable' could be seen as being 'inhibited', so could two dimensions called 'approach' and 'inhibition' be studied together as two sides of the same coin?

The above questions concern not only methods of investigation, but also the theoretical conceptualisation of temperament: that is, how psychologists decide what the relevant concepts are and what the study of temperament should include. As we will see shortly, since the outset researchers have focused their efforts on different aspects of temperament, since indeed it is a very broad concept, and they have different ways of conceptualising and measuring such dimensions for their work. In short, there is no consensus as such regarding how many dimensions there are that can characterise a child's temperament, due to the lack of a unanimous definition that has been brought forward to conceptualise an overarching concept. And arguably that is not really the goal of such research due to how broad the concept of temperament is. That is not to say that there is no convergence in the researchers' findings (in fact, the opposite may be argued), and certain common ground in study approaches can also be easily identified.

Dimensions of temperament

Although there is no agreement on the precise number of dimensions that cover the complex picture of what temperament is like, generally speaking, many reviews of the literature lead to a fairly clear picture. Many researchers have tended to investigate the aspects of temperament that conform, at least in approximate definition, to one or two of the three categories that John Bates (one of the prominent writers in this area) described back in 1989. These are:

1. *Emotional responses.* These refer to the child's general quality of mood (e.g. is she easy-going or difficult?), her reaction to new or unfamiliar people, objects or events (similar to the idea of 'approach' we considered in the example earlier; a longstanding series of studies has examined this as 'inhibition' – see later in this section), and her tolerance towards internal states and changes in these such as hunger and boredom. Thus other terms for this concept, reflecting both its broadness and researchers' focus, have included reactivity, emotionality (with positive versus negative valence), impulsivity, shyness and sociability and so forth.
2. *Attentional orientation.* This refers to how easily the child is distracted from any ongoing activity she is engaged in, or how easily she gets distressed, and can be comforted when distressed. Alternative terms thus include persistence (but also distractibility), attentional focusing and so on.
3. *Motor activity.* This refers to both the frequency and 'vigour' (or intensity) of the child's activity (similar to the idea of 'activity' we considered earlier) and the child's ability to moderate her activity if required. Thus motor activation, or more commonly activity level with effortful control (see later), have been used to coin such a concept.

These are clearly very broad categories that often contain a few to several dimensions which can be observed, or inferred, from children's behaviours. Some investigators may have also lifted dimensions from within just one or two of the categories, with their findings later reviewed under a theme of its own. For example, as mentioned previously, 'inhibition' by itself has been studied a great deal (see Kagan's work later). Others have conceptualised or measured separately positive and negative emotional responses as 'emotionality' (see Buss and Plomin below), where the positive describes a sociable and easy-going child and the negative pertains to a tendency towards intolerance, irritability and being easily frustrated (see Rothbart's theory later). In addition, as mentioned earlier, as children grow older, they can improve the ability to moderate or manage their responses; some have separately studied this aspect of the child (see Rothbart's effortful control).

So, what work has been done to produce such a large and variable 'list' of dimensions? The following gives an overview of some of the best-known research by a few key theorists, all with the aim of characterising at least one major part of the child's temperament repertoire.

Thomas and Chess's nine dimensions

Few reviews of childhood temperament could omit the pioneering contributions made by two child psychiatrists, Alexander Thomas and Stella Chess. The impetus for their highly influential and one of the best-known longitudinal studies, the New York Longitudinal Study

> **STOP AND THINK**
>
> **Going further**
>
> - With its complexity and the lack of agreement on structure, what do you think should be the optimum number of dimensions that temperament is considered in?
>
> One way to approach this is to consider a related and complex concept – our personality:
>
> - Would you consider your personality in a large or small number of dimensions?
> - What would be the advantages and disadvantages of having many or few dimensions?

(Thomas et al., 1963; Thomas and Chess, 1977), was their regular observations that traced later childhood behavioural difficulties to apparently far earlier appearances in infancy. This led them to ponder on the possibility of some underlying and enduring factors that determine differences between children's behaviour which also have links with pathological outcomes. In the early 1950s, they began longitudinal research, initially on a sample of 141 families, in order to develop a systemic theory to cover a wide range of traits for a wide range of ages (from infancy to adolescence) which could characterise children's temperament. They interviewed parents when the children were only 3 months old and followed up the families into the school years when direct assessments and observations of the children were conducted. The interview data led to an early nine-dimensional framework which has inspired a whole host of further theory developments and studies in this area right up to the present day. The nine dimensions and their brief descriptions can be found in Table 10.2 with those of the other theorists discussed here.

When further data were rated on these dimensions, Thomas and Chess found that certain characteristics clustered together (e.g. children who were higher in approach tended also to have a more positive quality of

Table 10.2 Temperament theories, their dimensions and descriptions.

Theorists	Dimension	Description
Thomas and Chess	Activity level	Ratio of active periods to inactive ones
	Rhythmicity	Regularity of body functions (e.g. sleep, hunger)
	Distractibility	Readiness to be distracted from a task
	Approach/withdrawal	Response to new objects, people and situations
	Adaptability	Ease to adapt to changes in environment
	Persistence	Length of time spent staying on a task
	Intensity of reaction	Energy level in gross motor activity
	Quality of mood	Balance of friendly, joyful behaviour vs reverse
	Threshold of responsiveness	Level of stimulation needed to evoke a response
Buss and Plomin	Emotionality	Tendency to be distressed with fear or anger
	Activity	Tempo, vigour and endurance in behaviour
	Sociability	Tendency to seek and feel gratified by social interaction and responsiveness towards others
Kagan	Behavioural inhibition	Tendency to approach/withdraw from novelties
Rothbart	Positive emotionality/surgency (extraversion)	Tendency to approach new experiences with positive emotions
	Negative affectivity (anxiety)	Tendency to respond to new experiences with fear or withdraw from them or other threat
	Attention span	Duration of orienting or interest
	Self-regulation/effortful control	Ability to regulate attention or behaviour or to soothe oneself

mood), enabling them to derive three types of temperament that characterise the children:

a) 'Easy' children (40% of their sample) are approachable and adaptable, positive in mood, and have regular body functions (rhythmicity) and mild intensity.
b) 'Slow-to-warm-up' children (15% of sample) are likely to withdraw from a new stimulus, but will adapt slowly to it, are negative in mood, and show mild reactions, but relatively regular biological functions.
c) 'Difficult' children (10% of sample) show high withdrawal and do not adapt easily to new experiences, are negative in mood and high in intensity, and have irregular body functions.

The last type has sparked the most interest and controversies, as the children in this group are at higher risk of adjustment problems later in childhood (Thomas et al., 1968). This fits with Thomas and Chess's suspicion that later difficulties have earlier underlying origins. It is worth noticing that 35% of children did not fit into any of the types; they reportedly showed a combination of two or all types' description. Furthermore, later work that attempted to replicate Thomas and Chess's model found problems in confirming those nine dimensions or reliably allocating children into the three types. You might have already noticed from Table 10.2 that, compared to the other theories, this earlier one has a rather large number of dimensions, and a close examination of the description of these dimensions suggests that some are related to each other. For example, a child who shows low 'persistence' is likely to be high in 'distractability'; if we cannot 'persist' well on a task, we are more easily 'distracted'. Indeed, these dimensions are statistically correlated with one another. When there is a large enough overlap between two dimensions, this implies some overall underlying factor (e.g. attention span) and a broader dimension may more appropriately describe them (indeed, severely impaired attention is an important aspect in abnormal development, notably ADHD; see later in this chapter and Chapter 17, Attention Deficit Hyperactivity Disorder).

Mounting evidence shows that the nine dimensions are not empirically distinct, even though the three temperament types have received empirical support through the application of sophisticated statistical techniques (see the review by Shiner et al., 2012). The lack of independence between dimensions is one of the reasons behind later frameworks that were developed with fewer, but broader, dimensions to describe different behavioural tendencies in children. We shall turn to these in the following parts of the chapter.

CASE STUDY

'Difficult' temperament?

Our 7-year-old son is very sensitive and throws many tantrums. He usually starts his day in a bad mood, causing immediate distress in trying to get him off to school. He is doing well in school, where he has an excellent teacher who runs a very structured classroom. But, at home, he makes a fuss about everything that doesn't go his way, spoiling dinner, games and bedtime. He seems to need a lot of attention, yet he often spoils it when we try to give it to him. When he's in a good mood, he is terrific. He's also very caring with a baby sister. But right now we are mostly angry at him. How can we turn things around?

The above description of a boy was written in a Q&A column (April 2015) to a 'resident' psychologist on the website Psych Central, a community of psychologists giving information and advice about mental health, family, parenting and relationship issues. In response, the practitioner (retired Dr Kalman Heller) explains different temperaments and raises the possibility that the child has a 'difficult' temperament, citing Thomas and Chess. He reassures the parent that the difficulties are not caused by 'bad parenting', but parents do play an important role in influencing the course of development (and if they allow the behaviour to 'run the house', it will get worse). Heller also recommends more 'structure', noting the difference it makes in school, through clearer limits and consistent reinforcement to create more 'predictable' environments (e.g. for getting ready for school) and anticipating situations that may be overly stimulating (e.g. holidays or birthdays) to help him prepare and unwind.

- Do you agree with the assessment of a difficult temperament for this boy?
- What about his recommendations for more 'structure'?

It is difficult to ascertain whether the child has a difficult temperament without knowing his history, especially his behavioural style when younger, as this information is an indicator of stability and continuity, which as we have seen are the key qualifiers for temperamental traits. Still, being hard to please, getting into bad moods easily and very intense emotional reactions are also the key traits of 'difficult' children, according to Thomas and Chess. Yet this difficulty seems to be specific to (or be more severe at) home and is perhaps directed at only the parents, since the child is capable of positive behaviour in school and with his sibling. This is not in line with context dependence, as we saw earlier; we could expect an inherently difficult temperament to be apparent across contexts, albeit being expressed differently. Nevertheless, *if* he is a difficult child, planning well-structured and monitored environments and avoiding overstimulation is probably sound as this temperament is also characterised by lowered adaptability to change and heightened withdrawal from novelty. We refer to the potential importance of school structure for the child's behaviour in a later chapter (see Chapter 14, 'Developmental psychology and education').

Source: http://psychcentral.com/lib/qa-coping-with-a-difficult-temperament/00010755

Buss and Plomin's EAS

Well known for their twin and other heredity-related studies, Arnold Buss and Robert Plomin developed a simpler model in 1984 and a related system of measures based on parental ratings (see the next section) to assess temperament, in response to the complexity and methodological issues of the early framework by Thomas and Chess. The model is widely known as the EAS, where E stands for Emotionality, A stands for Activity, and S stands for Sociability (their description can be found in Table 10.2). Buss and Plomin's work assessing the heritability of temperament was driven by a strong influence from adult personality theories with a genetic basis (that personality is inherited through genes). Not unlike Thomas and Chess, they sought to find aspects of temperament that appear early in infancy, since that indicates the likelihood of influence by genes and a foundation for later tendencies as personality traits. Buss and Plomin drew largely from the work of Hans Eysenck (1981), a prominent figure in personality research whose theory has two major dimensions, extraversion and neuroticism, that have been hugely influential in the field.

Extraversion is a measure of sociability and impulsivity, with 'extraverts' at one end of a spectrum depicting highly sociable and impulsive people who like excitement or tend to orient towards external stimulation, and 'introverts' being quiet, introspective people who prefer predictability and orient towards inner states at the other end of the spectrum. Neuroticism refers to the degree of emotional stability or instability, with people high on this trait exhibiting more anxiety or fear and those extremely neurotic displaying obsessive or compulsive behaviour (neurotic behaviour).

Obviously the range of behaviours that would be demonstrated by adult extraverts, introverts or neurotics may not be as easily identified in children, and some require an amount of decision making and control (remember the narrower range of behaviours displayed by very young infants in Table 10.1). However, conceptually it is not difficult to envisage, for example, that a child high in emotionality would become more 'neurotic' later on, or that a very 'sociable' child might grow up to be an 'extravert', when we consider the definitions of those concepts. With this broader approach along with the popularity of Eysenck's theory, Buss and Plomin proposed that their three dimensions can describe most variations in children's temperament and that these will also match later personality variations, as both temperament and personality are underpinned by the same innate origins that we inherit – our genes.

So has there been much support for Buss and Plomin's ambitious theory? It seems that there has. Firstly, by 1984 when they put forward the EAS framework, data from their series of studies on twins at age 4 had already shown good correlations between identical twins. A correlation of 1 means a perfect association between the pair. Their work revealed correlations of 0.63 and 0.62 for Emotionality and Activity respectively, if lower (0.53) for Sociability. Importantly, the figures for non-identical twins were not significant; they did not differ from zero statistically (a correlation of 0 means no association between the two) (Buss and Plomin, 1984). Bearing in mind that only identical twins share 100% of genetic material and non-identical twins are no more similar to each other than non-twin siblings, the result that only identical twins are similar for EAS indicates that, at least on these three dimensions at this age, temperament is likely to be influenced by a strong genetic component.

In addition, later Plomin, his colleague Emde and their collaborators (Emde et al., 1992; Plomin et al., 1993) reported further research on 100 pairs of identical twins and 100 pairs of non-identical twins at 14 and 20 months, also using the EAS measure. Each child's level of inhibition (see Kagan in the next section) was also assessed by independent observers. The correlations on both the EAS measure and inhibition were again consistently higher for identical twins than for non-identical twins, suggesting a strong genetic component in temperament development.

Twin studies aside, another line of work undertaken by Plomin and his team (Plomin et al., 1988) on the heritability of temperament is the Colorado Adoption Project, which followed up adopted children, and both their biological and adoptive parents and siblings, at ages 1 to 4 years. This design enabled the study of the effects of both genes and the environment and their interactions on development, and the longitudinal nature meant that age-to-age correlations could be charted. The correlations between measures of children at different ages as they got older was of particular interest as it is a fair indicator of stability, one of the critical features of temperament we covered earlier. Indeed, Plomin et al. found some promising year-on-year correlations: about 0.60 at ages 1 to 2 for Emotionality and Sociability, rising to near 0.65 at ages 2 to 3 for all of EAS, then the figure for Activity dropped to under 0.60 whereas the other two dimensions remained stable one year on (Plomin et al., 1988). Such findings show that, at least for this age range, children's behaviours at one age are good predictors of those at a later age, suggesting medium-term stability, even though different groups of behaviours show differing degrees of stability.

Buss and Plomin's (1984) three-dimensional model is still in use today, particularly in behavioural genetics studies that examine the degree to which behaviours are genetically and environmentally influenced. For instance, in a recent study by Ganiban et al. (2011), six types of sibling (monozygotic and dizygotic twins, full siblings in intact families, plus full-, half- and unrelated siblings in step-families) totalling over 700 pairs were rated with the EAS to study the contribution of child temperament (versus the environment) to parenting. It found that children's temperament contributes the most to parents' own negativity when the child had high levels of negative emotionality and sociability, which suggests that child-based traits have an enhanced impact on negative parenting when children demonstrate challenging characteristics.

Not only does Buss and Plomin's framework portray children's differences in temperament in a more simplified way, but also their research points to a strong genetic component in differences that tend to stay relatively stable through infancy to pre-school. Whether such differences will hold in the even longer term can

Some infants are said to be more 'positive', 'sociable' or 'easy' than others.

Source: Pearson Education Ltd/Shutterstock

only be answered by other studies following up children for a lengthy period of their development, and only that could support their argument that variations in childhood temperament will map onto later variations in personality. This is a theme that we will cover later in the chapter. Furthermore, one key drawback (as we will see in the section 'Measurements for temperament', page 290) that this approach shares with that of Thomas and Chess is its reliance on parental ratings of children's behavioural tendencies. It is partly in response to this that the next model has taken a very different approach to studying behaviour.

> **STOP AND THINK**
>
> **Reflection**
>
> With our ongoing study of the structure of temperament in terms of its dimensions, we have covered two influential models: Thomas and Chess's and Buss and Plomin's.
>
> - What are the contrasting and common features of these two models?
> - Which do you think is a better model to capture children's behavioural styles?

Kagan's behavioural inhibition

Although he did not intend to provide a framework to cover the entire set of behavioural tendencies that describe a child's temperament, Jerome Kagan has been widely known and acclaimed for his comprehensive approach to studying a specific response set in children called behavioural inhibition. Based on past longitudinal observations captured in his book, *Birth to Maturity* (Kagan and Moss, 1983), he was intrigued by the key discovery that the only psychological quality preserved from the first three years of life through to adulthood was the disposition that was then called 'passivity'. This concerns how a child reacts to novelty: does he approach strange or new objects, people and events quickly and eagerly, or does he withdraw and look fearful, clinging to his mother? For over four decades, Kagan's teams focused their efforts mostly on testing young children with methods that reveal how they react to new situations. Since responses to things already encountered may have been shaped by past experiences, the responses children show when *novel* things are presented can give a better idea of what their 'natural' behaviour is like in a given situation. Unsurprisingly then, like Buss and Plomin, Kagan's approach to inhibition also has its basis firmly grounded in the 'nature' side of the nature–nurture debate on development (see also 'Explanations for differences in temperament', pages 297–304).

In most of Kagan's research, laboratory-based measures of behaviour as well as of physiological functioning were taken. This is quite a departure from the methods used by the two approaches above: namely, parental reports and ratings (the merits and drawbacks of which are reviewed in detail in the section 'Measurements for temperament', page 290). From Kagan's laboratory work, he identified two groups which could be defined by their consistent profiling of behaviours from the second year of life. On one side are children who tend to be timid, cautious and restrained (about 15% of his sample, whom he called 'inhibited') and on the other those who are outgoing and spontaneous (also 15%, called 'uninhibited') or seemingly enjoy the same novel settings (Kagan, 1989). However, Kagan does not view inhibition as a 'spectrum', with inhibited and uninhibited children at the opposite ends (like, say, 'high' vs 'low' emotionality). He believes instead that these two groups refer to qualitatively distinct peoples. In other words, they are fundamentally different types of children, like Thomas and Chess's 'easy', 'difficult' and 'slow-to-warm-up' children. He found that only the responses of those 20% children who were most inhibited or uninhibited at 14 to 20 months reliably predicted their behaviour at 4 years of age. This led Kagan to believe that the two types each share similar kinds of genes (genotype) and a related environmental history, and thus share a similar set of behavioural and associated physiological characteristics that can be measured. Indeed, his physiological

> **Definitions**
>
> **Behavioural inhibition:** a concept Kagan has defined to characterise young children's behaviour in unfamiliar settings, mostly by independent observations, into two qualitatively distinct types: inhibited and uninhibited.
> **Inhibited:** tendency to be timid, cautious or restrained and to withdraw from novelty.
> **Uninhibited:** outgoing and spontaneous, and approaches novelty in the same settings.

measures, taken alongside behavioural responses concurrently, revealed that inhibited children had higher and more stable heart rates, larger pupil dilations, greater motor tension and higher levels of cortisol (a hormone usually secreted in a state of stress). This suggests lower 'thresholds' of reactivity in their limbic system, which is a brain structure known to support functions such as emotion, behaviour and long-term memory (Kagan et al., 1988). How neural systems may affect responses is covered later in 'Explanations for differences in temperament', pages 297–304.

In addition to the strong biological evidence for inhibition, Kagan's follow-up work also shows longer-term stability for this dimension. Figure 10.1 shows the indexes of inhibition for a group of 41 children who had been rated as consistently inhibited at 21 months, drawn from a larger sample based on their responses to unfamiliar objects and people in laboratories. These children were then followed up at 7½ years. The aggregate index at 7½ years was based on behaviour during play with unfamiliar children and was assessed by an examiner who did not know their inhibition status (i.e. blind testing). The correlation between the indexes was indeed significant (at 0.67) and although half of the originally inhibited children no longer displayed an extreme level of shyness at 7½ years, 80% still had not acquired the style of a typical uninhibited child, and 10% became very timid. Three-quarters of these children reportedly had one or more usual fears (e.g. being alone at home, speaking up in class), and a third (versus none in the uninhibited sub-sample) had a sibling who also had such fears, again suggesting a genetic basis for this behavioural profile (Kagan, 1989).

From Kagan's later studies that involved observations at even younger ages and longer-term follow-ups, similar findings were reported. Half of those who were highly inhibited at 4 months (higher levels of crying and motor activity) were still classified as highly inhibited at 8 years, and three-quarters of uninhibited 4-month-olds stayed in that category also at age 8 (Kagan et al., 1993b). The stability of inhibition has recently been reported to continue into individuals' adolescence and even early adulthood (Kagan and Herschkowitz, 2005; Kagan, 2013). Longer-term longitudinal work into wider temperamental traits is covered in detail in the last section of this chapter.

Thus far, we can see that Kagan's very concentrated research efforts on inhibition have yielded findings that show not only a likely biological basis for this function, but also long-term stability across development, mostly based on the direct observations of children's behaviours. Still, as Kagan was always aware, inhibition is only one aspect of the much larger group of temperamental qualities. By focusing on such a specific set of behaviours that infants display in only novel contexts, it is likely that this set does reflect largely innate physiological functioning underpinned by biological variables. Therefore, the question may be: should we accept that our understanding of children's behavioural styles can be reduced to such specific, discrete aspects? What about

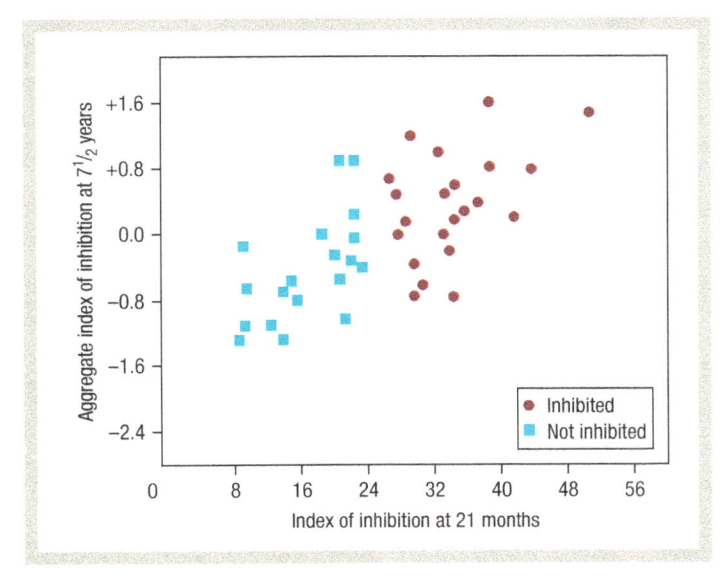

Figure 10.1 Plots of original index of inhibition at 21 months and aggregate index of inhibition at 7½ years.

Source: Kagan (1989)

the other qualities that we are aware of which children display regularly (such as irritability and in/attention)? We shall turn to one more theory that has attempted to be more inclusive in its approach.

Rothbart's additional 'effortful control'

In a recent and still evolving framework, the prolific researcher Mary Rothbart (Rothbart et al., 2000) has adapted elements from the earlier frameworks into newer dimensions (which can be found in Table 10.2). For example, we have discussed the fact that Thomas and Chess's related dimensions 'distractibility' and 'persistence' might be subsumed under one overall dimension of 'attention span' (though, in her later version, this concept was dissolved; Rothbart et al., 2001). Meanwhile, emotional responses have been split into 'positive' and 'negative' types, with the two relating to Kagan's 'uninhibited' and 'inhibited' types respectively, although for Rothbart *emotion* is emphasised rather than behaviour. Finally, Rothbart's model contains a dimension not previously emphasised by the other theorists whose work we have been reading – effortful control, or self-regulation. According to Rothbart, we do not simply differ in how we respond to situations, but also in how we can regulate or manage the responses. Hence a crucial feature of this dimension as distinct from others is that it involves *voluntary* ('effortful') suppression of responses so that other, more appropriate responses can be enacted (Rothbart and Bates, 1998).

Not surprisingly, then, the additional dimension of effortful control has received more interest than others, not least because of its implication that some self-consciousness is needed. This is interesting because, previously, we surmised that temperament is about some relatively 'basic' behaviours or emotions, almost with the assumption that they are 'natural' responses in infants without much conscious awareness. Nevertheless, research has found that despite its definition, effortful control is a relatively reliable trait that may also have a physiological basis. The precise testing procedure will be described in the next section, but it is important to note that children's performance on this measure is related to other indicators of effortful control, such as parental ratings of impulse control or coping with frustration (Rothbart et al., 2003). In fMRI research with adults (Botvinick et al., 2001), the tasks testing effortful control activate their frontal lobes, which are areas of the brain involved in executive functioning or resolving conflicting tendencies between different parts of the brain. Therefore it is possible that effortful control requires the child to reconcile competing tendencies: for example, delaying gratification from a treat for a greater reward or ignoring a distracter while trying to stay focused on a task. Mastering such control early in life may help the child to develop a vital executive function.

With regards to other dimensions on Rothbart's list, various studies have revealed that young children who score low or high on both positive and negative emotionality, attention span and effortful control tend to score similarly when they are reassessed several months to a few years on, even into adulthood (Ruff and Rothbart, 1996; Rothbart et al., 2000), but the stability (assessed by age-to-age correlations) is low to moderate (0.6 or below; Putnam et al., 2000). Still, through her vigorous questionnaire-, laboratory- (see below), observation-based research, Rothbart has enabled a detailed examination of temperament's structure (Shiner et al., 2012).

Being a relatively recently developed list of dimensions, Rothbart's theory offers a close resolution between the different frameworks that came before, and children differing on these dimensions (even on voluntary effortful control) tend also to show later differences (Rothbart, 2004). The significant contribution lies in its integrated biological and environmental approach to temperament (Rothbart, 2011; see also 'Explanations for differences in temperament', pages 297–304).

Measurements for temperament

We have just reviewed four approaches to the study of temperament which differ to varying degrees in terms of how they conceptualise temperament (the extent to which it is determined by genes), the number of dimensions

> **Definition**
>
> Effortful control: a concept Rothbart identified to characterise how people voluntarily suppress certain responses in order to substitute with other, usually more appropriate, ones as a process that is likely to be mediated by the system of frontal lobes known to be involved in resolving conflicting tendencies between different parts of the brain.

proposed, what kinds of response and behaviour define them and whether they run along a spectrum or denote qualitatively distinct types of children. Closely related to these approaches, researchers' methods of studying the behaviours of children that make up temperament have also differed in terms of time, resources, suitability of the method (for the dimensions defined) and reliability and validity (see Chapter 3, 'Research methods'). We will examine the most commonly used methods and evaluate their 'pros and cons' below.

Parental reports and ratings

Temperament has been, until relatively recently, most frequently assessed through standardised ('checklist') interviews with or questionnaires given to parents. For instance, we have seen that Thomas and Chess, the pioneering systematic investigators, initially interviewed parents of the sample of children when they were very young. Parents may also make 24-hour diary-type recordings of their infant's behaviours. Such a 'labour-intensive' form of reporting requires extensive exposure to the child, but can account for temporary fluctuations, such as sickness or stress, and obviously the parents would be the best candidates to notice such things. With recent advances in technology, the use of video-recordings in the home setting is also possible, which is not only convenient, but also allows others (such as researchers) to observe and rate the same behaviour. This relates to the method of third-party independent observations, and you will read about research where investigators either observe children live or chart their recorded behaviour in the home environment in the next section.

As research in the field of temperament evolved, 'checklists' of children's behaviours became available from previous research. There is now a very wide range of questionnaires that researchers can use, and more are continuing to be devised and adapted for the same purpose of measuring children's behavioural styles in a standardised format. Buss and Plomin, whose work we considered above, devised one of the most popular instruments, which they used to measure the EAS dimensions in a survey by parents' ratings for children under the age of 5 years (see Table 10.3). A more comprehensive range of behaviours is often measured by one of the 'Carey Questionnaires' (William Carey is a paediatrician who works with parents supporting different temperaments and writes widely about the area, such as his book *Understanding Your Child's Temperament*, 2005). Table 10.4 shows ten items from the original 97-item form (Fullard et al., 1978, 1984) for 1- to 3-year-olds, called the 'Toddler Temperament Scale' (TTS). The full measure has been frequently used for early childhood behaviour in large-scale projects (such as the Longitudinal Study of Australian Children, LSAC; Soloff et al., 2005), and short versions with a reduced number of items are also available (e.g. Lewis and Olsson, 2011).

Increasingly, since Rothbart's landmark proposal of and continuous work on effortful control as part of temperament's behavioural repertoire, the measurement she devised, the Child Behavior Questionnaire (CBQ; Rothbart et al., 1994; revised by Rothbart et al., 2001), has gained a great deal of currency, being deployed in much research since the 2000s (see below). The highly extensive multiscale form is designed for 3- to 7-year-olds and contains no fewer than 195 items in its original version across 15 scales or subsections from Activity Level, Approach and Attention to Sadness, Shyness and Smiling/Laughter. Reduced versions (short and 'very short' forms; Putnam and Rothbart, 2006) have also been developed and widely used. Table 10.5 presents a specimen of the items from the CBQ.

> **STOP AND THINK**
>
> **Going further**
>
> Concerning the EAS, TTS, and CBQ in Tables 10.3, 10.4 and 10.5:
>
> - Which one do you prefer?
> - Are there items or aspects you find to be problematic?
> - What do you think are the strengths and weakness of such questionnaires?

It is quite clear that either the items themselves or the entire scale, or both, are defined better in some checklists than others. For instance, some behaviours in the relatively generic EAS may be more or less 'typical' in the same child depending on the time and place, whereas the TTS presents a greater variety of contexts. The CBQ presents various scales, each pertaining to a subsidiary behaviour with both contextualised and generic items. Although these checklists

Table 10.3 The EAS survey for parental ratings by Buss and Plomin (1984).

Please circle the rating on each of the items for your child.

	Not typical				Very typical
1 Child tends to be shy	1	2	3	4	5
2 Child cries easily	1	2	3	4	5
3 Child likes to be with people	1	2	3	4	5
4 Child is always on the go	1	2	3	4	5
5 Child prefers playing with others rather than alone	1	2	3	4	5
6 Child tends to be somewhat emotional	1	2	3	4	5
7 When child moves about, he usually moves slowly	1	2	3	4	5
8 Child makes friends easily	1	2	3	4	5
9 Child is off and running as soon as he wakes up	1	2	3	4	5
10 Child finds people more stimulating than anything else	1	2	3	4	5
11 Child often fusses and cries	1	2	3	4	5
12 Child is very sociable	1	2	3	4	5
13 Child is very energetic	1	2	3	4	5
14 Child takes a long time to warm up to strangers	1	2	3	4	5
15 Child gets upset easily	1	2	3	4	5
16 Child is something of a loner	1	2	3	4	5
17 Child prefers quiet, inactive games to more active ones	1	2	3	4	5
18 When alone, child feels isolated	1	2	3	4	5
19 Child reacts intensely when upset	1	2	3	4	5
20 Child is very friendly with strangers	1	2	3	4	5

Table 10.4 Extracted items (97 in complete form) from the Toddler Temperament Scale by Fullard et al. (1978).

Using the scale shown below, please circle the figure that tells how often the child's recent and current behaviour has been like the behaviour described by each item.

	Almost never	Rarely	Usually does not	Usually does	Frequently	Almost always
1 The child gets to sleep at about the same time each evening (within ½ hour)	1	2	3	4	5	6
2 The child fidgets during quiet activities (storytelling, looking at pictures)	1	2	3	4	5	6
3 The child takes feedings quietly with mild expression of likes and dislikes	1	2	3	4	5	6
4 The child is pleasant (smiles, laughs) when first arriving in unfamiliar places	1	2	3	4	5	6
5 The child's initial reaction to seeing the doctor is acceptance	1	2	3	4	5	6
6 The child pays attention to game with parent for only a minute or so	1	2	3	4	5	6
7 The child's bowel movements come at different times from day to day	1	2	3	4	5	6
8 The child is fussy on waking up (frowns, complains, cries)	1	2	3	4	5	6
9 The child's initial reaction to a new babysitter is rejection (crying, clingy, etc.)	1	2	3	4	5	6
10 The child reacts to a disliked food even if it is mixed with a preferred one	1	2	3	4	5	6

Table 10.5 Specimen items (one from each scale; 195 in complete form) from the Child Behavior Questionnaire by Rothbart et al. (2001).

Parents to rate according to the trueness of each item in describing their child.

	Extremely untrue of your child						Extremely true of your child
Activity level Gross motor activity, including rate and extent of locomotion.							
Seems always in a big hurry to get from one place to another.	1	2	3	4	5	6	7
Anger/frustration Negative affectivity related to interruption of ongoing tasks or goal blocking.							
Has temper tantrums when s(he) doesn't get what s(he) wants.	1	2	3	4	5	6	7
Attentional focusing Capacity to maintain attentional focus on task-related channels.							
When picking up toys or other jobs, usually keeps at the task until it's done.	1	2	3	4	5	6	7
Discomfort Negative affectivity related to sensory qualities of stimulation, including intensity; rate; or complexities of light, movement, sound, and texture.							
Is not very bothered by pain.	1	2	3	4	5	6	7
Fear Negative affectivity, including unease, worry, or nervousness, which is related to anticipated pain or distress and/or potentially threatening situations.							
Is not afraid of large dogs and/or other animals.	1	2	3	4	5	6	7
High intensity pleasure Pleasure or enjoyment related to situations involving high stimulus intensity, rate, complexity, novelty, and incongruity.							
Likes going down high slides or other adventurous activities.	1	2	3	4	5	6	7
Impulsivity Speed of response initiation.							
Usually rushes into an activity without thinking about it.	1	2	3	4	5	6	7
Inhibitory control Capacity to plan and to suppress inappropriate approach responses under instructions or in novel or uncertain situations.							
Can lower his/her voice when asked to do so.	1	2	3	4	5	6	7
Low intensity pleasure. Pleasure or enjoyment related to situations involving low stimulus intensity rate, complexity, novelty, and incongruity.							
Rarely enjoys just being talked to.	1	2	3	4	5	6	7
Perceptual sensitivity Detection of slight, low-intensity stimuli from the external environment.							
Notices the smoothness or roughness of objects s(he) touches.	1	2	3	4	5	6	7
Positive anticipation Amount of excitement and anticipation for expected pleasurable activities.							
Gets so worked up before an exciting event that s(he) has trouble sitting still.	1	2	3	4	5	6	7
Sadness Negative affectivity and lowered mood and energy related to exposure to suffering, disappointment, and object loss.							
Cries sadly when a favourite toy gets lost or broken.	1	2	3	4	5	6	7
Shyness (versus social approach). Slow or inhibited (versus rapid) speed of approach and discomfort (versus comfort) in social situations.							
Often prefers to watch rather than join other children playing.	1	2	3	4	5	6	7
Smiling/laughter Positive affect in response to changes in stimulus intensity, rate, complexity, and incongruity.							
Laughs a lot at jokes and silly happenings.	1	2	3	4	5	6	7
Soothability (and falling reactivity) Rate of recovery from peak distress, excitement, or general arousal.							
Has a hard time settling down for a nap.	1	2	3	4	5	6	7

are convenient, there is the danger that parents distort their ratings due to misinterpretation of items or social desirability, whilst reports, diaries or interviews give parents the opportunity to substantiate or clarify behaviours, or to respond to questions and justify answers (in the case of interviews). This is not to overlook the fact that for both forms of measure, even though parents can take advantage of their knowledge of their child across many contexts, taking data from parents (particularly from parents alone) has been criticised as having major drawbacks.

There is a danger that relying on parents as observers, recorders *and* raters is unreliable due to various kinds of bias. First, parents' expectations about their child's behaviour rather than their actual behaviour may be reported. For instance, their perceptions of infant emotionality at 4 and 8 months have been found to predict further independent measures of emotionality at 8 and 12 months, respectively (Pauli-Pott et al., 2003). This suggests that this measure can be shaped by parents' perceptions. In fact, parental perceptions before the birth of their child can affect their later ratings of the child's temperament. Mothers' personality measured pre-birth has been found to predict their ratings of the babies' temperament (Vaughn et al., 1987), and anxious or depressed mothers tend to rate their babies as more difficult (Mebert, 1991). Recent research has found that, even when observing laboratory measures, mothers' own traits (those with more negative emotionality rated their child's negative traits higher) influence the extent to which they successfully encode analogous behaviours (Hayden et al., 2010).

Therefore, variation in parents' characteristics, perceptions and expectations can be a source of variation in their reports or ratings of that child's future temperament. Any stability in ratings of a child's temperament may in fact indicate the stability of his/her parental attributions. However, as you will read in the next section, no matter how biased they are, it has been argued that parents' personalities and attributions should form part of the equation that explains their child's behaviour. On the whole, the agreement (correlation) between parents' ratings and direct observations, which varied greatly in the past (between 0.28 and 0.69, depending on the dimension; Hagekull et al., 1984), has shown more moderate associations, with the same behaviours being observed by parents and researchers (e.g., Hayden et al., 2010; Mangelsdorf et al., 2000).

Parents may make more biased raters of their own children's temperament.
Source: Pearson Education Ltd/Brand X Pictures

Even nowadays, much research, and not only on temperament, still makes use of parental reporting (see Chapter 9 on attachment, for instance), though many researchers also use other forms of measurement to monitor reliability and validity, and reduce bias. Are these other forms really more objective? We will look at two more forms of measurement to explore this issue.

Independent observations

Earlier we read about Kagan's work in the laboratory, observing children's reactions to novel, unfamiliar situations, leading to the classification of two groups: inhibited versus uninhibited children. What sorts of things actually 'happen' in the laboratory? If physiological measures are taken, what equipment is 'attached' to the infants? What combination of responses or scores leads a child to be classed as 'inhibited' or 'uninhibited'?

In the Research Methods box, this kind of research procedure is documented. Meanwhile, not only Kagan but an increasing, if still limited, number of researchers since the 2000s have used laboratory or other out-of-home settings with independent raters (sometimes with parents as extra observers; e.g. Lo et al., 2014). Despite the 'unnatural' context, parents for the most part view their child's responses in such tasks as typical representations of his/her behaviour in other settings, even though the consistency tends to be higher for positive traits, probably reflecting social desirability concerns. Nevertheless, the use of such ratings is recommended as at least complementary to parental reports, even if this requires significant resources (only about 5% of child temperament is assessed by this method; reviewed by Lo et al., 2014). There are other forms of independent assessments that are relatively less 'labour intensive'. We will now consider one of these: how Rothbart investigates her construct of effortful control.

Experiment on effortful control: a spatial-conflict task (Rothbart et al., 2003)

Rothbart's team has found that what she identifies as effortful control can be tested as early as 2½ to 3 years of age. Her spatial-conflict task designed for infants is similar to, if less demanding than, those designed for adults. The task involves the child watching a computer screen showing two identical objects (say, two houses), one on the right and one on the left, each containing a figure that is meaningful to the object (say, a cartoon character) where the two figures look different from each other. During the task, a picture of a character identical to one of those inside a house appears – sometimes above the relevant house (a spatially compatible trial), sometimes above the house that contains the different character (a spatially incompatible trial). The child is asked to 'help' the appearing character to find his/her 'home' by touching the relevant character's house. Normally, in incompatible trials, the participant has an automatic impulse to reach for the same side of the screen as the appearing stimulus's picture. To execute the correct response the child participant has to suppress this impulse and replace it by reaching for the opposite side to the stimulus. The two types of trial are shown in Figure 10.2. It may seem like a really easy task – indeed, pre-schoolers do find it relatively easy – but this is not so for younger children. Marked improvements in performance tend to occur in the third year of life, leading investigators to concur with Rothbart that the basic functioning needed for this task denotes the early development of the neural system for this kind of executive function or 'effortful control' (Botvinick et al., 2001).

We can see from the example given (in Figure 10.2) of the spatial-conflict task that a relatively simple procedure administered by computers can measure performance, reflecting the amount of control younger children can garner to simultaneously suppress and enact different responses. An advantage of this general

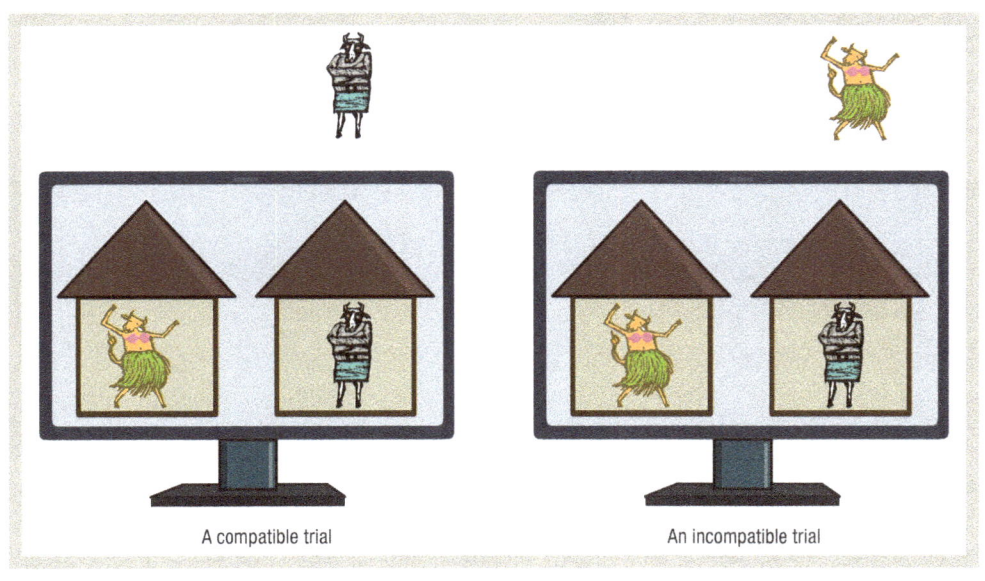

Figure 10.2
Example of stimulus used in spatial conflict task.
Source: Rothbart et al. (2003)

RESEARCH METHODS

Independent behavioural observations with objective physiological measures: Kagan

For a long time, Kagan has been conducting observational research on inhibition with babies as young as 4 months of age and toddlers of about 2 years (the most recent in Fox et al. (2015), where high levels of motor activity and distress at unfamiliar events at 4 months predicted inhibited behaviour at 14 months across three independent samples). In Kagan's laboratories, these children are exposed to a range of unfamiliar experiences and their behavioural and physiological responses are taken. Considering the young ages of these children, the experiences may include presenting them with new sights or sounds (e.g. colourful novel toys or moving mobiles for very young babies; popping a balloon, or meeting a stranger, animal or robot for the first time, for older infants). It is also possible to alter the appearance or behaviour of otherwise 'normal' objects or people in atypical ways, such as dressing them up in novel costumes. Electrodes are placed on the children's bodies and blood pressure cuffs on their arms to gauge heart rate and cardiovascular function (consideration is given to the fact that this procedure itself is also novel, and possibly stressful, at least at first). Saliva samples before and after the encounters may be taken as well as skin surface temperature for cortisol secretion and temperature changes.

In terms of behavioural indicators, observers are trained to look for any tensing of muscles, any movement of arms or legs with agitation, and any relevant vocalisation along with these (implying high reactivity/an inhibited child) instead of a relaxed posture, or even smiling and cooing with apparent pleasure (low reactivity/uninhibited) for smaller babies. During infancy, with increased muscle control and mobility, behaviours upon the presentation of novelty such as quick withdrawal, possibly with visible or audible reactions like grimacing or whimpering (inhibited), versus approaching or orienting with interest and even laughter (uninhibited), are noted.

As children enter pre-school ages, with their emerging linguistic ability, measures such as amounts of talking or smiling (versus quiet periods) during an interview with an unfamiliar adult or spontaneous play with an unfamiliar peer (versus staying back and watching) may be taken. For most sessions in most age groups, video-recordings are taken. Then more than one observer can gauge the same behaviours and responses, and any agreement (or disagreement) between the independent observations can be calculated statistically (called *inter-rater reliability*) or resolved. Parents can, of course, view and rate such responses as typical or atypical of their child's behaviour outside.

For longitudinal follow-ups, researchers like Kagan want to find out whether the 30% of babies who are classified in the extreme groups (those who are easily stressed and upset and those who are very comfortable or even delighted with the new experiences) become fearful, inhibited or outgoing, uninhibited children and youngsters (Kagan, 1998, 2003). Of course, with age we can also self-evaluate and self-report this aspect of our personality: whether we are reserved and shy, or sociable and confident people (as can be seen in the longitudinal research documented later in this chapter).

- How do you compare Kagan's assessments of inhibition with other methods of measuring you have learnt about?
- What do you see are the key strengths and limitations of his approach?

---

procedure is the fact that the child is not being presented live with any potential perceived threat (like unfamiliar situations), and with widespread accessibility to technology nowadays, many nursery-age children already have encounters with tasks and games in this medium.

It is possible then that (and this concerns performance-based tasks in general) performance can improve across trials (a 'practice' effect), and tests may favour children more familiar with computerised tasks. Furthermore, what is actually measured is indeed performance on something that is purported to need a certain functioning, rather than behaviours reported or observed. This is also a conceptual issue, however; as we have already discussed, temperament is a larger set of behaviours and therefore, despite the reliability and validity of the method of measurement, effortful control is still just one aspect of temperament.

In any case it is clear that parental reports, independent observation and experimentation 'tap' into different aspects (even if with certain overlapping), and thus use different assessment criteria, of child behaviour. Also, the former requires parents to provide their perceptions about their child in relation to many predefined characteristics, whereas in the latter observers are asked to focus on specific behaviours (either live or video-recorded) or children are asked to perform a specific function. We have already reviewed the issues in relying solely on parental reports for studying temperament. The use of observation or experimentation, particularly as the sole basis for studying this broad concept, is far from being justified since the validity of some such measures is inconclusive, even though spatial-conflict task performance correlates with some parental reports of effortful control (Rothbart et al., 2003). With advances in technology, testing and analysis, the ability to measure the correlates of individual differences in various aspects of temperament by questionnaire, observation and laboratory tasks should provide a stronger basis for further understanding (Rothbart et al., 2011).

Explanations for differences in temperament

The two sections above have essentially given an overview of the 'what' and 'how' of child temperament: first, what criteria behavioural styles have to satisfy to be seen as 'temperament', and what its likely structure is in terms of dimensions of behaviour; and secondly, how children may manifest such dispositions as temperamental traits, and how we may measure them. In this section, we will explore the 'why' of temperament: why is there such a range of behavioural styles among children? We will consider what may cause such differences and explore whether they are to do with what the child is born with and the influences she encounters before birth, or what she experiences afterwards. The nature–nurture debate is continued throughout this book. With regards to temperament, the debate is as complex as elsewhere, if not more so, not only because of the complexity of temperament itself, but also because of its increasingly complex manifestations with age.

STOP AND THINK

Reflection

Remind yourself of the cases described in the opening of the chapter. You noted earlier that the two boys do have differences and maybe similarities in behavioural style. We also gave you a little of their parents' and home background and in the last section we learnt that parents' perceptions may influence their children's behaviour.

- Do you think some of the behaviours shown by Sebastian and Luke are what they were born with?
- Which do you think are most likely to be a product of their genes?
- Are there behaviours that you think more likely to have been a consequence of their experiences?
- What might be the role of their parents' or siblings' responses to them and perceptions of them?
- What about the larger family structure and circumstances as a whole?

Genes and the biological

At the beginning of this chapter, we already stated that temperament is generally thought to have a genetic foundation and to be underpinned by inherited biology. Then at various points in the previous section, evidence supporting this was presented. Indeed, one of the clearest commonalities across the four theoretical approaches to temperament is (if not stated as part of the theory explicitly) the idea that some basic innate qualities will show very early on in life. We also read that: (1) these qualities are more similar between people who are related to each other closely by genes (twins, siblings) and (2) the physiological functioning during some responses is executed by certain parts of the brain (e.g. inhibition). We will look closely at the evidence for these main explanations that point to 'nature' as the key to differences in temperament between children. We will also examine some of the questions and limitations associated with these explanations.

Temperament's heredity

From Buss and Plomin's twins research in the previous section, we saw that identical twins are more alike in their temperament than non-identical twins, who in turn are no more alike than non-twin siblings. Similar findings have also been reported by more recent research (Ganiban et al., 2011; Goldsmiths et al., 1999; Stilberg et al., 2005). The work to date has been conducted by using both reporting by parents (who are likely to assume and predict behavioural similarities between their children and to treat them similarly; see also the section 'The environment', page 301), and independent observation. It is also possible to employ separate observers (who do not know that they are rating a twin) to observe twins along physiological measures. The convergence between these different types of research findings indicates a strong genetic foundation for temperament.

We also saw from Plomin's adoption research and Kagan's longitudinal research that some dimensions of temperament and inhibition are stable over infancy into older childhood, and even adolescence and adulthood. This implies an influence by heredity, since it would be very unlikely that anything else but genes would remain stable for such a long time. Since then, with increasing interest and resources, more longitudinal work has been possible. For example, the Australian Temperament Project (ATP), arguably the first of such large-scale studies, aimed to examine the relationship between child temperament and development into adolescence, particularly the risk of behavioural problems (Pedlow et al., 1993; Prior et al., 2000). The children of 2443 families recruited in the 1980s were assessed on an extensive range of measures similar to the CBQ (such as emotional, attentional and behavioural tests, reactivity and self-regulation). In the original cohort of 450 children, mothers' reports of rhythmicity, irritability, inflexibility and persistence (similar to Thomas and Chess's) along measures of cooperation/manageability and the tendency to approach/avoid contact (similar to Kagan's inhibition) were moderately stable from infancy to age 8 (Pedlow et al., 1993). It was also found that difficult temperament types predicted longer-term social behaviour and adjustment, such as anxiety in adolescence (Letcher et al., 2012). The Longitudinal Study of Australian Children (LSAC) 20 years on using similar measures found that the later cohort was no different on the incidences of behavioural problems, if they were slightly more easy-going and sociable and less anxious than the ATP cohort (Smart and Sanson, 2008). Similarly, their temperament type (reactive, avoidant and impulsive) predicted later anxiety and depressive symptoms (Lewis and Olsson, 2011).

More and longer-term large-scale longitudinal research will be reviewed later in this chapter. On the whole, though, there is now stronger and still growing evidence of consistency between early temperament and later behaviour over long periods of development, supporting the idea that genes are at least part of the explanation for temperament.

Biological make-up and neurological processes

We have reviewed the role of genes as part of the 'why' for children's temperament differences, but for 'how' this component can bring about differences as we observe behaviour, researchers have taken steps to study certain functioning systems underpinned by our biological make-up. For example, we already considered in some detail Kagan's research into children's inhibition, involving measuring their physiological functions. The pattern of findings shown by inhibited children led to a suggestion that the limbic system is relevant for their threshold of reactivity to novelty. In particular, Kagan's later studies (1998, 2003) revealed that individual differences in arousal in the organ *amygdala* (an inner brain structure that executes avoidance reactions; see Figure 10.3) contribute to children's differences in inhibition. In an inhibited child, novel stimuli excite the amygdala and its connections to the cortex (surface of the brain) and the rest of the nervous system very readily, which prepares the body to respond to stimuli perceived as threats. In an uninhibited child, the excitation level is expected to be much less extreme.

There is also longitudinal neurological evidence supporting Kagan's argument. In an article published in the prestigious journal *Science* in 2003, a study led by Kagan's colleague Carl Schwartz, in collaboration with Kagan and others (Schwartz et al., 2003), reported fMRI data from adults who had been categorised as inhibited

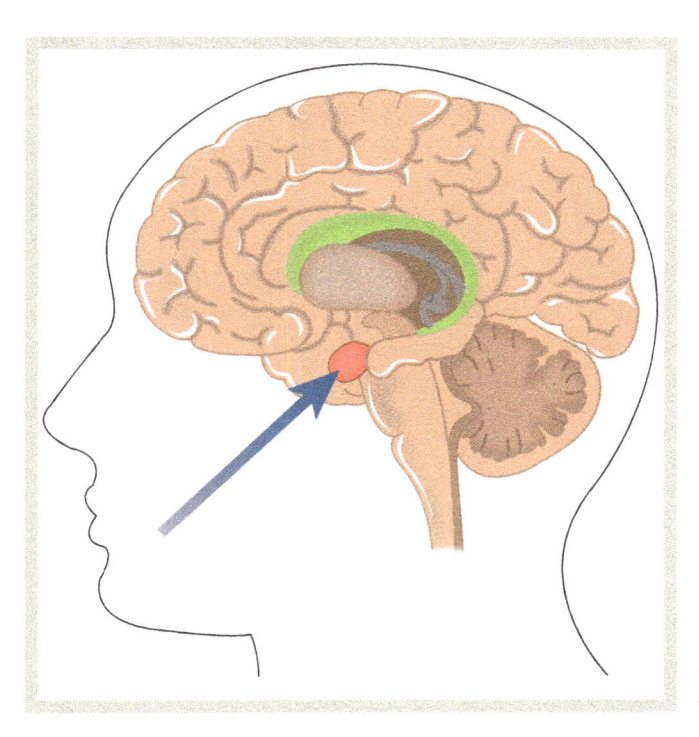

Figure 10.3 Location of the amygdala in the brain.

or uninhibited in their second year of life. It showed the inhibited toddlers, now as adults, had greater activity in the amygdala than did adults who had been former uninhibited toddlers. Furthermore, these two groups of adults were distinguishable by their patterns of physiological measures of the kind that we read about earlier (such as heart rate, cortisol level, pupil dilation and blood pressure). These findings are strong evidence for the stability of such temperament types with neurological data.

Since the amygdala is connected to the cerebral cortex, neural activity transmitted to other cortical regions has also been charted along behavioural and physiological measures. One region comprises the frontal lobes in the cortex, where shy/inhibited toddlers and pre-schoolers exhibit greater EEG activity in the right lobe versus the left lobe (Kagan and Herschkowitz, 2005), which has been linked with negative emotionality (Calkins et al. 1996). Those children categorised behaviourally as sociable and uninhibited show the opposite pattern (greater activity in the left frontal lobe). (In general, most individuals (neither uninhibited nor inhibited) exhibit similar activity across the two sides.) A pattern of greater activity in the left has predicted faster extinction of fear learning and an increased ability to down-regulate negative emotions or avoid attention to images conveying social threat, where the chronic activation of such a 'brain–body' withdrawal system is seen to be energy consuming, with the continued stress probably resulting in temperamental shyness (reviewed by Miskovic and Schmidt, 2012). Furthermore, shy/unsociable pre-schoolers tend to show greater general activation in the cerebral cortex (Henderson et al., 2001, 2004), a function indicating higher arousal in the face of any perceived threat.

STOP AND THINK

Going further

You have just read about more research into the heredity and biological basis of differences in children's behavioural patterns.

- What are the strengths of this volume of research?
- Do you think there is room for other (non-genetic or biological) factors?
- To what extent are you convinced that temperament is inherited and our behaviour is mediated by our biological make-up?

Further biological support comes from the studies of gene-controlled neurotransmitters. Higher levels of dopamine and serotonin, which are known to regulate responses to unfamiliar or new information, are found in inhibited children (Lakatos et al., 2003) as well as adolescents and adults (reviewed by Helfinstein et al., 2012). This reinforces the position that at least inhibition is related to overstimulation of genetically inherited biological systems, which result in associated physiology and observed behaviour.

Potential for change

The heritability and neurological evidence above, particularly from longitudinal work, is indeed very persuasive, not least with modern sophisticated physiological measures and neuroimaging technology charting patterns of 'internal' processes or functioning concurrent with children's and adults' behavioural responses. Thus it appears that at least some aspects of temperament, most notably reactivity towards novelty, or inhibition, are mediated by biology as underpinned by our genes. However, there are still a few uncertainties which are harder to resolve. The first concerns the issue of 'cause-and-effect'. It is impossible to ascertain whether even the clear neurological differences (particularly when measured in later childhood or adulthood) really 'cause' the behaviour observed or are a result of those habitual responses. This is particularly important in the face of the second issue, which is the evidence that temperament changes over time. Indeed, inhibition statuses, along with physiological patterns, have been found to change over the first four years of life (Fox et al., 2001). If our genes give us our biological make-up, which in turn controls our physiological and behavioural responses, then any observed changes imply that our biology is not stable. So, is it possible that our behaviour (especially early in life) can shape our biological make-up (i.e. apart from our genes)?

The key to understanding this seems to be that both temperament and 'biology' develop with age; it has been shown that temperament is most stable between 24 and 48 months, which also marks the turning point from which long-term predictions based on temperament are more reliable (Lemery et al., 1999). Intriguingly, it seems that there may be a 'window' for best stability, one possible reason being that certain features (and the relevant biological systems) are undeveloped or underdeveloped until this age. Consider effortful control, which improves between 2½ and 3 years and increases in stability thereafter, where the relevant brain sites (frontal lobes) have been identified in adults (Rothbart et al., 2003). Therefore, certain systems will only start to form and develop during infancy and go on to affect other systems (such as regulating emotionality). In fact, even heritability is relatively low in the neonatal versus infancy period, and the brain is quite 'plastic' (malleable) and biological systems can modify with experience, so that the 'starting point' of temperament may provide a 'reaction range' for further biological and behavioural outcomes (see Nigg, 2006a).

Kagan himself acknowledges that there is potential for change in temperament. There are always a small proportion of uninhibited children who acquire a more reserved demeanour because of intervening stressful experiences (Kagan, 1991). Similarly, certain highly inhibited children do not become consistently fearful later. Kagan used the case of a 'very inhibited' boy who, through conscious efforts, 'overcame' his inhibition as an example and emphasised that a child does not have to be a 'victim' of his biology. Moreover, change seems to be especially tied to mothering, with mothers who are not over-protective or demanding helping children become less reactive (Kagan et al., 1993a) – we will cover maternal factors in detail shortly. Thus even though our basic inherited tendencies will set in motion some directions and limits, change in behavioural outcomes is possible through effort and experience. This led Kagan to write that any predisposition inherited by genes is 'far from being a life sentence' (1999, p. 32).

The environment and parenting

In the above part, we were reflecting that despite evidence aplenty supporting the role of genes and biology in temperament, these should not be taken as definitively determining behavioural outcomes; experience too, can exert an impact, and thus change is possible. So what can provide the child with this kind of 'experience'? In this section we will explore two main non-genetic or non-biological mechanisms that can influence children's behavioural patterns directly as well as interacting with genetic and biological influences to produce behavioural differences in children.

The environment

The environment can include a great many things: the satisfaction (or otherwise) of the child's basic needs through nutrition or deprivation, which can seriously affect temperament (Wachs and Bates, 2001); the shared and non-shared environment between siblings; and many cultural factors. We will look at the latter two first, since a lot of the research on the shared environment concerns maternal variables and these will be covered later.

We have seen evidence of how parents' perceptions and expectations of children even before birth, and their own characteristics, can predict their children's behaviour. If we go one step further: our personality, mental state, perceptions and expectations all influence the way we behave towards others, and this certainly applies in the family environment. We commented in the introduction that parents often compare their children to each other. In the case of siblings, parents see them as more dissimilar than other observers do, and this in turn may influence their parenting. In particular, in the case of twins, parents may actually emphasise or encourage their unique features (if they still see them as more similar than they would see non-twins). There is evidence that mothers treat identical twins differently, and these differences further predict the twins' later behavioural adjustments (Deater-Deckard et al., 2001). Children themselves also respond to the differential treatment. Outside of the home, siblings try to distinguish themselves from each other, and this seems to be the case also for twins. In fact there has been evidence that temperament differences between twins increase with age (McCartney et al., 1990), even though it is impossible to ignore the significant amount of research, some of which we have read in this chapter, documenting similarities in temperament between twins.

Perhaps, if we are to examine how any development is fostered in the environment as opposed to being imbued as the inborn disposition, wider variables including culturally specific concepts of temperament and treatment of children should be explored. The Nature–Nurture box describes selected research on ethnic and gender variations in temperament. These findings and debates are useful for illustrating how what may appear to be innate, due to its early emergence, can still be at least partly fostered by parents and supported by a larger cultural system of norms, values and beliefs.

Maternal variables

We have just considered how the wider culture can influence the way we as parents and peers perceive and behave differently towards different children based on their group membership, and before that, how parents perceive and treat their individual children differently. Since the socialisation of children tends to begin at home, parental factors should feature prominently as external inputs to the child's behaviour. Here, we will examine how in particular the mother's characteristics and perceptions may influence her child's emerging temperament.

NATURE–NURTURE

Ethnic and gender differences in temperament

Some researchers have investigated whether children from different ethnic groups or the two sexes can have different temperaments. The key questions are: are differences due to ethnicity or sex? Are they because parenting differs between groups? Are there wider cultural differences that affect the behaviour of children (like some behaviours being encouraged or discouraged more than others in one sex or an ethnic group)?

Some of the earliest observations were again made by Kagan (Kagan et al., 1978). His team found that, compared to Caucasian infants of the same age, social class and childcare arrangement, Chinese infants aged 3 to 29 months were more subdued, shy and fearful in the novel laboratory situations. Their reactions were also associated with more stable heart rates than the Caucasians, leading to Kagan's biological explanations for inhibition among Chinese children. Kagan's work comparing Caucasian, Chinese and Japanese babies also found that Asian babies tend to score lower on many behavioural aspects including activity, vocal responses, irritability and whether they are also more easily soothed when upset and can better quiet themselves (Kagan et al., 1994).

While ethnic variations may imply genetically related racial differences, a better understanding of the groups' culture and of methodological issues in studying ethnic minority groups can give a better insight into their children's behavioural styles. For many Asian cultures, such as Japanese, their conceptions about new-borns are the opposite to those of the Western culture. Whilst the West encourages an active and verbal approach towards parenting to encourage their children to become autonomous and independent individuals, the Japanese believe that babies arrive as independent beings that are to be taught to rely on their mother, and close physical contact is encouraged, so many babies hardly leave their mother in the first year of life. We have also seen (in Chapter 9) that Japanese and Korean mothers tend to approach their babies rather than encourage their babies to approach them, as seen more in Western mothers (Jin et al., 2012). In addition, in East Asian cultures the expression of strong emotions is undesirable and discouraged, as it disrupts harmony within the family and between people. Strong emotions in children are likely to be curbed, and such early child-rearing practice may be part of the reason for the better self-regulation of emotions in Asian children (Rothbaum et al., 2000).

Parenting aside, other work has actually found relatively similar temperament styles between Caucasian and Asian babies (Hsu et al., 1981) and pre-schoolers (Windle et al., 1988). This suggests that differences observed may be a matter of biases, interpretation of behaviours and translation of questionnaires (in the case of parental reports), and the lack of experience in completing standard forms and tasks among some parents (Kohnstamm, 1989; see also 'Measurements for temperament', page 290). Research with multiple measures allowing for cultural variations in desirability of behaviour should therefore be promoted.

In fact, similar kinds of bias and practice can be said about gender differences in temperament. Some research (Calkins et al., 2002) has found boys to be more intense emotionally and girls more fearful but sociable. Recent work using multiple methods has reported a similar trend, with girls also showing lower activity than boys (Olino et al., 2013). Genetic and hormonal differences do exist between the sexes, and that much is granted by 'nature', but actual behavioural differences by gender tend to be small, and in strength rather than the nature of traits (Al-Hendawi and Reed, 2012), but they are perceived as larger by adults and even children themselves (you can read more about studies of such perceived differences in Chapter 11, 'Development of self-concept and gender identity').

We can easily imagine some common assumptions about the sexes, with boys seen as more boisterous, impulsive and irritable, and girls quieter and sensitive, but calmer and more cooperative. Such gender stereotypes and expectations can further influence child-rearing practice, parent–child relationships and the child's later friendships (see the next two chapters). An active, gregarious boy may receive attention and even encouragement to be even more physically demonstrative and emotionally explicit, whereas a quiet and shy boy may be ignored or even teased for being feminine or 'sissy'. There are cultural variations in the content of stereotypes and level of stereotyping, however; the way in which such perceptions and treatment influence children's self-concept, thinking and behaviour will be covered in detail in Chapter 11.

Since the 1970s, the now highly influential and respected researcher Judy Dunn has specialised in investigating children's close relationships within the family unit. Though not necessarily focusing exclusively on temperamental differences, one key identifiable aspect of some of her (particularly longitudinal) work is her approach of using intensive observations in the naturalistic home environment. Her early bout of studies from the 1970s with her colleague Carol Kendrick, summarised in a highly popular book, *Siblings: Love, Envy and Understanding*, in 1982, documents various aspects of family life when the parents and older child are expecting the arrival of a new sibling. As may be expected in this period of uncertainty, most children will show a pattern of behaviours such as demanding attention, anxiety and tearfulness, and disturbed sleep. However, importantly, Dunn and Kendrick found that such behaviours, which normally would be seen as temperamental characteristics of children, were actually related to the quality of the mother–child relationship. From their observations, over an extended period, of mother–child interactions in the home, they noted that the way in which the mother discussed the future arrival of a sibling or explained how this baby would have wants and needs was crucial. These variables rendered dramatically less important the initial observed differences in temperament between children, and led the researchers to conclude that behavioural styles of children should not be considered independently from the social situations in which they find themselves (Dunn and Kendrick, 1982).

Dunn and Kendrick's point reminds us of context dependence, which, as we discussed earlier in the chapter, is that a child's context can influence the expression of his temperament. A particular factor within the social context is *people*, in terms of the nature of the relationship that key people have with the child. Dunn and Kendrick's findings suggest that the more stable the relationship is between mother and child, the more stable the temperament characteristics will be for the child. Recent research further found that both parents' role (termed *co-parenting*) and the child's characteristics (i.e. negative reactivity) contribute to his behaviours across the transition to siblinghood. In negatively reactive children, supportive co-parenting (where parents support each other) appeared to be a protective factor, whilst when the parents engaged in high levels of undermining co-parenting (where they undermine each other) children displayed increases in externalising behaviour in this transition (Kolak and Volling, 2013).

The impressive work Dunn did looking into the intricacies of family relationships has prompted others to conduct more work into mother–infant interactions, and by extension, the characteristics of the mother. Typically the main caregiver, she 'affords' the baby its earliest interactions and relationship, and thus her personality and mental state will be important. For instance, Lynne Murray (Murray and Stein, 1991; Murray, 1992) conducted both laboratory experiments on mother–baby interactions as well as follow-ups to study behaviour of children with mothers who had postnatal depression (PND). In her laboratory (Murray and Stein, 1991), mothers were asked to engage in face-to-face interactions with their 1- to 2-month-old babies as they normally would before one of three different types of 'disruption' occurred. In one, an experimenter distracted the mother by starting a conversation with her so that she had to break her interaction with her baby. This was set up as a 'normal' disruption, since mothers' needs to attend to, say, the phone or the door are 'real-life' occurrences. The other two conditions were 'unnatural' disruptions in that either the mother was asked to continue to face her baby, but also stay still, expressionless and unresponsive ('still face' condition), or (via a live video-link) her otherwise normal expressions and responses were set out-of-sync with the baby (we learned earlier in the book that, from early on, mother and child already develop some synchronised behaviour like imitation).

The findings showed that in normal disruption, babies tended to be quiet and watch the interaction between mother and experimenter, but showed no distress. In unnatural disruptions, the baby would frown and move his arms about in an attempt to draw her attention, before being self-absorbed and passive later on after she showed the still-face expressions. Or the baby made short glances at the mother's face onscreen before turning away and becoming self-absorbed as well as distressed and avoidant. The patterns indicate that, even in such a controlled setting, very small babies are highly sensitive to the subtleties of their mothers' interaction with them.

How the first child behaves when his/her mother is expecting can depend on the mother–child relationship.

Source: Corbis/Tom Stewart

Later, in Murray's (1992) follow-up study, she recruited mothers with PND when their babies were 6 months old. One year on she found that their infants were less securely attached (see Chapter 9 for attachment security) and were more likely to present behavioural difficulties (including temper tantrums, eating difficulties and sleep disturbances) compared with a control group where the mothers were not depressed. We have seen above how responsive babies are to the subtle behaviour of their mother as early as the first month in life. If, due to her mental state, a mother cannot be as responsive as usual or enact normal interactions with her baby, this may explain the baby's problem behaviours later on. In fact, Murray's video data of mother–baby interactions in the second month revealed that depressed mothers were less likely to respond to their baby's signals and were more likely to express hostility to behaviours that non-depressed mothers would ignore. Perhaps depressed mothers' behaviour reflects their personal experiences and preoccupations due to their condition. Later research found that persistence and rhythmicity in infants are related to mothers' PND (Sugawara et al., 1999), and that depressive vulnerability in either mother or father is also associated with the child's negative affect and lack of effortful control (Pesonen et al., 2006). In a recent large-scale study of over 2000 families (Lee, 2013), mother-reported depression was the most predictive (over and above various variables such as family income and marital satisfaction) of susceptibility to the effects of child temperament on the mother–child interaction style (coded by warmth and responsiveness).

In sum, various factors and processes are at work to influence the relationship that the significant parent has with a child (see also Chapter 9) that can impact on the child's behavioural style. This is not to say that differences in temperament are 'caused' by parent–child variables alone, as we know that our genes and biology are highly relevant. Yet what is important is that genetic and biological contributions do not alone determine differences in temperament, and such differences should be understood in relation to their environment and social contexts. The interplay between these variables from 'nature' and 'nurture' is even clearer if we consider the longer-term development of temperament and its influence on other areas of development. These are the issues we will turn to in the final section.

Temperament in the long term

In order to evaluate the heritability, stability or biological component of temperament, we have already considered several longitudinal studies (from Thomas and Chess, through Plomin and Kagan, to Dunn and Murray). It is through such long-term work that the consistency of, and changes in, temperament can be explored, but how 'long term' can it go? We have seen that many aspects are quite stable, whilst others may change, and the behavioural manifestation of temperament can be different across time and space. So, if we consider that, many years later, when the child is grown up and some things are different about her while others remain, do we still regard her style of behaving as 'temperament'? If not, what else do we call it – her personality? And how much does earlier temperament have a bearing on it? These are the issues that we will explore in this final section. Moreover, related to these issues we will explore whether other developmental outcomes in the long term, including 'maladjustments', can also be traced back to differences in early temperament.

Developing personality?

Earlier we briefly cited the concept of adult 'personality' (as defined by Eysenck, whose work Buss and Plomin drew on). In fact, for older children many researchers already prefer to use this term to describe their behavioural style, perhaps because of the prevalent idea that temperament refers to 'basic' biologically driven responses. This clearly cannot describe the later-emerging, more conscious and controlled sets of behaviour and emotions. Still, as in the case of Eysenck's theory, many personality theories actually do carry the assumption that at least some of the adult dimensions have a genetic or biological foundation (Costa and McCrae, 1997). So, can we then say that children's temperament at least in part 'maps' on to their later personality?

Longitudinal research into adulthood

Although there is more longitudinal research now available on the development of temperamental traits, not many studies have specifically looked into whether these traits evolve into personality traits, particularly into adulthood, with sizable samples. The two Australian studies (ATP and LSAC) that we described earlier are examples of large-scale works that reported data from their cohort into adulthood. In the Lifespan box, one other such large-scale longitudinal project is described, which reports how the stability of temperamental measures taken in infancy/early childhood is related to personality types, psychological adjustment and social functioning in adulthood.

LIFESPAN

The Dunedin Multidisciplinary Health and Development Study

The Dunedin study has been an ongoing project looking at the health, development and behaviour of a cohort of babies who were recruited at birth (between 1 April 1972 and 31 March 1973) with parental consent, in Dunedin, New Zealand. The children were traced for follow-up at 3 years; at that point 1037 were assessed, and they were later re-assessed every two years, with a battery of psychological, medical and sociological measures. The latest follow-ups were carried out through to the participants' late 30s (still sampling over 950; Moffitt et al., 2007, 2013; Olsson et al., 2013).

At ages 3, 5, 7 and 9 years, each child participated in a standard set of cognitive and motor tasks, and in every other data-collection year they were evaluated by an examiner using rating scales on: lack of control (inability to modulate impulsive expression, lack of persistence in problem solving and sensitivity to stress); approach (like Kagan's inhibition – tendency, willingness or eagerness to explore new stimuli); and sluggishness (withdrawn, unresponsive social behaviour; Caspi and Silva, 1995). From such dimensions, five groups of children were identified:

- **under-controlled** (106 children) – high scores on lack of control;
- **inhibited** (80 children) – very high on lack of control and sluggishness;
- **confident** (281 children) – high scores on approach;
- **reserved** (151 children) – high scores on sluggishness;
- **well-adjusted** (405 children) – scores normative (not high or low) on all scales.

As children, participants were reassessed every other year until age 15 years. As part of the assessment in adulthood, from age 18 years, participants completed a version of the Multidimensional Personality Questionnaire (MPQ). This is a highly popular self-report instrument designed to assess individual differences in personality based on the current most dominant theory, the 'Big Five' (Costa and McCrae, 1997): extraversion–introversion, neuroticism–stability, agreeableness–disagreeableness, openness to experience–resistance to change, and conscientiousness–laxity. Apart from that, participants also had a full day of tests, interviews and examinations (e.g. physical examinations, psychiatric interviews). From age 21 years, such data have also been complemented by questionnaires mailed to parents, teachers and peers nominated by the participants (Caspi, 2000; Caspi et al., 2003).

Follow-ups (Caspi et al., 2003; Moffitt et al., 2007) have found, in particular, that 'under-controlled' 3-year-olds were more likely to self-rate as less agreeable and conscientious, and highly neurotic. They were reported to be impulsive, unreliable and antisocial, with more conflict with peers and at work. In contrast, 'inhibited' and 'reserved' 3-year-olds were more likely to grow up to see themselves as more introverted, with the inhibited being seen as more unassertive and depressed, and having less social support/friends and more problems in romantic relationships, and importantly, a tendency towards psychopathology (see also 'Temperament and other developmental and pathological outcomes', pages 307–9). These are in sharp contrast to once 'confident' or 'well-adjusted' children, who were more likely to become extraverted individuals open to experience.

In the most recent follow-ups (Olsson et al., 2013), moderate indirect effects of child social connectedness (measured by cooperative play, sharing and level of confidence at age 5) on adult wellbeing (defined by prosocial behaviour, social participation, sense of coherence and positive coping style) were found as mediated by its continuity through to adolescence. Curiously, a specific trait of temperament, self-control (similar to Rothbart's self-regulation, measured by parents' and teachers' reports, observation and own ratings), strongly predicted adult health and wealth, even after controlling for IQ and social class (Moffitt et al., 2013). As adults, children with poor control are more likely to have addiction issues, low income, poor saving habits/credit problems and social welfare dependence, higher crime conviction rates and lower parenting skill. The researchers further identified the early warning signs of troubled adulthood that arise in adolescence (age 13–21); those with poor self-control were more likely to 'make mistakes' (e.g. smoking, leaving school with no qualifications or becoming unplanned parents). This contrasts with a subset with high self-control, who had better outcomes, had never made such 'mistakes', and reported the highest life satisfaction at age 38 years. Meanwhile, self-control is identified as malleable and 'teachable', and this has important implications for targeted intervention programmes to enhance young children's self-control, which are likely to bring greater returns.

The scale and longevity of the Dunedin study is indeed impressive. Its findings suggest that temperament differences as identified by independent raters in childhood are linked not just to differences in self-rated personality, but also to peer-rated interpersonal functioning as well as independent reports of health and wealth more than three decades later. While being greatly persuasive as evidence of the 'mapping' of early temperament onto later personality and related pathology, it is important to bear in mind, again, that statistical links and 'likelihoods' (between early temperament traits and later outcomes) do not mean that individual infants all stay the same as they become adults. Indeed, there is considerable variation behind such group patterns, and the authors of the study use the key word 'probabilistic' to describe these relationships (Caspi, 2000, p. 170).

Furthermore, even 'continuity' does not imply 'cause'. It is said that, although continuity is more likely than change, it may be seen as a kind of 'person–environment transaction'. Even temperamental characteristics with genetic heritage may 'accumulate response strength' through repeated reinforcement. In the context of interpersonal interactions with others in developmental settings, people may be 'drawn in as accomplices' who maintain the characteristics' continuity until they become elaborated into cognitive structures which are more meaningfully understood as our personality (Caspi, 2000; Caspi et al., 2003). This rather indirect linkage between early temperament and adult personality, with factors and processes interacting over the life course, is better understood through the concept of 'goodness-of-fit' that follows.

STOP AND THINK

Reflection

- Can you think of any real-life 'micro' examples of this process of 'interaction' or 'transaction'?

For instance, consider again the cases of the 2-year-olds at the beginning of the chapter. Sebastian's parents allow him into their bed when he is unsettled and may give in to his demands for snacks.

- Who is affecting whose behaviour in this scenario?
- Could his parents' practices shape Sebastian's existing tendencies and therefore future behaviour?

Goodness-of-fit

Think back to the three infant temperament types classified by the pioneering researchers Thomas and Chess ('easy', 'slow-to-warm-up' and 'difficult'). Theirs and other studies have found a link between these early types and later differences in personalities (Rothbart and Bates, 1998). In particular, 'difficult' infants are more likely to have problematic adjustments whereas easy infants are less likely to do so. Still, that is not to claim that early temperament directly and definitively maps onto later personality. In fact, Thomas and Chess (1977) were the first to put forward the idea that because of the child's initial temperament type, parents are likely to foster an environment better suited to that type over another. An environment required to cope with a difficult child is likely to be different from an environment suitable for the easy type. Thus, any difficulty later could be a result of a 'mismatch' between the environment and the temperament expressed initially. Their term goodness-of-fit pertains to just this idea. This means that child temperament and the environment are inextricably interwoven, and both must be considered in their interplay as contributions to developmental outcomes. The 'bidirectional' and interactive effects, particularly between parenting and temperament, cover many aspects of the child (such as frustration, impulsivity and self-regulation) and are argued to fine-tune theoretical models of both parenting and temperament (Kiff et al., 2011). Negative emotionality, for instance, in infancy has an indirect effect on toddler self-regulation due to its impact on parent–child responsive interactions (Kim and Kochanska, 2012). That does not mean highly negative infants are consigned to being poorly controlled toddlers later; when in responsive relationships (particularly with mother's support), this type of infant can gain more self-regulation.

Indeed, Thomas and Chess (1990) had already argued that, over time, continuity and change are not mutually exclusive. A characteristic can remain stable for a period of time (say, infancy) then change. Such a characteristic may also be stable over a long time for one individual, but change for another. Because both can be observed in theirs and others' work, Thomas and Chess argue that it is more relevant to locate processes or mechanisms that result in stability or change for any pattern over time. These processes will be particularly critical when we consider the relationship between temperament and other areas of development, especially those outcomes that are seen as 'pathological'. Indeed, since the NYLS, many investigators have shifted from a focus on definition and measurement to the examination of relationships between temperament and psychopathology. These areas will mark the final part of this chapter.

Temperament and other developmental and pathological outcomes

Considering the various dimensions that temperament contains (such as emotionality, activity and self-regulation) and having touched on findings about its ability to predict later personal and interpersonal outcomes in adulthood, it is only logical to expect that such dimensions will have an impact on other areas (cognitive and social) of a child's medium-term development.

Cognitive functioning and social behaviour

For learning performance, cognitive functioning dimensions such as attentional orientation and effortful control are highly relevant, as they influence whether a child can spend enough time on-task or concentrate in class. Also, a child who is highly inhibited may be more reluctant to explore novel environments and activities, reducing the opportunity to learn new information. However, too much novelty seeking may be disruptive for structured learning activities. It has been established that children with low attention span and high impulsivity are more likely to experience problems in learning at home and in school (Tizard and Hughes, 1984). Later, self-directedness and persistence were found to be positively related to academic competence, achievement and intelligence, which

Definition

Goodness-of-fit: this concept defines how both genetic components as the innate part of temperament, and environmental forces will combine and interact over time to produce positive (through good 'fit') or negative (through bad 'fit') developmental outcomes.

were negatively related to novelty seeking in children with externalising problems (Copeland et al., 2004). Recent research has also found predictiveness of negative emotionality in at-risk (low-income, minority or with disability) pre-schoolers for later school adjustment and academic adjustment through their reduced persistence (Al-Hendawi and Reed, 2012). These findings point to the importance of self-regulation, attention and moderate levels of novelty seeking in learning and intellectual development.

It is paramount to bear in mind that much learning in school takes place within a social context, requiring positive child–teacher and peer interactions; the impact of chid temperament on social behaviour is important. It has been found that teacher-rated temperament is related to peer-rated social status in pre-school, with rejected children displaying difficult temperaments in terms of higher activity, distractibility and persistence, and both rejected and neglected children having lower adaptability and more negative mood than popular children (Walker et al., 2001). This suggests that a child's temperament may affect social behaviour, which in turn is evaluated by others, who act on it (to reject or neglect him). This is critical since those who are rejected or neglected may fail to develop the effective interpersonal skills needed for social interactions and relationships in school. Early temperament (in particular, high resistance to control and novelty stress), coupled with family stress, is also a prime predictor for later externalising problems in school (Schermerhorn et al., 2013), which is a key hindrance to learning and peer relationships; see also Chapter 12, 'Peer interactions and relationships').

In fact, temperamental differences are already at work earlier in childcare centres (Crockenberg, 2003). Children who respond negatively and intensely to novel events will become increasingly stressed during long days in such full-time care. When such children lack sufficient regulatory skills, they are more likely to experience conflict with peers or to withdraw from peer interaction, which in turn contributes to their stress. This may explain why it has been found that parents encountered greater difficulty in placing children with difficult temperaments in satisfactory day-care arrangements (Lerner and Galambos, 1985).

Chapter 9, Attachment and Early Social Experiences, covers an important area in emotional development, the quality of attachment of the child to the mother.

As attachment is nurtured from the first year of life by how the mother behaves towards her child, it may seem obvious that temperament is crucial in this relationship. However, there is little evidence that temperament is actually related to attachment. Instead, as we saw in Chapter 9, the two work in conjunction to produce later attachment and behaviour styles. This is possibly because, as explained earlier, the mother's interactions with her baby can lead to his behavioural differences, but mother's (and others') responsiveness to him also depends on his temperament traits – another example of 'goodness-of-fit' (Notaro and Volling, 1999; Kim and Kochanska, 2012).

Psychopathology

From the Dunedin study described earlier, it was found that temperament type predicts later personality, social functioning and 'tendency towards psychopathology', where the latter affects those classified as 'inhibited' and 'under-controlled' or lacking in 'self-control'. It is reported that, as young adults, children once classed as under-controlled (46%) or inhibited (53%) were more likely than well-adjusted (38%) children to be diagnosed with a psychiatric disorder. Depression featured more for the inhibited and alcohol dependence for the under-controlled, while suicide attempts were more concentrated in both (Caspi, 2000). Under-controlled individuals were also more likely to be repeat offenders in theft, assault or fraud than well-adjusted or inhibited individuals, perhaps because, as interview data suggest, the under-controlled perceived fewer social deterrents to crime (versus the inhibited, who feared getting caught). This is not dissimilar to how children low in self-control at age 5 were more likely to have addiction or substance dependence and criminality as adults, often after risky decisions or habits that started since adolescence. Very telling is also the fact that of the bottom-fifth self-control scorers, 22% (versus 7% in the top fifth) attempted or died by suicide (an indicator of deep unhappiness) by age 38 (Moffitt et al., 2013).

These findings are very illuminating, if alarming, since if taken at face value they imply that some characteristics at a young age already predispose children to maladjustment, an early death or a life of crime. It is again important to remind ourselves that these are all but 'risks' or links between measures, and that effect sizes tend to be small to medium statistically.

Also, 'a lot of development occurs after the age of three' (Caspi, 2000, p. 168) including those medium-term cognitive and social outcomes identified above which more directly contribute to later problems. For instance, under-controlled individuals tend to leave school earlier than well-adjusted individuals, and the former were also at greater risk of unemployment or job dismissal. The resultant socio-economic issues (e.g. poverty) lead in part to some of their maladjustments. This highlights again the degree of 'fit' between early temperamental characteristics and the socialisation context, which may modify the subsequent experiences in the environment.

Another area where recent research has explored its links with temperament is attention deficit hyperactivity disorder (ADHD), which refers to a range of problem behaviours associated with poor attention span (Likierman and Muter, 2005) (ADHD is discussed in detail in Chapter 17, 'Attention deficit hyperactivity disorder'). These include inattentiveness, impulsiveness, restlessness and hyperactivity, often hindering children from learning and socialising effectively. Based on such descriptions alone, it would seem that there is much overlap between ADHD and some temperament types (such as Thomas and Chess's 'difficult' type), except that ADHD requires a medical diagnosis. In diagnosing a child as having ADHD, a required number from a specified list of 'symptoms' must be exhibited for at least six months and to an extent that is unusual for that age. Only 1.7% of the UK population have this disorder, which makes it much rarer than 'difficult' temperament, which is found in approximately 10% of the population.

Still, the behavioural descriptions of ADHD, and in particular the assumed contribution of both biological and environmental factors (which include temperament), have been seen as an indication of conceptual and empirical overlap, and some studies have reported on the specific temperaments of children diagnosed with ADHD (e.g. Cho et al., 2008; Foley et al., 2008). For instance, parent-rated higher negative reactivity, activity and impulsivity and lower persistence, attentional focusing and inhibitory control feature more in ADHD versus normative samples, as well as higher novelty seeking and lower self-directedness, which in turn predicts the severity of ADHD symptoms. The Cutting Edge box summarises further recently published studies in this area. It seems that there is indeed some overlap, but the precise aspects or pattern of temperament dimensions and whether and how they are directly linked to ADHD sub-types remain to be seen. It is likely a child with a combination of traits pertaining to extreme levels of negative emotionality or approach with poor regulation is more at risk of developing ADHD.

Of course, as with other areas of development, temperament is no definitive 'cause' for such pathology, but it is likely that what underpins some aspects of temperament also underpins ADHD symptoms. This would be of particular interest to parents and professionals in reading early signs of the disorder and finding ways to improve its conditions.

CUTTING EDGE

Temperament of children with ADHD: recent findings

Some of the most influential work documented about the link between temperament and ADHD has come from Joel T. Nigg. As a clinical psychologist and prolific scientist, he has written over 100 peer-reviewed articles and a ground-breaking book *What Causes ADHD?* (2006b), which dissects the genetic, neural and environmental factors. His recent work (Nigg, 2010; Martel et al., 2009) focuses on multi-pathway processes that can be invoked from temperament or personality in relation to ADHD. From his relatively large clinical samples (over 100 with ADHD, with matched controls) he distinguishes between a control 'top-down' factor, involving cognitive and effortful control (conscientiousness), and an affective 'bottom-up' one, involving negative emotionality/neuroticism, agreeableness and reactive control as differentially and specifically related to the two key ADHD aspects, inattention and hyperactivity, respectively (although only in younger children; adolescents' personality–ADHD mapping differs slightly). However, he warns of the fact that many kinds of attention are still within normal range in ADHD (except cognitive control, among others) and that any such personality/temperament trait marker pertains to only a subset of the ADHD population due to the syndrome's heterogeneity.

His most recent research (Karalunas et al., 2014) involves refining such sub-types of childhood ADHD by using parent-rated temperament dimensions, physiological and MRI measures and clinical outcomes longitudinally in a community sample of 437 children with and without ADHD. The proposed novel sub-types ('mild'/normative emotion regulation, 'surgent'/extreme levels of positive approach motivation, and 'irritable'/extreme levels of negative emotionality, anger and poor soothability) showed stability over time (one year) and were distinguishable by unique patterns of physiology and clinical outcomes, despite being independent of existing clinical demarcation, including DSM-5 on symptom severity. The team suggests that this temperament-based typology provides a superior description of ADHD than current clinical criteria. The ongoing nature of the work means that stability of the sub-types will continue to be monitored.

Sources: Karalunas et al. (2014); Martel et al. (2009); Nigg (2010)

SUMMARY

From definitions to structure and measurements, not to mention explanations and development, temperament is a concept that is very far from being wholly understood. That is not to say that theorists and researchers are not at least striving for some common ground on which to approach temperament. Even if the number of dimensions that this construct should contain is disagreed upon, some key features like stability and continuity, context-dependence, early emergence and contextual variables are generally agreed to be critical, as the behavioural styles of children should not be transient, but at least relatively consistent over time and place. In addition, research has led to an understanding of how the expression of temperament changes over time with developments in other areas. These include children's developing mobility, executive functioning and effortful control and language.

Temperament is thought to be a relatively consistent set of tendencies to behave in certain ways, also referred to as traits, but the precise number of traits which exist is not agreed upon. Early work by John Bates focused on three broad categories of behaviours, each of which contained sub-categories of behaviour which could be observed. Later, Thomas and Chess developed a nine-dimensional framework, but several of those dimensions could be subsumed under fewer broader headings, leading to the development of simpler models such as Buss and Plomin's three-dimensional EAS model. Instead of studying the entire set of children's behavioural tendencies, Kagan focused specifically on behavioural inhibition. Most recently, the work of Rothbart has received considerable attention. Whilst she has built on previous research, her four-dimensional model includes effortful control – a new and significant dimension which focuses on children's ability to self-regulate.

The idea that genes and thus inherited biological processes can affect both a child's early temperament as well as his/her later personality is nothing new, and research evidence is also persuasive. However, two vital points must be borne in mind. First, evidence of genetic heritability does not mean that temperament is only inherited; the environment can mediate the eventual developmental outcomes. It is also important, secondly, to recognise that evidence of a biological basis does not mean that change in behavioural styles cannot happen; some neural systems are plastic during infancy. A new direction for research is to study mechanisms through which consistency and change occur.

Finally, with age, temperament and personality become increasingly complex in organisation and manifestation. Whilst some aspects of early temperament may be linked to later personality, there are great differences between the earliest behavioural responses and the later behaviours of children who are increasingly aware of their own characteristics and can monitor their behaviour and self-regulate. Nevertheless, research has revealed links between early temperament and later cognitive and interpersonal functioning, as well as pathology, right into adulthood. Some aspects of temperament, such as attentional orientation, persistence and effortful control, will clearly be important for learning and have been linked with intellectual development. Similarly, children with more difficult temperaments are likely to encounter social challenges. Having said all of this, it is important to be aware of the transaction which takes place between temperament and the environment, to appreciate that such links need not be causal. Further research in this field will incorporate these factors, allowing for a more complete picture of temperament and its relationship with other developmental outcomes and disorders.

REVIEW QUESTIONS

1. Discuss what might be the qualifying conditions for something to be considered a temperamental trait.
2. Compare and contrast at least two examples of the structure of temperament in terms of its behavioural dimensions.
3. What are the advantages and disadvantages of using parental reports or ratings and third-party behavioural observations in laboratories to measure temperamental traits?
4. Critically evaluate the extent to which temperament is genetically given versus environmentally driven.
5. Do differences in childhood temperament predict differences in personality of older children and adults?

RECOMMENDED READING

For more general information on understanding children's temperament, see:

Carey, W. B., with Jablow, M. M. (2005). *Understanding your Child's Temperament*. New York: Macmillan: Simon & Schuster.

Mervielde, I., & de Pauw, S. S. W. (2012). Models of child temperament. In M. Zentner & R. L. Shiner (Eds.), *Handbook of Temperament* (21–40). New York: Guilford Press.

Shiner, R. L., Buss, K. A., McClowry, S. G., Putnam, S. P., Saudino, K. J., & Zentner, M. (2012). What is temperament now? Assessing temperament research on the twenty-fifth anniversary of Goldsmith et al. (1987). *Child Development Perspectives*, 6, 436–444.

To learn more about temperament and siblings, and the ways in which family relationships influence temperament, see:

Dunn, J., & Kendrick, C. (1982). *Siblings: Love, Envy and Understanding*. Cambridge, MA: Harvard University Press.

To read more about how early temperament may be linked to later psychological pathology, see:

Nigg, J. T. (2006). Temperament and developmental psychopathology. *Journal of Child Psychology and Psychiatry*, 47, 395–422.

RECOMMENDED WEBSITES

Supported by b-di.com – 'Understanding Behavioural Individuality' – this is an organic website for general 'fact finding' and checking on updates concerning temperament research. It targets parents, practitioners and academics:
http://www.temperament.com

Thomas, Chess and Birch's (1970) article, The origin of personality (in *Scientific American*, 223 (2), 102–109) – a very comprehensive account of their original nine dimensions:
http://www.acamedia.info/sciences/sciliterature/origin_of_personality.htm

Website devoted to the Colorado Adoption Project, hosted by the Institute for Behavioral Genetics, containing the project's history, statistics and references for publications:
http://ibgwww.colorado.edu/cap/

Website devoted to the Longitudinal Study of Australian Children, hosted by the Australian Institute of Family Studies, with the latest news and publications:
http://www.growingupinaustralia.gov.au

Website devoted to the Dunedin Multidisciplinary Health and Development Study, hosted by the University of Otago, with the project's latest news and publications:
http://dunedinstudy.otago.ac.nz/

Chapter 11
Development of self-concept and gender identity

Learning outcomes

After reading this chapter, and with further recommended reading, you should be able to:

1. Recognise and define the different components of self-concept.
2. Critically evaluate the development of these different components and the factors that influence their development in children.
3. Critically describe children's understanding of their own and others' gender groups at different ages.
4. Outline the principles of the key theories that have been proposed to explain the development of gender identity.
5. Critically review the associated research that has been conducted for support of such theories.

Forms of self-awareness and identity

'I'm 5 years old . . . I'm a boy, and . . . I have brown hair, brown eyes . . . I'm fast! . . . I like to play, like all the time!' (5-year-old boy, in response to 'who are you?'; student's field notes)

'[I'd play with her cos] she's like me, we're both girls, we're like . . . the same . . .' (7-year-old white English girl in a London state primary school)

'I think she (pointing at the photo of a girl) won't like the same (food) as me cos only girls like to eat veggies!' (7-year-old English boy in a Greater London suburb)

- How has the 5-year-old boy described himself – would you say it is a superficial or deep description?
- Look at what the 7-year-old girl has said about her friend. Why is it important that her friend is a girl?
- Similarly, why does the 7-year-old boy infer such 'culinary habits' on specifically the opposite sex?

Introduction

The examples above are some of the typical responses from children of their age group in terms of how they would describe themselves to others or how they think about themselves and others. As we shall see later in the chapter, individual features (or 'attributes') such as those that the 5-year-old boy used in the form of age, gender, appearance and likes and dislikes tend to be some of the most prominent 'self-descriptions' by children at this age. Similarly, a clear preference for peers of the same sex, or making contrasting inferences about peers of their own and the opposite sex, as voiced by the two 7-year-olds, is fairly common among children at that age. Even adults would invariably draw on some of the individual and social group-based attributes and qualities to describe themselves. All of these are part and parcel of our senses of self and identity. In this chapter we first explore the definitions of self-concept and social identity. Then we move on to examine how the self-concept, and arguably the most dominant form of social identity – gender identity – develop across different stages of childhood, and the perspectives and theories that are used by academics to explain this development.

What are self-concept and social identity?

We have already had a glimpse of the 'ingredients' that make up a sense of self from the points of view of children. Let's spend a few moments on the question 'Who am I?' to explore this a little more.

> **STOP AND THINK**
>
> Consider the opening examples of children's answers to the question, 'Who am I?' What answer would you give now, as an adult, to the question, 'Who am I?'

It is quite likely that you would have thought about at least one of these items in your 'Who am I?' search: name, age, gender, birthplace and/or nationality, occupation, religion and parental status (if you have children). For some of us, it may be the case that one (or more) of the items on this list also makes us 'proud' (such as our job or being a parent). For others, an item or two may distinguish us as the same as (or different from) other people we know (such as our birthplace or nationality). Still others might have preferred to use abilities or interests, such as our dress sense, music taste or cooking and sporting skills, to mark ourselves out. Whatever they are on our 'Who am I?' list, and whether they are judged positively or negatively by others or ourselves, or in fact whether or not they can be observed by others, it is these characteristics, roles and ideas that we have built up and hold about ourselves that make up this jigsaw notion known as our self-concept.

Notice how some of these attributes, such as gender, age, race, ethnicity and nationality, are readily adopted by societies to categorise individuals into groups. Such groupings are often seen to share common characteristics, either external or internal, which we use to describe ourselves and others (as we have done in the exercise). However, we do not just describe each other; we also develop feelings towards our own group as well as other groups (such as a sense of belonging or preference, as we have seen in the case of the 7-year-old girl in the opening example). Moreover, sometimes, whether consciously or subconsciously, we make assumptions and evaluations of each other based on such group membership (as in the 7-year-old boy in the opening example), or how people think and behave in ways upheld as typical of members in such groups (such as being masculine or a 'typical man'). Our sense of social identity concerns all of these thinking (cognitive), feeling (affective) and behavioural components (Tajfel, 1978). The later part of the chapter will look closely at these concepts that concern the ever-important gender categories and associated identities.

As we have explored in the exercise and examples above, for many of us, those ingredients that build up our self-concepts and social identities serve as a kind of framework for thinking about our social world, structuring our experiences and guiding our social conduct and interpersonal interactions and relationships. Therefore, what we perceive of ourselves is highly central to our personality and behaviour. And we will see shortly how the self-concept forms very early in life and is influenced by a variety of factors, both cognitive and social, which makes it all the more important for us to try to understand its development.

Theories in the development of the self-concept

The influential theorist in self-concepts, Eleanor Maccoby (1980), once pointed out that a sense of self develops by 'degrees', in a gradual and cumulative manner. As every one of us develops ideas about who we are, those ideas are continually reviewed and

> **Definitions**
>
> **Self-concept:** ideas we have about ourselves, including our physical and mental qualities, and our emotional and behavioural attributes.
>
> **Social identity:** a sense of identity derived from our membership of social groups, including categorising ourselves as members, feelings of belonging, and behaviour consistent with what is expected of group members.

revised through childhood in the light of our cognitive development and social experiences. For example, any fast-growing toddler will become more and more aware of her own behaviour as well as *others'* responses to it, and may form her own perceptions and evaluations of it. All these inputs are likely to play a role in shaping her later, more competent, realistic and reflective concept of herself as she grows.

Children's self-concepts through the years

Before delving into the stages of development in self-concept, and the factors that influence it in children, it is a good idea to explore what kinds of attributes and qualities children actually have about themselves at different ages. The first opening example in this chapter shows us some of the commonest kinds of description that children give in response to asking themselves the question 'Who am I?' This open-ended question has been one of the most popular, if simplest, means of obtaining children's self-descriptions.

Susan Harter, a prominent researcher in the 1980s, reviewed studies in which children were asked about themselves involving, among others, the 'Who am I?' question. What she noticed is an apparent developmental pattern in which children at different ages predominantly use different kinds of attributes and qualities to describe themselves. For the youngest children (aged 5 years or younger), observations based on their physical or external characteristics, such as appearance or activities, feature the most in their self-descriptions. For older children, there is often a shift towards more 'internal' descriptions, such as relationships with others or their inner feelings, beliefs and attitudes. For instance, in Rosenberg's (1979) study of 8- to 18-year-olds in Baltimore, when asked about what kind of person they would like to become, 36% of the 8-year-olds' answers were to do with interpersonal traits (e.g. 'shy', 'friendly') versus 69% of the 14–16-year-olds. The oldest group (up to 18 years old) also made far more use of the inner qualities that were only available to themselves and referred more to self-control (e.g. 'I don't show my feelings') when concerned with such emotions, motivations, wishes and secrets. Some of the popular features of self-descriptions at different ages are summarised in Table 11.1.

Table 11.1 Children's self-descriptions at different ages.

Age	Self-descriptions	Examples
5 years or under	Physical features or facts, overt preference or possessions	'I've red hair.' 'A girl.' 'I like milk.' 'I've got a bike.'
5–9 years	More character references and gradually interpersonal traits	'I'm happy.' 'I'm brave.' 'Sometimes I'm shy.'
Beyond 10 years	Increasing qualifiers for above by considering private self-knowledge	'I try not to be selfish but I find it hard sometimes.'

Of course, there may be a big difference between how particularly older children may describe themselves to a stranger, such as a researcher, and how they really think and feel about themselves (and later studies that have used methods other than self-reporting will be reviewed).

Also, as children get older, their increasingly complex language will enable them to express themselves more thoroughly. Nevertheless, such research gives us a taste of the increasing complexity of the developing child's self-concept. Indeed, the development of our self-concept as unique individuals, at least in Western cultures, is seen as a lengthy and complex journey, which goes through at least several stages throughout childhood, and probably even more over our lifetime (Maccoby, 1980). So, where, or at what age, is the starting point of this journey? And how does this self-understanding become more complex over time?

The emerging sense of self: early self-awareness

An awareness of the self, or the realisation and establishment that we simply 'exist' as our own individual entity, is the very first constituent that emerges of our self-concept. It has been argued that in early infancy children do not have this basic awareness – they do not perceive themselves as distinct beings – as separate from other beings, with their own unique appearance, properties or agency (meaning that they can cause an effect on other objects or actors in their physical and social world, that they can 'make things happen'). Such self-awareness can be illustrated using a simple visual cue recognition technique commonly known as the 'rouge test' (see the Research Methods box).

RESEARCH METHODS

Early sense of self

Developed initially for research with apes, Lewis and Brooks-Gunn (1978, 1979) carried out a simple experiment with young children by asking mothers unobtrusively to apply a spot of rouge to their child's nose. Later the children's reactions to their self-image were monitored when they were put in front of a mirror; the assumption was that if they were able to recognise the image was that of themselves – possessing a sense of self – they would reach for the spot on their nose where the rouge had been applied. This response was rarely observed before the age of 15 months, even though at 1 year old, children were amused by what they saw in the mirror – without paying any attention to the rouge – as if they were laughing at another child whose nose had been painted on! It was not until the second half of the second year that most of the children showed signs that they knew definitely the spot was of interest as it was on their *own* nose.

There are other techniques for assessing self-awareness that rely more on verbal indicators, such as asking some children to name or describe photographs of themselves (Bullock and Lutkenhaus, 1990) and examining their use of relevant terms like 'I' and 'me' (Bates, 1990). On the whole, these studies have found that, as with the rouge test, children's self-awareness (the recognition that the self exists as a separate and distinct individual with its own attributes), as the essential first stepping stone in the development of self-concept, is achieved by the end of the second year (see Figure 11.1).

- Do you think the rouge test is a good way of assessing a child's self-recognition?

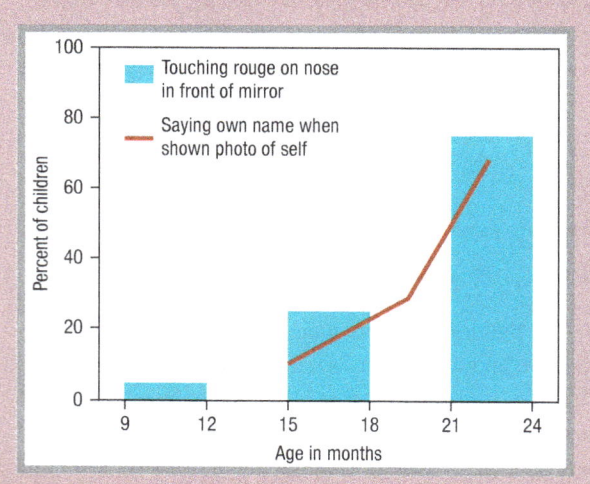

Figure 11.1 Self-recognition by the rouge test and self-naming from 9 to 24 months.
Source: Lewis and Brooks-Gunn (1978)

The key 'tool' of the rouge test is the mirror in which the infant recognises the reflection of his/her facial appearance. Could it be that familiarity with mirrors or emphasis on the *face* in social interactions may influence the development of this form of self-concept? A study by Keller et al. (2004) found that mutual eye contact and object stimulation (using objects to attract a child's attention) between parents and babies at 3 months predicted self-concept at 18–20 months and this might explain why infants of Cameroonian Nso farmers showed relatively low levels of self-recognition using the rouge test, compared with their Western counterparts. It is suggested that distal parenting (more object and face-to-face contexts), which is prevalent in the West and urban regions, facilitates this kind of (facial) recognition of others and self in infants compared with more proximal parenting (involving body stimulation and contact) in rural tribes.

Definition

Self-awareness: the first step in the development of self-concept; the recognition that we are distinct from others with physical and mental properties of our own.

The subjective or existential self

We have just seen how the earliest awareness of the self, the recognition that we exist as a separate and unique entity, has been studied in infancy. This early self-recognition was labelled as the 'self-as-subject', or the self 'I', by the pioneering American psychologist and philosopher,

William James (1892). This initial feature of the self as a 'subject' of experience is usually thought of in terms of its distinction from, or as a precursor to, the later feature of the self as an 'object' of knowledge (see the next section). James further articulated four conditions or elements for this existential self that refer to an awareness of: (1) our own agency in life events; (2) the uniqueness of our own experience as distinct from other people; (3) the continuity of our identity; (4) our own awareness, implying an element of self-reflexivity (that we are able to reflect on our awareness of the self).

Lewis (1990, 1991), of the rouge test, calls this aspect of the self the subjective self or existential self and argues that it endures through time and space, in line with James's original four elements. Even though, as we have explored in Lewis's studies, the child does not reach an elaborate understanding of the self until the second year of life, Lewis places the starting points of early existential understanding in the first few months of life. These early and basic starting points are rooted in numerous everyday interactions between the infant and the objects and people in their world. During such encounters, the infant learns that his actions can affect objects or people around him (their agency), that he is able to 'make' things happen, control objects and 'cause' others to respond. These can be very simple interactions such as an infant's attempts to move or manipulate a toy, or that, as he smiles, his mother smiles back or, when he cries, she coos and comforts. This is particularly true in the early months when parents spend a lot of time imitating the infant's behaviours, expressions and vocalisations (Meltzoff, 1990). It is through these experiences that the infant begins to separate the self from everything else (such as mother) and learn that this separate existence (as 'I') continues over time and across contexts.

The objective or categorical self

As cited earlier, James's configuration of the self consists of another key feature that he called the 'self-as-object', or the self as 'me'. This is more commonly known as the objective self or categorical self (Lewis, 1990). This aspect concerns the emerging process of defining the self in relation to the kinds of attributes and qualities that are commonly used to describe groupings of people, such as size, gender, ethnicity and relationship to others (as we explored briefly in the chapter's opening, with the concept of social identity, and will do so again later on). By this point of development, usually beyond 2 years of age, children have achieved self-awareness, or the existential or subjective self, and they begin to be able to place themselves within, or to become aware that they can be seen by others in relation to, a great array of social categories (like gender and race) that human societies tend to use to define the individuals living among them.

The exact process of how, and the degree to which, children make use of human social categories to define themselves and each other will be detailed in the second part of this chapter ('Understanding of gender categories', pages 322–42). For now, it is important just to note the key distinction between the categorical 'me' and the existential 'I'. The categorical self does not refer to basic properties such as agency, but emphasises our 'roles' as commonly seen in the wider social world, and their associated attributes in relation to other members in society (such as being a girl versus being a boy, being a child versus being a grown-up).

The looking-glass self

It has been pointed out that a child's emerging existential self and the later objective self are influenced by social factors, particularly the child's understanding of his/her relationships with other people and of other people's perception of themselves. Cooley and Mead were two of the key theorists who initially conceptualised this close relationship between an individual child's understanding and others' understanding of the self formally (Cooley, 1902; Mead, 1934). This idea, termed the 'looking-glass self', refers to the way others hold up a 'social mirror' in which we may see ourselves as we are 'reflected' by them, and from there, we build up our senses of the self from the views we come to understand that others may have of us.

> **Definitions**
>
> **Subjective or existential self:** the recognition of the self that is unique and distinct from others, endures over time and space, and has an element of self-reflexivity.
> **Objective or categorical self:** the recognition of the self as the person seen by others and defined by the attributes and qualities used to define groups of people.
> **Looking-glass self:** the sense of self we develop as we respond to interactions with others and see how others react to us. We see ourselves reflected in other people's behaviour towards us.

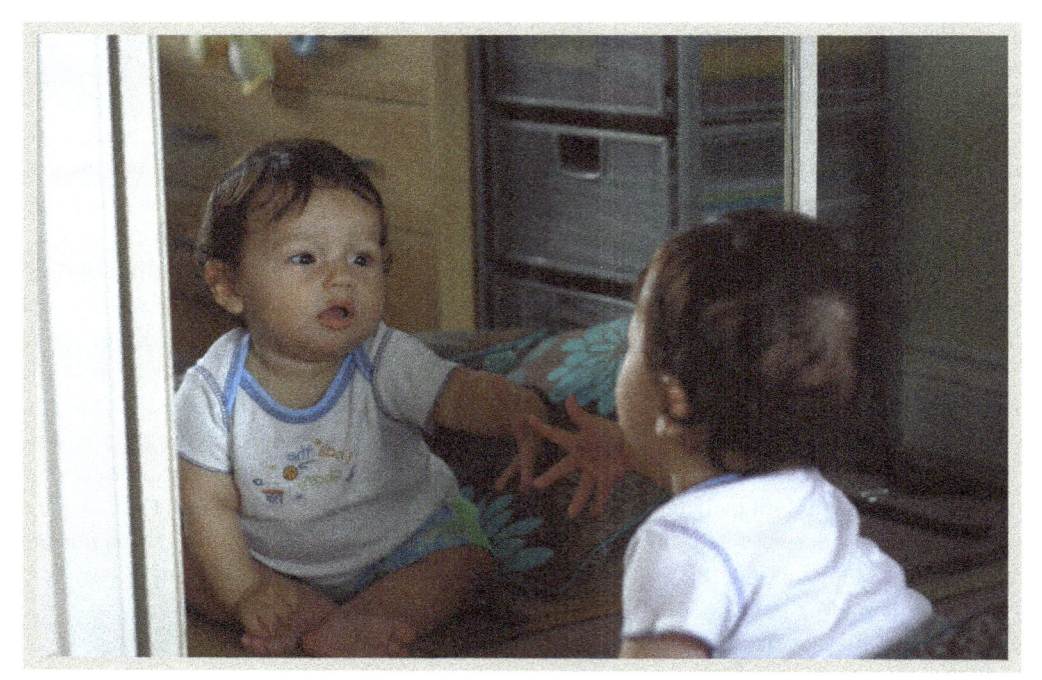

Infant looking at himself in the mirror and reaching towards reflected image.
Source: Lam

Within this view, the importance of social interactions is emphasised as the tool through which the self and the social world are inextricably linked. Through repeated social exchanges, such as games and play, most of which involve the use of language, children gradually come to realise and adopt some of the perspectives that others have of them, and with such knowledge they also become more able to reflect on themselves. According to Cooley and Mead, a child cannot develop a sense of self without interactions with others, in order to learn how those others view the world and the people within it – including the child himself or herself.

Despite the idea of self as being a unique individual, self-concept is inextricably linked with others, where various social inputs come into play as the child develops her notion of what she is 'like' compared to others. This comparison process can be evaluative as well – it involves value-laden judgements about one's qualities. We will explore this side of the self below.

Self-esteem

Apart from the common attributes and social roles and categories we use to describe ourselves, we also have a more reflective and evaluative feature of our self-concept. Remember how in the first exercise of the chapter we reflected on the things about ourselves that make us feel proud? Suffice it to say there are likely also things for which we do not feel very proud about ourselves. Children often reflect on and evaluate themselves, and such evaluations form an important part of their self-concept, their self-esteem.

Children's self-evaluations also go through stages of development, similar to the other features of the self. For instance, younger children tend to have more general or 'global' self-evaluations, such as how happy they are about themselves or how much they like the way they are. On entering early adolescence, their evaluations become increasingly differentiated, with separate judgements about their physical appearance, peer acceptance, and academic or athletic performance, and so forth. Susan Harter, as mentioned before with her work on children's self-descriptions, distinguished five areas in which children's self-evaluations may be measured: (1) scholastic competence – how competent the child considers herself to be at school; (2) athletic competence – the child's self-assessment of her competence in sporting activities;

Definition

Self-esteem: the evaluative and reflective features of our self-concept that can vary from high to low, and which draw in part on others' evaluations of ourselves.

(3) social acceptance – the child's self-assessment of popularity among her peers (see also the next chapter); (4) physical appearance – how good- or bad-looking the child thinks she is; (5) behavioural conduct – how acceptable the child thinks her behaviour is to others (Harter, 1987, 1990).

Harter also considers that our self-esteem functions as the discrepancy between two internal assessments of ourselves, our ideal self and our real self: that is, what we *would like* ourselves to be or think we *ought to be* versus what we think we *really are*. When there is little difference between the two selves, discrepancy is low, and self-esteem is generally high. When the discrepancy is high, self-esteem will be lower. The latter suggests that the child sees himself as failing to 'live up' to their ideals or standards. Obviously, such standards are not the same for everybody. A child who sees athletic competence as more important than academic competence and who does not do that well in his school work, but is reasonably sporty, will not suffer much from a low self-esteem. However, another child who achieves similar standards as the first child at school, but values academic competence as highly important, will have a lower self-esteem.

Developmentally, from junior school or later childhood at ages 8–10 onwards, children show increasing consistency (little fluctuation in the short term) in their self-esteem, and their judgements become increasingly more realistic, with an overall fall in self-esteem levels versus early childhood, as they are more and more aware of their positive as well as negative attributes (Harter, 2003). In the transition to adolescence, self-esteem becomes increasingly differentiated or 'compartmentalised' with newer areas (such as relationships and future career projections). Into adolescence, with the changing school (secondary or high school) environment accompanied by increased conflict in social roles, emotional changes and relationship complexity (Harter, 1998), a temporary decline in self-esteem is observed, although it tends to rise again towards adulthood with increasing maturity, control and coping ability (see also the Lifespan box for the continuity into adulthood). Social influences are a likely explanation, since older childhood self-judgements become increasingly closely matched with the evaluations of others (such as those by teachers; Marsh et al., 1998). The evaluations of others, therefore, function like elements of the looking-glass self, providing a reference point from which we reflect on ourselves and build up aspects of our self-concept. Here such influences bear more specifically on the evaluative aspects of the self.

Summing up: self-concept development

As we have seen, the child's self-concept, including self-esteem, is a highly significant part of her social development. This development seems to emerge from fairly rudimentary senses that gradually evolve into more complex understandings which are impacted by a multitude of factors, of which a few have been described above, most notably the social actors around the child, such as her parents and peers. The qualities, roles and evaluations taken on by the child also tend to become increasingly consistent with those expected by the social groups and institutions around her over time. In the next part of the chapter, we will draw attention to such relationships between the child's sense of self and one of the most pervasive systems involving a social group – gender.

LIFESPAN

Is self-esteem a stable psychological factor or does it change as we get older?

A paper published by Orth et al. in 2010 reports findings from the Americans' Changing Lives study, which followed up 3617 individuals (aged 25–40 years) for 16 years. The study collected data on, among other things, self-esteem, and the analysis revealed an interesting effect. Self-esteem increased fairly steadily during early to middle adulthood, before reaching a peak at around 60 years of age, then appeared to decline during older adulthood. When the authors investigated the data more closely, they found a few social group differences in the longer-term changes. For instance, women generally had lower self-esteem than men during young adulthood but, by older age, this difference gradually disappeared. There also appeared to be an effect of race, in that people who described themselves as 'black' saw a more dramatic fall in self-esteem towards late adulthood than did people who described themselves as 'white'. Education, too, played a part with more educated people reporting higher overall levels of self-esteem than less educated people, although for both groups their lifespan 'arcs' in self-esteem were the same (as in Figure 11.2).

- Why do you think is there a sharp fall in self-esteem around the age of 60 years for all the participants in this research study?

The authors noted that midlife is a time of relative stability in terms of work, family and romantic relationships. People increasingly occupy positions of power and status. This might in turn promote self-esteem. However, older adults may be experiencing a change in roles, such as an 'empty nest' (especially for women with their children leaving home), retirement and obsolete work skills in addition to health issues.

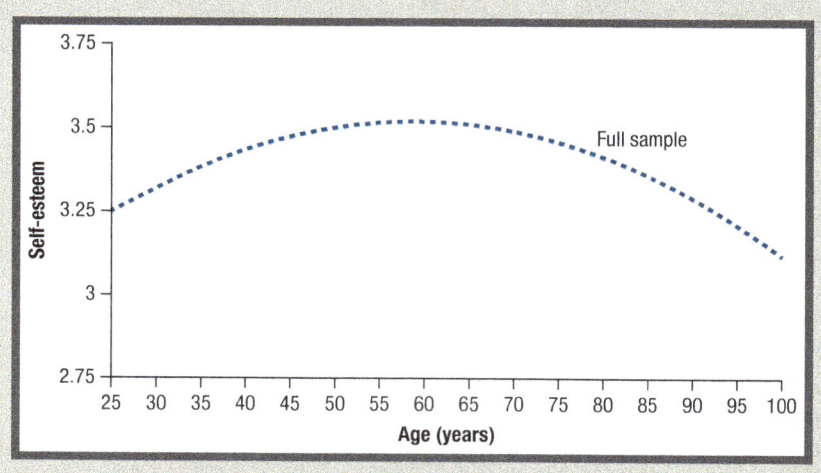

Figure 11.2 Changes in self-esteem through adulthood.
Source: Orth et al. (2010)

Understanding of gender categories: children's gender identity

We have seen how children gradually develop a sense of self across different ages. As the self-concept becomes more stable, children categorise and evaluate themselves and others along a wider range of social category systems, such as age, gender and race. As we have explored in the early part of the chapter, social categories are those groups in society that are seen to share common attributes, and social identities refer to the way we think and feel about, and behave towards, our own and others' social groups. Among all the possible social identities we have, our sense of gender identity starts to develop very early in life. Indeed, Lewis and Brooks-Gunn (1979), whose work (the rouge test) we read earlier, argue that gender is among the earliest, if not the earliest, social category systems a child learns, and that knowledge about this system is concurrently developed in relation to the child's sense of self and others. We will first explore the child's basic understanding of gender in this section.

Development of gender identity

How do children understand that they are a boy or a girl? And when and how do they realise that they will grow up to be a man or a woman? How do they identify (or even endorse) those behaviours, attitudes and expectations considered to be appropriate for their own gender in their society? These are some of the questions we will address below.

Gender identity, just like self-concept, has different levels and aspects, which develop gradually in stages. Children appear able to differentiate people by gender very early. By 9 to 12 months, they respond differently to photographs of male versus female faces (e.g. Brooks-Gunn and Lewis, 1981; Fagot and Leinbach, 1993) and to male and female strangers in person (Smith and Sloboda, 1986). Soon after, from about 12–18 months, they acquire a set of verbal labels for these categories ('mummy', 'daddy'). However, at 2 years, many children still do not know how to answer if asked directly whether they are a boy or a girl. This is helped if they are shown stereotypical pictures of boys and girls and asked which one(s) refer to them (Thompson, 1975). Nevertheless, by 3 years of age, most children can correctly label themselves by their gender (Weinraub et al., 1984).

Kohlberg's cognitive-developmental theory (1966, explained more fully later) describes gender identity development as a three-step learning process that results from the child's attempt to understand sex-role behaviour. The three steps are: gender labelling (when the child is aware of his/her own sex but believes it can change); gender stability (when the child is aware that sex is stable over time, i.e. if I am a boy now, then I will still be a boy in a year's time); and gender constancy or consistency (when the child is aware that his/her sex remains the same, regardless of time or circumstance, i.e. even if I dress as a girl, I am still a boy).

The correct labelling of oneself and others by gender is only the first step towards an understanding of gender identity, and research shows that at the age of 3 children are very much reliant upon external physical characteristics in the 'here and now' as they identify each other. When children at this age are faced with 'deeper' questions about their gender, such as 'When you were a baby, were you a little girl or little boy?' or 'When you grow up, will you be a mummy or daddy?', many are very confused. This aspect of gender identity, known as gender stability, refers to the understanding that our gender group membership is a permanent part of ourselves that remains the same through time. This is usually achieved by around 4 years of age (Slaby and Frey, 1975). However, at this age, recognition of gender groups largely relies on stereotypical features. This can be easily demonstrated by an experimental procedure where, for example, the picture of a stereotypical-looking boy (with short hair and shorts) is presented, and only the stereotypical elements (hair and clothing) are switched into those stereotypical of a girl (with long hair and a dress; see Figure 11.3). Although the transformation is performed in front of the child and is not taxing on memory, many pre-schoolers are confused, and say that the boy in the picture is a girl after the switch (Emmerich et al., 1977; Gouze and Nadelman, 1980).

Non-pictorial methods, such as hypothetical questioning (e.g. 'Can you be a girl if you really want to be?', 'If a boy lets his hair grow very long, is he still a boy?') may also be used. When children acknowledge that gender stays the same despite changes in appearance, gender constancy is achieved, and this tends to occur after 5 years of age. It seems odd that children who understand the permanency of gender can somehow be 'fooled' by the superficial changes, even though research with children in both Western and Eastern cultures has charted this trend (Munroe et al., 1984). This may be because gender constancy requires knowledge of biological sex differences, and indeed constancy is achieved earlier in children who understand the genital differences (as a marker of sex differences to children) between the sexes (Bem, 1989).

The fulfilment of all of gender labelling, stability and constancy may seem like a major milestone in the young child's development, but it is only a basic part of gender identity. A larger part is learning about what is associated with 'being' a boy or a girl, what being a member of a gender group is supposed to mean in various social contexts. In fact, around the time of gender labelling, about 2½ years (Kuhn et al., 1978), children have already begun building up basic ideas about the activities, abilities or preferences and, later, attitudes and expectations that are appropriate for, or typical of,

Definitions

Gender stability: the understanding that gender group membership is normally stable and permanent over time.
Gender constancy: the understanding that gender group membership is unchanged despite changes in appearance.
Gender labelling: correct identification of 'male' or 'female' of oneself and others.

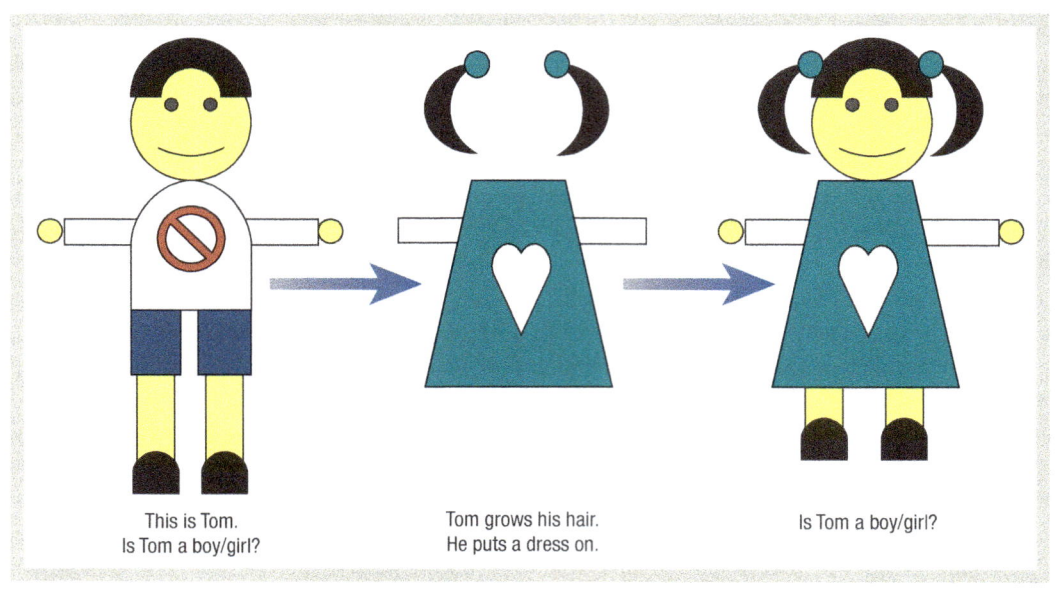

Figure 11.3 An example of the experimental transformation used for testing gender constancy in children.

their own and the other gender. These may surround adult daily activities, such as cooking and cleaning for women, repairing the house and car for men, or activities familiar to children, such as playing with dolls for girls and playing with trains for boys. Gender stereotypes also include beliefs about more subtle tendencies, such as 'girls cry and give kisses' and 'boys fight and don't cuddle'. Gender stereotyping also increases rapidly with age; before middle childhood (by the age of 5 years), children already associate various occupations and crude personality traits (such as 'strong', 'soft-hearted', 'cruel' and 'gentle') to men and women, and by the age of 8 to 9 years, their stereotypes are already very similar to those of adults (e.g. Best et al., 1977; Martin, 1993; Serbin et al., 1993).

Perhaps it is not surprising that children's stereotypes mimic those of adults. After all, in many societies, adults have clearly divided gender roles and stereotypes (most childcare is still conducted by women and men take on the heavier manual work, for instance) – children's beliefs may simply reflect the practical reality they witness. However, gender roles have, at least in post-industrial societies, been changing a great deal whilst children's beliefs have not always caught on, but seem simply to exaggerate common stereotypes. Apart from that, what is startling is that stereotyped behaviours are shown in children earlier than stereotyped beliefs are expressed, as the following will review.

Children's preference for gender-stereotyped toys and games is apparent by about 18 to 24 months, before they are able to label gender categories reliably, and this continues well into middle childhood (O'Brien, 1992). By the age of 3, before gender stability, children begin to profess a preference for peers of their own gender for play and friendships, and actually interact more with them. When they are in school, their regular friendship groups are almost exclusively composed of those of

Definition

Gender stereotypes: beliefs about what is appropriate for or typical of one's own or the other gender group.

STOP AND THINK

- How typical do you rate yourself as a member of your gender group? Alternatively, how masculine or feminine do you see yourself?
- Did you see yourself as a 'boyish' (or 'girlish') child? What criteria did you use?
- Do you think children nowadays think and behave in more or less gender-stereotyped ways compared with when you were a child?

their own sex, and this continues well into adolescence (Maccoby, 1988, 1990). While boys tend to prefer to play outdoors in less structured large-group activities (such as football and play-fighting; see also the next chapter), girls tend to socialise in pairs or smaller groups, or engage in more structured 'traditional' games (such as skipping and hopscotch).

It is important to view the above evidence with caution. Much of the research involved observations of behaviours or interactions in homes, classrooms or playgrounds and required researchers' categorisation and interpretation, and thus a level of bias may have drawn from the inputs. Furthermore, some of the differences observed are often quite small and many studies of infants under 2 years of age have not found many consistent behavioural differences between boys and girls (see reviews by Owen Blakemore et al., 2009; Maccoby, 1998, 2000). Still, the division between boys and girls in social interactions and the same-sex preference in friendships are such prevalent social phenomena that we cannot deny that gender exerts a strong force on children's identity and relationships.

Taken together, gender is a system of social categories that permeates children's lives from very early on. Even before they learn the gender labels or grasp the idea of their permanency, stereotyped behaviours and thinking are already apparent. So, what may explain this pervasive phenomenon? There are myriad arguments that are centred upon either the 'nature' or 'nurture' side of the debate, whilst others focus on the role played by the child. We will explore some of the major theories in the following sections.

By school age, children's peer groups consist of mostly same-sex peers and this continues into adolescence.
Source: Lam

Biological explanations for gender identity

It is of little surprise that many researchers have located biological factors as being responsible for gender differences. Men and women are clearly different in terms of their genetic make-up and physiology, and some such inherent differences may underpin the psychological differences observed between boys and girls.

The basic genetic sex difference (the male has an XY pair and the female an XX pair of chromosomes) means differential sex hormone production before birth and later in adolescence (the male with more testosterone and the female with more oestrogen). This leads to different body and physical attributes, including the male's larger average size, relatively greater physical strength and lung capacity and, arguably, more aggressive instincts. According to most biological accounts, gender differences in social role patterns have taken shape through the course of evolution as an outcome of humans' adaptation to their environment, with men and women being 'equipped' with such physical characteristics and instinctual tendencies for different functions. For instance, the gender division of hunters and gatherers is a result of the male's size and strength being better suited for the demands of the former, with the female's childbearing and breastfeeding abilities making her the 'natural' caregiver or homemaker. Sex differences in psychological functioning are, however, less clear and probably overstated (Hyde, 2005). Whilst there appears to be an effect of social influences on the development of aspects of self-esteem (women generally score higher on behavioural conduct and moral-ethical self-esteem; Gentile et al., 2009), other studies seem to demonstrate biological influences – for example, where men are better at mental rotation tasks and women are better at verbal tasks (Hausmann et al., 2009). However, performance in mental rotation tasks can be improved with priming and practice (Ortner and Sieverding, 2008), and as males have been inducted and expected to perform more of these tasks, this suggests that social opportunities to engage in 'masculine' tasks are a potential factor other than biological sex.

Parental investment theory

Some theorists, namely the sociobiologists, have taken the above ideas further to explain the contemporary behaviours, relationship patterns and even status disparity between the sexes. The logic of their reasoning, termed the parental investment theory (Wilson, 1972, 1978; Archer, 1992; Kendrick, 1994), is set around the specifics of male–female reproduction, which is seen as the primary goal of human survival – to pass on one's own genes. Reproduction is less 'costly' biologically to the male since he does not carry the unborn offspring or give birth. However, he does not have the important advantage of the female in being certain that any offspring born to her will possess her genes – unless he remains with his mate to preclude her from mating with other males. Therefore a 'trade' is struck whereby the sexes each assess and offer the other their relevant attributes; he needs to assess her reproductive capacity to bear his offspring and offer a level of commitment towards providing for and protecting those offspring, while she takes time in turn to assess his suitability as a reproductive partner with the requisite strength and resources to protect and provide for her and their offspring.

Sociobiologists argue that the reproductive trade-off has led to differential ideas about what is attractive or 'sought after' in males and females. For instance, greater emphasis is placed on youthfulness and physical attractiveness for the female, whereas traits such as ambition and competitiveness, associated with the pursuit of conquest and territory and resource guarding, are more valued for the male (Buss, 1987). It is debatable whether, related to this trade-off, women really take greater care in their appearance than men do in modern societies if we consider such phenomena as the 'metrosexual' male, but as we saw earlier, research shows that boys do engage in more activities that command dominance and competitiveness than girls do (see also the next chapter on play-fighting). However, whether such behaviours have their origin in biological sex differences evolved through a *very* long history of environmental changes is harder to ascertain.

Definition

Parental investment theory: a theory used to explain gender differences on the basis of biological sex differences. The theory states that reproduction has different implications for males and females and that men and women therefore look for different traits in each other, which through the course of evolution have been adapted as the modern-day observed gender role, behaviour and status differences.

Biological evidence

In order to ensure that the biologically given sex differences underpin children's psychological and behavioural outcomes, some signs of the biological impact should be shown before the child experiences socialisation, to pinpoint that it is inherited biology rather than learnt characteristics that is responsible for their role differences. This requires research in early infancy and makes definitive evidence difficult to obtain, at least in humans, as we know from earlier in the chapter and previous chapters that from a young age the infant is already very receptive and responsive to the social world around them. Therefore, some of the early evidence has come from research on animals that manipulated the sex hormones of offspring through the pregnant mothers. One common practice was where scientists administered doses of testosterone to pregnant monkeys prenatally and monitored the development of their female offspring (e.g. Young, 1964). Many found that the offspring displayed more 'rough-and-tumble' play and aggression towards each other compared with female offspring who had not received testosterone.

Short of being able to do the same to human participants for obvious ethical reasons, a smaller number of studies on children who received abnormal amounts of sex hormones due to their mothers' conditions or accidents and errors in the medical sciences have shed light on the discussion. The earliest cases were reported by Money and Ehrhardt (1972) who examined girls with congenital adrenal hyperplasia (CAH), a condition resulting from exposure to excessive levels of androgen (a male sex hormone) before birth as a treatment given to mothers prone to miscarriages. The girls were born

Definition

Congenital adrenal hyperplasia: congenital adrenal hyperplasia can affect both boys and girls. People with congenital adrenal hyperplasia lack an enzyme needed by the adrenal gland to make the hormones cortisol and aldosterone. Without these hormones, the body produces more androgen – a type of male sex hormone. This causes male characteristics to appear early (or inappropriately). About 1 in 10 000–18 000 children are born with congenital adrenal hyperplasia (MEDLINE Plus, 2010).

with male genitalia that were corrected surgically, and were raised as girls. Follow-ups showed that they saw themselves as more 'tomboyish' and played less with other girls compared with a matched sample who had not received treatment. Further research showed that girls with CAH due to genetic defects were more likely to play with boys' toys and were reported by their parents as being less interested in girls' activities (Berenbaum and Snyder, 1995). Such reports have been replicated across countries, including the UK, USA, Japan and Sweden (see a review by Owen Blakemore et al., 2009). However, we should bear in mind that the knowledge of their daughters' medial history might have affected the parents' attitudes, perception or behaviour, though under the circumstances it would be unlikely that they actually encouraged the masculine behaviours rather than the opposite. For other research involving sex hormones, see also the case studies in Chapter 3, 'Research methods'.

Money and Ehrhardt (1972), who wrote about the CAH cases, also treated and reported on a high-profile case that, many years later, was to become one of the most controversial in the medical and psychological professions and beyond (see the 'Nature–nurture' box).

The true story of the twins makes a compelling case for the role that biology plays in developing gender identity. It would appear that no matter what interventions are put in place, we simply cannot avoid the effects of the genes and biological mechanisms we are born with. However, similar to the studies of the girls who were exposed to excess hormones prenatally, the parents knew the biological sex of the twin, who was also already in his second year when he underwent reconstructive surgery. Also, hormonal and psychological therapies continued to his adolescence, despite his unease about the visits to the medical and psychiatric professionals (as documented in media coverage). These events could have raised the child's doubts about his assigned gender and his parents' behaviours towards him. Finally, even when findings converge with prescriptions of the biological accounts, published cases such as this are rare.

In general, any evidence of the direct effects of hormonal manipulation and biological dysfunction on gender identity in humans is harder to obtain, even though some reviewers have observed in normally developing individuals that male sex hormones have the strongest effects on play, aggression (Collaer and Hines, 1995) and sexual orientation (Patterson, 1995). Still, is gender identity all about play, aggressive instincts and sex? Many limitations of the biological accounts, and in particular the parental investment theory, concern their narrow scope, centred upon dominance and sexual behaviour. Much of the focus was placed on male physical strength and 'innate' aggressiveness to explain dominance when, even among animals, dominance can be strategic and learned, and is not always associated with strength and aggressiveness (Sayer, 1982). Even if biological instincts are directly responsible for such behaviours, as we reviewed earlier, gender *identity* consists of much more than just behaviour. It includes complex cognitive and affective processes, some of which involve conscious decision making, such as identifying ourselves with others of our own gender group, forming stereotypes and expectations based on such memberships, all of which vary across societies and can change over time.

NATURE–NURTURE

Gender realignment: the well-known case of 'the boy without a penis'

Documented in several televised programmes and a popular book (*As Nature Made Him: The Boy who was Raised as a Girl*; see Colapinto, 2013), apart from academic articles, is the case of a boy who was one of a set of identical twins, followed initially by Money and Ehrhardt (1972). Born as a normal male, at 7 months of age Bruce had most of his penis burnt off during a spoiled routine circumcision. It was not until nearly a year later that the confused and upset parents referred themselves to Dr John Money, who advised them to have him undergo radical surgical reconstruction, followed by years of hormonal therapy, to ultimately become a girl. The surgery went ahead when Bruce was 17 months old and the case was soon hailed as a 'success' story of nurture overcoming nature to shape one child's gender identity, when Money's initial follow-ups reported a well-adjusted 'Brenda' with feminine characteristics, if energetic and a little 'tomboyish'. In fact, this was the first case of gender reassignment ever performed on a developmentally normal child – Money had routinely conducted the procedure originally on hermaphrodites (individuals born with both male and female sexual organs) – leading doctors around the world to perform many more reassignments on infants with injured or abnormal genitalia. Bruce was the ultimate 'real-life' experiment to prove it was nurture, not nature, that determines gender identity – particularly when his twin brother could be a perfect matched 'control' raised as a boy.

The reality was rather more complicated. Money's publications on the case ceased in the late 1970s. Decades later, when the twin, now 'David', was a grown-up and cast aside his anonymity to the media, the story of a truly harrowing childhood was recounted. John described how he felt awkward around girls, was not interested in girls' activities but in running, fighting and climbing, and was later teased by his peers for his masculine mannerisms. A follow-up of David's teens, by Milton Diamond (1982), a biologist by training, told a story of isolation and depression, with a great deal of uncertainty about his gender. But it was not until the disturbed 14-year-old became suicidal that his parents decided to reveal the truth on the advice of a local psychiatrist, and he soon embarked on the painful journey of reverting his identity back in line with his biological sex.

As an adult, David married, adopted children and later cooperated with Diamond and others to participate in a follow-up (Diamond and Signmundson, 1997) and further media coverage (see the websites at the end of the chapter). However, depression plagued his adolescence and adulthood, among other issues, such as marital and financial difficulties and a history of clinical depression in the family (which also affected his mother and twin brother, who committed suicide when David was 36). In 2004, at the age of 38, two days after his wife told him that she wanted to separate from him, David took his own life.

- Do you think the twin's troubled gender identity was a result of biology?
- What other factors might have influenced his gender development?

Social learning theories of gender identity

We have seen the effects of biological sex on gender identity as well as their limitations as a sole explanation. We have identified that, as different societies hold different conceptions of gender-appropriate thinking and behaviour that can change over time, it is plausible that the social environment plays a part in forming children's gender identity. Almost an antithesis to biological accounts, one other early approach, social learning theories (Bandura, 1969, 1977; Mischel, 1966, 1970), proposes that children are 'shaped' into gender roles by the behaviour of adults and other children, and as such children are recipients of social information about what is appropriate for their own gender group in their own culture.

According to the premises of social learning theories, gender identity is acquired (rather than pre-programmed by genes) as a product of the child's accumulated learning experiences and socialisation, and the socialising 'agents' are the key players in a child's life – adults, peers and the media being the key sources. Social learning operates through two complementary processes called *reinforcement* and *modelling*. For reinforcement,

Definition

Social learning theories: an approach that explains gender identity development in terms of the child's accumulating learning experiences from their social environment, particularly through modelling others' behaviour and being rewarded for adopting approved mannerisms.

the child is rewarded for behaving in gender-appropriate ways and 'punished' for behaving in gender-inappropriate ways, according to the gender roles in their culture. So-called 'rewards' and 'punishment' are metaphoric and often do not come in a tangible, overt manner (treats or reprimands). The socialising agents' attention or encouragement, or the lack or withdrawal of them, already serve as effective rewards or punishment (such as parents offering their children toys seen as appropriate for their gender, or being more engaging when they play with these toys, and less so when the children pick up toys seen as more appropriate for the opposite sex).

The agents themselves often also demonstrate gender-role-appropriate behaviours (and therefore serve as 'models' for how to perform such behaviours) as well as the consequences of conforming to the gender norms in that culture. There are many everyday examples of gender-role demonstrations (such as fathers and mothers performing gender-typical chores in the home, and televised commercials showing the popularity and enjoyment of children engaging with gender-stereotyped toys). These socialising agents' actions and responses will, whether consciously or unconsciously, lead to gender-role learning in the child, as we will explore below.

Adults as socialising agents

> **STOP AND THINK**
>
> Think back to your childhood: the daily routines that your parents engaged in (work, household duties and pastimes) and their interactions with you (caring roles and play). Then talk to some parents about their daily activities, or observe them, or (if you are a parent yourself) reflect on your daily activities with your children.
>
> - How much of those are gender-typical behaviours?
> - Do the father and mother take part in such behaviours to different extents?
> - Has the pattern changed over the years?

Since its inception in the 1970s, the social learning approach to gender identity development has attracted a great deal of research, with the early period focusing on the behaviours and attitudes of adults towards children. For example, parents were observed to 'reward' gender-stereotyped behaviours and activities by infants of as young as 18 months, such as encouraging girls more for touching and cuddling than boys (Lewis, 1975),

Copying dad's behaviour is part of the gender-learning process.
Source: Lam

giving more encouragement to children for picking up gender-appropriate toys or engaging them for more gender-appropriate style of play or activities (e.g. Fagot, 1978; Caldera et al., 1989; Fagot and Hagan, 1991).

A series of studies since the 1970s, collectively known as the 'Baby X' experiments, illustrate some clear differences in the reactions towards, and expectations of, the same baby by adults simply due to her dress code or labelling by gender. Take the classic study by Will and colleagues (1976). The same baby girl was either dressed in blue and called 'Adam', or in pink and called 'Beth', when passed to some adult participants who were unaware of the purpose of the study. The adults were observed as they interacted with the infant, including their choice of toys (doll, train or 'gender-neutral' fish) that they handed to the baby. The results showed that the adults interacted differently with the baby depending on the colour of clothes and the name given ('Beth' was given the doll more often and received more smiles from the adults). Other Baby X studies vary in detail, such as the choice of toys, whether the baby was presented in person or via a video link, and the kinds of evaluation that adults had to make and so on, while retaining the same basic design. These studies reported similar patterns to that by Will et al. Both men and women were more likely to refer to the baby as 'big' and 'strong' when labelled as a boy versus 'small' and 'soft' when labelled as a girl (Rubin et al., 1974). They also encouraged the boy with more vigorous play and exploration, and treated the girl more gently and helped her more (Condry and Condry, 1976).

On the other hand, reviews of Baby X studies and similar research (Stern and Karraker, 1989; Golombok and Fivush, 1994; Maccoby, 2000; Golombok and Hines, 2002) noticed that some findings varied according to the kinds of measure used. Adults had less stereotypic responses if they were asked to evaluate the child's personality traits (e.g. how friendly or playful s/he was) compared with when they actually interacted with the child. This suggests that it is the adults' *behaviour* that bears out their existing gender stereotypes more, while their views (of the child) will be based more on the child's characteristics as they observed them.

Clearly, children do not only receive reinforcement through the behaviour and reactions of adults who hold gender-typed ideas. Even without such direct inputs, adults act as models of stereotyped behaviours which children observe and imitate. Studying children and their mothers, Fagot et al. (1992) reported that those with mothers who endorsed more traditional gender roles tended to gender-label objects earlier than those with mothers of more gender-egalitarian views. Reviewing a large body of work, it was noted that daily activity contexts (e.g. which parent does what at home) accounted for most of the variation in the modelling observed (Leaper, 2000). A recent study analysing parent–child (12-month-olds) interactions in Norway (Nordahl et al., 2014) has found noteworthy differences in mothers' and fathers' engagement. Fathers of boys showed more positive engagement than mothers of boys and fathers of girls, while mothers of both sexes were equally engaging. The researchers argue that child gender plays a greater role for fathers as they identify more with sons and perceive themselves as important role models to boys. On the other hand, mothers spend more time with their baby in the first year and have more experience and may be more organised and coherent with their emotional responses.

Therefore, the prior expectations and experiences of major adult role models can play a distinct role in how they interact with their young, who in turn may appropriate such behaviours. This is somewhat in line with a former meta-analysis (Lytton and Romney, 1991) that reported boys and girls to have similar experiences, if slightly more gender-stereotyped reinforcement by fathers (Lytton and Romney, 1991). This, in practice, is not really favouring social learning, as the majority of caregivers and educators are female. Theoretically speaking, if the strength of a child's gender identity was largely contingent on the rewards from, and his/her observations of, available adult models, then many children would have acquired a feminine identity. Moreover, whether through reinforcement or observation, what exactly is taken on board by the child, and how it gets 'translated' into gender-stereotyped behaviour, is far less clear-cut. Obviously, more forces are at work to foster gender development, and we will turn to these other agents next.

Peers as socialising agents

By middle childhood (by about age 5 and upwards), at least half of the child's waking hours will be spent in the social institution that is school, where most of the socialising agents are other children. All these agents bring with them their existing gender stereotypes as well as sharing such views (if sometimes also challenging those of each other), constructing and reproducing more. In fact, by 3 to 4 years of age, children already recognise the gender-appropriateness of play and activities, and criticise their peers for what they see as gender-inappropriate behaviour. The stereotypes that are re-created (such as 'daddies don't cook' and 'mummies don't drive cars') can in fact be even more rigid than those of adults (e.g. Fagot, 1977). As we saw earlier, both boys and girls like to play and associate more with those of their own sex. It is unsurprising that peers are such a dominant force in children's lives.

In a study that compared directly the behaviours of mothers, fathers and peers towards 3- to 5-year-olds' gender-appropriate and inappropriate play, Langlois and Downs (1980) found that peers had the strongest responses. Children were first instructed to play with highly gender-stereotyped toys for either boys or girls. Once the child was settled into play, the parent or peer was invited into the room to observe and interact with the child. Mothers displayed little differentiation in their responses towards their children, but fathers were rather more responsive towards gender-appropriateness; they were positive with their child in gender-appropriate play, but were more overtly hostile (making disparaging remarks or ridicule), particularly with sons, when they engaged in cross-gender play. Still, the peers' reactions towards gender-inappropriate play were the strongest of all, and also most negative when boys were playing with girls' toys.

Reviewing Baby X research, Stern and Karraker (1989) noted that, when children were asked to play with Baby X, they were more strongly influenced by information about the baby's alleged sex than were adults. The authors reason that, since children are themselves still learning about their own gender, they are prone to adopting more extreme attitudes. However, relatively recent reviews of other studies (e.g. Leman and Tenenbaum, 2014; Golombok and Hines, 2002; Owen Blakemore et al., 2009) have found few consistent differences in peer responses towards boys and girls, or towards gender-appropriate and inappropriate play or behaviour. Also similar to adult reinforcement and modelling, whether peers' responses translate later into more gender-stereotyped play and behaviour in children is difficult to study. Still, recent longitudinal research (Martin et al., 2013) found that the sex of school children's peers contributed the most to predict their friendships later, followed by activities (which are themselves gender-typed). So, it can be said that peers can both directly and indirectly influence children's gender development.

Researchers have also attempted to explore the real effects of agents by training adults or rewarding children to actively promote certain activities (such as cooperative play) and then measuring the children's behaviour at a later point. For example, Fagot (1985) found that girls were influenced by teachers and other girls, but not by boys, whereas boys were only influenced by other boys, and not by teachers or girls, preferring noisy rough-and-tumble play. This may be because cooperative activities involve 'feminine' behaviour (such as being quiet and sharing) to which girls are already more receptive than boys. In that case, children's 'selective' attention to different socialisation *content* (rather than socialising agents *per se*) should be studied. A recent study (Pahlke et al., 2014) has found that lessons fostering the ability to challenge sexism by teaching children aged 4–10 years to respond to undesirable/unfair bias (e.g. teasing about gender-role nonconformity) could lead to them being better able to identify sexism in the media and to respond to peers' sexist comments after a 6-month post-test period. This suggests that children are far from being passive vessels of gender and stereotyped information; they have the agency themselves also to either reproduce or resist stereotypes.

The media as a socialising agent

> **STOP AND THINK**
>
> When you next watch television with commercials, make notes of the behaviour and communication of the actors. How much of this can be called gender-stereotyped?

Since the beginning of the postwar years, the mass media, particularly televised media, have featured prominently in children's lives in industrialised countries. Children spend more time watching television and dealing in other digital media forms, particularly the internet, than they do interacting with their families and friends and even in school (Buckingham, 2003, 2013). Where the content of media is concerned, it is strongly stereotyped. Despite societal changes and political trends, in that adult broadcasters and actors of both sexes have become more equal in status, it is still the case that in series and commercials, even in children's programmes during primetime, many themes and roles are highly 'gendered', with some being more 'action-packed' or fantasy-based and others more sedentary or 'real-life', which might influence the viewing patterns of different children.

A study by Huston and colleagues has reported that, although the average time spent on watching television showed no sex differences, *what* boys and girls watched was very different from each other. Boys' interests were more uniform and 'action-oriented' and girls' were more diverse and 'people-oriented' (Huston et al., 1999). Later, Livingstone and Bovill (2001), in a large-scale European study, surveyed children's favourite shows between the ages of 6 and 16 years and found distinct developmental patterns of interests between boys and girls (Table 11.2). Both sexes were largely interested in cartoons until 9 or 10 years, when girls turned to soaps, and then this continued to 12–13 years before they turned to other series. In contrast, boys were equally likely to tune in to TV series or sports programmes at 12–13 years before sports became dominant from 15–16 years.

More recently, electronic media such as computer games and the internet have offered a highly attractive, or even addictive, source of entertainment (Larson, 2001). One study by Roberts and associates showed a consistent pattern where, between the ages of 8 and 18 years, boys spent three times as much time as girls did on video games (Roberts et al., 2004). This trend also held when comparing young adult male and female students (Li and Kirkup, 2007). If we consider the style and content or themes of popular video games (such as Super Mario, Call of Duty, and Football Manager 2010, all within the top 10 best-sellers on Amazon at time of writing), which are often masculine and action-oriented, these findings are perhaps not surprising. However, other games on the list include more feminine themes (such as Lego Harry Potter, Just Dance, and Dance on Broadway), so the gaming industry may have become wise to the needs of girl players. A more recent survey of over 1200 students (Greenberg et al., 2010) reports that, while boys play more and have more motives (such as fantasy gratification) for play than girls do, their preference for physical games declines in late adolescence as motives start weakening from the middle years.

Since the 2000s, the focus has shifted towards children's and young people's use of the internet both as a source of information and, particularly more recently, as a space for online or 'virtual' social networking. There have been claims that online interactions and behaviour often reflect and reinforce gender norms (such as beauty ideals for girls or 'macho' personas for boys) that can shape young people's identity. Educational psychologist Catherine Steiner-Adair, in her studies with over 1000 children on the impact of technology (Steiner-Adair and Barker, 2013), found that it is clear that the internet has amplified the worst gender stereotypes that have been around, and she advocates teaching children to deconstruct those potentially harmful gender 'codes'. Indeed, in social media (such as Facebook) young men and women do tend to conform to social roles and norms consistent with their gender (Haferkamp et al., 2012).

The above findings are informative to the extent that they show children are selectively attending to media content that contains material appropriate for their own sex. Yet an obvious and critical issue remains about the nature of the relationship between viewing, game playing or internet use and gender identity. Earlier studies only established a tenuous relationship between the two (Durkin, 1985). It was observed that TV in the 1970s and 1980s portrayed women more negatively or in gender-stereotypic behaviour and rarely cast them in a starring role. It appears that, although some things have changed in terms of the newer gaming industry catering for girls, others have stayed the same in terms of the content of much of the televised media, particularly that for the teen market in terms of female under-representation (Gerding and Signorielli, 2014). It could be that already stereotyped children, just like their adult counterparts, simply prefer to engage with such material to find confirmation of their own views, and thus they are just responding to pre-existing preferences and tendencies (see the Cutting Edge box for how young people may interpret media information). However, because *selective* attention and modelling

Table 11.2 Favourite TV shows by age and gender: a European study.

Age	Boys	Girls
6–7 years	Cartoons	Cartoons
9–10 years	Cartoons	Soap operas
12–13 years	TV series, sports	Soap operas
15–16 years	Sports	TV series

Source: After Livingstone and Bovill (2001)

CUTTING EDGE

Teenagers constructing gender identity through media representations of romantic/sexual relationships and alcohol consumption

In a recently published paper in the *Sociology of Health and Illness*, a research team in Scotland (Hartley et al., 2014) report findings from 13- to 15-year-olds that explored how their relationships and drinking behaviour were shaped by the quest for appropriate gender identity. Contrary to most other social developmental studies, the researchers used a 'qualitative' non-statistical approach with relatively few (just over 80) participants. They engaged the students in group discussions and in-depth individual interviews that tapped into sensitive topics, including sexual behaviour, smoking, drinking and illegal drug use, and how such behaviours came to be interpreted by the participants and related to how they talked about their own behaviours.

On examining what forms of sexual/romantic behaviour and alcohol use are considered gender-appropriate, the students appeared to integrate media portrayals into their own notions of gender-appropriate behaviour. For instance, several students reported that the media directly influenced their relationship expectations, citing American sitcoms as sources of role models as well as portrayals of relationship – even though they were aware that such were unlike 'real life'. Also, while boys thought that girls learned 'perfect' unrealistic relationship expectations from TV or movies, girls suggested that boys derived their expectations from pornography. Although the media appeared to influence less their expectations of drinking, teenagers might drink to help them 'connect' with the opposite sex in ways which were shaped by what is gender-appropriate as learned from the media portrayals; they believed that certain kinds of drinking-related sexual behaviour made them appear more or less feminine or masculine (e.g. boys being drunk related to promiscuous sex and physical aggression).

In sum, the processes of media influence seem to operate primarily through teenagers' presumptions about how their peers are influenced. Drawing on media content, they attempt to understand the roles and rules of relationships, and how one should behave, seemingly with the aim to belong and be accepted, by second-guessing their opposite-sex counterparts.

- Why do you think that the researchers focused on sexual/romantic relationships and drinking to engage the teenagers in their study?
- What may be the reason that the teenagers believed that others (particularly the opposite sex) are more strongly affected by the media?

As we read in the first part of this chapter on self-concepts, individuals become aware of their objective self, particularly in relation to common social categories such as gender as their social identity, through their relationships with others; Cooley's 'looking-glass self' suggests that people must consider themselves through the eyes of others. Moreover, the authors argue that, specific to their stage of development from childhood into adulthood, teenagers shift from largely single-sex to mixed-sex interactions (see the next chapter for details) and are increasingly required to negotiate their identities with a different peer group (i.e. the opposite sex). Finally, in the West, two of the most prevalent ways in which teenagers construct their identities in transition into adulthood (like rites of passage) are through the practices of drinking and engaging in sexual relationships. The authors further expected that these may demonstrate particular femininities and masculinities in particular social settings and interactions (as they indeed found from their data).

are happening, children should have some *cognition* (or awareness) of their own gender to guide them regarding *which* behaviour to take on board, and it is some of these processes that we will explore in the next approach.

Cognitive theories of gender identity

We have just considered the possibility that, in order for children to acquire a sense of gender identity, they ought to have some knowledge or awareness (cognition) of their own gender to steer them towards those agents of their own group. Indeed, the pioneer of the earliest cognitive theory of gender identity, Lawrence Kohlberg (1966), previously argued that 'our approach to the problems of sexual development starts directly with neither biology nor culture, but with cognition' (p. 82).

Drawing mainly on Piaget's school of thought (see Chapter 2, 'Theoretical perspectives'), Kohlberg (1966, 1969) saw gender identity development, like other cognitive development, as a constructive process; an active child is guided by reason or logic when dealing with gender-role knowledge. But where does this knowledge come from? 'How much' knowledge is needed for developing our sense of gender identity? According to Kohlberg, gender-role knowledge comes from children's encounters with the world around them – a process that he calls 'self-socialisation' (Maccoby and Jacklin, 1974). As for how much knowledge, we can find certain suggestions in Kohlberg's (1969) own cognitive-developmental theory. Interestingly, Kohlberg's theory also linked a child's cognitive capacity to his/her capacity for moral reasoning. These ideas and their role in managing behaviour in schools are explored in Chapter 15, 'Understanding bullying'.

Cognitive-developmental theory

Matching closely with Piaget's (1953) stage-based theory of intellectual development, Kohlberg expounded that the self-socialisation of gender identity develops gradually through three stages from early through middle childhood. In fact, the key milestones of the stages are concepts that we have earlier covered as gender labelling, stability and constancy, with each stage featured by a key (or rather, a lack of) cognitive skill (see Table 11.3). For example, in stage 2, the lack of conservation skills means that children are prone to being confused by physical transformation (as illustrated by the counter and liquid experiments in Chapter 3), including the transformation for testing gender constancy.

Unlike either the biological accounts or social learning theories, which see that the child's gender development is determined by her genes or the impact of socialising agents, this theory hinges on the assumption that the child's own role in seeking gender-role information is driven by her gender awareness and cognitive skills. Stage 3 skills are pivotal in Kohlberg's model because this is when the child is equipped with the fullest essential knowledge about her own gender group, that it is a differentiating, permanent and immutable part of her identity (gender labelling, stability and constancy all achieved).

Definition

Cognitive-developmental theory: a theory, derived by Kohlberg, that explains gender identity development by the child's developing cognitive skills in three stages, which underpin critical milestones in understanding about gender as gender labelling, gender stability and gender constancy.

Table 11.3 Stages in Kohlberg's (1969) cognitive-developmental theory.

Stage/age	Gender feature	Cognitive feature
Stage 1	Gender labelling	
2½–3½ years	Slow recognition of gender labels	Egocentrism
	Treat labels as personal terms	
Stage 2	Gender stability	
3½–4½ years	Gradually aware of gender durability	Poor conservation skills
	Dependent on physical cues	
Stage 3	Gender constancy	
4½–7 years	Understand gender is constant across time and contexts	Conservation skills achieved

Evidence supporting Kohlberg's theory has therefore come mainly from research that has identified a close relationship between the achievement of gender constancy and children's gender-appropriate or stereotyped behaviour or attitudes. For instance, Slaby and Frey (1975) examined pre-school children's level of gender constancy and attention towards same-gender models. They found that boys with a higher level of performance on gender constancy would pay more attention to male models than female ones, compared with those with a lower level of constancy. Similarly, Ruble et al. (1981) investigated the relationship between gender constancy and effects of commercials featuring gender-stereotyped toys. They found that gender constancy predicted children's responsiveness to the commercials, such that those who achieved constancy were more likely to play with the toys and judge that they were appropriate for their own gender compared with those who were not gender-constant.

Although such studies make a strong case for the importance of gender constancy, later research (e.g. Fagot, 1985; Carter and Levy, 1988) shows that, although gender constancy *helps* children to seek gender-appropriate information, it is not always *needed*. Indeed, as we reviewed earlier, gender-stereotyped tendencies (such as same-sex peer preference) are clearly apparent in pre-school – well before gender constancy is expected. Perhaps a lesser understanding of gender is already adequate. The next cognitive approach is one that takes this critical point into account.

Gender schema theories

Gender schema theorists do not dispute Kohlberg's point regarding the child's active role, but this relatively recent approach differs from his theory in its 'key' to explaining gender identity and stereotyping: simply, the knowledge of gender labels instead of acquiring gender constancy. Going by schema theorists (Bem, 1981; Martin and Halverson, 1981, 1983, 1987), once children can label social (gender) groups and crucially know to which group they belong (a boy or a girl), they are readily motivated to search the social environment for information about behaviours or values consistent with that group (to be like others in it) which build up or enrich their *schema*. A schema is a system of beliefs (including stereotypes) about attributes associated with social groups. They provide a set of cognitive structures that help the child to form evaluations of and make assumptions about each other, objects and situations based on social group membership.

Accordingly, simply knowing one's own and others' gender (gender labelling) alone is sufficient to construct and develop gender schemas, and further development of gender identity and stereotypes builds on this knowledge base. However, it is important to bear in mind that in the beginning, the young child's schemas are very basic, based on a simple 'ingroup/outgroup' dichotomy and the most typical characteristics of each sex. Then the child learns more about the ingroup, including gradually a grasp of deeper, less superficial characteristics, which help build up part of his self-concept (a more coherent sophisticated sense of self as we read earlier) before he then begins to pay attention to the outgroup (see Martin and Halverson, 1981, 1987).

To demonstrate the workings of the schemas, an example using toy choice is used here (see Figure 11.4). The child perceiver might first identify a toy as gender-appropriate (or inappropriate) on his own liking of a new toy. Then, with the key knowledge of his own gender, the child will attend to it/prefer it more if it is deemed appropriate to the ingroup, or in the case of a new object predict that others of the *ingroup* will like it (if he does himself). The first mapping shows that, for a common, stereotyped toy like a car, the child knows that this item is designed 'for boys', hence the awareness of his own gender group leads him to decide that playing with this object is 'for him' (Martin and Halverson, 1981). A similar cognitive operation that depends on the child's awareness of his own gender may apply to thinking about a new, non-stereotyped toy (in the second mapping). Clearly, the child's own liking of any new toy will depend on how attractive it is to him. Yet if he has to 'guess' if *other* children may like it (an inference-making process), he may base his predictions on his own liking *in combination with the gender group membership* of himself in relation to those about whom he is making the predictions. Here, if the perceiver is a boy and he likes the toy, he may infer that, since he likes it, other boys should like it as much as he does (and girls less so) – even though the toy itself remains novel and non-stereotyped (as was found by Martin et al. (1995) with children as young as 4 years of age for a range of attractive and

---

Definition

Gender schema: a system of beliefs about the attributes and behaviours associated with gender that help the child to form evaluations of, and to make assumptions about, each other and social objects and situations based on gender group memberships.

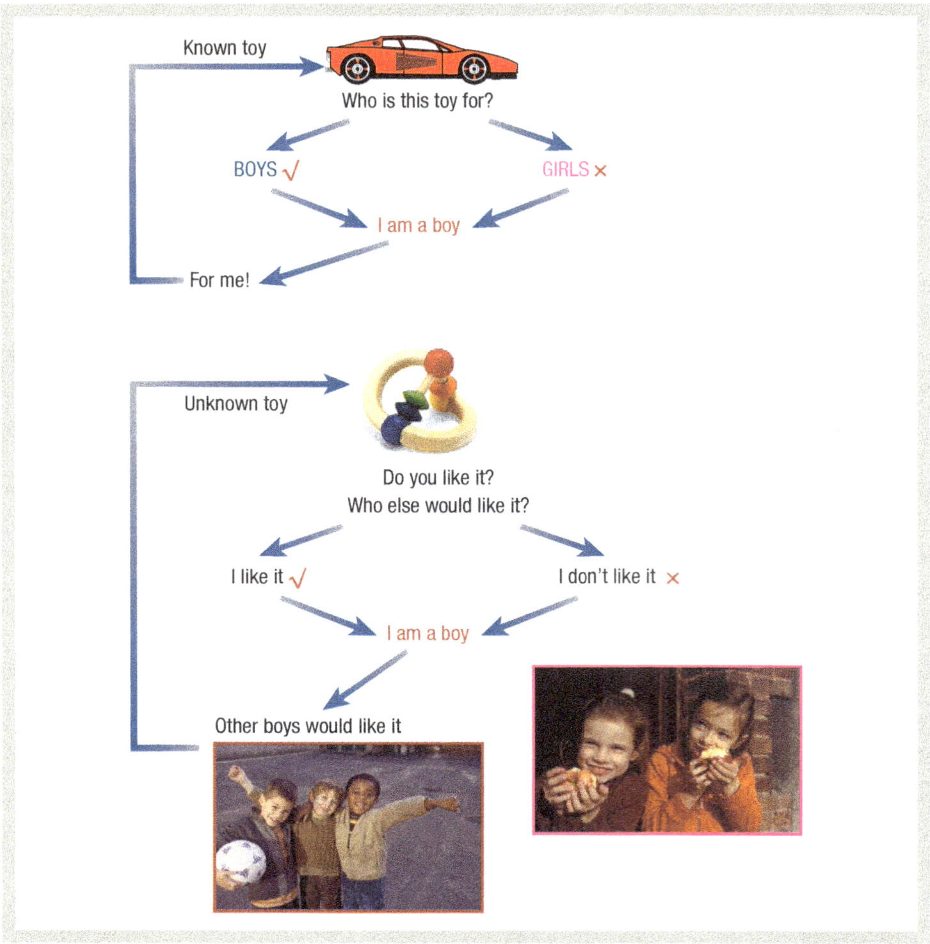

Figure 11.4 The workings of gender schemas for known and novel toys.

Sources: (a) Martin and Halverson (1987); (b) Martin et al. (1995)

non-attractive novel toy objects). The child is said to be generalising his own attributes *selectively* to others of his gender ingroup, effectively generating new stereotypes for an otherwise gender-neutral object.

In the original study, children were asked how much they liked the toys and how much other 'boys' and 'girls' would like them. One may argue that, perhaps by articulating the gender group labels, children might have been 'primed' to think along gender divisions. However, later research (Lam and Leman, 2003) found that the 'gendercentric' thinking pattern still held when only photographs of boys and girls were shown (without articulating the terms). In fact, not only was such inference making applied to toys (which are of obvious interest to children anyway, or as a genre of social 'objects' toys are more susceptible to being assigned new stereotypes since many toys are advertised as 'for boys' or 'for girls'); but also the pattern has been found to apply to inference making about some foods (Lam and Leman, 2009).

Gender schemas influence things from gender-segregated play and playmate preference (e.g. Fagot, 1985; Martin et al., 1999; Leman and Lam, 2008) and recall of stereotypic information (e.g. Ruble and Stangor, 1986; Carter and Levy, 1988; Liben and Signorella, 1993), to preferred occupation and adult family preferences (Signorella and Hanson Frieze, 2008). The general trend is that children process faster, remember better and prefer material that is consistent with gender schemas (beliefs about what is gender-appropriate, such as stories or descriptions about boys and girls that are stereotypical in character or behaviour) and are less efficient or willing to deal with inconsistent information, or may even distort the material (e.g. 'misremembering' or fabricating book content, for instance; Frawley, 2008). Moreover, children perform better at tasks labelled as being 'for' their gender ingroup (Davies, 1986). This has considerable practical implications in such areas as education, as children not only actively organise their thinking and behaviour around what is expected of their gender ingroup, but also are more motivated to do well in a newly stereotyped task (simply because it is said to be 'for' their own sex).

A key strength of the schematic approach to gender identity is that it can account for the rigidity with which longstanding gender stereotypes are upheld by children. This is because the theories denote that once children are aware of their own gender group membership and start to build their gender schemas, they will already attend to and take on board more information that confirms stereotypic beliefs (and attune less to what deviates from them). This, in turn, enriches the schema further, and the child becomes even more stereotyped. This way, the child would be already attentive to the gender-appropriateness *already learned* about those attributes that are displayed or behaviours performed by a socialising agent, rather than the sex of the agent *per se* – which is where the social learning approach fell short in explaining. These tenets fit particularly well with the basic assumption of a cognitive approach that projects the child as an 'active' participant in constructing her own gender knowledge structures (the schemas). Furthermore, this construction will be increasingly susceptible to stereotypes in the environment, and this will in turn shape the child's behaviours and values, and inform their future decisions.

Despite the merits mentioned, there are at least several key limitations with this popular approach to accounting for the development of gender identity. The first concerns the cognitive school of theories in general. Even though it is empowering to conceptualise the child as active in formatting his/her own gender identity, the idea of 'self-socialisation' is at best vague. Even information such as 'cars are for boys' is taken for granted as just a common gender stereotype in the social environment to be 'picked up' by children. This leaves a 'black box' of unknowns like *how* children pick up this kind of information; the approach concentrates on what happens at the processing level, having assumed that the child already holds this information. Therefore we know relatively little about *what* the child's schemas actually contain (what beliefs or ideas), even though we know quite well *how* schemas are supposed to 'work' (as illustrated earlier).

However, it is well established (see Chapter 3) that cognitive development occurs within, and depends on, the social context of the child and his/her co-participants (cf. Vygotsky, 1978b), which is particularly important for developing social identities including gender identity

Gender-inappropriate play? Going by the schematic approach, the knowledge of gender stereotypes should mean that this girl would avoid the type of stereotypic toys she is enjoying.
Source: Lam

(Lloyd and Duveen, 1992). Furthermore, if general cognitive skills (such as labelling and conservation, which do not differ between boys and girls) determine gender-typed thinking and behaviour, we would expect similar stereotyping tendencies in boys and girls. However, this is not the case; as we saw earlier, boys and men tend to be more stereotypic than girls and boys, perhaps as a result of the father–son interaction from early in life. A recent study also shows that, when children were afforded the chance to predict the sex of gender-ambiguous characters (in drawings) in their own words (rather than using closed-ended dichotomised descriptions), they explained the reasons for their gender assignments in more unconventional than stereotypic terms, particularly in the case of younger, pre-school children (Tenenbaum et al., 2010). Perhaps to truly understand how children play an 'active' role in constructing gender identity, procedures such as this that give them their own 'voice' in research should be sought more.

Finally, with advances in technology including infant eye tracking since the 2000s, the research poses challenges for the basic premise of the approach. By 18 months, infants already attend more to gender-appropriate but novel toys (Campbell et al., 2000). Although we should exercise caution when interpreting observational data of pre-verbal infants, it is intriguing that infants who cannot reliably identify each other by gender can 'assign' gender to novel objects. Unless stereotypic toys possess properties 'intrinsically' appealing to boys and girls (such as in their textures), other (cognitive or non-cognitive) factors ought to be considered.

A combined approach: social cognitive theory

Mindful of the shortcomings of social learning and cognitive approaches, as reviewed above, Kay Bussey and Albert Bandura (1999, 2004) proposed a combined social cognitive theory of gender development that was an attempt to offer a more comprehensive account of children's gender identity development. Social cognitive theory describes a three-factor model of personal factors, environmental factors and behavioural patterns influencing gender development. Bussey and Bandura argue that we learn about gender through three routes: tuition, enactive experience and modelling. Gender *tuition* occurs when, for instance, a mother teaches her daughter how to bottle-feed a baby or when a father teaches his son the rules of football or the different types of car on the road.

Enactive experience describes the reaction of others to the child's behaviours, which facilitates gender development by reinforcing stereotyped behaviours and disapproving of or sanctioning non-stereotyped behaviours. Most commonly experienced, Bussey and Bandura argue, is *gender modelling*, where children learn about gender-stereotyped behaviours simply through observing other people.

As with the social learning approach that describes the development of aggression in young children, the social cognitive theory of gender development describes four factors influencing the learning potential of observed behaviour. Bussey and Bandura argue that observation of behaviour alone is not enough for the child to model it. In order for observations to have an effect on learning, four key cognitive processes must be activated: attention, memory, production and motivation. Therefore, children must first notice that the information is related to gender and be able to process and store this information in memory (see Chapter 6, 'Memory and intelligence'). Afterwards, the child must practise (produce) the behaviour they have learned and be rewarded for it (motivation). With all four processes successfully in place, an example of say, a girl's observation of her aunt making the tea while her uncle watches football with her brother will become a gender learning experience, which can be reinforced when she offers to help her aunt or when her uncle suggests that she help out so that he and her brother can catch up on a game.

Social cognitive theory is a complex model describing gender development in children that provides a framework for understanding the complicated interactive nature of personal and environmental factors and biological patterns of behaviours. According to the theory, children monitor their behaviour and their emotional reaction to that behaviour – does the girl matching her behaviour to her aunt's feel any sense of pride or shame in helping to make the tea while her brother watches the football? If the girl feels a sense of pride, she will add this experience to her developing sense of self-efficacy in attaining this gender-desirable role. This self-efficacy will then be reinforced and developed through further exposure to

Definition

Self-efficacy: a person's belief about how effectively he or she can control herself, her thoughts or behaviours, particularly when intended to fulfil a personal goal.

situations where she can practise (making the tea), through social modelling (seeing her mother and friends making the tea) and through social persuasion (seeing other fathers persuading women to make the tea whilst they watch sport on TV).

Gender identity development: synthesis and transaction

> **STOP AND THINK**
>
> - Of the three major approaches that have been proposed to explain gender identity development, which one do you find the most convincing?
> - Why is that?

From what we have read of the major theoretical approaches, none alone can give a complete explanation for the complex and multidimensional 'jigsaw' that is the development of gender identity. It seems that there are biological forces in place that are irrepressible, where we simply cannot change some of the instincts and tendencies based on such forces. At the same time, it is clear that, from day one, the social forces are already at work. These operate through the way in which the child's life is structured by those closest to them. Their responses to, and expectations of, the child based on his or her gender can be both overtly and covertly conveyed, while at the same time the socialising agents themselves provide ready examples of gender-appropriate behaviour. Meanwhile, the child is not a passive recipient 'imbued' by the action of their genes or people around them. Children actively seek and make sense of information about the gender groups available in their social environment and, from there, build and refine a complex system of thinking that will guide their further discovery. This is helped by the understanding of crucial concepts, such as the knowledge of which group they belong to. Clearly, none of these processes works in isolation. Figure 11.5 offers a model of 'transaction' between the factors and processes inherent in the child and those found in the environment with which the child interacts.

Transaction here refers to the continual interactions between forces derived from the child's own characteristics (be they the inborn biological sex or later self-concept constructed by the child) and the environment in which he or she is placed (which contains socialising agents). One crucial point is that each stage of development itself will lead on to spiralling interactions. Following the diagram, this is not so much because of the physical differences between the sexes from birth (which do influence some behavioural tendencies), but because of the psychological attributions made by socialising agents in the child's immediate environment, based on seeing such physical cues. Such attributions influence the way adults and peers behave towards the child, who is also actively making sense of their behaviour, to build up an early sense of self. The child, however, will continue to seek more information about gender groups and may find confirmation for the gender-relevant attributes from

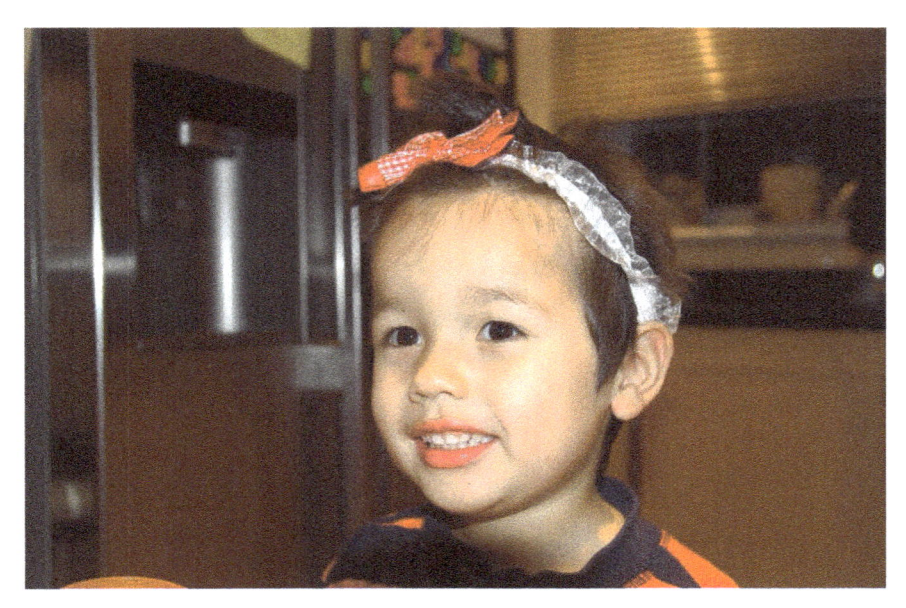

Figure 11.5 Gender-inappropriate play? Going by the schematic approach, the knowledge of stereotypes would mean that this boy would avoid the kind of stereotypic play or cross-dressing that he seems to be enjoying.

Source: Lam

the environment through the agents again. These inputs can then lead the child to differentiate further between the sexes in terms of these attributes.

Although it is in itself logical and plausible, the validity of transaction models such as this is difficult to test empirically, since it involves several interactions all happening at the same time. It is also difficult to apply the model to explain gender identity on an individual basis, especially in cases where a child has an 'atypical' identity. The Case Study box features one such case. What could possibly explain this kind of phenomenon?

It is noteworthy that, unlike the twins earlier, here is a case that concerns a boy who was born with the usual sets of male chromosomes, hormones and genitalia. It is then difficult to use biological explanations, unless there are unknown biological forces at work. The author raises the questions of how much hormones 'shape the brain' to be male or female and whether this development can be 'interrupted'. This opens up the possibilities of other kinds of input on gender identity. The parents apparently do not see the boy's gender identity as a 'problem' and lead a 'normal' life. Can this be seen as their 'condoning' gender-inappropriate behaviour, contrary to what we read earlier about social learning theories, where adults actively reinforce gender-appropriateness? However, since we read that their son's feminine tendencies started by the age of 2, should the parents have intervened by actively 'shaping' him into a boy and referring him to professionals earlier? There are no simple answers to such questions, or indeed a 'right' solution to such cases, but what they do highlight, as the author argues, is the complex of biopsychological processes that form our gender development.

Summing up: gender identity development

Undoubtedly, gender provides one of the most, if not the most, pervasive systems of classification in societies, and one that permeates most aspects of adults' and children's lives. Since infancy, children already recognise the basic male–female distinctions, and from

CASE STUDY

Gender identity disorder (abridged from original article)

Mistakes in God's Factory

In 2005 a 12-year-old German boy became the world's youngest person to start hormone treatments for a sex change.

Kim P. is 14 years old. She's had enough of psychiatrists who ask weird questions. She's had enough of doctors who reject her case because this fashion-conscious girl – previously called 'Tim' in her patient file – unsettles them.

She was born as a boy. Her body, chromosomes and hormones were all undoubtedly masculine. But she felt otherwise. For Kim it was clear from the beginning that, as she says, 'I wound up in the wrong body.'

At the age of 2, Tim tried on his older sister's clothes, played with Barbies and said, 'I'm a girl.' Her parents thought it was a phase, but at the age of 4 Tim was still bawling after every haircut. At last he ran into his room with a pair of scissors and hollered that he wanted to 'cut off my thing!' and it was clear to his parents that the problem was serious. From then on, at home, Tim went by the name 'Kim'. By age 8 there was nothing boyish about her. She played typical girl games with other girls, went to their birthday parties and even dressed up for the ballet. Her teachers praised her exemplary social skills. When she was teased in the schoolyard and called names like 'tranny' or 'queer', she walked away.

'We always saw Kim as a girl, but not as a problem,' says the father. 'In fact, our life was surprisingly normal.' Normal until Kim was 12, and experienced the first signs of puberty. She was overcome by panic when her voice began to drop. She had no interest in becoming one of those brawny creatures with gigantic hands and deep voices who dressed like women but looked unfeminine. Only hormones could prevent Kim from turning into Tim again, and time was of the essence.

'Hormone treatment! Gender adjustment! How could you possibly do this to the child?' the family's paediatrician barked at the father – in Kim's presence.

Then came the sessions at the state psychiatric hospital, where Kim would sit in green rooms with high ceilings, playing with experimental blocks, while her parents answered endless questionnaires.

Kim's is a classic case, according to Bernd Meyenburg. Gender identity disorders are not rare among children, and they often appear as soon as a child starts to speak. The problem goes away in about a quarter of these children. In about 2 to 10% of the cases, though, early gender identity disorders lead to transsexualism.

'From a purely medical standpoint we are dealing with the mutilation of a biologically healthy body,' says Meyenburg. But in Kim's case, says Meyenburg, 'it would have been a crime to let her grow up as a man. There are very few people in whom it's so obvious.'

Meyenburg has been studying transsexuality since the 1970s. In those days, orthodox psychiatry believed that adverse social circumstances – namely the parents – were to blame when someone felt out of place in his or her biological gender.

Even Meyenburg was long convinced that severe emotional trauma in childhood caused transsexualism. 'On the other hand,' he says, 'depression isn't exactly rare in mothers. Wouldn't that mean there should be far more transsexuals?' Meyenburg points out another inconsistency: 'There are cases in which you could poke around in the parents' relationship as long as you wish and still find nothing.'

Gender development in human beings is a complex of bio-psychological processes, and when something goes wrong, not everyone understands. The medical community in particular tends to impose order. Developmental psychologists long believed that children were born emotionally neutral, and that a person's perceived gender affiliation was the result of social influence. Experts still think a lot of gender-specific behaviour is learned, but they also believe some of it is pre-wired in the womb. The extent to which androgen or oestrogen shapes the brain to be male or female is debatable; the age at which gender identity is established is unknown. Whether the development of an identity can be interrupted during early childhood isn't clear.

'Nowadays we believe that it's both,' says Meyenburg – 'environment and biology.'

'From an emotional standpoint, Kim comes across as a healthy, happy and balanced child,' Meyenburg wrote in his report. She had never behaved like a boy, not even for a short period of time. 'There is no doubt that her wish is irreversible, because it has been evident since very early childhood.'

In the past, Meyenburg was strictly opposed to hormone treatment before a child came of age. He began to question the wisdom of his own rules when one of his patients resisted his advice and ordered hormones over the internet. She went abroad at 17 and had a sex change operation for a few thousand euros. Meyenburg was angry at the time. Today this woman, a law student, is one of his happiest patients.

Now Meyenburg allows his young patients to enter hormone treatment early, before puberty complicates a sex change. 'They simply suffer less,' he says.

Kim is already much closer to realising her dream. The first letter of her name has been changed in her record, and her school now treats her as a girl. Thanks to the hormones, her breasts are developing, like those of other girls in her class. She's allowed to use the girls' locker room during gym class.

One thing hasn't completely changed for Kim, though – heckling in the schoolyard. But now her best friend sticks up for her. Kim says she feels good about herself in spite of the taunts. 'My girlfriends see me as a completely normal person,' she says.

'It's out of the question for me,' says Kim, who still wants to get rid of the parts of her body that remind her that she was born as Tim. By law, in Germany, she'll have to wait until she's 18 to take the next step. Meanwhile, she resorts to wearing tight pants.

'I just happen to be a girl,' says Kim. She keeps a piggybank in her bedroom filled with change she has been saving for the operation – since the age of 5. Once it's over, her new life will start. 'In Paris,' she says, 'where no one knows me.'

Source: *Spiegel* online magazine, 26 January 2007 (translated from the German)

- What do you think is the explanation for Kim's gender identity?
- Do you agree with Bernd Meyenburg's assessment and decision to conduct hormone treatment (and later a sex change) on Kim?
- Do you think Kim will ever think of himself as a boy?

there, a more sophisticated understanding about gender group memberships develops. Gender identity is a multidimensional construct in that it encompasses all of the cognitive, affective and behavioural components, and none of the purely biologically, socially or cognitively oriented approaches alone can explain this spectrum of developments. An inclusive approach in the form of transactions between the innate, individual and environmental elements offers the most reasonable account. It is, however, difficult to obtain empirical evidence for the simultaneous transactions, and many atypical cases of gender identity development remain unresolved.

SUMMARY

This chapter has covered the development of children's self-concept and, related to this, their gender identity. First, we saw that self-concept develops by degrees, from an infant's rudimentary awareness of their own existence as separate from that of others, to a more evaluative and reflective sense of the self as the child recognises how they may be perceived by others. Accordingly, through the ages, children's self-descriptions develop from ones about the more physical, observable and measurable features to ones derived from interpersonal relationships and inner qualities. Notably, this gradual development is likely to be influenced by the social interactions in which the child engages with those around them. Over time, their perceptions and evaluations become increasingly consistent with what is expected by others.

The chapter then looked at the part of a child's self-concept that is derived from gender group membership. We saw that, by the second year in life, infants respond differently to male and female stimuli and, soon after, they learn the gender labels to identify others and themselves, although this is based on superficial features – even when children learn that gender is a permanent part of the self. It is not until children grasp that gender remains constant despite outward changes in middle childhood that they have a fuller understanding of their membership. Still, gender encompasses other aspects, particularly the knowledge of stereotypes and gender-appropriate behaviour.

Three major theoretical approaches were put forward to explain the development of gender identity. The biological accounts propose that the different role, status and behavioural patterns between the sexes originate from biological differences evolved over time as humans adapted to environmental demands. In contrast, social learning theorists argue that children acquire gendered behaviour and values by modelling on and reinforcement by parents, peers and the media. Cognitive theories concentrate on the child's role in seeking and processing gender material from the environment and, in doing so, constructing their own gender identity. Each approach has its merits and empirical support; especially strong are the medical cases for the biological accounts, experiments showing different responses by adults or peers to the same child labelled differently or gender-appropriate and inappropriate behaviour for social learning, and studies showing the effects of schemas on gendered behaviour and recall for schema theories. Each approach also has its drawbacks, such as the narrow list of behaviours explained by biological factors, the issue of selective attention or modelling for social learning theories, and newer research into pre-labelling infants' differential responses to stereotyped toys. A transaction model was suggested which integrates the approaches, though the assessment of its validity requires further extensive research.

It is indeed the case that there are still plenty of 'unknowns' to be discovered about children's development of self-concept and gender identity. Questions remain, such as what in the social environment is 'most' significant in facilitating the development of self-concepts and gender identities – parents, peers, school or the media? What makes male–female distinctions so 'intrinsically' salient to begin with? How do we integrate the different biological, environmental and individual-child factors and cognitive processes to explain cases of atypical gender identity development? A great deal of work has discovered much of the crucial foundational knowledge and explicated the workings of each branch of factors and processes. The direction for future ventures in the area is to find out how these branches operate in conjunction with each other.

REVIEW QUESTIONS

1. What are the major milestones towards the child's establishment of a self-concept? What abilities does each of them require and reflect?
2. 'A child's gender identity is neither biologically determined, acquired through their social environment nor constructed by the child him or herself.' Evaluate the validity of this statement.
3. How important is self-esteem to our overall self-concept and what may influence its development?
4. What are the key factors that determine a child's sense of gender identity? Are some stronger than others?
5. Compare and contrast two major theoretical approaches that have been used to explain the development of gender identity.

RECOMMENDED READING

To understand the development of the looking-glass self, read:

Tice, D. M., & Wallace, H. M. (2005). The reflected self: Creating yourself as (you think) others see you. In M. R. Leary & J. P. Tangney (Eds.), *Handbook of Self and Identity* (91–105). New York: Guilford Press.

To understand more on the development of self throughout childhood and adolescence, read:

Harten, S. (2005). The development of self-representations during childhood and adolescence. In M. R. Leary & J. P. Tangney (Eds.), *Handbook of Self and Identity* (610–642). New York: Guilford Press.

For an in-depth discussion on self and identity development:

Fischer, K. W., & Harter, S. (2001). *The Construction of the Self: A Developmental Perspective*. New York: Guildford Press.

For a classic article covering a range of issues on gender development:

Maccoby, E. E. (2000). Perspectives on gender development. *International Journal of Behavioral Development*, 24, 398–406.

For an extensive nature–nurture debate on gender development:

Lipp, R. A. (2005). *Gender, Nature, and Nurture* (2nd Ed.). Mahwah, NJ: Lawrence Erlbaum Associates.

For more extensive, integrated reviews of research on gender development:

Leman, P. H., & Tenenbaum, H. R. (Eds.) (2014). *Gender and Development*. New York: Psychology Press.

Owen Blakemore, J. E. O., Berenbaum, S. A., & Liben, L. S. (Eds.) (2009). *Gender Development*. Hove: Psychology Press.

RECOMMENDED WEBSITES

The Max Planck Institute for Human Development has a number of research centres devoted to understanding our development of the self and self-concept:

http://www.mpib-berlin.mpg.de/index.en.htm

The SELF Research Centre (the Self-concept Enhancement and Learning Facilitation Group) based at Oxford University encompasses 450 members from 45 countries across six continents and a network of satellite centres producing research on enhancing positive self-concept:

http://www.self.ox.ac.uk/index.htm

For further information on issues relating to gender identity and research:

http://www.gires.org.uk

For media coverage of the Reimer case, the twin who was born a boy and raised as a girl, see these BBC sites:

http://www.bbc.co.uk/sn/tvradio/programmes/horizon/dr_money_prog_summary.shtml
http://www.bbc.co.uk/news/health-11814300

For current issues related to gender and development, particularly practical and global issues such as inequalities, *Gender and Development* is the only journal dedicated to this focus:

http://www.genderanddevelopment.org

Chapter 12
Peer interactions and relationships

Learning outcomes

After reading this chapter, and with further recommended reading, you should be able to:

1. Describe the nature of the peer group at different ages and appreciate the potential importance of this social structure to a child's development.
2. Critically evaluate the significance of peer interactions, particularly play, for a child's social and cognitive development.
3. Understand the issues surrounding social status in peer groups, including acceptance, rejection and neglect, the factors that influence social status, and its consequences.
4. Critically evaluate the key functions of friendship for children, the factors that influence its formation and development, and its longer-term implications.
5. Compare and evaluate the research studies and related methods that have been used to study the above developments and how they may impact on findings.

Interaction in the playground

The following is an (abridged) extract of a skipping game observed in a junior school, in June 1970, by Iona Opie, author of the book *The People in the Playground*:

> . . . the boss (of the game – often the one who thought of playing it) was a girl called Mandy, and the five other skippers looked to her for instructions. She decided that they should play 'Down in the kitchen, Doin' a bit of stitchin', In comes a burglar, And knocks you Out.' Mandy jumped into the rope first. She was certainly a good skipper. The routine went smoothly for several changes, a new skipper coming into the rope at 'In' and leaving it at 'Out'. Then someone less skilful came in, stumbled, and had to take an end. Being a less skilful turner, as well, she dropped the rope. There was a restless rearrangement of the group and murmurs of 'Mandy, shall I?' They had a few more turns at this game, then Mandy said they would play a different one. They started skipping through the rope in a continuous line, Building Up Bricks, doing one skip, each, then two, then three, and so on. The clumsy 'ender' dropped the rope again. It is not customary to dismiss a player from a game. Mandy had to choose whether to let her continue as an incompetent turner or let her become a skipper again and even more certainly interrupt the flow of the game. She darted forward like a dervish. 'Stop dropping the rope!' she said, picking up the end and thrusting it into the girl's hand. 'We got to three.' . . .
>
> 'It isn't always easy to join in a game,' an 11-year-old girl explained to me. 'People are a bit fussy about who plays with them.' I asked a group of younger girls, 'What do you do if you want to join in a game and they won't let you?' 'You go and play the same game on your own somewhere else,' was the prompt response; and she meant 'with your own set of friends'. A solitary child trying to attach herself to a game is an unusual occurrence, and that child is likely to be an oddity of some kind. 'We usually play with our own friends,' they said. 'We usually play in a four, and that is usually enough for a game. If we need any more we go and ask some more people, people we know.' There is a centre ring of friends, and an outer ring who can be co-opted. The four friends come out to play as a group, and are thus insulated against any social problems. They have no need to wheedle or bludgeon their way into other groups or games. 'What if there's a new game that you've never seen before, and you want to learn it?' I asked. 'We watch, and if they say we can't join in we just watch, and soon they tell us to go away.'
>
> *Source:* Opie (1993, pp. 5–6)

Think about when you were learning games in the school playground.

- Did you find it easy to join in or did you find it difficult?
- Was it easier to join in if one of your friends was already playing that game?

Introduction

The opening example taken from the vivid descriptions in Iona Opie's book epitomises some of the key concepts and raises some important questions that will be addressed in this chapter. So far in this part of the book, we have covered the earliest social interactions and relationships which the child establishes with her family members and the factors which can influence this early social development. As the child grows older, the environments that she enters into, and learns from, expand to outside of the home and the number and types of people within the environments also grow. These people include adults other than the child's parents and caregivers, but importantly, as she continues her journey of socialisation and associated learning in more formalised settings, such as nursery or pre-school and then full-time school, social interactions and relationships that involve what will be her 'peer group' will take centre-stage in her day-to-day life.

This chapter overviews, examines and evaluates the kinds of interaction that children engage in with their peers and the relationships that they form with these other children through the course of their development. We will first take a look at the nature of children's peer groups from a young age to later in childhood, and the kinds of things that they do in such groups, particularly the key theme of play, from which children are seen to learn a lot about themselves and others, and which sets up a stage for other aspects of development including language and cognition. After that the chapter will go further to explore the more enduring relationships that children develop with their peers through development, including the significant issues, such as a child's 'place' or social status within a peer group, the functions of friendship and the factors that influence the course and consequences of these relationships.

The peer group and peer interactions

Children's peer groups have offered the basis for studying development for a long while. Yet what a peer group is and how we define a 'peer' could be subject to various interpretations. Generally speaking, a peer is another child of the same or similar age to a child, often within a year or so of his/her own age, and the peer group refers to children other than the child's family members (Salmon, 1992). In this sense the children's siblings are not 'peers', although quite often they are close enough in age and, of course, a key social influence in a child's life (Dunn and Kendrick, 1982).

> **Definition**
>
> Peer group: the other children or young people with whom a child or young person engages who are of a similar age and not family members.

Even though children interacting and playing with each other may look rather natural to the casual observer, it actually requires social skills and understanding that are not demanded (or demanded as much) by interactions with older, more competent people such as the parents and other adults. The unequal adult–child combination (also known as *vertical relationships*; see Hartup, 1989) functions with the adult being the provider of security and protection, enabling the child to gain knowledge and skills – as seen in the attachment relationship (see Chapter 9, 'Attachment and early social experiences'). Such provision and support is not found in the peer group (also known as *horizontal relationships*) since the children are similar in age and social powers, but each of them may have different needs, desires and wishes. This means that peer groups tend to be more difficult to sustain, because their interactions require a greater level of reciprocity, and each child will have to learn skills in the other's company, such as sharing and cooperation as well as conflict resolution and moderating competitions, if the peer group is to continue relatively harmoniously without hostility. Thus the way that children socialise within such groups is distinct from parental socialisation and, once a peer group is formed, children within it may develop their own norms, ideas and identities. In fact, the influence of the peer group on development has been suggested to be of utmost importance, over and above that of parental socialisation, by various renowned psychologists (Harris, 1998; Pinker, 2002).

Children's peer groups and interactions through the years

STOP AND THINK

You may find this question easier if you have had experiences with young children, or you might ask someone who has young children:

- How young are children when they start to 'engage' one another – take an interest or even attract another's attention in order to initiate interactions or actually play?

Infancy

Even though, when we think about the 'peer group', many of us tend to create a picture of friendship groups in school (the opening example is one such illustration), in reality infants already seem to take an interest in peers of their own age by the end of their first year in life. As early as 6 months of age, two babies when faced with each other may stare and make noises at and even reach for the other, to explore the other's body, hair or clothing, and such behaviours become more evident towards the end of this first year (Hay et al., 1983). However, it needs to be said that, although this might reflect how babies can be 'interested' in one another, infants this young still prefer to explore and interact with objects and will display this interest in human others often only when no toy objects are around. It is not until well into the second year that infants are seen in more frequent and elaborate interactions, in which longer sequences of initiating and responding behaviours ensue. Still, toddlers usually play with toys alongside each other (see the next subsection) rather than in a coordinated way that involves mutual imitation or continuous reciprocation. This is observed closer to age 2, but even then their interactions often end up in conflict (Hay and Ross, 1982). This may be due to the stage of development, where neither party has acquired the social skills to accommodate each other's differences for long.

Even young infants are already interested in their peers, but this interest is transient and they are more interested in objects at this stage.

Source: Lam

Early childhood/pre-school ages

Apart from their rapidly increasing physical mobility and social understanding, from 2 to 3 years old, many children in the West at least will go to day nurseries or play groups; thus their opportunities to 'practise' social interactions with same-age others also increase. There is evidence that, between 2 and 5 years of age, children play with increasing reciprocation and cooperation with each other. One of the first people to document this systematically was Mildred Parten (1932), who observed children in nurseries as part of her doctorate studies. She found that, while the younger 2- to 3- year-olds appeared more solitary, engaging in 'parallel' activities alongside each other rather than in so-called 'associative' or 'cooperative' activities *with* each other (see also 'Play', pages 351–8), the latter started to appear more and more often as children got older. Parten also defined several other categories (see Table 12.1), and the progression of children decreasing in alone-time without interacting with their peers towards increased social participation with them along this set of categories was later taken as the 'benchmark' that reflects children's development of social skills.

Over the years, however, research suggests that the emphasis on activity with others as a yardstick for more 'advanced' social skills is over-simplistic (Smith, 1978) as both older and younger children commonly engage in group and solitary play, while parallel play was stable with time. Later studies suggest that parallel play while being an onlooker of others' interactions serves as a transition where children can gradually bring themselves closer to joint activities and eventually proceed to join in as they acquire the appropriate entry skills (Fantuzzo et al., 1998; Rubin et al., 1998). Recent research in playgroup settings has found that both cooperative and parallel play tend to increase over time, particularly in the presence of mothers who were seen as skilful supervisors, implying the scaffolding role of adults at this stage (Mize and Pettit, 2010).

In sum, during the pre-school years children show an increase in tendency to participate in joint activities and with that the size of the peer group starts to increase. They still spend a great deal of time in parallel activities, but this appears to be able to serve the function of allowing children to learn about and easing them into a peer group's etiquette and activity if it is first coupled with observing the peers.

Middle childhood/school ages

While peer interactions seem to change in a notable, but gradual, way through early childhood, by the end of the first year in school children already have a very strong tendency for 'belonging' to a peer group. This may be because, by this time, children spend most of their day in school in a broad range of contexts, including some free play periods where interactions with peers are less closely followed, and even less structured and maintained by adults, compared with the earlier years in pre-school.

The dynamics of the peer group also evolve rapidly, in the sense that an emerging structure is apparent (often involving leadership and followers, as illustrated in the example at the start of the chapter), as the size of the group continues to grow and the activities and interactions within it become more complex. As mentioned above, peers within the group come with different backgrounds, interests, wishes and so on. The increase in exposure and exchanges will increase children's awareness of differing perspectives, and these interactions over time will further develop their ability to interpret and understand others' needs and motives, and to refine their social rules to accommodate others' roles and intentions (Denham et al., 2004; see also Chapter 8, 'Theory of mind').

At the same time, with the increasing freedom children enjoy for associating with only others they prefer, some 'chasm' quickly and clearly becomes apparent. In particular, boys and girls usually go separate ways in developing their peer groups with distinct structure and nature of interactions. In fact, by junior school years (age 7 years), boys are already far more likely to be observed to play in larger groups at team sports such as football, while girls form smaller close-knit units or 'cliques' that engage in more organised or 'traditional' activities, such as skipping, as we observed in

Table 12.1 Parten's categories of play behaviour in pre-school.

Category	Description
Unoccupied	Child not being involved in any activity
Onlooker	Child watching others but not joining in
Solitary	Child playing alone away from others
Parallel	Child playing alongside others with the same objects or in a similar activity as others without interacting with others
Associative	Child interacting with others while participating in the same activity
Cooperative	Child interacting with others in well-coordinated complementary ways that may involve sharing with and supporting each other

Source: Parten (1932)

the opening example (see also Lloyd and Duveen, 1992). As we explored earlier (see Chapter 11, Development of Self-concept and Gender Identity), by school age, peers provide some of the strongest socialising agents (often stronger than parents) of gender behaviours and stereotypes as they readily recognise the gender-appropriateness of activities and may even criticise each other for what is commonly seen as gender-inappropriate behaviours. Not surprisingly then, over time in school, children are more and more likely to associate with same-sex others in increasingly gender-stereotypical activities, with boys showing more competitiveness and girls striving for more collaboration and agreeableness generally (Leaper, 1991; see also Chapter 11).

Adolescence

With an even longer part of the weekday spent on the school grounds, and even more freedom than ever before to socialise with peers after school and often also at the weekend, adolescence is the time when the peer group exerts arguably the greatest influence on the teenager (examined in more detail in Chapter 13, 'Physical changes during adolescence'). Indeed, by mid-adolescence (13–14 years), most teenagers spend more time with peers than with any other set of social agents.

Through the journey from infancy to adolescence, the peer group evolves in obvious ways, and the key nature and functions of interactions within it transform progressively. They go from the kinds of exchange that parents have a key part in orchestrating in the early years, as they arrange visits to others' homes and nurseries, towards greater and greater autonomy on the part of the children as their social skills, choices and experiences expand and adults' supervision and guidance decline. This is not to say that the family does not matter; there is evidence that the family is still the primary reference point where advice for education, career and finance is concerned, and the peer group is sought for 'social' issues such as appearance and relationships (Sebald, 1989). Nevertheless, it can be said that the peer group has the key function of helping to bring the young person from being dependent on the family to being more independent.

Play

So far, we have identified the key features of children's interactions with peers over the course of development and some of the major functions that such groups and interactions serve. Some of the questions that remain concern the 'what' and the 'how'. While children engage with each other, exactly what 'kinds of things' do they do? How do they actually acquire or develop the skills which we have just seen that they acquire through doing such things? We all know that the commonest activity schoolchildren do with each other outside of class is play. Here we take a closer look at play in the context of social interactions.

STOP AND THINK

You may draw on your own experiences or observations of children for this exercise.

- What do you understand as 'play'? Do you still 'play'?
- If you do, how is your kind of play different from those you engaged in as a child?
- Why do you think they are different? Are there similarities too?

However you answered the questions in the Stop and Think box, one key theme that you may well have brought up concerning 'play' is that it is an activity that you *enjoy*. Researcher Jane Howard has spent a lot of time researching play behaviour in young children and has adopted a novel approach in defining its usefulness within an educational framework. She reported that what a child defined as play was no more complex than the belief that play was time away from the teacher (Howard et al., 2006)! Howard's work has also revealed that when learning is fun, more is learned by the child. This could be due to increased motivation of children within a fun environment. For instance, when children learn from play, it is different from many forms of learning, as they absorb information, knowledge or skills at least from something that they feel motivated to do (Göncü and Gaskins, 2007). This is one of many reasons why there has been such a push towards learning through play at least in nurseries and even in early years' school settings in the past few decades, so as to offer a 'natural' way through which children can learn.

As a dominant part of the interactions with peers, the complexity of peer play increases with age as well as the kinds of development that come with it. Saying that, it is plausible that even early play with a peer group is helpful for a child to acquire or practise social skills and

NATURE–NURTURE

Is play innate or learned?

With play being seen as an intrinsic part of childhood (and often beyond) in contemporary societies, many people tend to presume that play is something 'natural', which children 'just do'. Indeed, research shows that there is good reason for this. Some of this work has come from comparative psychology, as introduced in previous chapters, where animals are studied for behaviours similar to our own; in this case when engaged in various forms of play, especially social play. As the young of most mammals play socially, any research reporting parallels is useful to understanding the evolutionary origins and functions of play.

Of all social play, rough-and-tumble play is most frequently observed in non-humans. Maintaining such play requires players to read social cues appropriately, react swiftly and accurately to movements, and anticipate responses. Common play signals have evolved in many species that act as behavioural cues or honest reassurances that the behaviour is playful (and not aggression). This type of play is said to be cognitively and emotionally challenging in that it 'exaggerates the experience of loss of control, especially given the unpredictability that arises from having to use an implicit rule-structure (one that promotes reciprocity) to recover from instability in rapid sequences of behaviour that may last only a few seconds' (Pellis et al., 2014, p. 87). Various developmental benefits are suggested from such play, such as promoting social competence and emotional regulation, and growing evidence suggests that this helps shape the development of the prefrontal cortex, the area of the brain known for its role in executive function. Children who engage in lots of rough-and-tumble play are more socially confident in non-play situations and the same is true for rats and some primates. Yet there are many exceptions that do not play (such as most rodents) or that play but do not benefit in the same way, like the meerkat, and many animals deprived of the opportunity to play still develop normal social relationships (reviewed by Lewis Graham and Burghardt, 2010).

Research also looks at 'playful' expressions of animal and human infants in relation to various play contexts. For instance, humans associate play with laughter, especially in social situations. Tickling or wrestling, the easiest way to elicit laughter, is observed in all of humans, some primates and even rats, who give a chirrup when tickled that increases in frequency during rough-and-tumble or behaviour associated with positive rewards (see Lewis Graham and Burghardt, 2010). In this way, laughter has probably evolved from social play, and one key brain region, the hypothalamus, involved with the experience of pleasure, is seen to influence the proximal motivational aspects (e.g. physical contact) of social play. Evolutionary increases in hypothalamus size have been correlated with increases in the frequency of social, but not non-social play (Lewis Graham and Burghardt, 2010).

On the other hand, chimpanzees' play is punctuated by a variety of facial, vocal and body expressions, such as relaxed open-mouth displays, laughter-like soft, breathy pants or grunts, and numerous expressive behaviours including head bobs, hand claps and foot stomps, but also throwing and kicking. The latter group of behaviours are not exclusive to play and can be found in more aggressive contexts. Hence modalities of expressions with type of play (and non-play) vary. For instance, in social play the rate of 'play faces' is high, in solitary play the rate of body expressions is high, but mild-contact social play elicits the highest rates of play faces and other expressions (often hitting) – which are also matched by play partners and such matching increases with age (Ross et al., 2014). While this suggests that those behaviours are emotional expressions of joy that develop social functions through peer interactions in infant chimpanzees, it is unlikely that certain behaviours such as hitting are as benign in humans, or at least they are not promoted in children's socialisation with supervision by adults.

There are also other play behaviours that we quite clearly do not share with animals, particularly the more imaginative type (i.e. symbolic and make-believe play). This is probably because of a 'stark gap' in the expression of pretend behaviour even between our closest living primate cousins and us (Nielsen, 2012).

Nielsen reviews anecdotal reports claiming to show that great apes have the mental representational ability to pretend. These include a chimpanzee that started acting as if she was playing on a pull-toy after growing fond of such toys, but ceased after a few weeks, and small amounts of footage showing examples of pretence in captive chimpanzees and bonobos. The examples depart starkly from the frequency, richness and complexity noted in children by the age of 4 years. Such advanced imitation, pretence and other complex features (such as the construction of rules and meanings agreed by players) are argued to be some of the building blocks with which children rehearse social realities as critical developmental domains in the evolution of human culture, which are absent or not prevalent in non-human animals.

Taken together the comparative literature shows that non-human animals clearly play and that their play shares certain 'parallels' with ours, but there are also important differences in form and purpose. Play is not a unitary trait and nor does it serve a singular function (Pellis et al., 2014). In essence, play is not something that children (and animals) 'just do', or perhaps it is not just about what children do, but how they do it: the various seemingly 'natural', but complex, nuances of play can become the fundamental cornerstones to the development of cognitive, emotional and social skills.

cognitive understanding. In order to sustain play, a child will sometimes have to subdue his own agenda in the interest of the joint activity, and that requires an awareness of the peer's agenda, and the ability to regulate one's own behaviours and emotions (Gottman, 1986). As we saw in earlier chapters (Chapter 8, 'Theory of mind', and Chapter 10, 'Childhood temperament and behavioural development'), the prerequisite skills emerge during early childhood and play offers an arena to refine them. However, as we have learnt in the last section, children up to age 5 spend much of their time in solitary activities. We ought therefore to identify the kinds of play that are 'social' and 'non-social' and what kinds of learning can be included with them. As Parten (1932) labelled six categories of social interactions, later researchers have assembled these further, along with children's ages, into a few categories of play (Table 12.2).

Dolls' houses from the 1800s to the 2000s. Although the style of house has changed, role play with dolls' houses has been around for a few hundred years.

Source: Alamy Images/ClassicStock

Table 12.2 Categories of play.

Play/age group	Description	Examples
Functional (first 2 years)	Simple, physical activities with or without toy objects	Running, bouncing a ball, jumping over something
Symbolic (2–6 years)	Representing absent objects/events with available ones or own body	Pretending to eat from an empty dish or hand
Make-believe/ sociodramatic (2–6 years)	Acting out roles or pretend games involving real social roles or made-up imaginary ones	Playing house/ school or 'real-life' (e.g. hospital) or fictional scenarios
Constructive (3–6 years)	Creating or building a tangible object or representation of one	Using building blocks, drawing, making jigsaws
Games with rules (6 years up)	Structured games with publicly accepted rules	Football, other ball games, skipping, hopscotch

Sources: adapted from Piaget (1951); Smilansky (1968); Rubin et al. (1983, 1998)

Although solitary play involving functional activities and construction remains proportionately higher in frequency through the pre-school years, there is a noticeable rise in the amount of time spent on the more complicated form of social play, namely make-believe play. We will first look closely at this form of play and its related, but simpler, form of play, symbolic play, which emerges earlier in childhood, their major characteristics and the skills that they reflect in the sections below. We will also look at what has often been overlooked as a simpler 'physical' form of play, 'rough-and-tumble play', to examine its main features. Soon after, we will examine the learning and development that such play may foster, including language, cognitive and social skills, emotional development and group-order adjustment.

Symbolic play

The earliest systematic description and interpretation of young children's play, perhaps not surprisingly, came from Piaget, corresponding roughly with his stage theory of development (see Chapter 2, 'Theoretical perspectives'). Piaget (1951) observed and labelled three main stages of play in a developmental sequence (with some overlapping), where the simplest stage of play involving basic functional activities (in Table 12.2) was called 'sensorimotor' play.

The next stage, which starts from around 15 months and continues to around 6 years of age, was called symbolic play, also known as 'fantasy' or 'pretend' play. This form of play, as the term suggests, marks the beginnings of the child being able to 'symbolically' represent something, be it an object or an event, which is absent in their immediate setting. An example of this is a child pretending to drink from an empty cup, where there is no liquid inside, making the requisite slurping sound. The behaviours of gesturing and imitating a drinker suggest that the child has 'symbolic' understanding, that she knows that the key object (liquid) is not there, but she is mimicking the relevant act, one of the key milestones in her cognitive development. As children become more skilled, they may start to mimic a series of representational behaviours, such as pretending to 'pour the tea' besides drinking. These will not only involve a broader behavioural repertoire, and thus more representations, but quite likely also more use of language as children narrate more and more complicated series of acts (see Chapter 5, 'Language development'). This will be particularly the case when such play begins to involve more than one child, paving the way for more elaborate 'make-believe' play.

Make-believe play

Also known as role- or sociodramatic play (Smilansky, 1968), 'make-believe' play reflects an extended version of the development of representations in children's cognitive skills. Emerging often shortly after the simpler forms of symbolic play at 2 to 3 years old and becoming more

---

Definitions

Make-believe play: also known as sociodramatic or role play, play that involves two or more children acting out social roles, whether real-life or fictional ones, in pretend games, usually requiring negotiation and reciprocation with each other with agreed rules in the shared imaginary scenario.

Symbolic play: also known as fantasy or pretend play, play that involves 'symbolic' representation, where the child pretends that an absent object is present and acts out the relevant behaviours involving that object.

Rough-and-tumble play: also known as 'play-fighting', play that involves physical activity, often without objects, such as wrestling, tumbling, kicking and chasing; it is commonest during middle childhood among boys.

complex with the inclusion of peers, such play marks the key advances from earlier solo pretences. Until the end of the second year, the child's pretences are relatively inflexible in terms of the nature of the acts they represent and the choice of objects they use. For instance, most 18-month-olds can only mimic real actions that adults perform (such as drinking and serving tea) and use objects that are actually used for the actions (cups), and cannot act out imaginary events or substitute with other objects (such as using a hand to mimic the shape of a cup). The use of less realistic objects as the ones they represent in imaginary situations emerges from age 2 (Striano et al., 2001).

Furthermore, the involvement of peers in this form of 'social' play means that the child is a co-participant in acts that include not only herself, but also others. This may not begin with a 'real' peer at first, but she may 'serve tea' to a doll or act out a scene between two dolls before she plays out the scene with another child. Through this form of acting, she realises the different perspectives between the co-participants in the interactions. The benefits of involving peers do not stop here; having more children means having more ideas and roles. Often only one act or one set of acts can be thought and played out at one time by one child. With more children, the series of acts that are imagined can be combined as each child takes on a different role and builds on another's storylines, often spontaneously. This requires the skills of reciprocating the other's efforts and negotiating a plan of pretence (who plays what) with pre-assigned rules. In particular, when the child is involved with a peer with more sophisticated skills, she needs to 'raise the level' of pretence, whereby the play becomes richer, more diverse and sustained (Bornstein, 2006b). Such games depart more from real roles into fantasy with age and exposure to inputs from sources like comics and TV (see the Case Study box). The fact that children are aware that such play is 'make-believe' reflects their understanding of the distinction between the imaginary and reality (Rakoczy et al., 2004).

Rough-and-tumble play

So far in this section, we have focused on the kinds of play that involve more cognitive and social skills (such as language, imagination and negotiation) rather than physical skills, and which are 'higher up' on the play chart as

CASE STUDY

Lost babies

This example describes how two 6-year-old girls role-play at being two 'lost babies'.

Laura: We're the two lost babies, yeah
Aalliyah: Yeah we're the two lost babies . . .
Laura: Pretend we saw a boat
Aalliyah: No this is the boat, yeah. (*moving onto a low stool*) Now get behind. (*Both shuffle the 'boat' around the 'water' amid some argument about which way it should go*)
Laura: Pretend we were in a fight. (*play-fighting in boat*) Then something terrible happens.
Aalliyah: What?
Laura: Happens to the water and then I couldn't swim . . . (*both children fall out of the 'boat'. Laura moves Aalliyah face down on the 'water'*) Pretend you couldn't swim. Here's your help. (*throws a jumper over Aalliyah*)
Aalliyah: Get it off of me.
Laura: Pretend I'm the horrible one, yeah, and she's the good one . . . No you're still stuck in the water (*begins to cover Aalliyah with newspaper*)
Aalliyah: No more paper on me, your mum's gonna . . .
Laura: One more. Then you came out. You messed up all the papers.

Source: Open University (2003)

- What does this example of play show us?
- Can we use play to understand the experiences of children who perhaps might not be able to tell us what has happened to them?

The girls' play demonstrates imagination and spontaneity as they improvise both their script and props, and it is unlikely that they have experienced the situation they enact: being lost at sea and drowning. This shows how make-believe play offers the contexts for sharing and making sense of experiences that are fantasy rather than real life.

more advanced or 'mature' forms of play. However, just as many children continue to engage in solitary rather than joint activities; much play, in fact, involves the more gross physical activity without objects, particularly in the vastness of the school grounds. One often-overlooked activity is 'rough-and-tumble' play (Pellegrini and Smith, 1998) or 'play-fighting'. This form of play, more common among boys and commonest during school ages (10% versus 4% during pre-school and adolescence; Pellegrini, 2006), involves wrestling, chasing, kicking, tumbling or rolling on the ground, thus resembling real fighting. It does, however, differ from real fighting in that afterwards children continue playful interaction rather than going their own way, as they do after real fighting. Still, it is often misunderstood by certain well-meaning teachers, who break up the participants, or clamp down on it altogether on school grounds for fears that such activity can lead to aggressive behaviours (Tannock, 2011). Very occasionally this does happen, but often for a reason: either when a participant misinterprets another's acts (when a play-fighting advance is seen with hostile intent), or when one breaks some understood or agreed 'rule' or expectation of a game – both of which are more likely to be elicited by some children than others (see 'Peer groups and social status', pages 358–66). In fact, the understanding of such rules in this form of play is argued to serve certain social functions among the peer group, as we will examine below.

Play, learning and development

We have seen the critical characteristics that involve peer interactions in a few major forms of play and the skills that they reflect, which children realise as they play. A further potentially controversial question of interest not only to child psychologists, but also to educators and policy-makers, is: do children learn and develop skills from play? This is a difficult question because it is almost impossible to 'prove' that play actually 'causes' learning or development to take place rather than requiring and reflecting the child's existing skills repertoire. At the same time, there are certain clear relationships between a child's advances in play and achievements in numerous domains of development, and evidence of children lacking or lagging behind in some skills if they are deprived of certain forms of play.

Perhaps because of their complex representational nature, the bulk of research has examined the impact of symbolic and make-believe play. For instance, it has been noted that the gestures and sounds that are used for symbolic play appear at about the same time as children's first vocabulary, and that those who are skilled enough to link up a chain of acts (such as pouring and drinking tea) are also the first to link up words within their speech (Bates et al., 1987). Although it is plausible that the children already know the words before they use them to narrate their play, it is still possible that certain words that children hear will be learned (or learned more quickly) if they can 'connect' with what they can see, do, think or feel. Language delay also typically goes hand-in-hand with delays in play that involves imitation and symbolic functions (Bates et al., 1987). Similarly, past researchers observed (Smilansky, 1968) that immigrant and disadvantaged pre-schoolers who did not engage in sociodramatic play lagged behind in both language and cognitive skills. However, it is worth noting that the delays might be due to their general under-stimulation rather than the lack of certain play only. Recent research employing detailed analysis of longitudinal observations of pre-schoolers' sociodramatic play suggests that such play can facilitate not only productive language skills (in second language; Galeano, 2011) but also mathematical development (Emfinger, 2009). The role of more-able willing peers is championed in the case of language skills, in that they create and carry out the play initially before the child can engage with increasing participation in conversation in the weaker language (from receptive to productive skills) over time. Such play further involves many spontaneous numerate behaviours such as counting, adding, subtracting and representing number with signs or symbols (fingers and tally-marks, for instance). These offer children an avenue to practise, consolidate and internalise such skills by adopting roles and playing out scripts to make sense of the world (for more numerate behaviours, see Chapter 7, 'The development of mathematical thinking').

As the various forms and levels of pretend play emerge and develop at around the same age (4 to 5 years) as those of theory of mind (see Chapter 8), it has been said that such play promotes the child's understanding of others' perspectives. For elaborate sociodramatic play in particular, where playmates take complementary and reciprocal roles, with an agreed set of rules and symbolic meanings beyond everyday life (such as action heroes from movies), the need to hone their coordination and negotiation to sustain that shared fantasy world is even greater. There is evidence of a link between the skills in such play and theory of mind abilities (Taylor and Carlson, 1997), but such correlational work should be treated with caution (see Chapter 3, 'Research methods'). There has been experimental work, where children are 'trained' in complex pretend play (Dockett, 1998), and the children not only perform more pretend activities and excel in make-believe skills, but also show substantial improvements in theory of mind tasks compared to those who have not gone through training. Such studies are hard to come by and sample sizes often relatively small, but they do offer evidence that elements from the play can help develop social and cognitive skills over time.

Apart from its cognitive functions, Piaget (1951) went a step further regarding the usefulness of make-believe play. He noticed how some children used their representational skills to revisit events or situations that were anxiety provoking (such as a visit to the dentist). In so doing, the child is said to be more in control the second time and to come to terms with the experience better. In fact, long before then, others (such as Freud, 1920; see Chapter 2 for his theoretical perspective) had already explored how the inner world of a child's psyche could be revealed through play. Some observed how children re-enact difficult or troubling situations through pretend play as a vehicle to express and control their feelings. However, it is difficult to ascertain the precise mechanism of such play without much empirical evidence, even though its potential therapeutic value and emotional significance are noteworthy even today in its application to play therapy (Rucinska and Reijmers, 2015).

Besides rehearsing and consolidating representational skills, which is Piaget's position on play, Vygotsky (1978a) actually regarded make-believe play itself as a zone of proximal development (ZPD; Chapter 2) – a vital tool for extending cognitive and social skills. He saw such play contexts as liberating the child from situational constraints to explore novel ways of thinking, behaving and relating that would not be used in other activities which do not require imagination or rely on external stimuli. With assigned roles and rules, pretend play demands that they suppress their impulses to comply with such expectations, particularly as the child needs to think or plan with peers before or during play in such contexts. Children who display more sociodramatic play are seen as more socially competent, with their interactions lasting longer and attracting more additional peers to the group, compared to social play that does not include pretend elements (Creasey et al., 1998). Studies have shown that make-believe can enhance performance on cognitive tasks including attention (Ruff and Capozzoli, 2003), self-regulation (Elias and Berk, 2002) and emotional understanding (Lindsey and Colwell, 2003). Recent research by Lindsey and Colwell (2013) on different forms of play over a two-year period reported that the proportion of sociodramatic play observed in year 1 predicted children's emotional expressiveness and emotional knowledge and regulation (termed as *affective social competence*) a year later, after controlling for ASC skills at year 1.

STOP AND THINK

Revisit the case study of 6-year-old Aalliyah and Laura playing at 'lost babies'. Now, imagine them building a jigsaw puzzle together. Can you think of what kinds of skill they show in 'lost babies' that are not needed for playing the puzzle? And vice versa?

Less research has examined the functions of physical play such as rough-and-tumble play, perhaps because its 'obvious' benefits in physical development such as strengthening muscles and increasing fitness are taken for granted. At the same time, the play-fighting behaviour and interactions are very similar to those on show in the young of many mammal species (see also the Nature–nurture box on page 352), suggesting that this form of play can serve a social function from an evolutionary perspective (see Pellegrini, 2006).

It has been argued that rough-and-tumble play sets the path for establishing a 'dominance hierarchy' (Pellegrini and Smith, 1998), which is a stable 'pecking order' that denotes each member's position in conflict settings. The more dominant members are able to win over others in conflict and have an advantage over them in access to resources. Thus, rough-and-tumble play may

Definition

Dominance hierarchy: a relatively stable ordering of different-status members by their ability to win in conflict that signifies different access to resources, established by challenges through rough-and-tumble play.

be seen as a way for children to test and realise their own and others' strength and establish their positions with respect to this kind of dominance. In regular scuffles or arguments between children, there is often a consistent pattern of winners and losers that remains relatively stable through middle childhood. Then during adolescence play-fighting is often used (especially by boys) to challenge each other and attempt a rise in status within a 'safe' situation (without getting harmed in a 'real' fight). Interestingly, not only does rough-and-tumble play not generally lead to aggression, it can lead to continued affiliation (through further games) as it usually involves friends. Boys who play-fight tend to be popular (see 'Peer groups and social status', pages 358–66) and have a wider variety of strategies for solving social problems (reviewed by Pellegrini, 2006). Perhaps rough-and-tumble play affords the opportunities to practise initiating and maintaining more interactions with peers.

On the other hand, there is evidence to show that rough-and-tumble play with fathers, in the pre-school years, where fathers are less dominant in play, is associated with aggression and worse emotion regulation 5 years later, over and above the effects of initial aggression (Flanders et al., 2010). Other research has found that the 'soothing' techniques for such play in infancy are associated with early temperament, particularly effortful control (see Chapter 10). While infants with more positive affect engage in more rough-and-tumble, the use of distraction as a soothing method is associated with negative affect (Nakagawa and Sukigara, 2014). Considering that these studies refer to rough-and-tumble within an unequal parent–child dyad, if the home setting may act as a 'training ground' for later peer interactions, it is probable that later problems may occur if the child does not receive appropriate responses indicating boundaries for such play. Studies documenting observations of rough-and-tumble play in pre-school and teachers' views suggest that this is an evolving form of play where children may move into more complex behaviours as they mature and that, particularly for boys, it is an avenue for growth from a social perspective – learning the limits of physical play with others and about signalling and modulating emotions to appropriate levels (Lindsey and Colwell, 2013; Tannock, 2011).

Play, as a dominant and dynamic form of peer interactions, is multifaceted and multifunctional. Although the jury is out as to whether play 'causes' specific learning and development, it is clear that it is demanding on social and cognitive skills and can serve as a platform towards further interactions. It is noteworthy that, whether play is physical and vigorous or sedentary and symbolic, children have to engage themselves and each other as active co-participants in the process to sustain the shared activity. With advances in modern technology, particularly the electronic kinds, some of such active agency may not be as much in demand and it is worth pondering on the impact that it may have on the interactive learning we have just come across (see the Cutting Edge box).

Peer groups and social status

At this point, we have seen that the nature of the peer group and its interactions evolves with age, and evaluated some of the most influential forms of play along with their likely functions in learning and skills development. Meanwhile, researchers have noticed individual differences between children in their 'readiness' for this kind of social interaction, that some children seem to be 'better' than others at interacting with their peers or are more easily accepted into a peer group. In the same vein, some children find it particularly hard to join peer groups, or even get 'rejected' by others in such groups. Yet some other children seem to 'hang in the balance' in that they are neither strictly rejected nor welcomed by their peers at all. These phenomena are concerned with what is often referred to as children's peer social status. This is a way to look at the extent to which different children are accepted and liked (or rejected and disliked) by their peers. It is important to point out that, unlike friendship (which we will cover later), this kind of acceptance, liking or popularity among peers does not involve a mutual reciprocal relationship between two children, but rather only the peer group's perspective of a child and not the child's perspective of the group. Even a widely rejected child may still have a friend or two, if popular children are likely to have more friends since they are well liked by a much bigger pool of peers with whom they can make friends.

> **Definition**
>
> **Social status:** the extent of acceptance or likeability of individual children by the peer group, based on the group's general view of the individual.

CUTTING EDGE

Does gaming damage or 'teach' children about interactions?

A government poll in 2010 (reported in Williams, 2010) reports that one in six children under the age of 7 have 'difficulty talking' – a problem that worried families blame on their children's onscreen gaming experiences. Such reports are seen to peddle common fears about video games, that they are addictive and promote social isolation. Such fears are not groundless as research has shown the detriments of pathological gaming, including loneliness and social withdrawal, anxiety and depressive symptoms, potentially resulting from the displacement of 'real-world' social interactions (Lemmens et al., 2011; Schimmenti et al., 2013).

In direct contrast is a bulk of recent research documenting the positive long-lasting effects of gaming. These include the development of cognitive and perceptual skills, which educators harness for practical training (Eichenbaum et al., 2014), and bridging and bonding social 'capital' (building new relationships and strengthening existing ones) through online gaming user interactions (Kim et al., 2014). With the popularity of multiplayer online role-playing games over the last decade, some gamers engage in 'social' interactions that lead to the formation of online social groups and 'communities' (Hussain and Griffiths, 2014; see also 'Multimedia games and adolescent development' in Chapter 13, pages 397–8).

Tom Chatfield, who is a web designer/developer and regular contributor to *Guardian Technology*, argues that gaming life can be a place that is not so much about 'escaping the commitments and interactions that make friendships "real" as it is about a sophisticated set of satisfactions with their own increasingly urgent reality and challenges' (Chatfield, 2010). He describes a list of computer games involving virtual worlds, some of which offer users a chatroom where they can 'interact' with each other in virtual graphical locations, which they themselves have created and where you can 'have and do anything you liked'. Others involve players 'banding together' to earn greater rewards through accumulative 'achievement' points – only attainable by hundreds of hours of effort – while also lifting their individual score in the global rankings, which is seen as an 'awesome' engine for 'engaging a networked community'.

LAN (local area network) 'parties' have become quite common, with the largest hosted in 2007 at DreamHack in Jönköping, Sweden with 10 445 connected computers. A more recent phenomenon is that of Minecraft, where a graphically basic game involving construction blocks attracts likeminded adults and children who may be brought together through a LAN. Some parents note the positive effects, especially on children who would otherwise be dismissed as 'geeks' (reported by Mark Ward on BBC News in 2013).

Thus computing games, particularly online gaming, can be very creative and very sociable. As gaming has become an integral part of life for the twenty-first-century 'net generation' of children (and many adults), for whom communicating or socialising online is commonplace, some advocate that we need fresh perspectives to look into the subject (such as how to harness collaborative education within this venue) rather than just focusing on the negatives (Bekebrede et al., 2011; Kim et al., 2014).

- Have you played any computer games of the kind described above?
- Do you agree or disagree with Chatfield's analysis and comments? How strongly?
- How do 'virtual' interactions differ from 'real' ones when children play such games?

As Chatfield himself comments, virtual interactions cannot replace real ones, but some elements of game-play may be comparable to those in 'real life', such as how to collaborate and negotiate towards a shared goal. However, one key missing element is the true identity of the player (except in certain games where players may choose to disclose among known social circles). Within many LAN parties, a strong sense of identity seems to be asserted with each player generating an avatar by which they become known and which can have specific benefits, as it conceals social categories such as gender, ethnicity or attractiveness, which can affect peer status (see the following sections).

It is argued that some elements of interactive computer game-play may be comparable to those in real life.
Source: Pearson Education Ltd/Photodisc/Ryan McVay

Over the years, psychologists have investigated 'what makes' some children more or less accepted and liked than others. Research has investigated whether it is something to do with the accepted or rejected child himself or whether it is more to do with the peer group. Such work is obviously paramount, as a child's peer status could affect how she feels; no one wants to be rejected! And, of course, with very few peers accepting, or even some actively rejecting them, some children 'forgo' the opportunities for peer interactions and play that we considered earlier, and this can in turn impact on their learning and development. In the following we will review research that has identified these different types of children, their characteristics that may make them accepted, rejected or neglected, and the consequences that peer status can lead to.

There have been different methods for measuring children's social status over the years. Some of these involve directly asking members in a peer group to nominate others within the group whom they favour the most, or want to associate with the most. Similarly, they can also be asked to nominate those whom they least like or want least to associate with (e.g. each pupil in a class may be asked to name a few classmates by a researcher saying, 'Who in this class would you like to sit with/play with the most?' and 'Who in this class would you not like to sit/play with?'). Then those who receive the most nominations of 'most liked' and 'least liked' would be the most accepted and rejected, respectively (and those who receive few of either can be seen as the neglected children). Alternatively, children may be asked to evaluate each other within the peer group, by giving a rating on a Likert scale (from 1, most dislike, to 5, most like), for instance. Then each child will have a popularity/acceptance score.

Children may also be directly observed, say, in a school playground, over a set period of time, to see who interacts with whom, and how often, which gives an idea of how 'sought after' each child is by other children. The most 'popular' children would be those who are approached or engaged by the greatest number of other children, the 'rejected' children may approach their peers but are usually avoided by them, and the neglected ones are those who neither approach nor 'get approached' by others (see the Research Methods box on sociometry).

Peer acceptance

Accepted children are those who are typically most liked or chosen as playmates by their peers. Not surprisingly, attraction can be 'skin-deep' and physical appearance can make a child more popular; attractive and physically larger children (Dion and Berscheid, 1974) and adolescents (Boyatzis et al., 1998) tend to fall into this category. Still, other features that can be helped (by children) contribute to social status. Many accepted or popular children are academically and socially competent, in that they are able to communicate in a friendly, warm and sensitive way, and are generally more positive, cooperative and supportive compared to other children (Cillessen and Bellmore, 2004). In conflicts, such children excel at negotiation and compromise (Rose and Asher, 1999), and in joining in activities they are adept at adjusting their behaviour to 'fit in' (Rubin et al., 1998; Cillessen and Bellmore, 2004). Perhaps this is due to their better emotional understanding (Underwood, 1997) and perspective-taking skills (Fitzgerald and White, 2003). A recent longitudinal study (Santos et al., 2014) reports that personality and behavioural attributes characteristic of socially competent pre-schoolers (such as being attentive to peers and initiating interactions) are antecedents associated with higher sociometric status and reciprocal friendship. However, it should be borne in mind that at these ages (3–5 years) such status and relationships are far from stable (also see the 'Research methods' box for sociometric status).

More occasionally, and usually in later childhood or adolescence, children are identified as popular *due to* their belligerent or 'antisocial' behaviour being associated with being 'cool'. In particular, among boys, they tend to have good athletic skills, but will deliberately challenge authority or get into trouble and fights, which can enhance their status further, especially in a youth culture that values aggressive behaviour (Stormshak et al., 1999). Among girls, such 'antisocial popularity' tends to decline with age as they become increasingly socially aggressive and controlling while peers start to question and resent their manipulative tactics and reject them (Cillessen and Mayeux, 2004). A study of over 600 Dutch early adolescents (6th grade) reports that popularity and acceptance are functions of a complex profile of traits; while some may be popular by having both prosocial and antisocial behaviour and high extraversion, those showing lower levels of antisocial behaviour are more likely to be 'accepted' (more akin to friendships; see the final section of the chapter) by their peers (Wolters et al., 2014).

Peer rejection

Rejected children are the most concerning group as rejection is related to poor developmental outcomes (see later); hence this group has received more research. These are children who are least liked or are disliked the most or are least likely to be picked as playmates. Such unpopularity probably comes from a child's aggressive, disruptive or uncooperative behaviour. They may lack social skills in that they fail to take turns and interrupt play, for instance. Many also have poor control of their emotional expressions (Eisenberg et al., 1995). There is some evidence that such children also have poorer perspective-taking skills (Crick et al., 2002). This is manifest in how boys may misinterpret their peers' innocent and playful behaviour as having hostile intent – for example, in the case of play-fighting, as we read earlier – and respond in kind with aggression. Unlike the 'antisocial' kind of aggression that older popular children display, which enhances their peer status, these aggressive and

---

Definitions

Accepted children: children who are popular, accepted or well liked by the majority of other children in the peer group.

Rejected children: children who are unpopular, avoided as a playmate, least liked, or disliked by others in the peer group.

RESEARCH METHODS

Sociometry

How accepted a child within the peer group is can be identified as an 'index' of that child's relative standing, and this way of charting their social status is known as **sociometry**, or sociometric techniques. This may derive from peer nominations/ratings as being 'liked' or a playmate (but also the reverse), for example. Some studies use observations to mark the frequency of each child playing with another peer(s). The data obtained are at times used to plot a 'sociogram', which illustrates the pattern of overall interactions between children in the wider peer group, apart from individual children's sociometric 'status'. One of the early researchers to do this kind of charting was Anne Clark with colleagues in the 1960s (Clark et al., 1969). Figure 12.1 shows their sociogram based on the observations of free play in a US nursery. Each small circle (girl) or triangle (boy) represents a child in his/her group. The lines between them indicate the proportions of time the children play together. The large circles indicate the number of playmates each child has.

One of the first features that 'stands out' immediately from the sociogram is the two boys who are isolated (outside of the concentric circles). The rest of the group are socially linked in some way; in particular, all the other boys are part of a loose 'network' around a 'triad' of boys closely associated together. In contrast, the girls are relatively segregated as a larger gender group, although they have their own 'cliques' in the form of dyads and small groups. Hence finally, it is clear that they do not interact across gender much at all; there is only one boy–girl connection in the peer group. This is in line with other research in both nursery and school interactions (as we saw earlier and in Chapter 11).

- Do you think the sociometric approach is a good way to measure peer social status? Is the sociogram easy to understand?
- Are there differences between the different ways of collecting data about social status: peer nominations/ratings, teacher reports and direct observations?
- Which way do you think is the most accurate and which is most consistent?

As with using the different relevant data collection methods in other research topics, both reliability and validity (see Chapter 3, 'Research methods') depend in part on the informants who give or chart the data – here, the children and the researchers. Whilst the self/other-reporting methods (peer nominations and sometimes teacher ratings – which do not tend to align together; Santos et al., 2014) depend on the perspectives, memory and honesty of those who supply the data, direct observations depend on the skills

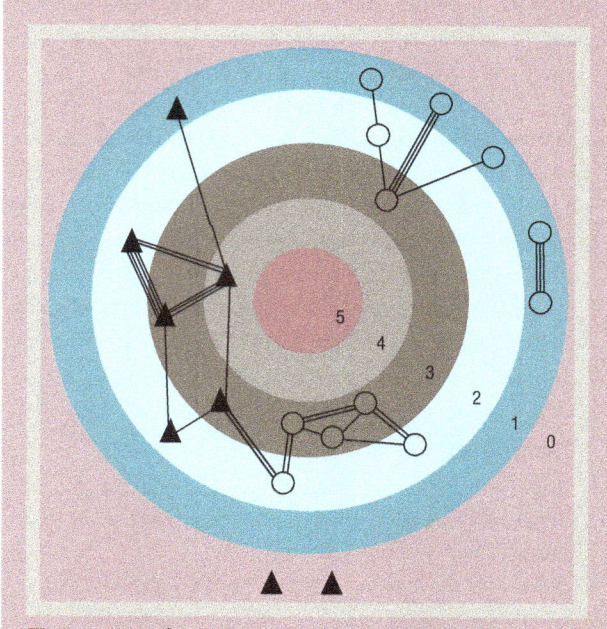

Figure 12.1 Sociogram of peer social status in a nursery.
Source: Clark et al. (1969)

Definition

Sociometry: a technique that charts the relative standing of children within their peer group, where data of their popularity/acceptance can be collected by self-reporting of peer preferences or observations of their interactions with each other.

and interpretations of the researchers who observe and document the children's interactions.

Worth noting is that relatively little is known about the behaviour of children assigned to different sociometric status groups in contexts outside of North America. The measures have been adopted for recent research in European countries such as Italy (Nelson et al., 2010), Portugal (Santos et al., 2014) and Romania (Soponaru et al., 2014). The patterns are generally in line with that of US children (e.g. higher-status children tend to show more sociability and less aggression). Yet it is important to note that in most pre-school to early school year contexts, sociometric status is not terribly stable and certain 'movement' between status groups over time is commonplace.

rejected children tend to be more antagonistic against their peers and get into conflicts that elicit the peers' hostility, which in turn confirm their own expectation that other people are hostile to them (Dodge et al., 1990).

On the other hand, rejection or unpopularity of some children may also arise from the characteristics opposite to those of aggression. These children are seen as 'withdrawn' in that they are passive, or timid even, or socially awkward. They may suffer from social anxiety, so much so that they fear the challenge of approaching their peer group as they hold negative expectations about how others will treat them and worry about being rejected, which itself then becomes a self-fulfilling prophecy (Ladd and Burgess, 1999). In fact, rejected and withdrawn children are often very aware that they are disliked (Harrist et al., 1997), but many rejected and aggressive children assume that others like them (Zakriski and Coie, 1996).

Indeed, some research has examined the 'heterogeneity' of peer rejection in relation to children's social prominence (their specific place or role, such as being leader, 'cool' or sporty, and so on); being 'liked' as a sociometric index does not convey one's position in certain social structures (Farmer et al., 2011). While few rejected children have high prominence, this type of child tends to be rated by others as having high levels of aggression (i.e. the aggressive rejected type), is likely to be identified as a 'bully' and is more likely to associate with other prominent peers.

However, although it is the case that many rejected children lack some social skills that are needed to interact effectively with peers, not all rejection is the *result* of lacking such skills. Sometimes children may react strongly to rejection by pre-existing popular cliques that exclude non-members, and in doing so they exhibit what is labelled as maladjusted behaviour (see also Chapter 15, 'Bullying'). These children may not lack such skills and may not be rejected in other contexts.

Peer neglect

There are certain children who are neither strongly liked nor strongly disliked, unlike either of the categories of children above. Not particularly aggressive or shy, many neglected children are nevertheless socially inept and unassertive, and tend to play by themselves or on the fringes of larger peer groups. Surprisingly, despite their rare interactions with others, many neglected children do not report feeling unhappy and lonely; neither are they that bothered about being neglected or ignored by their peers (McElhaney et al., 2008). It is possible that their peer status is simply a function of their personality; they may just prefer to be by themselves.

Many neglected children are in fact as 'well adjusted' as their peers, and may share characteristics even with their 'popular' counterparts. Some such children are skilled enough to join in with peer activities if they so wish (Harrist et al., 1997; Ladd and Burgess, 1999). Indeed, by behaviour profiling in recent research, neglected children are found to be generally not that distinguishable from average-status children, even if both types tend to have lower sociability than popular children (Nelson et al., 2010). As such, their 'neglected'

Definition

Neglected children: children who are neither accepted nor rejected, or not strongly liked or disliked, by their peer group.

status may be temporary if it is possible for them to 'raise' their level of popularity over time (Rubin et al., 1998). By this token, one may question, apart from some of the identified personality or behaviour correlates, how a child comes to be classified into a peer status in the first place, and how accurate, fair or consistent such a classification is (see the Research Methods box). The dynamics of a peer group, once a child has been recognised as a certain 'type', may be at play – which we will explore below.

Consequences of social status

We have identified a few major categories of children, according to their standing relative to their peers and how they come to be categorised. It is worth noting that once a child has been associated with a given status, this association may remain as the child is known by his 'reputation', even if the child's behaviour changes (Rubin et al., 1998). It can be particularly difficult for a child, who is known to be rejected, to try to be accepted even if he improves his social skills. This is because, once that problematic reputation is attached, his behaviour tends to be interpreted accordingly, whether or not it fits with this reputation.

Meanwhile, not all children fall into the popular, rejected or neglected categories; some are none of these. As we have read, children may be 'average' in that they are rated as having average popularity or acceptance and they arouse no strong feelings in others. Moreover, there is a minority of so-called 'controversial' children who are most liked by some peers *as well as* most disliked by others (Coie et al., 1983). As noted earlier, most children do show some status 'mobility', particularly neglected children whose status may be unstable. As they are not totally without social interaction, many neglected average and controversial children do not seem to be drastically disadvantaged by their status and manage to make friends (see 'Children's friendships', pages 366–75). However, even if neglected children do as well in school as popular children (Wentzel and Asher, 1995), they are prone to loneliness and depression (Cillessen et al., 1992) and may blame teachers for not dealing with their social dilemma (Galanaki, 2004). The link between depression and peer neglect is borne out by brain-imaging research showing that peer neglect and physical pain stimulate the same part of the brain (Eisenberger, 2003). At the other end, controversial children, typified by high sociability and aggression, fare little different from rejected children in terms of conflict and victimisation (Nelson et al., 2010). However, as adolescents, controversial and popular peers report the least loneliness, in contrast to their neglected and certain rejected counterparts (Woodhouse et al., 2012).

Not surprisingly, the most liked or popular children, perhaps due to their friendly and outgoing dispositions, tend to show the highest levels of sociability and cognitive ability and the lowest levels of aggressiveness and withdrawal, compared with other groups in later years. They also tend to enjoy higher academic success and are better adjusted in adult life (Bagwell et al., 1998). These outcomes may have more to do with their characteristics that have led them to become popular rather than being a direct benefit derived from their popular status. Also, the reason for their popularity is important within the peer context. As explained earlier, some older children's subcultures value certain 'antisocial' behaviour, such as challenging authority. Obviously such behaviour and the popularity that comes with it go against positive school adjustments (Allen et al., 2005). In reality, peer acceptance tends to be higher among students who display only a low level of antisocial behaviour (Wolters et al., 2014) and a higher level of academic achievement (Soponaru et al., 2014).

As recognised earlier, rejected children are most problematic; they form the group that suffers the greatest disadvantages, as they are most likely to experience a lack of regular social contact. For the rejected aggressive children, they spend more time arguing and fighting rather than in social play or conversation, and even if they play socially it is often in smaller groups with younger or other rejected children. As they are often unaware that they are disliked or even overestimate their popularity, this can make them increasingly unpopular over time (Hughes et al., 1997). Generally their interaction pattern tends to be the opposite to that of their popular peers through middle childhood, featuring more physical and relational aggression as well as victimisation (Nelson et al., 2010). By adolescence, these children often do poorly in school (Wentzel and Asher, 1995) and are at greater risk of so-called 'externalising problems', the negative 'acting out' of behaviours like interpersonal violence and delinquency. They are more likely to drop out of school due to adjustment difficulties such as playing truants or becoming bullies, and are also at risk of assembling in antisocial gangs (Cairns et al., 1988), as they tend to be attracted to one another and form their own social network (Woodhouse et al., 2012).

Indeed, there is evidence that rejected aggressive individuals are at risk of longer-term rejection and troubled relationships (Rubin et al., 1998). Excess aggressiveness is one of the few definite aspects of early functioning that predicts future emotional disturbances and behavioural problems (see Chapter 10). However, it should be noted that problematic interactions in earlier childhood can themselves be a 'sign' of some deeper maladjustment that is also reflected in later disturbances, rather than being a result of rejection which may have resulted from such maladjustment. For instance, there is some evidence that these rejected children have more attentional problems, which are in turn associated with academic performance as well as social interaction, warranting more support for this group to improve their attention skills (Wilson et al., 2011).

At the same time, the rejected, but withdrawn, children have a rather different set of outcomes. These children may have tried to gain acceptance by their peers and failed, before they eventually give up and become even more withdrawn and feel extremely lonely. This can happen as early as nursery, and as their feelings of loneliness rise and their self-esteem declines, their school achievement suffers, and many avoid school (Buhs and Ladd, 2001). Chronic rejection can lead to so-called 'rejection sensitivity', which is a heightened tendency to readily perceive, anxiously expect and overreact to overt or implied rejection; accompanied by defensive feelings, such expectations predict certain behavioural reactions like even more withdrawal (see Nesdale et al., 2014). Links have been found between social withdrawal and loneliness in shy children from middle childhood, and while social withdrawal is viewed even more negatively by older children this has clinical implications in adolescence (Woodhouse et al., 2012). These include 'internalising' problems such as social anxiety and depression. Since they distrust others, most withdrawn rejected children have few or no friends (see 'Children's friendships', pages 366–75), and these friends tend also to be withdrawn peers lacking in social skills and confidence (Rubin et al., 2006).

Both types of rejected children are at risk of peer harassment, but they would take on opposite roles due to their disposition. Aggressive rejected children tend to act as bullies (see Chapter 15), as they behave with hostility and read hostile intent into others' behaviour. Withdrawn children are particularly likely to be picked on as victims due to their insecure or fearful and submissive demeanour (Sandstrom and Cillissen, 2003). Excluded from 'normal' interactions, rejected children may continue to miss out on the opportunities presented by such exchanges to learn how to handle competitions, conflicts or cooperation without intervention. Recent research of 8- to 11-year-olds' feelings and behaviour

Neglected children may prefer to be alone or join in play if they wish.
Source: Bubbles Photolibrary/Loisjoy Thurston

Table 12.3 Characteristics and outcomes of accepted, rejected and neglected children.

Status type	Characteristics	Outcomes
Accepted	Physically attractive Warm and friendly character Interact positively and cooperatively Good at negotiation and compromise Adjust behaviour to join in play Good perspective-taking skills	High sociability Good cognitive skills Low aggressiveness Little social withdrawal Academic success Better adjusted as adults
Rejected aggressive	Aggressive, disruptive or uncooperative Poor control of emotions Lack etiquette for joining in play Poor perspective-taking skills Antagonistic and hostile/read hostile intent Unaware that they are disliked	Poor school performance At risk of school dropout, violence and delinquency Longer-term behavioural/emotional maladjustments and troubled relationships
Rejected withdrawn	Passive, timid or socially awkward Hold negative expectations of others Do not approach/hesitate to join peers Aware that they are disliked	Low self-esteem Poor school achievement and school avoidance Social anxiety/depression
Neglected	Socially inept and unassertive Play alone or on the fringes of large groups May not be unhappy/prefer to be alone May join in peer group and raise acceptance	Not always disadvantaged Can make some friends More prone to loneliness May trigger depression

on having just been rejected shows that they have neutral thoughts (the same as before rejection) but 'prevention' behaviours including crying or walking away (to avoid further rejection; Chiffriller and Kangos, 2014). This suggests that, although they feel confused and frustrated, they do not know how to promote themselves to be included, which leaves room for training 'promotion' thoughts and behaviours by these ages.

We have seen how different children have different propensities to interact effectively with peers due to their dispositions as well as the nature of the peer context. As such, they fall into several types of peer social status, which come with different developmental outcomes and susceptibility towards longer-term adjustment issues (the traits of major status groups and their possible outcomes are summarised in Table 12.3). These are important for interventions aimed at improving peer interactions and psychological adjustments of at-risk children, such as coaching attention or positive social skills and emotion understanding, and reinforcing friendly interaction and cooperation (DeRosier, 2007). As part of the pathway towards better adjustments, which are a positive outcome, children strike promising relationships with one another, or 'make friends'. In the final section of this chapter, we look at friendship as a special relationship between peers, its nature through development, the factors which influence it, and its functions and implications.

Children's friendships

> **STOP AND THINK**
>
> Think back to your own childhood when you remember the first 'friend' you had (of course, the definition of 'friend' differs between people, but in this case think of ones whom you had considered to be close enough to you that you claimed them as 'friends').
>
> - How old were you when you had this friend?
> - What made you see him/her as your 'friend'?
> - How long did the friendship last?

The vast majority of children, as we have seen, in one form or another regularly engage in meaningful interactions with their peers, and some peers are more 'sought after' than others. However, just being preferred the most by many other children is not quite the same as being a 'friend' to those children. Friendship refers to a *mutual* association or kinship between two (or more) children; both/all parties involved in the companionship want to be with the other(s) and are positive and cooperative towards each other. Epstein (1989) distinguished three bases for the selection of friends by children. The first basis is simply physical proximity: children are more likely to choose friends from the children they meet at home, in their street or in their pre-school or class at school. The second basis of friendship is sharing characteristics like age and sex. Boys are more likely to make friends with other boys of the same age and girls are more likely to make friends with other girls of the same age (see also Chapter 11 on gender relationships). Once a child has selected other children as friends based on these characteristics, Epstein argues that the friendships are more likely to continue if they share similar interests and attitudes. Within this special kind of relationship where the children choose to spend more time with each other than other peers, sensitivity, trust and closeness will tend to build up over time. Meanwhile, friends can also have more disagreement with each other than they do with other people, probably because they have more opportunities to disagree with those they spend more time with. However, with trust, understanding and other complex psychological elements involved in friendships, it is expected that disagreements can be resolved by negotiation or compromise to find a mutually acceptable solution. Disagreements with those who are not friends are less likely to be resolved with such an outcome.

Over the next subsections we will look closely at children's friendships across the age groups to review their differences in quality before we look into other factors that influence the development of friendships between different children. Finally, we will evaluate the research that investigates the functions of children's friendships and the developmental outcomes and long-term implications of these friendships.

Friendships through the years

Just as there are qualitative differences in peer interactions between the age groups in terms of complexity, so there are age differences in friendship quality, not surprisingly as friendships evolve from such interactions. We will look at the ages at which children see each other as friends, and the features of such friendships, before evaluating a stage model used to explain the age changes.

Early childhood/pre-school ages

Although there is evidence that toddlers already have play preference for some peers over others (Howes, 1983, 1987), it is difficult to ascertain that they consciously view the preferred peers as 'friends'. Though we have mentioned abstract and complex concepts like 'trust' and 'closeness', ask pre-schoolers to tell us who their friends are, and why those are their friends, and their responses tend to be very simple, such as 'they play with me' (Selman, 1980). This in part has something to do with their limited vocabulary, but it is indeed true that at such young ages children spend most of their time playing, as we saw earlier. At this stage, children regard friendships casually, as something that can start easily, and 'concretely' such as by seeing each other regularly even in passing, or sharing toys a lot, and thus such friendships will also end abruptly, such as when one party refuses to share or cannot play with the other.

Still, the stability of friendships increases even during this period; almost 20% of 3-year-olds spend more of their time with one other child, and this rises to over half at 4 years (Hinde et al., 1985). Compared to other companies, such pairs show more extended interaction, mutual liking, reciprocity and support, and less negative behaviour towards each other (Maguire and Dunn, 1997). Lastly, as we saw earlier and in Chapter 11, pre-schoolers already largely segregate themselves by gender, forming regular associations with only those of their own sex.

Middle childhood/school ages

With starting, or transferring, school being a critical and potentially stressful time at this stage, many children voice that having one or more friends is important

Definition

Friendship: a mutual reciprocal relationship between two or more people where both or all parties involved want to spend more time with the other(s) than other peers.

and explore various strategies (such as making requests, initiating groups and offering support) to build friendships (Danby et al., 2012). Thus although friendship in earlier school ages (around 5 to 8 years) is still based on common activities and physical proximity (Bigelow and La Gaipa, 1980), eventually a 'friend' is more than just a regular playmate, as someone who shares beliefs, rules, expectations about sanctions and so on. The progression reflects children's distinction of friendships from acquaintances or casual relationships, and a cognitive shift from a focus on the 'physical' to the 'psychological' (see Chapter 2, 'Theoretical perspectives'). This is when the 'deeper' elements of closeness and trust emerge, and children as friends recognise each other's personal qualities, needs and wants, where each party is expected to support the other in times of need. For instance, schoolchildren who think that one should help a friend when the friend is being teased by other peers, even if it may risk oneself being teased by others as well, are likely to have more friends than those who think that one should not help the friend in this scenario to avoid lowering one's own status (Rose and Asher, 2004). Indeed, violation of trust, including not helping a friend when help is needed and breaking a promise, is seen as a serious breach of friendship in this age group.

Behaviourally, children who claim to be friends with each other tend to talk more with each other, and are more tactile and affectionate, and supportive and cooperative towards each other than towards non-friends (Hartup, 2006). Because of such features, school-aged children's friendships are more selective than pre-schoolers' ones; they claim fewer but closer friends than pre-schoolers, particularly among girls, who value closeness and exclusivity more than boys do.

Adolescence

By the time children are 11–12 years old, they begin to value closeness or intimacy in friendship, where they share more of their 'inner feelings', including secrets, with their friends and are more knowledgeable and understanding about one another's feelings. In turn, they expect a friend to be loyal, faithful, trustworthy and supportive (Hartup, 2006). They work harder on compromise and negotiation towards maintaining exclusiveness as friends. As a result, friendships between adolescents tend to be more stable and enduring than those of younger children; only about 20% of friendships formed before the age of 11–12 years last as long as a year, versus 40% of those friendships formed three years later by the same individuals (Cairns and Cairns, 1994). As the adolescent focuses more on 'quality' rather than 'quantity' of friendship, the degree of selectivity becomes even higher and the number of 'best friendships' declines (from four to six in middle childhood to one or two in adolescence), particularly among girls (Hartup and Stevens, 1999).

Meanwhile, compared to younger children adolescents are also more 'realistic' about the durability of friendship; they acknowledge that their friends cannot fulfil all their needs and that friendships can change over time, in that friends can become closer or less close as people or circumstances change. For example, a girl who changes her status by getting a boyfriend will spend less time with her female friends and this can lead to their ending the friendships if those friends have not yet got boyfriends. Some also mature faster, or achieve higher academically or athletically, than their friends and if such achievement domains are important to the group, such status differences can mark the beginning of the end in some friendships (Akers et al., 1998). Yet they also surmise that good-quality friendships can adapt to change and last. Recent research has found that by early adolescence children report higher friendship quality if they feel that friends respond to their achievements by giving support and positive feedback (such as expressing joy or offering congratulations; Altermatt, 2011). This is particularly the case where adolescents have outperformed their friends, whose responses can be predicted by the friendship quality (as rated by children and other peers) – better friends are more likely to offer support or seek help rather than respond by going 'off-task' (not mentioning the achievement; Altermatt and Ivers, 2011).

Stages in children's conception of friendships

Looking at the features identified above of children's friendships at different age periods, from a developmental perspective it would seem that children's ideas of what friendships are 'about' go through a sequence of stages that reflect certain changes in their socio-cognitive understanding. The well-regarded American psychologist Robert Selman (1980) clearly advocates this school

> Mary and Sally have been friends since they were five year sold. A new girl, Rosie, starts in their class. Mary doesn't like Rosie much because she thinks Rosie is a show-off. One day Rosie invites Mary to go with her to the park, and this places Mary in a dilemma because she has already promised Sally that she will go to her house on that day. What will Mary do?
>
> Selman's stories and questions probe into the kind of friendship (e.g., how much trust and understanding) between the protagonists, and a comparison between striking new friendships (Mary and Rosie) and keeping old ones (Mary and Sally).

Figure 12.2 An example of a friendship dilemma by Selman (1980) (names and some features of story changed).

STOP AND THINK

- Do you agree with Selman's stages of friendship?
- Do you think some children may be capable of a more or less sophisticated notion of friendship at those ages?

of thought. He observed the age-related transformations in how children construe and interpret friendships, and related these to the development of social cognition. To do so, he interviewed many children and read them stories that were centred round a friendship 'dilemma'. Then he asked them some questions about the relationships between the characters in the story and how the dilemma should best be resolved (an example is given in Figure 12.2).

From his analysis of the responses provided by 3- to 15-year-old children, Selman summarised the key changes into four main stages in the development of their conceptions of friendship corresponding to their perspective-taking skills. These stages are listed in Table 12.4.

It is clear that Selman sees children's changing understanding of friendships as a linear progression from a focus on friends' physical characteristics (such as where they live, what they do) to their psychological attributes (from likes/dislikes to values). This is likened to the general development of social and cognitive abilities (as Piaget's theory; see Chapter 2), where a child's focus turns from the external to the internal, as he can increasingly take another's perspective, and the concern for more abstract notions of support and values in line with more sophisticated social understanding through adolescent development (see Chapter 13, Adolescence).

While Selman's stages make sense and are supported by data, studies that have explored children's associations in other ways have found that young children's meanings of friendships can be broader and deeper than what are in Selman's descriptions. For example, the sociologist William Corsaro spent several months in a nursery to document extensive 'natural' observations of children's activities and paid particular attention to how the children talked with one another when they referred to the word 'friend' (e.g. Corsaro, 1985). Corsaro identified six categories from such talk, where the most frequently invoked were when children used being 'friends' as a gateway to join in play, or as they played they mentioned that they were 'friends'. While

Table 12.4 Selman's (1980) stages of friendship definition.

Stage	Age (years)	Description
Momentary physical playmate	3–5	Define friends in terms of shared activities and geographical associations; friends are children they play with, live nearby or go to same school; refer to friends in here-and-now; no reference to personal characteristics/psychological attributes
One-way assistance	6–8	Friend is someone who helps you or does things that please you; need to become aware of each other's likes/dislikes; no reciprocal nature yet
Fairweather cooperation	9–12	Key feature is reciprocal understanding; evaluate friends' action/know friends can judge them and adapt or take account of each other's preferences. Disagreement/conflicts still end friendship
Mutual concern	11–15	Can take perspective of other people; friendship as a bond built over time and made strong/stable by mutual support, concern and understanding; compatible interests, values and personalities; fiercely protected; can withstand minor conflicts

these fit with the activity description appropriate for the age group in Selman's model, the other categories, less frequently observed, show children using friendship in abstract ways: to mark 'sides' in competitions (friends versus non-friends), exclude others from joint activities (only friends play), express concern for others (when a friend is absent) and use 'best friends' as a measure of their feelings, care and mutual concern for each other. In the example in Figure 12.3, the children's talk can be seen to show implicitly a more advanced level of understanding about friends even though both children are under the age of 4 years. One child felt the need to justify being away from her friend and the other felt the need to know. Such mutual concern is expected only from the later stages in Selman's model. Corsaro did mention that the children involved had a closer relationship than most others (and this is the only example in this category).

Since then, many researchers have used a similar approach to taking a detailed look at children's friendships. For instance, Susan Danby and associates involved 162 4- to 6-year-olds in Queensland, Australia, in video-recorded interactions, drawings and audio-recorded interviews. The latter were interpreted in terms of the strategies in friendship formation when starting school (Danby et al., 2012). The in-depth accounts provide rich insights into the children's sophisticated understanding that friendship is more than being together or sharing activity (e.g. it 'takes time' to know each other), including empathy of others' situation and appreciation of their competence. The intricacies of interactions in such research suggest that we should examine the context in which friendship is built by children, some of whom may develop an understanding beyond their years.

Factors influencing children's friendships

We have seen how the quality of children's friendship changes over the course of development; with age, most friendships tend to become more intimate, reciprocal and enduring, even though some children may acquire these features in their friendships a little younger. Apart from age, other factors can influence the nature of friendship. For instance, children in certain friendship groups may do things differently from those in other groups, or those from similar backgrounds who share some other characteristics may become friends more easily or stay friends for longer.

Personality and preferences

As the saying goes, 'birds of a feather flock together', and this certainly seems to be true for the formation of friendships. We tend to choose others like ourselves to be friends as we have the same frame of reference and are thus more likely to share each other's points of view. Children are no different and their friends also tend to

---

Jenny and Betty, not quite four years old, are climbing into a large wooden box. Betty has just returned to play with Jenny after having been with another girl for most of the morning.

Betty to Jenny:	I do like you, Jenny. I do.
Jenny to Betty:	I know it.
Betty to Jenny:	Yeah. But I just ran away from you. You know why?
Jenny to Betty:	Why?
Betty to Jenny:	Because I –
Jenny to Betty:	You wanted to play with Linda?
Betty to Jenny:	Yeah.
Jenny to Betty:	I ranned away with you. Wasn't that funny?
Betty to Jenny:	Yes.
Jenny to Betty:	Cause I wanted to know what happened.
Betty to Jenny:	I know you wanted – all the time you wanna know because you're my best friend.
Jenny to Betty:	Right.

Figure 12.3 An extract of 3-year-olds' talk about friendship.

Source: Corsaro (1985, p. 166)

resemble themselves in personality, social status, academic achievement, prosocial behaviour, interpersonal judgement and such (Haselager et al., 1998). This is particularly important for adolescents as they value mutual affirmation and cooperation even more highly. Their friends tend to be similar to themselves in identity status (see Chapter 13, Adolescence), academic orientation, political beliefs, attitudes to drugs and even law-breaking behaviour (Akers et al., 1998). Occasionally, a change in circumstances such as moving school or home can mean exploring friendships with those with alternative views. In early adolescence, some may forgo similarity in favour of a popular peer. However, once similarities in personality and preference are established, children tend to spend more time together, thus becoming even more alike in their attitudes, values, behaviour and achievements (Berndt and Keefe, 1995).

A recent set of studies in the Netherlands (Yu et al., 2013, 2014a, 2014b) reports that adolescents with different personality types differ in friendship quality ('resilient' friends show less conflict and more support and problem solving than over-controlling and under-controlled types), which in turn influences future behaviour and relationship quality (see the next section).

Gender group and identity

As we explored earlier in this chapter and in Chapter 11, Development of Self-concept and Gender Identity, by school age children already show preference for same-sex playmates and this tendency increases into adolescence. The friendships they build on, and get reinforced by, involve single-sex groups, and there are qualitative differences in these friendships (Lloyd and Duveen, 1992). As boys' interactions are often activity-based and competitive (like team sports), their friendship groups tend to be larger and more inclusive, but focus on competition or dominance in school or sporting achievements, and conflict is quite common. In contrast, girls' friendship groups tend to be smaller, and more exclusive and intensive, as they share emotional closeness and support via talking about their feelings (Maccoby, 2002). Such differences are linked to their gender identity and role expectations (see Chapter 11). More 'masculine' boys are less likely to have intimate friendships, and there is evidence that emotional management is linked to having fewer friends among boys. However, girls tend to have more friends if they can better manage to control their emotions, where that is critical for self-disclosure and agreeability (Dunsmore et al., 2008).

It is still important to emphasise that there are overall commonalities between boys' and girls' friendships; both value collaboration and cooperation among friends. Also, although boys' friendships differ in the style of communication and exchange, it does not mean that intimacy is less important. Boys' friendships have been likened to 'contradictions of masculine identities' (Frosh et al., 2002); as toughness and masculinity are inextricably linked, there is a discrepancy between their need for emotional closeness and difficulty in discussing it with male friends. This is borne out by a UK study (Betts and Stiller, 2013) where several gender differences are reported in the antecedents of 9–11-year-old children's relative importance in 'best' friendship networks. For instance, boys' friendship security (which often requires or enhances emotional closeness) is actually followed by a drop in their share of friendships in class – which does not apply to girls.

Friendship and technology

Earlier we examined the contemporary issues surrounding gaming and children's ability to communicate and interact with each other. Since the massive rise in computer use and access to the internet and other interactive technologies in the 1990s, children all over the industrialised world and beyond have been using these means to create and develop friendships. This medium can take the form of texts and calls by personal mobile phones, email, instant messaging, chatrooms, blogs and, most commonly among older children and adolescents, social networking sites (e.g. Facebook, Twitter). In the early days, the medium was particularly popular with boys, who often started on collaborative simulation games, like the ones we read about earlier, before moving on to visiting chatrooms, and studies suggest that such gaming experiences can promote the development of the masculine identity in teenage boys (Sanford and Madill, 2006).

Nowadays children use computer technology in much the same ways as they use other environments. Through online 'spaces' they explore issues that they may or may not discuss in 'real life', including peer and parental relationships and conflicts, and even private or sensitive issues such as sexuality, drug taking and eating disorders, particularly among teenagers. Perhaps due to the 'non-face-to-face' context of interactions, they feel less inhibited and 'open up' more. There is some evidence that instant messaging, which used to be teenagers' preferred form of virtual interaction, increased the feelings of intimacy and wellbeing between existing friends (Valkenburg and Peter, 2007). With Facebook being so popular, some research shows that much perceived social support is obtained from online friends (Akbulut and Günüç, 2012). Interestingly, the division of gender roles is as apparent online as it is in real life (girls being more verbal and boys more graphical in role play). However, when a cross-sex pair interacts, some boys adopt a more 'feminine' interacting style (Calvert et al., 2003). This may be due to the anonymity that 'frees' them from the need to behave in a stereotypical 'masculine' way.

Although the virtual contexts of the internet may afford more freedom and discretion to children who build their friendships in this medium, there are some hazards from such liaisons. The internet is not only for keeping in touch; some friendships are started this way, particularly in forums, gaming or networking sites. At times such friendships are then taken 'offline' where the friends meet face-to-face; parents may be rightly concerned about this. Online roles can be assumed or manipulated, and some 'friends' may have disingenuous motives other than making friends, including impostors who are adults befriending children online. There have indeed been high-profile cases where another child or an adult imposter has used the internet to befriend and abuse or harm a child, some with tragic ends (e.g. Halliday, 2014).

The often uncensored processes of 'e-communication' also mean that children are more likely to receive (sexual or racial) harassment, abuse or bullying from peers (Tynes et al., 2004). The details of this form of bullying, called *cyberbullying*, will be discussed later in the book (see Chapter 15, 'Understanding bullying'). Meanwhile, it is worth keeping in mind that although things may 'go wrong' between people in this medium, internet technology is but a set of useful 'tools' to develop friendships, and online friendships are unlikely to replace 'real' friendships. Recent studies show that more support from face-to-face friends is associated with fewer Facebook friendships (Akbulut and Günüç, 2012), and while some adolescents experiencing peer-related loneliness may increase Facebook use for social skills compensation, such use can actually increase the loneliness further over time (Teppers et al., 2014).

STOP AND THINK

Imagine your friend sends you an email or a text that makes you very unhappy or tells you some unwelcome news (say, they heard a mutual friend speak badly of you). Do you think that you would be unhappier or less unhappy if this was communicated to you in person? Why?

Functions and implications of children's friendships

Now that we have learnt about the nature of friendship in development, how children make and keep friends, and what may facilitate or hinder this process, this final section will focus on the functional question of what children's friendships are 'for' and what may be the implications of their having or not having good friends. Intuitively, it may seem obvious that having friends is better than having no friends; no one wants to be friendless or lonely! The crux of the matter is: how 'useful' is having friends (especially considering some of the more dubious or troublesome aspects of some kinds of friendship)? What is even more difficult is to show that any positive or negative outcome is *due to* having or not having friends. Here, we will evaluate some of the social, cognitive and longer-term psychological developments to which children's friendships are argued to contribute.

Self-concepts and evaluations

As we covered in depth in Chapter 11, one achievement of development is to establish a sense of self, or 'who we are'. Our self-concept frames how we think about the world, structures our social experiences and guides our social conduct, interactions and relationships. The 'objective self' concerns defining ourselves in relation to others – it is constructed in the context of social relationships, first with parents and then more and more with peers. We have also seen that what others think about and how they behave towards a child matters from infancy onwards, and increases in importance through adolescence. These are the reasons why being accepted, especially by those whom we care about or whose opinions we value – our friends – is so important as this gives us a positive sense of self. With friends, the child also explores the social role and identity she has (e.g. as a leader or follower, a boy or girl), and over time the norms of appearance, attitudes and behaviour will become absorbed into the child's self-concept.

'Belonging' is particularly significant for the adolescent's psychological wellbeing, as peer group pressure (see Chapter 13) has never been more salient than it is in adolescence. As commitment to crowds and cliques wanes towards later adolescence, and before mixed-sex friendships begin, friends become more sensitive to each other's personalities and strengths and weaknesses – a process that explores both the self and others, and supports self-development, identity and perspective taking (Savin-Williams and Berndt, 1990). Likewise, our self-esteem is very much bound up with people's, especially significant others', perceptions of our social standing and is related to the quality of our interactions since early in life (see Chapter 11). Recent research (Dehart et al., 2011) has found that implicit (unconscious, automatic) self-esteem is also related to implicit evaluations of significant others – friends as much as family or romantic partners – suggesting the importance of friends in our inner sense of self.

Problem solving, learning and cognitive development

Children do not just play and chat with their friends; in school they may interact in more formal capacities, such as working on a class-based task or other intellectual problems. There has been a great collection of evidence that collaboration with peers, particularly those who are friendly to oneself, can advance children's cognitive and social development (see Chapter 14, 'Development psychology and education'). Without adult instructions, two otherwise 'ignorant' (unknowing of the solution) children who are confronted with a problem, whether it is a perceptual, number or moral decision, can reach the solution eventually when neither has been able to achieve it alone. Starting from each having a partial or incomplete perspective, the children exchange their ideas through active discussion until a new approach combining those ideas arrives; learning is hence promoted this way as a joint discovery for greater cognitive development (Howe, 1993; Howe and Mercer, 2007).

There is even evidence that friends – compared with non-friends – perform more effectively in such tasks (Fonzi et al., 1997). This is because they tend to propose more ideas than non-friends and are better at sharing, negotiating and making compromises during potential conflicts, particularly within stable friendships that last through the school year as they display more sensitivity towards each other. More recent findings have been less conclusive on the issue, where friends' and non-friends' performance (in scientific reasoning tasks) within peer collaboration did not differ; what mattered was whether a collaboration was marred by conflict (Swenson and Strough, 2008) – even if friends are supposedly less likely to run into conflict. As collaborative learning is widely used in education, not just in 'normal' subjects, but from civics education to PE, more work is needed to discover how peers as 'critical friends' may become supporters or distractors (Anderson and Lubig, 2012; Koeboek and Knoppers, 2015).

School and psychological adjustments and future relationships

Apart from the obvious benefits for social and cognitive development, there are also more latent benefits of having friends. As friends are supposed to offer support, sensitivity and concern for one another, they should serve as a 'buffer' against stressful events such as family difficulties or maladaptive behaviours. Research implies that friendships can promote psychological wellbeing by reducing the need for antisocial acts; adolescents who are under family stress, but have close friends, are comparable in wellbeing to those who are not under such stress (Gauze et al., 1996).

Having close friends in school is conducive to better academic adjustment as school becomes a place where children enjoy interacting with others and they view school life in a more positive light (Berndt and Keefe, 1995). As we read earlier, children with low peer acceptance (which probably leads to a shortage of friends) are at risk of school avoidance and dropout. Recent research has upheld the trend, with the quality of friendship identified as early as in kindergarten associated with greater social skills (if high quality) and less problem behaviour (low quality) in school (Engle et al., 2011). The picture is similar for adolescents; although peer acceptance plays the most robust role, this factor together with the number of good friends and friendship quality all contributed to adjustment during the school transition (Kingery et al., 2011).

There are also arguments that good friendship (or lack thereof) in childhood lays the groundwork for later psychological health (or pathology) and even romantic relationships. We have read that sexuality, relationships, drugs and disorders are common topics between friends. Until recently, most studies had been retrospective reports, but an increasing number of longitudinal studies have now examined the potential impact that childhood friendships have on longer-term outcomes. As we have seen, excluded or rejected peers often experience depressed affect. Research shows that this easily escalates over time if they remain friendless, but for those who manage to befriend a few others, friendships have protective effects against this escalation (Bukowski et al., 2010). At the same time, for older children, belonging to 'cliques' with a high status is linked to an increase (over four years) of externalising problems, even if also a lower level of internalising problems (Witvliet et al., 2010). Likewise, adolescents of certain personality types (e.g. 'over-controlled'; see the Lifespan box) are more susceptible to the influence of friends' delinquency (e.g. vandalism, shoplifting), while others (resilient or under-controlled) are more likely to influence friends through their own delinquency (Yu et al., 2014a).

It may be that certain outcomes, apart from being products of individual tendencies – and children tend to select others with similar tendencies to be friends – are also a function of the processes through which friends can influence each other to engage in similar behaviours. We should also bear in mind that, although having friends is important for the various reasons identified earlier, in many friendships – even quality ones – there are both positive and negative features. Research tends to capture the positives (e.g. support and disclosure) that promote socio-emotional functioning, while the negatives, which can range from conflict and competition to jealousy and antagonism, are associated with symptoms of psychopathology (e.g. anxiety and depression; Kouwenberg et al., 2013). If we view childhood friendships as a 'training ground' for experimenting with positive and negative behaviours and seeing them through to their consequences, the same can be said of such friendships being avenues for children to learn about other relationships: emotional disclosure (to friends) can prepare the child or adolescent for relationships in the future (see the Lifespan box).

LIFESPAN

Stable childhood friendships – implications for adulthood?

As briefly reviewed in the previous section, a series of studies has reported adolescents' friendship characteristics as a function of their personality types in the Netherlands. These works, written by Rongjin Yu, are part of a larger longitudinal project, some of which formed part of her doctorate thesis (Yu et al., 2013, 2014a, 2014b). The 2014b paper, in particular, describes a 10-year follow-up study that traced Dutch youths in six waves of questionnaire data, from the ages of 12 or 16 years (as two cohorts), until they were young adults at 21 or 25 years (years 2001 to 2010). The aim was to investigate whether friendship quality in adolescence can be an (indirect) pathway through which personality types give continuity to romantic relationship quality in adulthood.

The researchers assessed 524 adolescents' personality using the popular Big Five dimensions (as described in Chapter 10, 'Child temperament and behavioural development'). In particular, they were interested to examine three personalities classified as 'resilients', 'under-controllers' and 'over-controllers' (Block and Block, 1980). Resilients are individuals characterised by a high level of ego-resiliency (tendency to respond flexibly to environmental demands) and a medium level of ego-control (tendency to contain rather than express motivational impulses). Over-controllers and under-controllers both have a low level of ego-resiliency, but over-controllers have a high level of ego-control and under-controllers have a low level of ego-control. Past research has found that a resilient personality bodes well with better friendships in adolescence (Van Aken and Semon Dubas, 2004) and romantic relationships in adulthood, but separately. The longitudinal nature of such research could bridge these differences over emerging adulthood.

Yu et al. found that resilients reported higher friendship quality, as indicated by more perceived support and less perceived dominance from, and less negative interaction with, their best friend. Moreover, perceived friendship quality gave an indirect linkage between personality types and romantic relationship quality. Resilients in both cohorts experienced higher level of support from their romantic partner as young adults predicted through the mean levels of support in their adolescent friendships, and less negative interaction with and less dominance from the adult romantic partner through the mean levels of negative interaction and dominance in their friendship in adolescence. The authors conclude that the impact that personality types could have on romantic relationship as adults is indirect – through friendship as adolescents – as individual differences in earlier friendship quality 'spill over' to romantic relationship quality in adulthood.

- What could the research find out about the relationship between adolescent friendships and later outcomes in adulthood?
- What was the study unable to show?

In Chapter 10, we read about longitudinal studies of even longer-term (middle adulthood) outcomes following up children or adolescents whose temperament or personality were assessed years earlier. However, Yu et al.'s work has measured not only the adolescent personality, but also the specifics of relationships experienced at several time-points. The researchers claim that no prior research had examined why adolescents with different personality types vary in their romantic relationship quality in adulthood – through linkages with friendship quality. The linkages suggest a 'natural' progression for romantic relationship development, in which youths practise principles of volition and reciprocity in friendships and later generalise related abilities and expectations to relationships of a different (romantic) kind.

Despite the strength of this work, both personality and relationship features relied on the use of 'single-informant' data (data by the participants themselves), which has obvious bias issues. Some of the larger-scale longitudinal studies we read of temperament involve participants' friends and partners. Importantly, despite being a prospective study, one still cannot draw causal inference. Although we know (from Chapter 10) that there is a certain genetic component to personality, environmental inputs (e.g. upbringing) still contribute a great deal as well; it could be that a series of early life events (say, parental separation or bereavement) had shaped certain aspects of personality as well as the relationship outlook of a person, but this was not captured by the data. Moreover, the degree of similarity between friends' and partners' personality may influence the quality of their relationship. Therefore, using multiple-informant data would indeed be enlightening.

SUMMARY

The phenomenon of peer socialisation marks the child's transition from having the nuclear family as his primary influences to a wider social world where others with characteristics more different from his own become his key influences. Since infancy, the child seems already to have a natural curiosity and basic need to engage his peers, although the skills required to enact more meaningful interactions will take some time to hone. These skills, such as perspective taking, turn taking, sharing and negotiation, will grow with age as the size and structure of the child's peer group and the nature of its interactions become larger or more complex.

As a key theme of peer interactions, play is also argued as natural and central to the child's day-to-day life, and as an activity useful for learning and development. As with other types of social interaction, the complexity of play also increases with age, from solitary and largely physical forms to the more collaborative and symbolic ones that incorporate pretend elements, objects, rules and reciprocation between two or more children. Although it is impossible to establish a causal link, play is nevertheless at least involved in enhancing language and other cognitive skills (such as theory of mind), promoting emotional understanding and leading to further social interactions with others. Even physical (non-symbolic) forms of play, such as rough-and-tumble between boys, can serve to establish and maintain an orderly hierarchy within a safe environment, leading possibly to other friendly interactions.

At the same time, there are individual differences in children's effectiveness for peer interactions. Due partly to their personal characteristics and partly to the peer context in which they find themselves, some children are more accepted by others and some are more likely to be rejected, whereas some are not strongly preferred or disliked by their peer group. These phenomena may result from children's social skills (sociability and aggression, for instance), preference (whether they want to be alone) and expectations (whether they expect to be accepted or rejected by others). Still, children's peer social status is associated with a host of positive and negative consequences, such as school achievement and psychological disturbances. Understanding such relationships helps with interventions aiming to improve interactions and adjustments of at-risk children.

As children engage more and more over time with peers whom they prefer, some forms of friendships evolve. Just as the complexity of peer interaction itself increases with age, so does the complexity of children's friendship. Older children tend to have more intimacy, sensitivity and mutual concern and understanding, and their friendship groups are smaller and more stable, than younger children. Similarities in personality, a common social group and identity (most notably gender) and technology may act to facilitate the formation and progress of friendship, although at times they may hinder these processes through stereotyped expectations and misunderstanding.

Children's experiences with their peer groups and friends have implications for several areas of their development; at least self-concept and identity, collaborative learning and social and cognitive skills, and quite possibly longer-term psychological adjustments (such as general well-being, school success and even psychopathology). These developmental outcomes are probably implicated through the child's continuing relationships that she builds and develops with others, even though the precise cause and effect cannot yet be ascertained.

The onus for researchers is to detect the processes within peer socialisation that lead to developmental, particularly long-term, consequences of both positive and negative kinds, and to identify effective methods that can maximise the potential for positive change and minimise the ill effects of any negative starting points, so that children can mutually benefit from each other in their peer group.

REVIEW QUESTIONS

1. What are the key features of children's interactions with peers at different ages through development and what are the key functions they serve?
2. How do children 'play' at different ages? What may they learn from it?
3. How do children become popular, rejected or neglected by their peers?
4. How can the ways we study children's interactions and relationships affect the outcomes we obtain from such research?
5. How do children make 'friends' at different ages? Do friendships in childhood have any significant impact on other developments or later life experiences?

RECOMMENDED READING

For a very wide variety of 'close-up' observations of children's peer interactions and children's own narratives:

Opie, I. (1993). *The People in the Playground*. Oxford: Oxford University Press.

Danby, S., Thompson, C., Theobald, M., & Thorpe, K. (2012). Children's strategies for making friends when starting school. *Australian Journal of Early Childhood*, 37, 63–71.

For different perspectives on play:

Göncü, A., & Gaskins, S. (2007). *Play and Development: Evolutionary, Sociocultural and Functional Perspectives*. Hove: Psychology Press.

Lewis Graham, K., & Burghardt, G. M. (2010). Current perspectives on the biological study of play: Signs of progress. *Quarterly Review of Biology*, 85, 393–418.

For various perspectives on the importance and functions of children's friendships:

Hartup, W. W. (2006). Relationships in early and middle childhood. In A. L. Vangelisti & D. Perlman (Eds.), *Cambridge Handbook of Personal Relationships* (171–190). New York: Cambridge University Press.

Bagwell, C. L., & Schmidt, M. E. (2011). *Friendships in Childhood and Adolescence*. New York: Guilford Publications.

RECOMMENDED WEBSITES

For a report on peer interactions and classroom learning (The Primary Review) by Christine Howe and Neil Mercer, Cambridge University, produced in 2007:

http://www.primaryreview.org.uk/Downloads/Int_Reps/4.Children_development-learning/Primary_Review_2–1b_briefing_Social_development_learning_071214.pdf

For information on children's play, including theory, research, policy and practice, the Children's Play Information Service (CPIS), part of the National Children's Bureau:

http://www.ncb.org.uk/cpis/home.aspx

For discussions on online gaming and virtual interactions and relationships:

http://www.guardian.co.uk/technology/2010/jan/10/playing-in-the-virtual-world

For a snapshot on the benefits and hazards of friendships (NYU Child Study Center):

http://www.aboutourkids.org/articles/do_kids_need_friends

For a suggestion of the problems that children without friends/experiencing rejection face:

http://www.nncc.org/Guidance/dc26_wo.friends1.html

Chapter 13
Adolescence

Learning outcomes

After reading this chapter, and with further recommended reading, you should be able to:

1. Describe and evaluate the notion of adolescence as a period of 'storm and stress', consider the modern principle of 'adolescence' and locate it within recent global social and economic change.
2. Describe the physiological and psychological changes that occur during puberty and what the implications are for the individual.
3. Understand the role of early childhood, peer and family relationships in forming friendships and romantic attachments during the teenage years.
4. Understand the implications of family structure, race and migration on the development of the teenager's sense of identity.
5. Describe the development of gender identity, sexuality and sex behaviour in the teenage years.

Teenage angst

'It's not fair!' How often do you remember you saying these words to your parents when you were a teenager? How often do you think you really meant those same words? From having a happy-go-lucky child playing with dolls and cars, dancing and playing in the garden, parents sometimes seem baffled by the seemingly overnight transition to moody, sarcastic teenager plagued by spots and a desperate need to express herself as an individual and be accepted by her friends.

- How does such a dramatic change seem to happen overnight?
- How do we as psychologists explain this change in behaviour and, apparently, personality?
- Does this change happen for all young people or for only a few? This chapter will explore the experiences of young people and the physical and psychological processes at work.

Introduction

So what is it like being a teenager? For some, every small detail was vitally important to us in our teenage years – having the right poster in our room, the right music to listen to, the right clothes and make-up was fundamental to our sense of identity and, of course, let's not forget the emotional pain and injustice we felt on discovering a spot or being ignored on the dance floor at the school disco! Is it really so hard being a teenager? Is puberty really such a dramatic force or do the teenage years simply represent a continuation of development, following a series of stages in advancing cognitive, behavioural and social skills?

This chapter describes the period of adolescence from a developmental psychology point of view. During adolescence there are important physical changes that prepare the body for reproduction and build strength in readiness for adulthood. The cognitive changes that begin in childhood continue in the teenage years, allowing the young person greater insight into the complex adult world of decision making and moral thinking. Both the physical and the cognitive changes in adolescence result in important social changes that support the young person's need for autonomy from the family unit and a greater reliance on friends and romantic partners. Adolescence is an important stage of development that spans the process of maturing from a dependent child to an independent adult, and the theories and process described in this chapter will help you to understand how crucial this period of development is.

A brief history of adolescence

Scientist Granville Stanley Hall wrote one of the most important, pivotal texts on 'adolescence' in 1904, two weighty volumes describing the biological, psychological and social aspects of adolescence, focusing on key differences, as he saw it, in the experiences of men and women. In Hall's volume, *Youth: Its Education, Regimen and Hygiene*, he coined the term 'storm and stress' to describe the emotional and physical volatility of adolescence. He saw the teenage years as being not a steady process of development but a more dramatic, unpredictable series of growth 'spurts' that the young person has to contend with. This phrase 'storm and stress' has made its way into common parlance and is often used to describe the experience of teenagers, but is it correct? Do all teenagers experience a turbulent adolescence or do most progress through this stage in much the same way as they did their childhood?

Daniel Offer wrote a pivotal book in 1969 entitled *The Psychological World of the Teenager* in which he disputes Hall's conclusions on adolescence. Offer disagrees with the idea that the teenage years are necessarily a period of mood swings and huge hormonal flux, and argues that these findings have always been reported in studies of teenagers with behavioural and emotional difficulties. He, in turn, conducted a number of studies on children who were not experiencing these problems and found that, although some young people do experience emotional upheaval or show disruptive behaviour, this is certainly not the norm. Further support for Daniel Offer's theory comes from Jeffrey Jenson Arnett who proposed that, although some teenagers experience conflict with their parents, mood disruptions and engage in high levels of risk behaviour, it is not experienced by all, and not by young people from all cultures (Arnett, 1999). Arnett found greater adolescent 'storm and stress' in industrialised cultures, but found those living in traditional cultures were much less likely to find adolescence so disrupting. However, he did find that as young people came into more contact with the cultural experiences of the industrialised nations (through geographical or cultural migration), so they were more likely to experience 'storm and stress'.

The introduction of compulsory education for children was pivotal in developing 'youth culture'. In the late nineteenth century, laws were passed in Europe to restrict child labour and schooling was made compulsory (Kett, 1977). Realistically, however, education could not be introduced when children were still needed as workers to keep business ventures afloat. The biggest change to European society over the last 150 years or so has been the increasing industrialisation of the way we live. As the steam engine and other important feats of engineering began to influence the way products were made, so people changed from working from home to working within specialised manufacturing units, mills and factories. Children and young adults were no longer needed as cheap, readily available labour and the increasingly complex nature of the work began to demand a more highly educated workforce.

In the years following the Second World War, changes in European society and periods of economic prosperity in the 1950s presented more opportunities for young people. Many young people, rather than simply leaving school for work or marriage, began to extend the length of time that they spent in education. The average age for young people to engage in adult 'real life' (such as joining the workplace and getting married) rose to approximately 25 years of age (Hartung and Sweeney, 1991). Daniel Offer wrote from the perspective of a world recovering from two wars – a world in a fragile economic state but also a technologically advancing one. His social world was one with a growing youth culture as more young people stayed on at school to learn the necessary skills for this new, highly industrialised workplace. Compare the world of the 1960s, too, to the world of the new millennium. More and more young people are staying on at college, studying for professional, vocational and academic qualifications. More than ever the workplace is requiring highly skilled employees, and the range and definition of those workplaces is increasing year on year. The world is changing and so the educational and skills needs of young people are increasing, and youth culture is expanding and diversifying at a rate never seen before (Hodkinson and Deicke, 2007, p. 15).

Definition

Storm and stress: described by G. S. Hall as the emotional and physical volatility of adolescence.

PHYSICAL CHANGES DURING ADOLESCENCE

The 1960s and 1970s were a great time for young people developing their sense of identity.
Source: Alamy Images/Pictorial Press Ltd

> **STOP AND THINK**
>
> Who is 'the adolescent'? Essentially, the adolescent is partly a socio-cultural construct and partly a biological one. Adolescence is the transition time between childhood (pre-puberty) and adulthood (complete physical maturation). In Europe, the period of adolescence is tightly connected to the physical changes of puberty: the transition to sexual maturity; and the legal age of cognitive maturity, accepting responsibility for decision making, 18 years.

Physical changes during adolescence

The key physical change during adolescence is the onset of puberty and the subsequent development of sexual maturity. Although puberty is mainly concerned with physical maturation, it also has a psychological effect on both boys and girls. First, the physical changes result in increases in height, weight and overall proportions, and changes in the ratio of fat to muscle occur. The girls' bodies start to increase the amount of fat present whilst the boys' bodies build more muscle weight. For girls, puberty usually occurs between 10 and 15–16 years of age. For boys, puberty usually occurs from 11 years of age to 17–18 years of age. During puberty, the girls experience many changes: the ovaries develop and begin to release eggs or *ova* and menstruation begins; they develop breasts and pubic hair. For the boys, the testes develop and release sperm, they develop facial, body and pubic hair and show penis growth (Tanner, 1990).

Trends in age at menarche (first menstruation)

Interestingly, the age at which young girls reach menarche or experience their first menstruation has changed a lot over the last 150 years (Tanner, 1990; see Table 13.1).

Table 13.1 Trends in age at menarche.

Year	Average age at menarche
1850	17 years
1900	14½–15 years
1950	13½–14 years
1990	12–13 years

> **Definition**
>
> Menarche: a woman's first menstrual period.

NATURE–NURTURE

What is responsible for the fall in age at menarche between 1850 and 1990?

Early-onset puberty is associated with many factors, biological and environmental. Sometimes these factors are clearly biological or environmental, but often the factors are so highly interlinked that it can be difficult to argue which is more dominant. For example, a young woman who has a diet high in fat and who takes little exercise will weigh more and begin puberty earlier than her counterpart who has a healthy diet and lifestyle. One of the reasons for this is that white fat cells release a hormone called leptin. If the girl has very low levels of fat, her leptin production will be poor and she will experience a delay in reaching reproductive maturity (Palmert et al., 1998).

Compare this predominantly biological factor in early onset of puberty with Anthony Bogaert's finding of a much more environmental factor in menarche. Bogaert published a paper in 2008 which examined the effect of family structure on timing of menarche. He reported data collected in a national study of Great Britain which showed that even when body mass index was taken into account, girls who had grown up in families without a father present had a much earlier experience of menarche than girls who grew up in an intact family. Why would this be the case? Is this because growing up in a home with only one parent means that these girls have been being raised in a more stressful home environment?

Belsky et al. (1991) proposed that early-onset puberty was actually an adaptive response to a stressful environment, preparing the young person for separation from the family unit. This train of thought represents a highly evolutionary psychology perspective on puberty, as Belsky suggests that becoming sexually mature allows the woman to begin reproduction quickly, passing on the genes to the next generation, before she dies. Although this theory may seem too biological for the average psychologist, Belsky's findings are supported by Surbey's (1990) study of 1200 women which found menarche five months earlier in girls with absent fathers than in girls from intact families. Other research also appears to confirm the environmental stress theory and has found that presence of a stepfather, family conflict and maternal mood disorders are all related to early menarche (Allison and Hyde, 2013).

This trend for earlier age at menarche has been demonstrated in all industrialised societies over the past 150 years, whilst non-industrialised societies have shown a much more stable pubertal age (Esrael and Yifru, 2013). However, non-industrialised societies that are becoming more prosperous are starting to show this trend for earlier menarche. A number of theories have been put forward to explain this trend. There is evidence that taller, fitter, well-nourished girls begin to menstruate earlier (Graber et al., 1994). In 2010, researchers reporting from the Avon Longitudinal Study of Childhood and Adolescence reported that a diet high in protein-rich animal foods such as meat and dairy is associated with an earlier menarche (Rogers et al., 2010).

Psychological issues and the timing of puberty

Why are we interested in the timing of *puberty* as psychologists? The onset of puberty can often be a difficult time for young people. For some, puberty begins between the ages of 10 and 12 years, and for others onset can be as late as age 14 or 15 years. The physical changes that occur can seem to happen quite quickly and often, too, the young person may feel 'out of sync' if he matures earlier or later than his peers. In particular, early-maturing girls have been found to exhibit significantly more behaviour problems than their peers (Caspi and Moffitt, 1991), but why is this?

For young women, the onset of puberty is usually most distinctly defined by menarche, the first menstruation. Parents and teachers will typically prepare the young girl for the practicalities of menarche and menstruation,

Definition

Puberty: the period of physical maturation from a child into an adult.

and many girls may read about menstruation in young women's magazines or hear about it from older siblings and friends. Very few teenage girls experience their first menstruation as a psychologically traumatic event; however, it may still come as a surprise to many of them (Brooks-Gunn, 1988b). For teenage boys, their first ejaculation (spermarche) may also come as a surprise. Few young boys receive the amount of information young girls receive on their own experience of puberty. They may be aware that ejaculations will occur from the penis, but few are told what to expect on the first occasion by their teachers or parents, from magazines or their friends (Gaddis and Brooks-Gunn, 1985).

Early research investigating the impact of the timing of puberty (relative to peers) revealed differences in the experience of men and women. For example, young men who matured earlier than their peers were often reported as more confident, independent and physically attractive than their later maturing peers. Early-maturing boys were also more likely to do well at school academically and athletically (Brooks-Gunn, 1988a). For young women, however, the reverse seemed to be true. Early-maturing girls reported significantly worse self-esteem and seemed less popular. They appeared depressed and lonely and were unlikely to do well at school during this time. The young women who matured later were seen to be much more popular with their peers and were rated much more physically attractive than their early-maturing peers (Ge et al., 1996). Early female maturers were also found to be more likely to engage in sexually promiscuous behaviour during adolescence, have more difficulties relating socially, report more emotional problems such as depression and anxiety, and experience more intense conflict with parents than did their peers (Susman et al., 1985). However, in recent years, the picture seems to be more complex than originally thought. Early maturation seems to be no longer as positive an experience for young men (Ge et al., 2001a) and in fact both early and late development seem to be problematic for young people (Williams and Dunlop, 1999).

The research now seems to show that early experience of puberty in young men results in the same or similar negative psychological experiences found in early maturing young women, including depression and anxiety, which may be expressed in aggressive, antisocial or other delinquent behaviours (Mendle and Ferrero, 2012).

Neurological changes during puberty

Two main changes occur in the brain before and after puberty. First, the axons (the long, thread-like part of the nerve cell) in the frontal cortex continue to be covered in a layer of myelin, the fatty tissue that speeds up the transmission of electrical impulses (Yakovlev and Lecours, 1967). This myelination results in faster transmission of information in the frontal cortex, the part of the brain that allows you to plan events, imagine the future or use reasoned arguments (see Figure 13.1).

The second change to the brain during puberty is a change in the number of synapses (the small spaces between the neurons) within the prefrontal cortex,

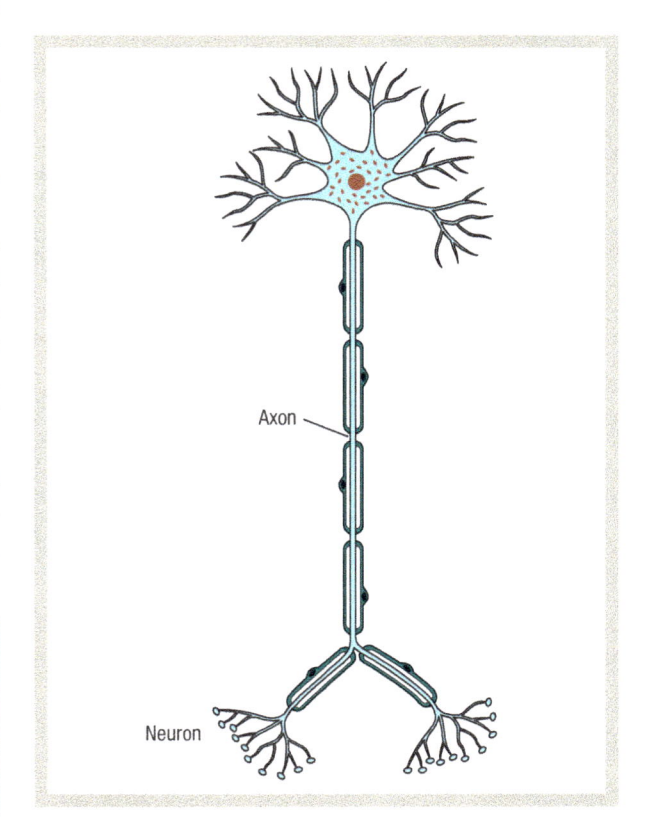

Figure 13.1 The axon.

> ### STOP AND THINK
> Why should experiencing early onset of puberty be so much more problematic in a young woman than in a young man? Consider this question from the perspective of current social roles for men and women.

the very front area of the brain. During infancy and childhood, the number of synapses in the prefrontal cortex increases rapidly (Huttenlocher, 1994). However, during puberty, there seems to be rapid reduction of these synapses, such that by adulthood, the brain has 41% fewer synapses than the new-born child (Abitz et al., 2007). It is thought that the rapid growth in synapses results in a surplus of connections within the brain. Synaptic pruning occurs in the first year of life and then again at puberty, and it is believed that this results in greater efficiency in the transmission of information in the brain (Blakemore and Choudhury, 2006).

The brain is composed of white matter and grey matter. White matter is mainly involved in transmitting information from the body to the cerebral cortex and is packed full of myelin-covered axons. Actions controlled by white matter include the regulation of body temperature, heart rate and blood pressure, but also the expression of emotions, the release of hormones and the regulation of food and water intake. Grey matter is mainly involved in muscle control, sensory perception, memory, emotions and speech. Using magnetic resonance imaging (MRI) techniques, researchers have noted that prior to adolescence, there is a significant increase in the amount of both white and grey matter, but that, following puberty, the amount of grey matter starts to decrease and is replaced by white matter (Sowell et al., 1999).

A longitudinal study conducted by Gogtay et al. (2004) demonstrates the decrease in grey matter from childhood to adulthood. Gogtay et al. conducted MRI scans of children every two years from the age of 5 until the child reached 20 years of age. Figure 13.2 shows the averaged changes the researchers found. Note that not all areas of the brain change at the same time, but that areas that deal with motor skills mature earlier than areas involved in more complex functions such as attention and memory (Siegler et al., 2010).

Definition

Synaptic pruning: the elimination of excess synapses.

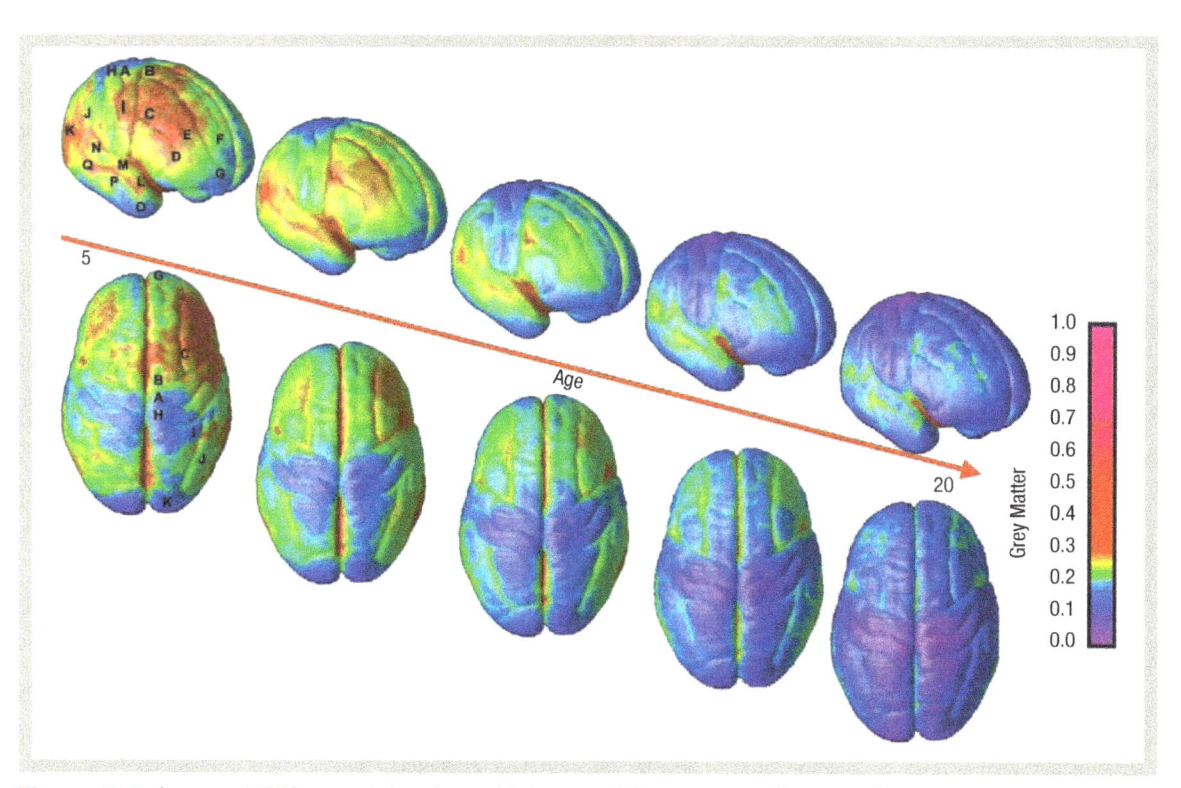

Figure 13.2 Averaged MRI scans taken from children aged 5 years up to 20 years of age, showing the decrease in grey matter over time.

Source: Gogtay et al. (2004)

How, then, do these changes in the brain affect the behaviour of the teenager? The changes to the frontal lobe might result in improvements in executive functions such as selective attention, decision making and response inhibition (Blakemore and Choudhury, 2006). This means that, by adulthood, our teenager will have developed the capacities for focusing on a task for longer, for making choices and for restraining themselves from doing something that they know is wrong or harmful. Another skill the teenager might develop is prospective memory – the ability to remember to do something in the future, such as phone their parents when they arrive at a friend's house after a long journey (Ellis, 1996; Ellis and Kvavilashvili, 2000). Interestingly, there is a 'dip' in performance on face recognition and emotion recognition tasks during early puberty, a function of the frontal cortex (Carey et al., 1980). Although ability to identify emotions in photographs of faces returns in late adolescence, there is a significant reduction in young teens' ability to read emotions and possibly, therefore, to read the situation they find themselves in (McGivern et al., 2002). Other tasks related to social cognition, such as theory of mind and the related ability to take another's perspective (see Chapter 8, 'Theory of mind'), appear to be affected during the teenage years, and although little research has been conducted yet to investigate this phenomenon, these are activities related to the frontal cortex (Blakemore and Choudhury, 2006). Some recent developments in adolescent brain research and their implications for education are discussed in Chapter 14, 'Developmental psychology and education'.

Cognitive development and changes in the teenage years

Cognitive development happens during the teenage years in much the same way as it has done through the childhood years. The main theorists defining cognitive development are Piaget, Erikson, Elkind and Kohlberg. We will take each theorist in turn and consider the implications of their theories for our understanding of the development in teen reasoning and decision making.

Jean Piaget (1896–1980): theory of cognitive development

Piaget's stage theory of cognitive development (Piaget, 1952b) has so far considered the *sensorimotor* stage of development (from birth to 2 years of age), the *pre-operational* stage of development (from age 2 years to age 7 years) and the *concrete operations* stage of development (from age 7 years to age 11 years). To summarise briefly the child's cognitive development prior to the teenage years (see Chapter 2, 'Theoretical perspectives', for more detail), in the *sensorimotor* stage we can see a child explore and seek to understand their environment through play and experimentation. The child learns that objects do not actually disappear when hidden (object permanence) and she will even seek to uncover a hidden object in order to resume playing with it.

During the *pre-operational* stage the child learns more about the environment and works out the relationship between cause and effect. In the early part of this stage, the child will learn that a toy out of reach might be brought to her by pulling on the attached string. Later on, the child develops more complex skills, such as learning the relationship between behaviour and emotion. The child learns that behaviour can have an effect on emotions not just for themselves but also for others. However, although the child can understand the effect her behaviour has had on another person, it is not until the child enters the stage of *concrete operations* that she can make hypothetical connections. Before the concrete operations stage, the child will not necessarily be able to anticipate possible outcomes of her behaviour, but Piaget believed that by the age of 11 years, most children are able to classify objects (e.g. into 'plant', 'animal', 'food', etc.) and to begin to consider simple logic problems. During this stage, the child also develops the ability to 'rotate' objects and problems mentally.

To complete the task, you need to be able to rotate the template mentally and hypothetically match it to one of the boxes. Prior to the concrete operations stage, a child will not be able to complete this task. However, once the child is aged approximately 10 or 11 years, she has developed enough cognitive skill to accomplish this task with ease. So by the time our young person enters into adolescence, she has already developed some quite complex cognitive abilities and is ready to build on them some more. Piaget theorised that around the age of 11 years, children entered the *formal operations* stage of

STOP AND THINK

Consider the puzzle below. Which of the boxes presented to the right of the dotted line are made from the template on the left?

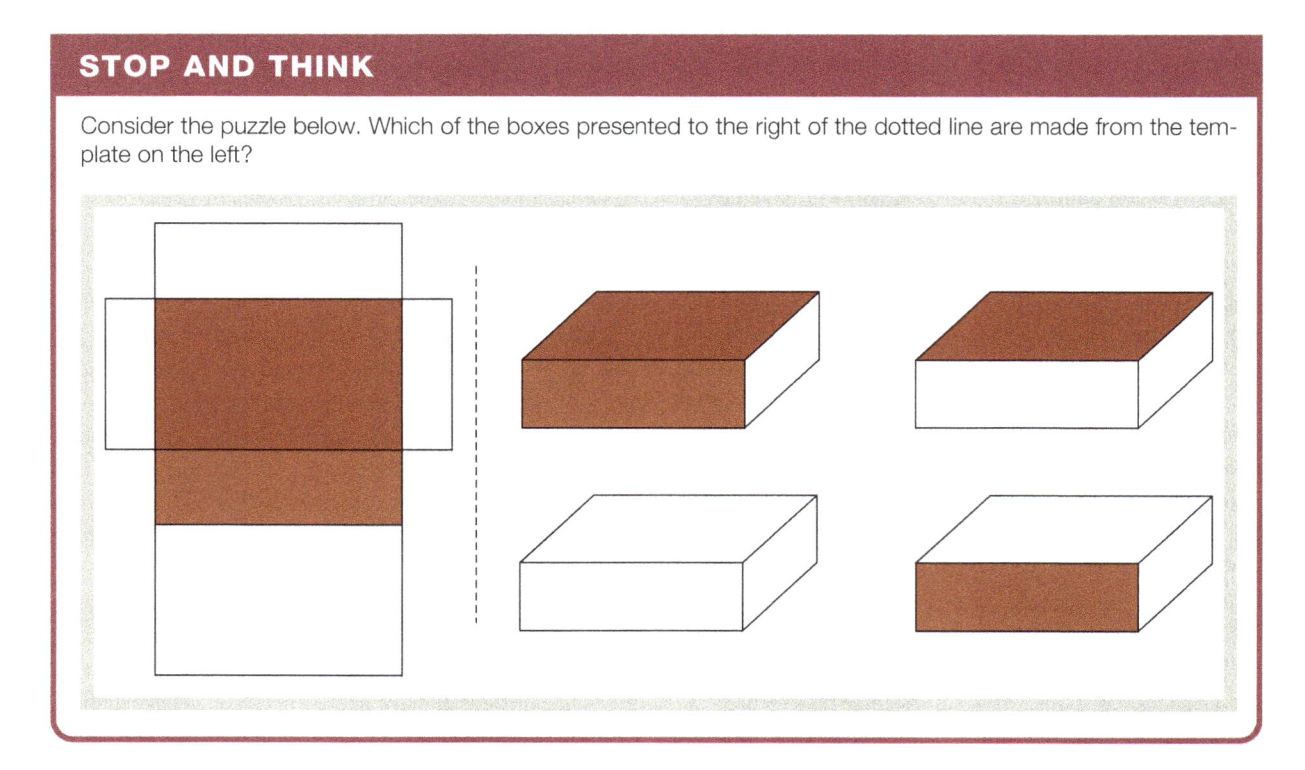

development and began to show much more adult-like thinking behaviour. During this stage, the child's abilities in abstract problem solving expand to include, for example, the use of letters instead of numbers in mathematical problems, and by the time they reach the age of 15 years, most children are able to solve simple algebraic equations.

During adolescence our young person becomes more idealistic and can make judgements on outcomes to hypothetical questions. Later on, the teenager also begins to be more methodical in their thinking and builds on their simple logic capabilities to deduce solutions. For example, they may find solving simple Su-Do-Ku matrices quite easy (see Figure 13.3).

During the formal operations stage, the young person develops hypothetico-deductive reasoning and propositional thought. Hypothetico-deductive reasoning is the ability to solve problems in a specific way. Our young person may look at a situation and develop a general theory or hypothesis about why it has occurred. He might then weigh up all the possible reasons for why this situation has occurred and use this information to deduce how the outcome might be affected. The young person then will apply these hypotheses and see what the outcome actually is in

Definition

Hypothesis: a proposed explanation for why or how two events might be related to each other.

Figure 13.3 Can you solve this Su-Do-Ku puzzle? Every row and every column must include the numbers 1–9 as must each smaller 3 × 3 block.

the real world. By this process, the young person is developing the ability to look at events and consider a number of possible reasons for it occurring. For instance, a young person engaged in the formal operations stage might view a news report of a break-out of war in a region. He might form hypotheses explaining why war has occurred and have views on possible outcomes. By keeping up-to-date with news reports, the young person will see how the outcome of war is affected by certain actions and develop a personal view on the causes of war. During this stage, the young person is using unique cognitive skills. He is starting to problem solve by using possibilities to test realities. Children who have not engaged in the formal operations stage of cognitive processing are unable to do this.

The second characteristic of the formal operations stage of cognitive development is propositional thought. The young person develops an ability to evaluate logic without needing real-life examples to back it up. For instance, in algebra class, the young person might develop the skills needed in mathematics to use symbols in place of numbers (see Chapter 7, 'The development of mathematical thinking') and answer hypothetical mathematical statements. He might also develop the ability to deduce truth from logical statements. For example, if Steve is taller than Carole and Kim is taller than Steve, who is the shortest person in the group? Children engaged in the concrete operations stage will not be able to do this task, but adolescents who have entered the formal operations stage of cognitive development will find this task relatively easy. Developing the ability for propositional thought is important for young people to be able to consider non-concrete concepts.

Evaluation

Although Piaget considered progression to the formal operations stage of cognitive development to be achieved by all, this just is not the case. Think about yourself: how able are you at logic puzzles or philosophical discussions? Are you better or worse at these tasks than your friends? A study by Keating (1980) indicated that only 40–60% of college students consistently use formal logic – which means that 40–60% of college students regularly fail Piaget's operational problems!

Erik H. Erikson (1902–94): theory of psychosocial development

A key developmental change that occurs during adolescence takes the form of a period of identity searching. Erikson's theory of psychosocial development (Erikson, 1963) describes life as a series of stages characterised by a crisis that the individual must resolve (see Chapter 2, 'Theoretical perspectives') (Erikson, 1968). During adolescence the young person engages in the identity versus role-confusion stage of development. Up until now, most of our psychological development has been influenced by the environment we were raised in and the parenting and schooling we have received. In the identity versus role-confusion stage, however, these aspects of cognitive development and change are up to our teenager. Forming an identity is vital if the young person is to know who she is, what she values and what she wants out of life.

To successfully develop a strong sense of identity, Erikson suggests that we need to look inwards at ourselves and work out who we are. We need to form personal values and a sense of life direction in order to choose our careers and our moral and religious beliefs. We need to think about what our friendships mean to us and what we want in the future from our relationships. If we are successful in this stage then we emerge into adulthood with *fidelity*: we have a strong sense of self and are able to stay true to ourselves. Without this we find ourselves unsure of what we want from life and may, for instance, have difficulty forging a career pathway.

Definitions

Propositional thought: the ability to consider a hypothetical concept without having to see the events actually happening in order to come to a conclusion.

Identity versus role-confusion stage of development: Erikson's description of the pursuit of a coherent sense of self during the teenage years. Role confusion can occur when the teenager is unable to put together aspects of him or herself (see Chapter 2).

Teenagers often look to each other for approval of their clothing or music choice, or their point of view.
Source: Pearson Education Ltd/Studio 8

Evaluation

Erikson believed that most of us have a good idea of who we are and what we want to be by around the age of 20. However, since Erikson published his work, society has changed and our entry into adulthood is now delayed until our mid-20s. The result of this is that we now have more time to work these things out. We stay in school for longer, spend more time getting settled in careers, and marry and have our children later than our parents and grandparents did (Heckhausen et al., 2010). Although a lot of identity searching is carried out through adolescence, many of us keep returning to thoughts about who we are and what we believe in throughout our adult lives. Even with a well-developed self, events out of our control, such as illness, redundancy or becoming a carer for a parent, can change our life plans and even challenge our beliefs about who we are.

David Elkind (1931–): theory of adolescent egocentrism

During the period of identifying the self, our young person may come across a number of cognitive hurdles. David Elkind published a paper in 1967 called 'Egocentrism in adolescence', in which he described the unique thinking of the teenager. Elkind believed that during the teen years the young person becomes focused predominantly on what others might think of him and develops a crushing preoccupation with himself – a situation he called adolescent egocentrism. There is no evidence to suggest that the young man *is* the centre of attention, but some adolescents certainly feel that they are. This overwhelming feeling encourages the adolescent to go to extreme lengths not to be embarrassed. This usually involves dressing the same as your peers, wearing your hair the same way and behaving in the same way.

One consequence of adolescent egocentrism is that in social situations the young person is constantly aware of the reactions of the people around him. The teenager makes the mistake of thinking that everyone is as interested as him in the way he looks and the way he acts – in fact, he creates an *imaginary audience*. The young person begins to focus more on this audience's opinion of him and it suddenly becomes very important to look a certain way, to wear certain clothes, to style your hair in a particular fashion – even if you are just popping to the shops for a pint of milk! During early adolescence

Definition

Adolescent egocentrism: the young person's preoccupation with himself, likened to being on a permanent social stage where he or she is the focus of attention.

there is usually a measurable drop in self-esteem as the young person's egocentrism makes him 'hyper-aware' of others' opinions. This fall in self-esteem does not last long, however, and many young people soon find that their self-esteem returns to levels seen in childhood and becomes generally stable throughout adulthood (Simmons and Blyth, 1987).

The belief that others are as interested in you as you are yourself can be likened to being on an imaginary stage where the audience is as critical or as approving as you are of yourself. The teenager believes that he or she will be and is the focus of attention in a social situation and for this reason the adolescent often develops a sense of self-consciousness. As the audience is self-created, a key member of that audience is actually the teenager himself. As he will know what details are critical in his appearance and behaviour, so he has a particularly tough audience to please.

Some teenagers crave privacy during these sometimes difficult years and parents can find it difficult to communicate with them at this time. Erikson argues that the sheer energy required to maintain this critical audience is exhausting to the young person and that the need for privacy might be a reaction to being under this constant scrutiny. By removing himself from a social environment, the teenager is giving himself time to relax from this intrusive period of self-inspection. Conversely, many teenagers strive for company during these years and form many close friendships and attempt romantic relationships. Just as they have the need for privacy and space when they are being critical of themselves, so they have the need for company when they are feeling good about themselves. Teenagers can spend a lot of time in front of the mirror perfecting their hair, skin and make-up, admiring their clothes and their fashion awareness, all in preparation for meeting and impressing their friends, girlfriends and boyfriends.

What is interesting, however, is that most groups of teenagers are quite different from groups of children and adults, in that each member of the group is often more concerned with being observed, being impressive and being accepted by the group than they are with observing the group, forming impressions and accepting others into the group! Thus, the groups of teenagers tend to be formed of individuals so conscious of looking right, wearing the right clothes and acting the right way that they barely form a group at all. As Elkind remarks in his essay on adolescent egocentrism, the young people in the group are both actor and audience (Elkind, 1967). Whilst the teenager fails to differentiate his own feelings over those of other people, he also starts to believe that his own particular beliefs and feelings are much more significant than any experienced by anyone before. This *personal fable* can be quite persuasive; the teenager believes that his life is unique or heroic or even has mythical qualities and, therefore, the experiences he has have never been experienced by anyone before. Only he can truly understand the meaning of song lyrics or poetry, or truly understand the real meaning of life. For some the *invincibility fable* dominates their thinking and they develop a strong sense that the bad things in the world will never happen to them. They do not truly believe they are immortal or immune, but there is a definite sense that they are protected from anything that could go wrong.

Evaluation

Aspects of these concepts can be useful in helping us understand some teen behaviour – the need for privacy and space, the pain of new love and the joys of friendships, the seemingly unfathomable risks taken. This stage in cognitive development does not last for long, as by the age of 15 or 16 years the teenager becomes more adept at distinguishing his own thoughts and needs from those of others and the imaginary audience starts to retreat. No longer does the teenager fear social groupings to the extent of the earlier years of adolescence, and slowly their self-esteem starts to return to pre-adolescence levels. As the teenager becomes more proficient in forming close personal relationships, so the personal fable weakens its grasp and the young person starts to see himself in a more realistic light. By comparing the opinion and reaction of a close friend, girlfriend or boyfriend to the teen's own opinions and interests, the teenager replaces the imaginary audience with a real one and establishes a true sense of self.

Lawrence Kohlberg (1927–87): theory of moral development

You may be able to see a pattern emerging in Erikson's and Piaget's theory of cognitive development and Elkind's discussion of adolescent egocentrism. Not only is the teenager becoming skilful in solving mathematical problems, but the young person is also developing an ability to solve ethical dilemmas and a sense of morality. Psychologist Lawrence Kohlberg also saw the connection, and from Piaget's theory of cognitive development comes Kohlberg's six-stage theory of moral development (Kohlberg, 1969). The implications of Kohlberg's ideas about moral development for managing children's behaviour in schools are explored in Chapter 14, 'Developmental psychology and education'. With his theory, Kohlberg wanted to illustrate the parallels between cognitive development generally and how we develop complexity in our consideration more specifically of moral and ethical issues. Kohlberg based his theory on his findings from research and interviews with groups of young children, teenagers and adults. In order to test the development of morality and the ability to solve ethical dilemmas, a number of studies were conducted. In each of these studies, participants were presented with a hypothetical situation and were then asked to make a decision. Kohlberg was not interested so much in the answer to the posed question, as in how the participant came to the answer. In analysing the reasoning for the answer, Kohlberg was able to categorise the answers into one of six stages. We will describe two example studies here. First, we will describe the 'Heinz dilemma' and then we will describe the 'Milgram study'. Consider each situation in turn. What would your answer be and, more importantly, how did you come to this decision?

'The Heinz dilemma'

A woman is near death from a particular form of cancer. There is one drug that the doctors think might save her. It is a form of radium that a pharmacist in the same town has recently discovered. The drug is expensive to make and the pharmacist is charging ten times what it cost to make the drug. The pharmacist paid £200 for the radium and is charging £2000 for a small dose of the drug. The sick woman's husband, Heinz, tried to borrow the money from everyone he knew but was only able to raise £1000, half of what he needed. He told the pharmacist that his wife was dying and asked him to sell the drug to him more cheaply or even to let him pay the remainder at a later date. The pharmacist, however, refused. Heinz was desperate for the drug and broke into the pharmacy to steal the drug for his wife. Should he have done that?

(adapted from Kohlberg, 1969)

Should Heinz have stolen the drug for his dying wife or not? What are the reasons behind your decision?

Kohlberg noted from his research that most people gave reasons for their decisions that could be easily fitted into one of six categories (Kohlberg, 1973). The categories reflect varying degrees of complexity in thought and social awareness. Kohlberg suggested these categories could be represented as a series of stages that individuals generally pass through as they mature. The stages are grouped together under three level headings reflecting Piaget's stages of cognitive development.

Level 1 Pre-conventional morality

- *Stage 1 Obedience and punishment*: this is the earliest stage of moral development. Rules are fixed and absolute and a decision is made to obey the rules only as a way of avoiding punishment. Young children tend to develop this way of thinking first, but adults are also capable of expressing this type of reasoning. In the Heinz experiment, if the participant says simply, *'No, Heinz should not have stolen the drug. It is wrong, stealing is a crime'*, then you may consider that this person's reasoning for their answer reflects stage 1 of moral reasoning.
- *Stage 2 Individualism and exchange*: this stage is only possible when a child or adult is able to consider hypothetically another person's point of view. If the participant says, *'Yes, Heinz should have stolen the drug, his wife needed it so what else could he do?'*, then this person is arguing that Heinz should do whatever best serves his needs. Moral reasoning in this stage purely supports the need of the individual.

Level 2 Conventional morality

- *Stage 3 Interpersonal relationships*: up to this point, the reasoning given in stages 1 and 2 has not considered any social role or responsibility of the players in our dilemma and one could argue that the person is reporting a very simplistic understanding of moral and ethical issues. In stage 3, the rationale for deciding whether or not Heinz should have stolen the drug becomes more complex and indicates that the person has developed a sense of socially defined expectation. People whose moral reasoning reflects the importance of conformity, being 'nice', and the importance of this in maintaining relationships are considered to be using stage 3 decision-making skills. In the Heinz experiment, if the participant reasons: *'Well of course it was theoretically wrong to steal the drug, but what* kind of husband would he be if he didn't steal the drug? His wife needed it and of course he would put her health over the monetary needs of the pharmacist', then the participant is using the role of husband and the social expectations of being a 'good husband' to support Heinz's behaviour.

- *Stage 4 – Maintaining social order*: at this stage of moral development, people begin to consider society as a whole when making judgements. The focus of their decision making is maintaining law and order by following the rules, doing one's duty and respecting authority. This is more complex than the simple obedience versus punishment morality explicit in stage 1 of Kohlberg's theory. Stage 1 thinking reflects the personal issue of right and wrong, whereas a person at stage 4 considers morality within a more global context. *'Heinz was wrong to steal the drug. I know his wife needed it and I know that I would have wanted to do the same thing, but we have laws for a reason, you know. We can't all go about stealing what we want. Where would society be if we all did that?'*

Level 3 Post-conventional morality

- *Stage 5 Social contract and individual rights*: the final two stages of morality Kohlberg rationalises as requiring 'high-level' cognitive abilities. Moral reasoning at these levels may begin to be seen during mid- to late adolescence and will continue to develop into adulthood. Decision making at this stage starts to take into account the differing values, opinions and beliefs of other people. During this stage, it is acknowledged that rules and laws are important for maintaining a society, but the members of that society should be able to define, agree and amend those rules. A person showing stage 5 moral reasoning might state: *'Heinz shouldn't have stolen the drugs because we have laws against that kind of thing, but hey, this is a pretty unique situation here. The pharmacist was charging too much for the drug and Heinz offered him a reasonable deal – pay half now and the remainder later. Perhaps the laws need to be changed so that a person can have access to this drug at a fair price – probably a law is needed to limit how much the pharmacist could charge for it.'*
- *Stage 6 – Universal principles*: the sixth stage of moral reasoning transcends the prescribed system of law and instead shows that a person is ready to make a moral judgement based on what he or she thinks are universal truths. *'This situation is completely unnecessary. People have the right to expect fair and reasonable treatment. If this pharmacist had discovered a cure for this woman's cancer, how could he live with himself putting his own greed first and denying someone treatment? The pharmacist's behaviour is inherently wrong – regardless of whether in a court of law he would be proved the victim here, he should not withhold such valuable treatment.'* This person's reasoning follows internalised notions of justice, of right and wrong, and the thought processes shown here reflect a greater sense of morality over the conventional sense of wisdom and law.

STOP AND THINK

Think of a moral dilemma that is currently being explored in your daily news bulletin.

- What arguments are being put forward by opposing sides of the debate?
- What phrases are people using to support their arguments?
- Are they concordant with stage 3 or stage 4 thinking, or does the debate reflect stage 5 or stage 6 thinking?

Evaluation

There are a number of criticisms we might level at Kohlberg's theory of moral development. Kohlberg's theory may describe moral development from the point of view of understanding the nature of justice, but what about other factors in that debate? Can we truly make a moral decision based on personal and societal notions of justice without caring about the issues or being compassionate? Perhaps more importantly, does a sense of moral reasoning actually translate into behaviour? Might we be able to discuss hypothetical situations from any one of the six stages Kohlberg describes, yet in reality perform only within the confines of, say, stage 3 or stage 4? Think of the Heinz dilemma: would you break into the pharmacy to steal the drug? Would you be hampered by your sense of social duty even though you could theoretically rationalise this act? Could you physically carry out the theft even though morally you had concerns about it? We may all be capable of deciding what we want or ought to do, but actually doing it is a very different matter.

The Milgram study (1974)

Let's see what happens when people are given the opportunity to carry through with an action rather than simply consider a situation from a hypothetical point of view. The following study was devised by a researcher, Professor Stanley Milgram, to assess how people responded to authority and to find out what their decision-making process was when in a situation that presented a real ethical dilemma. Participants were invited to a research institute to take part in a study that proposed to investigate the role of punishment in learning behaviour. Two participants were taken to a room where they had to select a folded piece of paper from a hat that had either the word 'teacher' or 'learner' written on it. The participant who had picked the piece of paper with 'learner' written on it was then strapped to a chair behind a screen by the researcher and attached to a device that would deliver electric shocks as the punishment for incorrect answers. The participant who had picked the piece of paper with 'teacher' written on it was asked to assist the researcher in strapping down the 'learner' and then taken to the other side of the screen. The 'teacher' was then introduced to the task. He or she had to read aloud pairs of words to the 'learner' then test the 'learner's' recall of those words. The 'teacher' was told that for every wrong answer, he or she should administer an electric shock to the 'learner' via the console on the table in front of the screen. As an example of the kind of shock the 'learner' would receive, the researcher attached the 'teacher' temporarily to the console and administered a low-level shock. During the task, each time the 'learner' answered correctly the 'teacher' confirmed the answer. When the 'learner' answered incorrectly the 'teacher' delivered an ever-increasing electric shock. As these shocks increased in intensity, the 'teacher' could hear the 'learner' respond in increasing levels of distress at the pain being caused. If the 'teacher' wavered and sought the researcher's advice on whether to continue the study, the researcher simply replied: '*you must continue*'. So what did the participants do?

The majority of the participants continued administering shocks to the 'learner'. Every time the 'learner' made an incorrect answer, each 'teacher' gave the 'learner' a shock more intense that the one before – right up to the maximum level of electric shock. Now, remember, this study was not actually about the role of punishment in learning behaviour but was designed to understand how people respond to authority. Thus, Milgram was not interested so much in *what* each participant did but *why* they did it. The 'teacher' was the only true participant in this study. The 'learner' was actually another researcher who was playing a part. He was not

---

LIFESPAN

Kohlberg's theory of moral development

As with other stage theories, do we all enter each stage and progress through learning about moral reasoning and developing our sense of ethical practice? Do we all progress to stage 6 during adolescence and begin making decisions based on our own innate sense of righteousness and justice (Kohlberg, 1981)? In practice, many adults commonly rationalise their decisions with statements that support stages 3 and 4 reasoning. Think about moral development as more of a lifespan approach to decision making. As a teenager, could you compare effectively the arguments used in tabloid newspapers with those of late-night current affairs programming and the broadsheet papers? Or do you need more life experience in order to appreciate the purpose of this debate and to understand the political and philosophical position of the writers and presenters of the newspapers and debate programmes? As an adult you are more able to judge the motive behind the headline debate – is the debate to decide on the election of a politician or is it to fight for a change to a rule or law?

actually attached to any equipment and therefore did not receive any of the electric shocks. Immediately after the 'teacher' had completed administering the shocks to the 'learner', Milgram took them aside and asked them what their reasons were for continuing with the study.

> **STOP AND THINK**
>
> So why did they do it? Look at the quotes presented below. Each of these reflects a person at each stage of moral development. See if you can allocate each rationale for why each 'teacher' continued with the experiment even when the 'learner' begged them to stop. (Correct answer is presented at the end of the chapter.)

Kohlberg argues that people tend to sit comfortably within one of the stages in their moral reasoning but will also draw on the arguments from the stages either side to support some of their decisions. Take the situation of the 'teacher' who generally uses stage 4 thinking. She may report that she continued with the study because she was '*told to*' and that the university had obviously sanctioned this experiment. However, if the responses from the 'learner' had prevented her from continuing with the study, she might have reported stage 5 reasoning: 'I thought this would be alright but it isn't. I can't continue.'

Evaluation

One of the criticisms of Kohlberg's theory is that it does not take into account the role of other people in the decision-making process. Kohlberg does not consider the effect that the behaviour of other people around you can have on your own moral reasoning. Milgram's initial study tested the moral decision making of people who were isolated by their role as 'teacher' and who were given full autonomy to punish the 'learner' for mistakes made. However, how realistic is this? To test this theory in a more 'natural' decision-making environment, Milgram set up a further study where the 'teacher' was joined by two other participants. These participants observed and commented on the 'teacher's' administration of punishment during the learning task but were not actually involved in giving the punishment itself. When the 'teacher' gave a 150 volt electric shock as punishment to the 'learner', the first observer expressed discomfort with the study and left the experiment. When the 'teacher' gave a 210 volt electric shock as punishment to the 'learner', the second observer followed the first in expressing his concern with the study and walked away. The observers were actually other researchers in the university and Milgram had deliberately introduced this twist to the study to see if the behaviour of the 'teacher' would be affected by the moral stance of the other participants. What Milgram found was that in 36 of the 40 cases, the behaviour of the observers affected the moral reasoning of the 'teacher' and the experiment was brought to a halt. Compare this to the studies where the 'teacher' acted alone – only 14 of the 40 cases brought the experiment to a halt.

Milgram concluded that moral reasoning and behaviour can be influenced by the behaviour of people around you. If members of your social group disapprove of

Quote	Which stage of reasoning?
'I was paid to do this. I felt bad about it but I had a job to do. I did what I was asked to do, I lived up to the deal.'	....
'You told me what to do and I did it. I figured you know what you're doing. It took a lot of self-control to do this. This is sanctioned by the School right? This is legal?'	....
'I did what I was told to do, you said to continue. I shocked the guy because he wasn't learning. I did it because I had to do it.'	....
'I'm not going to do it, I'm sorry. You've probably got reasons but ... I don't see any reason to shock someone because of an experiment. You have no right to do that, I won't be part of it.'	....
'It really bothered me, the other guy was getting hurt but I figured you knew what you were doing. You're a psychologist, you wouldn't hurt anyone. If I'd stopped I'd have ruined your experiment.'	....
'This is crazy, I thought this experiment was going to be good for society but this is crazy, I'll not continue.'	....

Source: taken from Rosenhan et al., 1976

your reasoning or actions, then you are more likely to change them to conform to the group's expectations. This study had enormous impact when it was published and in looking at his clearly presented research findings we can understand why researchers have since focused a lot of their energy on the effects of groups and peers on behaviour. The period of adolescence is a time of immense cognitive development. The young person is engaged in developing formal operational thought processes (Piaget, 1952). They are developing the ability to use hypothetical concepts to understand and predict the world, and the ability to use and understand logic and abstract thinking processes. They are experiencing more complex ways of thinking about moral issues and developing their skills in more intricate decision making.

These developments all help to create a sense of identity (Erikson, 1968). Teenagers have to decide who they are, what they value and what their life-goals are. This process continues into adulthood, but it is during adolescence that teenagers experience their main identity crisis. These cognitive changes and the conflict and struggle for autonomy are key features of adolescents' personal development and are influenced by the social relationships they have with their parents and peers. The next part of this chapter will help you understand the role other people have in the psychological development of the adolescent.

Social development in the teenage years

This part of the chapter discusses life in modern family units: the role of the family in adolescent development, families where racial heritage is mixed and families where the children may be adopted or not biologically related to parents. Many people – family, friends, teachers, pastors – and experiences are involved in the formation of our sense of self (Adamson et al., 1999).

A great deal of research has been carried out on the role of families in adolescent and young adult development. Research tells us that our ability to find intimacy in our adult relationships is dependent on our experiences of intimacy in our childhood and adolescent relationships (Collins et al., 1997). How this works is that the lessons learned in forming good relationships with our families and friends in childhood become the scaffold on which later competence in teen and adult relationships develops (Masten and Cicchetti, 2010). Parents who are overly punitive or harsh teach children that connecting to others can be risky, and so harsh parenting can be associated with difficulties in establishing healthy, stable romantic relationships as a young adult (Conger et al., 2000; Franz et al., 1991). In contrast, parents who are warm and proactive in their parenting teach children that relationships can be rewarding and fulfilling and prepare them well for adult relationships (Longmore et al., 2001).

Young people from different countries can describe what makes a good or bad parental relationship quite differently. For instance, teenagers in Canada consider their parents more tolerant than do teenagers in France or Italy. Italian adolescents consider their relationship with their parents to be strong whereas the French adolescents rated their relationship with their parents to be weak with little parental supervision (Claes et al., 2003). Whatever the perception of parenting style, what is really important is a good relationship between parents and teenagers with plenty of father involvement (Flouri and Buchanan, 2002).

Family structure can also influence how much emotional support a teenager receives. When a teenager grows up in a family with both parents present, there is less aggression between family members than when the father is absent or a non-biologically related male partner is present (Honess et al., 1997). Part of the reason for this finding seems to be due to the differences in quality of communication between teenagers and their parents in separated, divorced and intact families. A study by Lanz et al. (1999) showed that teenagers in non-intact families find it much harder to talk to their parents about their fears and worries when compared to intact biological and adoptive families. These teenagers were also much more likely to be involved in arguing and fighting with their friends and other teens at school (Palmer and Hollin, 2001).

Adoptive families

All children, teenagers and adults who have been adopted will spend some time thinking about their birth parents – what kind of people were they? Why did they give me up for adoption? Would I have been happy being raised by my birth parents? To find out whether the parenting

CASE STUDY

The impact of immigration on identity

For a teenage boy called Patrick, the quest for identity also includes an exploration of his racial and ethnic roots. Patrick's parents are happily married. His mother is from the Republic of Ireland and his father is from Sweden. Patrick was born in Sweden and the family moved to Dublin when Patrick was 7 years of age. Before the family moved to Dublin, Patrick's parents prepared him for the move by speaking in English and some Gaelic, showing him pictures of the city he was moving to and talking excitedly about the move. Now, at the age of 17, Patrick is beginning to take an interest in his family background and wants to know more about his Swedish heritage. Patrick's father talks about life in Sweden as a young boy and every three years or so Patrick, his mother and father have made the journey to Stockholm to visit their Swedish relatives, but Patrick has settled well into his new country and now considers himself Irish with a Swedish father.

- What role has having an Irish mother and a Swedish father had in shaping Patrick's identity?
- How might Patrick develop his sense of Swedish identity if he chooses to do so?
- Will he be able to maintain links with Sweden as he continues to live in Ireland?

experience of adolescents in adoptive families was different from that of non-adoptive adolescents, a study was conducted to look at parent–child relationships in different family structures – intact families, separated/divorced families and adoptive families. The research found that those adolescents who came from separated families had more difficulties in their relationships with their parents than the children from other family structures, but that those adolescents in adoptive families reported better communication with their adoptive parents than did the adolescents in the other families (Lanz et al., 1999).

Identity and immigration

National identity (whether you are British, French, Spanish or German, for instance) is an important aspect of identity. Maintaining your sense of national identity when travelling and once settled in your host nation is a difficult task but an important one, and research indicates that this is vital to securing a positive outcome in the 'new' country. Research into the experiences of Russian adolescents migrating to Finland in the late 1980s to early 1990s reveals that those teens with good self-esteem found their psychological adjustment to life in Finland much easier and they also reported less racial discrimination. Parents were valuable during this transition process by maintaining Russian traditions when in Finland and by helping to boost the teenagers' self-esteem and to protect them from discrimination (Jasinskaja-Lahti and Liebkind, 2001).

Those teenagers who make a good transition to their new country are less likely to experience discrimination and will make greater headway in learning the second language of that country. Research has found that parents who are supportive of their teenagers' needs and make efforts to continue with family traditions help their teenagers enormously in adapting to the new environment (Liebkind and Jasinskaja-Lahti, 2000; Jasinskaja-Lahti and Liebkind, 2001). In our case study example, by regaling the family with tales of his childhood, Patrick's father is keeping the memory of Patrick's birth nation alive. The family's regular visits to Stockholm reinforce their dual identity and will make any decision Patrick makes in the future, perhaps about returning to Sweden, easier and more informed.

Teenagers can go through a period of identifying more closely with one race over the other in the early stages of identity development, but usually, by the time they reach adulthood, many teenagers have developed a positive inclusive racial identity attitude and good self-esteem. In particular, adolescents who live with both parents are more likely to assimilate both identities into a coherent sense of self and are more likely to express racial pride and positive self-identity (Fatimilehin, 1999).

> **STOP AND THINK**
>
> Migration of families within Europe can be triggered by the search for employment, a desire to return to the ancestral home or a need to move to warmer or cooler climes. How might moves of this nature have a positive effect on the development of the young person?

Friends become increasingly important to the teenager.
Source: Pearson Education Ltd/Tudor Photography

Development of gender identity in the teenage years

In Chapter 11, Development of Self-concept and Gender Identity, we describe the formation of identity, including gender identity, during childhood. During puberty the young person's sense of gender identity intensifies (Basow and Rubin, 1999). Young teenagers start to develop a much stronger connection to the gender roles society has prepared them for and they become much more stereotyped in their attitudes and behaviour. For both boys and girls, the need to be an adult man and woman is intense, but the portrayal of stereotyped behaviour is much stronger in teenage girls, who perhaps feel less able to develop their more 'masculine' side than when they were children.

As teenagers begin the search for their identity and strive for autonomy from the family unit, so their friends and peers become increasingly central to and prevalent in their daily lives. Gender schema theory (Bem, 1981) is an information-processing approach that combines social learning theory with cognitive development theory. It begins with the premise that from birth we are socially conditioned to be either a boy or a girl. During our early years, we develop a strong identification with being a boy or a girl and start to align specific behaviours that we see being carried out by either boys or girls, and men or women, and by the time we reach school age, we very clearly 'know' what we can or cannot do as a boy or a girl. Some children identify *more* with being a boy than with being an individual: for example, rather than saying 'I am Billy', the child will say 'I am a boy'. This child is then said to have a strong gender schema of 'boy'.

This gender schema will then predict what toys Billy will play with (cars rather than dolls) based purely on what Billy thinks 'boys do'. If Billy does not have a strong gender schema then he will play with whatever toy he wants to play with, regardless of the gender association of that toy. In this case, Billy is 'gender aschematic'. During the teenage years, gender schema theory proposes that the growing time spent with same-sex friends has an increasing influence on the specificity and strength of the gender schema that our teen already has, which results in much more gender-stereotyped behaviour and gender identification.

Peers and their effect on gender identity

Gender identity appears to be an important factor in making strong friendships (Young and Sweeting, 2004). Research by Brutsaert (2006) demonstrates that our friends are much more likely to accept us if we have a strong sense of gender identity. Brutsaert states that if a person's gender identity matches their biological sex and the social norms associated with it then the level of peer acceptance experienced in school increases significantly. This effect seems to be particularly strong for boys' peer acceptance – boys who developed gender identities that did not support social norms and whose behaviour reflected more feminine-type behaviours were much less likely to be accepted by their peers.

This finding could reflect the very nature of peer groups in adolescence. Peer groups in early adolescence are generally gender homogeneous (boys belong to all-boy friendship groups and girls belong to all-girl friendship groups), and then develop over time into a more heterogeneous mix of boys and girls. Peer preference tends to lose its gender specificity and relates much more to the personality characteristics of the members of the group. Teens at age 16 years and at age 19 years demonstrate strong in-group bias over and above own-gender bias – something that is less identifiable in the younger adolescents (Eckes et al., 2005).

Why is peer acceptance important to young people? Certainly, risk behaviours such as smoking, drinking alcohol, taking drugs, stealing cars and damaging property have often been attributed to the notion of 'peer pressure' – a process that absolves the teenager of any personal responsibility for their actions and perhaps rather conveniently blames it on the faceless mass of 'youth'. Whilst it may be certain that peers do influence behaviour within a group of friends, it is simplistic to reason that the individual teenager is wholly unable to act without that influence. Teenagers consistently rate their own social group more positively than they do other social groups, and those who identify most with the group tend to show the most group member preference and are more likely to condone group behaviours (Tarrant et al., 2001). What happens, however, when the group no longer serves the needs of the teenager? In deciding whether to remain within the friendship group or whether to move into a different, more palatable group, an important factor is the attachment style a young person has with his or her parent. Girls tend be more socially anxious than boys, but generally teens who have experience of a secure childhood attachment tend to report good-quality friendships and show better group integration in adolescence (Zimmermann, 2004). Thus, this teenager is more likely to remain in the group as long as it satisfies his needs. If there is any conflict in the group then our teenager will be able to resolve it to his satisfaction and either become a key player in changing the focus of the group or be confident enough to walk away and join another peer group. The securely attached teenager is able to form strong friendships at any time in his life and will be able to integrate well into a different peer group if necessary. The avoidant attached or dismissive attached teenager, however, reports a much more shallow basis to his friendships, and is more likely to be influenced by the group's direction and less likely to walk away if the group becomes engaged in activity he knows is wrong.

STOP AND THINK

What if you experience a mismatch between your biological sex and your sense of personal gender? For example, a report from the Netherlands revealed that 1 in 11 900 men and 1 in 30 400 women over the age of 15 years report themselves as transsexual (Bakker et al., 2007).

How might the reactions of family, peers and other members of society affect a young person's ability to accept or cope with the fact that their biological sex and their personal sense of gender do not match?

Multimedia games and adolescent development

Much has been said in the popular press about the impact that television viewing and playing computer games have on the developing adolescent. Many examples of violence and aggression have been attributed to lone teenagers and their TV viewing habits or computer gaming hours, but is there any evidence to support this? A study by Aluja-Fabregat (2000) looked at personality variables in 470 Catalan 13–14-year-olds with varying degrees of contact with different types of film and television programming. Aluja-Fabregat found that students who watched more violent material were more likely to be rated as aggressive by their teachers. However, another study found that exposure to aggressive computer games was not related to aggression in 204 13–14-year-old students in England. In fact, total exposure hours to computer games accounted more for levels of aggression in the teenagers than the actual content of the computer games

Definitions

Peer preference: choosing friends who have similar interests to our own and who have a similar set of beliefs or outlook on life.

Peer pressure: when the friendship group convinces the young person to say or do something that they would not ordinarily say or do in order to gain positive regard or acceptance.

(Colwell and Payne, 2000). The data are complicated and more research is needed to unpack the connection between watching TV, playing computer games and teen aggression and violence.

If we look at a study conducted by Krahe and Moller (2004) in Germany, the authors found support for the notion that exposure to violent video games corresponded to increased expression of violence. What they discovered was that playing violent computer games changed the teenagers' acceptance of violence and aggression. The 231 13–14-year-olds were more likely to engage in the violent computer games if they were male and were then more likely to express more violence through hostility and the acceptance of a more aggressive social behavioural norm. Thus, what we can conclude from current research is that the playing of aggressive computer games affects teenagers by changing the young person's perspective on what is an acceptable level of violence. It is this shifting upwards of what they *think* is a normal level of aggression that is responsible for increasing levels of aggression in their interactions with each other.

Aggression, antisocial behaviour and bullying

Aggression, antisocial behaviour and bullying can be encountered at any time in life, but for our teenager, the effects can be particularly harmful. As we have discussed, one effect of adolescent egocentrism is the exaggerated experience of emotions and the high level of importance attributed to these emotions and others' behaviour by the teen. So whether the teen is the bully or the object of the bullying, the emotional and behavioural fallout are likely to be more severe at this age than at any other time. How does aggression and bullying in adolescence come about? Here we will briefly look at the social factors connected to bullying behaviour. (For a full discussion of the effects of bullying on the young person's development, see Chapter 15, 'Understanding bullying'.)

CUTTING EDGE

An example of how video games can affect teenage behaviour?

On 20 April 1999, in a town called Littleton in Jefferson County, Colorado, USA, two teenagers called Eric Harris and Dylan Klebold arrived at the gates of Columbine High School, and proceeded to kill and maim a number of pupils and teachers. Hours of media coverage were spent trying to search for the reasons why this killing had happened. Blame was levelled first at the type of music the teenagers liked to listen to and then at the violent type of video game they liked to play. It was easy for society to pinpoint the blame in this way, but were music and video games responsible for these teens' violent behaviour? Further investigation into the young men's lives reveals a catalogue of events that together may help us understand their actions.

Although Eric Harris and Dylan Klebold spent a lot of time listening to music and played violent video games together, it is simplistic to state that these alone were responsible for their violent actions. A combination of factors was probably to blame. The teenagers were becoming increasingly depressed and isolated, and parents and teachers had ignored their repeated pleas for help. The high school was blamed for allowing rivalry between the 'Goths', the 'Jocks' and the 'Christians' to escalate in the school by not taking reports of bullying and aggression seriously enough. Security was tightened up in American high schools following this event and attempts have been made to improve the relationships between the different social 'groups' within schools, but similar shootings have happened at other schools since, so much more research into understanding the triggers for these events is obviously needed.

Source: http://acolumbinesite.com

Social factors in bullying

A study by Barnow et al. (2005) of 168 adolescents revealed that adolescents who engaged in aggressive behaviour were more likely to report low self-esteem, be novelty seeking and, importantly, experience peer rejection. The authors found that parents can have a pivotal role in their children's bullying behaviour as significant correlations existed between teen aggression and delinquency and parents' antisocial behaviour, emotional rejection and low emotional warmth. Teenagers who report negative self-perception and negative parenting are also more likely to show antisocial behaviour (Ostgard-Ybrandt and Armelius, 2004). Bullying behaviour between the ages of 14 and 18 years also tends to be shown by teens whose parents have a low level of involvement in family life (Flouri and Buchanan, 2003) and, in boys in particular, poor parenting tends to relate to future criminality and contact with the police (Flouri and Buchanan, 2002).

Mental health in adolescence

Bullying (see Chapter 15, 'Understanding bullying') has been implicated as a main cause of poor mental health in adolescence. Approximately one in ten children aged 5 to 15 years experiences poor mental health, 11% of boys and 8% of girls (Government National Statistics published in the UK, 2004). Also responsible for poor mental health can be the adoption of poor-quality and passive coping strategies in the teenage years (see Table 13.2). The extreme outcomes of poor coping strategies in adolescence can be mood swings, frustration and periods of sadness and depression. In 2005, Quijada et al. reported on a study of Spanish teenagers which found that a little over 10% of young people aged 12–16 years could be scored as clinically depressed. This finding is not confined to Spain, or to this narrow age range. A study of Italian teenagers found a very similar prevalence of depression in young people from as young as 8 years to 17 years of age (Poli et al., 2003). This high figure is comparable with prevalence of depression in the adult population and demonstrates the importance of family monitoring of depressive symptoms in their teenager.

Depression seems to be becoming an increasing problem in the teenage population. A longitudinal study of mental health in the UK has revealed that there has been a substantial rise in depression and other emotional problems over the past 25 years regardless of sex, socio-economic status or family structure (intact, separated, adoptive and so on) (Collishaw et al., 2004). Depression in young people has also been researched in a large-scale longitudinal study conducted in Finland. In Pelkonen et al.'s study (2003) they found that approximately 13% of the young women had depression compared with 9% of the young men. Depression risk factors for the young women were related to low self-esteem and 'internal' factors such as dissatisfaction with school and family environment and having no close friends. The risk factors for the young men related also to low self-esteem but were also more concerned with 'external' factors such as difficulty resolving conflict at school and within the family environment, problems with the law and, again, having no close friends.

The influence of the family environment for both young men and young women in predicting depression appears to be both direct (parents have depression symptom histories) and indirect (parenting style and attachment). Given that our teenager benefits psychologically from social contact and direct approach coping strategies, it is important that families with a history of depression attempt to break the cycle and develop life skills that do not foster the development of depression in their teenagers. Outside the home, depression in teenagers can be triggered by events at school and other events outside their control with devastating consequences. In an Italian study of nearly 1000 adolescents, nearly 250 of the teenagers (mostly girls) reported having thoughts of suicide and self-harm. The teenagers cited bullying and aggression in school as

Definition

Depression: a common mental disorder that presents with depressed mood, loss of interest or pleasure, feelings of guilt or low self-worth, disturbed sleep or appetite, low energy, and poor concentration (World Health Organization).

causing the depression and, for the boys, bullying by their fathers. The causes of the depression in the girls reflected a poor family environment – the girls reported being exposed to aggressive behaviour from both their mothers and their fathers (Baldry and Winkel, 2003). In a smaller-scale English study, nearly 40% of the teenagers reported having been bullied at school and 50 of the 331 teenagers who took part in the study reported symptoms so severe that they satisfied the researchers that these teenagers could have a clinical diagnosis of stress (Mynard et al., 2000).

It is evident, then, that bullying is a fairly common and destructive part of adolescence. So what can be done to protect against the long-term effects? A multinational study conducted in Canada, France and Italy revealed that bullying, aggressive and antisocial behaviour could be mediated and even prevented with high levels of parental supervision, a politically liberal and socially tolerant family environment based on fairness and inclusion of all people regardless of race, religion or political party preference, low levels of family conflict and a strong positive attitude towards peers (Claes et al., 2005). Given that antisocial behaviour is linked to sensation-seeking behaviour (which includes impulsive decisions and behaviour which is not well thought through), it is important for parents and families to encourage empathy in adolescence and a positive attitude towards others (Garcia et al., 2005).

Concerns and coping

We already know that self-esteem can be affected during adolescence, but for most teenagers this is a transient change and one that is resolved by early adulthood. Those teenagers who grow up in families strong on communication and conflict resolution, for instance, are often able to manage the physical and psychological changes during puberty and are able to maintain and develop good social relationships (Aronen and Kurkela, 1998). However, some teenagers experience difficulties in coping with puberty and develop poor strategies for managing their emotions, relying on rumination and aggression to express their frustration, rather than attempting to distract themselves from their woes and to share their concerns with their friends and families (Hampel and Petermann, 2005).

The daily concerns of adolescents (spots, body shape, dating, studying and family relationships) can cause more worry than might be expected from an adult's perspective and need to be taken seriously in some cases. Seiffge-Krenke (2000) found that regardless of the severity of life events – whether they are daily hassles or major life events – teenagers each tend to choose a coping strategy and use it across the board, regardless of the situation and whether a different strategy might be more appropriate. See the different coping styles described by Carver et al. (1989) in Table 13.2. Thus, a passive coping

Table 13.2 Different styles of coping.

Active coping strategies	Passive coping strategies
Active coping: removing or avoiding the stressor	*Restraint coping*: putting your coping on hold until it can be of use
Planning: thinking about how to confront the stressor	*Resignation or acceptance*: accepting that the event has happened and is real
Seeking instrumental social support: seeking advice, information or help	*Focus on and venting of emotions*: becoming aware of the distress you are feeling and venting those feelings
Seeking emotional social support: getting sympathy from someone	*Denial*: denying the reality of the stressor
Suppression of competing activities: stop doing other things so that you can focus on dealing with the stressor	*Mental disengagement*: daydreaming, sleeping or other methods of distraction from the stressor
Religion: involving yourself in religious activity	*Behavioural disengagement*: stop trying to do the activity that the stressor is interfering with you doing
Positive reinterpretation and growth: making the best of it by learning from the situation	*Alcohol or drug use*: using alcohol and other drugs to disengage from the stressor
Humour: making jokes and using humour to reduce the distress	

Source: Carver et al. (1989)

strategy such as withdrawal might be used for coping with embarrassment over facial spots and imperfections, but could also be used for dealing with parental divorce, poor performance at school or relationship difficulties. The lack of complexity in their coping strategies, the use of passive coping strategies and the broad application of them are key factors in predicting poor psychological adaptation to different life events and high levels of anxiety and depression in teenagers. In the long term, teenagers who use active coping strategies are less likely to experience depression as adults, whereas those who use passive coping strategies are much more likely to experience depression later on in life.

With help, most teenagers can develop the ability to use various coping strategies but, without that help, some will hold on to the avoidant style of coping and, for them, the long-term prognosis for mental health is poor (Seiffge-Krenke and Klessinger, 2000). The role of families in developing coping strategies in their teenage son or daughter is not only important during the teenage years; it could also be vital earlier on in childhood. Teenagers who report secure attachments are much more likely to deal with their problems actively and to discuss their problems with their friends and family (Oliva et al., 2009). Most of these securely attached teenagers, whether male or female, young or heading into adulthood, report satisfaction with their parents and their parenting behaviours (Seiffge-Krenke and Beyers, 2005).

Sex and relationship behaviour in adolescence

Think about a typically developing young woman. Her parents think that she spends all her time on the phone talking with her friends about the boys at school. She seems to crave emotional intimacy and, at the moment, that need is being satisfied in her relationships with her friends. At what point, however, is she going to look to the boys for that intimacy and what type of relationship is she likely to have with them? Research shows that the type of attachment experienced as a young child often reflects the type of relationship a young person is likely to engage in. For instance, people who are described as securely attached are more likely to report longer-lasting relationships, and fewer extra-relational sex encounters and one-night stands, and to have more enjoyment of physical contact (Feeney and Noller, 1996). Compare this to the avoidant attached young person, who is statistically more likely to experience more extra-relational sex encounters and one-night stands. They are also less likely to have a truly close relationship and to have less enjoyment of physical contact. Thus, if a teenager feels close to her parents and feels able to talk to them about her boyfriends and relationships, she is more likely to experience a longer-lasting and more emotionally satisfying relationship than if she feels emotionally distant from her parents.

Should the teenager's parents be worrying about when she is going to engage in sexual behaviour? In a sample of 3000 Norwegian adolescents, Traeen et al. (1992a) found that by the time the teenager reached the age of 19 years, 69% of the women and 59% of the men had had sexual intercourse and most of them within a romantic relationship. Generally, the men had female partners of comparable age, but the women were more likely to have male partners nearly three years older than themselves. The men were more likely to report a larger number of sexual partners, but the women reported having more frequent sex. So given that (statistically speaking) a young woman is likely to have had sexual intercourse by the time she is 19 years of age, perhaps her parents should concern themselves more with educating her about the risks associated with sexual activity rather than the sexual activity itself.

> **STOP AND THINK**
>
> The data presented in the Research Methods box overleaf reveals the *average* age at first intercourse and *percentages* of the population who have lost their virginity by a certain age, but not *whom* the person first had sex with or what it was like.
>
> How might we find out more about teen early sex behaviour?

Risky sex behaviours

Sex during the teenage years can be a statistically risky business. Data collected in medical clinics and health drop-in centres show that 75% of newly diagnosed sexually transmitted infections are in adolescents and

RESEARCH METHODS

When do we experience first sexual intercourse?

The timing of first sex can actually be aligned to different times of the year depending on the relationship in which one is involved. For instance, teenagers who are involved in a romantic relationship are more likely to embark on first sex during the month of december whereas teenagers who are looking to lose their virginity in other contexts are more likely to choose to do so in the summer months.

(Levin et al., 2002)

Research into trends such as this and other factors relating to sexuality is often conducted by using *quantitative* methodologies (see Chapter 3, 'Research methods'). When researchers want to take a broad look at sex behaviour across the population, they will seek to ask as many people as possible about their experiences in sex. Studies are rarely longitudinal – researchers often do not look at the behaviour of the same people across a period of time – but are mostly cross-sectional in that they look at what people are doing in a 'snapshot' or a short period of time. The following study illustrates the value of a cross-sectional, large-scale study of sex behaviour.

The British National Surveys of Sexual Attitudes and Lifestyle publishes data from a large-scale study of the sexual behaviour of over 15 000 men and women (most recently collected between September 2010 and August 2012). This study revealed that:

- by the age of 16 years, 31% of young people have already engaged in heterosexual intercourse;
- over a lifetime men will have on average around 11 sexual partners and women will have 7 to 8;
- 7% of men and 16% of women have had a sexual experience with a partner of the same sex (Mercer et al., 2013).

---

young adults (Belsky et al., 1991). Diagnosis of sexually transmitted infections in the UK doubled from 669 000 to 1 333 000 between 1991 and 2001 in the under-20s. In particular, genital Chlamydia infection in women is increasing and is the most common sexually transmitted infection in the under-20s (Government National Statistics published in the UK, 2004).

Traeen et al.'s study into adolescent sexual behaviour in Norway (1992b) found that teenagers were more concerned about preventing pregnancy than about protection from sexually transmitted infections. Although 51% of the teenagers reported using a condom on first sexual intercourse, on most recent intercourse that behaviour had dropped to 31% and instead birth-control pill use had risen from 7% to 38%. Even those teenagers engaging in sex with a large number of partners were no more likely to use condoms than the teenagers with fewer partners. Edgardh (2002) noted that 74% of young Swedish men who regularly played truant from school were engaged in frequent sexual intercourse and they were three times as likely to have incurred a sexually transmitted infection as young men who regularly attended school. In Scotland, a study of 7630 14-year-olds tells us that 18% of the boys and 15% of the girls reported having had sexual intercourse and only 65% of them reported regular use of condoms. The authors found that those teenagers who had engaged in sexual intercourse were more likely to report low levels of parental monitoring (Henderson et al., 2002). Condom use has been shown to be much more likely if the young person reports that he or she intends to use a condom with a new partner, and reports that he or she has previously used condoms with other partners (Abraham et al., 1992). However, maintaining condom use in relationships, to prevent the transmission of infection, remains an elusive goal for most sexual health workers, health psychologists, researchers and government agencies.

SUMMARY

So, what does developmental psychology contribute to our understanding of adolescence? G. S. Hall described this time of life as one of 'storm and stress', yet Offer proposed that not all teenagers experience a turbulent period of growth and that many cope well with the changing demands of impending adulthood – a finding that has been supported in more recent research findings.

However, the teenage years are still characterised for all young people by some significant physical and cognitive changes. Onset of puberty can be a worry for many teenagers, especially if they feel asynchronous to their peers. The teenager's egocentrism and discomfort at the (imaginary) audience results in a skewed perception of life around them, and often the teen will concoct a quite fantastical personal fable when making sense of this sudden, perhaps overwhelming, awareness of the world around them. The cognitive changes appear to be a result of the neural changes occurring during the teenage years and, in particular, the period of synaptic pruning, although preparing an adult, efficient processing brain could account for some of the contrary behaviour of the young adolescent. All the physical and cognitive changes during the teenage years are intrinsic in forming the young person's sense of identity.

It is not just the physical changes which occur during puberty that are important, however; secure early childhood attachments combined with good relationships with friends and family during the teenage years are also pivotal in helping the teenager develop a strong sense of identity. We have seen that family structures are varied and each has its own strengths and weaknesses. Many teenagers in Europe live in homes where the parents have different racial heritage, and part of their search for identity includes a process of exploring and assimilating both racial identities into a coherent whole. Migration is a large part of life for some teenagers, and we have seen that the transition to a new country can be successfully achieved with support from the parents.

A crucial part of identity development is a sense of gender. Gender schema theory helps us to understand how gender identity develops during adolescence and how a sense of gender can play a pivotal part in the acceptance of a teenager by her peer group. Peers are important in shaping behaviour, but if a teenager does not like the direction his group is taking, then the confident teen will happily change his affiliation to the group and make new friends.

We have explored many aspects of teenage life: the highs and lows, the need for friends and family, coping with the physical changes, some of the risks of bullying and the passage into adult sexuality and sexual behaviour. For some the teenage years are turbulent and stressful, but for most they pass with only small periods of distress and successfully prepare the young person for full engagement with adult life.

ANSWERS TO PUZZLES

The Su-Do-Ku puzzle answer:

7	3	5	1	6	9	2	4	8
4	9	6	5	2	8	3	7	1
1	8	2	3	4	7	5	9	6
9	2	8	4	7	6	1	5	3
6	7	3	2	1	5	4	8	9
5	4	1	9	8	3	7	6	2
3	5	7	6	9	2	8	1	4
8	1	9	7	3	4	6	2	5
2	6	4	8	5	1	9	3	7

Correct answers to the moral stages task:

Quote	Which stage of reasoning?
'I was paid to do this. I felt bad about it but I had a job to do. I did what I was asked to do, I lived up to the deal.'	2
'You told me what to do and I did it. I figured you know what you're doing. It took a lot of self-control to do this. This is sanctioned by the School right? This is legal?'	4
'I did what I was told to do, you said to continue. I shocked the guy because he wasn't learning. I did it because I had to do it.'	1
'I'm not going to do it, I'm sorry. You've probably got reasons but … I don't see any reason to shock someone because of an experiment. You have no right to do that, I won't be part of it.'	6
'It really bothered me, the other guy was getting hurt but I figured you knew what you were doing. You're a psychologist, you wouldn't hurt anyone. If I'd stopped I'd have ruined your experiment.'	3
'This is crazy, I thought this experiment was going to be good for society but this is crazy, I'll not continue.'	5

Source: taken from Rosenhan et al., 1976

REVIEW QUESTIONS

1. Critically evaluate G. S. Hall's notion that adolescence is a period of 'storm and stress'.
2. Contrast the possible psychological experience of a young girl experiencing puberty ahead of her peers. How will this affect her relationship with her friends and her future dating behaviour?
3. Evaluate the role of early childhood, peer and family relationships in forming friendships and romantic attachments during the teenage years.
4. Describe the implications of family structure, race and migration for the development of the teenager's sense of identity.
5. Critically evaluate two psychological theories that describe the development of gender identity in the teenage years.

RECOMMENDED READING

For more information on the psychological effects surrounding puberty:

Oldehinkel, A. J., Verhuist, F. C., & Ormel, J. (2011). Mental health problems during puberty: Tanner stage-related differences in specific symptoms. The TRAILS study. *Journal of Adolescence*, 33 (4), 498–505.

For more information on how the changes to the frontal cortex affect and help us to understand the teenager's behaviour:

Blakemore, S. J., & Choudhury, S. (2006). Development of the adolescent brain: Implications for executive function and social cognition. *Journal of Child Psychology and Psychiatry*, 47 (3), 296–312.

Goddings, A-L., Dumontheil, I., Blakemore, S. J., et al. (2014). The relationship between pubertal status and neural activity during risky decision-making in male adolescents. *Journal of Adolescent Health*, 54 (2, Supplement), S84–S85.

For more information on the effect of migration on the teenager's experience of school:

Motti-Stefanidi, F., & Masten, A. S. (2013). School success and school engagement of immigrant children and adolescents: A risk and resilience developmental perspective. *European Psychologist*, 18 (2), 126–135.

For information on the role social networking sites are having in the young person's development:

Ekstrom, M., Olsson, T., & Shehata, A. (2014). Spaces for public orientation? Longitudinal effects of internet use in adolescence. *Information, Communication and Society*, 17 (2, Special Issue), 168–183.

RECOMMENDED WEBSITES

For more information on the TRAILS study:
http://www.trails.nl/en/

Society for Research on Adolescence:
http://www.s-r-a.org

Guide to the Longitudinal Study of Young People in England:
http://www.cls.ioe.ac.uk

European Association for Research on Adolescence:
http://www.earaonline.org

Section IV
Clinical/applied aspects

Chapter 14
Developmental psychology and education

Malcolm Hughes

Learning outcomes

After reading this chapter, and with further recommended reading, you should be able to:

1. Recount and evaluate the extent to which the main theories of developmental psychology and theories of learning have been applied in children's centres, schools, colleges and universities.
2. Assess the likely effectiveness of applying differing perspectives of educational theorists and practitioners in relation to key themes of teaching and learning.
3. Critically analyse the value of adopting developmentally appropriate approaches to educational systems and pedagogy.
4. Construct an argument about what to do for learners with special needs, and root that argument in a thoroughgoing knowledge of psychosocial development.

Edward – written by Elizabeth, his class teacher

Edward is a non-identical 7-year-old twin brother. Both boys, Edward and Richard, were taken into care soon after birth as their mother was a drug addict. The boys lived with foster parents until they were 2½. They now live with their maternal grandmother who they call 'Mum'. Both grandmother and her boyfriend are alcoholics. The grandmother's boyfriend sleeps in the same room as the boys. The boys are fiercely competitive and argue most of the time. They are very physical with each other and Edward has been known to self-harm. The boys have got persistently worse at home so grandmother is struggling more and more. They have set fire to furniture including a cot containing a baby.

In September 2009, the boys were placed in my class which lasted two-and-a-half weeks before they had to be separated. They were physically and mentally abusive to each other and Edward would be the same with other children in the class. At first the class was a very tense and scared group of people, adults and children alike, as the boys could fly off the handle at a moment's notice.

At break times Edward regularly falls out with other children and is rude and abusive to children and staff. Sometimes my headteacher is called four or five times a day to remove Edward. He is then brought back not long after in a terrible mood which makes him impossible to manage.

Recently a behaviour therapist observed Edward for an hour and claimed that he was 'angelic', that the school were doing a fantastic job and that there was nothing she need do. She also advised that Edward remain in the same class next year which would mean that his brother would go into the class above him.

Edward is the brighter of the twins. This is most apparent in maths and topic work. He can enjoy PE, PSHE and French but, as he cannot cooperate with other children, he misses a lot of these sessions or simply does not join in. It has been calculated that he is in the 92nd percentile for non-verbal communication, which the therapist said was his strength and should be exploited, but she did not tell me how or why. He is very good at mental arithmetic and enjoys his numeracy lessons.

This has been a very difficult year in which I have felt a range of emotions: guilt that I am not actually helping Edward and feeling that I am letting down my class; despair at being left to deal with Edward by myself; relief when he is away and then in turn shame that I feel that way. Most days I just feel like a failure.

- How do you feel about Edward, Richard and Elizabeth, based on Elizabeth's account?
- What action would you take next if you were the headteacher in this school?
- What advice would you offer Elizabeth?

▶

▶ **Introduction**

Edward, Richard and Elizabeth are real people, although their names have been changed; the story presented in the opening example is real and written 'from the heart'. Both Edward and his brother pose significant challenges to their teachers which can be traced back to problems during their psychological development. These circumstances – where a relatively young but highly committed and inspirational teacher feels she is a failure, is letting down her class and feels ashamed – reflect a dilemma in education. To what extent can learners' experience in schools and colleges – the educational provision – be varied to suit their psychological development? This chapter explores to what extent developmental psychology is and can be applied not only to relatively extreme cases such as Edward and his brother, but to the way education more generally is organised and delivered.

Behaviour in school is the result of many factors, internal and external to the child and to the school itself.
Source: Pearson Education Ltd/Shutterstock

There are three main sections to this chapter. Firstly, we explore the ways in which understanding education requires an understanding of children's personal, social and cultural influences. Secondly, we review the main theories of human development and learning, and develop arguments about how these theories have been both shaped and applied by teachers and developmental psychologists in a range of educational settings. Thirdly, we explore areas of educational provision – what we refer to as 'themes of developmentally appropriate provision' – that can, and some would argue should, inform the educational experiences of our children, young people and adult learners.

Understanding development within social contexts

As you have read in Nature–Nurture boxes throughout this book, children's development is affected in profound and complex ways by the circumstances – the culture – in which they grow up, and the case of Edward is no exception to this. Why does Edward behave as he does? What aspects of Edward's upbringing to date have had the strongest influence on Edward's development? How do different aspects of children's experiences relate to each other? Who is more influential: parents, teachers or peers? To try to answer such questions we can turn to a model developed by Urie Bronfenbrenner, discussed previously in Chapter 2, 'Theoretical perspectives'. Bronfenbrenner was a renowned psychologist and a co-founder of the *Head Start* programme for disadvantaged and challenging pre-school children. In his bio-ecological model, Bronfenbrenner mapped the many interacting social contexts that affect development (Bronfenbrenner, 1989; Bronfenbrenner and Evans, 2000). However, the *bio* aspect of the model recognises that people also bring their biological selves to the developmental process. The small child sitting in the middle of Figure 14.1 represents this very important idea. Remember from the example that Edward behaves

UNDERSTANDING DEVELOPMENT WITHIN SOCIAL CONTEXTS | 411

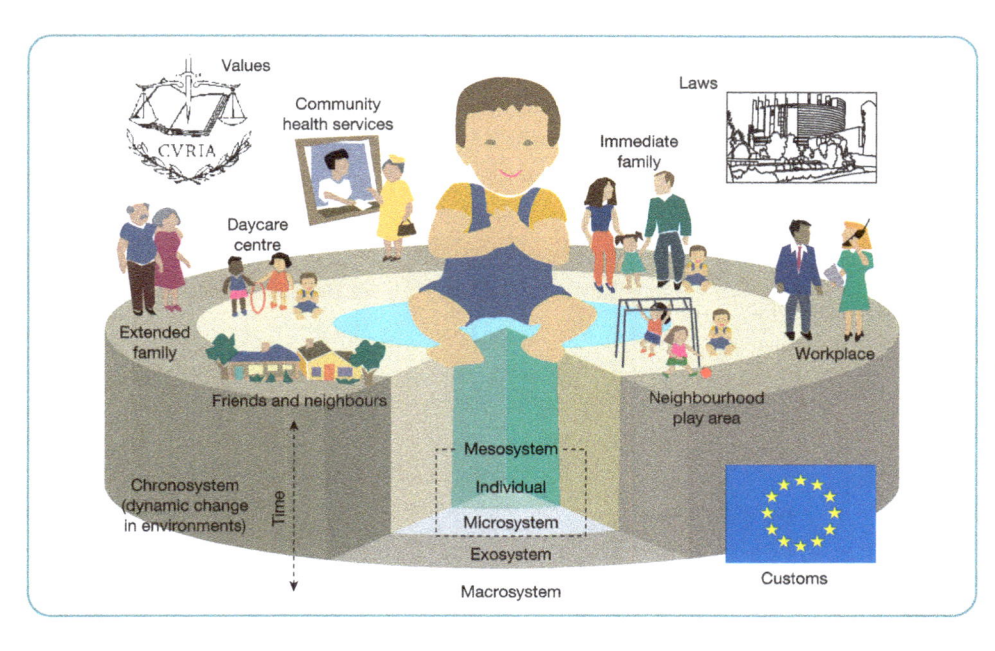

Figure 14.1 Urie Bronfenbrenner's bioecological model of human development.
Source: Berk, L.E. (1997). *Child Development* (4th edn). Boston: Allyn & Bacon. p. 25 © 1997 Pearson Education, Inc. Reproduced with permission of the author.

differently from his brother despite many genetic factors being similar (but not identical) and both boys sharing many defining social experiences. The *ecological* part of the model recognises that the social contexts in which we develop are ecosystems because they are in constant interaction and influence each other. Bronfenbrenner's model depicts the different cultural systems which 'surround' and influence a young child like Edward.

You can see that every child develops within a *microsystem* of his immediate relationships and activities, which make up the child's own 'little world'. Relationships within this world are reciprocal and interactive – they 'flow' in both directions (see Chapter 2). The child's behaviour affects the parents and the parents' behaviour influences the child. Microsystems exist and interact within a *mesosystem*, which is the set of interactions and relationships among all the elements of the microsystem – the family members interacting with each other or with the teacher. These are slightly more distant from the child because they do not involve him directly, but nevertheless they influence his life. Again, all these relationships are reciprocal.

The mesosystem of interacting microsystems also interact with the *exosystem*, the layer which includes all the social settings that affect the child, even though the child is not a direct member of the system: for example, teachers' relations with school managers; parents' jobs and social pursuits; the community's resources for health, employment or recreation; or a family's religious affiliation.

The *macrosystem* is the larger society – its values, laws, conventions, and traditions, all of which influence the conditions and experiences of the child's life. These systems help us to think about the many dynamic forces that interact to create the context for children's development.

We asked earlier, 'Who is more influential, teachers or friends?' Well, according to Bronfenbrenner's model, teachers are part of the child's mesosystem and friends are part of the microsystem. Therefore friends are closer to the child than teachers and certainly closer than local employers or national politicians. Perhaps one of the problems with Bronfenbrenner's model is that it is not explicit about how different ecologies (interactions of people within their environment) impact at different times during a lifespan. The exosystem will become more important in a child's life as she gets older (see Chapter 2). Put simply, earlier in life, homes and families will be more influential and so, when thinking about why Edward behaves as he does, this is an important idea to consider.

Study of Bronfenbrenner's bio-ecological model suggests that genetic, biological and social determinants are important factors in understanding why Edward behaves as he does. For example, as the children have been taken into care very soon after birth and their grandmother is an alcoholic, we might assume that there are some family problems that span generations; perhaps a genetic disposition. There could have been drug abuse and/or malnutrition during pregnancy affecting the boys' heath and development (see Chapter 4, 'Prenatal development and infancy'). There will almost certainly be an attachment problem (see Chapter 9, 'Attachment and early social experiences') as the children were separated from their mother as babies and their foster family at the age of 2. There may also be socio-economic problems, possibly violence or other traumatic experiences, and probably a lack of parenting capacity in the grandmother. All of this makes it clear that Edward's education is a problem which the teacher cannot solve alone, particularly as the problems are generated in life outside school. The boys need to be assessed thoroughly by a specialist in developmental and educational psychology.

What the example of Edward does demonstrate is that cognitive development, learning and academic achievement are not distinct from the socio-cultural factors that have a profound impact on our lives. Edward is described as bright by his teachers and so far there is no significant difference in language and reading, memory and intelligence, mathematical thinking or general academic attainment between Edward and the normal expectations for his age (see Chapter 6, 'Memory and intelligence'). So what aspects of his development have been most affected by bio-ecological factors? In Edward's case it is probably his temperament and emotional development; his self-concept and identity; his ability to engage in comfortable social interactions; and his capacity to make and maintain supportive relationships. In the longer term, impoverished and warped development in these areas will have an adverse impact on the academic achievement of learners if they continue to find engagement with teachers and peers so difficult. It is also true that Edward is having a significant impact on his classmates and teachers, but what else is affecting the experiences and development of the children in Elizabeth's class and in all the other classrooms of our schools, colleges and universities?

From your past reading – perhaps of Chapter 2 in particular – you should have a good idea of what theoretical frameworks might underpin the application of developmental psychology to classrooms. These are the sorts of understanding that would inform a specialist in developmental and educational psychology who was asked to assess Edward and to suggest care and teaching programmes that might help him. A number of names may already have sprung to mind – Piaget, Vygotsky, Bruner, Bowlby – and we have already discussed Bronfenbrenner.

All of these influential scientists have contributed to our understanding of the application of developmental psychology in educational settings, and so it is to the application of developmental theory in classrooms that we turn next.

STOP AND THINK

Reflection

Review the example of Edward at the start of the chapter.

- Why is Edward behaving as he is? Review the summaries of Chapter 9, Attachment and Early Social Experiences, and Chapter 10, Childhood Temperament and Behavioural Development. They will provide the language for you to frame a response.
- Why might the behaviour therapist have considered Edward to be 'angelic', given the accounts of the class teacher and other staff?

The application of developmental theory in classrooms

As discussed in Chapter 1, developmental psychology is concerned with helping to understand the various processes that determine our psychological make-up during important phases of human growth. Continuous processes such as maturation, growth and enhanced capacity mould the way we change and develop throughout our lives. However, as discussed in Chapter 2, Theoretical Perspectives, development is also commonly presented by psychologists in periods of time or stages. Many theoretical frameworks (for example, Jean Piaget's four stages of cognitive development, explained in Chapter 2) give an impression of distinctly separate stages closely linked to chronological age, and describe a very precise ordering of change (Piaget, 1972). Piaget's stage model is the most commonly applied set of theories in early years settings and schools in Europe, Australasia and North America. The Nature–Nurture box which follows highlights Piaget's contribution to education policy and practice, and shows how even Bronfenbrenner's bio-ecological

NATURE–NURTURE

Does cognitive development occur naturally or as the result of what happens to us?

According to Piaget, the 'power house' behind development from one stage to the next is maturation (Inhelder and Piaget, 1958). All of us have a genetic set of instructions for cognitive development that prepare us for certain changes at certain ages. According to Piaget's theory, you cannot teach a 7-year-old something that only a 15-year-old can learn, no matter how good your teaching skills or how diligent the pupil. In the same way, by the time the 7-year-old reaches age 15, biological maturation will make it easy for him to understand the world as a typical child of 15 understands it. This idea lies at the heart of developmentally appropriate education provision – an idea which will dominate much of the second part of this chapter.

Piaget's emphasis on the importance of maturation contrasts with the views of other theorists such as the psychologist Howard Gardner, who believe that there are few inherent or 'hard-wired' limits to development. They believe that development occurs as a reaction to other influences rather than as the blueprint of a particular genetic type. Furthermore Gardner and similarly minded theorists believe that environmental stimulation – what happens to us – can override any limits that might exist (Shih, 2013), that new-borns possess considerable inbuilt or easily developed cognitive capacities (see Chapter 4, 'Prenatal development and infancy') and that Piaget underestimated the power of what developmental psychologist Howard Gardner called the 'inborn cognitive architecture' – the already highly developed cognitive structures of the brain at birth (Gardner, 2006).

Piaget portrayed maturation as an active process in which children seek out information and stimulation in the environment that matches the maturity of their thinking. This contrasts with the view of other theorists such as the behaviourists (e.g. Pavlov, Skinner), whose theories and work are also explored in Chapter 2, who saw the environment as acting on the child through rewards and punishments and the child reacting to the environment, rather than seeing children as proactive agents of their own development.

---

model has been informed by earlier developmental scientists such as Piaget.

The separation and precise ordering which define stage theories is one of the criticisms of developmental theories, although the idea of different stages does provide a structure for the different phases of schooling and what is taught in each phase. For example, there may be an attempt to have developmental stages correspond with the key stages prescribed in a national curriculum for schools, or with age phases represented in school age groupings (there is more explanation of this later). For example, compulsory schooling in Sweden and Denmark begins at the age of 7. 'Primary' schooling is normally 6 to 13 years in Norway, 6 to 12 in Belgium and 5 to 11 or 12 in England and Wales (Woolfolk et al., 2013). Why are there differences in the stages of schooling across broadly similar cultures? How are developmental stages applied to schooling provision in the UK or in your country?

Implications of Piagetian theory for teaching and learning

So was Piaget right about these issues of cognitive development or are his theories flawed? This matters a great deal, given that Piaget has made a huge contribution to our understanding of children's cognitive development and to learning. Piaget has been so influential that if his theories are flawed then we would need to question much of the educational policy and practice that is built on them. What is the extent of Piaget's influence? Here is a 'top ten' of ways in which – in the author's opinion – Piaget's work has influenced education. It is worth noting that not all classroom practice is built on

Definition

Maturation: change over time which is naturally occurring and genetically programmed.

these important ideas. However, the authors cited in the list are amongst many scholars who quite recently have observed these aspects of Piaget's influence in contemporary educational settings.

1. Learning requires an active construction of knowledge rather than just passively listening, and learners should engage actively: learners 'doing' is better than teachers 'telling' (Harris, 2008; Chen et al., 2014).
2. Learning by discovery promotes the building of ideas, concepts and mental schemes (see Chapter 7, 'The development of mathematical thinking'). Some would argue that all real learning (what some educationalists call 'authentic learning') results from discovery rather than being shown or memorising by repetition (Yuliani and Saragih, 2015).
3. The construction of ideas should move from concrete and practical experiences to more abstract notions. Teachers should start with what a learner sees, feels or manipulates, and move to a construction of meaning made by the learner (Maschietto and Bussi, 2009).
4. A teacher's role is to 'make possible'; to aid the child in discovery, questioning and speculating (Janssen et al., 2014). 'The art of teaching is the art of assisting discovery' – Mark van Doren, poet and teacher.
5. Concept formation is vital for all learners regardless of subject or age (Hay, 2007; Goldstone and Day, 2012). As you will see later, concepts are the building bricks of knowledge and understanding.
6. The notion of age-related stages should not become a 'straitjacket'. Observations of what a child can do are much more useful than chronological age in deciding provision. However, deciding how rather than just what to teach should be more directly informed by understanding the significance of stages in children's cognitive development. Pupils' 'readiness' to learn can determine the type of learning experiences provided (Oliver et al., 2007; Akengin and Sevgi, 2013).
7. The interrelation between practical experience and learning language is explicitly necessary in the pre-operational thinking stage (Chapter 2), and remains an essential aspect of learning experiences later on (Vinther, 2005; Mistry and Barnes, 2013).
8. Thinking is a cumulative process. Lower-order ways of thinking exist first that prepare for higher-order thinking later. Secondary schools and colleges should not begin with each new student as 'a blank sheet', but view them as expert and experienced learners who may or may not choose to further invest effort in their future learning (Noyes, 2006; Yew et al., 2011).
9. Teachers and practitioners should set tasks matched to the needs of pupils in a school or college designed to accommodate individual needs and rates of learning. This becomes increasingly challenging as differences

Is children 'doing' better than teachers 'telling'?
Source: Pearson Education Ltd/Jules Selmes

across the ability range increase with age (Williams and Nicholas, 2006; Graves, 2011).
10. Schools and colleges should explicitly provide appropriate experiences to foster cognitive development and pupils' natural desire to learn rather than view the role of the taught curriculum as only the organisation of what knowledge and skills should be learned (Cottingham, 2005; Brown & Yi-Chin, 2013).

This is not an exhaustive list – all lists like this one are a personal selection by an author – but it does serve to show the practical application of one theory of developmental psychology in education in a way that, hopefully, can also be recognised from the personal experience of the reader. Of course, theory building and practical applications did not stop with Piaget. Others built on and developed his work to such an extent that these later ideas became known as neo-Piagetian theory.

> **STOP AND THINK**
>
> **Going further**
>
> It is argued by some commentators that Piaget gave greater attention to early and mid-childhood and showed insufficient interest in adolescence and emerging adulthood.
>
> - Do you agree?
> - Why do you think Piaget might have done this?
>
> To find out what might characterise cognitive maturation through adolescence, see Recommended Reading. Also review your study of Chapter 13, 'Adolescence'.
>
> - In what ways do you think the education of adolescents should differ from that of younger children?
> - Why do you think so?
> - What would you change about secondary schooling to make it more appealing or relevant to adolescents?
>
> Justify your answers by referring to theories and research you have read about.

Neo-Piagetian theory

Neo-Piagetian theory (e.g. Case, 1992, 1998) builds on the stages and changes in Piaget's cognitive development theory. The influential and highly thought of psychologist Professor Robbie Case (1945–2000) believed that changes within each stage resulted from changes in increased mental capacity. For example, the Piagetian conservation of number task (see Chapter 7) requires more than one cognitive strategy to be successful. In this task children are shown an array of counters or buttons in a line bunched up together or spread out. Their task is to recognise that the number remains the same regardless of changes in their arrangement. Young children fail because they are unable to hold different pieces of information in their short-term memory at the same time. Older primary-aged children hold information from previous experiences that allows them to go on to more complex tasks. Case's theory and its underpinning empirical research was a major advance in developmental psychology, integrating important aspects of the Piagetian stage theory and cognitive information-processing theory to capitalise on the strengths of each, and particularly to draw out from this incorporation implications for teaching methods used at different phases of schooling. According to Case, cognitive structures in infancy are sufficient for immediate responses to sensory-motor information – that is, what we see, hear and feel. In early childhood, cognition relates to creating internal representations of information; and in later childhood, transformations of those representations through experience (Case, 1985). Let's unpick this last complex and important idea.

Case believes that changes in development result from changes to information-processing capacity in working memory (see Chapter 6, 'Memory and intelligence') or what he calls *m space*. Growth in capacity, he argues, is linked to how well children can use their limited memory capacity. This involves four processes:

- *Stage 1 Encoding*: maturation of the brain enables increased speed of processing of working memory over time. The brain makes sense of what it 'sees'

> **Definitions**
>
> **Neo-Piagetian theory:** a recent interpretation of Piaget's theory in an information-processing framework that places greater emphasis on cognitive processes than maturation.
>
> **Information-processing theory:** the likening of human cognition to the working structures of a computer, with input, processing, memory, output, etc. that helps us 'conceptualise' what is happening in the brain.

much faster. If six sweets are placed in a line in groups of two, and young children (at Piaget's pre-operational stage) are asked, 'How many sweets are there?', they will count them one by one. Older children with their increased capacity will arrive at the answer faster and with fewer steps (recognising an array of six). Younger children cannot 'see' or make sense of the whole picture as yet.

- *Stage 2 Strategies*: these free up mental capacity. Case sees merit in the strategies used by children that Piaget referred to. Such strategies include how learners try to understand something new by fitting it into what they already know (assimilation). When this strategy becomes more expert and automatic, this leads to more 'cognitive room' to change existing schemes in response to a new situation (accommodation). (This links to point 2 in the 'top ten' list previously.)
- *Stage 3 Automatisation*: the automisation of knowledge leads to central conceptual structures. This allows more complex thinking which also frees up information-processing capacity and allows more advanced thinking. When ideas are fully formed, children can 'move up a level'. Pre-school children understand stories in one dimension (e.g. what the story line is); by the primary years, several sub-plots can be understood and combined into a main plot. By adolescence, children can handle multiple and overlapping storylines due to development in the conceptual structures in the higher, more forward parts of the brain.
- *Stage 4 Generalisation*: this involves moving from being quite task-specific to more general. Here children learn to apply what they know to other contexts, but this takes time. Take our example of conservation to illustrate this. A child pours liquid from one container to another and demonstrates understanding of the 'height' and 'width' of the liquid and begins to create understanding of how liquid is conserved. Once automatic, a central conceptual structure of conservation is formed that enables that general concept to be applied to other similar situations, not just liquid and containers.

Collaborating with his research students, many of whom were experienced schoolteachers, Case developed innovative teaching schemes and lesson designs, especially in mathematics. These lessons support successful learning by students, and exemplify and advance important principles of learning, like those put forward earlier in the 'top ten' of ways in which Piaget's work has influenced education and, later on in this chapter, how to conceive of developmentally appropriate learning and assessment tasks. Neo-Piagetian theory is still developing, but has already shown applications to explaining dyslexia and reading difficulties (Papadopoulos et al., 2012) and studies on academic skills using this approach have proved very valuable, for example, in the teaching of mathematics (Andrade and Vilela, 2013).

Critics of neo-Piagetian theory (like critics of Piaget's own theories) assert that the theory avoids the biological underpinnings of how the brain functions and places little emphasis on the social or cultural influences of cognition – such as those suggested in Bronfenbrenner's bio-ecological theory. However, information-processing theories offer applications to many educational settings. For example, the emphasis which information-processing theories place on memory helps to explain how younger learners' limited memory causes difficulties with many reading and problem-solving tasks. Secondly, teachers can encourage learners to actively engage with their learning (remember points 1 and 2 from the Piaget 'top ten' list) by teaching pupils strategies to kick-start various cognitive processes. For instance:

- 'self-questioning' ('What do I already know about this topic?', 'How have I solved problems like this before?');
- 'thinking aloud' while performing a task ('OK so far', 'This isn't making sense', 'I need to change strategies');
- writing down 'self-questions' and 'thinking aloud' statements;

Definitions

Assimilation: within Piagetian theory, this is the process of taking new information into existing knowledge structures.

Accommodation: within Piagetian theory, this is the revision of older knowledge structures to take account of new information.

Central conceptual structure: a well-formed mental scheme of a concept like 'horse' that can be generally applied to all horses and requires little more assimilation until we experience a zebra for the first time.

- making graphic representations (e.g. concept maps, flow charts, semantic webs) of one's thoughts and knowledge.

> **STOP AND THINK**
>
> **Reflection**
>
> - What examples from your own learning can you think of where you have been taught or have used cognitive strategies such as self-questioning and thinking aloud – sometimes referred to as meta-cognitive strategies?
> - Are you using any at the moment as you work your way through this chapter?
> - Does writing things down help? Why or why not?

These are just a few examples of strategies to encourage cognitive development when viewing the development of our capacity as information processors. We have acknowledged and celebrated the contribution made by Jean Piaget and neo-Piagetian theorists such as Robbie Case to our understanding of cognitive development, and demonstrated to some extent the application of their theories to schools and schooling. However, it is now timely to compare and contrast the application of Piaget's research and theories with that of another influential scientist, the Russian psychologist Lev Vygotsky.

Vygotsky's social-constructivist theory

Lev Vygotsky's social-constructivist approach (described in Chapter 2) offered a major alternative to Piaget in the period between 1920 and 1930, although his work did not appear in English and therefore gain wider recognition until the 1960s. Where Piaget took the view of the child as an 'experimental scientist', Vygotsky likened the child to an apprentice, where cognitive development and capacity is promoted through interaction with those who already possess cognitive capacity, knowledge and skills (Vygotsky, 1978b). It is through our social interactions with parents and teachers that we develop our intellectual capabilities. Development and learning occur from processes first on a social plane (i.e. between people) and then secondly on a psychological one (i.e. individually).

Group work is often used in university teaching, and in socio-cultural theory is key to development and learning.
Source: Pearson Education Ltd/Robert Harding/ Bananastock

It is not just parents or other 'significant' adults who can support learning in Vygotsky's theory. Supporting learners to competency also involves knowledgeable or skilful peers helping less advanced ones. This takes place in contemporary classrooms and playgrounds when learners work together, perhaps on a collaborative task in a process called cooperative learning. Most primary classrooms have furniture arranged in table groups to positively promote children's interaction with each other. If you spent ten minutes observing well-structured and organised group work, you might (hopefully!) see and hear children at any of these tables helping each other, learning from one another in pursuit of a common goal and without the direction of a teacher. This is a broader idea than Vygotsky's original view where there is a single child and another more expert child/adult. In cooperative learning, groups of children with varying degrees of expertise have been found to stimulate learning in each other (Doymus, 2008; Chen and Chang, 2014). Other research, while supportive of this, also indicates that cooperative learning is more effective when children have been trained in cooperative procedures (Pica, 2011) and the teacher has prior experience of working with children in this way (Oortwijn et al., 2008).

Implications of Vygotsky's theory for teaching and learning

There are implications of Vygotsky's work for education. One key factor is the role of the teacher in structuring learning. In the UK as long ago as 1992, Robin Alexander, Jim Rose and Chris Woodhead (known then as the 'Three Wise Men' of UK educational policy) criticised child-centred education (widely associated with the theories of Jean Piaget) and the notion of fixed-stage development, which they believed led to lowered expectations, inhibited teachers' interventions and confined the role of the teacher to 'facilitator'. They stated:

> More recent studies demonstrate what children, given effective teaching, can achieve . . . [The more recent studies] place proper emphasis on the teacher as teacher rather than facilitator. Such insights are, in our view, critical to the raising of standards in primary classrooms.
>
> (Alexander et al., 1992, p. 14)

Lev Vygotsky stressed intellectual development rather than structuring learning to match a stage of cognitive development. The activities selected in school are very important to challenge and extend learning, and should include meaningful and stimulating classroom activities pitched to be within each child's individual ability to cope – what has become known as 'personalised learning'. In particular, Vygotsky believed that teaching children at all stages should reflect many opportunities for pretend play for language development. This is seen as good practice in the early years, but much less so later on. In the same way as we selected our 'top ten' ways in which the work of Piaget is reflected in schools, we now present a 'top ten' of the ways we believe Vygotsky's work has influenced education:

1. Teachers can use language across the curriculum and in all phases of education to develop higher mental functions (Fenwick, 2010).
2. Pupils should be encouraged to talk aloud when engaged in problem-solving exercises (Steif et al., 2010).
3. Pupils develop their own cognitive capacity at their own pace, but this process requires access to rich and stimulating environments (O'Toole, 2008).
4. Teachers and practitioners should watch for states of developmental readiness (Jacobs et al., 2010).
5. Children advance their learning by pretend play. There should be bountiful opportunities for young children to do this (Porter, 2012; Swindells and Stagnitti, 2006).
6. It is the defining skill of a teacher to decide what kind of support is necessary, when to give the support and how much support is necessary for an individual – what has become known as 'personalised learning' (Courcier, 2007; Hosseini et al., 2013).
7. Packaging or 'chunking' learning should be a very common practice in many learning contexts – skilled teachers break down a task and adjust the methods of presentation (Allen, 2008).
8. Teachers should design collaborative tasks to encourage cooperative learning. Most European primary classrooms have furniture arranged in table groups to positively promote children's interaction with each other (Lwin et al., 2012).

Definition

Cooperative learning: working in small groups, acting together to meet a learning goal or goals.

9. Teachers should train learners in cooperative and reciprocal procedures so that learning is more effective (Treleaven et al., 2012).
10. High-quality teaching is as important as providing discovery learning opportunities in promoting a learner's development. Given effective teaching, all learners can achieve (Dunphy, 2009).

The Vygotsky 'top ten' summarises the effect of how many writers and researchers, including those cited in both the Piaget and the Vygotsky lists, believe developmental psychology has been and should be applied in many schools and colleges. To summarise, Piaget, the neo-Piagetian theorists, such as Robbie Case, and Lev Vygotsky represent the clearest links between developmental psychology and its application in educational settings. However, there is a complex and very important link and distinction between theories of developmental psychology and learning theories or how pupils learn best. Before considering how best to apply developmental psychology, let's try and tease out the distinction between developmental theory and learning theory in order to establish an important focus on developmental psychology.

CUTTING EDGE

Brain development in adolescence

There has been a recent surge of research on neurological development in adolescence (Chapter 13) that sheds new light on cognitive development during these years (Giedd, 2008). Research technologies, especially fMRI (functional magnetic resonance imaging) and PET scans (positron emission tomography) give us a much better understanding of how the brain develops, because these new technologies show how different parts of the brain work when performing a cognitive task (e.g. memorising, making decisions), by focusing on the connections or synapses between the neurons – the cells of the nervous system including the brain.

For years we have known about the over-production of these synaptic connections during prenatal development and through the first 18 months of life (see Chapter 4), but now it turns out that a new period of over-production also occurs in early adolescence (Giedd, 2008). Over-production peaks at about age 12 or so, but obviously that is not when we reach our cognitive peak. After 12, there follows a huge amount of synaptic pruning, in which the number of synapses is whittled down considerably. Interestingly, recent research using fMRI methods shows that synaptic pruning is more rapid among adolescents with high intelligence (Shaw et al., 2006; Steinberg, 2011). Why might this be? Well, synaptic pruning allows the brain to work more efficiently, as brain pathways become 'slicker'.

Another recent surprise for researchers has been in the growth of the cerebellum – a structure in the lower brain. This is perhaps the most surprising recent finding because the cerebellum is part of the lower brain and was thought to be involved only in basic functions such as major movement. Now, however, it turns out that the cerebellum is important for many higher functions as well, such as musicianship, mathematical problem solving, making decisions and appreciating humour (Strauch, 2003). In fact, the cerebellum is the last structure of the brain to stop growing, not completing its phase of over-production and pruning until the mid-20s. So, what can we conclude about brain development in adolescence and emerging adulthood on the basis of this new research?

1. The brain grows and changes a lot more than we understood in the past.
2. The neurological changes increase cognitive abilities substantially.
3. Although adolescents are more advanced in their thinking than children, their cognitive development is not yet mature.
4. Synaptic pruning that makes thinking faster and more efficient also makes thinking more rigid and less flexible so, for example, it becomes harder to learn a new language.
5. After adolescence, it is easier for people to make balanced judgements about complicated issues because they have a well-pruned set of connections in the brain that are quicker and slicker.

Moving from developmental theory to learning theory

Theories that have their roots in developmental psychology (Piaget, Vygotsky and others) are based upon the 'clinical observation' of behaviour which demonstrates individual capacity (or lack of capacity) in developed or developing cognitive processes. An example of this can be found in the Cutting Edge box. Clinical observation allows for the development of theories which can describe, analyse and predict the behaviour of individuals as they move through stages of development. These theories (as we have already seen in our examples of Piaget, Case and Vygotsky) inform curricular provision, the content and the structure of formal schooling, the layout of the classroom and therefore the development of approaches to teaching and learning for groups of pupils as well as individuals.

Learning theories arise in part from the application of developmental psychology to educational settings, and also from the observation and analysis of teaching and learning behaviours. These theories have a particular focus (not surprisingly) on how learners learn best and how teachers can become better teachers, and include the principles adopted during initial teacher training and the continuing professional development of teachers. Learning theories explain how learning happens and then promote strategies to improve the quality of learning experiences. How the brain works and how it develops during key developmental stages such as adolescence (see Chapter 13) are important matters of concern for those engaged in applying developmental psychology to education.

The Cutting Edge box begs the question of how this new information can and should be applied in educational contexts. The second part of this chapter should help provide an answer by considering what is meant by 'developmentally appropriate provision' in education – a fundamental idea in the application of developmental psychology – that can be considered as the match between the educational experience of the learner (the status of their cognitive development, perhaps the neurological surge or the speed of synaptic pruning) and the learner's ability to make the most of the experience. We will explore what we term the 'five themes of developmentally appropriate provision': developmentally appropriate curricula; developmentally appropriate teaching; developmentally appropriate activities; developmentally appropriate behaviour management; and developmentally appropriate schools.

Five themes of 'developmentally appropriate provision'

Developmentally appropriate curricula

The curriculum is what is taught in schools, colleges and universities, organised by age group (usually into academic years) and by subject. There is also something called 'the hidden curriculum': the values, attitudes and insights which are not overtly taught, but may be modelled and demonstrated by teachers and managers in institutions. The curriculum is usually organised into schemes of work informed by over-riding aims and detailed lists of learning objectives. Many examples of curricula are organised in spiral forms, so that pupils will come across similar subject content year on year, but with more complex or difficult ideas introduced. Further structure is usually given to curricula by grouping them into stages linked to school phases.

Since the 1980s, a statutory National Curriculum for schools in England has been developed. Many other countries have developed national curricula and the next Stop and Think box asks you to explore comparable arrangements in your own country or another country. The National Curriculum in England sets out the stages and core subjects that children will be taught during their time at school. Children aged 5 to 16 in 'maintained' or state schools should be taught the National Curriculum. The National Curriculum is organised into blocks of years called 'key stages'. There are four key stages as

> **Definition**
>
> Developmentally appropriate provision: when the educational experiences of learners are matched with the learners' ability to make the most of the experience.

well as an Early Years Foundation Stage (EYFS). The EYFS covers education for children before they reach 5 (compulsory school age). For each National Curriculum subject, there is a programme of study. The programmes of study describe the subject knowledge, skills and understanding which pupils are expected to develop during each key stage.

> **STOP AND THINK**
>
> **Going further**
>
> Review the structure of the National Curriculum for Schools in England at http://curriculum.qcda.gov.uk
>
> Use the internet to search for another country's national curriculum. Try to identify some similarities and differences between the two. To what causes would you ascribe any differences?

For example, the programmes of study for science were written by teams of subject experts and were based on research into progression in conceptual understanding within the science levels; a team from Liverpool University's Centre for Research in Primary Science and Technology, in partnership with Kings College London. So it could be argued that for some of the children, for some of the time, there is a good match between the state of individual cognitive development and the curriculum. However, it is recognised that, for other children, the mismatch between programmes of study and cognitive development is so great that some or all of the programmes should be disapplied. Disapplication is permitted for individual pupils for a temporary period, through a statement of special educational need, or to allow for curriculum development or experimentation (Department for Education and Science, 2006).

Why does disapplication occur? Most of the time disapplication happens because a pupil is finding it very difficult to make the same progress as other pupils –

> **Definition**
>
> **Disapplication:** the term used to indicate that a pupil or group of pupils need no longer be taught part or all of a programme of study.

there is a developmental gulf opening up. It may seem unlikely that that gulf can be bridged; it may be that attempts to do so are counterproductive, or that lack of development in a particular area has a damaging effect on other subject areas. Probably the biggest problem that older pupils have, and one of the greatest causes of disapplication, is poor reading skills (Duff et al., 2008; Ricketts et al., 2008).

A pupil's access to the curriculum depends to a large extent upon their ability to fluently and effortlessly read the many texts that are presented in the course of a timetable week. Cognitive capacity that is consumed with the difficulties of decoding and making sense of sometimes complex technical texts, leaves 'no room' for information processing, problem solving and the other higher-order cognitive capacities of analysis, argument, synthesis, etc. There are all sorts of reasons why some pupils fall behind with their reading development. Some are environmental and some may be related to brain structure or phonological development. These are summed up as the cognitive capacity to learn (Veraksa, 2011) and are how a number of experts describe 'intelligence' (see Chapter 6, 'Memory and intelligence'). One good example of this was a study by psychologist Mark Eckert and colleagues of 39 eleven-year-old children. The team found that temporal lobe asymmetry, hand preference, family history of reading disability and socio-economic status explained over half of the variance in phonological and verbal performance (Eckert et al., 2001).

One effect of the environment is the ability of parents, teachers and others to observe a child's readiness to read. Reading readiness is a term that in 1970s Britain informed the practice of schools and teachers, but oddly and, to begin with, in a negative way. It was suggested to teachers (and at this author's own training college in Cheltenham, England) that there was no point in pushing children to learn to read until they were ready, and the work of Piaget was the primary source of justification for this. Education lecturers made a connection between Piaget's stage 3, concrete operations (age 7 to 11 years), and children's more effortless acquiring of reading skills. Trainee teachers were taught that it was simply a pointless waste of time to give formal phonological training before many children were ready.

However, approaches to reading readiness have changed in the last 40 years. Teachers were and are

A 5-year-old reading to his 1½-year-old sister. Is it useful to start reading to children at a very young age?
Source: Lam

encouraged to look for signs that individual children are ready for formal instruction, usually phonological approaches with the development of 'phonemic' awareness being a consequence rather than a precursor of reading (Ashby et al., 2013). What are the signs of readiness to learn to read, then? Table 14.1 is an example of the kind of checklist that trainee teachers of Early Years and the Foundation Stage are encouraged to use. It will help you identify this aspect of developmentally appropriate curricula.

In this section, we have discussed how the Programmes of Study making up the National Curriculum in England are formally structured to take account of a cognitive developmental sequence that owes much to the theories of stage development put forward by Jean Piaget. We looked at how some children have aspects of the curriculum disapplied to them when a developmental gulf opens up that cannot be bridged. We also looked at the teaching of reading in terms of structuring the curriculum to take account of reading readiness, and what some of the signs of reading readiness might be. There's clearly an overlap here with ideas of 'developmentally appropriate teaching' and it is to that idea that we next turn.

STOP AND THINK

Reflection
- What do you think might be the outcomes of trying to teach children to read too early, before they show the signs of reading readiness?
- Think back to when you learned to read. When did you start and how did you learn? You may have to ask somebody in the family if you learned at a very early age!

Developmentally appropriate teaching

If curriculum is about what is taught then this section on developmentally appropriate teaching is about *how* it is taught. Teaching methods vary widely within and between formal subject areas. Effective developmentally appropriate teaching in physical education will be very different from mathematics. Even within mathematics, how teachers of mathematics design their teaching will

Table 14.1 Tick list of some signs of reading readiness.

Some signs of reading readiness – that formal reading instruction as part of the curriculum is developmentally appropriate. Observe some children over time at ages 3, 4 and 5. How many signs of reading readiness can you record?

A child . . .	Observed
displays a greater interest in books and takes pleasure in looking at them, though it may appear that they're looking primarily at the pictures	
acts as if a reader	
grips books the correct way up	
turns pages at the correct times	
discusses what is happening and will relate their own experiences, e.g. television programmes and advertisements	
understands that the reader is focusing on the print and that the print is transmitting a message	
conjectures on what is read and the meaning of the pictures	
enjoys stories being read again and again, and 'joins in' regularly	
determines meaning from context by saying things like, 'I am scared of cats too'	
can recognise their own name, brands (e.g. the McDonald's 'M') and other public signs	
asks, 'What does that say?'	
identifies and imitates sounds of letters including by identifying, 'Train starts with "t" – the same as my name!'	

vary – from enabling pupils to gain automatic recall of number bonds (50 + 70 = 120 is like 5 + 7 = 12) and multiplication facts (9 × 7 = 63) to the very different set of knowledge and understanding required in using the properties of common regular polygons to solve problems. There are obviously different ways of teaching different subjects, but what are the most common types of teaching?

In this section we are going to describe three broad types of teaching which are founded on the questioning technique used by the teachers: directive exposition; non-directive discovery; and interactive connection building. The kinds of question that teachers ask is a good way to recognise what is going on; how the teacher relates to the learners and the type of learning that might be taking place. Before exploring the types of teaching that are found in classrooms, it is worth thinking about how we know what kinds of teaching are happening. Much of the empirical evidence that underpins and is cited in this chapter comes from the systematic observation of classrooms. In the Research Methods box, information and discussion is provided about an observational methodology that is now often used in classrooms – the video camera.

Directive exposition

'Chalk and talk' instruction (now often done through PowerPoint presentation) occurs using a programme of

---

RESEARCH METHODS

Observation using classroom video

In Chapter 3, Research Methods, we discussed various research methods, including observation. The use of video cameras has enabled observational studies to capture more extensively behaviours in a particular setting, and has also allowed observations to be viewed by other people, leading to greater reliability and validity in the coding and interpretation of observations. In addition, it is very difficult to recover the details of classroom interactions and activity through field observation alone. More traditional recording methods of ethnography such as field notes and even audio recordings fail to pay sufficient attention to the detail of classroom practice and action. In addition, the potential for confusion or misunderstanding is still rife if audio alone is used to augment written notes, since the complexity of kinaesthetics and body language would be missed (Visnovska and Cobb, 2013).

The video camera is therefore a good tool with which to access detailed classroom behaviour, and detailed and repeated observation of video data provides the opportunity for a methodology fit for purpose in highly dynamic and interactionist contexts. Despite all of these positive aspects of using video, its most common criticism is the unnatural effects it can have on the classroom research subjects (Cowan, 2014).

In one study which used this method, a school was approached for permission for a classroom-based research project on how teachers used questioning when teaching using the school's interactive whiteboards (IWBs). The school was well equipped with digital display technologies linked to the internet available in all classrooms. The study asked the children and their teacher to engage in a collaborative task with a video camera; 'telling a story' of how teachers asked questions when using the interactive whiteboard over the period of a week (Hughes and Longman, 2006).

The locations chosen for the camera were often limited, whether due to the position of power sockets or to teachers' preferences. The typical positioning of the camera created problems for the researchers in using some of the data. For example, pupils/teachers often chose to use a corner or side position not normally taken by a teacher or by pupils. In some sense, the camera became a visitor in the classroom and was not accepted as part of the teaching and learning. Because of this constraint, the camera's viewpoint meant that in some lighting conditions the images and text on the IWB were not discernible. Teachers and pupils chose positions that attempted a panopticon of the whole classroom, 'so we could see everything that was happening'. The position of a small boom microphone on the camera meant a good deal of background classroom noise was picked up, which often masked the question and answer interactions.

Classrooms are difficult places to capture good-quality video data and, with hindsight, the teachers and children reported that they would do things very differently. Despite these difficulties, the children were able to capture something of what kinds of question their teachers asked during a school week, but this experience revealed some of the pitfalls and limitations of this method of data collection.

---

experiences that are structured to provide small amounts of learning about things, and demonstrations or modelling of the desired outcomes, which can be recorded, assessed and reinforced, and outcomes rewarded. Progress is driven by the structure of the lesson or part of lesson. Responses to closed questions are limited to one or two words. For example, 'Name the five largest castles in Wales' is a closed question with a correct set of responses. The answers can be found quickly, recovering the answers from memory, using a reference book or database of castles containing a field relevant to the area within the walls (or some similar dimension). Pupils can show their ability to memorise, to search text or to interrogate a database, but not much else.

Learning is passive, concerned with the limbic processing of information, and is associated with the psychology of behaviourism (see Chapter 2, 'Theoretical perspectives'). Teaching does not take account of preferred learning styles, or the learner's intuitive engagement with the learning process. This view of the teacher and teaching style broadly corresponds with the 'Teacher as Sage – the Sage-on-the-Stage' (Stinson and Milter, 1996) and the *Nuremberg Funnel* model (Kaiser, 1946) of delivering or transferring the curriculum. The Nuremberg funnel is a fictional device by which a teacher can easily and effortlessly pour into a learner's mind all the wisdom and knowledge required.

Traditional lectures do not lend themselves to much more than passive listening and recording of information.
Source: Pearson Education Ltd/123RF.com/stockbroker

Non-directive discovery

Discovery instruction is when teachers provide a range of experiences that are unstructured, but are informed by programmes of study considered appropriate for a non-linear and integrated curriculum. Progress is driven by the interests of the learners, and teachers will pursue a range of ideas concurrently and in partnership with pupils. The emphasis is on personal discovery and personal construction. Responses to open questions are unlimited. For example, 'What can you find out about castles?' is a very open question that gives enormous scope for pupils to gather huge amounts of information. ICT can make that gathering exercise very fast and can also produce large quantities of beautifully presented 'work'. However, it is very unlikely that the information gathered will be processed in a way that will provoke and allow learning to take place. Little notice is taken of cognitive processes.

Teachers negotiate the starting point in which knowledge and concepts of a particular subject are the learning intentions of the session, and provide vivid and powerful means to these ends. This approach provides for a common starting experience for pupils, and so can emphasise a social dimension to the learning. Learning is active, but constrained within the limitations of the pupils' perceptions of what is possible or known. Teachers provide opportunities and support for any curiosity shown to discover 'What would happen if . . .?' The learner has the ability to explore in a content-free environment, but this does not necessarily allow for the learner to stray beyond the confines of current knowledge. Learning defaults to conceptual connections that are most obvious within the chosen context. This style of relationship broadly corresponds with 'Teachers as Guide – the Guide-by-the-Side' (Stinson and Milter, 1996).

Interactive connection building

Using this method, teachers provide a 'programme' of experiences that are structured to provide wide-ranging opportunities for learning about things, and demonstrations or modelling of an approach to learning that draws out the connections between prior learning and new learning, and between different subject areas, which can be celebrated, assessed, reinforced and outcomes rewarded. Progress is inspired by the teacher, who can not only 'talk the talk', but also 'walk the walk' – specifically, the teacher can argue for the methods she uses and her approach to problem solving.

Responses to structured questions are focused and offer opportunities for argument. These are questions requiring learners to engage in one or more of the cognitive processes: criticism, synthesis, transformation, experiment, creation, incorporation, categorising, discarding, refining, sequencing, explaining and connecting. Teachers set out to engage the pupil in their own learning and to structure the experience. For example, we might ask the question 'Why do spiral stairs in castle towers often ascend in an anti-clockwise direction?' (There are some interesting theories around about this and one or two myths.) Teachers can then plan to use vivid materials and media to make the learning focus on making causal connections between observed phenomena. The emphasis on cognitive process provides the best opportunity out of the three approaches for developmentally appropriate teaching.

Learning is active and driven by teacher-imposed tasks which require a level of curiosity to discover 'What would happen if . . .?' The scope of media and resources used is expandable on any number of levels and in multiple forms of communication and information handling. Learning can occur in large leaps as seemingly unconnected ideas and facts can be brought together, sometimes by chance. The learner is empowered, but can become exhausted by the demands for creative thought and concentrated learning effort. This style of relationship broadly corresponds with the 'Teacher as demanding and inspirational coach'.

STOP AND THINK

Reflection

Think back to the teaching styles adopted by teachers you have had.

- What teaching styles did you experience?
- Which do you prefer? Why?

Finding connections looks to be very important in order to inspire learning, as does the style of teaching adopted, since this defines the question and answer interactions between the teacher and the class. One example of developmentally appropriate teaching is explored in the Case Study box. What aspects of this approach might make this example developmentally appropriate? Would this be a developmentally appropriate teaching technique at any age?

CASE STUDY

Developmentally appropriate teaching – a concept attainment lesson

Here is how a teacher helped his pupils aged 9 and 10 learn about a familiar concept, and practise thinking skills at the same time. The teacher began a lesson by saying that he had an idea in mind and wanted pupils to 'work out what it is'. He placed two signs on a table – 'examples' and 'non-examples'. Then he placed an apple in front of the 'examples' sign and a rock in front of the 'non-examples' sign.

He asked his pupils, 'What do you think the idea might be?' 'Things we eat!' was the first suggestion. The teacher wrote 'hypotheses' on the board and, after a brief discussion of the meaning of 'hypotheses,' listed 'things we eat' under this heading. Next he asked for other hypotheses. 'Living things' and 'Things that grow on plants' came next.

After some discussion about plants and living things, the teacher brought out a tomato for the 'examples' side and a carrot for the 'non-examples'. Animated reconsideration of all the hypotheses followed these additions and a new hypothesis – 'red things' – was suggested. Through discussion of more examples (peach, squash, orange) and non-examples (lettuce, artichoke, potato), the pupils narrowed their hypothesis to 'things with seeds in the parts you eat'.

The pupils had 'constructed' the concept of 'fruit' – foods with seeds in the edible parts (or, a more advanced definition, any engorged ovary, such as a pea pod, nut, tomato, pineapple, or the edible part of a plant developed from a flower).

This case study provides a description of a teacher adopting a developmentally appropriate style for 9- and 10-year-olds for two reasons. First, the concepts being employed are within the grasp of the learners (remember Vygotsky's zone of proximal development – ZPD – explained in Chapter 2), and the exemplars used by the teacher are within the experience of the learners (Piaget's approach to using concrete examples, moving then from concrete to abstract). Secondly, the process reflects the importance of teaching for the development of robust mental schemas (Piaget) for fruit rather than trying to construct 'fruit' from more random and disassociated experiences. Did you know (not just know about but 'know') how to define a fruit? Remember that the youngsters in this example are not just learning a definition of a fruit 'off by heart', but are constructing that meaning. The construction of meaning, according to developmental psychologists such as Piaget, Vygotsky and Robbie Case, is the key to understanding.

- **Try designing a lesson of your own to teach children of the same age about fruit, without using concept development. How might you go about this?**
- **Given what you know about Piaget and Vygotsky, try explaining to someone else the pros and cons of your lesson, and of the case study lesson described here.**

In this section, we have considered developmentally appropriate teaching and explored three broad models of teaching. Opportunities for applying developmentally appropriate teaching methods seem to be much greater in the type of teaching called 'interactive connection building', which explicitly explores cognitive processes such as transforming, explaining and connecting. However, we all know that progress in educational settings is not only about what the teacher does. Much of the activity associated with schooling and learning is about how the pupil or student engages with the ideas, concepts, skills and understandings of a particular programme of study in which they are occupied. So now we will explore learner activity and to what extent teachers can and should try to provide developmentally appropriate activities for pupils.

Developmentally appropriate activities

Learners engage in a wide range of activities in schools and colleges. Are some kinds of activity simply more appropriate at different developmental stages than at others? Can activities be pigeonholed in this way? Before attempting any such process we should first consider what kinds of learning activity people do engage in at school and college. What follows is a straightforward, but not definitive list with a word or two of explanation. Learners engage in:

- *Play*: usually unstructured interaction with objects and other people. This is how we find out about the world from a very early age. After the age of 6 or 7, play is not normally a planned-for activity (Hyvonen, 2008; McInnes et al., 2013) in education.
- *Practice*: a cognitive necessity to establish patterns of thought and behaviour, and to provide a level of automaticity. This activity is planned for at all stages of education (Webb and Vulliamy, 2007).
- *Listening and watching*: the principal 'diet' of school children and university undergraduates everywhere. Who was it who said, 'The lecture is the process by which the university notes of the lecturer become the university notes of the student, without bothering the brains of either'? However, remember that Vygotsky suggested that learning from the modelling of others who are more skilful or knowledgeable is an important and developmentally sound part of the learning experience (Horsthemke and Kissack, 2008; Lewin et al., 2008).
- *Problem solving*: this is at its best where it is a 'real' problem with a solution requiring an amount of steps appropriate to the cognitive development of those attempting the solution. Problems need to be carefully chosen to be do-able, perhaps within the capability (the ZPD) of the learner and with some support available (Middleton, 2009).
- *Discussion*: again this is dependent upon a set of skills that require certain cognitive competencies – for example, to empathise and reciprocate; to have developed a clear and positive self-concept; to be able to regulate responsive behaviour; and so forth. Can young children discuss? Evidence from some studies would suggest that this is a difficult activity for teachers to plan for (Flynn, 2007; Haynes and Murris, 2013).
- *Collaboration*: learners need to be working with those who have broadly similar levels of cognitive development, or the collaboration becomes a peer mentoring or teaching role. Such roles are not necessarily bad things. However, all learners need opportunities to adopt these roles and not be continually giving support or receiving peer mentoring (Watts and Youens, 2007).
- *Research, experimentation and investigation*: these activities have much in common with play in that they require active engagement, problem solving and moving from concrete experiences and observations to creating concepts and robust mental schemes. At best, research, experimentation and investigation can provoke the development of higher-order cognitive skills, such as analysis, evaluation, synergy, deduction and induction (Voogt et al., 2009; Clary and Wandersee, 2010).
- *Recording*: many learners find writing things down (or creating mind maps or concept maps), whilst listening to teachers' expositions or when reading text, to be very helpful. However, this depends upon a high level of cognitive activity and is perhaps best kept for older teenagers and emergent adult learners (Barrett et al., 2014).
- *Reporting*: this is one of the most cognitively demanding activities (requiring analysis, synthesis and interpretation), although sometimes delivery of the report can be little more than reading all the tiny text on a PowerPoint presentation (Harden, 2008).

So, which of these activities are appropriate at different stages of development or phases of schooling, or should we plan for all learners to engage in a wide variety of activities? Is baby Jack Davies exploring an object ('Is it a hat, is it a sandwich?') fundamentally the same activity as a 13-year-old absorbed in the pendulum experiment used by Piaget? Is discussion an appropriate activity for 5-year-olds, or are we mixing that up with playing at having a tea party in a 'Wendy House' (a very important activity, as Vygotsky lay great store by the importance of pretend play to advance learning)? What kind of learning is happening when pupils watch teachers modelling activities? Let's look to the teaching of science to explore some of these questions.

STOP AND THINK

Reflection

Can young children discuss things? In the last few years a movement has grown in the UK for teaching philosophy to children of 5 and 6 (check out the news reports archive on your favourite daily paper website). One example question for 5-year-olds is 'Why does the music sing so nicely?' Try answering that one with a group of your friends.

Activities in the teaching of science

Some would argue (e.g. Dori and Herscovitz, 2005; Pedrosa de Jesus and Coelho Moreira, 2009; Burns et al., 2014) that no other school subject promises so much active learning in conceptually complex contexts than science. What could be more enjoyable than imploding old oil cans by sucking out the air, or exploding rising gas bubbles and creating carbon rings on the school lab ceiling? Who has not looked in awe at the construction of a honeycomb or with fascination at the goings on in a glass-sided ants nest? Consider the pleasure in discovering the method of making hydrogen sulphide (H_2S). What about the sense of achievement in raising the heaviest weight by just a simple pull of a rope going through the right configuration of pulleys?

Compare all of this with the reaction of one 14-year-old called Tom. 'Why do we have to do writing all the time? Today we did writing in PE and 'home ec', and all we've done in science this year is copy writing from the board and drawing diagrams in our books. It's so boring and I can't wait to give it up' (author's unpublished journal note). Tom is not alone. When students can choose subjects they wish to study, the dropout rate for sciences is worrying (George, 2006; Stewart, 2013). What is the problem here? Look at Table 14.2. There is a representative checklist of some of the cognitive activities that are most relevant to the learning of science knowledge, skills and principles by the key scientific activities of investigation and experiment. Take a moment or two now to note down in the second column how often, in your experience, science lessons contained opportunities to develop each of these cognitive activities. Then use the final column to rank each activity by level of increasing cognitive complexity.

There is no right or wrong set of answers – you may not know what some of the cognitive activities are. However, it is likely that you estimated observation and recording to be amongst the most frequently occurring, but also as two of the least complex activities. What would that tell us? There is evidence to suggest that science lessons in the main do not provide for cognitively appropriate learning activities (EunJin, 2013) – learners may be too busy observing and recording – and there is little progression in the activities required, particularly for those considered less able (Hallam and Ireson, 2005; Yerrick et al., 2011).

Of course, whilst there may be an argument that says guided discovery through the social construction of knowing 'what, how and why' should underpin all stages of learning in science, there are clearly some processes that cannot and should not be formalised at too early a stage. These include conjecture, analysis (including pattern seeking) and formal, multilevel pre-test/post-test experimentation. However, effective teachers of science engage children in a variety of learning activities and part of the art of the teachers is to devise tasks that provide for cognitive development and progression without taking learners beyond their ability to cope. Psychologists can provide frameworks for developmentally appropriate learning activities in science (e.g. Lavonen et al., 2006; Zohar, 2006; Huan-Yu et al., 2009; Abdelaziz, 2013).

Psychologists also get heavily involved in developing and carrying out assessment activities on learners, particularly those learners who do not conform to the expected norms of cognitive development and learning.

Science teaching has the potential to be exciting and interactive.

Source: Pearson Education Ltd/Shutterstock.com/michaeljung

Table 14.2 Cognitive activities in science.

Alphabetical order	Estimate of incidence in science lessons	Level of increasing cognitive complexity
Analysis		
Application		
Communication		
Conceptualisation		
Conjecture		
Memorisation		
Observation		
Organisation		
Pattern seeking		
Practice		
Recall		
Recording		
Refinement		
Replication		
Schema forming		

Source: Christine Chin, David Brown. Student-generated questions: a meaningful aspect of learning in science. *International Journal of Science Education*, Volume 24, Number 5 (2002), pp. 521–549.

Assessing children's attainment and potential is an important application of developmental psychology in education and so it is to assessment that we next turn.

Developmentally appropriate assessment activities

All learning activities can, to a greater or lesser extent, be 'used' by teachers to assess how well a pupil is doing in achieving the learning that is envisaged, when designing and programming the activities. Assessment is an important strand of pedagogy – the science of teaching and learning – and there are three main phases of assessment: initial assessment, formative assessment and summative assessment.

Initial assessment

Distinguished educational psychologist Dr David Ausubel wrote:

> If I had to reduce all of educational psychology to just one principle, I would say this: The most important single factor influencing learning is what the learner already knows. Ascertain this and teach him accordingly.
>
> (Ausubel et al., 1978, p. 163)

It makes good sense for teachers to discover as much as possible about the developmental stage of a pupil before designing a programme of learning activities to take account of where she has got to. However, in school settings things are seldom so individual or personal. Broad assumptions are made that most children will have reached a certain stage of cognitive and emotional/moral development and that initial assessments are screening exercises to identify those who may fall outside of the expected norms and for whom special arrangements need to be made. Where individual differences from expected norms are identified as being acute (for example, an 18-month difference at the age of 7, so the child may be displaying behaviours expected of a typical child of 5½), this may trigger a set of diagnostic assessments, normally delivered by a developmental specialist such as an educational psychologist, who would then help teaching professionals to design a personal education plan including appropriate interventions. This may trigger part or parts of a national curriculum being disapplied from the child.

Assessment at the start of schooling or of a phase of schooling is common in European schools (Huber and Grdel, 2006; Pasztor, 2008), in many other developed countries (Bierman et al., 2008) and in the developing world (Marshall et al., 2012). What are sometimes called baseline assessments are used for making international comparisons (Tymms et al., 2004; Hasselgreen, 2005). In England, initial assessments are associated with the start of the Foundation Stage and Key Stage 1, and these are carried out by teacher observation of pupils engaged in a range of learning activities. Such assessments are concerned with process and what the child can do rather than assessing the worth of outcomes like a page of completed calculations or a written story. In parts of the UK, observations are linked with developmental targets called 'Stepping Stones' associated with the Six Areas of Learning and Development (see http://www.education.gov.uk for more information).

Remember, many of these kinds of assessment are by observation of what the child can do in a variety of play and activity situations. Learning and development are closely linked at these early stages, but later on teachers tend to rely on what other teachers report about the successful progress of individual pupils through the programmes of study, drawing on the Levels of Attainment set out in the National Curriculum for each subject. Written tests of what pupils can remember and do (the outcomes) become more common during the later primary years, and some of those tests provide summative and normative (see below) information which can be used as an initial assessment for a new phase of schooling. It is typical for pupils to enter secondary school armed with a set of level grades, and after some time and a test or two, usually in mathematics, pupils are often then grouped by ability for some, or all, of the curriculum.

Formative assessment

Formative assessment is the ongoing evaluation of how pupils are doing whilst engaged in learning activities of one kind or another. Judgements made by teachers help to formulate what will be the next set of ideas covered and which are the most appropriate activities through which to engage pupils in programmes of study. An important skill for teachers is to use opportunities where a pupil finds an activity difficult or admits that he doesn't understand, by adapting the activity to diagnose what the problem may be. What follows is an example of the kind of diagnostic conversation that can take place:

> **T:** How can you work out the number of squares in this array if there are 7 rows and 9 columns?
> **P:** I don't know, is it 16?
> **T:** That's interesting. How did you get 16?
> **P:** I just added the 7 and 9?
> **T:** OK, let's look at this array of 2 rows and 3 columns?
> **P:** That's easy, it's 6 squares.
> **T:** How did you get that?
> **P:** I just looked at it.
> **T:** Go on, anything else you can tell me?
> **P:** Well there are 2 lots of 3, which makes 6.
> **T:** What kind of sum is 2 lots of 3 to make 6?
> **P:** I don't know . . .

What is the teacher's diagnosis of the difficulty faced by the pupil? This youngster's schema for multiplication doesn't include the concept of 'lots of' to spark the retrieval of multiplication facts, irrespective of how automatic those facts are. As is very familiar to many teachers, this pupil doesn't know what sum to do because there's an important bit 'missing' from his multiplication schema and, therefore, the schema needs to be refined.

Formal diagnostic assessments are also carried out by educational psychologists and special educational needs teachers (sometimes referred to as SENCOs) who 'identify' there is a problem by using normative tests, such as tests of intelligence (see Chapter 6). These compare an individual pupil's results on an individual test with many thousands of other children of (usually) the same age, to place them within a statistical framework. Remember from our opening example about Edward: 'It has been calculated that [Edward] is in the 92nd percentile for non-verbal communication, which the therapist said was his strength and should be exploited, but she did not tell me how.'

Once a general problem has been identified by an educational psychologist or a SENCO, she may follow this up with a series of criteria-based tests where the performance of pupils is compared with statements (criteria) of what a pupil can or cannot understand in order to complete the elements of the test. By looking at the profile of criteria unsuccessfully met, an expert can diagnose the likely causes of under-performance and support the design of an intervention to remediate the difficulties. These processes are some of the most important applications of developmental psychology and theories of learning to education, and are worthy of additional study by following the references to assessment in the Recommended Reading at the end of the chapter.

Summative assessment

At the end of a topic (a defined part of a programme of study), a term, year or phase, summative assessment can take place. The content of an assessment summarises the substance of the programme of study – the expected learning outcomes – and provides information about how well an individual pupil has acquired and developed the understandings, skills and knowledge met during the topic, term, year or phase. Almost all these kinds of assessment are written tests, with full marks for complete and correct answers or no mistakes made. As pupils get older, the emphasis of school assessment moves away from what pupils can do and how they do it to what pupils can remember, or remember how or what to do. Straightforward scores are often generated which can be compared with other pupils and groups of pupils, with standards required by an accrediting body or with targets set by national organisations.

Examples of summative tests are the End of Key Stage Tests in England for pupils aged 7, 11 and 14 (now under considerable threat in their present form), the General Certificates of Secondary Education at age 16 (the end of compulsory schooling in Britain) and 'Finals' – examinations held at the end of three- or four-year undergraduate degree programmes at many British and European universities. These examinations mark and sometimes allow access to the next phase of education, or permit entrance to professions and membership of professional bodies.

All of this begs a question. How developmentally appropriate are different forms and types of assessment at any stage of schooling? A typical pattern in English schools and colleges is for children at 3 to 6 to be individually assessed by observation; children at 7 to 13 to be assessed by a combination of formative, diagnostic (in the best classrooms) and short written tests focused on recent learning experiences; and pupils/students aged 14–21 to be assessed on formal presentations, longer written examinations or the making of artefacts completed over a longer period of time. The Lifespan box compares the typical pattern of assessment practice in English schools with the defining age-related psychosocial theories of psychologist Erik Erikson (described in Chapter 2, 'Theoretical perspectives', and Chapter 13, 'Adolescence'). Remember that Erikson emphasised the emergence of the self, the search for identity, the individual's relationships with others and the role of culture throughout life (Erikson, 1963). Furthermore, Erikson suggests that children and adults at every age face a conflict between a potential positive outcome, such as learning to trust other people, and an unhealthy alternative like becoming wary and apprehensive. What effect may the form of assessment used have upon a person's self-image and view of society?

Are the methods of assessment used in schools and colleges developmentally appropriate, based on your reading of the Lifespan box? Why or why not? There is an obvious link between development, learning and assessment practice during infanthood and the early years of schooling, and up to puberty many teachers hold to the idea that achievement is more important than attainment. However, formal and statutory testing arrangements in England, and formerly in other parts of the United Kingdom, have reinforced in children's and parents' minds the idea that by the age of 11 or so the die is cast and, for policy-makers, any personal inferiority felt by some pupils is an unfortunate consequence of celebrating the attainment of other pupils and schools (Abbas, 2007; Tomlinson, 2008).

Summative assessments are often written tests.
Source: Pearson Education Ltd/Shutterstock.com/Captain Petolea

Definitions

Achievement: personal accomplishment of skills, knowledge and understanding in comparison to an individual's former achievement. A measure of personal progress.

Attainment: personal accomplishment of skills, knowledge and understanding in comparison to typical accomplishments. Comparisons are made with examination requirements or the attainments of others.

LIFESPAN

Comparison of the age-related stage theories of Erikson with forms and outcomes of assessments

Infancy to 12 months – trust versus mistrust

Assessments are made by medical practitioners, developmental experts and 'knowing' parents of 'milestones of development' during the sensorimotor stage: for example, weight gain; perceptual cognition through physical reactions to light, sound and orientation; and grasp reflex to deliberate use of opposing grasp. Baby record and baby book records are shared between parents (who often 'own' the record) and practitioners (Woods, 2006; Reich et al., 2010).

12 months to 3 years – autonomy versus shame

Parents, carers and educational practitioners maintain a reassuring, confident attitude, informally noting achievements in basic motor and cognitive skills. Assessments are by observation of attempts to master new skills. Care is taken not to highlight unsuccessful attempts as children may begin to feel shame; they may learn to doubt their abilities to manage the world on their own terms. Remember, Erikson believes that children who experience too much doubt at this stage will lack confidence in their own abilities throughout life (McGregor and Elliot, 2005; Webster, 2008).

3 to 6 years – initiative versus guilt

Observations by early years practitioners and teachers are compared to early years developmental stages in defined areas of learning and development. A personal profile is maintained in school and nursery and shared with parents. There are no formal comparisons with others and assessments are formative, criteria-referenced and diagnostic. The key idea is that pupils look for positive feedback and encouragement to engage with assessment tasks without any sense of failure. To make sure each pupil has a chance to experience success, practitioners assess in small steps and avoid competitive situations altogether. Assessment is tolerant of mistakes, especially when children are attempting to do something on their own (Yurick et al., 2012).

7 years to puberty – industry versus inferiority

Children confront an increased focus on outcomes, grades and performance as well as more academic, social and athletic competition on all fronts. Children move from pre-operational to concrete-operational thinking, so accept grades as concrete reflections of the actuality of their performance and poor comparative grades are a cause of feelings of inferiority. To encourage industry and avoid feelings of inferiority, pupils are encouraged to set their own achievable goals for the outcomes of assessments and to record their own progress. Teachers regularly praise and reward pupils for making the most progress rather than being the best (Corpus and Lepper, 2007).

Adolescence – identity versus role confusion – and young adulthood – intimacy versus isolation

Not all adolescents will move to formal thinking, and formal thinking may seldom be required at college and university. This means that students can still be successful by using pre-formal or perhaps concrete operational thinking to satisfy their examiners. A resilient sense of identity is based upon successful and meaningful attachments (Chapter 9, 'Attachment and early social experiences'). Adolescents (and those in emerging adulthood) need a lot of realistic feedback about their work and advice on how to improve, from those with whom they have formed robust attachments. When adolescents and young adults perform poorly, teachers and counsellors make sure they understand the consequences for themselves. Most importantly, because learners are 'trying on' roles (Morgan and Stevens, 2008), all those working with young people keep the roles separate from the person by realistically feeding back on performance without criticising the student (Currie et al., 2006; Scheeler et al., 2010).

> **Middle adulthood – generativity versus stagnation**
>
> There are no developmentally appropriate adaptations to the process of assessment for this stage. However, engagement with new learning and new ideas is essential to avoid stagnation, and assessment regimes encourage rather than hinder fresh engagement. Career change or resumption may require new engagement with formal or statutory assessment arrangements, and these might prove to be more difficult hurdles for those in middle adulthood (Bower et al., 2010).

> **Older adulthood – ego integrity versus despair**
>
> It is unlikely that many people will be subject to formal assessment practice at this stage, as learning activity is not usually subject to that kind of scrutiny, but there are examples where older people take up or continue learning activities in the arts, languages, painting and singing in choirs that can sometimes include a competitive aspect (Heuser, 2005; Kim et al., 2013). Those with ego integrity will often 'meet with Triumph and Disaster, And treat those two imposters just the same' (Rudyard Kipling, 'If').

During adolescence, a youngster may become informally established as a class clown, a victim, a bully, sporty, brainy, lazy or 'cool'; sometimes reinforced by formal reporting arrangements which include summative comments about attainment. However, there is a danger that most formal assessment is relatively impersonal (McLaughlin and Simpson, 2007) and summative because of large group sizes and students experiencing many different teachers during the school week (Mays, 2012). Even at college or university, assessment regimes are dominated by individual extended writing tasks and examination 'finals' (Smith and Miller, 2005; Smith, 2012). Perhaps these shortcomings flow from the scale and characteristics of classrooms and schools in many parts of the developed world. Large classes and many different teachers can contribute to problems with managing learning and assessment activities, so let's take a look at a major concern for teachers at all phases of schooling: behaviour management.

Developmentally appropriate behaviour management

Let's begin with a true story: William (age 26) had just taken up a deputy headship at a village primary school. His previous post had been in a secondary school in a local town where he was Head of Maths. It was his first lunchtime and he was on the 'deputy head prowl' to seek out the ne'er-do-wells and other assorted miscreants who can make the lunch hour a challenging time for school staff. In the entrance hall was a particularly attractive display of windmills made by some older children in the school as part of a science topic on gears and pulleys. The sails of many of the windmills rotated beautifully when a handle at the back or the side was turned. Also in the entrance hall was a little lad from the Reception class (4 to 5 years) who was having a fine old time turning the handles and looking inside to see how it worked. 'What the blazes do you think you are doing young man?' William bellowed in his best Head-of-Maths-now-Deputy-Head voice. A terrified face spun around, a lovingly constructed windmill crashed to the floor and the little lad scarpered, only to be found 10 minutes later hiding under the temporary classroom at the back of the school, still crying and inconsolable.

Was this appropriate behaviour management? Was this an act of behaviour management at all? Did the little chap need managing? What should William have done? Many years later when William told this story to a group of mature trainee teachers, one of them argued that the only behaviour here that needed managing was the teacher's, and that the outcomes of the behaviour were a broken windmill, a broken-hearted youngster, a broken relationship and an inauspicious start to a career as a primary school teacher. The 'windmill incident' – more embarrassing for 'William' as time goes by – begs the important question of what behaviours need managing in schools and how is this best done?

To secure robust moral and social development, behaviours and activities need to be managed and the way in which they are best managed depends upon the stage of development. Behaviours that need managing are those concerning both conduct and performance. Conduct issues relate to the way individuals and groups act and react towards others within the school or college community, and the buildings and resources that are the capital of the institution. These issues pertain to moral questions and decisions about what is right and wrong, and to acceptable or unacceptable social behaviour. We can draw on the theoretical ideas of Jean Piaget, Lawrence Kohlberg and Erik Erikson to help us understand the behaviour management needs of children at different stages in their development. Clearly, disruptive, damaging or violent behaviour in schools is viewed as unacceptable behaviour and is subject to a range of sanctions that are usually well rehearsed and understood (West et al., 2011) but there is a good deal of disagreement about what sanctions are appropriate and how unacceptable behaviour should be dealt with (Goodman, 2006).

Performance relates to the behaviour of individuals and how effectively they are engaging with the learning activities provided by the school in order to make their expected academic progress. Absorbed engagement with developmentally appropriate learning activities is considered successful activity provoked by intrinsic incentives or rewards (pleasant feelings and an improvement to self-image), or extrinsic incentives or rewards. Lack of engagement with learning activities can be deemed unsuccessful activity and so the intrinsic incentives are not satisfied and the extrinsic rewards are withheld. Successful performance behaviour is often rewarded and/or has its own rewards; unsuccessful performance behaviour is usually acknowledged, then new targets are set to take a 'first step to success' (Seeley et al., 2009). Of course, social competence and successful learning are associated, particularly for children with special educational needs (Wight and Chapparo, 2008).

STOP AND THINK

Going further

Analyse and discuss with some fellow students the implications of the two statements: 'Clearly, disruptive, damaging or violent behaviour in schools is viewed as unacceptable behaviour and is subject to a range of sanctions that are usually well rehearsed and understood' and 'Successful performance behaviour is often rewarded and/or has its own rewards; unsuccessful performance behaviour is usually acknowledged, then new targets are set to take a "first step to success"'.

This difference between conduct and performance is important in knowing how teachers and others should attempt to apply developmentally appropriate behaviour management. The little boy exploring the windmills was not engaged in bad behaviour, but was probably engaged in successful learning behaviour provoked by curiosity. This was successful behaviour 'rewarded' by being shouted at by a young teacher with a regrettable lack of confidence and understanding. Playing with the windmills was not bad behaviour and no sanction or punishment should have applied at all. He was getting his own reward by satisfying his curiosity and William could have further rewarded him by praising him and answering some of his questions – giving the little chap some 'teacher-time' would have been reward enough.

The first four stages of psychologist Lawrence Kohlberg's 'Six Stages of Moral Development' apply here and included in Table 14.3 is information about the application of developmental principles to classroom and school behaviour management practices in relation to each of the stages. Kohlberg allied a child's cognitive capacity (explored in Chapter 11, 'Development of self-concept and gender Identity') with the capacity for moral reasoning, and was more concerned with reasoning than

How best to manage bad classroom behaviour is the subject of much debate.
Source: Pearson Education Ltd/Shutterstock.com/racorn

Table 14.3 Kohlberg's six stages of moral development and developmentally appropriate behaviour management in relation to conduct.

	Level 1 Pre-conventional morality – to age 10	
Stage and title	**Kohlberg's description**	**How effective teachers manage behaviour**
Stage 1 Punishment-avoidance and obedience	Children will make moral decisions purely on the basis of self-interest. They will disobey rules if they think they can do so without getting caught.	Set clear rules about what is not acceptable behaviour (Woods, 2008). Children at this stage generally submit to authority so a reprimand will generally be accepted and all that is needed (Infantino and Little, 2005). Children obey rules to avoid being punished and expect their own and others' unacceptable behaviour to be punished (Kuhn et al., 2014).
Stage 2 Exchange of favours	Children recognise that others have needs, but prioritise their needs over those of others.	Teachers can agree with children a range of rewards and sanctions that would apply in certain circumstances (Roth et al., 2011). Children now seek rewards for their actions because they believe they should behave well for their own gains (Berg et al., 2013). Children also attempt to engage in negotiation, so a school-age child might be heard to say, 'I will be good if I can watch the TV programme afterwards' (Roth et al., 2011). Amongst other aspects of practice, effective teachers hold hard to the idea that good behaviour is the expected norm and will challenge unacceptable behaviour (Olive and Liu, 2005; Duncan-Andrade, 2007).
	Level 2 Conventional morality	
Stage 3 Good boy/good girl	Young people make decisions on the basis of what will please others and are very concerned to keep friends.	Teachers emphasise the effect of bad behaviour on others including themselves. Being reprimanded includes being faced with the effects and outcomes of behaviour, and sanctions include removal from the social setting in which the behaviour took place for the benefit of all (Gomes et al., 2011). This is where the 'cool-off space' is important and the giving of options to emphasise that consequences are fully understood (Elias and Schwab, 2006).
Stage 4 Law and order	Young people look to society as a whole for guidelines about moral decisions. They think of rules as absolute, inflexible and unchangeable.	What is considered unacceptable in the school or college is congruent with, and is understood by students in similar terms to, laws and sanctions found in wider society (Apel et al., 2009). Therefore, violent, abusive or racist activity is considered the same in school as out of school. Unlawful acts such as the selling of drugs andr stealing are dealt with by involving community support officers and the police service (Lyle and Hendley, 2007). Challenging behaviour is sometimes related to poor mental health and schools are often seen as the optimum setting to deliver inter-agency interventions (Spratt et al., 2006).
	Level 3 Post-conventional morality	
Stage 5 Social contract	Recognises that rules are social constructions – agreements that can be changed or ignored when necessary.	Does not readily apply in school and college settings.
Stage 6 Universal ethical principle	Adheres to a small number of universal abstract principles that transcend specific rules. Answers only to the inner conscience.	Does not readily apply in school and college settings.

children's understanding of right and wrong (Kohlberg, 1969). His research and theory about moral reasoning are explored fully in Chapter 13.

> **STOP AND THINK**
>
> **Reflection**
>
> - Is there anything here that helps us to understand how best to deal with and help Edward (the subject of the opening example in this chapter)? It may be worth flicking back and re-reading the sections dealing with his behaviour and engagement with learning tasks.
> - Do Kohlberg's stages and the commentary provided in Table 14.3 apply to Edward at all (remember he is 8) and will they ever apply? For example, can Edward empathise?
> - When do children develop the ability to empathise and how does this happen? (You may want to check back to Chapter 8, 'Theory of mind'.)

Table 14.3 seeks to highlight ways that teachers and counsellors work with children and young people which take account of many of the themes of development that have been presented in Section III of this book (Chapters 9–13). In an ideal world, there would not be any need for teachers to reprimand children, or for schools to use sanctions to modify the behaviour of the students, but sadly this is not the case. Indeed, some commentators reported at the start of this century that schools and colleges were increasingly challenged by the behaviour of some of their pupils and students (e.g. Derrington, 2005; Potts, 2006). One of the explanations for this trend was that large secondary schools found it increasingly difficult to offer developmentally appropriate experiences for their students (Newman, 2008). It is worth noting that any consensus that behaviour and discipline in schools worsened during the first decade of this century was considered by popular commentators to be a myth (e.g. Elliott, 2009); a view supported by empirical evidence from more authoritative sources (e.g. Wilkins et al., 2010). Our final section will now consider what is meant by developmentally appropriate schooling and schools. In the UK we seldom talk about developmentally appropriate provision, but in some northern European countries, creating developmentally appropriate schools is a national and political aspiration (Wetz, 2009). Denmark is one such country whose current provision makes a marked contrast with that of many other European countries, including the UK.

Developmentally appropriate schools

Learning from the Danish educational system

In search of developmentally appropriate schools, the author travelled to Denmark and spent a week visiting local schools, lecturing, questioning and having discussions in a teachers' training college in Skarup. The following account looks at the way that the Danish authorities have attempted to engage with the national aspiration for developmentally appropriate schools and includes a comparative commentary on equivalent UK provision, drawing on ideas that have emerged in this chapter.

An important review of schooling in Denmark arose out of a national 'conversation' in the early 1990s. The review's findings were enacted in an education Act (the Folkeskole Act of 1994) which gives emphasis to a national shared responsibility for the education and wellbeing of its young people. In England, the link between education and children's wellbeing was one adopted in 2002 in response to the tragic case of Victoria Climbie enshrined in the *Every Child Matters* programme (search for: https://www.education.gov.uk/consultations/downloadableDocs/EveryChildMatters.pdf). So far, it has been consistently reported that Every Child Matters seems to have had little effect upon the structure of schooling and schools or the nature of schooling in England (Payne, 2007; George and Clay, 2008; Mead, 2011).

In Denmark, the Folkeskole Act endorsed and required the design of a 12-year inclusive school experience for all children, with a commitment to a curriculum built on ideas of social relevance in a variety of schools which should be part of and accountable to the local community. Grouping children by ability was made unlawful. All schools are well resourced and have status. In contrast, the political, professional and popular discourse in the UK is about 'failing schools' (Thompson, 2011; Blaire, 2012; Stein, 2012). Different levels of resourcing are provided in private and state schools, and between areas where parents and local organisations (e.g. churches and businesses) contribute to school funds in formal and informal ways (Gillard, 2008). In impoverished underperforming schools, rolls (the headcount of pupils attending) fall as parents try to move their children into other schools reported or thought of as being better (Choi-wa, 2009; Thompson, 2011) or move house to a different area to 'win' places at 'good' schools during the transition from primary to secondary schooling (Serbin et al., 2013).

In Denmark, there are no transition difficulties, as primary and secondary provision is integrated into one Folkeskole (people's school) for all children aged from 6 to 16, with no more than 500 students in a school. In practice this means a two-form entry throughout (i.e. there are two classes of each age group). There are nine years of compulsory education with an optional additional year at age 16; children are divided into groups by age, but not by ability; and progression from one year to the next is automatic.

Most UK primary schools are one- or two-form entry, but after transition pupils enter secondary school of typically 1000 pupils or more. Indeed there are a growing number of super-sized schools of pupil rolls between 1500 and 3000 (Gillard, 2008; Hampton, 2014). The contrast between primary and secondary schooling is stark and transfer can be a significant ordeal for children (Mellor and Delamont, 2011), many of whom make negative progression in educational attainment and social development (Gottfredson and DiPietro, 2011).

Teaching practice throughout Danish schools is based on group work and learning together, which leads to ways of working required for the completion of a significant final-year project. Assessment is continuous and formative, and teachers are required not to give their students marks until they are 14 years of age. School status is linked not to public or statutory examination results, but to school ambience, the wellbeing of pupils, the quality of attachment relationships between teachers and pupils and the quality of learning experiences.

Much teaching practice at UK secondary schools and elsewhere in Europe is didactic (Kelemen, 2013; Meyer, 2007) and 'skewed' by teaching to the statutory tests and public examinations taken in Britain at 16 and 18 years (Greatorex and Malacova, 2006).

Assessments are generally summative and even from the first years of schooling form the basis for reports to parents which include attainment grades relative to other pupils of the same age (Robinson and Harris, 2013).

In Denmark, the class group remains the same throughout so that students have continuity with both their subject teachers (who have a four-year training programme in child development and are expected to teach three or four subjects) and their class group. The key person for all students is the *Klasslaerer* (class teacher or tutor), who stays with the group all the way, providing a consistent attachment for pupils (and families) through school to young adulthood. In the UK, the class teacher or form tutor usually changes every year in both primary and secondary schools. Although the primary school class teacher will teach his class for almost the whole curriculum (Eaude, 2014), at secondary school the form tutor may not teach her form for any subject (Tucker, 2013; Reid, 2006) and it is not out of the ordinary for teenagers to be taught by 11 or 12 different teachers in a week and for a teacher to teach 400 different pupils in a week (Wetz, 2009).

The foregoing comparative descriptions suggest that Danish folkeskoles represent developmentally appropriate schools, capable of delivering developmentally appropriate teaching and learning experiences, and appropriate programmes of study. These schools in Denmark contrast sharply with current provision in secondary schooling in the UK and other parts of Europe, where the application of developmental psychology to education is far less obvious. There are now increasingly urgent and powerful calls for this matter to be addressed by policymakers in the rest of Europe, and for the development of small 'different' secondary schools, particularly in areas of social and economic deprivation (Tasker, 2008; Corbett, 2013).

Think about the ideas of developmentally appropriate provision, and the learning and developmental theories we have explored. What binds all of this together? What are the connections you can make between theory and practice; between developmental psychology and educational provision; between principles in action and reacting to personal and profound need? We learn by making these kinds of connection. What are the connections between this chapter and Chapters 15, 16 and 17 on bullying, atypical development and ADHD?

STOP AND THINK

Going further

Responses to the case study – Edward

The same case study notes from the beginning of the chapter were sent to a number of professionals working within the children's workforce who were asked for their response, including any ideas about what could be done. We have provided just a taste of their responses here:

'He would be placed in a school for children with special needs, where pupils learn to know other pupils with different kinds of problems and learn to deal with other pupils' problems as well as with their own.'

(Lisbeth Jonsson, School Teacher, `Sotenäs Kompetenscentrum, Kungshamn, Sweden)

'This should not be a personal challenge for an individual teacher which results in a sense of failure but one where properly supported and resourced teaching teams address children's diagnosed learning and emotional needs in a carefully structured programme.'

(James Wetz, Secondary School Headteacher, Visiting Fellow, Bristol University)

'Try to arrange things so they have the maximum contact with areas of the curriculum that they enjoy, without skewing things too far away from the statutory obligations. If they are "statemented", I think they can be taught with less regard for the National Curriculum.'

(Michael Nicholson, Senior Lecturer in Education, University of the West of England)

'Conversations with Edward should be focused on solutions rather than analysing what has gone wrong – not productive. When children mimic inappropriate behaviours it is usually an indication that boundaries are not secure or clear for them.'

(Marie Walker, Lead Behaviour Support Teacher, Gloucestershire and Forest Pupil Referral Service)

During this chapter you have reflected on Edward's experience of school and considered whether there are ways in which the application of developmental psychology can shed some light on what troubles him, and what practically can be done to help him.

- how do these professionals' responses compare to your own judgements?
- Can you recognise the developmental or educational theories which underpin the different responses above?

SUMMARY

The chapter contains an analysis and evaluation of the extent to which the main theories of developmental psychology and learning have been applied in schools, colleges and universities, and has provided an assessment of the likely effectiveness of applying differing perspectives of educational theorists in relation to key themes of teaching and learning. Specifically, consideration was given to Urie Bronfenbrenner's mapping of the many interacting social contexts that affect development in his bio-ecological model of development (e.g. those which influence Edward). The model does not show how socio-cultural influences change over time. However, Jean Piaget framed one of the most influential age-related stage models of cognitive development.

His stage model, which is the most commonly applied set of theories in early years settings and schools, forms part of the 'nature versus nurture' debate. Critics complain that Piaget ignored young children's inborn cognitive architecture and that what happens to us is what really matters.

Robbie Case's information-processing theory argues that the development of working memory is a key cognitive development for learning, but, like Piaget's theory, it is criticised for giving too little emphasis to social and cultural influences. However, Lev Vygotsky emphasised the social construction of knowledge through interaction with more knowledgeable others. Ideas of the importance of the teachers, language development and cooperative learning provided the basis for a top ten of applications of Vygotsky's ideas. Critics claim that Vygotsky gave too little emphasis to the cognitive functioning of the brain and the Cutting Edge box provided information about recent attempts to understand what is happening in the brain at various important stages of learning.

The second part of the chapter built on ideas of how educational systems and pedagogy can be enhanced by adopting developmentally appropriate approaches. Five themes of 'developmentally appropriate provision' were explored. These comprised: curricula; teaching; learning and assessment activities; behaviour management; and the structure, size and organisation of schools. Observations of current practice evidenced in the research literature showed how effective teaching can be enhanced when principles of developmental psychology (e.g. information-processing models which encourage teachers to provide timely and high-quality formative assessment feedback) are used to enhance provision and determine high-quality learning experiences for all age groups.

The example of Edward and his brother Richard was used to construct an argument about what to do for learners with special needs which is rooted in a thorough-going knowledge of psycho-social development. Respondents and others who have commented, many at length, about the opening example of this chapter are unanimous in this respect: the case study represents a problem that the teacher cannot solve alone, particularly as the problems are generated in life outside school. The boys need to be assessed thoroughly by a specialist in developmental and educational psychology. There can be no better definition or summary of the need for the application of developmental psychology in education.

REVIEW QUESTIONS

1. Outline two of the main developmental theories that have impacted on classroom practice in Britain during the last 40 years. Which has been more influential, and why?
2. What is meant by developmentally appropriate provision in schools and colleges? Give examples from your own experience and from your wider reading, and critically evaluate its effectiveness.
3. Discuss some of the ways in which cognitive development and learning theories are connected.
4. Which learning theory can best inform the practice of teaching and support developmentally appropriate learning activities? Justify your answer with reference to educational practice that you have experienced, and from your wider reading.
5. Are assessment practices at your own institution developmentally appropriate? Justify your answer with reference to theory, research and educational practice.
6. Describe the experience of learners attending schools which reflect the principles of developmentally appropriate provision. Compare and contrast the experience of learners at such schools with that of learners at other schools.

RECOMMENDED READING

To find out what might characterise the connection between cognitive development and emotional development see:

Schwenck, C., Göhle, B., Hauf, J., Warnke, A., Freitag, C., & Schneider, W. (2014) Cognitive and emotional empathy in typically developing children: The influence of age, gender, and intelligence, *European Journal of Developmental Psychology*, 11 (1), 63–76.

For a full description and explanation of learning and teaching concepts, read Chapter 8 in:

Woolfolk, A., Hughes, M., & Walkup, V. (2013). *Psychology in Education* (2nd Ed.). Harlow: Pearson.

An important presentation of Robbie Case's historic research (and one to browse on your next trip to the library) is:

Case, R., & Okamoto, Y. (1996). *the role of Central Conceptual Structures in the Development of Children's thought*. Chicago, IL: University of Chicago Press.

One of the most useful sources for conceptualising how cognitive processes can inform teaching, learning and assessment, and which, as the title suggests, is a most useful revision of work by leading educational psychologist Benjamin Bloom, is:

Anderson, L. W., Krathwohl, D. R., Airasian, P. W., Cruikshank, K. A., Mayer, R. E., Pintrich, P. R., Raths, J., & Wittrock, M. C. (Eds.) (2001). *A Taxonomy for Learning, Teaching and Assessing: A Revision of Bloom's Taxonomy of Educational Objectives*. Boston, MA: Allyn & Bacon.

RECOMMENDED WEBSITES

For a comprehensive summary of over 50 theories of learning, see the website of educational psychologist, Dr Greg Kearsley:

http://tip.psychology.org/theories.html

If you disagree with his 'take' on any of the theories or find the website useful, why not email him at: **gkearsley@sprynet.com**

For helpful advice on the application of developmental psychology in classroom management, explore the 'behaviour 2 learn' website (formerly behaviour4learning). The site provides 'practical resources and information for trainee teachers, newly qualified teachers and those in the early phase of their career development. The materials . . . are drawn from a variety of sources, but each item has been carefully selected in order that it helps to inform and enhance the key idea that pupil behaviour is linked to the learning they experience':

http://www.behaviour2learn.co.uk/about

Watch the video (or search for 'Teaching with Bayley' – a series of videos by psychologist John Bayley) on how the application of developmental and behavioural psychology in challenging situations can prove to be very successful:

http://www.teachers.tv/videos/attention-seekers

Reference is made in this chapter to the Every Child Matters agenda. What is 'Every Child Matters' and where did it come from? What is the envisioned impact in educational and social service contexts? Explore the HM Government website at:

https://www.education.gov.uk/consultations/downloadableDocs/EveryChildMatters.pdf

One of the most important roles in applying developmental psychology in education is that of the 'educational psychologist'. 'Ed psychs' are responsible for understanding children's learning, emotional and behavioural difficulties, testing and diagnosis, developing learning plans and designing interventions. Find out more about the role at:

http://www.educational-psychologist.co.uk/roleofep.htm

or read:

Kelly, B., Woolfson, L. & Boyle, J. (2008). *frameworks for practice in educational psychology: a textbook for trainees and practitioners*. London: Jessica Kingsley.

Chapter 15
Understanding bullying

Elizabeth Nixon and Suzanne Guerin

Learning outcomes

After reading this chapter, and with further recommended reading, you should be able to:

1. Explain the issues in defining and investigating 'bullying' and reflect on different definitions of the behaviour.
2. Describe prevalence rates of bullying, gender-related trends in prevalence rates and the nature of involvement in bullying.
3. Discuss the development of bullying behaviour across early and middle childhood, and adolescence.
4. Identify the key features associated with cyberbullying and understand the distinctions between traditional forms of bullying and cyberbullying.
5. Critically evaluate key theoretical perspectives on bullying.
6. Compare the different types of intervention that have been developed to address the issue of bullying, and reflect on issues relating to their effectiveness.

Bullying in the press

'Merseyside schoolchildren as young as nine bullying each other on an unprecedented scale'

Liverpool Echo, 2 March 2014

'Campaign aims to combat bullying'

Marlborough Express (New Zealand), 4 March 2014

'Cyberbullying poses greater risk of suicide among young people, study suggests'

Globe and Mail (Canada), 11 March 2014

'District struggles to develop policy for handling bullying'

Palo Alto Online (California, USA), 13 March 2014

These newspaper headlines all appeared in the press within two weeks of each other in early 2014. Bullying is often discussed in the media, and stories can include reports of research studies or policy changes as well as stories of individual young people and their experiences of bullying. As we can see from the headlines, the specific issues being considered here reflect some of the challenges of responding to these behaviours effectively. But what types of message do these reports give us about bullying?

The article in the *Liverpool Echo* reports the common concern that increased access to technology, including the internet and smart phones, has had a significant impact on younger children's involvement in cyberbullying. The report also highlights the demand for support among young people, with the NSPCC reporting that in 2013 it supported over 300 young people who had experienced bullying online. This links to the report from the Canadian *Globe and Mail*, which reflects on the findings from recent research, published in the journal *Pediatrics*, in which 34 studies on the link between bullying and suicide were reviewed. The review article presents the contrasting views: 1) that suicide is a direct result of bullying or 2) that suicide is associated with pre-existing mental health issues. The authors of the research review stress the contribution of involvement in bullying as a risk factor for suicide, with cyberbullying being associated with a higher risk. The report on this research in the *Globe and Mail* includes comments from Debra Pepler, an international expert on bullying who has been researching this area since the 1990s. Pepler suggests that cyberbullying is a higher risk factor for suicide due to its public nature and potential intensity. Together, these media reports highlight the interest in this form of bullying and, given the interest in this behaviour, we will return to the topic of cyberbullying later in this chapter.

The other two media reports reflect another aspect of bullying that is central to the current chapter: strategies and programmes designed to tackle bullying and cyberbullying. The report from the *Marlborough Express* in New Zealand describes a local campaign that is targeting attitudes towards bullying, and particularly beliefs that bullying is acceptable. The campaign targets those younger than 19 years of age and focuses on getting young people involved in bullying prevention. In comparison the report from ▶

▶ California (*Palo Alto Online*) presents some of the challenges in tackling bullying. Anti-bullying policies play a key role in prevention and intervention but, as this report highlights, bringing all key stakeholders together to agree the content of policies can be difficult. A particular challenge in this setting relates to the fact that certain bullying behaviours are illegal under legislation relating to minority groups, but other bullying behaviours are not addressed within a legal framework. However, a more telling point in this report is the lack of reference to the involvement of young people in drafting the policy. Later in this chapter we will discuss the range of prevention and intervention strategies that have been developed to address the problem of bullying, including those that actively involve young people.

Introduction

Bullying is an important social issue that affects the lives of countless children and young people around the world. It is sometimes said that the exploitation of the weak by the strong is a long-standing feature of how nature works (Rigby, 2002). Some even argue that bullying can be understood as an expression of an evolutionary drive to dominate others socially in order to acquire additional resources or improve one's social standing (Volk et al., 2012). Notwithstanding these ideas about the possible evolutionary basis of bullying behaviours, being the victim or target of bullying is a grim daily reality that undermines children's healthy development. There appears to be a reliable relationship between being involved in bullying and impaired physical and mental health – these children tend to be unhappy and lonely and have low self-esteem, and to display various forms of psychological distress, including anxiety, depression and high levels of social dysfunction compared to children who are not involved in bullying (Juvonen and Graham, 2014). The negative effects of bullying are also not restricted to short-term effects. Children who are involved in bullying as victims and perpetrators are more likely to experience and display aggressive and violent behaviour later in life, even after controlling for other childhood risk factors (Ttofi et al., 2012).

There is little doubt that there is heightened awareness nowadays about bullying in the media, among parents, educators and policy-makers, although this may not necessarily reflect radical shifts in the prevalence of bullying. The first systematic research on the topic of school bullying was the pioneering work of Dan Olweus in Sweden and Norway in the early 1970s. Since that time, there has been a proliferation of research into the issue, some of which we will look at in this chapter. What has become clear is that bullying is a complex social process that can have extremely damaging consequences for both bullies and their victims. In this chapter, we consider how the problem of bullying is conceptualised and understood, and examine what can be done to reduce the scale and impact of the problem.

What is bullying?

In conducting research on any topic it is important to have a clear definition of the target behaviour(s). This is essential both to focus the research and to ensure that the potential for learning is maximised. In this section, we will consider the question: what is bullying? Different definitions of bullying and how they have evolved over time will be considered. In addition, we will explore the small body of research that has examined what bullying means to children and young people.

> **Definition**
>
> Bullying: an interaction which is intended to and does cause harm to a person who is seen as being less powerful than the perpetrator.

In the UK, the Department for Education (DfE) defines bullying as 'behaviour by an individual or group, repeated over time, that intentionally hurts another individual or group either physically or emotionally' (Department for Education, 2014a, p. 6). It is also stated that 'Bullying can take many forms (for instance, cyber-bullying via text messages or the internet), and is often motivated by prejudice against particular groups' (p. 6). This is an important definition as it forms the basis for the UK government's policy position on bullying in school. However, when we look at the different definitions of bullying that have been presented in research and policy documents, it is clear that the definition of bullying has changed significantly over the course of the last 20 years of research.

Early attempts at defining bullying

One area of change relates to the perpetrators of bullying behaviour, with early formulations focusing more on the group's rather than the individual's activities. For example, Lagerspetz et al. (1982) stressed the collective or group nature of bullying behaviours, while Erling Roland's (1989) definition included behaviours that were carried out by individuals or groups. Interestingly, Roland's formulation was one of the first to stress the power imbalance between bullies and victims, describing the victim of bullying as 'an individual who is not able to defend himself' (p. 21). David Lane (1989) also reported on changes in the types of behaviour that are cited in definitions, highlighting the move from more concrete behaviours such as physical and verbal aggression to more psychological forms such as exclusion.

A comprehensive summary of the criteria common to most definitions of bullying was provided by David Farrington, a forensic psychologist, whose research has explored the full range of human aggressive behaviour, from bullying to serious criminality. He defined bullying as:

> physical, verbal, or psychological attack or intimidation that is intended to cause fear, distress, or harm to the victim; an imbalance of power, with the more powerful child oppressing the less powerful one; absence of provocation by the victim; and repeated incidents between the same children over a prolonged period
>
> (Farrington, 1993, p. 384)

This definition summarises what are generally accepted to be the key elements of bullying behaviour, and the influence of these criteria can be clearly seen in the definition applied by the DfE mentioned above.

STOP AND THINK

Reflection

Take a few minutes and think about this definition of bullying. Does it reflect your own views of what bullying is? Imagine yourself in a school playground trying to establish whether or not an incident between two children constitutes bullying.

- What questions do you need to ask?
- Whose views are important to obtain?
- What might influence your ability to determine the true nature of the incident?

While there is general agreement among researchers about the definition of bullying, when we look at research which has asked children, young people and adults for their definitions of bullying, a more complicated picture emerges. As children and young people are the perpetrators, victims and witnesses of school bullying, it is important to consider how they conceptualise the behaviour. A number of studies have specifically explored these definitions and they have shown that children and young people have quite well-developed definitions of bullying (Arora, 1996).

Early conceptualisations of bullying described the behaviour as direct and physical.
Source: Pearson Education Ltd/Tudor Photography

Children and young people's definitions

One of the patterns that has emerged clearly from the research looking at children and young people's definitions of bullying is the range of behaviours that are incorporated. This is a key area of agreement between children's and researchers' definitions. One of the most important studies in this area was led by Peter Smith, and was coordinated across 14 countries (Smith et al., 2002). This study used cartoons of different behaviours to explore the views of over 1200 children and young people aged 8 and 14 years. The data showed that children distinguished among physical, verbal and psychological forms of bullying, and distinguished these from other behaviours. This study also highlighted age differences, which we will return to below.

However, just as there are areas of agreement, this is not consistent across all of the criteria highlighted by David Farrington above. Interestingly, studies where children are asked about their views using more open-ended methods such as interviews and focus groups (group-based interviews) often produce different results. One of the first interview studies of children's and young people's definitions of bullying was conducted by Kirsten Madsen (1996), who looked at groups of children and adults aged 5–6 years, 9–10 years, 15–16 years, and 18–29 years. All the groups were interviewed about their perceptions and definitions of bullying. Madsen found that children and young people rarely mentioned repetition (3%), intention (5%) or provocation (7.5%) as defining features of bullying. Another study, which involved interviews with 168 Irish 11- and 12-year-olds, also supported these findings (Guerin and Hennessy, 2002).

Developmental changes in definitions

In addition to looking at children's definitions of bullying, a number of key studies have considered developmental patterns in definitions from childhood to adulthood. Smith and Levan (1995) found that 6-year-olds were not able to distinguish between fighting and bullying, and Smith et al.'s (2002) 14-country study found that 8-year-olds were able to contrast aggressive and non-aggressive scenarios, but were not able to distinguish among the different forms of bullying. Claire Monks and Peter Smith (2006) later showed that 4- to 8-year-olds differentiated between aggressive and non-aggressive acts while adolescents and adults had a more sophisticated understanding of bullying, considering imbalance of power and repetition of behaviour in their definitions. Other research comparing children's, parents', teachers' and researchers' views supports the argument that differences exist between adult and child definitions, particularly around the nature of bullying as intentional (Smorti et al., 2003; Naylor et al., 2006). Thus, it is important to take on board the child's view, given the extent to which teachers (and indeed other adults) may not be aware of the level of bullying in a school.

The implications of a lack of consensus in definition

Given that there are areas of both agreement and disagreement between the individuals who are the victims, perpetrators and witnesses of bullying, and the experts whose work informs practice in tackling the behaviour, it is important to ask: what are the implications of disagreement? The most important implication relates to the way in which we tackle bullying. We discuss interventions later in this chapter, but it is fair to say that approaches where adults and children work together with a common understanding of what bullying is may have greater potential to succeed than approaches involving either group's perspective alone. If the two groups differ in their views of the behaviour that is supposed to be targeted, they may find themselves working at cross-purposes. As it is adults who act to implement interventions in schools, we must be careful that we do not address only those behaviours that fit with adult definitions.

While we began this section by stressing the importance of having a clear definition of target behaviours for the purpose of research (and indeed practice), it seems that this is not something that exists in bullying research. Throughout this book, you have come across other areas of research where developmental psychologists have different conceptualisations of certain constructs (think back to Chapter 6, Memory and Intelligence, for example, where different ideas about intelligence are discussed; or Chapter 10, Childhood Temperament and Behavioural Development, where different ideas about temperament are considered). However, it could be that it is more important to recognise the views of different groups than to attempt to decide who is right! This issue

CUTTING EDGE

Bullying in cyberworld

Despite the significant amount of research conducted on the nature of bullying, our awareness of the constellation of behaviours that make up this concept continues to develop. One of the most recent forms of the behaviour to be considered is cyberbullying.

While not as developed as the body of research on traditional bullying, cyberbullying research has developed significantly in recent years. As a result, a number of definitions have been proposed. For example, Kowalski et al. (2008) define it as 'bullying through email, instant messaging, in a chat room, on a website or gaming site, or through digital messages or images sent to a cellular phone' (p. 1), while Peter Smith and colleagues describe this subset of behaviour as 'an aggressive, intentional act, carried out by a group or individual, using electronic forms of contact, repeatedly and over time against a victim who cannot easily defend him or herself' (2008a, p. 376). Looking at these two definitions, we can see that while the first focuses more on the distinct behaviours that might be classified under this term, the second definition draws more on the criteria discussed in general definitions: that is, repetition, intention and an imbalance of power. An interesting paper published in 2012 has examined this pattern by exploring the views of adolescents in six European countries on definitions of cyberbullying. Menesini and colleagues (2012) examined views concerning three dimensions related to traditional bullying (intentional harm, repetition and power) and two dimensions relating to cyberbullying (anonymity and public versus private action). They concluded from their analysis of responses from 2257 young people that the imbalance of power was a clear defining dimension, followed by intention to harm and anonymity, highlighting the clear links to traditional bullying definitions.

As with traditional definitions of bullying above, it is important to ask how young people themselves define cyberbullying. A paper by Vanderbosch and Van Cleemput (2008) at the University of Antwerp reports the findings of a study that explored the views of a large sample of Belgian adolescents. Focus groups were used to explore the young people's views of cyberbullying. Many aspects of this group's definition were comparable to existing views, including intentionality and repeated occurrence. However, in one of the key findings they highlighted that the term 'cyberbullying' is aligned more with internet-based behaviours, rather than the broader forms of electronic media-based interactions described by Kowalski and colleagues above. Despite this finding, the term 'cyberbullying' is generally taken to refer to a broad range of electronic media-based behaviours, and it is this definition that will be applied in this chapter.

> **Definition**
>
> Traditional bullying: forms of bullying behaviour that involve physical, verbal or psychological attacks without the use of electronic media.

is further complicated by historical changes in definitions of bullying. We touched on this earlier but now turn to an example of how our understanding of bullying continues to change, as interest in cyberbullying has grown.

> **Definition**
>
> Cyberbullying: forms of bullying behaviour that use electronic media such as the internet, mobile phones, etc.

Involvement in bullying

A great number of studies have been conducted to explore how commonly bullying occurs (its prevalence) and the nature of children's involvement in bullying. These studies have generally presented participants with a definition of bullying and asked them to report their involvement based on that definition. However, as we have seen in the previous section, this may be problematic if bullying means something different

Cyberbullying is a relatively new form of bullying.
Source: Pearson Education Ltd/123RF.com/Ion Chiosea

to children than it does to adults or researchers. It is important to bear in mind that the majority of studies using researchers' definitions may not represent the extent and nature of bullying as it is experienced and perceived by children themselves.

Who is involved in bullying?

When we think about the people involved in bullying, what type of people do we think about? Many people might hold the stereotypes of the quiet, shy and academically orientated victim and the popular, physically developed and perhaps less academically orientated bully. However, looking at what we know about the types of children who are involved in these behaviours, the reality is more complex. Later in this chapter, we will consider the way in which children can be involved in bullying both directly and indirectly (as part of the group process); however, for now let us consider the characteristics of the groups most directly involved in the behaviour: bullies, victims and bully/victims.

Children and young people who bully others are generally referred to as bullies or perpetrators, while those who are bullied or victimised are generally referred to as victims. The term 'bully/victim' is used to refer to individuals who are involved both as bullies and victims. There has been a large body of literature on the characteristics of these groups, and studies have considered both personal characteristics (e.g. self-esteem) and family characteristics. Table 15.1 highlights just some of the patterns that have been identified.

One of the key challenges in this area is the extent to which findings from individual research studies might contradict each other. For example, in discussing patterns of self-esteem among children involved in bullying, O'Moore and Kirkham (2001) highlight some of the different patterns identified in research. However, reviewing the findings it appears that the most consistent pattern is that all of those involved in bullying have lower levels of self-esteem than those not involved in bullying while, within the participant group, bully/victims seem to show the lowest levels of self-esteem.

In relation to features of the family, the general pattern is that the families of bullies and bully/victims appear to show more conflict and less cohesion then families of victims and children not involved in bullying. However, a study by Stevens et al. (2002) highlighted an interesting pattern. While ratings of family functioning by children showed differences across the groups as highlighted in the table, ratings given by parents showed no differences.

So how do we draw a clear conclusion from this literature? On a simplistic level, there is evidence to suggest that children and young people who are involved in bullying show different patterns of personal and family functioning when compared to non-involved children and to each other. However, on a more intricate level, there is a need to consider whether there are causal relationships in these patterns. It is unclear whether participation in or exposure to bullying behaviour is caused by these factors, whether these factors are themselves the result of bullying or whether some common third factor is the cause. As many students know, establishing causation in human behaviour research is a major challenge (see Chapter 3, 'Research methods').

Definition

Bully/victims: children and young people who engage in bullying others and are bullied themselves.

Table 15.1 Key characteristics of different groups involved in bullying as identified by research.

Group	Personal characteristics	Family characteristics
Victims	Higher anxiety than children not involved.	More cohesion than bullies' families (Stevens et al., 2002).
	Higher depression and more health problems than those not involved and bullies (Kowalski and Limber, 2013).	High levels of conflict (Baldry and Farrington, 2000).
		Less authoritative parenting (Smith and Myron-Wilson, 1998).
Bullies	Lower self-esteem than children not involved (Kowalski and Limber, 2013).	Families show less cohesion (Bowers et al., 1992).
	Higher levels of emotional dysregulation than children not involved (Bettencourt et al., 2013).	Low maternal and paternal involvement (Flouri and Buchanan, 2003).
		More authoritarian parenting (Baldry and Farrington, 2000) and lack of supervision (Holt et al., 2009).
		More perceived family conflict (Stevens et al., 2002).
Bully/victims	Higher anxiety and depression than children not involved and bullies.	Similar levels of perceived family conflict to bullies (Stevens et al., 2002).
	Lower self-esteem than victims and those not involved.	Less warm and more overprotective parents in comparison with parents of uninvolved youth (Schwartz et al., 1997).
	More health problems than those not involved (Kowalski and Limber, 2013).	
	Higher levels of emotional dysregulation than children not involved (Bettencourt et al., 2013).	

Interestingly, very few studies have attempted to reflect on this issue from a qualitative perspective. While some qualitative studies ask children about their views of bullying generally, very few have asked children about their own experience of being involved. It is understandable that the challenges of doing this ethically might prevent a researcher from pursuing this topic. However, a small number of studies have looked at children's experiences in this way. Gamliel et al. (2003) report a study of six young American students, one of whom was identified as a bully, while Mishna (2004) focuses on the views of victims only, but does also explore parents' and teachers' views. There is no doubt that there are additional insights to be gained from talking to children about their experiences of being bullied and their own reasons for participating in bullying. However, this continues to be a gap in the existing literature. In a later study by Sawyer, Mishna and colleagues, 20 parents whose children had been the victims of bullying were interviewed (Sawyer et al., 2011). The findings showed that some parents found it difficult to identify specific incidents as bullying, particularly when the behaviours occurred among groups of friends. Also, some parents thought that bullying was a normal part of growing up, and that physical forms of bullying were more serious than other forms of bullying.

STOP AND THINK

Going further

Try to design and plan out an imaginary research project which would explore bullying from a qualitative perspective, interviewing bullies, victims and bully/victims.

- Using your knowledge of ethics in research (refer back to Chapter 3 if necessary), what ethical issues might you encounter and how could you overcome them?
- Consider your obligations to protect all of your participants; to obtain informed consent from children/parents/teachers; to maintain the anonymity and confidentiality of your participants. What are the challenges? How might you resolve them?

How prevalent is traditional bullying?

Since the late 1980s, studies of the extent and nature of bullying have been carried out in a range of countries. However, reviewing the prevalence of the behaviour reported in these studies highlights the challenge of

NATURE–NURTURE

Are some children biologically predisposed to become bullies?

Could the kind of qualities associated with bullying others be at least to some degree biologically inherited? What can behavioural genetics – the study of nature and nurture – tell us about the origins of bullying? In an early study by O'Connor et al. (1980) conducted in the USA, mothers of 54 pairs of identical twins (who share 100% of their genes) and mothers of 33 pairs of non-identical twins (who share 50% of their genes) rated their 8-year-old children on their tendency to bully others. The identical twin correlation (0.72) was substantially higher than the fraternal twin correlation (0.42). As we have seen previously, if genetic influence is important for a trait, identical twins will be more similar than fraternal twins. Therefore, this difference was interpreted as a sign of a genetic influence upon the predisposition to bully others.

Behaviour geneticists have been concerned for some time now about the heritability of aggressive behaviours, a central quality related to bullying. One impressive report was based on data from British and Swedish studies involving over 1500 twin pairs. This study found that identical twin correlations (ranging from 0.68 to 0.82) were greater than non-identical twin correlations (ranging from 0.41 to 0.44) for aggressive symptoms, again suggesting that a tendency towards aggressive behaviour is highly heritable (Eley et al., 1999). Yet there is still a long way to go to understand how genetics influence aggressive behaviour and to identify the particular biological pathways involved. It may be that particular aspects of temperament (such as self-regulation), which have a strong genetic base, may render the individual more likely to respond aggressively in social situations and that gene-controlled neurotransmitters, such as serotonin, have a role to play in this relationship.

Of course, at the heart of the nature–nurture debate and understanding genetic influence is the study of environmental influences. Beyond genetic influence, the roles of the family environment and parenting have been investigated with respect to involvement in bullying. In his book *Friends and Enemies: Peer Relations in Childhood*, Barry Schneider (2000) reviewed a number of studies examining the relationship between parenting behaviour and childhood aggression and peer acceptance. These studies consistently showed that parenting characterised by high levels of restrictiveness and harsh discipline (authoritarian parenting) was associated with aggressive behaviour in children. Of course, just because we have observed a relationship does not mean that we can assume that harsh parenting gives rise to aggressive behaviour. It is possible that the aggressive behaviour is a cause rather than an effect of punitive parenting.

One useful study adopted a prospective (forward-looking) approach to mapping early family experiences onto later involvement in bullying. Schwartz et al. (1997) studied the early family experiences of a group of 198 5-year-old boys. Four to five years later, aggressive behaviour and peer victimisation were assessed in school: 16 boys were identified as aggressive victims, 21 as non-aggressive victims, 33 as non-victimised aggressors and 128 as normative boys. Analysis of the early family experiences of the aggressive boys (both victimised and non-victimised groups) revealed some interesting patterns. Compared to the other groups, boys who emerged as aggressive victims were found to have had pre-school histories of experience with harsh, disorganised and potentially abusive home environments. Mother–child interactions were characterised by hostility and overly punitive and restrictive parenting. These children were also exposed to higher levels of marital conflict. In contrast, these experiences did not characterise the home experiences of non-victimised aggressors. However, the home environments of these children did incorporate exposure to aggressive and conflictual role models.

These authors concluded that observation of violence among adults may dispose a child towards aggressive behaviour, but only the experience of violence disposes a child towards the combination of peer victimisation and aggressive behaviour. This prospective study enables us to infer with greater confidence that harsh parenting is a likely contributory factor to children's aggressive behaviour. However, it is still possible that a third variable (such as biological vulnerabilities) leads to both particular family experiences and maladaptive social behaviour. Thus, it seems that bullying is a complex phenomenon that must be understood as a product of the characteristics of the individual bully and their family characteristics, as well as the broader social settings in which bullying incidents take place.

representing the patterns of involvement across groups of victims, bullies and bully/victims. In order to consider these patterns, we will consider prevalence for each of these three groups separately.

Prevalence of victimisation

The percentage of children bullied by others reported within eight studies has been summarised in Table 15.2.

As we can see from the table, these surveys across a range of countries have yielded considerable variations in the prevalence of victimisation. It is difficult to know whether these differences are real or reflect methodological or classification differences. The definitions for bullying vary across the studies, as do the time frames used and the age of the participants. Some studies report specifically how frequently bullying occurred (for example, at least once a week); others use less clearly defined time frames, such as 'regularly', 'frequently' or 'occasionally'. Other studies record whether children have ever been bullied, while some studies refer to the last school term or school year only. Thus, prevalence rates are not directly comparable across the studies. A general trend, however, is that many studies report greater involvement at less frequent levels with a lower proportion of children being bullied on a more frequent basis.

The most comprehensive cross-national study of bullying along with other health behaviours was the Health Behaviour of School-aged Children (HBSC) study of 207 334 children aged 11–15 years reported by Currie et al. (2012). This study found that 13% of 11-year-old children, 12% of 13-year-old children and 9% of 15-year-old children across 38 countries were bullied at least twice a month during the previous months. Rates of being bullied for 13-year-old girls ranged from 2% in Armenia and 4% in Sweden to 26% in Lithuania. Rates of being bullied for boys ranged from 5% in Armenia and 4% in Sweden to 30% in Lithuania. We can have greater confidence in the comparability of these rates, given that a standard questionnaire was administered across the different samples.

STOP AND THINK

Going further

Consider the high level of variation evident in the studies presented above and the possible explanations posed.

- Can you think of other possible reasons for these national differences?
- Are there factors within a social or cultural group that may increase or decrease the reported incidence of bullying?

Prevalence of bullying others

In examining the rates of perpetration of bullying, similar issues emerge in comparing findings across studies. The findings relating to perpetrators of bullying from the eight studies previously mentioned are reported in Table 15.3.

As with figures for reported involvement as a victim of bullying, there is significant variation in figures here, ranging from less than 1% to over 30%. Recognising the methodological variation in these studies, it is again useful to reflect on the multinational Health Behaviour of School-aged Children (HBSC) study (Currie et al., 2012). This study found that 8%, 11% and 12% of 11-, 13- and 15-year-olds, respectively, reported frequently perpetrating bullying against another. There was considerable variability across the countries: Romania, Lithuania and Austria were among the countries with

Table 15.2 Details of prevalence of being bullied in different countries from different published reports.

Authors	Country	Age range	Sample size	Prevalence of being bullied — Infrequently/at all	Prevalence of being bullied — Regularly
Olweus (1993)	Norway	7–16 years	130 000	Not reported	9% once a week or more
Whitney and Smith (1993)	England	8–11 years	2623	27% sometimes or more	10% once a week or more
		11–16 years	4135	10% sometimes or more	4% once a week or more
Rigby (1997)	Australia	9–18 years	5396	35% sometimes or more often	12.8% at least once a week
Tomas de Almeida (1999)	Portugal	6–9 years 10–11 years	2746 3270	Not reported Not reported	21.9% more than twice 21.6% more than twice (all referring to during last term)
Borg (1999)	Malta	9–14 years	6282	41.5% 'once or twice' and 'sometimes'	19% about 'once a week' and 'several times'
Wolke et al. (2001)	England	6–8 years	2377	Not reported	24.5% at least once a week 34.7% four or more times in past six months
	Germany	8 years	1538	Not reported	8% at least once a week 21% four or more times in past six months
Williams et al. (2009) [Growing up in Ireland study]	Ireland	9 years	8568	40% in the past year	Not reported
Currie et al. (2012) [HBSC study]	38 countries	11–15 years	207 334	Not reported	13%, 12% and 9% (for 11-, 13- and 15-year-olds respectively), at least twice in the past couple of months

the highest rates, while Wales, Sweden and Ireland were among the countries with the lowest rates.

Prevalence of bully/victims

One form of involvement in bullying which is important to consider is that of the bully/victim – as mentioned earlier, these are the children who both bully others and are bullied by others. There are two important reasons for including the category of bully/victim in research in bullying. The first is that failing to identify the number of bully/victims might mean that the involvement in bullying is over-estimated, as bully/victims are included in the figures for both bullies and victims. The second important reason is that, as discussed earlier in the section on characteristics, this group potentially differs from bullies, victims and uninvolved pupils in their experiences, background and later life adjustment. While these children share characteristics of both bullies and victims, bully/victims are not a simple average or composite of the bully and victim groups (Bowers et al., 1992). Though fewer in number than 'pure victims', these children appear to be at a higher risk for maladjustment across many domains of functioning (Schwartz et al., 2001; Kowalski and Limber, 2013). Table 15.4 summarises some of the studies that have reported the prevalence of this group.

Table 15.3 Details of prevalence of bullying others in different countries from different published reports.

Authors	Country	Age range	Sample size	Prevalence of bullying others Infrequently/at all	Regularly
Olweus (1993)	Norway	7–16 years	130 000	Not reported	7% once a week or more
Whitney and Smith (1993)	England	8–11 years	2623	12% sometimes or more	4% once a week or more
		11–16 years	4135	6% sometimes or more	1% once a week or more
Rigby (1997)	Australia	9–18 years	5396	23.9% sometimes or more often	4% at least once a week
Tomas de Almeida (1999)	Portugal	6–9 years	2746	Not reported	19.6% more than twice
		10–11 years	3270	Not reported	15.4% more than twice (all referring to during last term)
Borg (1999)	Malta	9–14 years	6282	34.7% 'once or twice' and 'sometimes'	14.2% about 'once a week' and 'several times'
Wolke et al. (2001)	England	6–8 years	2377	Reported as never/seldom so not included	14% four or more times in past six months 2.4% at least once a week
	Germany	8 years	1538	Reported as never/seldom so not included	17.1% four or more times in past six months 4.8% at least once a week
Williams et al. (2009)	Ireland	9 years	8568	13% in the past year	Not reported
Currie et al. (2012)	38 countries	11–15 years	207 334	Not reported	8%, 11% and 12% (for (11-, 13- and 15-year-olds respectively), at least twice in the past couple of months

Table 15.4 Details of prevalence of bully/victims in different countries from different published reports.

Authors	Country	Age range	Sample size	Prevalence of being a bully/victim
Olweus (1993)	Norway	7–16 years	130 000	1.9%
Whitney and Smith (1993)	England	8–11 years	2623	Not reported
		11–16 years	4135	
Rigby (1997)	Australia	9–18 years	5396	Not reported
Tomas de Almeida (1999)	Portugal	6–9 years	2746	Not reported
		10–11 years	3270	
Borg (1999)	Malta	9–14 years	6282	Not reported
Wolke et al. (2001)	England	6–8 years	2377	12%
	Germany	8 years	1538	13%
Williams et al. (2009)	Ireland	9 years	8568	10%
Currie et al. (2012)	38 countries	11–15 years	207 334	Not reported

This table highlights one of the main difficulties with understanding the prevalence of this type of involvement in bullying – that there is a high degree of inconsistency in reporting on the category of bully/victim. It is only more recently that this group seems to have been given attention. Schwartz et al. (2001) suggested that 4–8% of children are identified as bully/victims, although some studies report higher rates than this.

How prevalent is cyberbullying?

Given the focus of this chapter in part on cyberbullying as a specific form of bullying, it is important to consider the prevalence of this particular form of bullying. Over the last decade, a growing body of research is focusing specifically on this behaviour. Based on a survey of a small sample of 84 teens in the USA, Raskauskas and Stolz (2007) found that 49% of their participants had been victims of cyberbullying and 21% had cyberbullied another, at least once or twice over the previous school year. In another survey, conducted on a larger sample of 533 11–16 year olds in England, Smith et al. (2008a) found that a substantially lower proportion of young people than reported in the US study – 14.1% – had been cyberbullied over the previous school year. Bullying via instant messaging (9.9%) and picture phones (9.5%) was most common, followed by text message bullying (6.6%). Smith et al. (2008a) reported that 11.1% of London youth had cyberbullied another over the previous school year – again a substantially lower rate than reported by Raskauskas and Stolz (2007). Both studies found that most cyberbullies were also traditional bullies and many cybervictims had also been victimised by traditional forms of bullying. These studies suggest that traditional victims and bullies are likely to retain their roles across the context of the physical and the cyberworld. More recently, Popović-Ćitić and colleagues (2011) examined the prevalence of cyberbullying and victimisation among 387 11–15-year-olds in Serbia. They found that 20% of students had been bullied online, while 10% reported that they had cyberbullied another.

Based on these studies, what can we conclude about the prevalence of cyberbullying? Very little really, as the studies arrived at very different rates, with the American study showing a particularly divergent rate in comparison with the other two studies. What might account for the different rates of cyberbullying found across the studies? Do the differences relate to the samples included in the studies or variations in the survey methods used? Or perhaps the divergent findings reflect 'true' differences between American, British and Serbian youths' experiences of cyberbullying?

In fact, the three studies used a similar methodology in that participants were required to complete questionnaires. Raskauskas and Stolz (2007) asked students to consider the nature of bullying incidents (through text messages, picture phone or website) within the current school year and the frequency of those incidents (ranging from zero incidents to 16 or more). Smith et al. (2008a) presented participants with a series of questions on cyberbullying, including whether they had been cyberbullied and, if so, through which medium and how long ago this had happened (last week or month, this term, last school year, over a year ago and never). In the Serbian study, participants were asked whether or not they had performed or experienced any of a series of cyberbullying behaviours (such as sending offensive, rude and insulting messages through chat rooms, emails or text messaging, posting cruel rumours about a person in order to damage his or her reputation, or sharing someone's secret or embarrassing information online) since the beginning of the school year.

So, although using similar methodologies, the response categories across the three studies were not directly comparable. Furthermore, the sample in the US study was a small convenience sample recruited from two youth development events held at their school. Bias may exist in the sample because of the characteristics of young people who attend such events. In contrast, in the larger English and Serbian studies, participants were recruited from their classes in a range of secondary schools and it is likely that a broader range of participants were accessed than in the US study. Thus, methodological characteristics need to be considered when 'weighing up' the prevalence rates presented. We could also consider whether there is any further research to draw upon.

Based on a survey of 3767 middle school students (11–14-year-olds) in the USA, Kowalski and Limber (2007) found similar rates of cyberbullying to those reported by Smith et al. (2008a) – 11% of their participants had been victims of cyberbullying, 4% had cyberbullied another and 7% had both bullied another and been victimised electronically, at least once in the preceding months. Interestingly, almost half of the bully victims in this study did not know the identity of the perpetrator of the bullying. Thus it seems that the three studies based on larger samples yielded relatively similar prevalence rates of between 11 and 20%. These convergent findings make us feel more confident in what we know about the prevalence of cyberbullying.

Having considered definitions and prevalence of bullying, we now turn our attention to examining how involvement in bullying is associated with factors such as gender and age.

CUTTING EDGE

The impact of cyberbullying

What are the implications of involvement in cyberbullying? We know that peer victimisation is a precursor of children's internalising difficulties such as anxiety, depression and school avoidance (Reijntjes et al., 2010). However, skipping school may no longer make things easier for victims of bullying as children with mobile phones or internet access may now be subjected to electronic forms of bullying.

Cyberbullying can include (but is not limited to) harassing or threatening emails or text messages, defamatory websites and online polls on social networking sites in which individuals post mean or insulting comments about or images of others. Unlike traditional bullying that usually takes place during circumscribed periods of time (e.g. on the way to and from school or during school), these electronic forms of bullying can transcend school grounds and the school day and can potentially happen anytime and anywhere. As this area of research evolves, studies have changed from those initially focused upon establishing prevalence rates of cyberbullying, to studies examining relations between involvement in cyberbullying and more traditional forms of bullying, to more recent studies which examine the impact of cyberbullying on victims.

It is likely that the effects of cyberbullying are similar to those of traditional bullying. In one of the few studies on the effects of cyberbullying, Ybarra and Mitchell (2004) found that youths who are both online bullies and victims are most likely to experience serious psychosocial challenges, including problem behaviour, substance use, depressive symptoms and low school commitment. Online bully/victims (those who bully others online and are online victims themselves) were six times more likely to report emotional distress as a result of being the target of internet harassment, compared to those who are online victims only.

Some researchers believe that the long-term effects of cyberbullying are as bad if not worse than those that accompany traditional bullying because it is much more difficult to escape from cyberbullying – a child who is electronically bullied must cease to communicate electronically in order to escape from the bullying. This may have other implications for the child, such as becoming disconnected from his or her social network. Further, the public nature of cyberbullying increases the impact of the bullying – victims of cyberbullying can be potentially humiliated and denigrated in the view of thousands of individuals (Kowalski et al., 2008). However, much more research is needed to further understand the long-term impact of cyberbullying on victims.

Cyberbullying has been very present in the popular media, not least due to a number of cases of suicide that have been linked to cyberbullying. One example is the case of Ryan Halligan from Vermont in the USA, reported by Kowalski and colleagues (2008). Ryan died by suicide at 13 years of age following persistent bullying and humiliation by peers at school, which continued online. Towards the end of the school year, it was rumoured in instant messaging conversations and at school that Ryan was gay. Following his death, Ryan's father discovered that he had been cyberbullied in regard to these rumours. His father also discovered that Ryan had befriended one of the popular girls from school online, as a means to quash the 'gay' rumour. When Ryan approached the girl in person after the summer holidays, he discovered that she had joked about liking him and had circulated their private online conversations to her friends in order to humiliate him. Two weeks before his death just weeks into the new school year, Ryan wrote an instant message stating: 'Tonight is the night, I think I'm going to do it,' to which his 'friend' replied: 'It's about f** time.' Following Ryan's death,

Vermont enacted a Bullying Prevention Policy Law in May 2004 and later adopted a Suicide Prevention Law which provides measures to assist teachers and others to recognise and respond to depression and suicide risks among teens. Ryan's case has also been cited by legislators in other US states proposing legislation to curb cyberbullying (Halligan, 2009).

As technologies become increasingly prevalent in the lives of children and young people, we will undoubtedly hear and read more tragic stories such as these. However, research offers us important insights into this challenging issue. Hinduja and Patchin (2010) consider the existing research on bullying and suicidal ideation, before looking at the association between both traditional and cyberbullying and aspects of suicidal ideation and attempts. They conclude that both forms of the behaviour have a negative impact on suicide risk among young people. Building on this, van Geel and colleagues at the University of Leiden in the Netherlands conducted a meta-analysis of studies in this area, which was covered in the report from the Canadian media site *The Globe and Mail*. They identified 34 studies, with a combined sample of almost 285 000 individuals, examining the link between victimisation and suicidal ideation, and nine studies, with a combined sample of just over 70 000 participants, on the association between victimisation and suicide attempts. Supporting Hinduja and Patchin, they concluded that experience of victimisation is linked to both ideation and attempts, but that cyberbullying is more strongly associated with suicidal ideation (though they do caution that this conclusion is based on a small number of studies).

Perhaps it is not surprising that cyberbullying has been labelled an emerging public health problem due to the potential for devastating and even fatal effects for some victims. A very interesting editorial by Hertz et al. (2013) reports on an expert panel convened by the Centers for Disease Control and Prevention to discuss taking a public health approach to this issue. They highlight three themes from this expert discussion: 1) given the prevalence and potential impact of bullying, these behaviours represent a public health problem; 2) there is evidence of a strong relationship between bullying and suicide but it is important to recognise the influence of other mediating factors; and 3) the prevention of bullying and suicide could be informed by existing public-health-based approaches.

Gender patterns in involvement in bullying

Both boys and girls are frequently involved in bullying. Early research in bullying suggested that boys are more likely than girls to engage in bullying behaviour (Olweus, 1993; Whitney and Smith, 1993). In the recent HBSC study, boys reported bullying more and being victimised more than girls, although typically the size of these gender differences was very small (Currie et al., 2012). Others studies have found no consistent gender differences in rates of perpetration of bullying and victimisation (Williams et al., 2009). The research now suggests that there are gendered forms of bullying and when different types of bullying behaviour are assessed, prevalence rates for boys and girls are largely similar overall.

Boys are more likely to be physically bullied by other boys (rarely girls), and girls are more likely to be victimised through indirect bullying (by both boys and girls). Indirect bullying is distinct from physical and verbal bullying in that the actions may not be observed by the victim at the time, but nonetheless have intentional and negative consequences for the victim. Examples of indirect bullying include behaviours such as exclusion from a group, spreading rumours about somebody or turning people against someone. Kaukiainen and colleagues have defined indirect bullying as: 'a noxious behaviour in which the target person is attacked not physically or directly through verbal intimidation but in a more circuitous way through social manipulation' (1999, p. 83). Crick and Grotepeter (1995) applied the term 'relational aggression' to a similar construct, which they described

> **Definition**
>
> Indirect bullying: forms of bullying that may not be observed by the victim at the time, but nonetheless have intentional and negative consequences for the victim (e.g. spreading rumours).

Girls are more likely than boys to be the victims of indirect or relational bullying.
Source: Fotolia

as 'harming others through purposeful manipulation and damage of peer relationship' (p. 711). A number of studies have demonstrated that girls are subject to this indirect or relational bullying more frequently than boys are, and this difference is particularly apparent during early and middle childhood (Crick et al., 2002). In an interesting qualitative study conducted by Owens et al. (2000), focus groups with 54 teenage girls found that girls engage in indirect bullying to eliminate boredom, to seek attention, to ensure that they are a member of the 'in group', because of jealousy and to get revenge.

Over the last decade, however, well-established gender differences in relational aggression have been called into question. Two reviews of research found that boys are as likely as girls to engage in behaviours that damage the reputation of others, or to engage in exclusionary tactics. In addition, as children get older, it becomes less socially acceptable to use physical aggression against peers, and so both genders tend to resort to relational aggression when bullying others (Archer and Coyne, 2005; Card et al., 2008).

Definition

Relational bullying: forms of bullying whereby the bully manipulates children in the social setting of the victim, with the intention of causing harm or distress.

Gender patterns in cyberbullying

Are boys or girls more likely to be victims and perpetrators of cyberbullying? It seems that cyberbullying may also be an effective means for girls to achieve the kinds of goal highlighted above in the Owens et al. study, so we might expect girls to engage in cyberbullying more frequently than boys. The research does seem to indicate that this is the case: both Kowalski and Limber (2007) and Peter Smith et al. (2008a) found that girls outnumber boys in terms of the overall frequency with which cyberbullying occurs (both perpetration and victimisation). However, we must be cautious in drawing this conclusion, as contradictory evidence has also been found – Beran and Li (2007) and Hinduja and Patchin (2008) reported that no particular gender is more likely to be victims of cyberbullying.

Developmental patterns in involvement with bullying

When thinking about child development it is important to recognise that behaviours develop and change over time, and in considering bullying this is no less important. Looking back to the tables summarising prevalence patterns, it appears that there is evidence of patterns across age, with lower rates of participation apparent for older groups. So at what ages are children most likely to be involved in bullying? Research begins looking at bullying from early childhood within pre-school and kindergarten settings, although the number of studies of bullying with this age group is small relative to the number of studies on school-aged children. Nevertheless, it is useful to explore some of the research conducted with different age groups.

Bullying among pre-school children

One of the first things you will notice when reviewing studies with young children is a tendency to use aggression rather than bullying as a behavioural label. Claire Monks et al. (2004) suggest that, while many of the behaviours considered among this age group may be considered as bullying, it is difficult to determine the presence of an imbalance of power between the bully or aggressor and the victim – a factor that is central to most definitions of bullying. In addition, studying bullying during this early childhood period is difficult. Self-report measures – the most commonly used method of obtaining data on bullying – are difficult to administer to younger children. Therefore, studying bullying among younger age groups (3 to 7 years) demands more time-consuming and labour-intensive methods, such as direct observation and individual interviews.

Nevertheless, there is evidence that pre-school children can be perpetrators and victims of behaviours that would be called bullying among older children. For example, high rates of physical aggression have been seen particularly among pre-school boys. Typically, these episodes centre on contested toys or objects, and such incidents are referred to as instrumental aggression. Into the pre-school period and early childhood period, physical aggression declines and verbal aggression increases as children develop better means of communication with each other and the ability to internally regulate their emotional states (Underwood, 2002). Relational kinds of aggression (e.g. not letting others join a game) are evident among girls and less commonly among boys during early childhood (Crick et al., 1997). Of course, aggression and bullying are distinct concepts and attempts to distinguish these concepts within the research with younger children are rare (Rigby, 2002). However,

Instrumental aggression in pre-schoolers.
Source: Pearson Education Ltd/Shutterstock.com/2xSamara.com

there is clear evidence that early experiences of aggression, particularly physical aggression, are associated with later experiences (Barker et al., 2008) and, because of this, it is important to consider the studies of pre-school behaviour as part of the developmental continuum of bullying in children.

Bullying in middle childhood

Given the difficulties associated with studies of bullying in pre-schoolers, it is unsurprising that much of the research has been conducted with older children. The result is that the patterns of behaviour in this age group have been carefully examined. Over the course of middle childhood (7 to 12 years), it seems that the incidence of reported victimisation declines with age. In one review of studies, Peter Smith et al. (1999a) cited figures from several large-scale studies previously mentioned to note that a steady decline in bullying is evident for both boys and girls over this developmental stage (Olweus, 1993; Whitney and Smith, 1993; Rigby, 1997). This may be the result of children developing better social skills, which help them to interact more effectively with their peers. However, Smith et al. argued that bullying may be perceived differently by younger and older children – so results for groups that vary in age may not be directly comparable. Among perpetrators of bullying, however, there is little evidence of a change in the tendency to bully others – this seems to remain stable across middle childhood (Hanish and Guerra, 2004).

Bullying in adolescence

Looking finally to adolescence, the pattern of declining rates of victimisation appears to continue. In one study based in the USA, Tonya Nansel et al. (2001) found that 24% of 6th graders (age 11–12) had been bullied often, compared with 16% of 8th graders (age 13–14) and 9% of 10th graders (age 15–16). However, there may be an exception to this continued decline: Rigby (1997) documented a temporary rise in reported bullying that coincided with the transition to secondary school. This may be an example of how the social context in which children of a particular age find themselves is crucially important and may even take precedence over developmental factors. However, an interesting explanation for this pattern has been proposed by Anthony Pellegrini. He argues that aggression can serve a purpose during the transition between different school levels. Pellegrini and Bertini (2001) discuss the way in which adolescents, particularly males, may use aggression to establish dominance within the group during this transition, and suggest that this highlights the possible evolutionary function of bullying and aggression. We should, however, be cautious in how we interpret these perceived declines in bullying from early childhood to adolescence. It is possible that older children are simply less likely to report being the victim of bullying, for fear of being perceived as weak or vulnerable.

Developmental patterns in cyberbullying

In considering developmental patterns in cyberbullying, we might expect factors to do with the social environment to play an important role – one must have access to electronic communication tools in order to be a perpetrator or victim of cyberbullying. Kowalski and Limber (2007) found that children aged 6 to 8 years were less likely than children aged 9–11 years to have been cyberbullied – a trend that is somewhat at odds with that observed with more traditional forms of bullying. This may be because older children have more unsupervised access to the internet and mobile phones. This study also found that 8th graders (13–14-year-olds) cyberbullied others more frequently than 6th and 7th graders (11–13 years). However, in a recent review, Tokunaga (2010) highlighted the inconsistency within the research and pointed to the possibility of a complex relationship between age and frequency of cyberbullying victimisation. For example, Williams and Guerra (2007) found that rates of cyberbullying victimisation were lowest at age 10–11 (4.5%), peaked at ages 13–14 (12.9%), and declined from age 14 years onwards (9.9%). Much more research is needed to explore these patterns.

Considering the issues discussed in this section, it appears that bullying behaviours have their foundations in early childhood aggression and, from a peak in the school years, rates of victimisation appear to decrease over time. In comparison, rates of perpetration of bullying show less radical reductions over time. From an applied perspective, there is a clear need to consider the implications of these developmental patterns of bullying behaviour. Recognising related behaviours among

---

STOP AND THINK

Going further

This section has considered the influence of factors such as age and gender on involvement in bullying. However, there are other factors that might be influential. For example, we might consider whether involvement in bullying depends on whether children are in a racial/ethnic majority or minority group, or whether identifying with a sexual minority group has an impact. One of the implications of ethnicity- or sexuality-related bullying was highlighted in the media report from California presented at the outset of this chapter. While many forms of both traditional and cyberbullying are not prohibited in law, harassment/bullying on the basis of sexuality and ethnicity is likely to constitute a breach of the law.

One report that considers the experiences of lesbian, gay, bisexual and transgender (LGBT) youth in the USA is the 2011 *National School Climate Survey* (Kosciw et al., 2012), which surveyed just over 8500 students between the ages of 13 and 20 years. The authors report that over 80% of students experienced verbal harassment, while over one-third were physically harassed because of their sexual orientation. Interestingly, it was noted that reports of victimisation were lower when schools were described as having an inclusive curriculum and clear bullying/harassment policies that addressed sexual-identity-based harassment.

- For what reasons might children and young people from ethnic and sexual identity minority groups be susceptible to being the target of bullying?
- What implications does this have for prevention and intervention?

pre-schoolers may help prevent later problems, while recognising the potential function of these behaviours in adolescence may help educators to understand bullying among this group. It is also worth considering how bullying is a lifespan phenomenon that extends well beyond childhood and adolescence into adulthood. This is explored further in the Lifespan box.

Bullying as a group process

So far, we have been very much focused upon bullying as an individual-oriented phenomenon – research has been concentrated mainly on bullies and victims and, more recently, there has been an increased focus upon bully/victims. However, bullying is a social process, usually taking place within a group context. While many children report negative attitudes towards bullying, it is important to know how these children actually behave in bullying situations (Sutton and Smith, 1999). For example, do they join in? Do they actively encourage the bully (perhaps by shouting or cheering)? Do they passively accept the bullying (perhaps by being present but doing nothing about it or by being amused by the situation)? Do they stick up for the victims or tell somebody about it? Do they tackle the bully in any way?

Christine Salmivalli et al. (1996) wanted to address these questions and so developed the Participant Role Questionnaire (PRQ), in which each child assesses each classmate's as well as his or her own typical behaviour in bullying situations. Six roles were identified in bullying, which are outlined in Table 15.5.

The PRQ also enables bully/victims to be identified, as the secondary roles of the victimised children can also be analysed. A number of studies have utilised the PRQ to study the prevalence of these roles. In the UK, Sutton and Smith (1999) found the following prevalence rates: victims 18.1%, bullies 14.0%, assistants 7.3%, reinforcers 5.7%, defenders 27.5% and outsiders 11.9% of the sample, respectively. However, in this study, children (7 to 10 years) were only asked to rate classmates of the same sex. Findings from studies such as this illustrate that victimisation (being the victim of bullying) is not something that goes on exclusively between the bully and the victim. Most children in the class are affected in some way.

Salmivalli (2001) has also reported that these roles tend to be relatively stable and the most stable of all roles is that of the victim. Placing bullying in its group context enables better understanding of the perpetrator's motivation to bully, the lack of support provided to victims, the persistence of bullying across time, and the adjustment of victims (Salmivalli, 2010). For example, why is it that some peers become defenders of the victims while others become reinforcers or assistants to the bully? Much work remains to be done to answer these important questions, but emerging research suggests that there may be different individual characteristics associated with different participant roles. For example, in comparison with children classified into other roles, those classified as bullies, assistants and reinforcers have more positive attitudes to bullying and seem to lack empathetic understanding with victims (Pöyhönen and Salmivalli, 2008). Findings such as these could be useful in helping to determine *who* should be targeted by intervention programmes, *what* behaviours or attitudes need to be changed, and *how* those changes might be brought about.

Table 15.5 Participant roles with descriptions and examples of items from the PRQ.

Participant role	Description	Examples of items on questionnaire
Bully	Active, initiative-taking, 'ring-leader', bullying behaviours	Starts bullying; makes others join in the bullying
Assistant to bully	Following the bully, assisting him or her	Joins in the bullying; assists the bully
Reinforcer to bully	Providing bully with feedback that encourages him or her	Comes around to watch the situation; laughs
Defending victim	Takes sides with the victim	Says to the victim, 'Never mind'; tries to make others stop bullying
Staying outside	Withdrawing, not reacting to bullying	Is not usually present (in bullying situations); does not even know about the bullying
Victim	Target of systematic harassment	

Source: Salmivalli (2001)

LIFESPAN

Bullying in the workplace

Bullying is most commonly associated with childhood and the teenage years, and this is reflected in the research, which has primarily focused upon school contexts. However, bullying is not restricted to schooldays but can extend beyond adolescence into adulthood. As Smith (1997) points out, bullying can potentially occur whenever groups of people meet together. Research on bullying in adulthood has gained momentum in recent years and has focused on contexts such as the workplace and prisons. Here we will discuss bullying in the workplace, which is increasingly recognised as a serious issue, with detrimental implications for job-related and health-related outcomes for employees, including mental and physical health problems, stress, burnout, and reduced job satisfaction and commitment to their employer (Nielsen and Einarsen, 2012).

In the workplace, bullying takes on complex, subtle and indirect forms. Rayner and Hoel (1997) describe several different types of workplace bullying, including: threats to professional and personal status (e.g. humiliating, accusing someone of lack of effort, belittling opinion, name calling, insulting), isolation (e.g. preventing access to opportunities, withholding important information), overwork (e.g. giving unrealistic deadlines or an impossible workload) and destabilisation (e.g. removing responsibility, assigning meaningless tasks, failing to give credit when it is due and setting someone up to fail). Behaviours such as intimidation, public humiliation and unwanted physical contact can undermine the integrity and confidence of employees, increase absenteeism and reduce efficiency, with substantial costs to the victims, as well as to the organisation as a whole (Cowie et al., 2002).

Factors to do with the organisational climate can also contribute to bullying in the workplace. Vartia (1996) found that bullying is promoted by organisational features such as inadequate opportunities to influence matters concerning oneself at work, lack of reciprocal conversations about the tasks and goals of the work unit, poor mechanisms to exchange information among employees and a strained and competitive atmosphere. Organisations are now recognising the need for policies and procedures to protect their employees from bullying and harassment, as well as the need to create an organisational culture that does not facilitate bullying.

However, while organisational factors are no doubt important, the role of individuals must also be considered. There may be some continuity in the extent to which individuals are victimised in childhood and then go on to be victimised in adulthood. The same may be true for those who bully others. Very little research, however, has considered this issue. In one study, Smith et al. (2003) sought to examine whether being a victim of bullying at school would increase the likelihood of being a victim of bullying in the workplace. Over 5000 adults in various work settings completed an anonymous questionnaire on their school experiences in relation to bullying and their conditions and relationships at work. The study found that individuals who had been either a victim or a bully/victim at school were more likely to have been bullied at work in the last five years, compared with those who had not been a victim or a bully/victim at school. The authors concluded that being victimised at school increases one's risk of being victimised later in life in the workplace. One limitation of this study is that it is a retrospective study, meaning that it relied upon people's reports of their bullying experiences at school, rather than assessing their experiences at that time and then following them up later when they were adults. An additional issue relates to the ability to establish a causal link between early and later experiences, which is a challenge for all research in developmental psychology.

The conclusion arising from this study – that there is consistency in patterns of victimisation across different life stages (from childhood to adulthood) and across different contexts (from school to the workplace) – highlights the need to provide support and skills to those at risk of victimisation at a young age, in order to prevent continuity of victimisation experiences.

Bullying is a group process, in which children other than just bully and victim play a role.
Source: Pearson Education Ltd/Tudor Photography

Theoretical perspectives on bullying

So far in this chapter, we have drawn on research studies to inform our discussion of bullying. However, psychological theories can also make an important contribution to our understanding of the issue. Theories can form an important basis for anti-bullying prevention and intervention programmes. For example, if we believe that bullies lack particular social skills or empathy for others, interventions may be targeted at teaching children these skills. Alternatively, if we consider that bullying is a group process in which the bully's actions are reinforced by peer onlookers, interventions may target observers and peers who fail to intervene in bullying incidents. Different theories can be used to explain why some children bully others and why others are bullied. Some of these theories are drawn from work on aggression in children and have been applied to bullying; others have been developed specifically to explain bullying. While it is not possible to consider all of these, we will look at four in detail now. The theories are summarised in Table 15.6, with attention drawn to their origins and their focus.

Social-information processing model

One of the most influential perspectives on childhood aggression has been the social-information processing model of children's social adjustment proposed by Crick and Dodge (1994). This six-step model, illustrated in Figure 15.1, proposes that in their social interactions, children proceed through five stages in 'reading' different social situations before they respond in the sixth and final step of the model. This model was initially developed to understand the broad range of aggressive behaviours exhibited by children and young people. However, it has clear potential to be applied to the study of bullying behaviour.

For example, imagine you are a 9-year-old child who is playing a game alone at a table. A peer walks by, knocks into the table and the game falls to the floor. In stages 1 and 2 of the model, *encoding and interpretation of cues* take place. First, you select and attend to

> **Definition**
>
> Social-information processing: the way in which people make sense of information relating to social interactions and social contexts.

Table 15.6 Main features of four key theories of bullying.

Theory	Key references	Origins	Focus
Social-information processing theory	Crick and Dodge (1994)	Social cognition, aggressive behaviour	The bully's cognitive processing
Bullying and theory of mind	Sutton et al. (1999a, 1999b)	Bullying	The bully's social intelligence
Attribution theory	Graham and Juvonen (2001)	Social cognition	The victim's cognitive processing
Disinhibition	Suler (2004)	Online behaviour	Cyberbullying

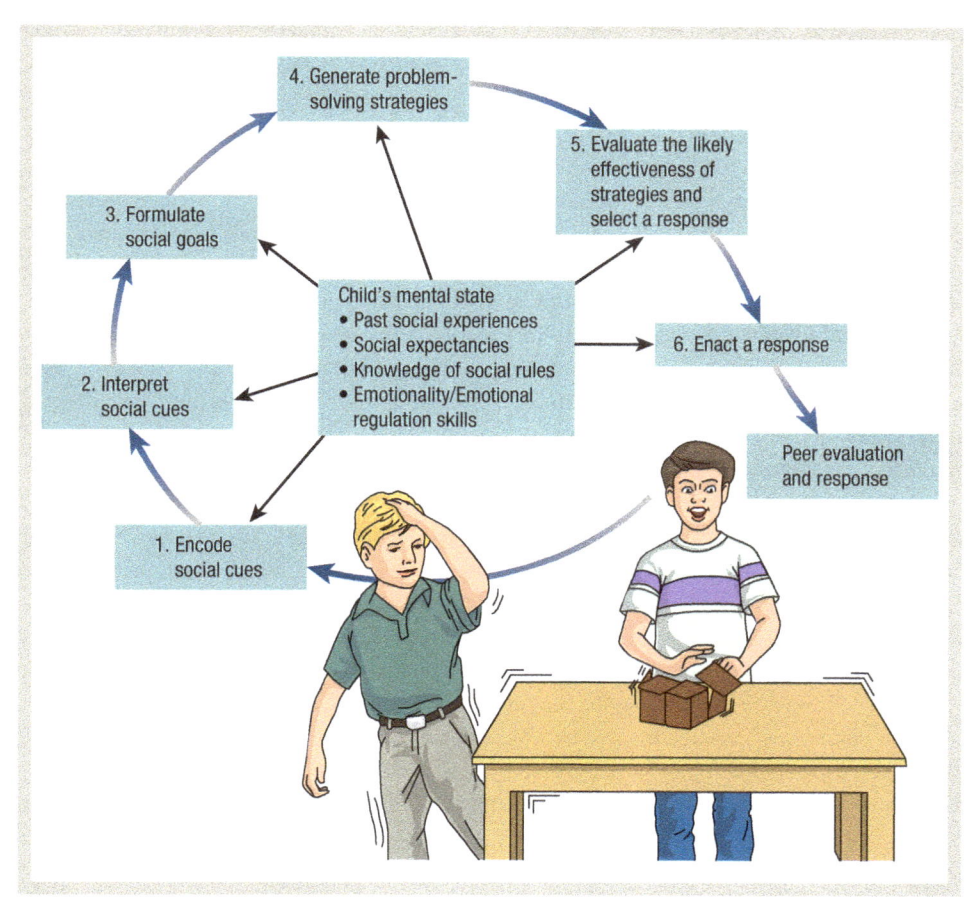

Figure 15.1
Representation of Crick and Dodge's model.
Source: Shaffer and Kipp (2010)

information (cues) about the social situation and then you interpret the cues to make sense of the social situation. In stage 1, the social cues you choose to attend to might be influenced by your ability to gather information from the setting. The interpretation of these cues in stage 2 might involve making assumptions about why particular events have occurred or the intention of the peer. For example, what happened? Why did this situation happen (causal attribution)? Did the peer mean to bump into the table or was it accidental (intent attribution)? What was the peer's reaction to the event? Other encoding that might take place at this stage includes attending to internal cues, such as emotional arousal. In stage 3 of the model, *clarification of goals* occurs, in which you formulate a goal or desired outcome for the situation. Do you want help picking up the game? Do you want the peer to apologise? Do you want to move on to a new game? Do you want to 'get even' with the provocateur?

In stage 4, it is hypothesised that children *access possible responses* to the situation from their memory store, and in stage 5, they *decide upon a response*. You might think about a range of possible responses to this situation or remember how you behaved in the past in response to similar experiences. Did a particular response in the past lead to a favourable or unfavourable outcome? In deciding what you do, you evaluate the likely outcomes of various responses (outcome expectations). You might ask yourself: what will happen if I hit the provocateur, or ignore him/her? Your moral values (e.g. beliefs that hitting somebody is a bad thing to do) may influence the response that you decide upon. In stage 6 of the model, the chosen *response is enacted*.

Crick and Dodge hypothesised that children who bully or are aggressive towards peers display patterns of social-information processing that are distinct from those of non-aggressive peers. One of the most widely studied components of their model is how children interpret social cues to infer the motives of others (intent attributions, stage 2 of the model) – for example, determining whether a peer acted with benign or hostile intent. Crick and

Dodge argue that physically aggressive children tend to display a hostile attributional bias when interpreting social cues. That is, they tend to attribute malicious intent to peer provocateurs even when such intent is not actually present. Crick et al. (2002) presented hypothetical vignettes to groups of aggressive and non-aggressive children aged 9 to 12 years. Each vignette described a provocation situation in which the intent of the behaviour of the provocateur was ambiguous. Children were asked to state whether the provocateur's behaviour was intentional (hostile) or benign (accidental). Results from the study found that sub-groups of aggressive children did process social information in distinctive ways from non-aggressive children. Children who were rated as being high on physical aggression exhibited more hostile attributions or explanations than did children rated as low on physical aggression. This study supports claims made by Crick and Dodge's social-information processing theory, which suggests that physically aggressive children display a hostile attributional bias when interpreting social cues.

The model also holds when examining relational aggression. Crick et al. (2002) found that relationally aggressive children exhibited hostile attributional biases for relational provocation situations (e.g. being the only one not invited to a classmate's birthday party), but not for instrumental provocation situations (e.g. getting pushed into mud). In contrast, physical aggression tended to be elicited by provocations of an instrumental nature, but not provocations of a relational nature. The authors conclude that hostile attributional biases of relationally aggressive children tend to be distinct from those of physically aggressive children. Also, the types of peer interaction that are provoking and likely to elicit hostile attributional biases (and subsequent aggressive acts) are specific to relational versus physical forms of aggression.

However, some studies do not find support for the idea that hostile attribution biases for relational events are associated with relational aggression (e.g. Nelson et al., 2008). In an effort to understand conflicting findings in the literature, Crick has suggested a *relational vulnerability model*. Specifically, she hypothesised that hostile attribution biases for relational provocations would only result in relationally aggressive behaviour among children who are *already vulnerable* when it comes to relationships. One way in which children may display relational vulnerability is if they are very sensitive (i.e. experience heightened emotional responses) when faced with an ambiguous or potentially provoking social situation. In support of this hypothesis, Crick and her team found that hostile attribution biases were associated with relational aggression among girls but only when levels of emotional sensitivity and previous experiences of peer relational victimisation were also high (Mathieson et al., 2011). Thus, it is the girls who are relationally victimised, and who demonstrate both hostile attributional biases and emotional distress in response to relational provocation, who are most likely to be relationally aggressive. Future research based on the social-information processing and relational vulnerability models is needed to identify further characteristics of girls and boys that may make them vulnerable to hostile attributions and different forms of aggressive behaviour.

In considering this theoretical approach, it is important to see that research suggesting that aggressive children exhibit social-information processing deficits has rarely focused on the bully *per se*. As discussed previously in the chapter, although bullies are aggressive by nature, they are more than that – they are aggressive people who seek to take advantage of less powerful people in situations in which they can be dominant (Rigby, 2002). In addition, it is important to remember that children come to social situations with a set of biologically predisposed capabilities (such as a tendency to be impulsive) and a database of memories of previous experiences, which also influence how they process social information and how they typically behave.

The second theoretical position, proposed by Sutton et al. (1999a), takes issue with the deficit view of Crick and Dodge and instead argues that bullies are skilled manipulators and better mind-readers than others.

Bullying and theory of mind

As we have seen, bullying is an antisocial and aggressive act but one that is often conducted in a social way and within a social setting. Sutton et al. (1999a, 1999b) suggest that, in order to truly understand bullying, we need to take account of the context in which bullying occurs,

Definition

Hostile attributional bias: the tendency for some people to attribute hostile intention to the actions of others in non-hostile situations.

the roles which different children assume within this context and the skills that may be of use to a bully. It seems plausible that a variety of mind-reading skills (involved in theory of mind; see Chapter 8, 'Theory of mind') are in operation when children bully others. As noted earlier in the chapter, bullying usually occurs in the presence of peers, who may take on one of a variety of roles (assistant to or reinforcer of the bully, defender of the victim, or uninvolved). Being an effective bully may involve firstly grasping and then manipulating the internal mental states – beliefs, thoughts and feelings – of all those involved. Thus, bullies may be at an advantage if they possess superior theory of mind skills to those of their victims and followers.

In order to test this, 193 children aged 7 to 10 years were presented with a version of the Participant Role Scale (Salmivalli et al., 1996) to ascertain the nature of their involvement in bullying. Children were classified as a bully, assistant to a bully, reinforcer, defender, outsider or victim. For those children who were identified in the bully role, teachers completed a questionnaire to assess the type of bullying (physical, verbal or indirect bullying). All children were then read 11 short stories in order to assess their understanding of mental states or emotions. Here is an example of one such story, which tapped into mental states:

> During the war, the Red army captured a member of the Blue army. They want him to tell them where his army's tanks are; they know they are either by the sea or in the mountains. They know that the prisoner will not want to tell them, he will want to save his army, and so he will certainly lie to them. The prisoner is very brave and very clever, he will not let them find his tanks. The tanks are really in the mountains. Now when the Red side asks him where his tanks are, he says: 'They are in the mountains.'
>
> (Happé, 1994, p. 150)

The children were then asked a series of questions such as: is it true what the prisoner said? Where will the army look for his tanks and why did the prisoner say what he said? Responses to the questions were scored from 0 (fail), to 1 (pass but without reference to a mental state), to 2 (pass including reference to a mental state or belief). For example, a child scored as 2 might respond in the following way: 'They will look by the sea because they think that the prisoner is lying to them.'

The findings from this study revealed that bullies had higher social cognition scores than any other group. Furthermore, it was the children who bullied others verbally, rather than indirectly or physically, who scored highest on the theory of mind stories. It may be that theory of mind skills are particularly adaptive in order to tease somebody effectively and know what names or taunts will be most hurtful. However, one could also argue that theory of mind is important even in physical bullying, as the bully will still have to choose an effective time and method, avoid detection, maximise the victim's vulnerability and minimise the chances of being hurt themselves.

More recent research has revealed mixed findings regarding superior theory of mind skills among those who perpetrate bullying against others. For example, among a sample of young children aged 4 to 6 years, Monks and colleagues (2005) found that aggressors did not show high levels of performance on tasks assessing theory of mind. However, it may be that the type of aggression typically shown by younger children does not rely to the same extent on good social cognitive skills as the types used by older children. Looking at older children, Shakoor et al. (2012) found that adolescent victims, bullies and bully/victim had poor theory of mind skills in early childhood. However, for the bullies, the association between theory of mind skills and bullying became insignificant, once other factors like family deprivation and child maltreatment were taken into account – for bullies with poor theory of mind, these family factors play a more influential role in children's risk of becoming bullies. This was not the case for victims or bully/victim – for these children poor theory of mind contributed to the risk of children becoming victims or bully/victims over and above family factors. The findings point to the importance of understanding early differences in social cognition among children who later become involved in bullying.

Renouf et al. (2010) expanded upon Sutton et al.'s theory by suggesting that the link between theory of mind skills and bullying behaviour might depend upon the type of bullying behaviour. Specifically, they

---

Definition

Theory of mind: being able to infer the full range of mental states (beliefs, desires, intentions, imagination, emotions, etc.) that cause action (Baron-Cohen, 2001).

believed that children with poor theory of mind skills who have difficulty taking into account another person's perspective may be likely to react aggressively during situations involving real or perceived threats (as is the case with children who display hostile attributional biases). These are known as *reactive aggressors*. On the other hand, children with high theory of mind skills may deliberately select aggressive behaviour in certain social situations because they expect to achieve personal gains. These are known as *proactive aggressors*. In line with this, the researchers expected to find superior theory of mind skills among proactive aggressors, and inferior theory of mind skills among reactive aggressors. This is indeed what they found. Low theory of mind skills were related to higher levels of reactive aggression among children, specifically among children who were frequently victimised by their peers. High theory of mind skills were found among children who engaged in frequent proactive aggression – these skills enable these proactive aggressors to plan and execute their behaviour, including weighing up the costs and benefits of using aggression, and anticipating how other people will react.

So what can be concluded from this research? Do bullies have superior theory of mind skills? The results of the studies do cast some doubt on the claims made by the social skills deficit model of aggression that bullies have poor social skills. Sutton et al.'s and others' findings lend support to the idea that bullies may not be socially inadequate in the way Crick and Dodge described. However, much more research is needed to explore the relation between specific theory of mind skills and bullying. Bullies with good theory of mind skills may still show deficits in particular areas: for example, in their beliefs involving moral emotions, such as guilt, shame and sympathy. Do bullies understand these emotions but not share them with others? Bullies may show a good awareness of others' emotional states but still demonstrate an unwillingness to feel empathy towards others. If this is the case, intervention strategies which aim to enhance the mind-reading skills of bullies may be misguided, if bullies already have these skills but do not have empathic capacities.

Definition

Empathy: the ability to identify with the emotions of others and to read the physical expression of emotions in others.

Understanding victimisation using attribution theory

The theories above focus on the actions, skills and intentions of the bully; however, they have little to say about the experiences and actions of the victims of bullying. In some ways, this reflects the common belief that bullying is the result of actions on the part of the bully. While it is not appropriate to suggest that victims should be blamed for being bullied, it is important to remember that bullying is a social behaviour that is the result of the dynamic interaction of the bully and the victim. It is important to consider what the role of the victim may be in this interaction.

There are many possible roles that have been considered in the literature on bullying. Looking at bullying from a behaviourist perspective, it could be that the reaction of the victim reinforces the bully. On the one hand, we might expect that displays of distress reinforce the bully whose aim is to hurt or upset the victim. On the other hand, researchers in Canada have argued that displays of anger on the part of the victim might provoke the bully further (Mahady-Wilton et al., 2000). In addition, researchers have identified different types of victim, with different roles in the interaction. For example, Stephenson and Smith (1989) proposed a particular type of victim – the provocative victim – whose behaviour in some way provoked the attention and indeed the anger of the bully. These examples highlight the complexity of the bully–victim dynamic and the need to reflect on the victim in this dynamic.

One theoretical approach that has been applied to victims of bullying is attribution theory. This explores the way in which a person explains or attributes cause to behaviours. We have already seen in the social-information processing theory how bullies tend to make hostile attributions. Extending this general theory, Graham and Juvonen (2001) have applied the framework to victims of bullying. They consider how victims of bullying explain the cause of their victimisation. They describe causes in terms of their locus (i.e. do they see the cause as being something inside them or outside them?), stability (i.e. does the cause change over time?) and controllability (i.e. can the cause be controlled?). They link the idea of the locus of attributions to self-esteem, suggesting that attributing the cause of bullying to something that is external to them (e.g. a lack of supervision by teachers) is less damaging to an individual's self-esteem than attributing the cause to something that is internal (e.g. because you are short). In this way, the authors frame these attributions as differing in terms of the level of self-blame attributed, and suggest that the cause which the victim assigns to the behaviour could increase or decrease the potential harm caused by the bullying.

Graham and Juvonen have conducted research on attributions of bullying. In studying young people's responses to statements regarding reasons for bullying, they identified four patterns or themes. These are summarised in Table 15.7, along with an overview of the characteristics of this attribution type and examples cited. They found that victims of bullying are more likely to attribute bullying to each of these causes, but that the type most associated with adjustment difficulties such as anxiety is characterological self-blame, which locates the cause within the person (thus reducing self-esteem), is uncontrollable (thus not manageable or resolvable) and is stable over time (so unlikely to improve).

In a partial test of this theory, Perren et al. (2013) investigated the role of self-blaming attributions in children's adjustment difficulties. Based on a two-year longitudinal study of 478 10-year-old children, the authors found that the link between peer victimisation and internalising difficulties (e.g. anxious, depressed and withdrawn behaviours) was greater among children who exhibited higher levels of self-blame (e.g. beliefs that 'I must have done something to make this happen'). In line with the theory, the authors conclude that victims' interpretations regarding the reasons or causes of victimisation are central to understanding how being bullied may affect children in different ways.

Considering the possible implications of this theory for understanding bullying, Graham and Juvonen discuss the extent to which young people could be supported to change the way in which they attribute the causes of their victimisation and thereby improve their ability to cope with victimisation. They also argue for the use of this approach to change the attributions of peers and therefore make them more likely to support the victim. This approach is interesting in the context of the current popularity of cognitive behavioural therapy (CBT) as a mental health intervention. CBT focuses on changing the way in which an individual thinks and behaves in relation to challenges. There is scope to explore the application of therapeutic models that support changing attribution styles in victims of bullying.

Understanding cyberbullying: disinhibition in online behaviour

The theories presented in this section can help us to understand cyberbullying at least to some extent. However, as we have seen, cyberbullying is distinct from traditional bullying in a number of important ways. To date, no specific theory of cyberbullying has been proposed (Tokunaga, 2010) and the development of theory in the area of cyberbullying has not kept pace with the proliferation of research in the area of cyberbullying, or with the proliferation of technology itself. Researchers in the area of cyberbullying have tended to draw upon theories explaining traditional bullying and/or theories explaining online behaviour more generally.

One important difference between traditional 'school-yard' bullying and cyberbullying relates to the anonymity afforded to the cyberbully. In one survey of over 3000 teenagers, half of the electronic victims reported not knowing the identity of the perpetrator (Kowalski and Limber, 2007). In another study, based on 1211 completed questionnaires, almost 40% of secondary school pupils and one-third of primary school pupils who were victims of cyberbullying reported not knowing the identity of the bully (Dehue et al., 2008). Anonymity in online interactions gives rise to what is known as the phenomenon of disinhibition. According to Suler (2004), when

Table 15.7 Attribution types in bullying.

Attribution type	Characteristics	Examples
Characterological self-blame	Internal Uncontrollability Stable over time	'If I were a cooler kid, this wouldn't happen to me'
Behavioural self-blame	Internal Personal control Can change over time	'I shouldn't have been there'
Threat from others	External	'These . . . kids pick on everyone'
Passivity	Not reported	'I would feel helpless'

Source: after Graham and Juvonen (2001, examples taken from p. 55)

Definition

Disinhibition: the tendency to behave in ways other than one might normally, showing a lack of restraint or regard for social norms.

people have the opportunity to separate their online actions from their in-person identity, they may feel less vulnerable about acting out and behaving in ways that they might not otherwise be willing to do if their identities were known. In effect, people dissociate themselves from their online persona and can avert responsibility for their online behaviour. As Kowalski et al. (2008) state: 'with electronic communication, [people] can hide behind an assumed identity and wreak havoc' (p. 64).

A second feature of online communication relates to invisibility, which also contributes to disinhibition. Given that interaction occurs via technology and not through face-to-face interaction, neither perpetrator nor victim is visible to the other. Bullies cannot see the emotional reaction of their victims (or of bystanders) and so the opportunity for their behaviours to be inhibited by the emotional responses of others is missing. As Kowalski and others suggest, it is as if some bullies fail to remember that they are actually communicating with another person. It is likely that this disinhibition effect contributes, at least in part, to the phenomenon of cyberbullying, but the relation between disinhibition and cyberbullying remains to be empirically tested.

More recently, a theory known as General Strain Theory (GSM) has been applied in research on cyberbullying (and traditional bullying). Briefly, this theory proposes that people experience strain in their lives, arising from an inability to achieve goals, a loss of positively valued stimuli and the introduction of negatively valued stimuli. As a result of strain, people experience negative emotional responses such as anger and frustration, and over time, individuals may become aggressive and prone to engaging in delinquent or criminal behaviour as a way of alleviating their frustration (Agnew, 1992). A number of studies have examined bullying as a source of strain, and also as an outcome of strain. It makes sense that bullying could occur as a response to strain – the individual seeks to relieve him or herself of negative feelings and bullying another may elicit feelings of power and superiority.

In support of this theory, Patchin and Hinduja (2011) found that youth who reported strain were significantly more likely to have engaged in cyberbullying and traditional bullying. Hinduja and Patchin (2007) also utilised GST to identify the strain consequences of being a victim of cyberbullying. They found that being victimised was a form of strain that was subsequently associated with school problems and engagement in delinquent behaviour offline. Drawing upon longitudinal data on youth in Korea, Jang et al. (2014) also found that being a victim of bullying off-line was significantly related to perpetrating bullying against others online. Consistent with GST, the authors proposed that those who are bullied off-line go on to cyberbully others as a means of externalising the strain they experience. This study demonstrates the potential usefulness of GST to explain linkages among different forms of involvement in bullying.

Where to from here in theorising bullying?

It is clear that the first two theories discussed are a world apart in their predictions about the social–cognitive processes of those who bully others. One theory predicts that bullies have deficient social–cognitive skills that manifest themselves in hostile attribution biases, which give rise to an increased likelihood of aggressive behaviour in response to ambiguous social situations. In contrast, the other theory predicts that bullies are good perspective-takers who can skilfully manipulate social situations.

Crick and Dodge (1999) argue that even if bullies are good mind-readers, other cognitive processes are operating which contribute to their engagement in negative behaviours. Sutton and his colleagues go further to state that perhaps bullies may perceive and interpret social cues very accurately (the first two stages of Crick and Dodge's model), but their process of response selection (stages 4–5) may be driven by distinct goals (stage 3) reflecting different values and beliefs. Bullies may attach more value to the rewarding outcomes of aggression and less value to the negative outcomes associated with aggression.

Deviant values and beliefs may well be influenced by the child's peer network or broader cultural context. The norms inherent within a peer or school culture may be as important as hostile attributions in predicting hostile responses among children. Taking this perspective demands that we pay attention to everybody's role in bullying, and do not focus exclusively on the bully. For example, what about the social–cognitive skills of those who defend the victims or those who remain uninvolved? What skills prevent these children from becoming bullies or victims? Could their skills be used to promote prosocial behaviour among other children or to provide positive social support to those involved in bullying?

Neither of these theories addresses the social skills of children and young people involved in cyberbullying. Theories of online behaviour provide some insights, but their contribution to understanding what goes on in the minds of those who bully others is limited.

However, perhaps answers can be found in moving from theories that seek to understand the behaviours to those that consider the context in which the behaviours occur? Theorists such as Urie Bronfenbrenner and Jacqueline and Richard Lerner consider the ecology of human development – that is, the complex context within which we grow and learn. Several researchers in the field of bullying have looked to the ecological perspective to understand bullying. Hong and Espelage (2012) highlight the evidence for bullying as a behaviour that is influenced by multiple social settings, including the home, school and community. They also stress the need for an ecological approach in tackling bullying, concluding that 'bullying is a complex social phenomenon that is embedded in a number of systems, which may inadvertently reinforce and maintain bullying interactions' (p. 319).

Given the outstanding questions outlined above regarding the nature of bullying, it is important to focus on the areas of bullying research that are less developed. Finding answers to questions such as these could have important implications for how anti-bullying interventions are designed, and it is to this that we will turn our attention in the next section.

> **STOP AND THINK**
>
> **Going further**
>
> - Based on your reading of the different theories of bullying, and about the nature of cyberbullying as opposed to traditional bullying, would you argue that cyberbullies are thugs or thinkers?
> - What other explanations of behaviour might help us to understand this relatively new form of bullying?

Tackling bullying: methods of intervention and prevention

Within the context of applied psychology, the goal of research is to apply knowledge and inform practice. In the same way, the drive to understand bullying was fuelled by the need to develop ways to address the problem in schools. Before the surge of interest in bullying in the 1990s, there were few resources available to help school principals and teachers with this. As with research on bullying, it was in Scandinavia, particularly in Norway, that new interventions for use in schools first developed. In 1983, the Norwegian government funded a nationwide campaign in all of its 3500 schools (Smith and Sharp, 1994). Since then, education authorities in more countries have moved to provide resources for dealing with bullying in schools. In the UK, the Department for Education has issued two documents for schools: *Preventing and Tackling Bullying: Advice for Headteachers, Staff and Governing Bodies* (Department for Education, 2014a) and *Supporting Children and Young People who are Bullied: Advice for Schools* (Department for Education, 2014b). These documents clarify the responsibility of schools to prevent bullying under the following legislation:

- Education and Inspections Act 2006
- Independent School Standard Regulations 2010
- Equality Act 2010
- Children Act 1989

The document *Preventing and Tackling Bullying* discusses both prevention of bullying, whereby schools work to create an atmosphere of respect among staff and pupils that promotes positive behaviour, and intervention, which considers disciplinary procedures while recognising that those involved in bullying may need support. Other common terms used to describe prevention and intervention programmes are proactive and reactive, respectively.

Two main approaches to intervention and prevention are described and discussed in policy documents and the research literature, and a significant body of research has considered the impact of these approaches. Firstly, educational approaches tend to focus on the education of class groups, whole schools, and other groups about what bullying is and its effects on those involved. An example of this approach is the internationally known Olweus Prevention Programme (www.olweus.org). These programmes generally focus on education and prevention in the school setting. Secondly, the participant approach focuses on direct intervention with those

> **Definitions**
>
> **Prevention:** acting to reduce the likelihood that a behaviour may occur.
> **Intervention:** acting to stop a behaviour from continuing.

individuals and groups that are actively involved in bullying. One example of this approach is the Support Group Method (Robinson and Maines, 2008; previously called the No-Blame Approach). In addition to these approaches, in recent years a third approach that seeks to address bullying in more creative ways, such as through utilising peer counselling or peer support, has emerged (e.g. Cowie and Wallace, 2000). The decision to implement one approach over another will often rest with the school and/or the Local Education Authority. Each of these approaches will now be discussed.

The educational approach

The main aim of this approach is to educate people about what bullying is, its effects and what to do about it. The educational approach can be used in a number of different ways, depending on who is to be educated. A classroom intervention focuses on the pupils within a classroom and may be implemented by the class teacher. On a wider level, a school-based intervention may involve educating the staff in the school, as well as the pupils. In addition, a school-based intervention will generally include the parents.

An educational curriculum is often used as part of the educational approach. Cowie and Sharp (1994) described two objectives of educational curricula: namely, raising awareness about bullying and challenging pupils' attitudes. A number of methods and resources are available for use as part of a classroom curriculum. Examples include quality circles, drama, videos, role-playing and literature. Quality circles refer to structured group meetings aimed at devising practical solutions to the problem of bullying. Through the quality circle process, pupils learn about the nature of bullying, formulate solutions and evaluate the advantages and disadvantages of putting a solution into practice (Cowie and Sharp, 1994).

The educational approach is evident in a number of anti-bullying interventions. Olweus (1993) included aspects of curriculum-based education at the class level in his intervention. This programme also included conference days and parent–teacher meetings to educate parents about bullying. The Sheffield project in England (Whitney et al., 1994) also used aspects of education in tackling bullying. Whitney et al. (1994) reported that schools were given the option of including aspects of classroom curricula, for example literature and video-based discussion, in their intervention.

There are also a number of 'Anti-bullying Packs', which have been developed as educational resources for schools. One of the most widely used packs in the UK was the *Don't Suffer in Silence* pack, published in 2000 by the Department for Education and Employment (Department for Education and Employment, 2000). This pack was updated in 2002 and included information for pupils, parents and teachers on what bullying is and what to do about it. In 2007, the Department of Children, Schools and Families (DCSF) published *Safe to Learn* (Department for Children, Schools and Families, 2007). With the establishment of the Department for Education and the move to the centralised GOV.UK website, these resources have been archived. However, many local authorities have developed their own resources: for example, Tower Hamlets published its *Anti-Bullying Resource Pack* in 2011 (see http://www.towerhamlets.gov.uk/lgsl/851–900/886_bullying_and_harassment_po.aspx).

A core feature of the educational approach is a comprehensive school policy on bullying. Whitney et al. (1994) described a school policy document as an 'essential framework within which other interventions could operate successfully and maintain continuity' (p. 21). Schools in Britain and Ireland are required to have anti-bullying policies, and Smith et al. (2008b) conducted a review of these policies in over 140 schools in one English county. This review involved identifying a set of key criteria for policies and assessing the extent of their inclusion in the schools' documentation. Criteria included: defining what constitutes bullying, specifying procedures for reporting and responding to bullying incidents, evaluating the school policy and outlining prevention strategies. Smith et al. found that, on average, 40% of the criteria were evident in schools' anti-bullying policies. In addition, they reported that few policies considered cyberbullying specifically. This highlights a continuing need for schools to review and update the policy documents that guide and govern responses to bullying.

A recent report by Thompson and Smith (2011) captures the learning from a nationwide study of the strategies used by schools to tackle bullying. Educational and curriculum-based approaches considered in this study included whole-school approaches (e.g. SEAL, which aims to promote social and emotional development) and classroom-based approaches (e.g. circle time, which consists of group discussion of issues in a friendly manner). This report highlights both the frequency with which the educational approach is adopted by schools and the role that this approach can play in the prevention of bullying in schools.

There are many benefits to the educational approach in addressing the problem of bullying. From a practical perspective, an educational curriculum can be included as part of the school's day-to-day curriculum, which may result in a long-running intervention, rather than one of limited duration. Also, this approach goes beyond those involved directly in the behaviour and can be extended to the whole school community. The inclusion of parents and the wider community might mean that there is a greater degree of consistency in the messages that young people receive about bullying. Finally, the implementation of an educational intervention may require less financial investment than some of the other approaches which will be considered later. There is a growing range of resources available for schools to use as part of an educational curriculum and there may be less need for specialised training for those involved in the implementation of these methods, unlike aspects of the participant approach which is considered next.

Conversely, there are some issues to be aware of with this broad approach. Firstly, if the programme is being delivered by a number of groups both inside and outside the school, it will require consistency in the delivery. This will result in training needs for key stakeholders such as school staff. This issue was noted as a challenge in relation to a number of approaches examined by Thompson and Smith (2011). Also, such an intervention, if it is to be included as part of the wider school curriculum, will have to be evaluated and updated on a regular basis in order to ensure its effectiveness. It is interesting to note that procedures for evaluating school anti-bullying policies were evident in only one-third of the schools included in Smith et al.'s review (2008b). Finally, it is important to recognise that the educational approach is more commonly used as a proactive or preventative measure in tackling bullying, and other techniques will be more beneficial when dealing directly with incidents.

The participant approach

This approach to tackling bullying differs from the educational approach in that it generally focuses directly on those involved in bullying, either as individuals or as groups. The methods by which this approach can be implemented range from those of a disciplinary approach, as seen in the use of sanctions, to more therapeutic approaches, as described below. Recently, restorative practice-based approaches (Morrison, 2006) have gained significant support. However, the common theme is that the school is called on to deal with the individuals directly involved in bullying – that is, both the bullies and the victims.

One of the most common methods of dealing with these individuals is through the use of discipline, including talking with the bully to raise their awareness of their behaviour and its effects, conveying disapproval for their actions and administering appropriate sanctions. The Olweus Programme (1993) includes serious talks with both the victim and the bully, which may subsequently involve meeting with their respective parents. Thompson and Smith (2011) examined schools' use of actions including reprimands, withdrawal of privileges, detention and removal from class, noting that these were used by over 90% of schools.

Methods have also been developed which focus on providing skills to those involved in bullying (both bullies and victims) to help them respond in difficult situations. Smith et al. (1994) described the use of interventions such as conflict resolution, peer counselling and assertiveness training. With the growing interest in cyberbullying, internet safety skills have become part of this repertoire and groups such as Kidscape in the UK provide information for adults and young people (www.kidscape.org.uk). A major advantage is that these methods provide pupils with the skills to deal with the problem, recognising the reality that, as an amount of bullying will probably always remain hidden, pupils must be equipped to deal with it.

There are also a number of more 'therapeutic' individual programmes that are becoming more common. The best examples of these are the Pikas method (originally the Method of Shared Concern, 1989) and Maines and Robinson's Support Group approach (originally the No Blame Approach, 1991). The Pikas method is a six-step technique of therapeutically intervening in bullying, which involves individual interviews with each of the people involved (bullies and victims), followed by a group meeting with those involved. These meetings are organised and facilitated by a trained adult (who is possibly either a counsellor or educational psychologist) and focused on developing a shared concern among the group for the victim. Pikas argued that one of the benefits of interviewing the victim is that it assists the therapist in identifying whether the pupil is a classic or a provocative victim.

This allows the therapist to adjust his/her interactions with the various individuals involved. The end stage of this process is a meeting between the bullies and the victims; however, the therapist decides when this is appropriate.

The Support Group (previously No Blame) approach is a method of tackling bullying first outlined by Maines and Robinson (1991), and then published as a resource pack (Maines and Robinson, 1992). Similar to the Pikas method, this seven-step approach tackles bullying by working to create a supportive group of students around the victim and, as the title states, no blame for the behaviour is attributed. The group's behaviour is seen as a problem that must be solved and the group is given the responsibility for solving it. This approach differs from the Pikas method in that, while the victim is interviewed to gain insight into the effects of the bullying, he or she is not included in the problem-solving process. As with the Pikas method, the process works through a series of group discussions with those involved in bullying the victim. During these discussions, the group is presented with the victim's perspective and asked if there are ways they could help. Again, follow-up meetings are used to reinforce positive decisions.

It is clear that a wide variety of methods are available for use as part of the participant approach, ranging from didactic discipline-based methods to more inclusive methods. Discussing these approaches as reactive techniques, Thompson and Smith (2011) note that sanctions/discipline and restorative techniques were most common, while the Support Group and Pikas methods were used in 10% and 5% of schools respectively. One of the benefits of participant approaches is that they target those involved in bullying directly. However, the challenge for these methods is that those involved must be identified. From the point of view of the implementation of such methods, there is also a question around who is responsible for facilitating the various methods. Pikas described a therapist facilitating the group. The training necessary to introduce these methods into schools may mean that schools are hesitant to introduce them and that they would only be used in serious cases where the individuals come into contact with an educational psychologist. However, the methods have been used as part of interventions that also include elements of the educational approach. This was the case with the Sheffield project (Whitney et al., 1994) where the Method of Shared Concern and peer counselling were both offered as options to schools involved in the study. Peer counselling or peer support is the next and final method of intervention to be considered in this chapter.

Peer support

In recognition of the fact that bullying often takes place in the presence of other children and young people but generally away from adults, Sonia Sharp (1996) argues that peers should be directly involved in prevention and intervention. Across the approaches already considered, children and young people have been actively involved in anti-bullying work to different extents; however, peer support (or peer counselling, as it is also known) represents an approach that maximises the involvement of peers in addressing bullying.

One of the main figures in the development of peer support programmes is Professor Helen Cowie, Director of the UK Observatory for Non-Violence (www.ukobservatory.com). She states that 'Peer support interventions recognize that pupils themselves have the potential to assume a helpful role in tackling a problem' (Cowie, 2000, p. 87). Cowie goes on to describe the mechanisms for peer support, whereby adults support young people in the development of listening skills and empathy, which they in turn use to support their classmates. A very useful textbook by Cowie and Wallace (2000) provides detailed guidance on the development and implementation of peer support programmes.

In their national study, peer-based approaches were a key method of proactively addressing bullying, with six different schemes examined including peer mentoring, peer mediation, buddy schemes and bystander training. An interesting finding, however, was that some of these schemes were more often recommended by local authorities than they were delivered by schools. Another development noted by the authors was the use of cyber-mentors in secondary schools, which involved online mentoring of students.

Similar to some of the more participatory approaches above, and in contrast to the educational approach, there has been limited large-scale systematic evaluation of peer support programmes. Peter Smith (2004) argues that, despite evidence of benefits in terms of the general school climate and more specifically for the pupils who work as supports, there is little evidence of a systematic positive effect on victims of bullying. While peer support may be seen to actively

Definition

Peer support: a method by which children and young people are trained to act as supports for others who are experiencing difficulties such as bullying.

CASE STUDY

The KiVa Anti-Bullying Programme in Finland

Bullying is an international phenomenon and it is not surprising that new approaches to tackling the behaviour are being developed around the world. One of the most recent new developments in school-based programmes is the KiVa Anti-Bullying programme (http://www.kivaprogram.net), which combines aspects of intervention and prevention as described above.

Commissioned by the Ministry of Education and Culture in Finland in 2006, the programme was developed by researchers and educators at the University of Turku. The programme draws on the work of Christine Salmivalli (2010) and focuses on the role and action of peer bystanders. Key elements of the programme are universal educational elements such as lessons, events and online activities for pupils, and guides for parents and teachers (Salmivalli and Poskiparta, 2012). The participant-focused elements involve discussions with those directly involved (victims and bullies) as well as working with possible peer supporters who are asked to support the pupil being bullied.

The KiVa programme has been evaluated using a randomised controlled trial, one of the most rigorous designs available to researchers (Karna et al., 2011), showing significant effects on both reports of victimisation and bullying others. While there is debate about the effectiveness of school-based programmes, with reviews suggesting that effects are modest, Juvonen and Graham (2014) describe KiVa as a promising programme. In addition, the uptake of the programme nationally in Finland suggests that there is significant support for the approach.

- Can you think of any ways in which researchers could establish the success or otherwise of an intervention like this one?
- What challenges might they face in assessing how well it has worked?

---

involve young people, there is no doubt that the demands of training and supporting the peer supporters represents a challenge for even the most committed schools.

STOP AND THINK

- How influential can children and young people be in tackling bullying themselves?
- What are the key elements for supporting them to do this effectively and safely?
- Can you see any negative effects of involving peers in tackling bullying?
- What might teachers and parents think of a programme that involves young people?

How successful have school-based interventions been?

Given the range of options available to schools wanting to address the problem of bullying, it is important to think about the effectiveness of these interventions. As mentioned earlier, one of the most widely known prevention and intervention programmes for bullying in school is the Olweus Prevention Programme (www.olweus.org). This programme was first described in detail as the basis for Dan Olweus's book *Bullying at School: What We Know and What We Can Do* (Olweus, 1993). Olweus (1994) reported the findings of an early large-scale evaluation of the effects of the intervention programme, which is generally referred to as the Bergen study, so named after the location in which the study was completed. Levels of bullying in participating schools were assessed before the intervention, and at a one- and two-year interval following the intervention. The results suggested that the intervention was a success, with involvement in bullying falling by approximately 50%.

However, few studies have been able to replicate such a dramatic impact on involvement. The Sheffield study in the UK (Whitney et al., 1994) reported changes after intervention of about 12–15% in the numbers of children bullying others and being bullied. Also of importance are the studies that have found an increase in bullying behaviour after intervention. Examples of studies showing an increase in involvement include one reported by Debra Pepler and colleagues, which evaluated a schools-based intervention in Canada (1994), and another by Earling Roland (1989), who reported the results of a study that implemented Olweus's intervention in another part of Scandinavia. However, a comprehensive review by Juvonen and Graham (2014) suggests that the inconsistencies in studies are more a reflection of differences in the research methods used to evaluate the programmes, citing challenges such as programme fidelity (i.e. has the programme been delivered as intended?) and a lack of randomised evaluations.

Merrell et al. (2008) conducted a meta-analysis – a statistical review of the body of literature on a particular effect – of school-based anti-bullying interventions. Overall 16 studies were included, including the Olweus Programme and variations on this approach. Together, the studies had over 15 000 participants and focused on a range of self-report and teacher-report outcomes. These outcomes included variables ranging from reports of participation in bullying, to witnessing bullying, to positive attitudes regarding bullying. Merrell and colleagues found that the effects included both positive and negative effects (which is in line with the individual studies reported above), but that the majority of studies did not report strong effects on bullying behaviour. They concluded that 'Although antibullying interventions appear to be useful in increasing awareness, knowledge, and self-perceived competency in dealing with bullying, it should not be expected that these interventions will dramatically influence the incidence of actual bullying and victimization behaviours' (Merrell et al., 2008, p. 41). The findings of this meta-analysis highlight the level of inconsistency in the research literature, whereby the significant changes reported following Olweus's original intervention have not been widely replicated – a finding that undermines to some extent the evidence for this programme.

Nevertheless, the debate about effectiveness continues and an interesting series of papers highlights the dynamic nature of this debate. Published in the *Journal of Experimental Criminology*, three papers by key authors in this area present the findings of a systematic review of research on schools-based interventions (Ttofi and Farrington, 2011), a commentary by other leading researchers (Smith et al., 2012), and finally a response by the original authors (Ttofi and Farrington, 2012). The overall theme of these papers suggests that school-based intervention is effective, but that factors such as the variation in programmes and the implications for different age groups need to be examined in more detail.

The challenge of tackling cyberbullying

The review of school policies on bullying described earlier highlighted a lack of consideration of cyberbullying as a specific form of bullying behaviour. While it could be argued that this is a reflection of this subtype's relatively recent emergence, it is also important to reflect on the additional challenges that cyberbullying incorporates. A paper by Australian researcher Marilyn Campbell (2005) reflects on some of the challenges of preventing and directly intervening in this area. These challenges include the need to raise awareness about these new forms of bullying behaviour among children and adults, and adults' lack of familiarity with the electronic media used in cyberbullying and the implications of this for their ability to supervise children and young people.

However, one of the key issues Campbell highlights is the lack of clarity around who is responsible for tackling cyberbullying. While many schools target traditional forms of bullying because they occur in the school environment and on the school grounds, these physical boundaries do not exist for cyberbullying. Campbell stresses the fact that this issue is further complicated by debates regarding the responsibility of phone and internet-service providers for intervening in these behaviours.

A more recent review of evidence in this area by Perren and colleagues (2012) provides a helpful overview and evaluation of different approaches to addressing cyberbullying. They conceptualise approaches under three headings:

1. Those that prevent cyberbullying by reducing the risk of exposure, such as school-based programmes, raising awareness and internet safety training.
2. Those that combat cyberbullying, such as blocking upsetting content, seeking support from peers and adults, and ignoring negative interactions.
3. Those that aim to reduce the negative effects of cyberbullying, such as promoting healthy forms of coping and providing effective support.

This framework provides a very useful overview of the ways in which we can work to tackle cyberbullying. However, most notably it highlights the lack of research in this area, with the authors noting only one experimental evaluation of a cyberbullying programme. Clearly there is a need to address this gap.

RESEARCH METHODS

Issues in researching bullying

As a rule, the findings of psychological research are only as reliable and valid as the research methods used to conduct the research. As a result, it is important to consider the way in which methodological issues might impact on our understanding of bullying.

If we consider the research that has been discussed in this chapter, it is clear that researchers working on the topic of bullying have drawn on a wide range of research methods from qualitative interviews to experimental evaluations. A number of the studies assessing the prevalence of bullying in school have used large-scale anonymous surveys, while more exploratory studies have tended to use qualitative methods. The preceding sections of this chapter have highlighted a third type of research method that is becoming more common, that of rigorous evaluation designs such as the randomised controlled trial. This design is one of the strongest available to researchers, allowing for causal conclusions to be drawn.

Each method comes with its benefits and limitations. Ahmad and Smith (1990) compared various survey methods, including anonymous and non-anonymous surveys. They observed lower rates of involvement when pupils had to write their names on the surveys and concluded that anonymous questionnaires were most suitable when examining involvement in bullying. It may be that people are more likely to report either victimisation or perpetration if they know that they cannot be later identified. More recently, a paper by Thomas et al. (2014) considered the way in which bullying and cyberbullying are assessed. They argue for a need to integrate these two areas, so that studies of bullying examine both traditional and newer forms of behaviour.

With respect to qualitative methods, these can be very effective in exploring group and individual perspectives on bullying, as we have seen in the research on children's definitions of bullying. These qualitative methods strive to elicit participants' perspectives in a manner which is not biased by the researchers' preconceived views. For other research purposes, however, such as the assessment of large-scale involvement in bullying, we do have to consider the practicality of using interviews and focus groups, which can be expensive and time consuming.

Aside from the relative merits of different methods of data collection, there are broader challenges in conducting research in this area. One of the most practical challenges is the fact that bullying is a behaviour that generally occurs if not in secret, then away from adults. The secrecy that surrounds bullying raises concerns about the validity of self-reported involvement and peer report, both of which have been used in research. However, it is generally believed that young people's reports are more accurate than adult reports. Ahmad and Smith (1990) reported that peer nominations showed better agreement with self-report questionnaires than teacher nominations did, suggesting that we should try to elicit reports from the individuals involved rather than relying upon teacher or parent report. Building on this, Thomas et al. (2014) conclude that there are fewer problems with using self-reports as compared to peer reports for establishing prevalence.

Another challenge relates to the variations in definitions of bullying discussed earlier. If people have different understandings about what constitutes bullying, then valid and reliable assessment of the nature and extent of bullying becomes difficult. In addition, it is challenging to design and deliver an appropriate intervention if individuals have distinct perspectives on the nature of the problem. Thomas et al. provide some insight into this issue in comparing definition-based measures and behaviour-based measures. They note that presenting a definition is problematic when there is variation in views of the behaviour. In contrast, however, presenting a list of behaviours excludes consideration of criteria such as repetition and intention. They call for researchers to operationalise the key criteria used to define bullying and to utilise these criteria in research to ensure accuracy.

Finally, thinking about future research on the topic of bullying, there is a huge need for longitudinal designs to be used. As we have seen, bullying is not just a problem that impacts upon children and young people. The behaviour extends across the life course, as discussed in the Lifespan box on page 461. Limited psychological research has utilised longitudinal designs to identify precursors to being a bully or a victim, or to understand the potential long-term negative consequences of bullying for both bullies and victims. A major review of longitudinal outcomes conducted by Ttofi et al. (2012) found that both victims and bullies were at higher risk of later violent and antisocial behaviour. Thus, we know that the negative effects of bullying have the potential to continue into adulthood. Much more longitudinal research is needed to trace the developmental pathways of both bullies and victims across the lifespan.

SUMMARY

In this chapter, we have explored the topic of bullying. Six learning outcomes were identified and, in this concluding section, we will revisit and consider each learning outcome in turn. Firstly, defining bullying and delineating the specific behaviours that constitute bullying has not been easy. However, most researchers generally accept that bullying involves repeated physical, verbal or psychological attack in the absence of provocation, which is intended to cause harm or distress to the victim. There is also assumed to be an imbalance of power between the bully and victim. However, a more complex picture emerges when children and young people are asked for their perspectives on what constitutes bullying, and adult and child definitions do not appear to be directly comparable. Eliciting children's and young people's conceptualisations of bullying is important since bullying most commonly occurs out of the sight of adults, and it is children and young people who perpetrate, witness and are the victims of bullying. Unlike adult definitions, elements such as repetition and intention are not central to young people's definitions. Such divergences in perspectives can have important implications for how we research bullying and how we design and evaluate effective prevention and intervention programmes. Moreover, with the emergence of new forms of bullying via electronic media, there is a need to adapt to these new media and continue to refine and update how we conceptualise bullying.

Secondly, findings arising from a range of studies on the prevalence of bullying indicate that it is a very common experience that affects many children's lives. Prevalence estimates for victimisation range from 4% to almost 42%, while rates for perpetration vary from 1% to 35%. However, there is also considerable inconsistency in prevalence rates across the studies, reflecting variation in the methods used within research and differences in how bullying is understood by children of different ages or perhaps across different cultural groups. Some clear gender patterns are also evident, particularly with regard to the types of bullying behaviour in which boys and girls engage. In looking at prevalence rates, we have seen a tendency to focus upon the involvement of bullies and victims, and, more recently, there has been a focus upon the bully/victim. Researchers have reminded us that bullying is a social and group-oriented phenomenon, so we should not ignore the fact that most children in a group are affected in some way by bullying. Six roles in bullying have been identified, and further understanding of these participant roles in bullying is needed, so that their implications for intervention can be considered.

Thirdly, we have considered developmental changes in bullying. Even very young children engage in aggressive behaviour. During the pre-school period and early childhood, physical aggression declines and verbal aggression increases. Relational kinds of aggression are also evident during this stage, particularly among girls. A steady decline in victimisation is evident from 7 to 12 years, and this continues into the period of adolescence. Among perpetrators of bullying, these behaviours appear to remain relatively stable across childhood and adolescence. However, we should be cautious in how we interpret the decline in victimisation throughout middle and later childhood and into adolescence – older children may be less likely to admit to being victimised for fear of being perceived as vulnerable.

Fourthly, in relation to cyberbullying, we have considered its distinctions from traditional forms of bullying. The prevalence of cyberbullying varies somewhat from study to study, but reliable estimates suggest that between 10% and 20% of young people have been victims, with some research suggesting that girls may be more likely than boys to become involved in it. Little research has documented developmental patterns in cyberbullying, although there are suggestions that it becomes more prevalent in the teenage years, possibly relating to older children having increased access to mobile phones and computers. However, with the even more recent changing patterns in access to technology (and younger children now having more ready access to the internet than previously) the assumption that cyberbullying is an issue for adolescents only is unfounded. Thus, cyberbullying may be distinct from other forms of bullying in terms of the gender and developmental patterns associated with it. Other important differences include the visibility of the bullying, where bullying via social networking sites may be observed by unlimited numbers of people, and the fact that cyberbullying via the internet or mobile phone could potentially happen at any time or in any place, in contrast to other forms of bullying which tend to occur during circumscribed periods of time. Some commentators suggest that, due to its relentless and public nature, the psychological impact of cyberbullying could be even greater than that experienced by victims of more traditional forms of bullying.

Fifthly, we have considered theoretical perspectives on bullying. Crick and Dodge's social-information processing model argues that children who are aggressive display a hostile attributional bias which increases the likelihood that a child will react to an ambiguous social situation with aggression. In stark contrast, Sutton and colleagues suggest that bullies are skilled manipulators who display competent theory of mind skills. Research based on the theories lends some support to both perspectives, and there has been debate in the literature about which is correct. In addition, the application of attribution theory to understanding how both bullies and victims explain the causes of bullying allows us to compare the different perspectives of those involved in the behaviour and to understand how bullying may differentially impact upon individuals. Critically reflecting upon the merits of these divergent perspectives could have important implications for how we address the problem of bullying. To date, no coherent theory of cyberbullying has been proposed, although theories of online behaviour have been utilised to understand cyberbullying. Specifically, anonymity often inherent in online interactions gives rise to disinhibition, where people are less likely to act in socially acceptable ways than they would if their identity was known. However, there has been little research to explore the role that disinhibition plays in cyberbullying.

Finally, the sixth learning outcome was concerned with interventions, and two broad approaches were described: educational approaches and participant approaches. A third approach – peer support or peer counselling – involves children directly in anti-bullying programmes. Each approach comes with advantages and disadvantages and, to date, there has been limited large-scale evaluation of many of the programmes. However, randomised controlled trials and meta-analyses of schools-based programmes are becoming more common. There continues to be ongoing debate as to the relative effectiveness of these approaches, which overall seem to have only a modest impact on rates of bullying. It is important to reflect upon the efficacy and potential for success of the various approaches along with considerations of the challenges and potential pitfalls of implementation.

REVIEW QUESTIONS

1. Based on the different perspectives on defining bullying, what are the key elements of the behaviour?
2. What are the key distinctions between bullies, victims and bully/victims?
3. How do variables such as gender and age affect involvement in bullying?
4. Compare and contrast the different theoretical positions that have been used to explain bullying.
5. What are the strengths and limitations of existing methods of preventing bullying in a school setting?
6. What are the additional challenges associated with understanding and addressing the problem of cyberbullying?

RECOMMENDED READING

For more on international trends in bullying, see:

Smith, P. K., Morita, Y., Junger-Tas, J., Olweus, D., Catalano, R., & Slee, P. (1999). *The Nature of School Bullying: A Cross-National Perspective*. London: Routledge.

Currie, C., Zanotti, C., Morgan, A., Currie, D., de Looze, M., Roberts, C., Samdel, O., Smith, O. R. F., & Barnekow, V. (Eds.) (2012) *Social Determinants of Health and Well-Being among Young People: Health Behaviour in School-Aged Children (HBSC) Study – International Report from the 2009/2010 Survey*. Copenhagen, Denmark: WHO Regional Office for Europe. [www.hbsc.unito.it/it/images/pdf/hbsc/prelims-part1.pdf]

For more on cyberbullying, see:

Kowalski, R. M., Limber, S. P., & Agatston, P. W. (2008). *Cyber Bullying*. Malden, MA: Blackwell.

For more on intervention and prevention, see:

Smith, P., Pepler, D., & Rigby, K. (2004). *Bullying in Schools: How Successful Can Interventions Be?* Cambridge: Cambridge University Press.

Salmivalli, C., & Poskiparta, E. (2012). KiVa Anti-bullying Program: Overview of evaluation studies based on a randomized controlled trial and national rollout in Finland. *International Journal of Conflict and Violence*, 6, 294–302.

For more on peer support, see:

Cowie, H., & Wallace, P. (2000). *Peer Support in Action: From Bystanding to Standing By*. London: Sage.

For more on bullying as a group process, see:

Salmivalli, C. (2010). Bullying and the peer group: A review. *Aggression and Violent Behaviour*, 15, 112–120.

For more on theories of bullying, see articles by:

Sutton, J., Smith, P. K., & Swettenham, J. (1999) and Crick, N., & Dodge, K. (1999) in *Social Development*, 8, 117–127.

RECOMMENDED WEBSITES

The website for the UK Department for Education; use the search function to find policy documents and resources on bullying. You can also follow the links to **www.teachernet.gov.uk**, which has additional information for teachers:
http://www.gov.uk

The website for a major UK-based charity with a commitment to reducing bullying and other forms of abuse – it contains information and resources for young people, parents and professionals:
http://www.kidscape.org.uk

The website for the UK Observatory for the Promotion of Non-violence, a national initiative which targets behaviours such as aggression and bullying, with the aim of promoting wellbeing:
http://www.ukobservatory.com

A website containing information on the Olweus Bullying Prevention Programme:
http://www.olweus.org/public/index.page

A website containing information on the KiVa Anti-Bullying Programme:
http://www.kivaprogram.net

Chapter 16
Atypical development
Shabnam Berry-Khan and Emma Rowley

Learning outcomes

After reading this chapter, and with further recommended reading, you should be able to:

1. Describe some of the key developmental difficulties and disorders associated with childhood, their prevalence and causes.
2. Compare and contrast the different approaches to developmental assessment, critically evaluate their strengths and weaknesses, and consider their predictive value for later development.
3. Show an awareness of the issues surrounding clinical diagnosis of a child's difficulties, and the positive and negative impact this may have on the child and family.
4. Understand the ways in which disorders of development can impact upon the child's emotional health, and consider the risk and protective factors associated with positive and negative outcomes.
5. Examine the research evidence to support different approaches to intervention.

Daniel

Daniel is a 3-year-old boy who lives with his mother, Linda, and his 18-month-old sister. Over the past few months, Linda has become increasingly concerned about Daniel's development: he has been slow to talk and uses only two words, 'car' and 'drink'. His younger sister has already overtaken him with her language, and is much better at getting what she wants, pointing and bringing things to her mother when she needs help. With Daniel, it is much more of a guessing game. Linda has to work hard just to get him to look at her, and he often just seems to ignore her when she calls him or tries to play with him. It can be very frustrating.

At playgroup, although he looks just like any other 3-year-old, Daniel stands out from the other children because of his behaviour. Every day he heads to the same corner, where he will sit, placing toy cars in a long line and peering at them closely. He doesn't play with the other children or join them for 'circle time', and cries when someone disturbs his play. He finds it hard to share or follow instructions, and needs a lot of support to join in with group activities.

- What could be the cause of Daniel's difficulties and what do they mean for his development?
- Will he be able to catch up and develop the skills he needs to learn and communicate?
- What will help him to do this?

Introduction

Child development is a complex and dynamic process, involving the interaction of a multitude of different genetic, neurological, emotional, behavioural and environmental factors. This chapter is designed to help you understand some of the ways in which a child's development can progress along an 'atypical' route and how, as developmental psychologists, we can use our assessment skills to identify and support children who may be experiencing developmental difficulties, within the context of the wider family, school and social system.

As the scenario above suggests, a child's progress through the different stages of development can be far from straightforward. As children grow and develop, they must each face their own individual challenges, building up a vast array of skills over time to become healthy, happy, fully functioning members of society.

Whilst most children will go on to achieve the expected developmental milestones, many others, just like Daniel in the example above, may face an uphill struggle from birth, experiencing significant difficulty in some or all areas of their development. So far in this book, we have looked in detail at some of the key areas of development, and the processes through which healthy, typically developing children acquire different skills, from learning and memory in infancy to the development of sophisticated 'theory of mind' understanding and formation of social relationships in childhood. But what ▶

▶ happens when children do not show this same pattern of skill acquisition? What if they are born with difficulties which mean that they will not develop at the same rate or in the same way as other children of their age? This chapter aims to introduce you to some of the important ways in which a child's development can follow an 'atypical' path, highlighting key areas of developmental disorder and disability in childhood, their causes and prevalence. Among the disabilities included are:

- developmental delay and disorder;
- learning disability;
- specific learning difficulties (e.g. dyslexia, dyspraxia);
- pervasive developmental disorders (e.g. autism spectrum disorder);
- genetic disorders (e.g. Down's syndrome, Turner's syndrome).

Then we will look at how we, as developmental psychologists, can apply our assessment and intervention skills within different settings to help understand the nature of a child's difficulties, and effectively support their ongoing development by using specific interventions such as behavioural, educational and therapeutic strategies. Finally, we will look at the impact of childhood disorder and disability on the growing child's emotional and mental health, and consider the wide-ranging impact of a child's disability on parents, siblings and the wider family system.

What is atypical development?

In the pre-school years, children typically develop a large number of skills in a relatively short period of time, from their first attempts at communication (e.g. crying and smiling), through to symbolic play, all the way to taking their first tentative steps. Whilst it is widely acknowledged that children tend to develop at their own pace, the range of skills they show largely follows a typical and predictable trajectory, with the acquisition of one skill providing a stepping stone to the next. This sequence of skills and abilities (often referred to as developmental milestones) provides a framework for our understanding of child development, allowing us to gauge the child's level of functioning from the behaviour, skills and abilities they demonstrate. Development that deviates significantly from this developmental sequence is considered 'atypical', and may be an early indication of possible difficulties in childhood.

Table 16.1 shows some of the typical developmental milestones from birth to 5 years, in the key areas of development. As Table 16.1 suggests, individual differences between children will mean that there is typically some variation (usually several months) in the age at which the different physical, cognitive, social and emotional milestones are reached. In the same way, the rate of development between different areas of skill varies considerably: some children may show early advances in one area, such as motor ability, while others may race ahead with language, their first words appearing much earlier than expected. Children who show early progress in one area do not necessarily show a similar rate of development across other areas. In fact, it is not uncommon to see a slowing down in the development of some skills during a burst of development in another, with the child using all of his biological and psychological resources to develop one skill at a time. Children with special needs often move through the different developmental stages in unusual and very uneven ways. For example, they may sit or walk at the usual age but show delay in their language skills. Parents, health visitors and other caregivers have the critical role of observing and charting the child's early development, keeping records of skill attainment and behaviour, which may later help to identify specific areas of need or difficulty. In the case of unusual or atypical development, this is often the first step in the identification and assessment process, assisting clinicians and child development specialists in determining the specific needs and/or possible developmental diagnosis relevant to the individual child.

Table 16.1 Developmental milestones chart.

Area of development	Milestone	Age range in typically developing children
Gross motor skills (physical movement)	Holds head steady in sitting position	1–4 months
	Sits independently	5–9 months
	Stands alone	9–16 months
	Walks alone	9–17 months
Fine motor skills and eye–hand coordination	Follows object with eyes	1–3 months
	Reaches out and grasps object	2–6 months
	Passes objects from hand to hand	4–8 months
	Builds a tower of two wooden blocks	10–19 months
	Copies a circle	24–40 months
Communication skills	Babbles 'dada', 'mama'	5–14 months
	Responds to familiar words	5–14 months
	First words spoken with meaning	10–23 months
	Shows need using gesture	11–19 months
	Uses two-word phrases	15–32 months
Personal and self-help skills	Feeds self with biscuit	4–10 months
	Drinks from cup	9–17 months
	Dry by day	14–36 months
	Bowel control	16–48 months
Social interaction	Smiles when talked to	1–2 months
	Plays peek-a-boo games	3–6 months
	Distinguishes between familiar adults	6–9 months
	Shows anxiety at separation	9–12 months
	Watches other children and copies play	24–36 months
Cognitive skills	Shows anticipation for expected events	0–3 months
	Imitates others' facial expressions	3–6 months
	Understands object permanence	6–9 months
	Basic trial and error and problem solving	6–9 months
	Understands cause-and-effect	12–18 months

Source: adapted from Cunningham, C. (1988) *Down's Syndrome: An Introduction for Parents.* Souvenir Press Ltd. Human Horizon Series.

Understanding the process of child development

The developmental milestones provide a helpful guide for parents and professionals alike, and can act as an important indicator of later developmental problems. However, progression through the different stages of development is not simply a matter of genetics or predetermined physical maturation (see Chapter 9, 'Attachment and early social experiences'). As well as being influenced by the child's genetic and neurological characteristics, it is also dependent upon the dynamic interactions between biological and environmental influences (see Figure 16.1; Sheridan, 2008).

These interactions between biology and environment result in a high level of variability in children's developmental outcomes. For example, a child growing up in a country in which war, conflict and food shortage are an

Figure 16.1 Influences on development.

Source: Sheridan, M. (2008) *From Birth to Five Years*, Routledge.

everyday reality may show a vastly different developmental profile from a child who lives in a safe, stable and economically secure part of the world. In the same way, a child experiencing abuse, neglect or growing up with parents with mental health difficulties may experience many more developmental challenges than the child who has a healthy, secure parental attachment relationship and grows up in a supportive environment. As we shall see in this chapter, in order to really understand a child's developmental difficulties, we must consider both the

NATURE–NURTURE

Epigenetics and our understanding of the great nature–nurture debate

How do our experiences and genes interact to shape development? And can this interaction lead to alterations in the brain development and behaviour of subsequent generations? Challenging the accepted science of genetics, recent studies suggest that we inherit much more from our mothers and fathers than just our genetic material, and that experiences early in development can in fact shape the activity of our DNA. This new research could radically change the way we understand childhood disorders, which may, perhaps, be traced back to 'epigenetic markers' left generations ago.

An example of this ground-breaking new area of research is the 2006 study by Professor Meaney at McGill University, Montreal, and Frances Champagne, a behavioural scientist at Columbia University in New York, which identified genetic changes in the adult offspring of rats, depending upon the level of maternal care received in infancy. Their research (Champagne et al., 2006) showed that those rats who were repeatedly groomed and tended to by their mothers during their first week of life were subsequently much better at coping with stressful situations than those who received little or no maternal contact in their early days.

Although the idea that early nurture has positive psychological effects on children is nothing new, Champagne et al.'s study suggests that there could be an underlying physiological change in these children, altering the expression of genes involved in reproductive behaviour, and thus allowing for the transmission of maternal behaviour across generations. Epigeneticists also think that socio-economic factors such as poverty may 'mark' children's genes, leaving them more prone to depression and addiction in later life, regardless of their own circumstances in adulthood.

These latest findings suggest that a so-called Lamarckian model of 'soft inheritance' is possible, in which parents can pass on characteristics acquired during their lifetime to their offspring. The exciting field of epigenetics is only just beginning to unfold, and as it does, it threatens to challenge all that we accept as true about the science of human inheritance.

Child development is affected by genetics, culture and context.
Source: Photolibrary/BSIP Medical

> **STOP AND THINK**
>
> Revisit the case study of Daniel at the beginning of this chapter.
>
> - Using Figure 16.1, can you identify any biological or environmental factors which may be impacting upon his developmental progress?
> - What else would you need to find out to explore the different influences on his development more fully?

sequences of development as well as the context within which this development takes place (see Figure 16.1).

Child development in context

Throughout this chapter, we will be looking at the way in which biological and genetic influences, as well as illness and disease, can impact upon a child's development. However, as we have learnt, of equal importance are the environmental influences of the child's past learning experiences, her immediate social and psychological environment (e.g. parents, siblings, schoolteachers and relatives) and the wider cultural, political, religious and social surroundings in which she grows and develops. Today, developmental psychologists have a much wider appreciation of the significance of environmental factors in shaping the child's development, and much research has been carried out to determine the extent to which these factors play a causal role in childhood difficulties (see Rutter et al.'s study from 2001 examining the effects of institutional deprivation on later childhood development).

One of the pioneers in this field, Urie Bronfenbrenner, highlights the role of environment or 'nurture' in shaping a child's development. His *ecological systems theory* (Bronfenbrenner, 1989) defines a series of five sociocultural systems or 'layers', ranging from family and school interactions to the beliefs, values and traditions of the child's culture and wider social system, which interact with each other to help shape the child's development. In this way, changes or difficulties in one layer will have a ripple effect, causing changes throughout the other layers or systems. Bronfenbrenner's theory has recently been renamed *bioecological systems theory*, to emphasise the role of the child's own biology – arguably one of the most fundamental environmental influences fuelling later development (see Chapter 2, 'Theoretical perspectives', for a full discussion of this theory).

Culture and developmental 'norms'

So far in this chapter, we have discussed a model of child development which is well established within Europe and large parts of the Western world: namely, the 'milestone approach', which maps neatly onto a Western model of healthcare and education, with its specific, culturally bound physical, cognitive and social targets. However, research suggests that different cultural expectations and child-rearing practices can strongly influence the rate and expression of children's development.

Consider, for example, the stage at which children are encouraged by their parents or caregivers to feed themselves. In the Western world, adults encourage their infants early on to learn self-feeding, even if learning to self-feed means making a mess. By contrast, in non-Western cultures, the adult's primary purpose in feeding the infant is to ensure that they have eaten an adequate meal with the minimum amount of waste or mess. As such, they may continue to spoon-feed their child for a much longer period than is considered the 'norm' in Europe. Similarly, babies in the West tend to spend much longer periods of time by themselves – sleeping

Developmental milestones across cultures

- Motor precocity of African infants who sit, crawl and walk at least two months earlier than Caucasian infants (Ainsworth, 1977; Geber and Dean, 1957; Capute et al., 1985)
- Delayed self-feeding and cutlery skills in African and South Asian children compared to US norms (Gokiert et al., 2007)
- Advanced attainment of pencil skills in Japanese children compared to British norms (Saida and Miyashita, 1979)
- Earlier reverse-style rolling skills in infants born in Hong Kong compared to Caucasian infants (Nelson et al., 2004)

Figure 16.2 Cultural differences in child development.

Table 16.2 Table of compulsory schooling in Europe.

Age	Country
4	Northern Ireland
5	Cyprus, England, Malta, Scotland, Wales
6	Austria, Belgium, Croatia, Czech Republic, Denmark, France, Germany, Greece, Hungary, Iceland, Republic of Ireland, Italy, Liechtenstein, Luxembourg, Netherlands, Norway, Portugal, Romania, Slovakia, Slovenia, Spain, Switzerland, Turkey
7	Bulgaria, Estonia, Finland, Latvia, Lithuania, Poland, Serbia, Sweden

Source: National Foundation for Educational Research (2013)

in separate rooms, and amusing themselves in playpens. As a result, they learn to use verbal communication to get the attention of adults (e.g. calling out to the parent or caregiver out of necessity), whereas babies from non-Western cultures, who spend much of their time in close physical contact with their parents, learn to use non-verbal communication such as hand gestures or changes in muscle tone or posture to get their needs met. Figure 16.2 summarises some of the research findings highlighting the variation in child development across cultures.

Across cultures, a powerful determinant of childhood skill development is the age at which formal schooling begins. Across Europe, the age of compulsory schooling ranges between 4 years of age (e.g. in Northern Ireland) and 7 years of age (e.g. in Finland and Bulgaria). In recent years, researchers have explored the relationship between early schooling and the cognitive, emotional and behavioural development of children. The findings are varied, with some studies concluding that early formal education may in fact impede children's natural skill development, and may have inadvertently contributed to the higher rates of learning needs in British children of school age (House, 2011). This may go some way to explaining the success of the Finnish education system, which sees very positive academic outcomes despite its relatively late statutory school attendance age of 7 years.

As developmental psychologists, a curiosity and awareness of the differences that exist across cultures in terms of child-rearing, social, cultural and religious practices is vital in understanding the individual child. Whilst comprehensive assessment of the effects of culture on children's wellbeing may not always be possible, careful consideration of issues of cultural identity and acknowledgement of the importance of culture in the child's behaviour and development may enable us to develop a more complete picture of the child, incorporating this information into an holistic formulation of his individual strengths and difficulties.

STOP AND THINK

Consider your own early development, or that of siblings or relatives. You may want to discuss this with someone who knew you as you were growing up.

- What family, cultural or religious beliefs helped influence your parents'/caregivers' ideas about child development?
- What impact did these ideas and beliefs have on your early experience and learning?

Statutory assessment of special educational needs in children

More than one-fifth of school-age children in England are said to have 'special educational needs' (SEN), amounting to around 1.7 million children. SEN refers to learning difficulties or disabilities, which range from problems in thinking and understanding, to physical or sensory difficulties and/or difficulties with speech and language. It can also include social problems, including how a child relates to and behaves with other people, or emotional and behavioural difficulties.

Often a child's special educational needs are picked up when parents or school staff notice that the child is falling behind his peers. At this point, the school may put in place additional support measures, such as extra support with reading, under a programme known as 'School Action'. Should more specialist support be needed, this programme is stepped up to 'School Action Plus'. Most children with additional needs fall within one of these two school-based programmes.

When the child requires support in a number of areas, and/or the school cannot provide all of the help the child needs, it may suggest that a statutory assessment of the child's special educational needs is carried out. This assessment, conducted by the Local Education Authority and contributed to by the child's family, school and healthcare team, is a detailed investigation to find out exactly what the child's special educational needs are, and what additional help the child needs when at school. Once this assessment has been completed, a document or 'Education, Health and Care Plan or EHCP' is produced, setting out the child's needs, and the minimum recommended support they require in order to access the school curriculum. Often the EHCP will include provision for one-to-one support for the child during lessons, as well as specialist therapy input, such as speech and language therapy, as part of the school day.

Once an EHCP has been issued, the child's school is obliged to use the additional funding it receives to put in place the suggested support. The level of support offered is reviewed each year in an 'annual review meeting', usually attended by the child's teacher, any therapists working with the child, as well as the child's parents. In England, around 13% of children with special educational needs have an Education, Health and Care Plan. Unfortunately, due to the cost involved in implementing the recommendations outlined in an EHCP, the number of formal plans being written is falling, despite an increase in the proportion of children known to have learning difficulties.

Holding all of these important contextual factors in mind, how might we identify when children are showing signs of atypical development? What might such an assessment look like, and who might be involved? What kinds of developmental problem do we see in children, and how can we offer support to enable them to lead a happy and fulfilling life? These are just some of the questions which we shall explore throughout the rest of this chapter.

Assessment

For the child with atypical development, the identification of differences in development is only the first step: once these have been identified, a journey begins in which parents and caregivers generally seek to understand what might be causing their child's difficulties. Although the process can vary enormously, parents, just like the parents of David in the case example (on page 488), often express their concerns to a health professional, who may refer the child for assessment. But what is assessment, and how can it be used to identify areas of difficulty? What are the approaches which clinicians use to better understand a child's developmental trajectory?

What is assessment?

General developmental assessment can take a variety of forms, and typically involves the gathering of information from a range of different sources, such as parents, teachers, specialist health visitors and other health professionals, as well as the use of a range of different assessment methods, from history taking and structured parent questionnaires to cognitive assessments and play-based observations. This holistic approach to information gathering ensures that there is as much information as possible available about the child's functioning and behaviour in all different areas of their life. This thorough and often time-consuming

Definition

Assessment: assessment is the process of collecting information on children, typically through observations, tests, clinician/teacher rating scales, etc., in order to make inferences about their development, typically within a school or clinical context.

CASE STUDY

Extract from a health visitor's referral letter to the community child development team

Dear Colleagues,
Re: David Thomas, DOB: 12/09/2011

Thank you for seeing this lovely 3-year-old boy who was brought to my clinic today by his parents. David has left-sided hearing loss and experiences recurrent ear infections. His speech is showing signs of significant delay, and his speech sounds for familiar objects are often unclear. Since he started nursery, his parents have noticed that David is behind his peers in a number of key areas, including his play skills, which they describe as rather 'babyish'. He is also reluctant to finger-feed, and still insists on his parents spoon-feeding him at each mealtime. He is not yet potty trained, and mum tells me that he doesn't yet appear aware of when he may have a full nappy.

Parents are naturally quite concerned, and wonder whether David may have more global difficulties with his development. I wonder if you could offer the family an assessment in your clinic.

---

process necessarily draws upon the skills of a range of different health professionals, including paediatricians, clinical psychologists, speech and language therapists, occupational therapists and physiotherapists, who may work jointly or in parallel to carry out assessments and bring together information crucial to the assessment process. By using different forms of assessment, we can begin to develop an understanding of the child's skills and abilities over a range of important developmental domains, from physical growth and development of motor skills like walking, running and jumping, to cognition (thinking and learning), communication and social development.

Why assess?

Psychological assessment is a complex, detailed, in-depth process. Broadly speaking, psychological assessments are used to:

- provide a diagnosis for a treatment plan;
- assess a particular area of functioning or disability, such as for school settings, to enable more appropriate support and intervention to be provided;
- assess treatment outcomes;
- help courts decide issues such as child custody or competency to stand trial;
- help assess job applicants or employees;
- provide career development counselling or training.

(Standards for Education and Training in Psychological Assessment, 2006)

In the case of child development assessments, the purpose is to understand the trajectory of development that a child is following in order to diagnose a disability and to inform future interventions.

Ethical dilemmas in the assessment and diagnosis of young children

Assessment of young children, when it is done in an appropriate way, can be an extremely useful way of providing information to caregivers, parents, teachers and clinicians about the child's skills, abilities and areas of difficulty. Within a clinical context, assessment can be used to help identify and, where appropriate, diagnose specific disorders of development. Western models of healthcare are based on diagnoses, although opinion varies widely as to the value and possible negative implications of giving young children a diagnostic label. How helpful it is to the client? Do clinicians do more harm than good by using labels?

Benefits of diagnosis include guiding appropriate treatment and making the process of assessment more efficient (Jellinek and McDermott, 2004), ensuring that diagnostic labels are based on scientifically sound evidence (American Psychological Association, 1994) and facilitating effective clinical practice by using treatments that work (Roth et al., 1996). The American Psychological Association (1995) has argued that diagnosis aids communication across health disciplines within the context of multidisciplinary teams. Pilgrim (2001) also states that having a diagnosis might be helpful for a client because the fact that the disorder is easily researchable can be useful, for example, when requesting additional support, such as from the education system. It is possibly for these reasons that only diagnostic methods of describing problems are accepted for insurance claims and in courts of law (Butler, 1998).

On the other hand, diagnoses can be problematic. For example, diagnostic categories can often overlap and, on their own, do not provide clinicians with a clear indication of a client's disorder (e.g. Johnstone, 2006); nor do they always capture the rare or complex symptoms of the disorder (Butler, 1998). In addition, diagnosis, as defined by the *Diagnostic and Statistics Manual* (DSM), is consistently found to have low reliability and validity (Aboraya et al., 2006). Jellinek and McDermott (2004) stated that clients' context needs to be known, otherwise the problem will not be understood. For example, a child's defiant behaviour can be indicative of a number of issues: to hide a learning difficulty, to gain attention from parents, to be accepted into a peer group or even in response to a stressful situation at home. As Boyle (2001) stated, without a context or further details about the problem's causes, a treatment plan is difficult to develop and is not likely to produce positive outcomes.

Finally, one of the most damaging problems with diagnosis is the social stigma that it can create. Social labels and categories given to groups of similarly perceived people assume certain characteristics and traits. These assumptions lead to expectations of an individual and can lead to stereotypes and prejudice (Devine, 1989). While stereotypes may contain a kernel of truth (Jones, 1997), individual differences must still be considered before category assumptions are applied.

Assessment methods

Now that we have understood what assessment is and why it is useful to clinicians, the following section introduces you to some of the common assessment methods that a psychologist (or paediatrician) might use as part of a generalised assessment of functioning within a child development context. These include:

- play-based assessment and observation;
- standardised cognitive assessment;
- developmental history taking.

Play-based assessment and observation

As earlier chapters suggest, play is one of the most fundamental ways in which a child can learn about herself and the world around her. It is through play that the child can practise, elaborate on and perfect skills before they become necessary for survival in adulthood (Rubin, 1982; Smidt, 2011). In this way, play represents an important tool for learning and developing personal resources for life.

Play provides a naturalistic opportunity for the child to test out and develop their sensory and motor skills (Piaget, 1962), social abilities (Rubin et al., 1989) and language (Caplan and Caplan, 1973). It is also a natural means of expression for most children, and it allows children to experience a wide range of emotions and situations. By observing how children play and what they play with, it is possible to gain a rich understanding of a child's developmental level, as well as obtaining important information about their cultural and social context. As such, clinical assessments may utilise formal and informal play-based assessment observations alongside other types of assessment to inform children's developmental profiles.

Bronfenbrenner argued that 'much of contemporary developmental psychology is the science of the strange behaviour of children in strange situations with strange adults for the briefest possible periods of time'. Accordingly, he considered that only 'experiments created as real are real in their consequences' and stressed that research should begin to focus on how children develop in settings representative of their actual world (i.e. in 'ecologically valid' settings). For instance, instead of studying children only in the laboratory, we should study them in their homes, schools and playgrounds (Bronfenbrenner, 2004).

Today, developmental psychologists continue to believe that, in order to be able to observe a child in a way that would indicate his true skills, we must seek to make the assessment process as relaxed, naturalistic and appealing to children as possible. When play is used, children are able to have the freedom to express themselves, focusing on a range of items and activities which are of interest to them, and with which they are happy to engage for a period of time. Assessments of play involve observations of how a child plays alone, with peers and with adults in free play or in specific games, as well as how she uses communication, problem solving and imaginative skills to enhance her play. Table 16.3 highlights the types of toy that can be used in a play assessment and what types of skill a child can demonstrate.

The way children play can be useful in understanding their developmental abilities and difficulties in a naturalistic way. However, there are some criticisms of using play to assess children's skills. A number of factors can confound play assessments, making it challenging to understand the true nature of a child's presentation. For example, if a child has a poor attention span and cannot complete a colour-matching puzzle, it may appear as if he is unable to match colours. Or if a child has a poor pincer grip and cannot hold a pencil effectively, she may appear not to be able to draw. Some children have a more passive temperament and so their social skills may look and possibly be less advanced than their peers. Equally, a child who wants a toy from a high shelf, but does not feel confident that someone will help her, might attempt to get the toy from the shelf themselves rather than ask for help.

How children play with age-appropriate toys can give you an insight into their cognitive abilities.
Source: Lam

Table 16.3 Examples of how toys and activities can be used to assess a child's development.

Toy/activity	Assessment/questions	Domain of skill displayed
Cause-and-effect toy (toys with buttons that result in immediate results, e.g. flashing lights or a sound)	Operates it? How?	Cognitive, motor
	Asks for help if stuck?	Communication
	Shows emotion on his face?	Social
	Involves others, directly (calls them over) or indirectly (looks at them)?	Communication, social
	Attention level?	Cognitive
	Moves on to something else?	Social, communication, cognitive
	Verbal or non-verbal?	Communication
Drawing	Pencil grip?	Motor
	Type of drawing?	Cognitive
	Attention level?	Cognitive, behaviour
	Shows drawings to others?	Social
	Brings others into activity?	Social
	Shares drawing tools?	Social

Toy/activity	Assessment/questions	Domain of skill displayed
Puzzles, problem-solving tasks (e.g. threading, colour matching)	Communicates needs?	Communication
	Able to complete?	Cognitive
	If the task cannot be done?	Communication, social, cognitive, behaviour
Physical play	Emotional expression?	Social, communication, behaviour
	Shares his enjoyment with others?	Social
	Able to regulate emotion after being aroused?	Social, behaviour
	Ability to transition to another task?	Social
	Movement and coordination?	Motor
Home corner, dolls, cars	Initiates play?	Social, cognitive
	Follows someone else's lead?	Social
	Builds on a story brought in by someone else?	Social, cognitive
	Tolerates intrusion from others?	Social
	Repetitive?	Behaviour
	Verbal or non-verbal?	Communication
Building blocks	Can replicate structures?	Cognitive
	Can stack?	Cognitive
	Shares blocks?	Social, behaviour
	Communication style?	Communication

Children who have experienced trauma may also express their play skills in an unusual way which can belie their actual skills and abilities. In other words, attention span, physical dexterity, personality, attachment style and emotional factors can interfere with a child's 'true' ability. In addition, it must be remembered that our understanding of play is based on Western child-rearing practices. Thus, an assumption is made that the child is familiar with the toy, and understands its purpose and function, and that this form of play is positively construed by parents.

It is possible that in large parts of the world, children do not have access to the Western toys used in such play assessments. As such, it would not be a fair assessment of a child's development if these same toys and activities were used to assess a child who had recently moved to the country from another part of the world. In this instance, it would be perfectly understandable if the child were to show uncertainty as to the function of a 'jack-in-the-box', perhaps become alarmed and upset by the 'popping-up' of the figure at the end of the play routine. Such play with toys may not be a 'practised skill' for this child because it is not considered a worthwhile activity by his parents. Caution must therefore be exercised in interpreting the play skills of children from different cultures, particularly if playing with toys in this way is not usually encouraged or understood. Finally, Russ (2004) states that play-based approaches need to be better supported by empirical studies. This is particularly important for European models of healthcare and education, which strive to offer the very best evidence-based, scientifically driven assessment and support for children with developmental difficulties.

STOP AND THINK

Think about the children you know.

- What does their play say about their level of cognitive and social development?
- Is their play affected by other factors, such as culture, anxiety or poor attention?
- Are their play skills different in different places, such as home and nursery? If so, in what ways?
- Could attachment style account for this difference in any way?

Standardised assessment

As we have seen, direct observation of young children at play can be one of the most valuable ways to gather information about key aspects of their cognitive, language, social, emotional and physical (or motor) development. This is because it enables us to gain a 'fly-on-the-wall' view of the child's development, communication and behaviour in a relaxed and familiar context, doing what comes most naturally to them – playing. With such an effective and naturalistic approach to assessments, it is easy to see why so many clinicians value observation of the child's play above other, more structured forms of assessment.

However, whilst play assessment is undeniably a vital part of the assessment process, it does not give us any way of accurately measuring the child's skills in an exact (quantitative) way over time, or systematically and reliably comparing their abilities to those of other children of a similar age. Providing this information can be helpful not only in monitoring an individual child's progress over time, but also in knowing what kinds of support, and at what level, a child may need within his school or nursery setting, according to his profile of strengths and difficulties.

Standardised assessment tools can provide a useful way of looking in greater detail at the different areas of a child's development. Complementing more informal parent report and observational methods, they offer a uniform way of comparing an individual child's level of functioning to that of a large sample of other children of the same age. The results of such assessments allow clinicians and parents to see more clearly whether there are specific areas of the child's development which fall below the expected or typical range (often referred to as the 'developmental norm'), and whether their specific profile of strengths and difficulties fits with a particular clinical diagnosis. Moreover, administration of the same test at key points in the child's developmental trajectory can give valuable information about progress and/or possible loss of skill in the major developmental domains, as well as allowing us to predict the child's level of functioning in later childhood.

Child development specialists use a wide range of different standardised measures, some of which aim to measure functioning in one specific area of development (e.g. language and communication), whilst others offer a comprehensive profile of the child's strengths and difficulties in all five key developmental domains (cognition, language, social–emotional, motor and adaptive behaviour). An assessment tool widely used across much of Europe and the USA is the Bayley Scales of Infant Development (Bayley-III; Bayley, 1969, 1993). This measure, which includes a core battery of five scales, can be used to assess children from as young as 1 month of age (although more typically children aged from 1 to 3 years). The Bayley uses a combination of interactive (mainly non-verbal) play-based tasks and parent questionnaires, designed to measure specific strengths and competencies, as well as identifying any areas of difficulty. It also provides a valid and reliable measure of a child's abilities, in addition to giving comparison data for children with high-incidence clinical diagnoses.

One of the key areas of the developmental assessment often undertaken by a developmental psychologist is cognitive assessment (the Stanford–Binet Intelligence Test and Wechsler Intelligence Scales are the most widely used measures in the world). This specialised form of testing is used to gain a more detailed understanding of the child's cognitive or intellectual ability, so as to identify specific areas of strength and difficulty, to help understand fluctuations in concentration and attention levels and identify specific learning difficulties (e.g. dyslexia), or more global impairment, often referred to as a learning disability. The test itself usually comprises a number of different tasks and activities (see the photo below and

A standardised developmental assessment uses interactive, play-based tasks to identify specific strengths and difficulties in children from as young as 1 year old.
Source: Pearson Education Ltd/Jules Selmes

ASSESSMENT

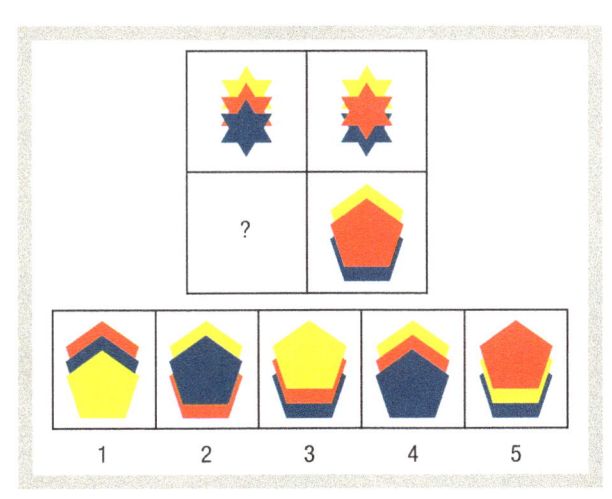

Figure 16.3a Matrix reasoning (a measure of fluid reasoning). The child is presented with a partially filled grid and asked to select the item that properly completes the matrix.

Figures 16.3a and 16.3b), which are administered by the clinician during one or more individual sessions with the child. Sub-tests are designed to measure abilities such as verbal and non-verbal fluid reasoning, receptive and expressive vocabulary, working memory and processing speed.

The sum of the child's performance on key tasks allows an overall intelligence quotient (IQ) score to be calculated. As with other standardised assessments, this overall score can be usefully compared to the test's own same-age sample norms, to give an indication of whether the child's thinking and learning skills are at the level expected for her age (or within the 'normal range').

IQ and the normal distribution curve

IQ scores in the general population are known to follow a normative distribution, which can be represented graphically as a bell-shaped curve (see Figure 16.4). As the graph shows, in a typical population, the largest percentage of scores fall within the 'average' range (between 85 and 115), whilst a much smaller number score moderately below (70–85; indicative of 'mild to moderate learning disability') or moderately above (115–130) the average range. Very high (above 130) and very low (below 70) scores are rare. Children gaining an IQ score of 70 or below are likely to have significant learning disability.

IQ is often expressed in 'percentiles' (or 'centiles' as they are sometimes called). Different from the percentage scores used to indicate the number of tasks the child completed correctly, the percentile rank of a score highlights the percentage of scores within the same age range which are the same or lower than the child's actual score. For example, a child with an overall IQ score of 100 has a percentile rank of 50. This means that the child has scored the same or higher than 50% of the children within his age range. By contrast, a child with an IQ score of 80 has a percentile rank of only 9, meaning that only 9% of children within her age range would score the same or lower (i.e. the majority of children tested would gain an IQ score above 80).

Unfortunately, there has been much criticism of the use of cognitive assessment or 'IQ testing' in the past. Historically, such assessments may have been carried out in order to make ruthless decisions about who might be eligible for limited resources and, in some cases, to exclude those with a lower score from being able to access particular educational and employment opportunities. Whilst most health and education professionals

Figure 16.3b Picture concepts (a non-verbal measure of fluid reasoning, perceptual organisation and categorisation). From each row of objects, the child selects objects that go together based on an underlying concept.

> **Definition**
>
> Intelligence quotient (IQ): devised by the German psychologist William Stern (1912), the intelligence quotient or IQ is a score derived from one of several different standardised tests designed to measure ability over a range of different cognitive tasks.

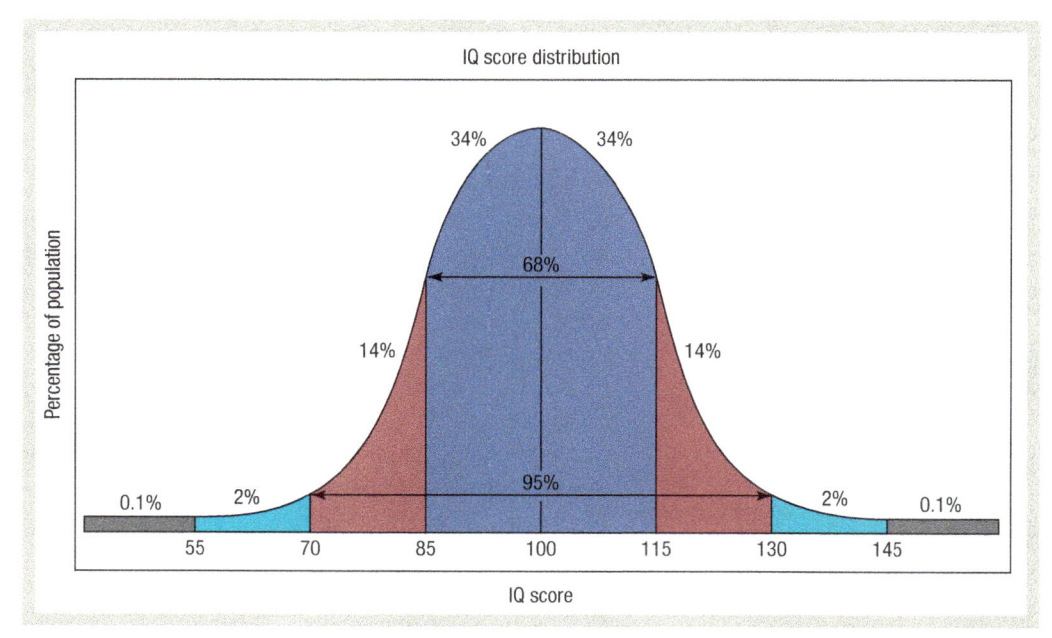

Figure 16.4 IQ scores across the general population.

would agree that these practices are no longer employed within a modern healthcare system, valid concerns remain about the usefulness of intelligence tests in accurately capturing a child's everyday functioning. Critics argue that the formats of many intelligence tests do not capture the complexity and immediacy of real-life situations, thus limiting their ability to predict non-test or non-academic intellectual abilities.

Best practice dictates that, just as with any other assessment, cognitive testing should not be used in isolation as a measure of a child's skills and abilities. Rather, it should form part of a comprehensive package of assessment which examines the child's full range of abilities across different settings, taking into consideration important individual, familial and contextual factors.

Developmental history assessment

As well as using play-based and standardised assessments to get a sense of the current abilities of a child, it is crucial to the assessment process that the history of the child's development is also considered and understood alongside the child's presentation at the time of investigation.

Developmental history taking is an assessment that typically asks parents or main caregivers to describe their child's behaviours, skills and abilities throughout the child's life from pregnancy through to their current age. A clinician will ask the informant a series of in-depth and specific questions relating to their child, eliciting information about the age at which the behaviour was shown, the quality of the behaviour and, if applicable, the frequency of its occurrence.

The clinician initially asks the parents for details about the child's early development using questions that are guided by the developmental milestones. These questions also focus on the child's current strengths and difficulties as a way to understand the carer's concerns and the child's current abilities. Clinicians also try to assess the child's abilities at around the ages of 5 to 7 (even if the child is older at the time of assessment), because a child would usually have developed a wide range of skills and behaviours by this age and the pattern of skills acquisition is clearer. In addition, the developmental profile at this age is somewhat predictive of future progress, so the details can be used to advise about prognosis (Bolton, 2001). This is also the age range at which children generally enter the education system in most countries within Europe, so it can act as a convenient anchor point for the parents' recall.

Interviewing parents or other informants about a child's early developmental history can be difficult and should be approached with two issues in mind. The first is that the ability for most parents to remember what their child did, at what age, for how long and to what extent can be challenging, particularly if they have other children or if the period of time was busy for them. Forewarning parents that they will be asked questions about their child's development to date can be useful to encourage them to think about their child's past and prepare for the interview. Asking questions about specific events such as birthdays, moving home or the birth of a sibling can help parents to anchor their memories and to describe their child at those times.

The second issue is that the professional should elicit from parents descriptive statements rather than evaluative ones about their child's development. This is aimed at distinguishing the parents' perceptions, which can be biased by anxiety and meaning, from more objective descriptions of what their child was like.

> **STOP AND THINK**
>
> As you might imagine from the example questions above, clinicians ask for in-depth, detailed and sometimes circumstantial, and therefore personal, information about and around a child's life to date.
>
> - How do you think a parent might feel about such questions?
> - How might a clinician make the developmental history-taking session less stressful for the parents?

Assessments by other health professionals

Far from being the preserve of psychologists and paediatricians, comprehensive assessment of a child's development necessarily involves a wide range of health professionals, who may work together with, or alongside, the multidisciplinary team to help develop a more complete understanding of the child's strengths and difficulties.

Given the wide range of factors to consider during a developmental assessment, it is common for colleagues from speech and language therapy, occupational therapy, physiotherapy and community nursing, as well as nursery and school staff, all to play a role in bringing together important information about the child's functioning. Like psychologists, allied health professionals use a range of different assessment techniques, observations and standardised measures to explore the child's skills and abilities. Whilst an exhaustive description of these assessments is beyond the scope of this chapter, the following section aims to summarise some of the ways in which the important contribution of these professionals is delivered.

Specialist health visitor

A specialist health visitor is a qualified nurse and health visitor with additional experience, knowledge and skills in the area of childhood disability. He works closely with the child and family within their own community, playing an important role in the early screening and detection of developmental difficulties. From the moment a difficulty is identified, the specialist health visitor works to link the child and family with the appropriate specialist services, supporting them through the process of assessment and diagnosis, offering advice and encouraging parents to take an active role in the child's care and decision-making process. Thus, coordination can be a key part of his role, focusing on current needs and anticipating future needs with physical health, mental health, social care and education colleagues.

Speech and language therapy

Speech and language therapists (sometimes referred to as speech and language pathologists) are a vital component of any child development team. As we learnt earlier, speech and language difficulties are some of the most common issues affecting young children, accounting for a large number of referrals to child health services. Alongside detailed medical history taking, speech and language therapists are intrinsically involved in the assessment of these difficulties, carrying out a range of assessments from informal games and observation to structured speech and language evaluation using standardised measures. The speech and language therapist can provide important information about structural difficulties affecting language production (e.g. in children suffering from cleft palate or other muscular abnormalities), difficulties of word production, expressive language and understanding, and those difficulties which may be part of a wider syndrome or disorder, such as those seen within the autism spectrum. In schools, speech and language therapists observe the child's use of language and communication in the familiar environment of the classroom to gain valuable insight into the nature and quality of the child's interactions and social initiations with their same-age peers. They would also seek teaching staffs' usually impartial perspectives as part of their assessment.

Occupational therapy

Occupational therapists work with young children from birth onwards, treating both physical and developmental disorders through purposeful activities that improve and develop important functional skills needed for everyday independence (e.g. feeding, brushing teeth and hair, and dressing). They may work with children with physical delay or disability where there are concerns regarding the development of fine and gross motor, visual–motor, oral–motor, self-care and motor planning skills, often where children have a limited sensory experience or lack normal motor control. In addition, they can provide specialist therapeutic input around sensory integration techniques which, some research suggests, can be particularly helpful in managing irregular levels of sensory stimulation with children with autism and other developmental disabilities (Schaaf and Miller, 2005). Following assessment, occupational therapists sometimes work together with clinical psychologists to help develop children's adaptive skills, particularly where a behavioural approach to skill acquisition may be useful.

Psychiatry

Psychiatrists, like their paediatric colleagues, commonly play an important role in the neuropsychological and developmental assessment of children presenting with developmental difficulties. Whilst they may carry out many of the same tasks as a paediatrician, their specialist knowledge of mental health difficulties means that they are ideally placed to carry out assessments where there is a question of psychiatric morbidity, such as psychosis, differential diagnosis or identification and diagnosis of complex neurological disorders such as epilepsy and Tourette's syndrome. Child and adolescent psychiatrists play an integral role in the prescribing and monitoring of medications to help control some of the serious symptoms of a number of developmental disorders.

Disorders of development

The identification of developmental difficulties as early as possible is key to the wellbeing of the child and her family. The previous section described how crucial it is to involve parents, education workers and health professionals in the assessment and measurement of developmental problems, and how different methods and approaches can be used to understand the child's developmental presentation.

As can be imagined, such a multifaceted assessment, across time and in different settings, can generate a lot of observational data. Given that there is no clear way to diagnose observed developmental behaviours, how this information is pulled together lies in the skill of the clinicians involved in the care of the child. But what disorders can children have? And what does it mean to be 'diagnosed' with a disorder? The following sections will describe these diagnoses:

- developmental delays, disorders and learning disabilities;
- specific learning difficulties (e.g. dyslexia, dyspraxia);
- pervasive developmental disorders;
- speech and language disorder;
- genetic disorders (e.g. Down's syndrome, Turner's syndrome);
- physical impairments (e.g. blindness, hearing impairment, cerebral palsy).

Developmental delay and disorder, and learning disability

Like Sandra in the Case Study box, many parents become aware of their child's developmental abilities when they see other children performing tasks that their child is apparently not yet able to do or only recently completed. We already know that for each developmental milestone and ability, there is a range of age in which we might see skills develop. However, when a child does not meet expected developmental milestones and there is no specific diagnosis or apparent explanation, a number of questions can be raised about the child's developmental trajectory: is it evidence of a delay in development, whereby the milestone will indeed be met given more time? Is it a sign of a disordered development, suggesting an inconsistent developmental pathway? Or are we looking at a global delay that may be indicative of a learning disability? The following subsections will tease apart the differences between delayed, disordered and disabled developments.

Developmental delay

A child who has a developmental delay exhibits slower-than-expected rate of attainment of developmental milestones, although progress still occurs in the anticipated sequence within each developmental domain. In other words, a child's speech and language, fine and gross motor skills, personal and social skills or a combination thereof develop slower than expected. While children are known to develop at different rates (e.g. it is considered that walking typically starts in a spread of ages between 8 months and 15 months), sometimes children can display abnormal delays in development.

Developmental disorder

A child who has a disordered developmental profile has gaps or 'scatter' in his attainment of developmental milestones. Progress occurs in a non-sequential pattern within the developmental domain in question. Sometimes this is referred to as a 'deviant' pattern of development. Adding to the confusion is the fact that a child with developmental disorder often has developmental delay as well: that is, not only have developments occurred in a non-standard order, but the developments that have occurred are also above the age range in which we would expect to see that skill first displayed.

A child with a disordered developmental pattern may first come to the attention of care providers when parents notice that a younger sibling has surpassed an older one in some areas. Yet, at the same time, the older child has successfully achieved some age-appropriate skills. This pattern offers evidence of gaps or scatter in the older child's skills. Sometimes a child's inability to perform certain tasks, while successfully completing others, is misinterpreted as non-compliance. As a result, the child may be at risk of punishment for not doing something that she actually cannot do or does not understand. Identifying disorder in a child's developmental pattern is particularly important for the early identification of developmental language disorders and autistic spectrum disorders, and for distinguishing these conditions from others such as a learning disability.

Global developmental disability and learning disability

A learning disability is an overall problem with receiving, processing, analysing and storing information. People with a learning disability (LD) find it harder than others to learn, understand and communicate. People at the milder end of the LD spectrum can gain an education, work and enter meaningful relationships. These experiences are more difficult for people with profound and multiple learning disabilities, who might need full-time help with every aspect of their lives, including eating, drinking, washing, dressing and toileting.

CASE STUDY

Parental perspectives on atypical development

I had my only child, Molly, two and a half years ago. I was therefore not an experienced mother and before Molly, I did not feel particularly inclined towards babies or children. My knowledge about children was somewhat limited. Molly was born at full term with a normal delivery. However, she was a restless and difficult-to-soothe child. But, to me, that's what children are like. It was not until I saw Molly with other children that I realised that something was not quite right. Children her age were speaking words clearly, not just babbling on occasion. They were sharing toys and playing with dolls, not casting them around the room or looking for a TV remote to chew on. I overheard another mother saying her child's quite good at kicking a ball. Molly only learnt to walk a few months ago! When the nursery key-worker said that Molly was less able than the other children her age, that's when I panicked. Molly's now got a general developmental assessment appointment tomorrow with a paediatrician. How could I have been so unaware of her difficulties?

Sandra, mother to Molly, 2 years 6 months old

It is possible that a child with a global developmental delay who does not receive support is then considered to have a learning disability at a later age. Typically, global delay that has not been 'caught up' by approximately 9 years of age is considered a learning disability.

There are approximately 1.5 million people with mild to profound LD in the UK (Department of Health, 2007). Two to three children in every 100 will have an LD, and those with IQ scores of 55 or less will generally have a physiological reason for their disability (Tervo, 2003). The US Department of Education (2001) states that 5% of all children in public schools have an LD. In Germany, the majority of children with LD attend one of the three 'special schools' in the system and statistics suggest that 5% of children attend a special school (Pixa-Kettner, 2005). According to Holland (2002), there are 80 000 children with LD in Denmark.

Aetiology

Developmental delays and disorders have a number of possible causes. They may be due to the neurological formation of the child's brain whilst in gestation, a premature birth, genetic and heredity disorders or infections. Sometimes, if a child is using his mental resources to learn a particular skill (e.g. speaking), he may avoid learning other skills in the meantime (e.g. walking).

> **Definition**
>
> Learning disability: 'a condition of arrested or incomplete development of the mind, which is especially characterised by impairment of skills manifested during the developmental period, which contribute to the overall level of intelligence, i.e. cognitive, language, motor and social abilities . . . Adaptive behaviour is always impaired' (ICD-10).

Speech and language delays may also be secondary issues reflecting other primary problems, such as audiological function, larynx, throat, mouth or nose difficulties, limited experience of communicating from parents or other adults, and learning problems.

Those children with more severe developmental problems are likely to be chromosomal and genetic-based, such as Down's syndrome and fragile X syndrome, or other abnormalities with the structure or development of the brain or spinal cord, such as cerebral palsy or spina bifida. Other causes can include prematurity, infections (e.g. congenital rubella or meningitis) and metabolic diseases (e.g. hypothyroidism). Whilst various tests can be done to identify the underlying cause, the cause typically remains undetermined.

Diagnostic assessment

In order to ensure a thorough and accurate assessment of a child's developmental abilities, it is imperative that the sources of information for the assessment are varied and widely drawn. Without such a comprehensive and careful assessment, it is unlikely that an accurate diagnosis will be made, owing to the subtleties in how a child's abilities present. This in turn will have an impact on the support made available to the child.

The diagnostic assessment of developmental problems uses a range of methods to elicit information about the child (see Table 16.4). These include parent interviews, formal testing of development, informal observations of the child in naturalistic environments such as home and school, questionnaire-derived measures and physical examinations including blood tests. Observing the child across time and in different environments is key to understanding how the environment may have an effect on the child's functioning, thus providing valuable information about the child's 'true' abilities.

Table 16.4 Assessment tools and approaches for assessing a child's development.

Standardised assessments	Non-standardised assessments	Interviews	Questionnaires	Physical examinations
• Wechsler cognitive assessments	• Play-based assessments	• Developmental history	• Bayley Scales of Infant Development	• Blood tests
• Griffiths Mental Development Scales	• Home-based assessments	• Schoolteachers	• Vinelands Adaptive Behaviour Scales	• Height
	• School observations			• Weight
				• Head circumference
				• Reflex response
				• Gait/posture

Specific learning difficulties

People can also have specific learning difficulties that can make learning more difficult. It does not mean that these individuals have a global learning problem; indeed, these specific difficulties can co-exist alongside the full range of cognitive abilities. Often, learning difficulties are grouped by their related school-area skill set or cognitive weakness. If a child is in school, it will probably be apparent if she is struggling with reading, writing, or maths, and so narrowing down the type of difficulty may well be easier. However, the more subtle forms of these difficulties may not be detected until later in a person's academic career. Table 16.5 outlines some of the more common specific learning problems that people can experience.

Autistic spectrum disorders

Autistic spectrum disorders (ASD; abbreviated to 'autism' from here) have gained much attention from academics and media alike, as well as the general public. After all, people with autism can be portrayed in a fascinating way, such as the girl who cannot speak but can calculate sums instantaneously, or how memory

Table 16.5 Common types of specific learning difficulty.

Diagnostic term	Learning difficulty	Learning problem
Dyslexia	Difficulty processing language	Problems reading, writing, spelling, speaking
Dyscalculia	Difficulty with maths	Problems doing maths problems, understanding time, using money
Dysgraphia	Difficulty with writing	Problems with handwriting, spelling, organising ideas
Dyspraxia (sensory integration disorder)	Difficulty with fine motor skills	Problems with hand–eye coordination, balance, manual dexterity
Auditory processing disorder	Difficulty hearing differences between sounds	Problems with reading, comprehension, language
Visual processing disorder	Difficulty interpreting visual information	Problems with reading, maths, maps, charts, symbols, pictures

LIFESPAN

Life course outcomes for siblings of adults with learning disabilities or mental illness

A study by Taylor et al. (2008) investigated the impact of having a sibling with either a learning disability or a mental illness on the psychological wellbeing of adults, following them in a longitudinal study from 18 years to 64 years of age. This paper is reported as part of the larger Wisconsin Longitudinal Study. The authors studied 268 adults who had siblings with mild intellectual disability and 83 adults who had siblings with mental illness, and compared them with the experiences of adults with siblings without intellectual disability or mental illness.

The data reveal that adults with a sibling with intellectual disability were more likely to live nearby the sibling and to have more regular contact with the family, compared with the adults without siblings with intellectual disabilities. The adults with siblings with mental illness, however, reported higher levels of psychological distress and poorer psychological wellbeing. These findings were more significant for adults whose sibling with the mental illness was male.

- Consider the findings of this study. Why are the adults with a sibling with intellectual disabilities more likely to live nearby that sibling and to have more frequent contact with the family?
- Why is this not the case for adults with a sibling with mental illness?
- Why do the adults with a sibling with mental illness report a more significant effect on their psychological wellbeing in adult life?

about train timetables can be so impressive in a boy who struggles to remember how to make a sandwich. We only need to mention the film *Rain Man* to conjure a popular culture picture of disorder and brilliance existing in one being. However, how people present with autism and the recent interest in autism is not always so positive or heart-warming. Indeed, many parents of young children in Europe will have heard of the reports linking the measles, mumps and rubella (MMR) inoculations with autism (and bowel disorders), as well as reports stating that the prevalence of the disorder is increasing (e.g. Wakefield et al., 1998; Fombonne, 2001). But what is autism and is there really an epidemic of it? This section will describe what is meant by autism and its associated behaviours, as well as describing the current understandings of the causes and the specific assessment tools that contribute to identifying the disorder.

Autism is a life-long neurodevelopmental condition that affects how a person communicates with, and relates to, those around them. The three main areas of difficulty which people with autism share are sometimes known as the 'triad of impairments' (see Figure 16.5):

- difficulty with communication;
- difficulty with social interaction;
- difficulties with imagination, flexibility of thinking and/or sensory sensitivities.

Criteria for the diagnosis of autism are set out in the ICD-10 (*International Classification of Diseases*, 10th revision) and the Diagnostic and fifth version of the *Statistical Manual of Mental Disorders* (DSM-V), and are based on behavioural characteristics and patterns of behaviours (see Table 16.6).

Prevalence rates of autism vary considerably due to definitions and assessment approaches. Recent estimates suggest that across the lifespan approximately 1 in 100 people in the UK have autism (National Autistic Society, 2013). Towards the end of the twentieth century, in Europe and the USA prevalence rates for autism ranged between 5 and 72 cases per 10 000 children (Sponheim and Skjeldal, 1998; Kadesjo et al., 1999). More recently, childhood estimates of autism are between 25 and 60 cases per 10 000 (Baird et al., 2006; Centers for Disease Control and Prevention [CDC], 2009), with UK autism rates across the sexes being 3.8 per 1000 boys and 0.8 per 1000 girls (Taylor et al., 2013). It is thought to affect four times as many males than females, although the reason for this is unknown. These statistics are generally considered consistent across the world (CDC, 2014), except in South Korea where childhood autism was considered to be 26.4 per 1000 primary-aged children (Kim et al., 2011).

While some feel that clinical signs can be seen in children as young as 6 to 12 months (Volkmar and Charwarska, 2008), children are more reliably diagnosed at age 3, although language development might interfere with diagnosis (e.g. when it is unclear whether language delay causes poor social interaction or whether social interaction would be problematic anyway).

Severity of autism symptoms can be affected by a range of additional factors, such as intellectual disabilities, attention deficit hyperactivity disorder and anxiety-based disorders (e.g. obsessive–compulsive disorder,

CASE STUDY

A referral to a child development centre from a paediatrician

Jack is a 26-month-old boy who I have been seeing under my general developmental clinic. He has not progressed beyond babbling yet and is not compensating for his lack of verbal communication skills with non-verbal skills, such as consistent eye contact, expressive facial affect and gesture. He seems to prefer doing things on his own terms. Mother reports that she does not always know whether he understands what is being asked of him or whether he is simply ignoring her because he can get quite fixated on spinning the wheels of his car or watching TV. Mother is therefore struggling to get him to do things he needs to do, such as getting ready to go out or going to bed, which typically results in tantrums.

I have spoken to Mother about my concerns regarding Jack's social communication skills and I would be grateful if you could see this little boy for further assessment in your clinic.

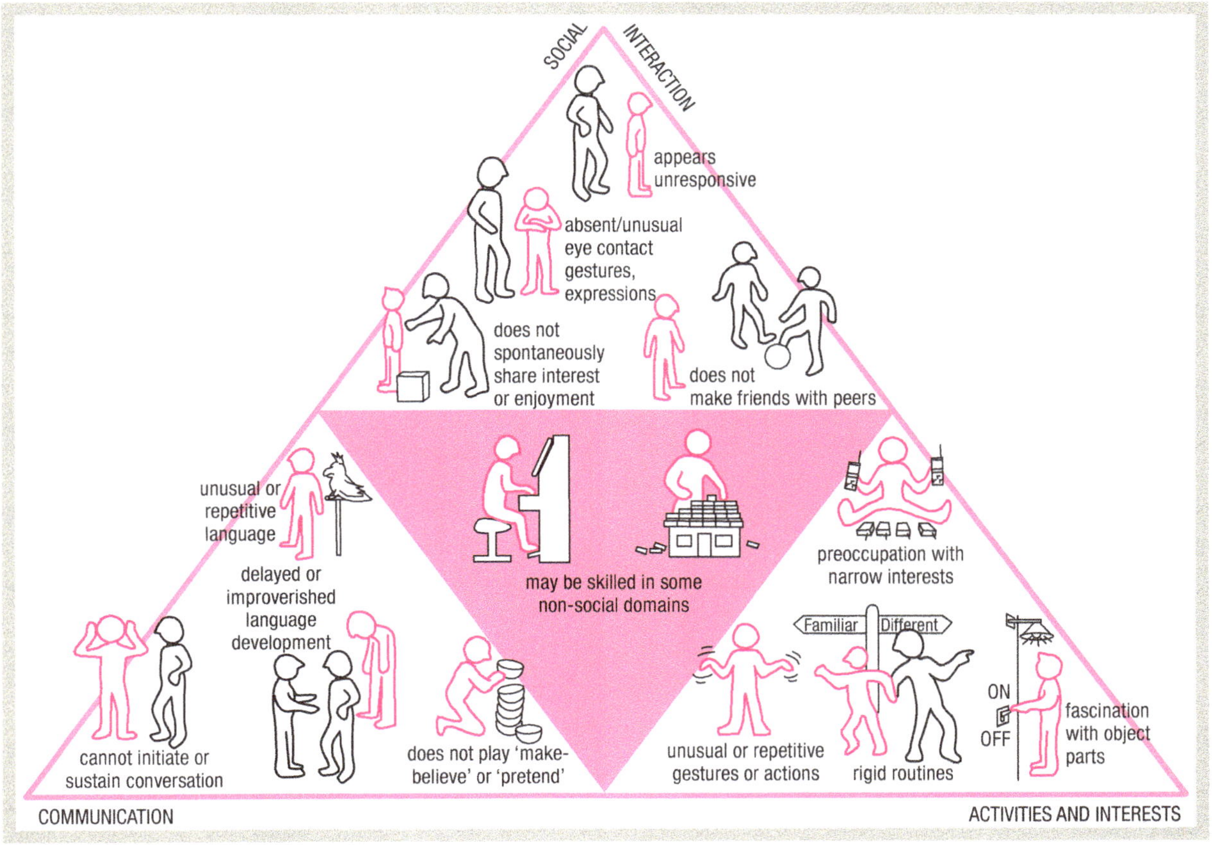

DISORDERS OF DEVELOPMENT | **501**

Figure 16.5 Triad of impairment

Source: Open University website

Table 16.6 Typical symptoms of autism in children.

Communication	Social interaction	Flexibility of thoughts

• Impairment in language development, especially comprehension, e.g. no babbling or gestures before 12 months, no single words by 18 months, no spontaneous two-word phrases by 24 months
• Non-verbal communication, including gestures, facial expressions and social smiling, limited in range and frequency:
  – unusual use of language
  – poor response to name
• Regression of verbal and social skills
	• Self-directed and wanting things to be on their own agenda/'in her own world'
	• Lack of interest in other children/odd approach to others
	• Limitation in, or lack of imitation of, actions (e.g. clapping during nursery rhymes)
	• Lack of showing toys or other objects to others
	• Limited recognition or responsiveness to others' emotions
	• Limited variety of imaginative play or pretence, especially social imagination (i.e. not being able to build on play directed by others)
	• Failure to initiate or sustain simple play with others
	• Inappropriate responses to adults (e.g. getting too close or not acknowledging them)
		• Motor mannerisms, e.g. flapping hands when excited
		• Repetitive play/preferring sameness
		• Inability to cope with change
		• Biting, hitting, or aggression to peers; oppositional to adults
		• Hyper- or hypo-sensitive to the body's sensory receptors
		• Compulsive behaviours (e.g. turning light switches on and off), regardless of scolding

OCD). Thus, it is not uncommon to see children with autism experience co-morbid problems (see Table 16.7).

The autism 'spectrum'

As with any disorder, the characteristics of autism can vary widely from person to person. Autism is conceptualised to describe a group of disorders that typically includes the disorders autism, Asperger syndrome and atypical autism (e.g. pervasive developmental disorders). The word 'spectrum' is used because the characteristics of the condition exist on a continuum of skills that vary considerably between individuals. As such, categorising people squarely into one diagnosis or another, or to say that someone is 'more autistic' than someone else, can be highly misleading. It might be more helpful to think about autism being a cluster of dimensions that can be grouped together in a multitude of different combinations to provide a picture that fits under the autism description.

The ICD and DSM diagnostic manuals are continually altering their definitions for autism, and attempting to categorise what is essentially a dimensional disorder is inevitably problematic. In fact, until May 2013, those who had symptoms that qualified for the different subgroups of autism under the DSM-IV were given their respective label, be it autistic disorder, high-functioning autism, Asperger syndrome or 'pervasive developmental delay (not otherwise specified)'. However, since the publication of the latest DSM-V diagnostic manual in May 2013, anyone who is considered to have autism features that meet the diagnostic threshold will be given the single diagnosis of 'autism spectrum disorder'. Those diagnosed prior to May 2013 are encouraged to use the pre-existing diagnosis, if they prefer, because as you will read later on, a developmental diagnosis and new labels can be emotionally difficult to adjust to. In addition to making label changes, the DSM-V has also reduced the triad of impairments to two categories: social communication and interaction, and restricted, repetitive patterns of behaviour, interests or activities.

Although the DSM is used by most countries, the main set of criteria used in the UK and in Europe is the World

Table 16.7 Co-morbidities with autism.

Area of difficulty	Frequency of co-morbid symptoms %
Developmental	
• Intellectual disability	40–80
• Language problems	50–63
• Attention, concentration, impulsivity, hyperactivity	59
• Motor delays	9–19
Psychiatric	
• Anxiety	43–84
• Depression	2–30
• Obsessive–compulsive disorders	37
• Tics, Tourette's	8–10
• Oppositional defiant behaviours	7
• General behaviour problems	3
Sensory	
• Tactile	80–90
• Auditory	5–47
Neurological	
• Seizures, epilepsy	5–49
Sleep	
• Sleep disruption	52–73
Gastro-intestinal	
• Food selectivity difficulties	30–90
• Gastro-oesophageal reflux, constipation	8–59

Source: adapted from Levy et al. (2009).

Health Organization's *International Classification of Diseases* (ICD). Consequently, it is unlikely that the redefined DSM-V autism classification will affect Europe greatly at present. The ICD was updated in 2015, which is likely to have a greater influence on European autism assessment and diagnosis. This chapter will continue to understand autism and its sub-groups as described in the ICD-10.

The reliability of sub-groups varies across studies, and their long-term relevance is uncertain (Szatmari, 2000). Although the term 'autistic spectrum disorder' does not appear in the ICD-10, professionals find that this term is much more easily understood by parents and professionals than the manual's term of 'pervasive developmental disorders' (PDD). The two terms, ASD and PDD, are now used almost synonymously.

To complicate the picture further, those with autism may, though not necessarily will, have a learning disability. Those who have Asperger syndrome tend to have average, or above average, cognitive function, but still have difficulty relating to other people and making sense of the world. It is likely that those with more severe and persevering autism symptoms will have a learning disability as well. Therefore, people with autism can present in different ways, where some are able to function in the world, supporting themselves, and others will need a lifetime of specialist support and professional input on a daily basis.

Children with atypical autism display difficulties from two domains of the triad of impairments. Children with atypical autism may have difficulties in the communication and social interaction domains of functioning, but not so clearly in the imagination or behaviours category of impairment. In other words, a child diagnosed under this sub-category of spectrum will have social communication problems, but much less overt difficulties in the rigid behaviours, special interests and imaginative domains.

While there are similarities with autism, children with Asperger syndrome have fewer problems with speaking and have an average, or above average, intelligence. They do not usually have the accompanying learning disabilities sometimes associated with autism, but they may have specific learning difficulties. These may include dyslexia and dyspraxia or other conditions

CUTTING EDGE

Early identification in babies as young as 2 months old

As you will have learnt from this chapter so far, children with autism make less eye contact than others of the same age and this feature can be central to the diagnosis of the disorder in children from 2 to 3 years of age upwards. But, according to Jones and Klin (2013), infants as young as 2 months can display signs of this condition. This makes their findings the earliest detection of autism symptoms to date.

Jones and Klin studied 110 infants from birth; 59 had a sibling with autism ('high-risk diagnosis' group) and the remaining 51 did not have a sibling with autism ('low-risk diagnosis' group). For ten regular intervals over the next two years, they used video images of children with their carers and eye-tracking equipment to see where the babies were looking. Their rationale was that babies have a predisposition towards making eye contact and that young babies look more at the eyes than at any part of the face, and they look more at the face than at any part of the body.

After the two years of data collection, 12 children from the high-risk diagnosis group were diagnosed with an ASD – all but two of them boys – and one male from the low-risk group was similarly diagnosed. Between 2 and 6 months of age, these 13 children were observed to look at eyes less and less over time. Yet, when the study began, these infants tended to gaze at eyes just as often as children who would not later develop autism. These are interesting results, although the expectation might have been that the babies who go on to develop autism would make noticeably less eye contact from birth.

If Jones and Klin's findings can be replicated, the implications for interventions can begin much earlier, thus changing the way health and education services currently manage children's and families' needs.

Source: http://www.nature.com/news/autism-symptoms-seen-in-babies-1.14117

such as attention deficit hyperactivity disorder (ADHD) and epilepsy. Children with Asperger syndrome will not have had a language difficulty prior to the age of 3 (often cited as the basic marker of difference compared with a high-functioning child with autism) and they are most typically diagnosed within the first few years of starting school because of their marked difficulties in social interaction and imagination or behaviours. With the right support and encouragement, people with Asperger syndrome can lead full and independent lives.

Aetiology

Although autism is behaviourally defined, it is widely accepted that autism has a biological basis sometimes as a result of a range of problems, such as tuberous sclerosis to rubella *in utero* and postnatal infection like encephalitis (Baird et al., 2003). Despite these clear organic associations, a specific medical cause is found in only a minority of people with autism (6–10% depending on the study), and more often in those with pronounced learning problems (e.g. Fombonne, 1999). Genes are thought to play a key role. For example, twin studies have shown that in monozygotic twins the chance of concordance for autism is 60%, with a greater concordance for some social impairment, compared with a much lower rate in dizygotic twins (Szatmari, 2003). The rate of autistic spectrum disorders in individual siblings is 2–6%, a marked increase above population rates. Autism has been associated with many cytogenetic abnormalities, especially on chromosome 15, and is also found in fragile X syndrome (Veenstra-Vanderweele and Cook, 2003).

Autism is also agreed to be a neurobiological disorder, despite results from structural brain scans not showing consistency of diagnostic markers. However, functional imaging has shown abnormalities of face processing (the area of the fusiform nucleus) in several studies (Baird et al., 2003). Neuroanatomists talk about the brains of people with autism forming at different rates from conception (e.g. Arndt et al., 2005), which results in faster then slower growths in certain parts of the brain relating to some cognitive functions typical in autism (Geschwind, 2009). Cognitive theorists, on the other hand, talk about 'mind blindness' (Baron-Cohen et al., 1985) in terms of limited understanding of own or others' thoughts and feelings, 'executive functioning' problems with respect to deficits in working memory, inhibition and planning (Kenworthy et al., 2008) and 'central coherence' weaknesses which explain difficulties in seeing the full picture (Happé and Frith, 2006).

Possibly due to a combination of more compelling research linking autism to organic causes and the 1994 outcry that the MMR vaccine is linked to autism, public anxiety has resulted in a dramatic fall in immunisation rates (NHS immunisation statistics, 2001). The epidemiological evidence is unconvincing (e.g. Fombonne and Cook, 2003), and the UK's Department of Health and Royal College of Paediatrics and Child Health have endorsed the safety of the MMR vaccine. Even so, parents of children with autism continue to express the view that the medical profession does not take their concerns about possible causes of autism seriously. Unfortunately, many professionals and business-minded people across the globe have tried to market 'miracle cures' for autism behaviours, such as secretin. These approaches have received wide publicity, but scientific methods, including double-blind trials, have not confirmed a curative effect.

Diagnostic assessment

The aim of assessment is to confirm a diagnosis, assess strengths and difficulties in the child and associated developmental and mental health impairments (co-morbidities), as well as assess for wider impacting factors, such as family needs. However, what makes autism different is the great variation in presentation, the wide range of skills and deficits and the high rate of associated behavioural, mental health and often subtle learning problems. It is for these reasons that the UK's National Autism Plan for Children (2006) recommends a range of professionals to be involved in the autism assessments of children. Diagnosis of autism can be a lengthy and emotional journey for all involved. Assessment includes a full developmental history and, later, a more specialised multidisciplinary diagnostic autism assessment would typically be conducted. The assessment would address the core domains of autism – social interaction, communication and behaviour – as well as looking at the individual child's overall cognitive ability, adaptive or self-help skills, motor development and sensory sensitivity. Such assessments can be completed by a range of different child health specialists, including paediatricians, psychologists, speech and language therapists, occupational therapists, educational and social work colleagues.

Professionals utilise a range of different methods and tools in order to assess the child for autism. Questionnaires are a useful way to gain qualitative data about the frequency and severity of symptoms. Parent interviews include the Autism Diagnostic Interview – Revised (ADIR) and Developmental, Dimensional and

Diagnostic Interview (3di). Observational measures, such as the semi-structured, standardised Autism Diagnostic Observation Schedule (ADOS), look at social behaviours, communication abilities and repetitive behaviours using the medium of play. The ADOS and ADI-R are based on DSM criteria and, as such, are typically used in research settings, as well as clinical settings, although the ADI-R is a lengthy and therefore less favourable clinical tool. These methods have arguably improved the accuracy and reliability of diagnoses.

> **STOP AND THINK**
>
> 'Everyone is on the autism spectrum somewhere.'
>
> - Do you believe this?
> - When you read the table of autism behaviours (Table 16.6), could you relate any of them to yourself or to people you know?

Rett syndrome

Rett syndrome is a rare pervasive neurodevelopmental disorder which affects significantly more females than males, making it the most common genetic cause of severe disability in females. A large proportion of people with Rett syndrome have a mutation, or fault, on the *MECP2* gene on the X chromosome. While it is a genetic (though not hereditary) disorder and so is present at birth, it is not usually detected until children are 1 year old because of the major developmental regression. Children will lose skills they have developed, and this regression can be accompanied by distress and anxiety, for both children and parents. People with Rett syndrome have severe and multiple disabilities, physical and learning, and become totally reliant on others for support throughout their lives.

For people with Rett syndrome, there are significant communication and mobility issues. Most will not speak and only 50% will walk in adulthood. Co-morbid physical health problems include epilepsy, chronic spinal curvature and breathing and feeding difficulties. However, due to improved treatment and care, people with Rett syndrome are living into their 50s and beyond (Rett Syndrome Association UK, 2010).

Childhood disintegrative disorder

Childhood disintegrative disorder (CDD), also known as Heller's syndrome and disintegrative psychosis, is also a rare pervasive neurodevelopmental disorder that affects the domains of communication, social interaction and motor skills. To date, there is no known cause for CDD.

Like Rett syndrome, CDD is characterised by the regression of functioning. However, onset is usually late at 3 years old and in some cases almost 6 years old (Fombonne, 2009). Therefore, until the age of 3, children will demonstrate age-appropriate levels of functioning in the expressive communication, receptive understanding, social skills, motor skills, play skills, self-care and toileting domains. CDD is likely if the acquired skills are then lost in at least two of these seven areas of functioning. In addition, children with CDD exhibit difficulties in at least two of the autism triad of impairment domains.

Genetic disorders

Genetic and chromosomal disorders are illnesses or developmental abnormalities arising as a result of *in utero* deviations or mutations in the child's genetic material, or where a large part of the genetic code has been disrupted. Whilst some mutations in a gene may cause few or no problems, other changes can cause serious illnesses such as sickle cell anaemia and cystic fibrosis. It is, as yet, unclear how most genetic abnormalities occur. Some appear to arise spontaneously, whilst others are probably a result of exposure to toxic substances, such as radiation. When parents are close relatives, the child faces an increased risk of having a genetic disorder, as there is a higher likelihood that both parents have the same abnormal genes. Having two such genes can lead to serious diseases or degenerative conditions, such as Tay-Sachs disease.

Chromosomal abnormalities can affect any of the 23 pairs of chromosomes (each of which is made up of around 4000 genes), including the sex chromosomes. Chromosomal abnormalities include having extra chromosomes (addition or duplication), missing chromosomes (deletion) or parts of one chromosome wrongly positioned on another. Some chromosomal abnormalities are so severe that they cause the death of the embryo or foetus before birth. Other abnormalities can cause physical deformities and difficulties, as well as some developmental disorders such as Down's syndrome (Trisomy 21) and fragile-X syndrome.

Table 16.8 summarises some of the most common chromosomal and genetic disorders in children, their incidence, signs and symptoms.

Table 16.8 Genetic developmental disorders.

Genetic disorder	Incidence	How is it diagnosed?	Physical features	Developmental difficulties
Down's syndrome (also known as Trisomy 21) Children with Down's syndrome inherit an extra copy of chromosome 21 from either the mother or father	The most common single cause of birth defects, affecting approximately one in every 660 infants of both sexes	• *In utero*, via amniocentesis • Following birth, diagnosis can be made based on distinctive physical features and blood test	Microcephaly (small head), flat facial profile, hypotonia (low muscle tone), small mouth and protruding tongue and upward slanted eyes. 40–50% of children present with heart problems, and a significant number also have some degree of vision and hearing loss.	All children with Down's syndrome experience a degree of learning disability, from mild to severe global difficulties. Delayed developmental milestones, including motor, functional and language skills.
Prader–Willi syndrome Genetic deletions (missing genetic material) on chromosome 15	Affects one in every 12,000–15,000 infants of both sexes	• Genetic testing (usually prompted by parental concerns about their child's feeding and motor development in the early years)	Hypotonia with a poor suck reflex, hypogonadism (immature development of sexual organs) and obesity (caused by excessive eating and preoccupation with food).	Children with Prader–Willi syndrome experience global developmental delay, developing into mild or moderate learning disability in later childhood. Behavioural difficulties and temper tantrums, particularly around food, due to excessive desire to eat.
Klinefelter syndrome A syndrome arising as a result of an extra X chromosome in most cells (XXY)	Affects one in 500–1,000 males	• Genetic testing (often only detected in later childhood, when child's testes and other sexual characteristics fail to develop and mature)	Few observable features, but immature testicular development. In later childhood and adolescence, boys show immature sexual development, including sparse body and facial hair, breast development and poor muscle development.	Boys with Klinefelter's syndrome often present with speech and language disorders, short attention span, specific learning difficulties and poor self-expression and communication skills.
Angelman syndrome Gene mutations on chromosome 15	Affects one in 15,000 infants	• Genetic testing (often only detected between 2 and 5 years, when characteristic behaviours and facial features become more evident)	Children with AS may have a small head, wide mouth, protruding tongue, sometimes associated with a prominent chin. AS is often associated with seizures and unusual bouts of laughter.	Children with AS typically show developmental delay, leading to severe learning disability as well as language and communication difficulties.

Neurofibromatosis Gene mutation on chromosome 17 (NF1 – 90% of cases) or 22 (NF2)	Affects one in 2,500–4,000 children, with the more severe form occurring in one in 40,000–50,000 births	• Concern often raised following identification of dermal neurofibromas • Diagnosis confirmed by blood test	Benign and malignant tumours of the central nervous system, 'café au lait' spots on the skin, dermal neurofibromas (showing as lumps under skin), brown spots on iris, occasional short stature and mild macrocephaly (large head size).	40–60% of children have some degree of learning difficulty (such as dyslexia) or generalised learning disability. Difficulties with concentration, coordination (affecting fine and gross motor skills), memory, visuo-motor and visuo-spatial skills, organisation and processing. Occasional language and social difficulties.
Turner syndrome Second X chromosome is absent or abnormal	A relatively common syndrome, affecting one in 2,500 girls	• Concern often raised due to noticeable physical characteristics • Diagnosis confirmed by genetic testing	Girls with Turner syndrome are typically of short stature, with a webbed neck, wide-spaced under-developed breasts and puffy hands and feet. Abnormalities of the eyes and bones. Amenorrhea.	Although girls with Turner syndrome generally have cognitive ability within the normal range, they show a relative weakness in visuo-spatial processing. For example, non-verbal reasoning and memory skills tend to be weaker than verbal reasoning and memory. Difficulties with peer relationships due to immaturity, shyness and social anxiety.
Williams syndrome Microdeletion of chromosome 7 at the elastin gene focus	Affects one in 20,000 infants	• A blood test (called the FISH technique) can detect whether the elastin gene is missing	Facial features include prominent cheeks, upturned nose, wide mouth, irregular teeth. Children may have a heart problem, typically supravalvular aortic stenosis, peripheral pulmonary artery stenosis or both. These heart murmurs are often present at birth. Some children develop hypercalcaemia, usually within the first two years of life. This may cause failure to thrive, feeding problems, irritability, vomiting, constipation and kidney problems.	Williams syndrome is associated with global developmental delay, leading to moderate to severe learning disability. Children may initially show delayed language development, although this becomes a relative strength in later childhood. Children are impulsive and disinhibited, with a chatty, outgoing personality. Despite this, they can have difficulties forming same-age friendships. They also show difficulties with visuo-spatial integration.

Speech and language disorder

We learnt earlier about the importance of early parent–infant interaction in promoting the young child's development of language (see Chapter 5, 'Language development'). In fact, it is difficult to over-estimate the crucial role that speech, language and communication play in enabling children to develop and lead fulfilling lives, access education and develop meaningful social relationships with others. Children acquire language and communication skills through naturalistic interactions with their world (Rossetti, 2001). Language acquisition is a robust biological attribute; however, as with other important areas of development, it is dependent on the powerful role of the environment and the availability of plentiful opportunities for the young child to interact with the world around him. Interference with a child's ability to interact normally can result in development and communication delay (Rossetti, 2001).

There is wide individual variation in the age and rate at which young children acquire language, although the majority of children are typically producing their first words at around 10 to 12 months. In their study, Fenson et al. (1993) report that, at the age of 16 months, 80% of children understand between 78 and 303 words. Between the ages of 2 and 3, parents often witness an 'explosion' in their child's speech, with a rapid increase in vocabulary and an ability to combine three or more words into sentences, and by the age of 5, most typically developing children have learned 90% of the grammar they will need throughout life.

Unfortunately, according to research, delayed speech and language development is the most common symptom of developmental disability in children under the age of 3, affecting one in every ten children in the UK (Lee et al., 2004), and accounting for a considerable proportion of referrals to child health services. Children who do not develop age-appropriate language skills are often described as having a speech and language delay or disorder. Such difficulties can be classified according to the specific area of impairment (see below), although children with language problems commonly present with several different overlapping areas of difficulty:

- receptive language (understanding and formulating spoken language);
- expressive language (processing and producing speech sounds);
- speech (articulation);
- dysfluency (hesitating or stumbling over words);
- using and understanding all aspects of language appropriately in different social contexts.

Understanding and formulating spoken language

Some children may not be able to understand the words being spoken to them and/or the grammatical rules of sentence construction (Bishop and Adams, 1992). These difficulties with understanding can have serious and wide-ranging implications when children reach school age, as they prevent children from accessing vital classroom learning opportunities (e.g. through class discussion or pair-work). They also make it hard to remember information given verbally, meaning that these children struggle to follow more than one instruction at a time and may need to have verbal instructions supplemented with a visual prompt, such as a photograph or picture, in order to understand better. Aside from the implications for learning, there are less obvious social consequences for this group, as they not only find it difficult to join their peers in conversation but also may fail to detect the subtle but important nuances of their peer-group's speech, leaving them at risk of low self-esteem, social isolation and bullying (see Jerome et al., 2002).

Processing and producing speech sounds

Children with speech and language difficulties may not be able to process effectively the speech sounds that make up words. This means they cannot identify which sounds come at the beginning of words or break up words into their component parts (Carroll and

---

Definition

Dysfluency: an abnormal degree of hesitation or stumbling over words, making speech difficult to understand. Stammering (or stuttering) is the most common form of dysfluency. The speech of people who are dysfluent may be hard to understand; it may seem jerky or disjointed and it does not flow easily from one word to the next.

Snowling, 2004). These skills are essential for children starting primary school, as this is the age at which they learn to read and to spell (tasks which involve linking sounds to letters and breaking up words to make them easier to read). Research shows that children who struggle to process speech sounds are at risk of literacy difficulties (Stackhouse and Wells, 1997; Goswami and Bryant, 2007).

An inability to produce speech sounds appropriately can have a significant impact upon a child's ability to make herself understood. As such, children with these problems may experience extreme frustration and difficulty in making their needs known, sharing information about themselves, answering questions and joining in with conversations with peers.

Using and understanding all aspects of language appropriately in different social contexts

Difficulties with pragmatic language – the ability to understand and use language in a social context – can cause significant problems with social interaction. Children may have difficulty knowing when and how to use their language in different social situations (Bishop et al., 2000), or knowing the differences in how to speak to adults or peers. They may not understand jokes or sarcasm, or may struggle with metaphorical language, taking well-known phrases literally (Leinonen and Letts, 1997). Consider, for example, the double meaning of popular phrases 'It's raining cats and dogs' or 'He threw the rule book out the window', both of which might mean very different things to a child (or adult) who does not have a social understanding of language. Such misunderstandings can cause children to respond in unusual and unpredictable ways to what might have appeared to be a perfectly normal comment, putting them at risk of social exclusion or appearing misbehaved to parents and teachers.

Aetiology

There are a wide range of different aetiological factors associated with speech and language problems in children. Some difficulties may be secondary to other causal factors, such as hearing impairment, motor disorder and acquired disorders resulting from neurological damage (e.g. strokes), whereas others occur in the context of a more complex developmental syndrome, such as autism, cerebral palsy or general learning disability.

A language disorder is said to be 'primary' when there appears to be no other underlying reason or recognised clinical syndrome to explain the child's difficulties. Primary problems or 'specific language impairment' can be characterised as those affecting the structural aspects of language (lexical knowledge, syntax and phonology), and those affecting mainly pragmatics and abstract understanding or 'higher-order functions'. The profiles of children with specific language impairment are dynamic over time, such that children with a particular pattern of difficulties may make improvements in some areas and not others, giving a different profile from year to year. In some cases, problems resolve naturally over time; however, for others, specialist intervention from child development services may be required.

Diagnostic assessment

Assessment of young children presenting with speech and language difficulties, as with any detailed developmental assessment, should be multidimensional, including a full developmental history, family history and hearing test, to rule out hearing impairment as a causal factor. As we discussed earlier, given the wide range of underlying factors which may contribute to developmental speech and language difficulties, a broad assessment, encompassing communication, both verbal and non-verbal, play and imagination, cognitive skills, attention and concentration, motor skills, emotional regulation and behaviour, is vital in ruling out alternative explanations for the child's difficulties, such as selective mutism or autism. In addition, formal assessment of global language function by a speech and language therapist (for example, using the Bus Story Test for pre-school children; Renfrew, 1991 – see Figure 16.6) can give an

> **Definition**
>
> Pragmatic language: pragmatics is a sub-field of linguistics devoted to the study of how context contributes to meaning. Specifically, it examines how the transmission of meaning depends not only on the linguistic knowledge (grammar and words used) of the speaker and listener, but also on the context of the utterance, knowledge about the subject matter, etc., all of which help to attribute meaning to language.

> The Bus Story Test is a fun assessment used by speech and language therapists to assess the age level of consecutive speech in children from 3 to 8 years. Children are told a story about a bus, which is read out to them alongside a series of twelve pictures. They must then retell the story in their own words.
>
> Their speech is assessed for information content, sentence length and grammatical usage, and an age-equivalent language score calculated.

Figure 16.6 The Bus Story Test.

Source: Renfrew (1991)

indication of overall language competence, whilst being a good prognostic indicator of long-term language functioning (Bishop and Edmundson, 1987).

Developmental speech and language difficulties are common, with an estimated prevalence of 3.8% (Shriberg, 1999). Fortunately, recent research suggests that, of those who are diagnosed, the majority of speech problems abate, whilst those who are more persistent often respond well to specialist intervention (Law et al., 2004). However, children with these kinds of difficulty are at a major disadvantage compared to their peers once they begin primary school, since they must learn within an environment where the medium for learning (which, in most education systems in Europe, is spoken language) is their biggest obstacle. The massive impact which speech and language disorder can have on a child's life and future development means that early recognition, understanding and multidisciplinary intervention are key to ensuring that the child is able to reach his full potential.

Therapy and intervention

The process of assessment and diagnosis of a child's developmental difficulties can be a difficult and emotionally overwhelming time for the whole family. Unlike in traditional medicine, there is rarely one prescribed treatment or approach which will make the child's symptoms improve or restore areas of skill that appear to have been lost or damaged. Rather, it is the role of the child health professional to help the child and family to understand and adjust to the child's diagnosis, whilst establishing a package of care aimed at supporting the child's specific developmental needs in the most appropriate way.

In the first instance, intervention may often be concerned with helping the parents and family of the child to understand the difficulties and/or diagnosis which has been given as well as setting aside time and space to think about what changes may need to be made to everyday life in order to accommodate a new way of doing things (e.g. relying on picture communication rather than speech), or to make room for specialist equipment to support the child's physical needs. Parents may also be concerned about behaviours their child shows which are difficult to understand, or which impact upon the everyday activities of the family, such as over-activity, hitting or pushing other children or limited awareness of danger. Still others may seek medical intervention for their child's condition, particularly if there are particular medications which have been shown to stabilise or improve their child's symptoms (e.g. epilepsy medication).

Given the wide range of difficulties which may arise within the context of a child's developmental difficulties, support and intervention, just like assessment, must be multifaceted, involving a range of professionals, according to the needs of the individual child and family. Within this system of professionals, there is a defined and important role for psychologists to play: offering therapy and support to identify and manage emotional responses to diagnosis, support around expectations of the child in terms of skill attainment and future progress, interventions for challenging behaviours, assessing for co-morbid mental health concerns in the child or family, and supporting the wider system around the child, including linking in with other professionals and systems, such as school.

The next section of this chapter will look at some of the ways in which developmental psychologists can offer support and intervention to the families of children with developmental difficulties. We shall focus on the following interventions:

- psychoeducation;
- psychopharmacotherapy;
- parent training and support;
- behavioural intervention;
- recognising the mental health needs of the child;
- supporting the wider system.

Psychoeducation

A key role for the child clinical psychologist in supporting families is in providing information and psychoeducation around the child's specific needs. Psychoeducation, as the name suggests, involves helping the child, family and wider social system (e.g. school staff) to understand the child's diagnosis and its associated symptoms and difficulties. This can take various forms, from individual discussion and guidance, provision of relevant child- or parent-friendly literature and electronic resources to psychoeducation groups for parents, aimed at providing information as well as an opportunity to share and seek support from other parents.

Psychoeducation is not only beneficial at the time of a child's diagnosis. It continues to play an important role throughout early childhood and beyond. Parents may seek support in thinking about ways to manage important developmental milestones (e.g. toilet training, feeding and establishing a sleep routine) and behavioural difficulties (e.g. hitting siblings, tantrums and over-activity) in the context of their child's developmental difficulties.

Psychopharmacotherapy

As we know from the earlier parts of this chapter, development problems typically require multidisciplinary assessment and input into fully understanding the different aspects of the child's difficulties. Part of this multidisciplinary input is also to consider how multidisciplinary teams support the behavioural symptoms that children with developmental problems can have. One type of treatment offered by medically trained colleagues is medication and its use is largely, though not exclusively, for the management of challenging behaviours.

Challenging behavioural problems, such as tantrums, aggression and self-injurious behaviours, in children with autism have been known to be reduced with risperidone, an antipsychotic drug (McCracken et al., 2002). Methylphenidate, branded as Ritalin, which is similar to amphetamines, can be prescribed to help reduce ADHD symptoms. Melatonin, a naturally occurring hormone that induces sleep, can be artificially altered with pharmaceuticals for children who have difficulties sleeping.

However, the role of medication in the treatment of child development problems is controversial. Johnstone (2006) states that there is no known biological cause for behaviour problems in child developmental problems, and thus it is unfounded and irresponsible, given the side-effects and unknown longer-term outcomes, to use medication as a first-choice treatment option. Side-effects can often be difficult for children and their families to manage and their impact should not be under-estimated (e.g. Hollander et al., 2006). Examples of common side-effects include confusion, suicidal thoughts, depression or withdrawal, as well as restlessness, irritability, sleeping problems, loss of appetite, weight loss, stomach ache, headache, rapid or irregular heartbeat, elevated blood pressure, and sometimes muscle twitches of the face and other parts of the body, which could lead to Tourette's syndrome, and possibly the suppression of growth. In addition, scientific trials to validate the effectiveness and safe use of drugs in developmental problems are poor (e.g. Esch and Carr, 2005; Broadstock et al., 2007).

More recently, medical and psychological research on behaviour management tends to agree that a combination of psychological interventions, such as parent training alongside medication can result in better behavioural outcomes for children with developmental problems (Aman et al., 2009).

Parent training and support

Parent training approaches have become increasingly popular in recent years, and many different systems – such as Incredible Years (Webster-Stratton, 2006), Bavolek's Nurturing programme (Bavolek, 2010), and 'Strengthening families, strengthening communities' (Steele et al., 2000) – have been developed over the years for parents to manage their child's behaviours. Overall, behavioural parent training programmes have been found to be very effective in reducing a range of children's behavioural symptoms (e.g. Barlow and Parsons, 2006). Techniques need to be clear and consistent, and include:

- praising positive behaviours that parents wish to see more of;
- ignoring completely unhelpful behaviours that parents wish to see less of (unless the child is doing something unsafe);

- rewards that motivate the child to behaviour positively;
- setting appropriate boundaries;
- outlining the consequences, such as time-out, for the child's unhelpful behaviours.

Although many of the ideas and techniques taught in behavioural parent training appear uncomplicated, many parents need careful teaching and support to learn and use them appropriately in the different situations that they find themselves in with their child. Therefore, assistance from a professional may be required to help parents develop their understanding of the principles of the approaches, as well as their child's idiosyncrasies.

With children with developmental problems, some of the techniques may be unrealistic and therefore unfair because of their difficulties, and so the implementation of techniques used would need to be adapted to fit more appropriately around the child's difficulties. For example, a child with a learning disability may require longer time to respond to commands (e.g. 'Come here, please') or to learn that praise is given to positive behaviours. A child with autism may not be able to retain spoken information and so a visual reminder of the request may be more effective. Using time-out techniques for five minutes may be too long for a child with an ADHD diagnosis and so a shorter time-out period may be just as effective.

In addition to offering parents direct behavioural approaches for their child's behaviours, emotional support should be offered to parents. Parents typically find themselves experiencing a range of different emotions regarding their child's diagnosis and associated difficulties (Barnett et al., 2006). Some of those feelings might be sadness for the loss of the child they were expecting, or uncertainty about what the future might hold for their child and their family. The grief response of and adjustment to a child's new and life-long diagnosis is a hugely emotional journey that can require professional understanding and support.

Behavioural intervention

Behavioural problems are common in children with disabilities (Rutter, 1970), representing a large proportion of referrals to specialist child mental health services. Research shows that, whilst the same behaviours that present in all children and young people may also present in children with developmental difficulties, certain patterns of behaviour are seen much more frequently in children with additional learning or developmental difficulties (World Health Organization, 1992).

Behavioural intervention can play a key role in the management of a wide range of common childhood difficulties, from over-activity and challenging behaviour to sleeping, feeding and toileting problems. Its flexibility and adaptability is well suited to the field of developmental disability, allowing the therapist to tailor interventions to the child's developmental level as well as train parents in the day-to-day management of their child's behaviour. Grounded in learning theory, interventions are built on the premise that most human behaviour is learned through the interaction between the child and her environment. In this way, behaviours which are reinforced (e.g. by social praise or tangible reward) tend to be repeated by the child and, conversely, those which are not reinforced become less frequent. Behavioural work with children thus focuses upon teaching and increasing specifically targeted positive behaviours, whilst reducing or eliminating those which are inappropriate or less adaptive.

As with any intervention, the implementation of a successful behavioural plan depends upon detailed and carefully conducted assessment, with the aim of understanding where, when and how often the target behaviour occurs, what it looks like and what the direct consequences might be, as well as identifying any factors that seem to influence the behaviour. This is sometimes called a functional analysis or behavioural ABC (antecedent, behaviour, consequence) assessment.

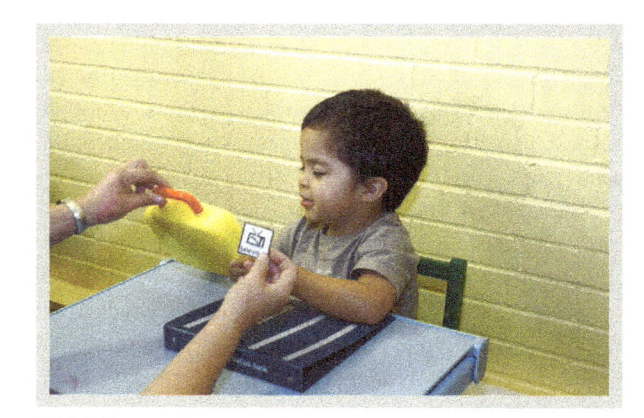

PECS (Picture Exchange Communication System): a system through which pictures and symbols are exchanged in place of spoken language, to aid communication in children with autism and other developmental disorders.

Source: Pearson Education Ltd/Jules Selmes

RESEARCH METHODS

Evidence-based practice versus practice-based evidence

Evidence-based practice (EBP) is the scientific approach to delivering rigorous research. The key role is to provide *efficacious* evidence with respect to the psychotherapies. From this evidence, guidelines are produced and therapists are required to practise accordingly. Examples of methods of EBP are clinical case descriptions, observational studies, process–outcome links, non-randomised outcome studies and randomised controlled trials (RCTs). Practice-based evidence (PBE), conversely, refers to the generation of advances in our knowledge through research conducted via the clinical work of practitioners within everyday clinical settings, to enhance treatment quality. The key role of evidence here is to increase the effectiveness of interventions in clinical settings. From this evidence, therapists can improve their practice and, in this way, services become more efficient. Examples of methods of PBE are clinical opinion, single case studies, sessional data, client feedback and practice research networks (PRNs).

Evidence-based practice is an important principle of applied science, and particularly specialist therapies. For one, it suggests that research findings (e.g. from a randomised controlled trial of treatment for anxiety) will have validity within a clinical setting. Clinicians can then apply such treatment approaches in their work with clients, with a much greater level of confidence in the potential for it to improve the client's symptoms. A commitment to evidence-based practice gives practitioners, and their clients, a greater certainty that a particular treatment or therapy approach has been shown to be helpful in similar instances, which is necessary in the current political and financial climates (Bower, 2003). EBP can also be used to protect professionals in legal matters by validating their use or alluding to incompetent clinical practice (Parry et al., 2003).

On the other hand, EBP fails and PBE gains ground when considering the true complexities of or subtle changes in psychological and cultural processes that underlie the mental distress of the individual. Parry (2000) states that EBP outcomes are based on diagnostically homogeneous samples which are not representative of real-life clients. One of the biggest successes of PBE has been the development of the practice research network. According to Margison et al. (2000), PRNs can be defined as a large number of clinicians who collaborate to collect and report data to help practising clinicians meet EBP and PBE agendas. PRNs adopt a naturalistic approach by gathering data from routine clinical settings rather than from RCTs; the clinicians use the same measures and tools in order to generate large datasets to allow comparisons between client populations, treatment, clinicians and services. Ultimately, the PRN will allow consensual setting of standards and benchmarking of outcomes to enhance delivery and services. In the UK, networks have already been set up in York, Leeds and London.

In sum, it seems that EBP is only going to be as good as the methodology it is based on. The limitations of the EBP approach are such that evidence supporting safe and effective therapy is driven from the practice side. On the other hand, PBE is only as good as the clinicians' training in practice *and* research. While the emphasis is on the applicability of evidence to clinical practice, PBE also has the scope to include more empirical components of evidence through its use of PRNs. Therefore, the PBE approach in psychotherapy *per se* is not sufficient without the rigour of a scientific approach, but such an inclusion makes this approach more appropriate for the needs of psychotherapy theory and practice.

In many cases, an assessment can identify specific learning tasks that may help to reduce a particular behaviour, where this is linked to some deficit in a skill. For example, a non-verbal child with autism may express his frustration at not being able to communicate his needs through aggressive or disruptive behaviour. Identifying and working to help the child acquire alternative skills (in this case, teaching the child more adaptive ways to communicate, e.g. via Makaton or PECS; see below), which are then rewarded, will encourage him to use alternative forms of communication in order to get his needs met.

As well as identifying gaps in the child's learning skills, a functional assessment may bring to light ways in which parents are unwittingly reinforcing and perpetuating problem behaviour: for example, the parents who get their daughter dressed for school every day to avoid her early morning tantrums, or the mother who allows her son to come in the living room and watch television when he can't sleep. Once these reinforcing patterns have been identified, the clinical psychologist can work with the child and family to think about alternative strategies to manage the behaviour, emphasising the importance of rewarding and encouraging appropriate behaviour, whilst ignoring or minimising that which is inappropriate or undesirable.

Behavioural interventions, like any other approach, must be tailored to the child's own developmental level. Targets should include a series of developmentally appropriate steps towards the desired behaviour, with an emphasis on rewarding and reinforcing each small milestone reached. Sometimes, the use of a concrete visual cue, such as a sticker reward chart or 'token economy' system, can help to involve the child in reaching her goal behaviour, whilst providing an easy way of monitoring progress (see Figure 16.7).

Given their central role, parents are ideally placed to carry out much of the behavioural work with their child with a developmental disability. Behavioural parent training, a common form of behavioural intervention, rests on the assumption that, if parents can be trained to use specific behavioural skills in managing their child within the home on a day-to-day basis, then they can effect significant changes in their child's behaviour. A number of different behavioural parent training courses have been built upon this fundamental premise, including the popular 'Incredible Years' parent training programme (Webster-Stratton, 2006).

STOP AND THINK

Thinking about the principles of learning theory, consider a change you would like to implement in your own life (e.g. eating more healthily/going to the gym).

- What are the reinforcing factors that will help motivate you to change your existing behaviour?
- What are the barriers to this change?

Recognising the mental health needs of the child

Mental health disorders in all children and adolescents are surprisingly common. They affect between one and two in ten of children and young people – with the most recent UK figure indicating that one in ten of 5–16-year-olds had a diagnosed mental health disorder, which amounts to one in three in an average classroom (Green et al., 2005).

According to CAMHEE (Child and Adolescent Mental Health in an Enlarged Europe, 2009), across Europe in general, on average one in every five children and

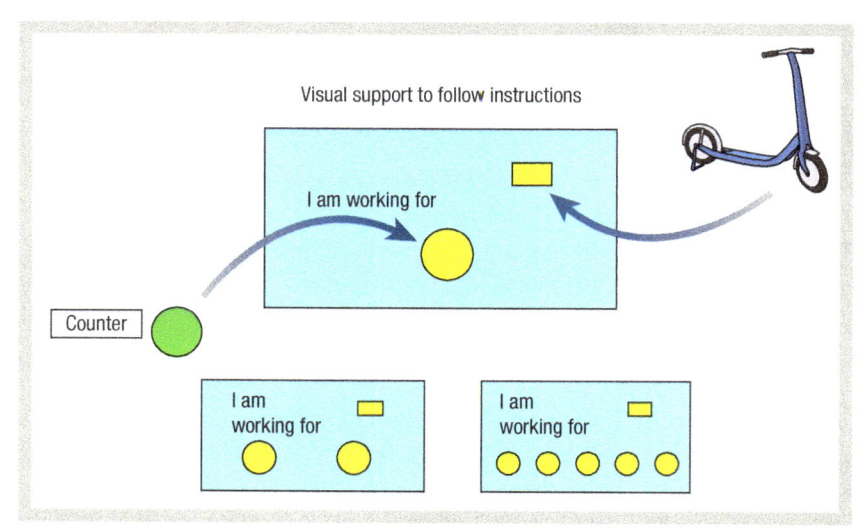

Figure 16.7 Visual support using behavioural techniques to encourage the child.

adolescents suffers from developmental, emotional or behavioural problems, and approximately one in eight have a clinically diagnosed mental disorder. Unfortunately, the fear is that new and applicant countries to Europe are facing higher rates of childhood psychological needs.

Figures of populations in the United States indicate that a mental illness occurs in between 13 and 20% of US children, where the greatest prevalence was observed in the 6- to 11-year-old category (Perou et al., 2013). In the same study, 8% of school-aged adolescents were reported as having at least 14 days of feeling mentally unwell in a month.

Like all children, those with a developmental disorder or learning disability may be faced with emotional challenges at key developmental stages. In fact, studies suggest that some emotional (or internalising) problems of childhood, such as fear, worry and shyness, are so common that they could be described as normal. Whilst, for many, such symptoms may improve over time with little need for outside help, the additional challenges faced by children and adolescents with developmental disabilities mean that they are at greater risk of developing more severe and enduring mental health difficulties, for which specialist intervention may be appropriate.

Research findings suggest that as many as one-third of children and young people with a learning disability experience mental health problems (Emerson et al., 2011), which is approximately three times more than in the general children population. In fact, a study by Corbett (1979) showed that, of a sample of children with severe learning disability, as many as 47% had some form of psychiatric disorder. Amongst those most at risk are children with an autism spectrum disorder and those with hyperkinesis (ADHD). Such findings are of great concern, given the evidence that mental health problems can contribute to poorer wellbeing, social inclusion and life opportunities of children (Quilgars et al., 2005). For children with a developmental disorder, these effects can be far reaching, having a particularly negative impact on the wellbeing of the wider family, and especially the mother (Baker et al., 2003; Hatton and Emerson, 2003).

Worryingly, emotional and mental health difficulties presenting in children with additional difficulties may often be overlooked by parents and the wider professional system. Diagnostic overshadowing, in which psychiatric symptoms may be wrongly attributed to a primary diagnosis of learning disability or developmental delay, is a common phenomenon, occurring even amongst the most experienced clinicians. Moreover, it may be much more difficult for parents and other caregivers to detect these symptoms in children who struggle to communicate verbally, and who already face a number of other additional challenges. Consequently, these children often have to wait some time before a mental health difficulty is recognised, placing them at risk of developing more severe symptoms and increased social withdrawal.

As professional awareness has increased, so too have we seen a rise in the number of specialist services offering emotional support and intervention to children with disabilities and their families. Often based within multidisciplinary teams, clinicians may work with the child or young person to address issues of poor self-esteem and self-image relating to their disability. Similarly, they may spend time exploring issues of identity and self-acceptance with children who have an awareness of themselves as 'different' from those in their peer group at school. Where children are experiencing distress as a result of their difficulties with social interaction and anxiety, the clinician's role may include teaching them important new social skills, or helping them with relaxation techniques to take control of the physical and emotional symptoms of stress and anxiety.

For many children with developmental difficulties, language and social interaction ability can prove to be a significant barrier to communication. Therapists often use creative approaches to engage with these children at the appropriate developmental level, using drawing, play, photographs and pictures. Moreover, they may spend time working with the family, school and wider system, to support them and increase their awareness of the child's concerns and difficulties, enabling them to put in place small changes to support the child's emotional needs, such as a 'circle of friends' to promote friendships and peer acceptance in a child experiencing feelings of loneliness and social isolation at school.

The wider systems

From assessment right through to intervention, working with children with developmental difficulties necessitates collaborative team working. Healthcare, education, mental health and medical professionals as well as parents/carers are all involved in the process. In some cases, social service involvement may be necessary in the case of child protection issues, and respite options may also be important in helping the families cope with their children's needs. The management and support around children with developmental problems can be vast and complex.

Given the different agencies that can be involved in the identification of a child with developmental difficulties, it is also important to think about who has raised the problem and what they are hoping to gain from such a thorough clinical assessment. Whose problem is it? In thinking about this question, it is imperative to hold the child and family in the centre of any debate to help guide how best to manage the referral, what the added value is of undertaking such an assessment for the child/family and where intervention should be placed.

Another important consideration when working with children's developmental problems is considering the needs of the families, especially fathers and siblings. Being a parent is a challenge even without having a child with special needs. When a family first learn about the child's disability, it is not uncommon for parents to re-evaluate some of the hopes and expectations they had for their child. How to manage this news alongside continuing to grow as a family and value each member and ensure that he has an equal share of family time becomes the focus. Fathers and siblings are typically marginalised members of the family due to their roles, but research suggests that the impact on these family members of living with a child or sibling who is developing atypically can be negative. For example, fathers can be excluded from key decisions about the child's care, and managing the emotional impact of having a child with such needs can be difficult to express, particularly if there are cultural or gender role factors preventing this (see Lamb, 2004). Siblings often have less time to spend with their parents and their choices can sometimes be limited due to the disability, resulting in expression of emotions that might be unhelpful to them (Deisinger, 2008). Considering the wider professional and family aspects is important in providing effective therapy to children with developmental needs.

Sharing your experiences with other parents can bring much needed emotional support when caring for a child with developmental difficulties.
Source: Getty Images

SUMMARY

This chapter has introduced us to the complex, multifaceted and often emotional process that child development professionals have to manage when posed questions like 'Why isn't my child talking yet?', 'Why does my child not play with other children?' and 'Did I do something wrong to cause my child's disability?'

The assessment of children's developmental pathways can be difficult, particularly in the absence of any scientific confirmation. Clinicians have to work in a multidisciplinary team to bring together observations from their expertise, over time and across different settings, to agree consensually about the developmental needs of the child, accurately and sensitively. Often through the assessment alone, professionals also learn a large amount of information about the family which helps inform the contextual aspects in which the developmental assessment is taking place.

However, as the chapter outlines, the needs of the child and her family do not stop with a diagnosis. A clinician's role is also very much about the development of a package of care that provides appropriate interventions to support the child and her family through what can be a distressing and challenging time. Often, offering support around current difficulties can give families something concrete and real to focus on, while also helping minimise natural fears about the present problems and future concerns for their child.

Finally, there are two key messages from health professionals for families with a child being assessed for atypical development problems. The first is that, like all children that are ever born, their child will make progress for the rest of their lives. It may not be as quickly as we might like, nor might it be to the same extent. Nonetheless, input from services and parents can facilitate this learning and, while it may be different, progress is a given.

The other message is that, aside from the atypical development difficulties, every child has his or her own personality, interests, likes and dislikes. Atypical development does not affect these characteristics and it does not necessarily stop a child from being happy. To remind parents that their child will feel and also give them huge amounts of pleasure is to state a fact – it is also a message of joy in times of upset and understandable worry.

REVIEW QUESTIONS

1. Discuss the different biological, social and cultural factors which influence the way in which a child develops. How might these factors interact with each other to contribute to developmental difficulties?
2. What advantages does a play-based form of assessment have over more structured assessments in helping us to understand a child's strengths and difficulties?
3. How can behavioural learning theory help us to understand and develop strategies to support positive behaviour in children with developmental difficulties?
4. In what way does the 'triad of impairments' help inform our thinking about the key strengths and deficits present in children with an autism spectrum disorder?

RECOMMENDED READING

For an evaluation of the evidence for many widely used child and adolescent mental health treatments:

Fonagy, P., Target, M., Cottrell, D., Phillips, J., & Kurtz, Z. (2005). *What Works for Whom? A Critical Review of Treatments for Children and Adolescents*. New York: Guilford.

For an overview of the practice of early childhood intervention:

Shonkoff, J. P., & Meisels, S. J. (Eds.) (2000). *Handbook of Early Childhood Intervention*. Cambridge: Cambridge University Press.

RECOMMENDED WEBSITES

The National Autistic Society is an established UK-based autism charity with information and advice for families and professionals:

http://www.autism.org.uk

Contact a Family provides support, advice and information for families with disabled children:

http://www.cafamily.org.uk

Mencap provides advice and support for young people and adults with learning disabilities:

http://www.mencap.org.uk

SIBS provides advice and support to children and young people who have a sibling with a disability, and for parents:

http://www.sibs.org.uk

Chapter 17
Attention deficit hyperactivity disorder (ADHD)

David Daley

Learning outcomes

After reading this chapter, and with further recommended reading, you should be able to:

1. Explain the key characteristics of ADHD.
2. Describe the complex presentation of ADHD.
3. Understand how ADHD develops and why certain individuals are more at risk of expressing ADHD.
4. Recognise the different treatment options available for ADHD.

Sam

Case study: ADHD medication can be tough, but it works

Sam Cook has been on medication since his attention deficit hyperactivity disorder was diagnosed three years ago. The 10-year-old from Hitchin, Hertfordshire, takes Concerta, a slow-release type of methylphenidate, once a day.

'We noticed a change almost straight away, and the school did as well,' his mother, Sarah, said. He used to be disruptive in class and upset other children. We tried a lot of things, taking him swimming to tire him out for example, but Sam is like a whirlwind, a Duracell bunny, and sometimes I cannot control his energy. He cannot keep still.

'The medication doesn't change him – he is still full of energy – but it takes that edge off him and makes him easier to manage. You can get through to him when he is on the medication.'

Ms Cook said that she had noticed a few side-effects from the drug. Sam was a bit more anxious than he used to be and his sleep had been disrupted slightly.

'It can be tough, but the medication has been good and it has made a massive difference. He is actually learning things at school and you can get through to him. The drug makes him more manageable,' she said.

Ms Cook said that she would continue to use drugs to treat her son's ADHD, and would pay for them privately if necessary. Not using the medication, she said, 'is not a road that I would even think about going down. It is not just Sam that is affected by his behaviour – it is everybody in that classroom. He was not able to deal with a classroom situation.'

Source: *The Times*, 24 September 2008; retrieved 18 October 2008 from http://www.timesonline.co.uk/tol/news/uk/health/article4813734.ece

- Have you read articles similar to this and wondered what the evidence is behind the headline?
- Many people now know someone with ADHD or may wonder if they themselves have it, but what is ADHD?
- How can psychology help children and adults affected by this condition?
- Do you think it is appropriate to medicate children with these types of difficulty?

Introduction

The focus of this chapter is on the experiences and problems of children with attention deficit hyperactivity disorder (ADHD) and their parents. We will aim to explain what ADHD

▶ is, explore what problems children with ADHD experience and discuss what other difficulties are commonly associated with having ADHD. In particular, this chapter focuses on four key issues. First, the complexity of ADHD and, secondly, its developmental course are explained. While it was originally conceived of as a disorder of childhood, there is now good evidence to suggest that the disorder is also present in pre-school children, adolescents and adults. Thirdly, the causes of ADHD are investigated. Where do the symptoms of ADHD come from and why are children with ADHD inattentive, impulsive and hyperactive? Focusing on the latest research findings from genetic and neuroscience studies, current theories which link abnormalities in parts of the brain with the unique symptoms of ADHD will be explored. Finally, treatments for ADHD are described. Whilst treatment with stimulant medication is currently the most widely used treatment option, the evidence base for alternative treatments will also be explored.

Natural inquisitiveness or a lack of impulse control?
Source: Getty Images/Martin Hospach

Introduction to attention deficit hyperactivity disorder

Attention deficit hyperactivity disorder (ADHD) is a highly prevalent and heterogeneous developmental disorder, meaning that the problems that children with ADHD have and the underlying causes of their behaviour can be very different. It is characterised by age-inappropriate levels of inattention and/or hyperactivity and impulsivity (DSM-V; American Psychiatric Association, 2013). Essentially, children with ADHD have levels of attention, concentration and activity characteristic of children much younger than them. If we were to examine very young children, then most 2-year-old children would appear to meet the criteria for ADHD (see the next section); however, by the age of 4 nearly all of those children would not meet these criteria as they demonstrate improved concentration and fewer instances of impulsive behaviour.

ADHD is typically associated with impairment across several domains of functioning (Daley, 2006), and children with ADHD typically have difficulty with their family at home and in the classroom as well as when playing with peers. At home, children with ADHD usually have a poor short-term memory (remembering things they are asked to do immediately). They have a very active brain, which means that they like to be kept busy, hate waiting and therefore will do anything to avoid being bored. Children with ADHD tend to talk and fidget when they are supposed to be sitting quietly, and interrupt when people are talking. In the classroom, ADHD children often become a focus for classroom disruption; they usually blurt out answers to questions rather than waiting until the teacher asks them for the answer. ADHD children find it difficult to listen to the teacher and therefore often miss instructions and announcements, and usually

> **Definition**
>
> **Heterogeneous developmental disorder:** a condition that might have many different causes that affects the normal development of the child.

find interfering with or pestering other children an excellent way of avoiding boredom. When playing with peers, ADHD children struggle to wait their turn, rarely attending to important rule changes in games, and they give up on the game very easily if they do not get what they want, making them less than ideal playmates.

Classification of ADHD

The disorder now known as ADHD has been the subject of many name changes over the years, from *hyperkinetic syndrome* to *attention deficit disorder* (ADD) to *ADD with hyperactivity* (American Psychiatric Association, 1994) to *hyperkinesis* (World Health Organization, 1992); as research into the disorder advances, the working definitions change. The most widely used diagnostic tool is the American Psychiatric Association's (APA's) *Diagnostic and Statistical Manual* (DSM), whose most recent edition (DSM-5) cites the syndrome named attention deficit hyperactivity disorder (ADHD). DSM-5 criteria for ADHD in childhood are that patients must have experienced a minimum of six symptoms of inattention (e.g. failing to sustain attention in tasks or play activities, not listening when being spoken to directly), or six symptoms of hyperactivity/impulsivity (e.g. talking excessively, fidgeting with hands or feet). The manual distinguishes between three sub-types of the disorder and recognizes ADHD in adulthood for the first time.

a. Predominantly inattentive type.
b. Predominantly hyperactive type.
c. Combined type.

In order to reach diagnosis according to the latest version of the DSM, symptoms must have onset before the age of 12 (rather than age 7, as in the previous edition, DSM-IV), must be pervasive across settings (e.g. home and school) and must be associated with substantial impairment in functioning (American Psychiatric Association, 2013).

Symptom structure of ADHD

It is widely accepted that ADHD consists of two key difficulties, which are inattention and hyperactive–impulsive behaviour (American Psychiatric Association, 2013). However, some researchers have questioned the validity of this claim. Several studies have used factor analysis to examine how the symptoms of ADHD cluster together. These studies in general confirm two distinct components to ADHD: inattention and hyperactivity–impulsivity. These findings gave rise to the distinction between the sub-types of ADHD in the DSM-IV and now in the DSM-5. However, the DSM-IV structure was devised using largely childhood samples; therefore, developmental concerns have been aired over the validity of diagnosing pre-schoolers and adults using a structure derived from children (Span et al., 2002). Although the same two-factor structure has been replicated in adult samples (Du Paul et al., 2001), Span et al. (2002) concluded from their data that adult ADHD symptoms were actually best described using a three-factor structure with separate factors for inattention, hyperactivity and impulsivity. However, the research methods used in these studies appear to affect the results obtained. In a college-student study, Glutting et al. (2005) found that the factor structure changed according to where symptom reports came from: analysis using parent-report measures demonstrated the DSM-IV two-factor structure,

---

STOP AND THINK

- Do any of the symptoms of ADHD sound familiar?
- Do you know anyone who struggles to pay attention or concentrate? Or perhaps you know someone who is very impulsive?
- How do you think these difficulties might impact on their lives?
- Do you think there are any advantages or disadvantages to being impulsive?

Definitions

DSM-5 criteria for ADHD in childhood: current classification for combined type ADHD requires a minimum of six out of nine symptoms of inattention and a minimum of six out of nine symptoms of hyperactivity/impulsivity to be present in the child. Symptoms of inattention include daydreaming, distractibility and disorganisation; symptoms of hyperactivity include restlessness and fidgeting; while symptoms of impulsivity include impatience and not being able to stop yourself from acting. In addition, there must be some impairment from symptoms in two or more settings (e.g. home and school) and clear evidence of significant impairment in social, school or work functioning.

Factor analysis: a statistical method that reduces large numbers of questionnaire items down to a smaller number of clusters or underlying factors.

CASE STUDY

James

Jennifer and Paul are young parents with three children. Their first son Harry is 8 years of age. He has always been a helpful and easy-going child, does well at school and has lots of friends. Their second son James is 6 years of age and is completely different. James finds it very difficult to sit still for more than a few minutes. He is very distracted and has difficulty watching his favourite television programme for more than a few minutes. James is also very impulsive, and rarely thinks before he acts. This means that he constantly interrupts other people's conversations and has had several accidents, including pulling a saucepan of hot water onto himself when he was 3 years of age. Unlike his older brother who is very patient, James finds waiting very difficult. He always wants everything straight away, and would rather give up on a game or activity than wait his turn. James also has memory difficulties and finds it difficult to remember instructions or lists. In many ways James behaves just like his younger brother Edward, who is 2½ years old.

Despite having a very popular older brother, James has very few friends. Other children find it very difficult to play with him, as he finds it hard to pay attention to rule changes in their games, always wants to go first and spoils the game if he has to wait. When he was younger, James didn't seem to care about his lack of friends, but now that he is a bit older, the lack of friends and the fact that no one invites him to birthday parties is beginning to make him feel sad.

James has recently been attending his local Child and Adolescent Mental Health Service and is currently being assessed for attention deficit hyperactivity disorder. His grandmother says that his dad was just like him when he was that age. She is also somewhat critical of the way that his mother deals with his behaviour, and feels that she is far too inconsistent.

- Why do you think that Harry and James, who are brothers, are so different?
- What do you think might be the causes of James' difficulties?
- Do you think that James will grow out of these problems without any help?

STOP AND THINK

- With such contradictory findings about the structure of ADHD in different samples and age groups, what do you think are some of the factors that might explain these differences?
- Do you think the way that some of these studies define ADHD might be relevant?
- Who do you think is the most reliable person to report on ADHD symptoms? Child, parent, teacher or peer? Why do you think so?

whilst self-report measures of symptoms revealed a three-factor solution, in line with the work of Span et al. (2002). Partly to address these concerns, the DSM-5 (American Psychiatric Association, 2013) now recognises ADHD in adulthood, which can be diagnosed with a lower threshold of five symptoms rather than six, to control for the developmental nature of ADHD.

ADHD across the lifespan

We will now consider ADHD across the lifespan, first by examining the prevalence of the disorder and then by considering ADHD in pre-school children, school-aged children and adolescents, and then in adulthood.

Prevalence and developmental span

It is estimated that ADHD affects about 4% of children in the UK (Daley, 2006) and 5–10% of children worldwide (Faraone et al., 2003), with approximately 40%

of children with ADHD continuing to meet diagnostic criteria into adulthood (Fischer et al., 1993). There have been many criticisms of the studies that have examined the prevalence of ADHD, as different studies report widely different prevalence rates. It is clear that the method of measuring ADHD as well as the respondent influences the prevalence: for example, mothers tend to report lower levels of ADHD symptoms than fathers do (Dave et al., 2008). Culture is also important. Sonuga-Barke et al. (1993) suggest that teachers' ratings of hyperactivity in children vary according to the child's ethnicity. In this study, the authors demonstrated that Asian children rated high in ADHD symptoms by their teachers were actually no more hyperactive or inattentive than British non-hyperactive children when rated by the researchers. Indeed, when British and Asian children who received the same high ADHD scores were examined, the researchers recorded that the Asian children displayed fewer hyperactive behaviours in the classroom than their British counterparts. Sonuga-Barke et al. interpreted this finding as suggesting that teachers have higher expectations of classroom behaviour for Asian children and that the ADHD ratings of Asian children were therefore biased. It appears that the Asian children have to display fewer hyperactive behaviours in the classroom than British children to be rated by their teacher as problematic.

ADHD in the pre-school years

A notable increase, over recent years, in the number of pre-school children coming to clinical attention with ADHD symptoms, and being prescribed medication for their ADHD symptoms (Zito et al., 2000), has driven researchers to examine ADHD in the pre-school period (Daley et al., 2009). Findings from this research suggest that children with pre-school ADHD symptoms share many of the characteristics associated with their school-aged counterparts. Typically, pre-school children with ADHD present with the same symptoms (Gadow and Nolan, 2002) and experience similar developmental impairment (Lahey et al., 1988) as well as similar neuropsychological deficits (Sonuga-Barke et al., 2003). Several studies have examined whether pre-school children who exhibit symptoms of ADHD continue to show them into school age, and the results generally confirm that children characterised as hyperactive during the pre-school years continue to manifest problems with impulsive behaviour, aggression and social adjustment

The challenge of diagnosis: is this child having fun for the camera or does he have ADHD?
Source: Corbis/Westend 61

in primary school. Pierce et al. (1999) found that symptoms of ADHD identified in pre-school boys predicted continuing problems in middle childhood. Consistent with these findings, Lahey et al. (2004) found that children who met full diagnostic criteria during their first assessment were likely to continue to meet diagnostic criteria for ADHD over the next three years.

Pre-school children at risk of ADHD are often given the label 'hyperactive'. Hyperactivity is a term that reflects the fact that every child demonstrates some inattention, impulsivity and hyperactive behaviours. In the pre-school period, we are most interested in children who exhibit extremely high levels of hyperactivity. Hyperactivity in pre-school children differs from

Definition

Hyperactive: a descriptive term that is frequently applied to children who have low levels of attention to a task, can behave impulsively and without consideration of the consequences and/or may be unable to sit quietly with other children.

the categorical concept of ADHD in that the clinical sub-group of children have such extreme scores for inattention, impulsivity and hyperactive behaviour that they are different from the rest of the population and warrant a clinical label.

The difference between hyperactivity and ADHD is mostly related to what we call impairment. Having high levels of symptoms does not mean that the child has ADHD. In order for a clinical label of ADHD, the child has to have very high levels of symptoms, those symptoms need to have been present for at least six months and the presence of symptoms needs to create other difficulties for the child. Within an ADHD context, impairment is usually considered as interference with school work (or school readiness in the pre-school years, such as being able to sit and listen to a story and take turns sharing toys). However, it can also be seen as impairment in children's peer relationships, where ADHD symptoms may prevent children from making friends or engaging in the same activities as their friends.

Interestingly, similar levels of impairment have been found both when children have been recruited from community samples without a formal diagnosis (Sonuga-Barke et al., 1994) and when children have been recruited from clinics or hospitals (DuPaul et al., 2001). Therefore, although pre-school children at risk of ADHD show extreme scores for hyperactivity (Daley and Thompson, 2007), they do not all necessarily go on to develop ADHD, as it appears that a whole range of environmental factors can enhance or reduce the risk of developing ADHD. For example, parents' responses to their children can either enhance or reduce the likelihood that a child with a genetic risk for ADHD will go on to develop the disorder (see 'Treatment for ADHD', pages 535–9, for a discussion of what can be done to change the developmental progression of ADHD).

ADHD in adulthood

While originally conceived as a disorder of childhood and adolescence, recent evidence suggests that there is scientific merit and clinical value in examining ADHD in adulthood (Daley, 2006). ADHD symptoms have been shown to persist into later life, with up to 40% of childhood cases continuing to meet full criteria in the adult years (Fischer et al., 1993). Adult ADHD appears to share many characteristics with the childhood disorder. Similar to their childhood counterparts, adults with ADHD display impairment in the interpersonal, vocational and cognitive domains. For example, adults with ADHD find their impulsivity and inattention make it harder to stay in romantic relationships and to keep their job, and they have a tendency to make unwise decisions. The memory problems associated with ADHD also make it more difficult for them to plan their lives (Dinn et al., 2001). In general, adults with ADHD tend to choose jobs and careers that suit their specific difficulties. You are therefore less likely to find ADHD individuals sitting in front of computer screens all day; instead, they tend to choose jobs which involve working outside, do not require sustained concentration and do involve a lot of movement and activity (construction work, agriculture, delivery work, etc.). Some individuals are able to capitalise on their difficulties and use them to their advantage: for example, in theory, an individual with ADHD would make a good trader on the stock market, as their impulsive nature would allow them to make the sort of rapid decisions that the job requires.

The adult and childhood disorders also appear to share a common neuropathology, which means that the same components of the brain that have been shown to control ADHD in childhood are also responsible for the control of ADHD in adulthood (Hesslinger et al., 2001). Adults with ADHD also demonstrate a similar response to drug treatment for ADHD as children with the disorder (Sachdev, 1999), which underlines the similarities between ADHD in childhood and ADHD in adulthood.

Differences in the rates of ADHD in adulthood found by some longitudinal studies, however, raise questions about the validity of the disorder in adults. Faraone (2000) claims that discrepancies in rates of ADHD in longitudinal studies can be explained by two important factors: first, psychiatric co-morbidity and the way ADHD is diagnosed; and secondly, the lack of developmentally appropriate ADHD symptoms in adulthood. The Diagnostic and Statistical Manual of Mental Disorders, one common method for diagnosing ADHD, relies on hierarchical diagnosis, whereby disorders rated higher up the hierarchy are allowed a wider range of symptoms and more associated problems than those

Definition

Psychiatric co-morbidity: the experience of two psychological conditions at the same time: for example, anxiety and depression or ADHD and conduct disorder.

LIFESPAN

In adulthood, those with ADHD are likely to pick jobs which allow plenty of opportunity for movement and activity. Which of these two jobs would be a better option?

Sources: Pearson Education Ltd/Studio 8

Source: Shutterstock.com/Dmitry Kalinovsky

rated lower down. Although this might seem like a reasonable method of diagnosing primary conditions whilst taking into account co-morbid, secondary conditions, the technique does have its problems. Faraone (2000) claims that reliance on hierarchical diagnoses can distort the diagnosis of ADHD in adulthood. He quotes an example from Mannuzza et al. (1993), who found very low levels of ADHD in a longitudinal study of adults who had been diagnosed with ADHD in childhood. The Mannuzza study applied a hierarchical rule, which excluded children whose primary referral had been conduct problems and aggression, even though they also had ADHD as a secondary condition. However, aggressive children with ADHD are statistically more likely to have a more persistent disorder than non-aggressive children with ADHD. Therefore, the low rate of ADHD at follow-up in adulthood in the Mannuzza study reflects the use of hierarchical diagnosis, which excluded lots of possible cases, thereby distorting the prevalence rate.

The DSM-IV had problems in accounting for development in the diagnosis of ADHD as, despite the different expectations for children and adults, it did not provide different diagnostic symptoms for adults. Faraone (2000) argued that the DSM-IV was developmentally insensitive for ADHD because, with time and maturity, children learn to inhibit or control some of their symptoms of ADHD. For example, while it is fairly typical to see young ADHD children running around a room and touching everything in sight, it is rare to see adults with ADHD behaving in the same way. Also, whilst school children are often required to sit and concentrate for long periods of time, many adults do not have to do so. In fact, as discussed previously, many individuals with ADHD specifically

STOP AND THINK

- What do you think the debate about the validity of ADHD in adulthood means for individuals with ADHD who reach adulthood?
- Do you think confusion over the number of symptoms needed to get or maintain a diagnosis might impact on their care?
- How do you think it would feel to be told that you no longer met criteria for ADHD, and therefore did not deserve further treatment, even though nothing had changed except your age?

choose jobs that involve lots of movement and activity (building work, delivery work, etc.). ADHD in adulthood is therefore more likely to present as irritability and mood swings, as well as risk-taking behaviour; yet the symptoms used to diagnose ADHD in adults do not emphasise these problems very well. While the new DSM-5 now recognises ADHD in adulthood, it still uses the items developed to identify ADHD in childhood, which may make it insensitive for identifying ADHD in adults.

We conclude that, despite some debate about the number of symptoms required to meet the criteria for ADHD in adults, in general ADHD as a disorder appears to be very similar at different developmental stages. Therefore, for the rest of this chapter we will focus on ADHD in childhood, and only refer to the pre-school or adult periods when the evidence base is different from that for children.

Co-morbidity and associated impairments in ADHD

It is widely accepted that ADHD is a co-morbid disorder, but what is actually meant by this is far from clear. Gillberg et al. (2004) point out that co-morbidity can mean a number of different things. First, co-morbidity can mean that there is a common underlying aetiology (or explanation) that leads to two or more different disorders. However, co-morbidity can also mean that one disorder leads to another, or even that two unrelated disorders co-occur. The term 'co-morbid' also implies that their entities are morbid conditions (i.e. diseases). In fact, the vast majority of co-morbidities with ADHD represent functional impairments and symptoms, which are not rooted in specific diseases (Gillberg et al., 2004). It therefore seems more prudent and more helpful to discuss associated problems with ADHD rather than co-morbidity.

ADHD appears to be associated with a wide variety of other psychiatric problems. Notable associations exist with oppositional defiant disorder (ODD), conduct disorder (CD), depression and anxiety. About 50–60% of children with ADHD meet the criteria for ODD, even in the pre-school period (Kadesjo et al., 2001). Busch et al. (2002) reported that ADHD children are more likely to demonstrate mood disorders such as depression, multiple anxiety disorders and substance use disorders. In adult cases, co-morbid conditions include mood disorders, antisocial behaviour disorders and substance use disorders. In addition to associations with other psychiatric disorders, children with ADHD are also more likely to experience a substantial array of associated developmental, social and health problems, which will be discussed here.

Motor coordination

Studies using balance assessment, tests of fine motor gestures, electronic or paper-and-pencil mazes often find children with ADHD to be less coordinated than children without ADHD (Mariani and Barkley, 1997). Indeed, as many as 60% of children with ADHD have some form of developmental coordination disorder (Kadesjo et al., 2001). The association between ADHD and poor motor coordination is probably linked to a common but as yet unclear neurological problem.

Reduced intelligence

Clinic-referred children with ADHD often have lower scores on intelligence tests than control groups, particularly in verbal intelligence (McGee et al., 1992). These differences range from 7 to 10 standard score points. Studies using both community samples and clinical samples (Sonuga-Barke et al., 1994; Peterson et al., 2001) have also found negative associations between ADHD and intelligence. The reason for lower levels of IQ in children with ADHD is less clear. Obviously being inattentive means that children with ADHD are less likely to learn from what is going on around them, which may explain the particularly low levels of verbal IQ, as children with ADHD may find it harder to listen, remember and therefore learn new words that are being used by people around them. However, having conducted lots of IQ tests on young children with ADHD, I do wonder how accurate these IQ tests are. Children with ADHD find it very difficult to concentrate and focus on an IQ test, and often just give the first answer that comes into their head, rather than taking time to work out the answer.

Impaired academic functioning

The vast majority of clinic-referred children with ADHD have difficulty with school performance, often doing much worse at school than other children with the same level of IQ and ability. ADHD children frequently score lower on standardised achievement tests (Hinshaw, 1994), a feature found even in pre-school children with ADHD (Barkley et al., 2002), suggesting that the disorder may influence school readiness. The reason for this is not clear, but it has been found that pre-schoolers who express ADHD symptoms are much more likely to experience difficulties with knowing their numbers, colours and shapes (Mariani and Barkley, 1997). At school, ADHD children often struggle with schoolwork and social interaction (Nijmeijer et al., 2008), whilst adolescents with ADHD are also likely to experience academic attainment difficulties (Daley and Birchwood, 2010) and social problems (Greene et al., 1997).

The research reviewed so far supports the notion that ADHD individuals experience academic problems. However, are these academic problems the result of factors directly related to ADHD (symptoms, underlying processes) or are they the result of factors that are indirectly related to ADHD? Because of the close association between ADHD and CD (antisocial tendency), there has been a body of research investigating the outcomes of individuals with these conditions. The research suggests that ADHD+CD individuals experience both future academic and future offending problems; however, it is their ADHD behaviours that predict only future academic problems, and their CD behaviours that predict future criminal behaviour. Frick et al. (1991) investigated children with a diagnosis of ADHD+CD and found that CD was only related to academic problems because of its close ties with ADHD, whereas only ADHD was the significant predictor of academic performance. This evidence suggests that conduct problems in children with ADHD do not explain the difficulties experienced in school. Other explanations must exist for the association between ADHD and problems with academic disadvantage.

ADHD, IQ and academic attainment

Could IQ be the root of the academic disadvantage? Research has shown that negative associations exist between ADHD and intelligence (McGee et al., 1992),

This child is concentrating hard on completing the jigsaw, something a child with ADHD might have difficulties in doing.
Source: Pearson Education Ltd/Jules Selmes

and – although the link between IQ and achievement is an age-old debate – evidence suggests that psychometric intelligence predicts future achievement (Watkins et al., 2007). Studies that demonstrate the link between ADHD and academic under-achievement have controlled for differences in intelligence within the sample (Diamantopoulou et al., 2007), or matched experimental and control groups for IQ level (Barry et al., 2002), suggesting that ADHD individuals perform academically at a lower level than would be predicted by their IQ. However, whilst ADHD individuals have been shown to score lower than controls on IQ tests, the evidence does not yet suggest that ADHD is the primary cause of their impaired academic performance.

Social problems

Children with ADHD face serious social problems to the extent that some researchers are surprised that they are not included in the criteria for the disorder. Clark et al. (1988) in an observational study reported much higher levels of aggression, less coordinated play and much less conversation from ADHD children when they played with a non-ADHD child, as compared to two non-ADHD children playing together. Children with ADHD are often rejected by their peers and have fewer friends than their non-ADHD peers (Hinshaw and Melnick, 1995), as highlighted by our case vignette at the start of this chapter. There are many possible explanations for why ADHD children have few friends, the most likely being that they are difficult to play with, they find it hard to attend to the subtle changes in the rules of games, they do not wait their turn and they react very negatively to having to wait and to losing, all of which make them less than ideal playmates. As a result, ADHD children tend to choose other ADHD children as playmates. This often means that they lack children within their friendship circles who can model attention, concentration and positive behaviours. Unfortunately, as a general rule, these social difficulties are often resistant to psychosocial and drug interventions and therefore continue into adolescence and adulthood.

Accident proneness

Studies have identified that children with ADHD are said to be more accident-prone by parents, relative to children without ADHD (DiScala et al., 1998). ADHD children are more likely than their non-ADHD peers to have to visit accident and emergency units, even during the pre-school period. Knowledge about safety does not appear to be lower in these children, implying that interventions aimed at increasing knowledge about safety may have little impact (Mori and Peterson, 1995). The higher accident rate is generally considered to be the result of impulsivity and a lack of forethought (not thinking before you act), both of which would allow a child with ADHD to jump off a high wall without thinking about the fact that they might break their arm or leg! It is also worth remembering that ADHD children are also more likely to lack motor coordination, so a greater tendency to be clumsy may also explain higher accident rates in ADHD.

Sleep problems

Studies report an association between ADHD and sleep disturbances (Gruber et al., 2000). Corkum et al. (1999) found that sleep problems occurred twice as often in ADHD as in non-ADHD children. The sleep problems the children experience are mainly more behavioural problems at bedtime, taking a longer time to fall asleep, instability of sleep duration, tiredness at wakening or frequent night waking. Parents of children with ADHD report that their children require significantly less sleep than their non-ADHD siblings, and that they fall asleep much later than would be expected for their developmental age, but also wake earlier. Again, the association between ADHD and sleep difficulties is likely to be shared neurological processes in the brain.

It is easy to see why ADHD is often viewed as such a complex disorder, as it is often associated with a wide range of other associated problems. The reason why ADHD children often have so many other difficulties is not yet clear, but these other difficulties often share similar genetic, environmental or biological explanations.

What causes ADHD?

Everyone seems to have a theory as to what causes ADHD and most people are wrong! In this section, we will examine the evidence base for a range of explanations about what causes ADHD. We will then delve a little deeper, not only to discover the underlying causes of ADHD, but also in an attempt to explain why children with ADHD engage in inattentive, impulsive and hyperactive behaviours rather than being quiet and focused.

Genetics and other biological factors

ADHD is a highly heritable disorder (Thapar et al., 1999). The genetics of ADHD have been demonstrated in many family, twin and adoption studies. Parents and siblings of children with ADHD have been found to have a two- to eight-fold increased risk for ADHD (Biederman, 2005). Relatives of adopted ADHD children have been shown to have lower rates of ADHD than biological relatives of non-adopted ADHD children, and similar rates to the relatives of non-ADHD children (Sprich et al., 2000).

The genetics of ADHD are very complex. The genetic risk associated with ADHD appears to be related to many different bits of genetic code scattered across lots of different genes and, to be honest, we probably still do not fully understand the genetics of ADHD. Typically, molecular genetics studies have established an association with

> **Definition**
>
> Molecular genetics: the field of biology that studies the structure and function of genes at a molecular level. It focuses on how genes are transferred from generation to generation.

a single dopamine transporter gene (Cook et al., 1995), specifically implicating the 7-repeat allele of the human dopamine receptor *D4* gene (Brookes et al., 2006).

However, other genes have also been implicated, including *SNAP 25* (synaptosomal associated protein gene), *DBH* (dopamine beta-hydroxylase gene) and *DRD5* (dopamine receptor genes), but the influence of each gene on its own on ADHD is very small. Therefore, we can conclude that the real genetic influence of ADHD is probably a complex set of gene-by-gene interactions, which may differ across individuals and which may prove very difficult to untangle.

Other biological risk factors include maternal smoking during pregnancy and obstetric complications. The link between mothers smoking during pregnancy and their children being more at risk of developing ADHD is the result of the way that nicotine influences the various neurotransmitter systems in our body. For example, prenatal nicotine exposure has been shown to produce reductions in norepinephrine (Seidler et al., 1992), while drug treatments that act on and enhance the norepinephrine system have been shown to be effective at treating ADHD. Other complications, including children still being in the womb well beyond the date at which they should have been born, low birth weight and foetal distress, are all thought to be implicated in ADHD (Banerjee et al., 2007).

Environment

While the genetic influences on ADHD have been widely reported (Thapar et al., 2007), it is vital not to under-estimate the importance of the environment in general and the social environment in particular. Even processes that are predominantly influenced by genetics can be moderated by environment. For example, how tall we are is mostly determined by our genes. If you are tall then it is very likely that you have a tall parent and/or grandparent. Even so, during the twentieth century the population has become much taller as a result of better nutrition, which is an environmental influence.

The power of the social environment has been clearly demonstrated by several studies that have examined the

---

NATURE–NURTURE

Genetic and environmental influences

In relation to ADHD, the debate is less about 'nature versus nurture' and more about nature *and* nurture. It would be simplistic and misleading even to attempt to consider whether ADHD was caused by nature (genetics) or nurture (environment). The reality is that both genetics and environment interact to allow children at risk of developing ADHD to display the symptoms of the disorder. We now know that ADHD is a genetic disorder, and about 70% of the risk of having ADHD can be explained through genetics. That still leaves a large role for environment (see the sections on environment and diet in this chapter). The way in which genes and environment interact is complex and best explained through a couple of key examples.

1. *Simple gene–environment interaction*. If an adult with ADHD decides to have a family then their children are at an increased risk of inheriting some of the key genetic material which increases their risk of developing ADHD. At the same time, ADHD in adulthood is also more likely to make that parent more chaotic, disorganised and reactive, creating the perfect environment for their children who carry the genetic risk for ADHD to develop the disorder.
2. *Nurture can change nature*. Just because genes play a strong role in determining one's susceptibility, this does not mean that environment cannot change the outcome. In ADHD, the role of nurture in changing the outcome is widely seen. Take, for example, an inattentive child who struggles in maths class but who excels in PE class, or the ADHD child who cannot remember his homework but never forgets a song lyric. Same child, same genes – different environments, different outcomes. Nurture 'influencing' nature. By training parents to change the way they parent their ADHD children, we are trying not to change the child's genes, but to alter the environment that the child exists in, as a way of changing their ADHD symptoms.

causal role that early adverse experience associated with institutional deprivation plays in determining developmental outcomes. Findings consistently highlight the elevated rates of inattention/over-activity among children raised in deprived institutional care, both in the short term and in the longer term into early adolescence (Stevens et al., 2008). One possible connection between early deprivation and ADHD symptoms may be via reactions to stress. There is a growing interest in the way in which individuals with ADHD respond to stress. Some children with ADHD have displayed an atypical cortisol response to stress, in which their cortisol levels decrease following a stressor. These responses are primarily governed by part of the brain called the hypothalamic–pituitary–adrenal (HPA) axis. One possibility is that regulation of the HPA axis involves an under-functioning behavioural inhibition system that results in poor response inhibition – one of the central deficits of ADHD.

Parenting

While ADHD is highly heritable, a key environmental risk factor is parenting; chaotic or disorganised parenting is likely to bring about ADHD in genetically predisposed individuals (Johnston and Mash, 2001). Further support for the importance of parenting comes from intervention studies, where improvements in ADHD symptoms have come about when parents have been taught alternative parenting skills (Sonuga-Barke et al., 2001). Other family–environment risk factors have been identified, including chronic family conflict, decreased family cohesion and exposure to parental psychopathology, particularly ADHD.

Diet

While there is a common consensus that diet, particularly sugar and food additives, is one of the major causes of ADHD, there is very little scientific evidence to support this notion. Research studies from the 1980s did suggest a link between diet and ADHD; however, more recent research has failed to establish any real connection between diet and ADHD. Sugar consumption is also anecdotally linked in parents' minds to ADHD; however, there is no scientific evidence to link sugar consumption in children and ADHD behaviour. In fact, Kummel et al. (1996) reviewed all 12 studies that had examined the relationship between sugar consumption and ADHD and concluded that sugar ingestion does not lead to any untoward behaviour in children with ADHD or in children without ADHD.

The influence of artificial food additives and colours on ADHD is more complicated. Bateman et al. (2004) demonstrated that artificial food additives and colours were associated with higher ratings of hyperactive behaviour in pre-school children. McCann et al. (2007) replicated these findings in pre-school children and also extended their study to older children, obtaining similar results. However, all these studies used children in the general population who did not have ADHD, and McCann et al. (2007) conclude that the adverse influence of additives and colours is not just seen in children with extreme hyperactivity (i.e. ADHD) but can also be seen in the general population, no matter what level of hyperactivity the child had. These findings suggest that food additives and colours do not cause ADHD, but actually make all children more hyperactive.

Neuropsychology of ADHD

Studies examining the neuropsychology of ADHD provide an opportunity to understand the relationship between underlying biological processes and the symptoms of ADHD. For many years, it was accepted that ADHD symptoms were the result of cognitive dysregulation (Nigg, 2001), that the ADHD child's behaviour resulted from insufficient forethought, planning and control. Evidence to support this viewpoint came from many studies using neuropsychological tests, which demonstrated that ADHD children performed less well on these tests than did children without ADHD (Inoue et al., 1998).

A summary of ADHD as a disorder of cognitive dysregulation suggested that the relationship between biology and behaviour in ADHD was mediated by an

Definition

Cognitive dysregulation: a term used to describe the set of deficits in higher-order cognitive processes (e.g. planning and working memory) that individuals with ADHD exhibit.

inability to inhibit responding (Sonuga-Barke, 2002). In contrast to the dominant view, Sonuga-Barke et al. (1994) offered an alternative view of ADHD, not as a disorder of cognitive dysregulation but as a motivational style. This viewed ADHD as a functional response by the child, aimed at avoiding delay. This alternative viewpoint of ADHD was based on studies by Sonuga-Barke et al. (1994) which showed that most of the neuropsychological evidence to support the notion that ADHD is a result of cognitive dysregulation was confounded by the child having to wait. To demonstrate this, Sonuga-Barke et al. (1994) asked ADHD and non-ADHD children to participate in the matching familiar figures test – a computer-based task where children have to match a picture of an ordinary object with one of six variants. Sonuga-Barke et al. (1994) found the same results as previous studies. ADHD children made more impulsive responses and more errors. However, the researchers pointed out that all these studies involved trial constraints where as soon as one trial ended the next began. In other words, ADHD children made more impulsive responses because it allowed them to complete the task quicker and therefore escape delay. When Sonuga-Barke et al. (1994) re-ran their study in a context where how quickly the child completed the task made no difference to when the next task was presented (i.e. there was no time constraint), ADHD children performed no differently from non-ADHD children.

Results of these studies led to the development of the *delay aversion hypothesis* (Sonuga-Barke et al., 1996), which characterised the influence of delay on behaviour dependent upon whether or not the child has control over his environment. When the child is in control of his environment, he can choose to minimise delay by acting impulsively – for example, by skipping the queue at the end of the slide! When the child is not in control of his environment, or at least where he is expected to behave in certain ways or face sanctions, the child would choose to distract himself from the passing of time. For example, in a classroom context during literacy lessons the child could achieve this either by daydreaming (inattention) or by fidgeting (hyperactivity).

Traditionally, these two different accounts of ADHD have both sought to explain the disorder independently. However, a study by Solanto et al. (2001) compared the measurement of both of these hypotheses in a head-to-head study. Results of this study showed that measures used to test each hypothesis were uncorrelated, demonstrating that they measured different components of the ADHD construct. Both sets of measures were correlated with ADHD and, when combined, were highly diagnostic, correctly distinguishing 87.5% of cases from non-cases (i.e. classifying ADHD children from non-ADHD children).

These results suggested that both accounts appeared to help to explain ADHD, but that neither explanation was the single theory of ADHD which both theoretical camps had been searching for. Based on these findings, Sonuga-Barke (2002) proposed his dual pathway model of ADHD. This model proposed two possible routes between biology and ADHD behaviour (see Figure 17.1): one via cognitive dysregulation and the other via motivational style. This was subsequently developed into a three pathway model by Sonuga-Barke et al. (2010), which also included time perception, as ADHD children are very poor at estimating and replicating intervals of time.

Time discrimination involves being able to distinguish between different lengths or intervals of time. There is some evidence to suggest that individuals with ADHD have difficulties with this which might explain their impulsive behaviour. Smith et al. (2002) examined time discrimination tasks in ADHD and non-ADHD control children. In this study, children with and without ADHD were presented with two circles on a screen and had to estimate which of the two was presented for the longest interval of time. The study found that ADHD

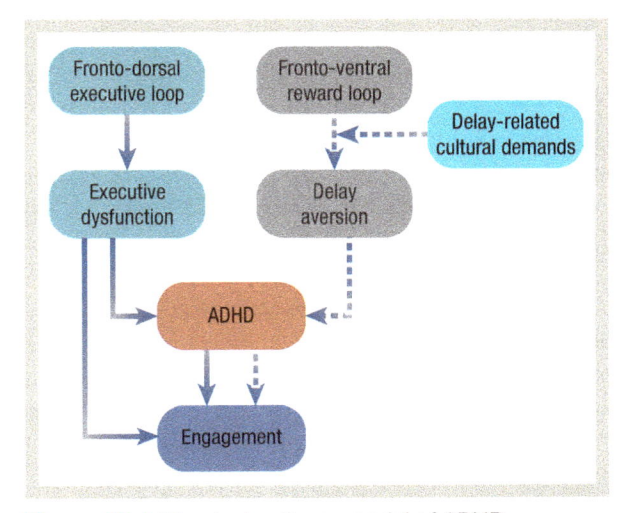

Figure 17.1 The dual pathway model of ADHD.

Source: adapted from Sonuga-Barke, E.J.S. (2002). *Behavioural and Brain Research*, 130, 29–36.

children found it very difficult to distinguish between the two, a finding supported by Rubia et al. (2007). Smith et al. (2002) suggest that time discrimination difficulties may be more central to ADHD than previously thought. However, it is not yet clear how time discrimination might actually impact on ADHD children's symptoms, or even on their experience of time. To date, the research evidence has focused on examining very small differences in time, rather than longer intervals of time. If time discrimination is implicated in ADHD, then it might be that ADHD children are less good at judging the passing of time; therefore, if a parent asks the child to 'wait a minute', as parents often do, the ADHD child might have more difficulty in working out how long that actually is.

Clinically, these models suggest that there may be merit in targeting different sub-types of ADHD with specific treatments, as well as allowing the development of novel interventions – for example, aimed at reducing aversion to delay (Sonuga-Barke, 2002). Sonuga-Barke (2004) has suggested ways in which a greater understanding of the influence of delay aversion on the development of ADHD could be used to develop alternative interventions. His suggestions include the use of delay fading, a technique to reorganise systematically the child's delay experience, as a means of increasing tolerance for delay and reducing ADHD symptoms. For example, most ADHD children have a very negative view of waiting. If you or I wanted to get great concert tickets, we would join the very long queue and wait our turn, and getting the tickets would justify the long wait. An ADHD individual would want the tickets just as much as anyone else, might join the long queue but would most likely not wait long enough to get their reward for waiting (the tickets). Therefore, for ADHD children one simple way to reduce delay aversion is to ensure that very short tolerance to delay is positively rewarded. Parents can achieve this by simply asking their ADHD child to wait for a short period (1–2 minutes) before they give their child a simple reward such as a chocolate bar or ice cream. Over time, this will help the ADHD child to understand that waiting does sometimes also have a positive outcome. Parents and teachers might also be able to help ADHD children by either not giving younger children instructions in intervals of time (e.g. yes, I will get that for you in two minutes) and ensuring they model intervals of time correctly for older children. Modelling time intervals correctly would involve not saying you are going to be there in two minutes when in fact you know it is going to take you at least ten minutes!

Other neuropsychological theories

Cognitive dysregulation and delay aversion are the dominant neuropsychological theories of ADHD, but other neuropsychological explanations also exist and may be highly relevant for some ADHD children.

Working memory

While we have focused in general on cognitive dysregulation as an explanation for ADHD symptoms, one component of this dysregulation – working memory (WM) – might be especially important in helping us to understand ADHD. Martinussen et al. (2005) conducted a meta-analysis of findings examining the quality of working memory in children with ADHD. Their results suggest that working memory processes are impaired in children with ADHD, which may help to explain the academic difficulties that children with ADHD experience, as well as the many reports from parents of how their children with ADHD are so forgetful (Daley, 2006).

Definition

Working memory: the part of memory that is critical to conscious thought because it permits internal representation of information (e.g. rules) to guide decision making and overt behaviour (responses) during an activity, so that behaviour is not dominated by the immediate sensory cues in the environment (for a review, see Baddeley, 1986).

This child is learning that waiting can have its rewards.
Source: Getty Images/Geri Lavrov

Therefore, our examination of the neuropsychology of ADHD indicates that some ADHD symptoms result from cognitive dysregulation and are presumed to be beyond the control of the individual. Other symptoms may result from delay aversion – a functional response by the individual to their environment, which results in them making decisions which suit their own individual needs rather than the needs of their parents, teachers or society.

Treatment for ADHD

Interventions for ADHD are a relatively controversial topic, and dominated by the results of two large American studies, the Multi-modal Treatment Study of ADHD (MTA) (Jensen et al., 2001) and the Preschool ADHD Treatment Study (PATS) (Kollins et al., 2006). The controversy surrounds whether or not it is appropriate to medicate children with ADHD. On one hand, medication appears to yield significant improvements in symptoms (Konrad et al., 2006). However, a number of concerns have been raised regarding the use of psycho-stimulant medication for children with ADHD, especially younger children. These range from ethical objections to using medication to modify children's behaviour (Perring, 1997) to concerns about the lack of evidence for the long-term effectiveness of the medication (Pelham et al., 1998). Side-effects of medication have also been a cause of concern. Research has indicated that pre-school children seem to be at increased risk of developing short-term side-effects such as appetite suppression or sleeplessness (Ghuman et al., 2001), and there is also a lack of research evidence regarding the long-term effects of medication on pre-school children's physical and neurological development (Sonuga-Barke et al., 2003).

How does medication for ADHD work?

When most parents of children with ADHD are told that the most common drug therapy for ADHD is stimulant medication, they tend to laugh nervously and point out that their child is already over-stimulated and what they need is a drug to calm them down. The reality is that the most common and effective drug therapy for ADHD is a drug called methylphenidate (brand names include Ritalin, Equasym and Concerta). This drug is an amphetamine, and therefore a stimulant. Methylphenidate is a norepinephrine and dopamine reuptake inhibitor, which means that it increases the level of the dopamine neurotransmitter in the brain. While we do not fully understand why methylphenidate works for individuals with ADHD, the most common explanation is that ADHD is in part the result of a dopamine imbalance in the brain.

Evidence for drug treatments

The MTA study set out to compare the efficacy of medication management, psychosocial intervention, which included parent training and help for the child's teacher, combined intervention (medication and psychosocial intervention) and routine community care. Results of the MTA

STOP AND THINK

- What do you think about using medication for ADHD?
- Does our understanding of what causes ADHD make medication use more or less acceptable?
- If ADHD is the result of cognitive dysregulation and beyond the control of the individual, does this make medication use more or less acceptable than if ADHD is the result of delay aversion and a functional response by the individual that best suits their own individual needs?

Definitions

Psycho-stimulant medication: psycho-stimulant medications, used for their ability to balance chemicals in the brain that prohibit the child from maintaining attention and controlling impulses, may be used to reduce the major characteristics of ADHD.

Norepinephrine: a neurotransmitter that influences parts of the brain where attention and responding actions are controlled. It underlies the fight-or-flight response and directly increases heart rate, triggering the release of glucose from energy stores and increasing blood flow to skeletal muscles.

Dopamine: a neurotransmitter that occurs in a wide variety of animals, including both vertebrates and invertebrates.

study suggested that medical management alone was significantly more effective for the core symptoms of ADHD compared with psychosocial treatment alone and routine community care (Jensen et al., 2001). In addition, psychosocial intervention did not significantly improve outcomes when combined with medical treatment. The results of this study influenced recommendations made in the British NICE report (National Institute of Health and Clinical Excellence, 2008) on interventions for ADHD, which recommended medication as the front-line intervention, to be followed by psychosocial intervention, if necessary.

However, later analysis using different outcome measures of ADHD symptoms indicated the superiority of combined intervention over medical management alone in the long term (Swanson et al., 2001), while analysis of different groups within the data showed large effects for psychosocial intervention in certain groups and settings (Swanson et al., 2002). However, the relevance of the MTA study results to intervention in clinical settings remains unclear. The study compared a drug intervention tailored to each child's needs to a psychosocial intervention much less tailored to children's needs (Greene and Ablon, 2001).

The psychosocial intervention used could never be replicated clinically, as it involved a multitude of individual sessions for the child, summer camps, additional classroom help, support for the child's teacher, and group and individual sessions for the child's parents (Green and Ablon, 2001). More important is the fact that no theoretical rationale for the content of the behavioural intervention has ever been published. It seems to have been developed from little bits of interventions developed by individuals involved in the study, all mixed up together. While never formally tested, it is possible that elements of the intervention were also counterproductive (Morrell and Murray, 2003), as what was taught directly to parents may not have supported what teachers were told to do in the classroom, for example.

A weakness of the MTA is that it did not include pre-school children. The lack of a rigorous trial on pharmacological intervention for pre-school children with ADHD was the rationale for PATS (Kollins et al., 2006). This was a multicentre, randomised, placebo-controlled trial designed to evaluate the five-week efficacy and 40-week safety of methylphenidate in pre-school children with ADHD. The protocol involved eight phases, one of which was parent training. Children aged 3 to 5½ years ($n = 303$) were recruited. The study found side-effects that were similar to those found in older children, with the most common being decreased appetite, emotional outbursts, difficulty falling asleep and weight loss (Wigal et al., 2006). There was also an overall slowing of growth, although the children were heavier than expected at baseline based on population levels. The effect of the medication on behaviour was lower than in the MTA (which investigated older children), based on both parent and teacher ratings, although overall the results suggest that medication may be useful for some pre-school children, but should be used with caution.

Psychosocial interventions

As an alternative to drug therapy, psychosocial treatment with parent training (PT) is considered a suitable first-level treatment for young children presenting with signs of ADHD (Conners et al., 2001). Due to some evidence of the efficacy of these interventions with school-age children with ADHD, an increasing number of empirical studies have, since the 1990s, evaluated the outcomes of PT intervention for pre-school age children with ADHD, and such interventions appear to be notably successful for this age group (Hartman et al., 2003). Following PT intervention, improvements have been found in parent–child interaction (Pisterman et al., 1989), in compliance and on-task behaviour (Sonuga-Barke et al., 2001) and in parent-reported ADHD symptoms and child behaviour problems (Jones et al., 2007). However, concern has been raised as to whether such parenting interventions are sufficiently targeting ADHD symptoms, following meta-analysis evidence that effect sizes for behavioural interventions (including parenting interventions) drop to near zero when analysing data from informants who are probably blind to treatment allocation (Sonuga-Barke et al., 2013). These results question whether it is the effort of participating in an intervention rather than the content of the intervention that might make unblinded parents rate improvement in ADHD symptoms in their children at the end of intervention.

The strongest evidence for PT is with pre-school children and this probably reflects the premise that early intervention, before the child's transition to school and before the child's symptoms become associated with secondary problems such as academic failure, aggressive behaviour and conduct problems, provides the best opportunity to alter the developmental course of the disorder (Daley, 2006). When considering effective PT treatments for ADHD during the pre-school period, three interventions have been shown to be effective and are worthy of further discussion.

New Forest Parent Training Programme (NFPP)

The NFPP (Sonuga-Barke et al., 2001) is a parent-based intervention package specifically designed to address the core symptoms of ADHD, as well as target key parenting skills. The intervention entails eight one-hour individual sessions delivered by specially trained therapists, and focuses on four intervention components: 1) psycho-education; 2) parent–child relationships, including positive parenting, extension of language to promote emotional self-regulation and play; 3) behaviour training to encourage consistent limit setting; and 4) attention training to help parents work on improving their child's attention.

The Triple-P Positive Parenting Programme

The Standard Behavioural Family Intervention (SBFI) (Sanders et al., 2000) consists of an average of 10 one-hour sessions with a practitioner on an individual basis. This programme teaches 17 core child management strategies, including 10 strategies to promote child competence and development (e.g. physical affection, attention and praise) and 7 strategies to promote effective limit setting and managing disruptive behaviour (e.g. rule setting, directed discussion and time-out). A six-step planned activities routine is also introduced to parents to promote the generalisation and maintenance of parenting skills (e.g. planning ahead and joint decision making).

Incredible Years (IY) Parent Training Programme

The IY Programme (Webster-Stratton and Hancock, 1998) is a group-based parenting intervention, available in a range of formats. Skills taught on the 12-week basic programme include: 1) how to establish a positive relationship with their child through play and child-centred activities; 2) encouraging praise, reward and incentives for appropriate behaviours; 3) guidance in the use of effective limit setting and clear instruction giving; and 4) strategies for managing non-compliance.

RESEARCH METHODS

Randomised control trial designs

Efficacy trials are usually the first attempt to evaluate an intervention. They are usually conducted within university settings and apply lots of exclusion criteria to the types of participant who can be included in the study. The researchers also usually apply rigorous control over how the intervention is delivered. Effectiveness trials are usually conducted once some evidence exists to support the efficacy of the intervention. Such trials are usually conducted in more 'real-world' settings, with participants recruited from clinical services, and are usually delivered by clinic staff. They still, however, apply lots of exclusion criteria, often making it difficult to translate the results of these trials into everyday clinical work.

For example, Jones et al. (2007) examined the efficacy of the Incredible Years parenting intervention for pre-school children with conduct problems and ADHD. In this study, a health visitor identified children who were at risk of developing conduct problems and ADHD when they were 3 years of age. Children and their parents were then randomised either to an intervention group where the parent received the intervention immediately or to a 'waiting list' control group where the parents had to wait to receive the intervention six months later. The study then examined whether ADHD symptoms in the children whose parents received the intervention were less noticeable after six months than those whose parents had to wait. By randomly allocating parents to intervention or a waiting list control, it is easier to establish whether any changes in child behaviour were due to the intervention rather than other explanations. The researchers found that those children whose parents had received the intervention displayed significantly fewer symptoms of ADHD than the children whose parents were on the waiting list.

Parents acquire these skills through facilitator-led group discussion, brainstorming, videotape modelling, role-play, shared problem solving and rehearsal of taught intervention techniques through home assignments. Parents attend the group for 2.5 hours per week for 12 weeks.

Why are these interventions successful at targeting pre-school ADHD?

Whilst the NFPT contains some of the key elements of a child and parents (CP) intervention, it has the added advantage of being directly informed by key aetiological theories of ADHD, and therefore addresses the core symptoms of ADHD. The programme contains psychoeducation about ADHD, games aimed at tackling cognitive dysregulation and inhibitory dysfunction, and strategies aimed at reducing delay aversion. However, despite the fact that Triple-P and IY are interventions developed to treat and prevent conduct problems, they appear to be effective at reducing ADHD in pre-school children. This success may be attributed, at least in part, to the sound theoretical grounding of these interventions. Effective PT interventions draw from the principles of social learning theory and highlight the reciprocal nature of parent–child interaction. Parents acquire behaviour management techniques, such as effective use of praise, using language to describe feelings, giving clear, concise instructions, effective limit setting and the use of non-violent discipline techniques, all within the context of positive, sensitive and responsive parenting. It is well documented that sensitive, responsive parenting in the early years provides the foundation for the development of child self-regulation skills (Hughes et al., 1998). Children with ADHD have particular difficulties with self-regulation skills such as listening, attending and controlling their temper (Daley and Thompson, 2007). Therefore, providing parents with effective strategies, tailored to their child's individual needs, promotes child self-regulation and can be instrumental in reducing symptoms of ADHD. The inclusion of strategies to promote more effective coping, problem-solving and communication skills may also help parents to deal with the day-to-day stressors associated with parenting a child with ADHD.

Is there a robust evidence base to support parent training for ADHD?

The evidence base supporting the interventions reviewed above has several methodological issues that warrant further discussion. First, in terms of the measures used to assess the symptoms of pre-school ADHD, the NFPP trial was particularly robust. The evaluation measured child ADHD symptoms using the Parental Account of Children's Symptoms (Taylor et al., 1991) – a well-validated structured clinical interview – as well as an objective observation measure of child attention and task switching (Sonuga-Barke et al., 2001). The evaluation of the IY programme relied exclusively on parent-report measures, and included the hyperactivity sub-scale of the Strengths and Difficulties Questionnaire (SDQ; Goodman, 1997) and the Conners Parent Rating Scale (Conners, 1994). The SDQ and Conners have been used extensively in treatment outcome studies and are highly reliable and valid instruments (Goodman, 1997). It should be noted, however, that the IY evaluation was conducted within the context of a larger trial – the North Wales Sure Start Trial. The trial evaluated the IY on a community sample of pre-school children at risk of developing conduct problems (see Hutchings et al., 2007). Direct observations of parent–child interactions were included in the assessment battery of the main trial, but did not directly measure the core symptoms of ADHD.

Secondly, the design of the NFPP study was particularly robust as it included a comparison intervention group (with no specific parenting strategies provided), in addition to a standard waiting list control group. With such a design, one can be more confident in concluding that intervention outcomes are due to the components of the intervention as opposed to contact with therapists/services. Whilst the Triple-P evaluation did examine two intervention groups against a waiting list control group, one of these interventions was simply a more enhanced version of the other, and therefore they shared much of their therapeutic content. The IY trial only compared the intervention group with a standard control group.

Thirdly, given the pervasiveness of impairment across situations, the use of multiple informants is strongly recommended in ADHD research. All evaluations reviewed here relied solely on the reports of one parent. However, the NFPP study did include objective observation of child on-task behaviour, which is at least independent of parental report.

Finally, establishing the long-term stability of intervention outcomes is of particular salience to PT research. There is some evidence to suggest that PT programmes are not entirely successful with every family, especially in the long term. Unfortunately, the positive effects of many prevention programmes decline rapidly after intervention (Serketich and Dumas, 1996). In this context, the IY evaluation was particularly robust, demonstrating 18-month stability of intervention effects (Jones et al., 2008), whereas the Triple-P reported 12-month stability (Bor et al., 2002), whilst for NFPT, outcome stability was only reported 15 weeks after programme completion (Sonuga-Barke et al., 2001).

The evidence base for parent training with older children with ADHD is much weaker, with fewer clear results, as there is a degree of variability in its effectiveness in the management of childhood ADHD (Anastopoulos et al., 1993). Age again appears to be a factor, with interventions being more effective for younger children with problems relating to compliance, rule following, defiance and aggression. What is urgently needed is robust evidence that parent training is effective in routine clinical samples of children aged between 6 and 12 years with a diagnosis of ADHD.

To summarise, psychosocial intervention is a valuable treatment alternative to stimulant medication during the pre-school years, especially when intervention is tailored to the problems that children with ADHD experience, when it is delivered in a timely way (i.e. early) and when the interventions are informed by theories about the aetiology of ADHD. For older children, the findings are less clear and much less certain, and for now drug therapy will probably remain the front-line treatment for these children.

Future directions in ADHD research

We will end this chapter with my personal view of what some of the current hot topics are in ADHD, and what might be more widely accepted in the future. Only time will tell whether I am correct or just wildly optimistic!

Self-help interventions

Despite the availability of effective interventions, the prevalence of ADHD creates a need that far exceeds available personnel and resources. In many parts of the UK, parents often have to travel long distances to access services provided at inconvenient times, leading to high levels of non-engagement or non-completion. A Cochrane review (Montgomery et al., 2006) concluded that self-help interventions were worth considering in clinical practice targeting child behaviour problems. They could reduce the amount of time therapists have to devote to each case, increase access to intervention and release clinician time to concentrate on more complex cases. For families, self-administered interventions significantly reduce or eliminate costs, transport and timing difficulties. Families can complete the intervention in their own home, in their own time and at their own pace. Evidence supports the efficacy of self-help intervention for childhood behaviour problems, either on its own or in combination with telephone support (Morawska and Sanders, 2006) or media support (Sanders et al., 2008). A self-help intervention for adults with ADHD that included help with planning and organisation has already been evaluated (Stevenson et al., 2003) and has demonstrated significant reductions in ADHD symptoms and improvements in organisation skills and self-esteem. A recent pilot trial of a self-help book for parents of children with ADHD (Daley and O'Brien, 2013) showed that self-help intervention reduced parents' ratings of ADHD symptoms, and enhanced parenting self-esteem, but did not change objective measures of ADHD (see previous comments about the Sonuga-Barke et al. (2013) meta-analysis, page 536). The challenge ahead will be to translate and test current efficacious therapist-led interventions for ADHD in effective self-help formats.

Variability in reaction time

One of the most striking findings from neuropsychological studies using children with ADHD is that their performance on tests which involve reaction time is very variable. This variability in reaction time performances is called *intra-subject variability* (ISV), and it is not specific to ADHD but can also be seen in other mental health difficulties and even in older adults.

A U-shaped function characterises the relationship between ISV in cognitive performance and age across the lifespan. As well as being studied in theories of typical development, intra-subject variability is a measure often employed when studying clinical populations. For example, increased intra-subject (also known as between participants or individual differences) variability characterises performance of the elderly and that of patients with dementia, head injury, schizophrenia and ADHD. Studies of ADHD in particular have extensively pursued intra-subject variability and have consistently shown that ADHD children are more variable in their performance than controls (Klein et al., 2006). What is yet to be determined is whether or not this profile of performance on reaction time tests equates to anything clinically useful. For example, do ISV scores on a reaction time test predict how inattentive a child with ADHD will be in a classroom?

Working memory training

Given the relative importance of working memory deficits in ADHD, it makes sense that an intervention aimed at improving working memory should reduce ADHD symptoms. Klingberg et al. (2005) reported results of a randomised control trial of a computerised working memory intervention for children with ADHD. The intervention focused on getting children to engage in computer tasks that involved practising working memory. Children in the intervention group were rated as having significant reductions in ADHD symptoms post-intervention and three months after the end of intervention. While the exciting results of this study warrant replication and expansion, the possibility that ADHD symptoms can be reduced by practising working memory games similar to those on Nintendo Brain Training is of great potential. It offers another form of intervention which does not depend on a therapist, it provides something concrete that the child with ADHD can engage in directly to help reduce her ADHD symptoms, and it is likely to be a more acceptable form of intervention for adolescents with ADHD than parent training or drug treatment.

Increasing the use of technology in ADHD treatments

Despite living in a technologically advanced world, most of the assessments and treatments used clinically for ADHD have not changed much in the last 20 to 30 years. The NIHR MindTech cooperative which has recently been established at the University of Nottingham aims to enhance the use of new technology in the diagnosis and treatment of all mental health problems (see www.mindtech.org.uk). One interesting development is the evaluation of objective measures of ADHD to aid clinical diagnosis. QB-Test is an objective measure of ADHD symptoms that combines a neuropsychological test of attention and impulsivity with a motion-sensitive camera that can detect the level of hyperactivity in the child while they are undertaking the test (Wehmeier et al., 2011). Current investigations underway at the University of Nottingham involve investigating the diagnostic utility of QB-Test as well as evaluating in a randomised controlled trial whether use of QB-Test speeds up the time taken to make an accurate diagnosis of ADHD as well as enhancing clinician confidence in the diagnoses they have made.

CUTTING EDGE

The quality of life of children with ADHD: a recent publication

A recent systematic review of the literature examining quality of life (QoL) of children with ADHD by Danckaerts et al. (2010) has drawn some interesting conclusions. ADHD is associated with such a wide range of deficits and associated problems that it has been linked to very low levels of QoL in previous studies. This systematic review set out to address three main questions:

1. What is the impact of ADHD on QoL?
2. What are the relationships between ADHD symptoms, functional impairment and mediators and moderators of QoL in ADHD?
3. Does the treatment of ADHD impact on QoL?

The broad search strategy examined 1445 articles which, after inspection and the application of strict inclusion criteria, were reduced to 36 articles on which the systematic review was based. Inclusion criteria included peer-reviewed articles published in one of five European languages, of any design, which included at least some empirical data on QoL in children with ADHD and used a QoL measure.

Results showed that QoL was impaired in children with ADHD, with parents of children with ADHD rating their children's QoL as being at 1.5 standard deviations lower than that of non-ADHD children. Also, QoL decreases as symptom severity increases, or where it is complicated by the presence of other difficulties or psychosocial stressors. There was some evidence that drug treatments improved QoL, but these effects were small. Finally, and most interestingly, there was evidence that parents and children assessed QoL differently.

Children with ADHD rated their own QoL less negatively than their parents and do not always see themselves as functioning less well than healthy controls. The review concludes that future research needs to distinguish QoL effects from those related only to symptoms and functional impairment, and to study the differences between child and parent perceptions of ADHD and its impact on QoL.

Neurofeedback

Neurofeedback is a neurobehavioural treatment aimed at acquiring self-control over certain brain activity patterns and implementing these skills in daily life situations. It has recently been examined as a new treatment for ADHD. Gevensleben et al. (2009) randomly allocated children to either 36 sessions of neurofeedback or an attention skills training control condition. Results showed that children in the neurofeedback group were rated by both teachers and parents as having significantly fewer symptoms of ADHD compared to the control group. A recent meta-analysis that explored the impact efficacy of neurofeedback for ADHD found that unblended parental ratings supported the efficacy of neurofeedback, but more blinded measures did not (Sonuga-Barke et al., 2013) While these results warrant further replication and expansion, and the costs of neurofeedback need to be evaluated, neurofeedback looks like a promising future intervention for ADHD if studies can demonstrate that it leads to real reductions in ADHD symptoms rather than just changing parents' perceptions of ADHD symptoms.

SUMMARY

Our conclusions at the end of this introduction to ADHD are that the disorder is both complex and fascinating; that ADHD is a disorder with multiple probable causes, most of which interact with each other, so that no two individuals with ADHD are likely to have developed the disorder for exactly the same set of reasons; that ADHD is a lifetime disorder, recognisable from very early in the pre-school period, and remains a problem for some individuals through into adulthood; that it rarely occurs on its own, and is associated with a wide range of other associated problems; that both genetics and environment are very important in increasing the likelihood that an individual will develop ADHD; and, more importantly, that the role of neuropsychological deficits such as inhibitory control, delay aversion, working memory deficits, etc. helps us to understand the links between what happens in the ADHD brain and ADHD behaviours. Many treatments are available for ADHD. Drug treatments are effective for most older children, but they are less effective and have greater side-effects for young children. Psychological treatments in the form of parent training are very effective for younger children, but there is less evidence for their utility in older children.

REVIEW QUESTIONS

1. Is ADHD a lifetime disorder? Discuss.
2. What are the causes of ADHD?
3. Explain how the symptoms of ADHD (inattention, impulsivity and hyperactivity) develop.
4. Compare and contrast the various treatment options available for ADHD.

RECOMMENDED READING

For a more advanced text which would expand in greater detail the ideas introduced in this chapter:

Banaschewski, T., Coghill, D., Danckaerts, M., Döpfner, M., Rohde, L., Sergeant, J. A., Sonuga-Barke, E. J. S., Taylor, E., & Zuddas, A. (2010). *Attention-Deficit Hyperactivity Disorder and Hyperkinetic Disorder*. Oxford: Oxford University Press.

A book written for parents but which explains in simple terms the key strategies that parents need to use to help their children with ADHD:

Laver-Bradbury, C., Weeks, A., Thompson, M., Daley, D., & Sonuga-Bakre, E. J. S. (2010). *Step by Step Help for Children with ADHD*. London: Jessica Kingsley.

A paper which describes the randomised control trial of a parenting intervention for ADHD:

Sonuga-Barke, E. J. S., Daley, D., Thompson, M., Laver-Bradbury, C., & Weeks, A. (2001). Parent-based therapies for preschool attention-deficit/hyperactivity disorder: A randomized, controlled trial with a community sample. *Journal of the American Academy of Child and Adolescent Psychiatry*, 40, 402–408.

A paper which develops the ideas on the neuropsychology of ADHD:

Sonuga-Barke, E. J. S. (2002) Psychological heterogeneity in AD/HD: A dual pathway model of behaviour and cognition. *Behaviour and Brain Research*, 130, 29–36.

RECOMMENDED WEBSITES

UK Attention Deficit Disorder Information and Support Service – people-friendly information and resources about ADHD to anyone who needs assistance – parents, sufferers, teachers or health professionals:

http://www.addiss.co.uk

Website of the American Academy of Child and Adolescent Psychiatry, a resource site for parents and professionals on a whole range of child psychiatry disorders including ADHD:

http://www.aacap.org

Official website of the American National Institute of Mental Health and its section on ADHD:

http://www.nimh.nih.gov/health/publications/attention-deficit-hyperactivity-disorder

Glossary

Accepted children: children who are popular, accepted or well liked by the majority of other children in the peer group.

Accommodation: within Piagetian theory, this is the revision of older knowledge structures to take account of new information.

Achievement: personal accomplishment of skills, knowledge and understanding in comparison to an individual's former achievement. A measure of personal progress.

Additive composition: the property of numbers that allows any to be defined as the sum of two other numbers.

Additive relations: relations between quantities defined within a part–whole schema.

Adolescent egocentrism: the young person's preoccupation with himself, likened to being on a permanent social stage where he or she is the focus of attention.

Adult Attachment Interview: a semi-structured interview method for probing into an adult's early childhood relationship experiences with attachment figures and assessing the extent to which she integrates such experiences into her current relationships.

Algebra: a domain of mathematics that involves representing quantities and relations by letters, rather than numbers, and operating on these in ways that respect the properties of the operations and the relations.

Analogical reasoning: a method of problem solving which makes use of the similarity of a new problem to some previously solved problem.

Animacy: the concept of animacy refers to an understanding of the difference between living (animate) and non-living (inanimate) things.

Apgar scale: a rating scale for the condition of the new-born.

Assessment: assessment is the process of collecting information on children, typically through observations, tests, clinician/teacher rating scales, etc., in order to make inferences about their development, typically within a school or clinical context.

Assimilation: within Piagetian theory, this is the process of taking new information into existing knowledge structures.

Asynchronous development: the situation that arises when a child is performing at a more advanced stage in one developmental skill and a less advanced stage in a second developmental skill: for example, the child may be performing well in Piaget's conservation of liquids task but less well in Kohlberg's Heinz dilemma task measuring moral development.

Attachment: a strong, enduring, affectionate bond an infant shares with a significant individual, usually the mother, who knows and responds well to the infant's needs.

Attachment security: the readiness of an infant to use the primary caregiver to derive a sense of security that can be reflected in her pattern of attachment behaviours.

Attachment types: patterns of behaviour observed in the Strange Situation denoting differing security of attachment to the primary caregiver as a safe base from which to explore.

Attainment: personal accomplishment of skills, knowledge and understanding in comparison to typical accomplishments. Comparisons are made with examination requirements or the attainments of others.

Attention: the part of our cognitive processes which controls ability to focus efficiently on specific things and ignore others.

Autobiographical memory: an individual's personal memory for their life experiences and events and for information about themselves.

Behavioural inhibition: a concept Kagan has defined to characterise young children's behaviour in unfamiliar settings, mostly by independent observations, into two qualitatively distinct types: inhibited and uninhibited.

Belief-desire stage of theory of mind: the ability to make a mental representation of the world.

Bully/victims: children and young people who engage in bullying others and are bullied themselves.

Bullying: an interaction which is intended to and does cause harm to a person who is seen as being less powerful than the perpetrator.

Cardinal numbers: numbers used in counting, to denote how many items are in a set.

Cardinality: the property of being represented by a cardinal number.

Case study: the detailed investigation of the experience of one person or of a small group of people.

Categorisation: the grouping or organisation of items based on their similarity.

Category: a set of sounds or words perceived as belonging to the same group (e.g. all instances of the sound /s/ or all words relating to female humans).

Central coherence: the ability to put together information in context to form a whole picture (Frith, 1989).

Central conceptual structure: a well-formed mental scheme of a concept like 'horse' that can be generally applied to all horses and requires little more assimilation until we experience a zebra for the first time.

Classical conditioning: describes the process of learning an association between two stimuli.

Cognitive-developmental theory: a theory, derived by Kohlberg, that explains gender identity development by the child's developing cognitive skills in three stages, which underpin critical milestones in understanding about gender as gender labelling, gender stability and gender constancy.

Cognitive dysregulation: a term used to describe the set of deficits in higher-order cognitive processes (e.g. planning and working memory) that individuals with ADHD exhibit.

Cognitive interview: a technique developed specifically for interviewing witnesses in legal situations, using principles of memory from cognitive psychology, to maximise the amount of information which is accurately recalled.

Cohort: a cohort is a group of people who are defined by having something collectively in common.

Colic: a condition where babies cry for long periods of time (most commonly in the first three months of life) without obvious reason, but possibly due to trapped wind or infant temperament.

Common fractions: notations for rational numbers that use the form a/b, in which b can have any value.

Concepts: mental representations upon which categories are based.

Confound variables: extraneous factors in a research study that are not specifically measured or manipulated and that may affect the results of that study.

Congenital adrenal hyperplasia: congenital adrenal hyperplasia can affect both boys and girls. People with congenital adrenal hyperplasia lack an enzyme needed by the adrenal gland to make the hormones cortisol and aldosterone. Without these hormones, the body produces more androgen – a type of male sex hormone. This causes male characteristics to appear early (or inappropriately). About 1 in 10,000–18,000 children are born with congenital adrenal hyperplasia (MEDLINE Plus, 2010).

Conservation: the principle that the shape or appearance of something can change without there being a change in quantity.

Constructivism: a philosophy of learning founded on the premise that, by reflecting on our experiences, we construct our own understanding of the world we live in (Piaget, 1967).

Context-dependence: related sets of behaviour or expressions depending on settings.

Continuity: related ranges of behaviour appropriate to age.

Continuous development: change that occurs at a steady pace, perhaps showing a constant, consistent improvement or growth.

Continuous perspective: development is a continuous, life-long experience which does not follow specific steps and stages, but early experiences are built upon and skills expanded continuously.

Continuous quantities: quantities to which one must apply a unit of measurement in order to determine their magnitude, such as length, mass, time, etc.

Cooperative learning: working in small groups, acting together to meet a learning goal or goals.

Counting all: term used to describe behaviour in addition tasks whereby children join sets and start counting from one, e.g. when adding seven and five tokens, they count all the items in the first set starting from one and then continue counting as they point to the items in the second set.

Counting on: term used to describe behaviour in addition tasks whereby children start counting from the number after the value of one set, e.g. when adding seven and five tokens, they point to an item in the second set and start to count from 8.

Co-variation or isomorphism of measures problems: multiplicative reasoning problems in which there is a fixed ratio between two quantities or two measures. For example, there is usually a fixed ratio between the number of sweets you buy and the price you pay.

Covert attention: the act of mentally focusing on one of several possible stimuli.

Creativity: the ability to think in new or different ways or to come up with original ideas, concepts or solutions.

Critical period: the time period that was thought to be critical for the formation and development of any attachment relationship, hypothesised to be 6 months to 3 years, beyond which it is seen as highly difficult for such a bond to be formed.

Critical period hypothesis: the suggestion that there is a specific period of time in the early part of a child's life (suggestions about when this begins and ends vary), during which language learning should occur in order to develop normally.

Cross-sectional research design: a method of collecting data that administers a test or series of tests to a participant or group of participants on one occasion only.

Cues: stimuli which assist with the retrieval of information from memory by providing a hint or by helping to recreate something of the original encoding environment.

Cyberbullying: forms of bullying behaviour that use electronic media such as the internet, mobile phones, etc.

Decades: values in a numeration system with a base 10 that include one or more groups of 10 units. In English, twenty, thirty, forty, etc. up to ninety are the number labels for decades.

Deception: (1) the deliberate act of creating false knowledge in your participants for the purpose of influencing the outcomes of the research study; (2) trying to make someone else believe that something is true when in fact it is false (Baron-Cohen, 2001).

Decimal fractions: fractions in which the denominator is a power of 10. Decimal fractions can be expressed as a/b, but they can also have a different notation: $8/10$ can also be expressed as 0.8.

Defence mechanisms: coping styles used during moments of anxiety brought on by unresolved libidinous urges.

Demand characteristics: when a participant anticipates what the researcher wants from them and changes their behaviour to conform to that perceived desirable performance.

Dendrites: the branches or extensions at the top of neurons that allow contact with other neurons and so form neural networks.

Denominator: in the common notation of fractions (a/b), the denominator is b, which can also be conceived as the divisor in the division represented by the a/b notation.

Depression: a common mental disorder that presents with depressed mood, loss of interest or pleasure, feelings of guilt or low self-worth, disturbed sleep or appetite, low energy, and poor concentration (World Health Organization).

Desire stage of theory of mind: the ability to detect in someone a strong feeling of wanting to have something or wishing for something to happen.

Developmentally appropriate provision: when the educational experiences of learners are matched with the learners' ability to make the most of the experience.

Disapplication: the term used to indicate that a pupil or group of pupils need no longer be taught part or all of a programme study.

Discontinuous development: change that occurs in what appear to be great bursts of achievement following a period of steady consolidation of perhaps knowledge or skill.

Discrete quantities: quantities which can be counted using natural numbers –1, 2, 3, etc.

Discriminate: in speech-sound perception, to be able to tell the difference between speech sounds of a language.

Disinhibition: the tendency to behave in ways other than one might normally, showing a lack of restraint or regard for social norms.

Divergent thinking: the type of thinking which is usually the product of creativity and is therefore original.

Dividend: in division, the quantity that is being divided.

Divisor: in division, the quantity by which another quantity (the dividend) is to be divided.

DNA (deoxyribonucleic acid): strings of biochemical material that provide the code for genes.

Dominance hierarchy: a relatively stable ordering of different-status members by their ability to win in conflict that signifies different access to resources, established by challenges through rough-and-tumble play.

Dopamine: a neurotransmitter that occurs in a wide variety of animals, including both vertebrates and invertebrates.

DSM-5 criteria for ADHD in childhood: current classification for combined type ADHD requires a minimum of six out of nine symptoms of inattention and a minimum of six out of nine symptoms of hyperactivity/impulsivity to be present in the child. Symptoms of inattention include daydreaming, distractibility and disorganisation; symptoms of hyperactivity include restlessness and fidgeting; while symptoms of impulsivity include impatience and not being able to stop yourself from acting. In addition, there must be some impairment from symptoms in two or more settings (e.g. home and school) and clear evidence of significant impairment in social, school or work functioning.

Dyscalculia: impaired number comprehension, number production or calculation. When attributed to brain damage, it is known as acquired dyscalculia. With no evidence of brain damage, and a discrepancy between number abilities and general intelligence, it is known as developmental dyscalculia.

Dysfluency: an abnormal degree of hesitation or stumbling over words, making speech difficult to understand. Stammering (or stuttering) is the most common form of dysfluency. The speech of people who are dysfluent may be hard to understand; it may seem jerky or disjointed and it does not flow easily from one word to the next.

Dyslexia: a learning difficulty which affects a person's ability to read despite otherwise normal levels of intelligence.

Early emergence: in infancy, product of biology and/or environment since birth.

EEG (electroencephalogram): record of brain activity recorded by means of electrodes placed around the scalp.

Effortful control: a concept Rothbart identified to characterise how people voluntarily suppress certain responses in order to substitute with other, usually more appropriate, ones as a process that is likely to be mediated by the system of frontal lobes known to be involved in resolving conflicting tendencies between different parts of the brain.

Ego: our conscious decision-making process.

Egocentric: understanding the world only from your own perspective and finding it difficult to understand the point of view of another person.

Empathy: the ability to identify with the emotions of others and to read the physical expression of emotions in others.

Encoding: the first stage of information processing in memory, where information is taken in via the senses.

Encoding specificity principle: a principle which states that memory is improved when contextual information present at the time of encoding is also available at the time of retrieval.

Episodic memory: memory for specific events or occurrences, including details of time, place and emotions associated with it.

Ethology: the study of behaviour in its natural setting. Ethologists do not conduct experiments on behaviour in non-naturalistic settings; they prefer to observe and catalogue behaviour as it occurs naturally and without intervention from the researcher.

Exosystem: the social settings that do not immediately impact on a person, but surround them and are important to their welfare.

Experimental methods: the manipulation of events to see if change in one variable effects change in another variable.

Explicit: explicit knowledge is that which has been stated clearly and in detail, and where there is no room for misunderstanding, confusion or doubt.

Factor analysis: a statistical method that reduces large numbers of questionnaire items down to a smaller number of clusters or underlying factors.

False belief: the wrongly held belief that something is true.

Familiarisation: a procedure for testing infant perceptual and cognitive skills by presenting an item for a set number of times or trials and then comparing infant interest in the familiar item with interest in a novel one.

Folk psychology: the information that ordinary people have about the mind and how it works. It is usually based in a common set of traditions and customs that are used to explain people's emotions and behaviour.

Friendship: a mutual reciprocal relationship between two or more people where both or all parties involved want to spend more time with the other(s) than other peers.

G: an abbreviated way of referring to general intelligence, the common factor believed by some to underpin performance on all intelligence tests.

Gaze following: the ability to follow where another person is looking and to look in the same direction.

Gender constancy: the understanding that gender group membership is unchanged despite changes in appearance.

Gender labelling: correct identification of 'male' or 'female' of oneself and others.

Gender schema: a system of beliefs about the attributes and behaviours associated with gender that help the child to form evaluations of, and to make assumptions about, each other and social objects and situations based on gender group memberships.

Gender stability: the understanding that gender group membership is normally stable and permanent over time.

Gender stereotypes: beliefs about what is appropriate for or typical of one's own or the other gender group.

Goodness-of-fit: this concept defines how both genetic components as the innate part of temperament and environmental forces will combine and interact to over time to produce positive (through good 'fit') or negative (through bad 'fit') developmental outcomes.

Habituation-recovery: a procedure for testing infant perceptual and cognitive skills by repeatedly presenting an item until the infant's interest drops to some criterion or set level, then presenting a novel item to see if the infant shows refreshed interest and so can distinguish it from the familiar one.

Heterogeneous developmental disorder: a condition that might have many different causes that affects the normal development of the child.

High-amplitude sucking (HAS) method: a procedure for testing infant auditory skills (especially in regard to speech and music), in which infants suck on a dummy or pacifier to maintain a sound if interested.

Holophrase: a single word which expresses some more complex idea.

Hostile attribution bias: the tendency for some people to attribute hostile intention to the actions of others in non-hostile situations.

Hyperactive: a descriptive term that is frequently applied to children who have low levels of attention to a task, can behave impulsively and without consideration of the consequences and/or may be unable to sit quietly with other children.

Hypothesis: a proposed explanation for why or how two events might be related to each other.

Id: our biological impulses.

Identity versus role-confusion stage of development: Erikson's description of the pursuit of a coherent sense of self during the teenage years. Role diffusion can occur when the teenager is unable to put together aspects of him or herself (see Chapter 2).

Implicit: implicit knowledge comes from an understanding of what is meant or suggested even when it has not been directly stated.

Imprinting: a process in which new-borns of most species will recognise and seek proximity with the first object they encounter (usually the primary caregiver) following the activation of a trigger during a critical period after birth.

Indirect bullying: forms of bullying that may not be observed by the victim at the time, but nonetheless have intentional and negative consequences for the victim (e.g. spreading rumours).

Induction: a type of reasoning where a factual conclusion is reached on the basis of empirical evidence, but need not necessarily be true.

Infanticide: intentionally causing the death of an infant.

Infantile amnesia: a phenomenon whereby memories from the first three or four years of life are relatively scarce.

Information-processing theory: the likening of human cognition to the working structures of a computer, with input, processing, memory, output, etc. that helps us 'conceptualise' what is happening in the brain.

Informed consent: agreeing to take part in a study whilst knowing as far as possible the details of the study methodology, including all possible risks and benefits of taking part.

Inhibited: tendency to be timid, cautious or restrained and to withdraw from novelty.

Innate behaviour: behaviour that appears instinctive, and is natural and not learned; behaviour or abilities that we are born with.

Intelligence quotient (IQ): devised by the German psychologist William Stern (1912), the intelligence quotient or IQ is a score derived from one of several different standardised tests designed to measure ability over a range of different cognitive tasks.

Internal working model: the mental representation about oneself, others and their relationships on which one's expectations about future relationships are based.

Intervention: acting to stop a behaviour from continuing.

Interview: the interview is conducted by the researcher following either a strict list of questions (a closed or structured interview) or an open format that evolves from the answers the respondent gives (an open interview).

IQ: abbreviation for intelligence quotient – a score obtained from an individual's performance on tests designed to measure intelligence.

Language acquisition device: a hypothetical cognitive structure predisposed towards the acquisition of language and sensitive to rule-based regularities in everyday speech, therefore allowing for the development of grammar and syntax.

Lateralisation: the principle that some specific psychological functions are located in one or the other side of the brain's two cortical hemispheres.

Learning disability: 'a condition of arrested or incomplete development of the mind, which is especially characterised by impairment of skills manifested during the developmental period, which contribute to the overall level of intelligence, i.e. cognitive, language, motor and social abilities . . . Adaptive behaviour is always impaired' (ICD-10).

Longitudinal research method: a method of collecting data that administers a test or series of tests to the same participant or group of participants on a number of occasions.

Looking-glass self: the sense of self we develop as we respond to interactions with others and see how others react to us. We see ourselves reflected in other people's behaviour towards us.

Macrosystem: the cultural values, laws, customs and resources available to a person.

Make-believe play: also known as sociodramatic or role-play, play that involves two or more children acting out social roles, whether real-life or fictional ones, in pretend games, usually requiring negotiation and reciprocation with each other with agreed rules in the shared imaginary scenario.

Maternal deprivation hypothesis: the notion that later serious deleterious outcomes will result from the lack of a consistent attachment figure in early childhood.

Maternal sensitivity: the emotional sensitivity of the mother to recognise her child's cues and to respond to them promptly, appropriately and consistently.

Maturation: change over time which is naturally occurring and genetically programmed.

Mean: a statistical term which refers to the numerical average of a set of numbers. To calculate the mean, add all of the numbers in the set and divide by the number of items in the set.

Median: the mid-point in the range of scores that the participants received on a measure. If we place our participants' maths scores in ascending order (5, 5, 5, 7, 8), we can see that the score at the mid-point in the range from 5 to 8 is the third 5 and the median score is therefore 5.

Menarche: a woman's first menstrual period.

Mesosystem: the connections between elements of the microsystem.

Meta-analysis: a method of statistical analysis which combines the results of many studies to identify an overall effect or change, often in an attempt to overcome problems of small sample sizes in research.

Metacognition: a person's knowledge or awareness of their own cognition; sometimes referred to as 'knowledge about knowledge' or 'cognition about cognition'.

Meta-representation: (1) the ability to separate reality from fantasy, e.g. during pretend play (Leslie, 1987); (2) additionally, knowing the difference between what might be represented in a photograph or painting of an object and what the reality of that object might be (Perner, 1991).

Microsystem: the activities and interactions immediately surrounding a person.

Mind-mindedness: the ability of a parent to see and treat her child as an individual with his own thoughts and feelings, through her interactions with him, using talk to refer to mental states.

Mnemonics: memory aids which are used to assist with the learning or memorisation of information.

Modal: the most frequently obtained score that the participants received on a measure. In our example, the most frequently obtained score is 5 (5, 5, 5, 7, 8) and the modal score is therefore 5.

Molecular genetics: the field of biology that studies the structure and function of genes at a molecular level. It focuses on how genes are transferred from generation to generation.

Monotropism: the idea that any child only forms a strong attachment to one person.

Myelinisation: the growth of fatty insulating coating along the axon of the neuron.

Naming insight: the realisation that all things have names, leading to a fundamental change in the way children think about the world.

Natural numbers: the set of counting numbers. Does not include negative numbers, but some people include zero as a natural number. The cardinality of a finite set will be a natural number.

Nature: the role of genetics in forming our behaviour, our personality or any other part of ourselves.

Neglected children: children who are neither accepted nor rejected, or not strongly liked or disliked, by their peer group.

Neo-Piagetian theory: a recent interpretation of Piaget's theory in an information-processing framework that places greater emphasis on cognitive processes than maturation.

Neural tube: hose-shaped structure forming the basis of the brain and spinal cord in the embryo.

Neurogenesis: the production of neurons in the embryo.

Neuroimaging: techniques which provide images of the structure and/or functioning of the brain.

Neuronal migration: the movement of neurons to appropriate locations in the brain and body.

Norepinephrine: a neurotransmitter that influences parts of the brain where attention and responding actions are controlled. It underlies the fight-or-flight response and directly increases heart rate, triggering the release of glucose from energy stores and increasing blood flow to skeletal muscles.

Numerator: in the common notation of fractions (a/b), the numerator is a, which can also be conceived as the dividend in the division represented by the a/b notation.

Numerical calculation: the arithmetic operations that children carry out to find the answer to a problem.

Nurture: the role of family, society, education and other social factors in forming our behaviour, our personality or any other part of ourselves.

Object permanence: knowing that even when something has disappeared from view, it has not necessarily actually disappeared.

Objective or categorical self: the recognition of the self as the person seen by others and defined by the attributes and qualities used to define groups of people.

Observation study: the researcher views behaviour in either a laboratory or a natural setting and records events that take place. The researcher generally tries not to influence events unless this is a necessary feature of the study design.

Operant conditioning: the process that describes how behaviours can be encouraged or inhibited by the effective use of reward or punishment.

Ordinality: in set theory, this is the use of numbers to measure the position of a number in an ordered set.

Overt attention: the act of directing the senses towards a particular stimulus.

Parental investment theory: a theory used to explain gender differences on the basis of biological sex differences. The theory states that reproduction has different implications for males and females and that men and women therefore look for different traits in each other, which through the course of evolution have been adapted as the modern-day observed gender role, behaviour and status differences.

Participant confidentiality: the treatment of any data collected on a participant to prevent the identification of the participant.

Partitioning: the process of dividing a whole into parts.

Peer group: the other children or young people with whom a child or young person engages who are of a similar age and not family members.

Peer preference: choosing friends who have similar interests to our own and who have a similar set of beliefs or outlook on life.

Peer pressure: when the friendship group convinces the young person to say or do something that they would not ordinarily say or do in order to gain positive regard or acceptance.

Peer support: a method by which children and young people are trained to act as supports for others who are experiencing difficulties such as bullying.

Phoneme: the smallest units of sound in a language.

Phonology: the sound system of a particular language.

Pilot study: a small-scale, preliminary run of a study that aims to test, for example, the appropriateness of the measurement tools, methods used and then the quality of the data collected. A pilot study is usually conducted to refine the full-scale run of a study.

Placenta: the organ which connects to the wall of the mother's uterus, and which connects to the foetus by the umbilical cord. It allows for the uptake of nutrients by the foetus, and for the elimination of waste.

Plasticity: the ability of the brain to reorganise neural pathways either to recover lost functioning due to damage, or in response to learning from new experiences.

Play sensitivity: responsiveness to the infant during play through cooperation and motivation by accepting her initiative, adapting play to her cognitive capability and responding to her emotional expressions.

Positivism: (concept) a system recognising only that which can be scientifically verified or logically proved, and therefore rejecting metaphysics and theism (Oxford Dictionaries, 2008).

Pragmatic language: pragmatics is a sub-field of linguistics devoted to the study of how context contributes to meaning. Specifically, it examines how the transmission of meaning depends not only on the linguistic knowledge (grammar and words used) of the speaker and listener, but also on the context of the utterance, knowledge about the subject matter, etc., all of which help to attribute meaning to language.

Pragmatics: the part of language concerned with its use in social contexts.

Preferential looking method: a procedure for testing infant perceptual and cognitive skills by observing infant viewing preferences for two or more items.

Prevention: acting to reduce the likelihood that a behaviour may occur.

Procedural memory: implicit, unconscious long-term memory for skills or how to do things.

Product of measures problems: multiplicative reasoning problems that involve three variables, where the third one is the product of the first two.

Propositional thought: the ability to consider a hypothetical concept without having to see the events actually happening in order to come to a conclusion.

Proto-declarative pointing: the ability to point at the same object of interest as another person.

Prototype: a person or a thing that serves as an example of a type.

Proximity seeking: a set of typical behaviours displayed by children to draw the attention of the primary caregiver towards themselves or reach her when separated, with the goal of restoring proximity.

Psychiatric co-morbidity: the experience of two psychological conditions at the same time: for example, anxiety and depression or ADHD and conduct disorder.

Psycho-stimulant medication: psycho-stimulant medications, used for their ability to balance chemicals in the brain that prohibit the child from maintaining attention and controlling impulses, may be used to reduce the major characteristics of ADHD.

Puberty: the period of physical maturation from a child into an adult.

Qualitative methods: methods that describe and define concepts, *without* the use of numbers, and are usually conducted with smaller participant numbers.

Quantitative methods: use a systematic approach for collecting data that have or are assigned a numerical value.

Quantity: a property of magnitude or multitude used to express how much or how many of something there is.

Quotient: in division, the number of times by which the dividend is divisible by the divisor.

Ratio: expresses the magnitude of one quantity relative to another.

Rational numbers: numbers which can be expressed as a simple fraction.

Referential words: common nouns used to denote real objects.

Rehearsal: the repetition of information in a deliberate attempt to aid memory.

Rejected children: children who are unpopular, avoided as a playmate or least liked or disliked by others in the peer group.

Relational bullying: forms of bullying whereby the bully manipulates children in the social setting of the victim, with the intention of causing harm or distress.

Relational calculation: the operations of thought that children must carry out in order to handle the relations between quantities in the problem.

Relations: the positions, associations, connections, or status of one person, thing or quantity with regard to another or others; relational statements have an implied converse, so that (for example) if *A* is greater than *B*, then *B* must be less than *A*.

Representational stage of theory of mind: the ability to know that someone may believe something is true even when it is not and understand that the mistake happens because they are relying on incorrect or false knowledge.

Repression: a psychological defence mechanism which allows uncomfortable memories to be stored in the unconscious mind.

Research: (a) the systematic investigation into and study of materials, sources, etc., in order to establish facts and reach new conclusions; (b) an endeavour to discover new or collate old facts, etc. by the scientific study of a subject or by a course of critical investigation (Oxford Dictionaries, 2008).

Retrieval: the third stage of information processing in memory, by which information is brought back out of storage and recalled.

Rough-and-tumble play: also known as 'play-fighting', play that involves physical activity, often without objects, such as wrestling, tumbling, kicking and chasing; it is commonest during middle childhood among boys.

Schemes of action: representations of actions that can be applied to a variety of objects leading to predictable outcomes independent of the objects.

Scripts: mental representations which we have of certain types of event, which include our general expectations of such events based on prior experience.

Seeing leads to knowing: the principle that a person's belief/knowledge about a situation depends partly on what they have seen.

Self-awareness: the first step in the development of self-concept; the recognition that we are distinct from others with physical and mental properties of our own.

Self-concept: ideas we have about ourselves, including our physical and mental qualities, and our emotional and behavioural attributes.

Self-efficacy: a person's belief about how effectively he or she can control herself, her thoughts or behaviours, particularly when intended to fulfil a personal goal.

Self-esteem: the evaluative and reflective features of our self-concept that can vary from high to low, and which draw in part on others' evaluations of ourselves.

Semantic memory: long-term memory for facts, concepts and meanings.

Semantically related: words which have something in common in terms of their meaning.

Semantics: the part of language concerned with the meanings of words and parts of words.

Sensitive period: revised from critical period, the timeframe that is most conducive to forming strong attachment compared to other times in the child's life.

Separation anxiety: the anxiety a child experiences when separated from the mother or primary carer.

Separation protest: a set of typical behaviours displayed by the infant to register a form of protest against their caregiver's departure.

Shaken baby syndrome: a type of child abuse which occurs when a baby is vigorously shaken; it can result in neurological damage and may be fatal.

Shaping: a process by which children's utterances move closer to correct speech as the result of positive reinforcement, which leads to a series of successive approximations.

Social identity: a sense of identity derived from our membership of social groups, including categorising ourselves as members, feelings of belonging, and behaviour consistent with what is expected of group members.

Social-information processing: the way in which people make sense of information relating to social interactions and social contexts.

Social learning theories: an approach that explains gender identity development in terms of the child's accumulating learning experience from their social environment, particularly through modelling others' behaviour and being rewarded for adopting approved mannerisms.

Social status: the extent of acceptance or likeability of individual children by the peer group, based on the group's general view of the individual.

Sociometry: a technique that charts the relative standing of children within their peer group, where data of their popularity/acceptance can be collected by self-reporting of peer preferences or observations of their interactions with each other.

Stability: similar level relative to other same-age peers over time.

Stage theories: theories based on the idea that we progress through a pattern of distinct stages over time. These stages are defined by the acquisition or presence of abilities and we generally pass through them in a specified order and during a specified age range.

Stimulus (plural stimuli): anything which elicits or evokes a response, such as a sound, a picture, a taste or a smell.

Storage: the second stage of information processing in memory, by which information is retained for short or long periods of time.

Storm and stress: described by G. S. Hall as the emotional and physical volatility of adolescence.

Strange Situation: a seven-part staged procedure employed to observe the behaviours and interactions between a child and the primary caregiver in a controlled laboratory setting, from which the type of attachment security between the dyad can be deduced.

Stranger anxiety: the wariness or fear of an infant when encountering those who are unfamiliar, often characterised by the seeking of proximity to the caregiver.

Subjective or existential self: the recognition of the self that is unique and distinct from others, endures over time and space, and has an element of self-reflexivity.

Suggestibility: how susceptible someone is to ideas or information presented by others.

Superego: our sense of morality and social norms.

Symbolic play: also known as fantasy or pretend play, play that involves 'symbolic' representation, where the child pretends that an absent object is present and acts out the relevant behaviours involving that object.

Synapse: the gap between neurons across which the neural signal is passed.

Synaptic pruning: the elimination of excess synapses.

Synaptogenesis: rapid growth of dendrites to form neural connections or synapses.

Syntax: the part of language concerned with the rules which govern how words can be combined to make sentences.

Telegraphic speech: speech consisting of phrases of a small number of words (usually nouns, verbs and adjectives) combined to make sense, but without complex grammatical forms.

Temperament: a general underlying set of tendencies to behave in a particular way. It should show stability, continuity, context-dependence and early emergence.

Teratogen: an environmental hazard to prenatal development.

Thalamocingulate division: part of the human brain suggested within Paul MacLean's 'Triune Brain' theory (that we have three brains, each developed from the preceding ones through evolution) as important in family-related behaviour.

Theorems in action: propositions held to be true which are only implicitly known to the person who holds them.

Theory: a statement that we use to understand the world about us with three important component parts: it defines, explains and predicts behaviour.

Theory of mind: being able to infer the full range of mental states (beliefs, desires, intentions, imagination, emotions, etc.) that cause action (Baron-Cohen, 2001).

Tool for thinking: a culturally developed system of signs that allows the user to represent something and operate on the representations in order to reach a conclusion about the represented reality.

Top-down processing: when the processing of information coming in via the senses is heavily influenced by prior knowledge.

Traditional bullying: forms of bullying behaviour that involve physical, verbal or psychological attacks without the use of electronic media.

Transformations: changes in the number of a set resulting from an event (e.g. an increase in the number of marbles you have due to winning a game). May also refer to changes of position (e.g. if you walked 2 km away from a house, your position changes).

Transitivity: a property of relations where new logical conclusions about one relation can be reached on the basis of premises about two other relations. For example, if $A = B$ and $B = C$, then $A = C$.

Uninhibited: outgoing and spontaneous, and approaches novelty in the same settings.

Variables: has different meanings in different contexts. Here it is understood as quantities that we can measure through counting or using conventional measuring tools.

Visual recognition memory: memory for a visual stimulus which has been seen before. This type of memory can be assessed from very early in life and so is often used in infant memory research.

Vocabulary spurt: a point in language development where the rate of acquisition of new words is thought to accelerate rapidly.

Whole numbers: also referred to as directed numbers. The natural numbers together with the negatives of the non-zero natural numbers ($-1, -2, -3, \ldots$).

Working memory: the part of memory that is critical to conscious thought because it permits internal representation of information (e.g. rules) to guide decision making and overt behaviour (responses) during an activity, so that behaviour is not dominated by the immediate sensory cues in the environment.

Zygote: the single cell formed from the union of sperm and ovum.

Bibliography

Abbas, T. (2007). British South Asians and pathways into selective schooling: Social class, culture and ethnicity. *British Educational Research Journal*, 33 (1), 75–90.

Abdelaziz, H. (2013). From physical benchmarks to mental benchmarks: A four dimensions dynamic model to assure the quality of instructional activities in electronic and virtual learning environments. *Turkish Online Journal of Distance Education (TOJDE)*, 14 (2), 268–281.

Abitz, M., Nielsen, R. D., Jones, E. G., Laursen, H., Graem, N., & Pakkenberg, B. (2007). Excess of neurons in the human newborn mediodorsal thalamus compared with that of the adult. *Cerebral Cortex*, 17 (11), 2573–2578.

Aboraya, A., Rankin, E., France, C., El-Missiry, A., & John, C. (2006). The reliability of psychiatric diagnosis revisited: The clinician's guide to improve the reliability of psychiatric diagnosis. *Psychiatry*, 3 (1), 41–50.

Abraham, C., Sheeran, P., Spears R., & Abrams, D. (1992). Health beliefs and promotion of HIV-preventive intentions among teenagers: A Scottish perspective. *Health Psychology*, 11 (6), 363–370.

Adams, R. J., & Courage, M. C. (1998). Human newborn colour vision: Measurements with chromatic stimuli varying in excitation purity. *Journal of Experimental Child Psychology*, 68, 22–34.

Adams, R. J., & Courage, M. L. (2002). A psycho-physical test of the early maturation of infants' mid- and longwavelength retinal cones. *Infant Behaviour and Development*, 25, 247–254.

Adamson, L., Hartman S. G., & Lyxell, B. (1999). Adolescent identity – a qualitative approach: Self-concept, existential questions and adult contacts. *Scandinavian Journal of Psychology*, 40 (1), 21–31.

Agnew, R. (1992). Foundation for a general strain theory of crime and delinquency. *Criminology*, 30, 47–87.

Adolph, K. E. (2000). Specificity of learning: Why infants fall over a veritable cliff. *Psychological Science*, 11, 290–295.

Ahmad, Y. S., & Smith, P. K. (1990). Behavioural measures review No. 1: Bullying in schools. *Newsletter of the ACPP*, 12, 26–27.

Ahmed, A., & Ruffman, T. (1998). Why do infants make A not B errors in a search task, yet show memory for the location of hidden objects in a nonsearch task? *Developmental Psychology*, 34, 441–453.

Ainsworth, M. (1963). The development of infant–mother interaction among the Ganda. In B. M. Foss (Ed.), *Determinants of Infant Behavior*, Vol. 2 (67–104). London: Methuen.

Ainsworth, M. (1967). *Infancy in Uganda: Infant Care and the Growth of Love*. Baltimore, MD: Johns Hopkins University Press.

Ainsworth, M. D. S. (1977). Infant development and mother–infant interaction among Ganda and American families. In P. H. Leiderman, S. R. Tulkin, & A. Rosenfeld (Eds.), *Culture and Infancy* (49–68). New York: Academic Press.

Ainsworth, M., & Bell, S. (1969). Some contemporary patterns of mother–infant interaction in the feeding situation. In A. Ambrose (Ed.), *Stimulation in Early Infancy* (133–170). London and New York: Academic Press.

Ainsworth, M. D. S., & Bell, S. M. (1970). Attachment, exploration, and separation: Illustrated by the behaviour of one-year-olds in a strange situation. *Child Development*, 41, 49–67.

Ainsworth, M., & Bell, S. M. (1974). Mother–infant interactions and the development of competence. In K. Connolly & J. Bruner (Eds.), *The Growth of Competence* (97–118). London: Academic Press.

Ainsworth, M. D. S., Blehar, M. C., Waters, E., & Wall, S. (1978). *Patterns of Attachment: A Psychological Study of the Strange Situation*. Hillsdale, NJ: Erlbaum.

Akbulut, Y., & Günüç, S. (2012). Perceived social support and Facebook use among adolescents. *International Journal of Cyber Behavior, Psychology and Learning*, 2, 30–41.

Akengin, H., & Sevgi, S. (2013). An experimental research on readiness levels of students in terms of geographical concepts, and on development of these concepts. *Education*, 133 (4), 481–494.

Akers, J., Jones, R., & Coyl, D. (1998). Adolescent friendship pairs: Similarities in identity status development, behaviors, attitudes, and interests. *Journal of Adolescent Research*, 13, 178–201.

Alati, R., Macleod, J., Hickman, M., Sayal, K., May, M., et al. (2008). Intrauterine exposure to alcohol and tobacco use and childhood IQ: Findings from a parental offspring comparison within the Avon Longitudinal

Study of Parents and Children. *Pediatric Research*, 64, 659–666.

Alati, R., Smith, G. D., Lewis, S. J., Sayal, K., Draper, E. S., Golding, J., Fraser, R., & Gray, R. (2013). Effect of prenatal alcohol exposure on childhood academic outcomes: Contrasting maternal and paternal associations in the ALSPAC Study. *Plos One*, 8(10), 1–9, e74844.

Alexander, R., Rose, J., & Woodhead, C. (1992). Curriculum organization and classroom practice in primary schools: A discussion paper. London: DES.

Al-Hendawi, M., & Reed, E. (2012). Educational outcomes for children at-risk: The influence of individual differences in children's temperaments. *International Journal of Special Education*, 2, 64–74.

Allen, C., Porter, M., McFarland, F., Marsh, P., & McElhaney, K. (2005). The two faces of adolescents' success with peers: Adolescent popularity social adaptation, and deviant behavior. *Child Development*, 76, 747–760.

Allen, P. (2008). Managing knowledge in technical demonstration plans: A template. *Knowledge Management Research and Practice*, 6 (3), 245–253.

Allison, C. M., & Hyde, J. S. (2013). Early menarche: Confluence of biological and contextual factors. *Sex Roles*, 68, 55–64.

Altermatt, E. R. (2011). Capitalising on academic success: Students' interactions with friends as predictors of school adjustment. *Journal of Early Adolescence*, 31, 174–203.

Altermatt, E. R., & Ivers, I. E. (2011). Friends' responses to children's disclosure of an achievement-related success: An observation study. *Merrill-Palmer Quarterly*, 57, 429–454.

Aluja-Fabregat, A. (2000). Personality and curiosity about TV and films violence in adolescents. *Personality and Individual Differences*, 29 (2), 379–392.

Aman, M. G., McDougle, C. J., Scahill, L., Handen, B., Arnold, L. E., Johnson, C., Stigler, K. A., Bearss, K., Butter, E., Swiezy, N. B., Sukhodolsky, D. D., Ramadan, Y., Pozdol, S. L., Nikolov, R., Lecavalier, L., Kohn, A. E., Koenig, K., Hollway, J. A., Korzekwa, P., Gavaletz, A., Mulick, J. A., Hall, K. L., Dziura, J., Ritz, L., Trollinger, S., Yu, S., Vitiello, B., & Wagner, A. (2009). Medication and parent training in children with pervasive developmental disorders and serious behavior problems: Results from a randomized clinical trial. *Journal of the American Academy of Child and Adolescent Psychiatry*, 48 (12), 1143–1154.

American Psychiatric Association (1994). *Diagnostic and Statistical Manual of Mental Disorders* (4th Ed.). Washington, DC: APA.

American Psychiatric Association (1995). *Diagnostic and Statistical Manual of Mental Disorders*, Fourth Edition–Primary Care Version (DSM-IV®–PC). Washington DC: APA.

American Psychiatric Association (2013). *Diagnostic and Statistical Manual of Mental Disorders* (5th Ed.). Arlington, VA: American Psychiatric Publishing.

Anastopoulos, A. D., Shelton, T. L., DuPaul, G. J., & Guevremont, D. C. (1993). Parent training for attention deficit hyperactivity disorder: Its impact on parent functioning. *Journal of Abnormal Child Psychology*, 21, 581–596.

Anderson, D. L., & Lubig, J. (2012). The missing link: Peer conferencing in civics education. *Social Studies*, 103, 201–205.

Andrade, T., & Vilela, D. (2013).Contributions from sociology of science to mathematics education in Brazil: Logic as a system of beliefs. *Cultural Studies of Science Education*, 8 (3), 709–724.

Anzures, G., Quinn, P. C., Pascalis, O., Slater, A. M., & Lee, K. (2010). Categorization, categorical perception, and asymmetry in infants' representation of face race. *Developmental Science*, 13 (4), 553–564.

Aoyama, S., Toshima, T., Saito, Y., Konishi, N., Motoshige, K., Ishikawa, N., Nakamura, K., & Kobayashi, M. (2010). Maternal breast milk odour induces frontal lobe activation in neonates: A NIRS study. *Early Human Development*, 86, 541–545.

Apel, R., Pogarsky, G., & Bates, L. (2009). The sanctions–perceptions link in a model of school-based deterrence. *Journal of Quantitative Criminology*, 25 (2), 201–226.

Apgar, V. (1953). A proposal for a new method of evaluation in the newborn infant. *Current Research in Anaesthesia and Analgesia*, 32, 260–267.

Apperly, I. A. (2008). Beyond simulation-theory and theory-theory: Why social cognitive neuroscience should use its own concepts to study theory of mind. *Cognition*, 107 (1), 266–283.

Archer, J. (1992). Childhood gender roles: Social context and organisation. In H. McGurk (Ed.), *Childhood Social Development: Contemporary Perspectives* (31–61). Hillsdale, NJ: Erlbaum.

Archer, J. & Coyne, S. M. (2005). An integrated review of indirect, relational, and social aggression. *Personality and Social Psychology Review*, 9, 212–230.

Aries, P. (1960). *L'Enfant et la vie familiale sous l'Ancien Régime*. Paris: Plon. Translated into English by Robert Baldick as *Centuries of Childhood: A Social History of Family Life*.

Arndt, T. L., Stodgell, C. J., & Rodier, P. M. (2005). The teratology of autism. *International Journal of Developmental Neuroscience*, 23 (2), 189–199.

Arnett, J. J. (1999). Adolescent storm and stress, reconsidered. *American Psychologist*, 54 (5), 317–326.

Aronen, E. T., & Kurkela, S. A. (1998). The predictors of competence in an adolescent sample: A 15-year followup study. *Nordic Journal of Psychiatry*, 52 (3), 203–212.

Arora, C. M. J. (1996). Defining bullying: Towards a clearer general understanding and more effective intervention strategies. *School Psychology International*, 17, 317–329.

Ashby, J., Dix, H., Bontrager, M., Dey, R., & Archer, A. (2013). Phonemic awareness contributes to text reading fluency: Evidence from eye movements. *School Psychology Review*, 42 (2), 157–170.

Askew, M., Brown, M., Rhodes V., Wiliam D., & Johnson D. (1997). *Effective Teachers of Numeracy in Primary Schools: Teachers' Beliefs, Practices and Pupils' Learning*. British Educational Research Association Conference, 10–14 September.

Astington, J. (1994). *The Child's Discovery of the Mind*. Cambridge, MA: Harvard University Press.

Atkinson, J. (2000). *The Developing Visual Brain*. Oxford: Oxford University Press.

Atkinson, J., & Braddick, O. (1981). Acuity, contrast sensitivity and accommodation in infancy. In R. N. Aslin, J. R. Alberts, & M. R. Petersen (Eds.), *Development of Perception: Psychobiological Perspectives: Vol. 2, The Visual System* (245–277). New York: Academic Press.

Atkinson, R. C., & Shiffrin, R. M. (1968). Human memory: A proposed system and its central processes. In K. W. Spence & J. T. Spence (Eds.), *The Psychology of Learning and Motivation: Advances in Research and Theory* (Vol. 2, 742–775). New York: Academic Press.

Ausubel, D., Novak, J., & Hanesian, H. (1978). *Educational Psychology: A Cognitive View*. New York: Holt, Rinehart, & Winston.

Baddeley, A. D. (1986). *Working Memory*. Oxford: Clarendon.

Baddeley, A. D. (1992). Working memory. *Science*, 255, 556–559.

Baddeley, A. D. (1998). *Working Memory*. Oxford: Oxford University Press.

Baddeley, A. (2003). Working memory: Looking back and looking forward. *Nature Reviews Neuroscience*, 4, 829–839.

Baddeley, A. D., & Hitch, G. (1974). Working memory. In G. H. Bower (Ed.), *The Psychology of Learning and Motivation* (Vol. 8, 47–90). San Diego, CA: Academic Press.

Bagwell, C. L., Newcomb, A. F., & Bukowski, W. M. (1998). Preadolescent friendship and peer rejection as predictors of adult adjustment. *Child Development*, 69, 140–153.

Baillargeon, R. (2004). Infants' reasoning about hidden objects: Evidence for event-general and event-specific expectation. *Developmental Science*, 7, 391–424.

Baillargeon, R., & DeVos, J. (1991). Object permanence in young infants: Further evidence. *Child Development*, 62, 1227–1246.

Baillargeon, R., Scott, R. M., & He, Z. (2010). False-belief understanding in infants. *Trends in Cognitive Science*, 14 (3), 110–118.

Baird, G. E., Cass, H., & Slonims, V. (2003). Diagnosis of autism. *British Medical Journal*, 327, 488–493.

Baird, G., Simonoff, E., Pickles, A. et al. (2006). Prevalance of disorders on the autism spectrum in a population cohort of children in South Thames: The Special Needs and Autism Project (SNAP). *Lancet*, 368, 210–215.

Baker, B. L., McIntyre, L. L., Blacher, J., Crnic, K., Edelbrock, C., & Low, C. (2003). Pre-school children with and without developmental delay: Behavioural problems and parenting stress over time. *Journal of Intellectual Disability Research*, 471, 217–230.

Bakker, A., van Kesteren, P. J. M., Gooren, L. J. G., & Bezemer, P. D. (2007). The prevalence of transsexualism in the Netherlands. *Acta Psychiatrica Scandinavica*, 87 (4), 237–238.

Bakker, S. (1999). Educational assessment in the Russian Federation. *Assessment in Education: Principles, Policy and Practice*, 6 (2), 291–303.

Baldry, A. C., & Farrington, D. P. (2000). Bullies and delinquents: Personal characteristics and parental styles. *Journal of Community and Applied Social Psychology*, 10, 17–31.

Baldry, A. C., & Winkel, F. W. (2003). Direct and vicarious victimization at school and at home as risk factors for suicidal cognition among Italian adolescents. *Journal of Adolescence*, 26 (6), 703–716.

Bandura, A. (1969). Social learning theory of identificatory processes. In D. A. Goslin (Ed.), *Handbook of Socialization Theory and Research* (213–262). Chicago, IL: Rand McNally.

Bandura, A. (1977). *Social Learning Theory*. Englewood Cliffs, NJ: Prentice Hall.

Bandura, A. (1989). Social cognitive theory. In R. Vasta (Ed.), *Annals of Child Development: Vol. 6, Theories of Child Development: Revised Formulations and Current Issues* (1–60). Greenwich, CT: JAI Press.

Bandura, A., & Walters, R. H. (1963). *Social Learning and Personality Development*. New York: Holt, Rinehart, & Winston.

Banerjee T. D., Middleton, F., & Faraone, S. V. (2007). Environmental risk factors for attention-deficit hyperactivity disorder. *Acta Pædiatric*, 9, 1269–1274.

Banich, M. T. (2004). *Cognitive Neuroscience and Neuropsychology*. Boston, MA: Houghton Mifflin.

Barker, E. D., Boivin, M., Brendgen, M., Fontaine, N., Arseneault, L., Vitaro, F., Bissonnette, C., & Tremblay, R. E. (2008). Predictive validity and early predictors of peer-victimization trajectories in preschool. *Archives of General Psychiatry*, 65, 1185–1192.

Barkley, R. A., Fischer, M., Smallish, L., & Fletcher, K. (2002). The persistence of attention-deficit/hyperactivity disorder into young adulthood as a function of reporting source and definition of disorder. *Journal of Abnormal Psychology*, 111 (2), 279–289.

Barlow, J., & Parsons, J. (2006). Group-based parent training programme for improving emotional and behavioural adjustment in 0–3 year old children (Cochrane Review). In *The Cochrane Library*, Issue 2. Oxford: Update Software.

Barnett, D., Clements, M., Kaplan-Estrin, M., McCaskill, J. W., Hunt, K., Butler, C. M., Schram, J. L., & Janisse, H. C. (2006). Maternal resolution of child diagnosis: Stability and relations with child attachment across the toddler to preschooler transition. *Journal of Family Psychology*, 20 (1), 100–107.

Barnett, D., Ganiban, J., & Cicchetti, D. (1999). Maltreatment, negative expressivity, and the development of Type D attachments from 12 to 24 months of age. In J. E. Vondra & D. Barnett (Eds.), *Atypical attachment in infancy and early childhood among children at developmental risk. Monographs of the Society for the Research in Child Development*, 64 (3), Serial No. 258, 97–118.

Barnow, S., Lucht, M., & Freyberger, H.J. (2005). Correlates of aggressive and delinquent conduct problems in adolescence. *Aggressive Behavior*, 31 (1), 24–39.

Baron-Cohen, S. (1989). Are autistic children behaviourists? An examination of their mental-physical and appearance-reality distinctions. *Journal of Autism and Developmental Disorders*, 19, 579–600.

Baron-Cohen, S. (1992). Out of sight or out of mind: Another look at deception in autism. *Journal of Child Psychology and Psychiatry*, 33, 1141–1155.

Baron-Cohen, S. (1995). *Mindblindness: An Essay on Autism and Theory of Mind*. Cambridge, MA: MIT Press/Bradford Books.

Baron-Cohen, S. (2001). Theory of mind and autism: A review. Special Issue of the *International Review of Mental Retardation*, 23 (169).

Baron-Cohen, S. (2008). 100 words: Autism. *British Journal of Psychiatry*, 193, 321.

Baron-Cohen, S., Leslie, A. M., & Frith, U. (1985). Does the autistic child have a 'theory of mind'? *Cognition*, 21, 37–46.

Baron-Cohen, S., Wheelwright S., Hill J., Raste Y., & Plumb, I. (2001). The 'Reading the Mind in the Eyes' Test revised version: A study with normal adults, and adults with Asperger syndrome or high-functioning autism. *Journal of Child Psychology and Psychiatry*, 42, 241–251.

Barone, L., & Lionetti, F. (2011). Attachment and emotional understanding: A study on late-adopted pre-schoolers and their parents. *Child: Care, Health and Development*, 38, 690–696.

Barr, R. G. (2004). Early infant crying as a behavioural state rather than a signal. *Behavioural and Brain Sciences*, 27 (4), 460.

Barrett, M., Swan, A., Mamikonian, A., Ghajoyan, I., Kramarova, O., & Youmans, R. (2014). Technology in note taking and assessment: The effects of congruence on student performance. *International Journal of Instruction*, 7 (1), 49–58.

Barry, T. D., Lyman, R. D., & Klinger, L. G. (2002). Academic underachievement and attention-deficit/hyperactivity disorder: The negative impact of symptom severity on school performance. *Journal of School Psychology*, 40, 259–283.

Bartgis, J. P., Thomas, D. G., Lefler, E. K., & Hartung, C. M. (2008). The development of attention and response inhibition in early childhood. *Infant and Child Development*, 17, 491–502.

Basow, S. A., & Rubin, L. R. (1999). Gender influences on adolescent development. In N. G. Johnson & M. C. Roberts (Eds.), *Beyond Appearance: A New Look at Adolescent Girls* (25–52). Washington, DC: APA.

Bateman, B., Warner, J. O., Hutchinson, E., Dean, T., Rowlandson, P., Gant, C., Grundy, J., Fitzgerald, C., & Stevenson, J. (2004). The effects of a double blind, placebo controlled, artificial food colourings and benzoate preservative challenge on hyperactivity in a general population sample of preschool children. *Archives of Diseases in Childhood*, 89, 506–511.

Bates, E. (1990). Language about me and you: Pronominal reference and the emerging concept of self. In E. Cicchetti & M. Beeghly (Eds.), *Self in Transition: Infancy to Childhood* (165–183). Chicago, IL: University of Chicago Press.

Bates, E., O'Connell, B., & Shore, C. (1987). Language and communication in infancy. In J. D. Osofsky (Ed.), *Handbook of Infant Development* (2nd Ed., 149–203). New York: Wiley.

Bates, J. E. (1989). Concepts and measures of temperament. In G. A. Kohnstamm, J. E. Bates, & M. K. Rothbart (Eds.), *Temperament in Childhood* (3–26). Chichester: Wiley.

Bauer, P. J. (2007). Recall in infancy: A neuro-developmental account. *Current Directions in Psychological Science*, 16, 142–146.

Baumrind, D. (1991). Parenting styles and adolescent development. In R. M. Lerner, A. C. Petersen, & J. Brooks-Gunn (Eds.), *Encyclopedia of Adolescence* (Vol. 2, 746–758). New York: Garland.

Bavolek, S. J. (2010). The art and science of raising healthy children. Available at: http://www._nurturingparenting.com/research_validation/articles_for_professionals.php.

Bayley, N. (1969). *Bayley Scales of Infant Development*. New York: Psychological Corp.

Bayley, N. (1993). *Bayley Scales of Infant Development* (2nd Ed.). San Antonio, TX: Psychological Corp.

Bayley, N. (2005). *Bayley Scales of Infant Development* (3rd Ed.). Oxford: Harcourt Assessment.

BBC (2014). *Baby P: The Untold Story*. Broadcast on BBC 1, 15 October 2014. http://www.bbc.co.uk/mediacentre/latestnews/2014/bbc-one-doc-charts-untold-story-of-babyp.

Beaman, R., & Wheldall, K. (2000). Teachers' use of approval and disapproval in the classroom. *Educational Psychology*, 20 (4), 431–446.

Beals, D. E., De Temple, J. M., & Dickinson, D. K. (1994). Talking and listening that support early literacy development of children from low-income families. In D. K. Dickinson (Ed.), *Bridges to Literacy: Children, Families and Schools* (19–40). Cambridge, MA: Blackwell.

Becker, J. (1993). Young children's numerical use of number words: Counting in many-to-one situations. *Developmental Psychology*, 19, 458–465.

Beebe, B., Lachmann, F., Markese, S., & Bahrick, L. (2012a). On the origins of disorganized attachment and internal working models: Paper I, A dyadic systems approach. *Psychoanalytic Dialogues*, 22, 253–272.

Beebe, B., Lachmann, F., Markese, S., Buck, K. A., Bahrick, L. E., Chen, H., Cohen, P., Andrews, H., Feldstein, S., & Jaffe, J. (2012b). On the origins of disorganized attachment and internal working models: Paper II, An empirical microanalysis of 4-month mother–infant interaction. *Psychoanalytic Dialogues*, 22, 352–374.

Behne, T., Liszkowski, U., Carpenter, M., & Tomasello, M. (2012). Twelve-month-olds' comprehension and production of pointing. *British Journal of Developmental Psychology*, 30 (3), 359–375.

Beijersbergen, M. D., Juffer, F., Bakermans-Kranenburg, M. J., & van IJzendoorn, M. H. (2012). Remaining or becoming secure: Sensitive support predicts attachment continuity from infancy to adolescence in a longitudinal adoption study. *Developmental Psychology*, 48, 1277–1282.

Beitchman, J., Wilson, B., Brownlie, E. B., Walters, H., & Lancee, W. (1996). Long term consistency in speech/language profiles: 1. Developmental and academic outcomes. *Journal of American Academy of Child and Adolescent Psychiatry*, 35 (6), 804–814.

Bekebrede, G., Warmelink, H. J. G., & Mayer, I. S. (2011). Reviewing the need for gaming in education to accommodate the net generation. *Computers and Education*, 57, 1521–1529.

Bell, M. A. (2002). Power changes in infant EEG frequency bands during a spatial working memory task. *Psychophysiology*, 39, 450–458.

Bell, S. M., & Ainsworth, M. D. (1972). Infant crying and maternal responsiveness. *Child Development*, 43 (4), 1171–1190.

Belsky, J. (1988). The 'effects' of infant day care reconsidered. *Early Child Research Quarterly*, 3, 235–272.

Belsky, J. (1992). Consequences of child care for children's development. A deconstructionist view. In A. Booth (Ed.), *Child Care in the 1990s: Trends and Consequences* (83–94). Hillsdale, NJ: Erlbaum.

Belsky, J., & Steinberg, L. D. (1978). The effects of day care: A critical review. *Child Development*, 49, 929–949.

Belsky, P., Steinberg, L., & Draper, P. (1991). Childhood experience, interpersonal development, and reproductive strategy: An evolutionary theory of socialization. *Child Development*, 62, 647–670.

Bem, S. L. (1981). Gender schema theory: A cognitive account of sex-typing. *Psychological Review*, 88, 354–364.

Bem, S. L. (1989). Genital knowledge and gender constancy in preschool children. *Child Development*, 60, 649–662.

Bender, B. G., & Levin, J. R. (1976). Motor activity, anticipated motor activity, and young children's associative learning. *Child Development*, 47, 560–562.

Benoit, D., & Parker, K. C. H. (1994). Stability and transmission of attachment among three generations. *Child Development*, 65, 1444–1456.

Benedict, H. (1979). Early lexical development: Comprehension and production. *Journal of Child Language*, 6, 183–200.

Beran, T., & Li, Q. (2007). The relationship between cyberbullying and school bullying. *Journal of Student Wellbeing*, 1, 15–33.

Berenbaum, S. A., & Snyder, E. (1995). Early hormonal influences on childhood sex-typed activity and playmate preferences: Implications for the development of sexual orientation. *Developmental Psychology*, 31, 31–42.

Berg, J., Morris, P., & Aber, L. (2013). Two-year impacts of a comprehensive family financial rewards program on children's academic outcomes: Moderation by likelihood of earning rewards. *Journal of Research on Educational Effectiveness*, 6 (4), 295–338.

Bergman, K., Sarkar, P., O'Connor, T. G., Modi, N., & Glover, V. (2007). Maternal stress during pregnancy predicts cognitive ability and fearfulness in infancy. *Journal of the American Academy of Child and Adolescent Psychiatry*, 46, 1454–1463.

Berko, J. (1958). The child's learning of English morphology. *Word*, 4, 150–177.

Bermejo, V., Morales, S., & deOsuna, J. G. (2004). Supporting children's development of cardinality understanding. *Learning and Instruction*, 14, 381–398.

Berndt, T. J., & Keefe, K. (1995). Friends' influence on adolescents' adjustment to school. *Child Development*, 66, 1312–1329.

Bernstein, D. M., Thornton, W. L., & Somerville, J. A. (2011). Theory of mind through the ages: Older and middle-aged adults exhibit more errors than do younger adults on a continuous false belief task. *Experimental Aging Research*, 37 (5), 481–502.

Best, D. L., Williams, J. E., Cloud, J. M., Davis, S. W., Robertson, L. S., Edwards, J. R., Giles, H., & Fowles, J. (1977). Development of sex-trait stereotypes among young children in the United States, England, and Ireland. *Child Development*, 48, 1375–1384.

Bettencourt, A., Farrell, A., Liu, W. & Sullivan, T. (2013). Stability and change in patterns of peer victimization and aggression during adolescence. *Journal of Clinical Child and Adolescent Psychology*, 42, 429–441.

Betts, L. R., & Stiller, J. (2013). Centrality in children's best friend networks: The role of social behaviour. *British Journal of Developmental Psychology*, 32, 34–49.

Beuhring, T., & Kee, D. W. (1987). Developmental relationships among metamemory, elaborative strategy use and associative memory. *Journal of Experimental Child Psychology*, 44, 377–400.

Biederman, J. (2005). Attention-deficit/hyperactivity disorder: A selective overview. *Biological Psychiatry*, 57, 1215–1220.

Bierman, K. L., Domitrovich, C. E., Nix, R. L., Gest, S. D., Welsh, J. A., Greenberg, M. T., Blair, C., Nelson, K. E. and Gill, S. (2008). Promoting academic and social-emotional school readiness: The Head Start REDI Program. *Child Development*, 79 (6), 1802–1817.

Bigelow, B. J., & La Gaipa, J. J. (1980). The development of friendship values and choice. In H. C. Foot, A. J. Chapman, & J. R. Smith (Eds.), *Friendship and Social Relations in Children* (15–44). Chichester: Wiley.

Birch, E., & Petrig, B. (1996). FPL and VEP measures of fusion, stereopsis and stereoacuity in normal infants. *Vision Research*, 36 (9), 1321–1327.

Bishop, D. V. and Adams, C. (1992). Comprehension problems in children with specific language impairment: Literal and inferential meaning. *Journal of Speech and Hearing Research*, 35 (1), 119–129.

Bishop, D. V., Chan, J., Adams, C., Hartley, J., & Weir, F. (2000). Conversational responsiveness in specific language impairment: Evidence of disproportionate pragmatic difficulties in a subset of children. *Development and Psychopathology*, 12 (2), 177–199.

Bishop, D. V. M., & Edmundson, A. (1987). Specific language impairment as a maturational lag: Evidence from longitudinal data on language and motor development. *Developmental Medicine and Child Neurology*, 29, 442–459.

Bjorklund, D. F., & Jacobs, J. W. (1985). Associative and categorical processes in children's memory: The role of automaticity in the development of free recall. *Journal of Experimental Child Psychology*, 39, 599–617.

Blaire, E. (2012). Does their ethical justification disappear if they were not previously failing schools? *Prospero*, 18 (2), 14–21.

Blakemore, S. J., & Choudhury, S. (2006). Development of the adolescent brain: Implications for executive function and social cognition. *Journal of Child Psychology and Psychiatry*, 47 (3), 296–312.

Blass, T. (2000). *Obedience to Authority: Current Perspectives on the Milgram Paradigm*. New York: Psychology Press.

Block, J. H., & Block, J. (1980). The role of ego-control and ego-resiliency in the organization of behaviour. In W. A. Collins (Ed.), *Development of Cognition, Affect, and Social Relations* (39–101). Hillsdale, NJ: Erlbaum.

Bogaert, A. F. (2008). Menarche and father absence in a national probability sample. *Journal of Biosocial Science*, 40 (4), 623–636.

Boller, K., Rovee-Collier, C., Borovsky, D., O'Connor, J., & Shyi, G. (1990). Developmental nature of changes in the time-dependent nature of memory retrieval. *Developmental Psychology*, 26 (5), 770–779.

Bolton, P. (2001). Developmental assessment. *Advances in Psychiatric Treatment*, 7, 32–40.

Bor, W., Sanders, M. R., & Markie-Dadds, C. (2002). The effect of the Triple-P Positive Parenting Programme on pre-school children with co-occurring disruptive behaviours and attention/hyperactive difficulties. *Journal of Abnormal Child Psychology*, 30, 571–587.

Borg, M. G. (1999). The extent and nature of bullying among primary and secondary schoolchildren. *Educational Research*, 41, 137–153.

Bornstein, M. H. (2006a). Hue categorization and colour naming: Physics to sensation to perception. In N. J. Pitchford & C. P. Biggam (Eds.), *Progress in Colour Studies: Vol. 2, Psychological Aspects* (35–68). Amsterdam: John Benjamin.

Bornstein, M. H. (2006b). Social relationships in early symbolic play. In A. Göncü & S. Gaskins (Eds.), *Play and Development: Evolutionary, Sociocultural and Functional Perspectives* (101–129). London: Erlbaum.

Borovsky, D., & Rovee-Collier, C. (1990). Contextual constraints on memory retrieval at six months. *Child Development*, 61, 1569–1583.

Botvinick, M. M., Braver, T. S., Barch, D. M., Carter, C. S., & Cohen, J. D. (2001). Conflict monitoring and cognitive control. *Psychological Review*, 108, 624–652.

Bouchard, T. J., Jr., Lykken, D. T., McGue, M., Segal, N. L., & Tellegen, A. (1990). Sources of human psychological differences: The Minnesota Study of Twins Reared Apart. *Science*, 250 (4978), 223–228.

BouJaoude, S. (2002). Balance of scientific literacy themes in science curricula: The case of Lebanon. *International Journal of Science Education*, 24 (2), 139–156.

Boulton, M. G. (1983). *On Being a Mother: A Study of Women with Preschool Children*. London: Tavistock.

Bower, E., English, C., Choi, D., Cedfeldt, A., & Girard, D. (2010). Education to return nonpracticing physicians to clinical activity: A case study in physician re-entry. *Journal of Continuing Education in the Health Professions*, 30 (2), 89–94.

Bower, P. (2003). Efficacy in evidence-based practice. *Journal of Clinical Psychology and Psychotherapy*, 10, 328–336.

Bowers, L., Smith, P. K., & Binney, V. (1992). Cohesion and power in the families of children involved in bully/victim problems at school. *Journal of Family Therapy*, 14 (4), 371–387.

Bowlby, J. (1944). Forty-four juvenile thieves: Their characters and home life. *International Journal of Psychoanalysis*, 25, 1–57; 207–228.

Bowlby, J. (1951). *Maternal Care and Mental Health: Report to the World Health Organization*. New York: Shocken Books.

Bowlby, J. (1953). *Child Care and the Growth of Love*. Harmondsworth: Penguin.

Bowlby, J. (1958). The nature of the child's tie to his mother. *International Journal of Psychoanalysis*, 39, 350–373.

Bowlby, J. (1969). *Attachment and Loss: Vol. 1, Attachment*. New York: Basic Books.

Bowlby, J. (1973). *Attachment and Loss: Separation*. New York: Basic Books.

Bowlby, J. (1980). *Attachment and Loss: Loss, Sadness and Depression*. New York: Basic Books.

Bowlby, J. (1982). *Attachment and Loss: Vol. 1, Attachment* (2nd Ed.). New York: Basic Books.

Bowlby, R. (2007). Babies and toddlers in non-parental daycare can avoid stress and anxiety if they develop a lasting secondary attachment bond with one carer who is consistently accessible to them. *Attachment and Human Development*, 9, 307–319.

Boyatzis, C., Baloff, P., & Durieux, C. (1998). Effects of perceived attractiveness and academic success on early adolescent peer popularity. *Journal of Genetic Psychology*, 158, 337–344.

Boyd, D., & Bee, H. (2006). *Lifespan Development* (4th Ed.). Boston, MA: Allyn & Bacon.

Boyle, M. (2001). Abandoning diagnosis and (cautiously) adopting formulation. British Psychological Society Centenary Conference, 28–31 March, Glasgow.

Boynton, P., & Anderson, I. (2009). Baby P – what is our response?, *The Psychologist*, 22, 2, 8–9.

Brainerd, C. J., & Reyna, V. F. (1990). Gist is the gist: Fuzzy-trace theory and the new intuitionism. *Developmental Review*, 10, 3–47.

Brainerd, C. J., & Reyna, V. F. (2001). Fuzzy-trace theory: Dual processes in memory, reasoning and cognitive neuroscience. *Advances in Child Development and Behavior*, 28, 41–100.

Brainerd, C. J., & Reyna, V. F. (2004). Fuzzy-trace theory and memory development. *Developmental Review*, 24 (4), 396–439.

Brainerd, C. J., Reyna, V. F., & Forrest, T. J. (2002). Are young children susceptible to the false-memory illusion? *Child Development*, 73, 1363–1377.

Breakwell, G. M., Hammond, S., Fife-Schaw, C., & Smith, J. A. (2006). *Research Methods in Psychology* (3rd Ed.). London: Sage.

Brehmer, Y., Li, S. C., Muller, V., von Oertzen, T., & Lindenberger, U. (2007). Memory plasticity across the lifespan: Uncovering children's latent potential. *Developmental Psychology*, 32 (2), 465–478.

Bremner, G., & Fogel, A. (2001). *Blackwell Handbook of Infant Development*. Oxford: Blackwell.

Brent, R. L., & Fawcett, L. B. (2007). Developmental toxicology, drugs and foetal teratogenesis. In E. A. Reece & J. C. Hobbins (Eds.), *Clinical Obstetrics: The Foetus and Mother* (215–235). Oxford: Blackwell.

Brewin, C. R. (2007). Autobiographical memory for trauma: Update on four controversies. *Memory*, 15 (3), 227–248.

Broadstock, M., Doughty, C., & Eggleston, M. (2007). Systematic review of the effectiveness of pharmacological treatments for adolescents and adults with autism spectrum disorder. *Autism*, 11 (4), 335–348.

Brody, G. H., Beach, S. R. H., Philibert, R. A., Chen, Y. F., Lei, M. K., Murray, V. M., & Brown, A. C. (2009). Parenting moderates a genetic vulnerability factor in longitudinal increases in youths' substance use. *Journal of Consulting and Clinical Psychology*, 77, 1–11.

Broerse, J., Peltola, C., & Crassini, B. (1983). Infants' reactions to perceptual paradox during mother–infant interactions. *Developmental Psychology*, 19, 310–316.

Bronfenbrenner, U. (1979). Beyond the deficit model in child and family policy. *Teachers College Record*, 81 (1), 95–104.

Bronfenbrenner, U. (1986). Ecology of the family as a context for human development: Research perspectives. *Developmental Psychology*, 22 (6), 723–742.

Bronfenbrenner, U. (1989). Ecological systems theory. In R. Vasta (Ed.), *Annals of Child Development* (Vol. 6, 187–249). Boston, MA: JAI Press, Inc.

Bronfenbrenner, U. (2004). *Making Human Beings Human: Biological Perspectives on Human Development*. London: Sage.

Bronfenbrenner, U., & Evans, G. (2000). Developmental science in the 21st century: Emerging questions, theoretical models, research designs and empirical findings. *Social Development*, 9, 115–125.

Bronfenbrenner, U., & Morris, P. A. (1998). The ecology of developmental processes. In R. M. Lerner (Ed.), *Handbook of Child Psychology: Vol. 1, Theoretical Models of Human Development* (535–584). New York: Wiley.

Brookes, K., Xu, X., Chen, W., Zhou, K., Neale, B., Lowe, N., Aneey, R., Franke, B., Gill, M., Ebstein, R., Buitelaar, J., Sham, P., Campbell, D., Knight, J., Andreou, P., Altink, M., Arnold, R., Boer, F., Buschgens, C., Butler, L., Christiansen, H., Feldman, L., Fleischman, K., Fliers, E., Howe-Forbes, R., Goldfarb, A., Heise, A., Gabriels, I., Korn-Lubetzki, I., Marco, R., Medad, S., Minderaa, R., Mulas, F., Muller, U., Mulligan, A., Rabin, K., Rommelse, N., Sethna, V., Sorohan, J., Uebel, H., Psychogiou, L., Weeks, A., Barrett, R., Craig, I., Banaschezski, T., Sonuga-Barke, E., Eisenberg, J., Kuntsi, J., Manor, I., McGuffin, P., Miranda, A., Oades, R. D., Plomin, R., Roeyers, H., Rothenberger, A., Sergeant, J., Steinhausen, H. C., Taylor, E., Thompson, M., Faraone, S. V., Asherson, P., & Johansson, L. (2006). The analysis of 51 genes in DSM-IV combined type attention deficit hyperactivity disorder: Association signals in DRD4, DAT1 and 16 other genes. *Molecular Psychiatry*, 11, 934–953.

Brooks-Gunn, J. (1988a). Antecedents and consequences of variations in girls' maturational timing. *Journal of Adolescent Health Care*, 9, 365–373.

Brooks-Gunn, J. (1988b). The impact of puberty and sexual activity upon the health and education of adolescent girls and boys. *Peabody Journal of Education*, 64, 88–113.

Brooks-Gunn, J., & Lewis, M. (1981). Infant social perception: Responses to pictures of parents and strangers. *Developmental Psychology*, 17, 647–649.

Brosnan, Mark J. (2008). Digit ratio as an indicator of numeracy relative to literacy in 7-year-old British schoolchildren. *British Journal of Psychology*, 99 (1), 75–85.

Brousseau, G., Brousseau, N., & Warfield, V. (2007). Rationals and decimals as required in the school curriculum, Part 2: From rationals to decimals. *Journal of Mathematical Behavior*, 26, 281–300.

Brown, A. M., & Lindsey, D. T. (2013). Infant colour vision and colour preferences: A tribute to Davida Teller. *Visual Neuroscience*, 30 (5–6), 243–250.

Brown, A. M., & Miracle, J. A. (2003). Early birocular vision in human infants: Limitations on the generality of the superposition hypothesis. *Vision Research*, 43, 1563–1574.

Brown, C., & Yi-Chin, L. (2013). The influence of developmentally appropriate practice on children's cognitive development: A qualitative metasynthesis. *Teachers College Record*, 115 (12), 1–36.

Brown, G., McBride, B., Shin, N., & Bost, K. (2007). Parenting predictors of father–child attachment security: Interactive effects of father involvement and fathering quality. *Fathering*, 5, 197–219.

Browne, J. V. (2008). Chemosensory development in the foetus and newborn. *Newborn and Infant Nursing Reviews*, 8 (4), 180–186.

Brown, M. (1981). Number operations. In K. Hart (Ed.), *Children's Understanding of Mathematics: 11–16* (23–47). Windsor: NFER-Nelson.

Bruck, M., & Ceci, S. J. (1997). The nature of applied and basic research on children's suggestibility. In N. Stein, P. A. Ornstein, B. Tversky, & C. J. Brainerd (Eds.), *Memory for Everyday and Emotional Events* (83–111). Hillsdale, NJ: Erlbaum.

Brutsaert, H. (2006). Gender-role identity and perceived peer group acceptance among early adolescents in Belgian mixed and single-sex schools. *Gender and Education*, 18 (6), 635–649.

Bryan, K. L. (1995). *The Right Hemisphere Language Battery* (2nd Ed.). Kibworth: Far Communications.

Bryant, P., Morgado, L., & Nunes, T. (1992). Children's understanding of multiplication. Paper presented at the Conference on Psychology of Mathematics Education, Tokyo, Japan, in T. Nunes, & P. Bryant, (1996). *Children Doing Mathematics*. Oxford: Blackwell.

Bryant, P., Nunes, T., Evans, D., Campos, T., & Bell, D. (2008). The number line as a teaching tool. American Educational Research Association Annual Meeting. New York, 24–28 March.

Buckingham, D. (2003). Multimedia childhoods. In M. J. Kehily & J. Swann (Eds.), *Children's Cultural Worlds* (183–228). Milton Keynes: Open University/Chichester: Wiley.

Buckingham, D. (2013). *Children Talking Television: The Making of Television Literacy* (Critical Perspectives on Literacy and Education). Abingdon: Routledge.

Buhs, E. S., & Ladd, G. W. (2001). Peer rejection as antecedent of young children's school adjustment: An examination of mediating processes. *Developmental Psychology*, 37, 550–560.

Bukatko, D., & Daehler, M. W. (2004). *Child Development: A Thematic Approach*. New York: Houghton Mifflin.

Bukowski, W. M., Laursen, B., & Hoza, B. (2010). The snowball effect: Friendship moderates escalations in depressed affect among avoidant and excluded children. *Development and Psychopathology*, 22, 749–757.

Bullock, M., & Lutkenhaus, P. (1990). Who am I? Self-understanding in toddlers. *Merrill-Palmer Quarterly*, 36, 217–238.

Burman, E. (2007). *Deconstructing Developmental Psychology* (2nd Ed.). London: Routledge.

Burns, M., Pierson, E., & Reddy, S. (2014). Working together: How teachers teach and students learn in collaborative learning environments. *International Journal of Instruction*, 7 (1), 17–32.

Busch, B., Biederman, J., Cohen, L. G., Sayer, J. M., Monuteaux, M. C., Mick, E., Zallen, B., & Faraone, S. V. (2002). Correlates of ADHD among children in pediatric and psychiatric clinics. *Psychiatric Services*, 53, 1103–1111.

Buss, A. H., & Plomin, R. (1984). *Temperament: Early Developing Personality Traits*. Hillsdale, NJ: Erlbaum.

Buss, D. M. (1987). Selection, evocation, and manipulation. *Journal of Personality and Social Psychology*, 53, 1214–1221.

Bussey, K., & Bandura, A. (1999). Social cognitive theory of gender development and differentiation. *Psychological Review*, 106, 676–713.

Bussey, K., & Bandura, A. (2004). Social cognitive theory of gender development and functioning. In A. H. Eagly, A. E. Beall, & R. J. Sternberg (Eds.), *The Psychology of Gender* (2nd Ed., 92–119). New York: Guilford Press.

Butler, G. (1998). Clinical formulation. In A. S. Bellock & M. Hersen (Eds.), *Comprehensive Clinical Psychology* (1–23). Oxford: Pergamon.

Butler, P. (2011). Baby P effect puts record number of 'at risk' children in care. *Guardian*, 8 September. Available at: http://www.theguardian.com/society/2011/sep/08/baby-p-effect-child-protection.

Buttelmann, D., Carpenter, M., & Tomasello, M. (2009). Eighteen-month-old infants show false-belief understanding in an active helping paradigm. *Cognition*, 112, 337–342.

Buyse, E., Verschueren, K., & Doumen, S. (2011). Preschoolers' attachment to mother and risk for adjustment problems in kindergarten: Can teachers make a difference? *Social Development*, 20, 33–50.

Cairns, R. B., & Cairns, B. D. (1994). *Lifelines and Risks: Pathways of Youth in Our Time*. Cambridge: Cambridge University Press.

Cairns, R. B., & Cairns, B. D. (2008). Aggression and attachment: The folly of separatism. In A. C. Bohart & D. J. Stipek (Eds.), *Constructive and Destructive Behavior: Implications for Family, School, and Society* (3rd Ed., 21–48). New York: APA.

Cairns, R. B., Cairns, B. D., Neckerman, H. J., Gest, S. D., & Gariépy, J. L. (1988). Social networks and aggressive behavior: Peer acceptance or peer rejection? *Developmental Psychology*, 24, 815–823.

Caldera, Y. (2004). Paternal involvement and infant-father attachment: A Q-set study. *Fathering*, 2, 191–210.

Caldera, Y. M., Huston, A. C., & O'Brien, M. (1989). Social interactions and play patterns of parents and toddlers with feminine, masculine, and neutral toys. *Child Development*, 60, 70–76.

Calkins, S., Dedmon, S., Gill, K., Lomax, L., & Johnson, L. (2002). Frustration in infancy: Implications for emotion regulation, physiological processes, and temperament. *Infancy*, 3, 175–197.

Calkins, S. D., Fox, N. A., & Marshall, T. R. (1996). Behavioral and physiological antecedents of inhibited and uninhibited behavior. *Child Development*, 67, 523–540.

Calvert, S., Mahler, B., Zehnder, S., Jenkins, A., & Lee, M. (2003). Gender differences in preadolescent children's online interactions: Symbolic modes of self-presentation and self-expression. *Applied Developmental Psychology*, 24, 627–644.

Campbell, A., Shirley, L., Heywood, C., & Crook, C. (2000). Infants' visual preference for sex-congruent babies, children, toys and activities: A longitudinal study. *British Journal of Developmental Psychology*, 18, 479–498.

Campbell, M. A. (2005). Cyber-bullying: An old problem in a new guise? *Australian Journal of Guidance and Counselling*, 15, 68–76.

Campos, J. J., Hiatt, S., Ramsay, D., Henderson, C., & Svejda, M. (1978). The emergence of fear on the visual cliff. In M. Lewis & L. Rosenblaum (Eds.), *The Origins of Affect* (149–182). New York: Plenum.

Capel, S., Zwozdiak-Myers, P., & Lawrence, J. (2004). Exchange of information about physical education to support the transition of pupils from primary and secondary school. *Educational Research*, 46 (3), 283–300.

Caplan, F., & Caplan, T. (1973). *The Power of Play*. New York: Doubleday.

Capute, A. J., Shapiro, B. K., Palmer, F. B., Ross, A., & Wachel, R. C. (1985). Normal gross motor development: The influences of race, sex and socioeconomic status. *Development Medicine and Child Neurology*, 27, 635–643.

Card, N. A., Stucky, B. D., Sawalani, G. M. & Little, T. D. (2008). Direct and indirect aggression during childhood and adolescence: A meta-analytic review of gender differences, intercorrelations, and relations to maladjustment. *Child Development*, 79, 1185–1229.

Carey, S. (2002). The origin of concepts: Continuing the conversation. In N. L. Stein, P. J. Bauer, & M. Rabinowitz (Eds.), *Representation, Memory and Development: Essays in Honour of Jean Mandler* (43–52). Mahwah, NJ: Erlbaum.

Carey, S. (2004). Bootstrapping and the origin of concepts. *Daedalus*, 133 (1), 59–69.

Carey, S., Diamond, R., & Woods, B. (1980). The development of face recognition: A maturational component. *Developmental Psychology*, 16, 257–269.

Carey, W. B. with Jablow, M. M. (2005). *Understanding Your Child's Temperament*. New York: Macmillan, Simon & Schuster.

Carlson, E., Sampson, M., & Sroufe, A. (2003). Implications of attachment theory and research for developmental- behavioral pediatrics. *Journal of Developmental and Behavioral Pediatrics*, 24, 364–379.

Carlson, E., Sroufe, A., & Egeland, B. (2004). The construction of experience: A longitudinal study of representation and behavior. *Child Development*, 75, 66–83.

Carlson, V. J., & Harwood, R. L. (2003). Attachment, culture, and the caregiving system: The cultural patterning of everyday experiences among Anglo and Puerto Rican mother–infant pairs. *Infant Mental Health Journal*, 24, 53–73.

Carpenter, T. P., & Moser, J. M. (1982). The development of addition and subtraction problem solving. In T. P. Carpenter, J. M. Moser & T. A. Romberg (Eds), *Addition and Subtraction: A Cognitive Perspective* (10–24). Hillsdale, NJ: Erlbaum.

Carpenter, T. P., Ansell, E., Franke, M. L., Fennema, E., & Weisbeck, L. (1993). Models of problem solving: A study of kindergarten children's problem-solving processes. *Journal for Research in Mathematics Education*, 24, 428–441.

Carpenter, T. P., Hiebert, J., & Moser, J. M. (1981). Problem structure and first grade children's initial solution processes for simple addition and subtraction problems. *Journal for Research in Mathematics Education*, 12, 27–39.

Carr, S. B., & Coustan, D. R. (2006). Drugs, alcohol abuse and effects in pregnancy. In E. A. Reece & J. C. Hobbins (Eds.), *Clinical Obstetrics: The Foetus and Mother* (88–94). Oxford: Blackwell.

Carroll, J. M., & Snowling, M. J. (2004). Language and phonological skills in children at high risk of reading difficulties. *Journal of Child Psychology and Psychiatry*, 45 (3), 631–640.

Carter, D. B., & Levy, G. D. (1988). Cognitive aspects of early sex-role development: The influence of gender schemas on preschoolers' memories and preferences for sex-typed toys and activities. *Child Development*, 59, 782–792.

Carver, C. S., Scheier, M. F., & Weintraub, J. K. (1989). Assessing coping strategies: A theoretically based approach. *Journal of Personality and Social Psychology*, 56, 267–283.

Case, R. (1985). *Intellectual Development: Birth to Adulthood.* New York: Academic Press.

Case, R. (1992). Neo-Piagetian theories of child development. In R. J. Sternberg & C. A. Berg (Eds.), *Intellectual Development* (161–196). New York: Cambridge University Press.

Case, R. (1998). The development of conceptual structures. In W. Damon (Series Ed.) & D. Kuhn & R. S. Siegler (Vol. Eds.), *Handbook of Child Psychology: Vol. 2, Cognition, Perception, and Language* (5th Ed., 745–764). New York: Wiley.

Casella, R. (2002). Where policy meets the pavement: Stages of public involvement in the prevention of school violence. *International Journal of Qualitative Studies in Education*, 15 (3), 349–372.

Casey, B. J., Giedd, J. N., & Thomas, K. M. (2000). Structural and functional brain development and its relation to cognitive development. *Biological Psychology*, 54, 241–257.

Cashon, C. H., & Cohen, L. B. (2000). Eight-month-old infants' perception of possible and impossible events. *Infancy*, 1, 429–446.

Caspers, K., Paradiso, S., Yuvuis, R., Troutman, B., Arndt, S., & Philibert, R. (2009). Association between the serotonin transporter promoter polymorphism (5-HTTLPR) and adult unresolved attachment. *Developmental Psychology*, 45, 64–76.

Caspi, A. (2000). The child is father of the man: Personality continuities from childhood to adulthood. *Journal of Personality and Social Psychology*, 78, 158–172.

Caspi, A., & Moffitt, T. E. (1991). Individual differences are accentuated during periods of social change: The sample case of girls at puberty. *Journal of Personality and Social Psychology*, 61, 157–168.

Caspi, A., & Moffitt, T. E. (2006). Gene-environment interactions in psychiatry: Joining forces with neuroscience. *Nature Reviews: Neuroscience*, 7, 583–590.

Caspi, A., & Silva, P. A. (1995). Temperamental qualities at age three predict personality traits in young adulthood: Longitudinal evidence from a birth cohort. *Child Development*, 66, 486–498.

Caspi, A., Harrington, H., Milne, B., Amell, J. W., Theodore, R. F., & Moffitt, T. E. (2003). Children's behavioural styles at age 3 are linked to their adult personality traits at 26. *Journal of Personality*, 71, 495–514.

Catherwood, D. (1993). The haptic processing of texture and shape by 7- to 9-month-old infants. *British Journal of Developmental Psychology*, 11, 299–306.

Catherwood, D. (1993). The robustness of infant haptic memory: Testing its capacity to withstand delay and haptic interference. *Child Development*, 64, 702–710.

Catherwood, D., Cramm, A., & Foster, H. (2003). Asymmetry in infant hemispheric readiness after exposure to a visual stimulus. *Developmental Science*, 6, 62–66.

Catherwood, D., Skoien, P., Green, V., & Holt, C. (1996). Assessing the primal moments in infant encoding of compound visual stimuli. *Infant Behavior and Development*, 19, 1–11.

Cattell, R. B. (1940). A culture-free intelligence test. I. *Journal of Educational Psychology*, 31 (3), 161–179.

Ceci, S. J., & Bruck, M. (1993). Suggestibility of the child witness: An historical review and synthesis. *Psychological Bulletin*, 113, 403–439.

Centers for Disease Control and Prevention, CDC (2009). *Health, United States, 2008, with Special Feature on the Health of Young Adults*. US Department of Health and Human Services, CDC, National Center for Health Statistics, March 2009, DHHS Publication No. 2009-1232. Available at: http://www.cdc.gov/nchs/data/hus/hus08.pdf.

Centers for Disease Control and Prevention, CDC (2014). *Health, United States, 2013, with Special Feature on Prescription Drugs*. US Department of Health and Human Services, CDC, National Center for Health Statistics, May 2014, DHHS Publication No. 2014-1232. Available at: http://www.cdc.gov/nchs/data/hus/hus13.pdf.

Cernoch, J. M., & Porter, R. H. (1985). Recognition of maternal axillary odours by infants. *Child Development*, 56, 1593–1598.

Chabert, R., Guitton, M. J., Amram, D., Uziel, A., Pujol, R., Lallemant, J. G. and Puel, J. L. (2006). Early maturation of evoked otoacoustic emissions and medial olivocochlear reflex in preterm neonates. *Pediatric Research*, 59, 305–308.

Chae, S. S. C. (2003). Adaptation of a picture-type creativity test for pre-school children. *Language Testing*, 20 (2), 179–188.

Champagne, F. A., Weaver, I. C., Diorio, J., Dymov, S., Szyf, M. and Meaney, M. J. (2006). Maternal care associated with methylation of the estrogen receptor-alpha1b promoter and estrogen receptor-alpha expression in the medial preoptic area of female offspring. *Endocrinology*, 147 (6), 2909–2915.

Chatfield, T. (2010). Why playing in the virtual world has an awful lot to teach children. *Guardian*, 10 January 2010. Available at: http://www.guardian.co.uk/technology/2010/jan/10/playing-in-thevirtual-world.

Chen, C., & Chang, C. (2014). Mining learning social networks for cooperative learning with appropriate learning partners in a problem-based learning environment. *Interactive Learning Environments*, 22 (1), 97–124.

Chen, J., Chen, M., & Sun, Y. (2014). A tag based learning approach to knowledge acquisition for constructing prior knowledge and enhancing student reading comprehension, *Computers and Education*, 70, 256–268.

Chen, Z., Sanchez, R. P., & Campbell, T. (1997). From beyond to within their grasp: The rudiments of analogical problem-solving in 10- to 13-month-olds. *Developmental Psychology*, 33, 790–801.

Chiffriller, S. H., & Kangos, K. A. (2014). Children's reactions when ignored and rejected: A second look. *North American Journal of Psychology*, 16, 241–252.

Child and Adolescent Mental Health in an Enlarged Europe, CAMHEE (2009). *Child and Adolescent Mental Health in Enlarged EU: Development of Effective Policies and Practices (2007–2009)*. European Commission – DG Health and Consumers. Available at: www.camhee.eu.

Chisholm, K. (1998). A three-year follow-up of attachment and indiscriminate friendliness in children adopted from Romanian orphanages. *Child Development*, 69, 1092–1106.

Chisholm, K., Carter, M. C., Ames, E. W., & Morison, S. J. (1995). Attachment security and indiscriminately friendly behavior in children adopted from Romanian orphanages. *Development and Psychopathology*, 7, 283–294.

Chiu, C.-Y. P., Schmithorst, V. J., Brown, R. D., Holland, S. K., & Dunn, S. (2006). Making memories: A cross-sectional investigation of episodic memory encoding in childhood using fMRI. *Developmental Neuropsychology*, 29 (2), 321–340.

Cho, S. C., Hwang, J. W., Lyoo, E. K., Yoo, H. J., Kin, B. N., & Kim, J. W. (2008). Patterns of temperament and character in a clinical sample of Korean children with attention-deficit hyperactivity disorder. *Psychiatry and Clinical Neurosciences*, 62, 160–166.

Choi-wa, D. H. (2009). Human resource management in Hong Kong preschools: The impact of falling rolls on staffing. *International Journal of Educational Management*, 23 (3), 217–226.

Chugani, H. T., Phelps, M. E., & Johnson, J. C. (1987). Positron emission tomography study of human brain functional development. *Annals of Neurology*, 22, 487–497.

Cichetti, D., & Barnett, D. (1991). Attachment organization in maltreated preschoolers. *Development and Psychopathology*, 4, 397–411.

Cillissen, A. H. N., & Bellmore, A. D. (2004). Social skills and interpersonal perception in early and middle childhood. In P. K. Smith & C. H. Hart (Eds.), *Blackwell Handbook of Childhood Social Development* (355–374). Malden, MA: Blackwell.

Cillessen, A. H. N., & Mayeux, L. (2004). From censure to reinforcement: Developmental changes in the association between aggression and social status. *Child Development*, 75, 147–163.

Cillessen, A. H. N., van I. Jzendoorn, H. W., van Lieshout, C. F. M., & Hartup, W. W. (1992). Heterogeneity among peer-rejected boys: Subtypes and stabilities. *Child Development*, 63, 893–905.

Claes, M., Lacourse, E., Bouchard, C., & Perucchini, P. (2003). Parental practices in late adolescence, a comparison of three countries: Canada, France and Italy. *Journal of Adolescence*, 26 (4), 387–399.

Claes, M., Lacourse, E., Ercolani, A. P., Pierro, A., Leone, L., & Presaghi, F. (2005). Parenting, peer orientation, drug use, and antisocial behavior in late adolescence: A crossnational study. *Journal of Youth and Adolescence*, 34 (5), 401–411.

Clark, A. H., Wyon, S. M., & Richards, M. P. M. (1969). Free-play in nursery school children. *Journal of Child Psychology and Psychiatry*, 10, 205–216.

Clark, M. L., Cheyne, J. A., Cunningham, C. E., & Siegel, L. S. (1988). Dyadic peer interaction and task orientation in attention deficit disordered children. *Journal of Abnormal Child Psychology*, 16, 1–15.

Clarke-Stewart, A. (1988). The 'effects' of infant day care reconsidered: Risks for parents, children and researchers. *Early Childhood Research Quarterly*, 3, 292–318.

Clarke-Stewart, K. A., Goosens, F. A., & Allhusen, V. D. (2001). Measuring infant mother attachment: Is the Strange Situation enough? *Social Development*, 10, 143–69.

Clarkson, T. W., Magos, L., & Myers, G. J. (2003). The toxicology of mercury: Current exposures and clinical manifestations. *New England Journal of Medicine*, 349, 1731–1737.

Clary, R., & Wandersee, J. (2010). Scientific caricatures in the earth science classroom: An alternative assessment for meaningful science learning. *Science and Education*, 19 (1), 21–37.

Clasien de Schipper, J., Tavecchio, L. W. C., & Van Ijzendoorn, M. H. (2008). Children's attachment relationships with day care caregivers: Associations with positive caregiving and the child's temperament. *Social Development*, 17, 454–470.

Clay, A. W., Bloomsmith, M. A., Bard, K. A., Maple, T. L., & Marr, M. J. (2015). Long-term effects of infant attachment organization on adult behaviour and health in nursery-reared, captive chimpanzees (Pan troglodytes). *Journal of Comparative Psychology*, advance online publication, 129 (2), 145–59.

Clements, W. A., & Perner, J. (1994). Implicit understanding of belief. *Cognitive Development*, 9, 377–396.

Coie, J. D., Dodge, K. A., & Coppotelli, H. (1983). Dimensions and types of social status: A cross-age perspective. *Developmental Psychology*, 18, 557–570.

Colapinto, J. (2013). *As Nature Made Him: The Boy who was Raised as a Girl*. Harper Perennial (eBook).

Cole, P. M., Barrett, K. C., & Zahn-Waxler, C. (1992). Emotion displays in two-year-olds during mishaps. *Child Development*, 63 (2), 314–324.

Collaer, M. L., & Hines, M. (1995). Human behavioral sex differences: A role for gonadal hormones during early development? *Psychological Bulletin*, 118, 55–107.

Collins, W. A., Hennighausen, K. H., Schmit, D. T., & Sroufe, L. A. (1997). Developmental precursors of romantic relationships: A longitudinal analysis. In S. Shulman (Ed.), *New Directions for Child Development* (69–84). San Francisco, CA: Jossey-Bass.

Collishaw, S., Maughan, B., Goodman, R., & Pickles, A. (2004). Time trends in adolescent mental health. *Journal of Child Psychology and Psychiatry*, 45 (8), 1350–1362.

Colombo, J. (2001). The development of visual attention in infancy. *Annual Review of Psychology*, 52, 337–367.

Colombo, J., & Mitchell, D. W. (1990). Individual and developmental differences in infant visual attention: Fixation time and information processing. In J. Colombo and J. W. Fagen (Eds.), *Individual Differences in Infancy* (193–227). Hillsdale, NJ: Erlbaum.

Colwell, J., & Payne, J. (2000). Negative correlates of computer game play in adolescents. *British Journal of Psychology*, 91, 295–310.

Condry, J., & Condry, S. (1976). Sex differences: A study in the eye of the beholder. *Child Development*, 47, 812–819.

Conger, R. D., Cui, M., Bryant, C. M., & Elder, G. H. (2000). Competence in early adult romantic relationships: A developmental perspective on family influences. *Journal of Personality and Social Psychology*, 79, 224–237.

Conners, C. K. (1994). The Conners rating scales: Use in clinical assessment, treatment planning and research. In M. Maruish (Ed.), *Use of Psychological Testing for Treatment Planning and Outcome Assessment* (467–497). Hillsdale, NJ: Erlbaum.

Conners, C. K., March, J. S., Frances, A., Wells, K. C., & Ross, R. (2001). Treatment of attention deficit hyperactivity disorder: Expert consensus guidelines. *Journal of Attention Disorders*, 4, 7–128.

Consortium of Institutions for Development and Research in Education in Europe, CIDREE (2007).

The education of 4- to 8-year-olds: Re-designing school entrance phase. Swiss Coordination Centre for Research in Education. Available at: http://www.cidree.org/fileadmin/files/pdf/publications/YB_7_The_Education_of_4-8-Year-Olds_1_.pdf.

Conway, M. (2007). 10,000 autobiographical memories: Results of the BBC's National Memory Survey. Keynote Address to the Annual Conference of the British Psychological Society, York, 21–23 March.

Cook, E. H., Vandenbergh, D. J., Stein, M. A., Cox, N. J., Yan, S., Krasowski, M. D., Uhl, G. R., & Leventhal, B. L. (1995). Molecular genetic analysis of the dopamine transporter in attention-deficit/hyperactivity disorder (ADHD). *American Journal of Human Genetics*, 57 (4), A189.

Cooley, C. H. (1902). *Human Nature and the Social Order*. New York: Scribner.

Copeland, W., Landry, K., Stanger, C., & Hudziak, J. J. (2004). Multi-informant assessment of temperament in children with externalizing behavior problems. *Journal of Clinical Child and Adolescent Psychology*, 33, 547–556.

Corbett, J. A. (1979). Psychiatric morbidity and mental retardation. In F. E. James and R. P. Smith (Eds.), *Psychiatric Illness and Mental Handicap* (11–25). London: Gaskell Press.

Corbett, M. (2013). What we know and don't know about small schools. *Our Schools/Our Selves*, 22 (2), 99–104.

Corkum, P., Moldofsky, H., Hogg-Johnson, S., Humphries, T., & Tannock, R. (1999). Sleep problems in children with attention-deficit/hyperactivity disorder: Impact of subtype, comorbidity, and stimulant medication. *Journal of the American Academy of Child and Adolescent Psychiatry*, 38, 1285–1293.

Corpus, J. H., & Lepper, M. R. (2007). The effects of person versus performance praise on children's motivation: Gender and age as moderating factors. *Educational Psychology*, 27 (4), 487–508.

Correa, J., Nunes, T., & Bryant, P. (1998). Young children's understanding of division: The relationship between division terms in a noncomputational task. *Journal of Educational Psychology*, 90, 321–329.

Corsaro, W. (1985). *Friendship and Peer Culture in the Early Years*. Norwood, NJ: Ablex.

Costa, P. T., & McCrae, R. R. (1997). Longitudinal stability of adult personality. In R. Hogan, J. Johnson, & S. Briggs (Eds.), *Handbook of Personality Psychology* (269–290). San Diego, CA: Academic Press.

Cottingham, M. (2005). Developing spirituality through the use of literature in history education. *International Journal of Children's Spirituality*, 10 (1), 45–60.

Courage, M. L., Reynolds, G. D., & Richards, J. E. (2006). Infants' attention to patterned stimuli: Developmental change from 3 to 12 months of age. *Child Development*, 77, 680–695.

Courcier, I. (2007). Teachers' perceptions of personalised learning. *Evaluation and Research in Education*, 20 (2), 59–80.

Cowan, K. (2014). Multimodal transcription of video: Examining interaction in early years classrooms. *Classroom Discourse*, 5 (1), 6–21.

Cowan, N. (1999). An embedded-processes model of working memory. In A. Miyake & P. Shah (Eds.), *Models of Working Memory: Mechanisms of Active Maintenance and Executive Control* (62–101). Cambridge: Cambridge University Press.

Cowan, R., & Daniels, H. (1989). Children's use of counting and guidelines in judging relative number. *British Journal of Educational Psychology*, 59, 200–210.

Cowie, H. (2000). Bystanding or standing by: Gender issues in coping with bullying. *Aggressive Behavior*, 26, 85–97.

Cowie, H., & Sharp, S. (1994). How to tackle bullying through the curriculum. In S. Sharp & P. K. Smith (Eds.), *Tackling Bullying in Your School: A Practical Handbook for Teachers* (41–78). London: Routledge.

Cowie, H., & Wallace, P. (2000). *Peer Support in Action: From Bystanding to Standing By*. London: Sage.

Cowie, H., Naylor, P., Rivers, I., Smith, P. K., & Pereira, B. (2002). Measuring workplace bullying. *Aggression and Violent Behaviour*, 7, 33–51.

Cox, M. J., Owen, M. T., Henderson, V. K., & Margand, N. A. (1992). Prediction of infant–father and infant–mother attachment. *Developmental Psychology*, 28, 474–483.

Craig, C. M., & Lee, D. N. (1999). Neonatal control of sucking pressure: Evidence for an intrinsic tau guide. *Experimental Brain Research*, 124, 371–382.

Crain, W. (2005). *Theories of Development: Concepts and Applications* (5th Ed.). Englewood Cliffs, NJ: Pearson Prentice Hall.

Cramer, K., Post, T., & Currier, S. (1993). Learning and teaching ratio and proportion: Research implications. In D. T. Owens (Ed.), *Research Ideas for the Classroom: Middle Grades Mathematics* (159–178). New York: Macmillan.

Creasey, G. L., Jarvis, P. A., & Berk, L. E. (1998). Play and social competence. In O. N. Saracho & B. Spodek (Eds.), *Multiple Perspectives on Play in Early Childhood Education* (116–143). Albany, NY: State University of New York Press.

Crick, N. R., & Dodge, K. A. (1994). A review and reformulation of social-information processing mechanisms in children's social adjustment. *Psychological Bulletin*, 115, 74–101.

Crick, N. R., & Dodge, K. A. (1999). 'Superiority' is in the eye of the beholder: A comment on Sutton, Smith and Swettenham. *Social Development*, 8, 128–131.

Crick, N. R., & Grotepeter, J. K. (1995). Relational aggression: Gender and social psychological adjustment. *Child Development*, 66, 710–722.

Crick, N. R., Casas, J. F., & Mosher, M. (1997). Relational and overt aggression in preschool. *Developmental Psychology*, 33, 589–600.

Crick, N. R., Casas, J. F., & Nelson, D. A. (2002). Toward a more comprehensive understanding of peer maltreatment: Studies of relational victimization. *Current Directions in Psychological Science*, 11, 98–101.

Crick, N. R., Grotepeter, J. K., & Bigbee, M. A. (2002). Relationally and physically aggressive children's intent attributions and feelings of distress for relational and instrumental peer provocations. *Child Development*, 73, 1134–1142.

Crockenberg, S. (2003). Rescuing the baby from the bathwater: How gender and temperament (may) influence how child care affects child development. *Child Development*, 74, 1034–1038.

Crook, C. (1987). Taste and olfaction. In P. Salapatek & L. Cohen (Eds.), *Handbook of Infant Perception: Vol. 1, From Sensation to Perception* (237–264). New York: Academic Press.

Crooks T. (2002). Educational assessment in New Zealand schools. *Assessment in Education: Principles, Policy and Practice*, 9 (2), 237–253.

Csibra, G., & Johnson, M. H. (2007). Investigating event-related oscillations in infancy. In M. de Haan (Ed.), *Infant EEG and Event-Related Potentials* (289–304). Hove: Psychology Press.

Csibra, G., Davis, G., Spratling, M. W., & Johnson, M. H. (2000). Gamma oscillations and object processing in the infant brain. *Science*, 290, 1582–1585.

Cuevas, K., & Bell, M. A. (2011). EEG and ECG from 5 to 10 months of age: Developmental changes in baseline activation and cognitive processing during a working memory task. *International Journal of Psychophysiology*, 80, 119–128.

Cunningham, P. (2006). Early years teachers and the influence of Piaget: Evidence from oral history. *Early Years: An International Journal of Research and Development*, 26 (1), 5–16.

Currie, C., Zanotti, C., Morgan, A., Currie, D., de Looze, M., Roberts, C., Samdel, O., Smith, O.R.F. & Barnekow, V. (Eds.) (2012). *Social Determinants of Health and Well-being among Young People. Health Behaviour in School-Aged Children (HBSC) Study: International report from the 2009/2010 survey*. Copenhagen, Denmark: WHO Regional Office for Europe. http://www.hbsc.unito.it/it/images/pdf/hbsc/prelims-part1.pdf

Currie, D., Kelly, D. and Pomerantz, S. (2006). 'The geeks shall inherit the earth': Girls' agency, subjectivity and empowerment. *Journal of Youth Studies*, 9 (4), 419–436.

Daley, D. (2006). Attention deficit hyperactivity disorder: A review of the essential facts. *Child Care Health and Development*, 32, 193–204.

Daley, D., & Birchwood, J. (2010). ADHD and academic performance: Why does ADHD impact on academic performance and what can be done to support ADHD children in the classroom? *Child Care Health and Development*, 26, 455–464.

Daley, D., & O'Brien, M. (2013). A small scale randomized controlled trial of the Self-help version of the New Forest Parent Training Programme for children with ADHD symptoms. *European Child and Adolescent Psychiatry*, DOI: 10.1007/s00787-013-0396-8.

Daley, D., & Thompson, M. (2007). Parent training for ADHD in preschool children. *Advances in ADHD*, 2, 11–16.

Daley, D., Jones, K., Hutchings, J., & Thompson, M. (2009). Attention deficit hyperactivity disorder in pre-school children: Current findings, recommended interventions and future directions. *Child: Care, Health and Development*, 35, 754–766.

Damaraju, E., Caprihan, A., Lowe, J. R., Allen, E. A., Calhoun, V. D., & Phillips, J. P. (2014). Functional connectivity in the developing brain: A longitudinal study from 4 to 9 months of age. *NeuroImage*, 84, 169–180.

Danby, S., Thompson, C., Theobald, M., & Thorpe, K. (2012). Children's strategies for making friends when starting school. *Australian Journal of Early Childhood*, 37, 63–71.

Danckaerts, M. E., Brensinger, C. M., Ralph, L. N., Seward, D. A., Bilker, W. B., & Siegel, S. J. (2010). Psychiatric health care provider attitudes towards implantable medication. *Psychiatry Research*, 15 (177), 167–171.

Dannemiller, J. L., & Stephens, B. R. (1988). A critical test of infant pattern preference models. *Child Development*, 59, 210–216.

Daurignac, E., Houdé, O., & Jouvent, R. (2006). Negative priming in a numerical Piaget-like task as evidenced by ERP. *Journal of Cognitive Neuroscience*, 18, 730–736.

Dave, S., Nazareth, I., Senior, R., & Sherr, L. (2008). A comparison of father and mother report of child behaviour on the Strengths and Difficulties Questionnaire. *Child Psychiatry and Human Development*, 39, 399–413.

Davidson, R. J. (1994). Asymmetric brain function, affective style and psychopathology: The role of early experience and plasticity. *Development and Psychopathology*, 6, 741–758.

Davies, D. R. (1986). Children's performance as a function of sex-typed labels. *British Journal of Social Psychology*, 25, 173–175.

De Haan, M. (2008). Brain function. *Encyclopaedia of Infant and Early Development*, 225–236.

De Haan, M., & Johnson, M. H. (2003). *The Cognitive Neuroscience of Development*. London: Psychology Press.

De Schipper, J. C., Tavecchio, L. W. C., Van IJzendoorn, M. H., & Van Zeijl, J. (2004). Goodness-of-fit in center day care: Relations of temperament, stability and quality of care with the child's problem behavior and well-being in day care. *Early Childhood Research Quarterly*, 19, 257–272.

de Schonen, S., & Mathivet, E. (1990). Hemispheric asymmetry in a face discrimination tasks in infants. *Child Development*, 61, 1192–1205.

de Villiers, J. G., & de Villiers, P. A. (2000). Linguistic determinism and the understanding of false beliefs: Children's reasoning and the mind. In P. Mitchell & K. J. Riggs (Eds.), *Children's Reasoning and the Mind* (191–228). Hove: Psychology Press/Taylor & Francis UK.

de Wolff, M. S., & van Ijzendoorn, M. H. (1997). Sensitivity and attachment: A meta-analysis on parental antecedents of infant attachment. *Child Development*, 68, 571–591.

Deary, I. J., Leaper, S. A., Murray, A. D., Staff, R. T., & Whalley, L. J. (2003). Cerebral white matter abnormalities and lifetime cognitive change: A 67-year follow-up of the Scottish Mental Survey of 1932. *Psychology and Ageing*, 18, 140–148.

Deary, I. J., Whalley, L. J., Lemmon, H., Crawford, J. R., & Starr, J. M. (2000). The stability of individual differences in mental ability from childhood to old age: Follow-up of the 1932 Scottish Mental Survey. *Intelligence*, 28, 357–375.

Deary, I. J., Whiteman, M. C., Starr, J. M., Whalley, L. J., & Fox, H. C. (2004). The impact of childhood intelligence on later life: Following up the Scottish Mental Surveys of 1932 and 1947. *Journal of Personality and Social Psychology*, 86 (1), 130–147.

Deater-Deckard, K., Pike, A., Petrill, S. A., Cutting, A. L., Hughes, C., & O'Connor, T. G. (2001). Nonshared environmental processes in social-emotional development: An observational study of identical twin differences in the preschool period. *Developmental Science*, 4, F1–F6.

DeCasper, A. J., & Fifer, W. P. (1980). Of human bonding: Newborns prefer their mothers' voices. *Science*, 208, 1174–1176.

DeCasper, A. J., & Spence, M. J. (1986). Prenatal maternal speech influences newborns' perceptions of speech sounds. *Infant Behavior and Development*, 9, 133–150.

DeCasper, A., Lecanuet, J. P., Busnel, M. C., Granier-Deferre, C., & Maugeais, R. (1994). Foetal reactions to recurrent maternal speech. *Infant Behaviour and Development*, 17, 159–164.

Dehaene, S. (1992). Varieties of numerical abilities. *Cognition*, 44, 1–42.

Dehaene, S. (1997). *The Number Sense*. London: Penguin.

Dehaene, S., DehaeneLambertz, G., & Cohen, L. (1998). Abstract representations of numbers in the animal and human brain. *Trends in Neurosciences*, 21, 355–361.

Dehart, T., Pelham, B., Fiedorowicz, L., Carvallo, M., & Gabriel, S. (2011). Including others in the implicit self: Implicit evaluation of significant others. *Self and Identity*, 10, 127–135.

Dehue, F., Bolman, C., & Völlink, T. (2008). Cyberbullying: Youngsters' experiences and parental perception. *CyberPsychology and Behaviour*, 11, 217–223.

Deisinger, J. A. (2008). Issues pertaining to siblings of individuals with autism spectrum disorders. In A. Rotatori (Ed.), *Autism and Developmental Disabilities: Current Practices and Issues* (Advances in Special Education, Vol. 18) (135–155). Bingley: Emerald Group.

Dejin-Karlsson, E., Hanson, B. S., Estergren, P. O., Sjoeberg, N.-O, & Marsal, K. (1998). Does passive smoking in early pregnancy increase the risk of small-for-gestational-age infants? *American Journal of Public Health*, 88, 1523–1527.

Deloache, J. S., & Brown, A. L. (1983). Very young children's memory for the location of objects in a large-scale environment. *Child Development*, 54, 888–897.

Denham, S. A., von Salish, M., Olthof, T., Kochanoff, A., & Caverly, S. (2004). Emotional and social development in childhood. In P. K. Smith & C. H. Hart (Eds.), *Blackwell Handbook of Childhood Social Development* (307–328). Malden, MA: Blackwell.

Denison, S., Reed, C., & Xu, F. (2013). The emergence of probabilistic reasoning in very young infants. *Developmental Psychology*, 49 (2), 243–249.

Dennett, D. (1978). *Brainstorms: Philosophical Essays on Mind and Psychology*. Cambridge, MA: Bradford Books/MIT Press.

Department for Children, Schools and Families (2007). *Safe to Learn: Embedding Antibullying Work in Schools*. Nottingham: DCSF Publications.

Department for Education (2014a). *Preventing and Tackling Bullying: Advice for Headteachers, Staff and Governing Bodies*. London: Department for Education. https://www.gov.uk/government/publications/preventing-and-tackling-bullying

Department for Education (2014b). *Supporting Children and Young People who are Bullied: Advice for Schools*. London: Department for Education. https://www.gov.uk/government/uploads/system/uploads/attachment_data/file/292505/supporting_bullied_children_advice.pdf

Department for Education and Employment (2000). *Bullying: Don't Suffer in Silence*. London: The Stationery Office.

Department for Education and Science (2006). *Disapplication of the National Curriculum (Revised) Guidance*. London: DfES.

Department of Health (2007). *Developing a Speech and Language Strategy for the Community: Thinking beyond Sure Start to the Challenge of the Mainstream*. London: Department of Health.

DeRosier, M. E. (2007). Peer-rejected and bullied children: A safe schools initiative for elementary school students. In J. E. Zins, M. J. Elias, & C. A. Maher (Eds.), *Bullying, Victimization, and Peer Harassment* (257–276). New York: Haworth.

Derrington, C. (2005). Perceptions of behaviour and patterns of exclusion: Gypsy Traveller students in English secondary schools. *Journal of Research in Special Educational Needs*, 5 (2), 55–61.

Devine, P. G. (1989). Stereotypes and prejudice: Their automatic and controlled components. *Journal of Personality and Social Psychology*, 56 (1), 5–18.

Devís-Devís, J. (1997). Policy, practice, and reconversion in Spanish educational reform: Teaching and teacher education in physical education. *Curriculum Journal*, 8 (2), 213–230.

Diamantopoulou, S., Rydell, A., Thorell, L. B., & Bohlin, G. (2007). Impact of executive functioning and symptoms of attention deficit hyperactivity disorder on children's peer relations and school performance. *Developmental Neuropsychology*, 32 (1), 521–542.

Diamond, A. (2009a). The interplay of biology and the environment broadly defined. *Developmental Psychology*, 45, 1–8.

Diamond, A. (2009b). All or none hypothesis: A global deficit mode that characterizes the brain and mind. *Developmental Psychology*, 45, 130–138.

Diamond, A., Cruttenden, L., & Neiderman, D. (1994). AB with multiple wells: 1: Why are multiple wells sometimes easier than two wells? Memory or memory + inhibition. *Developmental Psychology*, 30, 192–205.

Diamond, A., Prevor, M. B., Callender, G., & Druin, D. P. (1997). Prefrontal cortex cognitive deficits in children treated early and continuously for PKU. *Monographs of the Society for Research in Child Development*, 62, 1–205.

Diamond, M. (1982). Sexual identity, monozygotic twins reared in discordant sex roles and a BBC follow-up. *Archives of Sexual Behavior*, 11, 181–186.

Diamond, M., & Sigmundson, H. K. (1997). Sex reassignment at birth. *Pediatric and Adolescent Medicine*, 151, 298–304.

Dinn, W. M., Robbins, N. C., & Harris, C. L. (2001). Adult attention deficit/hyperactivity disorder: Neuropsychological correlates and clinical presentation. *Brain Cognition*, 46, 114–121.

Dion, K., & Berscheid, E. (1974). Physical attractiveness and peer perception among children. *Sociometry*, 37, 1–12.

Dirix, C. E., Nijhuis, J. G., Jongsma, H. W., & Hornstra, G. (2009). Aspects of foetal learning and memory. *Child Development*, 80 (4), 1251–1258.

DiScala, C., Lescohier, I., Barthel, M., & Li, G. H. (1998). Injuries to children with attention deficit hyperactivity disorder. *Paediatrics*, 6, 1415–1421.

Dixon, L. Q., Zhao, J., Shin, J. Y., Wu, S., Su, J. H., Burgess-Brigham, R., Gezer, M. U., & Snow, C. (2012). What we know about second language acquisition: A synthesis from four perspectives. *Review of Educational Research*, 82 (1), 5–60.

Dobson, V., & Teller, D. Y. (1978). Assessment of visual acuity in infants. In J. C. Armington, J. Krauskopf, & B. R. Wooten (Eds.), *Visual Psychophysics and Physiology* (385–396). New York: Academic Press.

Dockett, S. (1998). Constructing understandings through play in the early years. *International Journal of Early Years Education*, 6, 105–106.

Dodge, K. A., Coie, J. D., Pettit, G. S., & Price, J. M. (1990). Peer status and aggression in boys groups: Developmental and contextual analysis. *Child Development*, 61, 1289–1309.

Doherty-Sneddon, G. (2008). The great baby signing debate. *The Psychologist*, 21 (4), 300–303.

Dori, Y., & Herscovitz, O. (2005). Case-based long-term professional development of science teachers. *International Journal of Science Education*, 27 (12), 1413–1446.

Doymus, K. (2008). Teaching chemical equilibrium with the jigsaw technique. *Research in Science Education*, 38 (2), 249–260.

Dozier, M., Stovall, K. C., Albus, K. E., & Bates, B. (2001). Attachment for infants in foster care: The role of caregiver state of mind. *Child Development*, 72, 1467–1477.

Dromi, E. (1987). *Early Lexical Development*. Cambridge: Cambridge University Press.

Dubois, J., Dehaene-Lambertz, G., Kulikova, S., Poupon, C., Hüppi, P. S., & Hertz-Pannier, L. (2014). The early development of brain white matter: A review of imaging studies in foetuses, newborns and infants. *Neuroscience*, 276, 48–71.

Duff, F. J., Fieldsend, E., Bowyer-Crane, C., Hulme, C., Smith, G., Gibbs, S., & Snowling, M. J. (2008). Reading with vocabulary intervention: Evaluation of an instruction for children with poor response to reading intervention. *Journal of Research in Reading*, 31 (3), 319–336.

Duncan-Andrade, J. (2007). Gangstas, Wankstas, and Ridas: Defining, developing, and supporting effective teachers in urban schools. *International Journal of Qualitative Studies in Education*, 20 (6), 617–638.

Dunn, J., & Kendrick, C. (1982). *Siblings: Love, Envy and Understanding*. Cambridge, MA: Harvard University Press.

Dunn, L., & Herwig, J. E. (1992). Play behaviors and convergent and divergent thinking skills of young children attending full-day preschool. *Child Study Journal*, 22 (1), 23–38.

Dunphy, E. (2009). Early childhood mathematics teaching: Challenges, difficulties and priorities of teachers of young children in primary schools in Ireland. *International Journal of Early Years Education*, 17 (1), 3–16.

Dunsmore, J., Noguchi, R., Garner, P., Casey, E., & Bhullar, N. (2008). Gender-specific linkages of affective social competence with peer relations in preschool children. *Early Education and Development*, 19, 211–237.

DuPaul, G. J., McGoey, K. E., Eckert, T. L., & Vanbrakle, J. (2001). Preschool children with attention-deficit/hyperactivity disorder: Impairments in behavioural, social, and school functioning. *Journal of the American Academy of Child and Adolescent Psychiatry*, 40, 508–522.

Durkin, K. (1985). Television and sex-role acquisition: III effects. *British Journal of Social Psychology*, 24, 191–210.

Eaude, T. (2014). What makes primary classteachers special? Exploring the features of expertise in the primary classroom. *Teachers and Teaching*, 20 (1), 4–18.

Eckert, M. A., Lombardino, L. J. and Leonard, C. M. (2001). Planar asymmetry tips the phonological playground and environment raises the bar. *Child Development*, 72 (4), 988–1002.

Eckes, T., Trautner, H. M., & Behrendt, R. (2005). Gender subgroups and intergroup perception: Adolescents' views of own-gender and other-gender groups. *Journal of Social Psychology*, 145 (1), 85–111.

Edelson, D. C. (2001). Learning-for-use: A framework for the design of technology-supported inquiry activities. *Journal of Research in Science Teaching*, 38 (3), 355–385.

Edgardh, K. (2002). Sexual behaviour and early coitarche in a national sample of 17-year-old Swedish boys. *Acta Paediatrica*, 91, 985–991.

Eichenbaum, A., Bavelier, D., & Shawn Green, C. (2014). Video games: Play that can do serious good. *American Journal of Play*, 7, 50–72.

Eimas, P. D. (1975). Auditory and phonemic coding of the cues for speech: Discrimination of the [r-l] distinction by young infants. *Perception and Psychophysics*, 18, 341–347.

Eimas, P. D., Siqueland, E. R., Jusczyk, P. W., & Vigorito, J. (1971). Speech perception in infants. *Science*, 171, 303–306.

Eisenberg, L. (1999). Experience, brain and behaviour: The impact of a head start. *Pediatrics*, 103, 1031–1035.

Eisenberg, N., Fabes, R. A., Murphy, B., Maszk, P., Smith, M., & Karbon, M. (1995). The role of emotionality, regulation, and social functioning: A longitudinal study. *Child Development*, 66, 1360–1384.

Eisenberger, N. (2003). Does rejection hurt? An fMRI study of social exclusion. *Science*, 302, 290–292.

Eke, R., & Lee, J. (2004). Pace and differentiation in the Literacy Hour: Some outcomes of an analysis of transcripts. *Curriculum Journal*, 15 (3), 219–231.

Eley, T. C., Lichtenstein, P., & Stevenson, J. (1999). Sex differences in the etiology of aggressive and nonaggressive anti-social behaviour: Results from two twin studies. *Child Development*, 70, 155–168.

Elias, C. L., & Berk, L. E. (2002). Self-regulation in young children: Is there a role for sociodramatic play? *Early Childhood Research Quarterly*, 17, 1–17.

Elias, M. J., & Schwab, Y. (2006). From compliance to responsibility: Social and emotional learning and classroom management. In C. Evertson & C. S. Weinstein (Eds.), *Handbook for Classroom Management: Research, Practice, and Contemporary Issues* (309–341). Mahwah, NJ: Erlbaum.

Elicker, J., Englund, M., & Sroufe, L. A. (1992). Predicting peer competence and peer relationships in childhood from early parent-child relationships. In R. D. Parke & G. W. Ladd (Eds.), *Family–Peer Relationships: Modes of Linkage* (77–106). Hillsdale, NJ: Erlbaum.

Elkind, D. (1967). Egocentrism in adolescence. *Child Development*, 38 (4), 1025–1034.

Elliott, A. (2009). Myth: 'Behaviour and discipline in schools today are far worse than in the past'. *Times Educational Supplement*, 4864, 34–35.

Ellis, J. (1996). Prospective memory or the realisation of delayed intentions: A conceptual framework for research. In M. Brandimonte, G. O. Einstein, & M. A McDaniel (Eds.), *Prospective Memory: Theory and Applications* (1–22). Hillsdale, NJ: Erlbaum.

Ellis, J., & Kvavilashvili, L. (2000). Prospective memory in 2000: Past, present and future directions. *Applied Cognitive Psychology*, 14, S1–S9.

Emde, R. N., Gaensbauer, T. G., & Harmon, R. J. (1976). Emotional expression in infancy: A biobehavioural study. *Psychological Issues: Monograph Series*, 10 (37).

Emde, R. N., Plomin, R., Robinson, J., Corley, R., De-Fries, J., Fulker, D. W., Reznick, J. S., Campos, J., Kagan, J., & Zahn-Waxler, C. (1992). Temperament, emotion, and cognition at fourteen months: The MacArthur longitudinal twin study. *Child Development*, 63, 1437–1455.

Emerson, E., Hatton, C., Robertson, J., et al. (2011). *People with Learning Disabilities in England: Improving Health and Lives*. Learning Disabilities Observatory.

Emfinger, K. (2009). Numerical conceptions reflected during multiage child-initiated pretend play. *Journal of Instructional Psychology*, 36, 326–334.

Emmerich, W., Goldman, K. S., Kirsh, B., & Sharabany, R. (1977). Evidence for a transitional phase in the development of gender constancy. *Child Development*, 48, 930–936.

Emory, E. K., Emory, U., & Toomey, Kay A. (1988). Environmental stimulation and human foetal responsivity in late pregnancy. In W. P. Smotherman & S. R. Robinson (Eds.), *Behavior of the Foetus* (141–161). Caldwell, NJ: Telford Press.

Engle, J. M., McElwain, N. L., & Lasky, N. (2011). Presence and quality of kindergarten children's friendships: Concurrent and longitudinal associations with child adjustment in the early school years. *Infant and Child Development*, 20, 365–386.

Epstein, J. L. (1989). The selection of friends: Changes across the grades and in different school environments. In T. J. Berndt & G. W. Ladd (Eds.), *Peer Relationships in Child Development* (158–187). New York: Wiley.

Ericsson, K. A., Krampe, R. Th., & Tesch-Römer, C. (1993). The role of deliberate practice in the acquisition of expert performance. *Psychological Review*, 100, 363–406.

Ericsson, K. A., Nandagopal, K., & Roring, R. W. (2005). Giftedness viewed from the expert performance perspective. *Journal for the Education of the Gifted*, 28 (3), 287–311.

Erikson, E. H. (1950). *Childhood and Society*. New York: Norton.

Erikson, E. H. (1963). *Childhood and Society* (2nd Ed.). New York: Norton.

Erikson, E. H. (1968). *Identity, Youth and Crisis*. New York: Norton.

Erikson, E. H. (1974). *Dimensions of a New Identity*. New York: Norton.

Erikson, P. S., Perfileva, E., Bjork-Erikson T., Alborn, A., Nordborg, C., Peterson, D., & Gage, F. (1998). Neurogenesis in the adult hippocampus. *Nature Medicine*, 4, 1313–1317.

Eriksson, M., Marschik, P. B., Tulviste, T., Almgren, M., Pereira, M. P., Wehberg, S., Marjanovic-Umek, L., Gayraud, F., Kovacevic, M., & Gellego, C. (2012). Differences between girls and boys in emerging language skills: Evidence from 10 language communities. *British Journal of Developmental Psychology*, 30 (2), 326–343.

Erzar, T., & Erzar, K. K. (2008). 'If I commit to you, I betray my parents': Some negative consequences of the intergenerational cycle of insecure attachment for young adult romantic relationships. *Sexual and Relationship Therapy*, 23 (1), 25–35.

Esch, B. E., & Carr, J. E. (2005). Secretin as a treatment for autism: A review of the evidence. *Journal of Autism and Developmental Disorders*, 34 (5), 543–556.

Esrael, A., & Yifru, B. (2013). Age at menarche among in-school adolescents in Sawla town, South Ethiopia. *Ethiopian Journal of Health Sciences*, 23 (3), 189–200.

EunJin, B. (2013). Exploring impacts of the EED 420 science methods course on pre-service elementary teachers' views regarding the nature of science. *International Electronic Journal of Elementary Education*, 5 (3), 219–232.

Evans, M. A. (2010). Language performance, academic performance and signs of shyness: A comprehensive review. In K. H. Rubin & R. Coplan (Eds.), *The Development of Shyness and Social Withdrawal* (179–212). New York: Guilford Press.

Eysenck, H. J. (1981). *A Model for Personality*. Berlin: Springer.

Fagan, J. F. (1970). Memory in the infant. *Journal of Experimental Child Psychology*, 9, 217–226.

Fagan, J. F. (1973). Infants' delayed recognition memory and forgetting. *Journal of Experimental Child Psychology*, 14, 453–476.

Fagot, B. I. (1977). Consequences of moderate crossgender behavior in preschool children. *Child Development*, 48, 902–907.

Fagot, B. I. (1978). The influence of sex of child on parental reactions to toddler children. *Child Development*, 49, 459–465.

Fagot, B. I. (1985). Beyond the reinforcement principle: Another step toward understanding sex role development. *Developmental Psychology*, 21, 1097–1104.

Fagot, B. I., & Hagan, R. (1991). Observations of parent reactions to sex-stereotyped behaviors: Age and sex effects. *Child Development*, 62, 617–628.

Fagot, B. I., & Leinbach, M. D. (1993). Gender-role development in young children: From discrimination to labelling. *Developmental Review*, 13, 205–224.

Fagot, B. I., Leinbach, M. D., & O'Boyle, C. (1992). Gender labelling, gender stereotyping, and parenting behaviors. *Developmental Psychology*, 28, 225–230.

Fantuzzo, J., Coolahan, K., & Mendez, J. (1998). Contextually relevant validation of peer play constructs with African American Head Start children: Penn Interactive Play Scale. *Early Childhood Research Quarterly*, 13, 411–431.

Fantz, R. L. (1956). A method for studying early visual development. *Perceptual and Motor Skills*, 6, 13–15.

Fantz, R. L. (1964). Visual experience in infants: Decreased attention to familiar patterns relative to novel ones. *Science*, 146, 668–670.

Faraone, S. V. (2000). Attention deficit hyperactivity disorder in adults: Implications for theories of diagnosis. *Current Directions in Psychological Science*, 9, 33–36.

Faraone, S. V., Sergeant, J., Gillberg, C., & Biederman. (2003). The worldwide prevalence of ADHD: Is it an American condition? *World Psychiatry*, 2 (2), 104–113.

Farmer, T. W., Hall, C. M., Leung, M-C., Estell, D. B., & Brooks, D. (2011). Social prominence and the heterogeneity of rejected status in late elementary school. *School Psychology Quarterly*, 26, 260–274.

Farrington, D. P. (1993). Understanding and preventing bullying. In M. Tonry & N. Morris (Eds.), *Crime and Justice: An Annual Review of Research*, 17 (381–458). Chicago, IL: University of Chicago Press.

Fatimilehin, I.A. (1999). Of jewel heritage: Racial socialization and racial identity attitudes amongst adolescents of mixed African-Caribbean/White parentage. *Journal of Adolescence*, 22 (3), 303–318.

Fearon, R. M., Van Ijzendoorn, M. H., Fonagy, P., Bakermans-Kranenburg, M. J., Schuengel, C., & Bokhorst, C. L. (2006). In search of shared and nonshared environmental factors in security of attachment: A behavior-genetic study of the association between sensitivity and attachment security. *Developmental Psychology*, 42, 1026–1040.

Feeney, J. A., & Noller, P. (1996). *Adult Attachment*. Thousand Oaks, CA: Sage.

Feigenson, L., & Halberda, J. (2008). Conceptual knowledge increases infants' memory capacity. *Proceedings of National Academy Sciences*, 105 (29), 9926–9930.

Feng, Y., & Walsh, C. A. (2001). Protein–protein interactions, cytoskeletal regulation and neuronal migration. *Nature Reviews Neuroscience*, 2, 408–416.

Fenson, L., Dale, P. S., Reznick, J. S., Bates, E., Thale, D. J., & Pethick, S. J. (1994). Variability in early communicative development. *Monographs of the Society for Research in Child Development*, 59 (5), 174–179.

Fenson, L., Dale, P., Reznick, J. S., Thal, D., Bates, E., Hartung, J. P., Pethick, S., & Reilly, J. S. (1993). *Macarthur Communicative Development Inventories: User's Guide and Technical Manual*. San Diego, CA: Singular Publishing.

Fenwick, L. (2010). Initiating and sustaining learning about literacy and language across the curriculum within secondary schools. *Australian Journal of Language and Literacy*, 33 (3), 268–283.

Ferrier, S., Dunham, P., & Dunham, F. (2000). The confused robot: Two-year-olds' responses to breakdowns in conversation. *Social Development*, 9 (3), 337–347.

Field, T. (2010). Touch for socioemotional and physical well-being: A review. *Developmental Review*, 30, 367–383.

Field, T. M., Cohen, D., Garcia, R., & Greenberg, R. (1984). Mother–stranger face discrimination by the newborn. *Infant Behavior and Development*, 7, 19–25.

Field, T. M., Woodson, R. W., Cohen, D., Greenberg, R., Garcia, R., & Collins, K. (1983). Discrimination and imitation of facial expressions by term and preterm neonates. *Infant Behavior and Development*, 6, 485–489.

Fifer, W., Monk, C., & Grose-Fifer, J (2001). Prenatal development and risk. In G. Bremner & A. Fogel (Eds.), *Blackwell Handbook of Infant Development* (505–542). Oxford: Blackwell.

Fight Crime Invest in Kids (2006). *Cyber Bully: Preteen*. Princeton, NJ: Opinion Research Corporation.

Filloy, E., & Rojano, T. (1989). Solving equations: The transition from arithmetic to algebra. *For the Learning of Mathematics*, 9, 19–25.

Finlay, D., & Ivinskis, A. (1984). Cardiac and visual responses to moving stimuli presented either successively or simultaneously to the central and peripheral visual fields in 4-month-old infants. *Developmental Psychology*, 20, 29–36.

Fischer, K. W. and Bidell, T. R. (2006). Dynamic development of action and thought. In R. M. Lerner (Ed.), *Handbook of Child Psychology: Vol. 1, Theoretical Models of Human Development* (6th Ed., 313–399). New York: Wiley.

Fischer, M., Barkley, R. A., Fletcher, K. E., & Smallish, L. (1993). The adolescent outcome of hyperactive children: Predictors of psychiatric, academic, social, and emotional adjustment. *Journal of the American Academy of Child and Adolescent Psychiatry*, 32, 324–332.

Fitzgerald, D., & White, K. (2003). Linking children's social worlds: Perspective-taking in parent–child and peer contexts. *Social Behaviour and Personality*, 31, 509–522.

Flanagan, C. (1999). *Early Socialisation: Sociability and Attachment*. London: Routledge.

Flanders, J. L., Simard, M., Paquette, D., Parent, S., Vitaro, F., Pihl, R. O., & Seguin, J. R. (2010). Rough-and-tumble play and the development of physical aggression and emotion regulation: A five-year follow-up study. *Journal of Family Violence*, 25, 357–367.

Flavell, J. H., Miller, P. H., & Miller, S. A. (2002). *Cognitive Development*. Upper Saddle River, N.J: Prentice Hall.

Flouri, E., & Buchanan, A. (2002). What predicts good relationships with parents in adolescence and partners in adult life: Findings from the 1958 British birth cohort. *Journal of Family Psychology*, 16 (2), 186–198.

Flouri, E., & Buchanan, A. (2003). The role of mother involvement and father involvement in adolescent bullying behavior. *Journal of Interpersonal Violence*, 18 (6), 634–644.

Flynn, N. (2007). Good practice for pupils learning English as an additional language: Lessons from effective literacy teachers in inner-city primary schools. *Journal of Early Childhood Literacy*, 7 (2), 177–198.

Foley, M., McClowry, S. G., & Castellanos, F. (2008). The relationship between attention deficit hyperactivity disorder and child temperament. *Journal of Applied Development Psychology*, 29, 157–169.

Fombonne, E. (1999). The epidemiology of autism: A review. *Psychological Medicine*, 29, 769–786.

Fombonne E. (2001). Is there an epidemic of autism? *Pediatrics*, 109, 411–412.

Fombonne, E. (2009). Epidemiology of pervasive developmental disorders. *Pediatric Research*, 65 (6), 591–598.

Fombonne, E., & Cook, E. H. (2003). MMR and autistic enterocolitis: Consistent epidemiological failure to find an association. *Molecular Psychiatry*, 8, 133–134.

Fonzi, A., Schneider, B. H., Tani, F., & Tomada, G. (1997). Predicting children's friendship status from their dyadic interaction in structured situations of potential conflict. *Child Development*, 68, 496–506.

Forman, E. A., & McPhail, J. (1993). Vygotskian perspective on children's collaborative problem-solving activities. In E. A. Forman, N. Minick, & C. A. Stone (Eds.), *Contexts for Learning* (323–347). New York: Cambridge University Press.

Fox, N., Henderson, H., Rubin, K., Calkins, S., & Schmidt, L. (2001). Continuity and discontinuity of behavioral inhibition and exuberance: Psychophysiological and behavioral influences across the first four years of life. *Child Development*, 72, 1–21.

Fox, N. A., Snidman, N., Haas, S. A., Degan, K. A., & Kagan, J. (2015). The relations between reactivity at 4 months and behavioral inhibition in the second year: Replication across three independent samples. *Infancy*, 20, 98–114.

Francis, D. D., Diorio, J., Plotsky, P. M., & Meaney, M. J. (2002). Environmental enrichment reverses the effects of maternal separation on stress reactivity. *Journal of Neuroscience*, 22, 7840–7843.

Franklin, A., & Davies, I. R. L. (2004). New evidence for infant colour categories. *British Journal of Developmental Psychology*, 22, 349–377.

Franklin, A., Catherwood, D., Alvarez, J., & Axelson, E. (2010). Hemispheric asymmetries in categorial perception of orientation in infants and adults. *Neuropsychologia*, 48, 2648–2657.

Franklin, A., Drivonikou, G. V., Bevis, L., Davies, I. R. L., Kay, P., & Regier, T. (2008). Categorical perception of colour is lateralized to the right hemisphere in infants, but to the left hemisphere in adults. *Proceedings of the National Academy of Sciences*, USA, 105, 3221–3225.

Franz, C. E., McClelland, D. C., & Weinberger, J. (1991). Childhood antecedents of conventional social accomplishment in midlife adults: A 35-year prospective study. *Journal of Personality and Social Psychology*, 60, 586–595.

Frawley, T. J. (2008). Gender schema and prejudicial recall: How children misremember, fabricate, and distort gendered picture book information. *Journal of Research in Childhood Education*, 22, 291–303.

Freeman, N. H., Antonuccia, C., & Lewis, C. (2000). Representation of the cardinality principle: Early conception of error in a counterfactual test. *Cognition*, 74, 71–89.

Freeman, N. H., Lewis, C., & Doherty, M. (1991). Preschoolers' grasp of a desire for knowledge in false belief reasoning: Practical intelligence and verbal report. *British Journal of Developmental Psychology*, 9, 139–157.

Freud, S. (1920). *A General Introduction to Psychoanalyis*, New York: Boni & Liveright.

Freud, S. (1933). *New Introductory Lectures on Psychoanalysis* (Trans. W. J. H. Sprott). New York: Norton.

Freud, S. (1949). *An Outline of Psychoanalysis* (Trans. J. Stratchley; originally published 1940). New York: Norton.

Freud, S. (1995). Beyond the pleasure principle (originally published 1920). In J. Strachey (Ed.), *The Standard Edition of the Complete Psychological Works of Sigmund Freud*, Vol. XVII. London: The Hogarth Press.

Frick, P. J., Kamphaus, R. W., Lahey, B. B., Loeber, R., Christ, M. A. G., Hart, E. L., & Tannenbaum, L. E. (1991) Academic underachievement and the disruptive behaviour disorders. *Journal of Consulting and Clinical Psychology*, 59 (2), 289–94.

Friedman, J. M., & Polifka, J. E. (1998). *The Effects of Neurologic and Psychiatric Drugs on the Foetus and Nursing Infant*. Baltimore, MD: Johns Hopkins University Press.

Friedman, S. (1972). Habituation and recovery of visual response in the alert human newborn. *Journal of Experimental Child Psychology*, 13, 339–349.

Friedman, S., & Sigman, M. (Eds.) (1981). *Preterm Birth and Psychological Development*. New York: Academic Press.

Frith, U. (1989). *Autism: Explaining the Enigma*. Oxford: Blackwell.

Frosh, S., Phoenix, A., & Pattman, R. (2002). *Young Masculinities*. Basingstoke: Palgrave Macmillan.

Frydman, O., & Bryant, P. E. (1988). Sharing and the understanding of number equivalence by young children. *Cognitive Development*, 3, 323–339.

Frydman, O., & Bryant, P. (1994). Children's understanding of multiplicative relationships in the construction of quantitative equivalence. *Journal of Experimental Child Psychology*, 58, 489–509.

Fullard, W., McDevitt, S. C., & Carey, W. (1978). *Toddler Temperament Scale*. Philadelphia, PA: Department of Educational Psychology, Temple University.

Fullard, W., McDevitt, S. C., & Carey, W. B. (1984). Assessing temperament in one- to three-year-old children. *Journal of Pediatric Psychology*, 9, 205–217.

Gaddis, A., & Brooks-Gunn, J. (1985). The male experience of pubertal change. *Journal of Youth and Adolescence*, 14, 61–69.

Gadow, K., & Nolan, E. (2002). Differences between preschool children with ODD, ADHD, and ODD & ADHD symptoms. *Journal of Child Psychology and Psychiatry*, 43, 191–201.

Galanaki, E. (2004). Teachers and loneliness: The children's perspective. *School Psychology International*, 25, 92–105.

Galeano, R. (2011). Scaffolding productive language skills through sociodramatic play. *American Journal of Play*, 3, 324–355.

Gallese, V., Rochat, M., Cossu, G., & Sinigaglia, C. (2009). Motor cognition and its role in the phylogeny and ontogeny of action and understanding. *Developmental Psychology*, 45, 103–113.

Gallimore, R., & Weisner, R. S. (1977). My brother's keeper: Child and sibling caretaking. *Current Anthropology*, 18, 169–190.

Gallistel, C. R., & Gelman, R. (1992). Preverbal and verbal counting and computation. *Cognition*, 44, 43–74.

Gamliel, T., Hoover, J. H., Daughtry, D. W., & Imbra, C. M. (2003). A qualitative investigation of bullying. The perspectives of fifth, sixth and seventh graders in a USA parochial school. *School Psychology International*, 24, 405–420.

Ganger, J., & Brent M. R. (2004). Reexamining the vocabulary spurt. *Developmental Psychology*, 40 (4), 621–632.

Ganiban, J. M., Ulbricht, J., Saudino, K. J., Reiss, D., & Neiderhiser, J. (2011). Understanding child-based effects on parenting: Temperament as a moderator of genetic and environmental contributions to parenting. *Developmental Psychology*, 47, 676–692.

Garcia, J. J. M., Collado, E. N., & Gomez, J. L. G. (2005). Psychological risk and protective factors for antisocial behavior in adolescents. *Actas Espanolas De Psiquiatria*, 33 (6), 366–373.

Gardner, H. (1993). *Multiple Intelligences*. New York: Basic Books.

Gardner, H. (2006). *Changing Minds: The Art and Science of Changing Our Own and Other People's Minds*. Boston, MA: Harvard Business School Press.

Gauthier, I., Williams, P., Tarr, M. J., & Tanaka, J. (1998).Training 'greeble' experts: A framework for studying expert object recognition processes. *Vision Research*, 38, 2401–2428.

Gauze, C., Bukowski, W. M., Aquan-Assee, J., & Sippola, L. K. (1996). Interactions between family environment and friendship and associations with self-perceived well-being during early adolescence. *Child Development*, 67, 2201–2216.

Gazelle, H., & Spangler, T. (2007). Early childhood anxious solitude and subsequent peer relationships: Maternal and cognitive moderators. *Journal of Applied Developmental Psychology*, 28, 515–535.

Ge, X., Conger, R. D., & Elder, G. H., Jr. (1996). Coming of age too early: Pubertal influences on girls' vulnerability to psychological distress. *Child Development*, 67, 3386–3400.

Ge, X., Conger, R. D., & Elder, G. H., Jr. (2001a). The relation between puberty and psychological distress in adolescent boys. *Journal of Research on Adolescence*, 11, 49–70.

Geber, M., & Dean, M. R. C. P. (1957). Gesell tests on African children. *Pediatrics*, 20 (6), 1055–1065.

Gelman, R., & Butterworth, B. (2005). Number and language: How are they related? *Trends in Cognitive Sciences*, 9, 6–10.

Gelman, R., & Gallistel, C. R. (1978). *The Child's Understanding of Number*. Cambridge, MA: Harvard University Press.

Gelman, R., & Meck, E. (1983). Preschoolers' counting: Principles before skill. *Cognition*, 13, 343–359.

Gentile, B., Dolan-Pascoe, B., Twenge, J. M., Maitino, A., Grabe, S., & Wells, B. E. (2009). Gender differences in domain-specific self-esteem: A meta-analysis. *Review of General Psychology*, 13 (1), 34–45.

George, R. (2006). A cross-domain analysis of change in students' attitudes toward science and attitudes about the utility of science. *International Journal of Science Education*, 28 (6), 571–589.

George, R., & Clay, J. (2008). Reforming teachers and uncompromising 'standards': Implications for social justice in schools. *FORUM: For Promoting 3–19 Comprehensive Education*, 50 (1), 103–112.

Gerding, A., & Signorielli, N. (2014). Gender roles in tween television programming: A content analysis of two genres. *Sex Roles*, 70, 43–56.

Gerstadt, C. L., Hong, Y. J., & Diamond, A. (1994). The relationship between cognition and action: Performance of 3.5–7 year olds on Stroop-like day–night test. *Cognition*, 53, 129–153.

Gervai, J., Novak, A., Lakatos, K., Toth, I., Danis, I., Ronai, Z., Nemoda, Z., Sasvani-Szekely, M., Bureau, J. F., Bronfman, E., & Lyons-Rubh, K. (2007). Infant genotype may moderate sensitivity to maternal affective communications: Attachment disorganization, quality of care, and the DRD4 polymorphism. *Social Neuroscience*, 2, 307–319.

Geschwind, D. H. (2009). Autism: The ups and downs of neurolin. *Biological Psychiatry*, 66 (10), 904–905.

Gesell, A. (1933). Maturation and the patterning of behavior. In C. Murchison (Ed.), *A Handbook of Child Psychology* (2nd Rev. Ed.). Worcester, MA: Clark University.

Gevensleben, H., Holl, B., Albrecht, B., Schlamp, D., Kratz, O., Studer, P., Wangler, S., Rothenberger, A., Moll, G. H., & Heinrich, H. (2009). Distinct EEG effects related to neurofeedback training in children with ADHD: A randomized controlled trial. *International Journal by Psychophysiology*, 74, 149–157.

Ghetti, S., Edelstein, R. S., Goodman, G. S., Cordon, I. M., Quas, J. A., Alexander, K. W., Redlich, A. D., & Jones, D. P. H. (2006). What can subjective forgetting tell us about memory for childhood trauma? *Memory and Cognition*, 34 (5), 1011–1025.

Ghuman, J. K., Ginsburg, G. S., Subramaniam, G., Ghuman, H. S., Kau, A. S., & Ma, R. (2001). Psychostimulants in preschool children with attention-deficit/hyperactivity disorder: Clinical evidence from a developmental disorders institution. *Journal of the American Academy of Child and Adolescent Psychiatry*, 40, 516–524.

Giaschi, D., Narasimhan, S., Solski, A., Harrison, E., & Wilcox, L. M. (2013). On the typical development of stereopsis: Fine and coarse processing. *Vision Research*, 89, 65–71.

Gibson, E., & Walk, R. D. (1960). The 'visual cliff'. *Scientific American*, 202, 64–71.

Giedd, J. N. (2008). The teen brain: Insights from neuroimaging. *Journal of Adolescent Health*, 42 (4), 335–343.

Giedd, J. N., Blumenthal, J., Jeffries, N. O., Rajapaske, J. C., Vaituzis, C., & Liu, H. (1999). Development of the corpus callosum during childhood and adolescence: A longitudinal MRI study. *Progress in Neuro-Psychopharmacology and Biological Psychiatry*, 23, 571–588.

Gilbert, S. F. (2000). *Developmental Biology* (6th Ed.). Sunderland, MA: Sinauer.

Giles, A., & Rovee-Collier, C. (2011). Infant long-term memory for associations formed during mere exposure. *Infant Behaviour and Development*, 34, 327–338.

Gillard, D. (2008). Blair's academies: The story so far. *FORUM: For Promoting 3–19 Comprehensive Education*, 50 (1), 11–22.

Gillberg, C., Gillberg, C. I., Rasmussen, P., Kadesjo, B., Soderstrom, H., Rastam, M., Johnson, M., Rothenberger, A., & Niklasson, L. (2004). Coexisting disorders in ADHD: Implications for diagnosis and intervention. *European Journal of Adolescent Psychiatry*, 13, 180–192.

Gillies, R. M. (2000). The maintenance of co-operative and helping behaviours in co-operative groups. *British Journal of Educational Psychology*, 70 (1), 97–111.

Ginsberg, H. P. (1997). *Entering the Child's Mind: The Clinical Interview in Psychological Research and Practice*. Cambridge: Cambridge University Press.

Gluckman, P., Hanson, M., & Beedle, A. (2007). Early life events and their consequences for later disease: A life history and evolutionary perspective. *American Journal of Human Biology*, 19, 1–19.

Glutting, J. J., Youngstrom, E. A., & Watkins, M. W. (2005). ADHD and college students: Exploratory and confirmatory factor structures with student and parent data. *Psychological Assessment*, 17 (1), 44–55.

Gogtay, N., Giedd, J. N., Lusk, L., Hayashi, K. M., Greenstein, D., Vaitusis, A. C., Nugent, T. F. III, Herman, D. H., Clasen, L. S., Toga, A. W., Rapoport, J. L., & Thompson, P. M. (2004). Dynamic mapping of human cortical development during childhood through early adulthood. *PNAS*, 101, 8174–8179.

Gojman, S., Millan, S., Carlson, E., Sanchez, G., Rodarte, A., Gonzalez, P., & Hernandez, G. (2012). Intergenerational relations of attachment: A research synthesis of urban/rural Mexican samples. *Attachment and Human Development*, 14, 553–566.

Gokiert, R. J., Chow, W., Parsa, B., & Vandenberghe, C. (2007). *Community Cross-Cultural Lessons: Early Childhood Developmental Screening and Approaches to Research and Practice*. Community–University Partnership for the Study of Children, Youth, and Families, University of Alberta, Edmonton.

Goldberg, S. (2000). *Attachment and Development*. London: Arnold.

Goldfarb, W. (1947). Variations of adolescent adjustment of institutionally reared children. *American Journal of Orthopsychiatry*, 17, 449–457.

Goldfield, E. C., & Wolff, P. H. (2002). Motor development in infancy. In A. Slater & M. Lewis (Eds.), *Introduction to Infant Development* (6–82). Oxford: Oxford University Press.

Golding, J., Prembey, M., Jones, R., & ALSPAC team (2001). ALSPAC – The Avon Longitudinal Study of Parents and Children I. Study Methodology. *Paediatric and Perinatal Epidemiology*, 15, 74–87.

Goldsmiths, H. H., Buss, A. H., Plomin, R., Rothbart, M. K., Thomas, A., Stella, C., Hinde, R. A., & McCall, R. B. (1987). Roundtable: What is temperament? Four approaches. *Child Development*, 58, 505–529.

Goldsmiths, H. H., Lemery, K. S., Buss, K. A., & Campos, J. J. (1999). Genetic analyses of focal aspects of infant temperament. *Developmental Psychology*, 35, 972–985.

Goldstone, R., & Day, S. (2012). Introduction to 'New conceptualizations of transfer of learning'. *Educational Psychologist*, 47 (3), 149–152.

Goleman, D. (1995). *Emotional Intelligence*. New York: Basic Books.

Golombok, S., & Fivush, R. (1994). *Gender Development*. Cambridge: Cambridge University Press.

Golombok, S., & Hines, M. (2002). Sex differences in social behavior. In P. K. Smith & C. H. Hart (Eds.), *Blackwell Handbook of Childhood Social Development* (117–136). Malden, MA: Blackwell.

Gomes, M., Mortimer, E., & Kelly, G. (2011). Contrasting stories of inclusion/exclusion in the chemistry classroom. *International Journal of Science Education*, 33 (6), 747–772.

Göncü, A., & Gaskins, S. (2007). *Play and Development: Evolutionary, Sociocultural and Functional Perspectives*. Hove: Psychology Press.

Goodman, J. (2006). School discipline in moral disarray. *Journal of Moral Education*, 35 (2), 213–230.

Goodman, R. (1997). The Strengths and Difficulties Questionnaire: A research note. *Journal of Child Psychology, Psychiatry, and Allied Disciplines*, 38, 581–586.

Goodman, R. (2000). *Children of the Japanese State*. Oxford: Oxford University Press.

Gopnick, A., & Meltzoff, A. (1987). The development of categorization in the second year and its relation to other cognitive and linguistic developments. *Child Development*, 58, 1523–1531.

Gopnik, A., Slaughter, V., & Meltzoff, A. N. (1994). Changing your views: How understanding visual perception can lead to a new theory of the mind. In C. Lewis & P. Mitchell (Eds.), *Children's Early Understanding of Mind: Origins and Development* (157–181). Hillsdale, NJ: Erlbaum.

Gorard, S., Taylor, C., & Fitz, J. (2002). Does school choice lead to 'spirals of decline'? *Journal of Education Policy*, 17 (3), 367–384.

Goswami, U. (2006). The foundations of psychological understanding. *Developmental Science*, 9, 545–550.

Goswami, U., & Bryant, P. (2007). Children's cognitive development and learning. *Primary Review*, 2/1a, 1–4.

Gottfredson, D., & DiPietro, S. (2011). School size, social capital, and student victimization. *Sociology of Education*, 84 (1), 69–89.

Gottman, J. M. (1986). The world of coordinated play: Same- and cross-sex friendship in young children. In J. M. Gottman & J. G. Parker (Eds.), *Conversations of Friends: Speculations on Affective Development* (139–191). Cambridge: Cambridge University Press.

Gouze, K. R., & Nadelman, L. (1980). Constancy of gender identity for self and others in children between the ages of three and seven. *Child Development*, 51, 275–278.

Graber, J. A., Brooks-Gunn, J., Paikoff, R. L., & Warren, M. P. (1994). Prediction of eating problems and disorders: An eight year study of adolescent girls. *Developmental Psychology*, 30 (6), 823–834.

Grafenhain, M., Behne, T., Carpenter, M., & Tomasello, M. (2009). One-year-olds' understanding of non-verbal gestures directed to a third person. *Cognitive Development*, 24 (1), 23–33.

Graham, S., & Juvonen, J. (2001). An attributional approach to peer victimisation. In J. Juvonen & S. Graham (Eds.), *Peer Harassment in School: The Plight of the Vulnerable and Victimized* (49–72). New York: Guilford Press.

Graham, S. A., & Kilbreath, C. S. (2007). It's a sign of the kind: Gestures and words guide infants' inductive inferences. *Developmental Psychology*, 43, 1111–1123.

Grattan, M. P., De Vos, E., Levy, J., & McClintock, M. K. (1992). Asymmetric action in the human newborn: Sex differences in patterns of organization. *Child Development*, 63, 273–289.

Graven, S. N., & Browne, J. V. (2008). Sleep and brain development: The critical role of sleep in foetal and early neonatal brain development. *Newborn and Infant Nursing Reviews*, 8 (4), 173–179.

Graves, M. F. (2011). Vocabulary instruction: Matching teaching methods to the learning task and the time available for instruction. *California Reader*, 44 (3), 4–8.

Greatorex, J., & Malacova, E. (2006). Can different teaching strategies or methods of preparing pupils lead to greater improvements from GCSE to A level performance? *Research Papers in Education*, 21 (3), 255–294.

Gréco, P. (1962). Quantité et quotité: Nouvelles recherches sur la correspondance terme-a-terme et la conservation des ensembles. In P. Gréco & A. Morf (Eds.), *Structures numeriques elementaires: Etudes d'Epistemologie Genetique*, Vol. 13 (35–52). Paris: Presses Universitaires de France.

Green, H., McGinnity, A., Meltzer, H., et al. (2005). *Mental Health of Children and Young People in Great Britain 2004*. London: Palgrave.

Greenberg, B. S., Sherry, J., Lachlan, K., Lucas, K., & Holmstrom, A. (2010). Orientations to video games among gender and age groups. *Simulation and Gaming*, 41, 238–259.

Greene, R. W., & Ablon, J. S. (2001). What does the MTA study tell us about effective psychosocial treatments for ADHD? *Journal of Clinical Child Psychology*, 30, 114–121.

Greene, R. W., Biederman, J., Faraone, S. V., Sienna, M., & Garcia-Jetton, J. (1997). Adolescent outcome of boys with attention deficit/hyperactivity disorder and social disability: Results from a 4-year longitudinal follow-up study. *Journal of Consulting and Clinical Psychology*, 65, 758–767.

Grieg, A., Taylor, J., & MacKay, T. (2007). *Doing Research with Children* (2nd Ed.). London: Sage.

Griffiths, C. C. B. (2007). Pragmatic abilities in adults with and without dyslexia: A pilot study. *Dyslexia*, 13, 276–296.

Grossmann, K. E. (1985). *Die Qualität der Beziehung zwischen Eltern und Kind. Grundlagen einer psychisch gesunden Entwicklung* (The quality of the relationship between parents and child: The basis for healthy psychological development). *Praxis der Psychotherapie und Psychosomatik*, 30, 44–54.

Grossmann, K., Grossmann, K. E., Fremmer-Bombik, E., Kindler, H., Scheueueu-Englisch, H., & Zimmerman, P. (2002). The uniqueness of the child–father attachment relationship: Fathers' sensitive and challenging play as a pivotable variable in a 16-year longitudinal study. *Social Development*, 11, 307–331.

Grossmann, K. E., Grossmann, K., & Schwan, A. (1986). Capturing the wider view of attachment: A reanalysis of Ainsworth's strange situation. In C. E. Izard & P. E. Read (Eds.), *Measuring Emotions in Infants and Children* (Vol. 2, 124–171). New York: Cambridge University Press.

Grossman, T., Gliga, T., Johnson, M. H., & Mareschal, D. (2009). The neural basis of perceptual category learning in human infants. *Journal of Cognitive Neuroscience*, 21 (12), 2276–2286.

Gruber, R., Sadeh, A., & Raviv, A. (2000). Instability of sleep patterns in children with attention-deficit/hyperactivity disorder. *Journal of the American Academy of Child and Adolescent Psychiatry*, 39, 495–501.

Guerin, S., & Hennessy, E. (2002). Pupils' definitions of bullying. *European Journal of Psychology of Education*, 17, 249–261.

Gwiazda, J., & Birch, E. E. (2001). Perceptual development: Vision. In E. B. Goldstein (Ed.), *Handbook of Perception* (636–668). Oxford: Blackwell.

Haferkamp, N., Eimler, S., Papadakis, A. M., & Kruck, J. V. (2012). Men are from Mars, women are from Venus? Examining gender differences in self-presentation on social networking sites. *Cyberpsychology, Behavior and Social Networking*, 15 (2), 91–98.

Hagekull, B., Bohlin, G., & Lindhagen, K. (1984). Validity of parental reports. *Infant Behaviour and Development*, 7, 77–92.

Hagen, E. H. (2002). Depression as bargaining: The case postpartum. *Evolution and Human Behaviour*, 23, 323–336.

Hahn, W. K. (1987). Cerebral lateralisation of function: From infancy through childhood. *Psychological Bulletin*, 101, 376–392.

Hainline, L. (1998). The development of basic visual abilities. In A. Slater (Ed.), *Perceptual Development: Visual, Auditory and Speech Perception in Infancy* (5–50). Hove: Psychology Press.

Haith, M. M. (1998). Who put the cog in infant cognition? Is rich interpretation too costly? *Infant Behavior and Development*, 21, 167–179.

Hale, C. M., & Tager-Flusberg, H. (2003). The influence of language on theory of mind: A training study. *Development Science*, 6, 346–359.

Hall, G. S. (1904). Youth: Its education, health and regime. In S. Goodman & S. Wheeler (2005). *The Project Gutenberg EBook of Youth: Its Education, Regimen, and Hygiene by G. Stanley Hall*. October.

Hallam, S., & Ireson, J. (2005). Secondary school teachers' pedagogic practices when teaching mixed and structured ability classes. *Research Papers in Education*, 20 (1), 3–24.

Halliday, J. (2014). Teenage computer engineer pleads guilty to murdering Breck Bednar, 14. *Guardian* (online), UK news, 25 November. Available at: http://www.theguardian.com/uk-news/2014/nov/25/breck-bednar-14-murder-lewis-daynes

Halliday, J. L., Watson, L. F., Lumley, J., Danks, D. M., & Sheffield, L. J. (1995). New estimates of Down syndrome risks at chorionic villus sampling, amniocentesis and live birth in women of advanced maternal age from a uniquely defined population, *Prenatal Diagnosis*, 15, 455–465.

Halligan, J. (2009). *Ryan's story: In memory of Ryan Patrick Halligan 1989–2003*. Available at: http://www.ryanpatrickhalligan.org/laws/laws.htm.

Hamilton, C. E. (1994). Continuity and discontinuity of attachment from infancy through adolescence. *Child Development*, 71, 690–694.

Hampel, P., & Petermann, F. (2005). Age and gender effects on coping in children and adolescents. *Journal of Youth and Adolescence*, 34 (2), 73–83.

Hampton, M. (2014). Life changing language: Progress in language learning in the lower secondary school. *English 4–11*, 50, 19–33.

Hane, A. A., Fox, N. A., Henderson, H. A., & Marshal, I. J. (2008). Behavioural reactivity and approach–withdrawal bias in infancy. *Developmental Psychology*, 44, 1491–1496.

Hanish, L. D., & Guerra, N. G. (2004). Aggressive victims, passive victims, and bullies: Developmental continuity or developmental change? *Merrill-Palmer Quarterly*, 50, 17–38.

Hannon, E. E., & Trehub, S. E. (2005). Metrical categories in infancy and adulthood. *Psychological Science*, 16, 48–55.

Happé, F. (1994). An advanced test of theory of mind: Understanding of story characters' thoughts and feelings by able autistic, mentally handicapped, and normal children and adults. *Journal of Autism and Developmental Disorders*, 24, 129–154.

Happé, F., & Frith, U. (2006). The weak coherence account: Detail-focused cognitive style in autism spectrum disorders. *Journal for Autism Development and Disorder*, 36 (1), 5–25.

Harden, R. M. (2008). Death by PowerPoint: The need for a 'fidget index'. *Medical Teacher*, 30 (9–10), 833–835.

Hariri, A. R., & Forbes, E. E. (2007). Genetics of emotion regulation. In J. J. Gross (Ed.), *Handbook of Emotion Regulation* (110–134). New York: Guilford Press.

Harlow, H. (1958). The nature of love. *American Psychologist*, 13, 673–685.

Harlow, H., & Harlow, M. (1969). Effects on various mother–infant relationships on rhesus monkey behaviours. In B. M. Foss (Ed.), *Determinants of Infant Behaviour* (Vol. 4, 15–36). London: Methuen.

Harlow, H., & Zimmerman, R. R. (1959). Affectional responses in the infant monkey. *Science*, 130, 421–432.

Haroaian, L. (2000). Sexual competency development in sexually permissive and sexually restrictive societies. *Electronic Journal of Human Sexuality*, 3 (1).

Harris, A. (2008). Leading innovation and change: Knowledge creation by schools for schools. *European Journal of Education: Research, Development and Policies*, 43 (2), 219–228.

Harris, G. (1997). Development of taste perception and appetite regulation. In G. Bremner, A. Slater, & G. Butterworth (Eds.), *Infant Development: Recent Advances* (9–30). Hove: Psychology Press.

Harris, J. R. (1998). *The Nurture Assumption: Why Children Turn Out the Way They Do*. New York: Free Press.

Harrist, A. W., Zaia, A. F., Bates, J. E., Dodge, K. A., & Pettit, G. S. (1997). Subtypes of social withdrawal in early childhood: Sociometric status and social-cognitive differences across four years. *Child Development*, 68, 278–294.

Hart, B., & Risley, T. R. (1995). *Meaningful Differences in the Everyday Experiences of Young American Children*. Baltimore, MD: Brookes.

Hart, K., Brown, M., Kerslake, D., Kuchermann, D., & Ruddock, G. (1985). *Chelsea Diagnostic Mathematics Tests: Fractions 1*. Windsor: NFER-Nelson.

Harter, S. (1987). The determinations and mediational role of global self-worth in children. In N. Eisenberg (Ed.), *Contemporary Topics in Developmental Psychology* (219–242). New York: Wiley Interscience.

Harter, S. (1990). Processes underlying adolescent self-concept formation. In R. Montemayor, G. R. Adams, & T. P. Gullotta (Eds.), *From Childhood to Adolescence: A Transitional Period?* (205–239). Newbury Park, CA: Sage.

Harter, S. (1998). The development of self-representations. In W. Damon & N. Eisenberg (Eds.), *Handbook of Child Psychology: Social, Emotional and Personality Development* (5th Ed., 553–617). New York: Wiley.

Harter, S. (2003). The development of self-representations during childhood and adolescence. In M. R. Leary & J. P. Tangney (Eds.), *Handbook of Self and Identity* (610–642). New York: Guilford Press.

Hartley, J. E. K., Wight, D., & Hunt, K. (2014). Presuming the influence of the media: Teenagers' constructions of gender identity through sexual/romantic relationships and alcohol consumption. *Sociology of Health and Illness* (early view online). DOI: 10.1111/1467-9566.12107.

Hartman, R. R., Stage, S. A., & Webster-Stratton, C. (2003). A growth curve analysis of parent training outcomes: Examining the influence of child risk factors (inattention, impulsivity, and hyperactivity problems), and parental and family risk factors. *Journal of Child Psychology and Psychiatry and Allied Disciplines*, 44, 388–398.

Hartshorn, K., Rovee-Collier, C., Gerhardstein, P. C., Bhatt, R. S., Wondoloski, T. L., Klein, P., Gilch, J., Wurtzel, N., & Campos-de-Carvalho, M. (1998). Ontogeny of long-term memory over the first year-and-a-half of life. *Developmental Psychobiology*, 32, 69–89.

Hartung, B., & Sweeney, K. (1991). Why adult children return home. *Social Science Journal*, 28, 467–480.

Hartup, W. W. (1989). Social relationships and their developmental significance. *American Psychologist*, 44 (2), 120–126.

Hartup, W. W. (2006). Relationships in early and middle childhood. In A. L. Vangelisti & D. Perlman (Eds.), *Cambridge Handbook of Personal Relationships* (171–190). New York: Cambridge University Press.

Hartup, W. W., & Stevens, N. (1999). Friendships and adaptation across the life span. *Current Directions in Psychological Science*, 8, 76–79.

Hasebrink, U., Livingstone, S., & Haddon, L. (2008). *Comparing Children's Online Opportunities and Risks across Europe: Cross-national Comparisons for EU Kids Online*. London: EU Kids Online (Deliverable D3.2).

Haselager, J. T., Hartup, W. W., van Lieshout, C. F. M., & Riksen-Walraven, J. M. A. (1998). Similarities between friends and nonfriends in middle childhood. *Child Development*, 69, 1198–1208.

Hasselgreen, A. A. H. (2005). Assessing the language of young learners. *Language Testing*, 22 (3), 337–354.

Hatch, J.A. (Ed.) (1995). *Qualitative Research in Early Childhood Settings*. Westport, CT and London: Praeger.

Hatten, M. E. (2002). New directions in neuronal migration. *Science*, 297, 1660–1663.

Hatton, C., & Emerson, E. (2003). Families with a person with intellectual disabilities: Stress and impact. *Current Opinion in Psychiatry*, 16, 497–501.

Hausmann, M., Schoofs, D., Rosenthal, H. E. S., & Jordan, K. (2009). Interactive effects of sex hormones and gender stereotypes on cognitive sex differences: A psychobiosocial approach. *Psychoneuroendocrinology*, 34 (3), 389–401.

Hay, D. (2007). Using concept maps to measure deep, surface and non-learning outcomes. *Studies in Higher Education*, 32 (1), 39–57.

Hay, D., & Ross, H. (1982). The social nature of early conflict. *Child Development*, 53, 105–113.

Hay, D., Nash, A., & Pederson, J. (1983). Interactions between six-month-old peers. *Child Development*, 54, 557–562.

Hayden, E. P., Durbin, C. E., Klein, D. N., & Olino, T. M. (2010). Maternal personality influences the relationship between maternal reports and laboratory measures of child temperament. *Journal of Personality Assessment*, 92, 586–593.

Hayne, H. (2004). Infant memory development: Implications for childhood amnesia. *Developmental Review*, 24 33–73.

Haynes, J., & Murris, K. (2013). The realm of meaning: Imagination, narrative and playfulness in philosophical exploration with young children. *Early Child Development and Care*, 183 (8), 1084–1100.

Heath, C., & Hindmarsh, J. (1997). Analysing interaction: Video, ethnography and situated conduct. In J. A. Hughes & W. Sharrock (Eds.), *The Philosophy of Social Research* (99–121). London: Longman.

Heckhausen, J., Wrosch, C., & Schulz, R. (2010). A motivational theory of lifespan development. *Psychological Review*, 117, 32–60.

Held, R., & Hein, A. (1963). Movement produced stimulation in the development of visually guided behaviour. *Journal of Comparative and Physiological Psychology*, 56, 872–876.

Helfinstein, S. M., Fox, N. A., & Pine, D. S. (2012). Approach-withdrawal and the role of the striatum in the temperament of behavioral inhibition. *Developmental Psychology*, 48, 815–826.

Henderson, H. A., Fox, N. A., & Rubin, K. H. (2001). Temperamental contributions to social behavior: The moderating roles of frontal EEG asymmetry and gender. *Journal of the American Academy of Child and Adolescent Psychiatry*, 40, 68–74.

Henderson, H., Marshall, P., Fox, N., & Rubin, K. (2004). Psychophysiological and behavioral evidence for varying forms and functions of non-social behavior in preschoolers. *Child Development*, 75, 236–250.

Henderson, M., Wight, D., Raab, G., Abraham, C., Buston, K., Hart, G., & Scott, S. (2002). Heterosexual risk behaviour among young teenagers in Scotland. *Journal of Adolescence*, 25 (5), 483–494.

Hepper, P. G. (1988). Foetal 'soap' addiction. *Lancet*, June, 1347–1384.

Hepper, P. G. (1992). Fetal psychology. An embryonic science. In J. G. Nijhuis (Ed.), *Fetal Behaviour. Developmental and Perinatal Aspects* (129–156). Oxford: Oxford University Press.

Hepper, P. G. (1996). Foetal memory does it exist? *Acta Paediatrica*, Supplement 416, 16–20.

Hepper, P. G. (2002). Prenatal development. In A. Slater & M. Lewis (Eds.), *Introduction to Infant Development* (39–60). Oxford: Oxford University Press.

Hepper, P. G., & Leader, L. R. (1996). Foetal habituation. *Fetal and Maternal Medicine Review*, 8, 109–123.

Hernandez-Reif, M., Field, T., del Pino, N., & Diego, M. (2000). Less exploring by mouth occurs in newborns of depressed mothers. *Infant Mental Health Journal*, 21, 204–210.

Hertz, M. F., Donato, I. & Wright, J. (2013). Editorial: Bullying and suicide – A public health approach. *Journal of Adolescent Health*, 53, S1–S3.

Hesslinger, B., Thiel, T., Van Elst, L. T., Hennig, J., & Ebert, D. (2001). Attention-deficit disorder in adults with or without hyperactivity: Where is the difference? A study in humans using short echo H-1-magnetic resonance spectroscopy. *Neuroscience Letters*, 304, 117–119.

Hetherington, E. M., & Stanley-Hagan, M. (2002). Parenting in divorced and remarried families. In M. H. Bornstein (Ed.), *Handbook of Parenting* (2nd Ed., Vol. 3, 287–315). Mahwah, NJ: Erlbaum.

Heuser, L. (2005). We're not too old to play sports: The career of women lawn bowlers. *Leisure Studies*, 24 (1), 45–60.

Hiebert, J., & Tonnessen, L. H. (1978). Development of the fraction concept in two physical contexts: An exploratory investigation. *Journal for Research in Mathematics Education*, 9 (5), 374–378.

Hinde, R. A. (1989). Temperament as an intervening variable. In G. A. Kohnstamm, J. E. Bates, & M. K. Rothbart (Eds), *Temperament in Childhood* (27–33). Chichester: Wiley.

Hinde, R. A., Titmus, G., Easton, D., & Tamplin, A. (1985). Incidence of 'friendship' and behavior toward strong associates versus nonassociates in preschoolers. *Child Development*, 56, 234–245.

Hinduja, S., & Patchin, J. W. (2007). Offline consequences of online victimization: School violence and delinquency. *Journal of School Violence*, 6, 89–112.

Hinduja, S. & Patchin, J. W. (2010). Bullying, cyberbullying and suicide. *Archives of Suicide Research*, 14, 206–221.

Hinduja. S., & Patchin, J. W. (2008). Cyberbulling: An exploratory analysis of factors related to offending and victimization. *Deviant Behaviour*, 29, 129–156.

Hinojosa, T., Sheu, C. F., & Michel, G. F. (2003). Infant hand preference for grasping objects contributes to the development of a hand-use preference for manipulating objects. *Developmental Psychobiology*, 43, 328–334.

Hinshaw, S. P. (1994). *Attention Deficits and Hyperactivity in Children*. Thousand Oaks, CA: Sage.

Hinshaw, S. P., & Melnick, S. M. (1995). Peer relationships in boys with attention deficit hyperactivity disorder with and without co-morbid aggression. *Development and Psychopathology*, 7, 267–647.

Hodges, J., & Tizard, B. (1989). Social and family relationships of ex-institutional adolescents. *Journal of Child Psychology and Psychiatry*, 30, 77–98.

Hodkinson, P., & Deicke, W. (2007). *Youth Cultures: Scenes, Subcultures and Tribes*. Routledge: New York.

Hoicka, E., & Akhtar, N. (2012). Early humour production. *British Journal of Developmental Psychology*, 30 (4), 586–603.

Hoicka, E., & Gattis, M. L. (2012). Acoustic differences between humorous and sincere communicative intentions. *British Journal of Developmental Psychology*, 30(4), 531–549.

Holland, R. (2002). *Vouchers Help the Learning Disabled*. Chicago, IL: The Heartland Institute.

Hollander, E., Wasserman, S., Swanson, E. N., Chaplin, E., Schapiro, M. L., Zagursky, K., & Novotny, S. (2006). A double-blind placebo-controlled pilot study of olanzapine in childhood/adolescent pervasive developmental disorder. *Journal of Child and Adolescent Psychopharmacology*, 16 (5), 541–548.

Holmes, D. (1990). The evidence for repression: An examination of sixty years of research. In J. Singer (Ed.), *Repression and Dissociation: Implications for Personality, Theory, Psychopathology, and Health* (85–102). Chicago, IL: University of Chicago Press.

Holt, M. K., Kaufman Kantor, G., & Finkelhor, D. (2009). Parent/child concordance about bullying involvement and family characteristics related to bullying and peer victimization. *Journal of School Violence*, 8, 42–63.

Holyoak, K. J., Junn, E. N., & Billman, D. O. (1984). Development of analogical problem-solving skill. *Child Development*, 55, 2042–2055.

Home Office and Department of Health (1992). *Memorandum of Good Practice on Video Recorded Interviews with Child Witnesses for Criminal Proceedings*. London: HMSO.

Honess, T. M., Charman, E. A., Zani, B., Cicognani, E., Xerri, M. L., Jackson, A. E., & Bosma, H. A. (1997). Conflict between parents and adolescents: Variation by family constitution. *British Journal of Developmental Psychology*, 15, 367–385.

Hong, J. S., & Espelage, D. L. (2012). A review of research on bullying and peer victimization in school: An ecological system analysis. *Aggression and Violent Behaviour*, 17, 311–322.

Hoogeven, L., van Hell, J. G., & Verhoeven, L. (2012). Social-emotional characteristics of gifted accelerated and non-accelerated students in the Netherlands. *British Journal of Educational Psychology*, 82 (4), 585–605.

Horsthemke, K., & Kissack, M. (2008). Vorleben: Educational practice beyond prescription. *Journal of Curriculum Studies*, 40 (3), 277–288.

Horwitz, S. M., Irwin, J. R., Briggs-Gowan, M. J., Bosson, H. J., Mendoza, J., & Carter, A. S. (2003). Language delay in a community cohort of young children. *Journal of the American Academy of Child and Adolescent Psychiatry*, 42 (8), 932–940.

Hosseini, S., Tawil, A., Jahankhani, H., & Yarandi, M. (2013). Towards an ontological learners' modelling approach for personalised e-learning. *International Journal of Emerging Technologies in Learning*, 8 (2), 4–10.

House, R. (2011). *Too Much, Too Soon? Early Learning and the Erosion of Childhood*. Stroud: Hawthorn Press.

Howard, J., Jenvey, V., & Hill, C. (2006). Children's categorisation of play and learning based on social context. *Early Child Development and Care*, 176 (3 & 4), 379–393.

Howe, C. (1993). Peer interaction and knowledge acquisition. *Social Development* (Special issue), 2 (3).

Howe, C., & Mercer, N. (2007). *Children's Social Development, Peer Interaction and Classroom Learning (Primary Review Research Survey 2/1b)*. Cambridge: University of Cambridge Faculty of Education.

Howe, M. L., & Courage, M. L. (1997). The emergence and early development of autobiographical memory. *Psychological Review*, 104, 499–523.

Howes, C. (1983). Patterns of friendship. *Child Development*, 54, 1041–1053.

Howes, C. (1987). Social competence with peers in young children: Developmental sequences. *Developmental Review*, 7, 252–272.

Hsu, C. C., Soong, W. T., Stigler, J. W., Hong, C. C., & Liang, C. C. (1981). The temperamental characteristics of Chinese babies. *Child Development*, 52, 1337–1340.

Hsu, V. C., & Rovee-Collier, C. (2006). Memory reactivation in the second year of life. *Infant Behavior and Development*, 29 (1), 91–107.

Huan-Yu, L., Shian-Shyong, T., Jui-Feng, W., & Jun-Ming, S. (2009). Design and implementation of an object oriented learning activity system. *Journal of Educational Technology and Society*, 12 (3), 248–265.

Huber, S. G., & Grdel, B. (2006). Quality assurance in the German school system. *European Educational Research Journal*, 5 (3–4), 196–209.

Hudson, B. (2006). User outcomes and children's services reform: Ambiguity and conflict in the policy implementation process. *Social Policy and Society*, 5 (2), 227–236.

Hughes, C. (1999). Identifying critical social interaction behaviors among high school students with and without disabilities. *Behavior Modification*, 23, 41–60.

Hughes, C., Jaffee, S. R., Happe, F., Taylor, A., Caspi, A., & Moffitt, T. E. (2006). Origins of individual differences in theory of mind: From nature to nurture? *Child Development*, 76 (2), 356–370.

Hughes, C., White, A., Sharpen, J., & Dunn, J. (1998). Antisocial, angry, and unsympathetic: 'Hard to manage' preschoolers' peer problems and possible cognitive influences. *Journal of Child Psychology and Psychiatry*, 41, 169–179.

Hughes, J., & Sharrock, W. (1997). *The Philosophy of Social Research*. London: Longman.

Hughes, J., Cavell, T., & Grossman, P. (1997). A positive view of self: Risk or protection for aggressive children? *Development and Psychopathology*, 9, 75–94.

Hughes, M. (1981). Can preschool children add and subtract? *Educational Psychology*, 3, 207–219.

Hughes, M. W. H., & Longman, D. (2006). Whole class teaching strategies and interactive technology: Towards a connectionist classroom. British Educational Research Association Conference, University of Warwick, 5–7 September 2006.

Hunting, R. P., & Sharpley, C. F. (1988). Fractional knowledge in preschool children. *Journal for Research in Mathematics Education*, 19 (2), 175–180.

Hussain, Z., & Griffiths, M. D. (2014). Qualitative analysis of online gaming: Social interaction, community, and game design. *International Journal of Cyber Behavior, Psychology and Learning*, 4, 41–57.

Huston, A. C., Wright, J. C., Marquis, J., & Green, S. B. (1999). How young children spend their time: Television and other activities. *Developmental Psychology*, 35, 912–925.

Hutchings, J., Bywater, T., Daley, D., Gardner, F., Jones, K., Eames, C., Tudor-Edwards, R., & Whitakker, C. (2007). A pragmatic randomised control trial of a parenting intervention in Sure Start services for children at risk of developing conduct disorder. *British Medical Journal*, 334, 678–682.

Huttenlocher, J., Haight, W., Byrk, A., Seltzer, M., & Lyons, T. (1991). Early vocabulary growth: Relation to language input and gender. *Developmental Psychology*, 27 (2), 236–248.

Huttenlocher, P. R. (1990). Morphometric study of human cerebral cortex development. *Neuropsychologia*, 28, 517–527.

Huttenlocher, P. R. (1994). Synaptogenesis in human cerebral cortex. In G. Dawson & K. W. Fischer (Eds.), *Human Behaviour and the Developing Brain* (137–152). New York: Guildford.

Hyde, J. S. (2005). The gender similarities hypothesis. *American Psychologist*, 60 (6), 581–592.

Hyvonen, P. (2008). Teachers' perceptions of boys' and girls' shared activities in the school context: Towards a theory of collaborative play. *Teachers and Teaching: Theory and Practice*, 14 (5–6), 391–409.

Imbo, I., & Vandierendonck, A. (2007). The development of strategy use in elementary school children: Working memory and individual differences. *Journal of Experimental Child Psychology*, 96, 284–309.

Infantino, J., & Little, E. (2005). Students' perceptions of classroom behaviour problems and the effectiveness of different disciplinary methods. *Educational Psychology*, 25 (5), 491–508.

Inhelder, B., & Piaget, J. (1958). *The Growth of Logical Thinking from Childhood to Adolescence*. New York: Basic Books.

Inoue, K., Nadaoka, T., Oiji, A., Morioka, Y., Totsuka, S., Kanbayashi, Y., & Hukui, T. (1998). Clinical evaluation of attention-deficit hyperactivity disorder by objective quantitative measures. *Child Psychiatry and Human Development*, 28, 179–188.

Isabella, R. A. (1993). Origins of attachment: Maternal interactive behavior across the first year. *Child Development*, 64, 605–621.

Isabella, R. A. (1995). The origins of the infant–mother attachment: Maternal behavior and infant development. *Annals of Child Development*, 10, 57–81.

Izard, C. E. (1994). Innate and universal facial expressions: Evidence from developmental and cross-cultural research. *Psychological Bulletin*, 115, 288–299.

Jacobs, E., Miller, L., & Tirella, L. (2010). Developmental and behavioral performance of internationally adopted preschoolers: A pilot study. *Child Psychiatry and Human Development*, 41 (1), 15–29.

James, W. (1890). *The Principles of Psychology*. New York: Holt.

James, W. (1961). *Psychology: The Briefer Course* (originally published 1892). New York: Harper & Row.

James, W. (1892). *Psychology*. American science series, briefer course. New York: Henry Holt & Co.

Jang, H., Song, J. & Kim, R. (2014). Does the offline bully-victimization influence cyberbullying behavior among youths? Application of General Strain Theory. *Computers in Human Behaviour*, 31, 85–93.

Janssen, F., Westbroek, H., & Driel, J. (2014). How to make guided discovery learning practical for student teachers. *Instructional Science*, 42 (1), 67–90.

Jasinskaja-Lahti, I., & Liebkind, K. (2001). Perceived discrimination and psychological adjustment among Russian-speaking immigrant adolescents in Finland. *International Journal of Psychology*, 36 (3), 174–185.

Jellinek, M. S., & McDermott, J. (2004). Formulation: Putting the diagnosis into a therapeutic context and treatment plan. *Child and Adolescent Psychiatry*, 43 (7), 913–916.

Jensen, P. S., Hinshaw, S. P., Kraemer, H. P. et al. (2001). ADHD comorbidity findings from MTA study: Comparing comorbid subgroups. *Journal of the American Academy of Child and Adolescent Psychiatry*, 40, 147–158.

Jerome, A. C., Fujiki, M., Brinton, B., & James, S. L. (2002). Self-esteem in children with specific language impairment. *Journal of Speech, Language and Hearing Research*, 45, 700–714.

Jin, M. K., Jacobvitz, D., Hazen, N., & Jung, S. H. (2012). Maternal sensitivity and infant attachment security in Korea: Cross-cultural validation of the Strange Situation. *Attachment and Human Development*, 14, 33–44.

Johnson, M. H. (2001). Functional brain development in infancy. In G. Bremner & A. Fogel (Eds.), *Blackwell Handbook of Infant Development* (169–190). Oxford: Blackwell.

Johnson, M. H. (2002). The development of visual attention in early infancy: A cognitive neuroscience perspective. In M. H. Johnson, Y. Munakata, & R. O. Gilmore (Eds.), *Brain Development and Cognition: A Reader* (134–150). Oxford: Blackwell.

Johnson, M. H., Munakata, Y., & Gilmore, R. O. (Eds.) (2002). *Brain Development and Cognition: A Reader*. Oxford: Blackwell.

Johnston, C., & Mash, E. J. (2001). Families of children with attention-deficit/hyperactivity disorder: Review and recommendations for future research. *Clinical Child and Family Psychology Review*, 4, 183–207.

Johnstone, L. (2006). Controversies and debates about formulation. In R. Dallos and L. Johnstone (Eds.), *Formulation in Psychology and Psychotherapy*. Abingdon: Taylor & Francis.

Jokela, M., Power, C., & Kivimäki, M. (2009). Childhood problem behaviours and injury risk over the life course. *Journal of Child Psychology and Psychiatry*, 50, (12), 1541–1549.

Jones, J. M. (1997). *Prejudice and Racism* (2nd Ed.). New York: McGraw-Hill.

Jones, K., Daley, D., Hutchings, J., Bywater, T., & Eames, C. (2007). Efficacy of the Incredible Years intervention for children with ADHD. *Child: Care Health and Development*, 33, 749–756.

Jones, K., Daley, D., Hutchings, J., Bywater, T., & Eames, C. (2008). Efficacy of the Incredible Years intervention for children with conduct problems and ADHD: Long-term follow-up. *Child: Care, Health and Development*, 34, 380–390.

Jones, W., & Klin, A. (2013). Attention to eyes is present but in decline in 2–6-month-old infants later diagnosed with autism. *Nature*, 504 (7480), 423–431.

Jordan, F. M., & Murdoch, B. E. (1993). A prospective study of the linguistic skills of children with closed-head injury. *Aphasiology*, 7, 503–512.

Jorgensen, K. (1999). Pain assessment and management in the newborn infant. *Journal of Perianesthesia Nursing*, 14, 349–356.

Joseph, J. (2001). Separated twins and the genetics of personality differences: A critique. *American Journal of Psychology*, 114, 1–30.

Jusczyk, P. W., Houston, D., & Goodman, M. (1998). Speech perception during the first year. In A. Slater (Ed.), *Perceptual Development: Visual, Auditory and Speech Perception in Infancy* (357–388). Hove: Psychology Press.

Juvonen, J. & Graham, S. (2014). Bullying in schools: The power of bullies and the plight of victims. *Annual Review of Psychology*, 65, 159–185.

Kadesjo, B., Gillberg, C., & Hagberg, B. (1999). Brief report: Autism and Aspergers syndrome in seven-year-old children. *Journal of Autism and Developmental Disorder*, 29, 327–331.

Kadesjo, C., Kadesjo, B., Hagglof, B., & Gillberg, C. (2001). ADHD in Swedish 3- to 7-year-old children. *Journal of the American Academy of Child and Adolescent Psychiatry*, 40, 1021–1028.

Kagan, J. (1989). Temperamental contributions to social behaviour. *American Psychologist*, 44, 668–674.

Kagan, J. (1991). Continuity and discontinuity in development. In S. E. Brauth, W. S. Hall, & R. J. Dooling (Eds.), *Plasticity of Development* (11–26). Cambridge, MA: MIT Press.

Kagan, J. (1994). *Galen's Prophecy*. New York: Basic Books.

Kagan, J. (1998). Biology and the child. In N. Eisenberg (Ed.), *Handbook of Child Psychology: Vol. 3, Social, Emotional, and Personality Development* (5th Ed., 177–236). New York: Wiley.

Kagan, J. (1999). The concept of behavioral inhibition. In L. A. Schmidt & J. Schulkin (Eds.), *Extreme Fear, Shyness, and Social Phobia: Origins, Biological Mechanisms, and Clinical Outcomes* (3–13). New York: Oxford University Press.

Kagan, J. (2003). Behavioral inhibition as a temperamental category. In R. J. Davidson, K. R. Scherer, & H. H. Goldsmith (Eds.), *Handbook of Affective Science* (320–331). New York: Oxford University Press.

Kagan, J. (2008). In defense of qualitative changes in development. *Child Development*, 79, 1606–1624.

Kagan, J. (2013). Temperamental contributions to inhibited and uninhibited profiles. In P. D. Zelazo (Ed.), *The Oxford Handbook of Developmental Psychology: Vol. 2, Self and Others* (142–164). New York: Oxford University Press.

Kagan, J., & Herschkowitz, N. (2005). *A Young Mind in a Growing Brain*. Mahwah, NJ: Erlbaum.

Kagan, J., & Moss, H. A. (1983). *Birth to Maturity: A Study in Psychological Development* (2nd Ed.). Newhanen, CT: Yale University Press.

Kagan, J., Arcus, D., & Snidman, N. (1993a). The idea of temperament: Where do we go from here? In R. Plomin & G. E. McClearn (Eds.), *Nature, Nurture and Psychology* (197–210). Washington, DC: American Psychological Association.

Kagan, J., Arcus, D., Snidman, N., Feng, W. Y., Hendler, J., & Greene, S. (1994). Reactivity in infants: A cross-national comparison. *Developmental Psychology*, 30, 342–345.

Kagan, J., Kearsley, R., & Zelazo, P. (1978). *Infancy: Its Place in Human Development*. Cambridge, MA: Harvard University Press.

Kagan, J., Reznick, J. S., & Snidman, N. (1988). Childhood derivatives of high and low reactivity in infancy. *Child Development*, 69, 1483–1493.

Kagan, J., Snidman, N., & Arcus, D. (1993b). On the temperamental qualities of inhibited and uninhibited children. In K. H. Rubin & J. B. Asendorpf (Eds.), *Social Withdrawal, Inhibition, and Shyness in Childhood* (19–28). Hillsdale, NJ: Erlbaum.

Kaiser, F. (1946). *Der Nürnberger Trichter*. Nuremberg: Sebaldus-Verlag.

Kalter, H. (2003). Teratology in the 20th century: Environmental causes of congenital malformations in humans and how they were established. *Neurotoxicology and Teratology*, 25, 131–282.

Kamii, C., & Clark, F. B. (1995). Equivalent fractions: Their difficulty and educational implications. *Journal of Mathematical Behavior*, 14, 365–378.

Karalunas, S. L., Fair, D., Musser, E. D., Aykes, K., Iyer, W. P., & Nigg, J. T. (2014). Subtyping attention-deficit/ hyperactivity disorder using temperament dimensions: Toward biologically based nosologic criteria. *JAMA Psychiatry*, 71, 1015–1024.

Kärnä, A., Voeten, M., Little, T., Poskiparta, E., Kalijonen, A., & Salmivalli, C. (2011). A large-scale evaluation of the KiVa Antibullying Program: Grades 4–6. *Child Development*, 82, 311–330.

Karmiloff-Smith, A. (1998). Development itself is the key to understanding developmental disorders. *Trends in Cognitive Sciences*, 2, 389–398.

Karmiloff-Smith, A. (1999). The connectionist infant: Would Piaget turn in his grave? In A. Slater & D. Muir (Eds.), *The Blackwell Reader in Developmental Psychology* (43–52). Oxford: Blackwell.

Kaufman, B. A. (1994). Day by day: Playing and learning. *International Journal of Play Therapy*, 3 (1), 11–21.

Kaufman, J., Csibra, G., & Johnson, M. H. (2003a). Representing occluded objects in the infant brain. *Proceedings Royal Society London B* (Suppl.), 270, S140–S143.

Kaufman, J., Mareschal, D., & Johnson, M. H. (2003b). Graspability and object perception in infants. *Infant Behaviour and Development*, 26, 516–528.

Kaukiainen, A., Bjorkqvist, K., Lagerspetz, K., Osterman, K., Salmivalli, C., Rothberg, S., & Ahlbo, A. (1999). The relationships between social intelligence, empathy, and three types of aggression. *Aggressive Behaviour*, 25, 81–89.

Kave, G., & Yafe, R. (2014). Performance of younger and older adults on tests of word knowledge and word retrieval: Independence or interdependence of skills? *American Journal of Speech-Language Pathology*, 23 (1), 36–45.

Kave, G., Knafo, A., & Gilboa, A. (2010). The rise and fall of word retrieval across the lifespan. *Psychology and Aging*, 25 (3), 719–724.

Kavšek, M., Yonas, A., & Granrud, C. E. (2012). Infants' sensitivity to pictorial depth cues: A review and meta-analysis of looking studies. *Infant Behaviour and Development*, 35, 109–128.

Kaye, K. (1977). Toward the origin of dialogue. In H. R. Schaffer (Ed.), *Studies in Mother–Infant Interaction* (89–117). London: Academic Press.

Kaye, K., & Brazelton, T. B. (1971). Mother–infant interaction in the organisation of sucking. Society for Research in Child Development, Minneapolis, MN, 1–4 April.

Kaye, K., & Wells, A. J. (1980). Mothers' jiggling and the burst–pause pattern in neonatal feeding. *Infant Behaviour and Development*, 3, 29–46.

Keating, D. (1980). Thinking processes in adolescence. In J. Adelson (Ed.), *Handbook of Adolescent Psychology* (211–246). New York: Wiley.

Keil, F. C. (2006). Cognitive science and cognitive development. In W. Damon & R. Lerner (Series Eds.) and D. Kuhn & R. S. Siegler (Vol. Eds.), *Handbook of Child Psychology: Vol. 2, Cognition, Perception, and Language* (609–635). New York: Wiley.

Keil, F. C. (2008). Space – the primal frontier? Spatial cognition and the origins of concepts. *Philosophical Psychology*, 21, 241–250.

Kelemen, G. (2013). Improving teachers' professional training. *Journal Plus Education/Educatia Plus*, 9 (2), 27–32.

Keller, H., Yovsi, R., Borke, J., Kärtner, J., Jensen, H., & Papaligoura, Z. (2004). Developmental consequences of early parenting experiences: Self-recognition and self-regulation in three cultural communities. *Child Development*, 45, 1745–1760.

Keller, K., Troesch, L. M., & Grob, A. (2013). Shyness as a risk factor for second language acquisition of immigrant pre-schoolers. *Journal of Applied Developmental Psychology*, 34, 328–335.

Kendrick, W. (1994). *A Thing About Men, and a Thing About Women*. New York: Simon & Schuster.

Kenworthy, L., Yerys, B. E., Anthony, L. G., & Wallace, G. L. (2008). Understanding executive control in autism spectrum disorders in the lab and in the real world. *Neuropsychology Review*, 18 (4), 320–338.

Kessler, R. C., Chiu, W. T., Demler, O., & Walters, E. E. (2005). Prevalence, severity, and comorbidity of twelve-month DSM-IV disorders in the National Comorbidity Survey Replication (NCS-R). *Archives of General Psychiatry*, 62 (6), 617–627.

Ketelaars, M. P., van Weerdenburg, M., Verhoeven, L., Cuperus, J. M., & Jansonius, K. (2010). Dynamics of the theory of mind construct: A developmental perspective. *European Journal of Developmental Psychology*, 7 (1), 85–103.

Kett, J. F. (1977). *Rites of Passage: Adolescence in America, 1790 to the Present*. New York: Basic Books.

Kida, T., & Shinohara, K. (2013). Gentle touch activates the prefrontal cortex in infancy: An NIRS study. *Neuroscience Letters*, 541, 63–66.

Kieren, T. E. (1993). Rational and fractional numbers: From quotient fields to recursive understanding. In T. Carpenter, E. Fennema, & T. A. Romberg (Eds.), *Rational Numbers: An Integration of Research* (49–84). Hillsdale, NJ: Erlbaum.

Kiff, C. J., Lengua, L. J., & Zalewski, M. (2011). Nature and nurturing: Parenting in the context of child temperament. *Clinical Child and Family Psychology Review*, 14, 251–301.

Kim, J., Kim, M., & Kim, J. (2013). Social activities and health of Korean elderly women by age groups. *Educational Gerontology*, 39 (9), 640–654.

Kim, S., & Kochanska, G. (2012). Child temperament moderates effects of parent–child mutuality on self-regulation: A relationship-based path for emotionally negative infants. *Child Development*, 83, 1275–1289.

Kim, Y. S., Leventhal, B. L., Koh, Y. J., et al. (2011). Prevalence of autism spectrum disorders in a total population sample. *American Journal of Psychiatry*, 168 (9), 904–912.

Kim, Y-Y., Kim, M-H., & Oh, S. (2014). Emerging factors affecting the continuance of online gaming: The roles of bridging and bonding social factors. *Cluster Computing*, 17, 849–859.

Kingery, J. N., Erdley, C. A., & Marshall, K. C. (2011). Peer acceptance and friendship as predictors of early adolescents' adjustment across the middle school transition. *Merrill-Palmer Quarterly*, 57, 215–243.

Kisilevsky, B. S., Hains, S. M., Brown, C. C., Lee, C. T., Cowperthwaite, B., Stutzman, S. S., Swansburg, M. L., Lee, K., Xie, X., Huang, H., Ye, H. H., Zhang, K., & Wang, Z. (2009). Foetal sensitivity to properties of maternal speech and language. *Infant Behaviour and Development*, 32, 59–71.

Klapper, J. (2003). Taking communication to task? A critical review of recent trends in language teaching. *Language Learning Journal*, 27 (1), 33–42.

Klaus, M. H., Kennell, J. H., & Klaus, P. H. (1995). *Bonding: Building the Foundations of Secure Attachment and Independence*. Reading, MA: Addison-Wesley.

Klein, C., Wendling, K., Huettner, P., Ruder, H., & Peper, M. (2006). Intra-subject variability in attention-deficit hyperactivity disorder. *Biological Psychiatry*, 60 (10), 1088–1097.

Klingberg, T., Fernell, E., Olesen, P. J., Johnson, M., Gustafsson, P., Dahlstrom, K., Gillberg, C. G., Forssberg, H., & Westerberg, H. (2005). Computerized training of working memory in children with ADHD: A randomized, controlled trial. *Journal of the American Academy of Child and Adolescent Psychiatry*, 44, 177–186.

Knoblauch, K., Bieber, M. L., & Werner, J. S. (1998). M- and L-cones in early infancy: I. VEP responses to receptor-isolating stimuli at 4- and 8-weeks of age. *Vision Research*, 38, 1753–1764.

Kochanska, G., & Kim, S. (2013). Early attachment organization with both parents and future behaviour problems: From infancy to middle childhood. *Child Development*, 84, 283–296.

Kochanska, G., Gross, J. N., Lin, M. H., & Nichols, K. E. (2002). Guilt in young children: Development, determinants, and relations with a broader system of standards. *Child Development*, 73 (2), 461–482.

Koeboek, J., & Knoppers, A. (2015). The role of perceptions of friendships and peers in learning skills in physical education. *Physical Education and Sport Pedagogy*, 20, 231–249.

Kohlberg, L. (1963). The development of children's orientations towards a moral order I. Sequence in the development of moral thought. *Vita Humana*, 6, 11–33. Reprinted in *Human Development* (2008), 51, 8–20.

Kohlberg, L. (1966). A cognitive-developmental analysis of children's sex-role concepts and attitudes. In E. E. Maccoby (Ed.), *The Development of Sex Differences* (82–173). London: Tavistock.

Kohlberg, L. (1969). Stage and sequence: The cognitive-developmental approach to socialization. In D. A. Goslin (Ed.), *Handbook of Socialization Theory and Research* (347–480). Chicago, IL: Rand McNally.

Kohlberg, L. (1973). The claim to moral adequacy of a highest stage of moral judgment. *Journal of Philosophy*, 70 (18), 630–646.

Kohlberg, L. (1976). Moral stages and moralization: The cognitive-developmental approach. In T. Lickona (Ed.), *Moral Development and Behavior: Theory, Research and Social Issues* (31–53). New York: Holt, Rinehart, & Winston.

Kohlberg, L. (1981). *Essays on Moral Development: Vol. 1, The Philosophy of Moral Development*. San Francisco, CA: Harper & Row.

Kohnstamm, G. A. (1989). Temperament in childhood: Cross-cultural and sex differences. In G. A. Kohnstramm, J. E. Bates, & M. K. Rothbart (Eds.), *Temperament in Childhood* (321–356). Chichester: Wiley.

Kolak, A. M., & Volling, B. L. (2013). Coparenting moderates the association between firstborn children's temperament and problem behaviour across the transition to siblinghood. *Journal of Abnormal Psychology*, 27, 355–364.

Kollins, S., Greenhill, L., Swanson, J., Wigal, S., Abikoff, H., McCracken, J., Riddle, M., McGough, J., Vitiello, B., Wigal, T., Skrobala, A., Posner, K., Ghuman, J., Davies, M., Cunningham, C., & Bauzo, A. (2006). Rationale, design, and methods of the Preschool ADHD Treatment Study (PATS). *Journal of the American Academy of Child and Adolescent Psychiatry*, 45, 1275–1283.

Konrad, K., Neufang, S., Hanisch, C., Fink, G. R., & Herpertz-Dahlmann, B. (2006). Dysfunctional attentional networks in children with attention deficit/hyperactivity disorder: Evidence from an event-related functional magnetic resonance imaging study. *Biological Psychiatry*, 59, 643–651.

Kornilaki, E. (1999). *Young Children's Understanding of Multiplicative Concepts: A Psychological Approach*. London: University of London.

Kornilaki, E., & Nunes, T. (2005). Generalising principles in spite of procedural differences: Children's understanding of division. *Cognitive Development*, 20, 388–406.

Kosciw, J. G., Greytak, E. A., Bartkiewicz, M. J., Boesen, M. J. & Palmer, N. A. (2012). *The 2011 National School Climate Survey: The Experiences of Lesbian, Gay, Bisexual and Transgender Youth in Our Nation's Schools*. New York: The Gay, Lesbian & Straight Education Network, www.glsen.org.

Kouwenberg, M., Rieffe, C., & Banerjee, R. (2013). Developmetrics: A balanced and short Best Friend Index for children and young adolescents. *European Journal of Developmental Psychology*, 10, 634–641.

Kowalski, R. M., & Limber, S. P. (2007). Electronic bullying among middle school students. *Journal of Adolescent Health*, 41, S22–S30.

Kowalski, R. M. & Limber, S. P. (2013). Psychological, physical, and academic correlates of cyberbullying and traditional bullying. *Journal of Adolescent Health*, 53, S13-S20.

Kowalski, R., Limber, S., & Agatston, P. (2008). *Cyber Bullying: Bullying in the Digital Age*. Malden, MA: Blackwell.

Krahe, B., & Moller, I. (2004). Playing violent electronic games, hostile attributional style, and aggression-related norms in German adolescents. *Journal of Adolescence*, 27 (1), 53–69.

Kramer, A. F., & Willis, S. L. (2003). Cognitive plasticity and aging. *Psychology of Learning and Motivation*, 43, 267–302.

Krampe, R. Th., & Ericsson, K.A. (1996). Maintaining excellence: Deliberate practice and elite performance in young and older pianists. *Journal of Experimental Psychology: General*, 125, 331–359.

Krebs, G., Squire, S., & Bryant, P. (2003). Children's understanding of the additive composition of number and of the decimal structure: What is the relationship? *International Journal of Educational Research*, 39, 677–694.

Kuczaj, S. (1982). The acquisition of word meaning in the context of the development of the semantic system. In C. Brainerd & M. Pressley (Eds.), *Progress in Cognitive Development Research: Vol. 2, Verbal Processes in Children* (95–123). New York: Springer.

Kuhl, P., & Rivera-Gaxiola, M. (2008). Neural substrates of language acquisition. *Annual Review of Neuroscience*, 31, 511–534.

Kuhn, D., Nash, S. C., & Brucken, L. (1978). Sex role concepts of two- and three-year-olds. *Child Development*, 49, 445–451.

Kuhn, E., Phan, J., & Laird, R. (2014). Compliance with parents' rules: Between-person and within-person predictions. *Journal of Youth and Adolescence*, 43 (2), 245–256.

Kumada, T., Komuro, Y., Li, Y., Littner, Y., & Komuro, H. (2011). Neuronal cell migration in foetal alcohol syndrome. In V. R. Preedy et al. (Eds.), *Handbook of Behaviour, Food and Nutrition* (2915–2930). New York: Springer.

Kummel, D. A., Seligson, F. H., & Guthrie, H. A. (1996). Hyperactivity: Is candy causal? *Critical Review in Food Science*, 36, 31.

Ladd, G. W., & Burgess, K. B. (1999). Charting the relationship trajectories of aggressive, withdrawn, and aggressive/withdrawn children during early grade school. *Child Development*, 70, 910–929.

Lagercrantz, H., & Changeux, J.-P. (2009). The emergence of human consciousness: From fetal to neonatal life. *Pediatric Research*, 65, 255–260.

Lagercrantz, H., & Changeux, J.-P. (2010). Basic consciousness of the newborn. *Seminars in Perinatology*, 34, 201–206.

Lagerspetz, K., Björkqvist, K., Berts, M., & King, E. (1982). Group aggression among school children in three schools. *Scandinavian Journal of Psychology*, 23, 45–52.

Lahey, B. B., Pelham, W. E., Loney, J., Kipp, H., Ehrhardt, A., Lee, S. S., Willcutt, E. G., Hartung, C. M., Chronis, A., & Massetti, G. (2004). Three year predictive validity of DSM-IV attention deficit hyperactivity disorder in children diagnosed at 4–6 years of age. *American Journal of Psychiatry*, 161, 2014–2020.

Lahey, B. B., Pelham, W. E., Stein, M. A., Loney, J., Trapani, C., Nugent, K., Kipp, H., Schmidt, E., Lee, S., Cale, M., Gold, E., Hartung, C. M., Willcutt, E., & Baumann, B. (1988). Validity of DSM IV attention deficit/hyperactivity disorder for younger children. *Journal of the American Academy of Child and Adolescent Psychiatry*, 37, 695–702.

Lakatos, K., Nemoda, Z., Birkas, E., Ronai, Z., Kovacs, E., Ney, K., Toth, I., Sasvari-Szekely, M., & Gervai, J. (2003). Association of D4 dopamine receptor gene and serotonin transporter promoter polymorphisms with infants' response to novelty. *Molecular Psychiatry*, 8, 90–97.

Lam, V. L., & Leman, P. J. (2003). The influence of gender and ethnicity on children's inferences about toy choice. *Social Development*, 12, 269–287.

Lam, V. L., & Leman, P. J. (2009). Children's gender- and ethnicity-based reasoning about foods. *Social Development*, 18, 478–496.

Lamb, M. (1987). Introduction: The emergent American father. In M. E. Lamb (Ed.), *The Father's Role: Crosscultural Perspectives* (3–25). Hillsdale, NJ: Erlbaum.

Lamb, M. E. (1997). The development of father–infant relationships. In M. E. Lamb (Ed.), *The Role of the Father in Child Development* (3rd Ed., 104–120). New York: Wiley.

Lamb, M. E. (1998). Nonparental child care: Context, quality, correlates, and consequences. In I. E. Sigel & K. A. Renninger (Eds.), *Handbook of Child Psychology: Vol. 4, Child Psychology in Practice* (5th Ed., 73–133). New York: Wiley.

Lamb, M. E. (2004). *The Role of the Father in Child Development*. London: Wiley.

Lamon, S. J. (1996). The development of unitizing: Its role in children's partitioning strategies. *Journal for Research in Mathematics Education*, 27, 170–193.

Lane, D. A. (1989). Bullying in school: The need for an integrated approach. In E. Roland & E. Munthe (Eds.), *Bullying: An International Perspective* (x–xiv). London: David Fulton.

Langer, A. (2003). Forms of workplace literacy using reflection-with-action methods: A scheme for inner-city adults. *Reflective Practice*, 4 (3), 317–333.

Langlois, J. H., & Downs, A. C. (1980). Mothers, fathers, and peers as socialization agents of sex-typed play behaviors in young children. *Child Development*, 51, 1237–1247.

Lanz, M., Iafrate, R., Rosnati, R., & Scabini, E. (1999). Parent–child communication and adolescent self-esteem in separated, intercountry adoptive and intact non-adoptive families. *Journal of Adolescence*, 22 (6), 785–794.

Larson, R. W. (2001). How US children and adolescents spend time: What it does (and doesn't) tell us about their development. *Current Directions in Psychological Science*, 10, 160–164.

Laville, S. (2009). Tracey Connelly: The story of a woman defined by abuse. *Guardian*, 11 August. Available at: http://www.theguardian.com/society/2009/aug/11/tracey-connelly-baby-p-mother

Lavonen, J., Juuti, K., Aksela, M., & Meisalo, V. (2006). A professional development project for improving the use of information and communication technologies in science teaching. *Technology, Pedagogy and Education*, 15 (2), 159–174.

Law, J., Garrett, Z., & Nye, C. (2004). Speech and language therapy interventions for children with primary speech and language delay or disorder. *Cochrane Collaboration Database of Systematic Reviews*, 2009, 4, CD004110.

Le Corre, M., & Carey, S. (2007). One, two, three, nothing more: An investigation of the conceptual sources of verbal number principles. *Cognition*, 105, 395–438.

Le Doux, J. (1999). *The Emotional Brain*. London: Phoenix.

Leach, F. (2003). Learning to be violent: The role of the school in developing adolescent gendered behaviour. *Compare*, 33 (3), 385–400.

Leader, L. R., Baille, P., & Martin, B. (1982). The assessment and significance of habituation to a repeated stimulus by the human foetus. *Early Human Development*, 7, 211–219.

Leaper, C. (1991). Influence and involvement in children's discourse: Age, gender and partner effects. *Child Development*, 62, 797–811.

Leaper, C. (2000). Gender, affiliation, assertion, and the interactive context of parent–child play. *Developmental Psychology*, 36, 381–393.

Leary, M. R. (2008). *Introduction to Behavioural Research Methods* (5th Ed.). Boston, MA: Pearson.

Lecompte, V., & Moss, E. (2014). Disorganized and controlling patterns of attachment, role reversal, and caregiving helplessness: Links to adolescents' externalizing problems. *American Journal of Orthopsychiatry*, 84, 591–589.

Lee, E. J. (2013). Differential susceptibility to effects of child temperament on maternal warmth and responsiveness. *Journal of Genetic Psychology*, 174, 429–449.

Lee, L., Stemple, J., Glaze, L., & Kelchner, L. (2004). Quick screen for voice and supplementary documents for identifying pediatric voice disorders. *Language, Speech, and Hearing Schools*, 35, 318–319.

Leech, D., & Campos, E. (2003). Is comprehensive education really free? A case-study of the effects of secondary school admissions policies on house prices in one local area. *Journal of the Royal Statistical Society: Series A (Statistics in Society)*, 166 (1), 135–154.

Leinonen, E., & Letts, C. (1997). Why pragmatic impairment? A case study in the comprehension of inferential meaning. *European Journal of Disorders of Communication*, 32, 35–52.

Leman, P. J., & Lam, V. L. (2008). The influence of race and gender on children's conversations and playmate choices. *Child Development*, 79, 1329–1343.

Leman, P. J., & Tenenbaum, H. R. (Eds.) (2014). *Gender and Development*. New York: Psychology Press.

Lemery, K. S., Goldsmith, H. H., Klinnert, M. D., & Mrazek, D. A. (1999). Developmental models of infant and childhood temperament. *Developmental Psychology*, 35, 189–204.

Lemmens, J. S., Valkenburg, P. M., & Peter, J. (2011). Psychosocial causes and consequences of pathological gaming. *Computers in Human Behavior*, 27, 144–152.

Lenneberg, E. (1967). *Biological Foundations of Language*. New York: Wiley.

Lenroot, R. K., & Giedd, J. N. (2006). Brain development in children and adolescents: Insights from anatomical magnetic resonance imaging. *Neuroscience and Behavioural Reviews*, 30, 718–729.

Leo, I., & Simion, F. (2009). Face processing at birth: A Thatcher Illusion Study. *Developmental Science*, 12, 492–498.

Lerner, J. V., & Galambos, N. L. (1985). Maternal role satisfaction, mother–infant interaction and child temperament. *Developmental Psychology*, 21, 1157–1164.

Leroux, G., Spiess, J., Zago, L., Rossi, S., Lubin, A., Turbelin, M. R., Mazoyer, B., Tzourio-Mazoyer, N., Houde, O., & Joliot, M. (2009). Adult brains don't fully overcome biases that lead to incorrect performance during cognitive development: An fMRI study in young adults completing a Piaget-like task. *Developmental Science*, 12, 326–338.

Leslie, A. M. (1987). Pretence and representation: The origins of 'theory of mind'. *Psychological Review*, 94, 412–426.

Leslie, A. M. (1994). Pretending and believing: Issues in the theory of ToM. *Cognition*, 50, 211–238.

Leslie, A. M., & Frith, U. (1988). Autistic children's understanding of seeing, knowing, and believing. *British Journal of Developmental Psychology*, 6, 315–324.

Leslie, A. M., & Thaiss, L. (1992). Domain specificity in conceptual development: Neuropsychological evidence from autism. *Cognition*, 43, 225–251.

Lester, B. M., Hoffman, J., & Brazelton, T. B. (1985). The rythmic structure of mother–infant interaction in term and preterm infants. *Child Development*, 56, 15–27.

Letcher, P., Sanson, A., Smart, D., & Toumbourou, J. W. (2012). Precursors and correlates of anxiety trajectories from childhood to late adolescence. *Journal of Clinical Child and Adolescent Psychology*, 41, 417–432.

Letcher, P., Smart, D., Sanson, A., & Toumbourou, J. (2009). Psychosocial precursors and correlates of differing internalizing trajectories from 3 to 15 years. *Social Development*, 18, 618–646.

Levin, J. R. (1976). What have we learned about maximising what children learn? In J. R. Levin and V. L. Allen (Eds.), *Cognitive Learning in Children: Theories and Strategies* (105–134). New York: Academic Press.

Levin, J. R., & Nolan, J. F. (2000). *Principles of Classroom Management: A Professional Decision-Making Model*. Boston, MA: Allyn & Bacon.

Levin, M. L., Xu, X. H., & Bartkowski, J. P. (2002). Seasonality of sexual debut. *Journal of Marriage and the Family*, 64, 871–884.

Levinson, S. C. (1983). *Pragmatics*. Cambridge: Cambridge University Press.

Levy, S. E., Mandell, D. S., & Schultz, R. T. (2009). Autism. *Lancet*, 374, 1627–1638.

Lewin, C., Somekh, B., & Steadman, S. (2008). Embedding interactive whiteboards in teaching and learning: The process of change in pedagogic practice. *Education and Information Technologies*, 13 (4), 291–303.

Lewis, A., & Mayer, R. (1987). Students' miscomprehension of relational statements in arithmetic word problems. *Journal of Educational Psychology*, 79, 363–371.

Lewis, A. J., & Olsson, C. A. (2011). Early life stress and child temperament style as predictors of childhood anxiety and depressive symptoms: Findings from the Longitudinal Study of Australian Children. *Depression Research and Treatment*, vol. 2011, Article ID 296026, 1–9.

Lewis, M. (1975). The development of attention and perception in the infant and young child. In W. M. Cruickshank & D. P. Hallahan (Eds.), *Perceptual and Learning Disabilities in Children* (Vol. 2, 137–162). Syracuse, NY: Syracuse University Press.

Lewis, M. (1990). Social knowledge and social development. *Merrill-Palmer Quarterly*, 36, 93–116.

Lewis, M. (1991). Ways of knowing: Objective self-awareness of consciousness. *Developmental Review*, 11, 231–243.

Lewis, M., & Brooks-Gunn, J. (1978). Self-knowledge and emotional development. In M. Lewis & L. A. Rosenblum (Eds.), *The Development of Affect* (205–226). New York: Plenum Press.

Lewis, M., & Brooks-Gunn, J. (1979). *Social Cognition and the Acquisition of Self*. New York: Plenum Press.

Lewis Graham, K., & Burghardt, G. M. (2010). Current perspectives on the biological study of play: Signs of progress. *Quarterly Review of Biology*, 85, 393–418.

Li, N., & Kirkup, G. (2007). Gender and cultural differences in internet use: A study of China and the UK. *Computers and Education*, 48 (2), 301–317.

Li, Z., van Aelst, L., & Cline, H. T. (2000). Rho GTPases regulate distinct aspects of dendritic arbor growth in Xenopus central neurons in vivo. *Nature Neuroscience*, 3, 217–225.

Libet, B., Wright, E. W., Feinstein, B., & Pearl, D. K. (1979). Subjective referencing of the timing for a conscious experience. *Brain*, 102, 193–224.

Liben, L. S., & Signorella, M. L. (1993). Gender-schematic processing in children: The role of initial interpretations of stimuli. *Developmental Psychology*, 29, 141–149.

Lickenbrock, D. M., Braungart-Rieker, J. M., Ekas, N. V., Zentall, S. R., Oshio, T., & Planalp, E. M. (2013). Early temperament and attachment security with mothers and fathers as predictors of toddler compliance and noncompliance. *Infant and Child Development*, 22, 580–602.

Liddell, C., & Rae, G. (2001). Predicting early grade retention: A longitudinal investigation of primary school progress in a sample of rural South African children. *British Journal of Educational Psychology*, 71 (3), 413–428.

Liebkind, K., & Jasinskaja-Lahti, I. (2000). Acculturation and psychological well-being among immigrant adolescents in Finland: A comparative study of adolescents from different cultural backgrounds. *Journal of Adolescent Research*, 15 (4), 446–469.

Likierman, H., & Muter, V. (2005). *ADHD and ADD*. Website ADHD Treatment Options – OmniMedicalSearch.com, retrieved 23 July 2010.

Liley, A. W. (1972). The foetus as a personality. *Australian and New Zealand Journal of Psychiatry*, 6, 99–103.

Lindsey, E. W., & Colwell, M. J. (2003). Preschoolers' emotional competence: Links to pretend and physical play. *Child Study Journal*, 33, 39–52.

Lindsey, E. W., & Colwell, M. J. (2013). Pretend and physical play: Links to preschoolers' affective social competence. *Merrill-Palmerly Quarterly*, 59, 330–360.

Lipkin, P. H. (2005). Towards creation of a unified view of the neurodevelopment of the infant. *Mental Retardation and Developmental Disabilities Research Reviews*, 11, 103–106.

Livingstone, S., & Bovill, M. (2001). *Children and Their Changing Media Environment: A European Comparative Study*. Mahwah, NJ: Erlbaum.

Lloyd, B., & Duveen, G. (1992). *Gender Identities and Education: The Impact of Starting School*. London: Harvester Wheatsheaf.

Lo, S. L., Vroman, L. N., & Durbin, E. (2014). Ecological validity of laboratory assessments of child temperament: Evidence from parent perspectives. *Psychological Assessment*, online first publication, October, 1–11.

Locke, A., Ginsborg, J., & Peers, I. (2001). Development and disadvantage: Implications for the early years and beyond. *International Journal of Language and Communication Disorders*, 37 (1), 3–15.

Locke, J. (1690). *Concerning Human Understanding*. Retrieved 14 October 2010 from http://arts.cuhk.edu.hk/Philosophy/Locke/echu/.

Lodge, C. (2002). Tutors talking. *Pastoral Care in Education*, 20 (4), 35–37.

Loftus, E. F. (1993). The reality of repressed memories. *American Psychologist*, 48 (5), 518–537.

Longmore, M. A., Manning, W. D., & Giordano, P. C. (2001). Preadolescent parenting strategies and teens' dating and sexual initiation: A longitudinal analysis. *Journal of Marriage and Family*, 63, 322–335.

Lorberbaum, J. P., Newman, J. D., Horwitz, A. R., Dubno, J. D., Lydiard, R. B., Hamner, M. B., Bohning, D. E., & George, M. S. (2002). A potential role for thalamocingulate circuitry in human maternal behaviour. *Biological Psychiatry*, 51, 431–445.

Lorenz, K. (1952). *King Solomon's Ring*. New York: Crowell.

Lorenz, K. (1966). *On Aggression*. London: Methuen.

Louis, J., Cannard, C., Bastuji, H., & Challamel, M. J. (1997). Sleep ontogenesis revisited: A longitudinal 24-hour home polygraphic study on 15 normal infants during the first 2 years of life. *Sleep*, 20, 323–333.

Love, J., Harrison, L., Sagi-Schwartz, A., van IJzendoorn, M., Ross, C., Ungerer, J., Raikes, H., Brady-Smith, C., Boller, K., Brooks-Gunn, J., Constantine, J., Kisker, E., Paulsell, D., & Chazan-Cohen, R. (2003). Child care quality matters: How conclusions may vary with context. *Child Development*, 74, 1021–1033.

Lummaa, V., Vuorisalo, T., Barr, R. G., & Lehtonen, L. (1998). Why cry? Adaptive significance of intensive crying in human infants. *Evolution and Human Behaviour*, 19, 193–202.

Lwin, S., Goh, C., & Doyle, P. (2012). 'I'm going to split you all up': Examining transitions to group/pair work in two primary English classrooms. *Language and Education: An International Journal*, 26 (1), 19–33.

Lyle, S., & Hendley, D. (2007). Can portfolios support critical reflection? Assessing the portfolios of Schools Liaison Police Officers. *Journal of In-Service Education*, 33 (2), 189–207.

Lyons-Ruth, K., Bronfman, E., & Parsons, E. (1999). Maternal frightened, frightening or atypical behavior and disorganized infant attachment patterns. In J. E. Vondna and D. Barnett (Eds.), *Atypical Attachment in Infancy and Early Childhood among Children at Developmental Risk. Monographs of the Society for Research in Child Development*, 64 (3), Serial No. 258, 67–96.

Lyons-Ruth, K., Repacholi, B., McLeod, S., & Silva, E. (1991). Disorganized attachment behavior in infancy: Short-term stability, maternal and infant correlates and risk-related subtypes. *Development and Psychopathology*, 3, 377–396.

Lytton, H., & Romney, D. M. (1991). Parents' differential socialization of boys and girls: A meta-analysis. *Psychological Bulletin*, 109, 267–296.

Maas, W. (2000). Early detection of speech and language delays in the Netherlands: The case for integrating primary and secondary prevention. *Child: Care, Health and Development*, 26 (2), 150–162.

Maccoby, E. E. (1980). *Social Development, Psychological Growth and the Parent–Child Relationship*. New York: Harcourt Brace Jovanovich.

Maccoby, E. E. (1988). Gender as a social category. *Developmental Psychology*, 24, 755–765.

Maccoby, E. E. (1990). Gender and relationships: A developmental account. *American Psychologist*, 45, 513–520.

Maccoby, E. E. (1998). *The Two Sexes: Growing up Apart, Coming Together*. Cambridge, MA: Harvard University Press.

Maccoby, E. E. (2000). Perspectives on gender development. *International Journal of Behavioral Development*, 24, 398–406.

Maccoby, E. E. (2002). Gender and group process: A developmental perspective. *Current Directions in Psychological Science*, 11, 54–58.

Maccoby, E. E., & Jacklin, C. N. (1974). *The Psychology of Sex Differences*. Stanford, CA: Stanford University Press.

Macdonald, H. (2002). Perinatal care at the threshold of viability. *Pediatrics*, 110, 1024–1027.

MacFarlane, A. (1975). Olfaction in the development of social preferences in the human neonate. In *Parent–Infant Interaction* (CIBA Foundation Symposium No. 33) (103–117). Amsterdam: Elsevier.

MacLean, P. D. (Ed.) (1990). *The Triune Brain in Evolution: Role in Paleocerebral Functions*. New York: Plenum.

Madsen, K. C. (1996). Differing perceptions of bullying and their practical implications. *Education and Child Psychology*, 13, 14–22.

Maguire, M., & Dunn, J. (1997). Friendships in early childhood and social understanding. *International Journal of Behavioral Development*, 21, 669–686.

Mahady-Wilton, M. M., Craig, W. M., & Pepler, D. J. (2000). Emotional regulation and display in classroom victims of bullying: Characteristic expressions of affect, coping styles and relevant contextual factors. *Social Development*, 9, 226–246.

Main, M., & Cassidy, J. (1988). Categories of responses to reunion with the parent at age 6: Predictable for infant classifications and stable over a 1-month period. *Developmental Psychology*, 24, 415–426.

Main, M., & Goldwyn, R. (1994). Adult attachment and classification system. Unpublished manuscript. University of California, Berkeley.

Main, M., & Hesse, E. (1990). Parents' unresolved traumatic experiences are related to infant disorganized attachment status: Is frightened and/or frightening parental behavior the linking mechanism? In M. T. Greenberg, D. Cicchetti, & E. M. Cummings (Eds.), *Attachment During the Preschool Years: Theory, Research and Intervention* (161–182). Chicago, IL: University of Chicago Press.

Main, M., & Solomon, J. (1990). Procedures for identifying disorganized/disoriented infants during the Ainsworth Strange Situation. In M. Greenberg, D. Cicchetti, & M. Cummings (Eds.), *Attachment in the Preschool Years: Theory, Research and Intervention* (121–160). Chicago, IL: University of Chicago Press.

Main, M., Kaplan, N., & Cassidy, J. (1985). Security in infancy, childhood, and adulthood: A move to the level of representation. In I. Bretherton & E. E. Waters (Eds.), *Growing Points of Attachment Theory and Research. Monographs of the Society for Research in Child Development*, 50, 66–104.

Maines, B., & Robinson, G. (1991). Don't beat the bullies! *Educational Psychology in Practice*, 7, 168–172.

Maines, B., & Robinson, G. (1992). *The No-Blame Approach*. Bristol: Lucky Duck.

Maines, B., & Robinson, G. (1998). The no-blame approach to bullying. In D. Shorrocks-Taylor (Ed.), *Directions in Educational Psychology* (281–295). London: Whurr.

Mamede, E. P. B. d. C. (2007). The effects of situations on children's understanding of fractions. Unpublished Ph.D. thesis, Oxford Brookes University, Oxford.

Mamede, E. (2009). Early years mathematics. The case of fractions. In V. Durand-Guerrier, S. Soury-Lavergne, & F. Arzarello (Eds.), *CERME 6, Proceedings of the Sixth Congress of the European Society for Research in Mathematics Education* (2607–2616). Lyon: Institut National de Recherche Pédagogique.

Mamede, E., & Nunes, T. (2008). Building on children's informal knowledge in the teaching of fractions. In *Proceedings of the Joint Meeting of PME32 and PME-N*, 3, 345–352.

Mamede, E., Nunes, T., & Bryant, P. (2005). The equivalence of ordering of fractions in part-whole and quotient situations. In W. Chick & J. L. Vincent (Eds.), *Proceedings of the 29th Conference of the International*

Group for the Psychology of Mathematics Education (3-281-3-288), Melbourne: PME.

Mampe, B., Friederici, A. D., Christophe, A., & Wermke, K. (2009). Newborns' cry melody is shaped by their native language. *Current Biology*, 19, 1994–1997.

Mandler, J. M. (2003). Conceptual categorization. In D. H. Rakison & L. M. Oakes (Eds.), *Early Category and Concept Development: Making Sense of the Blooming, Buzzing Confusion* (103–131). Oxford: Oxford University Press.

Mandler, J. M., & McDonough, L. M. (1993). Concept formation in infancy. *Cognitive Development*, 8, 291–318.

Mangelsdorf, S. C., Schoppe, S. J., & Buur, H. (2000). The meaning of parental reports: A contextual approach to the study of temperament and behavior problems. In V. J. Molfese & D. L. Molfese (Eds.), *Temperament and Personality Across the Life Span* (121–140). Mahwah, NJ: Erlbaum.

Mannuzza, S., Klein, R. G., Bessler, A., Malloy, P., & La-Padula, M. (1993). Adult outcome of hyperactive boys: Educational achievement, occupational rank, and psychiatric status. *Archives of General Psychiatry*, 50, 565–576.

Margison, F. R., McGrath, G., Barkham, M., Mellor-Clark, J., Audin, K., Connell, J., & Evans, C. (2000). Measurement and psychotherapy: Evidence-based practice and practice-based evidence. *British Journal of Psychiatry*, 177, 123–130.

Mariani, M., & Barkley, R. A. (1997). Neuropsychological and academic functioning in preschool children with attention deficit hyperactivity disorder. *Developmental Neuropsychology*, 13, 111–129.

Marland, M. (2002). From 'form teacher' to 'tutor': The development from the fifties to the seventies. *Pastoral Care in Education*, 20 (4), 3–11.

Marsh, H. W., Craven, R., & Debus, R. (1998). Structure, stability, and development of young children's self-concepts: A multicohort-multioccasion study. *Child Development*, 69, 1030–1053.

Marshall, J., Chinna, U., Hok, U., Tinon, S., Veasna, M., & Nissay, P. (2012). Student achievement and education system performance in a developing country. *Educational Assessment, Evaluation and Accountability*, 24 (2), 113–134.

Martel, M. M., Nigg, J. T., & von Eye, A. (2009). How do trait dimensions map onto ADHD symptom domains? *Journal of Abnormal Child Psychology*, 37, 337–348.

Martin, C. L. (1993). New directions for investigating children's gender knowledge. *Developmental Review*, 13, 184–204.

Martin, C. L., & Halverson, C. F. (1981). A schematic processing model of sex typing and stereotyping in children. *Child Development*, 52, 1119–1134.

Martin, C. L., & Halverson, C. F. (1983). The effects of sex-typing schemas on young children's memory. *Child Development*, 54, 563–574.

Martin, C. L., & Halverson, C. F. (1987). The role of cognition in sex role acquisition. In D. B. Carter (Ed.), *Current Conceptions of Sex Roles and Sex Typing: Theory and Research* (123–137). New York: Praeger.

Martin, C. L., Eisenbud, L., & Rose, H. (1995). Children's gender-based reasoning about toys. *Child Development*, 66, 1453–1471.

Martin, C. L., Fabes, R. A., Evans, S. M., & Wyman, H. (1999). Social cognition on the playground: Children's beliefs about playing with girls versus boys and their relations to sex segregated play. *Journal of Social and Personal Relationships*, 16, 751–771.

Martin, C. L., Kornienko, O., Schaefer, D. F., Hanish, L. D., Fabes, R. A., & Goble, P. (2013). The role of sex of peers and gender-typed activities in young children's peer affiliative networks: A longitudinal analysis of selection and influence. *Child Development*, 81, 921–937.

Martinussen, R., Hayden, J., Hogg-Johnson, S., & Tannock, R. (2005). A meta-analysis of working memory impairments in children with attention-deficit/hyperactivity disorder. *Journal of the American Academy of Child and Adolescent Psychiatry*, 44, (4), 377–384.

Marzano, R. J., & Marzano, J. S. (2003). The key to classroom management. *Educational Leadership*, 61 (1), 6–13.

Maschietto, M., & Bussi, M. B. (2009). Working with artefacts: Gestures, drawings and speech in the construction of the mathematical meaning of the visual pyramid. *Educational Studies in Mathematics*, 70 (2), 143–157.

Masten, A. S., & Cicchetti, D. (2010). Developmental cascades. *Development and Psychopathology*, 22, 491–495.

Mathieson, L. C., Murray-Close, D., Crick, N. R., Woods, K. E., Zimmer-Gembeck, M., Geiger, T. C. & Morales, J. R. (2011). Hostile intent attributions and relational aggression: The moderating roles of emotional sensitivity, gender, and victimization. *Journal of Abnormal Psychology*, 39, 977–987.

Mays, D. (2012). Tackling illiteracy in Year 7 of the comprehensive school. *Support For Learning*, 27 (3), 123–128.

Mayseless, O. (2006). *Parenting Representations: Theory, Research and Clinical Implications*. New York: Cambridge University Press.

McBryde, C., Ziviani, J., & Cuskelly, M. (2004). School readiness and factors that influence decision making. *Occupational Therapy International*, 11 (4), 193–208.

McCann, D., Barrett, A., Cooper, A., Crumpler, D., Dalen, L., Grimshaw, K., Kitchin, E., Lok, K., Porteous, L., Prince, E., Sonuga-Barke, E. J. S., Warner, J. O., & Stevenson, J. (2007). Food additives and hyperactive behaviour in 3 year-old and 8/9-year-old children in the community: A randomised, double-blinded, placebo-controlled trial. *The Lancet*, 370 (9598), 1560–1567.

McCartney, K., Harris, M. J., & Bernieri, F. (1990). Growing up and growing apart: A developmental meta-analysis of twin studies. *Psychological Bulletin*, 107, 226–237.

McCarty, M. E., & Ashmead, D. H. (1999). Visual control of reaching and grasping in infants. *Developmental Psychology*, 35, 620–631.

McCarty, M. E., Clifton, R. K., & Collard, R. R. (1999). Problem-solving in infancy: The emergence of an action plan. *Developmental Psychology*, 35, 1091–1101.

McClearn, G. E., Johansson, B., Berg, S., Pedersen, N. L., Ahern, F., Petrill, S. A., & Plomin, R. (1997). Substantial genetic influence on cognitive abilities in twins 80 years old or more. *Science*, 276 (5318), 1560–1563.

McCormick, M. C., McCarton, C., Tonascia, J., & Brooks-Gunn, J. (1993). Early educational intervention for very low birth weight infants: Results from the Infant Health and Development Program. *Journal of Pediatrics*, 123, 527–533.

McCracken, J. T., McGough, J., Shah, B., Cronin, P., Hong, D., Aman, M. G., Arnold, E., Lindsay, R., Nash, P., Hollway, J., McDougle, C. J., Posey, D., Swiezy, N., Kohn, A., Scahill, L., Martin, A., Koenig, K., Volkmar, F., Carroll, D., Lancor, A., Tierney, E., Ghuman, J., Gonzalez, N. M., Grados, M., Vitiello, B., Ritz, L., Davies, M., Robinson, J., & McMahon, D. (2002). Risperidone in children with autism and serious behavioral problems. *New England Journal of Medicine*, 347 (5), 314–321.

McCrink, K., & Wynn, K. (2004). Large number addition and subtraction by 9-month-old infants. *Psychological Science*, 15, 776–781.

McCune-Nicolich, L., & Bruskin, C. (1982). Combinatorial competency in symbolic play and language. In D. J. Pepler & K. H. Rubin (Eds.), *The Play of Children: Current Theory and Research* (Vol. 6, 30–45). New York: Karger.

McElhaney, K. B., Antonishak, J., & Allen, J. P. (2008). 'They like me, they like me not': Popularity and adolescents' perceptions of acceptance predicting social functioning over time. *Child Development*, 79 (3), 720–731.

McGee, R., Williams, S., & Feehan, M. (1992). Attention deficit disorder and age of onset of problem behaviours. *Journal of Abnormal Child Psychology*, 20 (5), 487–502.

McGivern, R. F., Andersen, J., Byrd, D., Mutter, K. L., & Reilly, J. (2002). Cognitive efficiency on a match to sample task decreases at the onset of puberty in children. *Brain and Cognition*, 50, 73–89.

McGregor, H. A., & Elliot, A. J. (2005). The shame of failure: Examining the link between fear of failure and shame. *Personality and Social Psychology Bulletin*, 31 (2), 218–231.

McInnes, K., Howard, J., Crowley, K., & Miles, G. (2013). The nature of adult–child interaction in the early years classroom: Implications for children's perceptions of play and subsequent learning behaviour. *European Early Childhood Education Research Journal*, 21 (2), 268–282.

McLaughlin, P., & Simpson, N. (2007). The common first year programme: Some lessons from a construction science course. *Teaching in Higher Education*, 12 (1), 13–23.

McPherson, S., Fairbanks, L., Tiken, S., Cummings, J. I., & Back-Madruga, C. (2002). Apathy and executive function in Alzheimer's disease. *Journal of the International Neuropsychological Society*, 8, 373–381.

Mattson, S. N., Crocker, N., & Nguyen, T. T. (2011). Fetal alcohol spectrum disorders: Neuropsychological and behavioral features. *Neuropsychological Review*, 21 (2), 81–101.

Mead, G. H. (1934). *Mind, Self and Society*. Chicago, IL: University of Chicago Press.

Mead, N. (2011). The impact of Every Child Matters on trainee secondary teachers' understanding of professional knowledge. *Pastoral Care in Education*, 29 (1), 7–24.

Meaney, M. J. (2001). Maternal care, gene expression, and the transmission of individual differences in stress reactivity across generations. *Annual Review of Neuroscience*, 24, 1161–1192.

Mebert, C. J. (1991). Dimensions of subjectivity in parents' ratings of infant temperament. *Child Development*, 62, 352–361.

MEDLINE Plus (2010). http://www.nichd.nih.gov/health/topics/Congenital_Adrenal_Hyperplasia.cfm.

Mehler, J., Jusczyk, P. W., Lambertz, G., Halsted, N., Bertoncini, J., & Amieltison, C. (1988). A precursor of language acquisition in young infants. *Cognition*, 29, 143–178.

Meins, E. (2013). Sensitive attunement to infants' internal states: Operationalizing the construct of mind-mindedness. *Attachment and Human Development*, 15, 524–544.

Meins, E., Fernyhough, C., Arnott, B., Leekam, S. R., & de Rosnay, M. (2013). Mind-mindedness and theory of mind: Mediating roles of language and perspectival symbolic play. *Child Development*, 84, 1777–1790.

Meins, E., Fernyhough, C., Arnott, B., Turner, M., & Leekam, S. R. (2011). Mother- versus infant-centred correlates of maternal mind-mindedness in the first year of life. *Infancy*, 16, 137–165.

Meins, E., Fernyhough, C., de Rosnay, M., Arnott, B., Leekam, S. R., & Turner, M. (2012). Mind-mindedness as a multidimensional construct: Appropriate and nonattuned mind-related comments independently predict infant–mother attachment in a socially diverse sample. *Infancy*, 17, 393–415.

Meins, E., Fernyhough, E., Fradley, E., & Tuckey, M. (2001). Rethinking maternal sensitivity: Mothers' comments on infants' mental processes predict security of attachment at 12 months. *Journal of Child Psychology and Psychiatry*, 42, 637–648.

Meins, E., Fernyhough, E., Wainwright, R., Das Gupta, M., Fradley, E., & Tuckey, M. (2002). Maternal mind-mindedness and attachment security as predictors of theory of mind understanding. *Child Development*, 73, 1715–1726.

Melhuish, E. C., Mooney, A., Martin, S., & Lloyd, E. (1990). Type of childcare at 18 months – I. Differences in interactional experience. *Journal of Child Psychology and Psychiatry*, 31, 849–859.

Mellor, D., & Delamont, S. (2011). Old anticipations, new anxieties? A contemporary perspective on primary to secondary transfer. *Cambridge Journal of Education*, 41 (3), 331–346.

Meltzoff, A. N. (1990). Foundations for developing a concept of self: The role of imitation in relating self to other and the value of social mirroring, social modelling, and self practice in infancy. In D. Cicchetti & M. Beeghly (Eds.), *The Self in Transition: Infancy to Childhood* (139–164). Chicago, IL: University of Chicago Press.

Meltzoff, A. N. (1995). Understanding the intentions of others: Reenactment of intended acts by 18-month-old children. *Developmental Psychology*, 31, 838–850.

Meltzoff, A. N., & Moore, M. K. (1977). Imitation of facial and manual gestures by human neonates. *Science*, 198, 75–78.

Mendle, J., & Ferrero, J. (2012). Detrimental psychological outcomes associated with pubertal timing in adolescent boys. *Developmental Review*, 32, 49–66.

Menesini, E., Nocentini, A., Palladino, B. E., Frisén, A., Berne, S., Ortega-Ruiz, R., Calmaestra, J., Scheithauer, H., Schultze-Krumbholz, A., Luik, P., Naruskov, K., Blaya, C., Berthaud, J., & Smith, P. K. (2012). Cyberbullying definition among adolescents: A comparison across six European countries. *Cyberpsychology, Behavior, and Social Networking*, 15, 455–463.

Mennes, M., van den Bergh, B., Lagae, L., & Stiers, P. (2009). Developmental brain alterations in 17 year old boys are related to antenatal maternal anxiety. *Clinical Neurophysiology*, 120, 1116–1122.

Mercer, C. H., Tanton, C., Prah, P., Erens, B., Sonnenberg, P., Clifton, S., Macdowall, W., Lewis, R., Field, N., Datta, J., Copas, A. J., Phelps, A., Wellings, K., & Johnson, A. M. (2013). Changes in sexual attitudes and lifestyles through the lifecourse and trends over time: Findings from the British National Surveys of Sexual Attitudes and Lifestyles (Natsal). *Lancet*, 382, 1781–1794.

Meristo, M., Falkman, K. W., Hjelmquist, E., Tedoldi, M. Surian, L., & Siegal, M. (2007). Language access and theory of mind reasoning: Evidence from deaf children in bilingual and oralist environments. *Developmental Psychology*, 43, (5), 1156–1169.

Merrell, K. W., Gueldner, B. A., Ross, S. W., & Isava, D. M. (2008). How effective are school bullying intervention programs? A meta-analysis of intervention research. *School Psychology Quarterly*, 23, 26–42.

Merriwether, A. M., & Liben, L. S. (1997). Adult's failures on Euclidean and projective spatial tasks: Implications for characterizing spatial cognition. *Journal of Adult Development*, 4, 57–69.

Mervis, C. B., Mervis, C. A., Johnson, K. E., & Bertrand, J. (1992). Studying early lexical development: The value of the systematic diary method. In C. Rovee-Collier and L. P. Lipsitt (Eds.), *Advances in Infancy Research* (Vol. 7, 291–378). Norwood, NJ: Ablex.

Meyer, M. A. (2007). Didactics, sense making, and educational experience. *European Educational Research Journal*, 6 (2), 161–173.

Michie, S. (1984). Why preschoolers are reluctant to count spontaneously. *British Journal of Developmental Psychology*, 2, 347–358.

Middleton, H. (2009). Problem-solving in technology education as an approach to education for sustainable development. *International Journal of Technology and Design Education*, 19 (2), 187–197.

Milan, S., Zona, K., & Snow, S. (2013). Pathways to adolescent internalizing: Early attachment insecurity as a lasting source of vulnerability. *Journal of Clinical Child and Adolescent Psychology*, 42, 371–381.

Milgram, S. (1974). *Obedience to Authority: An Experimental View*. New York: Harper Collins.

Miljkovitch, R., Danet, M., & Bernier, A. (2012). Intergenerational transmission of attachment representations in the context of single parenthood in France. *Journal of Family Psychology*, 26, 784–792.

Miller, K. (1984). Measurement procedures and the development of quantitative concepts. In C. Sophian (Ed.), *Origins of Cognitive Skills: The Eighteenth Annual Carnegie Symposium on Cognition* (193–228). Hillsdale, NJ: Erlbaum.

Milne, R., & Bull, R. (1999). *Investigative Interviewing: Psychology and Practice*. Chichester: Wiley.

Milne, R., & Bull, R. (2002). Back to basics: A componential analysis of the original cognitive interview mnemonics with three age groups. *Applied Cognitive Psychology*, 16, 743–753.

Mischel, W. (1966). A social learning view of sex differences in behavior. In E. E. Maccoby (Ed.), *The Development of Sex Differences* (56–81). London: Tavistock.

Mischel, W. (1970). Sex typing and socialization. In P. H. Mussen (Ed.), *Carmichael's Manual of Child Psychology* (Vol. 2, 3–72). New York: Wiley.

Mishna, F. (2004). A qualitative study of bullying from multiple perspectives. *Children and Schools*, 26, 234–247.

Miskovic, V., & Schmidt, L. A. (2012). New directions in the study of individual differences in temperament: A brain–body approach to understanding fearful and fearless children. *Monographs of the Society for Research in Child Development*, 77 (2), 28–38.

Mistry, M., & Barnes, D. (2013). The use of Makaton for supporting talk, through play, for pupils who have English as an Additional Language (EAL) in the Foundation Stage. *Education 3–13*, 41 (6), 603–616.

Mize, J., & Pettit, G. S. (2010). The mother–child as socialisation context: A short-term longitudinal study of mother–child–peer relationship dynamics. *Early Child Development and Care*, 180, 1271–1280.

Mo, Z., & Zecevic, N. (2008). Is *Pax6* critical for neurogenesis in the human foetal brain? *Cerebral Cortex*, 18, 1455–1465.

Moffitt, T. E., Caspi, A., Harrington, H., Milne, B. J., Melchior, M., Goldberg, D., & Poulton, R. (2007). Generalized anxiety disorder and depression: Childhood risk factors in a birth cohort followed to age 32. *Psychological Medicine*, 37, 441–452.

Moffitt, T. E., Poulton, R., & Caspi, A. (2013). Lifelong impact of early self-control: Childhood self-discipline predicts adult quality of life. *American Scientist*, 101, 352–359.

Molfese, V., Modglin, A., & Molfese, D. (2003). The role of environment in the development of reading skills: A longitudinal study of preschool and school-age measures. *Journal of Learning Disabilities*, 36, 59–67.

Molina, J. C., Chotro, M. G., & Dominguez, H. D. (1995). Foetal alcohol learning resulting from contamination of the prenatal environment. In J. P. Lecanuet, W. P. Fifer, N. A. Krasnegor, & W. P. Smotherman (Eds.), *Foetal Development: A Psychobiological Perspective* (419–438). Hillsdale, NJ: Erlbaum.

Money, J., & Ehrhardt, A. A. (1972). *Man and Woman/Boy and Girl*. Baltimore, MD: Johns Hopkins University Press.

Moni, K., van Kraayenoord, C., & Baker, C. (2002). Students' perceptions of literacy assessment. *Assessment in Education: Principles, Policy and Practice*, 9 (3), 319–342.

Monks, C. P., & Smith, P. K. (2006). Definitions of 'bullying': Age differences in understanding of the term, and the role of experience. *British Journal of Developmental Psychology*, 24, 801–821.

Monks, C. P., Smith, P. K., & Swettenham, J. (2004). Aggressors, victims, and defenders in preschool: Peer, self-, and teacher reports. *Merrill-Palmer Quarterly*, 49, 453–469.

Monks, C. P., Smith, P. K., & Swettenham, J. (2005). Psychological correlates of peer victimisation in preschool: Social cognitive skills, executive function and attachment profiles. *Aggressive Behavior*, 31, 571–588.

Monnier, C., & Bonthoux, F. (2011). The semantic-similarity effect in children: Influence of long-term knowledge on verbal short-term memory. *British Journal of Developmental Psychology*, 29 (4), 929–941.

Montgomery, A., Bjornstad, G., & Dennis, J. (2006). Media based behavioural treatments for behaviour problems in children. *Cochrane Database of Systematic Reviews*, 1. Art. No.: CD002206. DOI: 10.1002/14651858.

Moore, K. L., & Persaud, T. V. N. (2003). *The Developing Human: Clinically Oriented Embryology*. Philadelphia, PA: Saunders.

Moore, K. L., Persaud, T. V. N., & Shiota, K. (2000). *Colour Atlas of Clinical Embryology*. Philadelphia, PA: W. B. Saunders.

Morawska, A., & Sanders, M. R. (2006). Self-administered behavioural family interventions for parents of toddlers. Part 1: Efficacy. *Journal of Consulting and Clinical Psychology*, 74, 10–19.

Morgan, K., & Hayne, H. (2006). The effect of encoding time on retention by infants and young children. *Infant Behaviour and Development*, 29, 599–602.

Morgan, S., & Stevens, P. (2008). Transgender identity development as represented by a group of female-to-male transgendered adults. *Issues in Mental Health Nursing*, 29 (6), 585–599.

Mori, L., & Peterson, L. (1995). Knowledge of safety of high and low active-impulsive boys: Implications for child injury prevention. *Journal of Clinical Child Psychology*, 24, 370–376.

Morrell, J., & Murray, L. (2003). Parenting and the development of conduct disorder and hyperactive symptoms in childhood: A prospective longitudinal study from 2 months to 8 years. *Journal of Child Psychology and Psychiatry*, 44, 489–508.

Morrison, B. (2006). School bullying and restorative justice: Toward a theoretical understanding of the role of respect, pride, and shame. *Journal of Social Issues*, 62, 371–392.

Morrongiello, B. A., Fenwick, K. D., Hillier, L., & Chance, G. (1994). Sound localization in newborn human infants. *Developmental Psychobiology*, 27, 519–538.

Morton, J., & Johnson, M. H. (1991). Conspec and Conlearn: A two-process theory of infant face recognition. *Psychological Review*, 98, 164–181.

Mou, Y., Province, J. M., & Luo, Y. (2014). Can infants make transitive inferences? *Cognitive Psychology*, 68, 98–112.

Müller, U., & Giesbrecht, J. (2008). Methodological and epistemological issues in the interpretation of infant cognitive development. *Child Development*, 79 (6), 1654–1658.

Müller-Lyer, F. C. (1890). Review (untitled). *American Journal of Psychology* – Stable URL: http://www.jstor.org/stable/1411109 (Accessed: 16/08/2010), 3(2), 207–208.

Mumtaz, S., & Humphreys, G. (2001). The effects of bilingualism on learning to read English: Evidence from the contrast between Urdu-English bilingual and English monolingual children. *Journal of Research in Reading*, 24 (2), 113–134.

Munroe, R. H., Shimmin, H. S., & Munroe, R. L. (1984). Gender understanding and sex role preference in four cultures. *Developmental Psychology*, 20, 673–682.

Murray, L. (1992). The impact of post-natal depression on infant development. *Journal of Child Psychology and Psychiatry*, 33, 543–561.

Murray, L., & Cooper, P. J. (1997). Postpartum depression and child development. *Psychological Medicine*, 27 (2), 253–260.

Murray, L., & Stein, A. (1991). The effects of postnatal depression on mother–infant relations and infant development. In M. Woodhead, R. Carr, & P. Light (Eds.), *Becoming a Person* (144–166). London: Routledge.

Mynard, H., Joseph, S., & Alexander, J. (2000). Peer victimisation and posttraumatic stress in adolescents. *Personality and Individual Differences*, 29 (5), 815–821.

Naito, M. (2003). The relationship between theory of mind and episodic memory: Evidence for the development of autonoetic consciousness. *Journal of Experimental Child Psychology*, 85, 312–336.

Nakagawa, A., & Sukigara, M. (2014). The effects of soothing techniques and rough-and-tumble play on the early development of temperament: A longitudinal study of infants. *Child Development Research*, Article ID 741373, 1–19 (online article publication).

Nakagawa, M., Lamb, M. E., & Miyaki, K. (1992). Antecedents and correlates of the Strange Situation behavior of Japanese infants. *Journal of Cross-Cultural Psychology*, 23, 300–310.

Nakano, T., Watanabe, H., Homae, F., & Taga, G. (2009). Prefrontal cortical involvement in young infants' analysis of novelty. *Cerebral Cortex*, 19, 455–463.

Nansel, T. R., Overpeck, M. D., Pilla, R. S., Ruan, W. J., Simmons-Morton, B., & Scheidt, P. (2001). Bullying behaviour among US youth: Prevalence and association with psychosocial adjustment. *Journal of the American Medical Association*, 285, 2094–2100.

Nathanielsz, P. (1999). *Life in the Womb: The Origin of Health and Disease*. Ithaca, NY: Promethean Press.

National Autistic Society (2013). Myths, facts and statistics. Available at: http://www.autism.org.uk/about-autism/myths-facts-and-statistics/statistics-how-many-people-have-autism-spectrum-disorders.aspx

National Foundation for Educational Research (2013). Compulsory age of starting school in European countries. Available at: http://www.nfer.ac.uk/shadomx/apps/fms/fmsdownload.cfm?file_uuid=3B48895C-E497-6F68-A237-BCD7AB934443&siteName=nfer

National Initiative for Autism: Screening and Assessment (2003). *National Autism Plan for Children*. London: National Autistic Society.

National Institute for Health and Clinical Excellence (2008). *Attention Deficit Hyperactivity Disorder: Diagnosis and Management of ADHD in Children, Young People and Adults*. London: NICE.

Naylor, P., Cowie, H., Cossin, F., de Bettencourt, R., & Lemme, F. (2006). Teachers' and pupils' definitions of bullying. *British Journal of Educational Psychology*, 76, 553–576.

Nazzi, T., Floccia, C., & Bertoncini, J. (1998). Discrimination of pitch contours by neonates. *Infant Behavior and Development*, 21, 779–784.

Nelson, C. A. (2002a). Neural development and lifelong plasticity. In R. M. Lerner, F. Jacobs, & D. Wertleib (Eds.), *Handbook of Developmental Science* (Vol. 1, 31–60). Thousand Oaks, CA: Sage.

Nelson, C. A. (2002b). The ontogeny of human memory: A cognitive neuroscience perspective. In M. H. Johnson., Y. Munakata, & R. O. Gilmore (Eds.), *Brain Development and Cognition: A Reader* (151–178). Oxford: Blackwell.

Nelson, C. A., Thomas, K. M., & de Hann, M. (2006). *Neuroscience of Cognitive Development: The Role of Experience and the Developing Brain*. Hoboken, NJ: Wiley.

Nelson, D. A., Mitchell, C., & Yang, C. (2008). Intent attribution and aggression: A study of children and their parents. *Journal of Abnormal Child Psychology*, 36, 793–806.

Nelson, D. A., Robinson, C. C., Hart, C. H., Albano, A. D., & Marshall, S. J. (2010). Italian preschoolers' peer-status linkages with sociability and subtypes of aggression and victimisation. *Social Development*, 14, 698–721.

Nelson, E. A. S., Yu, L. M., Wong, D., Wong, H. Y., & Yim, L. (2004). Rolling over in infants: Age, ethnicity, and cultural differences. *Developmental Medicine and Child Neurology*, 46, 706–709.

Nelson, K. and Gruendel, J. (1981). Generalised event representations: Basic building blocks of cognitive development. In M. E. Lamb and A. L. Brown (Eds.), *Advances in Developmental Psychology* (Vol. 1, 21–46). Hillsdale, NJ: Erlbaum.

Nesdale, D., Zimmer-Gembeck, M. J., & Roxburgh, N. (2014). Peer group rejection in childhood: Effects of rejection ambiguity, rejection sensitivity, and social acumen. *Journal of Social Issues*, 70, 12–28.

Neuman, W. L. (2007). *Basics of Social Research: Qualitative and Quantitative Approaches* (2nd Ed.). London: Pearson.

Newman, C., Atkinson, J., & Braddick, O. (2001). The development of reaching and looking preferences in infants to objects of different sizes. *Developmental Psychology*, 37, 561–572.

Newman, G. E., Herrmann, P., Wynn, K., & Keil, F. C. (2008). Biases towards internal features in infants' reasoning about objects. *Cognition*, 107, 420–432.

Newman, M. (2008). Big or small: Does the size of a secondary school matter? *FORUM: For Promoting 3–19 Comprehensive Education*, 50 (2), 167–176.

Newschaffer, C. J., Croen, L. A., Daniels, J., Giarelli, E., Grether, J. K., Levy, S. E., Mandell, D. S., Miller, L. A., & Pinto-Martin, J. (2007). The epidemiology of autism spectrum disorders. *Annual Review of Public Health*, 28, 235–258.

NHS immunisation statistics, England: 2001–02. Retrieved November 6 from http://www.dh.gov.uk/en/_Publicationsandstatistics/_Statistics/_StatisticalWorkAreas/_Statisticalhealthcare/_DH_4016228.

Nichols, S., & Stich, S. (2003). *Mindreading: An Integrated Account of Pretence, Self-awareness and Understanding of Other Minds*. Oxford: Oxford University Press.

Nielsen, M. (2012). Imitation, pretend play, and childhood: Essential elements in the evolution of human culture? *Journal of Comparative Psychology*, 126, 170–181.

Nielsen, M. B. & Einarsen, S. (2012). Outcomes of exposure to workplace bullying: A meta-analytic review. *Work and Stress: An International Journal of Work, Health and Organisations*, 26, 309–332.

Nigg, J. T. (2001). Is ADHD a disinhibitory disorder? *Psychological Bulletin*, 127, 571–598.

Nigg, J. T. (2006a). Temperament and developmental psychopathology. *Journal of Child Psychology and Psychiatry*, 47, 395–422.

Nigg, J. T. (2006b). *What Causes ADHD? Understanding What Goes Wrong and Why*. New York: Guilford Press.

Nigg, J. T. (2010). Attention-deficit/hyperactivity disorder: Endophenotypes, structure, and etiological pathways. *Current Directions in Psychological Science*, 19, 24–29.

Nijmeijer, J. S., Minderaa, R. B., Buitelaar, J. K., Mulligan, A., Hartman, C. A., & Hoekstra, P. J. (2008). Attention deficit/hyperactivity disorder and social dysfunctioning. *Clinical Psychology Review*, 28, 692–708.

Nilsson, L., & Hamberger, L. (1990). *A Child is Born*. New York: Delacorte.

Niswander, K. R., & Evans, A. T. (1996). *Manual of Obstetrics*. Boston, MA: Little Brown.

Nordahl, K. B., Janson, H., Manger, T., & Zachrisson, H. D. (2014). Family concordance and gender differences in parent–child interaction at 12 months. *Journal of Family Psychology*, 28, 253–259.

Notaro, P. C., & Volling, B. L. (1999). Parental responsiveness and infant–parent attachment: A replication study with fathers and mothers. *Infant Behaviour and Development*, 22, 345–352.

Novillis, C. F. (1976). An analysis of the fraction concept into a hierarchy of selected subconcepts and the testing of the hierarchical dependencies. *Journal for Research in Mathematics Education*, 7, 131–144.

Nowakowski, R. S., & Hayes, N. L. (2002). General principles of CNS development. In M. H. Johnson, Y. Munakata, & R. O. Gilmore (Eds.), *Brain Development and Cognition: A Reader* (57–82). Oxford: Blackwell.

Noyes, A. (2006). School transfer and the diffraction of learning trajectories. *Research Papers in Education*, 21 (1), 43–62.

Nunes, T., & Bryant, P. (1996). *Children Doing Mathematics*. Oxford: Blackwell.

Nunes, T., & Bryant, P. (2010). Insights from everyday knowledge for mathematics education. In D. Preiss & R. Sternberg (Eds.), *Innovations in Educational Psychology* (51–78). New York: Springer.

Nunes, T., & Moreno, C. (2002). An intervention program to promote deaf pupils' achievement in numeracy. *Journal of Deaf Studies and Deaf Education*, 7, 120–133.

Nunes, T., & Schliemann, A. D. (1990). Knowledge of the numeration system among pre-schoolers. In L. S. T. Wood (Ed.), *Transforming Early Childhood Education: International Perspectives* (135–141). Hillsdale, NJ: Erlbaum.

Nunes, T., Bryant, P., Burman, D., Bell, D., Evans, D., & Hallett, D. (2008a). Deaf children's informal knowledge of multiplicative reasoning. *Journal of Deaf Studies and Deaf Education*, 14, 260–277.

Nunes, T., Bryant, P., Evans, D., & Bell, D. (2010). The scheme of correspondence and its role in children's mathematics. *British Journal of Educational Psychology, Monographs Series II*, 1(1), 1–18.

Nunes, T., Bryant, P., Evans, D., Bell, D., Gardner, S., Gardner, A., & Carraher, J. N. (2007a). The contribution of logical reasoning to the learning of mathematics in primary school. *British Journal of Developmental Psychology*, 25, 147–166.

Nunes, T., Bryant, P., Evans, D., Bell, D., & Hallett, D. (2008b). Developing deaf children's understanding of additive composition. American Educational Research Association Annual Meetings, New York, 24–28 March.

Nunes, T., Bryant, P., Pretzlik, U., Bell, D., Evans, D., & Wade, J. (2007b). La compréhension des fractions chez les enfants. In M. Merri (Ed.), *Activité humaine et conceptualisation*. Toulouse: Presses Universitaires du Mirail.

Nunes, T., Bryant, P., Pretzlik, U., & Hurry, J. (2006). *Fractions: Difficult but Crucial in Mathematics Learning*. London Institute of Education, London: ESRC-Teaching and Learning Research Programme, Research Briefing Number 13.

Nunes, T., Bryant, P., Sylva, K., & Barros, R. (2009). *Development of Maths Capabilities and Confidence in Primary School (No. Research Report DCSF-RR118)*. London: Department for Children, Schools and Families. Retrieved 7 November 2010 from http://publications.dcsf.gov.uk/eOrderingDownload/DCSF-RB118.pdf.

Nunes, T., Schliemann, A. D., & Carraher, D. W. (1993). *Street Mathematics and School Mathematics*. New York: Cambridge University Press.

Nwokah, E. E., Burnette, S. E., & Graves, K. N. (2013). Joke telling, humour creation, and humour recall in children with and without hearing loss. *Humor: International Journal of Humor Research*, 26 (1), 69–96.

O'Brien, M. (1992). Gender identity and sex roles. In V. B. Van Hasselt & M. Hersen (Eds.), *Handbook of Social Development: A Lifespan Perspective* (325–345). New York: Plenum Press.

O'Connor, M., Foch, T., Todd, S., & Plomin, R. (1980). A twin study of specific behavioural problems of socialisation as viewed by parents. *Journal of Abnormal Child Psychology*, 8, 189–199.

Offer, D. (1969). *The Psychological World of the Teenager: A Study of Normal Adolescent Boys*. New York: Basic Books.

Ohlsson, S. (1988). Mathematical meaning and applicational meaning in the semantics of fractions and related concepts. In J. Hiebert & M. Behr (Eds.), *Number Concepts and Operations in the Middle Grades* (53–92). Reston, VA: National Council of Mathematics Teachers.

Okamoto, Y., Curtis, R., Jabagchourian, J. J., & Weckbacher, L. M. (2006). Mathematical precocity in young children: A neo-Piagetian perspective. *High Ability Studies*, 17 (2), 183–202.

O'Leary, C., Zubrick, S. R., Taylor, C. L., Dixon, G., & Bower, C. (2009). Prenatal alcohol exposure and language delay in 2-year-old children: The importance of dose and timing on risk. *Pediatrics*, 123 (2), 547–554.

Olino, T. M., Durbin, C. E., Klein, D. N., Hayden, E. P., & Dyson, M. W. (2013). Gender differences in young children's temperament traits: Comparisons across observational and parent-report methods. *Journal of Personality*, 81, 119–129.

Oliva, A., Jimenez, J. M., & Parra, A. (2009). Protective effect of supportive family relationships and the influence of stressful life events on adolescent adjustment. *Anxiety, Stress and Coping*, 22 (2), 137–152.

Olive, M., & Liu, Y.-J. (2005). Social validity of parent and teacher implemented assessment-based interventions for challenging behaviour. *Educational Psychology*, 25, (2–3), 305–312.

Oliver, L. N., Dunn, J. R., Kohen, D. E., & Hertzman, C. (2007). Do neighbourhoods influence the readiness to learn of kindergarten children in Vancouver? A multilevel analysis of neighbourhood effects. *Environment and Planning A*, 39 (4), 848–868.

Oller, D. K. (1980). The emergence of the sounds of speech in infancy. In G. Yeni-Komshian, J. F. Ferguson & C. A. Ferguson (Eds.), *Child Phonology: 1 Production* (93–112). New York: Academic Press.

Olsson, C. A., McGee, R., Nada-Raja, S., & Williams, S. M. (2013). A 32-year longitudinal study of child and adolescent pathways to well-being in adulthood. *Journal of Happiness Studies*, 14, 1069–1083.

Olweus, D. (1993). *Bullying at School: What We Know and What We Can Do*. Oxford: Blackwell.

Olweus, D. (1994). Bullying at school: Basic facts and effects of a school-based intervention programme. *Journal of Child Psychology and Child Psychiatry*, 35 (7), 171–1190.

O'Moore, A. M., & Kirkham, C. (2001). Self-esteem and its relationship to bullying behaviour. *Aggressive Behavior*, 27, 269–283.

Onishi, K. H., & Baillargeon, R. (2005). Do 15-month-old infants understand false beliefs? *Science*, 308, 255–258.

Oortwijn, M., Boekaerts, M., & Vedder, P. (2008). The impact of the teacher's role and pupils' ethnicity and prior knowledge on pupils' performance and motivation to cooperate. *Instructional Science*, 36 (3), 251–268.

Open University (2003). *U212 Childhood, Video 3, Band 3, Pretend play*. Milton Keynes: Open University.

Opie, I. (1993). *The People in the Playground*. Oxford: Oxford University Press.

Orekhova, E. V., Stroganova, T. A., & Posikera, I. N. (2001). Alpha activity as an index of cortical inhibition during sustained internally controlled attention in infants. *Clinical Neurophysiology*, 112, 740–749.

Orekhova, E. V., Stroganova, T. A., Posikera, I. N., & Elam, M. (2006). EEG theta rhythm in infants and preschool children. *Clinical Neurophysiology*, 117, 1047–1062.

Organisation for Economic Co-operation and Development (2006). *Starting Strong II: Early Childhood Education and Care*. Paris: OECD.

Orth, U., Trzesniewski, K. H., & Robins, R. W. (2010). Self-esteem development from young adulthood to old age: A cohort-sequential longitudinal study. *Journal of Personality and Social Psychology*, 98 (4), 645–658.

Ortner, T. M., & Sieverding, M. (2008). Where are the gender differences? Male priming boosts spatial skills in women. *Sex Roles*, 59 (3–4), 274–281.

Osborn, M. (2001). Constants and contexts in pupil experience of learning and schooling: Comparing learners in England, France and Denmark. *Comparative Education*, 37 (3), 267–278.

Osborne, J., Simon, S., & Collins, S. (2003). Attitudes towards science: A review of the literature and its implications. *International Journal of Science Education*, 25 (9), 1049–1079.

Oshima, J., Oshima, R., Murayama, I., Inagaki, S., Takenaka, M., Nakayama, H., & Yamaguchi, E. (2004). Design experiments in Japanese elementary science education with computer support for collaborative learning: Hypothesis testing and collaborative construction. *International Journal of Science Education*, 26 (10), 1199–1221.

Osler, A. (2000). Children's rights, responsibilities and understandings of school discipline. *Research Papers in Education*, 15 (1), 49–67.

Ostgard-Ybrandt, H., & Armelius, B. A. (2004). Self-concept and perception of early mother and father behavior in normal and antisocial adolescents. *Scandinavian Journal of Psychology*, 45 (5), 437–447.

Ostoja, E., McCrone, E., Lehn, L., Reed, T., & Sroufe, L.A. (1995). Representations of close relationships in adolescence: Longitudinal antecedents from infancy through childhood. Paper presented at the biennial meeting of the Society for Research in Child Development, Indianapolis, IN, March.

O'Toole, L. (2008). Understanding individual patterns of learning: Implications for the well-being of students. *European Journal of Education: Research, Development and Policies*, 43 (1), 71–86.

Oxford Dictionaries (2008). *Concise Oxford English Dictionary* (11th Ed., revised). Oxford: Oxford University Press.

Owen Blakemore, J. E. O., Berenbaum, S. A., & Liben, L. S. (Eds.) (2009). *Gender Development*. Hove: Psychology Press.

Owens, L., Shute, R., & Slee, P. (2000).'I'm in and you're out . . .': Explanations for teenage girls' indirect aggression. *Psychology, Evolution and Gender*, 2, 19–46.

Pace, C. S., Zavattini, G. C., & Alessio, M. D. (2012). Continuity and discontinuity of attachment patterns: A short-term longitudinal pilot study using a sample of late-adopted children and their adoptive mothers. *Attachment and Human Development*, 14, 45–61.

Pahlke, E., Bigler, R. S., & Martin, C. L. (2014). Can fostering children's ability to challenge sexism improve critical analysis, internalization, and enactment of inclusive, egalitarian peer relationships? *Journal of Social Issues*, 70, 115–133.

Palmer, E. J., & Hollin, C. R. (2001). Sociomoral reasoning, perceptions of parenting and self-reported delinquency in adolescents. *Applied Cognitive Psychology*, 15 (1), 85–100.

Palmert, M. R., Radovik, S., & Boepple, P. A. (1998). Leptin levels in children with central precocious puberty. *Journal of Clinical Endocrinology and Metabolism,* 83 (7), 2260–2265.

Pantev, C., Ross, B., Fujioka, T., Trainor, L., Schulte, M., & Schulz, M. (2003). Music and learning-induced cortical plasticity. In G. Avanzini, D. Miciacchi, L. Lopez, & M. Majno (Eds), *The Neurosciences and Music: Mutual Interactions and Implications of Developmental Functions*. Annals of the New York Academy of Sciences (438–450).

Papadopoulos, T., Georgiou, G., & Parrila, R. (2012). Low-level deficits in beat perception: Neither necessary nor sufficient for explaining developmental dyslexia in a consistent orthography. *Research in Developmental Disabilities*, 33 (6), 1841–1856.

Papatheodorou, T. (2002). How we like our school to be: Pupils' voices. *European Educational Research Journal*, 1 (3), 445–467.

Pardini, M., & Nichelli, P.F. (2009). Age-related decline in mentalizing skills across adult life span. *Experimental Aging Research*, 35, 98–106.

Parker, J. G., & Asher, S. R. (1987). Peer relations and later personal adjustment: Are low accepted children at risk? *Psychological Bulletin*, 102, 357–389.

Parry, G. (2000). Evidence-based psychotherapy: An overview. In N. Rowland and S. Goss (Eds), *Evidence-based Counselling and Psychological Therapies: Research and Applications* (57–76). London: Routledge.

Parry, G. D., Cape, J., & Pilling, S. (2003). Clinical practice guidelines in clinical psychology and psychotherapy. *Journal of Clinical Psychology and Psychotherapy*, 10, 337–357.

Parsons, L. M., & Osherson, D. (2001). New evidence for distinctive brain systems for deductive and probabilistic reasoning. *Cerebral Cortex*, 11, 954–965.

Parten, M. B. (1932). Social participation among preschool children. *Journal of Abnormal and Social Psychology*, 27, 243–269.

Pascalis, O., & Slater, A. (Eds.) (2003). *The Development of Face Processing in Infancy and Early Childhood*. New York: Nova Science.

Pasztor, A. (2008). The children of guest workers: Comparative analysis of scholastic achievement of pupils of Turkish origin throughout Europe. *Intercultural Education*, 19 (5), 407–419.

Patchin, J. W. & Hinduja, S. (2006). Bullies move beyond the schoolyard: A preliminary look at cyberbullying. *Youth Violence and Juvenile Justice*, 4, 148–169.

Patchin, J. W. & Hinduja, S. (2011). Traditional and non-traditional bullying among youth: A test of General Strain Theory. *Youth and Society*, 43, 727–751.

Paterson, S. J., Brown, J. H., Gsodi, M. K., Johnson, M.H., & Karmiloff-Smith, A. (1999). Cognitive modularity and genetic disorders. *Science Magazine*, 286, 2355–2358.

Patterson, C. J. (1995). Sexual orientation and human development: An overview. *Developmental Psychology*, 31 (Special issue: Sexual orientation and human development), 3–11.

Pauli-Pott, U., Mertesacker, B., Bade, U., Haverkock, A., & Beckmann, D. (2003). Parental perceptions and infant temperament development. *Infant Behavior and Development*, 26, 27–48.

Payne, L. (2007). A 'Children's Government' in England and child impact assessment. *Children and Society*, 21 (6), 470–475.

Pedlow, R., Sanson, A., Prior, M., & Oberklaid, F. (1993). Stability of maternally reported temperament from infancy to 8 years. *Developmental Psychology*, 29, 998–1007.

Pedrosa de Jesus, H., & Coelho Moreira, A. (2009). The role of students' questions in aligning teaching, learning and assessment: A case study from undergraduate sciences. *Assessment and Evaluation in Higher Education*, 34 (2), 193–208.

Pelham, W. E., Wheeler, T., & Chronis, A. (1998). Empirically supported psycho-social treatments for attention deficit hyperactivity disorder. *Journal of Clinical Child Psychology*, 27, 189–204.

Pelkonen, M., Marttunen, M., & Aro, H. (2003). Risk for depression: A 6-year follow-up of Finnish adolescents. *Journal of Affective Disorders*, 77 (1), 41–51.

Pellegrini, A. D. (2006). The development and function of rough-and-tumble play in childhood and adolescence: A sexual selection theory perspective. In A. Göncü & S. Gaskins (Eds.), *Play and Development: Evolutionary, Sociocultural and Functional Perspectives* (77–98). London: Erlbaum.

Pellegrini, A. D., & Bertini, M. (2001). Dominance in early adolescent boys: Affiliative and aggressive dimensions and possible functions. *Merrill-Palmer Quarterly*, 47, 142–163.

Pellegrini, A. D., & Smith, P. K. (1998). Physical activity play: The nature and function of a neglected aspect of play. *Child Development*, 69, 577–598.

Pellis, S. M., Pellis, V. C., & Himmler, B. T. (2014). How play makes for a more adaptable brain: A comparative and neural perspective. *American Journal of Play*, 73–98.

Pennington, B. F. (2002). Genes and brain: Individual differences and human universals. In M. H. Johnsom, Y. Munakata, & R. O. Gilmore (Eds.), *Brain Development and Cognition: A Reader* (494–508). Oxford: Blackwell.

Pennington, B. F., McGrath, L. M., Rosenberg, J., Barnard, H., et al. (2008). Gene–environment interactions in reading disability and attention-deficit/hyperactivity disorder. *Developmental Psychology*, 45, 77–89.

Pepler, D. J., Craig, W. M., Zieglier, S., & Charach, A. (1994). An evaluation of an anti-bullying intervention in Toronto schools. *Canadian Journal of Community Mental Health*, 13 (2), 95–110.

Perner, J. (1991). *Understanding the Representational Mind*. Cambridge, MA: MIT Press.

Perner, J., & Ruffman, T. (1995). Episodic memory and autonoetic consciousness: Developmental evidence and a theory of childhood amnesia. *Journal of Experimental Child Psychology*, 59 (3), 516–548.

Perner, J., & Ruffman, T. (2005). Infants' insight into the mind: How deep? *Science*, 308, 214–216.

Perner, J., Kloo, D., & Gornik, E. (2007). Episodic memory development: Theory of mind is part of re-experiencing experienced events. *Infant and Child Development*, 16, 471–490.

Perner, J., Leekam, S. R., & Wimmer, H. (1987). Three-year-olds' difficulty with false-belief: The case for a conceptual deficit. *British Journal of Developmental Psychology*, 5, 125–137.

Perou, R., Bitsko, R. H., Blumberg, S. J., et al. (2013). Mental health surveillance among children: United States, 2005–2011. Centers for Disease Control and Prevention, *Supplements*, 62 (02), 1–35. Available at: http://www.cdc.gov/mmwr/preview/mmwrhtml/su6202a1.htm?s_cid=su6201a2_w

Perren, S., Ettekal, I. & Ladd, G. (2012). The impact of peer victimisation on later maladjustment: Mediating and moderating effects of hostile and self-blaming attributions. *Journal of Child Psychology and Psychiatry*, 64, 46–55.

Perren, S., Corcoran, L., Cowie, H., Dehue, F., Garcia, D., McGuckin, C., Sevcikova, A., Tsatsou, P. & Völlink, T. (2012). Tackling cyberbullying: Review of empirical evidence regarding successful responses by students, parents, and schools. *International Journal of Conflict and Violence*, 6, 283–293.

Perring, C. (1997). Medicating children: The case of Ritalin. *Bioethics*, 1, 228–240.

Peskin, J., & Ardino, V. (2003). Representing the mental world in children's social behavior: Playing hide-and-seek and keeping a secret. *Social Development*, 12, 496–512.

Pesonen, A.-K., Raikkonen, K., Heinonen, K., Jarvenpaa, A.-L., & Strandberg, T. E. (2006). Depressive vulnerability in parents and their 5-year-old child's temperament: A family system perspective. *Journal of Family Psychology*, 20, 648–655.

Pesonen, A., Raikkonen, K., Strandberg, T., Kelitikangas-Jarvinen, L., & Jarvenpaa, A. (2004). Insecure adult attachment style and depressive symptoms: Implications for parental perceptions of infant temperament. *Infant Mental Health Journal*, 25, 99–116.

Peterson, B. S., Pine, D. S., Cohen, P., & Brook, J. S. (2001). Prospective, longitudinal study of tic, obsessive-compulsive, and attention-deficit/hyperactivity disorders in an epidemiological sample. *Journal of the American Academy of Child and Adolescent Psychiatry*, 40, 685–695.

Piaget, J. (1932). *The Moral Judgment of the Child*. London: Kegan Paul, Trench, Trubner, & Co.

Piaget, J. (1951). *Play, Dreams and Imitation in Childhood*. London: Routledge & Kegan Paul.

Piaget, J. (1952a). *The Child's Conception of Number*. London: Routledge.

Piaget, J. (1952b). *The Origins of Intelligence in Children* (originally published 1932). New York: International Universities Press.

Piaget, J. (1953). *The Origins of Intelligence in Children*. London: Routledge and Kegan Paul.

Piaget, J. (1954). *The Construction of Reality in the Child*. New York: Basic Books.

Piaget, J. (1958). *The Growth of Logical Thinking from Childhood to Adolescence*. New York: Basic Books.

Piaget, J. (1962). *Play, Dreams, and Imitation in Childhood*. New York: Norton.

Piaget, J. (1967). *Biologie et connaissance* (Biology and Knowledge). Paris: Gallimard.

Piaget, J. (1972). *The Child's Conception of the World* (originally published 1926). Towota, NJ: Littlefield Adams.

Piaget, J. (1981). *Intelligence and Affectivity*. New York: Basic Books.

Piaget, J., and Inhelder, B. (1956). *The Child's Conception of Space*. London: Routledge.

Piaget, J., Inhelder, B., & Szeminska, A. (1960). *The Child's Conception of Geometry*. New York: Harper & Row.

Pica, R. (2011). Helping children cooperate. *YC: Young Children*, 66 (6), 60–61.

Piccardi, L., Leonzi, M., D'Amico, S., Marano, A., & Guariglia, C. (2014). Development of navigational working memory: Evidence from 6 to 10 year old children. *British Journal of Developmental Psychology*, 32 (2), 205–217.

Pierce, E. W., Ewing, L. J., & Campbell, S. B. (1999). Diagnostic status and symptomatic behaviour of hard to manage preschool children in middle childhood and early adolescence. *Journal of Clinical Child Psychology*, 28, 44–57.

Pikas, A. (1989). The common concern method for the treatment of mobbing. In E. Roland & E. Munthe (Eds.), *Bullying: An International Perspective* (91–104). London: David Fulton.

Pilgrim, D. (2001). Disordered personalities and disordered concepts. *Journal of Mental Health*, 10 (3), 253–265.

Pinel, J. J. (2008). *Biopsychology*. Boston, MA: Pearson.

Pinker, S. (2002). *The Blank Slate: The Modern Denial of Human Nature*. London: Allen Lane.

Pisterman, S., McGrath, P., Firestone, P., Goodman, J. T., Webster, I., & Mallory, R. (1989). Outcome of parent-mediated treatment of preschoolers with attention deficit disorder with hyperactivity. *Journal of Consulting and Clinical Psychology*, 57, 628–635.

Pixa-Kettner, U. (2005). Parenting with intellectual disability in Germany: Results of a new nationwide study. *Journal of Applied Research in Intellectual Disabilities*, 21 (4), 315–319.

Plomin, R., & DeFries, J. C. (1980). Genetics and intelligence: Recent data. *Intelligence*, 4 (1), 15–24.

Plomin, R., DeFries, J. C., & Fulker, D. W. (1988). *Nature and Nurture during Infancy and Early Childhood*. Cambridge: Cambridge University Press.

Plomin, R., Emde, R. N., Braungart, J. M., Campos, J., Corley, R., Fulker, D. W., Kagan, J., Reznick, J. S., Robinson, J., Zahn-Waxler, C., & DeFries, J. C. (1993). Genetic change and continuity from fourteen to twenty months: The MacArthur longitudinal twin study. *Child Development*, 64, 1354–1376.

Poli, P., Sbrana, B., Marcheschi, M., & Masi, G. (2003). Self-reported depressive symptoms in a school sample of Italian children and adolescents. *Child Psychiatry and Human Development*, 33 (3), 209–226.

Popović-Ćitić, B., Djurić, S. & Cvetković, V. (2011) The prevalence of cyberbullying among adolescents: A case study of middle schools in Serbia. *School Psychology International*, 32, 412–424.

Porter, N. (2012). Promotion of pretend play for children with high-functioning autism through the use of circumscribed interests. *Early Childhood Education Journal*, 40 (3), 161–167.

Posada, G., Carbonell, O. A., Alzate, G., & Plata, S. J. (2004). Through Colombian lenses: Ethnographic and conventional analyses of maternal care and their associations with secure base behavior. *Developmental Psychology*, 40, 508–518.

Posada, G., Jacobs, A., Richmond, M. Carbonell, O., Alzate, G., Bustamante, M., & Quiceno, J. (2002). Maternal caregiving and infant security in two cultures. *Developmental Psychology*, 38, 67–78.

Posner, M. I., & Rothbart, M. K. (1981). The development of attentional mechanisms. In J. H. Flowers (Ed.), *Nebraska Symposium on Motivation* (Vol. 28, 1–52). Lincoln, NE: University of Nebraska Press.

Pothier, Y., & Sawada, D. (1983). Partitioning: The emergence of rational number ideas in young children. *Journal for Research in Mathematics Education*, 14, 307–317.

Potts, A. (2006). Schools as dangerous places. *Educational Studies*, 32 (3), 319–330.

Power, M., & Prasad, S. (2003). Schools for the future: Inner city secondary education exemplar. *Architectural Research Quarterly*, 7 (3–4), 262–279.

Power, S., & Clark, A. (2000). The right to know: Parents, school reports and parents' evenings. *Research Papers in Education*, 15 (1), 25–48.

Pöyhönen, V. & Salmivalli, C. (2008). New directions in research and practice addressing bullying: Focus on defending behavior. In D. Pepler & W. Craig (Eds.) *Understanding and Addressing Bullying: An International Perspective* (pp. 26–43). Bloomington, IN: Author House.

Premack, D., & Woodruff, G. (1978). Does the chimpanzee have a 'theory of mind'? *Behavioral and Brain Sciences*, 4, 515–526.

Pressley, M. (1982). Elaboration and memory development. *Child Development*, 53, 296–309.

Prior, M., Sanson, A., Smart, D., & Oberklaid, F. (2000). Does shy-inhibited temperament in childhood lead to anxiety problems in adolescence? *Journal of the American Academy of Child and Adolescent Psychiatry*, 39, 461–468.

Psillos, D. (2004). An epistemological analysis of the evolution of didactical activities in teaching–learning sequences: The case of fluids. *International Journal of Science Education*, 26 (5), 555–578.

Purves, D., Brannon, E. M., Cabeza, R., Huettel, S. A., LaBar, K. S., Platt, M. L., & Woldorff, M. G. (2008). *Principles of Cognitive Neuroscience*. Sunderland, MA: Sinauer.

Putnam, S. P., & Rothbart, M. K. (2006). Development of short and very short forms of the children's behaviour questionnaire. *Journal of Personality Assessment*, 87, 103–113.

Putnam, S. P., Samson, A. V., & Rothbart, M. K. (2000). Child temperament and parenting. In V. J. Molfese & D. L. Molfese (Eds.), *Temperament and Personality Across the Life Span* (255–277). Mahwah, NJ: Erlbaum.

Pye, C. (1986). Quiche Mayan speech to children. *Journal of Child Language*, 13, 85–100.

Quijada, R. E., Montoya, C. M., Laserna, P. A., Toledo, A. P., Marco, E. M., & Rabadan, F. E. (2005). Depression prevalence in adolescents. *Actas Espanolas De Psiquiatria*, 33 (5), 298–302.

Quilgars, D., Searle, B., & Keung, A. (2005). Mental health and well-being. In J. Bradshaw & E. Mayhew (Eds.), *The Well-Being of Children in the UK* (134–160). London: Save the Children.

Quinn, P. C. (2002). Categorization. In A. Slater & M. Lewis (Eds.), *Introduction to Infant Development* (115–130). Oxford: Oxford University Press.

Quinn, P. C. (2004). Development of subordinate-level categorization in 3- to 7-month-old infants. *Child Development*, 75, 886–899.

Quinn, P. C (2008). In defense of core competencies, quantitative change, and continuity. *Child Development*, 79, 1633–1638.

Quinn, P. C., & Eimas, P. D. (1996). Perceptual cues that permit categorical differentiation of animal species by infants. *Journal of Experimental Child Psychology*, 63, 189–211.

Quinn, P. C., & Johnson, M. H. (2000). Global-before-basic object categorization in connectionist networks and 2-month-old infants. *Infancy*, 1, 31–46.

Quinn, P. C., Westerlund, A., & Nelson, C. A. (2006). Neural markers of categorization in 6-month-old infants. *Psychological Science*, 17, 59–67.

Quinn, P. C., Yahr, J., Kuhn, A., Slater, A. M., & Pascalis, O. (2002). Representation of the gender of human faces by infants: A preference for female. *Perception*, 31, 1109–1121.

Rahman, A., Lovel, H., Bunn, J., Igbal, A., & Harrington, R. (2004). Mothers' mental health and infant growth: A case-control study from Rawalpindi, Pakistan. *Child: Care, Health, and Development*, 30, 21–27.

Rainey, D., & Murova, O. (2004). Factors influencing education achievement. *Applied Economics*, 36 (21), 2397–2404.

Rakison, D. H. (2000). When a rose is just a rose: The illusion of taxonomies in infant categorization. *Infancy*, 1, 77–90.

Rakison, D., & Butterworth, G. (1998). Infants' use of object parts in early categorization. *Developmental Psychology*, 34, 49–62.

Rakoczy, H., Tomasello, M., & Striano, T. (2004). Young children know that trying is not pretending: A test of the 'behaving-as-if' construal of children's early concept of pretense. *Developmental Psychology*, 40, 388–399.

Ramus, F. (2002). Language discrimination by newborns: Teasing apart phonotactic, rhythmic, and intonational cues. *Annual Review of Language Acquisition*, 2, 85–115.

Ramus, F. (2006). Genes, brain, and cognition: A roadmap for the cognitive scientist. *Cognition*, 101, 247–269.

Raskauskas, J., & Stolz, A.D. (2007). Involvement in traditional and electronic bullying among adolescents. *Developmental Psychology*, 43, 564–575.

Rauschecker, J. P., & Henning, P. (2000). Crossmodal expansion of cortical maps in early blindness. In J. Kaas (Ed.), *The Mutable Brain* (243–259). Singapore: Harwood Academics.

Rayner, C., & Hoel, H. (1997). A summary review of literature relating to workplace bullying. *Journal of Community and Applied Psychology*, 7, 181–191.

Read, M. (1968). *Children of their Fathers: Growing up among the Ngoni of Malawi*. New York: Holt, Rinehart, & Winston.

Read, V. (2010). *Developing Attachment in Early Years Settings: Nurturing Secure Relationships from Birth to Five Years*. London: Routledge.

Reece, E. A., & Hobbins, J. C. (Eds.) (2006). *Clinical Obstetrics: The Foetus and Mother*. Oxford: Blackwell.

Rees, J. M., Lederman, S. A., & Kiely, J. L. (1996). Birth weight associated with lowest neonatal mortality: Infants of adolescent and adult mothers. *Pediatrics*, 98, 1161–1166.

Reich, S., Bickman, L., Saville, B., & Alvarez, J. (2010). The effectiveness of baby books for providing pediatric anticipatory guidance to new mothers. *Pediatrics*, 125 (5), 997–1002.

Reid, K. (2006). An evaluation of the views of secondary staff towards school attendance issues. *Oxford Review of Education*, 32 (3), 303–324.

Reijntjes, A., Kamphuis, J. H., Prinzie, P. & Telch, M. J. (2010). Peer victimization and internalizing problems in children: A meta-analysis of longitudinal studies. *Child Abuse and Neglect*, 34, 244–252.

Reijneveld, S. A., van der Wal, M. F., Brugman, E., Hira Sing, R. A., & Verloove-Vanhorick, S. P. (2004). Infant crying and abuse. *The Lancet*, 364, 1340–1342.

Renfrew, C. (1991). *The Bus Story: A Test of Continuous Speech*. Oxford: Headington.

Renouf, A., Brendgen, M., Séguin, J.R., Vitaro, F., Boivin, M., Dionne, G., Tremblay, R.E. & Pérusse, D. (2010). Interactive links between theory of mind, peer victimization, and reactive and proactive aggression. *Journal of Abnormal Psychology*, 38, 1109–1123.

Resnick, L., & Ford, W. W. (1981). *The Psychology of Mathematics for Instruction*. Hillsdale, NJ: Erlbaum.

Resnick, L. B., Nesher, P., Leonard, F., Magone, M., Omanson, S., & Peled, I. (1989). Conceptual bases of arithmetic errors: The case of decimal fractions. *Journal for Research in Mathematics Education*, 20, 8–27.

Rett Syndrome Association UK (2010). *What is Rett Syndrome?* Retrieved 6 November 2010 from http://www.rettuk.org/rettuk-public/rettuk/about-rett-syndrome/what-is-rett-syndrome.

Reyna, V. F., Holliday, R. E., & Marche, T. (2002). Explaining the development of false memories. *Developmental Review*, 22, 436–489.

Reynolds, G. D., Guy, M. W., & Zhang, D. (2011). Neural correlates of individual differences in infant visual attention and recognition memory. *Infancy*, 16 (4), 368–391.

Reznick, J. S., & Goldfield, B. A. (1992). Rapid change in lexical development in comprehension and production. *Developmental Psychology*, 28, (3), 406–413.

Rheingold, H. L., & Adams, J. L. (1980). The significance of speech to newborns. *Developmental Psychology*, 16 (5), 397–403.

Richards, C. A., & Sanderson, J. A. (1999). The role of imagination in facilitating deductive reasoning in 2-, 3- and 4-year-olds. *Cognition*, 72, B1–9.

Richards, J. E. (2010). The development of attention to simple and complex visual stimuli in infants: Behavioural and psychophysiological measures. *Developmental Review*, 30 (2), 203–219.

Richardson, K. (1994). Interactions in development. In J. Oates (Ed.), *The Foundations of Child Development* (211–258). Milton Keynes: Open University/Oxford: Blackwell.

Ricketts, J., Bishop, D. V. M., & Nation, K. (2008). Investigating orthographic and semantic aspects of word learning in poor comprehenders. *Journal of Research in Reading*, 31 (1), 117–135.

Ridley, M. (1995). *Animal Behavior: An Introduction to Behavioral Mechanisms, Development and Ecology* (2nd Ed.). Cambridge, MA: Blackwell Scientific.

Rigby, K. (1997). Attitudes and beliefs about bullying among Australian school children. *Irish Journal of Psychology*, 18, 202–220.

Rigby, K. (2002). *New Perspectives on Bullying*. London: Jessica Kingsley.

Rittle-Johnson, B., Siegler, R. S., & Alibali, M. W. (2001). Developing conceptual understanding and procedural skill in mathematics: An iterative process. *Journal of Educational Psychology*, 93 (2), 46–36.

Rivkees, S. A., & Hao, H. (2000). Developing circadian rhythmicity. *Seminars in Perinatology*, 24 (4), 232–242.

Roberts, D. F., Foehr, U. G., Rideout, V., & Brodie, M. (2004). *Kids and Media in America*. Cambridge: Cambridge University Press.

Robertson, J., & Robertson, J. (1989). *Separation and the Very Young*. London: Free Association Books.

Robinson, G., & Maines, B. (2008). *Bullying: A Complete Guide to the Support Group Method*. London: Sage.

Robinson, K., & Harris, A. (2013). Racial and social class differences in how parents respond to inadequate achievement: Consequences for children's future achievement. *Social Science Quarterly*, 94 (5), 1346–1371.

Rogers, I. S., Northstone, K., Dunger, D. B., Cooper, A. R., Ness, A. R., & Emmett, P. M. (2010). Diet throughout childhood and age at menarche in a contemporary cohort of British girls. *Public Health Nutrition*, 13 (12), 2052–2063.

Roland, E. (1989). Bullying: The Scandinavian research tradition. In D. P. Tattum & D. A. Lane (Eds.), *Bullying in School* (21–32). Stoke-on-Trent: Trentham Books.

Rosch, E. (1978). Principles of categorization. In E. Rosch & B. B. Lloyd (Eds.), *Cognition and Categorization* (27–48). Hillsdale, NJ: Erlbaum.

Rose, A. J., & Asher, S. R. (1999). Children's goals and strategies in response to conflicts within a friendship. *Developmental Psychology*, 35, (1), 69–79.

Rose, A. J., & Asher, S. R. (2004). Children's strategies and goals in response to help-giving and help-seeking tasks within a friendship. *Child Development*, 75, 749–763.

Rose, S. A. (1981). Developmental changes in infants' retention of visual stimuli. *Child Development*, 52, 227–233.

Rose, S. A., Feldman, J. F., & Jankowski, J. J. (2004a). The effect of familiarization time, retention interval, and context change on adults' performance in the visual paired comparison task. *Developmental Psychobiology*, 44, 146–155.

Rose, S. A., Feldman, J. F., & Jankowski, J. J. (2004b). Infant visual recognition memory. *Developmental Review*, 24, 74–100.

Rose, S., Feldman, J. F., & Jankowski, J. J. (2005). Dimensions of cognition in infancy. *Intelligence*, 32, 245–262.

Rosenberg, M. (1979). *Conceiving the Self*. New York: Basic Books.

Rosenhan, D. L., Moore, B. S., & Underwood, B. (1976). The social psychology of moral behaviour. In T. Lickona (Ed.), *Moral Development and Behavior* (241–252). New York: Holt, Rinehart, & Winston.

Rosenstein, D., & Oster, H. (1988). Differential facial responsiveness to four basic tastes in newborns. *Child Development*, 59, 1555–1568.

Rosenzweig, M. R. (1984). Experience, memory and the brain. *American Psychologist*, 39, 365–376.

Rosenzweig, M. R., Breedlove, S. M., & Watson, N. V. (2005). *Biological Psychology: An Introduction to Behavioural and Cognitive Neuroscience*. Sunderland, MA: Sinauer.

Ross, K. M., Bard, K. A., & Matsuzawa, T. (2014). Playful expressions in one-year-old chimpanzee infants in social and solitary play contexts. *Frontiers in Psychology: Cognitive Science*, 5, ArtID: 741.

Rossetti, L. M. (2001). *Communication Intervention: Birth to Three* (2nd Ed.). Albany, NY: Singular Thomson Learning/Delmar Publishing.

Roth, A., Fonagy, P., & Parry, G. (1996). Psychotherapy research, funding, and evidence-based practice. In A. Roth and P. Fonagy (Eds.), *What Works for Whom? A Critical Review of Psychotherapy Research* (37–56). New York: Guilford Press.

Roth, G., Kanat-Maymon, Y., & Bibi, U. (2011). Prevention of school bullying: The important role of autonomy-supportive teaching and internalization of prosocial values. *British Journal of Educational Psychology*, 81 (4), 654–666.

Rothbart, M. (2004). Temperament and the pursuit of an integrated developmental psychology. *Merrill-Palmer Quarterly*, 50, 492–505.

Rothbart, M. K. (2011). *Becoming Who We Are: Temperament and Personality in Development*. New York: Guilford Press.

Rothbart, M. K., & Bates, J. E. (1998). Temperament. In D. William & N. Eisenberg (Eds.), *Handbook of Child Psychology: Vol. 3, Social, Emotional, and Personality Development* (5th Ed., 105–176). Hoboken, NJ: Wiley.

Rothbart, M. K., & Bates, J. E. (2006). Temperament. In W. Damon & R. Lerner (Series Eds.), & N. Eisenberg (Vol. Ed.), *Handbook of Child Psychology: Vol. 3, Social, Emotional, and Personality Development* (6th Ed., 99–166). New York: Wiley.

Rothbart, M., Ahadi, S., & Evans, D. (2000). Temperament and personality: Origins and outcomes. *Journal of Personality and Social Psychology*, 78, 83–116.

Rothbart, M. K., Ahadi, S. A., & Hersey, K. L. (1994). Temperament and social behaviour in childhood. *Merrill-Palmer Quarterly: Journal of Developmental Psychology*, 40, 21–39.

Rothbart, M. K., Ahadi, S. A., Hershey, L. L., & Fisher, P. (2001). Investigations of temperament at three to seven years: The children's behavior questionnaire. *Child Development*, 72, 1394–1408.

Rothbart, M. K., Ellis, L. K., & Posner, M. I. (2011). Temperament and self-regulation. In K. D. Vohs & R. F. Baumeister (Eds.), *Handbook of Self-Regulation: Research, Theory, and Applications* (441–460). New York: Guilford Press.

Rothbart, M. K., Ellis, L. K., Rosario Rueda, M., & Posner, M. I. (2003). Developing mechanisms of temperamental effortful control. *Journal of Personality*, 71, 1113–1144.

Rothbaum, F., Pott, M., Azuma, H., Miyake, K., & Weisz, J. (2000). The development of close relationships in Japan and the United States: Paths of symbiotic harmony and generative tension. *Child Development*, 71, 1121–1142.

Rovee-Collier, C. K., & Boller, K. (1995). Interference or facilitation in infant memory? In F. N. Dempster & C. J. Brainerd (Eds.), *Interference and Inhibition in Cognition* (61–104). San Diego, CA: Academic Press.

Rovee-Collier, C., & Cuevas, K. (2009). Multiple memory systems are unnecessary to account for infant memory development: An ecological model. *Developmental Psychology*, 45, 160–174.

Rovee-Collier, C., Sullivan, M., Enright, M., Lucas, D., & Fagen, J. W. (1980). Reactivation of infant memory. *Science*, 208, 1159–1161.

Rubia, K., Smith, A., & Taylor, E. (2007). Performance of children with attention deficit hyperactivity disorder (ADHD) on a biological marker test battery for impulsiveness. *Child Neuropsychology*, 13 (3), 276–304.

Rubin, J. Z., Provenzano, F. J., & Luria, Z. (1974). The eye of the beholder: Parents' views on sex of newborns. *American Journal of Orthopsychiatry*, 44, 512–519.

Rubin, K., Bukowski, W., & Parker, J. (1998). Peer interactions, relationships and groups. In N. Eisenberg & W. Damon (Eds.), *Handbook of Child Psychology,*

Vol. 3: Social, Emotional and Personality Development (619–700). New York: Wiley.

Rubin, K., Wojslawowicz, J., Rose-Krasnor, L., Booth-LaForce, C., & Burgess, K. (2006). The best friendships of shy/withdrawn children: Prevalence, stability and relationship quality. *Journal of Abnormal Child Psychology*, 34, 143–157.

Rubin, K. H. (1982). Non-social play in preschoolers: Necessarily evil? *Child Development*, 53, 651–657.

Rubin, K. H., Fein, G. G., & Vandenberg, B. (1983). Play. In E. M. Hetherington (Ed.), *Handbook of Child Psychology: Vol. 4, Socialization, Personality, and Social Development* (4th Ed., 693–744). New York: Wiley.

Rubin, K. H., Hymel, S., & Mills, R. S. L. (1989). Sociability and social withdrawal in childhood: Stability and outcomes. *Journal of Personality*, 57, 237–255.

Ruble, D. N., & Stangor, C. (1986). Stalking the elusive schema: Insights from developmental and social-psychological analyses of gender schemas. *Social Cognition*, 4, 227–261.

Ruble, D. N., Balaban, T., & Cooper, J. (1981). Gender constancy and the effects of sex-typed televised commercials. *Child Development*, 52, 667–673.

Rucinska, Z., & Reijmers, E. (2015). Enactive account of pretend play and its application to therapy. *Frontiers in Psychology*, 6, 1–5.

Ruff, H. A., & Capozzoli, M. C. (2003). Development of attention and distractibility in the first 4 years of life. *Developmental Psychology*, 39, 877–890.

Ruff, H. A., & Rothbart, M. E. (1996). *Attention in Early Development: Themes and Variations*. Oxford: Oxford University Press.

Rummelhart, D. E., McClelland, J. L., & the PDP Research Group (1986). *Parallel Distributed Processing: Explorations in the Microstructure of Cognition: Vol. 1, Foundations*. Cambridge, MA: MIT Press.

Russ, S. W. (2004). *Play in Child Development and Psychotherapy: Toward Empirically Supported Practice*. Hillsdale, NJ: Erlbaum.

Ruthsatz, J., Detterman, D., Griscom, W. S., & Cirullo, B. A. (2008). Becoming an expert in the musical domain: It takes more than just practice. *Intelligence*, 36, 330–338.

Rutter, M. (1970). The description and classification of infantile autism. *Proceedings of the Indiana University Colloquium on Infantile Autism*. Springfield, IL: Charles C. Thomas.

Rutter, M. (1987). Temperament, personality and personality disorder. *British Journal of Psychiatry*, 150, 443–458.

Rutter, M., Kreppner, J., & O'Connor, T. (2001). Specificity and heterogeneity in children's responses to profound institutional privation. *British Journal of Psychiatry*, 179, 97–103.

Rutter, M., Silberg, J., O'Connor, T., & Simonoff, E. (1999). Genetics and child psychiatry: II empirical research findings. *Journal of Child Psychology and Psychiatry*, 40, 19–55.

Rymer, R. (1992). *Genie: A Scientific Tragedy*. New York: Harper Collins.

Saab, N., van Joolingen, W. R., & van Hout-Wolters, B. H. A. M. (2005). Communication in collaborative discovery learning. *British Journal of Educational Psychology*, 75 (4), 603–621.

Sachdev, P. (1999). Attention deficit hyperactivity disorder in adults. *Psychological Medicine*, 29, 507–514.

Sacks, H., Schegloff, E. A., & Jefferson, G. (1974). A simplest systematics for the organisation of turn-taking for conversation. *Language*, 50, 696–735.

Saffran, J. R., Loman, M. M., & Robertson, R. R. W. (2000). Infant memory for musical experiences. *Cognition*, 77, B15–B23.

Sagi, A., Koren-Karie, N., Gini, M., Ziv, Y., & Joels, T. (2002). Shedding further light on the effects of various types and quality of early child care on infant–mother attachment relationships: The Haifa study of early child care. *Child Development*, 73, 1166–1186.

Saida, Y., & Miyashita, M. (1979). Development of fine motor skill in children: Manipulation of a pencil in children aged 2 to 6 years old. *Journal of Human Movement Studies*, 5, 104–113.

Sainsbury, M., Whetton, C. Mason, K., & Schagen, I. (1998). Fallback in attainment on transfer at age 11: Evidence from the Summer Literacy Schools evaluation. *Educational Research*, 40 (1), 73–81.

Salmivalli, C. (2001). Group view on victimisation. Empirical findings and their implications. In J. Juvonen & S. Graham (Eds.), *Peer Harassment in School: The Plight of the Vulnerable and Victimized* (398–419). New York: Guilford Press.

Salmivalli, C. (2010). Bullying and the peer group: A review. *Aggression and Violent Behaviour*, 15, 112–120.

Salmivalli, C. & Poskiparta, E. (2012). KiVa Antibullying Program: Overview of evaluation studies based on a randomized controlled trial and national rollout in Finland. *International Journal of Conflict and Violence*, 6, 294–302.

Salmivalli, C., Lagerspetz, K., Bjorkqvist, K., Österman, K., & Kaukiainen, A. (1996). Bullying as a group process: Participant roles and their relations to social status within the group. *Aggressive Behaviour*, 22, 1–15.

Salmon, P. (1992). The peer group. In J. C. Coleman (Ed.), *The School Years: Current Issues in the Socialisation of Young People* (2nd Ed.). London: Routledge.

Sambeth, A., Pakarinen, S., Ruohio, K., Fellman, V., van Zuijen, T. L., & Huotilainen, M. (2009). Change detection in newborns using a multiple deviant paradigm: A study using magnetoencephalography. *Clinical Neuropsychology*, 120, 530–538.

San Juan, V., & Wilde Astington, J. (2012). Bridging the gap between implicit and explicit understanding: How language development promotes the processing and representation of false belief. *British Journal of Developmental Psychology*, 30 (1), 105–122.

Sanders, M. R., Markie-Dadds, C., Tully, L. A., & Bor, W. (2000). The triple P-positive parenting program: A comparison of enhanced, standard, and self-directed behavioral family intervention for parents of children with early onset conduct problems. *Journal of Consulting and Clinical Psychology*, 68 (4), 624.

Sanders, M. R., Calam, R., Durand, M., Liversidge, T., & Carmont, S. A. (2008). Does self-directed and web-based support for parents enhance the effects of viewing a reality television series based on the triple P Positive Parenting Programme? *Journal of Child Psychology and Psychiatry*, 49, 924–932.

Sandstrom, M. J., & Cillessen, A. H. N. (2003). Sociometric status and children's peer experiences: Use of the daily diary method. *Merrill-Palmer Quarterly*, 49, 427–452.

Sanford, K., & Madill, L. (2006). Resistance through video game play: It's a boy thing. *Canadian Journal of Education*, 29, 287–306.

Santos, A. J., Vaughn, B. E., Peceguina, I., & Daniel, J. R. (2014). Longitudinal stability of social competence indicators in a Portuguese sample: Q-sort profiles of social competence, measures of social engagement, and peer sociometric acceptance. *Developmental Psychology*, 50, 968–978.

Sarnecka, B. W., & Gelman, S. A. (2004). Six does not just mean a lot: Preschoolers see number words as specific. *Cognition*, 92, 329–352.

Sauter, D. A., Panattoni, C., & Happe, F. (2013). Children's recognition of emotions from vocal cues. *British Journal of Developmental Psychology*, 31 (1), 97–113.

Savin-Williams, R. C., & Berndt, T. J. (1990). Friendship and peer relations. In S. S. Feldman & G. R. Elliott (Eds.), *At the Threshold: The Developing Adolescent* (277–307). Cambridge, MA: Harvard University Press.

Sawyer, J. L., Mishna, F., Pepler, D. & Wiener, J. (2011). The missing voice: Parents' perspectives of bullying. *Children and Youth Services Review*, 33, 1795–1803.

Saxe, G. (1981). Body parts as numerals: A developmental analysis of numeration among the Oksapmin in Papua New Guinea. *Child Development*, 52, 306–316.

Saxe, G., Guberman, S. R., & Gearhart, M. (1987). Social and developmental processes in children's understanding of number. *Monographs of the Society for Research in Child Development*, 52, 100–200.

Sayer, J. (1982). *Biological Politics: Feminist and Antifeminist Perspectives*. London: Tavistock.

Schaaf, R. C., & Miller, L. J. (2005). Occupational therapy using a sensory integrative approach for children with developmental disabilities. *Mental Retardation and Developmental Disability Research Review*, 11, 143–148.

Schaal, B., Marlier, L., & Soussignan, R. (2000). Human foetuses learn odours from their pregnant mother's diet. *Chemical Senses*, 25, 729–737.

Schaffer, H., & Emerson, P. (1964). The development of social attachments in infancy. *Monographs of the Society for Research in Child Development*, 29 (3), Serial No. 94.

Scheeler, M., Macluckie, M., & Albright, K. (2010). Effects of immediate feedback delivered by peer tutors on the oral presentation skills of adolescents with learning disabilities. *Remedial and Special Education*, 31 (2), 77–86.

Schermerhorn, A. C., Bates, J. E., Goodnight, J. A., Lansford, J. E., Dodge, K. A., & Pettit, G. S. (2013). Temperament moderates associations between exposure to stress and children's externalizing problems. *Child Development*, 84, 1579–1593.

Schiefflin, B. B., & Ochs, E. (1983). A cultural perspective on the transition from prelinguistic to linguistic communication. In R. M. Golinkoff (Ed.), *The Transition From Prelinguistic to Linguistic Communication* (115–131). Hillsdale, NJ: Erlbaum.

Schimmenti, A., Caretti, V., & La Barbera, D. (2013). Internet gaming disorder or internet addiction? A plea for conceptual clarity. *Clinical Neuropsychiatry: Journal of Treatment Evaluation*, 11, 145–146.

Schneider, B. H. (2000). *Friends and Enemies: Peer Relations in Childhood*. London: Arnold.

Schneider, B. H., Atkinson, L., & Tardif, C. (2001). Child–parent attachment and children's peer relations: A quantitative review. *Developmental Psychology*, 37, 87–100.

Schuengel, G., Bakermans-Kranenburg, M. J., & van IJzendoorn, M. H. (1999). Attachment and loss: Frightening maternal behavior linking unresolved loss and disorganized infant attachment. *Journal of Consulting and Clinical Psychology*, 67, 54–63.

Schuetze, P., & Zeskind, P. S. (1997). Relation between reported maternal caffeine consumption during pregnancy and neonatal state and heart rate. *Infant Behavior and Development*, 20, 559–562.

Schulkin, J. (2000). Theory of mind and mirroring neurons. *Trends in Cognitive Sciences*, 4 (7), 252–254.

Schwartz, C. E., Wright, C., Shin, L., Kagan, J., & Raugh, S. (2003). Inhibited and uninhibited infants 'grown up': Adult amygdalar response to novelty. *Science*, 300, 1952–1953.

Schwartz, D., Dodge, K. A., Pettit, G. S., & Bates, J. E. (1997). The early socialisation of aggressive victims of bullying. *Child Development*, 68, 665–675.

Schwartz, D., Proctor, L. J., & Chien, D. H. (2001). The aggressive victim of bullying: Emotional and behavioural dysregulation as a pathway to victimisation by peers. In J. Juvonen & S. Graham (Eds.), *Peer Harassment in School: The Plight of the Vulnerable and Victimized* (147–174). New York: Guilford Press.

Sebald, H. (1989). Adolescents' peer orientations: Changes in the support system during the past decades. *Adolescence*, 24, 936–946.

Seeley, J., Small, J., Walker, H., Feil, E., Severson, H., Golly, A., & Forness, S. (2009). Efficacy of the first step to success intervention for students with attention-deficit/hyperactivity disorder. *School Mental Health*, 1 (1), 37–48.

Seidler, F. J., Levin, E. D., Lappi, S. E., & Slotkin, T. A. (1992). Fetal nicotine exposure ablates the ability of postnatal nicotine challenge to release norepinephrine from rat brain regions. *Developmental Brain Research*, 69, 288–291.

Seiffge-Krenke, I. (2000). Causal links between stressful events, coping style, and adolescent symptomatology. *Journal of Adolescence*, 23 (6), 675–691.

Seiffge-Krenke, I., & Beyers, W. (2005). Coping trajectories from adolescence to young adulthood: Links to attachment state of mind. *Journal of Research on Adolescence*, 15 (4), 561–582.

Seiffge-Krenke, I., & Klessinger, N. (2000). Long-term effects of avoidant coping on adolescents' depressive symptoms. *Journal of Youth and Adolescence*, 29 (6), 617–630.

Selman, R. L. (1980). *The Growth of Interpersonal Understanding*. New York: Academic Press.

Selman, R. L. (2003). *The Promotion of Social Awareness: Powerful Lessons from the Partnership of Developmental Theory and Classroom Practice*. New York: Russell Sage.

Sen, M. G., Yonas, A., & Knill, D. C. (2001). Development of infants' sensitivity to surface contour information for spatial layout. *Perception*, 30, 167–176.

Serbin, L. A., Powlishta, K. K., & Gulko, J. (1993). The development of sex typing in middle childhood. *Monographs of the Society for Research in Child Development*, 58, Serial No. 232.

Serbin, L., Stack, D., & Kingdon, D. (2013). Academic success across the transition from primary to secondary schooling among lower-income adolescents: Understanding the effects of family resources and gender. *Journal of Youth and Adolescence*, 42 (9), 1331–1347.

Serketich, W. J., & Dumas, J. E. (1996). The effectiveness of behavioural parent training to modify antisocial behaviour in children: A meta-analysis. *Behaviour Therapy*, 27, 171–186.

Seymour, P. H. K., Aro, M., & Erskine, J. M. (2003). Foundation literacy acquisition in European orthographies. *British Journal of Psychology*, 94, 143–174.

Shaffer, D. R., & Kipp, K. (2010). *Development Psychology: Childhood and Adolescence*. Belmont, CA: Wadsworth.

Shahar, S. (1990). *Childhood in the Middle Ages*. London: Routledge.

Shahin, A. J., Roberts, L. E., Chau, W., Trainer, L. J., & Miller, L. M. (2008). Music training leads to the development of timbre-specific gamma band activity. *NeuroImage*, 41, 113–122.

Shakoor, S., Jaffee, S. R., Bowes, L., Ouellet-Morin, I., Andreou, P., Happé, F., Moffitt, T. E. & Arseneault, L. (2012). A prospective longitudinal study of children's theory of mind and adolescent involvement in bullying. *Journal of Child Psychology and Psychiatry*, 53, 254–261.

Sharp, C. (2002). School starting age: European policy and recent research. Local Government Association Seminar 'When should our children start school?'. London, 1 November.

Sharp, S. (1996). The role of peers in tackling bullying. *Educational Psychology in Practice*, 11, 17–22.

Shaw, P., Greenstein, D., Lerch, J., Clasen, L., Lenroot, R., Gogtay, N., & Evans, A. (2006). Intellectual ability and cortical development in children and adolescents. *Nature*, 440, 676–679.

Sheridan, M. (2008). *From Birth to Five Years*. Oxford: Routledge.

Shih, C. (2013). Assisting people with disabilities in actively performing designated occupational activities with battery-free wireless mice to control environmental stimulation. *Research in Developmental Disabilities*, 34 (5), 1521–1527.

Shiner, R. L., Buss, K. A., McClowry, S. G., Putnam, S. P., Sandino, K. J., & Zentner, M. (2012). What is temperament now? Assessing progress in temperament research on the twenty-fifth anniversary of Goldsmith et al. (1987). *Child Development Perspectives*, 6, 436–444.

Shreeve, A., Boddington, D., Bernard, B., Brown, K., Clarke, K., Dean, L., Elkins, T., Kemp, S., Lees, J. Miller, D., Oakley, J., & Shiret, D. (2002). Student perceptions of rewards and sanctions. *Pedagogy, Culture and Society*, 10 (2), 239–256.

Shriberg, E. (1999). Phonetic consequences of speech disfluency. In J. Ohala, Y. Hasegawa, M. Ohala, D. Granveille, & A. Bailey (Eds.), *Proceedings of the XIVth International Congress on Phonetic Sciences* (Vol. 1, 619–622). Berkeley, CA: Department of Linguistics, University of California at Berkeley.

Shulman, S., Elicker, J., & Sroufe, L. A. (1994). Stages of friendship growth in preadolescence as related to attachment history. *Journal of Social and Personal Relationships*, 11, 341–361.

Siegal, M., & Beattie, K. (1991). Where to look first for children's knowledge of false beliefs. *Cognition*, 38, 1–12.

Siegler, R. S. (1996). *Emerging Minds: The Process of Change in Children's Thinking*. New York: Oxford University Press.

Siegler, R., DeLoache, J., & Eisenberg, N. (2010). *How Children Develop* (3rd Ed.). New York: Worth.

Signorella, M. L., & Hanson Frieze, I. (2008). Interrelations of gender schemas in children and adolescents: Attitudes, preferences, and self-perceptions. *Social Behavior and Personality*, 36, 941–954.

Simmons, R. G., & Blyth, D. A. (1987). *Moving into Adolescence: The Impact of Pubertal Change and School Context*. Hawthorne, NY: Aldine de Gruyter.

Simpson, A., & Riggs, K. J. (2005). Inhibitory and working memory demands of the day–night task in children. *British Journal of Developmental Psychology*, 23, 471–486.

Simpson, S., Vitiello, B., Wells, K., Wigal, T., & Wu, M. (2001). Clinical relevance of the primary findings of the MTA: Success rates based on severity of ADHD and ODD symptoms at the end of treatment. *Journal of the American Academy of Child and Adolescent Psychiatry*, 40, 168–179.

Skinner, B. F. (1957). *Verbal Behaviour*. East-Norwalk, CT: Appleton-Century-Crofts.

Slaby, R. G., & Frey, K. S. (1975). Development of gender constancy and selective attention to same-sex models. *Child Development*, 46, 849–856.

Slater, A., & Johnson, S. P. (1999). Visual sensory and perceptual abilities of the newborn: Beyond the blooming, buzzing confusion. In A. Slater & S. P. Johnson (Eds.), *The Development of Sensory, Motor and Cognitive Capacities* (121–141). Hove: Psychology Press.

Slater, A., & Lewis, M. (2002). *Introduction to Infant Development*. Oxford: Oxford University Press.

Slater, A. M., & Morison, V. (1985). Shape constancy and slant perception at birth. *Perception*, 14, 337–344.

Slater, A. M., Mattock, A., & Brown, E. (1990). Size constancy at birth: Newborn infants reponses to retinal and real size. *Journal of Experimental Child Psychology*, 49, 314–322.

Slater, A., Morison, V., & Rose, D. (1983). Perception of shape by the newborn baby. *British Journal of Developmental Psychology*, 1, 135–142.

Slobin, D. (1972). Children and language: They learn the same way around the world. *Psychology Today*, July, 71–76.

Smart, D., & Sanson, A. (2008). Do Australian children have more problems today than twenty years ago? *Family Matters*, 79, 50–57.

Smidt, S. (2011). *Playing to Learn: The Role of Play in the Early Years*. London: Routledge.

Smilansky, S. (1968). *The Effects of Sociodramatic Play on Disadvantaged Preschool Children*. New York: Wiley.

Smith, A., Taylor, E., Warner Rogers, J., Newman, S., & Rubia, K. (2002). Evidence for a pure time perception deficit in children with ADHD. *Journal of Child Psychology and Psychiatry*, 43, 529–542.

Smith, A. D. (2009). On the use of drawing tasks in neuropsychological assessment. *Neuropsychology*, 23 (2), 231–239.

Smith, M. (2012). Can online peer review assignments replace essays in third year university courses? And if so, what are the challenges? *Electronic Journal of E-Learning*, 10 (1), 147–158.

Smith, S. N., & Miller, R. (2005). Learning approaches: Examination type, discipline of study, and gender. *Educational Psychology*, 25 (1), 43–53.

Smith, P. K. (1978). A longitudinal study of social participation in preschool children: Solitary and parallel play re-examined. *Developmental Psychology*, 14, 517–523.

Smith, P. K. (1997). Bullying in life-span perspective: What can studies of school bullying and workplace bullying learn from each other? *Journal of Community and Applied Psychology*, 7, 249–255.

Smith, P. K. (2004). Bullying: Recent developments. *Child and Adolescent Mental Health*, 9, 98–103.

Smith, P. K., & Levan, S. (1995). Perceptions and experiences of bullying in younger pupils. *British Journal of Educational Psychology*, 65, 489–500.

Smith, P. K. & Myron-Wilson, R. (1998). Parenting and school bullying. *Child Psychology and Psychiatry*, 3, 405–417.

Smith, P. K., & Sharp, S. (1994). The problem of school bullying. In P. K. Smith & S. Sharp (Eds.), *School Bullying: Insights and Perspectives* (2–19). London: Routledge.

Smith, P. K., & Sloboda, J. (1986). Individual consistency in infant–stranger encounters. *British Journal of Developmental Psychology*, 4, 83–91.

Smith, P. K., Cowie, H., Olafsson, R., & Liefooghe, A. (2002). Definitions of bullying: A comparison of terms used, and age and sex differences, in a 14-country international comparison. *Child Development*, 73, 1119–1133.

Smith, P. K., Cowie, H., & Sharp, S. (1994). Working directly with pupils involved in bullying situations. In P. K. Smith & S. Sharp (Eds.), *School Bullying: Insights and Perspectives* (193–212). London: Routledge.

Smith, P. K., Madsen, K. C., & Moody, J.C. (1999a). What causes the age decline in reports of being bullied at school? Towards a developmental analysis of risks of being bullied. *Educational Research*, 41, 267–285.

Smith, P. K., Mahdavi, J., Carvalho, M., Fisher, S., Russell, S., & Tippett, N. (2008a). Cyberbullying: Its nature and impact in secondary school pupils. *Journal of Child Psychology and Psychiatry*, 49, 376–385.

Smith, P. K., Morita, Y., Junger-Tas, J., Olweus, D., Catalano, R., & Slee, P. (1999b). *The Nature of School Bullying: A Cross-National Perspective*. London: Routledge.

Smith, P. K., Salmivalli, C. & Cowie, H. (2012). Effectiveness of school-based programs to reduce bullying: A commentary. *Journal of Experimental Criminology*, 8, 433–441.

Smith, P. K., Singer, M., Hoel, H., & Cooper, C. L. (2003). Victimization in the school and the workplace: Are there any links? *British Journal of Psychology*, 94, 175–188.

Smith, P. K., Smith, C., Osborn, R., & Samara, M. (2008b). A content analysis of school anti-bullying policies: Progress and limitations. *Educational Psychology in Practice*, 24, 1–12.

Smolak, L. (1986). *Infancy*. Englewood Cliffs, NJ: Prentice Hall.

Smorti, A., Menesini, E., & Smith, P. K. (2003). Parents' definitions of children's bullying in a five-country comparison. *Journal of Cross-Cultural Psychology*, 34 (4), 417–432.

Snow, C. (1994). Beginning from baby-talk: Twenty years of research on input and interaction. In C. Galloway and B. Richards (Eds.), *Input and Interaction in Language Acquisition* (3–12). London: Cambridge University Press.

Snowling, M. (2000). *Dyslexia*. Oxford: Blackwell.

Sobel, D. (2000). *Galileo's Daughter: A Drama of Science, Faith and Love*. London: Fourth Estate Limited.

Sokolov, E. N. (1963). *Perception and the Conditioned Reflex*. Oxford: Pergamon.

Solanto, M. V., Abikoff, H., Sonuga-Barke, E., Schachar, R., Logan, G. D., Wigal, T., Hechtman, L., Hinshaw, S., & Turkel, E. (2001). The ecological validity of delay aversion and response inhibition as measures of impulsivity in AD/HD: A supplement to the NIMH multi-modal treatment study of AD/HD. *Journal of Abnormal Child Psychology*, 29, 215–228.

Soloff, C., Lawrence, D., & Johnstone, R. (2005). Longitudinal study of Australian children, technical paper no. 1: Sample design, Australian Institute of Family Studies, Melbourne, Australia. Available at: http://www.aifs.gov.au/growingup/pubs/technical/tp1.pdf.

Soltis, J. (2004). The signal functions of early infant crying. *Behavioural and Brain Sciences*, 27, 443–490.

Sonuga-Barke, E. J. S. (2002). Psychological heterogeneity in AD/HD: A dual pathway model of behaviour and cognition. *Behavioural Brain Research*, 130, 29–36.

Sonuga-Barke, E. J. S. (2004). On the reorganization of incentive structure to promote delay tolerance: A therapeutic possibility for AD/HD? *Neural Plasticity*, 11, 23–28.

Sonuga-Barke, E., Bitsakou, P., & Thompson, M. (2010). Beyond the dual pathway model: Evidence for the dissociation of timing, inhibitory, and delay-related impairments in attention-deficit/hyperactivity disorder. *Journal of the American Academy of Child and Adolescent Psychiatry*, 49, 345–355.

Sonuga-Barke, E., Brandeis, D., Cortese, S., Daley, D., Ferrin, M., Holtmann, M., Stevenson, J., Danckaerts, M., Van Der Oord, S., Dopfner, M., Dittmann, R. W., Simonoff, E., Zuddas, A., Banaschewski, T., Buitelaar, J., Coghill, D., Hollis, C., Konofal, E., Lecendreux, M., Wong, I. C., & Sergeant, J. (2013). Nonpharmacological interventions for ADHD: Systematic review and meta-analyses of randomized controlled trials of dietary and psychological treatments. *American Journal of Psychiatry*, 170, 275–289.

Sonuga-Barke, E. J. S., Dalen, L., & Remmington, B. (2003). Do executive deficits and delay aversion make independent contributions to preschool attention deficit/hyperactivity disorder? *Journal of the American Academy of Child and Adolescent Psychiatry*, 42, 1335–1342.

Sonuga-Barke, E. J. S., Daley, D., Thompson, M., Laver-Bradbury, C., & Weeks, A. (2001). Parent-based therapies for preschool attention-deficit/hyperactivity disorder: A randomized, controlled trial with a community sample. *Journal of the American Academy of Child and Adolescent Psychiatry*, 40, 402–408.

Sonuga-Barke, E. J. S., Lamparelli, M., Stevenson, J., Thompson, M., & Henry, A. (1994). Behaviour problems and pre-school intellectual attainment: The associations of hyperactivity and conduct problems. *Journal of Child Psychology and Applied Disciplines*, 35 (5), 949–960.

Sonuga-Barke, E. J. S., Minocha, K., Taylor, E. A., & Sandberg, S. (1993). Interethnic bias in teachers ratings of childhood hyperactivity. *British Journal of Developmental Psychology*, 11, 187–200.

Sonuga-Barke, E. J. S, Williams, E., Hall, M., & Saxton, T. (1996). Hyperactivity and delay aversion. III: The effects on cognitive style of imposing delay after errors. *Journal of Child Psychology and Psychiatry*, 37, 189–194.

Sophian, C. (1988). Limitations on preschool children's knowledge about counting: Using counting to compare two sets. *Developmental Psychology*, 24, 634–640. 230.

Soponaru, C., Tincu, C., & Iorga, M. (2014). The influence of the sociometric status of students on academic achievement. *Journal of Academic Emergency Medicine Case Reports/Akademik Acil Tip Olgu sunumlari Dergisi (Acil Tip Uzmanlari Dernegi)*, 149–168.

Sowell, E. R., Thompson, P. M., Holmes, C. J., Batth, R., Jernigan, T. L., & Toga, A. W. (1999). Localizing age related changes in brain structure between childhood and adolescence using statistical parametric mapping. *NeuroImage*, 6, 587–597.

Span, S. A., Earlywine, M., & Strybel, T. Z. (2002). Confirming the factor structure of attention deficit hyperactivity disorder symptoms in adult, nonclinical samples. *Journal of Psychopathology and Behavioural Assessment*, 24 (2), 129–136.

Spelke, E. S. (1979). Perceiving bimodally specified events in infancy. *Developmental Psychology*, 15, 626–636.

Spelke, E. (2000). Core knowledge. *American Psychologist*, 55, 1233–1242.

Spielhofer, T., Benton, T., & Schagen, S. (2004). A study of the effects of school size and single-sex education in English schools. *Research Papers in Education*, 19 (2), 133–159.

Sponheim, E., & Skjeldal, O. (1998). Autism and related disorders: Epidemiological findings in a Norwegian study using diagnostic criteria. *Journal of Autism and Developmental Disorder*, 28, 217–227.

Spratt, J., Shucksmith, J., Philip, K., & Watson, C. (2006). Interprofessional support of mental well-being in schools: A Bourdieuan perspective. *Journal of Interprofessional Care*, 20 (4), 391–402.

Sprich, S., Biederman, J., Crawford, M. H., Mundy, E., & Faraone, S. V. (2000). Adoptive and biological families of children and adolescents with ADHD. *Journal of the American Academy of Child and Adolescent Psychiatry*, 39, 1432–1437.

Sroufe, L. A., Carlson, E., & Schulman, S. (1993). Individuals in relationships: Development from infancy through adolescence. In D. C. Funder, R. D. Parke, C. Tomlinson-Keasey, & K. Widaman (Eds.), *Studying Lives Through Time: Personality and Development* (315–342). Washington, DC: APA.

Stackhouse, J., & Wells, B. (1997). *Children's Speech and Literacy Difficulties: A Psycholinguistic Framework*. London: Singular Publishers.

Stams, G. J. M., Juffer, F., & van IJzendoorn, M. H. (2002). Maternal sensitivity, infant attachment, and temperament in early childhood predict adjustment in middle childhood: The case of adopted children and their biologically unrelated parents. *Developmental Psychology*, 38, 806–821.

Standards for Education and Training in Psychological Assessment (2006). Position of the Society for Personality Assessment: An Official Statement of the Board of Trustees of the Society for Personality Assessment. *Journal of Personality Assessment*, 87, 355–357.

Stark, R. E. (1980). Stages of speech development in the first year of life. In G. Yeni-Komshian, J. F. Ferguson & C. A. Ferguson (Eds.), *Child Phonology: 1 Production* (73–90). New York: Academic Press.

Stark, R. E. (1981). Infant vocalisation: A comprehensive view. *Infant Mental Health Journal*, 2, 118–128.

Stattin, H., & Magnusson, D. (1990). *Pubertal Maturation in Female Development* (Vol. 2). Hillsdale, NJ: Erlbaum.

Steele, M., Hodges, J., Kaniuk, J., Hillman, S., & Henderson, K. (2003). Attachment representations and adoption: Associations between maternal states of mind and emotion narratives in previously maltreated children. *Journal of Child Psychotherapy*, 29, 187–205.

Steele, M., Marigna, M. R., Tello, J. and Johnston, R. (2000). *Strengthening Families, Strengthening Communities: An Inclusive Programme*. Facilitator Manual. London: Race Equality Unit.

Steffe, L. P., von Glaserfeld, E., Richards, J., & Cobb, P. (1983). *Children's Counting Types: Philosophy, Theory and Application*. New York: Praeger.

Steif, P., Lobue, J., Kara, L., & Fay, A. (2010). Improving problem solving performance by inducing talk about salient problem features. *Journal of Engineering Education*, 99 (2), 135–142.

Stein, L. (2012). The art of saving a failing school. *Phi Delta Kappan*, 93 (5), 51–55.

Steinberg, L. (2011). Demystifying the adolescent brain. *Educational Leadership*, 68 (7), 41–46.

Steiner-Adair, C., & Barker, T. H. (2013). *The Big Disconnect: Protecting Childhood and Family Relationships in the Digital Age*. New York: Harper Collins.

Stemmer, B., & Joanette, Y. (1998). The interpretation of narrative discourse of brain-damaged individuals within the framework of a multilevel discourse model. In M. Beeman & C. Chiarello (Eds.), *Right Hemisphere Language Comprehension: Perspectives from Cognitive Neuroscience* (329–348). London: Erlbaum.

Stephenson, P., & Smith, D. (1989). Bullying in the junior school. In D. P. Tattum & D. A. Lane (Eds.), *Bullying in School* (45–57). Stoke-on-Trent: Trentham Books.

Stern, M., & Karraker, K. H. (1989). Sex stereotyping of infants: A review of gender labelling studies. *Sex Roles*, 20, 501–522.

Stern, W. (1912). *The Psychological Methods of Intelligence Testing*. Baltimore, MD: Warwick & York.

Sternberg, R. J. (1985). *Beyond IQ: A Triarchic Theory of Human Intelligence*. New York: Cambridge University Press.

Stevens, S. E., Sonuga-Barke, E. J. B., Kreppner, J. M., Beckett, C., Castle, J., Colvet, E., Groothues, C., Hawkins, A., & Rutter, M. (2008). Inattention/overactivity following early severe institutional deprivation: Presentation and associations in early adolescence. *Journal of Abnormal Child Psychology*, 36, 385–398.

Stevens, V., De Bourdeaudhuij, I., & Van Oost, P. (2002). Relationship of the family environment to children's involvement in bully/victim problems at school. *Journal of Youth and Adolescence*, 31, 419–428.

Stevenson, C. S., Stevenson, R. J., & Whitmont, S. (2003). A self-directed psychosocial intervention with minimal therapist contact for adults with attention deficit hyperactivity disorder. *Clinical Psychology and Psychotherapy*, 10, 93–101.

Stewart, G. (2013). 'How not to give up on a science career.' *Chronicle of Higher Education* 60 (13): A30.

Stilberg, J., San Miguel, V., Murelle, E., Prom, E., Bates, J., Canino, G., Egger, H., & Eaves, L. (2005). Genetic environmental influences on temperament in the first year of life: The Puerto Rico Infant Twin Study (PRINTS). *Twin Research and Human Genetics*, 8, 328–336.

Stinson, J., & Milter, R. (1996). Problem-based learning in business education: Curriculum design and implementation issues. In L. Wilkerson & W. Gijselaers (Eds.), *Bringing Problem-Based Learning to Higher Education: Theory and Practice* (33–42). San Francisco, CA: Jossey-Bass.

Stormshak, E. A., Bierman, K. L., Bruschi, D., Dodge, K. A., & Coie, J. D. (1999). The relation between behavior problems and peer preference in different classroom contexts. *Child Development*, 79, 169–182.

Stouthamer-Loeber, M. (1986). Lying as a problem behavior in children: A review. *Clinical Psychology Review*, 6, 267–289.

Strachan, T., & Read, A. (2003). *Human Molecular Genetics*. New York: Wiley.

Strathearn, L. (2011). Maternal neglect: Oxytocin, dopamine and the neurobiology of attachment. *Journal of Neuroendrocrinology*, 23, 1054–1065.

Strathearn, L., Fonagy, P., Amico, J. A., & Montague, P. R. (2009). Adult attachment predicts mother's brain and oxytocin response to infant cues. *Neuropsychopharmacology*, 34, 2655–2666.

Strauch, B. (2003). *The Primal Teen: What the New Discoveries about the Teenage Brain Tell Us about Our Kids*. New York: Anchor.

Streeter, L. (1976). Language perception of 2-month-old infants shows effects of both innate mechanisms and experience. *Nature*, 259, 39–41.

Streissguth, A. P., Barr, H. M., Sampson, P. D., & Bookstein, F. L. (1994). Prenatal alcohol and offspring development: The first fourteen years. *Drug and Alcohol Dependence*, 36, 89–99.

Streri, A., & Spelke, E. S. (1988). Haptic perception of objects in infancy. *Cognitive Psychology*, 20, 1–23.

Striano, T., Tomasello, M., & Rochat, P. (2001). Social and object support for early symbolic play. *Developmental Science*, 4, 442–455.

Sugawara, M., Sakamoto, S., Kitamura, T., Toda, M. A., & Shima, S. (1999). Structure of depression symptoms in pregnancy and the postpartum period. *Journal of Affective Disorders*, 54, 161–169.

Sugita, Y. (2004). Experience in early infancy is indispensable for colour perception. *Current Biology*, 14, 1267–1271.

Suler, J. (2004). The online disinhibition effect. *Cyber Psychology and Behaviour*, 7, 321–326.

Suomi, S. J., & Harlow, H. F. (1972). Social rehabilitation of isolate-reared monkeys. *Developmental Psychology*, 6, 487–496.

Surbey, M. (1990). Family composition, stress, and human menarche. In F. Bercovitch & T. Zeigler (Eds.), *The Socio-endocrinology of Primate Reproduction* (71–97). New York: Liss.

Surian, L., & Leslie, A. M. (1999). Competence and performance in false belief understanding: A comparison of autistic and normal 3-year-old children. *British Journal of Developmental Psychology*, 17, 141–155.

Susman, E. J., Nottleman, E. D., Inoff-Germain, G. E., Loriaux, D. L., & Chrousos, G. P. (1985). The relation of relative hormonal levels and physical development and social–emotional behavior in young adolescents. *Journal of Youth and Adolescence*, 14, 245–264.

Sutherland, P., Badger, R., & White, G. (2002). How new students take notes at lectures. *Journal of Further and Higher Education*, 26 (4), 377–388.

Suttle, C. M., Banks, M. S., & Graf, E. W. (2002). FPL and sweep VEP to tritan stimuli in young human infants. *Vision Research*, 42, 2879–2891.

Sutton, J., & Smith, P. K. (1999). Bullying as a group process: An adaptation of the participant role approach. *Aggressive Behaviour*, 25, 97–111.

Sutton, J., Smith, P. K., & Swettenham, J. (1999a). Social cognition and bullying: Social inadequacy or skilled manipulation? *British Journal of Developmental Psychology*, 17, 435–450.

Sutton, J., Smith, P. K., & Swettenham, J. (1999b). Bullying and 'theory of mind': A critique of the 'social skills deficit' view of anti-social behaviour. *Social Development*, 8, 117–127.

Swanson, J. M., Kraemer, H. C., Hinshaw, S. P., Arnold, L. E., Conners, C. K., Abikoff, H. B., Clevenger, W., Davies, M., Elliott, G. R., Greenhill, L. L., Hechtman, L., Hoza, B., Jensen, P. S., March, J. S., Newcorn, J. H., Owens, E. B., Pelham, W. E., Schiller, E., Severe, J. B., Simpson, S., Vitiello, B., Wells, K., Wigal, T., & Wu, M. (2001). Clinical relevance of the primary findings of the MTA: Success rates based on severity of ADHD and ODD symptoms at the end of treatment. *Journal of the American Academy of Child and Adolescent Psychiatry*, 40, 168–179.

Swanson, J. M., Arnold, L. E., Vitiello, B., Abikoff, H. B., Wells, K. C., Pelham, W. E., March, J. S., Hinshaw, S. P., Hoza, B., Epstein, J. N., Elliott, G. R., Greenhill, L. L., Hechtman, L., Jensen, P. S., Kraemer, H. C., Kotkin, R., Molina, B., Newcorn, J. H., Owens, E. B., Severe, J., Hoagwood, K., Simpson, S., Wigal, T., & Hanley, T. (2002). Response to commentary on the multimodal treatment study of ADHD (MTA): Mining the meaning of the MTA. *Journal of Abnormal Child Psychology*, 30, 327–332.

Swenson, L. M., & Strough, J. (2008). Adolescents' collaboration in the classroom: Do peer relationships or gender matter? *Psychology in the Schools*, 45, 715–728.

Swindells, D., & Stagnitti, K. (2006). Pretend play and parents' view of social competence: The construct validity of the Child-Initiated Pretend Play Assessment. *Australian Occupational Therapy Journal*, 53 (4), 314–324.

Swinson, J., & Cording, M. (2002). Assertive discipline in a school for pupils with emotional and behavioural difficulties. *British Journal of Special Education*, 29 (2), 72–75.

Szatmari, P. (2000). The classification of autism, Asperger's syndrome, and pervasive developmental disorder. *Canadian Journal of Psychiatry*, 45, 731–738.

Szatmari, P. (2003). The causes of autism spectrum disorders. *British Medical Journal*, 326, 173–174.

Szücs, D. (2005). The use of electrophysiology in the study of early development. *Infant and Child Development*, 14, 99–102.

Tajfel, H. (1978). *Differentiation between Social Groups: Studies in the Social Psychology of Intergroup Relations*. London: Academic Press.

Takahashi, K. (1990). Are the key assumptions of the 'strange situation' procedure universal? A view from Japanese research. *Human Development*, 33, 23–30.

Tallon-Baudry, C., Bertrand, O., Peronnet, F., & Pernier, J. (1998). Induced gammaband activity during the delay of a visual short-term memory task in humans. *Journal of Neuroscience*, 18, 4244–4254.

Tanner, J. M. (1990). *Foetus into Man: Physical Growth from Conception to Maturity* (2nd Ed.). Cambridge, MA: Harvard University Press.

Tannock, M. (2011). Observing young children's rough-and-tumble play. *Australasian Journal of Early Childhood*, 36, 13–20.

Tardif, T., Fletcher, P., Liang, W., Zhang, Z., Kaciroti, N., & Marchman, V. A. (2008). Baby's first 10 words. *Developmental Psychology*, 44 (4), 929–938.

Tarrant, M., North, A. C., Edridge, M. D., Kirk, L. E., Smith, E. A., & Turner, R. E. (2001). Social identity in adolescence. *Journal of Adolescence*, 24 (5), 597–609.

Tasker, M. (2008). Smaller schools: A conflict of aims and purposes? *FORUM: For Promoting 3–19 Comprehensive Education*, 50 (2), 177–184.

Taylor, B., Jick, H., & McLaughlin, D. (2013). Prevalence and incidence rates of autism in the UK: Time trend from 2004–2010 in children aged 8 years. *BMJ Open*, 3 (10), e003219.

Taylor, E., Sandberg, S., Thorley, G., & Giles, S. (1991). *The Epidemiology of Childhood Hyperactivity*. Oxford: Oxford University Press.

Taylor, J. (2008). Could you care for a baby? *Sky News*. Retrieved 25 October 2010 from http://blogs.news.sky.com/eyewitnessblog/Post:c7fa863b-8ad9-495f-9abfa71db34f5964.

Taylor, J. L., Greenberg, J. S., Seltzer, M. M., & Floyd, F. J. (2008). Siblings of adults with mild intellectual deficits or mental illness: Differential life course outcomes. *Journal of Family Psychology*, 22 (6), 905–914.

Taylor, M., & Carlson, S. M. (1997). The relation between individual differences in fantasy and theory of mind. *Child Development*, 68, 20–27.

Teller, D. Y. (1998). Spatial and temporal aspects of colour vision. *Vision Research*, 38, 3275–3282.

Teller, D. Y., & Bornstein, M. H. (1987). Infant colour vision and colour perception. In P. Salapatek & L. Cohen (Eds.), *Handbook of Infant Perception: Vol. 2, From Perception to Cognition* (185–236). Orlando, FL: Academic Press.

Tenenbaum, H. R., Hill, D. B., Joseph, N., & Roche, E. (2010). 'It's a boy because he's painting a picture': Age differences in children's conventional and unconventional gender schemas. *British Journal of Developmental Psychology*, 101, 137–154.

Teppers, E., Luyckx, K., Klimstra, T. A., & Gooseens, L. (2014). Loneliness and Facebook motives in adolescence: A longitudinal inquiry into directionality of effect. *Journal of Adolescence*, 37, 691–699.

Tervo, R. (2003). Identifying patterns of developmental delays can help diagnose neurodevelopmental disorders. *A Pediatric Perspective*, 13 (3), 3–15.

Teuber, H. L., & Rudel, R. G. (1962). Behaviour after cerebral lesions in children and adults. *Developmental Medicine and Child Neurology*, 3, 3–20.

Thapar, A., Holmes, J., Poulton, K., & Harrington, R. (1999). Genetic basis of attention deficit and hyperactivity. *British Journal of Psychiatry*, 174, 105–111.

Thapar, A., Langley, K., Owen, M. J., & O'Donovan, M. C. (2007). Advances in genetic findings on attention deficit/hyperactivity disorder. *Psychological Medicine*, 37, 1681–1692.

Thatcher, R. W. (1991). Maturation of human frontal lobes: Physiological evidence for staging. *Developmental Neuropsychology*, 7, 397–419.

Thatcher, R. W., Lyon, G. R., Rumsey, J., & Krasnegor, J. (1996). *Developmental Neuroimaging*. San Diego, CA: Academic Press.

Thelen, E., & Smith, L. (Eds.) (1994). *A Dynamic Systems Approach to the Development of Cognition and Action*. Cambridge, MA: MIT Press.

Thomas, A., & Chess, S. (1977). *Temperament and Development*. New York: Brunner/Mazel.

Thomas, A., & Chess, S. (1990). Continuities and discontinuities in temperament. In L. N. Robins & M. Rutter (Eds.), *Straight and Devious Pathways from Childhood to Adulthood* (205–290). New York: Cambridge University Press.

Thomas, A., Chess, B., & Birch, H. G. (1968). *Temperament and Behaviour Disorders in Children*. New York: New York University Press.

Thomas, A., Chess, S., Birch, H. G., Hertzig, M. E. & Korn, S. (1963). *Behavioral Individuality in Early Childhood*. Oxford: New York University Press.

Thomas, H. J., Connor, J. P., & Scott, J. G. (2014). Integrating traditional bullying and cyberbullying: Challenges of definition and measurement in adolescents – a review. *Educational Psychology Review* [Online early].

Thompson, F. & Smith, P. K. (2011). *The Use and Effectiveness of Anti-Bullying Strategies in Schools*. Research Report DFE-RR098. London: Department for Education.

Thompson, H. (2011). Criminalizing kids: The overlooked reason for failing schools. *Dissent*, 58 (4), 23–27.

Thompson, P. W. (1993). Quantitative reasoning, complexity, and additive structures. *Educational Studies in Mathematics*, 3, 165–208.

Thompson, P. (1994). The development of the concept of speed and its relationship to concepts of rate. In G. Harel & J. Confrey (Eds.), *The Development of Multiplicative Reasoning in the Learning of Mathematics* (181–236). Albany, NY: State University of New York Press.

Thompson, R. A. (2000). The legacy of early attachments. *Child Development*, 71, 145–52.

Thompson, S. K. (1975). Gender labels and early sex role development. *Child Development*, 46, 339–347.

Tizard, B. (1977). *Adoption: A Second Chance*. London: Open Books.

Tizard, B., & Hodges, J. (1978). The effect of early institutional rearing on the development of eight-year-old children. *Journal of Child Psychology and Psychiatry*, 19, 99–118.

Tizard, B., & Hughes, M. (1984). *Young Children Learning: Talking and Thinking at Home and at School*. London: Fontana.

Tizard, B., & Rees, J. (1975). The effect of early institutional rearing on the behaviour problems and affectional relationships of four-year-old children. *Journal of Child Psychology and Psychiatry*, 16, 61–74.

Tocci, S. (2000). *Down Syndrome*. New York: Franklin Watts.

Tokunaga, R. S. (2010). Following you home from school: A critical review and synthesis of research on cyberbullying victimization. *Computers in Human Behaviour*, 26, 277–287.

Tomkins, C. A., Bloise, C., Timko, M., & Baumgartner, A. (1994). Working memory and inference revision in brain-damaged and normally ageing adults. *Journal of Speech and Language*, 37, 896–912.

Tomas de Almeida, A. M. (1999). Portugal. In P. K. Smith, Y. Morita, J. Junger-Tas, D. Olweus, R. Catalano, & P. Slee (Eds.), *The Nature of School Bullying: A Cross-National Perspective* (174–186). London: Routledge.

Tomlinson, S. (2008). Gifted, talented and high ability: Selection for education in a one-dimensional world. *Oxford Review of Education*, 34 (1), 59–74.

Toppelberg, C., & Shapiro, T. (2000). Language disorders: A 10-year research update review. *Journal of American Academy Child and Adolescent Psychiatry*, 39 (2), 143–152.

Traeen, B., Lewin, B., & Sundet, J. M. (1992a). The real and the ideal-gender differences in heterosexual behavior among Norwegian adolescents. *Journal of Community and Applied Social Psychology*, 2 (4), 227–237.

Traeen, B., Lewin, B., & Sundet, J. M. (1992b). Use of birth-control pills and condoms among 17–19-year-old adolescents in Norway-contraceptive versus protective behavior. *Aids Care: Psychological and Socio-medical Aspects of AIDS/HIV*, 4 (4), 371–380.

Trainor, L. J., & Heinmiller, B. M. (1998). The development of evaluative responses to music: Infants prefer to listen to consonance over dissonance. *Infant Behaviour and Development*, 21, 77–88.

Trainor, L. J., Shahin, A., & Roberts, L. E. (2003). Effects of musical training on auditory cortex in children. In G. Avanzini, C. Faienze, D. Miciacchi, L. Lopez, & M. Majno (Eds.), The neurosciences and music: Mutual interactions and implications of developmental functions. *Annals NY Academy of Sciences*, 999, 520–521.

Trehub, S. E., Schneider, B. A., Thorpe, L. A., & Judge, P. (1991). Observational measures of auditory sensitivity in early infancy. *Developmental Psychology*, 27, 40–49.

Trehub, S. E., Thorpe, L. A., & Morrongiello, B. A., (1985). Infants' perception of melodies: Changes in a single tone. *Infant Behaviour and Development*, 8, 213–223.

Treleaven, L., Sykes, C., & Ormiston, J. (2012). A dissemination methodology for learning and teaching developments through engaging and embedding. *Studies in Higher Education*, 37 (6), 747–767.

Trudeau, N., Poulin-Dubois, D., and Joanette, Y. (2000). Language development following brain injury in early childhood: A longitudinal case study. *International Journal of Language and Communication Disorders*, 35 (2), 227–249.

Ttofi, M. M. & Farrington, D. P. (2011). Effectiveness of school-based programs to reduce bullying: A systematic and meta-analytic review. *Journal of Experimental Criminology*, 7, 27–56.

Ttofi, M. M. & Farrington, D. P. (2012). Bullying prevention programs: The importance of peer intervention, disciplinary methods and age variations. *Journal of Experimental Criminology*, 8, 443–462.

Ttofi, M. M., Farrington, D. P. & Lösel, F. (2012). School bullying as a predictor of violence later in life: A systematic review and meta-analysis of prospective longitudinal studies. *Aggression and Violent Behaviour*, 17, 405–418.

Tucker, S. (2013). Pupil vulnerability and school exclusion: Developing responsive pastoral policies and practices in secondary education in the UK. *Pastoral Care in Education*, 31 (4), 279–291.

Tulving, E. (1983). *Elements of Episodic Memory*. New York: Oxford University Press.

Tversky, A., & Kahneman D. (1973). Availability: A heuristic for judging frequency and probability. *Cognitive Psychology*, 5, 207–232.

Tymms, P., Merrell, C., & Jones, P. (2004). Using baseline assessment data to make international comparisons. *British Educational Research Journal*, 30 (5), 673–689.

Tynes, B., Reynolds, L., & Greenfield, P. M. (2004). Adolescence, race and ethnicity on the Internet: A comparison of discourse in monitored vs. unmonitored chat rooms. *Journal of Applied Developmental Psychology*, 25, 667–684.

Tyler, K., & Jones, B. D. (2002). Teachers' responses to the ecosystemic approach to changing chronic problem behaviour in schools. *Pastoral Care in Education*, 20 (2), 30–39.

Tymms, P., Merrell, C., & Jones, P. (2004). Using baseline assessment data to make international comparisons. *British Educational Research Journal*, 30 (5), 673–689.

Underwood, M. (1997). Peer social status and children's understanding of the expression and control of positive and negative emotions. *Merrill-Palmer Quarterly*, 43, 610–634.

Underwood, M. K. (2002). Sticks and stones and social exclusion: Aggression among girls and boys. In P. K. Smith & C. H. Hart (Eds.), *Blackwell Handbook of Childhood Social Development* (533–548). Oxford: Blackwell.

US Department of Education (2001). *The 23rd Annual Report to Congress on the Implementation of the Individuals with Disabilities Education Act*.

Valkenburg, P. M., & Peter, J. (2007). Preadolescents' and adolescents' online communication and their closeness to friends. *Developmental Psychology*, 43, 267–277.

Valkenburg, P. M., & Vroone, M. (2004). Developmental changes in infants' and toddlers' attention to television entertainment. *Communication Research*, 31, 288–311.

Van Aken, M. A., & Semon Dubas, J. (2004). Personality type, social relationships, and problem behavior in adolescence. *European Journal of Developmental Psychology*, 1, 331–348.

van den Boom, D. C. (1994). The influence of temperament and mothering on attachment and exploration: An experimental manipulation of sensitive responsiveness among lower-class mothers with irritable infants. *Child Development*, 65, 1457–1477.

Van der Meer, A. L. H., Van der Weel F. R., & Lee D. N. (1996). Lifting weights in neonates: Developing visual control of reaching. *Scandinavian Journal of Psychology*, 37, 424–436.

Van der Meer, A. L. H., Fallet, G., & van der Weel, F. R. (2008). Perception of structured optic flow and random visual motion in infants and adults: A high-density EEG study. *Experimental Brain Research*, 186, 493–502.

Van Geel, M., Vedder, P. & Tanllon, J. (2014). Relationship between peer victimization, cyberbullying, and suicide in children and adolescents: A meta-analysis. *Journal of the American Medical Association: Pediatrics* [Online early]

van IJzendoorn, M. H. (1995). The association between adult attachment representations and infant attachment, parental responsiveness, and clinical status: A meta-analysis on the predictive validity of the Adult Attachment Interview. *Psychological Bulletin*, 113, 404–410.

van IJzendoorn, M. H., & deWolff, M. S. (1997). In search of the absent father: Meta-analyses of infant–father attachment – a rejoinder to our discussants. *Child Development*, 68, 604–609.

van IJzendoorn, M. H., & Kroonenberg, P. M. (1988). Cross-cultural patterns of attachment: A meta-analysis of the Strange Situation. *Child Development*, 59, 147–156.

van IJzendoorn, M. H., Vereijken, C. M. J. L., Bakermans- Kranenburg, M. J., & Riksen-Walraven, J. M. (2004). Assessing attachment security with the attachment Q Sort: Meta-analytic evidence for the validity of the Observer AQS. *Child Development*, 75, 1188–1213.

Vanderbosch, H., & Van Cleemput, K. (2008). Defining cyberbullying: A qualitative research into the perceptions of youngsters. *Cyberpsychology and Behavior*, 11, 499–503.

Van Herwegen, J., Rundblad, G., Davelaar, E. J., & Annaz, D. (2011). Variability and standardised test profiles in typically developing children and children with Williams Syndrome. *British Journal of Developmental Psychology*, 29 (4), 883–894.

Varley, W. H., Levin, J. R., Severson, R. A., & Wolff, P. (1974). Training imagery production in young children through motor involvement. *Journal of Educational Psychology*, 66, 262–266.

Vartia, M. (1996). The sources of bullying: Psychological work environment and organizational climate. *European Journal of Work and Organizational Psychology*, 5, 203–214.

Vaughn, B. E., Bradley, C. F., Joffe, L. S., Seifer, R., & Barglow, P. (1987). Maternal characteristics measured prenatally are predictive of ratings of temperamental 'difficulty' on the Carey Infant Temperament Questionnaire. *Developmental Psychology*, 23, 152–161.

Veenman, S., Kenter, B., & Post, K. (2000). Cooperative learning in Dutch primary classrooms. *Educational Studies*, 26 (3), 281–302.

Veenstra-Vanderweele, J., & Cook, E. (2003). Genetics of childhood disorders: Autism. *Journal of the American Academy of Child and Adolescent Psychiatry*, 42, 116–118.

Venezia, M., Messinger, D. S., Thorp, D., & Mundy, P. (2004). The development of anticipatory smiling. *Infancy*, 6 (3), 397–406.

Veraksa, N. E. (2011). Development of cognitive capacities in preschool age. *International Journal of Early Years Education*, 19 (1), 79–87.

Vergnaud, G. (1982). A classification of cognitive tasks and operations of thought involved in addition and subtraction problems. In T. P. Carpenter, J. M. Moser and T. A Romberg (Eds.), *Addition and Subtraction: A Cognitive Perspective* (60–67). Hillsdale, NJ: Erlbaum.

Vergnaud, G. (1983). Multiplicative structures. In R. Lesh & M. Landau (Eds.), *Acquisition of Mathematics Concepts and Processes* (128–175). London: Academic Press.

Vergnaud, G. (2009). The theory of conceptual fields. *Human Development*, 52, 83–94.

Verschaffel, L. (1994). Using retelling data to study elementary school children's representations and solutions of compare problems. *Journal for Research in Mathematics Education*, 25, 141–165.

Veugelers, W., & Vedder, P. (2003). Values in teaching. *Teachers and Teaching: Theory and Practice*, 9 (4), 377–389.

Victora, C. G., Horta, B. L., Loret de Mola, C., Quevedo, L., Pinheiro, R. T., Gigante, D. P., Goncalves, H., & Barros, F. F. (2015). Association between breastfeeding and intelligence, educational attainment and income at 30 years of age: A prospective birth cohort study from Brazil. *The Lancet Global Health*, 3 (4), e199–e205.

Vinther, J. (2005). Cognitive processes at work in CALL. *Computer Assisted Language Learning*, 18 (4), 251–271.

Visnovska, J., & Cobb, P. (2013). Classroom video in teacher professional development program: Community documentational genesis perspective. *ZDM*, 45 (7), 1017–1029.

Volk, A. A., Camilleri, J. A., Dane, A. V. & Marini, Z. A. (2012). Is adolescent bullying an evolutionary adaptation? *Aggressive Behaviour*, 38, 222–238.

Volkmar, F. R., & Chawarska, K. (2008). Autism in infants: An update. *World Psychiatry*, 7, 19–21.

Von Hofsten, C. (1982). Eye–hand coordination in newborns. *Developmental Psychology*, 18, 450–461.

Von Hofsten, C. (1984). Developmental changes in the organization of pre-reaching movements. *Developmental Psychology*, 20, 378–388.

Voogt, J., Tilya, F., & van den Akker, J. (2009). Science teacher learning of MBL-supported student-centered science education in the context of secondary education in Tanzania. *Journal of Science Education and Technology*, 18 (5), 429–438.

Vygotsky, L. S. (1962). *Thought and Language*. Cambridge, MA: MIT Press.

Vygotsky, L. S. (1978a). Mind in society: The development of higher psychological processes, in M. Cole, V. John-Steiner, S. Scribner, & E. Souberman (Eds.), *The Development of Higher Psychological Processes*. Harvard, MA: Harvard University Press.

Vygotsky, L. S. (1978b). *Mind in Society: The Development of Higher Mental Processes*. Cambridge, MA: Harvard University Press.

Wachs, T. D., & Bates, J. E. (2001). Temperament. In G. Bremner & A. Fogel (Eds.), *Blackwell Handbook of Infant Development* (465–501). Oxford: Blackwell.

Wakefield, A. J., Murch, S. H., Anthony, A., Linnell, J., Casson, D. M., Malik, M., Berelowitz, M., & Dhillon, A. P. (1998). Ileal-lymphoide-nodular hyperplasia, non-specific colitis and pervasive developmental disorder in children. *The Lancet*, 351 (9103). Retracted.

Walford, G. (2001). Funding for religious schools in England and the Netherlands. Can the piper call the tune? *Research Papers in Education*, 16 (4), 359–380.

Walker, S., Berthelsen, D., & Irving, K. (2001). Temperament and peer acceptance in early childhood: Sex and social status differences. *Child Study Journal*, 31, 177–192.

Wang, Z., & Shah, P. (2014). The effect of pressure on high- and low-working memory students: An elaboration of the choking under pressure hypothesis. *British Journal of Educational Psychology*, 84 (2), 226–238.

Ward, M. (2013). Why Minecraft is more than just another video game. *BBC News Magazine* (online), 7 September. Available at: http://www.bbc.co.uk/news/magazine-23572742

Warneken, F., & Tomaselo, M. (2006). Altruistic helping in human infants and young chimpanzees. *Science*, 311, 1301–1303.

Warneken, F., & Tomasello, M. (2009). Varieties of altruism in children and chimpanzees. *Trends in Cognitive Science*, 13, 397–402.

Watkins, M. W., Lei, P. W., & Canivez, G. L. (2007). Psychometric intelligence and achievement: A cross-lagged panel analysis. *Intelligence*, 35 (1), 59–68.

Watson, J. B. (1930). *Behaviorism* (Rev. Ed.). Chicago, IL: University of Chicago Press.

Watts, B., & Youens, B. (2007). Harnessing the potential of pupils to influence school development. *Improving Schools*, 10 (1), 18–28.

Watts, T. J. (2008). The pathogenesis of autism. *Clinical Medicine: Pathology*, 1, 99–103.

Weaver, I. C. G., Cervoni, N., Champagne, F. A., D'Alessio, A. C., Sharma, S., Seeki, J. R., Dymov, S., Szyf, M., & Meaney, M. J. (2004). Epigenetic programming by maternal behaviour. *Nature Neuroscience*, 7, 847–854.

Webb, R., & Vulliamy, G. (2007). Changing classroom practice at Key Stage 2: The impact of New Labour's national strategies. *Oxford Review of Education*, 33 (5), 561–580.

Webster, J. (2008). From childhood through adolescence: Journey of the spirit. *NAMTA Journal*, 33 (3), 64–78.

Webster-Stratton, C. (2006). *The Incredible Years: Trouble-Shooting Guide for Parents of Children Aged 2–8*. Seattle: The Incredible Years.

Webster-Stratton, C., & Hancock, L. (1998). Parent training for young children with conduct problems. Content, methods and therapeutic process. In C. E. Schaefer (Ed.), *Handbook of Parent Training* (98–152). New York: Wiley.

Wechsler, D. (1992). *Wechsler Intelligence Scale for Children III*. San Antonio, TX: The Psychological Corporation.

Wegerif, R., Littleton, K., Dawes, L., Mercer, N., & Rowe, D. (2004). Widening access to educational opportunities through teaching children how to reason together. *International Journal of Research and Method in Education*, 27 (2), 143–156.

Wehmeier, P. M., Schacht, A., Wolff, C., Otto, W. R., Dittmann, R. W., & Banaschewski, T. (2011). Neuropsychological outcomes across the day in children with attention-deficit/hyperactivity disorder treated with atomoxetine: Results from a placebo-controlled study using a computer-based continuous performance test combined with an infra-red motion-tracking device. *Journal of Child and Adolescent Psychopharmacology*, 21 (5), 433–444.

Wehmeier, P. M., Schacht, A., Ulberstad, F., Lehman, M., Schneider-Fresenius, C., Lehmkuhl, G., Dittman, R., & Banaschewski, T. (2012). Does atomoxetine improve executive function, inhibitory control, and hyperactivity? Results from a placebo-controlled trial using quantitative measurement technology. *Journal of Clinical Psychopharmacology*, 32, 653–661.

Weinraub, M., Clemens, L. P., Sockloff, A., Ethridge, R., Gracely, E., & Myers, B. (1984). The development of sex-role stereotypes in the third year: Relationships to gender labelling, gender identity, sex-typed toy preference, and family characteristics. *Child Development*, 55, 1493–1503.

Wellings, F., Nanchahal, K., Macdowall, W., McManusk S., Erens, B., Mercer, C. H., Johnson, A. M., Copas, A. J., Korovessis, C., Fenton, F. A., & Field, J. (2001). Sexual behaviour in Britain: Early heterosexual experience. *The Lancet*, 358 (9296), 1843–1850.

Wellman, H., & Estes, D. (1986). Early understanding of mental entities: A re-examination of childhood realism. *Child Development*, 57, 910–923.

Wellman, H. M., Cross, D., & Watson, J. (2001). Meta-analysis of theory of mind development: The truth about false-belief. *Child Development*, 72, 655–684.

Wentzel, K. R., & Asher, S. R. (1995). The academic lives of neglected, rejected, popular, and controversial children. *Child Development*, 66, 754–763.

Werker, J. (1989). Becoming a native listener. *American Scientist*, 77, 54–59.

Werker, J. F., & Tees, R. C. (1984). Cross-language speech perception: Evidence for perceptual reorganization during the first year of life. *Infant Behaviour and Development*, 7, 49–63.

West, A., Mattei, P., & Roberts, J. (2011). Accountability and sanctions in English schools. *British Journal of Educational Studies*, 59 (1), 41–62.

Wetz, J. (2009). *Urban Village Schools: Putting Relationships at the Heart of Secondary School Organisation and Design*. London: Calouste Gulbenkian Foundation.

White, B., & Held, R. (1966). Plasticity of sensori-motor development in the human infant. In J. F. Rosenblith & W. Allinsmith (Eds.), *The Causes of Behaviour* (60–70). Boston, MA: Allyn & Bacon.

Whitney, I., & Smith, P. K. (1993). A survey of the nature and extent of bullying junior/middle and secondary schools. *Educational Research*, 35, 3–25.

Whitney, I., Rivers, I., Smith, P. K., & Sharp, S. (1994). The Sheffield project: Methodology and findings. In P. K. Smith & S. Sharp (Eds.), *School Bullying: Insights and Perspectives* (20–56). London: Routledge.

Wigal, T., Greenhill, L., Chuang, S., McGough, J., Vitiello, B., Skrobala, A., Swanson, J., Wigal, S., Abikoff, H., Kollins, S., McCracken, J., Riddle, M., Posner, K., Jaswinder, G., Davies, M., Thorp, B., & Stehli, A. (2006). Safety and tolerability of methylphenidate in preschool children with ADHD. *Journal of the American Academy of Child and Adolescent Psychiatry*, 45, 1294–1303.

Wight, M., & Chapparo, C. (2008). Social competence and learning difficulties: Teacher perceptions. *Australian Occupational Therapy Journal*, 55 (4), 256–265.

Wilkins, K., Caldarella, P., Crook-Lyon, R., & Young, K. (2010). The civil behaviours of students: A survey of school professionals. *Education*, 130 (4), 540–555.

Will, J. A., Self, P. A., & Datan, N. (1976). Maternal behavior and perceived sex of infant. *American Journal of Orthopsychiatry*, 46, 135–139.

Williams, J., Greene, S., Doyle, E., Harris, E., Layte, R., McCoy, S., McCrory, C., Murray, A., Nixon, E., O'Dowd, T., O'Moore, M., Quail, A., Smyth, E., Swords, L. & Thornton, M. (2009) *Growing up in Ireland: National Longitudinal Study of Children. The Lives of 9-year-olds*. Dublin: Government of Ireland.

Williams, J. M., & Dunlop, L. C. (1999). Pubertal timing and self-reported delinquency among male adolescents. *Journal of Adolescence*, 22, 157–171.

Williams, M., & Gersch, I. (2004). Teaching in mainstream and special schools: Are the stresses similar or different? *British Journal of Special Education*, 31 (3), 157–162.

Williams, K., & Guerra, N. (2007). Prevalence and predictors of Internet bullying. *Journal of Adolescent Health*, 41, S14–S21.

Williams, P., & Nicholas, D. (2006). Testing the usability of information technology applications with learners with special educational needs (SEN). *Journal of Research in Special Educational Needs*, 6 (1), 31–41.

Williams, R. (2010). Parents too busy to help children learn to talk. *Guardian*, 4 January 2010. Available at: http://www.guardian.co.uk/society/2010/jan/04/parents-busy-children-learn-talk.

Wilson, B. J., Petaja, H., & Mancil, L. (2011). The attention skills and academic performance of aggressive/rejected and low aggressive/popular children. *Early Education and Development*, 22, 907–930.

Wilson, J. D. (1972). Recent studies on the mechanism of action of testosterone. *New England Journal of Medicine*, 287, 1284–1291.

Wilson, J. D. (1978). Sexual differentiation. *Annual Review of Physiology*, 40, 279–306.

Wimmer, H., & Perner, J. (1983). Beliefs about beliefs: Representation and constraining function of wrong beliefs in young children's understanding of deception. *Cognition*, 13, 41–68.

Windle, M., Iwawaki, S., & Lerner, R. M. (1988). Cross-cultural comparability of temperament among Japanese and American preschool children. *International Journal of Psychology*, 88, 547–567.

Winkler, I., Haden, G. P., Ladinig, O., Sziller, I., & Honing, H. (2009). Newborn infants detect the beat in music. *Proceedings of the National Academy of Sciences USA*, 106, 2468–2471.

Witvliet, M., van Lier, P. A. C., Brendgen, M., Koot, H. M., & Vitaro, F. (2010).Longitudinal associations between clique membership status and internalizing and externalizing problems during late childhood. *Journal of Clinical Child and Adolescent Psychology*, 39, 693–704.

Wolff, P. H. (1966). The causes, controls and organization of behaviour in the neonate. *Psychological Issues*, 5 (1), 1–105.

Wolff, P. H. (1968a). The serial organisation of sucking in the young infant. *Paediatrics*, 42, 943–956.

Wolff, P. H. (1968b). Sucking patterns of infant mammals. *Brain, Behaviour and Evolution*, 1, 354–367.

Wolke, D., Woods, S., Stanford, K., & Schulz, H. (2001). Bullying and victimisation of primary school children in England and Germany: Prevalence and school factors. *British Journal of Psychology*, 92, 673–696.

Wolters, N., Knoors, H., Cillessen, A. H. N., & Verhoeven, L. (2014). Behavioral, personality, and communicative predictors of acceptance and popularity in early adolescence. *Journal of Early Adolescence*, 34, 585–605.

Wong, W. K., Chan, T. W., Chou, C. Y., Heh, J. S., & Tung, S. H. (2003). Reciprocal tutoring using cognitive tools. *Journal of Computer Assisted Learning*, 19 (4), 416–428.

Woodhouse, S. S., Dykas, M. J., & Cassidy, J. (2012). Loneliness and peer relations in adolescence. *Social Development*, 21, 273–293.

Woods, L. (2006). Children and families: Evaluating the clinical effectiveness of neonatal nurse practitioners – an exploratory study. *Journal of Clinical Nursing*, 15 (1), 35–44.

Woods, R. (2008). When rewards and sanctions fail: A case study of a primary school rule-breaker. *International Journal of Qualitative Studies in Education*, 21 (2), 181–196.

Woolfolk, A., Hughes, M., & Walkup, V. (2008). *Psychology in Education*. Harlow: Pearson Education.

Woolfolk, A., Hughes, M., & Walkup, V. (2013). *Psychology in Education* (2nd Ed.). Harlow: Pearson Education.

World Health Organization (1992). *ICD-10 Classification of Mental and Behavioural Disorders*. Geneva: WHO.

Wynn, K. (1992). Evidence against empiricist accounts of the origins of numerical knowledge. *Mind and Language*, 7, 315–332.

Wynn, K. (1998). Psychological foundations of number: Numerical competence in human infants. *Trends in Cognitive Science*, 2, 296–303.

Xu, F., & Spelke, E. (2000). Large number discrimination in 6-month-old infants. *Cognition*, 74, B1–B11.

Yakovlev, P. A., & Lecours, I. R. (1967). The myelogenetic cycles of regional maturation of the brain. In A. Minkowski (Ed.), *Regional Development of the Brain in Early Life* (3–70). Oxford: Blackwell.

Ybarra, M. L., & Mitchell, K. J. (2004). Online aggressor/ targets, aggressors and targets: A comparison of associated youth characteristics. *Journal of Child Psychology and Psychiatry*, 45, 1308–1316.

Yerrick, R., Schiller, J., & Reisfeld, J. (2011). 'Who are you callin' expert?': Using student narratives to redefine expertise and advocacy lower track science. *Journal of Research in Science Teaching*, 48 (1), 13–36.

Yew, E., Chng, E., & Schmidt, H (2011). Is learning in problem-based learning cumulative? *Advances in Health Sciences Education*, 16 (4), 449–464.

Young, R., & Sweeting, H. (2004). Adolescent bullying, relationships, psychological well-being, and gender-atypical behavior: A gender diagnosticity approach. *Sex Roles*, 50, 525–537.

Young, R. D. (1964). Effect of prenatal drugs and neonatal stimulation on later behavior. *Journal of Comparative and Physiological Psychology*, 58, 309–311.

Younger, B. A.,, & Cohen, L. B. (1986). Developmental changes in infants' perception of correlations among attributes. *Child Development*, 57, 803–815.

Yu, R., Branje, S., Keijsers, L., Koot, H. M., & Meeus, W. (2013). Pals, problems, and personality: The moderating role of personality in the longitudinal association between adolescents' and best friends' delinquency. *Journal of Personality*, 81, 499–509.

Yu, R., Branje, S. J. T., Keijsers, L., & Meeus, W. H. (2014a). Personality types and development of adolescents' conflict with friends. *European Journal of Personality*, 28, 156–167.

Yu, R., Branje, S., Keijsers, L., & Meeus, W. H. (2014b). Personality effects on romantic relationship quality through friendship quality: A ten-year longitudinal study in youths. *PLoS ONE*, 9, e102078, 1–12.

Yuliani, K., & Saragih, S. (2015). The development of learning devices based guided discovery model to improve understanding concept and critically thinking mathematically ability of students at Islamic Junior High School of Medan, *Journal of Education and Practice*, 6 (24), 116–128.

Yurick, A., Cartledge, G., Kourea, L., & Keyes, S. (2012). Reducing reading failure for kindergarten urban students: A study of early literacy instruction, treatment quality, and treatment duration. *Remedial and Special Education*, 33 (2), 89–102.

Zakriski, A., & Coie, J. (1996). A comparison of aggressive-rejected and nonaggressive-rejected children's interpretation of self-directed and other-directed rejection. *Child Development*, 67, 1048–1070.

Zemach, I., Cheng, S., & Teller, D. Y. (2007). Infant colour vision: Prediction of infants' spontaneous colour preferences. *Vision Research*, 47, 1368–1381.

Zentall, S. R., Braungart-Rieker, J. M., Ekas, N. V., & Lickenbrock, D. M. (2012). Longitudinal assessment of sleep–wake regulation and attachment security with parents. *Infant and Child Development*, 21, 443–457.

Zimmer, E. Z., Fifer, W. P., Kim, Y.-I., Rey, H. R., Chao, C. R., & Myers, M. M. (1993). Response of the premature fetus to stimulation by speech sounds. *Early Human Development*, 33, 207–215.

Zimmerman, C. (2000). The development of scientific reasoning skills. *Developmental Review*, 20, 99–149.

Zimmermann, P. (2004). Attachment representations and characteristics of friendship relations during adolescence. *Journal of Experimental Child Psychology*, 88 (1), 83–101.

Zito, J. M., Safer, D. J., dosReis, S., Gardner, J. F., Boles, M., & Lynch, F. (2000). Trends in the prescribing of psychotropic medications to preschoolers. *Journal of the American Medical Association*, 283, 1025–1030.

Zohar, A. (2006). Connected knowledge in science and mathematics education. *International Journal of Science Education*, 28 (13), 1579–1599.

Zoia, S., Blason, L., D'Ottavio, G., Bulgheroni, M., Pezzetta, E., Scabar, A., & Castiello, U. (2002). Evidence of early development of action planning in the human foetus: A kinematic study. *Experimental Brain Research*, 176, 217–226.

Index

Note: Page numbers in **bold** indicate Glossary items.

5-HTT gene 76
5-HTTLPR gene 75–6
A not B error 104–5
abstract thought 39–40
accepted children (acceptance by peers) 358, 360–1, 364–6, **543**
accommodation (revision of older structures) 99, 416, **543**
achievement 431, **543**
action potential 78
addiction 308
additive composition of numbers 189–93, **543**
additive relations 180, **543**
ADD (attention deficit disorder) 523
ADD (attention deficit disorder) with hyperactivity 523
ADHD (attention deficit hyperactivity disorder) 285, 521–41
   across the lifespan 524–8
   and temperament 309–10
   case study (James) 524
   case study (Sam Cook) 521
   characteristics of 522–3
   classification 523
   cognitive dysregulation hypothesis 532–5
   cultural differences in assessment 524–5
   delay aversion hypothesis 533–5
   diagnostic criteria 523–4, 526–8
   DSM-5 diagnostic criteria 523–4, 526–8
   effect on children's quality of life 540–1
   hyperactivity in pre-school children 525–6
   in adulthood 523, 524–5, 526–8
   in the pre-school years 525–6
   models of 532–5
   neuropsychological theories 532–5
   prevalence 524–5
   subtypes 523
   symptom structure 523–4
ADHD comorbidity and associated impairments 526, 528–30
   accident-proneness 530
   antisocial behaviour disorders 528
   anxiety disorders 528
   autism 504
   conduct disorder (CD) 528
   depression 528
   impaired academic functioning 529
   motor coordination disorders 528
   oppositional defiant disorder (ODD) 528
   psychiatric co-morbidity 526, 528
   reduced intelligence scores 528, 529
   sleep problems 530
   social problems 529–30
   substance use disorders 528
   time discrimination difficulties 533–5
   working memory impairment 534
ADHD research, study design 537
ADHD research directions 539–41
   neurofeedback 541
   self-help interventions 539, 540
   technology for diagnosis and treatment 540
   variability in reaction time 539–40
   working memory training 540
ADHD risk factors 530–5
   biological risk factors 530–1
   chaotic or disorganised parenting 532
   diet 532
   environmental factors 531–2
   genetic factors 530–1
   maternal smoking during pregnancy 531
   obstetric complications 531
   prenatal exposure to nicotine 531
ADHD treatment 535–9
   medical management of symptoms 535–6
   parent training 536–9
   psychosocial interventions 536–9
   psycho-stimulant medication 521, 535–6
adolescence 379–403
   adoptive families 394–5
   aggression 397–400
   antisocial behaviour 398–400
   attachment and internal working model (IWM) 271–2
   bullying 398–400, 459
   changes in social cognition 385
   cognitive development and changes 385–94
   computer games and teen aggression 397–8
   coping strategies 399, 400–1
   depression risk factors 399–400
   development of gender identity 396–7
   development of youth culture 380–1
   egocentrism theory (Elkind) 388–9
   features of brain development 419
   formal operations stage (Piaget) 385–7
   friendships 368
   history of 380
   identity vs role-confusion stage (Erikson) 20, 22, 387–8, **547**
   impact of immigration on identity 395–6
   influence of family structure 394–5
   influence of friendships in adulthood 374–5
   influence of personality on relationships 374–5
   invincibility fable 389
   media influence on gender identity 331–4
   mental health issues 399–401
   moral development theory (Kohlberg) 389–94
   neurological changes 383–5
   peer groups and interactions 351
   peer pressure 397
   peers and gender identity 396–7
   personal fable 389
   physical changes during 381–5
   psychological issues at puberty 382–3
   relationship with parents 394–5
   risky sex behaviours 401–2
   self-consciousness 389
   self-esteem 389, 399
   self-evaluations 320–1
   separated families 394–5
   sex and relationship behaviour 401–2
   social development 394–9
   storm and stress 380
   suicidal thoughts and self-harm 399
   timing of first sex 401, 402
   timing of puberty 381–3
adolescent egocentrism theory (Elkind) 388–9, **543**

INDEX

adopted children 256
adoptive families 394–5
Adult Attachment Interview (AAI) 272–4, **543**
adults as socialising agents 329–30, 331
affective social competence 357
aggression
    and computer games 397–8
    contributory factors 450–1
    during adolescence 397–400
Ainsworth, Mary D. S. 7, 28–30, 47, 56–7, 58, 257–63, 264, 271, 272, 273
alcohol, prenatal effects 84
alcohol dependence 308
Alexander, Robin 418
algebra 205, 206, **543**
Americans' Changing Lives study 321
amygdala 298–9
anal stage of development (Freud) 18
analogical reasoning 108–9, **543**
anencephaly 79–80
Angelman syndrome 506
animacy 107, **543**
animal research on attachment 253–5
antisocial behaviour
    and social status 361, 364–5
    genetic factors 76
    teenagers 398–400
antisocial behaviour disorders and ADHD 528
anxiety, defence mechanism (Freud) 18–19
anxiety disorders, comorbidity with ADHD 528
Apgar score 86, **543**
Arnett, Jeffrey Jenson 380
Asperger syndrome 239, 241, 502–4
assent 64
assessment 487, **543**
    developmentally appropriate activities 429–33
assimilation 99, 416, **543**
asynchronous development 10, **543**
attachment 7, 247–75, **543**
    and childcare 263–70
    animal research 253–5
    beyond infancy 270–5
    Bowlby's early attachment theory 27–8, 249–52, 255–7
    critical period for 251, 253, 256
    cultural differences 255
    definition 27, 248–9
    effects of institutionalisation on young children 252, 256
    hospitalisation of young children 252
    impact of day care 268–70
    in adulthood 272–5
    in different family structures 274
    influences on early attachment patterns 76
    insecure-avoidant type 259–60, 262–3, 264, 270–4
    insecure-disorganised type 260, 261, 263, 264, 271–4
    insecure-resistant/ambivalent type 259–60, 262–3, 264, 270–4
    intergenerational patterns 272–5
    internal working model (IWM) 270–4
    later childhood and adolescence 271–2
    maternal deprivation hypothesis (Bowlby) 251–7
    measurement 257–63
    microanalysis of mother–baby interaction 261
    mind-mindedness in a parent 266–7
    monotropism 249, 253, 256
    mother as primary caregiver 263–7
    mother–infant dyads 247–8
    phases (Bowlby) 251
    potential consequences of maternal pathology 264–6
    proximity seeking 249–50, 251, 253
    role of the father 267–8, 274
    secure attachment 257–63, 264, 270–4, **543**
    sensitive period for 256, 268
    separation protest 250–1
    Strange Situation experiment 258–63, 271, 272, 273, 274
    stranger anxiety 250–1, 256–7
attachment security 257–63, 264, 270–4, **543**
attachment styles 121
attachment types 29–30, 258–63, **543**
attainment 431, **543**
attention **543**
    and memory 151
    in infants 101–2
attention deficit hyperactivity disorder see ADHD
attribution, hostile attribution bias 464
attribution theory, and victimisation 462, 466–7
atypical autism 502–3
atypical development 481–517
    assessment 486–9
    assessment by other health professionals 495–6
    assessment methods 489–96
    assessment types 487–8
    auditory processing disorder 499
    autistic spectrum disorders (ASD) 499–505
    behavioural interventions 512–14
    case study (Daniel) 481
    case study (David) 488
    case study (Molly) 497
    cerebral palsy 498
    childhood disintegrative disorder (CDD) 505
    chromosomal abnormalities 505
    context of child development 485
    cultural differences in child development 485–6
    definition 482–3
    developmental delay 496–8
    developmental disorder 496–8
    developmental history assessment 494–5
    developmental milestones 482–3, 485–6
    developmental 'norms' 485–6
    disintegrative psychosis 505
    disorders of development 496–510
    Down's syndrome (Trisomy 21) 498, 505–6
    dyscalculia 499
    dysgraphia 499
    dyslexia 499
    dyspraxia (sensory integration disorder) 499
    environmental factors in development 485
    ethical dilemmas related to assessment 488–9
    fragile X syndrome 498, 505
    genetic disorders 505–7
    global developmental disability 497–8
    Heller's syndrome 505
    influences on development 483–7
    insecure-disorganised attachment 260, 261, 263, 264, 271–4
    learning disability 496–8
    occupational therapy 496
    outcomes for siblings of adults with 499
    parent training and support 511–12
    parental perspective 497
    play-based assessment and observation 489–91
    problems caused by diagnosis 489
    psychiatric assessment 496
    psychoeducation 511
    psychopharmacotherapy 511
    reasons for assessment 488
    recognising the mental health needs of the child 514–15
    Rett syndrome 505
    special educational needs (SEN) assessment 486–7
    specialist health visitor support 495
    specific learning difficulties 499
    speech and language disorder 508–10
    speech and language therapy 495
    spina bifida 498
    standardised assessment 492–4
    Tay-Sachs disease 505
    therapy and intervention 510–16
    visual processing disorder 499
    wider systems involvement 515–16
audition in infants 95–6
    appraisal of audition 95
    auditory system 95
    coherence of sound perception 95–6
    detection of basic speech sounds 96
    detection of musical patterns 96, 97
auditory processing disorder 499
Australian Temperament Project (ATP) 298, 305
Ausubel, Dr David 429
autism 80
Autism Diagnostic Interview - Revised (ADI-R) 504–5
Autism Diagnostic Observation Schedule (ADOS) 505

autistic spectrum disorders (ASD) 499–505
    aetiology 504
    beliefs and mental states 239–41
    case of Gary McKinnon 241
    co-morbidities 500, 502
    diagnostic assessment 504–5
    diagnostic criteria 500–1, 502–4
    early identification in babies 503
    empathy impairment 239
    executive function 239
    features of 499–501
    group of disorders 502–4
    and personal responsibility 241
    poor central coherence 239
    systemising 239
    and theory of mind 239–41
autobiographical memory 146, 157, **543**
autonomy vs shame stage (Erikson) 20–1
Avon Longitudinal Study of Childhood and Adolescence 382
Avon Longitudinal Study of Parents and Children (ALSPAC) 55–6, 66, 214
axon and terminals 78
axons, myelinisation (myelination) 80–1, 383

baby buggy orientation, and parent–infant interaction 115
baby signing 133
Baby X experiments 330, 331
Baddeley, Alan 152
Bandura, Albert 34–5, 328, 338
Baron-Cohen, Simon 222, 224, 226–8, 230, 235
Bates, John 283
Bavolek's Nurturing programme 511
Bayley Scales of Infant Development 492, 498
Beebe, Beatrice 261
behavioural inhibition 288–90, 294–5, 296, **543**
behaviourist perspective 221
behaviourist theories on development 31–5
belief-desire stage of theory of mind 224–6, **544**
Bell, Sylvia 56–7
Belsky, Jay 268–9
Berko Gleason, Jean 137
Big Five personality dimensions 305, 374
Binet, Alfred 164–5
bio-ecological theory (Bronfenbrenner) 41–3, 410–12, 413, 485
biological perspectives on development 24–30
birth 85–6
    Apgar score of the neonate 86
    assessment of the neonate's health 86
    birth weight for gestational age 86
    complications 86
    initiation 85–6
    low birth weight babies 86
    pre-term babies 86
    small-for-gestational-age (SGA) babies 86
    stages of labour 86
Blakemore, Owen 327
Bogaert, Anthony 382
Bouchard, Thomas 5–6
Bowlby, John 27–8, 58, 117, 267, 268, 269

    early attachment theory 27–8, 249–52, 255–7
    internal working model (IWM) 270–4
    maternal sensitivity 263–7
    role of the father 267–8
Bowlby, Sir Richard 269
brain
    areas involved with language 125–6
    changes during puberty 383–5
    development in adolescence 419
    features and landmarks 78–9
    functions of white and grey matter 384
    postnatal development 88–90
    prenatal development 77–81
brain plasticity 89, 126, 300, **549**
    and musical training 97
    critical periods 90
British National Surveys of Sexual Attitudes and Lifestyle 402
British Picture Vocabulary Scale 166
Broca, Pierre Paul 125
Broca's aphasia 125
Broca's area 125–6
Bronfenbrenner, Urie 41–3, 410–12, 413, 469, 485, 489–90
Brosnan, Dr Mark 26
bully/victims 448–9, 452–4, **544**
bullying 443–77, **544**
    aggressive rejected children 363, 364–6
    among pre-school children 458
    and self-esteem 448, 449, 466–7
    and suicide 455–6
    and theory of mind 462, 464–6
    anti-bullying approaches 469–76
    as a group process 460, 462
    attribution theory and victimisation 462, 466–7
    based on ethnicity or sexuality 459
    bullies 448–9
    bully/victims 448–9, 452–4, **544**
    challenge of defining 444–7
    children and young people's definitions 446
    context of the behaviours 468–9
    contributory factors in aggressive behaviour 450–1
    developmental changes in definitions 446
    developmental patterns in involvement 457–9
    during adolescence 398–400
    ecological perspective 469
    educational approach to anti-bullying 470–1
    evaluation of school-based interventions 473–4
    experiences of LGBT youth 459
    forms prohibited by law 459
    gender patterns in involvement 456–7
    hostile attribution bias 464
    implications of lack of consensus in definition 446–7
    in adolescence 459
    in middle childhood 458
    in the workplace 461
    indirect bullying 456–7

    involvement in 447–9
    issues in researching 475–6
    KiVa Anti-Bullying programme (Finland) 473
    legal responsibility of schools 469
    methods of intervention and prevention 469–76
    Olweus Prevention Programme 469, 471, 473–4
    participant approach to anti-bullying 471–2
    participant roles 460, 462
    peer support (peer counselling) approach 472, 473
    Pikas method (Method of Shared Concern) 471–2
    prevalence of bully/victims 452–4
    prevalence of bullying others 451–3
    prevalence of traditional bullying 449–54
    prevalence of victimisation 451, 452
    relational bullying 456–7
    reports in the press 443–4
    social factors 399
    social-information processing model 462–4, 468
    Support Group Method 470, 471, 472
    tackling 469–76
    theoretical perspectives 462–9
    victims 448–9, 451, 452
    who is involved 448
    see also cyberbullying
Bus Story Test 509–10
Buss, Arnold 283, 284, 286–8, 298
Bussey, Kay 338

caffeine, prenatal effects 84
Campbell, Marilyn 474
cardinal numbers 178–9, **544**
cardinality 178–9, **544**
Carey, Susan 183–5, 186
Carey, William 291
Carey Questionnaires 291
Case, Robbie 415–17
case studies 58–60, **544**
    Baby P and other child abuse cases 265–6
    complexity of understanding relations 177
    developmentally appropriate teaching 426
    'difficult' temperament 285–6
    early memory in everyday life 147
    early pragmatics in everyday life 141
    Gary McKinnon (autism and personal responsibility) 241
    gender identity disorder 340–1
    Genie (language development) 127
    health visitor's referral letter to child development team 488
    impact of immigration on identity 395–6
    interpreting IQ 165
    James (ADHD assessment) 524
    KiVa Anti-Bullying programme (Finland) 473
    Little Albert (emotional conditioning) 32
    make-believe play ('lost babies') 355

case studies (*continued*)
  parental perspective on atypical development 497
  referral to a child development centre 500
  risks of alcohol consumption during pregnancy 84
  Stanford prison case study 59–60, 65
  when to end the study 59–60, 65
categorical self 319, **549**
categorisation **544**
  and language development 132–3
  in infancy 105–7
category **544**
  of speech sounds or words 119
Cattell's Culture Fair Intelligence Test (CCFIT) 168
central coherence 239, **544**
central conceptual structures 416, **544**
Centre for Child Mental Health 269
cerebellum, growth in adolescence 419
cerebral palsy 498
Champagne, Frances 484
Chatfield, Tom 359
Chess, Stella 283–6, 307
child abuse 118–19
  cases 264–6
  online risks 372
  sexual abuse 160
Child Behaviour Questionnaire (CBQ) 291, 293
child-centred education 418
childcare
  and attachment 263–70
  effects on children 28
childhood disintegrative disorder (CDD) 505
Chomsky, Noam 124–5, 126, 129
chromosomal abnormalities 505
chromosomes 74–5
circadian rhythms 81
classical conditioning 31, 32, **544**
classification 39
Climbie, Victoria 436
coercion of research participants 64
cognition, definition 99
cognitive abilities in infancy 99–101
cognitive behavioural therapy (CBT) 467
cognitive development
  and semantic development 132–3
  contemporary models 99–101
cognitive development theories 99
cognitive development theory (Piaget) 35–41
cognitive-developmental theory (Kohlberg) 334–5, **544**
cognitive dysregulation **544**
cognitive functioning and social behaviour 307–8
cognitive interviews 162–3, **544**
cognitive perspective on development 35–41
cohort **544**
cohort effects 62–3
colic in babies 118, **544**
Colorado Adoption Project 287
Columbine High School killings (1999) 398

common fractions 207–8, **544**
communication
  in infancy 116–19
  pre-verbal communication 116–19
  repairing faulty communications 139–40
computer games and teen aggression 397–8
concepts 105, 107, **544**
concerns and coping 400–1
Concerta 521, 535
concrete operations stage (Piaget) 36, 39
conduct disorder (CD) 528
confound variables 49, 54, **544**
congenital adrenal hyperplasia (CAH) 326–7, **544**
congenital rubella 498
Connelly, Peter (Baby P) 265–6
Connners Parent Rating Scale 538
consent 64, 65, 66
Conservation of Liquid task 9
conservation principle 38–9, **544**
constructivism 48, 49, **544**
context-dependence **544**
  of temperament 282
continuity **544**
continuous development 9–10, **544**
continuous perspective on development 15–16, **544**
continuous quantities 201, **544**
Conway, Martin 157
cooperative learning (group work) 417–18, **544**
co-parenting 303
coping strategies, in teenagers 399, 400–1
Corsaro, William 369–70
cortex of the brain 78
cortisol 85
counting all 192, **544**
counting on 192, **544**
court, children giving evidence in 162–3
co-variation or isomorphism of measures problems 202, **544**
covert attention 101, **545**
Cowie, Helen 472
creativity **545**
  and intelligence 167
Crick, N. 462–4, 468
criminal behaviour 308
critical period 27, **545**
  brain plasticity 90
  for attachment 251, 253, 256
critical period hypothesis **545**
  language development 126, 127
cross-sectional research design 50–1, **545**
crying
  in infants, effects of 117–19
  in neonates 130
cues 157–8, **545**
culture-fair intelligence testing 167–8
cutting edge
  biological influences on intellectual ability 26
  brain development in adolescence 419
  cyberbullying 447
  development of theory of mind 231

  early diagnosis of autism in babies 503
  EU Kids Online project 67
  impact of cyberbullying 455–6
  influences on teen aggression 398
  Math Wars (approaches to teaching mathematics) 214
  media influence on teenage gender identity construction 333
  memory functions and classroom performance 163
  origins of disorganised attachment 261
  quality of life of children with ADHD 540–1
  second language acquisition in immigrant children 134
  social aspects of onscreen gaming 359–60
  temperament of children with ADHD 309–10
  theory applied to real-life situations 163
  using EEG and neuroscience to explore infant cognition 100
cyberbullying 372, **545**
  challenge of tackling 474
  definition 447
  developmental patterns 459–60
  disinhibition in online behaviour 462, 467–8
  gender patterns in involvement 457
  impact of 455–6
  prevalence 454–5
  reports in the press 443
  research 447
  suicide cases 455–6
cybermentors in schools 472
cycles of attention 121–22

D4 dopamine receptor gene 531
Danby, Susan 370
Danish educational system 436–7
Darwin, Charles 25
day care, impact on attachment 268–70
DBH gene 531
decades 189, **545**
deception 226, **545**
  difficulty in children with autism 241
  in research studies 64–5
decimal fractions 207–8, **545**
deductive reasoning 39, 108–10
defence mechanisms 18–19, **545**
demand characteristics **545**
  for research participants 64
dendrites 78, **545**
denial (defence mechanism) 19
denominator 208, **545**
depression 308, **545**
  and peer neglect 364, 365
  comorbidity with ADHD 528
  risk factors in adolescence 399–400
  toddler's response to depressed mother 224
descriptive research 48
desire stage of theory of mind 225, **545**
despair in older adulthood 23
developmental delay 496–8

Developmental, Dimensional and Diagnostic Interview (3di) 504–5
developmental disorder 496–8
developmental milestones 482–3
developmental psychology
   attachment 7
   continuous vs discontinuous development 9–10
   debates 4–11
   defining 'typical' development 11
   definition 3
   early view of children as mini-adults 4
   evaluation of theories 10
   history of 4–11
   importance of early experiences 7
   influence of early philosophers 4–6
   nature vs nurture debate 4–7
   stage theories of development 7–9
developmental theory, and learning theories 420
developmentally appropriate provision **545**
   in education 420–39
Diagnostic and Statistical Manual of Mental Disorders see DSM
Diamond, Milton 328
Digit Span test 166
disapplication of elements of a study programme 421, **545**
discontinuous development 9–10, **545**
discrete quantities 201, **545**
discriminate (between speech sounds) 119, **545**
disinhibition **545**
   in online behaviour 462, 467–8
disintegrative psychosis 505
displacement (defence mechanism) 19
divergent thinking 168, **545**
dividend (in division) 201, **545**
divisor 201, **545**
DNA (deoxyribonucleic acid) 74, 84, **545**
Dodge, K. 462–4, 468
dominance hierarchy **545**
   through rough-and tumble play 357–8
dopamine 78, 254–5, 300, 535, **545**
Down's syndrome (Trisomy 21) 85, 498, 505–6
DRD4 gene 76
DRD5 gene 531
drugs, prenatal effects 84
DSM 489, 500, 502–3, 522, 523
   diagnosis of ADHD in adults 526–8
DSM-5 criteria for ADHD in childhood 523–4, **545–6**
Dunedin Multidisciplinary Health and Development Study 305–6
Dunn, Judy 302–3
dyscalculia 183, 499, **546**
dysfluency 508, **546**
dysgraphia 499
dyslexia 80, 416, 499, 503, **546**
   and pragmatic competence 139
   and working memory 139
Dyslexia Adult Screening Test (DAST) 139
dyspraxia (sensory integration disorder) 499, 503

early emergence **546**
   of temperament 282
early experiences, importance of 7
EAS model of temperament (Buss and Plomin) 283, 284, 286–8
EAS survey for parental ratings 291–2
Eckert, Mark 421
ecological systems theory 485
ecological validity of research 35
ectoderm 79
education 409–39
   achievement and attainment 431
   age of commencement of schooling 486
   application of developmental theory 412–19
   application of learning theories 420
   approach to anti-bullying 470–1
   child-centred education 418
   cooperative learning (group work) 417–18
   Danish educational system 436–7
   developmentally appropriate activities 426–9
   developmentally appropriate assessment activities 429–33
   developmentally appropriate behaviour management 433–6
   developmentally appropriate curricula 420–2, 423
   developmentally appropriate provision 420–39
   developmentally appropriate schools 436–7
   developmentally appropriate teaching 422–6
   directive exposition (chalk and talk) teaching 423–4
   disapplication of elements of a study programme 421
   formative assessment 430
   influence of Piaget's stage model 36, 412–15, 418, 421–2
   information-processing theory 415–17
   interactive connection building 425–6
   learners with special needs (Edward case study) 409–12, 430, 436, 438, 439
   legal responsibility to deal with bullying 469
   National Curriculum 430
   neo-Piagetian theory 415–19
   non-directive discovery 424–5
   personalised learning 418
   science teaching activities 428–9
   social-constructivist theory 417–19
   special educational needs assessments 430
   summative assessment 431
   teaching styles 422–6
   understanding difficult behaviour 409–12, 430, 436, 438, 439
educational approach to anti-bullying 470–1
EEG (electroencephalogram) 73, **546**
   exploring infant cognition 100
   mapping infant brain activity 89–90
   visually evoked potentials in infants 92

effortful control (Rothbart) 283, 284, 290, **546**
   spatial conflict task 295–7
ego 18–19, **546**
ego intensity vs despair stage (Erikson) 20, 23
egocentric **546**
egocentrism 37, 138–9, 388–9
eight ages of man (Erikson) 19–24
Elkind, David, theory of adolescent egocentrism 388–9
emotional intelligence 167
empathy 466, **546**
   development of 224–6
   impairment in autism 239
empiricist view of number competence 183–5
E_{mx} genes 80
enactive experience 338
encoding (memory) 147, **546**
encoding specificity principle 157–8, **546**
endoderm 79
enriched parallel individuation 184
environment (nurture)
   influence on early development 74–6
   interaction with genes 75–6
   see also nature–nurture question
epigenetics 75, 484
epilepsy 496
   and autism 504
episodic memory 146, 148, 154, **546**
Equasym 535
Erikson, Erik H. 7, 19–24
   age-related stage theories compared with assessment outcomes 432–3
   behaviour management 434
   eight ages of man 19–24
   theory of psychosocial development 387–8
ethical issues
   dilemmas in assessment and diagnosis of young children 488–9
   in research 59–60
ethical working practice 63–6
ethology 25–7, 253, **546**
EU Kids Online project 67
evaluative research 48
Every Child Matters programme 436
evidence-based practice (EBP) 513
evoked otoacoustic emissions (EOAE) 95
executive function in people with autism 239
existential self 318–19, **551**
exosystem (Bronfenbrenner) 42, 411, **546**
experimental methods 53, **546**
explanatory research 48
explicit knowledge 128, 231, **546**
explicit memories 150
exploratory research 48
extinction of a behaviour 33
extraversion 286
Eysenck, Hans 286–7, 304

Facebook 371–2
factor analysis 523
Fagan, Joseph 148

false belief 128, **546**
false-belief tasks 230–5
    and theory of mind 226–9, 238–9
    children with autism 240
false memories 159, 160–2
familiarisation 92, 93, **546**
family structure, influence in adolescence 394–5
Fantz, Robert 148, 149
Farrington, David 445, 446
father, as attachment figure 267–8, 274
foetal alcohol spectrum disorders 84
foetal alcohol syndrome (FAS) 84
folic acid (vitamin B9) 84
folk psychology 221–2, **546**
food additives and colours, effects on children 532
forebrain 78, 79
forgetting 159–63
formal operations stage (Piaget) 36, 39–40, 385–7
formative assessment 430
fractions 206–15
fragile X syndrome 498, 504, 505
Freud, Anna 19
Freud, Sigmund 17–19, 20, 41
    revelations from pretend play 357
friendships 366–76, **546**
    adolescence 368
    and psychological wellbeing 373–5
    and self-evaluation 372–3
    bases for selection of friends 367
    definition of friendship 367
    early childhood/pre-school years 367
    factors influencing 370–2
    functions and implications 372–5
    functions in school 373–5
    gender group and identity 371
    hierarchy 225
    influence on future relationships 374–5
    influence on self-concept 372–3
    learning and cognitive development 373
    middle childhood/school ages 367–8
    online gaming 371–2
    personality and preferences 370–1
    problem solving 373
    social media 371–2
    stages in children's conception of 368–70
    technology and friendship 371–2
    through the years 367–70
frontal lobe 78, 79
functional magnetic resonance imaging (fMRI) studies 117, 153–4, 290, 298–9, 419
functional reasoning 205
fuzzy trace theory (FTT) 161, 163

G (general intelligence) 166, 170, **546**
gaming online
    friendships 371–2
    social aspects 359–60
Ganda people, Uganda 258
gaze following 222–4, **546**

gender constancy 323–4, **546**
gender differences
    language development 138
    temperament 302
gender identity 322–42
    adults as socialising agents 329–30
    and childhood friendships 371
    Baby X experiments 330, 331
    biological evidence 326–8
    biological explanations 325–8
    cognitive-developmental theory 334–5
    cognitive theories 334–40
    development in adolescence 396–7
    development of 322–5
    gender identity disorder 340–1
    gender reassignment 340–1
    gender schema theories 335–8
    influence of peers 396–7
    media as a socialising agent 331–4
    parental investment theory 325–6
    peers as socialising agents 330–1
    self-efficacy 338–9
    social cognitive theory 338–40
    social learning theories 328–34
    synthesis and transaction 339–40
    theories of 325–42
    transsexuality 340–1
    twin studies 327–8
gender labelling 323, **546**
gender modelling 338
gender reassignment 327–8, 340–1
gender roles 324
gender schema 335–8, 396, **546**
gender stability 323, 324, **546**
gender stereotypes 302, 323–5, 329–31, 338, **546**
General Certificates of Secondary Education 431
General Strain Theory 468
generativity vs stagnation stage (Erikson) 20, 22–3
genes
    expression of 74–5
    influence on early attachment patterns 76
    influence on early development 74–6
    see also nature–nurture question
    inheritance of 74
    interaction with environment 75–6
    versions of (alleles) 74, 76
genetic disorders 505–7
    effects on prenatal development 85
genital stage of development (Freud) 18
genotype 75
Gesell, Arnold 24–5, 41
gifted children 168, 170
Ginsberg, Herbert P. 49
global developmental disability 497–8
Goldfarb, William 252, 256
goodness-of-fit between influences 306–7, **546**
Gopnik, Alison 132–3
Gréco, Pierre 180
Griffiths Mental Development Scales 498

group membership 316
guilt 21

habituation-recovery method 92, 93, **547**
Hall, Granville Stanley 380
Halligan, Ryan 455–6
Harlow, Harry 253–4
Harris, Eric 398
Harris, Judith 6
Harter, Susan 317, 320–1
Health Behaviour of School-aged Children (HBSC) study 451–2
Heinz experiment (Kohlberg) 390–2
Heller, Dr Kalman 285–6
Heller's syndrome 505
heterogeneous developmental disorder 522, **547**
heuristics 108–9
high-amplitude sucking (HAS) method 95, 96, **547**
hindbrain 78, 79
hippocampus 78, 103
history-graded influences on development 16
holophrases 136, **547**
horizontal relationships 346
hospitalisation of young children 252
hostile attribution bias 464, **547**
Howard, Jane 351
Hughes, Martin 193
human development, influence of nature and nurture 74–6
Human Genome Project 75
humour and language 140
hyperactive **547**
hyperactivity in pre-school children 525–6
hyperkinesis 523
hyperkinetic syndrome 523
hypotheses 386–7, **547**
hypothetico-deductive reasoning 386
hypothyroidism 498

ICD-10 (*International Classification of Diseases*, 10th revision) 500, 502–3
id 18–19, **547**
ideal self 321
identity and immigration 395–6
identity vs role-confusion stage (Erikson) 20, 22, 387–8, **547**
imitation of behaviour 34–5
immigration
    and identity 395–6
    second language acquisition 134
implicit **547**
implicit knowledge 128, 231
implicit memories 150
imprinting 26–7, 28, 253–4, **547**
Incredible Years (IY) Parent Training Programme 511, 514, 537–9
indirect bullying 456–7, **547**
induction (inductive reasoning) 108–10, 184, 185, **547**
industrialised societies, trend for earlier age at menarche 381–2
industry vs inferiority stage (Erikson) 20, 21–2

INDEX

infant-directed speech 122, 123, 124, 140
infant perception 73, 91–8
    audition 95–6
    smell (olfactory) perception 97–8
    taste (gustatory) perception 97–8
    touch 96–7
    vision 91–5
infanticide 118, **547**
infantile amnesia 157, 159, **547**
infants
    attention 101–2
    basic knowledge and understanding 104–5
    categorisation 105–7
    cognitive abilities 99–101
    crying, nature of sounds produced 130–1
    learning 102–4
    memory 102–4
    motor abilities 98–9
    non-verbal early communication 116–19
    object permanence 104–5
    peer interactions 349
    reasoning and problem solving 108–10
    social interactions 121–22
    vocalisation stages 131
inferiority, feeling of 21–2
information-processing theory 415–17, **547**
informed consent 64, 65, 66, **547**
inhibited behaviour 288–90, 294–5, 296, **547**
initiative vs guilt stage (Erikson) 20, 21
innate (natural or instinctive) differences in children 56–7
innate behaviour 25, **547**
instinctive behaviour patterns 25
institutionalisation, effects on young children 252, 256
integrative perspectives in developmental psychology 41–3
intellectual ability, biological influences 26
intelligence
    and creativity 167
    heredity and environment interactions over time 170
    in children 164–72
    nature–nurture question 169, 170
    nature of 164
    role in cognition 145
    twin research 169
    types of intelligence 166–7
intelligence quotient (IQ) 164–6, 493–4, **547**
intelligence testing approaches 164–70
    challenges for children with ADHD 528
    culture-fair intelligence testing 167–8
    gifted children 168, 170
    IQ (intelligence quotient) 164–6, 493–4, **547**
    multiple intelligences approach 166–7
interactionist view
    language development 126–7
    number competence 181–2, 185
internal working model (IWM) 270–4, **547**
inter-rater reliability 296
intervention 469, **547**
interview method 57–8, **547**

intimacy vs isolation stage (Erikson) 20, 22
intra-subject variability (ISV) 539–40
introversion 286
inventories in developmental psychology 52
invincibility fable 389
IQ see intelligence quotient
isolation in young adulthood 22
isomorphism of measures problems 202

James, William 87, 100, 101, 319
jokes 140

Kagan, Jerome 283, 284, 288–90, 294–5, 296, 298, 300, 301–2
Kendrick, Carol 302–3
Kidscape 471
KiVa Anti-Bullying programme (Finland) 473
Klebold, Dylan 398
Klinefelter syndrome 506
Kohlberg, Lawrence
    behaviour management 434–6
    cognitive-developmental theory 323, 334–5
    interview method 58
    theory of moral development 389–94
Kuhl, Patricia 130

Lamarckian model of 'soft inheritance' 484
LAN (local area network) parties 359–60
Lane, David 445
language
    and categorisation 106
    definition 116
    features of 116
    pre-verbal communication 116–19
    rules of 116
    speech and language disorder 508–10
language acquisition device (LAD) 124–5, 126, 129, **547**
language components 119–20
    phonology 119
    pragmatics 119, 120
    semantics 119–20
    syntax 119, 120
language development
    and theory of mind 230–5
    babbling stage 131
    canonical babbling stage 131
    categorisation 132–3
    combining three and four words 137–8
    combining two words 136–7
    egocentrism 138–9
    effects on the brain 89
    gender differences 138
    growth of vocabulary in infancy 131–2
    holophrases 136
    humour 140
    infant social interactions 121–22
    learning the meanings of words 133
    mismatch error 135–6
    modulated babbling stage 131
    naming insight 132
    overextension error 135
    overlap error 135
    phonological development 128–31

pragmatics development 138–41
production and comprehension 136
referential word learning 134–6
repairing faulty communications 139–40
second language acquisition 134
semantic development 131–6
signing for babies 133
single-word utterances 136
speech-sound perception 128–9, 130
speech-sound production 129–31
syntactic development 136–8
telegraphic speech 137
turn taking in conversation 140
underextension error 134–5
understanding non-verbal vocalisations 140
using children's errors to understand 134–6
vocal play stage 131
language development theories 122–7
    brain areas involved with language 125–6
    critical period hypothesis 126, 127
    interactionist accounts 126–7
    learning theory 122–4
    nativist account 124–6
    social learning theory 123–4
latent stage of development (Freud) 18
lateralisation of brain functions 125, 140, **547**
learning and development through play 351–8
learning disability 496–8, **547**
learning in infancy 102–4
learning theories
    application in education 420
    accounts of language development 122–4
    perspectives on development 31–5
Lenneberg, Eric 126
Lerner, Jacqueline 469
Lerner, Richard 469
LGBT youth, experiences of bullying 459
lifespan perspective 15–16
    ADHD in adulthood 527
    Avon Longitudinal Study of Parents and Children (ALSPAC) 55–6
    bullying in the workplace 461
    Dunedin Multidisciplinary Health and Development Study 305–6
    Erikson's age-related stage theories compared with assessment outcomes 432–3
    influence of childhood friendships in adulthood 374–5
    intergenerational patterns of attachment 274
    Kohlberg's theory of moral development 392
    memory strategy use in adulthood 155–6
    multiplicative reasoning in later childhood 205
    musical brain 97
    outcomes for siblings of adults with learning disabilities or mental illness 499
    pragmatics and working memory 139
    self-esteem changes with age 321–2
    theory of mind through adulthood 236
    word retrieval across the lifespan 17

Locke, John 4, 5
logical thought 39
longitudinal research design 51–2, **547**
Longitudinal Study of Australian Children (LSAC) 298, 305
long-term memory 102
looking-glass self 319–20, **547**
Lorenz, Konrad 25–7, 253

MacArthur–Bates Communicative Development Inventories (CDI) 52–3, 54, 61
Maccoby, Eleanor 316–17, 325
MacLean, Paul 117
macrosystem (Bronfenbrenner) 42, 411, **547**
Madsen, Kirsten 446
Main, Mary 263, 271, 272–3
Makaton 514
make-believe/sociodramatic play 354–5, **548**
Maslach, Christina 60
maternal deprivation, effects of 27
maternal deprivation hypothesis (Bowlby) 251–7, **548**
maternal drug use, effects on the developing child 84
maternal sensitivity 29–30, 263–7, **548**
maternal smoking during pregnancy, ADHD risk factor 531
mathematical thinking
    additive composition of numbers 189–93
    additive reasoning 193–8
    additive relations 180
    cardinal concept of number (cardinality) 178–9
    Change problems 194–6, 198
    Combine problems 194–6, 198
    Compare problems 197–8
    counting as a tool for comparing quantities 187–8
    co-variation problems 202
    division 201–2
    dyscalculia 183
    empiricist view 183–5
    fractions 206–15
    interactionist view (Piaget) 181–2, 185, 186
    interest in development of 175–6
    isomorphism of measures problems 202
    learning to count to 100 188–9
    multiplicative reasoning 198–206
    nativist view 182–3
    nature of 177–9
    number system as a tool for thinking 186–93
    numerical calculation 195
    one-to-many correspondence problems 199–201
    ordinality 179–80
    partitioning 206–13
    power of mathematics 175
    product of measures problems 202–6
    quantity 178–9
    ratio 199–201
    rational numbers 198, 206–15
    reasoning and solving problems with numbers 193–206
    relational calculation 195
    relations 196–8
    sharing 208–13
    sharing problems 201–2
    theorems in action 195, 198
    theories of understanding number 181–6
    transformations 196–8
    transitivity 177
    understanding number 179–81
    understanding relations 177–8
    variables 198
mathematics teaching approaches 214
maturation 24–5, 413, **548**
Maxi and the chocolate task 226, 230, 235
McKinnon, Gary 241
mean (average) 50, 156, **548**
MECP2 gene 505
media as a socialising agent 331–4
medial temporal lobe 154
median score 50, **548**
medications, prenatal effects 84
Meins, Elizabeth 266–7
melatonin 511
Meltzoff, Andrew 132–3
memory
    component processes 146–8
    definitions 146
    encoding stage 147
    episodic memory 148
    individual differences in babies 103
    procedural memory 147–8
    retrieval stage 147
    role in cognition 145
    storage stage 147
    strategy use in adulthood 155–6
    types of 146
    types of information 147–8
    see also working memory
memory in children 60–1, 148–63
    cognitive interviews 162–3
    developments in encoding 150–6
    developments in retrieval 157–8
    developments in storage 156–7
    false memories 159, 160–2
    forgetting 159–63
    fuzzy trace theory (FTT) 161, 163
    infant memory 102–4, 148–50
    infantile amnesia 157, 159
    influence of prior knowledge and expectations 158–9, 162
    influence on classroom performance 163
    memory development with age 150–9
    repression of memories 160
menarche **548**
    trend for earlier age at 381–2
meningitis 498
mental age concept 164–6
mesoderm 79
mesosystem (Bronfenbrenner) 42, 411, **548**
meta-analysis 169, 229, **548**

metacognition 100, **548**
meta-representational ('pretend') play 223–4, 236–7, **548**
Method of Loci memory technique 155–6
methylphenidate 511, 521, 535
Meyenburg, Bernd 341
microsystem (Bronfenbrenner) 42, 411, **548**
midbrain 78, 79
Milgram study (1974), moral decision-making 392–4
mind-mindedness in a parent 266–7, **548**
Minecraft online game 359
Minnesota twin study 5–6
mirroring neurons 237
mistrust 20
MMR (measles, mumps and rubella) vaccine and autism 500, 504
mnemonics 153, 155–6, **548**
MOAO gene 76
mobile conjugate reinforcement paradigm 103, 104, 158
mode (modal score) 50, **548**
modelling in social learning theory 328–30
molecular genetics 530, **548**
Money, Dr John 327–8
Monks, Claire 446, 458, 465
monotropism 249, 253, 256, **548**
moral decision-making, Milgram study (1974) 392–4
moral development theory (Kohlberg) 389–94
Moray House Test 170
Moro reflex 87
mother
    as primary caregiver 263–7
    influence on child's temperament 301, 302–4
mother–infant interaction 247–8
    attachment behaviour 117–18
    cycles of attention 121–22
    turn taking in feeding 121
motherese (infant-directed speech) 122, 123, 124, 140
motor abilities in infancy 98–9
Motz, Anna 266
Müller-Lyer illusion 175, 177
Multidimensional Personality Questionnaire (MPQ) 305
Multi-modal Treatment Study of ADHD (MTA) 535–6
multiple classification 204
Murray, Lynne 303–4
music perception in infants 96, 97
musical ability, nature–nurture debate 54
myelinisation (myelination) of axons 80–1, 88, 383, **548**

naming insight 132, **548**
National Adult Reading Test 170
National Curriculum for Schools in England 420–2, 423, 430
national identity 395–6
nativist view
    language development 124–6
    understanding number 182–3

natural numbers 195, **548**
nature **548**
nature–nurture question
    as a continuum 6–7
    attachment 254–5
    attachment 30
    causes of ADHD 531
    cognitive development 413
    debate in developmental psychology 4–7
    definition of 'nature' 4
    definition of 'nurture' 4
    development of mathematical thinking 181, 186
    epigenetics 484
    ethnic and gender differences in temperament 301–2
    fall in age at menarche 382
    gender reassignment 327–8
    influences on early attachment patterns 76
    influences on early development 74–6
    intelligence studies of twins 169
    musical ability 54
    play 352–3
    postnatal brain development 90
    speech–sound perception 130
    temperament 297
    theory of mind twin studies 238
    understanding the meaning of numbers 186
    why some children become bullies 450–1
near-infrared spectroscopy (NIRS) 98, 104
negative reinforcement 32, 33
neglected children (neglect by peers) 360, 363–6, **548**
neonate
    movement and reflexes 87
    perceptions and abilities 87
    sleep states 87
    states of arousal or alertness 87
neo-Piagetian theory 415–19, **548**
neural plate 79, 80
neural tube **548**
    defects 84
    formation in the embryo 79–80
neurofeedback 541
neurofibromatosis 507
neurogenesis 80, **548**
neuroimaging techniques 153–4, **548**
neurological changes at puberty 383–5
neuronal differentiation in the prenatal brain 80–1
neuronal migration in the prenatal brain 80, 81, **548**
neurons 78
neuropsychology of ADHD 532–5
neuroscience
    mapping infant brain activity 89–90
    models of infant cognition 99–100
neuroticism 286
neurotransmitters 76, 78, 300
New Forest Parenting Programme (NFPP) 537, 538–9

New York Longitudinal Study 283–6
nicotine, effects of prenatal exposure 84, 531
Nigg, Joel T. 309–10
NIHR MindTech cooperative 540
Nintendo Brain Training 540
No-Blame Approach (Support Group Method) 470, 471, 472
'noble savage' view of the child 4
non-normative influences on development 16
non-nutritive suck rate 95, 96, 149–50
non-verbal vocalisations, understanding 140
norepinephrine 531, 535, **548**
norms and typicality 61–2
North Wales Sure Start Trial 538
number, demonstration of understanding 179–81
numerator 208, **548**
numerical calculation **548**
Nuremburg funnel model of teaching 424
nurture 4, **548** *see also* nature–nurture question

object permanence 37, 100, 104–5, **548**
objective self 319, **549**
observation study 56–7, **549**
obsessive–compulsive disorder (OCD) 500, 502
occipital lobe 78, 79
occupational therapy 496
Offer, Daniel 380
Oksapmin people (New Guinea) 188
Olweus, Dan 444
Olweus Prevention Programme 469, 471, 473–4
open interview 57
operant conditioning 31–4, **549**
Opie, Iona 347–8
oppositional defiant disorder (ODD) 528
oral stage of development (Freud) 18
ordinality 179–80, **549**
over-controlled personality type 374–5
overt attention 101, **549**
oxytocin 254–5

paired-associate tasks 153
parallel individuation 183–4
parent–infant interaction, baby buggy orientation 115
Parental Account of Children's Symptoms 538
parental investment theory 325–6, **549**
parietal lobe 78, 79
Parten, Mildred 8, 350, 353
partial reinforcement 34
participant confidentiality 66, **549**
Participant Role Questionnaire (PRQ) 460
Participant Role Scale 465
partitioning 206–13, **549**
paternal attachment 267–8, 274
Pattern Construction test 166
patterns of attachment (Ainsworth) 28–30
Pavlov, Ivan 31, 35, 41
PAX-6 gene 75

PECS (Picture Exchange Communication System) 512, 514
peer, definition 348
peer group 348, **549**
peer groups and interactions
    adolescence 351
    associative activities 350
    cooperative activities 350
    early childhood/pre-school ages 350
    features of 348–9
    friendships 366–76
    gender differences in childhood 350–1
    infancy 349
    middle childhood/school ages 350–1
    parallel activities 350
    peers as socialising agents 330–1
    play 351–8
    playground interactions 347
    social status 358–66
    theory of mind development 229
    through the years 349–51
peer preference 397, **549**
peer pressure 397, **549**
peer support (peer counselling) **549**
    approach to bullying 472, 473
Pelka, Daniel 265–6
Pelligrini, Anthony 459
Pepler, Debra 443, 474
personal fable 389
personalised learning 418
personality development 304–7
personality types 374–5
pervasive developmental disorders (PDD) 502, 503
PET scans 419
phallic stage of development (Freud) 18–19
phenotype 75
phenylketonuria (PKU) 75
phonemes 96, 119, **549**
phonological development 128–31
phonology 119, **549**
Piaget, Jean 41, 47, 58, 334
    animacy concept in infancy 107
    behaviour management 434
    cognitive development in infancy 99, 100, 101
    cognitive development theory 7, 9, 10, 15, 35–41, 385–7
    development of mathematical thinking 179, 180
    egocentrism 138–9
    influence on education policy and practice 36, 412–15, 418, 421–2
    interactionist view of number competence 181–2, 185, 186
    language acquisition 126, 129
    language development 133
    memory in infants 146
    object constancy in infants 94
    object permanence in infancy 104
    on make-believe play 357
    reasoning in infancy 108, 109
    view of the neonate 87
Pikas method (Method of Shared Concern) 471–2

INDEX

pilot study 52, **549**
Pinker, Steven 6
placenta 86, **549**
plasticity of the brain 89, 90, 97, 126, 300, **549**
play 351–8
    categories of 353–6
    constructive play 354
    definition 351
    establishment of dominance hierarchy 357–8
    functional play 354
    functions of 352–3
    games with rules 354
    in animals 352–3
    make-believe/sociodramatic play 354–5
    role in learning and development 351–8
    rough-and-tumble play 352, 354, 355–6, 357–8
    social and non-social 353–4
    solitary play 353–4
    symbolic play 354
play-based assessment and observation 489–91
play sensitivity 268, **549**
pleasure/pain motivation (Freud) 17–19
Plomin, Robert 283, 284, 286–8, 298
pointing, communicative function 133
positive reinforcement 31, 32
positivism 48–9, **549**
postnatal brain development 88–90
    connecting and pruning the brain 88
    critical periods for brain plasticity 90
    developmental neuroscience 89–90
    effects of language development 89
    lateralisation 89
    left and right brain development 89
    mapping infant brain activity 89–90
    myelinisation of neurons 88
    nature and nurture 90
    synaptic pruning 88
    synaptogenesis 88, 90
postnatal depression (PND) 303–4
post-traumatic amnesia 159–60
power relationships in research studies 64
practice-based evidence (PBE) 513
Prader–Willi syndrome 506
pragmatic language **549**
    difficulty with 509
pragmatics 119, 120, 138–41, **549**
predictive research 48
preferential looking method 91–3, 148, **549**
prefrontal cortex 154
    role in learning and memory 103–4
prenatal abilities and behaviours 82–3
    foetal learning 82–3
    foetal sleep and waking cycles 81–2
    foetal vision 83
    habituation 82
    hearing and auditory memory 82–3
    memory 82
    perception 82
    reflex responses in the foetus 81
    sense of smell 82
    sense of taste 82
    sense of touch 82
    startle reflex 82
prenatal development
    influence of nature and nurture 74–6
    physical development 77–8
prenatal development of the brain 77–81
    brain features and landmarks 78–9
    neural tube formation in the embryo 79–80
    neurogenesis 80
    neuronal differentiation in the prenatal brain 80–1
    neuronal migration in the prenatal brain 80, 81
    stages of development 79–81
    synaptic 'pruning' 81
    synaptogenesis 80, 81
prenatal developmental risk factors 83–5
    environmental pollutants and toxins 85
    environmental teratogens 83–5
    genetic errors 85
    maternal disease 84
    maternal drug use 84
    maternal malnutrition 83–4
    maternal psychological state 85
    maternal stress 85
preoperational thought stage (Piaget) 36, 37–9
Preschool ADHD Treatment Study (PATS) 535, 536
prevention 469, **549**
private self 224
problem solving in infancy 108–10
procedural memory 146, 147–8, **549**
product of measures problems 202–6, **549**
projection (defence mechanism) 19
propositional thought 387, **549**
pro-social behaviours 224
proto-declarative pointing 222–4, **549**
prototypes 105, 177–8, **549**
proximity seeking 249–50, 251, 253, **549**
psychiatric assessment of developmental disorders 496
psychiatric co-morbidity **549**
    in ADHD 526
psychoanalysis 160
    perspective on development 17–24, 221
psychoeducation 511
psychopathology, and temperament 308–10
psychopharmacotherapy 511
psychosexual development, theory of 17–19
psychosis 496
psycho-social development theory (Erikson) 19–24, 387–8
psycho-stimulant medications 521, 535–6, **549**
puberty 382, **550**
    changes in brain white and grey matter 384
    neurological changes 383–5
    timing and psychological issues 382–3
    trends in age at menarche 381–2
public self 224
punishment 33

QB-test 540
qualitative methods 49, 56–60, 65, **550**
quantitative methods 49, 52–6, **550**
quantity 178–9, **550**
questionnaires 52
quotient 201, **550**

ratio 199–201, **550**
rational numbers 198, 206–15, **550**
rationalization (defence mechanism) 19
Reading the Mind in the Eyes Test 236
real self 321
reasoning
    in adults 108
    in infancy 108–10
recall memory 102–3
recognition memory 102
referential words 131, 134–6, **550**
reflexes, in neonates 87
regression (defence mechanism) 19
rehearsal and memory 152, 153, **550**
reinforcement 31–4
    in social learning theory 328–30
rejected children (rejection by peers) 358, 360–1, 363, 364–6, **550**
rejection sensitivity 365
relational bullying 456–7, **550**
relational calculation **550**
relational vulnerability model 464
relations 177–8, **550**
REM sleep
    in neonates 87
    in the foetus 81–2
representational stage of theory of mind 226–9, 235–7, **550**
repression (defence mechanism) 19, 160, **550**
research 48, **550**
    reasons for carrying out 48
research methods 47–67
    appraising infant abilities 93
    assent 64
    assessment of pre-verbal children 128
    case studies 58–60, 65
    children's understanding of cardinality 178
    coercion of participants 64
    cohort effects 62–3
    confound variables 49, 54
    consent 64, 65, 66
    constructivism 48, 49
    cross-sectional research design 50–1
    debriefing participants 65
    deception in research studies 64–5
    demand characteristics 64
    early sense of self (rouge test) 318
    ecological validity 35
    ethical issues 59–60
    ethical working practice 63–6
    evidence-based practice versus practice-based evidence 513
    experimental methods 53
    independent observations with objective physical measures 296
    infant visual recognition memory 149
    informed consent 64, 65, 66
    interpretation and use of data 54–6

inter-rater reliability 296
interviews 57–8
issues in researching bullying 475–6
longitudinal research design 51–2
methods in developmental psychology research 50–67
norms and typicality 61–2
observation study 56–7
observation using classroom video 423–4
online research projects 67
participant confidentiality 66
physical and psychological safety of participants 65–5
pilot study 52
positivism 48–9
power relationships 64
qualitative methods 49, 56–60
quantitative methods 49, 52–6
questionnaires 52
randomised control trial designs 537
research path for theory of mind 235
safety considerations 65–6
sexual behaviour research 402
sociometry 362–3
Strange Situation experiment 259
surveys 52
target research groups 62–3
types of studies 48
understanding theoretical paradigms 48–9
use of inventories in developmental psychology 52
visual paired comparison (VPC) tasks 149
when to end the study 59–60, 65
working with children 60–7
resilient personality type 374–5
retrieval (memory) 147, **550**
Rett syndrome 505
reversibility of equations 39
Right Hemisphere Language Battery 139
risperidone 511
Ritalin 511, 535
Robertson, James 58–9, 65–6, 252
Robertson, Joyce 58–9, 65–6, 252
Roland, Erling 445
role-confusion 22
Romanian orphanage children (1980s) 256–7
Rose, Jim 418
Rothbart, Mary 283, 284, 290, 291, 293, 295–7
rouge test 317–18
rough-and-tumble play 352, 354, 355–6, 357–8, **550**
Rousseau, Jean-Jacques 4, 5
rubella, teratogenic effects 84
Rymer, Russ 127

Sally–Anne task 226–8, 230, 235
Salmivalli, Christine 460, 465, 473
sarcasm 229
scaffolding concept 41
scalar reasoning 205

schemes of action 181, **550**
Schneider, Barry 450
school shootings 398
Schwartz, Carl 298–9
science teaching activities 428–9
Scottish mental surveys 170
scripts (memory) 146, 158–9, 162, **550**
second-order states in theory of mind 229
Second World War, social upheaval caused by 257
seeing leads to knowing 223–4, **550**
self-as-object (self as 'me') 319
self-as-subject (self 'I') 318–19
self-awareness 315, 317–18, 319, **550**
rouge test 318
self-concept 315–22, **550**
and friendships 372–3
categorical self 319
children's self-concept at different ages 317–20
definition 316
early self-awareness 317–18, 319
existential self 318–19
ideal self 321
looking-glass self 319–20
objective self 319
real self 321
self-as-object (self as 'me') 319
self-as-subject (self 'I') 318–19
subjective self 318–19
theories of development 316–22
self-consciousness, in adolescence 389
self-efficacy 34, 338–9, **550**
self-esteem 320–2, **550**
and bullying 448, 449, 466–7
changes with age 321–2
in adolescence 389, 399
self-evaluation 320–1
and friendships 372–3
self-reflexivity 319
Selman, Robert 368–70
semantic development 131–6
semantic memory 146, **550**
semantically related words 120, **550**
semantics 119–20, **550**
sensitive period **550**
for attachment 256, 268
sensorimotor intelligence stage (Piaget) 36–7, 99, 100
sensory memory 102
separated families 394–5
separation anxiety 27–8, 57, **550**
separation protest 250–1, **550**
Strange Situation experiment 258–63
seriation 39
serotonin 76, 78, 300
set-based quantification 185
shaken baby syndrome 118–19, **550**
shame 21
shaping **550**
behaviour 33
process in language development 123–4
sharing 208–13
Sharp, Sonia 472
shop task 189–93

signing
for babies 133
in deaf children, and theory of mind 230
simulation theory (ST) of theory of mind 235, 237
Six Areas of Learning and Development 430
Skinner, B. F. 31–4
sleep–wake cycles in the foetus 81–2
Smarties task 228, 230
smell (olfactory) perception in infants 97–8
smiling in babies 118
Smith, Peter 446, 447, 457, 458, 472
SNAP25 gene 531
social anxiety in children 363, 365–6
social aspect of language, pragmatics 119, 120
social aspects of onscreen gaming 359–60
social behaviour, influence of temperament 307–8
social cognitive theory 338–40
social-constructivist theory (Vygotsky) 417–19
social contexts of development 410–12
social identity 315–22, **550**
social-information processing **551**
model of bullying 462–4, 468
social learning theory 34–5, **551**
account of language development 123–4
social media 371–2
social situations, ability to 'read' 224–5
social status 358–66, **551**
acceptance by peers 358, 360–1, 364–6
aggressive rejected children 361, 363, 364–6
and antisocial behaviour 361, 364–5
classification issues 363–4
consequences of 364–6
controversial category 364
definition 358
neglected children (neglect by peers) 360, 363–6
rejection by peers 358, 360–1, 363, 364–6
sociometry 362–3
sociocultural theory (Vygotsky) 41
sociometry 362–3, **551**
Soltis, Joseph 118
Sonic Hedgehog gene 85
spatial-conflict task 295–7
special educational needs (SEN) assessment 486–7
specialist health visitor support 495
specific learning difficulties 499
speculative research 48
speech and language disorder 508–10
aetiology 509
diagnostic assessment 509–10
pragmatic language difficulties 509
speech and language therapy 495, 509–10
spermarche 383
spina bifida 80, 498
Sroufe, Alan 271
stability **551**

INDEX

stage theories of development 7–9, 14–15, **551**
stagnation in middle adulthood 22–3
Standard Assessment Tests in schools 26
Standard Behavioural Family Intervention (SBFI) 537
Stanford–Binet Intelligence Test 165, 166, 492
Stanford prison case study 59–60, 65
startle reflex
    in neonates 87
    in the foetus 82
Steiner-Adair, Catherine 332
Stern, William 165, 493
stimulus (plural stimuli) 148, **551**
storage (memory) 147, **551**
storm and stress in adolescence 380, **551**
Strange Situation experiment 29, 57, 258–63, 271, 272, 273, 274, **551**
stranger anxiety 28, 57, 250–1, 256–7, **551**
    Strange Situation experiment 258–63
Strengths and Difficulties Questionnaire (SDQ) 538
stress, effects on gene expression 75–6
structured interview 57
subjective self 318–19, **551**
substance dependence 308
substance use disorders and ADHD 528
sucking reflex in neonates 87
Su-Do-Ku puzzles 386, 403
suggestibility 161–2, **551**
suicide and attempted suicide 308
    and bullying 455–6
summative assessment 431
superego 18–19, **551**
Support Group Method 470, 471, 472
suprachiasmatic nuclei 81
surveys 52
symbolic play 354, **551**
synapses 78, **551**
synaptic over-production 419
synaptic pruning **551**
    after birth 88
    during puberty 383–4
    in adolescence 419
    in the prenatal brain 81
synaptogenesis **551**
    in the prenatal brain 80, 81
    after birth 88, 90
syntactic development 136–8
syntax 119, 120, **551**
systematic problem solving 40
systemising, in autism spectrum conditions (ASC) 239

tabula rasa view of the child's mind 4
taste perception in infants 96–8
Tay-Sachs disease 505
telegraphic speech 137, **551**
temperament 279–311, **551**
    and biological make-up 298–300
    and pathological outcomes 307–10
    and personality development 304–7
    and second language acquisition 134
    and social behaviour 307–8

approaches to study 280
Bates's dimensions 283
Buss and Plomin's EAS model 283, 284, 286–8
children with ADHD 309–10
context-dependence 282
continuity 281–2
definition 280–2
'difficult' temperament 285–6
dimensions of 283–90
early emergence of 282
ethnic and cultural differences 301–2
explanations for differences in 297–304
family influences 301–4
gender differences 302
genes and the biological influences 297–300
goodness-of-fit between influences 306–7
heritability 297–8
in the long term 304–10
independent observations 294–5, 296
influence of environment 301–2
Kagan's behavioural inhibition 283, 284, 288–90, 294–5, 296
longitudinal research into adulthood 304–6
maternal variables 301, 302–4
measurements 290–7
neurological processes 298–300
parental reports and ratings 291–4
persistence over time 280–2
potential for change 300
psychopathology 308–10
Rothbart's 'effortful control' 283, 284, 290, 295–7
stability 281
studying and measuring 282–97
Thomas and Chess's nine dimensions 283–6
temporal lobe 78, 79
teratogens 83–5, **551**
Test Reception of Grammar 166
testosterone exposure in the womb, influence of 26
thalamocingulate division of the brain 117, **551**
thalidomide 84
theorems in action 195, 198, **551**
theoretical perspectives on development 14–44
    attachment theory 27–8
    behaviourist theories 31–5
    bioecological theory 41–3
    biological perspectives 24–30
    classical conditioning 31, 32
    cognitive development theory 35–41
    cognitive perspective 35–41
    continuous perspective 15–16
    ethology 25–7
    integrative perspectives 41–3
    learning perspectives 31–5
    lifespan perspective 15–16
    maturational theory 24–5
    operant conditioning 31–4
    patterns of attachment 28–30

psychoanalytic perspective 17–24
psychosexual development theory 17–19
psycho-social theory of development 19–24
social learning theory 34–5
sociocultural theory 41
stage theories 14–15
theory 14, **551**
    evaluation of theories 10
theory of mind 128, 154, 221–42, **551**
    ability to keep secrets 231
    ability to lie 231
    ability to 'read' social situations 224–5
    and bullying 462, 464–6
    and language development 230–5
    belief-desire stage 224–6
    children with autism 239–41
    cognitive skills used 222
    debates about origin of 238–9
    deception 226
    definition 222
    desire stage 225
    development of empathy 224–6
    development of 'mind-reading' skills 222–4
    developmental perspective 230–5
    false belief tasks 226–9, 230–5, 238–9
    folk psychology 221–2
    gaze following 222–4
    in deaf children 230
    meta-representational ('pretend') play 223–4
    pro-social behaviours 224
    proto-declarative pointing 222–4
    public self and private self 224
    representational account 235–7
    representational stage 226–9
    research path 235
    second-order states 229
    seeing leads to knowing 223–4
    simulation theory (ST) 235, 237
    theories of 235–9
    theory-theory (TT) account 235–7
    through adulthood 236
theory-theory (TT) account of theory of mind 235–7
Thomas, Alexander 283–6, 307
Three Mountains study (Piaget) 37–8, 40
Tizard, Barbara 256
Toddler Temperament Scale (TTS) 291, 292
tool for thinking 186–93, **551**
top-down processing 153, **551**
touch
    and wellbeing 96
    to learn about objects 96–7
Tourette's syndrome 496, 511
traditional bullying 447, **551** *see also* bullying
transformations **551**
transitive inference 109–10
transitivity 177, **551**
transsexuality 340–1
triarchic theory of intelligence 167
Triple-P Positive Parenting Programme 537, 538–9

Triune Brain theory 117
trust vs mistrust stage (Erikson) 20
turn taking in conversation 140
turn taking in feeding 121
Turner syndrome 507
twin studies 5–6
    bullying 450–1
    gender identity 327–8
    intelligence 169
    temperament 298
    theory of mind 238
Twitter 371

under-controlled personality type 374–5
uninhibited behaviour 288–90, 294–5, 296, **551**

variables 198, **552**
Vergnaud, Gérard 195–6, 198
vertical relationships 348
Vinelands Adaptive Behaviour Scales 498
vision in infants 91–5
    appraisal methods 91–3
    coherence 92–3
    colour categorisation 94
    colour vision 93–4
    depth (3-D) perception 94
    object constancy 94
    recognising emotional expressions 93
    shapes 93
    visual system 91, 92
    'whole' view of objects 94–5
'visual cliff' depth illusion 94
visual cortex 83
visual paired comparison (VPC) task 148, 149
visual processing disorder 499
visual recognition memory 148–9, **552**
vocabulary spurt 131–2, **552**
Vygotsky, Lev 41
    influence on education policy and practice 417–19, 427
    on make-believe play 357
    scaffolding concept 41
    social-constructivist theory 417–19
    sociocultural theory 41
    zone of proximal development (ZPD) 41, 357, 427

Watson, J. B. 4, 7
Watson, John 32
Weber function 182–3
Wechsler Adult Intelligence Scales 166
Wechsler cognitive assessments 498
Wechsler Intelligence Scales 492
Wechsler Memory Scale 170
Werker, Janet 129
Wernicke, Carl 125
Wernicke's area 125–6
whole numbers 195, **552**
Whorfian hypothesis 106
will, development of 21
Williams syndrome 166–7, 507
Wisconsin Longitudinal Study 499
Woodhead, Chris 418
working memory 102, 147, 152, 155, **552**
    and pragmatics 139
    impairment in ADHD
World Health Organization 252
Wug Test 137

youth culture, development of 380–1
Yu, Rongjin 374–5

Zeedyk, Suzanne 115
zone of proximal development (ZPD) 41, 357, 427
zygote 77, **552**